Lecture Notes in Computer Science 9366

Commenced Publication in 1973
Founding and Former Series Editors:
Gerhard Goos, Juris Hartmanis, and Jan van Leeuwen

More information about this series at http://www.springer.com/series/7409

Marcelo Arenas · Oscar Corcho
Elena Simperl · Markus Strohmaier
Mathieu d'Aquin · Kavitha Srinivas
Paul Groth · Michel Dumontier
Jeff Heflin · Krishnaprasad Thirunarayan
Steffen Staab (Eds.)

The Semantic Web – ISWC 2015

14th International Semantic Web Conference
Bethlehem, PA, USA, October 11–15, 2015
Proceedings, Part I

 Springer

Editors

Marcelo Arenas
Pontificia Universidad Católica de Chile
Santiago de Chile
Chile

Oscar Corcho
Universidad Politecnica de Madrid
Boadilla del Monte
Spain

Elena Simperl
University of Southampton
Southampton
UK

Markus Strohmaier
Department of Computational Social Science
Gesis Leibniz-Institut
Köln, Nordrhein-Westfalen
Germany

Mathieu d'Aquin
The Open University
Milton Keynes
UK

Kavitha Srinivas
IBM Research
Yorktown Heights, NY
USA

Paul Groth
Elsevier Labs.
Amsterdam
The Netherlands

Michel Dumontier
School of Medicine
Stanford University
Stanford, CA
USA

Jeff Heflin
Lehigh University
Bethlehem, PA
USA

Krishnaprasad Thirunarayan
Wright State University
Dayton, OH
USA

Steffen Staab
University of Koblenz-Landau
Koblenz, Rheinland-Pfalz
Germany

ISSN 0302-9743   ISSN 1611-3349   (electronic)
Lecture Notes in Computer Science
ISBN 978-3-319-25006-9   ISBN 978-3-319-25007-6   (eBook)
DOI 10.1007/978-3-319-25007-6

Library of Congress Control Number: 2015950869

LNCS Sublibrary: SL3 – Information Systems and Applications, incl. Internet/Web, and HCI

Springer Cham Heidelberg New York Dordrecht London

Printed on acid-free paper

Springer International Publishing AG Switzerland is part of Springer Science+Business Media (www.springer.com)

Preface

Since its inception in the last decade, the Semantic Web has experienced a steady and continuous development toward its original vision, both in terms of research and of technology development and applications. Many of the research results presented in the initial conferences have now matured and been taken up in commercial settings, giving rise to new research problems that are now being explored. Large-scale initiatives, such as some of the most popular datasets in the linked open data cloud, are now considered as commodities and are part of many services that are being used on a daily basis, not only inside our research community but also in other research areas.

The International Semantic Web Conference (ISWC) has continued to be the premier venue for presenting innovative systems, applications, and research results related to the Semantic Web. In this edition, we aimed at making it even more clear that the Semantic Web is not only about using the well-known W3C recommendations RDF, RDF Schema, and/or OWL, and dealing with their associated challenges, but generally about the combination of semantics, data, and the Web.

This volume contains the proceedings of ISWC 2015, with papers accepted into the various tracks for which specific calls for papers had been issued. Besides the usual research track, this year we split the Replication, Benchmark, Data and Software track and the Semantic Web In-Use track from previous editions into three more specialized tracks, covering: Empirical Studies and Experiments, In-Use and Software, and Data Sets and Ontologies.

We received a very good response to all our calls from a truly international community of researchers and practitioners. The statistics on the submissions and accepted papers were:

- Research track: 172 papers submitted, with 38 of them accepted
- Empirical Studies and Experiments track: 23 papers submitted, with seven of them accepted
- In-Use and Software track: 33 papers submitted, with 14 of them accepted
- Data Sets and Ontologies track: 35 papers submitted, with eight of them accepted

All submitted papers were reviewed by at least three Program Committee (PC) members. In the case of the research track, the review process for each paper was also overviewed by a senior PC member, whose job was to drive discussions among reviewers when their points of view diverged, to make sure that clear questions were sent to the authors so as to give them the opportunity to reply to reviewers during the rebuttal period, and to provide a final meta-review with a summary of the strongest and weakest aspects of each of the papers. Finally, the acceptance and rejection of papers were decided via phone conferences between PC chairs and senior PC members that lasted two consecutive days.

This year's edition also had two additional innovations. On the one hand, we encouraged authors to include pointers to any additional material that supports the scientific claims made in their papers (e.g., extended technical reports, source code, datasets, links to applications). This proposal was received well among authors, who made an extra effort to make such additional material available for reviewers first, and if their paper was accepted, to make it available together with their camera-ready version of the paper. Such additional material has been uploaded into a variety of systems, including figshare, zenodo and institutional repositories of universities and research centers.

The second request introduced by PC chairs was the suggestion to reviewers to sign their reviews if they wished, following recent trends on open reviewing, so as to pave the way for having a more transparent review process for our conference. The number of signed reviews was still very low, which suggests that there is a need to continue discussions on whether this open review model is applicable for a conference like ISWC or should be left to journals, which have a longer review process.

ISWC 2015 also included a Doctoral Consortium track for PhD students from the Semantic Web community, giving them the opportunity not only to present their work but also to discuss in detail their research topics and plans and to receive extensive feedback from leading scientists in the field. The Doctoral Consortium was very efficiently run by Fabio Ciravegna and María-Esther Vidal.

Another unique aspect of the International Semantic Web Conferences is the Semantic Web Challenge. In this competition, practitioners and scientists are encouraged to showcase useful and leading-edge applications of Semantic Web technology. This year the Semantic Web Challenge was organized by Sean Bechhofer and Kostis Kyzirakos. It consisted of two main tracks, the Open track, focused on end-user applications, and the Big Data track, which follows on the success of the Billion Triple Data track from previous editions.

The ISWC program was further enriched by keynote talks given by leading figures from both the academic and business world. Specifically, Michael Atkin, Andrew McCallum, and Ian Horrocks.

As in previous ISWC editions, the conference program also included an extensive Tutorial and Workshop Program, with eight tutorials and 24 workshops, which were co-ordinated by Miriam Fernández and Krzysztof Janowicz.

We would like to thank Jeff Z. Pan and Serena Villata for chairing an excellent Poster and Demo Session, and Vinay Chaudhri and Tony Shaw for co-ordinating the Industry Track, a forum for the latest discussions and demonstrations of semantic applications in the commercial world. The Industry Track serves as a complement to the In-Use and Software Track and shows just how far semantics are expanding through the enterprise.

The conference also included a Lightning Talk session, where ISWC attendees could at very short notice get five minutes of attention from the audience, to report on anything they have done, plan to do, like or dislike about the Semantic Web.

We are also much indebted to Krishnaprasad Thirunarayan, our proceedings chair, who provided invaluable support in compiling the printed proceedings and exhibited super-human patience in allowing the other chairs to stretch deadlines to the absolute limit. Many thanks also to Matthew Horridge and Nadeschda Nikitina, our student coordinators, and to Juan Sequeda, our publicity chair.

As has been the case for the past few years, ISWC 2015 also contributed to the linked data cloud, by providing semantically characterized data on aspects of the conference. This would not have been possible without the efforts of our metadata chair, Heiko Paulheim.

We would like to give a special thank you to the local organization chair, Jeff Heflin and his team, who did a brilliant job in taking care of the local arrangements and ensuring that anything the Organizing Committee needed was promptly made available. We would also like to thank the generous contribution from our sponsors and the fine work of the sponsorship chairs, Michelle Cheatham and Carlos Pedrinaci. Finally, we are indebted to Andrei Voronkov and his team for providing the sophisticated and convenient service of EasyChair and to Alfred Hofmann, Anna Kramer, and their team at Springer for being most helpful with publishing the proceedings.

October 2015

Marcelo Arenas
Oscar Corcho
Elena Simperl
Markus Strohmaier
Mathieu d'Aquin
Kavitha Srinivas
Michel Dumontier
Paul Groth
Steffen Staab

Conference Organization

General Chair

Steffen Staab   Universität Koblenz-Landau, Germany

Local Chair

Jeff Heflin   Lehigh University, USA

Research Track Chairs

Marcelo Arenas   Pontificia Universidad Católica de Chile, Chile
Oscar Corcho   Universidad Politécnica de Madrid, Spain

Empirical Studies and Experiments Track Chairs

Elena Simperl   University of Southampton, UK
Markus Strohmaier   Universität Koblenz-Landau, Germany

In-Use and Software Track Chairs

Mathieu d'Aquin   The Open University, UK
Kavitha Srinivas   IBM T.J. Watson Research Center, USA

Data Sets and Ontologies Chairs

Michel Dumontier   Stanford University, USA
Paul Groth   Elsevier Labs, The Netherlands

Industry Track Chairs

Vinay Chaudhri   SRI International, USA
Tony Shaw   Dataversity, USA

Workshop and Tutorial Chairs

Miriam Fernandez   The Open University, UK
Krzysztof Janowicz   University of California, Santa Barbara, USA

Demos and Posters Chairs

Jeff Z. Pan   University of Aberdeen, UK
Serena Villata   Inria, France

Doctoral Consortium Chairs

Fabio Ciravegna   University of Sheffield, UK
María-Esther Vidal   Universidad Simón Bolívar, Venezuela

Proceedings Chair

Krishnaprasad Thirunarayan   Wright State University, USA

Semantic Web Challenge Chairs

Sean Bechhofer   University of Manchester, UK
Kostis Kyzirakos   Centrum Wiskunde and Informatica, The Netherlands

Sponsorship Chairs

Michelle Cheatham   Wright State University, USA
Carlos Pedrinaci   The Open University, UK

Metadata Chair

Heiko Paulheim   University of Mannheim, Germany

Publicity Chair

Juan Sequeda   Capsenta Labs, USA

Assistant to General Chair

Ulrich Wechselberger   Universität Koblenz-Landau, Germany

Student Coordinators

Matthew Horridge   Stanford University, USA
Nadeschda Nikitina   University of Oxford, UK

Senior Program Committee: Research Track

Harith Alani   KMI, The Open University, UK
Lora Aroyo   VU University, The Netherlands

Sören Auer	University of Bonn, Germany
Philipp Cimiano	Bielefeld University, Germany
Philippe Cudré-Mauroux	University of Fribourg, Switzerland
Birte Glimm	University of Ulm, Germany
Lalana Kagal	MIT, USA
Spyros Kotoulas	IBM, Ireland
David Martin	Nuance Communications, USA
Axel-Cyrille Ngonga	Universität Leipzig, Germany
Natasha Noy	Google, USA
Jeff Z. Pan	The University of Aberdeen, UK
Axel Polleres	Vienna University of Economics and Business, Austria
Marta Sabou	KMI, The Open University, UK
Uli Sattler	University of Manchester, UK
Juan F. Sequeda	Capsenta Labs, USA
Tania Tudorache	Stanford University, USA
Antoine Zimmermann	Ecole des Mines de Saint Etienne, France

Program Committee: Research Track

Faisal Alkhateeb	Yarmouk University, Jordan
Pramod Anantharam	Kno.e.sis Center, Wright State University, USA
Kemafor Anyanwu	North Carolina State University, USA
Medha Atre	University of Pennsylvania, USA
Isabelle Augenstein	The University of Sheffield, UK
Nathalie Aussenac-Gilles	IRIT CNRS, France
Payam Barnaghi	University of Surrey, UK
Andrew Bate	University of Oxford, UK
Christian Bizer	University of Mannheim, Germany
Roi Blanco	Yahoo! Research, Spain
Eva Blomqvist	Linköping University, Sweden
Kalina Bontcheva	University of Sheffield, UK
Paolo Bouquet	University of Trento, Italy
Loris Bozzato	Fondazione Bruno Kessler, Italy
Adrian M.P. Brasoveanu	MODUL University Vienna, Austria
Carlos Buil Aranda	Pontificia Universidad Católica de Chile, Chile
Paul Buitelaar	Insight - National University of Ireland, Galway, Ireland
Gregoire Burel	The Open University, UK
Jean-Paul Calbimonte	EPFL, Switzerland
Diego Calvanese	KRDB Research Centre, Free University of Bozen-Bolzano, Italy
Amparo E. Cano	Knowledge Media Institute, The Open University, UK
Iván Cantador	Universidad Autónoma de Madrid, Spain
Irene Celino	CEFRIEL, Italy
Pierre-Antoine Champin	LIRIS, France
Gong Cheng	Nanjing University, China

Geert-Jan Houben	TU Delft, The Netherlands
Julia Hoxha	Institute of Applied Informatics and Formal Description Methods, Karlsruhe Institute of Technology, Germany
Bo Hu	Fujitsu Laboratories of Europe, UK
Wei Hu	Nanjing University, China
Eero Hyvönen	Aalto University, Finland
Ali Intizar	National University of Ireland, Ireland
Krzysztof Janowicz	University of California, Santa Barbara, USA
Mustafa Jarrar	Birzeit University, Palestine
Ernesto Jimenez-Ruiz	University of Oxford, UK
Hanmin Jung	KISTI, South Korea
Jaap Kamps	University of Amsterdam, The Netherlands
C. Maria Keet	University of Cape Town, South Africa
Matthias Klusch	DFKI, Germany
Jacek Kopecky	University of Portsmouth, UK
Manolis Koubarakis	National and Kapodistrian University of Athens, Greece
Markus Krötzsch	Technische Universität Dresden, Germany
Werner Kuhn	UCSB, USA
Agnieszka Lawrynowicz	Poznan University of Technology, Poland
Freddy Lecue	IBM Research, USA
Chengkai Li	University of Texas at Arlington, USA
Lei Li	Florida International University, USA
Nuno Lopes	IBM Research, Smarter Cities Technology Centre, Dublin, Ireland
Vanessa Lopez	IBM Research, Ireland
David Martin	Nuance Communications, USA
Diana Maynard	University of Sheffield, UK
Robert Meusel	University of Mannheim, Germany
Nandana Mihindukulasooriya	Universidad Politécnica de Madrid, Spain
Alessandra Mileo	National University of Ireland, Galway, INSIGHT Centre for Data Analytics, Ireland
Iris Miliaraki	Yahoo Labs, Spain
Riichiro Mizoguchi	Japan Advanced Institute of Science and Technology, Japan
Dunja Mladenic	Jozef Stefan Institute, Slovenia
Boris Motik	University of Oxford, UK
Enrico Motta	Knowledge Media Institute, The Open University, UK
Ekawit Nantajeewarawat	Sirindhorn International Institute of Technology, Thammasat University, Thailand
Nadeschda Nikitina	Oxford University, UK
Andriy Nikolov	fluid Operations AG, Germany
Lyndon Nixon	MODUL University, Austria
Jeff Z. Pan	The University of Aberdeen, UK

Bijan Parsia	University of Manchester, UK
Terry Payne	University of Liverpool, UK
Carlos Pedrinaci	The Open University, UK
Sujan Perera	Kno.e.sis Center, Wright State University, USA
Silvio Peroni	University of Bologna and ISTC-CNR, Italy
Robert Piro	University of Oxford, UK
Dimitris Plexousakis	Institute of Computer Science, FORTH, Greece
Valentina Presutti	STLab (ISTC-CNR), Italy
Freddy Priyatna	Universidad Politécnica de Madrid, Spain
Jorge Pérez	Universidad de Chile, Chile
Guilin Qi	Southeast University, China
Yves Raimond	BBC, UK
Ganesh Ramakrishnan	IIT Bombay, India
Maya Ramanath	IIT Delhi, India
Chantal Reynaud	LRI, Université Paris-Sud, France
Mariano Rico	Universidad Politécnica de Madrid, Spain
Giuseppe Rizzo	EURECOM, France
Marco Rospocher	Fondazione Bruno Kessler, Italy
Matthew Rowe	Lancaster University, UK
Sebastian Rudolph	Technische Universität Dresden, Germany
Harald Sack	Hasso Plattner Institute for IT Systems Engineering, University of Potsdam, Germany
Hassan Saif	The Open University - Knowledge Media Institute, UK
Francois Scharffe	LIRMM, University of Montpellier, France
Ansgar Scherp	Kiel University and Leibniz Information Center for Economics, Kiel, Germany
Stefan Schlobach	Vrije Universiteit Amsterdam, The Netherlands
Daniel Schwabe	Pontifical Catholic University of Rio de Janeiro, Brazil
Monika Solanki	Aston Business School, Aston University, UK
Dezhao Song	Thomson Reuters, USA
Milan Stankovic	Sépage and STIH, Université Paris-Sorbonne, France
Markus Strohmaier	University of Koblenz-Landau, Germany
Rudi Studer	Karlsruher Institut für Technologie (KIT), Germany
Gerd Stumme	University of Kassel, Germany
Vojĕtch Svátek	University of Economics, Prague, Czech Republic
Valentina Tamma	Science, University of Liverpool, UK
Kerry Taylor	CSIRO and Australian National University, Australia
Matthias Thimm	Universität Koblenz-Landau, Germany
Krishnaprasad Thirunarayan	Kno.e.sis Center, Wright State University, USA
Ioan Toma	STI Innsbruck, Austria
Raphaël Troncy	EURECOM, France
Anni-Yasmin Turhan	TU Dresden, Germany
Jacopo Urbani	Vrije Universiteit Amsterdam, The Netherlands
Jacco van Ossenbruggen	CWI and VU University Amsterdam, The Netherlands
María-Esther Vidal	Universidad Simon Bolivar, Venezuela
Daniel Vila Suero	Universidad Politécnica de Madrid, Spain

Haofen Wang	East China University of Science and Technology, China
Kewen Wang	Griffith University, USA
Zhichun Wang	Beijing Normal University, China
Fouad Zablith	American University of Beirut, Lebanon
Qingpeng Zhang	Rensselaer Polytechnic Institute, USA

Additional Reviewers

Aggarwal, Nitish
Angles, Renzo
Banda, Fredah
Bedathur, Srikanta
Beek, Wouter
Bertossi, Leopoldo
Bortoli, Stefano
Braghin, Stefano
Buil Aranda, Carlos
Butt, Anila Sahar
Carral, David
Catasta, Michele
Chekol,
    Melisachew Wudage
Chen, Lu
Cheng, Long
David, Jérôme
Davis, Brian
Denaux, Ronald
Doerfel, Stephan
Dou, Dejing
Dragisic, Zlatan
Ecke, Andreas
Ell, Basil
Flouris, Giorgos
Fundulaki, Irini
Färber, Michael
Gillani, Syed
Guéret, Christophe
Hammar, Karl
Hentschel, Christian
Huan, Gao
Jayaram, Nandish
Jimenez-Ruiz, Ernesto

Joshi, Amit
Kaminski, Mark
Kapahnke, Patrick
Keskisärkkä, Robin
Kim, Eunkyung
Kirrane, Sabrina
Knuth, Magnus
Kondylakis, Haridimos
Kosmerlj, Aljaz
Kämpgen, Benedikt
Lalithsena, Sarasi
Lefort, Laurent
Loebe, Frank
Lu, Chun
Martinez-Prieto,
    Miguel A.
Masopust, Tomas
Mazzola, Luca
Meroño-Peñuela, Albert
Meusel, Robert
Mirrezaei, Iman
Mongiovì, Misael
Nenov, Yavor
Niebler, Thomas
Novalija, Inna
Nuzzolese,
    Andrea Giovanni
Palmonari, Matteo
Piro, Robert
Porrini, Riccardo
Potoniec, Jedrzej
Ratcliffe, David
Ravindra, Padmashree
Reddy, Dinesh

Rei, Luis
Rezk, Martin
Ritze, Dominique
Rizzo, Giuseppe
Sanchez Ayte, Adam
Savenkov, Vadim
Schalk, Andrea
Schlobach, Stefan
Schmidt, Andreas
Sengupta, Kunal
Shekarpour, Saeedeh
Solimando, Alessandro
Steyskal, Simon
Taheri, Aynaz
Tamma, Valentina
Tiddi, Ilaria
Todorov, Konstantin
Tommasi, Pierpaolo
Tonon, Alberto
Tran, Trung-Kien
Tzitzikas, Yannis
Unbehauen, Joerg
Vrgoc, Domagoj
Wang, Cong
Wang, Wenbo
Wang, Zhe
Wu, Jiewen
Wu, Tianxing
Xiao, Guohui
Zappa, Achille
Zhang, Gensheng
Zhang, Xiaowang
Zheleznyakov, Dmitriy
Zhuang, Zhiqiang

Sponsors

Platinum Sponsors

Elsevier

Gold Sponsors

Fujitsu
Google
iMinds
Ontotext
Systap
Yahoo! Labs

Silver Sponsors

Franz Inc.

Contents – Part I

Research Task

Querying with SPARQL

Querying Linked Data

Linked Data

Instance Matching, Entity Resolution and Topic Generation

RDF Data Dynamics

Ontology Extraction and Generation

Knowledge Graphs and Scientific Data Publication

Contents – Part II

In-Use and Software Track

SPARQL and Querying Linked Data

Linked Data

Ontology-Based Data Access

Ontology and Instance Alignment

Knowledge Graphs

Data Processing, IoT, Sensors

Data Sets and Ontologies Track

Empirical Studies and Experiments Track

Experiments

Evaluation

Empirical Studies

Querying with SPARQL

SPARQL with Property Paths

Egor V. Kostylev[1], Juan L. Reutter[2], Miguel Romero[3],
and Domagoj Vrgoč[2]($\boxtimes$)

[1] University of Oxford, Oxford, UK
egor.kostylev@cs.ox.ac.uk
[2] PUC Chile and Center for Semantic Web Research, Santiago, Chile
{jreutter,dvrgoc}@ing.puc.cl
[3] University of Chile and Center for Semantic Web Research, Santiago, Chile
mromero@dcc.uchile.cl

Abstract. The original SPARQL proposal was often criticized for its inability to navigate through the structure of RDF documents. For this reason property paths were introduced in SPARQL 1.1, but up to date there are no theoretical studies examining how their addition to the language affects main computational tasks such as query evaluation, query containment, and query subsumption. In this paper we tackle all of these problems and show that although the addition of property paths has no impact on query evaluation, they do make the containment and subsumption problems substantially more difficult.

1 Introduction

Following the initial proposal for the SPARQL 1.0 query language [22] a lot of work been done by the theory community to study its basic properties. A seminal paper by Pérez et al. [16] gave us a clean theoretical foundation for the study of the language, and by now we understand very well the complexity of query evaluation [12,17], as well as the issues related to basic static analysis tasks such as containment and equivalence [12,20,21].

However, with the growth of RDF data available on the Web, also came the need for features not present in the original proposal. One such feature should allow to navigate though RDF documents and discover how different resourses are connected. This becomes apparent when considering applications such as linked data where the local topology of the document often does not provide sufficient information, and long chains have to be followed to obtain the desired answer. For this reason the W3C included *property paths* in the specification of SPARQL 1.1 [10], an extension of the original language with several important features.

Intuitively, a property path searches through the RDF graph for a sequence of IRIs that form a path conforming to an regular expression. For example, to infer that one property is a subclass of another we could ask a query $(?x, \text{subclass}^*, ?y)$ and check if our pair is in the answer. Here the property path is given by the regular expression subclass^*, which specifies that we can traverse an arbitrary number of subclass property links in order to reach $?y$ from $?x$.

© Springer International Publishing Switzerland 2015
M. Arenas et al. (Eds.): ISWC 2015, Part I, LNCS 9366, pp. 3–18, 2015.
DOI: 10.1007/978-3-319-25007-6_1

Although some work has been done on SPARQL with different forms of navigation [1–3, 8, 9, 14, 18, 24], little is known about the language that has property paths as specified in the latest standard [10]. Therefore, our goal is to study theoretical aspects of SPARQL with this functionality. In particular, in this paper we focus on the fundamental problems of query evaluation, containment, and subsumption. The first one is key for understanding the properties of any query language, while the other two are of fundamental importance in query optimization, ontological reasoning, and managing incomplete information.

So far, these problems have been studied for fragments of SPARQL that allow only basic operators such as AND, UNION, SELECT, and OPTIONAL (abbreviated as OPT in this paper) [9, 12, 20]. It is therefore interesting to see how property paths mix with the previous results on core SPARQL. A natural approach here would be to use techniques from the field of graph databases. After all, RDF triples closely resemble edges in a labelled graph, and property paths are similar to *regular path queries* [5]. However, we will show that this cannot be done directly, as not only RDF data model is richer than usual graphs [13], but also the SPARQL 1.1 standard allows for negation in property paths, which is known to make things more difficult [11, 15]. Another challenge is the presence of the OPT operator (which is not usually included in graph database query languages) and the way it interacts with property paths. We will show that techniques for SPARQL without property paths [12, 20] cannot be straightforwardly adapted to deal with the general language. To this end, we develop new techniques that merge the approaches of [5, 20] and use them to obtain matching complexity bounds for the considered problems.

We begin in Section 3 with a formalisation of property paths according to the latest specification [10]. We also pinpoint the differences between the resulting language and known formalisms, and discuss the difficulties they impose on possible adaptations of known techniques for solving the considered problems. Then, in Section 4, we study evaluation, containment, and subsumption for SPARQL with property paths that do not allow for optional matching. In particular, using techniques from automata theory we show that in this case property paths do not increase the complexity of evaluation, but have a significant effect on containment and subsumption. Finally, in Section 5 we study the full language, with both property paths and optional matching. Blending standard SPARQL and graph databases techniques we can show that adding OPT usually makes evaluation more difficult, but almost always leaves the complexity of the optimisation problems intact.

2 Preliminaries

RDF Graphs. Let **I**, **L**, and **B** be countably infinite disjoint sets of *IRIs*, *literals*, and *blank nodes*, respectively. The set of *RDF terms* **T** is $\mathbf{I} \cup \mathbf{L} \cup \mathbf{B}$. An *RDF triple* is a triple (s, p, o) from $\mathbf{T} \times \mathbf{I} \times \mathbf{T}$, where s is called *subject*, p *predicate*, and o *object*. An *(RDF) graph* is a finite set of RDF triples.

SPARQL Syntax. SPARQL is the standard pattern-matching language for querying RDF graphs. In what follows we build on the formalisation of the language proposed in [17]; in particular, we consider two-placed OPT and adopt set semantics of queries, leaving three-placed optional and the multiplicities of the answers as defined in the standard for future work. For now we also concentrate on the core fragment and introduce property paths in a separate section.

Formally, let $\mathbf{V}$ be an infinite set $\{?x, ?y, \ldots\}$ of *variables*, disjoint from $\mathbf{T}$. SPARQL *(graph) patterns* are defined recursively as follows:

1. a triple in $(\mathbf{I} \cup \mathbf{L} \cup \mathbf{V}) \times (\mathbf{I} \cup \mathbf{V}) \times (\mathbf{I} \cup \mathbf{L} \cup \mathbf{V})$ is a pattern, called *triple pattern*;
2. if P_1 and P_2 are patterns, then P_1 AND P_2, P_1 OPT P_2, and P_1 UNION P_2 are patterns, called AND-, OPT-, and UNION-*patterns*, respectively.

The set of all variables appearing in a pattern P is denoted by $\mathsf{var}(P)$.

In this paper we do not consider FILTER operator, leaving it for future work. It is also known that arbitrary graph patterns (even without FILTER) may have counter-intuitive behaviour and bad computational properties [17]. That is why we concentrate on a restricted class of graph patterns, which is widely used, has expected behaviour and better computational properties [17,20]—namely, well designed patterns [17,19]. Formally, a graph pattern P is *well designed* if it is UNION-free and each of its OPT-subpatterns P_1 OPT P_2 is such that all the variables in $\mathsf{var}(P_2)$ appearing in P outside this subpattern are also in $\mathsf{var}(P_1)$.

The class of well designed patterns, denoted $\mathcal{AO}$-SPARQL, is the main class for this paper. However, we also consider its restrictions and extensions. In particular, the subclass of $\mathcal{AO}$-SPARQL that allows only for AND-subpatterns is denoted $\mathcal{A}$-SPARQL. It corresponds to conjunctive queries without non-distinguished (existential) variables. These classes extend with UNION operator on the top level to $\mathcal{AOU}$-SPARQL and $\mathcal{AU}$-SPARQL: for example, the patterns in the former have the form P_1 UNION $\ldots$ UNION P_ℓ where all the P_i are in $\mathcal{AO}$-SPARQL.

Finally, we also consider the SELECT operator which acts as a result modifier of a graph pattern. In particular, SELECT *queries* are expressions of the form

$$\text{SELECT } X \text{ WHERE } P,$$

with P a graph pattern and *distinguished (projection) variables* X a subset of $\mathsf{var}(P)$. A class of SELECT queries with patterns from a class introduced above is denoted by adding $\mathcal{S}$ to the prefix; for example, $\mathcal{AOS}$-SPARQL stands for SELECT queries with well designed patterns. Note that patterns can be seen as queries with all the variables distinguished, so we use "query" as a general term.

SPARQL Semantics. The semantics of graph patterns is defined in terms of *mappings*, that is, partial functions from variables $\mathbf{V}$ to RDF terms $\mathbf{T}$. The *domain* $\mathsf{dom}(\mu)$ of a mapping μ is the set of variables on which μ is defined. Two mappings μ_1 and μ_2 are *compatible* (written as $\mu_1 \sim \mu_2$) if $\mu_1(?x) = \mu_2(?x)$ for all variables $?x$ that are in both $\mathsf{dom}(\mu_1)$ and $\mathsf{dom}(\mu_2)$. If $\mu_1 \sim \mu_2$, then $\mu_1 \cup \mu_2$ denotes the mapping obtained by extending μ_1 according to μ_2 on all the variables in $\mathsf{dom}(\mu_2) \setminus \mathsf{dom}(\mu_1)$.

Given two sets of mappings M_1 and M_2, the *join*, *union*, and *difference* of M_1 and M_2 are defined respectively as follows:

$M_1 \bowtie M_2 = \{\mu_1 \cup \mu_2 \mid \mu_1 \in M_1, \mu_2 \in M_2, \text{ and } \mu_1 \sim \mu_2\},$
$M_1 \cup M_2 = \{\mu \mid \mu \in M_1 \text{ or } \mu \in M_2\},$
$M_1 \setminus M_2 = \{\mu_1 \mid \mu_1 \in M_1 \text{ and there is no } \mu_2 \in M_2 \text{ such that } \mu_1 \sim \mu_2\}.$

Based on this, the *left outer join* of M_1 and M_2 is defined as

$$M_1 \ {\supset\!\!\!\bowtie}\ M_2 = (M_1 \bowtie M_2) \cup (M_1 \setminus M_2).$$

For a triple pattern P and a mapping μ we write $\mu(P)$ for the triple obtained from P by replacing each variable $?x \in \mathsf{dom}(\mu)$ by $\mu(?x)$. The *evaluation* $[\![P]\!]_G$ of a graph pattern P over a graph G is defined as follows:

1. if P is a triple pattern, then $[\![P]\!]_G = \{\mu : \mathsf{var}(P) \to \mathbf{T} \mid \mu(P) \in G\}$,
2. if $P = P_1$ AND P_2, then $[\![P]\!]_G = [\![P_1]\!]_G \bowtie [\![P_2]\!]_G$,
3. if $P = P_1$ OPT P_2, then $[\![P]\!]_G = [\![P_1]\!]_G \ {\supset\!\!\!\bowtie}\ [\![P_2]\!]_G$,
4. if $P = P_1$ UNION P_2, then $[\![P]\!]_G = [\![P_1]\!]_G \cup [\![P_2]\!]_G$.

Finally, the *evaluation* $[\![Q]\!]_G$ of a query Q of the form SELECT X WHERE P is the set of all projections $\mu|_X$ of mappings μ from $[\![P]\!]_G$ to X, where the *projection* of μ to X is the mapping that coincides with μ on X and undefined elsewhere.

3   Property Paths in SPARQL

Property paths are a new feature introduced in SPARQL 1.1 [10] to allow for navigational querying over RDF graphs. Intuitively, a property path views an RDF document as a labelled graph where the predicate IRI in each triple acts as an edge label. It then extracts each pair of nodes connected by a path such that the word formed by the edge labels along this path belongs to the language of the expression specifying the property path. Property paths resemble regular path queries studied in graph databases [4], but these formalisms have important differences both in syntax and semantics. In this section we define the new SPARQL operator according to the specification and compare the resulting extension with known query languages.

3.1   Property Path Expressions

We start with the definition of property path expressions, following the SPARQL 1.1 specification [10]. We use adopted syntax in spirit of graph database languages, but note that the standard sometimes uses different symbols for operators; for example, inverse paths e^- and alternative paths $e_1 + e_2$ from our definition are denoted there by $\hat{}\,e$ and $e_1 \mid e_2$, respectively.

Definition 1. Property path expressions *are defined by the grammar*

$$e ::= a \mid e^- \mid e_1 \cdot e_2 \mid e_1 + e_2 \mid e^+ \mid e^* \mid e? \mid !\{a_1, \ldots, a_k\} \mid !\{a_1^-, \ldots, a_k^-\},$$

where $a, a_1, \ldots, a_k$ *are IRIs in* $\mathbf{I}$. *Expressions of the last two forms (i.e., starting with* !*) are called* negated property sets.

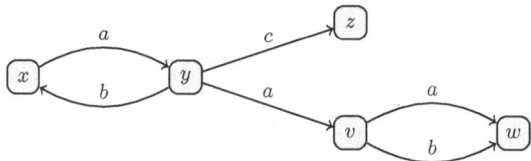

Fig. 1. Example RDF graph G

When dealing with singleton negated property sets brackets may be omitted: for example, $!a$ is a shortcut for $!\{a\}$. Besides the forms in Definition 1 the SPARQL 1.1 specification includes a third version of the negated property sets $!\{a_1, \ldots, a_k, b_1^-, \ldots, b_\ell^-\}$, which allows for negating both normal and inverted IRIs at the same time. We however do not include this extra form in our formalisation, since it is equivalent to the expression $!\{a_1, \ldots, a_k\} + !\{b_1^-, \ldots, b_\ell^-\}$.

The set of all property path expressions is denoted by **PP**. Their normative semantics is given in the following definition.

Definition 2. *The evaluation $[\![e]\!]_G$ of a property path expression e over an RDF graph G is a set of pairs of RDF terms from* **T** *defined as follows:*

$$
\begin{aligned}
[\![a]\!]_G &= \{(s,o) \mid (s,a,o) \in G\}, \\
[\![e^-]\!]_G &= \{(s,o) \mid (o,s) \in [\![e]\!]_G\}, \\
[\![e_1 \cdot e_2]\!]_G &= [\![e_1]\!]_G \circ [\![e_2]\!]_G, \\
[\![e_1 + e_2]\!]_G &= [\![e_1]\!]_G \cup [\![e_2]\!]_G, \\
[\![e^+]\!]_G &= \bigcup_{i \geq 1} [\![e^i]\!]_G, \\
[\![e^*]\!]_G &= [\![e^+]\!]_G \cup \{(a,a) \mid a \text{ is a term in } G\}, \\
[\![e?]\!]_G &= [\![e]\!]_G \cup \{(a,a) \mid a \text{ is a term in } G\}, \\
[\![!\{a_1, \ldots, a_k\}]\!]_G &= \{(s,o) \mid \exists a \text{ with } (s,a,o) \in G \text{ and } a \notin \{a_1, \ldots, a_k\}\}, \\
[\![!\{a_1^-, \ldots, a_k^-\}]\!]_G &= \{(s,o) \mid (o,s) \in [\![!\{a_1, \ldots, a_k\}]\!]_G\},
\end{aligned}
$$

where $\circ$ is the usual composition of binary relations, and e^i is the concatenation $e \cdot \ldots \cdot e$ of i copies of e.

Intuitively, two IRIs are connected by a negated property set if they are subject and object of a triple in the graph whose predicate is not mentioned in the set under negation. Note that, according to Definition 2, the expression $!\{a_1^-, \ldots, a_k^-\}$ retrieves the inverse of $!\{a_1, \ldots, a_k\}$, and thus it respects the direction: a negated inverted **IRI** returns all pairs of nodes connected by some other inverted IRI. To exemplify, consider the RDF graph G from Figure 1. We have that $[\![!a]\!]_G = \{(y,x),(y,z),(v,w)\}$ as we can find a forward looking predicate different from a for any of these pairs. Note that there is an a-labelled edge between v and w, but since there is also a b-labelled one, the pair (v,w) is in the answer. On the other hand, $[\![!a^-]\!]_G = \{(x,y),(z,y),(w,v)\}$, because we can traverse a backward looking predicate (either b^- or c^-) between these pairs.

Note that $!\{a_1, \ldots, a_k\}$ is not equivalent to $!a_1 + \ldots + !a_k$. To see this consider again the graph G from Figure 1. We have $[\![!a]\!]_G = \{(y,x),(y,z),(v,w)\}$ and $[\![!b]\!]_G = \{(x,y),(y,z),(y,v),(v,w)\}$, while $[\![!\{a,b\}]\!]_G = \{(y,z)\}$.

Property path expressions resemble navigational query languages for graph databases. Indeed, syntactically, property paths without negated property sets are nothing more than the well studied *2-way regular path queries (2RPQs)* [5], the default core navigational language for graph databases, with the only minor exception that the empty 2RPQ ε is not expressible as a property path expression (see [4] for a good survey on graph database query languages). However, negated property sets are a unique feature which has not been properly studied before in the SPARQL literature, as far as we are aware (safe [24], where nSPARQL⁻ language is introduced, which provides much more expressive navigational facilities than property paths, but no evaluation or optimisation bounds are given, and [1,2], where PSPARQL is studied, whose navigational operator is incomparable with property paths). Note that if we were working with graph databases, where predicates come from a finite alphabet Σ, then one could easily replace $!a$ with a disjunction of all other symbols in Σ. But since we are dealing with RDF graphs, which have predicates from the infinite set of IRIs **I**, we cannot treat this feature in such a naive way. Nevertheless, we can still show that deciding whether a pair of IRIs belongs to the evaluation of a property path expression e over an RDF graph G is as easy as computing the answers of 2RPQs—the problem is in low polynomial time. The idea of the algorithm is in the same spirit as the ideas of standard algorithms for evaluation of 2RPQs [4,7] and their extensions [1,2,18]: we construct from G and e two nondeterministic finite automata A_e and A_G of special type that can account for negated property sets, and then check that the cross product of these two automata is nonempty.

Proposition 1. *For every property path e and RDF graph G the problem of deciding whether a pair (a, b) of terms belongs to $[\![e]\!]_G$ can be solved in time $O(|G| \cdot |e|)$.*

3.2 Queries with Property Paths

SPARQL 1.1 incorporates property path expressions on the atomic level by means of triples with RDF terms or variables on the subject and object positions, but property path expressions on the predicate position. Formally, we have the following definition.

Definition 3. *A* property path pattern *is a triple in* $(\mathbf{I} \cup \mathbf{L} \cup \mathbf{V}) \times \mathbf{PP} \times (\mathbf{I} \cup \mathbf{L} \cup \mathbf{V})$.

Note, however, that property path patterns are incomparable with triple patterns, because they allow for property path expressions in predicate positions, but forbid variables in these positions. We use the notion of *atomic patterns* as a general term for triple and property path patterns.

The classes of queries introduced in Section 2 incorporate navigational functionality by allowing arbitrary atomic patterns as graph patterns, along with complex operator patterns. In our notation this is reflected by letter $\mathcal{P}$ in names of the classes. For example $\mathcal{AOUSP}$-SPARQL is the maximal language considered in this paper, which allows for AND, OPT, UNION, SELECT operators and arbitrary atomic patterns. Remember, however, that all the patterns we consider are (unions of) well designed patterns, assuming that for fragments with property paths this notion stays exactly the same as in Section 2.

To complete the formalization of SPARQL with property paths we need to define the semantics.

Definition 4. *For a property path pattern $P = (u, e, v)$ and an RDF graph G the evaluation $[\![P]\!]_G$ of P over G is the set of mappings*

$$\{\mu : \mathsf{var}(P) \to \mathbf{T} \mid (\mu(u), \mu(v)) \in [\![e]\!]_G\},$$

assuming that mappings μ extends to terms t from $\mathbf{T}$ as identity, that is, $\mu(t) = t$.

Having this definition at hand, the semantics of graph patterns and queries with property paths is exactly the same as in Section 2.

Since property paths resemble 2RPQs, SPARQL with property paths has a lot in common with other graph database languages, such as *conjunctive 2RPQs* (*C2RPQs*), which extend 2RPQs with conjunction and existential quantification, and *unions of C2RPQs* (*UC2RPQs*), further extending 2RPQs with union on the top level (see again [4]). However, there are some important differences.

First, SPARQL with property paths allows for both property path patterns and triple patterns, which may have a variable in the middle position. This is not possible in (U)C2RPQs.

Second, the UNION operator in SPARQL behaves differently from union in classical databases and UC2RPQs. In particular, it is *not null-rejecting*, that is, the patterns constituting a union may have different sets of variables, and, hence, the mappings in the evaluation may have different domains, even if the query is OPT-free.

The third and most important difference is the presence of optional matching in SPARQL. This unique SPARQL feature requires complete rethinking of many standard results in database theory, and, as we will see, results on property paths are not an exception.

In the rest of the paper we study properties of the SPARQL classes with property paths. It is convenient to start in the next section with classes without OPT and then continue in Section 5 with the ones incorporating this operator.

4 Properties of Classes without Optional Matching

The fundamental properties of query languages considered in this paper are complexity of query answering and optimisation problems, such as containment and subsumption. We begin the study of these properties with OPT-free classes of SPARQL with property paths.

4.1 Query Evaluation

We start with the most important fundamental problem for query languages—query evaluation. According to [23], this problem is formalised for any class $\mathcal{X}$-SPARQL defined in the previous sections as follows.

> EVALUATION($\mathcal{X}$-SPARQL)
> **Input:** An RDF graph G, $\mathcal{X}$-SPARQL query Q, and mapping μ.
> **Question:** Does μ belong to $[\![Q]\!]_G$?

As discussed above, the class $\mathcal{AUS}$-SPARQL without optional matching and property paths is just the class of unions of conjunctive queries, for which the evaluation problem is well known to be **NP**-complete. Without selection, that is, without non-distinguished variables, it is in **PTIME**. Based upon Proposition 1, we can show that adding property paths to OPT-free SPARQL does not affect the complexity of query evaluation, same as adding 2RPQs to conjunctive queries.

Proposition 2. *The following holds:*

- EVALUATION($\mathcal{X}$-SPARQL) *is* **NP**-*complete for* $\mathcal{X} \in \{\mathcal{ASP}, \mathcal{AUSP}\}$;
- EVALUATION($\mathcal{AUP}$-SPARQL) *is in* **PTIME**.

4.2   Query Containment

In this section we consider query containment for OPT-free SPARQL with property paths. This is one of the fundamental problems for static analysis of query languages [23], which asks whether all the answers of one query are among answers of another for any input RDF graph.

Formally, a query Q_1 is *contained* in a query Q_2, denoted by $Q_1 \subseteq Q_2$, if for every RDF graph G we have $[\![Q_1]\!]_G \subseteq [\![Q_2]\!]_G$. Then, the corresponding decision problem is defined as follows for classes of queries $\mathcal{X}_1$-SPARQL and $\mathcal{X}_2$-SPARQL.

> CONTAINMENT($\mathcal{X}_1$-SPARQL,$\mathcal{X}_2$-SPARQL)
> **Input:** Queries Q_1 from $\mathcal{X}_1$-SPARQL and Q_2 from $\mathcal{X}_2$-SPARQL.
> **Question:** Is $Q_1 \subseteq Q_2$?

It is known that containment of 2RPQs and C2RPQs without projection is **PSPACE**-complete [6], and **EXPSPACE**-complete if projection is allowed. Given the resemblance of 2RPQs and property paths, it is natural to ask whether the techniques of [6] and [5] can be reused in the context of SPARQL with property paths. It turns out that, to some extend, this is indeed the case, but the nature of triples in RDF graphs and the presence of negated property sets oblige us to rework most of their definitions, including the key one—"canonical database", in order to adapt them to the SPARQL scenario. The following examples illustrate the main challenges that arise and ideas how to overcome them.

Example 1. Consider $\mathcal{ASP}$-SPARQL queries

$$Q_1 = \mathsf{SELECT}\ ?x, ?y, ?z\ \mathsf{WHERE}\ (?x, !a, ?y)\ \mathsf{AND}\ (?x, !a, ?z),$$
$$Q_2 = \mathsf{SELECT}\ ?x, ?y, ?z\ \mathsf{WHERE}\ (?x, ?v, ?y)\ \mathsf{AND}\ (?x, ?v, ?z).$$

One can easily check that Q_1 is not contained in Q_2. However, a counterexample for this fact requires a graph in which images of $?x$ and $?y$ are connected by a different property than those of $?x$ and $?z$. It means that we cannot treat $!a$ just as a usual RDF term, but we need to allow each occurrence of a negated property set to be witnessed by a fresh term.

Example 2. Consider now $\mathcal{ASP}$-SPARQL queries

$$Q_3 = \mathsf{SELECT}\ ?x, ?y\ \mathsf{WHERE}\ (?x, ?v, ?y),$$
$$Q_4 = \mathsf{SELECT}\ ?x, ?y\ \mathsf{WHERE}\ (?x, !a, ?y).$$

Again, Q_3 is not contained in Q_4. This time, however, counterexamples are formed by triples of the form (b, a, c), for IRIs b and c. Thus, we cannot just construct a canonical graph by *freezing* every variable in the query on the left of the possible containment, because counterexamples may need to be formed by mapping some of these variables to negated IRIs from the query on the right.

Taking into account these ideas, we can rework the machinery in [5] so that the notion of canonical graphs is adapted to SPARQL queries with full property paths, including the limited negation. Then, using automata techniques, we can prove results similar to [5] for containment of OPT-free SPARQL with property paths—it is EXPSPACE-complete in general and PSPACE-complete if the right-hand side query is a pattern without projection.

Theorem 1. *The following holds:*

- CONTAINMENT($\mathcal{X}_1$-SPARQL,$\mathcal{X}_2$-SPARQL) *is* EXPSPACE-*complete for* $\mathcal{X}_1 \in \{\mathcal{AP}, \ldots, \mathcal{AUSP}\}$ *and* $\mathcal{X}_2 \in \{\mathcal{ASP}, \mathcal{AUSP}\}$;
- CONTAINMENT($\mathcal{X}_1$-SPARQL,$\mathcal{X}_2$-SPARQL) *is* PSPACE-*complete for* $\mathcal{X}_1 \in \{\mathcal{AP}, \ldots, \mathcal{AUSP}\}$ *and* $\mathcal{X}_2 \in \{\mathcal{AP}, \mathcal{AUP}\}$.

To conclude, we note that in the first case the space used depends exponentially only on the size of each of the union-free subpatterns and not on the number of these subpatterns. This property is crucial for the results of Section 5.3 (in particular, Theorem 3).

4.3   Query Subsumption

Query containment is a way of specifying that one query is more general than another, which is common across different query formalisms. However, the unique SPARQL feature is the ability to return partial answers, and Pérez et al. argued in [17] that it is more natural to compare SPARQL queries for subsumption, that is, to check whether for any answer to one query there is a more elaborate answer to the other one on any input RDF graph.

Formally, a mapping μ is *subsumed* by a mapping μ', denoted by $\mu \sqsubseteq \mu'$, if $\mathsf{dom}(\mu)$ is contained in $\mathsf{dom}(\mu')$ and $\mu \sim \mu'$. A query Q_1 is *subsumed* by a query Q_2 (written as $Q_1 \sqsubseteq Q_2$) if for every RDF graph G it holds that for each $\mu_1 \in [\![Q_1]\!]_G$ there exists $\mu_2 \in [\![Q_2]\!]_G$ such that $\mu_1 \sqsubseteq \mu_2$. The corresponding decision problem for classes of queries $\mathcal{X}_1$-SPARQL and $\mathcal{X}_2$-SPARQL is defined as follows.

SUBSUMPTION($\mathcal{X}_1$-SPARQL,$\mathcal{X}_2$-SPARQL)
   Input: Queries Q_1 from $\mathcal{X}_1$-SPARQL and Q_2 from $\mathcal{X}_2$-SPARQL.
   Question: Is $Q_1 \sqsubseteq Q_2$?

Although the notion of subsumption becomes more natural when dealing with the OPT operator, for completion we still study this problem for the case of OPT-free SPARQL queries with property paths. We also find it interesting that the complexity of subsumption ends up being higher than the complexity of containment for some of the classes.

Before stating the results on subsumption, we give some intuition behind them and compare subsumption with containment. For a query Q_1 from $\mathcal{ASP}$-SPARQL to be subsumed by a query Q_2 from the same class it is necessary that the set of distinguished variables of Q_1 is a subset of the distinguished variables of Q_2. Moreover, $Q_1 \sqsubseteq Q_2$ if and only if for every RDF graph G and mapping μ_1 in $[\![Q_1]\!]_G$ one can obtain μ_1 from some μ_2 in $[\![Q_2]\!]_G$ by projecting out the distinguished variables of Q_2 that are not distinguished in Q_1. The first obvious consequence of this observation is that in this case the subsumption problem for $\mathcal{ASP}$-SPARQL is not more difficult than the containment problem, because $Q_1 \sqsubseteq Q_2$ if and only if Q_1 is contained in SELECT X WHERE P_2, with X the set of output variables of Q_1 and P_2 the pattern of Q_2. However, rather surprisingly, the limited projection inherent to the subsumption problem is enough to make the problem EXPSPACE-hard even for patterns from $\mathcal{AP}$-SPARQL, which do not have non distinguished variables.

Proposition 3. *The problem* SUBSUMPTION($\mathcal{X}_1$-SPARQL,$\mathcal{X}_2$-SPARQL) *is* EXPSPACE-*complete for* $\mathcal{X}_1, \mathcal{X}_2 \in \{\mathcal{AP}, \ldots, \mathcal{AUSP}\}$.

5   Properties of Classes with Optional Matching

In this section we consider query evaluation, containment, and subsumption for SPARQL classes that allow for both the OPT operator and property paths. In addition to the difficulties from the previous section, such as negated property sets and non-null-rejecting union, we have to deal with mixture of optional matching and property paths. To overcome these difficulties we develop non-trivial compositions of the usual SPARQL and graph databases techniques, as well as invent new ones.

5.1   Query Evaluation

Complexity bounds for query evaluation of SPARQL classes with (well designed) optional matching that do not use property paths are by now well understood [12,17]. In particular, the problem is coNP-complete for graph patterns, that is, queries with all the variables distinguished, and jumps to Σ_2^p if arbitrary SELECT clauses are allowed. In this section we show that adding property paths to the set of allowed operators preserves these bounds. To this end, we develop a characterisation similar to the one in [12], by adapting the notions of OPT normal form and pattern trees to work with property path patterns.

A graph pattern P is in OPT *normal form* if no OPT operators appear in AND-subpatterns of P. It was shown in [17, Proposition4.11] that every well designed graph pattern without property path patterns can be transformed to an equivalent pattern in OPT normal form in polynomial time by means of a set of rewriting rules that "push" AND inside OPT (recall that well designed patterns have neither UNION nor SELECT clauses). It is straightforward to check that these rules are correctly applicable to graph patterns that allow for property paths, so in what follows we assume that all patterns are in OPT normal form (in particular, AND-patterns are just AND combinations of atomic patterns).

Each graph pattern P in OPT normal form can be intuitively represented as a *pattern tree* $Tree(P)$, that is, a rooted tree with nodes labelled by sets of atomic (i.e., triple and property path) patterns which is recursively constructed as follows:

- if P is an AND-pattern then $Tree(P)$ consists of a single node labelled with the set of all atomic patterns in this AND-pattern;
- if $P = P_1$ OPT P_2 then $Tree(P)$ is obtained from $Tree(P_1)$ and $Tree(P_2)$ by adding an edge form the root of the former to the root of the latter.

In other words, the labels of nodes in pattern trees correspond to conjunctions of atomic patterns, while edges represent the structure of optional matching. For a node n in a pattern tree, $\mathsf{and}(n)$ denotes the AND pattern consisting of the atomic patterns in its label, and $\mathsf{var}(n)$ denotes the set of all variables in these patterns; these notations propagate to sets of nodes and subtrees of pattern trees. In fact, we are interested only in subtrees containing the root of the original tree, so in what follows we assume this restriction without mentioning it explicitly. A node in a pattern tree is a *child* of a subtree T if it is not in T but its parent is.

It is important to note that pattern trees are unordered, so different patterns may have the same representation. However, we disregard this syntactical mismatch, because such patterns are always equivalent. This follows from the fact that for well designed patterns $((P_1$ OPT $P_2)$ OPT $P_3)$ is equivalent to $((P_1$ OPT $P_3)$ OPT $P_2)$ (this was stated in [16] and proved in [12] for patterns without property paths, but a generalisation to our case is straightforward).

Example 3. Consider the pattern

$$(((((?x, a + b, ?y) \text{ AND } (?x, c^*, ?y)) \text{ OPT } (?x, a, ?z)) \text{ OPT } (?x, b, ?w)).$$

The tree representing this pattern is as follows.

$$\{(?x, a + b, ?y), (?x, c^*, ?y)\}$$

$$\{(?x, a, ?z)\} \qquad\qquad \{(?x, b, ?w)\}$$

Another interesting property of pattern trees is that for each variable the set of all nodes with this variable in the labels is always connected. This is a vivid illustration of the well-designedness property of patterns. Moreover, every pattern tree $Tree(P)$ (and hence every well-designed pattern) can be normalised to an equivalent tree T' (called *NR normal form* [12]) such that $\mathsf{var}(n') \not\subseteq \mathsf{var}(n)$

for every edge (n, n') in T', that is, such that every node introduces a new variable in comparison to the parent of this node. Transformation to NR normal form can be done in polynomial time by adding the label of every node without new variables to the labels of its children and then removing all such nodes from the tree. In what follows we assume all well designed patterns and corresponding pattern trees to be in NR normal form.

An intuitive coNP algorithm for evaluation of well designed patterns with property paths works in the same way as the one described in [12] for the case without property paths. It consists in the following two steps. Since the input pattern is in NR normal form, the input mapping μ uniquely defines a subtree T'_μ such that $\mathsf{dom}(\mu) = \mathsf{var}(T'_\mu)$. So, on the first step we need to check for the input graph that $\mu(\mathsf{and}(T'_\mu)) \subseteq G$, that is, all the patterns in the subtree under μ indeed materialise in the input graph G. This check can be done in polynomial time, because by Proposition 1 property paths have tractable evaluation. On the second and more difficult step we need to guarantee that μ cannot be consistently extended to the variables of any child of T'_μ in T'. This can be done in coNP by guessing a counterexample (i.e., an extension) for one of these children.

Same as for patterns without property paths, this algorithm can be extended to union and selection in a straightforward way. In the latter case the complexity jumps one level of the polynomial hierarchy, because we have to guess the values of non-distinguished variables. Combining these results with matching lower bounds for the classes without property paths [12,17] we obtain the following proposition.

Proposition 4. *The following holds:*
- EVALUATION($\mathcal{X}$-SPARQL) *is Σ_2^p-complete for* $\mathcal{X} \in \{\mathcal{AOSP}, \mathcal{AUOSP}\}$;
- EVALUATION($\mathcal{X}$-SPARQL) *is* coNP-*complete for* $\mathcal{X} \in \{\mathcal{AOP}, \mathcal{AUOP}\}$.

The focus of this paper is SPARQL with well designed optional matching, and we leave a comprehensive study of SPARQL with property paths and arbitrary nesting of other operators considered in this paper for future work. However, as a final remark in this section, we note that it is not difficult to show PSPACE-completeness of evaluation for this class, that is, the same complexity as for any subclass of this class that allows for arbitrary optional matching [21].

5.2   Query Containment

Now we move to the containment problem of SPARQL with property paths. As shown in [20], without them the problem CONTAINMENT($\mathcal{X}_1$-SPARQL,$\mathcal{X}_2$-SPARQL) is NP-complete for any $\mathcal{X}_1$-SPARQL that allows for optional matching and for $\mathcal{X}_2$-SPARQL $= \mathcal{AO}$-SPARQL, that is for the class of well designed patterns. If $\mathcal{X}_2$-SPARQL also allows for union, then the complexity becomes Π_2^p-complete (again, for the full range of $\mathcal{X}_1$-SPARQL), and the problem is undecidable if $\mathcal{X}_2$-SPARQL allows for arbitrary selection. Thus we focus on the most general case where we can hope for decidability: checking whether a query in $\mathcal{AOUSP}$-SPARQL is contained in a query in $\mathcal{AOUP}$-SPARQL. Our main result is that this problem is also decidable, specifically, EXPSPACE-complete.

As we saw in the previous subsection, the techniques developed in [12,17] for checking evaluation can be extended to work with property paths with relatively little effort. Later we will see that similar strategy works for subsumption, because it can be reduced to checking containment of OPT-free queries, which is extensible to classes with property paths. However, the situation is different for containment. It is not clear how to apply the known techniques (e.g., the one in [20, Theorem3.7]) to state the problem in terms of containment of OPT-free queries. To overcome this, we develop a new characterization of containment that reduces the problem to a weaker form of containment between OPT-free queries. Then we take advantage of the automata techniques developed in Section 4.

In what follows we first present our new characterisation for containment for queries without property paths (which we believe is of independent interest) and then adapt it to the general case. We start with a definition.

Definition 5. *Let*

$$Q_1 = \mathsf{SELECT}\, X\ \mathsf{WHERE}\ P \quad and \quad Q_2 = P^1\, \mathsf{UNION}\ \ldots\ \mathsf{UNION}\, P^k$$

be queries from $\mathcal{AOSP}$-SPARQL and $\mathcal{AOUP}$-SPARQL respectively, with P, P^i well designed patterns. A good extension E of Q_1 over Q_2 is an AND *pattern*

$$\mathsf{and}(\mathit{Tree}(P))\ \mathsf{AND}\ \mathsf{and}(n_1)\ \mathsf{AND}\ldots\mathsf{AND}\,\mathsf{and}(n_m),$$

where $m \leq k$ and every n_j is obtained from a child of a subtree T_j of one of $\mathit{Tree}(P^1),\ldots, \mathit{Tree}(P^k)$ with $\mathsf{var}(T_j) = X$ by renaming all variables not in X to fresh ones. The support $\mathsf{sup}(E)$ *of E is the set of all the subtrees T_j.*

Our new characterisation of containment for the case without property paths is based on the following lemma.

Lemma 1. *Let*

$$Q_1 = \mathsf{SELECT}\, X\ \mathsf{WHERE}\ P \quad and \quad Q_2 = P^1\ \mathsf{UNION}\ldots\mathsf{UNION}\ P^k$$

be a $\mathcal{AOUS}$-SPARQL and $\mathcal{AOU}$-SPARQL queries respectively. Then $Q_1 \nsubseteq Q_2$ if and only if there is a good extension E over Q_2 of some $\mathcal{AOS}$-SPARQL query with a pattern P^* such that $\mathit{Tree}(P^*)$ is a subtree of one of the trees representing components of P and distinguished variables $X^* = X \cap \mathsf{var}(P^*)$ that satisfies the following conditions:
- (C1) *for each child n of $\mathit{Tree}(P^*)$, there is no homomorphism h from $\mathsf{and}(n)$ to E such that $h(?x) =\,?x$ for all variables $?x$ in $\mathsf{var}(n) \cap \mathsf{var}(E)$, and*
- (C2) *for each subtree T of one of $\mathit{Tree}(P^1),\ldots, \mathit{Tree}(P^k)$ with $\mathsf{var}(T) = X^*$ that is not in $\mathsf{sup}(E)$ there is no homomorphism h from $\mathsf{and}(T)$ to E such that $h(?x) =\,?x$, for all variables $?x$ in $\mathsf{var}(T) \cap \mathsf{var}(E)$.*

The intuition behind Lemma 1 is as follows. A good extension E satisfying conditions (C1) and (C2) gives us a witness for non-containment: it suffices to consider the "frozen RDF graph" G of E obtained by replacing each variable

$?x$ by a fresh IRI a_x and the mapping μ with $\mu(?x) = a_x$, for all $?x \in X^*$ and undefined for other $?x$. Then conditions (C1) and (C2) are a convenient way of stating that $\mu \in [\![Q_1]\!]_G$ and $\mu \notin [\![Q_2]\!]_G$.

Observe that the size of a good extension is polynomial in the size of Q_1 and Q_2. Thus, Lemma 1 gives us an alternative proof for Π_2^p-membership of containment of a query in a pattern if both of them do not use property paths. Indeed to find a counterexample for containment we need to guess a good extension and then call for a coNP oracle to check conditions (C1) and (C2).

To extend the characterisation of Lemma 1 to queries with property paths we need the following auxiliary notation. We write $P_1 \preceq P_2$ for patterns P_1 and P_2 if for each RDF graph G and mapping $\mu_1 \in [\![P_1]\!]_G$ there is a mapping $\mu_2 \in [\![P_2]\!]_G$ such that $\mu_1 \sim \mu_2$.

We analyse the complexity of containment in the presence of property paths by means of the following generalised statement.

Lemma 2. *Let*

$$Q_1 = \mathsf{SELECT}\,X\,\mathsf{WHERE}\,P \quad and \quad Q_2 = P^1\,\mathsf{UNION}\ldots\mathsf{UNION}\,P^k$$

be a $\mathcal{AOUSP}$-SPARQL and $\mathcal{AOUP}$-SPARQL queries respectively. Then $Q_1 \not\subseteq Q_2$ if and only if there is a good extension E over Q_2 of some $\mathcal{AOSP}$-SPARQL query with a pattern P^* such that $Tree(P^*)$ is a subtree of one of the trees representing components of P and distinguished variables $X^* = X \cap \mathsf{var}(P^*)$ that satisfies $E \not\preceq (N\,\mathsf{UNION}\,S)$, where

(C1′) *N is a union of all $\mathsf{and}(n)$ for children n of $Tree(P^*)$, and*

(C2′) *S is a union of all $\mathsf{and}(T)$ for subtrees T of trees $Tree(P^1), \ldots, Tree(P^k)$ with $\mathsf{var}(T) = X^*$ that are not in $\mathsf{sup}(E)$.*

Using techniques developed in Section 4.2, the condition $E \not\preceq (N\,\mathsf{UNION}\,S)$ can be checked in EXPSPACE. This gives us an EXPSPACE upper bound for containment of $\mathcal{AOUSP}$-SPARQL and $\mathcal{AOUP}$-SPARQL queries. Moreover, the matching lower bound can be derived from Proposition 3.

Theorem 2. *The problem* CONTAINMENT($\mathcal{X}_1$-SPARQL,$\mathcal{X}_2$-SPARQL) *is* EXPSPACE-*complete for $\mathcal{X}_1 \in \{\mathcal{AOP}, \ldots, \mathcal{AOUSP}\}$ and $\mathcal{X}_2 \in \{\mathcal{AOP}, \mathcal{AOUP}\}$.*

5.3   Query Subsumption

The last problem we study in this paper is subsumption of SPARQL queries with property paths. Letelier et al. [12,20] proved Π_2^p-completeness of this problem for all the classes with optional matching but without property paths, even if arbitrary selection is allowed. Moreover, they provide the following very simple and useful characterisation for the subsumption of $\mathcal{AO}$-SPARQL patterns: a pattern P_1 is subsumed by a pattern P_2 if and only if for every subtree T_1' of $Tree(P_1)$ there is a subtree T_2' of $Tree(P_2)$ such that $\mathsf{var}(T_1') \subseteq \mathsf{var}(T_2')$ and there is a homomorphism from $\mathsf{and}(T_2')$ to $\mathsf{and}(T_1')$ that is the identity on $\mathsf{var}(T_1')$. This idea extends to patterns with union in the usual way—the subsumption holds if and only if for every component of the first pattern there is a subsuming one in the second.

How can this characterisation be extended to deal with property paths? The immediate idea is just to replace homomorphism with containment of corresponding OPT-free queries. However, in the presence of union this simple strategy does not always work. Indeed, the pattern $(?x, (a + b), ?y)$ is subsumed by the pattern $(?x, a, ?y)$ UNION $(?x, b, ?y)$ (in fact, they are equivalent), but not in any of its components.

As we see, the problem is the disjunction introduced by property paths, and our characterisation needs to account for this. By doing so we arrive at the following characterisation. A pattern P_1 is subsumed by a pattern P_2 if and only if for every subtree T'_1 of $Tree(P_1)$ the AND-pattern $and(T'_1)$ is subsumed in the union of all AND-patterns $and(T'_2)$, where T'_2 ranges over subtrees of $Tree(P_2)$ with $var(T'_1) \subseteq var(T'_2)$. With this characterisation we avoid dealing with optional matching, and can thus solve subsumption by the techniques introduced in the previous section. As an illustration, we can use this characterisation in the example above to show that $Q_1 \sqsubseteq Q_2$, by choosing the same query $(?x, a, ?y)$ UNION $(?x, b, ?y)$. By extending this characterisation for all queries with arbitrary selection we obtain our last theorem.

Theorem 3. *The problem* SUBSUMPTION($\mathcal{X}_1$-SPARQL,$\mathcal{X}_2$-SPARQL) *is* EXPSPACE-*complete for* $\mathcal{X}_1, \mathcal{X}_2 \in \{\mathcal{AOP}, \ldots, \mathcal{AOUSP}\}$.

6   Conclusions

At a first glance it was not clear whether one could combine techniques from graph databases and the Semantic Web to study SPARQL with property paths. Indeed, on the one hand, graph database techniques failed short for such study, because RDF data allows for predicates from an infinite alphabet and property paths may have negation. On the other hand, even if the machinery developed to study SPARQL without property paths proved to be inspirational for this work, the characterisations provided in the literature were too specific to be used in the general case. In this paper we have shown how these two classes of techniques can be generalised and combined to reason about SPARQL queries that allow for property path patterns. In particular, we developed algorithms for evaluating such queries and deciding their containment and subsumption. Finally we would like to note that many of the upped bounds obtained here (e.g., all EXPSPACE and Π_2^p bounds) match the lower bounds for more restricted classes of queries.

As for future work, the main direction we would like to tackle is the addition of the FILTER operator to the language, since so far this feature of SPARQL has not been comprehensively considered in the literature. We have some preliminary results showing that the techniques from Section 5.2 can be extended to work in this setting. Another interesting direction is to study the fragments with property paths and full power of optional matching, that is, that allow for three-placed and not well designed OPTIONAL.

Acknowledgments. Reutter, Romero and Vrgoč were supported by the Millennium Nucleus Center for Semantic Web Research Grant NC120004.

References

1. Alkhateeb, F.: Querying RDF(S) with regular expressions. Ph.D. thesis, Université Joseph Fourier, Grenoble (2008)
2. Alkhateeb, F., Baget, J.F., Euzenat, J.: Extending SPARQL with regular expression patterns (for querying RDF). J. Web Sem. **7**(2), 57–73 (2009)
3. Arenas, M., Conca, S., Pérez, J.: Counting beyond a Yottabyte, or how SPARQL 1.1 property paths will prevent adoption of the standard. In: WWW 2012, pp. 629–638 (2012)
4. Barceló Baeza, P.: Querying graph databases. In: PODS 2013, pp. 175–188 (2013)
5. Calvanese, D., De Giacomo, G., Lenzerini, M., Vardi, M.Y.: Containment of conjunctive regular path queries with inverse. In: KR 2000, pp. 176–185 (2000)
6. Calvanese, D., De Giacomo, G., Lenzerini, M., Vardi, M.Y.: Reasoning on regular path queries. ACM SIGMOD Record **32**(4), 83–92 (2003)
7. Consens, M., Mendelzon, A.: GraphLog: a visual formalism for real life recursion. In: PODS 1990, pp. 404–416 (1990)
8. Chekol, M.W.: Static Analysis of Semantic Web Queries. Ph.D. thesis, Université de Grenoble (2012)
9. Chekol, M.W., Euzenat, J., Genevès, P., Layaïda, N.: SPARQL Query Containment under RDFS Entailment Regime. In: IJCAR 2012 (2012)
10. SPARQL 1.1 Query Language. http://www.w3.org/TR/sparql11-query
11. Kostylev, E.V., Reutter, J.L., Vrgoč, D.: Containment of Data Graph Queries. In: ICDT 2014, pp. 131–142 (2014)
12. Letelier, A., Pérez, J., Pichler, R., Skritek, S.: Static analysis and optimization of semantic web queries. ACM TODS 38(4) (2013)
13. Libkin, L., Reutter, J.L., Vrgoč, D.: Trial for RDF: adapting graph query languages for RDF data. In: PODS 2013, pp. 201–212 (2013)
14. Losemann, K., Martens, W.: The Complexity of Regular Expressions and Property Paths in SPARQL. ACM TODS 38(4) (2013)
15. Neven, F., Schwentick, T., Vianu, V.: Finite state machines for strings over infinite alphabets. ACM TOCL **5**(3), 403–435 (2004)
16. Pérez, J., Arenas, M., Gutierrez, C.: Semantics and Complexity of SPARQL. In: ISWC 2006, pp. 30–43 (2006)
17. Pérez, J., Arenas, M., Gutierrez, C.: Semantics and complexity of SPARQL. ACM TODS 34(3) (2009)
18. Pérez, J., Arenas, M., Gutierrez, C.: nSPARQL: A navigational language for RDF. J. Web Sem. **8**(4), 255–270 (2010)
19. Picalausa, F., Vansummeren, S.: What are real SPARQL queries like? In: SWIM 2011 (2011)
20. Pichler, R., Skritek, S.: Containment and equivalence of well-designed SPARQL. In: PODS 2014, pp. 39–50 (2014)
21. Schmidt, M., Meier, M., Lausen, G.: Foundations of SPARQL query optimization. In: ICDT 2010, pp. 4–33 (2010)
22. Prud'hommeaux, E., Seaborne, A.: SPARQL query language for RDF. W3C Recommendation (January 15, 2008). http://www.w3.org/TR/rdf-sparql-query/
23. Vardi, M.Y.: The Complexity of Relational Query Languages. In: STOC (1982)
24. Zhang, X., Van den Bussche, J.: On the Power of SPARQL in Expressing Navigational Queries. The Computer Journal (2014)

Recursion in SPARQL

Juan L. Reutter$^{(\boxtimes)}$, Adrián Soto, and Domagoj Vrgoč

PUC Chile and Center for Semantic Web Research, Santiago, Chile
{jreutter,dvrgoc}@ing.puc.cl, assoto@uc.cl

Abstract. In this paper we propose a general purpose recursion operator to be added to SPARQL, formalize its syntax and develop algorithms for evaluating it in practical scenarios. We also show how to implement recursion as a plug-in on top of existing systems and test its performance on several real world datasets.

1 Introduction

The Resource Description Framework (RDF) has emerged as the standard for describing Semantic Web data and SPARQL as the main language for querying RDF. After the initial proposal of SPARQL, and with more data becoming available in the RDF format, users found use cases that required exploring the structure of the data in more detail. In particular queries that are inherently recursive, such as traversing paths of arbitrary length, have lately been in demand. This was acknowledged by the W3C committee with the inclusion of property paths in the latest SPARQL 1.1. standard [12], allowing queries to navigate paths connecting two objects in an RDF graph.

However, in terms of expressive power, several authors have noted that property paths fall short when trying to express a number of important properties related to navigating RDF documents (cf. [6,7,22]), and that a more powerful form of recursion needs to be added to SPARQL to address this issue. As a result various extensions of property paths have been proposed (see e.g. [4,14,17,22]), but to the best of our knowledge no attempt to add a general recursion operator to the language has been made.

To illustrate the need for such an operator we consider the case of tracking provenance of Wikipedia articles presented by Missier and Chen in [19]. They use the PROV standard [24] to store information about how a certain article was edited, whom was it edited by and what this change resulted in. Although they store the data in a graph database, all PROV data is easily representable as RDF using the PROV-O ontology [27]. The most common type of information in this RDF graph tells us when an article A_1 is a revision of an article A_2. This fact is represented by adding a triple of the form $(A_1,$ prov:wasRevisionOf, $A_2)$ to the database. These revisions are associated to user's edits with the predicate prov:wasGeneratedBy and the edits can specify that they used a particular article with a prov:used link. Finally, there is a triple $(E,$ prov:wasAssociatedWith, $U)$ if the edit E was made by the user U. A snapshot of the data, showing provenance of articles about Edinburgh, is depicted in Figure 1.

© Springer International Publishing Switzerland 2015
M. Arenas et al. (Eds.): ISWC 2015, Part I, LNCS 9366, pp. 19–35, 2015.
DOI: 10.1007/978-3-319-25007-6_2

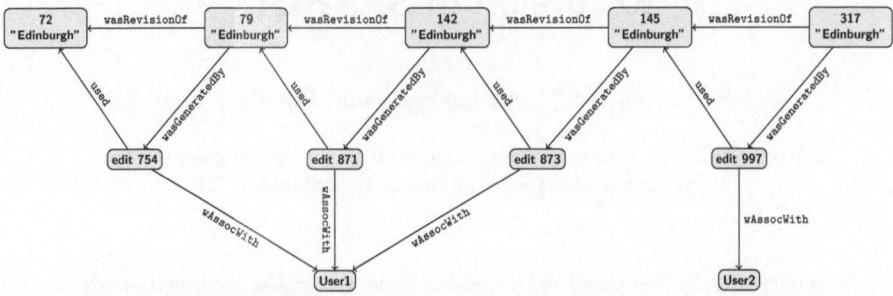

Fig. 1. RDF database of Wikipedia traces. The abbreviation `wAssocWith` is used instead of `wasAssociatedWith` and the `prov:`prefix is omitted from all the properties.

A natural query to ask in this context is the history of revisions that were made by the same user: that is all pairs of articles (A, A') such that A is linked to A' by a path of `wasRevisionOf` links and where all of the revisions along the way were made by the same user. For instance, in Figure 1 we have that the article 145 "Edinburgh" is a revision of the article 72 "Edinburgh" and all the intermediate edits were made by User1. Such queries abound in version control systems (for instance when tracking program development in svn or Git) and can be used to detect which user introduced errors or bugs, when the data is reliable, or to find the latest stable version of the data. Since these queries can not be expressed with property paths [6, 17], nor by using standard SPARQL functionalities (as provenance traces can contain links of arbitrary length), a general purpose recursion operator seems like a natural addition to the language.

One reason why recursion in SPARQL was not considered previously could be the fact that in order to compute recursive queries we need to apply the query to the result of a previous computation. However, typical SPARQL queries do not have this capability as their inputs are RDF graphs but their outputs are mappings. This hinders the possibility of a fixed point recursion as the result of a SPARQL query cannot be subsequently queried. One can avoid this by using **CONSTRUCT** queries, which output RDF graphs, and indeed [15] has proposed a way of defining a fixed point like extension for SPARQL based on this idea.

In this paper we extend the recursion operator of [15] to function over a more widely used fragment of SPARQL and study how this operator can be implemented in an efficient way on top of existing SPARQL engines. We begin by showing what the general form of recursion looks like and how to evaluate it. After arguing why full fledged recursion is unlikely to perform well on real world data, we consider a restriction called *linear recursion,* which is widely used in the relational context [1, 10], and show that it can express almost any use case found in practice. Next, we develop an elegant algorithm for evaluating this class of recursive queries and show how it can be implemented on top of an existing SPARQL system. For our implementation we use Apache Jena framework [13] and we implement recursive queries as an add-on to the ARQ SPARQL query engine. We use Jena TDB version 2.12.1, which allows us not to worry about queries whose intermediate results do not fit into main memory, thus resulting in a highly reliable system. Lastly, we test how this implementation performs on YAGO, LMBD and PROV records of Wikipedia revision history.[1]

Related Work. The most common recursive functionality available for SPARQL are property paths. These are either implemented fully [11,13], or with some limitations that ensure they can be efficiently evaluated [26]. Several extensions of property paths have also been considered by the research community [3,4,14,22] and although some of them can simulate certain recursive tasks, they still fail to express arbitrary recursive queries. There were also some attempts to allow recursion as a programming language construct [5,20], however they do not view recursion as a part of the language, but as an outside add-on. Regarding attempts to implement a full-fledged recursion as a part of SPARQL, both [25] and [15] propose a syntax of the recursion operator similar to the one used here, however, neither of the two describes specific algorithms for its execution, nor do they analyse its performance, but instead focus on expressive power.

2   Preliminaries

RDF Graphs and Datasets. RDF graphs can be seen as edge-labeled graphs where edge labels can be nodes themselves, and an RDF dataset is a collection of RDF graphs. Formally, let $\mathbf{I}$ be an infinite set of *IRIs*[2]. An *RDF triple* is a tuple (s, p, o) from $\mathbf{I} \times \mathbf{I} \times \mathbf{I}$, where s is called the *subject*, p the *predicate*, and o the *object*. An *RDF graph* is a finite set of RDF triples, and an *RDF dataset* is a set $\{G_0, \langle u_1, G_1 \rangle, \ldots, \langle u_n, G_n \rangle\}$, where $G_0, \ldots, G_n$ are RDF graphs and $u_1, \ldots, u_n$ are distinct IRIs. The graph G_0 is called the *default graph*, and $G_1, \ldots, G_n$ are called *named graphs* with *names* $u_1, \ldots, u_n$, respectively. For a dataset D and IRI u we define $\mathsf{gr}_D(u) = G$ if $\langle u, G \rangle \in D$ and $\mathsf{gr}_D(u) = \emptyset$ otherwise. Given two datasets D and D' with default graphs G_0 and G_0', we define the union $D \cup D'$ as the dataset with the default graph $G_0 \cup G_0'$ and $\mathsf{gr}_{D \cup D'}(u) = \mathsf{gr}_D(u) \cup \mathsf{gr}_{D'}(u)$ for any IRI u. Union of datasets without default graphs is defined in the same way, i.e., as if the default graph was empty.

SPARQL Syntax. We assume the familiarity with syntax and semantics of SPARQL 1.1 query language. However, we do recall two particular features that will be used: the GRAPH operator and the CONSTRUCT result form.

We assume all variables come from an infinite set $\mathbf{V} = \{?x, ?y, \ldots\}$ of *variables*. The official syntax for SPARQL 1.1 queries considers several operators such as OPTIONAL, UNION, FILTER, GRAPH and concatenation via the point symbol (.) to construct what is known as *graph patterns*. Users then use a result form such as SELECT or CONSTRUCT to form either result sets or RDF graphs from the matchings of a graph pattern. We assume that readers are familiar with graph patterns, we just note the syntax of the GRAPH operator: if P is

---

[1] The implementation, test data and complete formulation of used queries can be found in the online appendix available at http://web.ing.puc.cl/~jreutter/Recsparql.html.

[2] For clarity of presentation we do not include literals or blank nodes in our definitions.

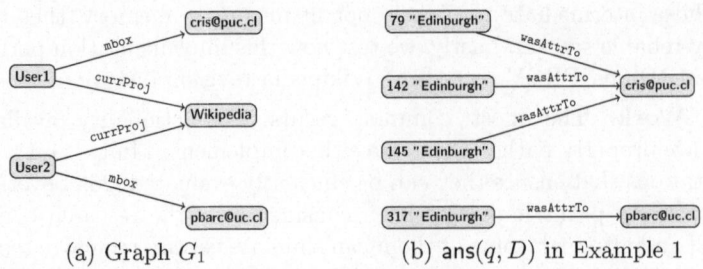

(a) Graph G_1 (b) ans(q, D) in Example 1

Fig. 2. Graphs used for Example 1. The prefixes `foaf:` and `prov:` are omitted.

a graph pattern and $g \in \mathbf{I} \cup \mathbf{V}$ then (GRAPH g P) is a graph pattern, called a GRAPH-*pattern*. The expression (GRAPH g P) allows us to determine which graph from the dataset we will be matching the pattern P to. For instance if we use an IRI in place of g the pattern will be matched against the named graph with the corresponding name (if such a graph exists in the dataset), and in the case that g is a variable, P will be matched against all the graphs in the dataset.

Although SELECT queries over graph patterns seem to be the most popular use of SPARQL, as the results of such queries are not RDF graphs, we will use the CONSTRUCT operator as a base for recursion. A SPARQL CONSTRUCT query, or *c-query* for short, is an expression

$$\text{CONSTRUCT } H \text{ } DS \text{ WHERE } P,$$

where H is a set of triples from $(\mathbf{I} \cup \mathbf{V}) \times (\mathbf{I} \cup \mathbf{V}) \times (\mathbf{I} \cup \mathbf{V})$, called a *template*; DS is a set of expressions of the form FROM NAMED $u_1, \ldots,$ FROM NAMED u_n, with each $u_i \in \mathbf{I}$ and $i \geq 0$, called a *dataset clause*[3]; and P is a graph pattern.

The idea behind the CONSTRUCT operator is that the mappings matched to the pattern P are used to construct an RDF graph according to the template H. Since all the patterns in the template are triples we will end up with an RDF graph as desired.

Example 1. Let G and G_1 be the graphs in Figure 1 and Figure 2, respectively. We want to query both graphs to obtain a new graph where each article is linked to the email of a user who modified it. Assuming we have a dataset with default graph G and that the IRI identifying G_1 is `http://db.ing.puc.cl/mail`, this would be achieved by the following SPARQL CONSTRUCT query q:

```
PREFIX prov: <http://www.w3.org/ns/prov#>
PREFIX prov: <http://xmlns.com/foaf/0.1>
CONSTRUCT {?article prov:wasAttributedTo ?mail}
FROM NAMED <http://db.ing.puc.cl/mail>
WHERE {
    ?article prov:wasGeneratedBy ?comment .
    ?comment prov:wasAssociatedWith ?usr .
    GRAPH <http://db.ing.puc.cl/mail> {?usr foaf:mbox ?mail}}
```

---

[3] For readability we assume the default graph as given.

The result $\mathsf{ans}(q, D)$ of evaluating q over D is depicted in Figure 2. The construct FROM NAMED is used to specify that the dataset needs to include the graph G_1 associated with the IRI `http://db.ing.puc.cl/mail`.

SPARQL Semantics. The semantics of graph patterns is defined in terms of *mappings* [12]; that is, partial functions from variables $\mathbf{V}$ to IRIs $\mathbf{I}$. Given a dataset D, and a graph G amongst the graphs of D, we denote the *evaluation* of a graph pattern P over D with respect to G as $[\![P]\!]_G^D$. The evaluation $[\![P]\!]^D$ of a pattern P over a dataset D with default graph G_0 is $[\![P]\!]_{G_0}^D$. The full definition of $[\![P]\!]^D$ and $[\![P]\!]_G^D$ can be found in the SPARQL standard, here we just note the semantics of GRAPH-patterns, for which we need some notation.

The *domain* $\mathsf{dom}(\mu)$ of a mapping μ is the set of variables on which μ is defined. Two mappings μ_1 and μ_2 are *compatible* (written as $\mu_1 \sim \mu_2$) if $\mu_1(?x) = \mu_2(?x)$ for all variables $?x$ in $\mathsf{dom}(\mu_1) \cap \mathsf{dom}(\mu_2)$. If $\mu_1 \sim \mu_2$, then we write $\mu_1 \cup \mu_2$ for the mapping obtained by extending μ_1 according to μ_2 on all the variables in $\mathsf{dom}(\mu_2) \setminus \mathsf{dom}(\mu_1)$. Given two sets of mappings M_1 and M_2, the *join* and *union* between M_1 and M_2 are defined respectively as follows:

$$M_1 \bowtie M_2 = \{\mu_1 \cup \mu_2 \mid \mu_1 \in M_1, \ \mu_2 \in M_2 \text{ and } \mu_1 \sim \mu_2\},$$
$$M_1 \cup M_2 = \{\mu \mid \mu \in M_1 \text{ or } \mu \in M_2\}$$

Let us now define the semantics of GRAPH-patterns. Consider a GRAPH-pattern $P = (\mathsf{GRAPH} \ g \ P')$. Then

$$
[\![P]\!]_G^D = \begin{cases} [\![P']\!]_{\mathsf{gr}_D(g)}^D & \text{if } g \in \mathbf{I} \\[2mm] \bigcup_{u \in \mathbf{I}} \left([\![P']\!]_{\mathsf{gr}_D(u)}^D \bowtie \{\mu_{g \mapsto u}\} \right) & \text{if } g \in \mathbf{V} \end{cases}
$$

where $\mu_{g \mapsto u}$ is the mapping with domain $\{g\}$ and where $\mu_{g \mapsto u}(g) = u$.

Next we recall the semantics of SPARQL queries. Let q be a SPARQL query and D a dataset. The answer $\mathsf{ans}(q, D)$ of q over D depends on the form of q:

- If q is a SELECT query, then $\mathsf{ans}(q, D)$ is the answer to q as defined in the SPARQL standard [12].
- If q is a c-query $q = \mathsf{CONSTRUCT} \ H \ DS \ \mathsf{WHERE} \ P$, then let $u_1, \ldots, u_n$ be the IRIs in DS and $G_1, \ldots, G_n$ the graphs associated to these IRIs; and consider the dataset $D' = D \cup \{\langle u_1, G_1 \rangle, \ldots, \langle u_n, G_n \rangle\}$. We define:

$$\mathsf{ans}(q, D) = \{\mu(t) \mid \mu \in [\![P]\!]^{D'}, t \text{ is a triple in } H \text{ and } \mu \text{ is defined on } \mathit{vars}(t)\}.$$

3 Adding Recursion to SPARQL

The most basic example of a recursive query in RDF is reachability: given a resource x, compute all the resources that are reachable from x via a path of arbitrary length. These queries, amongst others, motivated the inclusion of property paths into the recent SPARQL 1.1 standard [12]. However, as several authors subsequently pointed out, property paths fall short when trying to express queries that involve more complex ways of navigating RDF documents (cf. [4,7,8,22]) and as a result several extensions have been brought forward to combat this problem [2,14,17,22]. Almost all of these extensions are also based on the idea of computing paths between nodes in a recursive way, and thus share a number of practical problems with property paths. Most importantly, these queries need to be implemented using algorithms that are not standard in SPARQL databases, as they are based on automata-theoretic techniques, or clever ways of doing Breadth-first search on the graph structure of RDF documents.

3.1 A Fixed Point Based Recursive Operator

We have decided to implement a different approach: a much more widespread recursive operator that allows us compute the fixed point of a wide range of SPARQL queries. Before proceeding with the formal definition we illustrate the idea behind such queries by means of an example.

Example 2. Recall graph G from Figure 1. In the Introduction we made a case for the need of a query that could compute all pairs of articles (A, A') such that A is linked to A' by a path of wasRevisionOf links and where all of the revisions along the way were made by the same user. We can compute this with the following recursive query.

```
PREFIX prov: <http://www.w3.org/ns/prov#>
WITH RECURSIVE http://db.ing.puc.cl/temp AS {
    CONSTRUCT {?newversion ?user ?oldversion}
    FROM NAMED <http://db.ing.puc.cl/temp>
    WHERE{{
        ?newversion prov:wasRevisionOf ?oldversion .
        ?newversion prov:wasGeneratedBy ?edit .
        ?edit prov:used ?oldversion .
        ?edit prov:wasAssociatedWith ?user}
    UNION{
            GRAPH <http://db.ing.puc.cl/temp>
            {?newversion ?user ?intversion . ?intversion ?user ?oldversion}}}
}
SELECT ?newversion ?oldversion
FROM <http://db.ing.puc.cl/temp>
WHERE {?newversion ?user ?oldversion}
```

Let us explain how this query works. The second line specifies that a temporary graph named http://db.ing.puc.cl/temp is to be constructed according to the query below which consists of a UNION of two subpatterns. The first pattern does not use the temporary graph and it simply extracts all triples (A, U, B) such that A was a revision of B and U is the user generating this revision. All these triples should be added to the temporary graph.

Then comes the recursive part: if (A, U, B) and (B, U, C) are triples in the temporary graph, then we also add (A, U, C) to the temporary graph. We continue iterating until a fixed point is reached, and finally we obtain a graph that contains all the triples (A, U, A') such that A is linked to A' via a path of revisions of arbitrary length but always generated by the same user U. Finally, the SELECT query extracts all such pairs of articles from the constructed graph.

As hinted in the example, the following is the syntax for recursive queries. It is based on the recursive operator that is part of SQL.

Definition 1 (Syntax of recursive queries). *A recursive SPARQL query, or just recursive query, is either a SPARQL query or an expression of the form*

$$\text{WITH RECURSIVE } t \text{ AS } \{q_1\} \; q_2, \tag{1}$$

where t is an IRI from $\mathbf{I}$, q_1 is a c-query, and q_2 is a recursive query. The set of all recursive queries is denoted rec-*SPARQL.*

Note that in this definition q_1 is allowed to use the temporary graph t, which leads to recursive iterations. Furthermore, the query q_2 could be recursive itself, which allows us to compose recursive definitions. As usual with this type of queries, semantics is given via a fixed point iteration.

Definition 2 (Semantics of recursive queries). *Let q be a recursive query of the form (1) and D an RDF dataset. If q is a non recursive query then* $\mathsf{ans}(q, D)$ *is defined as usual. Otherwise the answer* $\mathsf{ans}(q, D)$ *is equal to* $\mathsf{ans}(q_2, D_{LFP})$, *where D_{LFP} is the least fixed point of the sequence $D_0, D_1, \ldots$ with $D_0 = D$ and*

$$D_{i+1} = D \cup \{\langle t, \mathsf{ans}(q_1, D_i)\rangle\}, \; \textit{for } i \geq 0.$$

In other words, D_1 is the union of D with a temporary graph t that corresponds to the evaluation of q_1 over D, D_2 is the union of D with a temporary graph t that corresponds to the evaluation of q_1 over D_1, and so on until $D_{i+1} = D_i$. Note that the temporary graph is completely rewritten after each iteration. This definition suggests the following pseudocode for computing the answers of a recursive query q of the form (1) over a dataset D[4]:

1. Initialize a temporary RDF graph named after the IRI t as $G_{\text{Temp}} = \emptyset$.
2. While $\mathsf{ans}(q_1, D \cup \{\langle t, G_{\text{Temp}}\rangle\}) \neq G_{\text{Temp}}$ do:
   - Set $G_{\text{Temp}} = \mathsf{ans}(q_1, D \cup \{\langle t, G_{\text{Temp}}\rangle\})$
3. Output $\mathsf{ans}(q_2, D \cup \{\langle t, G_{\text{Temp}}\rangle\})$

Obviously this definition only makes sense as long as such fixed point exists. From the Knaster-Tarski theorem [16] it easily follows that the fixed point exists as long as queries used to define recursion are monotone. For the sake of presentation, here we ensure this condition by disallowing explicit negation (such as NOTEXISTS or MINUS) and optional matching from our c-queries (note that under construct queries, this fragment is known to be equivalent to queries defined by union of well designed graph patterns [15]). It was also shown in [15] that the existence of a fixed point can be guaranteed even when q_1 belongs to a rather technical fragment that does allow a limited form of negation and optional matching that extends beyond the use of unions of well designed patterns.

---

[4] For readability we assume that t is not a named graph in D. If this is not the case then the pseudocode needs to be modified to meet the definition above.

3.2 Complexity Analysis

Recursive queries can use either the SELECT or the CONSTRUCT result form, so there are two decision problems we need to analyze. For SELECT queries we define the problem SELQUERYANS, that receives as an input a recursive query Q using the SELECT result form, a tuple $\bar{a}$ of IRIs from $\mathbf{I}$ and a dataset D, and asks whether $\bar{a}$ is in $\mathsf{ans}(Q, D)$. For CONSTRUCT queries the problem CONQUERYANS receives a recursive query Q with a CONSTRUCT result form, a triple (s, p, o) over $\mathbf{I} \times \mathbf{I} \times \mathbf{I}$ and a dataset D, and asks whether this triple belongs to $\mathsf{ans}(Q, D)$.

Proposition 1. SELQUERYANS *is* PSPACE-*complete and* CONQUERYANS *is* NP-*complete. The complexity of* SELQUERYANS *drops to* Π_2^p *if one only considers* SELECT *queries given by unions of well-designed graph patterns.*

Thus, at least from the point of view of computational complexity, our class of recursive queries are not more complex than standard select queries [21] or construct queries [15]. We also note that the complexity of similar recursive queries in most data models is typically complete for exponential time; what lowers our complexity is the fact that our temporary graphs are RDF graphs themselves, instead of arbitrary sets of mappings or relations.

For databases it is also common to study the data complexity of the query answering problem, that is, the same decision problems as above but considering the input query to be fixed. We denote these problems as SELQUERYANS(Q) and CONQUERYANS(Q), for select and construct queries, respectively. As we see, the problem remains in polynomial time for data complexity, albeit in a higher class than for non recursive queries (see again [21] or [15]).

Proposition 2. *Both the problem* SELQUERYANS(Q) *and the problem* CONQUERYANS(Q) *are* PTIME-*complete. They remain* PTIME-*hard even for queries without negation or optional matching.*

However, even if theoretically the problems have the same combined complexity as queries without recursion and are polynomial in data complexity, any implementation of the above algorithm is likely to run excessively slow due to a high demand on computational resources (computing the temporary graph over and over again) and would thus not be useful in practice. For this reason, instead of implementing full-fledged recursion, we decided to support a fragment of recursive queries based on what is commonly known as *linear recursive queries* [1,10]. This restriction is common when implementing recursive operators in other database languages, most notably in SQL [23], but also in graph databases [8], as it offers a wider option of evaluation algorithms while maintaining the ability of expressing almost any recursive query that one could come up with in practice. For instance, as demonstrated in the following section, linear recursion captures all the examples we have considered thus far and it can also define any query that uses property paths. Furthermore, it can be implemented in an efficient way on top of any existing SPARQL engine using a simple and easy to understand algorithm. Next we formally define this fragment.

4   Realistic Recursion in SPARQL

The concept of *linear recursion* has become popular in the industry as a restriction for fixed point operators in relational query languages, because it presents a good tradeoff between the expressive power of recursive operators and their practical applicability. Let Q be the query WITH RECURSIVE t AS $\{q_1\}$ q_2, where t is an IRI from **I**, q_1 is a c-query, and q_2 is a recursive query. We say that Q is *linear* if for every dataset D, the answer $\mathsf{ans}(Q, D)$ of the query corresponds to the least fixed point of the sequence given by

$$D_0 = D, \quad D_{-1} = \emptyset,$$
$$D_{i+1} = D_i \cup \{\langle t, \mathsf{ans}(q_1, (D \cup D_i \setminus D_{i-1}))\rangle\}.$$

In other words, a recursive query is linear if, in order to compute the i-th iteration, we only need the original dataset plus the tuples that were added to the temporary graph t in the previous iteration. Considering that the final size of t might be comparable to the original dataset, linear queries save us from evaluating the query several times over an ever increasing dataset.

Most of the recursive extensions proposed for SPARQL are linear: from property paths [12] to nSPARQL [22], SPARQLeR [14] or Trial [17], and even our example. Unfortunately it is undecidable to check if a recursive query is linear (under usual complexity-theoretic assumptions) [9], so one needs to impose syntactic restrictions to enforce this condition. This is what we do next.

4.1   Linear Recursive Queries

Our queries are made from the union of a graph pattern that does not use the temporary IRI, denoted as p_{base} and a graph pattern p_{rec} that does mention the temporary IRI. Formally, a *linear recursive query* is an expression of the form

WITH RECURSIVE t AS {

        CONSTRUCT H DS WHERE p_{base} UNION p_{rec} } q_{out} (2)

with H and DS a construct template and dataset clause as usual, with p_{base} and p_{rec} graph patterns such that only p_{rec} is allowed to mention the IRI t and with q_{out} a linear recursive query. We further require that the recursive part p_{rec} mentions the temporary IRI only once. In order to describe our algorithm, we shall abuse the notation and speak of q_{base} to denote the query CONSTRUCT H DS WHERE p_{base} and q_{rec} to denote the query CONSTRUCT H DS WHERE p_{rec}, respectively.

This simple yet powerful syntax resembles the design choices taken in most SQL commercial systems supporting recursion [23] and even graph databases [8].

For example, the query in example 2 is not linear, because the temporary IRI is used twice in the pattern. Nevertheless, it can be restated as the following query that uses one level of nesting:

```
PREFIX prov: <http://www.w3.org/ns/prov#>
WITH RECURSIVE http://db.ing.puc.cl/temp1 AS {
    CONSTRUCT {?newversion ?user ?oldversion}
    FROM NAMED <http://db.ing.puc.cl/temp1>
    WHERE{
        {?newversion prov:wasRevisionOf ?oldversion .
        ?newversion prov:wasGeneratedBy ?edit .
        ?edit prov:used ?oldversion .
        ?edit prov:wasAssociatedWith ?user}
    UNION
        {}}
}
WITH RECURSIVE http://db.ing.puc.cl/temp2 AS {
    CONSTRUCT {?newversion ?user ?oldversion}
    FROM NAMED <http://db.ing.puc.cl/temp1>
    FROM NAMED <http://db.ing.puc.cl/temp2>
    WHERE{
        GRAPH <http://db.ing.puc.cl/temp1> {?newversion ?user ?oldversion}
    UNION{
        GRAPH <http://db.ing.puc.cl/temp1> {?newversion ?user ?intversion}.
        GRAPH <http://db.ing.puc.cl/temp2> {?intversion ?user ?oldversion}}}
}
SELECT ?newversion ?oldversion
FROM <http://db.ing.puc.cl/temp>
WHERE {?newversion ?user ?oldversion}
```

We wrote the union in the first query for clarity, but in general either p_{base} or p_{rec} can be empty. The idea of this query is to first dump all meaningful triples from the graph into a new graph `http://db.ing.puc.cl/temp1`, and then use this graph as a basis for computing the required reachability condition, that will be dumped into a second temporary graph `http://db.ing.puc.cl/temp2`[5].

Note that these queries are indeed linear, and thus we can perform the incremental evaluation that we have described above. The separation between base and recursive query also allows us to keep track of changes made in the temporary graph without the need of computing the difference of two graphs. We have decided to implement what is known as *seminaive evaluation*, although several other alternatives have been proposed for the evaluation of these types of queries (see [10] for a good survey). Our algorithm is presented in Algorithm 1.

So what have we gained? By looking at Algorithm 1 one realizes that in each iteration we only evaluate the query over the union of the dataset and the intermediate graph G_{temp}, instead of the previous algorithm where one needed the whole graph being constructed (in this case G_{ans}). Furthermore, q_{base} is evaluated only once, using q_{rec} in the rest of the iterations. Considering that the temporary graph may be large, and that no indexing scheme could be available, this often results in a considerable speedup for query computation. As we see next, the computational complexity is also reduced.

Complexity Analysis. We can find some explanation of why linear recursive queries behave better in practice when revisiting the computational complexity of the query answering problem, which shows a reduction in data complexity.

Theorem 1. *If Q is a linear recursive query, SelQueryAns(Q) and ConQueryAns(Q) are NLogSpace-complete.*

---

[5] One can show that in this case the nesting in this query can be avoided.

Algorithm 1. Computing the answer for linear recursive queries of the form (2)

Input: Query Q of the form (2), dataset D
Output: Evaluation $\mathsf{ans}(Q, D)$ of Q over D

1: Set $G_{\text{temp}} = \mathsf{ans}(\boldsymbol{q}_{\text{base}}, D)$ and $G_{\text{ans}} = G_{\text{temp}}$
2: Set $size = |G_{\text{ans}}|$
3: **loop**
4:     Set $G_{\text{temp}} = \mathsf{ans}(\boldsymbol{q}_{\text{rec}}, D \cup \{(t, G_{\text{temp}})\})$
5:     Set $G_{\text{ans}} = G_{\text{ans}} \cup G_{\text{temp}}$
6:     **if** $size = |G_{\text{ans}}|$ **then**
7:         **break**
8:     **else**
9:         $size = |G_{\text{ans}}|$
10:    **end if**
11: **end loop**
12: **return** $\mathsf{ans}(\boldsymbol{q}_{\text{out}}, D \cup \{\langle t, G_{\text{ans}}\rangle\})$

---

5 Experimental Evaluation

Our implementation of linear recursive queries was carried out using the Apache Jena framework [13] as an add-on to the ARQ SPARQL query engine. The version used was Jena TDB 2.12.1 as it allows the user to run queries either in main memory, or using disk storage when needed. As previously mentioned, since the query evaluation algorithms we develop make use of the same operations that already exist in current SPARQL engines, we can use those as a basis for the recursive extension to SPARQL we propose. In fact, as we show by implementing recursion on top of Jena, this capability can be added to an existing engine in an elegant and non-intrusive way[6].

We test our implementation using three different datasets. The first one is Linked Movie Database (LMDB) [18], an RDF dataset containing information about movies and actors[7]. The second dataset we use is a part of the YAGO ontology [28] and consists of all the facts that hold between instances. For the experiments the version from March 2015 was used. The last dataset is based on Missier and Chen's database of Wikipedia traces [19] we described previously. We chose 3 of their datasets, but since they are very small we enlarge them by taking disjoint copies of the same data until it reached the desired size. Since these datasets contain only the traces and nothing else we also added 30% of random unrelated triples to simulate the database containing other pieces of information. We grew 4 different datasets out of the provenance traces, of 50, 100, 150 and 200 Mb of size approximately. We refer to these datasets as PROV1,

---

[6] The implementation we use is available at http://web.ing.puc.cl/~jreutter/Recsparql.html.
[7] We use the data dump available at http://queens.db.toronto.edu/~oktie/linkedmdb/.

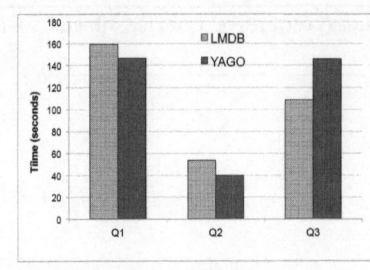

dataset ╲ query	Q1	Q2	Q3
LMDB	37349	1172	14568
YAGO	25404	480	9416

(b) The number of output tuples

Dataset	PROV1	PROV2	PROV3	PROV4
Time(sec)	12.3	22.8	33.8	46.5
No. tup.	220950	441900	667269	883800

(a) Query times on LMDB and YAGO

(c) Query from Section 4 on PROV datasets

Fig. 3. Running times and the number of output tuples for the three datasets.

PROV2, PROV3 and PROV4, respectively[8]. All the experiments were run on a MacBook Air with an Intel Core i5 1.3 GHz processor and 4GB of main memory.

5.1 Query Evaluation

Because of the novelty of our approach it was impossible to compare our times against other implementations, or run standard benchmarks to test the performance of our queries. Furthermore, while our formalism is similar to that of recursive SQL, all of the RDF systems that we checked were either running RDF natively, or running on top of a relational DBMS that did not support recursion as mandated by the SQL standard. OpenLink Virtuoso does have a *transitive closure* operator, but this operator can only compute transitivity when starting in a given IRI. Our queries were more general than this, and thus we could not compare them. For this reason we invented several queries that are very natural over the considered datasets and tested their performance. As all property paths can be expressed by linear recursive queries we will also test our implementation against current SPARQL systems in the following subsection.

We start our round of experiments with movie-related queries over both LMDB and YAGO. Since YAGO also contains information about movies, we have the advantage of being able to test the same queries over different real datasets (only the ontology differs). We use three different queries, all of them similar to that of Example 2. The first query Q1 returns all the actors in the database that have a finite Bacon number[9], meaning that they co-starred in the same movie with Kevin Bacon, or another actor with a finite Bacon number. A similar notion, well known in mathematics, is the Erdős number. Note that Q1 is a property path query. To test recursive capabilities of our implementation we use another two queries, Q2 and Q3, that apply various tests along the paths computing the Bacon number. The query Q2 returns all actors with a finite Bacon number such that all the collaborations were done in movies with the same director. Finally the query Q3 tests if an actor is connected to Kevin

---

[8] The datasets are available at http://web.ing.puc.cl/~jreutter/Recsparql.html.

[9] See http://en.wikipedia.org/wiki/Six_Degrees_of_Kevin_Bacon.

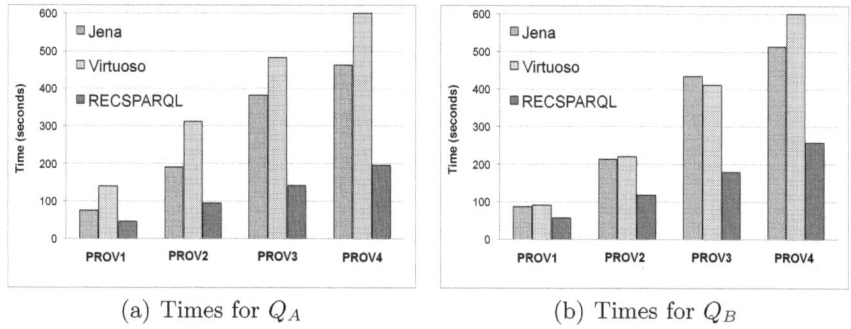

(a) Times for Q_A (b) Times for Q_B

Fig. 4. Evaluation time of Q_A and Q_B in our implementation is comparable to that of Jena or Virtuoso. For PROV4 both queries reported more than 600 seconds in Virtuoso.

Bacon through movies where the director is also an actor (not necessarily in the same movie). The structure of queries Q2 and Q3 is similar to the query from Example 2 and cannot be expressed using property paths either. The results of the evaluation can be found in Figure 3(a). As we can see the running times, although high, are reasonable considering the size of the datasets and the number of output tuples (Figure 3(b)).

The next round of experiments pushes our implementation to compute inherently recursive queries. For this we use the query from Example 2 that finds all pairs of Wikipedia articles whose revision history can be attributed to the same user. As we implement linear recursion, the version of the query presented in Section 4 is used. Figure 3(c) shows the running time of this query on the datasets derived from Wikipedia traces described before; it illustrates that running times are quite low when we take the number of computed tuples into consideration.

5.2   Comparison with Property Paths

Since to the best of our knowledge no SPARQL engine implements general recursive queries, we cannot really compare the performance of our implementation with the existing systems. The only form of recursion mandated by the latest language standard are property paths, so in this section we test how our implementation stacks against popular systems when executing property paths.

Every property path query is easily expressible using linear recursion. However, it is not fair to compare our recursive implementation of property paths to the one in current systems, as they specialize in executing this type of recursive queries, while the recursive operator we introduced is aimed at expressing a wide variety of queries that lie beyond the scope of property paths. For this reason highly efficient systems like Virtuoso will run queries they are optimized for much faster. For instance to run the query Q1 from Subsection 5.1 that computes all actors with a finite Bacon number in LMDB or YAGO Virtuoso takes less than 10 seconds, while our implementation takes much longer. Part of the difference in running times could be attributed to the fact that in this particular case our implementation runs queries on disc, while Virtuoso can perform them in main memory, but the main detractor is the fact that Virtuoso is designed to be efficient at property paths that are given a starting point, while recursive queries are not since they can express more general queries.

To have a somewhat fair comparison we will use property path queries that compute all pairs of IRIs connected by a specified property path. We use the PROV datasets introduced above and in Figure 1 and test for the existence of property paths `wasRevisionOf*` and `(wasGeneratedBy/used)*`. We refer to these queries as Q_A and Q_B.[10] Figure 4 presents the time each of the queries takes on the four PROV datasets of increasing size. We test the recursive implementation of property paths against the one in Jena and Virtuoso. As we can see our implementation is quite competitive with systems that specialize in property paths when we need to compute the entire relation. We can also see that Jena runs faster than Virtuoso in this case and we believe that this is due to the fact that Jena implements property paths in a way that returns all pairs of nodes that are connected by the specified query, while for Virtuoso we need to run the query from every possible starting point.

5.3   Limiting the Number of Iterations

In practical scenarios users are often interested in running recursive queries only for a predefined number of iterations. For instance, very long paths between nodes are seldom of interest and in a many use cases we will be interested in using property paths only up to depth four or five. For this reason we propose the following syntax to restrict the depth of recursion to a user specified number:

$$\text{WITH RECURSIVE } t \text{ AS } \{$$
$$\text{CONSTRUCT} H \ DS \text{ WHERE } p_{\text{base}} \text{ UNION } p_{\text{rec}}$$
$$\} \text{ MAXRECURSION } k \ q_{\text{out}} \tag{3}$$

Here all the keywords are the same as when defining linear recursion, and $k \geq 1$ is a natural number. The semantics of such queries is defined using Algorithm 1, where the loop between steps 4 and 12 is executed precisely $k - 1$ times.

It is straightforward to see that every query defined using recursion with predefined number of iterations can be rewritten in SPARQL by explicitly specifying each step of the recursion and joining them using the union operator. The question then is, why is specifying the recursion depth beneficial?

One apparent reason is that it makes queries much easier to write and understand. The second reason we would like to argue for is that, when implemented using Algorithm 1, recursive queries with a predetermined number of steps result in faster query evaluation times than evaluating an equivalent query with lots of joins. The intuitive reason behind this is that computing q_{base}, although expensive initially, acts as a sort of index to iterate upon, resulting in fast evaluation

---

[10] Note that in Virtuoso we need to specify the starting point of a property path. This is done by extracting each node from a unique triple containing it.

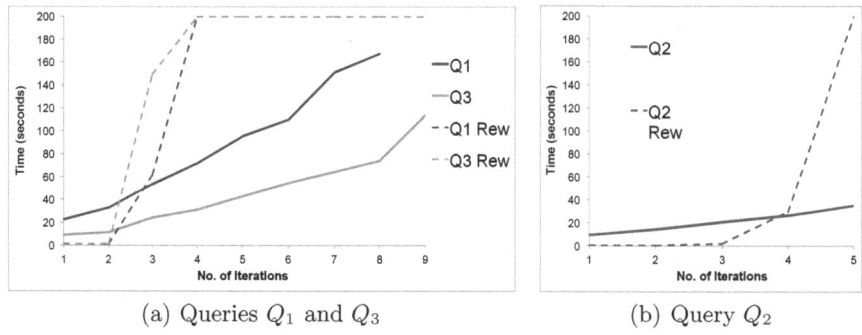

(a) Queries Q_1 and Q_3 (b) Query Q_2

Fig. 5. Limiting the number of iterations for Q_1, Q_2 and Q_3 over LMDB. Recursion dominates manually written SPARQL joins when several iterations are required.

times as the number of iterations increases. On the other hand, for even a moderately complex query using lots of joins, the execution plan will seldom be optimal and will often resort to simply trying all the possible matchings to the variables, thus recomputing the same information several times.

We substantiate this claim by running two rounds of experiments on LMDB and YAGO using queries Q1,Q2 and Q3 from Subsection 5.1 and running them for an increasing number of steps. In the first round we evaluate each of the queries using Algorithm 1 and run it for a fixed number of steps until the algorithm saturates. In the second round we use a SPARQL rewriting of a recursive query where the depth of recursion is fixed and evaluate it in Jena.

Figure 5 shows the results over LMDB. The results for YAGO show the same trend, so we do not include them. As we can see, the initial cost is much higher if we are using recursive queries, however as the number of steps increases we can see that they show much better performance and in fact, the queries that use only SPARQL operators time out after a small number of iterations.

6 Conclusion

As illustrated by several use cases, there is a need for recursive functionalities in SPARQL that go beyond the scope of property paths. To tackle this issue we propose a recursive operator to be added to the language and show how it can be implemented efficiently on top of existing SPARQL systems. We concentrated on linear recursive queries which have been well established in SQL practice and cover almost all interesting use cases and show how to implement them as an extension to Jena framework. Our tests show that, although very expressive, these queries run in reasonable time even on a machine with limited computational resources. We also include a command that allows to run recursive queries for a limited number of steps and show that the proposed implementation outperforms equivalent queries specified using only SPARQL operators. We believe all of this to be a good indicator of the usefulness of the recursion operator and why it should be a potential candidate for inclusion in the next SPARQL standard.

Acknowledgements. This work was funded by the Millennium Nucleus Center for Semantic Web Research Grant NC120004. We would like to thank Aidan Hogan, Egor Kostylev, James Cheney and the reviewers for helpful comments.

References

1. Abiteboul, S., Hull, R., Vianu, V.: Foundations of Databases. A-W (1995)
2. Alkhateeb, F., Baget, J.-F., Euzenat, J.: Extending SPARQL with regular expression patterns (for querying RDF). J. Web Sem. **7**(2), 57–73 (2009)
3. Alkhateeb, F., Euzenat, J.: Constrained regular expressions for answering rdf-path queries modulo RDFS. IJWIS **10**(1), 24–50 (2014)
4. Anyanwu, K., Sheth, A.: ρ-Queries: enabling querying for semantic associations on the semantic web. In: WWW (2003)
5. Atzori, M.: Computing recursive SPARQL queries. In: ICSC, pp. 258–259 (2014)
6. Barceló, P., Pérez, J., Reutter, J.L.: Relative Expressiveness of Nested Regular Expressions. In: AMW, pp. 180–195 (2012)
7. Bourhis, P., Krötzsch, M., Rudolph, S.: How to best nest regular path queries. In: Proceedings of the 27th International Workshop on Description Logics (2014)
8. Consens, M., Mendelzon, A.: Graphlog: A visual formalism for real life recursion. In: PODS, pp. 404–416 (1990)
9. Gaifman, H., Mairson, H., Sagiv, Y., Vardi, M.Y.: Undecidable optimization problems for database logic programs. JACM **40**(3), 683–713 (1993)
10. Green, T.J., Huang, S.S., Loo, B.T., Zhou, W.: Datalog and recursive query processing. Foundations and Trends in Databases **5**(2), 105–195 (2013)
11. Gubichev, A., Bedathur, S.J., Seufert, S.: Sparqling kleene: fast property paths in RDF-3X. In: GRADES (2013)
12. Harris, S., Seaborne, A.: SPARQL 1.1 query language. W3C Recommendation, 21 (2013)
13. The Apache Jena Manual (2015). http://jena.apache.org
14. Kochut, K.J., Janik, M.: SPARQLeR: extended sparql for semantic association discovery. In: Franconi, E., Kifer, M., May, W. (eds.) ESWC 2007. LNCS, vol. 4519, pp. 145–159. Springer, Heidelberg (2007)
15. Kostylev, E.V., Reutter, J.L., Ugarte, M.: CONSTRUCT queries in SPARQL. In: ICDT, pp. 212–229 (2015)
16. Libkin, L.: Elements of Finite Model Theory. Springer (2004)
17. Libkin, L., Reutter, J., Vrgoč, D.: Trial for RDF: adapting graph query languages for RDF data. In: PODS, pp. 201–212. ACM (2013)
18. Linked movie database. http://linkedmdb.org/
19. Missier, P., Chen, Z.: Extracting prov provenance traces from wikipedia history pages. In: EDBT/ICDT 2013 Workshops, pp. 327–330 (2013)
20. Motik, B., Nenov, Y., Piro, R., Horrocks, I., Olteanu, D.: Parallel materialisation of datalog programs in centralised, main-memory RDF systems. In: AAAI (2014)
21. Pérez, J., Arenas, M., Gutierrez, C.: Semantics and complexity of SPARQL. ACM Transactions on Database Systems 34(3) (2009)
22. Pérez, J., Arenas, M., Gutierrez, C.: nSPARQL: A navigational language for RDF. J. Web Sem. **8**(4), 255–270 (2010)

23. PostgreSQL.   http://www.postgresql.org/docs/current/interactive/queries-with.html

24. PROV Model Primer (2013). http://www.w3.org/TR/2013/NOTE-prov-primer-20130430/

25. Shaw, M., Detwiler, L.F., Noy, N.F., Brinkley, J.F., Suciu, D.: vSPARQL: A view definition language for the semantic web. J. Biomedical Informatics, 44 (2011)

26. Open Link Virtuoso (2015). http://virtuoso.openlinksw.com/

27. W3C. PROV-O: The PROV Ontology (2013). http://www.w3.org/TR/prov-o/

28. YAGO: A High-Quality Knowledge Base. http://www.mpi-inf.mpg.de/departments/databases-and-information-systems/research/yago-naga/yago/

Federated SPARQL Queries Processing with Replicated Fragments

Gabriela Montoya[1,2]($\boxtimes$), Hala Skaf-Molli[1], Pascal Molli[1],
and Maria-Esther Vidal[3]

[1] LINA – Nantes University, Nantes, France
{gabriela.montoya,hala.skaf,pascal.molli}@univ-nantes.fr
[2] Unit UMR6241 CNRS, Nantes, France
[3] Universidad Simón Bolívar, Caracas, Venezuela
mvidal@ldc.usb.ve

Abstract. Federated query engines provide a unified query interface to
federations of SPARQL endpoints. Replicating data fragments from different Linked Data sources facilitates data re-organization to better fit
federated query processing needs of data consumers. However, existing
federated query engines are not designed to support replication and replicated data can negatively impact their performance. In this paper, we formulate the source selection problem with fragment replication (SSP-FR).
For a given set of endpoints with replicated fragments and a SPARQL
query, the problem is to select the endpoints that minimize the number of
tuples to be transferred. We devise the FEDRA source selection algorithm
that approximates SSP-FR. We implement FEDRA in the state-of-the-art
federated query engines FedX and ANAPSID, and empirically evaluate
their performance. Experimental results suggest that FEDRA efficiently
solves SSP-FR, reducing the number of selected SPARQL endpoints as
well as the size of query intermediate results.

Keywords: Linked data · Federated query processing · Source selection · Fragment replication

1 Introduction

SPARQL endpoints enable to consume RDF data exploiting the *expressiveness*
of the SPARQL query language. Nevertheless, recent studies reveal that existing
public SPARQL endpoints main limitation is availability [4].

In distributed databases [17], a common practice to overcome availability problems is to replicate data near data consumers. Replication can be
achieved by complete dataset replication, active caching, pre-fetching or fragmentation [13].

RDF data consumers can replicate *subsets* of RDF datasets or *replicated
fragments*, and make them accessible through SPARQL endpoints. This will
provide the support for an efficient RDF data re-organization according to the
needs and *computational resource capacity* of data consumers, while these data

© Springer International Publishing Switzerland 2015
M. Arenas et al. (Eds.): ISWC 2015, Part I, LNCS 9366, pp. 36–51, 2015.
DOI: 10.1007/978-3-319-25007-6_3

can be still *accessed* using SPARQL endpoints. Unfortunately, although SPARQL endpoints can *transparently* access replicated fragments, as well as maintain their *consistency* [13], federated query engines are not tailored to exploit the benefits of replicated fragments.

Federated SPARQL engines [1],[6],[9],[18],[21] allow data consumers to execute SPARQL queries against a federation of SPARQL endpoints. However, these engines are just designed to select the SPARQL endpoints that ensure both a complete answer and an efficient execution of the query. In presence of replication, existing federated query engines may retrieve data from every relevant endpoint, and produce a large number of intermediate results that trigger many requests to the endpoints. Thus, federated query engines may exhibit poor *performance* while *availability* of the selected SPARQL endpoints is negatively impacted.

Although the problem of managing RDF data *overlapping* during federated query processing has been addressed in [12],[20], the problem of managing *replication* in a federation of RDF datasets still remains open. DAW [20] is able to detect overlapping between datasets and optimize source selection based on that. However, because DAW is not designed to manage data replication, there is no support for explicitly define and use replicated fragments. In consequence, DAW may select redundant data sources and generate a high number of intermediate results as we will report in our experiments.

In this paper, we build a replication-aware SPARQL federated query engine by integrating into state-of-the art federated query engines FedX [21] and ANAPSID [1], a source selection strategy called FEDRA that solves the source selection problem with fragment replication (SSP-FR). For a given set of SPARQL endpoints with replicated fragments and a SPARQL query, the problem is to minimize the number of transferred data from endpoints to the federated query engines, while preserving answer completeness and reducing data redundancy.

We empirically study federated query engines FedX and ANAPSID extended with FEDRA and DAW on synthetic and real datasets. The results suggest that FEDRA efficiently reduces intermediate results and data redundancy.

The paper is organized as follows. Section 2 describes background and motivations. Section 3 defines replicated fragments and presents the source selection problem for fragment replication. Section 4 presents the FEDRA source selection algorithm. Section 5 reports our experimental results. Section 6 summarizes related works. Finally, conclusions and future works are outlined in Section 7.

2   Background and Motivations

Existing SPARQL federated query engines do not support replicated data. To illustrate, we replicated the DBpedia dataset and defined two federations. The first is composed of one mirror of DBpedia, and the second of two identical mirrors of DBpedia. We used FedX [21] and ANAPSID [1] to execute the query in Figure 1a against both federations. In the first federation, these engines produced the same query answers. On the other hand, for the second federation, these

(a) DBpedia Query

```
select distinct ?p ?m ?n ?d where {
  ?p  dbprop:name ?m .
  ?p  dbprop:nationality ?n .
  ?p  dbprop:doctoralAdvisor ?d .
}
```

(b) Query Execution

#DBpedia Replicas	Execution Time (ms)		# Results	
	FedX	ANAPSID	FedX	ANAPSID
1	1,392	22,972	8,921	8,921
2	215,907	≥ 1,800,000	418	8,921

Fig. 1. DBpedia query and its execution time and number of results against one and two replicas of DBpedia for FedX and ANAPSID

query engines have no knowledge about the relationships among the mirrors of DBpedia, and they contact both data sources. In this way, performance in terms of execution time and number of results, is seriously degraded as depicted in Figure 1b.[1]

Furthermore, if the DAW approach were used, resources of data providers and consumers would be used to compute and download data summaries. DAW could select different DBpedia data sources per triple pattern, and execute thus the join between retrieved data at the federated engine level.

Of course, if federated query engines would know that one endpoint is the mirror of the other, the source selection pruning could be done more efficiently, i.e., only one source would be selected to execute the query. This problem is even more challenging if we consider that one endpoint can partially replicate data from several RDF datasets, i.e., only fragments of several datasets are replicated.

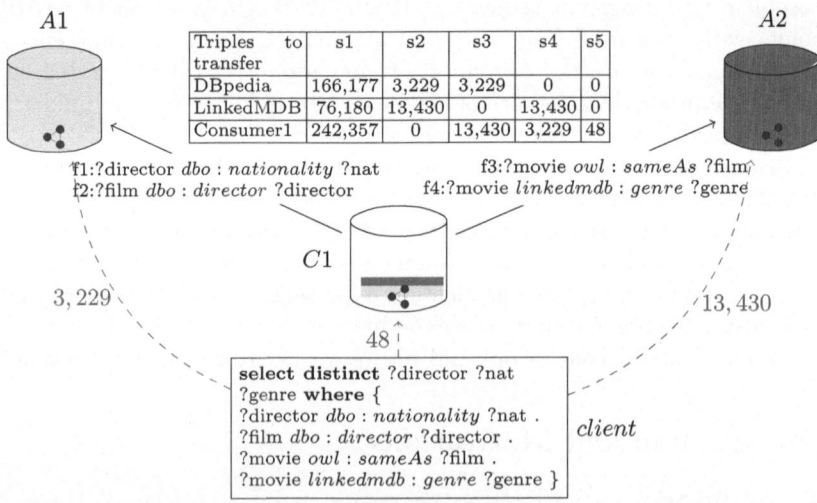

Fig. 2. Client defines a federation composed of DBpedia (A1), LinkedMDB (A2), and one Consumer (C1) endpoints with four replicated fragments

---

[1] FedX retrieves less results with two mirrors of DBpedia because it reaches the endpoints maximum number of result rows.

Suppose a Web application poses federated queries against endpoints $A1$ (DBpedia) and $A2$ (LinkedMDB). In order to speed up the queries, a data consumer endpoint $C1$ with replicated fragments has been installed as in Figure 2. Fragments are defined as simple CONSTRUCT SPARQL queries with one triple pattern. Fragments allow for the re-organization of RDF data *on* $C1$ to better address needs of data consumers..

Even in this simple setup, processing our running query against a federation including $A1$, $A2$, and $C1$ raises the problem of source selection with fragment replication (SSP-FR). There are at least five options to select sources for executing this query; these choices produce different number of transferred tuples as shown in Figure 2: (i) If no information about replicated fragments is available, all sources may be selected to retrieve data for all the triple patterns. The number of intermediate results is given in the solution $s1$. This will be the behavior of a federated query engine like FedX that ensures answer completeness.[2] (ii) Endpoints $A1$ and $A2$ could be chosen, in this case the number of intermediate results is given in $s2$. The number of intermediate results in $s2$ is less than $s1$ since some joins could be executed at $A1$ and $A2$. (iii) Another choice may be to use the $C1$ endpoint in combination with either $A1$ or $A2$ ($s3, s4$). This produces the same number of intermediate results as in $s2$, but they have the advantage of accessing less public endpoints. (iv) A last choice could be to use the $C1$ endpoint to retrieve data for all the triple patterns ($s5$). This solution profits from replicated fragments to execute opportunistic joins at $C1$; thus, it is able to achieve the *best* performance in terms of the number of intermediate results.

As the number of transferred tuples increases, the availability of the contacted SPARQL endpoints can be affected. A replication aware federated query engine could select the best sources to reduce the size of intermediate results while preserving answer completeness. In this paper, we formally address the following problem: Given a SPARQL query and a set of relevant SPARQL endpoints with replicated fragments, choose the SPARQL endpoints to contact in order to produce a complete query answer and transfer the minimum amount of data. We aim to develop an algorithm that produces solution $s5$ whenever possible, providing as output the sources to be used by a federated query engine.

3   Definitions and Problem Description

This section introduces definitions and the source selection problem with fragment replication (SSP-FR).

3.1   Definitions

Fragments are used to replicate RDF data. The data of a fragment is defined by means of the dataset public endpoint, or *authoritative endpoint*, and a CONSTRUCT query with *one* triple pattern.

---

[2] In order to preserve joins between different endpoints, each triple pattern should be posed to each endpoint individually.

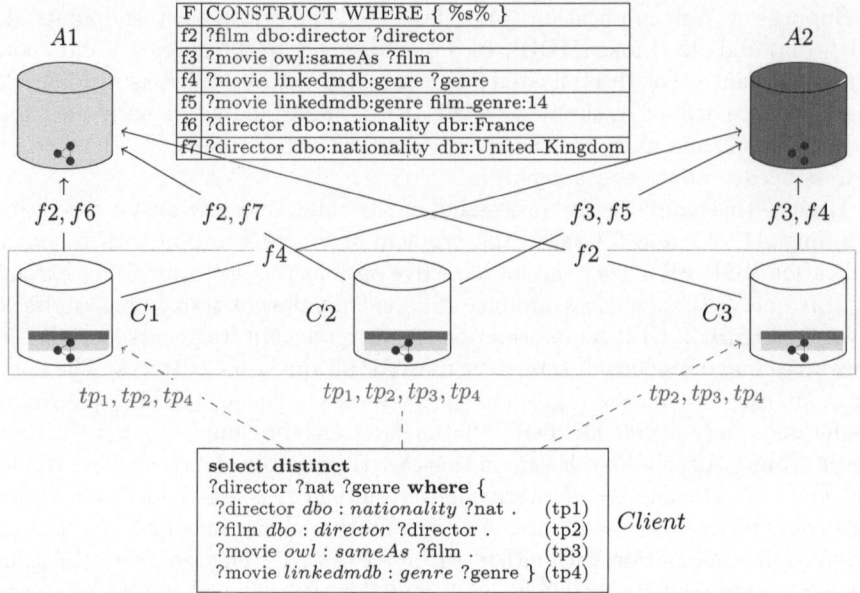

F	CONSTRUCT WHERE { %s% }
f2	?film dbo:director ?director
f3	?movie owl:sameAs ?film
f4	?movie linkedmdb:genre ?genre
f5	?movie linkedmdb:genre film_genre:14
f6	?director dbo:nationality dbr:France
f7	?director dbo:nationality dbr:United_Kingdom

Fig. 3. Client defines a federation composed of $C1, C2$, and $C3$ that replicates fragments $f2 - f7$

Definition 1 (Fragment). *A fragment is a tuple $f = \langle u, s \rangle$*
  - *u is the non-null URI of the authoritative endpoint where f is available;*
  - *s is a CONSTRUCT query with one triple pattern.*

Without loss of generality, s is limited to one triple pattern as in [13],[22]; this reduces the complexity of *fragment containment* problem as described in Definition 2. Additionally, we assume replicated fragments comprise RDF data accessible from public endpoints, i.e., the authoritative endpoints of the replicated fragments are disjoint with data consumer endpoints. This will allow data consumers to re-organize RDF data replicated from different public endpoints to fit in this way, their needs and requirements.

In this work, we make the following assumptions: (i) Fragments are replicated from public endpoints, and there is just one level of replication. (ii) Fragments are read-only and perfectly synchronized; the fragment synchronization problem is studied in [13], while querying fragments with divergence is addressed in [16]. (iii) For the sake of simplicity, we suppose that RDF data accessible through the endpoints are described as fragments.

To illustrate, consider the federation given in Figure 3. This federation extends the setup in Figure 2. Suppose three Web applications pose queries against DBpedia and LinkedMDB. To speed up query processing, data consumer endpoints: $C1$, $C2$, and $C3$ with replicated fragments have been configured.

At startup, the federated query engine loads the fragments description for each of the federation endpoints, and computes both the *fragment* and *containment* mappings. The **fragment mappings** is a function that maps fragments to a set of endpoints; the **containment mapping** is based on *containment* relation ($f_l \sqsubseteq f_k$) described in the Definition 2.

Two fragments loaded from two different endpoints Ci, Cj that have the same authoritative endpoint and equivalent construct queries are concatenated in the fragment mapping. For example, the federated engine loads fragments $\langle http://dbpedia.org/sparql, \ ?film \ db:director \ ?director\rangle$ from $C1, C2, C3$, computes equivalence, and adds in its fragment mapping $\langle http://dbpedia.org/sparql, \ ?film \ db:director \ ?director\rangle \rightarrow \{ C1, C2, C3 \}$.

Query containment and equivalence have been studied extensively. We adapt the definition given in [11] for the case of a triple pattern query.

Definition 2 (Triple Pattern Containment). *Let $TP(D)$ denote the result of execution of the triple pattern TP against an RDF dataset D. Let TP_1 and TP_2 be two triple patterns. We say that TP_1 is contained in TP_2, denoted by $TP_1 \sqsubseteq TP_2$, if for any RDF dataset D, $TP_1(D) \subseteq TP_2(D)$. We say that TP_1 is equivalent to TP_2, denoted by $TP_1 \equiv TP_2$, if $TP_1 \sqsubseteq TP_2$ and $TP_2 \sqsubseteq TP_1$.*

In the case of triple patterns, testing containment [10] amounts to finding a substitution of the variables in the triple patterns.[3] $TP_1 \sqsubseteq TP_2$, iff there is a substitution θ such that applying θ to TP_2 returns the triple pattern TP_1. Testing triple pattern containment has a complexity of $O(1)$. Solving the decision problem of triple pattern containment between TP_1 and TP_2, $TP_1 \sqsubseteq TP_2$, requires to check if $TP1$ imposes at least the same restrictions as TP_2 on the subject, predicate, and object positions, i.e., TP_1 should have at most the same number of unbounded variables as TP_2.

For the federation in Figure 3, $f5 \sqsubseteq f4$ because $f4$ and $f5$ share the same authoritative endpoint and there is a substitution θ defined as $\theta(?genre) = film\_genre : 14$, $\theta(?movie) = ?movie$, and applying θ to $f4$ returns $f5$. After identifying a substitution θ for all pair-wise fragments, it is straightforward to compute a **containment mapping** for a federation of SPARQL endpoints.

We can rely on fragment descriptions and the containment property to determine relevant fragments to a query. Relevant fragments contain relevant RDF data to each of the triple patterns of the query. A fragment is *relevant* to a query Q, if it is relevant to *at least one* triple pattern of the query.

Definition 3 (Fragment Relevance). *Let f be a fragment defined by a triple pattern TP_1. Let TP_2 be a triple pattern of a query Q. f is relevant to Q if $TP_2 \sqsubseteq TP_1$ or $TP_1 \sqsubseteq TP_2$.*

Table 1a shows the relevant fragments to the triple patterns in query Q, and the endpoints that provide these fragments. For example, the triple pattern $tp1$ has two relevant fragments: $f6$ and $f7$, and triple pattern $tp4$ has two relevant fragments: $f4$ and $f5$. Fragment $f4$ can produce the complete answer of $tp4$ because $f5 \sqsubseteq f4$, while both $f6$ and $f7$ are required to answer $tp1$.

---

[3] The substitution operator preserves URIs and literals, only variables are substituted.

Table 1. SSP-FR for query Q over a federation of $C1$, $C2$, and $C3$ of Figure 3

(a) Relevant Fragments to Q

	Q triple pattern	RF	Endpoints
tp_1	?director dbo:nationality ?nat	f6	C1
		f7	C2
tp_2	?film dbo:director ?director	f2	C1,C2,C3
tp_3	?movie owl:sameAs ?film	f3	C2,C3
tp_4	?movie linkedmdb:genre ?genre	f4	C1,C3
		f5	C2

(b) Answer completeness preservation

TP	$D_0(tp)$	$D_1(tp)$	$D_2(tp)$
tp_1	{C1,C2}	{C1,C2}	{C1,C2}
tp_2	{C1,C2,C3}	{C1}	{C3}
tp_3	{C2,C3}	{C2}	{C3}
tp_4	{C1,C2,C3}	{C3}	{C3}
Triples to transfer	421,675	170,078	8,953

3.2 Source Selection Problem with Fragment Replication (SSP-FR)

Given a SPARQL query Q, a set of SPARQL endpoints E, the set of fragments F that have been replicated by at least one endpoint in E, a fragment mapping *endpoints()*, a containment mapping $\sqsubseteq$.

The Source Selection Problem with Fragment Replication (SSP-FR) is to assign to each triple pattern in Q, the set of endpoints from E that need to be contacted to answer Q. A solution of SSP-FR corresponds to a mapping D that satisfies the following properties:

1. **Answer completeness preservation:** sources selected in D do not reduce the query engine answer completeness.
2. **Data redundancy minimization:** *cardinality(D(tp))* is minimized for all triple pattern tp in Q, i.e., redundant data is minimized.
3. **Data transfer minimization:** executing the query using the sources selected in D minimizes the number of transferred data.

We illustrate SSP-FR on running query Q of Figure 3. Table 1a presents relevant fragments for each triple pattern. Table 1b shows three $D(tp)$ that ensure the completeness preservation property. It may seem counterintuitive that these three $D(tp)$ do ensure the completeness preservation property, as they do not include existing DBpedia triples for *dbo:nationality* predicate with object different from *dbr:France* and *dbr:United_Kingdom*, but as they are not included in endpoints in E, these triples are inaccessible to the federation. Even if D_1 and D_2 minimize the number of selected endpoints per triple pattern, only D_2 minimizes the transferred data. Indeed, executing $tp1, tp2, tp3$ against replicated fragments that are located in the same data consumer endpoint will greatly reduce the size of intermediate results.

The approach proposed by Saleem et al. [20] is not designed for solving SSP-FR. Indeed, it does not take into account replicated data, and may produce a solution as D_1. The FEDRA algorithm exploits properties of the replicated fragments and is able to find solution D_2.

4 FEDRA: An Algorithm for SSP-FR

The goal of FEDRA is to reduce data transfer by taking advantage of the replication of relevant fragments for several triple patterns on the same endpoint.

Algorithm 1. FEDRA Source Selection algorithm

Require: Q: SPARQL Query; F: set of Fragments; endpoints : Fragment → set of Endpoint; $\sqsubseteq$: TriplePattern × TriplePattern
Ensure: selectedEndpoints: map from TriplePattern to set of Endpoint.
1: **function** SOURCESELECTION(Q,F,endpoints,$\sqsubseteq$)
2:   triplePatterns ← get triple patterns in Q
3:   R, E ← $\emptyset$, $\emptyset$
4:   **for each** tp ∈ triplePatterns **do**
5:     R(tp) ← RELEVANTFRAGMENTS(tp, F)   ▷ Relevant fragments as in Definition 3
6:     R(tp) ← {{f : f ∈ R(tp) : tp $\sqsubseteq$ f}} $\bigcup$ {{f} : f ∈ R(tp) : f $\sqsubseteq$ tp ∧ ¬(∃g : g ∈ R(tp) : f $\sqsubset$ g $\sqsubseteq$ tp)}
7:     E(tp) ← { ($\bigcup$ endpoints(f) : f ∈ fs) : fs ∈ R(tp) }
8:   basicGP ← get basic graph patterns in Q
9:   **for each** bgp ∈ basicGP **do**
10:     UNIONREDUCTION(bgp, E)   ▷ endpoints reduction for multiple fragments triples
11:     BGPREDUCTION(bgp, E)   ▷ endpoints reduction for the bgp triples
12:   **for each** (tp, E(tp)) ∈ E **do**
13:     selectedEndpoints(tp) ← for each set in E(tp) include one element
14:   **return** selectedEndpoints

Algorithm 2. Union reduction algorithm

Require: tps : set of TriplePattern; E : mapping from TriplePattern to set of set of Endpoint
15: **procedure** UNIONREDUCTION(tps, E)
16:   triplesWithMultipleFragments ← { tp : tp ∈ tps ∧ cardinality(E(tp)) > 1 }
17:   **for each** tp ∈ triplesWithMultipleFragments **do**
18:     commonSources ← ($\bigcap$ f : f ∈ E(tp))   ▷ get sources in all subsets in E(tp)
19:     **if** commonSources ≠ $\emptyset$ **then**
20:       E(tp) ← { commonSources }

Algorithm 1 proceeds in four main steps: I. Identify relevant fragments for triple patterns, a Basic Graph Pattern (BGP) triple pattern can be contained in one fragment or a union of fragments (lines 5-6). II. Localize relevant replicated fragments on the endpoints, e.g., Figure 4 (line 7). III. Prune endpoints for the unions (line 10). IV. Prune endpoints for the BGPs using a set covering heuristic (line 11).

Next, we illustrate how Algorithm 1 works on our running query Q and data consumer endpoints $C1, C2, C3$ from Figure 3.[4]

First, for each triple pattern, FEDRA computes relevant fragments in $R(tp)$, and groups them if they provide the same relevant data. For tp1, $R(tp1) \rightarrow \{\{f6\}, \{f7\}\}$. For tp4, as $f5 \sqsubseteq f4$, $f5$ is safely removed at line 6, and $R(tp4) \rightarrow \{\{f4\}\}$. Second, FEDRA localizes fragments on endpoints in $E(tp)$. For tp1, $E(tp1) \rightarrow \{\{C1\}, \{C2\}\}$. For tp4, $E(tp4) \rightarrow \{\{C1, C3\}\}$. Figure 4 shows the execution plans encoded in $R(tp)$ and $E(tp)$. Triple patterns like tp1, with more than one relevant fragment, represent unions in the execution plan.

Procedure UNIONREDUCTION (cf. Algorithm 2) prunes non common endpoints, if possible, to access triple patterns from as few endpoints as possible. In our running example, it is not possible because there is no common endpoint that replicates both $f6$ and $f7$. However, if, for example, $f7$ were also replicated at $C1$, then only $C1$ would be selected to execute tp1.

---

[4] As DBpedia is not included in the federation for processing Q, only fragments $f6$ and $f7$ are available to retrieve data for tp_1 and the engine will not produce all the answers that would be produced using DBpedia.

Algorithm 3. Basic graph pattern reduction algorithm

Require: tps : set of TriplePattern; E : mapping from TriplePattern to set of set of Endpoint
21: **procedure** BGPREDUCTION(tps, E)
22:     triplesWithOneFragment ← { tp : tp ∈ tps ∧ cardinality(E(tp)) = 1 }
23:     (S, C) ← minimal set covering instance using triplesWithOneFragment◁E
24:     C' ← MINIMALSETCOVERING(S, C)
25:     selected ← get endpoints encoded by C
26:     **for each** tp ∈ triplesWithOneFragment **do**
27:         E(tp) ← E(tp) ∩ selected

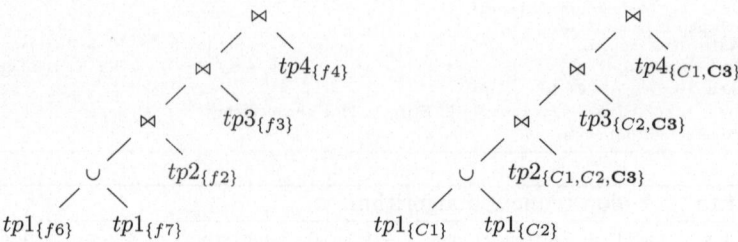

Fig. 4. Execution plan encoded in data structures R (left) and E (right); multiple subsets represent union of different fragment (ex. {f6}, {f7}); elements of the subset represent alternative location of fragments (ex. {C1,C3}); bold sources are the selected sources after set covering is used to reduce number of selected sources

Procedure BGPREDUCTION (cf. Algorithm 3) transforms the join part of $E(tp)$ (cf. Figure 4) into a set covering problem (cf. line 23). Each triple pattern is an element of the set to cover, e.g., tp2, tp3, tp4 correspond to s2, s3, s4 (cf. Figure 5a). And for each endpoint in $E(tp)$, we include the subset of triple patterns associated with that endpoint, e.g., for endpoint C1 we include the subset {s2,s4} as relevant fragments tp2 and tp4 are replicated by C1 (cf. Figure 5b). Line 24 relies on an existing heuristic [14] to find the minimum set covering. In our example, it computes $C'=\{\{s2,s3,s4\}\}$. Line 25 computes the selected endpoints, in our example, selected={ C3 }.

Finally, (Algorithm 1, line 13) chooses among endpoints that provide the same fragment and reduces data redundancy. For query Q, the whole algorithm returns D_2 of Table 1b.

Proposition 1. *Algorithm 1 has a time complexity of $O(n.m^2)$, with n the number of triple patterns in the query, m the number of fragments, k the number of endpoints, l the number of basic graph patterns in the query, and $m \gg k \land k \gg l$ holds.*

The upper bound given in Proposition 1 is unlikely to be reached, as it requires for all fragments to be relevant for each of the triple patterns. In practice (e.g., experiments from Section 5), even for high number of fragments (> 450), the source selection time remains low (< 2 secs).

Theorem 1. *If all the RDF data accessible through the endpoints of a federation are described as replicated fragments, FEDRA source selection does not reduce query engine answer completeness.*

(a) S instances

Triple Patterns (Tps)	E(tp)	S
tp2: ?film $dbo : director$?director	{{C1,C2,C3}}	{ s_2
tp3: ?movie $owl : sameAs$?film	{{C2,C3}}	s_3
tp4: ?movie $linkedmdb : genre$?genre	{{C1,C3}}	s_4}

(b) C instance

C1	C2	C3
↓	↓	↓
{{s_2,s_4},{s_2,s_3},{s_2,s_3,s_4}}		

Fig. 5. Set covering instances of S and C of BGP reduction Algorithm 3 for the query Q (Figure 3)

Table 2. Dataset characteristics: version, number of different triples (# DT), and predicates (# P)

Dataset	Version date	# DT	# P
Diseasome	19/10/2012	72,445	19
Semantic Web Dog Food	08/11/2012	198,797	147
DBpedia Geo-coordinates	06/2012	1,900,004	4
LinkedMDB	18/05/2010	3,579,610	148
WatDiv1	-	104,532	86
WatDiv100	-	10,934,518	86

5   Experimental Study

The goal of the experimental study is to evaluate the effectiveness of FEDRA. We compare the performance of federated SPARQL queries using FedX, DAW+FedX, FEDRA+FedX, ANAPSID, DAW+ANAPSID, and FEDRA+ANAPSID.

We expect to see that FEDRA selects less sources than DAW, and transfers less data from endpoints to the query engines.

Datasets and Queries: We use the real datasets: Diseasome, Semantic Web Dog Food, LinkedMDB, and DBpedia Geo-coordinates. Further, we consider two instances of the Waterloo SPARQL Diversity Test Suite (WatDiv) synthetic dataset [2,3] with 10^5 and 10^7 triples. Table 2 shows the characteristics of these datasets. The datasets are hosted on local Linked Data Fragment (LDF) servers.

We generate 50,000 queries from 500 templates for the WatDiv federation. We remove the queries that caused engines to abort execution, and queries that returned zero results. For the real datasets, we generate more than 10,000 queries using PATH and STAR shaped templates with two to eight triple patterns, that are instantiated with random values from the datasets. We include the DISTINCT modifier in all the queries, in order to make them susceptible to a reduction in the set of selected sources without changing the query answer.

For each dataset, we setup a ten consumer SPARQL endpoint federation (ten as in [20]). A consumer SPARQL endpoint is implemented using Jena Fuseki 1.1.1[5]. Each consumer endpoint selects 100 random queries. Each triple pattern

---

[5] http://jena.apache.org/, January 2015.

of the query is executed as a SPARQL construct query with the LDF client[6]. The results are stored locally if not present in at least three consumer endpoints and a fragment definition is created. This replication factor of three was set to avoid federations where all the fragments were replicated by all the endpoints.

In order to measure the number of transferred data, the federated query engine accesses data consumer endpoints through a proxy.

Implementations: FedX 3.0[7] and ANAPSID[8] have been modified to call FEDRA and DAW [20] source selection strategies during query processing. Thus, each engine can use the selected sources to perform its own optimization strategies. FEDRA and DAW[9] are implemented in both Java 1.7 and Python 2.7.3. Thus, FEDRA and DAW are integrated in FedX (Java) and ANAPSID (Python), reducing the performance impact of including these new source selection strategies. Proxies are implemented in Java 1.7. using the Apache HttpComponents Client library 4.3.5[10]. We used R[11] to compute the Wilcoxon signed rank test [24].

Evaluation Metrics: *i) Number of Selected Sources (NSS):* is the sum of the number of sources that have been selected per triple pattern. *ii) Number of Transferred Tuples (NTT):* is the number of tuples transferred from all the endpoints to the query engine during a query execution.

Further informations (implementation, results, setups details, tests p-values) are available at https://sites.google.com/site/fedrasourceselection.

5.1   Data Redundancy Minimization

To measure the reduction of the number of selected sources, 100 queries were randomly chosen, and the source selection was performed for these queries for each federation using ANAPSID and FedX with and without FEDRA or DAW. For each query, the sum of the number of selected sources per triple pattern was computed. Boxplots are used to present the results (Figure 6). Both FEDRA and DAW significantly reduce the number of selected sources, however, the reduction achieved by FEDRA is greater than the achieved by DAW.

To confirm it, we formulated the null hypothesis: "FEDRA selects the same number of sources as DAW does", and performed a Wilcoxon signed rank test, p-values were inferior or equal to 1.4e-05 for all federations and engines. These low p-values allow for rejecting the null hypothesis that DAW and FEDRA reduction are similar, and accepting the alternative hypothesis that FEDRA reduction is greater than the one achieved by DAW. FEDRA source selection strategy identifies the relevant fragments and endpoints that provide the same data. Only one

---

[6] https://github.com/LinkedDataFragments, March 2015.
[7] http://www.fluidops.com/fedx/, September 2014.
[8] https://github.com/anapsid/anapsid, September 2014.
[9] We had to implement DAW as its code is not available.
[10] https://hc.apache.org/, October 2014.
[11] http://www.r-project.org/

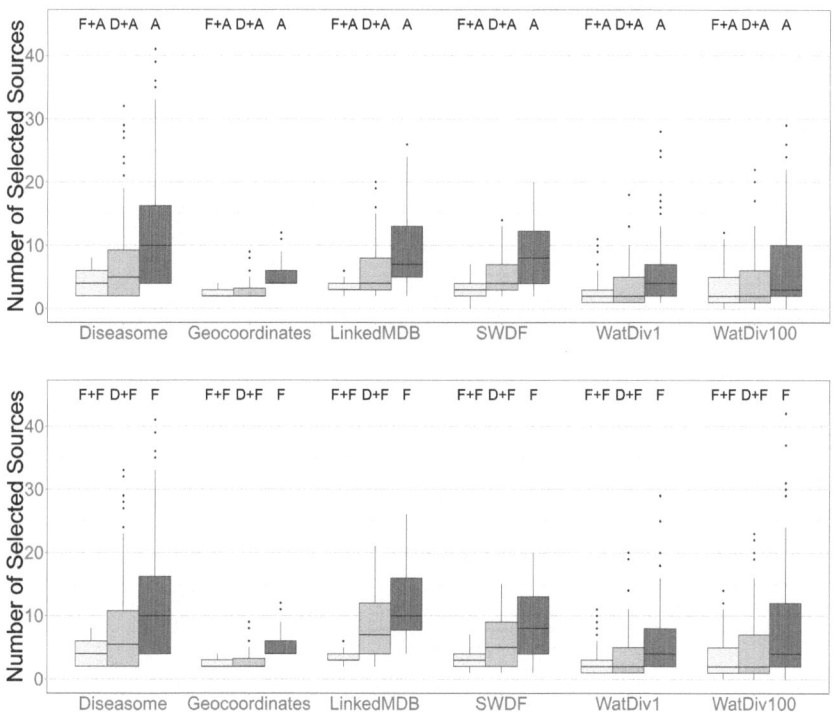

Fig. 6. Number of Selected Sources for execution of ANAPSID (A) and FedX (F) using FEDRA (F+), DAW (D+), and the engine source selection

of them is actually selected; in consequence, a huge reduction on the number of selected sources of up to 400% per query is achieved.

5.2   Data Transfer Minimization

To measure the reduction in the number of transferred tuples, queries were executed using proxies that measure the number of transmitted tuples from endpoints to the engines. Because queries that timed out have no significance on number of transferred tuples, we removed all these queries from the study.[12] Results (Figure 7) show that FEDRA source selection strategy leads to executions with considerably less intermediate results in all the federations except in the SWDF federation. In some queries of the SWDF federation, FEDRA+FedX sends exclusive groups that include BGPs with triple patterns that do not share a variable, i.e., BGPs with Cartesian products; in presence of Cartesian product, large intermediate results may be generated. Queries with Cartesian products counters FEDRA positive impact over other queries.

---

[12] Up to six queries out of 100 queries did not successfully finish in 1,800 seconds, details available at the web page.

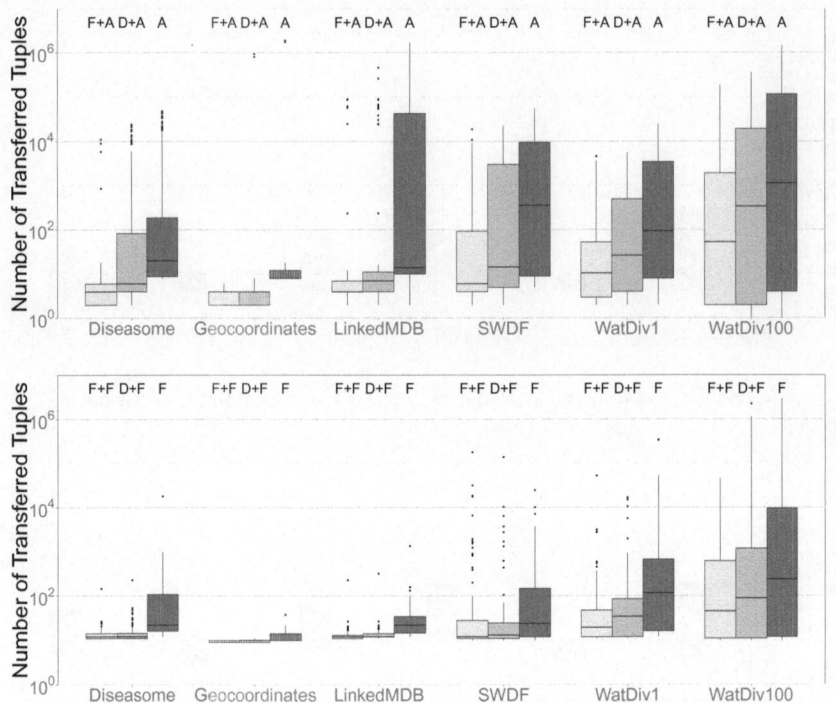

Fig. 7. Number of Transferred Tuples during execution with ANAPSID (A) and FedX (F) using FEDRA (F+), DAW (D+), and the engine source selection

Despite that, globally FEDRA shows an effective reduction of the number of transferred tuples. To confirm it, we formulated the null hypothesis: "using sources selected by FEDRA leads to transfer the same number of tuples as using sources selected by DAW"; and performed a Wilcoxon signed rank test, p-values were inferior or equal to 0.002 for all federations and engines except SWDF federation + FedX engine. In consequence, for all combinations of federation and engines except SWDF+FedX, we can reject the null hypothesis DAW and FEDRA number of transferred tuples are similar and accept the alternative hypothesis that FEDRA achieves a greater reduction of the number of transferred tuples than DAW. The reduction of the number of transferred tuples is mainly due to FEDRA source selection strategy aims to find opportunities to execute joins in the endpoints, and mostly, it leads to a significant reduction of the intermediate results size of up to four orders of magnitude.

6   Related Work

In distributed databases, data fragmentation and replication improve data availability and query performance [17]. Data fragmentation is tailored for representative queries; fragments are smartly allocated and replicated across servers for balancing workload and reducing size of intermediate results. Linked Data [7] is intrinsically a federation of autonomous participants where federated queries are unknown to a single participant, and a tight coordination of data providers is difficult to achieve. Consequently, federated query engines cannot rely on properties ensured by an allocation algorithm. SSP-FR challenge is to best use fragment localities to reduce intermediate results in a given federation.

Recently, the Linked Data fragments approach (LDF) [22, 23] proposes to improve Linked Data availability by moving query execution load from servers to clients. A client is able to execute locally a restricted SPARQL query by downloading fragments required to execute the query from an LDF server through a simple HTTP request. This strategy allows clients to cache fragments locally and decreases the load on the LDF server. LDF chooses a clear tradeoff by shifting query processing to clients, at the cost of slower query execution. In experiments, we present how to federate several SPARQL consumer endpoints that replicate fragments from LDF servers. Re-organizing fragments on data consumers opens the opportunity to process federated queries even with LDF servers.

Col-graph [13] enables data consumers to materialize triple pattern fragments and to expose them through SPARQL endpoints to improve data quality. A data consumer can update her local fragments and share updates with data providers and consumers. Col-graph proposes a coordination free protocol to maintain the consistency of replicated fragments. Currently, FEDRA can process federated queries over Col-graph collaboration networks if the topology of Col-graph is restricted to two layers without cycles. FEDRA does not yet consider divergence between fragments produced by concurrent editing, but it is addressed in [16].

HiBISCuS [19] source selection approach has been proposed to reduce the number of selected sources. The reduction is achieved by annotating sources with their authority URIs, and pruning sources that cannot have triples that match any of the query triple patterns. HiBISCuS differs from our aim of both selecting sources that are required to the answer, and avoiding the selection of sources that only provide redundant replicated fragments. While not directly related to replication, HiBISCuS index could be used in conjunction with FEDRA to perform join-aware source selection in presence of replicated fragments.

Recently, QBB [12] and DAW [20] propose duplicate-aware strategies for selecting sources for federated query engines. Both approaches use sketches to estimate the overlapping among sources. DAW uses a combination of Min-Wise Independent Permutations (MIPs) [8], and triple selectivity information to estimate the overlap between the results of different sources. Based on how many new query results are expected to be found, sources that are below predefined benefits, are discarded and not selected. Compared to DAW, FEDRA does not require to compute data summaries because FEDRA relies on fragment definitions and fragment containment to manage replication. Computing containments based on fragment descriptions is less expensive than computing data summaries; moreover, data updates are more frequent than fragment description updates. FEDRA minimizes the number of endpoints and data transfer and produces complete query answers. Consequently, if DAW and FEDRA could find the same number of sources to execute a query, FEDRA source selection considers the query basic graph patterns to delegate join execution to the endpoints and reduce intermediate results size. This key feature cannot be achieved by DAW as it performs source selection only at the triple pattern level.

7 Conclusions

In this paper, we illustrated how replicating fragments allow for data reorganization from different data sources to better fit query needs of data consumers. Then, we proposed a replication-aware federated query engine by extending state-of-art federated query engine ANAPSID and FedX with FEDRA, a source selection strategy that approximates SSP-FR.

FEDRA exploits fragment localities to reduce intermediate results. Experimental results demonstrate that FEDRA achieves significant reduction of intermediate results while preserving query answer completeness.

This work opens several perspectives. First, we made the assumption that replicated fragments are perfectly synchronized and cannot be updated. We can leverage this assumption and manage the problem of federated query processing with divergence [16].

Several variants of SSP-FR can also be developed. SSP-FR does not differentiate between endpoints and the cost of accessing endpoints is considered the same. Finally, SSP-FR and FEDRA can be extended to solve the source selection problem where the number of public endpoint accesses is minimized [16].

References

1. Acosta, M., Vidal, M., Lampo, T., Castillo, J., Ruckhaus, E.: ANAPSID: An Adaptive Query Processing Engine for SPARQL Endpoints. In: Aroyo et al. [5], pp. 18–34
2. Aluç, G., Hartig, O., Özsu, M.T., Daudjee, K.: Diversified Stress Testing of RDF Data Management Systems. In: Mika et al. [15], pp. 197–212
3. Aluç, G., Ozsu, M.T., Daudjee, K., Hartig, O.: chameleon-db: a Workload-Aware Robust RDF Data Management System. University of Waterloo, Tech. Rep. CS-2013-10 (2013)
4. Buil-Aranda, C., Hogan, A., Umbrich, J., Vandenbussche, P.-Y.: SPARQL web-querying infrastructure: ready for action? In: Alani, H., et al. (eds.) ISWC 2013, Part II. LNCS, vol. 8219, pp. 277–293. Springer, Heidelberg (2013)
5. Aroyo, L., Welty, C., Alani, H., Taylor, J., Bernstein, A., Kagal, L., Noy, N., Blomqvist, E. (eds.): ISWC 2011, Part I. LNCS, vol. 7031. Springer, Heidelberg (2011)
6. Basca, C., Bernstein, A.: Avalanche: putting the spirit of the web back into semantic web querying. In: Polleres, A., Chen, H. (eds.) ISWC Posters&Demos. CEUR Workshop Proceedings, vol. 658. CEUR-WS.org. (2010)
7. Bizer, C., Heath, T., Berners-Lee, T.: Linked Data - The Story So Far. Int. J. Semantic Web Inf. Syst. 5(3), 1–22 (2009)
8. Broder, A.Z., Charikar, M., Frieze, A.M., Mitzenmacher, M.: Min-Wise Independent Permutations. J. Comput. Syst. Sci. 60(3), 630–659 (2000)

9. Görlitz, O., Staab, S.: SPLENDID: SPARQL Endpoint Federation Exploiting VOID Descriptions. In: Hartig, O., Harth, A., Sequeda, J. (eds.) COLD (2011)
10. Gutierrez, C., Hurtado, C.A., Mendelzon, A.O., Pérez, J.: Foundations of Semantic Web databases. J. Comput. Syst. Sci. **77**(3), 520–541 (2011)
11. Halevy, A.Y.: Answering queries using views: A survey. VLDB J. **10**(4), 270–294 (2001)
12. Hose, K., Schenkel, R.: Towards benefit-based RDF source selection for SPARQL queries. In: Virgilio, R.D., Giunchiglia, F., Tanca, L. (eds.) SWIM, p. 2. ACM (2012)
13. Ibáñez, L.D., Skaf-Molli, H., Molli, P., Corby, O.: Col-Graph: towards writable and scalable linked open data. In: Mika et al. [15], pp. 325–340
14. Johnson, D.S.: Approximation algorithms for combinatorial problems. In: Aho, A.V., et al. (eds.) ACM Symposium on Theory of Computing, pp. 38–49. ACM (1973)
15. Mika, P. (ed.): ISWC 2014, Part I. LNCS, vol. 8796. Springer, Heidelberg (2014)
16. Montoya, G., Skaf-Molli, H., Molli, P., Vidal, M.E.: Fedra: Query Processing for SPARQL Federations with Divergence. Tech. rep., Université de Nantes (May 2014)
17. Özsu, M.T., Valduriez, P.: Principles of distributed database systems. Springer (2011)
18. Quilitz, B., Leser, U.: Querying distributed rdF data sources with SPARQL. In: Bechhofer, S., Hauswirth, M., Hoffmann, J., Koubarakis, M. (eds.) ESWC 2008. LNCS, vol. 5021, pp. 524–538. Springer, Heidelberg (2008)
19. Saleem, M., Ngonga Ngomo, A.-C.: HiBISCuS: hypergraph-based source selection for SPARQL endpoint federation. In: Presutti, V., d'Amato, C., Gandon, F., d'Aquin, M., Staab, S., Tordai, A. (eds.) ESWC 2014. LNCS, vol. 8465, pp. 176–191. Springer, Heidelberg (2014)
20. Saleem, M., Ngonga Ngomo, A.-C., Xavier Parreira, J., Deus, H.F., Hauswirth, M.: DAW: duplicate-AWare federated query processing over the web of data. In: Alani, H., et al. (eds.) ISWC 2013, Part I. LNCS, vol. 8218, pp. 574–590. Springer, Heidelberg (2013)
21. Schwarte, A., Haase, P., Hose, K., Schenkel, R., Schmidt, M.: FedX: Optimization Techniques for Federated Query Processing on Linked Data. In: Aroyo et al. [5], pp. 601–616
22. Verborgh, R., Hartig, O., Meester, B.D., Haesendonck, G., Vocht, L.D., Sande, M.V., Cyganiak, R., Colpaert, P., Mannens, E., de Walle, R.V.: Querying Datasets on the Web with High Availability. In: Mika et al. [15], pp. 180–196
23. Verborgh, R., Sande, M.V., Colpaert, P., Coppens, S., Mannens, E., de Walle, R.V.: Web-Scale querying through linked data fragments. In: Bizer, C., et al. (eds.) WWW Workshop on LDOW 2014. CEUR Workshop Proceedings, vol. 1184. CEUR-WS.org (2014)
24. Wilcoxon, F.: Individual comparisons by ranking methods. In: Breakthroughs in Statistics, pp. 196–202. Springer (1992)

FEASIBLE: A Feature-Based SPARQL Benchmark Generation Framework

Muhammad Saleem[1](✉), Qaiser Mehmood[2], and Axel-Cyrille Ngonga Ngomo[1]

[1] Universität Leipzig, IFI/AKSW, PO 100920, 04009 Leipzig, Germany
{saleem,ngongangomo}@informatik.uni-leipzig.de
[2] Insight Center for Data Analytics, National University of Ireland, Galway, Ireland
qaiser.mehmood@insight-centre.org

Abstract. Benchmarking is indispensable when aiming to assess technologies with respect to their suitability for given tasks. While several benchmarks and benchmark generation frameworks have been developed to evaluate triple stores, they mostly provide a one-fits-all solution to the benchmarking problem. This approach to benchmarking is however unsuitable to evaluate the performance of a triple store for a given application with particular requirements. We address this drawback by presenting FEASIBLE, an automatic approach for the generation of benchmarks out of the query history of applications, i.e., query logs. The generation is achieved by selecting prototypical queries of a user-defined size from the input set of queries. We evaluate our approach on two query logs and show that the benchmarks it generates are accurate approximations of the input query logs. Moreover, we compare four different triple stores with benchmarks generated using our approach and show that they behave differently based on the data they contain and the types of queries posed. Our results suggest that FEASIBLE generates better sample queries than the state of the art. In addition, the better query selection and the larger set of query types used lead to triple store rankings which partly differ from the rankings generated by previous works.

1 Introduction

Triple stores are the data backbone of many Linked Data applications [9]. The performance of triple stores is hence of central importance for Linked-Data-based software ranging from real-time applications [8,13] to on-the-fly data integration frameworks [1,15,18]. Several benchmarks (e.g., [2,4,7,9,16,17]) for assessing the performance of the triple stores have been proposed. However, many of them (e.g., [2,4,7,17]) rely on synthetic data or on synthetic queries. The main advantage of such synthetic benchmarks is that they commonly rely on data generators that can produce benchmarks of different data sizes and thus allow to test the scalability of triple stores. However, they often fail to reflect reality. In particular, previous works [5] point out that artificial benchmarks are typically highly structured while real Linked Data sources are most commonly weakly structured.

© Springer International Publishing Switzerland 2015
M. Arenas et al. (Eds.): ISWC 2015, Part I, LNCS 9366, pp. 52–69, 2015.
DOI: 10.1007/978-3-319-25007-6_4

Moreover, synthetic queries most commonly fail to reflect the characteristics of the real queries sent to applications [3,11]. Thus, synthetic benchmark results are rarely sufficient to detect the most suitable triple store for a particular real application. The DBpedia SPARQL Benchmark (DBPSB) [9] addresses a portion of these drawbacks by evaluating the performance of triple stores based on real DBpedia query logs. The main drawback of this benchmark is however that it does not consider important data-driven and structural query features (e.g., number of join vertices, triple patterns selectivities or query execution times etc.) which greatly affect the performance of triple stores [2,6] during the query selection process. Furthermore, it only considers SELECT queries. The other three basic SPARQL query forms, i.e., ASK, CONSTRUCT, and DESCRIBE are not included.

In this paper we present FEASIBLE, a benchmark generation framework able to generate benchmarks from a set of queries (in particular from query logs). Our approach aims to generate customized benchmarks for given use cases or needs of an application. To this end, FEASIBLE assumes that it is given a set of queries well as the number of queries (e.g., 25) to be included into the benchmark as input. Then, our approach computes a sample of the selected subset that reflects the distribution of the queries in the input set of queries. The resulting queries can then be fed to a benchmark execution framework to benchmark triple stores. The contributions of this work are as follows:

1. We present the first structure and data-driven feature-based benchmark generation approach from real queries. By comparing FEASIBLE with DBPSB, we show that considering data-driven and structural query features leads to benchmarks that are better approximations of the input set of queries.
2. We present a novel sampling approach for queries based based on exemplars [10] and medoids.
3. Beside SPARQL SELECT, we conduct the first evaluation of 4 triple stores w.r.t. to their performance on ASK, DESCRIBE and CONSTRUCT queries separately.
4. We show that the performance of triple stores varies greatly across the four basic forms of SPARQL query. Moreover, we show that the features used by FEASIBLE allow for a more fine-grained analysis of our benchmarking results.

The rest of this paper is structured as follows: We begin by providing an overview of the key SPARQL query features that need to be considered while designing SPARQL benchmarks. Then, we compare existing benchmarks against these key query features systematically (Section 3) and point out the weaknesses of current benchmarks that are addressed by FEASIBLE. Our benchmark generation process is presented in Section 4. A detailed comparison with DBPSB and an evaluation of the state-of-the-art triple stores follows thereafter. The results are then discussed and we finally conclude. FEASIBLE is open-source and available online at https://code.google.com/p/feasible/. A demo can be found at http://feasible.aksw.org/.

2   Preliminaries

In this section, we define key concepts necessary to understand the subsequent sections of this work. We represent each basic graph pattern (BGP) of a SPARQL query as a directed hypergraph (DH) according to [14]. We chose this representation because it allows representing property-property joins, which previous works [2,6] do not allow to model. The DH representation of a BGP is formally defined as follows:

Definition 1. *Each basic graph patterns BGP_i of a SPARQL query can be represented as a DH $HG_i = (V, E, \lambda_{vt})$, where*

- *$V = V_s \cup V_p \cup V_o$ is the set of vertices of HG_i, V_s is the set of all subjects in HG_i, V_p the set of all predicates in HG_i and V_o the set of all objects in HG_i;*
- *$E = \{e_1, \ldots, e_t\} \subseteq V^3$ is a set of directed hyperedges (short: edge). Each edge $e = (v_s, v_p, v_o)$ emanates from the triple pattern $<v_s, v_p, v_o>$ in BGP_i. We represent these edges by connecting the head vertex v_s with the tail hypervertex (v_p, v_o). We use $E_{in}(v) \subseteq E$ and $E_{out}(v) \subseteq E$ to denote the set of incoming and outgoing edges of a vertex v;*
- *λ_{vt} is a vertex-type-assignment function. Given a vertex $v \in V$, its vertex type can be 'star', 'path', 'hybrid', or 'sink' if this vertex participates in at least one join. A 'star' vertex has more than one outgoing edge and no incoming edge. A 'path' vertex has exactly one incoming and one outgoing edge. A 'hybrid' vertex has either more than one incoming and at least one outgoing edge or more than one outgoing and at least one incoming edge. A 'sink' vertex has more than one incoming edge and no outgoing edge. A vertex that does not participate in any join is of type 'simple'.*

The representation of a complete SPARQL query as a DH is the union of the representations of query's BGPs. As an example, the DH representation of the query in Figure 1a is shown in Figure 1b. Based on the DH representation of SPARQL queries we can define the following features of SPARQL queries:

Definition 2 (Number of Triple Patterns). *From Definition 1, the total number of triple patterns in a BGP_i is equal to the number of hyperedges $|E|$ in the DH representation of the BGP_i.*

Definition 3 (Number of Join Vertices). *Let $ST = \{st_1, \ldots, st_j\}$ be the set of vertices of type 'star', $PT = \{pt_1, \ldots, pt_k\}$ be the set of vertices of type 'path', $HB = \{hb_1, \ldots, hb_l\}$ be the set of vertices of type 'hybrid', and $SN = \{sn_1, \ldots, sn_m\}$ be the set of vertices of type 'sink' in a DH representation of a SPARQL query, then the total number of join vertices in the query $\#JV = |ST| + |PT| + |HB| + |SN|$.*

Definition 4 (Join Vertex Degree). *Based on the DH representation of SPARQL queries, the join vertex degree of a vertex v is $JVD(v) = |E_{in}(v)| + |E_{out}(v)|$, where $E_{in}(v)$ resp $E_{out}(v)$ is the set of incoming resp. outgoing edges of v.*

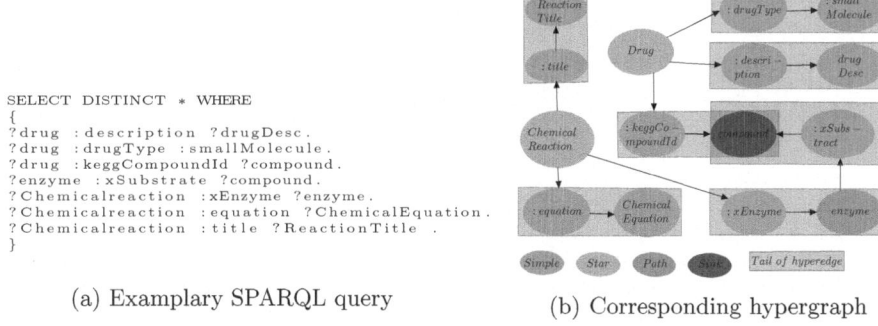

```
SELECT DISTINCT * WHERE
{
?drug   :description ?drugDesc.
?drug   :drugType :smallMolecule.
?drug   :keggCompoundId ?compound.
?enzyme :xSubstrate ?compound.
?Chemicalreaction :xEnzyme ?enzyme.
?Chemicalreaction :equation ?ChemicalEquation.
?Chemicalreaction :title ?ReactionTitle .
}
```

(a) Examplary SPARQL query

(b) Corresponding hypergraph

Fig. 1. DH representation of the SPARQL query. Prefixes are ignored for simplicity

Definition 5 (Triple Pattern Selectivity). *Let tp_i be a triple pattern and d be a relevant source for tp_i. Furthermore, let N be the total number of triples in d and N_m be the total number of triples in d that matches tp_i, then the selectivity of tp_i w.r.t. d is $Sel(tp_i, d) = N_m/N$.*

According to previous works [2,6], a SPARQL query benchmark should vary the queries it contains w.r.t. the following *query characteristics*: number of triple patterns, number of join vertices, mean join vertex degree, query result set sizes, mean triple pattern selectivities, join vertex types ('star', 'path', 'hybrid', 'sink'), and SPARQL clauses used (e.g., LIMIT, OPTIONAL, ORDER BY, DISTINCT, UNION, FILTER, REGEX). In addition, a SPARQL benchmark should contain (or provide options to select) all four SPARQL query forms (i.e., SELECT, DESCRIBE, ASK, and CONSTRUCT). Furthermore, the benchmark should contain queries of varying runtimes, ranging from small to reasonably large query execution times. In the next section, we compare state-of-the-art SPARQL benchmarks based on these query features.

3   A Comparison of Existing Benchmarks and Query Logs

Different benchmarks have been proposed to compare triple stores for their query execution capabilities and performance. Table 1 provides a detailed summary of the characteristics of the most commonly used benchmarks as well as of two real query logs. All benchmark executions and result set computations were carried out on a machine with 16 GB RAM and a 6-Core i7 3.40 GHz CPU running Ubuntu 14.04.2. All synthetic benchmarks were configured to generate 10 million triples. We ran LUBM [7] on OWLIM-Lite as it requires reasoning. All other benchmarks were ran on virtuoso 7.2 with NumberOfBuffers = 1360000, and MaxDirtyBuffers = 1000000. As query logs, we used (1) the portion of the DBpedia 3.5.1 query log (a total of 3,159,812 queries) collected between April 30th, 2010 and July 20th, 2010[1] as well as (2) the portion of the Semantic Web Dog Food (SWDF) query log (a total of 1,414,391 queries) gathered between

---

[1] We chose this query log because it was used by DBPSB.

Table 1. Comparison of SPARQL benchmarks and query logs (**F-DBP** = FEASIBLE Benchmarks from DBpedia query log, **DBP** = DBpedia query log, **F-SWDF** = FEASIBLE Benchmark from Semantic Web Dog Food query log, **SWDF** = Semantic Web Dog Food query log, **TPs** = Triple Patterns, **JV** = Join Vertices, **MJVD** = Mean Join Vertices Degree, **MTPS** = Mean Triple Pattern Selectivity, **S.D.** = Standard Deviation). Runtime(ms)

		LUBM	BSBM	SP2Bench	WatDiv	DBPSB	F-DBP	DBP	F-SWDF	SWDF
	#Queries	15	125	12	125	125	125	130466	125	64030
Forms (%)	SELECT	100	80	91.67	100	100	95.2	97.9	92.8	58.7
	ASK	0	0	8.33	0	0	0	1.93	2.4	0.09
	CONSTRUCT	0	4	0	0	0	4	0.09	3.2	0.04
	DESCRIBE	0	16	0	0	0	0.8	0.02	1.6	41.1
Clauses (%)	UNION	0	8	16.67	0	36	40.8	7.97	32.8	29.3
	DISTINCT	0	24	41.6	0	100	52.8	4.1	50.4	34.18
	ORDER BY	0	36	16.6	0	0	28.8	0.3	25.6	10.67
	REGEX	0	0	0	0	4	14.4	0.2	16	0.03
	LIMIT	0	36	8.33	0	0	38.4	0.4	45.6	1.79
	OFFSET	0	4	8.33	0	0	18.4	0.03	20.8	0.14
	OPTIONAL	0	52	25	0	32	30.4	20.1	32	29.5
	FILTER	0	52	58.3	0	48	58.4	93.3	29.6	0.72
	GROUP BY	0	0	0	0	0	0.8	7.6E-6	19.2	1.34
Results	Min	3	0	1	0	197	1	1	1	1
	Max	1.3E+4	31	4.3E+7	4.1E+9	4.6E+6	1.4E+6	1.4E+6	3.0E+5	3.0E+5
	Mean	4.9E+3	8.3	4.5E+6	3.4E+7	3.2E+5	5.2E+4	404	9091	39.5
	S.D.	1.1E+4	9.03	1.3E+7	3.7E+8	9.5E+5	1.9E+5	1.2E+4	4.7E+4	2208
BGPs	Min	1	1	1	1	1	1	0	0	0
	Max	1	5	3	1	9	14	14	14	14
	Mean	1	2.8	1.5	1	2.69	3.17	1.67	2.68	2.28
	S.D.	0	1.70	0.67	0	2.43	3.55	1.66	2.81	2.9
TPs	Min	1	1	1	1	1	1	0	0	0
	Max	6	15	13	12	12	18	18	14	14
	Mean	3	9.32	5.9	5.3	4.5	4.8	1.7	3.2	2.5
	S.D.	1.81	5.17	3.82	2.60	2.79	4.39	1.68	2.76	3.21
JV	Min	0	0	0	0	0	0	0	0	0
	Max	4	6	10	5	3	11	11	3	3
	Mean	1.6	2.88	4.25	1.77	1.21	1.29	0.02	0.52	0.18
	S.D.	1.40	1.80	3.79	0.99	1.12	2.39	0.23	0.65	0.45
MJVD	Min	0	0	0	0	0	0	0	0	0
	Max	5	4.5	9	7	5	11	11	4	5
	Mean	2.02	3.05	2.41	3.62	1.82	1.44	0.04	0.96	0.37
	S.D.	1.29	1.63	2.26	1.40	1.43	2.13	0.33	1.09	0.87
MTPS	Min	3.2E-4	9.4E-8	6.5E-5	0	1.1E-5	2.8E-9	1.2E-5	1.0E-5	1.0E-5
	Max	0.432	0.045	0.53	0.011	1	1	1	1	1
	Mean	0.01	0.01	0.22	0.004	0.119	0.140	0.005	0.291	0.0238
	S.D.	0.074	0.01	0.20	0.002	0.22	0.31	0.03	0.32	0.07
Runtime	Min	2	5	7	3	11	2	1	4	3
	Max	3200	99	7.1E+5	8.8E+8	5.4E+4	3.2E+4	5.6E+4	4.1E+4	4.1E+4
	Mean	437	9.1	2.8E+5	4.4E+8	1.0E+4	2242	30.4	1308	16.1
	S.D.	320	14.5	5.2E+5	2.7E+7	1.7E+4	6961	702.5	5335	249.6

May 16th, 2014 and November 12th, 2014. Note that we only considered queries (called *cleaned queries*) which produce at least 1 result after the query execution (130,466 queries from DBpedia and 64,029 queries from SWDF).[2] In the following, we compare these benchmarks and query logs w.r.t. the features shown in Table 1.

LUBM was designed to test the triple stores and reasoners for their reasoning capabilities. It is based on a customizable and deterministic generator for synthetic data. The queries included in this benchmark commonly lead to query results sizes ranges from 2 to 3200, query triple patterns ranges from 1 to 6, and all the queries consist of a single BGP. LUBM includes a fixed number of SELECT queries (i.e., 15) where none of the clauses shown in Table 1 is used.

The Berlin SPARQL Benchmark (BSBM) [4] uses a total of 125 query templates to generate any number of SPARQL queries for benchmarking. Multiple use cases such as explore, update, and business intelligence are included in this benchmark. Furthermore, it also includes many of the important SPARQL clauses of Table 1. However, the queries included in this benchmark are rather simple with an average query runtime of 9.1 ms and a largest query result set size of 31.

SP²Bench mirrors vital characteristics (such as power law distributions or Gaussian curves) of the data in the DBLP bibliographic database. The queries given in benchmark are mostly complex. For example, the mean (across all queries) query result size is above one million and the query runtimes are in the order of 10^5 ms (see Table 1).

The Waterloo SPARQL Diversity Test Suite (WatDiv) [2] addresses the limitations of previous benchmarks by providing a synthetic data and query generator to generate large number of queries from a total of 125 queries templates. The queries cover both simple and complex categories with varying number of features such as result set sizes, total number of query triple patterns, join vertices and mean join vertices degree. However, this benchmark is restricted to conjunctive SELECT queries (single BGPs). This means that non-conjunctive SPARQL queries (e.g., queries which make use of the UNION and OPTIONAL features) are not considered. Furthermore, WatDiv does not consider other important SPARQL clauses, e.g., FILTER and REGEX. However, our analysis of the query logs of DBpedia3.5.1 and SWDF given in table 1 shows that 20.1% resp. 7.97% of the DBpedia queries make use of OPTIONAL resp. UNION clauses. Similarly, 29.5% resp. 29.3% of the SWDF queries contain OPTIONAL resp. UNION clauses.

While the distribution of query features in the benchmarks presented so far is mostly static, the use of different SPARQL clauses and triple pattern join types varies greatly from data set to data set, thus making it very difficult for any synthetic query generator to reflect real queries. For example, the DBpedia and SWDF query log differ significantly in their use of DESCRIBE (41.1% for SWDF vs 0.02% for DBpedia), FILTER (0.72% for SWDF vs 93.3% for DBpedia) and UNION (29.3% for SWDF vs 7.97% for DBpedia) clauses. Similar variations have been

---

[2] The datadumps, query logs and cleaned queries for both datasets can be downloaded from project home page

reported in [3] as well. To address this issue, the DBpedia SPARQL Benchmark (DBPSB) [9] (which generates benchmark queries from query logs) was proposed. However, this benchmark does not consider key query features (i.e., number of join vertices, mean join vertices degree, mean triple pattern selectivities, the query result size and overall query runtimes) while selecting query templates. Note that previous works [2,6] pointed that these query features greatly affect the triple stores performance and thus should be considered while designing SPARQL benchmarks.

In this work we present FEASIBLE, a benchmark generation framework which is able to generate a customizable benchmark from any set of queries, esp. from query logs. FEASIBLE addresses the drawbacks on previous benchmark generation approaches by taking all of the important SPARQL query features of Table 1 into consideration when generating benchmarks. In the following, we present our approach in detail.

4   FEASIBLE Benchmark Generation

The benchmark generation behind our approach consists of 3 main steps. The first step is the cleaning step. Thereafter, the features of the queries are normalized. In a final step, we then select a sample of the input queries that reflects the cleaned input queries and return this sample. The sample can be used as seed in template-based benchmark generation approaches such as DBSBM and BSBM.

4.1   Data Set Cleaning

The aim of the data cleaning step is to remove erroneous and zero-result queries from the set of queries used to generate benchmarks. This step is not of theoretical necessity but leads to practically reliable benchmarks. To clean the input data set (here query logs), we begin by excluding all syntactically incorrect queries. The syntactically correct queries which lead to runtime errors[3] as well as queries which return zero results are removed from the set of relevant queries for benchmarking. We attach all 9 SPARQL clauses (e.g., UNION, DISTINCT) and 7 query features (i.e., runtime, join vertices, etc.) given in Table 1 to each of the queries. For the sake of simplicity we call these 16 (i.e., 9+7) properties *query features* in the following. All unique queries are then stored in a file[4] and given as input to the next step.

4.2   Normalization of Feature Vectors

The query selection process of FEASIBLE requires distances between queries to be computed. To ensure that dimensions with high values (e.g., the result set size) do not bias the selection, we normalize the query representations to ensure

---

[3] The runtime errors were measured using Virtuoso 7.2.

[4] A sample file can be found at http://goo.gl/YUSU9A

that all queries are located in a unit hypercube. To this end, each of the queries gathered from the previous step is mapped to a vector of length 16 which stores the corresponding *query features* as follows: For the SPARQL clauses, which are binary (e.g., UNION is either used or not used), we store a value 1 if that clause in used in the query. Otherwise we store a 0. All non-binary feature vectors are normalized by dividing their value with the overall maximal value in the data set. Therewith, we ensure that all entries of the query representations are values between 0 to 1.

4.3 Query Selection

The query selection process is based on the idea of exemplars used in [10] and is shown in Algorithm 1. We assume that we are given (1) a number $e \in \mathbb{N}$ of queries to select as benchmark queries as well as (2) a set of queries L with $|L| = n >> e$, where L is the set of all cleaned and normalized queries. The intuition behind our selection approach is to compute an e-sized partition $\mathcal{L} = \{L_1, \ldots, L_e\}$ of L such that (1) the average distance between the points in two different elements of the partition is high and (2) the average distance of points within a partition is small. We can then select the point closest to the average of each L_i (i.e., the medoid of L_i) to be a prototypical example of a query from L and include it into the benchmark generated by FEASIBLE. We implement this intuition formally by (1) selecting e exemplars (i.e., points that represent a portion of the space) that are as far as possible from each other, (2) partitioning L by mapping every point of L to one of these exemplars to compute a partition of the space at hand and (3) selecting the medoid of each of the partitions of space as a query in the benchmark. In the following, we present each of these steps formally. For the sake of clarity, we use the following running example: $L = \{q_1 = [0.2, 0.2], q_2 = [0.5, 0.3], q_3 = [0.8, 0.5], q_4 = [0.9, 0.1], q_5 = [0.5, 0.5]\}$ and assume that we need a benchmark with $e = 2$ queries. Note for the sake of simplicity, we used feature vectors of length 2 instead of 16.

Selection of Exemplars. We implement an iterative approach to the selection of exemplars (see lines 1-7 of Algorithm 1). We begin by finding the average $\tilde{L} = \frac{1}{n} \sum_{q \in L} q$ of all representations of queries $q \in L$. In our example, this point has the coordinates $[0.58, 0.32]$. The first exemplar X_1 is the point of L that is closest to the average and is given by $X_1 = \arg\min_{x \in L} d(\tilde{L}, x)$, where d stands for the Euclidean distance. In our example, this is the query q_2 with a distance of 0.08. We follow an iterative procedure to extending the set $\mathcal{X}$ of all exemplars: We first find $\eta = \arg\max_{y \in L \setminus \mathcal{X}} \left(\sum_{x \in \mathcal{X}} d(x, y) \right)$. η is the point that is furthest away from all exemplars. In our example, that is the query q_4 with a distance of 0.45 from q_2. We then add η to $\mathcal{X}$ and repeat the procedure for finding η until $|\mathcal{X}| = e$. Given that $e = 2$ in our example, we get the set $\mathcal{X} = \{q_2, q_4\}$ as set of exemplars.

Algorithm 1. Query Selection Approach

Data: Set of queries L; Size of the benchmark e
Result: Benchmark (set of queries) B

1 $\tilde{L} = \frac{1}{|L|} \sum\limits_{q \in L} q$;

2 $X_1 = \{\arg\min\limits_{x \in L} d(\tilde{L}, x)\}$;

3 $\mathcal{X} = \{X_1\}$;

4 **for** $i = 2; i \le e; i++$ **do**

5 $\quad X_i = \{\arg\max\limits_{y \in L \setminus \mathcal{X}} d(y, \mathcal{X})\}$;

6 $\quad \mathcal{X} = \mathcal{X} \cup \{X_i\}$;

7 **end**

8 $\mathcal{L} = \emptyset$;

9 **for** $i = 1; i \le e; i++$ **do**

10 $\quad L_i = \{X_i\}$;

11 $\quad \mathcal{L} = \mathcal{L} \cup \{L_i\}$;

12 **end**

13 **for** $i = 1; i \le e; i++$ **do**

14 $\quad L_i = \{q \in L \setminus \mathcal{X} : X_i = \arg\min\limits_{X \in \mathcal{X}} d(X, q)\}$

15 **end**

16 $B = \emptyset$;

17 **for** $i = 1; i \le e; i++$ **do**

18 $\quad \tilde{L}_i = \frac{1}{|L_i|} \sum\limits_{q \in L_i} q$;

19 $\quad b_i = \arg\min\limits_{q \in L_i} d(\tilde{L}_i, q)$;

20 $\quad B = B \cup \{b_i\}$;

21 **end**

22 **return** B;

Selection of Benchmark Queries. Let $\mathcal{X} = \{X_1, \ldots, X_e\}$ the set of all exemplars. The selection of benchmark queries begins with partitioning the space according to $\mathcal{X}$. The partition L_i is defined as $L_i = \{q \in L : \forall j \ne i : d(q, X_i) \le d(q, X_j)\}$ ((see lines 8-15 of Algorithm 1). It is simply the set of queries that are closer to X_i than to any other exemplar. In case of a tie, i.e., $d(q, X_i) = d(q, X_j)$ with $i \ne j$, we assign q to $\min(i, j)$. In our example, we get the following partition: $\mathcal{X} = \{\{q_1, q_2, q_3, q_5\}, \{q_4\}\}$. Finally, we perform the selection of prototypical queries from each partition (see lines 17-22 of Algorithm 1). For each partition L_i we begin by computing the average $\tilde{L}_i$ of all representations of queries in L_i. We then select the query $b_i = \arg\min\limits_{q \in L_i} d(\tilde{L}_i, q)$. The set B of benchmark queries is the set of all queries b_i over all L_i. Note that $|B| = e$. In our example, q_4 being the only query in the second partition means that q_4 is selected as representative for the second partition. The average of the first partition is located at $[0.5, 0.375]$. The query q_2 is the closest to the average, leading to q_2 being selected as representative for the first partition. Our approach thus returns a benchmark with the queries $\{q_2, q_4\}$ as result.

Figures 2a and 2b show Voronoi diagrams of the results of our approach for benchmarks of size 125 and 175 derived from the DBpedia 3.5.1 query log presented in Table 1 along the two dimensions with the highest entropy. Note that some of the queries are superposed in the diagram.

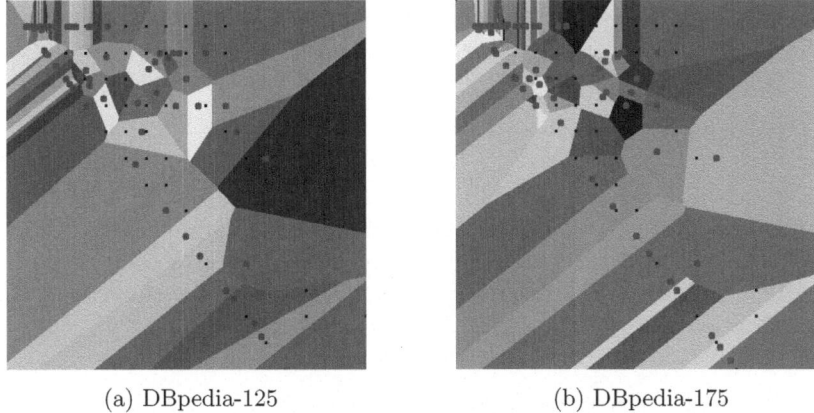

| (a) DBpedia-125 | (b) DBpedia-175 |

Fig. 2. Voronoi diagrams for benchmarks generated by FEASIBLE along the two axes with maximal entropy. Each of the red points is a benchmark query. Several points are superposed as the diagram is a projection of a 16-dimensional space unto 2 dimensions.

5   Complexity Analysis

In the following, we study the complexity of our benchmark generation approach. We denote the number of features considered during the generation process with d. e is the number of exemplars and $|L|$ the size of the input data set. *Reading and cleaning* the file can be carried out in $O(|L|d)$ as each query is read once and the features are extracted one at a time. We now need to *compute the exemplars*. We begin by computing the average A of all queries, which can be carried out using $O(|L|d)$ arithmetic operations. Finding the query that is nearest to A has the same complexity. The same approach is used to detect the other exemplars, leading to an overall complexity of $O(e|L|d)$ for the computation of exemplars. *Mapping each point* to the nearest exemplar has an a-priori complexity of $O(e|L|d)$ arithmetic operations. Given that the distances between the exemplars and all the points in L are available from the previous step, we can simply look up the distances and thus gather this information in $O(1)$ for each pair of exemplar and point, leading to an overall complexity of $O(e|L|)$. Finally, *the selection of the representative in the cluster* demands averaging the elements of the cluster and selecting the query that is closest to this point. For each cluster of size $|Cl|$, we need $(d|Cl|)$ arithmetic operations to find the average point. The holds for finding the query nearest to the average. Given that the sum of the sizes of all the clusters is $|L|$, we can conclude that the overall complexity of the selection step is $O(d|L|)$. Overall, the worst-case complexity of our algorithm is thus $O(d|L||E|)$.

In the best case, no queries passes the cleaning test, leading to no further processing and to the same complexity as reading the data, which is $O(|L|d)$. The same best-case complexity holds when a benchmark is generated. Here, the filtering step returns exactly e queries, leading to the exemplar generation step being skipped and thus to a complexity of $O(|L|d)$.

6   Evaluation and Results

Our evaluation comprises two main parts. First, we compare FEASIBLE with DBPSB w.r.t. how well the benchmarks represent the input data. To this end, we use the composite error function defined below. In the second part of our evaluation, we use FEASIBLE benchmarks to compare triple stores w.r.t. their query execution performance.

6.1   Composite Error Estimation

The benchmarks we generate aim to find typical queries for a given query log. From the point of view of statistics, this is equivalent to computing a subset of a population that has the same characteristics (here mean and standard deviation) as the original population. Thus, we measure the quality of the sampling approach of a benchmark by how much the mean and standard deviation of the features of its queries deviates from that of the query log. We call μ_i resp. σ_i the mean resp. the standard deviation of a given distribution w.r.t. to the ith feature of the said distribution. Let B be a benchmark extracted from a set of queries L. We use two measures to compute the difference between B and L, i.e., the error on the means E_μ and deviations E_σ

$$E_\mu = \frac{1}{k} \sum_{j=1}^{k} (\mu_i(L) - \mu_i(B))^2 \text{ and } E_\sigma = \frac{1}{k} \sum_{j=1}^{k} (\sigma_i(L) - \sigma_i(B))^2. \qquad (1)$$

We define a composite error estimation E as the harmonic mean of E_μ and E_σ:

$$E = \frac{2E_\mu E_\sigma}{E_\mu + E_\sigma}. \qquad (2)$$

6.2   Experimental Setup

Data sets and Query Logs: We used the DBpedia 3.5.1 (232.5M triples) and SWDF (294.8K triples) data sets for triple store evaluation. As queries (see Section 3), we used 130,466 cleaned queries for DBpedia and 64,029 cleaned queries for SWDF.

Benchmarks for Composite Error Analysis: In order to compare FEASIBLE with DBPSB, we generated benchmarks of sizes 15, 25, 50, 75, 100, 125, 150, and 175 queries from the DBpedia 3.5.1 query log. Recall this is exactly the same query log used in DBPSB. DBPSB contains a total of 25 query templates derived from 25 real queries. A single query was generated per query template in order to generate a benchmark of 25 queries. Similarly, 2 queries were generated per query template for a benchmark of 50 queries and so on. The 15-query benchmark of DBPSB was generated from the 25-query benchmark by randomly choosing 15 of the 25 queries. We chose to show results on a 15-query benchmark because LUBM contains 15 queries while SP^{2}Bench contains 12. We also generated benchmarks of the same size (15-175) from SWDF to compare FEASIBLE's composite errors as well as the performance of triple stores across different data sets.

Triple Stores: We used four triple stores in our evaluation: (1) *Virtuoso Open-Source Edition version 7.2* with NumberOfBuffers = 680000, MaxDirtyBuffers = 500000; (2) *Sesame Version 2.7.8* with Tomcat 7 as HTTP interface and native storage layout. We set the spoc, posc, opsc indices to those specified in the native storage configuration. The Java heap size was set to 6GB; (3) *Jena-TDB (Fuseki) Version 2.0* with a Java heap size set to 6GB and (4) *OWLIM-SE Version 6.1* with Tomcat 7.0 as HTTP interface. We set the entity index size to 45,000,000 and enabled the predicate list. The rule set was empty and the Java heap size was set to 6GB. Ergo, we configured all triple stores to use 6GB of memory and used default values otherwise.

Benchmarks: Most of the previous evaluations were carried out on SELECT queries only (see Table 1). Here, beside evaluating the performance of triples stores on SELECT evaluation, we also wanted to compare triple stores on the other three forms of SPARQL queries. To this end, we generated DBpedia-ASK-100 (100-ASK-query benchmark derived from DBpedia) and SWDF-ASK-50 (50-ASK-query benchmark derived from SWDF)[5] and compared the selected triple stores for their ASK query processing performances. Similarly, we generated DBpedia-CONSTRUCT-100 and SWDF-CONSTRUCT-23, DBpedia-DESCRIBE-25 and SWDF-DESCRIBE-100, and DBpedia-SELECT-100 and SWDF-SELECT-100 benchmarks to test the selected systems for CONSTRUCT, DESCRIBE, and SELECT queries, respectively. Furthermore, we generated DBpedia-Mix-175 (DBpedia benchmark of 175 mix queries of all the four query forms) and SWDF-Mix-175 to test the selected triple stores for their general query processing performance.

Benchmark Execution: The evaluation was carried out one triple store at a time on one machine. First, all data sets were loaded into the selected triple store. Once the triple store had completed the data loading, the 2-phase benchmark execution phase began: (1) *Warm-up Phase:* To measure the performance of the triple store under normal operational conditions, a warm-up phase was used where random queries from the query log were posed to triple stores for 10 minutes; (2) *Hot-run Phase:* During this phase, the benchmark query mixes were sent to the tested store. We kept track of the average execution time of each query as well as of the number of query mixes per hour (QMpH). This phase lasted for two hours for each triple store. Note that the benchmark and the triple

---

[5] We chose to select only 50 queries because the SWDF log we used does not contain enough ASK queries to generate a 100-query benchmark.

store were run on the same machine to avoid network latency. We set the query timeout to 180 seconds. The query was aborted after that and maximum time of 180 seconds was used as the query runtime for all queries which timed out. All the data (data dumps, benchmarks, query logs, FEASIBLE code) to repeat our experiments along with complete evaluation results are available at the project website.

6.3   Experimental Results

Composite Error. Table 2 shows a comparison of the composite errors of DBPSB and FEASIBLE for different benchmarks. Note that DBPSB queries templates are only available for the DBpedia query log. Thus, we were not able to calculate DBPSB's composite errors for SWDF. As an overall composite error evaluation, FEASIBLE's composite error is 54.9% smaller than DBPSB. The reason for DBPSB's error being higher that FEASIBLE's lies in the fact that it only considers the number of query triple patterns and the SPARQL clauses UNION, OPTIONAL, FILTER, LANG, REGEX, STR, and DISTINCT as features. Important query features (such as query result sizes, execution times, triple patterns and join selectivities, and number of join vertices) were not considered when generating the 25 query templates.[6] Furthermore, DBPSB only includes SELECT queries. The other three SPARQL query forms, i.e., CONSTRUCT, ASK, and DESCRIBE are not considered. In contrast, our approach considers all of the query forms, SPARQL clauses, and query features reported in Table 1.[7] It is important to mention that FEASIBLE's overall composite error across both data sets is only 0.038.

Table 2. Comparison of the Mean E_μ , Standard Deviation E_σ and Composite E errors for different benchmark sizes of DBpedia and Semantic Web Dog Food query logs. FEASIBLE outperforms DBPSB across all dimensions.

Benchmark	FEASIBLE			DBPSB			Benchmark	FEASIBLE		
	E_μ	E_σ	E	E_μ	E_σ	E		E_μ	E_σ	E
DBpedia-15	0.045	0.054	0.049	0.139	0.192	0.161	SWDF-15	0.019	0.043	0.026
DBpedia-25	0.041	0.054	0.046	0.113	0.139	0.125	SWDF-25	0.034	0.051	0.041
DBpedia-50	0.045	0.056	0.050	0.118	0.132	0.125	SWDF-50	0.036	0.052	0.043
DDBpedia-75	0.053	0.061	0.057	0.096	0.095	0.096	SWDF-75	0.035	0.051	0.042
DDBpedia-100	0.054	0.064	0.059	0.130	0.132	0.131	SWDF-100	0.036	0.050	0.042
DDBpedia-125	0.054	0.064	0.058	0.088	0.082	0.085	SWDF-125	0.034	0.048	0.040
DBpedia-150	0.055	0.064	0.059	0.107	0.124	0.115	SWDF-150	0.033	0.046	0.038
DBpedia-175	0.055	0.065	0.059	0.127	0.144	0.135	SWDF-175	0.033	0.045	0.038
Average	**0.050**	**0.060**	**0.055**	0.115	0.130	0.121	Average	0.032	0.048	0.039

---

[6] Queries templates available at: http://goo.gl/1oZCZY
[7] See FEASIBLE online demo for the customization of these features

Triple Store Performance. Figure 3 shows a comparison of the selected triple stores in terms of *queries per second* (QpS) and *query mixes per hour* (QMpH) for different benchmarks generated by FEASIBLE. Table 3 shows the overall rank-wise query distributions of the triple stores. Our ranking is partly different from the DBPSB ranking. Overall, (for mix DBpedia and SWDF benchmarks of 175 queries each, Figure 3e to Figure 3g), Virtuoso ranks first followed by Fuseki, OWLIM-SE, and Sesame. Virtuoso is 59% faster than Fuseki. Fuseki is 1.7% faster than OWLIM-SE, which in turn 16% faster than Sesame.[8]

A more fine-grained look at the evaluation reveals surprising findings: On ASK queries, Virtuoso is clearly faster than the other frameworks (45% faster than Sesame, which is 16% faster than Fuseki, which is in turn 96% faster than OWLIM-SE, see Figure 3a). The ranking changes for CONSTRUCT queries: While Virtuoso is still first (87% faster than OWLIM-SE), OWLIM-SE is now faster that 14% faster than Fuseki, which in turn is 42% faster than Sesame (Figure 3b). The most drastic change occurs on the DESCRIBE benchmark, where Fuseki ranks first (66% faster than Virtuoso, which is 86% faster than OWLIM-SE, which in turns 47% faster than Sesame, see Figure 3c). Yet another ranking emerges from the SELECT benchmarks, where Virtuoso is overall 55% faster than OWLIM-SE, which is 41% faster than Fuseki, which in turns 11% faster than Sesame (Figure 3d). These results show that the performance of triple stores varies greatly across the four basic SPARQL forms and none of the system is the sole winner across all query forms. Moreover, the ranking also varies across the different datasets (see, e.g., ASK benchmark for DBpedia and SWDF). Thus, our results suggest that (1) a benchmark should comprise a mix of SPARQL ASK, CONSTRUCT, DESCRIBE, and SELECT queries that reflects the real intended usage of the triple stores to generate accurate results and (2) there is no universal winner amongst triple stores, which points again towards the need to create customized benchmarks for applications when choosing their backend. FEASIBLE addresses both of these requirements by allowing users to generate dedicated benchmarks from their query logs.

Some interesting observations were revealed by the rank-wise queries distributions of triple stores shown in Table 3: First, none of the system is sole winner or loser for a particular rank. Overall, Virtuoso's performance mostly lies in the higher ranks, i.e., rank 1 and 2 (68.29%). This triple store performs especially well on CONSTRUCT queries. Fuseki's performance is mostly in the middle ranks, i.e., rank 2 and 3 (65.14%). In general, it is faster for DESCRIBE queries and is on a slower side for CONSTRUCT and queries containing FILTER and ORDER BY clauses. While OWLIM-SE's performance is usually on the slower side, i.e., rank 3 and 4 (60.86 %), it performs well on complex queries with large result set sizes and complex SPARQL clauses. Finally, Sesame is either fast or slow. For example, for 31.71% of the queries, it achieve the rank 1 (second best after Virtuoso) and but achieves rank 4 on 23.14% of the queries (second worse after OWLIM-SE). In general Sesame is very efficient on simple queries with small

---

[8] Note the percentage improvements are calculated from the QMpH values as A is (1-QMpH(A)/QMpH(B)*100) percent faster than B.

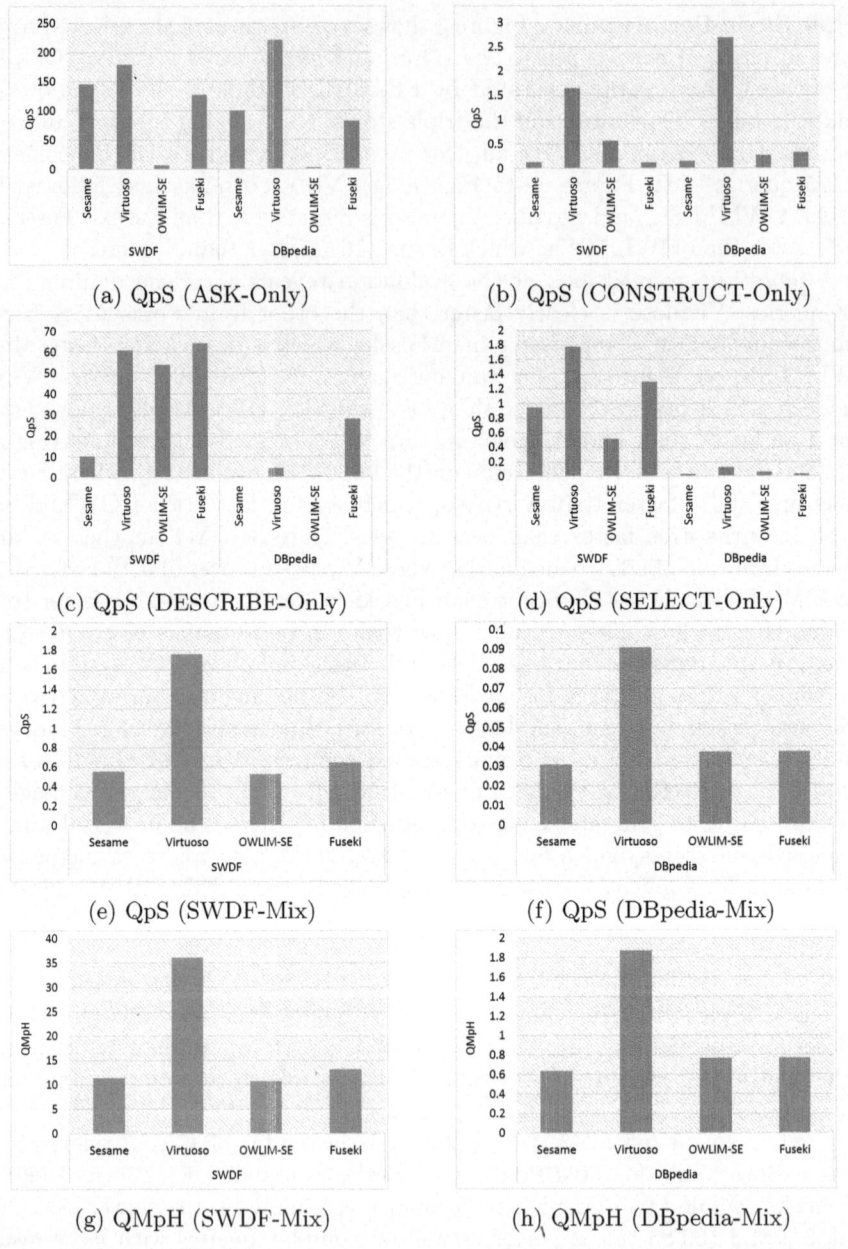

(a) QpS (ASK-Only)

(b) QpS (CONSTRUCT-Only)

(c) QpS (DESCRIBE-Only)

(d) QpS (SELECT-Only)

(e) QpS (SWDF-Mix)

(f) QpS (DBpedia-Mix)

(g) QMpH (SWDF-Mix)

(h) QMpH (DBpedia-Mix)

Fig. 3. Comparison of the triple stores in terms of Queries per Second (QpS) and Query Mix per Hour (QMpH), where a Query Mix comprise of 175 distinct queries.

Table 3. Overall rank-wise ranking of triple stores. All values are in percentages.

Triple Store	SWDF				DBpedia				Overall			
	1st	2nd	3rd	4th	1st	2nd	3rd	4th	1st	2nd	3rd	4th
Virtuoso	38.29	24.57	21.71	15.43	54.86	18.86	15.43	10.86	46.57	21.71	18.57	13.14
Fuseki	17.14	39.43	32.00	11.43	24.00	34.86	24.00	17.14	20.57	37.14	28.00	14.29
OWLIM-SE	10.29	30.29	21.14	38.29	13.14	24.57	25.14	37.14	11.71	27.43	23.14	37.71
Sesame	37.71	12.00	29.14	21.14	25.71	16.57	32.57	25.14	31.71	14.29	30.86	23.14

result set sizes, a small number of triple triple patterns, and a few SPARQL clauses. However, it performs poorly as soon as the queries grow in complexity. These results shows yet another aspect of the importance of taking structural and data-driven features into consideration while generating benchmarks as they allow deeper insights into the type of queries on which systems perform well or poorly.

Finally, we also looked into the number of query timeouts during the complete evaluation. Most of the systems time out for SELECT queries. Overall, Sesame has the highest number of timeouts (43) followed by Fuseki (32), OWLIM-SE (22), and Virtuoso (14). For Virtuoso, the timeout queries have at least one triple pattern with an unbound subject, an unbound predicate and an unbound object (i.e., a triple pattern of the form ?s ?p ?o). The corresponding result sets were so large that they could not be computed in 3 minutes. The other three systems mostly timeout for the same queries. OWLIM-SE generally performs better for complex queries with large result set sizes. Fuseki has problems with queries containing FILTER (12/32) and ORDER BY clauses (11/32 queries). Sesame's performance is slightly worse for complex queries containing many triple patterns and joins as well as complex SPARQL clauses. Note that Sesame also times out for 8 CONSTRUCT queries. All the timeout queries for each triple store are provided at the project website.

7   Conclusion

In this paper we presented FEASIBLE, a customizable SPARQL benchmark generation framework. We compared FEASIBLE with DBPSB and showed that our approach is able to produce high-quality (in terms of their composite error) benchmarks. In addition, our framework allows users to generate customized benchmarks suited for a particular use case, which is of utmost importance when aiming to gather valid insights into the real performance of different triple stores for a given application. This is demonstrated by our triple store evaluation, which shows that the ranking of triple stores varies greatly across different types of queries as well as across datasets. Our results thus suggest that all of the four query forms should be included in the future SPARQL benchmarks. For the sake of future work, we have started converting linked data query logs into RDF and made available through the LSQ [12] endpoint. Beside the key queries characteristics discussed in Table 1, we have attached many of the SPARQL 1.1 features to each of the query. We will extend FEASIBLE to query the LSQ SPARQL endpoint directly so as to gather queries for the benchmark creation process.

Acknowledgments. This work was partially supported by projects GeoKnow (GA: 318159) and SAKE (Grant No. 01MD15006E).

References

1. Acosta, M., Vidal, M.-E., Lampo, T., Castillo, J., Ruckhaus, E.: ANAPSID: an adaptive query processing engine for SPARQL endpoints. In: Aroyo, L., Welty, C., Alani, H., Taylor, J., Bernstein, A., Kagal, L., Noy, N., Blomqvist, E. (eds.) ISWC 2011, Part I. LNCS, vol. 7031, pp. 18–34. Springer, Heidelberg (2011)
2. Aluç, G., Hartig, O., Özsu, M.T., Daudjee, K.: Diversified stress testing of RDF data management systems. In: Mika, P., et al. (eds.) ISWC 2014, Part I. LNCS, vol. 8796, pp. 197–212. Springer, Heidelberg (2014)
3. Arias, M., Fernández, J.D., Martínez-Prieto, M.A., de la Fuente, P.: An empirical study of real-world SPARQL queries. CoRR (2011)
4. Bizer, C., Schultz, A: The berlin SPARQL benchmark. IJSWIS (2009)
5. Duan, S., Kementsietsidis, A., Srinivas, K., Udrea, O: Apples and oranges: a comparison of RDF benchmarks and real RDF datasets. In: SIGMOD (2011)
6. Görlitz, O., Thimm, M., Staab, S.: SPLODGE: systematic generation of SPARQL benchmark queries for linked open data. In: Cudré-Mauroux, P., et al. (eds.) ISWC 2012, Part I. LNCS, vol. 7649, pp. 116–132. Springer, Heidelberg (2012)
7. Guo, Y., Heflin, J.: LUBM: A benchmark for OWL knowledge base systems. JWS (2005)
8. Kamdar, M., Iqbal, A., Saleem, M., Deus, H., Decker, S.: Genomesnip: fragmenting the genomic wheel to augment discovery in cancer research. In: CSHALS (2014)
9. Morsey, M., Lehmann, J., Auer, S., Ngonga Ngomo, A.-C.: DBpedia SPARQL benchmark – performance assessment with real queries on real data. In: Aroyo, L., Welty, C., Alani, H., Taylor, J., Bernstein, A., Kagal, L., Noy, N., Blomqvist, E. (eds.) ISWC 2011, Part I. LNCS, vol. 7031, pp. 454–469. Springer, Heidelberg (2011)
10. Ngonga Ngomo, A.-C., Auer, S.: LIMES - a time-efficient approach for large-scale link discovery on the web of data. In: IJCAI (2011)
11. Picalausa, F., Vansummeren, S.: What are real SPARQL queries like? In: SWIM (2011)
12. Saleem, M., Ali, I., Hogan, A., Mehmood, Q., Ngonga Ngomo, A.-C.: LSQ: the linked SPARQL queries dataset. In: ISWC (2015)
13. Saleem, M., Kamdar, M.R., Iqbal, A., Sampath, S., Deus, H.F., Ngonga Ngomo, A.-C.: Big linked cancer data: Integrating linked TCGA and pubmed. JWS (2014)
14. Saleem, M., Ngonga Ngomo, A.-C.: HiBISCuS: hypergraph-based source selection for SPARQL endpoint federation. In: Presutti, V., d'Amato, C., Gandon, F., d'Aquin, M., Staab, S., Tordai, A. (eds.) ESWC 2014. LNCS, vol. 8465, pp. 176–191. Springer, Heidelberg (2014)
15. Saleem, M., Ngonga Ngomo, A.-C., Xavier Parreira, J., Deus, H.F., Hauswirth, M.: DAW: duplicate-aware federated query processing over the web of data. In: Alani, H., et al. (eds.) ISWC 2013, Part I. LNCS, vol. 8218, pp. 574–590. Springer, Heidelberg (2013)

16. Schmidt, M., Görlitz, O., Haase, P., Ladwig, G., Schwarte, A., Tran, T.: FedBench: a benchmark suite for federated semantic data query processing. In: Aroyo, L., Welty, C., Alani, H., Taylor, J., Bernstein, A., Kagal, L., Noy, N., Blomqvist, E. (eds.) ISWC 2011, Part I. LNCS, vol. 7031, pp. 585–600. Springer, Heidelberg (2011)

17. Schmidt, M., Hornung, T., Lausen, G., Pinkel, C: Sp2bench: a SPARQL performance benchmark. In: ICDE (2009)

18. Schwarte, A., Haase, P., Hose, K., Schenkel, R., Schmidt, M.: FedX: optimization techniques for federated query processing on linked data. In: Aroyo, L., Welty, C., Alani, H., Taylor, J., Bernstein, A., Kagal, L., Noy, N., Blomqvist, E. (eds.) ISWC 2011, Part I. LNCS, vol. 7031, pp. 601–616. Springer, Heidelberg (2011)

Querying Linked Data

LDQL: A Query Language for the Web of Linked Data

Olaf Hartig[1] and Jorge Pérez[2][✉]

[1] Hasso-Plattner-Institute for IT Systems Engineering, Potsdam, Germany
http://olafhartig.de/
[2] Department of Computer Science, Universidad de Chile, Santiago, Chile
jperez@dcc.uchile.cl

Abstract. The Web of Linked Data is composed of tons of RDF documents interlinked to each other forming a huge repository of distributed semantic data. Effectively querying this distributed data source is an important open problem in the Semantic Web area. In this paper, we propose LDQL, a declarative language to query Linked Data on the Web. One of the novelties of LDQL is that it expresses separately (i) patterns that describe the expected query result, and (ii) Web navigation paths that select the data sources to be used for computing the result. We present a formal syntax and semantics, prove equivalence rules, and study the expressiveness of the language. In particular, we show that LDQL is strictly more expressive than the query formalisms that have been proposed previously for Linked Data on the Web. The high expressiveness allows LDQL to define queries for which a complete execution is not computationally feasible over the Web. We formally study this issue and provide a syntactic sufficient condition to avoid this problem; queries satisfying this condition are ensured to have a procedure to be effectively evaluated over the Web of Linked Data.

1 Introduction

In recent years an increasing amount of structured data has been published and interlinked on the World Wide Web (WWW) in adherence to the Linked Data principles [3]. These principles are based on standard Web technologies. In particular, (i) the Hypertext Transfer Protocol (HTTP) is used to access data, (ii) HTTP-based Uniform Resource Identifiers (URIs) are used as identifiers for entities described in the data, and (iii) the Resource Description Framework (RDF) is used as data model. Then, any HTTP URI in an RDF triple presents a *data link* that enables software clients to retrieve more data by looking up the URI with an HTTP request. The adoption of these principles has lead to the creation of a globally distributed dataspace: the *Web of Linked Data.*

The emergence of the Web of Linked Data makes possible an *online execution* of declarative queries over up-to-date data from a virtually unbounded set of data sources, each of which is readily accessible without any need for implementing source-specific APIs or wrappers. This possibility has spawned

© Springer International Publishing Switzerland 2015
M. Arenas et al. (Eds.): ISWC 2015, Part I, LNCS 9366, pp. 73–91, 2015.
DOI: 10.1007/978-3-319-25007-6_5

research interest in approaches to query Linked Data on the WWW as if it was a single (distributed) database. For an overview on query execution techniques proposed in this context refer to [12].

The main contribution of this paper is the proposal of LDQL, a novel query language for the Web of Linked Data. The most important feature of LDQL is that it clearly separates query components for selecting query-relevant regions of the Web of Linked Data, from components for specifying the query result that has to be constructed from the data in the selected regions. The most basic construction in LDQL are tuples of the form $\langle L, Q \rangle$ where L is an expression used to select a set of relevant documents, and Q is a query intended to be executed over the data in these documents as if they were a single RDF repository. In an abstract setting one can use several formalisms to express L and Q. In our proposal, for the former part we introduce the notion of *link path expressions* that are a form of nested regular expressions (with some other important features) used to navigate the link graph of the Web. For the latter, we use standard SPARQL graph patterns. To begin evaluating these queries one needs to specify a set of seed URIs. The language also possesses features to dynamically (at query time) identify new seed URIs to evaluate portions of a query. Additionally, such queries can be combined by using conjunctions, disjunctions, and projection. We present a formal syntax and semantics for LDQL, propose some rewrite rules, and study its expressive power.

While there does not exist a standard language for expressing queries over Linked Data on the WWW, a few options have been proposed. In particular, a first strand of research focuses on extending the scope of SPARQL such that an evaluation of SPARQL queries over Linked Data has a well-defined semantics [9, 11,14,18]. A second strand of research focuses on navigational languages [7,14]. Although these languages have different motivations, a commonality of all these proposals is that, in contrast to LDQL, the definition of query-relevant regions of the Web of Linked Data and the definition of query-relevant data within the specified regions are mixed.

As our second main contribution we compare LDQL with three previously proposed formalisms for querying the Web of Linked Data: *SPARQL under reachability-based query semantics* [11], *NautiLOD* [7], and *SPARQL Property Path patterns under context-based semantics* [14]. We formally prove that LDQL is strictly more expressive than every one of these. We show that for every query Q in the previous languages, one can effectively construct an LDQL query which is equivalent to Q. Moreover, for every one of the previous languages, there exists an LDQL query that cannot be expressed in that language. These results show that LDQL presents an interesting expressive power.

The downside of the expressiveness provided by LDQL is the existence of queries for which a complete execution is not feasible in practice. To capture this issue formally, we define a notion of *Web-safeness* for LDQL queries. Then, the obvious question that arises is how to identify LDQL queries that are Web-safe. Our last technical contribution is the identification of a sufficient syntactic condition for Web-safeness.

The rest of the paper is structured as follows. Section 2 introduces a data model that provides the basis for defining the semantics of LDQL. In Section 3 we formally define the syntax and semantics of LDQL and show some simple algebraic properties. In Section 4 we compare LDQL with the three mentioned languages, and in Section 5 we focus on Web-safeness. Section 6 concludes the paper and sketches future work. Proofs of the formal results in this paper can be found in an extended version of the paper [13].

A preliminary version of some of the results in this paper have been presented in a workshop [10]. This paper is a substantial extension of [10] refining the definition of LDQL and introducing important changes to the syntax and the semantics of the language. Moreover, the comparison with previous proposals was not discussed in [10].

2 Data Model

In this section we introduce a structural data model that captures the concept of a Web of Linked Data formally. As usual [7,9,11,14,18], for the definitions and analysis in this paper, we assume that the Web is fixed during the execution of any single query.

We use the RDF data model [5] as a basis for our model of a Web of Linked Data. That is, we assume three pairwise disjoint, infinite sets $\mathcal{U}$ (URIs), $\mathcal{B}$ (blank nodes), and $\mathcal{L}$ (literals). An *RDF triple* is a tuple $\langle s, p, o \rangle \in \mathcal{T}$ with $\mathcal{T} = (\mathcal{U} \cup \mathcal{B}) \times \mathcal{U} \times (\mathcal{U} \cup \mathcal{B} \cup \mathcal{L})$. For any RDF triple $t = \langle s, p, o \rangle$ we write uris(t) to denote the set of all URIs in t.

Additionally, we assume another infinite set $\mathcal{D}$ that is disjoint from $\mathcal{U}$, $\mathcal{B}$, and $\mathcal{L}$, respectively. We refer to elements in this set as *documents* and use them to represent the concept of Web documents from which Linked Data can be extracted. Hence, we assume a function, say data, that maps each document $d \in \mathcal{D}$ to a finite set of RDF triples data(d) $\subseteq \mathcal{T}$ such that the data of each document uses a unique set of blank nodes.

Given these preliminaries, we are ready to define a *Web of Linked Data*.

Definition 1. A Web of Linked Data is a tuple $W = \langle D, adoc \rangle$ that consists of a set of documents $D \subseteq \mathcal{D}$ and a partial function $adoc : \mathcal{U} \to D$ that is surjective.

Function *adoc* of a Web of Linked Data $W = \langle D, adoc \rangle$ captures the relationship between the URIs that can be looked up in this Web and the documents that can be retrieved by such lookups. Since not every URI can be looked up, the function is partial. For any URI $u \in \mathcal{U}$ with $u \in \mathrm{dom}(adoc)$ (i.e., any URI that can be looked up in W), document $d = adoc(u)$ can be considered the authoritative source of data for u in W (hence, the name *adoc*). To accommodate for documents that are authoritative for multiple URIs, we do not require injectivity for function *adoc*. However, we require surjectivity because we conceive documents as irrelevant for a Web of Linked Data if they cannot be retrieved by any URI lookup in this Web.

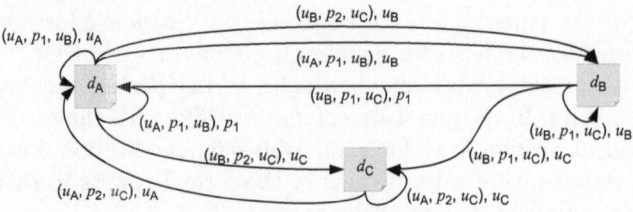

Fig. 1. The link graph $\mathcal{G}_{W_{ex}}$ of our example Web of Linked Data W_{ex}.

Let $W = \langle D, adoc \rangle$ be a Web of Linked Data. W is said to be finite [11] if its set D of documents is finite. In this paper we assume that every Web of Linked Data is finite. Given documents $d, d' \in D$ and a triple $t \in data(d)$, we say that a URI $u \in uris(t)$ establishes a *data link* from d to d', if $adoc(u) = d'$. As a final concept, we formalize the notion of a *link graph* associated to W. This graph has documents in D as nodes, and directed edges representing data links between documents. Each edge is associated with a label that identifies both the particular RDF triple and the URI in this triple that establishes the corresponding data link. These labels shall provide the basis for defining the navigational component of our query language.

Definition 2. The **link graph** of a Web of Linked Data $W = \langle D, adoc \rangle$, is a directed, edge-labeled multigraph, $\mathcal{G}_W = \langle D, E_W \rangle$, with set of edges $E_W \subseteq D \times (\mathcal{T} \times \mathcal{U}) \times D$ defined as $E_W = \{\langle d_{src}, (t, u), d_{tgt} \rangle \mid t \in data(d_{src}), u \in uris(t) \text{ and } d_{tgt} = adoc(u)\}$.

For a link graph edge $e = \langle d_{src}, (t, u), d_{tgt} \rangle$, tuple (t, u) is the label of e. Moreover, we sometimes write $e \in \mathcal{G}_W$ to denote that e is an edge in the link graph $\mathcal{G}_W$.

Example 1. As a running example for this paper assume a simple Web of Linked Data $W_{ex} = \langle D_{ex}, adoc_{ex} \rangle$ with three documents, d_A, d_B, and d_C (i.e., $D_{ex} = \{d_A, d_B, d_C\}$). The data in these documents are the following sets of RDF triples:

$$data(d_A) = \{\langle u_A, p_1, u_B \rangle, \qquad data(d_B) = \{\langle u_B, p_1, u_C \rangle\};$$
$$\langle u_B, p_2, u_C \rangle\}; \qquad data(d_C) = \{\langle u_A, p_2, u_C \rangle\};$$

and for function $adoc_{ex}$ we have: $adoc_{ex}(u_A) = d_A$, $adoc_{ex}(u_B) = d_B$, $adoc_{ex}(u_C) = d_C$, and $adoc_{ex}(p_1) = d_A$ (i.e., $dom(adoc_{ex}) = \{u_A, u_B, u_C, p_1\}$). This Web contains 10 data links. For instance, URI u_A in the RDF triple $\langle u_A, p_2, u_C \rangle \in data(d_C)$ establishes a data link to document d_A. Hence, the corresponding edge in the link graph of W_{ex} is $\langle d_C, (\langle u_A, p_2, u_C \rangle, u_A), d_A \rangle$. Figure 1 illustrates the link graph $\mathcal{G}_{W_{ex}}$ with all 10 edges.

3   Definition of LDQL

This section defines our Linked Data query language, LDQL. LDQL queries are meant to be evaluated over a Web of Linked Data and each such query is built from two types of components: *Link path expressions* (*LPEs*) for selecting que-ry-relevant documents of the queried Web of Linked Data; and SPARQL graph patterns for specifying the query result that has to be constructed from the data in the selected documents. For this paper, we assume that the reader is familiar with the definition of SPARQL [8], including the algebraic formaliza-tion introduced in [2,16]. In particular, for SPARQL graph patterns we closely follow the formalization in [2] considering operators AND, OPT, UNION, FILTER, and GRAPH, plus the operator BIND defined in [8]. We begin this section by introducing the most basic concept of our language, the notion of link patterns. We use link patterns as the basis for navigating the link graph of a Web of Linked Data.

3.1 Link Patterns

A link pattern is a tuple in $(\mathcal{U} \cup \{\_,+\}) \times (\mathcal{U} \cup \{\_,+\}) \times (\mathcal{U} \cup \mathcal{L} \cup \{\_,+\})$. Link patterns are used to match link graph edges in the context of a designated *context* URI. The special symbol $+$ denotes a placeholder for the context URI. The special symbol $\_$ denotes a wildcard that will drive the direction of the navigation. Before formalizing how link graph edges actually match link patterns, we show some intuition. Consider the link graph of Web W_{ex} in Example 1 (see Fig. 1), and the link pattern $\langle +, p_1, \_ \rangle$. Intuitively, in the context of URI u_{A}, the edge with label $(\langle u_{\mathrm{A}}, p_1, u_{\mathrm{B}} \rangle, u_{\mathrm{B}})$ from document d_{A} to document d_{B}, matches the link pattern $\langle +, p_1, \_ \rangle$. Notice that in the matching, the context URI u_{A} takes the place of symbol $+$, and u_{B} takes the place of the wildcard symbol $\_$. Notice that u_{B} also denotes the direction of the edge that matches the link pattern. On the other hand, the edge with label $(\langle u_{\mathrm{A}}, p_1, u_{\mathrm{B}} \rangle, u_{\mathrm{A}})$ from d_{A} to d_{A}, does not match $\langle +, p_1, \_ \rangle$; although u_{B} can take the place of the wildcard symbol $\_$, the direction of the edge is not to u_{B}. That is, when matching an edge labeled by (t, u) we require URI u to be taking the place of a wildcard in the link pattern. When more than one wildcard symbol is used, the link pattern can be matched by edges pointing to the direction of any of the URIs taking the place of a wildcard. For instance, in the context of u_{A}, the link pattern $\langle \_, p_2, \_ \rangle$ is matched by edges $\langle d_{\mathrm{A}}, (\langle u_{\mathrm{B}}, p_2, u_{\mathrm{C}} \rangle, u_{\mathrm{B}}), d_{\mathrm{B}} \rangle$ and $\langle d_{\mathrm{A}}, (\langle u_{\mathrm{B}}, p_2, u_{\mathrm{C}} \rangle, u_{\mathrm{C}}), d_{\mathrm{C}} \rangle$. The next definition formalizes this notion of matching.

Definition 3. A link graph edge with label $(\langle x_1, x_2, x_3 \rangle, u)$ **matches** a link pattern $\langle y_1, y_2, y_3 \rangle$ in the context of a URI u_{ctx} if the following two properties hold:

1. there exists $i \in \{1, 2, 3\}$ such that $y_i = \_$ and $x_i = u$, and
2. for every $i \in \{1, 2, 3\}$ either $y_i = +$ and $x_i = u_{\mathrm{ctx}}$, or $y_i = x_i$, or $y_i = \_$.

One of the rationales for adopting the notion of a context URI and the $+$ symbol in our definition of link patterns, is to support cases in which link graph navigation has to be focused solely on data links that are *authoritative*. A data link represented by link graph edge $\langle d_{\mathrm{src}}, (t, u), d_{\mathrm{tgt}} \rangle \in \mathcal{G}_W$ is authoritative in a Web of Linked Data $W = \langle D, adoc \rangle$ if $d_{\mathrm{src}} = adoc(u')$ for some URI $u' \in \mathrm{uris}(t)$. Thus, if we fix a context URI u_{ctx}, a link pattern that uses the $+$ symbol allows us to follow only authoritative data links from document $d_{\mathrm{ctx}} = adoc(u_{\mathrm{ctx}})$.

3.2   LDQL Queries

The most basic construction in LDQL queries are tuples of the from $\langle L, P \rangle$ where L is an expression used to select a set of documents from the Web of Linked Data, and P is a SPARQL graph pattern to query these documents as if they were a single RDF dataset. In an abstract setting, one can use any formalism to specify L as long as L defines sets of RDF documents. In our proposal we use what we call *link path expressions* (LPEs) that are a form of nested regular expressions [17] over the alphabet of link patterns. Every link path expression begins its navigation in a context URI, traverses the Web, and returns a set of URIs; these URIs are used to construct an RDF dataset with all the documents to be retrieved by looking up the URIs. This dataset is passed to the SPARQL graph pattern to obtain the final evaluation of the whole query. Besides the basic constructions of the form $\langle L, P \rangle$, in LDQL one can also use AND, UNION and projection, to combine them. We also introduce an operator SEED that is used to dynamically change, at query time, the seed URI from which the navigation begins. The next definition formalizes the syntax of LDQL queries and LPEs.

Definition 4. The syntax of LDQL is given by the following production rules in which lp is an arbitrary link pattern, $?v$ is a variable, P is a SPARQL graph pattern (as per [2]), V is a finite set of variables, and U is a finite set of URIs:

$$q := \langle lpe, P \rangle \mid (\text{SEED } U \ q) \mid (\text{SEED } ?v \ q) \mid (q \text{ AND } q) \mid (q \text{ UNION } q) \mid \pi_V q$$

$$lpe := \varepsilon \mid lp \mid lpe/lpe \mid lpe|lpe \mid lpe^* \mid [lpe] \mid \langle ?v, q \rangle$$

Any expression that satisfies the production q is an **LDQL query**, any expression that satisfies the production lpe is a **link path expression** (**LPE**), and any LDQL query of the form $\langle lpe, P \rangle$ is a **basic LDQL query**.

Before going into the formal semantics of LDQL and LPEs, we give some more intuition about how these expressions are evaluated in a Web of Linked Data W. As mentioned before, the most basic expression in LDQL is of the form $\langle lpe, P \rangle$. To evaluate this expression over W we will need a set S of *seed* URIs. When evaluating $\langle lpe, P \rangle$, every one of the seed URIs in S will trigger a navigation of link graph $\mathcal{G}_W$ via the link path expression lpe starting on that seed. That is, the seed URIs are passed to lpe as *context* URIs in which the LPE should be evaluated. These evaluations of lpe will result in a set of URIs that are used to construct a dataset over which P is finally evaluated.

Regarding the navigation of link graph $\mathcal{G}_W$, the most basic form of navigation is to follow a single link graph edge that matches a link pattern lp. When a navigation via a link pattern lp is triggered from a context URI u, we proceed as follows. We first go to the authoritative document for u, that is $adoc(u)$, and try to find outgoing link graph edges that match lp in the context of u (as explained in Section 3.1). Every one of these matches defines a new context URI u' from which the navigation can continue. More complex forms of navigation are obtained by combining link patterns via classical regular expression operators such as concatenation /, disjunction |, and recursive concatenation $(\cdot)^*$.

The nesting operator $[\cdot]$ is used to test for existence of paths. When a context URI u is passed to an expression $[lpe]$, it checks whether $\mathcal{G}_W$ contains a path from $d_{\text{ctx}} = adoc(u)$ that matches lpe. If such a path exists, the navigation can continue from the same context URI u. The most involved form of navigation is by using the expression $\langle ?v, q \rangle$ with q an LDQL query. To evaluate this expression from context URI u one first has to pass u as a seed URI for q and recursively evaluate q from that seed. This evaluation generates a set of solution mappings, and for every one of these mappings its value on variable $?v$ is used as the new context URI from which the navigation continues. Finally, note that our notion of LPEs does not provide an operator for navigating paths in their inverse direction. The reason for omitting such an operator is that traversing arbitrary data links backwards is impossible on the WWW.

To formally define the semantics of LDQL we need to introduce some terminology. We first define a function $\text{dataset}_W(\cdot)$ that from a set of URIs constructs an RDF dataset with all the documents pointed to by those URIs in W. Formally, given a Web of Linked Data $W = \langle D, adoc \rangle$ and a set U of URIs, $\text{dataset}_W(U)$ is an RDF dataset (as per [2,8]) that has the set of triples $\{t \in \text{data}(adoc(u)) \mid u \in U \cap \text{dom}(adoc)\}$ as default graph. Moreover, for every URI $u \in U \cap \text{dom}(adoc)$, $\text{dataset}_W(U)$ contains the named graph $\langle u, \text{data}(adoc(u)) \rangle$.

Example 2. Consider the Web W_{ex} in Example 1 and the set of URIs $U = \{u_{\text{A}}, u_{\text{C}}\}$. Then $\text{dataset}_{W_{\text{ex}}}(U)$ has $\{\langle u_{\text{A}}, p_1, u_{\text{B}} \rangle, \langle u_{\text{B}}, p_2, u_{\text{C}} \rangle, \langle u_{\text{A}}, p_2, u_{\text{C}} \rangle\}$ as default graph, and two named graphs, $\langle u_{\text{A}}, \{\langle u_{\text{A}}, p_1, u_{\text{B}} \rangle, \langle u_{\text{B}}, p_2, u_{\text{C}} \rangle\} \rangle$ and $\langle u_{\text{C}}, \{\langle u_{\text{A}}, p_2, u_{\text{C}} \rangle\} \rangle$.

In the formalization of the semantics of LDQL, we use the standard join operator $\bowtie$ over sets of solution mappings [8,16]. We also make use of the semantics of SPARQL graph patterns over datasets as defined in [2]. In particular, given an RDF dataset $\mathfrak{D}$, an RDF graph G in $\mathfrak{D}$, and a SPARQL graph pattern P, we denote by $[\![P]\!]_G^{\mathfrak{D}}$ the evaluation of P over G in $\mathfrak{D}$ [2, Definition 13.3].

We are now ready to formally define the semantics of LDQL and LPEs. Given a Web of Linked Data W and a set S of URIs, we formalize the evaluation of LDQL queries over W from the seed URIs S, as a function $[\![\cdot]\!]_W^S$ that given an LDQL query, produces a set of solution mappings. Similarly, the evaluation of LPEs over W from a context URI u, is formalized as a function $[\![\cdot]\!]_W^u$ that given an LPE, produces a set of URIs.

Definition 5. Given a finite set $S \subseteq \mathcal{U}$, the S**-based evaluation** of LDQL queries over a Web of Linked Data $W = \langle D, adoc \rangle$, denoted by $[\![\cdot]\!]_W^S$, is defined recursively as follows:

$$[\![\langle lpe, P\rangle]\!]_W^S = [\![P]\!]_G^{\mathfrak{D}} \quad \text{where } \mathfrak{D} = \text{dataset}_W\left(\bigcup_{u\in S}[\![lpe]\!]_W^u\right) \text{ with default graph } G,$$

$$[\![(\text{SEED } U\ q)]\!]_W^S = [\![q]\!]_W^U,$$

$$[\![(\text{SEED } ?v\ q)]\!]_W^S = \bigcup_{u\in\mathcal{U}}\left([\![q]\!]_W^{\{u\}} \bowtie \{\mu_u\}\right) \quad \text{where } \mu_u = \{?v \mapsto u\} \text{ for all } u \in \mathcal{U},$$

$$[\![(q_1\ \text{UNION}\ q_2)]\!]_W^S = [\![q_1]\!]_W^S \cup [\![q_2]\!]_W^S,$$

$$[\![(q_1\ \text{AND}\ q_2)]\!]_W^S = [\![q_1]\!]_W^S \bowtie [\![q_2]\!]_W^S,$$

$$[\![\pi_V q]\!]_W^S = \{\mu \mid \text{there exists } \mu' \in [\![q]\!]_W^S \text{ such that } \mu \text{ and } \mu' \text{ are}$$
$$\text{compatible and } \text{dom}(\mu) = \text{dom}(\mu') \cap V\}.$$

Now for the semantics of LPEs, given a context URI $u_{\text{ctx}} \in \text{dom}(adoc)$, the u_{ctx}-**based evaluation** of LPEs over W, denoted by $[\![\cdot]\!]_W^{u_{\text{ctx}}}$, is defined recursively as follows:

$$[\![\varepsilon]\!]_W^{u_{\text{ctx}}} = \{u_{\text{ctx}}\},$$

$$[\![lp]\!]_W^{u_{\text{ctx}}} = \{u \in \mathcal{U} \mid \text{there exist a link graph edge } \langle d_{\text{src}}, (t, u), d_{\text{tgt}}\rangle \in \mathcal{G}_W, \text{ with}$$
$$d_{\text{src}} = adoc(u_{\text{ctx}}), \text{ that matches } lp \text{ in the context of } u_{\text{ctx}}\},$$

$$[\![lpe_1/lpe_2]\!]_W^{u_{\text{ctx}}} = \{u \in [\![lpe_2]\!]_W^{u'} \mid u' \in [\![lpe_1]\!]_W^{u_{\text{ctx}}}\},$$

$$[\![lpe_1|lpe_2]\!]_W^{u_{\text{ctx}}} = [\![lpe_1]\!]_W^{u_{\text{ctx}}} \cup [\![lpe_2]\!]_W^{u_{\text{ctx}}},$$

$$[\![lpe^*]\!]_W^{u_{\text{ctx}}} = \{u_{\text{ctx}}\} \cup [\![lpe]\!]_W^{u_{\text{ctx}}} \cup [\![lpe/lpe]\!]_W^{u_{\text{ctx}}} \cup [\![lpe/lpe/lpe]\!]_W^{u_{\text{ctx}}} \cup \ldots,$$

$$[\![[lpe]]\!]_W^{u_{\text{ctx}}} = \{u_{\text{ctx}} \mid [\![lpe]\!]_W^{u_{\text{ctx}}} \neq \emptyset\},$$

$$[\![\langle ?v, q\rangle]\!]_W^{u_{\text{ctx}}} = \{u \in \mathcal{U} \mid \text{there exists } \mu \in [\![q]\!]_W^{\{u_{\text{ctx}}\}} \text{ such that } \mu(?v) = u\}.$$

Moreover, if $u_{\text{ctx}} \notin \text{dom}(adoc)$, then $[\![lpe]\!]_W^{u_{\text{ctx}}} = \emptyset$ for every LPE.

Example 3. Let lpe_{ex} be the LPE $\langle\_, p_1, \_\rangle^*/[\langle\_, p_2, \_\rangle]$. This LPE selects documents that can be reached via arbitrarily long paths of data links with predicate p_1 and, additionally, have some outgoing data link with predicate p_2. For our example Web W_{ex} and context URI u_{A}, the LPE selects documents $d_{\text{A}} = adoc_{\text{ex}}(u_{\text{A}})$ and $d_{\text{C}} = adoc_{\text{ex}}(u_{\text{C}})$. More precisely, we have $[\![lpe_{\text{ex}}]\!]_{W_{\text{ex}}}^{u_{\text{A}}} = \{u_{\text{A}}, u_{\text{C}}\}$. Note that document d_{B} can also be reached via a p_1–path, but it does not pass the p_2–related test.

Example 4. Consider a set of URIs $S_{\text{ex}} = \{u_{\text{A}}\}$ and a basic LDQL query $\langle lpe_{\text{ex}}, B_{\text{ex}}\rangle$ whose LPE is lpe_{ex} as introduced in Example 3 and whose SPARQL graph pattern is a basic graph pattern that contains two triple patterns, $B_{\text{ex}} = \{\langle ?x, p_1, ?y\rangle, \langle ?x, p_2, ?z\rangle\}$. Given that we have $[\![lpe_{\text{ex}}]\!]_{W_{\text{ex}}}^{u_{\text{A}}} = \{u_{\text{A}}, u_{\text{C}}\}$ (cf. Example 3), $\text{dataset}_{W_{\text{ex}}}([\![lpe_{\text{ex}}]\!]_{W_{\text{ex}}}^{u_{\text{A}}})$ has the default graph $\{\langle u_{\text{A}}, p_1, u_{\text{B}}\rangle, \langle u_{\text{B}}, p_2, u_{\text{C}}\rangle, \langle u_{\text{A}}, p_2, u_{\text{C}}\rangle\}$ (cf. Example 2). Then, according to the query semantics, the result of query $\langle lpe_{\text{ex}}, B_{\text{ex}}\rangle$ over W_{ex} using seeds S_{ex} consists of a single solution mapping, namely $\mu = \{?x \mapsto u_{\text{A}}, ?y \mapsto u_{\text{B}}, ?z \mapsto u_{\text{C}}\}$.

Example 5. Consider an LDQL query $q_{\text{ex}} = (\text{SEED } ?x\ \langle\varepsilon, \langle ?x, p_1, ?w\rangle\rangle)$ whose subquery is a basic LDQL query that has a single triple pattern as its SPARQL graph pattern. Additionally, let $q'_{\text{ex}} = \langle lpe_{\text{ex}}, \{\langle ?x, p_1, ?y\rangle, \langle ?x, p_2, ?z\rangle\}\rangle$ be the basic LDQL query introduced in Example 4, and let q''_{ex} be the conjunction of these two queries; i.e., $q''_{\text{ex}} = (q_{\text{ex}}\ \text{AND}\ q'_{\text{ex}})$. By Example 4 we know that

$[\![q'_{\text{ex}}]\!]^{S_{\text{ex}}}_{W_{\text{ex}}} = \{\mu\}$ with $\mu = \{?x \mapsto u_A, ?y \mapsto u_B, ?z \mapsto u_C\}$. Furthermore, based on the data given in Example 1, it is easy to see that $[\![q_{\text{ex}}]\!]^{S_{\text{ex}}}_{W_{\text{ex}}} = \{\mu_1, \mu_2\}$ with $\mu_1 = \{?x \mapsto u_A, ?w \mapsto u_B\}$ and $\mu_2 = \{?x \mapsto u_B, ?w \mapsto u_C\}$. For the S_{ex}-based evaluation of q''_{ex} over W_{ex}, the result sets $[\![q_{\text{ex}}]\!]^{S_{\text{ex}}}_{W_{\text{ex}}}$ and $[\![q'_{\text{ex}}]\!]^{S_{\text{ex}}}_{W_{\text{ex}}}$ have to be joined. Thus, we need to compute $\{\mu_1, \mu_2\} \bowtie \{\mu\}$, which results in a single mapping $\mu' = \mu_1 \cup \mu = \{?x \mapsto u_A, ?w \mapsto u_C, ?y \mapsto u_B, ?z \mapsto u_C\}$.

3.3   Algebraic Properties of LDQL Queries

As a basis for the discussion in the next sections, we show some simple algebraic properties. We say that LDQL queries q and q' are semantically equivalent, denoted by $q \equiv q'$, if $[\![q]\!]^S_W = [\![q']\!]^S_W$ holds for every Web of Linked Data W and every finite set $S \subseteq \mathcal{U}$.

Lemma 1. *The operators* AND *and* UNION *are associative and commutative.*

Lemma 2. *Let q_1, q_2, q_3 be LDQL queries, the following semantic equivalences hold:*

$$(q_1 \text{ AND } (q_2 \text{ UNION } q_3)) \equiv ((q_1 \text{ AND } q_2) \text{ UNION } (q_1 \text{ AND } q_3)) \qquad (1)$$

$$\pi_V(q_1 \text{ UNION } q_2) \equiv (\pi_V q_1 \text{ UNION } \pi_V q_2) \qquad (2)$$

$$(\text{SEED } U \ (q_1 \text{ UNION } q_2)) \equiv ((\text{SEED } U \ q_1) \text{ UNION } (\text{SEED } U \ q_2)) \qquad (3)$$

$$(\text{SEED } ?v \ (q_1 \text{ UNION } q_2)) \equiv ((\text{SEED } ?v \ q_1) \text{ UNION } (\text{SEED } ?v \ q_2)) \qquad (4)$$

Lemma 1 allows us to write sequences of either AND or UNION without parentheses. Our next result shows the power of the construction $\langle ?v, q \rangle$. In particular, it shows the somehow surprising finding that link patterns lp, concatenation $/$, disjunction $|$, and the test $[\cdot]$, are just *syntactic sugar* as they can be simulated by using ε, $\langle ?v, q \rangle$ and $(\cdot)^*$.

Proposition 1. *For every LDQL query q, there exists an LDQL query q' s.t. $q \equiv q'$ and every LPE in q' consists only of the symbol ε, the construction $\langle ?v, q \rangle$, and operator $(\cdot)^*$.*

Proof (Sketch). The proof is based on a recursive translation of link path expressions beginning with link patterns. For instance, a link pattern of the form $\langle +, p, \_ \rangle$ is encoded by $\langle ?v, \langle \varepsilon, (\text{GRAPH } ?u \ (?u, p, ?v)) \rangle \rangle$, and we can similarly encode all types of link patterns. To encode $/$ we make use of $\langle ?v, q \rangle$ and the operator AND inside q as follows. Consider an LPE $r = r_1/r_2$. It can be shown that r is equivalent to $\langle ?v, q \rangle$ where q is:

$$(\ \langle r_1, (\text{GRAPH } ?x \ \{ \ \}) \rangle \text{ AND } (\text{SEED } ?x \ \langle r_2, (\text{GRAPH } ?v \ \{ \ \}) \rangle) \ ).$$

Similarly, to encode $|$ we make use of UNION and to encode $[\cdot]$ we use projection.

Although not strictly necessary, we decided to keep link patterns and operators $/$, $|$, and $[\cdot]$ since they represent a natural and intuitive way of expressing navigation paths.

4 Comparison with Previous Linked Data Query Formalisms

In this section, we compare LDQL with alternative formalisms to query Linked Data on the WWW. There are some general query languages for the WWW (proposed before the advent of Linked Data) that are related to our proposal; in particular, WebSQL [15], which is similar in spirit to LDQL but different in the features that the languages posses. Two main novelties of LDQL compared with WebSQL are the possibility to dynamically select seed URIs at query time, and the traversal of links according to properties of the queried documents that can be defined in the same LDQL query. Neither of these are expressible in WebSQL. While a complete formal comparison between LDQL and WebSQL is certainly very interesting, we leave it for future work and, instead, focus on three more recent proposals of query formalisms for the Web of Linked Data [7,11,14]. We formally show that LDQL is strictly more expressive than every one of them.

4.1 Comparison with Property Paths Under Context-Based Query Semantics

Property paths (PPs for short) were introduced in SPARQL 1.1 as a way of adding navigational power to the language [8]. PPs are a form of regular expressions that are evaluated over a single (local) RDF graph; a PP expression is used to retrieve pairs $\langle a, b \rangle$ of nodes in the graph such that there is a path from a to b whose sequence of edge labels belongs (as a string) to the regular language defined by the expression. The syntax of PP expressions is given by the following grammar[1], where $p, u_1, u_2, \ldots, u_k$ are URIs.

$$pe := p \mid !(u_1|u_2|\cdots|u_k) \mid pe/pe \mid pe|pe \mid pe^*$$

A PP-pattern is defined as a tuple of the form $\langle \alpha, pe, \beta \rangle$ where pe is a PP expression, and α and β are in $\mathcal{U} \cup \mathcal{L} \cup \mathcal{V}$.

In [14] the authors adapted the semantics of PP-patterns so that they can be used to query the Web of Linked Data. The proposed query semantics is called *context-based semantics* [14]. To define this semantics, the authors first introduce the notion of a *context selector* for a Web of Linked Data W. This context selector is a function $C^W(\cdot)$ that given a URI $u \in \text{dom}(adoc)$ returns the RDF triples in $\text{data}(adoc(u))$ that have u in the subject position. Formally, for every URI $u \in \text{dom}(adoc)$ we have $C^W(u) = \{\langle s, p, o \rangle \in \text{data}(adoc(u)) \mid s = u\}$. To simplify the exposition, the authors extended the definition of $C^W(\cdot)$ to also handle URIs not in $\text{dom}(adoc)$, and literals and blank nodes. For any such RDF term a they define $C^W(a)$ as the empty set.

---

[1] In [14] the reverse path construction ^pe is also considered. We do not consider it here as the form of navigation of these reverse paths does not represent a traversal of the link graph.

The context-based semantics for PPs over the Web of Linked Data in [14] is a bag semantics that follows closely the semantics for PPs defined in the normative semantics of SPARQL 1.1 [8]. Hence, both semantics use a procedure, the *ArbitraryLengthPath* procedure [8], to define the semantics of the $(\cdot)^*$ operator. It was shown in [1] that for sets semantics, the normative semantics of PPs can be defined by using standard techniques for regular expressions. To make the comparison with LDQL, in this paper we adapt the context-based semantics for PPs presented in [14] by following the techniques in [1], and consider only sets of mappings. To this end, we define a function $[\![\cdot]\!]^{\text{ctxt}}_W$, that given a PP-pattern, returns its evaluation under context-based semantics over the Web of Linked Data W. In the definition, for a solution mapping μ and an RDF term α, we use the notation $\mu[\alpha]$ with the following meaning: $\mu[\alpha] = \mu(\alpha)$ if $\alpha \in \text{dom}(\mu)$, and $\mu[\alpha] = \alpha$ in the other case. Similarly, $\mu[\langle s, p, o\rangle] = \langle \mu[s], \mu[p], \mu[o]\rangle$.

$$[\![(\alpha, p, \beta)]\!]^{\text{ctxt}}_W = \{\mu \mid \text{dom}(\mu) = \{\alpha, \beta\} \cap \mathcal{V} \text{ and } \mu[\langle\alpha, p, \beta\rangle] \in C^W(\mu[\alpha])\}$$

$$[\![(\alpha, !(u_1|\cdots|u_k), \beta)]\!]^{\text{ctxt}}_W = \{\mu \mid \text{dom}(\mu) = \{\alpha, \beta\} \cap \mathcal{V} \text{ and exists } p \text{ s.t.}$$
$$\mu[\langle\alpha, p, \beta\rangle] \in C^W(\mu[\alpha]) \text{ and } p \notin \{u_1, \ldots, u_k\}\}$$

$$[\![(\alpha, pe_1/pe_2, \beta)]\!]^{\text{ctxt}}_W = \pi_{\{\alpha, \beta\} \cap \mathcal{V}}\left([\![(\alpha, pe_1, ?v)]\!]^{\text{ctxt}}_W \bowtie [\![(?v, pe_2, \beta)]\!]^{\text{ctxt}}_W\right)$$

$$[\![(\alpha, pe_1|pe_2, \beta)]\!]^{\text{ctxt}}_W = [\![(\alpha, pe_1, \beta)]\!]^{\text{ctxt}}_W \cup [\![(\alpha, pe_2, \beta)]\!]^{\text{ctxt}}_W$$

$$[\![(\alpha, pe^*, \beta)]\!]^{\text{ctxt}}_W = \{\mu \mid \text{dom}(\mu) = \{\alpha, \beta\} \cap \mathcal{V}, \mu[\alpha] = \mu[\beta] \text{ and } \mu[\alpha] \in \text{terms}(W)\} \cup$$
$$[\![(\alpha, pe, \beta)]\!]^{\text{ctxt}}_W \cup [\![(\alpha, pe/pe, \beta)]\!]^{\text{ctxt}}_W \cup [\![(\alpha, pe/pe/pe, \beta)]\!]^{\text{ctxt}}_W \cup \cdots$$

A *PP-based SPARQL query* [14] is an expression formed by combining PP-patterns using the standard SPARQL operators AND, UNION, OPT, FILTER and so on, following the standard semantics for these operators [2]. Our next results show that LDQL is strictly more expressive than PP-based SPARQL queries under context-based semantics.

Theorem 1. *There exists an LDQL query that cannot be expressed as a PP-based SPARQL query under context-based semantics.*

Proof (Sketch). One can show that LDQL query $q = \left(\text{SEED } U \ \langle\langle+, p, \_\rangle, (?x, ?x, ?x)\rangle\right)$ with $U = \{u\}$ cannot be expressed by PPs under context-based semantics because this semantics is "blind" to triples that are not authoritative. For instance, in a Web $W = \langle\{d, d'\}, adoc\rangle$ with $\text{data}(d) = \{\langle u, p, u'\rangle\}$, $\text{data}(d') = \{\langle u', p, u\rangle, \langle u, u, u\rangle\}$, $adoc(u) = d$ and $adoc(u') = d'$, the evaluation of q is the solution mapping $\{?x \mapsto u\}$. Notice that the only authoritative triple in d' is $\langle u', p, u\rangle$ as $d' = adoc(u') \neq adoc(u)$. Hence, one can prove that PP-based SPARQL queries under context-based semantics cannot access triple $\langle u, u, u\rangle$ in d', and thus, will never have $\{?x \mapsto u\}$ as solution.

Theorem 2. *Let $\alpha, \beta \in \mathcal{U} \cup \mathcal{L} \cup \mathcal{V}$. Then, for every PP-pattern $\langle\alpha, pe, \beta\rangle$, there exists an LDQL query q such that $[\![\langle\alpha, pe, \beta\rangle]\!]^{\text{ctxt}}_W = [\![q]\!]^{\emptyset}_W$ for every Web of Linked Data W.*

Proof (Sketch). In the proof we provide a translation scheme from PPs to LDQL. One major complication is that PPs can retrieve literals and, in general, values that are not in dom(*adoc*), which are difficult to handle by LPEs. For every PP-pattern $\langle ?x, pe, ?y \rangle$ we construct an LDQL query $Q_{pe}(?x, ?y)$. For example, for $\langle ?x, pe_1/pe_2, ?y \rangle$, our query is $\pi_{\{?x,?y\}}(Q_{pe_1}(?x, ?z) \text{ AND } Q_{pe_2}(?z, ?y))$, and for $\langle ?x, !(u_1 | \cdots | u_k), ?y \rangle$ the translation is (SEED $?x \langle \varepsilon, ((?x, ?p, ?y) \text{ FILTER } (?p \neq u_1 \wedge \cdots \wedge ?p \neq u_k)) \rangle \rangle$). To handle pe^* we need to use the construction $\langle ?v, q \rangle$ of LPEs, plus $(\cdot)^*$.

4.2   Comparison with NautiLOD

NautiLOD is a navigation language to traverse Linked Data on the WWW and to perform actions (such as sending emails) during the traversal [7]. We compare LDQL with NautiLOD without action rules. The syntax of NautiLOD expressions (without actions) is given by the following grammar (where $p \in \mathcal{U}$ and P is a SPARQL graph pattern).

$$ne := p \mid p\,\hat{}\, \mid \langle \_ \rangle \mid ne/ne \mid ne|ne \mid ne^* \mid ne[(\text{ASK } P)]$$

In terms of our data model[2], the semantics of NautiLOD expressions over a Web of Linked Data $W = \langle D, adoc \rangle$ from URI $u \in$ dom(*adoc*) is defined recursively as follows.

$$[\![p]\!]_W^u = \{ u' \mid \langle u, p, u' \rangle \in \text{data}(adoc(u)) \}$$
$$[\![p\,\hat{}\,]\!]_W^u = \{ u' \mid \langle u', p, u \rangle \in \text{data}(adoc(u)) \}$$
$$[\![\langle \_ \rangle]\!]_W^u = \{ u' \mid \langle u, p, u' \rangle \in \text{data}(adoc(u)) \text{ for some } p \in \mathcal{U} \}$$
$$[\![ne_1/ne_2]\!]_W^u = \{ u'' \mid u'' \in [\![ne_2]\!]_W^{u'} \text{ for some } u' \in [\![ne_1]\!]_W^u \text{ with } u' \in \text{dom}(adoc) \}$$
$$[\![ne_1 | ne_2]\!]_W^u = [\![ne_1]\!]_W^u \cup [\![ne_2]\!]_W^u$$
$$[\![ne^*]\!]_W^u = \{ u \} \cup [\![ne]\!]_W^u \cup [\![ne/ne]\!]_W^u \cup [\![ne/ne/ne]\!]_W^u \cup \cdots$$
$$[\![ne[(\text{ASK } P)]]\!]_W^u = \{ u' \mid u' \in [\![ne]\!]_W^u, \; u' \in \text{dom}(adoc) \text{ and } [\![P]\!]_{\text{data}(adoc(u'))} \neq \emptyset \}$$

We next show that for every NautiLOD expression there exists an equivalent LDQL query. Notice that the evaluation of a NautiLOD expression is a set of URIs, whereas the evaluation of an LDQL query is a set of mappings. Thus, to formally state our result we compare NautiLOD with LDQL queries that have a single *free variable*. Let $q(?x)$ be an LDQL query with $?x$ as free variable. We say that $q(?x)$ and a NautiLOD expression *ne* are equivalent if for every Web of Linked Data $W = \langle D, adoc \rangle$ and URIs u, u' with $u \in$ dom(*adoc*) it holds that $u' \in [\![ne]\!]_W^u$ if and only if $\{?x \mapsto u'\} \in [\![q(?x)]\!]_W^{\{u\}}$.

Theorem 3. *For every NautiLOD expression ne, there exists an LDQL query $q(?x)$, with $?x$ a free variable, that is equivalent to ne.*

---

[2] In [7], all URIs have an assigned set of RDF triples (which may be empty). In our data model one can have URIs not in dom(*adoc*). Hence, to properly capture the semantics of NautiLOD in terms of our data model we have to introduce conditions of the form "$u' \in$ dom(*adoc*)."

Proof (Sketch). The proof begins with a simple translation that replaces every $p \in \mathcal{U}$ in a NautiLOD expression by a link pattern $\langle +, p, \_ \rangle$. For instance, the expression p_1/p_2^* is translated into $\langle +, p_1, \_ \rangle / \langle +, p_2, \_ \rangle^*$. To translate $\langle \_ \rangle$ and $[(\textsc{ask } P)]$ we use $\langle ?v, q \rangle$. The complete translation poses several other complications (as described in the extended version [13]). In particular, the last step of NautiLOD expressions must be translated by using a SPARQL pattern and not an LPE. For this we use the following property. Given a regular expression r that does not generate the empty word, one can always write r as $r_1/a_1 | \cdots | r_k/a_k$ where the a_i's are base symbols of the alphabet. Thus, we can translate r by using LPEs to translate the r_i's as outlined above; next, translate the a_i's by using a method similar to the proof of Theorem 2, and finally use UNION for |.

Along the same lines of Theorem 1 one can prove the following result.

Theorem 4. *There exists an LDQL query $q(?x)$ that cannot be expressed in NautiLOD.*

4.3 Comparison with SPARQL Under Reachability-Based Query Semantics

In [11] the author introduces a family of reachability-based query semantics based on which SPARQL graph patterns can be used as a query language for Linked Data on the WWW. Similar to how the scope of the SPARQL part of a basic LDQL query is restricted to particular documents, reachability-based semantics restrict the scope of SPARQL queries to documents that can be reached by traversing a well-defined set of data links. To specify what data links belong to such a set, the notion of a *reachability criterion* is used; that is, a function $c: \mathcal{T} \times \mathcal{U} \times \mathcal{P} \rightarrow \{\text{true}, \text{false}\}$ where $\mathcal{P}$ denotes the set of all SPARQL graph patterns. Then, given such a reachability criterion c, a finite set S of URIs and a SPARQL graph pattern P, a document $d \in \mathcal{D}$ is *(c, S, P)-reachable* in a Web of Linked Data $W = \langle D, adoc \rangle$ if any of the following two conditions holds:

1. There exists a URI $u \in S$ such that $adoc(u) = d$; or
2. there exists a link graph edge $\langle d_{\text{src}}, (t, u), d_{\text{tgt}} \rangle \in \mathcal{G}_W$ such that (i) d_{src} is (c, S, P)-reachable in W, (ii) $c(t, u, P) = \text{true}$, and (iii) $d_{\text{tgt}} = d$.

Notice how the second condition restricts the notion of reachability by ignoring data links that do not satisfy the given reachability criterion c. Concrete examples of reachability criteria are c_{All}, c_{None}, and c_{Match} [11], where c_{All} selects all data links, and c_{None} ignores all data links; i.e., $c_{\text{All}}(t, u, P) = \text{true}$ and $c_{\text{None}}(t, u, P) = \text{false}$ for all tuples $\langle t, u, P \rangle \in \mathcal{T} \times \mathcal{U} \times \mathcal{P}$. In contrast to such an all-or-nothing strategy, criterion c_{Match} returns true for every data link whose triple matches a triple pattern of the given graph pattern; formally, $c_{\text{Match}}(t, u, P) = \text{true}$ if and only if there exists some solution mapping μ such that $\mu[tp] = t$ for an arbitrary triple pattern tp that is contained in P.

Given the notion of a reachability criterion, it is possible to define a family of (reachability-based) query semantics for SPARQL. To this end, let c be a reachability criterion, let S be a finite set of URIs, and let P be a SPARQL graph pattern. Then, for any Web of Linked Data $W = \langle D, adoc \rangle$, the S-based evaluation of P over W under c-semantics, denoted by $[\![P]\!]_W^{\mathsf{R}(c,S)}$, is the set of solution mappings $[\![P]\!]_G$ where G is the RDF graph that consists of all triples from all documents that are (c, S, P)-reachable in W.

While there exist an infinite number of possible reachability criteria, in this paper we focus on c_{All}, c_{None}, and c_{Match}. The following two results show that LDQL is strictly more expressive than SPARQL graph patterns under any of these three query semantics.

Theorem 5. Let $c \in \{c_{\mathsf{All}}, c_{\mathsf{None}}, c_{\mathsf{Match}}\}$. For every SPARQL graph pattern P there exists an LDQL query q such that $[\![P]\!]_W^{\mathsf{R}(c,S)} = [\![q]\!]_W^S$ for every Web W and $S \subseteq \mathcal{U}$.

Proof (Sketch). We only sketch the case of c_{All}-semantics. In this case, one can prove that the LPE $lpe^{c_{\mathsf{All}}} = \langle \_, \_, \_ \rangle^*$ simulates the reachability criterion c_{All}, and, thus, $[\![P]\!]_W^{\mathsf{R}(c_{\mathsf{All}},S)} = [\![\langle lpe^{c_{\mathsf{All}}}, P \rangle]\!]_W^S$. One can also find LPEs to simulate c_{None} and c_{Match}.

Theorem 6. Let $c \in \{c_{\mathsf{All}}, c_{\mathsf{None}}, c_{\mathsf{Match}}\}$. There exists an LDQL query q for which there does not exist a SPARQL pattern P such that $[\![P]\!]_W^{\mathsf{R}(c,S)} = [\![q]\!]_W^S$ for every W and $S \subseteq \mathcal{U}$.

5   Web-Safeness of LDQL Queries

In this section we study the "Web-safeness" of LDQL queries, where, informally, we call a query *Web-safe* if a complete execution of the query over the WWW is possible in practice (which is not the case for all LDQL queries as we shall see). To provide a more formal definition of this notion of Web-safeness we make the following observations. While the mathematical structures introduced by our data model capture the notion of Linked Data on the WWW formally (and, thus, allow us to provide a formal semantics for LDQL queries), in practice, these structures are not available completely for the WWW. For instance, given that an infinite number of strings can be used as HTTP URIs [6], we cannot assume complete information about which URIs are in the domain of the partial function *adoc* (i.e., can be looked up to retrieve some document) and which are not; in fact, disclosing this information would require a process that systematically tries to look up every possible HTTP URI and, thus, would never terminate. Therefore, it is also impossible to guarantee the discovery of every document in the set D (without looking up an infinite number of URIs). Consequently, any query whose execution requires a complete enumeration of this set is not feasible in practice. Based on these observations, we define *Web-safeness* of LDQL queries as follows.

Definition 6. An LDQL query q is **Web-safe** if there exists an algorithm that, for any finite Web of Linked Data $W = \langle D, adoc \rangle$ and any finite set S of URIs, computes $[\![q]\!]_W^S$ by looking up only a finite number of URIs without assuming an a priori availability of any information about the sets D and $\mathrm{dom}(adoc)$.

Example 6. Recall our example queries q_{ex}, q'_{ex}, and q''_{ex} (cf. Example 5). For query $q_{ex} = \big(\textsc{seed}\ ?x\ \langle\varepsilon, \langle?x, p_1, ?z\rangle\rangle\big)$, any URI $u \in \mathcal{U}$ may be used to obtain a nonempty subset of the query result as long as a lookup of u retrieves a document whose data includes RDF triples that match $\langle u, p_1, ?z\rangle$. Therefore, without access to D or $\mathrm{dom}(adoc)$ of the queried Web $W = \langle D, adoc\rangle$, the completeness of the computed query result can be guaranteed only by checking each of the infinitely many possible HTTP URIs. Hence, query q_{ex} is *not* Web-safe. In contrast, although it contains q_{ex} as a subquery, query $q''_{ex} = (q_{ex}\ \textsc{and}\ q'_{ex})$ is Web-safe, and so is $q'_{ex} = \langle lpe_{ex}, B_{ex}\rangle$. Given u_A as seed URI, a possible execution algorithm for q'_{ex} may first compute $[\![lpe_{ex}]\!]_W^{u_A}$ by traversing the queried Web W based on lpe_{ex}. Thereafter, the algorithm retrieves documents by looking up all URIs $u \in [\![lpe_{ex}]\!]_W^{u_A}$ (or simply keeps these documents after the traversal); and, finally, the algorithm evaluates pattern B_{ex} over the union of the RDF data in the retrieved documents. If W is finite (i.e., contains a finite number of documents), the traversal process requires a finite number of URI lookups only, and so does the retrieval of documents in the second step; the final step does not look up any URI. To see that q''_{ex} is also Web-safe we note that after executing subquery q'_{ex} (e.g., by using the algorithm as outlined before), the execution of the other (non-Web-safe) subquery q_{ex} can be reduced to a finite number of URI lookups, namely the URIs bound to variable $?x$ in solution mappings obtained for subquery q'_{ex}. Although any other URI may also be used to obtain solution mappings for q_{ex}, such solution mappings cannot be joined with any of the solution mappings for q'_{ex} and, thus, are irrelevant for the result of q''_{ex}.

The example illustrates that there exists an LDQL query that is not Web-safe. In fact, it is not difficult to see that the argument for the non-Web-safeness of query q_{ex} as made in the example can be applied to any LDQL query of the form $(\textsc{seed}\ ?x\ q)$ where subquery q is a (satisfiable) basic LDQL query; that is, none of these queries is Web-safe. However, the example also shows that more complex queries that contain such non-Web-safe subqueries may still be Web-safe. Therefore, we now show properties to identify LDQL queries that are Web-safe even if some of their subqueries are not. We begin with queries of the forms $\langle lpe, P\rangle$, $\pi_V q$, $(\textsc{seed}\ U\ q)$, and $(q_1\ \textsc{union}\ \ldots\ \textsc{union}\ q_n)$.

Proposition 2. *An LDQL query q is Web-safe if any of the following properties holds:*

1. *Query q is of the form $\langle lpe, P\rangle$ and lpe is Web-safe, where we call an LPE Web-safe if either (i) it is of the form $\langle?v, q'\rangle$ and LDQL query q' is Web-safe, or (ii) it is of any form other than $\langle?v, q'\rangle$ and all its subexpressions (if any) are Web-safe LPEs;*
2. *Query q is of the form $\pi_V q'$ or $(\textsc{seed}\ U\ q')$, and subquery q' is Web-safe; or*
3. *Query q is of the form $(q_1\ \textsc{union}\ \ldots\ \textsc{union}\ q_n)$ and each q_i $(1 \le i \le n)$ is Web-safe.*

It remains to discuss LDQL queries of the form $(q_1$ AND ... AND $q_m)$. Our discussion of query q''_{ex} in Example 6 suggests that such queries can be shown to be Web-safe if all non-Web-safe subqueries are of the form (SEED $?v$ q) and it is possible to execute these subqueries by using variable bindings obtained from other subqueries. A necessary condition for this execution strategy is that the variable in question (i.e., $?v$) is guaranteed to be bound in every possible solution mapping obtained from the other subqueries.

To allow for an automated verification of this condition we adopt Buil-Aranda et al.'s notion of strongly bound variables [4]. To this end, for any SPARQL graph pattern P, let sbvars(P) denote the set of strongly bound variables in P as defined by Buil-Aranda et al. [4]. For the sake of space, we do not repeat the definition here. However, we emphasize that sbvars(P) can be constructed recursively, and each variable in sbvars(P) is guaranteed to be bound in every possible solution for P [4, Proposition 1]. To carry over these properties to LDQL queries, we use the notion of strongly bound variables in SPARQL patterns to define the following notion of strongly bound variables in LDQL queries; thereafter, in Lemma 3, we show the desired boundedness guarantee.

Definition 7. The set of **strongly bound variables** in an LDQL query q, denoted by sbvars(q), is defined recursively as follows:

1. If q is of the form $\langle lpe, P \rangle$, then sbvars(q) = sbvars(P).
2. If q is of the form $(q_1$ AND $q_2)$, then sbvars(q) = sbvars(q_1) $\cup$ sbvars(q_2).
3. If q is of the form $(q_1$ UNION $q_2)$, then sbvars(q) = sbvars(q_1) $\cap$ sbvars(q_2).
4. If q is of the form $\pi_V q'$, then sbvars(q) = sbvars(q') $\cap V$.
5. If q is of the form (SEED U q'), then sbvars(q) = sbvars(q').
6. If q is of the form (SEED $?v$ q'), then sbvars(q) = sbvars(q') $\cup \{?v\}$.

Lemma 3. *Let q be an LDQL query. For every finite set S of URIs, every Web of Linked Data W, and every solution mapping $\mu \in [\![q]\!]^S_W$, it holds that* sbvars(q) $\subseteq$ dom(μ).

We are now ready to show the following result.

Theorem 7. *An LDQL query of the form $(q_1$ AND q_2 AND ... AND $q_m)$ is Web-safe if there exists a total order $\prec$ over the set of subqueries $\{q_1, q_2, ..., q_m\}$ such that for each subquery q_i $(1 \leq i \leq m)$, it holds that either (i) q_i is Web-safe or (ii) q_i is of the form (SEED $?v$ q) where q is Web-safe and $?v \in \bigcup_{q_j \prec q_i}$ sbvars(q_j).*

Proof (Sketch). We prove Theorem 7 based on an iterative algorithm that generalizes the execution of query q''_{ex} as outlined in Example 6. That is, the algorithm executes the subqueries $q_1 ... q_m$ sequentially in the order $\prec$ such that each iteration executes one of the subqueries by using the solution mappings computed during the previous iteration.

With the results in this section we have all ingredients to devise a procedure to show Web-safeness for a large number of queries (including queries that are arbitrarily nested). However, as a potential limitation of such a procedure we note that Theorem 7 can be applied only in cases in which all non-Web-safe subqueries are of the form (SEED $?v$ q). For instance, the theorem cannot be applied to show that an LDQL query of the form $\big(q_1$ AND $(q_2$ UNION (SEED $?x$ $q_3))\big)$ is Web-safe if $?x \in$ sbvars(q_1) and q_1, q_2 and q_3 are Web-safe. On the other hand, for the semantically equivalent query $\big((q_1$ AND $q_2)$ UNION $(q_1$ AND (SEED $?x$ $q_3))\big)$ we can show Web-safeness based on Theorem 7 (and Proposition 2). Fortunately, we may leverage the following fact to improve the effectiveness of applying Theorem 7 in the procedure that we aim to devise.

Fact 1. If an LDQL query q is Web-safe, then so is any LDQL query q' with $q' \equiv q$.

As a consequence of Fact 1, we may use the equivalences in Lemma 2 to rewrite a given query into an equivalent query that is more suitable for testing Web-safeness based on our results. To this end, we introduce specific normal forms for LDQL queries:

Definition 8. An LDQL query is in **union-free normal form** if it is of the form $(q_1$ AND ... AND $q_m)$ with $m \geq 1$ and each q_i $(1 \leq i \leq m)$ is either (i) a basic LDQL query or (ii) of the form $\pi_V q$, (SEED U q) or (SEED $?v$ q) such that subquery q is in UNION-free normal form. An LDQL query is in **union normal form** if it is of the form $(q_1$ UNION ... UNION $q_n)$ with $n \geq 1$ and each q_i $(1 \leq i \leq n)$ is in UNION-free normal form.

The following result is an immediate consequence of Lemma 2.

Corollary 1. *Every LDQL query is equivalent to an LDQL query in* UNION *normal form.*

In conjunction with Fact 1, Corollary 1 allows us to focus on LDQL queries in UNION normal form without losing generality. We are now ready to specify our procedure that applies the results in this paper to test a given LDQL query q for Web-safeness: First, by using the equivalences in Lemma 2, the query has to be rewritten into a semantically equivalent LDQL query $q_{\mathsf{nf}} = (q_1$ UNION ... UNION $q_n)$ that is in UNION normal form. Next, the following test has to be repeated for every subquery q_i $(1 \leq i \leq n)$; recall that each of these subqueries is in UNION-free normal form; i.e., $q_i = (q_1^i$ AND ... AND $q_{m_i}^i)$. The test is to find an order for their subqueries $q_1^i, \dots, q_{m_i}^i$ that satisfies the conditions in Theorem 7. Every top-level subquery q_i $(1 \leq i \leq n)$ for which such an order exists, is Web-safe (cf. Theorem 7). If all top-level subqueries are identified to be Web-safe by this test, then q_{nf} is Web-safe (cf. Proposition 2), and so is q (cf. Fact 1).

The given conditions are sufficient to show Web-safeness of LDQL. It remains open whether there exists a (decidable) sufficient *and* necessary condition for Web-safeness.

6   Concluding Remarks and Future Work

LDQL, the query language that we introduce in this paper, allows users to express queries over Linked Data on the WWW. We defined LDQL such that navigational features for selecting the query-relevant documents on the Web are separate from patterns that are meant to be evaluated over the data in the selected documents. This separation distinguishes LDQL from other approaches to express queries over Linked Data.

We focused on expressiveness, by comparing LDQL with previous formalisms, and on the notion of Web-safeness. Several topics remain open for future work. One of them is the complexity of query evaluation. A classical complexity analysis is easy to perform if we assume that all the data and documents are available as if they were in a centralized repository, and that they can be processed via a RAM machine model. We conjecture that under this model, the data complexity of evaluating LDQL will be polynomial. Nevertheless, a more interesting complexity analysis should consider a model that captures the inherent way of accessing the Web of Linked Data via HTTP requests, the overhead of data communication and transfer, the distribution of data and documents, etc. A more practical direction for future research on LDQL is the development of approaches to actually implement LDQL queries efficiently.

Acknowledgments. Pérez is supported by the Millennium Nucleus Center for Semantic Web Research, Grant NC120004, and Fondecyt grant 1140790.

References

1. Arenas, M., Conca, S., Pérez, J.: Counting beyond a yottabyte, or how SPARQL 1.1 property paths will prevent adoption of the standard. In: WWW 2012, pp. 629–638 (2012)
2. Arenas, M., Gutierrez, C., Pérez, J.: On the semantics of SPARQL. In: Semantic Web Information Management - A Model-Based Perspective, chap. 13, pp. 281–307. Springer (2009)
3. Berners-Lee,   T.:   Linked   Data   (2006).   http://www.w3.org/DesignIssues/LinkedData.html
4. Buil-Aranda, C., Arenas, M., Corcho, O.: Semantics and optimization of the SPARQL 1.1 federation extension. In: Antoniou, G., Grobelnik, M., Simperl, E., Parsia, B., Plexousakis, D., De Leenheer, P., Pan, J. (eds.) ESWC 2011, Part II. LNCS, vol. 6644, pp. 1–15. Springer, Heidelberg (2011)
5. Cyganiak, R., Wood, D., Lanthaler, M.: RDF 1.1 Concepts and Abstract Syntax. W3C Recommendation, February 2014
6. Fielding, R., Gettys, J., Mogul, J.C., Frystyk, H., Masinter, L., Leach, P.J., Berners-Lee, T.: Hypertext Transfer Protocol - HTTP/1.1, June 1999
7. Fionda, V., Pirrò, G., Gutierrez, C.: NautiLOD: A Formal Language for the Web of Data Graph. ACM Transactions on the Web **9**(1), 5:1–5:43 (2015)
8. Harris, S., Seaborne, A., Prud'hommeaux, E.: SPARQL 1.1 Query Language. W3C Recommendation, March 2013

9. Harth, A., Speiser, S.: On completeness classes for query evaluation on linked data. In: Proc. 26th AAAI Conf. (2012)
10. Hartig, O.: LDQL: a language for linked data queries. In: AMW 2015 (2015)
11. Hartig, O.: SPARQL for a web of linked data: semantics and computability. In: Simperl, E., Cimiano, P., Polleres, A., Corcho, O., Presutti, V. (eds.) ESWC 2012. LNCS, vol. 7295, pp. 8–23. Springer, Heidelberg (2012)
12. Hartig, O.: An Overview on Execution Strategies for Linked Data Queries. Datenbank-Spektrum **13**(2) (2013)
13. Hartig, O., Pérez, J.: LDQL: A Query Language for the Web of Linked Data (Extended Version). CoRR abs/1507.04614 (2015). http://arxiv.org/abs/1507.04614
14. Hartig, O., Pirrò, G.: A context-based semantics for SPARQL property paths over the web. In: Proc. 12th Extended Semantic Web Conf. (2015)
15. Mendelzon, A.O., Mihaila, G.A., Milo T.: Querying the world wide web. In: PDIS (1996)
16. Pérez, J., Arenas, M., Gutierrez, C.: Semantics and complexity of SPARQL. In: Cruz, I., Decker, S., Allemang, D., Preist, C., Schwabe, D., Mika, P., Uschold, M., Aroyo, L.M. (eds.) ISWC 2006. LNCS, vol. 4273, pp. 30–43. Springer, Heidelberg (2006)
17. Pérez, J., Arenas, M., Gutierrez, C.: nSPARQL: A Navigational Language for RDF. J. Web Sem. **8**(4), 255–270 (2010)
18. Umbrich, J., Hogan, A., Polleres, A., Decker, S.: Link Traversal Querying for a Diverse Web of Data. Semantic Web Journal (2014)

Opportunistic Linked Data Querying Through Approximate Membership Metadata

Miel Vander Sande[✉], Ruben Verborgh, Joachim Van Herwegen,
Erik Mannens, and Rik Van de Walle

Multimedia Lab, Ghent University – iMinds,
Gaston Crommenlaan 8 Bus 201, 9050 Ledeberg-Ghent, Belgium
{miel.vandersande,ruben.verborgh,joachim.vanherwegen,
erik.mannens,rik.vandewalle}@ugent.be

Abstract. Between URI dereferencing and the SPARQL protocol lies a largely unexplored axis of possible interfaces to Linked Data, each with its own combination of trade-offs. One of these interfaces is Triple Pattern Fragments, which allows clients to execute SPARQL queries against low-cost servers, at the cost of higher bandwidth. Increasing a client's efficiency means lowering the number of requests, which can among others be achieved through additional metadata in responses. We noted that typical SPARQL query evaluations against Triple Pattern Fragments require a significant portion of membership subqueries, which check the presence of a specific triple, rather than a variable pattern. This paper studies the impact of providing approximate membership functions, i.e., Bloom filters and Golomb-coded sets, as extra metadata. In addition to reducing HTTP requests, such functions allow to achieve full result recall earlier when temporarily allowing lower precision. Half of the tested queries from a WatDiv benchmark test set could be executed with up to a third fewer HTTP requests with only marginally higher server cost. Query times, however, did not improve, likely due to slower metadata generation and transfer. This indicates that approximate membership functions can partly improve the client-side query process with minimal impact on the server and its interface.

Keywords: Linked data · Querying · Availability · Scalability · SPARQL

1 Introduction

For a long period of time, querying Linked Data has been a story of two extremes, with Linked Data documents on the one side and the SPARQL protocol on the other. Currently, neither of them is able to drive real-world applications on the Web. On the one hand, public SPARQL endpoints are limited in number and suffer from frequent downtime [4,22]. Their resource consumption is hard to predict, caused by the expressiveness of the language and individual user demand.

For Johan De Smedt. Thanks to Daniel P. Miranker for his suggestions on Bloom filters.

This downtime results in insufficient reliability for client applications. Linked Data documents, on the other hand, are more predictable, but link-traversal-based query methods are significantly slower and result sets have varying levels of completeness, both of which are undesired traits for user applications. The issues with these two query solutions hint at a need for other client/server trade-offs.

Linked Data Fragments (LDF) [25] aim to analyse such trade-offs by proposing an uniform view on all interfaces to RDF. This reveals a complete spectrum between Linked Data documents and the SPARQL protocol, in which the state-of-the-art of Linked Data publishing can be advanced. This axis can be explored in the following two dimensions.

- **Selector**: allowing different, more complex questions for the server
- **Metadata**: extending the response with more information clients can use

In prior work, Triple Pattern Fragments (TPF) [25] were introduced as an alternative API with low-server cost. This interface offers a single triple pattern as selector and includes an estimated number of total matching triples as metadata. SPARQL queries can be evaluated client-side by combining several TPFs, using the metadata for optimization. Higher query execution time and more bandwidth are accepted in exchange for a small load on the server, thereby striking a more sustainable load balance between client and server. Recently, an algorithm that reduces bandwidth was proposed within the same server restrictions [23]. Another direction for improvement is to have servers support other features along the selector and/or metadata dimensions in addition to TPF.

In this paper, we explore the metadata dimension by adding approximate membership functions (AMF) as a composable feature for Linked Data Fragments APIs. An AMF is a space-efficient data structure that is able to indicate whether a set contains an item. False positives can occur with a fixed probability, but false negatives can not. This work studies their applicability as a server-side feature in addition to TPF, in order to reduce the number of HTTP requests during client-side SPARQL query execution. We study two different AMF techniques: Bloom filters [3] and Golomb-Coded Sets (GCS) [19]. Concretely, we present *i)* an in-depth comparison between different client-side algorithms with or without Bloom and GCS; *ii)* a vocabulary to describe approximate membership functions as metadata for self-descriptive APIs; *iii)* an evaluation of opportunistic querying, where we strive for result completeness first and validate their correctness later.

First, we present the preliminary concepts and related work in Section 2. Then, we discuss the motivation, research questions and hypotheses for this work in Section 3. Next, Section 4 shows how the TPF interface is extended with AMF metadata. After that, we demonstrate how the client benefits from this in Section 5, and how it enables a more opportunistic form of querying in Section 6. Finally, we evaluate the query algorithms with and without AMF metadata in Section 7, and conclude in Section 8.

2 Core Concepts and Related Work

2.1 SPARQL Query Evaluation Using Traditional Web APIs

Linked Data can be published on the Web using different APIs, of which data dumps and SPARQL endpoints are highly common [5]. The Linked Data Fragments conceptual framework [25] enables the analysis and comparison of Web APIs by abstracting each API according to how it provides access to parts of a certain dataset. Each such part is called a *Linked Data Fragment* (LDF), which consists of data, metadata, and controls. The *data* is a set of those triples of the dataset that match a given interface-dependent selector. The *metadata* set consists of triples that describe the dataset and/or the current fragment or related fragments. Finally, the *controls* are hypermedia links and/or forms that allow clients to retrieve other fragments of the same or other datasets.

Both data dumps and SPARQL endpoint responses can be considered LDFs. A data dump of a dataset employs all triples in that dataset, usually in a compressed archive, as the data. The metadata set contains data such as publication date and/or license. No controls are present, because all available data is contained within the archive. The main drawback of dumps that they cannot be queried "live": they need to be downloaded in their entirety to evaluate queries.

The SPARQL protocol [6] exposes RDF graphs on the Web using the SPARQL query language [10]. Each response to a CONSTRUCT or DESCRIBE query can be seen as an LDF, where the data consists of the RDF triples in the dataset that match the query. The metadata and control sets are empty; controls are implicitly in the SPARQL protocol. An advantage of SPARQL endpoints is their expressiveness: clients can ask very specific questions about a dataset. However, public SPARQL endpoints suffer from a two-sided availability problem: the majority of datasets is not published as a SPARQL endpoint (543 opposed to 9960 datasets)[1], and endpoints that are on the Web experience frequent downtime [4].

2.2 SPARQL Query Evaluation Using Triple Pattern Fragments

In addition to describing existing interfaces, LDF also allows defining new interfaces with different characteristics. The Triple Pattern Fragments (TPF) interface [24,25] combines the desirable characteristics of data dumps (low server-side cost) and SPARQL endpoints (live queryable). Clients can ask a server for triple patterns; in response, the server sends a TPF, consisting of the triples of the dataset matching the triple pattern (paged to keep the fragment size reasonably small), metadata expressing the total number of matching triples, and controls to retrieve all other TPFs of the same dataset. Complex SPARQL queries are evaluated by clients, which split a query into triple patterns and use the metadata in fragments to determine an efficient execution order. The advantage of TPFs is that they only require low processing power on the server side, and are thus less expensive to host with high availability [25]. The drawback is that

---

[1] http://stats.lod2.eu

SPARQL queries have longer query times than on a SPARQL endpoint. More than 600,000 crawled RDF files are available as TPFs through the LOD Laundromat [21]. DBpedia, arguably the most well-known dataset on the Semantic Web, has an official TPF interface with 99.999% availability [26].

TPFs move the query planning problem to the client. It is up to the client to make optimal use of metadata exposed by the server. The originally proposed query planning algorithm is greedy [25]. Assuming a Basic Graph Pattern (BGP) query, the client downloads results for the triple pattern with the lowest cardinality, based on the count metadata. Possible mappings for each resulting triple are bound to each remaining pattern, of which the one with lowest cardinality is subsequently requested from the server.

Van Herwegen et al. improve the greedy algorithm [23], aiming to minimize the number of HTTP calls by making global instead of local decisions. This is achieved by downloading two triple patterns separately in case this requires fewer HTTP calls. Multiple estimation techniques, based on the intermediate results of the algorithm, are used to predict which query path is least expensive. If the current path is suboptimal, the algorithm continues from the new path. This decrease in HTTP requests results, however, in more computational work for the client because of the more complex join process.

This paper seeks to provide an optimized balance between server-side cost and query execution time by extending the TPF interface with additional metadata, as we will discuss in Sections 4 to 6. The goal is to maintain a low per-request cost for the server, while reducing the number of requests clients need to execute to evaluate typical queries.

2.3 Approximate Membership Techniques

In the following, we summarize the Approximate Membership Function (AMF) families of Bloom filters and Golomb-Coded Sets. Both offer approximate membership assessment with a predefined false positive probability, but with different size and speed. Recall and precision are important parameters of an AMF f. Given the set of actual members M and a set of elements T for which we want to test membership, the set of positively tested elements $P_T = \{t \in T : f(t) = \text{true}\}$. We define $recall_f(T) = |M \cap P_T|/|M|$ and $precision_f(T) = |M \cap P_T|/|P_T|$. Both Bloom filters and Golomb-Coded Sets have 100% recall, i.e., all valid members of M will always be identified, but less than 100% precision.

Bloom Filters. A Bloom filter [3] is a bitmap of m bits populated using k different hash functions, initialized with all bits set to 0. An item is added by calculating k locations in the bitmap, which are set to 1. Each one is calculated by using a different hash function to ensure randomness. An item can be tested by calculating k locations using the same hash functions. Hence, both insertion and testing are $O(k)$. The result of a bit-wise AND of those locations in the filter determines if the item is a member. If false, the item is *definitely* not in the set. If true, the item *might* be in the set, because of false positives.

For a desired false positive probability rate p, the bit-size of a Bloom filter is proportional to its number of members n. The required size is $m = -n \cdot \log_2 e \cdot$

$\log_2 p$. For a given m, the optimal number of hashes k that minimizes false positive probability can be calculated with $k = m/n \cdot \ln 2$. Despite their compact representation, their size can be too large for network transfer. A solution is using compressed Bloom filters [15], at the cost of compression and decompression delays.

Golomb-Coded Sets. Golomb-coded sets (GCS) [19] provide a cleaner variation of compressed Bloom filters. The outputs of a single hash function are considered a uniformly distributed list of values instead of a bitmap. The differences between all values form a geometrically distribution with a parameter p. Golomb-coding is applied since it is an optimal encoding for discrete geometric distributions [8].

In terms of size, GCS approaches the theoretical minimum of $m = -n \cdot \log_2 p$ more closely than the equivalent Bloom filter. Compared to compressed Bloom filters, GCS have a minimal size overhead for the same p, but they are more easily chunked and indexed to deal with uncompressed size issues. Compared to plain Bloom filters, the query time is magnitudes slower due to decompression. However, this drawback can be minimized by including an index to quickly find areas of interest in the filter.

2.4   Query Evaluation with Approximate Membership

In the context of RDF querying, approximate membership functions are included in several related works, covering *i)* query routing in networks, *ii)* selectivity estimation for optimizing joins, *iii)* evolutionary querying, and *iv)* local database indexes.

Query routing applies Bloom filters in caches and indexes for peer-to-peer, MapReduce or cloud clusters, and Linked Data networks. Most systems [7,14,20] construct a *data summary* of neighboring nodes or clusters to make a query forwarding decisions. Some algorithms exchange these filters between nodes to maintain their network [11]. This is common in combination with Distributed Hash Tables (DHT) [11,27], where a DHT is used for data routing and Bloom filters for efficient communication between nodes.

More directly applicable is *selectivity estimation* of query patterns, e.g., graph patterns, to improve join performance. One approach is to group different chain-patterns, i.e. two distinct triple patterns connected by a single variable, according to their frequency [13]. A Bloom filter tests in what frequency group a chain pattern resides, which optimizes the pattern execution order. Other applications include representing equivalent classes to optimize hash joins, ranges of values for merge joins [16], and distributed n-way joins [2]. Although these works inspire future directions, many require more than a single triple pattern and have high demands for the server. Highly relevant is the proposal to extend the ASK query response [12] with combinations of bindings, i.e. two variables in a triple pattern, to improve source selection in SPARQL query federation frameworks. Bloom filters from different sources indicate overlap and save redundant requests. However, the benefit in a single-server setup is unclear.

Evolutionary querying is an alternative way of SPARQL query processing. Possible solutions are first guessed, and then incrementally refined. Oren et al. use a combination of fingerprinting and Bloom filters to rapidly evaluate approximate answers against large RDF datasets [17]. Although this is a centralized solution, it advocates *anytime* answers, which is in line with the opportunistic querying presented in this paper. The algorithm is initiated with random values, which returns initial results fast, but with low accuracy.

Finally, in the area of databases, Bloom filters are an efficient technique to prevent unnecessary disk access [18]. In such cases, the size of the filter and its impact on transfer delays are not applicable.

3   Problem Statement

3.1   Analysis of Query Execution Using Triple Pattern Fragments

The required time for a client evaluate certain SPARQL queries against TPF interfaces can still be unacceptable for responsive applications. A dominant factor in this time is the high number of HTTP requests. Therefore, by analyzing the nature of these requests, we can locate possible areas for changing the client/server trade-offs in the interface. To this end, we executed sample SPARQL queries from the WatDiv benchmark [1] against a TPF interface using the greedy algorithm [25]. WatDiv consists of 20 query templates grouped in four categories, namely linear (L), star (S), snowflake-shaped (F) and complex (C).[2]

The execution logs revealed a high number of requests for triple patterns without variables, i.e. testing the *membership* of a specific triple in the dataset. The templates L2, L4, and F3 respectively produced 50%, 51% and 74% membership subqueries. For S5, F5, C1, and C2, this proportion even reached 95% to 98%. Furthermore, the absolute number of requests of some of these templates is high (e.g., F3 needed 1,335 membership subqueries). A third of query templates is thus affected; the remaining 13 templates produced no membership subqueries at all. While these numbers do not allow generalized conclusions, they are certainly an important indication that a reduction of membership subqueries can have a considerable influence on the number of HTTP requests—and thus the overall query execution time.

3.2   Research Questions and Hypotheses

In the TPF interface, metadata is crucial for clients to evaluate SPARQL queries efficiently. By estimating the total number of matches per triple pattern, patterns with higher selectivity can be followed first [23,25]. If we augment this metadata, clients might be able to make more informed decisions and hence reduce the number of membership subqueries required to evaluate a SPARQL

---

[2] The 20 WatDiv templates are graphically displayed at http://db.uwaterloo.ca/ watdiv/basic-testing.shtml. Note that the number of templates per category does not necessarily reflect actual query distributions for specific datasets.

query, at the cost of higher per-request costs. This paper studies the impact of adding approximate membership functions to fragments in order to reduce the amount of HTTP requests. In this regard, we pose the following research question:

Question 1: To what extent can approximate membership metadata for TPFs reduce the number of HTTP requests necessary to evaluate SPARQL queries?

Probabilistic queries also enable new ways of generating results: uncertain results can be returned early, and validated later on. We investigate this as follows:

Question 2: To what extent can approximate membership metadata for TPFs reduce the time to achieve complete recall of SPARQL query results?

Adding such metadata requires AMFs to be generated on the server side, the impact of which should be investigated:

Question 3: What is the overhead of generating approximate membership metadata on the server CPU load at runtime?

The answers to these questions validate our exploration of the metadata dimension using AMFs. Concretely, we test the following hypotheses about the effectiveness of an interface I', which adds an AMF feature to the baseline TPF interface I. First, given the presence of AMFs, the client should be able to omit a portion of requests over HTTP, hence:

Hypothesis 1: The number of HTTP requests required to evaluate minimum a third of the WatDiv queries against I' can be significantly reduced.

Next, as stated above, the reduction in HTTP requests has a direct impact on the overall execution time, thus:

Hypothesis 2: The time to achieve complete recall when executing WatDiv queries against I' is significantly reduced on average.

Finally, we do not expect much extra load on the server, since an AMF using a non-cryptographic hash function can be computed fast:

Hypothesis 3: The interface I' increases server CPU usage only slightly compared to I for the same queries.

4   Extending the TPF Interface with AMF Metadata

The TPF interface responds with RDF documents and is self-descriptive [25], meaning that *i)* extensions to the TPF interface are features of a composable API, ensuring backward-compatibility; *ii)* clients can discover at runtime which features are supported. Therefore, servers can add an interface feature, e.g., AMFs as extra metadata, without any interference. This section introduces a generic ontology to express membership functions such as AMFs, followed by its implementation as a feature on top of the TPF interface.

We created a membership modeling ontology, which we publish and maintain at http://semweb.mmlab.be/ns/membership and denote with the prefix ms in the remainder of this paper. It defines `ms:Function` for generic functions and its subclasses `ms:ApproximateMembershipFunction` and `ms:HashFunction`. To allow for Bloom filters and Golomb-coded sets, the former has `ms:BloomFilter` and `ms:GolombCodedSet` as subclasses. Finally, `ms:hashFunction` associates instances of these classes with hash functions that can be instances of algorithms such as `ms:MD5` or `ms:MurmurHash3`.

Using this ontology, we define an interface feature that provides AMF metadata in the metadata graph of responses. In regular TPFs, each fragment contains a `void:triples` statement expressing the approximate total number of triples in the dataset that match the TPF's triple pattern [24]. For instance, each page of the TPF for the pattern "`?x rdf:type foaf:Person`" contains a metadata triple stating there are 96,300 matching triples in the dataset. Given a page size of 100 data triples, these data triples would be spread across 963 pages. Suppose that during the execution of a certain SPARQL query, the client arrives at a list of 215 potential mappings for "`?x rdf:type foaf:Person`". In order to verify with a minimum number of HTTP requests whether these mappings are valid, the 215 TPFs for the corresponding triples need to be downloaded, checking which mappings result in a triple that exists within the dataset.

By defining an interface feature that allows this fragment to contain an AMF, the clients can determine approximately whether a certain `?x` results in a triple of the dataset. Listing 1 shows an example AMF for the triple pattern "`?x rdf:type foaf:Person`". In this case, it is a Bloom filter with two specific Murmur functions as hash functions. The hash functions themselves are not detailed in the listing, but their parameters need to be explicitly available (either in the response or by dereferencing their URL). Listing 1 explicitly specifies that the members of the collection are the triples of the fragment, and that the AMF has been built by using the subject of these triples. This allows the client to interpret how exactly this AMF can be used. For instance, if the triple `dbp:Elvis_Presley rdf:type dbo:Artist` is part of the dataset, then the full URI of `dbp:Elvis_Presley` must yield a positive value in the membership function. Note that the false positive rate is also specified, allowing a client to estimate the certainty of each result. Finally, the AMF data itself has been made available in base64-encoded form.

This metadata allows a client to unambiguously recreate the AMF and verify the approximate membership of elements. Note that this self-descriptive approach does not require a contract between the client and the server, e.g., no hash function has to be agreed upon silently. Furthermore, clients that do not use this metadata feature, such as the original TPF client [25], will not be affected by it and can thus continue to use the interface. It is up to the server's discretion whether or not to provide an AMF on a page. If it is present, an AMF-aware client can use it; if not, the original algorithm without AMFs can be followed. This lets the server choose freely what metadata to include—based on, for instance, the computational effort to create the AMF.

```
<#metadata> foaf:primaryTopic <#fragment>.
<#metadata> {
    <#fragment> void:triples 96300.            # existing count metadata
    _:membershipFunction a ms:BloomFilter;  # AMF metadata
        ms:hashSize 524288;
        ms:hashFunction <MyMurmur1>, <MyMurmur2>;
        ms:memberCollection [
            ms:sourceCollection <#fragment>;
            ms:projectedProperty rdf:subject
        ];
        ms:falsePositiveRate 0.05;
        ms:falseNegativeRate 0.0;
        ms:binaryRepresentation "QmF...ZTY"^^xsd:base64Binary.
}
```
Listing 1. The self-descriptive AMF metadata in the TPF fragment for `?x rdf:type foaf:Person` allows the client to interpret and evaluate approximate membership.

To facilitate implementation, the AMF interface feature is the subject of a specification in the Hydra W3C Community Group, which is available at http://www.hydra-cg.com/spec/latest/linked-data-fragments/membership-metadata/.

5   SPARQL Query Execution with AMF-enabled TPFS

In order to explain the algorithm to query TPFs with AMF metadata, we will consider the following example query for DBpedia:

```
SELECT ?p ?c WHERE {
    ?p a <http://dbpedia.org/ontology/Artist>.              # tp₁
    ?p <http://dbpedia.org/ontology/birthPlace> ?c.         # tp₂
    ?c <http://www.w3.org/2000/01/rdf-schema#label> "York"@en.  # tp₃
}
```

Query 1. This SPARQL query finds artists born in cities named "York".

Given a regular TPF interface, the algorithms presented in Section 2.2 will compute results for each BGP B by recursively evaluating and binding each triple pattern $tp_i \in B$ in an order determined by the count metadata in their respective fragments. For example, by fetching the first page of the TPFs for Query 1 where $B = \{tp_1, tp_2, tp_3\}$, we obtain the count metadata $\{(tp_1, 96\,300), (tp_2, 625\,811), (tp_3, 2)\}$. Therefore, we start iterating over tp_3, which will supply values for ?c. This leads to 2 subqueries $B' = \{tp_1, tp_2\}$ where the remaining triple patterns are bound to concrete values of ?c (note that tp_1 is unaffected because it does not contain ?c). For instance, for ?c = dbp:York, we obtain count metadata $\{(tp_1, 96\,300), (tp_2', 207)\}$. Query execution thus continues with the smallest fragment tp_2', which results in 207 subqueries $B'' = \{tp_1'\}$ in which tp_1 is bound

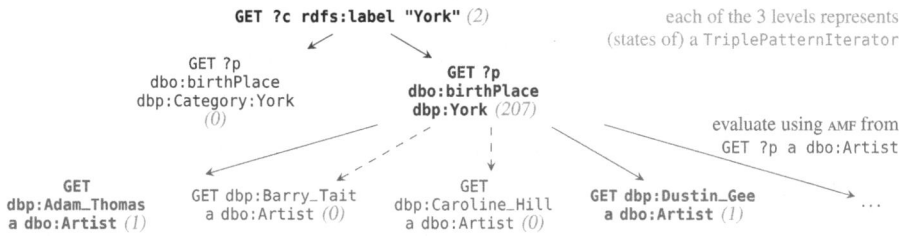

Fig. 1. The triple patterns of Query 1 with the least number of matches at each stage become nodes in the evaluation tree. Note how the third level of consists entirely of membership subqueries (single triples), and can thus be evaluated with the help of an AMF.

to possible values of ?p. These 207 subqueries are indeed membership queries, because they check the presence of a concrete triple without variables, e.g., "dbp:Adam_Thomas rdf:type dbo:Artist". All values of ?p that result in a match are solution mappings to the query. This process leads to an evaluation tree, as shown in Figure 1.

An efficient way to realize such evaluation trees are iterator pipelines [9], which allow for *incremental* query results. In existing TPF algorithms [23,25], two principal iterator types are responsible for SPARQL query evaluation over TPFs: a TriplePatternIterator for triple patterns and a GraphPattern-Iterator for BGPs. The whole of Section 5 is executed by a GraphPattern-Iterator, which chains together TriplePatternIterators for each of the three levels in the tree. Each TriplePatternIterator reads solution mappings from the iterator above it and tries to extend them with mappings for a given triple pattern. For instance, the iterator at level 2 with pattern "?p dbo:birthPlace ?c" receives mappings for ?c from the iterator at level 1. For each ?c, it tries to find mappings for ?p, which are then passed on to level 3. Finally, the TriplePattern-Iterator on level 3 with pattern "?p rdf:type dbo:Artist" either confirms or rejects mappings depending on whether the triple for a given ?p exists. This produces a total of 207 requests, which amount to 98% of the total HTTP traffic.

Algorithm 1 presents an extension of the original TriplePatternIterator [25] to make use of AMF metadata. When a TriplePatternIterator is initiated, the corresponding TPF for its initial triple pattern is requested (line 2). This fragment typically already resides in the client cache, since it was formerly requested by a GraphPatternIterator for count metadata. If the response contains AMF metadata, a *membership test function* is created and assigned to the iterator (line 4). In our example, this translates to a request for the TPF for "?p rdf:type dbo:Artist", which contains an AMF for all mappings of ?p. If no AMF metadata is found, we assign a constant function *True* that always returns true (possible match), so that a verification request is always necessary.

When GetNext is called, the TriplePatternIterator first reads an upstream mapping μ_s from its source iterator I_s (line 14). Then, we test whether the triple (pattern) tp' resulting from this mapping is present in the current AMF. If the

1 Function TriplePatternIterator.Init()
> **Data**: A source iterator self.I_s; A triple pattern self.tp

2 | $f_{tp} \leftarrow$ GET TPF for self.tp;

3 | **if** f_{tp} contains AMF metadata **then**

4 | | self.membership_test $\leftarrow f_{tp}$.metadata.amf;

5 | **else**

6 | | self.membership_test $\leftarrow True$ where $\forall x : True(x) =$ **true**;

7 | **end**

8 | self.current_fragment $\leftarrow \emptyset$;

9 end

10 Function TriplePatternIterator.GetNext()
> **Output**: The next mapping μ_n or **nil** when no such mappings are left

11 | $\mu \leftarrow$ **nil**;

12 | **while** $\mu =$ **nil do**

13 | | **while** self.current_fragment does not contain unread triples **do**

14 | | | self.$\mu_s \leftarrow$ self.I_s.GetNext();

15 | | | **return nil** if self.$\mu_s =$ **nil**;

16 | | | $tp' \leftarrow$ self.μ_s[self.tp];

17 | | | **if** self.membership_test$(tp') =$ **true then**

18 | | | | self.current_fragment $\leftarrow$ GET TPF for tp';

19 | | | **end**

20 | | **end**

21 | | $t \leftarrow$ an unread data triple from self.current_fragment;

22 | | $\mu \leftarrow$ a mapping μ' with dom$(\mu') =$ vars(self.tp) and μ'[self.tp] $= t$;

23 | **end**

24 | **return** $\mu \cup$ self.μ_s;

25 end

Algorithm 1. A TriplePatternIterator with support for AMF metadata

test returns **true**, we have a true positive or false positive, so the TPF corresponding to tp' is fetched and assigned to the iterator. For instance, if the mapping $\{?p =$ Adam_Thomas$\}$ returns **true**, we retrieve the TPF for "dbp:Adam_Thomas rdf:type dbo:Artist" to verify whether this triple is a true or false positive. If the test returns **false**, tp' is a true negative and need not be checked. For instance, if the mapping $\{?p =$ Barry_Tait$\}$ returns **false**, we are sure the corresponding TPF is empty, so we do not need to perform the HTTP request.

For each negative AMF result, this proposed extension of the algorithm saves an HTTP request. Depending on the type of query, cumulative savings can be extensive, as with Query 1. The positive results, however, still need to be verified in case false positives would have occurred. While we cannot eliminate the verification HTTP calls without endangering the correctness (precision) of query results, it is possible to further reduce the query time, as we will discuss in the next section.

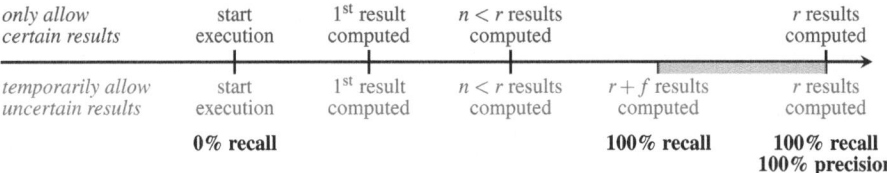

Fig. 2. This SPARQL query execution timeline compares regular and opportunistic query execution, assuming r total query results and f false positives. Note how both approaches achieve 100% recall and precision at a shared point in the end, but there exists a period during which only opportunistic execution reaches 100% recall (shaded).

6   Opportunistic Query Results

In general, query execution does not necessarily end when all valid results have been obtained; it could be that the engine still spends some time to rule out possible result candidates before being able to decide that the result set is in fact complete. Due to the approximate nature of AMFs, it is possible that at a certain point during line 1, the in-memory result set R already contains all r valid results. However, they cannot be returned yet, because R can still contain a number of false positives f. Only after the membership of all positive results of the AMF has been verified against the TPF interface, the f false positives can be discarded and all r matches can be returned safely.

For some use cases, it might be acceptable to *temporarily* consider incorrect results, especially if we are able to indicate which results can be trusted and which results cannot. If at first, we optimistically assume that all positive matches of the AMF are actual matches (i.e., we disregard the false positive rate), the client is able to reach 100% recall earlier, temporarily tolerating a precision below 100%. For each of those approximate matches, the client can express the probability that it is valid, namely $1 - p$ with p the false-positive rate of the AMF. As membership subqueries progress, the client can update the probability for true positives from $1 - p$ to 1, and retract false positives by setting their probability to 0. This opportunistic method of providing query results is important if fast results and eventual full precision are preferred over slower results with immediate precision. At no point in time, incorrect query results are presented as correct results of the query.

Figure 2 compares regular querying and opportunistic querying. Note in particular how both approaches eventually reach 100% recall and precision *at the same time*. In other words, even though the opportunistic algorithm temporarily allows uncertain results and thus a precision of less than 100%, the application eventually obtains the accurate result set. Also, the application that receives the result knows at each moment in time whether a result is certain or not, and can thus decide to either use it or not.

As an example, consider an application that displays photos of artists based on the results a certain SPARQL query. After a few HTTP calls, the query client returns 50 matches, all of which have a probability of 99%. The application can decide to already start downloading photos of the 50 matching artists, without displaying them to the user yet. Once 48 of the 50 matches are confirmed, the 48 photos can be displayed immediately; only 2 photos need to be discarded. The user thus sees the photos faster than if they had only been retrieved after full precision was achieved. This example indicates that opportunistic query answering has direct concrete uses in Web applications.

7 Evaluation

In the following, we discuss our evaluation of executing SPARQL queries against TPF interfaces with an AMF feature. From these experiments, we aim to assess whether AMFs are a valuable asset in the metadata dimension. We first describe the experiments and their setup. Then, we discuss their results to validate the three hypotheses of Section 3.2.

7.1 Experimental Setup

We extended the existing implementations of the TPF client[3] and server[4] to support both Bloom filters and Golomb-coded sets. The server is configured by specifying the AMF and the desired false positive probability. We chose the 32-bit MurMurHash3 hash function for GCS and FNV-1 for the Bloom filter. The server calculates a membership function on the fly for each request for a triple pattern with a single variable.

We ran the experiments with different false positive probabilities p: $1/1024 \approx$ 0.1%, $1/128 \approx 1\%$, and $1/64 \approx 1.6\%$. In each experiment, we executed 250 queries generated from 125 diverse WatDiv SPARQL templates on three interfaces: *i)* regular TPF interface *ii)* TPF with Bloom filters, and *iii)* TPF with GCS. All three cases were tested with both the original and the optimized client; the last two setups were tested with and without opportunistic querying. All experiments were run on a single Amazon EC2 machine with an 8-core Intel Xeon E2680 v2 CPU and 15GB DDR3 RAM, using a query timeout of 3 minutes and the WatDiv 100M triples dataset from [1]. The HTTP requests were routed through an NGINX cache instance to enable HTTP caching and to enforce a realistic Web bandwidth of 1Mbps per request. We published the full result logs online.[5]

7.2 HTTP Requests

Tables 1 to 4 summarize the results of the experiments. They compare each AMF-enabled setup against a regular TPF client/server setup, grouping each of the 250 queries on whether they resulted in an *equal, lower,* or *higher* measurement for *i)* number of requests, *ii)* time to first result, *iii)* time to 100% recall (i.e., with

---

[3] https://github.com/LinkedDataFragments/Client.js/tree/amq

[4] https://github.com/LinkedDataFragments/Server.js/tree/amq

[5] https://github.com/LinkedDataFragments/TPF-Membership-Metadata-Results

Table 1. Comparison of regular TPF versus TPF with Bloom filter setup (greedy TPF algorithm)

metric	# requests			1ˢᵗ result time (s)			100% recall time (s)			total time (s)		
queries in group	equal	lower	higher	equal	lower	higher	equal	lower	higher	equal	lower	higher
p=1/1024	81 qrs.	126 qrs.	43 qrs.	177 qrs.	0 qrs.	73 qrs.	152 qrs.	3 qrs.	95 qrs.	154 qrs.	1 qry.	95 qrs.
orig. group avg.	2,953	45,213	24,312	1	–	7	96	134	67	96	42	67
avg. difference		–15,217	+10		–	+6		–41	+23		–32	+22
p=1/128	79 qrs.	134 qrs.	37 qrs.	173 qrs.	0 qrs.	77 qrs.	150 qrs.	3 qrs.	97 qrs.	153 qrs.	1 qry.	96 qrs.
orig. group avg.	1,469	44,712	23,623	0	–	7	97	134	66	98	42	66
avg. difference		–14,210	+5		–	+5		–28	+24		–32	+23
p=1/64	80 qrs.	129 qrs.	41 qrs.	174 qrs.	0 qrs.	76 qrs.	152 qrs.	3 qrs.	95 qrs.	156 qrs.	1 qry.	93 qrs.
orig. group avg.	2,340	44,842	24,626	1	–	7	96	134	66	97	42	66
avg. difference		–13,341	+15		–	+4		–41	+21		–33	+21

Table 2. Comparison of regular TPF versus TPF with GCS setup (greedy TPF algorithm)

metric	# requests			1ˢᵗ result time (s)			100% recall time (s)			total time (s)		
queries in group	equal	lower	higher	equal	lower	higher	equal	lower	higher	equal	lower	higher
p=1/1024	83 qrs.	123 qrs.	44 qrs.	195 qrs.	0 qrs.	55 qrs.	160 qrs.	0 qrs.	90 qrs.	167 qrs.	0 qrs.	83 qrs.
orig. group avg.	2,271	45,598	26,919	1	–	10	94	–	70	91	–	72
avg. difference		–11,761	+18		–	+8		–	+15		–	+16
p=1/128	83 qrs.	132 qrs.	35 qrs.	196 qrs.	0 qrs.	54 qrs.	154 qrs.	0 qrs.	96 qrs.	153 qrs.	0 qrs.	97 qrs.
orig. group avg.	2,152	45,924	21,168	1	–	11	96	–	67	98	–	66
avg. difference		–11,594	+5		–	+8		–	+16		–	+16
p=1/64	81 qrs.	122 qrs.	47 qrs.	199 qrs.	0 qrs.	51 qrs.	167 qrs.	2 qrs.	81 qrs.	164 qrs.	2 qrs.	84 qrs.
orig. group avg.	2,930	45,032	26,602	1	–	11	91	122	72	93	122	70
avg. difference		–10,521	+31		–	+7		–3	+13		–3	+12

opportunistic querying enabled), and *iv)* total query execution time. The number of queries per group is indicated, together with their average measurement value in the regular setup, and the average decrease or increase in respectively the *lower* and *higher* groups. For example, the top-left value cell of Section 7.1 shows that, for Bloom filters with $p = 1/1024$, 126 queries had a lower number of HTTP requests; for each of these 126 queries, the regular setup needed on average 45,213 requests, whereas the AMF-enabled setup required 15,217 fewer requests.

Our experiments show that, with $p = 1/1024$, AMF metadata decreases the number of HTTP calls for roughly half of all considered queries (Bloom: 126 queries or 50.4%; GCS: 123 queries or 49.2%). As expected from the analysis in Section 3, those queries that benefit from improvements are queries with relatively many HTTP requests: the average number of requests per query in the *lower* group is 45,213 (GCS: 45,598), compared to 2,953 (GCS: 2,271) for queries that do not improve. The improvements let us conclude that a substantial number of

Table 3. Comparison of regular TPF versus TPF with Bloom filter setup (optimized TPF algorithm)

metric	# requests			1ˢᵗ result time (s)			100% recall time (s)			total time (s)		
queries in group	equal	lower	higher	equal	lower	higher	equal	lower	higher	equal	lower	higher
p=1/1024	82 qrs.	155 qrs.	13 qrs.	166 qrs.	0 qrs.	84 qrs.	200 qrs.	0 qrs.	50 qrs.	173 qrs.	0 qrs.	77 qrs.
orig. group avg.	1,590	18,240	11,387	1	–	5	120	–	71	110	–	69
avg. difference		–4,920	+2		–	+5		–	+21		–	+18

Table 4. Comparison of regular TPF versus TPF with GCS setup (optimized TPF algorithm)

metric	# requests			1st result time (s)			100% recall time (s)			total time (s)		
queries in group	equal	lower	higher	equal	lower	higher	equal	lower	higher	equal	lower	higher
p=1/1024	87 qrs.	147 qrs.	16 qrs.	199 qrs.	0 qrs.	51 qrs.	203 qrs.	0 qrs.	47 qrs.	209 qrs.	0 qrs.	41 qrs.
orig. group avg.	*2,743*	*18,326*	*10,816*	*1*	*–*	*9*	*120*	*–*	*74*	*114*	*–*	*88*
avg. difference		*−1,154*	*+3*		*–*	*+5*		*–*	*+14*		*–*	*+11*

these 45,000+ requests per query were membership subqueries; the AMF-based query algorithm manages to decrease their number by 15,217 (GCS: 11,761) on average. 43 queries (GCS: 43) result in a slightly higher number of requests, albeit negligible compared to the total number: 10 versus 24,312 (GCS: 18 / 26,919). Note that in general, the number of requests per query is very high because of the potentially high number of results in the WatDiv dataset. While numbers of this scale clearly highlight query patterns, many real-world queries can be evaluated with tighter constraints.

A similar pattern arises with the optimized TPF algorithm [23], which consumes fewer HTTP requests overall because of full client-side joins, but has potentially longer query times for the same reason. Even more queries benefit from lower request numbers: 155 (62%) for Bloom and 147 (58.8%) for GCS. We see a reduction of roughly the same ratio, both with Bloom filters and GCS, although the absolute request numbers are lower.

The observations generalize to the cases for $p = 1/128$ and $p = 1/64$, albeit with slightly different observations. As is expected from a higher number of false positives, we see a decreasing average gain with increasing p. Interestingly, we see the number of queries with fewer HTTP requests increase slightly for higher p values; we assume this is correlated with the smaller response size, which allows for a higher throughput.

The above results confirm a substantial positive impact on the number of HTTP requests, validating Hypothesis 1.

7.3   Query Execution Time

In all cases (excluding 1 or 2 exceptions), both the first result times and total query times remain the same or even increase, contrarily to what we had expected. As Tables 1 and 2 indicate, about one in three queries have their execution time prolonged with about 20 seconds, or a third of their time. This prolongation is higher for Bloom filters than GCS, which see a more limited effect absolutely (18 seconds) and proportionally (about a quarter). The cause of these elevated query times is likely the increased response size: since the server automatically sends AMFs for all patterns with one variable (even if the client does not use the AMF), the server-side computation time and client-side retrieval time increase. Given a connection of 1Mbps and on-the-fly AMF generation, as in this experiment, the decreased number of requests is apparently insufficient for the considered queries and dataset to result in temporal gains. This is confirmed by the fact that GCS performs better, as GCS representations are encoded more efficiently.

Interestingly, higher false-positive probabilities do not have a profound effect on query time. For the given constrains, the higher number of requests seems to be compensated by the decreased complexity of generating, transferring, and interpreting AMFs. This is an indication that further experimentation with low probabilities might be beneficial.

The prolonged total query time also hinders the effectiveness of opportunistic querying. Whereas its goal is to achieve full recall earlier—at the expense of temporarily allowing <100% precision—the slower overall execution prevented a globally positive result. The potential benefit of opportunistic querying is evidenced by the 3 queries that, with Bloom filters, achieve 100% recall 41 seconds—about a third—earlier. Since opportunistic results have no negative influence on query time, the increased recall times for ±95 queries must be entirely due to the slower speed of the AMF approach under the 1Mbps and on-the-fly constraints. Should we succeed in speeding up AMF generation and/or transfer time, we could expect to see a broader influence of opportunistic results. Furthermore, the number of false positives that needed to be revoked was either 0 or 1 for all of the considered queries, revealing a low temporary impact on precision.

The obtained results for execution time thus invalidate Hypothesis 2, as we were not able to decrease the time to full recall in general. Further research will need to assess the relation of this observation to on-the-fly generation and bandwidth, and perhaps also even higher false positive rates.

7.4   Server Impact

Finally, we measured the average CPU load during query execution for two different AMF configurations and two different false positive probabilities. Compared to the normal server CPU usage (9.2%), the AMF configurations show an increase of 1.6% ($p = 1/1024$), 2% ($p = 1/128$) and 5.7% ($p = 1/64$) for Bloom, and 1% ($p = 1/1024$), 1.6% ($p = 1/128$), and 1.9% ($p = 1/64$) for GCS. This is a very acceptable overhead which does not impact the server's low-cost nature. Bloom has a higher impact than GCS because of the many hashes it needs to calculate, which apparently outweigh the overhead of Golomb compression. Note that all AMF metadata is created at query time and can still benefit from precomputation and/or caching. Given the limited increase, the aforementioned numbers validate Hypothesis 3.

8   Conclusions

The Triple Pattern Fragments API enables client-side SPARQL execution on low-cost servers, at the cost of higher execution time and bandwidth usage. In this paper, we studied the effect of incorporating approximate membership metadata as an interface feature. In particular, we aimed at reducing HTTP requests by avoiding expensive triple membership checks. We observed that, for one third of a set of diverse query types, most of the request overhead are in fact membership subqueries. At the expense of one extra request to fetch the approximate membership metadata, potentially many more could be saved. Indeed, the experimental results confirm a drastic decrease in requests for half of the 250 randomly generated WatDiv queries, while others experience little overhead thanks to local caching. Furthermore, this addition does not affect the low-cost nature of the server, which only has a limited load increase. However, there is a computational overhead on the client for queries that are not improved. An intelligent client should minimize this, by deciding when to use membership metadata based on the query type.

Despite the reduction of requests, the total execution time is higher on average because of long delays introduced to generate AMFs. Therefore, we conclude that this metadata is not suitable for real-time computation. We therefore recommend to pre-compute or pre-cache it in advance. A strong benefit of HTTP caching has been proven for TPF querying [25] due to the limited possible number of requests, and this mechanism can be applied efficiently to TPFs with augmented metadata. While Bloom filters are preferred for lower computation time, the smaller size of Golomb-coded sets would prevail in the presence of caching. To prevent the overhead of generating and transferring AMFs, they could be served in a separate resource that clients explicitly request when needed.

While positive membership tests introduce a slight overhead, this can be compensated by enabling opportunistic querying. Our results show that retracting results after validation is rare and only effects a small number of results. Therefore, it makes sense to design Web applications that can deal with temporarily imprecise results.

A major advantage of adding AMF metadata to the TPF interface is that it happens transparently and in a self-descriptive way. The server can choose freely whether or not to add metadata to a certain response; clients can reactively use metadata when possible, or ignore it when they do not support or need it. Where count metadata has proven crucial for the initial design of TPF querying [25], this first exploration of a new metadata feature was proven an interesting direction. In the future, we could imagine different such types of join optimizations, based on optional selectivity information that servers send as metadata to help clients make intelligent decisions. Studying their impact on real-world scenarios such as human-crafted knowledge bases can shape further directions.

References

1. Aluç, G., Hartig, O., Özsu, M.T., Daudjee, K.: Diversified stress testing of RDF data management systems. In: Mika, P., Tudorache, T., Bernstein, A., Welty, C., Knoblock, C., Vrandečić, D., Groth, P., Noy, N., Janowicz, K., Goble, C. (eds.) ISWC 2014, Part I. LNCS, vol. 8796, pp. 197–212. Springer, Heidelberg (2014)
2. Basca, C., Bernstein, A.: Avalanche: putting the spirit of the Web back into semantic web querying. In: Scalable Semantic Web Knowledge Base Systems, pp. 64–79 (2010)

3. Bloom, B.H.: Space/time trade-offs in hash coding with allowable errors. Communications of the ACM **13**(7), 422–426 (1970)
4. Buil-Aranda, C., Hogan, A., Umbrich, J., Vandenbussche, P.-Y.: SPARQL webquerying infrastructure: ready for action? In: Alani, H., Kagal, L., Fokoue, A., Groth, P., Biemann, C., Parreira, J.X., Aroyo, L., Noy, N., Welty, C., Janowicz, K. (eds.) ISWC 2013, Part II. LNCS, vol. 8219, pp. 277–293. Springer, Heidelberg (2013)
5. Ermilov, I., Martin, M., Lehmann, J., Auer, S.: Linked open data statistics: collection and exploitation. In: Klinov, P., Mouromtsev, D. (eds.) KESW 2013. CCIS, vol. 394, pp. 242–249. Springer, Heidelberg (2013)
6. Feigenbaum, L., Williams, G.T., Clark, K.G., Torres, E.: SPARQL 1.1. protocol. Recommendation, w3c, March 2013. http://www.w3.org/TR/sparql11-protocol/
7. Filali, I., Bongiovanni, F., Huet, F., Baude, F.: A survey of structured P2P systems for RDF data storage and retrieval. In: Hameurlain, A., Küng, J., Wagner, R. (eds.) Transactions on Large-Scale Data- and Knowledge-Centered Systems III. LNCS, vol. 6790, pp. 20–55. Springer, Heidelberg (2011)
8. Gallager, R., Van Voorhis, D.C.: Optimal source codes for geometrically distributed integer alphabets. Transactions on Information Theory **21**(2), 228–230 (1975)
9. Graefe, G.: Query evaluation techniques for large databases. ACM Computing Surveys **25**(2), 73–169 (1993)
10. Harris, S., Seaborne, A.: SPARQL 1.1 query language. Recommendation, w3c, March 2013. http://www.w3.org/TR/sparql11-query/
11. Heine, F.: Scalable P2P based RDF querying. In: Proceedings of the 1st International Conference on Scalable Information Systems (2006)
12. Hose, K., Schenkel, R.: Towards benefit-based RDF source selection for SPARQL queries. In: Proc. of the 4th International Workshop on Semantic Web Information Management, pp. 1–8 (2012)
13. Huang, H., Liu, C.: Estimating selectivity for joined RDF triple patterns. In: Conference on Information and Knowledge Management, pp. 1435–1444 (2011)
14. Li, J., Vuong, S.: Ontsum: a semantic query routing scheme in P2P networks based on concise ontology indexing. In: Advanced Information Networking and Applications, May 2007
15. Mitzenmacher, M.: Compressed Bloom filters. Transactions on Networking **10**(5) (2002)
16. Neumann, T., Weikum, G.: Scalable join processing on very large RDF graphs. In: Proceedings of the International Conference on Management of Data, pp. 627–640. ACM (2009)
17. Oren, E., Guéret, C., Schlobach, S.: Anytime query answering in RDF through evolutionary algorithms. In: Sheth, A.P., Staab, S., Dean, M., Paolucci, M., Maynard, D., Finin, T., Thirunarayan, K. (eds.) ISWC 2008. LNCS, vol. 5318, pp. 98–113. Springer, Heidelberg (2008)
18. Pu, X., Wang, J., Luo, P., Wang, M.: Aweto: efficient incremental update and querying in RDF storage system. In: Proceedings of the 20th International Conference on Information and Knowledge Management, pp. 2445–2448. ACM (2011)
19. Putze, F., Sanders, P., Singler, J.: Cache-, hash-, and space-efficient Bloom filters. Journal of Experimental Algorithmics **14**(4) (2009)
20. Ravindra, P., Hong, S., Kim, H., Anyanwu, K.: Efficient processing of RDF graph pattern matching on MapReduce platforms. In: Proceedings of the 2nd International Workshop on Data Intensive Computing in the Clouds, pp. 13–20 (2011)

21. Rietveld, L., Verborgh, R., Beek, W., Vander Sande, M., Schlobach, S.: Linked data-as-a-service: the semantic web redeployed. In: 12th Extended Semantic Web Conference (2015)
22. Schmachtenberg, M., Bizer, C., Paulheim, H.: Adoption of the linked data best practices in different topical domains. In: Mika, P., Tudorache, T., Bernstein, A., Welty, C., Knoblock, C., Vrandečić, D., Groth, P., Noy, N., Janowicz, K., Goble, C. (eds.) ISWC 2014, Part I. LNCS, vol. 8796, pp. 245–260. Springer, Heidelberg (2014)
23. Van Herwegen, J., Verborgh, R., Mannens, E., Van de Walle, R.: Query execution optimization for clients of triple pattern fragments. In: Extended Semantic Web Conference, June 2015
24. Verborgh, R.: Triple Pattern Fragments. Unofficial draft, Hydra w3c Community Group. http://www.hydra-cg.com/spec/latest/triple-pattern-fragments/
25. Verborgh, R., et al.: Querying datasets on the web with high availability. In: Mika, P., Tudorache, T., Bernstein, A., Welty, C., Knoblock, C., Vrandečić, D., Groth, P., Noy, N., Janowicz, K., Goble, C. (eds.) ISWC 2014, Part I. LNCS, vol. 8796, pp. 180–196. Springer, Heidelberg (2014)
26. Verborgh, R., Mannens, E., Van de Walle, R.: Initial usage analysis of DBpedia's triple pattern fragments. In: Proc. of the 5th Workshop on Usage Analysis and the Web of Data (2015)
27. Zhang, X., Chen, L., Wang, M.: Towards efficient join processing over large RDF graph using MapReduce. In: Ailamaki, A., Bowers, S. (eds.) SSDBM 2012. LNCS, vol. 7338, pp. 250–259. Springer, Heidelberg (2012)

Networks of Linked Data Eddies: An Adaptive Web Query Processing Engine for RDF Data

Maribel Acosta[1](✉) and Maria-Esther Vidal[2]

[1] Institute AIFB, Karlsruhe Institute of Technology, Karlsruhe, Germany
maribel.acosta@kit.edu
[2] Universidad Simón Bolívar, Caracas, Venezuela
mvidal@ldc.usb.ve

Abstract. Client-side query processing techniques that rely on the materialization of fragments of the original RDF dataset provide a promising solution for Web query processing. However, because of unexpected data transfers, the traditional optimize-then-execute paradigm, used by existing approaches, is not always applicable in this context, i.e., performance of client-side execution plans can be negatively affected by live conditions where rate at which data arrive from sources changes. We tackle adaptivity for client-side query processing, and present a network of Linked Data Eddies that is able to adjust query execution schedulers to data availability and runtime conditions. Experimental studies suggest that the network of Linked Data Eddies outperforms static Web query schedulers in scenarios with unpredictable transfer delays and data distributions.

1 Introduction

The Linking Open Data cloud has experienced an impressive growth over the last decade [11], and consequently, the number of Linked Data applications is progressively increasing [6]. Although this situation evidences the success of Linked Open Data movements, it also encourages the Semantic Web community to urgently develop computational tools that effectively manage Linked Data.

Managing Linked Data usually requires accessing RDF datasets through specific Web access interfaces, e.g., SPARQL endpoints [5] or Triple Pattern Fragments (TPFs) [15]. SPARQL endpoints allow users to pose any SPARQL query against SPARQL servers, whereas TPFs are specific for triple-patterns, and their evaluations can be paged and retrieve metadata about the fragment page size, and the approximated fragment size. Further, SPARQL query engines implement data management techniques and execute queries against these Web access interfaces. Examples include federated query engines for SPARQL endpoints [1,7,12], and the client-side SPARQL query engine [15] against TPF servers.

Despite these developments, the Web-alike characteristics of Linked Data sources impose fundamental challenges on Linked Data management. The lack of statistics about selectivities and data distributions, unpredictable data transfer rates and server workload, can negatively impact the effectiveness of query

ⓒ Springer International Publishing Switzerland 2015
M. Arenas et al. (Eds.): ISWC 2015, Part I, LNCS 9366, pp. 111–127, 2015.
DOI: 10.1007/978-3-319-25007-6_7

engines against Linked Data, even in presence of the innovative querying capabilities offered by SPARQL endpoints and TPFs. This problem is mainly generated because existing Linked Data query engines implement execution query strategies that rely in some way, on the traditional *optimize-then-execute* paradigm, instead of following adaptive query strategies that adjust query executions to unexpected data source conditions. Thus, our main research problem is to devise adaptive query processing techniques that exploit properties of Linked Data technologies, and opportunistically adjust schedulers according to data availability and runtime conditions. Thus, query plans will be changed on a tuple-by-tuple basis, and answers will be produced as soon as they become available.

Adaptive query processing strategies have been extensively studied in the context of heterogeneous databases [3,4,10]. They can be divided into intra- and inter-operator solutions, and routing operators. Additionally, adaptivity can be implemented at different granularity levels: Fine-grained granularity indicates adaptation of small processes, e.g., per-tuple basis; while granularity is coarse-grained whenever adaptivity is attempted for large processes. Intra-operator techniques implement fine-grained granularity adaptivity, even in the context of a fixed query plan. Contrary, inter-operator techniques re-schedule initial plans based on: uncertainties in the execution cost, size of intermediate results, and unexpected delays. Finally, eddies [9] are routing operators that continuously reorder a query execution, by routing each intermediate tuple through the query operators in a variety of orders that simulate different query plans. Routing policies determine the routing destination of intermediate tuples. Eddies can be executed in a distributed fashion to avoid bottlenecks of a centralized eddy [13].

Building on these query processing strategies, we devise a novel client-side query processing engine that builds a network of Linked Data Eddies (nLDE) to opportunistically execute SPARQL queries against TPF servers. First, an nLDE relies on TPF metadata [15] to identify an initial bushy tree plan that reduces intermediate results. Leaves of the plan are grouped in star-shaped subtrees and internal nodes represent adaptive physical operators. Thus, intra-operator adaptivity is initially achieved. Simultaneously, eddies are created and empowered with Linked Data metadata to route tuples through the adaptive operators by following a pipeline strategy. We propose an innovative eddy routing policy that considers well-known SPARQL optimization heuristics [14]. In our approach, eddies are autonomous and any of them can produce query answers from tuples that have been already routed through all the nLDE adaptive operators. In this way, nLDE addresses adaptivity by executing different plans per tuple.

We empirically study the effectiveness of our network of Linked Data Eddies engine (nLDE engine) on SPARQL queries against RDF data exposed via TPF servers. Under the assumption of networks with no delays, we compare our query optimization techniques and adaptive strategies with the current TPF client. Experimental outcomes suggest that nLDE plans conduce to execution schedulers able to overcome drawbacks caused by the lack of data distributions even for queries with large intermediate results. Furthermore, we study the performance of our nLDE engine in presence of data transfer delays. The observed

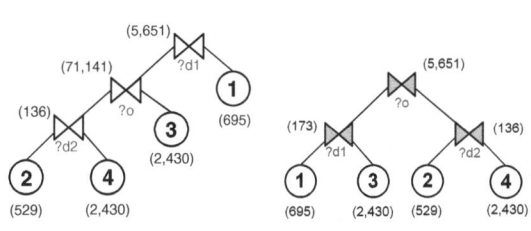

Metrics	Left-linear	Bushy tree
Execution Time (sec.)	318.90	3.03
Results	1,398	5,651
Requests	1,693	67

(a) Left-linear plan   (b) Bushy tree plan   (c) Execution results

Fig. 1. Different query plans to execute the query from Listing 1.1. The number of intermediate results produced by each operator are enclosed in parenthesis.

results confirm that routing adaptive query processing strategies provide a flexible solution for Linked Data management in unpredictable environments.

This paper comprises five additional sections. The following section illustrates a motivating example. We then define our approach in Section 3, and Section 4 presents experimental results. The related work is summarized in Section 5. Finally, we conclude in Section 6 with an outlook to future work.

2   Motivating Example

Consider the query from Listing 1.1 to *retrieve the drugs classified as DBpedia and Yago alcohols that share same routes of administration* to be executed using the TPFs for the English version of DBpedia.[1] The page size of these fragments is 100 and further metadata for each triple pattern is shown in Listing 1.1.

Listing 1.1. SPARQL query against DBpedia to retrieve information about resources classified as alcohols. Prefixes are used as in http://prefix.cc/

```
0 SELECT * WHERE {
1 ?d1 dcterms:subject dbpedia:Category:Alcohols.  # Count:   695
2 ?d2 rdf:type yago:Alcohols.                      # Count:   529
3 ?d1 dbprop:routesOfAdministration ?o.            # Count:  2430
4 ?d2 dbprop:routesOfAdministration ?o. }          # Count:  2430
```

We executed the query from Listing 1.1 using first the current TPF client[2], which follows a combination of *left-linear* plans with Nested Loop Joins to evaluate the query, as depicted in Figure 1(a). In this approach, the triple pattern with the smallest cardinality (Count) is executed first; in our example, this corresponds to tp_2 with approximately 529 results. For each binding of tp_2, the TPF client instantiates the next triple pattern, in our example this would be tp_4, and retrieves all the resulting fragments. The execution continues with this strategy

---

[1] http://fragments.dbpedia.org/2014/en
[2] https://github.com/LinkedDataFragments/Client.js

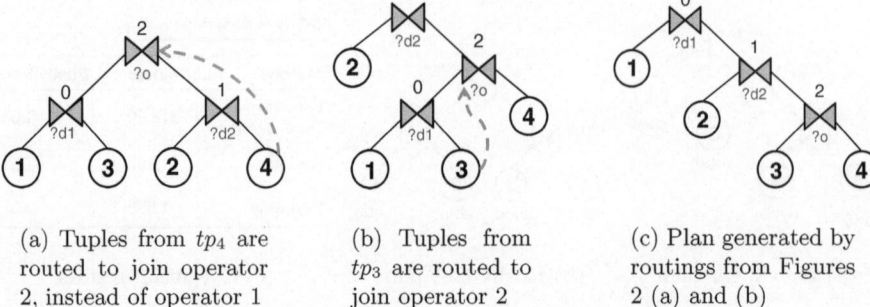

(a) Tuples from tp_4 are routed to join operator 2, instead of operator 1

(b) Tuples from tp_3 are routed to join operator 2

(c) Plan generated by routings from Figures 2 (a) and (b)

Fig. 2. Diverse execution plans generated by re-ordering the execution of operators during query execution. Dashed lines represent routing of tuples to operators.

for each tuple of the intermediate results. The results of executing the example SPARQL query are reported in the table of Figure 1(c). The execution stopped after 318.90 seconds, produced 1,398 results, and performed 1,693 requests.

Consider now executing the example query with the plan depicted in Figure 1(b). The shape of this plan corresponds to a *bushy tree* in which several subtrees can be executed simultaneously, reducing the number of intermediate results. For instance, the left-linear plan in Figure 1(a) for the example query produces $136 + 71, 141 = 71, 277$ intermediate results, while the bushy tree plan in Figure 1(b) for the same query produces $173 + 136 = 309$ intermediate results. Moreover, joining the results with a symmetric operator is less expensive in this case considering the cardinalities and page size of the fragments. For instance, joining tp_2 and tp_4 with a Nested Loop Join results in ~ 535 requests (6 requests to retrieve the fragment of tp_2 plus 529 requests for each binding), while performing a Symmetric Hash Join generates only ~ 31 requests (6 requests for tp_2 plus 25 requests for tp_4). The execution of the bushy tree plan successfully finalized in 3.03 seconds, and produced 5,651 results[3] with 67 requests.

These results were obtained under the assumption of a network with no delays. However, even efficient plans, like the one from Figure 1(b), can be affected under the presence of data transfer delays. To illustrate, consider that the source that resolves tp_2 becomes very slow; then, tuples retrieved for tp_4 can be routed to another join operator as depicted in Figure 2(a). The result of re-routing tuples from tp_4 is a new plan shown in Figure 2(b), in which the delayed source is evaluated at the end. The plan can further change, as depicted in Figure 2(c). We executed the plan from Figure 2(a) on a network with a total delay[4] of 1.99 seconds. When implementing the adaptivity presented in Figure 2, all the results were produced in 3.86 seconds, which suggests that adaptivity was

---

[3] The same number of results was obtained when executing the query against the DBpedia endpoint at http://dbpedia.org/sparql.

[4] Sum of all elapsed waiting times between receiving a fragment page i and the subsequent page $i + 1$.

able to hide 1.16 seconds of the total delay. We tackle adaptivity in Linked Data management, and propose a client-side query engine that builds a network of routing operators able to adjust execution schedulers to this type of scenarios.

3   Our Approach

We devise a query processing engine tailored to issue SPARQL queries in which RDF sources are accessed in a triple-pattern fashion. In particular, we focus on optimizing and executing queries against Triple Pattern Fragment (TPF) servers [15]. The main components of our engine are: i) The **query optimizer**, tailored to reduce the number of intermediate results and requests posed to the data source; and ii) The **adaptive routing query engine** that implements a network of eddies, able to dynamically adapt the optimized plan according to current execution conditions, e.g., network delays or unpredictable selectivities.

3.1   Query Optimizer

We propose a query optimizer to devise physical plans that can be efficiently executed against TPF servers, and make use of the metadata provided in each fragment. Given a query Q, our optimizer (see Algorithm 1) starts retrieving metadata for each triple pattern in Q (lines 1-2); in particular, it selects the estimated number of triples or cardinality of the fragment (*count*) and the number of triples accessed per fragment page (*pagesize*). Then, the algorithm orders the triple patterns according to their *count* value (line 3). Following our example query Q from Listing 1.1, triple patterns are ordered as follows: $Q' = \langle tp_2, tp_1, tp_3, tp_4 \rangle$.

The optimizer then proceeds in three phases as follows. In the first phase, the algorithm groups triple patterns as *star-shaped groups* (SSGs), i.e., sets of triple patterns that share one variable;[5] SSGs can be efficiently executed against RDF data [16]. The optimizer starts by selecting the first triple pattern of the list Q' (line 6), i.e., s is the pattern with the smallest cardinality, which in our example is tp_2. Then, s is joined with a triple pattern tp'_i in Q' that shares variables in common. If the number of accesses to retrieve the fragment of tp'_i is less than the estimated number of instances in s, then the optimizer places a Symmetric Hash Join ($\bowtie_{SHJ}$), otherwise a Nested Loop Join ($\bowtie_{NL}$) is placed (lines 10-13). For instance, as shown in Section 2, $(tp_2 \bowtie_{NL} tp_4)$ results in 535 requests, while $(tp_2 \bowtie_{SHJ} tp_4)$ generates only 31 requests. The value *count* of the star is updated (line 14) with an estimation of the number of intermediate results that will be generated, i.e., *cardinalityEstimation*. In the absence of selectivity factors of triple patterns, we empirically tested different estimators (sum, product, and maximum) to approximate *cardinalityEstimation*; we selected the sum since it provided a more realistic estimation. This stage is completed when all triple patterns in Q belong to a SSG. The result of this stage is the set S with SSGs, which in our running example would be: $S = \{(tp_2 \bowtie_{SHJ} tp_4), (tp_1 \bowtie_{SHJ} tp_3)\}$.

---

[5] A star-shaped group can be composed of only one triple pattern.

Algorithm 1. Physical Optimizer

Input: Query $Q = \{tp_1, tp_2, ..., tp_n\}$
Output: Bushy tree plan P_Q for Q
// **Get triple pattern metadata**
1 **for** $tp_i \in Q$ **do**
2 | $(tp_i.count, tp_i.pagesize) \leftarrow getMetadata(tp_i)$
    // **Order** Q **such that** $tp'_i.count \leq tp'_{i+1}.count$
3 $Q' \leftarrow \langle tp'_1, tp'_2, ..., tp'_n \rangle$
    // **Phase 1: Build index star-shaped groups (SSG)**
4 $\mathcal{S} \leftarrow \emptyset$
5 **while** $Q'.length() > 0$ **do**
6 | $s \leftarrow Q'.getFirst()$
7 | $vars_s \leftarrow vars(s)$
8 | **for** $tp'i$ in Q' **do**
9 | | **if** $|vars_s \cap vars(tp'_i)| = 1$ **then**
10 | | | **if** $(tp'_i.count/tp'_i.pagesize) \leq s.count$ **then**
11 | | | | $s \leftarrow (s \bowtie_{SHJ} tp'_i)$
12 | | | **else**
13 | | | | $s \leftarrow (s \bowtie_{NL} tp'_i)$
14 | | | $s.count \leftarrow cardinalityEstimation(s.count, tp'i.count)$
15 | | | $Q'.remove(tp'i)$
16 | $\mathcal{S} \leftarrow \mathcal{S} \cup \{s\}$
    // **Phase 2: Build bushy tree to combine SSGs with common variables**
17 $P_Q \leftarrow \mathcal{S}$
18 **do**
19 | $P'_Q \leftarrow P_Q$
20 | Select s_i and s_j from P_Q such that $vars(s_i) \cap vars(s_j) \neq \emptyset$
21 | $P_Q \leftarrow P_Q - \{s_i, s_j\}$
22 | $P_Q \leftarrow P_Q \cup \{(s_i \bowtie_{SHJ} s_j)\}$
23 **while** $P'_Q \neq P_Q$
    // **Phase 3: Place joins between SSGs with no common variables**
24 **do**
25 | Select s_i and s_j from P_Q
26 | $P_Q \leftarrow P_Q - \{s_i, s_j\}$
27 | $P_Q \leftarrow (P_Q \bowtie_{SHJ} s_j)$
28 **while** $|P_Q| > 1$
29 **return** P_Q

In the second phase, the optimizer builds bushy tree plans by combining subtrees created so far, e.g., the star-shaped groups identified previously. In order to join two subtrees, the subtrees must share at least one variable in common (line 20). Following the running example, subtrees $(tp_2 \bowtie_{SHJ} tp_4)$ and $(tp_1 \bowtie_{SHJ} tp_3)$ are joined since they share the variable ?o. All subtrees are joined in this stage with Symmetric Hash Join operators; which allows for executing different subtrees of the plan simultaneously. This stage finishes when no subtrees can be further combined (line 23). The outcome is a set of bushy trees P_Q.

Finally, in the third stage, subtrees that could not be joined before (since they share no variable in common) are combined. For the example query, our algorithm managed to build the efficient plan from Figure 1(b). In general, the optimizer produces a bushy tree plan P_Q for Q that allows for reducing intermediate results, and opportunistically places join operators aiming at reducing the number of requests to the sources.

3.2 Adaptive Routing Query Engine

The plan P_Q devised by the optimizer is then executed by the adaptive query engine designed to operate in unpredictable environments. Our query engine performs *routing operator* adaptivity [9], able to change the order of the initial plan according to the current conditions of execution. Tuples generated during query execution can be routed to physical operators following a different order than the one designated by the optimizer, but respecting the relationships between operators in P_Q. In our engine, adaptivity is performed on a tuple-based basis.

In order to perform this routing adaptivity, physical operators used to execute the plan P_Q should follow a *pipelining* strategy [9], i.e., able to produce tuples incrementally as soon as data from a source become available. This type of operators are denominated *adaptive operators*. Considering that P_Q contains n adaptive operators, each operator is identified with a different label from 0 to $n - 1$. For example, in Figure 2, the label of the Join operator between tp_1 and tp_3 is 0. In addition, each operator has a priority initially given by the execution order induced by P_Q, but operator priorities are updated as the execution goes on. In the following we define an adaptive operator in our query engine.

Definition 1 (Adaptive Operator). *Given an initial query plan P_Q for a query Q, an adaptive operator o is a physical non-blocking operator in P_Q. Each operator o in P_Q is annotated with two numbers denoted by label(o) and priority(o), such that:*

  – *label(o) corresponds to an identifier of o in P_Q and is unique;*
  – *priority(o) represents the priority of o in P_Q and induces the order in which o has to be executed in P_Q.*

During query execution, tuples are sent from adaptive operators to eddies. An eddy [2] is an operator that serves as a tuple router, that dynamically flows tuples through plan operators. To do so, eddies rely on tuple annotations denominated *Ready* and *Done* vectors. The *Ready* vector of a tuple indicates operators eligible to process that tuple. In our running example, tuples resulting from tp_1 should be processed by operators 0 and 2, but not by operator 1 – according to the plan from Figure 2(a); therefore, the *Ready* vector of these tuples is 101. The *Done* vector of a tuple indicates the operators that have already processed that tuple. For instance, if a tuple has only been processed by operator 1, then its *Done* vector is 010. All tuples that flowed into an eddy e are introduced into a routing buffer RB_e, and are routed to the next adaptive operator following a routing policy RP_e (cf. Section 3.3). Operators that have not processed a tuple t in RB_e are computed by performing the bitwise operation $Ready_t - Done_t$; then, one adaptive operator is selected by its priority according to the implemented routing policy RP_e. Figure 3 illustrates the components RB_e and RP_e of an eddy. In this example, the tuple $t = \{$d1=dbpedia:Bupranolol, o="Oral, topical"$\}$ in RB_e is annotated with $Ready=101$ and $Done=100$; RP_e decides to route the tuple to operator 2 since it is the only operator that has not processed t yet.

Eddies in our approach are enhanced with the capability of directly outputting results when a tuple has been processed by all operators. This allows for

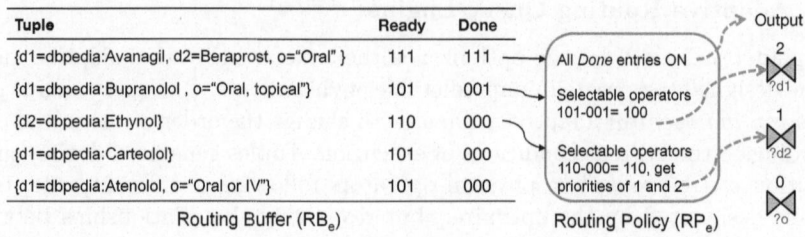

Fig. 3. Eddy operator e: Tuples are inserted into the Routing Buffer (RB_e), annotated with *Ready* and *Done* vectors. The Routing Policy (RP_e) selects the operator to route tuple t. Eddy outputs a tuple when it has been processed by all operators (*Done*=111)

pipelining final results efficiently. In contrast, in the distributed eddies proposed by Tian and DeWitt [13], final results are routed to an intermediary eddy (*eddy sink*). When queries produce large amount of results, the eddy sink could become a bottleneck, while in our approach the final output is produced in parallel by several autonomous eddies. In the following, we provide a definition of an eddy.

Definition 2 (Eddy Operator). *Given an initial query plan P_Q with n adaptive operators. An eddy e to execute P_Q is defined as a 2-tuple=(RB_e, RP_e) where RB_e corresponds to a routing buffer and RP_e is a routing policy. RB_e contains a set of tuples generated during the execution of P_Q. Each tuple t in RB_e is annotated with a pair of n-bit vectors named $Ready_t$ and $Done_t$, such that:*

- *A value of ON in the entry i of the $Ready_t$ vector of t indicates that t should be processed by the adaptive operator o such that $label(o) = i$.*
- *A value of ON in the entry i of the $Done_t$ vector of t indicates that t has been already processed by the adaptive operator o such that $label(o) = i$.*
- *t is produced as an output of the evaluation of P_Q when all entries in its $Done_t$ vector are ON (e is autonomous).*

RP_e is a function to route tuples from the eddy e to adaptive operators of P_Q. RP_e receives a tuple t in RB_e and outputs the identifier $label(o)$ of the adaptive operator o where t will be sent to.

Our query engine implements an adaptive network to execute query plans, called *network of Linked Data Eddies* (nLDE). An nLDE is composed of a set of adaptive operators and a set of eddies that dynamically send tuples among each other, constructing a bipartite graph G (see Figure 4). The number of adaptive operators is given by the plan to be executed. An eddy can get "clogged" when non-selective queries are executed against sources, and the transfer rate is faster than what the eddy is able to process. In order to avoid a "clogged" eddy, several eddies can be part of an nLDE such that the workload is distributed. This is particularly important when executing non-selective queries in which large amounts of intermediate results (tuples) have to travel through the network. Future work could focus on studying the optimal number of eddies in a network given the characteristics of a query, or even creating eddies on demand.

Figure 4 depicts an nLDE with two eddies for the query plan from Figure 2(a) of our running example. Edges in graph G from eddies to adaptive operators indicate that tuples were sent through these routes. Assuming that Eddy 0 is the one depicted in Figure 3, the nLDE contains an edge from Eddy 0 to operators 2 and 1 since tuples {d1=dbpedia:Bupranolol, o="Oral, topical"} and {d2=dbpedia:Ethynol} were routed to these operators, respectively. Analogously, an edge from an adaptive operator to an eddy indicates that at least a tuple was sent through that route. For instance, Figure 4 depicts an edge from the Join operator with label 0 to the Eddy 0. When inspecting the routing buffer of Eddy 0 (Figure 3), the tuple {d1=dbpedia:Bupranolol, o="Oral, topical"} is annotated with $Done=001$, indicating that this tuple was only processed by the operator with label 0, therefore this operator was the one that sent the tuple to Eddy 0.

Besides eddies and adaptive operators, nLDE takes into consideration the characteristics of SPARQL queries and properties of Linked Data sets accessed to resolve different portions of a query. This information is denominated *Triple Pattern Descriptor* (TD) and consists of annotating the triple patterns from the query with metadata. A TD is then exploited by eddies in an nLDE to devise efficient routes to process RDF data. Figure 4 illustrates the TD for our running example: Triple patterns of the query are annotated with their corresponding cardinality (number of triples) and with the position of joins (e.g., joins by subject-subject and object-object) with other patterns. However, one important factor when executing queries is the selectivity of operators: Operators with high selectivity produce less intermediate results. Due to skewed data distribution in RDF datasets, selectivity may vary depending on the RDF resources that are being processed and cannot be *a priori* estimated by solely analyzing triple pattern cardinalities. We propose therefore an eddy routing policy (cf. Section 3.3) tailored for RDF data that considers not only the productivity of operators but also the position of joins in SPARQL queries [14] to favor the routing of tuples to join operators where the estimated selectivity is high. In the following, we define a network of Linked Data Eddies and its components.

Definition 3 (Network of Linked Data Eddies). *Given a query Q and a query plan P_Q for Q, a network of Linked Data Eddies for P_Q is a 2-tuple $nLDE = (G, TD)$, where G is a bipartite graph $G = (E \cup O, V)$ and TD is a triple pattern descriptor. E is a set of eddy operators, O is the set of adaptive physical operators in P_Q, and V is a set of directed edges, such that:*

- $V \subseteq (E \times O) \cup (O \times E)$.
- *If (e, o) belongs to V then the eddy e has routed at least one tuple to the adaptive operator o.*
- *If (o, e) belongs to V then the adaptive operator o has sent at least one tuple to the eddy e.*

TD corresponds to a set of pairs $(tp, \mathcal{M}_{tp})$, where tp is a triple pattern of Q and $\mathcal{M}_{tp}$ corresponds to metadata of tp. Example of metadata properties could be: join position, RDF data source, cardinality, and fragment page size.

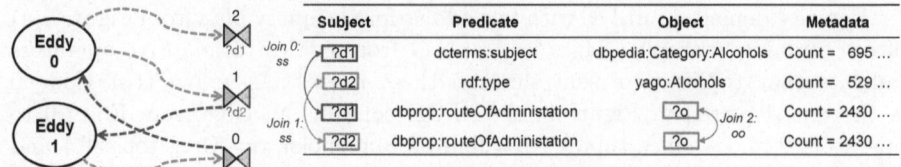

Fig. 4. Network of Linked Data Eddies (nLDE). Eddies and adaptive operators constitute a bipartite graph G. Edges in G represent routing paths of tuples. The Triple Pattern Descriptor (TD) of an nLDE maintains information about triple patterns from the query: metadata and operator position, e.g., subject-subject (ss), object-object (oo)

In order to ensure the correct processing of tuples, eddies and adaptive operators should respect a set of rules. For instance, eddies cannot route a tuple to an arbitrary operator, but it has to consider the processing history of the tuple – given by its *Ready* and *Done* vectors. This restriction is defined in the following.

Definition 4 (Routing Rule from Eddy to Adaptive Operator). *Given an eddy operator $e = (RB_e, RP_e)$ and a set of adaptive operators O in an nLDE, RP_e routes tuples from RB_e according to the following rule:*

– *e can route a tuple t in RT_e to an adaptive operator $o \in O$ with identifier $label(o) = i$ only if $Ready_t[i] = ON$ and $Done_t[i] = OFF$; the set of operators that meet these conditions for t are denominated 'eligible operators of t'.*

Note that an adaptive operator has no restrictions on selecting an eddy to send a tuple to. However, before sending a tuple to an eddy, the adaptive operator has to build the *Ready* and *Done* vectors of the tuple. The correct creation of the *Ready* vector ensures that the tuple will not be processed more than once by an adaptive operator. Furthermore, the correct creation of the *Done* vector guarantees that the tuple will be processed by all the corresponding operators. In the following, we present the rules to create *Ready* and *Done* vectors of tuples.

Definition 5 (Rules to Create Ready and Done Vectors). *Given an adaptive operator o in an nLDE and a set of eddy operators E. Consider a tuple t produced by a binary operator o when combining tuples t_i and t_j. The tuple t is sent to an eddy operator $e \in E$ respecting the following rules:*

– *$Ready_t$ corresponds to the bitwise OR logical operation of the Ready vectors of t_i and t_j,*
– *$Done_t$ corresponds to the bitwise OR logical operation of the Done vectors of t_i, t_j, and the identifier of o represented by $label(o)$.*

In case the operator o is unary, $Done_t$ is updated by performing the bitwise OR logical operation with $label(o)$, while $Ready_t$ remains the same.

The execution of a query Q with an nLDE satisfies the following property:

Property 1 (Soundness). Given a query Q and a network of Linked Data Eddies $nLDE = (G = (E \cup O, V), TD)$ for a query plan P_Q. A tuple t produced by an eddy $e \in E$ belongs to the set of answers of the query Q if and only if all the entries of the $Done_t$ vector are equal to ON.

3.3   Routing Policies

Routing Policy from Eddy to Adaptive Operator. Tuples in the routing buffer of an eddy are processed following a strategy first-come, first-served (FCFS), i.e., oldest tuples are attended first. When a tuple t is routed from an eddy, the routing policy selects among the 'eligible operators of t' the one with the highest priority. Operator priorities are initialized according to the plan devised by the optimizer: Operators with the highest priority value should be executed first. In our running example, operators 0 and 1 have higher priority values than operator 2. During query execution, the priority of operator o with $label(o) = i$ is updated as follows: $priority(i) = 1 - \frac{\#tuples\ received\ from\ i}{\#tuples\ routed\ to\ i}$. Measuring the ratio of tuples produced vs. consumed by an operator allows for estimating its selectivity. When join operators exhibit similar performance, an operator is chosen over the others based on the join position specified in the triple pattern descriptor (TD) of the nLDE, following the HEURISTIC 2 by Tsialiamanis et al. [14]. Additionally, our routing policy respects the following restrictions: 1) Tuples are not routed to non-symmetric operators, otherwise the number of requests to sources could be increased; 2) Tuples are not routed to operators that do not share variables in common, to avoid the generation of large amount of tuples in the network.

Routing Policy from Adaptive Operator to Eddy. As explained in Section 3.2, there are no restrictions when routing tuples to eddies. However, when several eddies are part of an nLDE, it is important to design routing policies from adaptive operators that allow for distributing the workload among several eddies. In this work, we implement a simple routing policy in which an operator randomly chooses an eddy following a uniform distribution, i.e., all eddies have the same probability to be selected. We empirically tested this policy and observed that it is able to fairly spread tuples among eddies in the network.

4   Experimental Results

We empirically assess the effectiveness of a client-side network of Linked Data Eddies (nLDE engine) to adapt query execution schedulers to unknown data distributions and unexpected data transfer delays. The client-side Web query engine of Triple Pattern Fragments (TPF client) [15] is used as the baseline of the study. Below we describe the configuration settings used in our experiments.

Datasets and Query Benchmarks[6]: TPFs for the English version of DBpedia are used as RDF data servers. We designed two benchmarks of queries by

---

[6] Benchmarks 1 and 2 are available at http://people.aifb.kit.edu/mac/nlde/.

analyzing triple patterns and sub-queries answerable for DBpedia. Benchmark 1 comprises 20 queries composed of basic graph patterns of between 4 and 14 triple patterns; these queries are non-selective and produce a large number of intermediate results. Benchmark 2 is composed of a total of 25 queries that have basic graph patterns of between three and six triple patterns; five queries about topics in five domains: *Historical, Life Sciences, Music, Sports,* and *Movies.*

Implementations: We implement proxies to configure data transfer delays. Both the nLDE engine and proxies are implemented in Python 2.7.6. We evaluate our experiments on a network with no delays, and in a fast network which is simulated with a gamma distribution ($\alpha = 1$, $\beta = 0.3$) of response latency resulting in an average latency of 0.3 secs. The setting 'nLDE (No Policy)' represents the basic query optimization (no adaptivity): The plan devised by the optimizer does not change. Experiments were executed on a Debian Wheezy 64 bit machine with CPU: 2x Intel(R) Xeon(R) CPU E5-2670 2.60GHz (16 physical cores), and 256GB RAM. Timeout was set to 1,800 secs.

Evaluation Metrics: The following metrics are computed separately for each benchmark. *i) Execution Time:* Elapsed time spent by a query engine to complete the execution of a query. It is measured as the absolute wall-clock system time as reported by the Python `time.time()` function. *ii) Number of Requests:* Total number of requests submitted to the servers during query execution. *iii) Number of Answers:* Total number of answers produced during the execution of a query plan. Queries were run five times and we report on the average time.

4.1 Effectiveness of nLDE Optimization Techniques

The goal of this study is to determining the impact that query selectivity and size of intermediate results have on the performance of client-side query engines in networks with no delays. We compare the nLDE engine with the TPF client on queries of Benchmark 1 and Benchmark 2. To compare the query optimization and execution techniques of both engines under the same conditions, the nLDE engine does not follow any routing policy, i.e., intermediate tuples are processed following the plan originally produced by the nLDE optimizer (Algorithm 1). Queries in Benchmark 1 are non-selective and produce a large number of results, while Benchmark 2 comprises very selective queries that produce a small number of results. Given the selectivity of queries in Benchmark 1, the timeout at 1,800 secs. is reached in some of the queries. Thus, we present the number of answers produced before timing out, in addition to the execution time. Figures 5(a) and (b) report on *Execution Time* and *Number of Answers* in logarithmic scale, respectively. We can observe that plans generated by the nLDE engine not only speed up the execution time, but they are able to produce more answers for the executed queries. The nLDE engine only consumes more time than the TPF client in queries Q5, Q8, Q10, and Q11, but as reported in Figure 5(b), the TPF client produces less number of answers than the nLDE engine in these queries. These results suggest that bushy trees comprised of

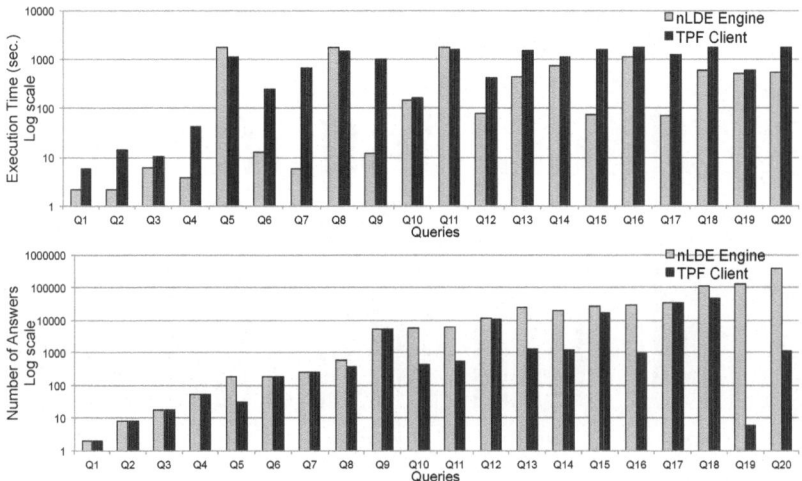

Fig. 5. Results for queries of Benchmark 1 for nLDE engine and TPF client; 20 non-selective queries against TPFs for the English version of DBpedia. a) Execution Time in secs. (log. scale), b) Number of Answers (log. scale). No delays in data transfer

star-shaped groups in conjunction with the nLDE adaptive operators, provide efficient execution schedulers to access TPF servers. Furthermore, we evaluate the overhead that these engines may cause to the data servers during query execution. Results of the execution of queries of Benchmark 2 are presented on Figures 6(a) and (b); because both engines produce all answers for each query, we just report on execution time and the number of requests submitted by each of the engines to the TPF servers. As can be seen, nLDE bushy plans speed up query schedulers by up to one order of magnitude, while they submit less requests to the TPF servers in the majority of the queries. The reason for this is that left-linear plans as the ones generated by the TPF client in conjunction with Nested Loop Join operators, may produce a large number of intermediate results that conduce to large number of requests to the TPF servers. In contrast, bushy plans composed of star-shaped groups minimize the number of intermediate results and in consequence, submit a small number of requests to the TPF servers. Thus, the nLDE engine is able to retrieve data from the TPF servers in a more efficient fashion, providing in this way, an effective approach for Linked Data management even in ideal scenarios of simple queries (Benchmark 2) and networks with no delays.

4.2 Adaptivity of the nLDE Engine

The goal of this study is to evaluate the performance of the routing policies implemented by the nLDE engine. Networks with delays allow for evaluating the adaptivity of engines to unpredictable changes. We simulate a fast network where data transfer rates are configured to respect a gamma distribution with $\alpha = 1$, $\beta = 0.3$. Further, we compare the execution time of the nLDE engine

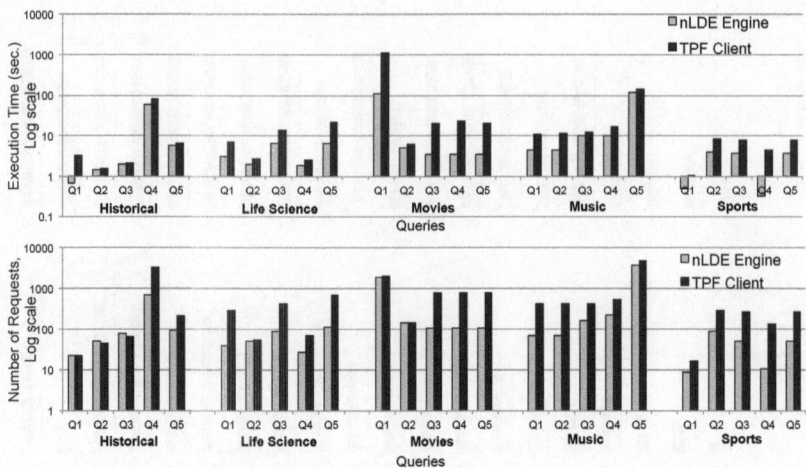

Fig. 6. Results for queries of Benchmark 2 in nLDE and TPF client; 25 Selective Queries against TPFs for the English version of DBpedia; Five Queries per Domain. a) Execution Time in secs. (log. scale), b) Number of Requests (log. scale)-No delays

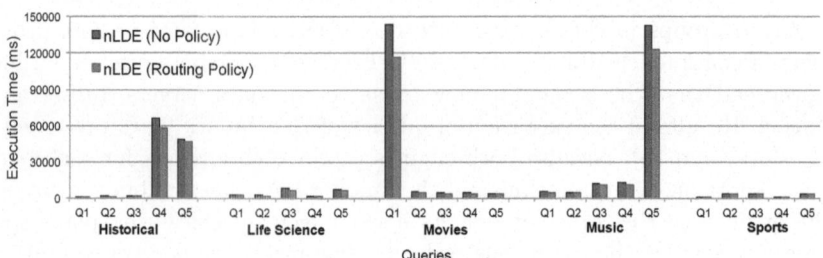

Fig. 7. Results for queries of Benchmark 2 in nLDE with No Routing Policy and nLDE with our Routing Policy. 25 Selective Queries against TPFs for the English version of DBpedia; Five Queries per Domain. Execution Time in msecs. Fast network simulated with a Gamma distribution ($\alpha = 1$, $\beta = 0.3$) of delays

when intermediate tuples are executed following the original plan (No Policy) and when execution schedulers are adapted to the data transfer rates according to our Routing Policy. Both instances of the nLDE engine produce the same number of query answers and server requests, so we report on *Execution Time* in milliseconds in Figure 7. As can be observed, the nLDE engine with the routing policy exhibits better performance than the nLDE engine with no policy. It is important to highlight that this scenario is quite troublesome for a routing policy. When queries produce a small number of intermediate results the policy might not have enough information to devise an efficient routing. Additionally, when network is fast with a relative low latency the policy has to be lightweight enough to process tuples arriving with fast rates. Despite of these conditions and the overhead caused by routing intermediate results, the nLDE engine with our routing policy is able to faster produce the complete results of the studied queries. We hypothesize that even better performance will be observed in slower networks and in presence of messy data distributions.

5   Related Work

We analyze the *adaptivity granularity* achieved by Web query processing approaches that rely on HTTP interfaces to access RDF data.

SPARQL endpoints exploit SPARQL expressiveness and efficiently access RDF data. Nevertheless, they may suffer from typical Web-publishing problems, i.e., connections may be slow or may, in the extreme, become unavailable. Existing federated engines, e.g., ANAPSID [1], FedX [12], and SPLENDID [7], implement adaptivity and mitigate in some way, the impact of these problems. In FedX and SPLENDID, adaptation is *coarse-grained* granularity, supporting the generation of fixed logical query plans according to the available endpoints. In addition, ANAPSID implements a *fine-grained* granularity adaptivity, and provides an intra-operator strategy and non-blocking operators. Thus, ANAPSID detects when SPARQL endpoints become unavailable, and opportunistically produces results as quickly as data arrives from the endpoints. Although these adaptive query processing techniques may empower SPARQL endpoints, because the *optimize-then-execute* paradigm is followed, completeness of the query results or query execution efficiency is not always achieved. Contrary, our network of Linked Data Eddies implements *routing operator* strategies able to change the logical query plan according to the conditions of the RDF data sources.

Hartig et al. [8] propose a Linked Data traversal approach and provide an inter-operator approach where source selection and link traversal are interleaved during query execution time. A non-blocking iterator model that relies on an asynchronous pipeline of iterators is used for traversing relevant links. Iterators are executed in an order heuristically determined, e.g., the most selective iterators are executed first. Further, the query engine is able to adapt the execution to source availability by on-the-fly detecting whenever an HTTP server stops responding. This approach adapts execution schedulers to uncontrollable network conditions; nevertheless, in presence of arbitrary data distributions, plans cannot be adapted and performance may be negatively impacted.

Finally, Verborgh et al. [15] propose a novel HTTP interface to access RDF data that rely on *Linked Data Fragments* (*LDF*) which can be easily generated by RDF data providers. Verborgh et al. also present a client-side Web query processing strategy for *Linked Data Fragments* of triple patterns (TPFs). This client-side query engine enhances Web clients with the capability of executing SPARQL queries and implements the non-blocking iterator model proposed by Hartig et al. [8] to adapt the query execution scheduler to different cardinality distribution of the retrieved TPF servers. Adaptivity is implemented at the level of TPF pages by interleaving TPF server selection with TPF requests to ensure thus that requests of more selective pages are executed first. Although TPF clients may effectively adapt query schedulers to TPFs with arbitrary data distributions, data transfer delays can negatively impact their performance. In contrast, the nLDE engine relies on both metadata provided by TPFs and novel routing techniques to identify efficient query plans that reduce execution time and number of requests. Therefore, the nLDE engine dynamically adapts execution schedulers to changing conditions of the TPF servers.

6   Conclusions and Future Work

We have defined the nLDE engine, a client-side query processing engine that builds a network of Linked Data Eddies to efficiently access TPF servers. The nLDE engine implements adaptivity at intra-operator levels as well as routing strategies that allow for the adaptation of execution schedulers to real-world conditions. Reported experimental results suggest that the nLDE engine is able to generate plans that not only increase the number of answers produced, but also reduce execution time and number of server requests. Moreover, in presence of unexpected data transfer delays, the nLDE engine is able to route intermediate results according to data availability and produce answers as soon as they are retrieved from the servers. In the future, we plan to define different routing policies and cost models that better estimate selectivity of TPFs.

References

1. Acosta, M., Vidal, M.-E., Lampo, T., Castillo, J., Ruckhaus, E.: ANAPSID: an adaptive query processing engine for SPARQL endpoints. In: Aroyo, L., Welty, C., Alani, H., Taylor, J., Bernstein, A., Kagal, L., Noy, N., Blomqvist, E. (eds.) ISWC 2011, Part I. LNCS, vol. 7031, pp. 18–34. Springer, Heidelberg (2011)
2. Avnur, R., Hellerstein, J.M.: Eddies: continuously adaptive query processing. In: SIGMOD, pp. 261–272 (2000)
3. Babu, S., Bizarro, P.: Adaptive query processing in the looking glass. In: CIDR, pp. 238–249 (2005)
4. Deshpande, A., Ives, Z.G., Raman, V.: Adaptive query processing. Foundations and Trends in Databases $1(1)$, 1–140 (2007)
5. Feigenbaum, L., Williams, G., Clark, K., Torres, E.: SPARQL 1.1 protocol (2013)
6. Fundulaki, I., Auer, S.: Linked Open Data - Introduction to the special theme. ERCIM News $2014(96)$ (2014)
7. Görlitz, O., Staab, S.: SPLENDID: SPARQL endpoint federation exploiting VOID descriptions. In: COLD Workshop (2011)
8. Hartig, O.: Zero-knowledge query planning for an iterator implementation of link traversal based query execution. In: Antoniou, G., Grobelnik, M., Simperl, E., Parsia, B., Plexousakis, D., De Leenheer, P., Pan, J. (eds.) ESWC 2011, Part I. LNCS, vol. 6643, pp. 154–169. Springer, Heidelberg (2011)
9. Hellerstein, J.M., Franklin, M.J., Chandrasekaran, S., Deshpande, A., Hildrum, K., Madden, S., Raman, V., Shah, M.A.: Adaptive query processing: Technology in evolution. IEEE Data Eng. Bull. $23(2)$, 7–18 (2000)
10. Laddhad, K., Sudarshan, S.: Adaptive query processing. Technical Report 05329014, Kanwal Rekhi School of Information Technology, Indian Institute of Technology, Bombay, Mumbai (2006)

11. Schmachtenberg, M., Bizer, C., Paulheim, H.: Adoption of the linked data best practices in different topical domains. In: Mika, P., Tudorache, T., Bernstein, A., Welty, C., Knoblock, C., Vrandečić, D., Groth, P., Noy, N., Janowicz, K., Goble, C. (eds.) ISWC 2014, Part I. LNCS, vol. 8796, pp. 245–260. Springer, Heidelberg (2014)

12. Schwarte, A., Haase, P., Hose, K., Schenkel, R., Schmidt, M.: FedX: optimization techniques for federated query processing on linked data. In: Aroyo, L., Welty, C., Alani, H., Taylor, J., Bernstein, A., Kagal, L., Noy, N., Blomqvist, E. (eds.) ISWC 2011, Part I. LNCS, vol. 7031, pp. 601–616. Springer, Heidelberg (2011)

13. Tian, F., DeWitt, D.J.: Tuple routing strategies for distributed eddies. In: VLDB, pp. 333–344 (2003)

14. Tsialiamanis, P., Sidirourgos, L., Fundulaki, I., Christophides, V., Boncz, P.A.: Heuristics-based query optimisation for SPARQL. In: EDBT, pp. 324–335 (2012)

15. Verborgh, R., et al.: Querying datasets on the web with high availability. In: Mika, P., Tudorache, T., Bernstein, A., Welty, C., Knoblock, C., Vrandečić, D., Groth, P., Noy, N., Janowicz, K., Goble, C. (eds.) ISWC 2014, Part I. LNCS, vol. 8796, pp. 180–196. Springer, Heidelberg (2014)

16. Vidal, M.-E., Ruckhaus, E., Lampo, T., Martínez, A., Sierra, J., Polleres, A.: Efficiently joining group patterns in SPARQL queries. In: Aroyo, L., Antoniou, G., Hyvönen, E., ten Teije, A., Stuckenschmidt, H., Cabral, L., Tudorache, T. (eds.) ESWC 2010, Part I. LNCS, vol. 6088, pp. 228–242. Springer, Heidelberg (2010)

Substring Filtering for Low-Cost Linked Data Interfaces

Joachim Van Herwegen$^{(\boxtimes)}$, Laurens De Vocht, Ruben Verborgh,
Erik Mannens, and Rik Van de Walle

Multimedia Lab, Ghent University – iMinds,
Gaston Crommenlaan 8 Bus 201, 9050 Ledeberg-Ghent, Belgium
joachim.vanherwegen@ugent.be

Abstract. Recently, Triple Pattern Fragments (TPFS) were introduced
as a low-cost server-side interface when high numbers of clients need to
evaluate SPARQL queries. Scalability is achieved by moving part of the
query execution to the client, at the cost of elevated query times. Since
the TPFS interface purposely does not support complex constructs such as
SPARQL filters, queries that use them need to be executed mostly on the
client, resulting in long execution times. We therefore investigated the
impact of adding a literal substring matching feature to the TPFS interface, with the goal of improving query performance while maintaining low
server cost. In this paper, we discuss the client/server setup and compare
the performance of SPARQL queries on multiple implementations, including Elastic Search and case-insensitive FM-index. Our evaluations indicate that these improvements allow for faster query execution without
significantly increasing the load on the server. Offering the substring feature on TPF servers allows users to obtain faster responses for filter-based
SPARQL queries. Furthermore, substring matching can be used to support
other filters such as complete regular expressions or range queries.

Keywords: Linked data · SPARQL · String matching · Regular
expressions

1 Introduction

The publication of RDF data on the Web is often presented as a dichotomy [6]:
either the entire dataset is made available in a downloadable data dump, or fine-
grained query-level access is provided through a public SPARQL endpoint [7].
In the first case, users need to download the entire dataset—even if they are
only interested in a specific part of it—and are then free to use it locally in any
way they see fit. Commonly, this means ingesting the triples in a local triple
store and setting up a private SPARQL endpoint. While this approach is most
straightforward for data publishers and offers most freedom for data consumers,
it also comes with a high burden in terms of needed bandwidth, device capacity,
and technical ability of the data consumer. Especially given the rise of mobile
devices to browse the Web, offline querying of datasets is not viable as the only

© Springer International Publishing Switzerland 2015
M. Arenas et al. (Eds.): ISWC 2015, Part I, LNCS 9366, pp. 128–143, 2015.
DOI: 10.1007/978-3-319-25007-6_8

solution. Furthermore, if datasets change often, synchronizing them with the latest version becomes a challenge.

In the second case, public SPARQL endpoints allow users to execute all of their queries on the server against live data, without having to worry about huge downloads or updates. However, since all work is shifted to the server, the endpoint's load increases drastically, causing an increase in server cost and potential overloads and subsequent downtime if many complex queries are executed. Even though most public servers pose certain limits to query execution, the low availability of SPARQL endpoints is a prominent issue [3], and high load is a potential availability risk. Furthermore, from an economic perspective, not all data publishers on the public Web are willing and/or able to pay for a computational infrastructure that allows third parties to execute complex queries free of charge, given that they already provide the data itself for free. Whether or not the duties of a publisher include live queryable access, the fact is that only a minority attempts to host a public SPARQL endpoint [6,20].

Recently, the Triple Pattern Fragments (TPFs) interface was introduced as an alternative to bridge the gap between the low server load of datasets and the functionality of a full SPARQL endpoint. TPFs limit the functionality of the server to triple pattern requests; more complex SPARQL queries are executed by a *client-side* query processor that decomposes them into triple patterns. Clients combine intermediary results received from the server locally to find results to larger queries. This greatly reduces the server load by shifting querying partially to the client, at the expense of increased query times and bandwidth. While basic graph pattern queries can be executed efficiently with TPFs, other query constructs potentially lead to slow queries. The TPF interface, however, is self-describing, meaning we can transparently add new features to it. While they might make individual requests more expensive, the number of requests—and thereby the total sum of all request costs—might be significantly reduced.

In this paper, we investigate a server-side interface feature that allows SPARQL queries with certain FILTER patterns to be executed more efficiently. With the regular TPF interface, all filters have to be evaluated client-side, since only exact triple patterns have server-side support. Concretely, this means that clients first have to download all triples that match the remainder of the query, after which the filter can be applied to these results. This works sufficiently for filters with low selectively, which SPARQL endpoints typically also execute at the end. However, if the filter is the only part of a query that has a high selectivity, the client cannot solve this query efficiently, since the filter can only be used on triples that were already downloaded from the server. For this reason, we introduce *substring matching* as a server-side interface, allowing the user to request all literal objects that contain a given string pattern.

In Section 2 we discuss related work, especially regarding query interfaces and pattern matching, and show how it is related to our current work. Section 3 explains the benefit of adding a substring feature to servers that publish LDFs, and Section 4 presents two implementations. We then extend the client-side query algorithm in Section 5 to make use of the substring feature and examine its impact on performance and server load in Section 6. We conclude in Section 7 and look at how this work can be extended in the future.

2   Related Work

This paper defines a server-side interface feature for substring search on RDF object literals. To place the contribution in context, we first discuss the multiple available interfaces to access Linked Data, followed by an introduction to the indexing algorithm used later on.

2.1   Web APIs to Linked Data

Linked Data can be published on the Web using different Application Programming Interfaces (APIs). The Linked Data Fragments conceptual framework [25,27] enables the analysis and comparison of Web APIs by abstracting each API according to how it provides access to parts of a given dataset. Each such part is called a *Linked Data Fragment* (LDF), which consists of data, metadata, and controls. The *data* is a set of those triples of the dataset that match a given interface-dependent selector. The *metadata* set consists of triples that describe the dataset and/or the current fragment or related fragments. Finally, the *controls* are hypermedia links and/or forms that allow clients to retrieve other fragments of the same or other datasets.

In addition to describing existing interfaces, LDFs also allow defining new interfaces with different characteristics. Below, we discuss three types of interfaces using the LDF conceptual framework.

Data Dumps. A data dump of a dataset is an LDF whose *data* consists of all triples in that dataset, usually in a compressed archive. The *metadata* set typically contains data such as publication date and/or license. No *controls* are present, because all available data is contained within the archive. Data dumps are prevalent on the Web: LODstats mentions more than 1,700 data dumps [6], and the LOD Laundromat contains more than 600,000 datasets crawled from the Web [20]. Their main drawback is that they cannot be queried "live", i.e., they need to be downloaded in their entirety before typical SPARQL queries can be evaluated over them. Since data dumps can become quite large (several gigabytes are not an exception), they are impractical for most use cases—especially if data changes often and needs to remain up-to-date. Furthermore, setting up and maintaining a query interface on top of a data dump requires a technical background and significant computational power, so this is out of reach for typical desktop users as well as all mobile users.

SPARQL Endpoints. The SPARQL protocol [7] exposes RDF graphs on the Web using the SPARQL query language [13]. Each response to a CONSTRUCT or DESCRIBE query can be seen as an LDF, where the *data* consists of the RDF triples in the dataset that match the query. The *metadata* and *control* sets are empty; controls are given implicitly through the SPARQL protocol. The main advantage of SPARQL endpoints is their expressiveness: clients can ask very specific questions about a dataset and retrieve only the results they are interested in. However, public SPARQL endpoints suffer from a two-sided availability problem: the majority of datasets is not published as a SPARQL endpoint [6], and those endpoints that are on the Web experience frequent downtime [3]. Furthermore, SPARQL endpoints have a high per-request cost [25] and are thus relatively expensive to host.

Triple Pattern Fragments. The Triple Pattern Fragments (TPF) interface [24,25] was designed to combine the desirable characteristics of data dumps (low server-side cost) and SPARQL endpoints (live queryable). Clients can ask a server for triple patterns; in response, the server sends a TPF, consisting of *data* triples matching the triple pattern (paged to reduce response sizes), *metadata* expressing the total number of matching triples, and *controls* to retrieve all other TPFs of the same dataset. Complex SPARQL queries are evaluated by clients, which split a query into triple patterns and use the metadata in fragments to determine an efficient execution order. The advantage of TPFs is that they only require low processing power on the server side, and are thus less expensive to host with high availability [25]. The drawback is that SPARQL queries have longer (but more consistent) query times than on a SPARQL endpoint. More than 600,000 datasets are available as TPFs through the LOD Laundromat [20]. DBpedia, the most well-known dataset on the Semantic Web, has an official TPF interface with 99.999% availability [26].

TPFs move the query planning problem to the client. It is up to the client to make optimal use of all metadata exposed by the TPF server, which in the default case consists of the estimated amount of matched triples for a triple pattern. Since a TPF server only supports triple patterns, complex SPARQL structures such as filters also have to be computed client-side. This can be done by checking all resulting triples against the filters in the SPARQL query. The originally proposed query planning algorithm is a greedy algorithm [25]. Assuming a Basic Graph Pattern (BGP) query, the client starts by downloading results for the smallest triple pattern in the BGP, based on the count estimate metadata sent by the server. The values of each resulting triple are bound to each remaining pattern. The client then requests the smallest of these bound patterns from the server, and continues binding results to unbound patterns until all patterns have been bound. This process is started multiple times if there are multiple unconnected BGP's. Computationally this method is quite fast: most of the time the client is simply waiting on the server response. The downside is that the client can become stuck in local optima, causing it to execute more requests than a theoretically optimal solution.

Van Herwegen et al. proposed an improvement to the greedy algorithm [22], which tries to find a solution using a minimum number of HTTP calls, avoiding local optima. This is achieved by downloading two triple patterns separately from the server and joining them on the client if this requires fewer HTTP calls. Multiple estimation techniques, based on the intermediate results of the algorithm, are used to predict which query path is least expensive. If the current path is suboptimal, the algorithm will change it at runtime and continue from the new path. This decrease in HTTP requests results, however, in more computational work for the client because of the more complex local joining process.

2.2 Burrows-Wheeler Transform and FM-Index

The Burrows-Wheeler Transform (BWT) [4] was created to transform data so that it can be compressed more easily without any loss [19]. It is used in multiple fields, such as bio-informatics [15].

An FM-index is an index on a BWT-transformed dataset to find substrings in the data by adding some additional metadata [10]. Brisaboa et al. show how an FM-index can even be used to perform substring matching in a list of strings instead of a single string, returning all strings that contain a given substring [2]. In Section 4.3, we extend this technique to also allow for case-insensitive matches.

Ferguson shows that it is even possible to execute regular expressions on data stored using an FM-index [8]. In his paper, he describes a system called FEMTO, which can index large datasets while still maintaining adequate performance.

2.3 HDT (Header Dictionary Triples)

HDT [9] is a data storage format that optimizes the space required to store large RDF datasets by storing its URIs and literals separately in a compressed dictionary and storing identifier triplets that reference this compressed data. Multiple dictionaries are supported by HDT; we are particularly interested in the dictionary that uses an FM-index to store the object literals, thus allowing full-text search on triple objects [1,16].

2.4 Full-Text Search in Triple Stores

HDT is not the only way to support full-text search on triples: there exist multiple other implementations supporting the same functionality or even more [5,17]. Minack et al. [18] performed an extensive comparison of multiple of these implementations in complete triple stores (unfortunately not including HDT since it is a data structure and not a triple store). They concluded that most standard triple stores have sufficient support for full-text search, but that there are still areas where performance is inadequate.

3 Problem Statement

A common use case for substring matching is when we know the name of an entity we are looking for, but we do not know its URI. As an example, Listing 1

```
SELECT ?movie
WHERE {
  ?movie dbpedia-owl:starring [ rdfs:label ?name ].
  FILTER REGEX(?name, "Matthias Schoenaerts", "i")
}
```

Listing 1. SPARQL query to find all movies with Matthias Schoenaerts

contains a query that returns all movies starring the actor Matthias Schoe-naerts. We assume the user did not know the exact URI that was necessary, and used string matching to find the URI that corresponds to the person called "Matthias Schoenaerts". Since TPF servers only support exact triple pattern lookups, a client-side algorithm would need to execute the filter locally on all triples joined by the previous two triple patterns. The first pattern has 200,000 matches and the second one more than 12,000,000, meaning that any solution would need at least 200 calls (assuming a page size of 100) to obtain results for the first pattern, and then another 200,000 to map them to their label.

However, if it were possible to filter all literals in the dataset first, we would only obtain 20 results that would then need to be mapped to the previous pat-terns, resulting in a total of 40 HTTP requests instead of 200,000. In general, the ability to solve substring matches is especially useful when all of the triple patterns have a low selectivity and the string pattern selectivity is quite high. For this example, the string pattern in Listing 1 is highly selective since there are only 20 results. These observations lead us to the following research question.

Question 1: How does the performance of queries with FILTER patterns improve if the TPF interface is extended with substring search on literals?

Extending the interface means that clients are able to send more complex requests, which could mean a higher per-request cost for servers. At the time, however, an increased expressivity of requests could lead to a reduction in the number of requests needed to evaluate a particular SPARQL query. This brings us to a second research question:

Question 2: What is the server-side impact of adding support for substring search to the interface, i.e., can we still maintain the low-cost properties associated with the TPF interface?

Ultimately, the results of this research should help data publishers decide whether the costs of adding substring search are worth the expressivity and the possible improvement in query performance they bring.

Question 3: For which scenarios and types of queries is it beneficial to add a substring search interface to the server?

Based on the above research questions, we propose the following hypotheses:

Hypothesis 1: The HTTP requests required to solve typical queries with highly selective REGEX FILTERs can be greatly reduced when a substring search is present in addition to a TPF interface.

```
PREFIX void:  <http://rdfs.org/ns/void#>
PREFIX foaf:  <http://xmlns.com/foaf/0.1/>
PREFIX hydra: <http://www.w3.org/ns/hydra/core#>

<#about> {
    <#about> foaf:primaryTopic <#fragment>.
    <#fragment> void:subset <http://example.org/mydataset>;
    <http://example.org/mydataset> hydra:search [
        hydra:template "http://example.org/mydataset{?substring}";
        hydra:mapping [ hydra:variable "substring";
                        hydra:property hydra:freetextQuery ]
    ].
}
```

Listing 2. Self-descriptive hypermedia controls in a TPF fragment explain how substring matching can be accessed (TriG syntax).

Hypothesis 2: Queries with REGEX FILTERs that are *not* highly selective are unaffected by the presence of a substring search interface.

Hypothesis 3: The cost to offer substring matching is limited such that substring requests can be executed at an acceptable time cost on a typical server.

4   Server-Side Interface

To support substring search, Section 4.1 defines an interface feature that can work in conjunction with the TPF interface. We evaluated two different techniques to filter through the data: an internal FM-index and an external Elasticsearch[1] index, which can be found in Section 4.2 and 4.3, respectively.

4.1   Extension of the TPF Interface

The TPF interface has been designed in a self-descriptive and extensible manner, so clients can discover what capabilities are supported [25]. Given a single URI to any resource of the interface, the client can fetch it with HTTP GET, asking for an RDF representation. In this representation, the clients will find hypermedia controls, which explain that "this interface can be queried by triple pattern" [24]. This avoids a hard-wired client/server contract. For example, if we visit the resource http://fragments.dbpedia.org/2014/en in a Web browser, we will see an HTML form with fields *subject*, *predicate*, *object*, and this form instructs the browser how to create HTTP requests against the interface. This same information is conveyed in the RDF-based representation of the same resource, using the Hydra Core Vocabulary [14,24].

    Since we aim to provide a substring search interface feature, we should similarly inform human and machine clients of this functionality and how they can

---

[1] http://www.elastic.co/

perform such requests. Listing 2 shows an example form in RDF for an example fragment of the dataset http://example.org/mydataset/. In this particular case, it states that substring search is supported on this dataset, and that it can be performed by appending the search string to http://example.org/mydataset? substring=. That way, with this resource as a starting point of their query process, clients can decide to use substring search during query execution. Should this not be supported, clients can decide to fall back to other features supported by the server, such as possibly TPF.

In order to explain the exact type of support for substring matching as implemented by the server, subproperties of hydra:freetextQuery might be defined, such as ex:substringQuery or ex:caseInsensitiveSubstringQuery. This then requires the client to understand such extensions; therefore, it might be beneficial to always additionally list the base property hydra:freetextQuery so that more generic clients can still interpret the hypermedia controls and thus use the interface. Note that due to this self-descriptive mechanism, no hard-coded contract between clients and servers is necessary, and conventions (such as ?substring=) need not be standardized but can transparently vary between servers. Implementers can consult the LDF substring feature specification[2] for a detailed explanation on how to optimally describe the interface.

4.2   Elasticsearch

Elasticsearch is a search server based on the text indexing engine Lucene [12]. It provides a full-text search engine with an HTTP interface and schema-free JSON documents. The fact that it has a Web interface out-of-the-box and is particularly designed for use in such scenarios, made it an obvious choice as a back-end. Elasticsearch being a versatile search solution and inheriting Lucene's extensive capabilities, it is not trivial to tweak its configuration. It is very strict about data types and forces developers to think from the beginning about how text queries will be performed against the underlying data.

The use case mentioned in this paper—searching for arbitrary-length exact substrings in texts of varying sizes—is not provided by ElasticSearch by default. For example, when searching for the actor name "Will Smith", ElasticSearch' standard tokenizer would match sentences such as *"Will Mr. and Ms. Smith be an awesome movie?"*, even though this is not an exact substring match and thus not a desired result in our use case.

Therefore, it is necessary to force ElasticSearch' analyzer to keyword-tokenize each text literal and apply an n-gram analyzer to each of them. The result is a huge index file, about the size of the original dataset. Furthermore, generic n-gram matching is very costly: instead of query times in the order of milliseconds, query times were in the order of dozens of seconds. Configuring ElasticSearch to work with only prefixes using edge-n-grams, effectively dropping certain results, mitigated the issue of extremely long query processing times. One could argue that most users would input prefix queries and expect a text search engine to

---

[2] http://www.hydra-cg.com/spec/latest/linked-data-fragments/substring-search/

behave in that way. Whatever the assumption might be, for use in a query scenario as explained before, results need to be exact and complete.

In ElasticSearch, important choices have to be made to optimize query time, index size, the number of desired matches, and the nature of the returned matches given the text search query and the use case. This makes choosing it for a generic use case where the end-user or application can not be reckoned with at least more debatable than initially expected. The evaluation in Section 6 shines some light on this aspect.

4.3   Case-Insensitive FM-Index

HDT already included support for substring search by using an FM-index. One simply has to edit the config file to make sure the correct type of dictionary is used when generating the HDT file. The problem here was that default FM-index only supports case-sensitive substring search, while we wanted case-insensitive searching as well. We will start by briefly explaining the existing algorithms, followed by our changes to FM-index to make it case-insensitive.

Burrows-Wheeler Transform. As mentioned in Section 2.2, BWT is a technique developed to transform a string in such a way that identical characters appear next to each other more often after transformation, while still allowing for a reverse transformation to the original string [4]. Strings that have sequences of identical characters are a lot easier to compress when using methods like *move-to-front transform* and *run-length encoding*.

The BWT creates n permutations of a string with length n by cyclically shifting the characters in the string. These strings are sorted and placed in a matrix, with each row corresponding to one of the permuted strings. The first column then corresponds to a sorted list of all characters in the original string. Since it is impossible to generate the original string from this list, the BWT actually stores the last column of the matrix, assuming certain characters are more likely to precede certain other characters, causing the BWT result to have multiple identical characters next to each other. From this string it actually is possible to go back to the original.

FM-Index. An FM-index adds metadata to a BWT-transformed string so that it can be used for full-text search without actually reverting back to the original string. The extra metadata consists of two parts: an array C containing for each character the amount of characters that precede it in the sorted string, and a matrix Occ containing for every character c and every position i how many times c occurs up to position i in the BWT string. Note that this metadata can be calculated at runtime and does not need to be stored with the BWT string.

Using these additional elements it is possible to count the number of times a pattern occurs in $\mathcal{O}(p)$ time with p being the length of the pattern. Actually locating the pattern matches in the string takes $\mathcal{O}(p + occ \log_\epsilon u)$ with occ being the number of occurrences and u the length of the string.

FM-Index as a Dictionary. As mentioned before, it is possible to generate HDT files that use an FM-index to store the literal objects. Brisaboa et al. [2] describe an adaptation of FM-index to store a list of n strings instead of a single string, by concatenating all strings and separating them with $n+1$ occurrences of a separator character s_1 (corresponding to the ASCII value 1). Since the BWT sorts all the prefix strings, the first $n+1$ characters will be s_1, with the first one being the last s_1 of the concatenation and the remaining occurrences of s_1 sorted based on the strings they precede, which is the same order of the concatenated strings if these are sorted in advance. HDT uses the positions of each s_1 to internally assign IDs to the object literals, meaning that ID 1 corresponds to string 1 after sorting the strings.

When converting a part of a BWT string to an original string, it is only possible to do this backwards since for every character we only know which character precedes it. Since the IDs correspond to the position of the *first* character of a string, going backwards would give us the wrong result. As the strings are sorted in the same order as the IDs, simply starting at position ID + 1 will give us the result for a given ID.

Case-Insensitive BWT. Sadakane [21] introduces a way to use case-insensitive searching in a BWT string by changing the algorithm in such a way that lower- and upper-case characters are interpreted as identical. Once the suffix substrings have been sorted, substrings starting with the same character will be next to each other, even if the character has a different casing. This method can even be extended to treat all kinds of symbols as identical, such as accented characters.

Case-Insensitive FM-Index. Some changes are needed to adapt a case-insensitive BWT for an FM-index. After concatenating the (case-insensitively) sorted strings, we replace the last s_1 with s_{255} instead to make sure that if the last two strings are identical (when ignoring casing) they remain in the same order after generating the BWT string. Previously this was not a problem since it was impossible to have identical strings in the concatenation, but now, if we did not append this character, the ordering of their IDs would be reversed.

Some changes also had to be made to the lookup algorithm to take the different casings into account. The values in the C table are also combined: $C(\text{A}) = C(\text{a})$, which now corresponds to the number of characters preceding the A and a characters. Similarly, the Occ matrix values were also merged to count the number of occurrences of A and a characters.

Since we do not actually change the casing of the strings, no information is lost and all objects can still be obtained from the triple store. We do need to introduce an extra step to still support case-sensitive searching by effectively verifying if the resulting strings match the case of the pattern.

5   Client-Side Query Algorithm

To make use of the substring functionality of the TPF server we updated the query execution algorithm as described by Verborgh et al. [25]. This is a greedy algorithm focusing on BGP queries and evaluating all other query constructs (filters, unions, etc.) after the BGP parts are resolved. Since evaluating FILTERs on the server is only advantageous if these are executed *before* the corresponding BGPs, it was necessary to change this ordering.

To make use of this new feature to solve SPARQL queries, we adapted how the client handles regular expression filters. Regular expression filters obviously support much more than simple string matching, so we first check if the query we want to execute contains an expression that can be translated into a pattern matching problem. If the query contains such a filter, we evaluate whether it would be efficient to solve that filter before the BGP parts are executed. The standard greedy algorithm starts by finding the triple pattern with the lowest number of results, then binding these results to the next smallest pattern and so on until all results are bound. For our implementation, we also check if one of the substring expressions has at least 100 times less results than the smallest pattern (100 being the page size). This is still a greedy implementation, albeit one that takes advantage of the server-side substring feature.

6   Evaluation

6.1   Experimental Setup

We compare multiple situations to evaluate the impact of the substring feature. We want measure how the performance changed on both client and server on substring queries, we want to make sure we did not hurt the performance on non-substring queries, and we also want to compare the FM-index implementation against adding an external index such as Elasticsearch.

We executed both client and server on the same machine (Intel Core i5-3230M CPU at 2.60GHz with 8GB of RAM) while the Elasticsearch index was located on a different server (12 Intel Xeon E5-2640 CPU cores at 2.50GHz with hyperthreading, 64GB of RAM) in the same network with a ping time of < 1ms with the DBpedia2014 dataset without abstracts[3]. The Elasticsearch index is on a different server due to the extra memory requirements for the index. All results can be found online[4] as well as the server[5] and client[6] code.

We performed the following tests:

1. With both Elasticsearch and FM-index, request all objects containing a specific keyword through the TPF interface, meaning these have to be requested one page at a time. The keywords are sampled from the list created by Freitas et al.[11] in such a way that their number of results are spread out.

---

[3] http://wiki.dbpedia.org/Downloads2014
[4] http://github.com/LinkedDataFragments/TPF-Substring-Results/
[5] http://github.com/LinkedDataFragments/Server.js/tree/feature-substring-search
[6] http://github.com/LinkedDataFragments/Client.js/tree/substring

```
SELECT ?person ?city WHERE {
  ?club a dbpedia-owl:SoccerClub;
        dbpedia-owl:ground ?city.
  ?player dbpedia-owl:team ?club;
          dbpedia-owl:birthPlace ?city.
  ?city dbpedia-owl:country dbpedia:Spain.
}
```

Listing 3. SPARQL query: Spanish soccer players

2. Evaluate the query in Listing 1 against a regular TPF server and a TPF server with a substring feature using an FM-index. We used the actor "Johnny Depp", who has many substring matches, to have more robust results.
3. Perform a query not containing any substring requirements on both the original as the FM-indexed version of TPF. For this we used the query in Listing 3.

6.2 Results

Elasticsearch and FM-Index. The results of the keyword test can be seen in full in Table 1 and visualized in Figure 1. The differences in results are due to the fact that our Elasticsearch configuration uses prefix matching. We did not configure the Elasticsearch index for full substring search since it performs a lot worse there, both in lookup speed and index size. It is clear that FM-index performs really well here, scaling linearly with the amount matches because an increase in matches also results in an increase in pages that need to be requested from the server.

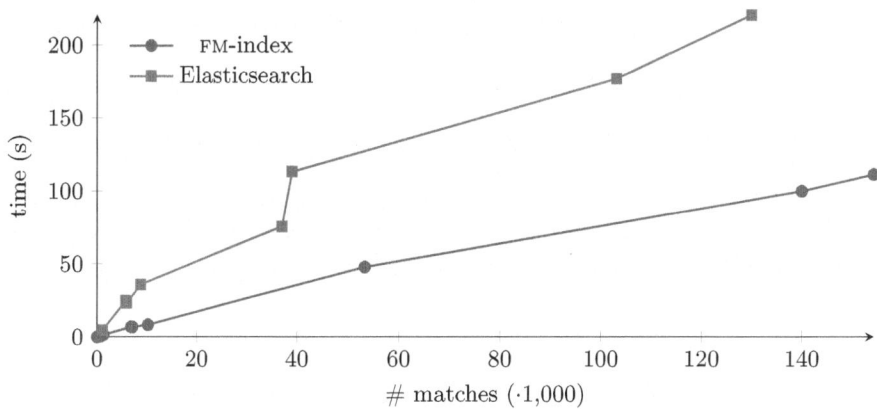

Fig. 1. Number of matches and query time for the keywords in Table 1.

Table 1. FM-index and Elasticsearch comparison.

keyword	FM-index		Elasticsearch	
	# matches	time (ms)	# matches	time (ms)
laptop	1,280	1,552	1,089	4,536
tools	6,795	6,900	5,679	24,758
photography	7,030	6,802	5,903	23,209
landing	10,211	8,302	8,735	35,863
computer	53,316	47,817	39,052	113,262
politician	139,952	100,052	103,159	176,938
sun	154,439	111,451	129,868	220,656
car	965,159	785,423	627,020	1,225,449

Table 2. Original implementation and FM-index comparison. CPU and memory strictly refer to the server process.

	"Johnny Depp"		Spanish soccer	
	original	FM-index	original	FM-index
http calls	304,154	174	91,658	91,694
time (ms)	1,189,706	1,352	329,287	319,065
average cpu (%)	58.98	40.67	42.34	45.12
average ram (mb)	3,664	3,563	440	3,290

Original Implementation and FM-Index. The results of the two implementations are found in Table 2 for both the query where having substring search is an advantage and the query where it has no influence at all. The results for the "Johnny Depp" query speak for themselves: where the original implementation needs to iterate over all the actors, the FM-index can first find the correct actor and iterate over his movies, having more than 100 times fewer HTTP calls.

The results of the second query are also positive: although more memory is required to store the FM-index during execution, there is no loss in performance, both implementations have the same results.

Data Size. Besides those evaluations there is also a difference in storage required: the original HDT file is 6.4GB while the updated HDT file with FM-index is 8.2GB in size. The Elasticsearch index for the original HDT file is 52.7GB. FM-index obviously has a big advantage here due to the fact that it is embedded in the data itself while Elasticsearch has to duplicate the data.

7   Conclusions

In this paper we discuss how the Triple Pattern Fragments interface can be extended by adding a substring pattern matching feature to the server, either by an internal FM-index or external Elasticsearch index. We extended the FM-index implementation of HDT to also support case-insensitive searches and updated the TPF server interface to make use of this functionality.

Our evaluations show that the new interface greatly increases the performance for certain queries (validating Hypothesis 1) without harming unrelated query results (validating Hypothesis 2). Also, the server can execute these substring queries quite fast (validating Hypothesis 3). The FM-index also performed better than the external Elasticsearch index, but since the functionality of both systems is not identical—because of the extra features in Elasticsearch—this can not be used to conclude that one is strictly better than the other.

The type of SPARQL queries that benefit from the substring interface are obviously those with a text-centric component. One possible application are *auto-completion* widgets, in which terms are suggested to an end user based on preliminary text input. Other applications include so-called *reconciliation* tasks, in which Linked Data identifiers are sought for a large corpus of text strings [23]. Such tasks currently rely on public SPARQL endpoints, on which they need to launch relatively costly queries, yet they can be implemented with the substring interface feature at lower cost and thus improved reliability.

In the future we would like to improve these results by using the FEMTO system described in Section 2.2 to also allow regular expressions besides simple pattern matching. It would also be interesting to see what the effect would be when the updated interface was used in the improved query algorithm described by Van Herwegen et al.[22] to further enhance query results. Besides partially replacing regular expression filters, we would also like to use the FM-index to support other filters, such as date ranges by finding all literals that match a specific date template. This would follow the TPF principle of solving complex problems by using simple building blocks.

Another interesting direction to explore is the combination of the substring interface feature with other interfaces than TPF. As we explained in Section 4, clients can dynamically discover support for substring matching, analogous to how they can dynamically discover support for TPF. Suppose a dataset is offered through a SPARQL interface, then the TPF interface can still be helpful. After all, support for substring search in SPARQL engines is not always available with high performance (even though derived features, such as prefix search or `bif:contains` might be supported). Therefore, SPARQL queries that rely on text filters might be evaluated by decomposing them on the client side into a substring search (evaluated on the substring interface) and a regular SPARQL query (evaluated on the SPARQL endpoint) in which the filter has been replaced by a list of matching substring values. An alternative is that the SPARQL endpoint is configured as a client of the substring interface; i.e., that it has access to this interface to evaluate complex text filters.

References

1. Arias Gallego, M., Corcho, O., Fernández, J.D., Martínez-Prieto, M.A., Suárez-Figueroa, M.C.: Compressing semantic metadata for efficient multimedia retrieval. In: Bielza, C., Salmerón, A., Alonso-Betanzos, A., Hidalgo, J.I., Martínez, L., Troncoso, A., Corchado, E., Corchado, J.M. (eds.) CAEPIA 2013. LNCS, vol. 8109, pp. 12–21. Springer, Heidelberg (2013). http://dx.doi.org/10.1007/978-3-642-40643-0_2
2. Brisaboa, N.R., Cánovas, R., Claude, F., Martínez-Prieto, M.A., Navarro, G.: Compressed string dictionaries. In: Pardalos, P.M., Rebennack, S. (eds.) SEA 2011. LNCS, vol. 6630, pp. 136–147. Springer, Heidelberg (2011)
3. Buil-Aranda, C., Hogan, A., Umbrich, J., Vandenbussche, P.Y.: SPARQL web-querying infrastructure: ready for action? In: Proceedings of the 12th International Semantic Web Conference, November 2013. http://link.springer.com/chapter/10.1007/978-3-642-41338-4_18
4. Burrows, M., Wheeler, D.J.: A block-sorting lossless data compression algorithm. Tech. Rep. SRC-RR-124, Digital Equipment Corporation (1994)
5. Erling, O., Mikhailov, I.: RDF support in the virtuoso DBMS. In: Pellegrini, T., Auer, S., Tochtermann, K., Schaffert, S. (eds.) Networked Knowledge - Networked Media. SCI, vol. 221, pp. 7–24. Springer, Heidelberg (2009)
6. Ermilov, I., Martin, M., Lehmann, J., Auer, S.: Linked open data statistics: collection and exploitation. In: Klinov, P., Mouromtsev, D. (eds.) KESW 2013. CCIS, vol. 394, pp. 242–249. Springer, Heidelberg (2013). http://dx.doi.org/10.1007/978-3-642-41360-5_19
7. Feigenbaum, L., Williams, G.T., Clark, K.G., Torres, E.: SPARQL 1.1 protocol. Recommendation, World Wide Web Consortium, March 2013. http://www.w3.org/TR/sparql11-protocol/
8. Ferguson, M.P.: FEMTO: fast search of large sequence collections. In: Kärkkäinen, J., Stoye, J. (eds.) CPM 2012. LNCS, vol. 7354, pp. 208–219. Springer, Heidelberg (2012). http://dx.doi.org/10.1007/978-3-642-31265-6_17
9. Fernández, J.D., Martínez-Prieto, M.A., Gutiérrez, C., Polleres, A., Arias, M.: Binary RDF representation for publication and exchange (HDT). Journal of Web Semantics 19, 22–41, March 2013. http://dx.doi.org/10.1016/j.websem.2013.01.002
10. Ferragina, P., Manzini, G.: Opportunistic data structures with applications. In: Proceedings of the 41st Annual Symposium on Foundations of Computer Science, pp. 390–398 (2000)
11. Freitas, A., Curry, E., O'Riain, S.: A distributional approach for terminological semantic search on the linked data web. In: Proceedings of the 27th Annual ACM Symposium on Applied Computing, pp. 384–391 (2012)
12. Gormley, C., Tong, Z.: Elasticsearch: The Definitive Guide. O'Reilly (2014)
13. Harris, S., Seaborne, A.: SPARQL 1.1 query language. Recommendation, World Wide Web Consortium, March 2013. http://www.w3.org/TR/sparql11-query/
14. Lanthaler, M., Gütl, C.: Hydra: a vocabulary for hypermedia-driven web APIs. In: Proceedings of the 6th Workshop on Linked Data on the Web, May 2013. http://ceur-ws.org/Vol-996/papers/ldow2013-paper-03.pdf
15. Li, R., Yu, C., Li, Y., Lam, T.W., Yiu, S.M., Kristiansen, K., Wang, J.: SOAP2: an improved ultrafast tool for short read alignment. Bioinformatics 25(15), 1966–1967 (2009)

16. Martínez-Prieto, M.A., Fernández, J.D., Cánovas, R.: Querying rdf dictionaries in compressed space. ACM SIGAPP Applied Computing Review **12**(2), 64–77 (2012)
17. Minack, E., Sauermann, L., Grimnes, G., Fluit, C., Broekstra, J.: The sesame luce-nesail: RDF queries with full-text search. NEPOMUK Consortium, Technical Report 1 (2008)
18. Minack, E., Siberski, W., Nejdl, W.: Benchmarking fulltext search performance of RDF stores. In: Aroyo, L., Traverso, P., Ciravegna, F., Cimiano, P., Heath, T., Hyvönen, E., Mizoguchi, R., Oren, E., Sabou, M., Simperl, E. (eds.) ESWC 2009. LNCS, vol. 5554, pp. 81–95. Springer, Heidelberg (2009)
19. Nelson, M.: Data compression with the Burrows-Wheeler transform. Dr. Dobb's Journal **9**, 46–50 (1996)
20. Rietveld, L., Verborgh, R., Beek, W., Vander Sande, M., Schlobach, S.: Linked data-as-a-service: the semantic web redeployed. In: Gandon, F., Sabou, M., Sack, H., d'Amato, C., Cudré-Mauroux, P., Zimmermann, A. (eds.) ESWC 2015. LNCS, vol. 9088, pp. 471–487. Springer, Heidelberg (2015)
21. Sadakane, K.: A modified Burrows-Wheeler transformation for case-insensitive search with application to suffix array compression. In: Proceedings of the Data Compression Conference, p. 548 (1999)
22. Van Herwegen, J., Verborgh, R., Mannens, E., Van de Walle, R.: Query execution optimization for clients of triple pattern fragments. In: Gandon, F., Sabou, M., Sack, H., d'Amato, C., Cudré-Mauroux, P., Zimmermann, A. (eds.) ESWC 2015. LNCS, vol. 9088, pp. 302–318. Springer, Heidelberg (2015)
23. van Hooland, S., Verborgh, R., De Wilde, M., Hercher, J., Mannens, E., Van de Walle, R.: Evaluating the success of vocabulary reconciliation for cultural heritage collections. Journal of the American Society for Information Science and Technology **64**(3), 464–479 (2013). http://freeyourmetadata.org/publications/freeyourmetadata.pdf
24. Verborgh, R.: Triple Pattern Fragments. Unofficial draft, Hydra w3c Community Group. http://www.hydra-cg.com/spec/latest/triple-pattern-fragments/
25. Verborgh, R., et al.: Querying datasets on the web with high availability. In: Mika, P., et al. (eds.) The Semantic Web – ISWC 2014. LNCS, vol. 8796, pp. 180–196. Springer, Heidelberg (2014). http://linkeddatafragments.org/publications/iswc2014.pdf
26. Verborgh, R., Mannens, E., Van de Walle, R.: Initial usage analysis of DBpedia's triple pattern fragments. In: Proceedings of the 5th Workshop on Usage Analysis and the Web of Data, June 2015
27. Verborgh, R., Vander Sande, M., Colpaert, P., Coppens, S., Mannens, E., Van de Walle, R.: Web-scale querying through linked data fragments. In: Proceedings of the 7th Workshop on Linked Data on the Web, April 2014. http://events.linkeddata.org/ldow2014/papers/ldow2014_paper_04.pdf

Linked Data

Linked Data

LinkDaViz – Automatic Binding of Linked Data to Visualizations

Klaudia Thellmann$^{(\boxtimes)}$, Michael Galkin, Fabrizio Orlandi, and Sören Auer

University of Bonn & Fraunhofer IAIS, Bonn, Germany
klaudia.thellmann@iais.fraunhofer.de, {galkin,orlandi}@iai.uni-bonn.de,
auer@cs.uni-bonn.de

Abstract. As the Web of Data is growing steadily, the demand for user-friendly means for exploring, analyzing and visualizing Linked Data is also increasing. The key challenge for visualizing Linked Data consists in providing a clear overview of the data and supporting non-technical users in finding suitable visualizations while hiding technical details of Linked Data and visualization configuration. In order to accomplish this, we propose a largely automatic workflow which guides users through the process of creating visualizations by automatically categorizing and binding data to visualization parameters. The approach is based on a heuristic analysis of the structure of the input data and a comprehensive visualization model facilitating the automatic binding between data and visualization parameters. The resulting assignments are ranked and presented to the user. With LinkDaViz we provide a web-based implementation of the approach and demonstrate the feasibility by an extended user and performance evaluation.

1 Introduction

The amount of data published as Linked Data is continuously increasing, but for end users it is still cumbersome to exploit and difficult to appraise the value of this data. A reason for this is that we still lack comprehensive means for user-friendly and engaging exploration and visualization of Linked Data.

Visualization is one of the most challenging but at the same time rewarding aspects of exploring Linked Data. We have a plethora of data modalities (factual, temporal, spatial, statistical, schema and meta data) and vocabularies for all of these. At the same time there is a vast variety of visualization and exploration techniques [4], most of which are limited either in generality [5] or usability for non-technical users [6,10]. Thus, the key challenge of Linked Data visualization consists in hiding the technical details of Linked Data and visualization configurations and finding a balance between generality and usability. This can be accomplished by automatizing the process of producing visualizations, which would greatly facilitate the interaction with data by end users [2,13].

In this article we present our approach LinkDaViz which supports the user in selecting and configuring visualizations by automatically binding Linked Data to visualizations. The approach is based on an analysis of the input data structure and a comprehensive visualization model comprising structural and layout

© Springer International Publishing Switzerland 2015
M. Arenas et al. (Eds.): ISWC 2015, Part I, LNCS 9366, pp. 147–162, 2015.
DOI: 10.1007/978-3-319-25007-6_9

options. The binding problem between the data and the visualization is reduced to an assignment problem involving cost functions and heuristics. The resulting assignments are ranked and the highest ranking visualization instantiations presented to the user. The user can further refine and configure these visualization instances.

The contributions of this work are in particular:

- a method for visualization-oriented input data analysis aiming at discovering structures relevant for visualization,
- a formal visualization model, comprising structural and layout options,
- a visualization recommendation algorithm that automatically binds the selected data properties to visualization parameters,
- an implementation of the approach with the LinkDaViz web application.

The LinkDaViz visualization tool simplifies the interaction with datasets unknown to a user in ways unforeseen by the publisher. We demonstrate the feasibility of our approach with an extensive user study and an evaluation of scalability and effectiveness.

2   Related Work

Most existing approaches are only usable by a technical audience or limited to certain domains or data representations [4]. In order to hide complexity of data selection and visualization configuration, the focus of visualization approaches has been shifting towards automation [2,5,13].

Klimek et al. [6] implemented a workflow (Payola) based on the Linked Data Visualization Model (LDVM) [2], which consists of various analyzers for automatically classifying datasets and transformers for mapping the data to visualization abstractions. However, the amount of manual configuration and the necessary transformation steps between different abstractions might be considered a shortcoming by non-technical users.

Voigt et al. [14] propose a generic approach for visualization configuration in form of a faceted browser (Vizboard). The user creates a weighted query on abstract visualization features, which is used to automatically compute the visualization suggestions to be presented to the user. LinkDaViz implements a different mechanism for automatically suggesting visualization without expecting the user to know beforehand how he intends to visualize the data.

Mutlu et al. [8] developed an approach for automatically mapping data to visualizations that have a similar input structure as a given RDF Data Cube. LinkDaViz follows a similar mapping approach, but is not limited to the Data Cube vocabulary and has a more generic matching based on bipartite graph matching.

Bikakis et al. [1] propose rdf:SynopsViz, which comprises features such as on-the-fly hierarchy construction, statistics, faceted browsing and measuring data quality through dataset metadata. Bindings for a user-selected visualization (five types of charts, timeline or treemap) are computed automatically based on a

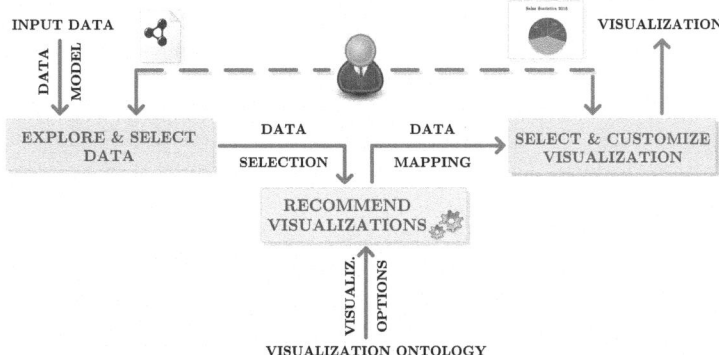

Fig. 1. The Linked Data Visualization Workflow.

selection of classes and properties. LinkDaViz supports any data types (not only numeric and dates), offers selection of data properties of different nesting depth, and automatically recommends visualizations, and not only bindings to a manually selected visualization.

With LinkDaViz we aim to find a balance between generality and ease of use. Hence, we aim at improving on existing approaches and supporting the user in selecting and configuring visualizations for arbitrary Linked Data through automatic visualization recommendation and intuitive customization.

3   Approach

In this section, the workflow for visualizing Linked Data is described formally. The goal of the workflow is to support users in selecting and configuring visualizations by providing a largely automatic visualization workflow. The visualization workflow is based on the assumption that the user does not necessarily know how to choose and manually configure visualizations for a certain dataset, but can decide whether a proposed visualization configuration is reasonable. Thus, the challenge is to compute a ranked list of visualization configurations from a subset of a dataset selected by a user for its visualization. It is not in the scope of this work to guess what part of a dataset the user might be interested in, but to provide assistance in visualizing a previously specified subset of the data.

The task of finding configurations for a visualization can be modeled as an assignment problem which describes how the selected data can be mapped to the visualization's input parameters. The assignment problem can then be solved using a weighted bipartite graph matching algorithm.

3.1   Visualization Workflow

The visualization workflow (depicted in Figure 1) guides the user through the process of visualizing data and starts with the exploration of a dataset. After the user has selected the part of the dataset to be visualized, a ranked list of recommended visualizations is computed. When one of the recommendations is selected, the resulting visualization is displayed, ready for customization.

For each workflow step, a different representation of data is needed, starting with the input data model, which is structured in a tree-like fashion suited for the exploration of data. The LinkDaViz ontology contains a description of the visualization's structural and layout parameters and the scales of measurement used for specifying what types of input data can be mapped to a visualization's parameters. The purpose of the ontology is to serve as a basis for the recommendation algorithm so it provides only the information necessary for computing visualization mappings. The data selected for visualization constitutes a subset of the input data and serves, together with the visualization options extracted from the visualization ontology, as input for the recommendation algorithm.

The following subsections contain a detailed description of the data representations, the formalization of visualizations and the recommendation algorithm.

3.2 Input Data Model

The input data model is a abstract description of the input for the LinkDaViz tool and is automatically generated for the selected dataset during the data exploration and selection phase of the visualization workflow. In order to obtain the model, a tree representation of the input dataset is built automatically level by level as the user browses through the classes and their appendant properties. The input data model consists of a finite set DS of datasets and a set of trees $Trees(ds)$ for each dataset $ds \in DS$. Each tree $T \in Trees(ds)$ is a directed tree $T = (V, E, r)$ with a root node $r \in V$ corresponding to an RDF class, and is defined by a set of nodes V and a set of edges E. For instance, the dataset depicted in Figure 2 contains statistics about European countries and can be modeled as two trees T_1, T_2 with root nodes $r_1 = $ Country and $r_2 = $ EU-Member.

The set of nodes V consists of inner nodes representing RDF object properties $O \subset V$ and leaf nodes representing RDF data properties $D \subset V$:

$$V = \{r\} \,\dot\cup\, D \,\dot\cup\, O \tag{1}$$

where for every edge $(v, w) \in E$, $v \notin D$ (that is, data properties are leaves).

For instance, the data properties nodes of tree T_1 from the first level are $D_1 = \{$ Name, Population, Area, Code$\}$ and one object node $O_1 = \{$Capital$\}$. Each data property node $d \in D$ has a scale $s_{data}(d)$ and a role $r_{data}(d)$, which are used in the computation of mappings to visualization options.

Data Scales. The scales of measurement are divided into categorical (*Nominal, Ordinal*) and quantitative (*Interval, Ratio*) scales and are used to categorize data properties [11]:

$$S = \{Nominal, Ordinal, Interval, Ratio\} \tag{2}$$

The only requirement for *Nominal* data properties is to have distinguished values, for instance gender: *male* and *female*.

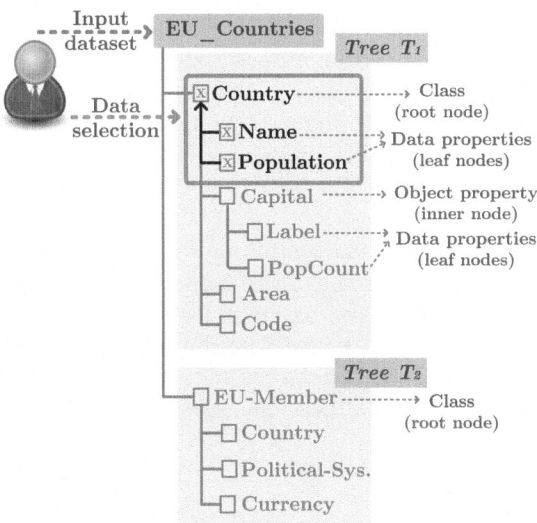

Fig. 2. Input Data Model.

Ordinal data properties additionally have an order between their values, like the values *always, sometimes, never* of a Likert scale. For properties of *Ordinal* scales, no notion of numerical difference is implied, even if the values are expressed as numbers.

In case of *Interval* or *Ratio* data properties, it makes sense to compute the numerical difference between their values. The difference between *Interval* and *Ratio* is that for *Ratio* values, zero is absolute. For instance, temperature can be measured using the *Interval* scale Celsius or the *Ratio* scale Kelvin, which in contrast to Celsius has an absolute zero point.

Based on these definitions, the hierarchy of scales can be defined as follows:

$$Nominal \longleftarrow Ordinal \longleftarrow Interval \longleftarrow Ratio \qquad (3)$$

with *Nominal* being the most generic and *Ratio* the most specific scale [12].

The categorization of data properties is performed heuristically depending on the data types of the data property values. Numbers are categorized as *Ratio*, dates as *Interval* and strings as *Nominal* data. For example, the scales of the data properties nodes $\texttt{Name}, \texttt{Population} \in D_1$ are $s_{data}(\texttt{Name}) = Nominal$ and $s_{data}(\texttt{Population}) = Ratio$.

Data Roles. Data property nodes $d \in D$ also may have the role $r_{data}(d) \in R$ which can be that of an independent variable (*Domain*) or of a dependent variable (*Range*):

$$R = \{Domain, Range, none\} \qquad (4)$$

This is needed because due to the structure of some visualizations, only independent variables can be reasonably assigned to some of their input parameters, while for others only dependent variables are appropriate. Hence, this information can be used to exclude certain unreasonable mappings.

The roles that can be associated to the data properties Name, Population $\in D_1$ are $r_{data}(\text{Name}) = Domain$ and $r_{data}(\text{Population}) = Range$. The roles of a data property can be extracted for instance from the metadata provided by the RDF Data Cube vocabulary.

Data Selection. The tree-like representation of the input data allows the user to browse the dataset and select some of the properties for visualization. The data selection $T_s = (V_s, E_s, r_s)$ is used as input for the recommendation algorithm and is a subtree of a tree $T \in Trees(ds)$ from a dataset $ds \in DS$ from the input data model, with T_s containing a subset $V_s \subseteq V$ of the nodes of T and all of the edges $E_s = E \cap V_s \times V_s$ between these, and with the same root $r_s = r \in V$ as T:

$$V_s = \{r_s\} \mathbin{\dot\cup} D_s \mathbin{\dot\cup} O_s \tag{5}$$

with $D_s \subset D$ and $O_s \subset O$.

For instance, the data selected from the EU-Countries dataset in figure 2 consists of two data property nodes from tree T_1, namely Name, Population $\in V$. This selection is a subtree of T_1 with the same root node $r_s = r_1 = $ Country and the edges $E_s = E_1 \cap V \times V = \{(\text{Country}, \text{Name}), (\text{Country}, \text{Population})\}$.

3.3 Visualization Model

A visualization model is introduced for formally describing the options defining the structure and the layout of a visualization and a mapping specifying the configuration of the visualization options. The visualization model *VM* is composed of sets of structural and layout options *SO* respectively *LO* and a set of all possible mappings M of a data selection T_s to a visualization *vis*:

$$VM = (SO, LO, M) \tag{6}$$

Structural Options. The purpose of the structural options $so \in SO$ of a visualization is to define the skeleton of the visualization. For instance, the structure of a column chart is defined by the following options: $SO = \{horizontal\ axis,\ vertical\ axis,\ groups\}$. A structural option $so \in SO$ is described by a name $n_{vis}(so) \in \Sigma^*$, a set of scales $s_{vis}(so) \in \mathcal{P}(S)$, a role $r_{vis}(so) \in R$ and a cardinality $c_{vis}(so) \in C$, with Σ^* being the set of strings in a given alphabet and $C = \{(0, 1), (0, *), (1, 1), (1, *)\}$ being the set of possible cardinalities, and S and R as in section subsection 3.2.

A structure option $so \in SO$ has a set of scales $s_{vis}(so) \subset S = \{Nominal,\ Ordinal,\ Interval,\ Ratio\}$, which represent the kinds of input data that can be mapped to it. For instance the scales of a column charts structural options are $s_{vis}(vertical\ axis) = \{Interval,\ Ratio\}$, $s_{vis}(horizontal\ axis) = \{\ Nominal\}$ and

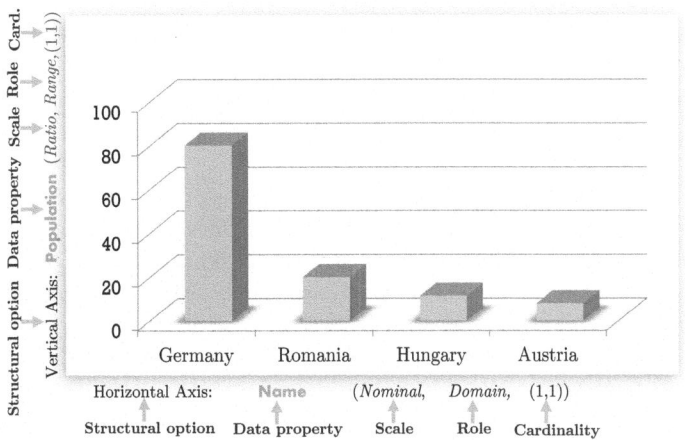

Fig. 3. Example of a structural options mapping.

$s_{vis}(\ groups) = \{Nominal\}$, which results in the following pattern describing the kinds of input data that can be mapped to a column chart:

$$\underbrace{horizontal\ axis}_{Nominal} \times \underbrace{groups^?}_{Nominal} \longrightarrow \underbrace{vertical\ axis}_{Ratio} \tag{7}$$

The role $r_{vis}(so) \in R$ of a structure option is used to restrict the data properties to independent or dependent variables that can be mapped to visualization options in order to ensure that the data conforms to the structure of the visualization. $R = \{Domain,\ Range,\ none\}$. For instance the roles of a column charts structural options are $r_{vis}(vertical\ axis) = \{Range\}$, $r_{vis}(horizontal\ axis) = r_{vis}(groups\ ) = \{Domain\}$, which results in the following pattern:

$$\underbrace{horizontal\ axis\ \times\ groups^?}_{domain} \longrightarrow \underbrace{vertical\ axis}_{range} \tag{8}$$

The roles of the selected data properties Name and Population, are $r_{vis}(\texttt{Name}) = \{Domain\}$ and $r_{vis}(\texttt{Population}) = \{Range\}$. This results in the following distribution of roles:

$$\underbrace{horizontal\ axis}_{domain\ =\ Name} \longrightarrow \underbrace{vertical\ axis}_{range\ =\ Population} \tag{9}$$

Which means that each European country has a population count as value, which is projected as a vertical bar in a column chart.

Finally, the cardinality $c_{vis}(so) \in C$ indicates if a structure option is required or optional and if it is single or multi-valued. The cardinality is indicated by affixing ? for cardinality $(0, 1)$, $*$ for $(0, *)$ and $+$ for $(1, *)$ to the scale of measurement, with no affix indicating cardinality $(1, 1)$. For instance, the

cardinalities of the structural options of column charts are: $c_{vis}(horizontal$
$axis) = c_{vis}(groups) = (1,1)$ and $c_{vis}(vertical\ axis) = (1,1)$, which results in
the pattern:

$$\underbrace{horizontal\ axis}_{Required} \times \underbrace{groups^?}_{Optional} \longrightarrow \underbrace{vertical\ axis}_{Required} \tag{10}$$

Layout Options. The layout options LO allow the user to refine the style of the
visualization. As they don't have any influence on the recommendation, they are
not formally described in detail. For instance, a column chart's layout can be
specified by the following options: $LO = (number\ grid\ lines,\ v\text{-}axis\ label,\ h\text{-}axis$
label, stacked columns)

Options Mapping. An options mapping $m = (m_{SO}, m_{LO})$ of the data selection T_s
to the visualization is composed of a structural options mapping $m_{SO} \subseteq SO \times D_s$
assigning data property nodes to structural options and a layout options mapping $m_{LO} = \{(lo_1, value\ 1), (lo_2, value\ 2), \ldots, (lo_m, value\ m)\}$ assigning values
to layout options $lo_i \in LO$ for $i \in \{1, \ldots, m\}$, $m \in \mathbb{N}$. The structural options
mapping must conform to the cardinality constraints of each structural option as
explained above. Initially, a computed suggestion can be assigned to the structural options, and predefined default values from the visualization ontology to
the layout options.

   An example of a possible mapping of the selected data properties from the
EU-Countries example in subsection 3.2 to a column chart's structural options
would be $m = (\{(vertical\ axis, \texttt{Population}), (horizontal\ axis, \texttt{Name})\}, \{(number$
$grid\ lines, 9), (v\text{-}axis\ label, \texttt{Population Count}), (h\text{-}axis\ label, \texttt{Country}), (stacked$
columns, $\texttt{false})\})$. This mapping is depicted in Figure 3 and results in a statistical visualization of the population count of European countries. Because no
grouping values were specified the optional structural option *groups* is left out.

3.4   Visualization Recommendation

In order to suggest possible visualization configurations, a recommendation algorithm has been introduced, which automatically binds the selected data properties to visualization options. For each visualization, the assignment of data
properties to the visualization's structural options is modelled as a weighted
bipartite graph matching problem and solved by the graph matching algorithm introduced by Kuhn and Munkres[3,7]. The optimal solutions of these
graph matching problems are then ranked to produce a list of recommended
visualizations.

Assignment Problem. The assignment problem for a visualization is defined as
follows: Given the set $D_s = \{d_1, d_2 \ldots d_m\} \subset V_s$ of data properties from the data
selection T_s and the set of structural options $SO = \{so_1, so_2 \ldots so_n\}$, find a valid
structural options mapping m_{SO} with maximum possible number of assigned
structure options and minimal cost.

The lower the cost of a mapping, the better it conforms to the input data the visualization expects, and thus the higher the likeliness that it corresponds to what the user envisioned. A high number of assigned data properties ensures that a large part of the selected data can be visualized.

The cost w_{ij} of mapping the data property d_j to the structural option so_i is the sum of three penalties, namely scales, roles and optionals penalty, which are introduced in more detail below.

$$w_{ij} = w_{ij}^{scale} + w_{ij}^{opt} + w_{ij}^{role} \tag{11}$$

Scales Penalty. The amount of the scales penalty w_{ij}^{scale} as displayed in Figure 4a indicates how well a data property's scale $s_{data}(d)$ matches a structural options's scales $s_{vis}(so)$. The higher the penalty the more unfitting the match of the data property d and the structural option so. When $s_{data}(d)$ is contained in $s_{vis}(so)$ this indicates a perfect match, so $w_{ij}^{scale} = 0$. In contrast, an invalid match is given a high penalty $w_{ij}^{scale} = w_{inv}$, for example $w_{inv} = 1000$.

The values of the penalties are chosen in a way to increase the likeliness of computing meaningful mappings.

For instance, it is more appropriate to map an *Interval* data property to a *Nominal* structural option than a *Ratio* property, because less information is lost for the *Interval* property, as *Interval* is more general than *Ratio* (cf. subsection 3.2).

		Structural Option		
Scales Penalty		*Nominal*	*Interval*	*Ratio*
Data Property	*Nominal*	0	w_{inv}	w_{inv}
	Interval	30	0	w_{inv}
	Ratio	40	30	0

(a) Scales penalties overview.

	Structural Option	
Optional Penalty	*Optional*	*Required*
	50	0

(c) Optionals penalties overview.

		Structural Option		
Role Penalty		*Domain*	*Range*	-
Data Property	*Domain*	0	w_{inv}	20
	Range	w_{inv}	0	20
	-	20	20	0

(b) Roles penalties overview.

			Structural Option		
Cost Matrix			so_1	so_2	so_3
			horizontal axis	vertical axis	groups
Data Property	d_1	*Name*	0	1000	50
	d_2	*Population*	1000	0	50

(d) Cost matrix example.

Fig. 4. Penalties overview and cost matrix example.

Roles Penalty. The roles penalty w_{ij}^{role} is added if the structural option has a defined role and the data property's role is not known, which might result in an incorrect match, or if the option has no role specified but the data property's role is known (see Figure 4b). In the latter case, it might be beneficial to favor mapping properties to the options whose roles are known by penalizing the mappings to the options with no associated roles. In both cases the role penalty has a higher significance than the scale penalty: $w_{ij}^{role} < w_{ij}^{scale}$ for non-perfect mappings ($w_{ij}^{scale} > 0$). In the cases in which either both sides' roles are known or not known, no role penalty is added.

Optionals Penalty. In case of optional structural options, an optionals penalty w_{ij}^{opt} is introduced to ensure that required structural options are preferred in the mapping, thus reducing the likeliness of producing an invalid mapping (see Figure 4 c). Therefore, the optional penalty must be greater than the greatest scale penalty of valid assignments (which is 40): $w_{ij}^{opt} = 50 < w_{ij}^{scale}$ for valid mappings ($w_{ij}^{scale} < w_{inv}$).

Cost Matrix. In order to solve an assignment problem a cost matrix $W = (w_{ij})_{i=1...n, j=1...m}$ is computed for all available visualizations by adding the scale penalty w_{ij}^{scale}, the optional penalty w_{ij}^{opt} and the role penalty w_{ij}^{role}. For the formal description, a square matrix is more favorable, which can be achieved by padding the weight matrix with zeroes (dummy values)[3]. From here on, it is assumed that the matrix is square: $n = m$

The cost matrix W for computing the mapping $m_{SO} = \{(vertical~axis,$ Population), (*horizontal axis*, Name)$\}$ of a column charts structural options $SO = (horizontal~axis, vertical~axis, groups)$ and the data selection $D = \{$Name, Population$\}$ from the EU-Countries is depicted in Figure 4 d.

The column entries from each row are composed of the sum of the scale weight, role and optional penalty. For instance, the mapping of data property d_1 = Name $\in D$ to the structural option $s_{vis}(s_1)$ = *horizontal axis* has the cost $w_{11} = w_{11}^{scale} + w_{11}^{role} + w_{11}^{opt} = 0$. Because the scales $s_{data}(d_1) = s_{vis}(s_1) = $ *categorical* and the roles $r_{data}(d_1) = r_{vis}(s_1) = $ *domain* match, no penalties are added. As the structural option cardinality $c_{vis}(horizontal~axis) = (1,1)$ indicates that this option is required, no optionals penalty is added.

Mapping. Given the cost matrix $W = (w_{ij})_{i=1...n, j=1...n}$ as input for the bipartite graph matching algorithm a maximal mapping from the selected data T_s to the structural visualization options SO, is computed. That is a permutation π of $\{1, 2, \ldots, n\}$ is determined with maximum value of

$$w_{m_{SO}} = \sum_{i=1}^{n} w_{i,\pi(i)} \qquad (12)$$

Ranking. After computing a mapping for each visualization, the mappings are ranked and the highest ranking one is presented to the user along with the other recommendations as alternative visualizations.

A mapping m_{SO} is excluded from the result list if its cost is higher than a threshold $w_{m_{SO}} \geq w_{inv}$ or if it has unassigned required structural options: $\nexists$ *data property* such that $\nexists(so_i, data~property) \in m_{SO}$ and $c^v(so_i) \in \{(1,1),(1,*)\}$.

A mapping m_{SO_1} is ranked higher than a mapping m_{SO_2} if m_{SO_1} has a larger number of assigned structural options than m_{SO_2}, that is, $|m_{SO_1}| > |m_{SO_2}|$ and if m_{SO_1} has a lower cost than m_{SO_2}: $w_{m_{SO_1}} < w_{m_{SO_2}}$.

4   Implementation

Architecture. In order to guide the user through the process of visualizing Linked Data, a JavaScript based web-application, LinkDaViz[1], has been developed. The application receives data in RDF or tabular format as input. It consists of a frontend module for exploring and selecting data and configuring visualizations, and a back-end module for computing visualization recommendations (see Figure 5). The frontend module is realized using *Ember.js*[2], an open-source JavaScript client-side MVC framework, and consists of a component for querying and categorizing data, the visualization widgets library and a component for configuring a visualization. The selected input dataset is queried and categorized by determining the scale and role of each data property. The visualization widgets library contains configurable visualizations for statistical, temporal and geographical data (e.g. charts based on *D3/Dimple*[3], maps based on *Leaflet*[4]) and visualizations for previews (e.g. tables). The component for configuring visualizations is in charge of initializing and triggering the rendering of the recommended visualizations.

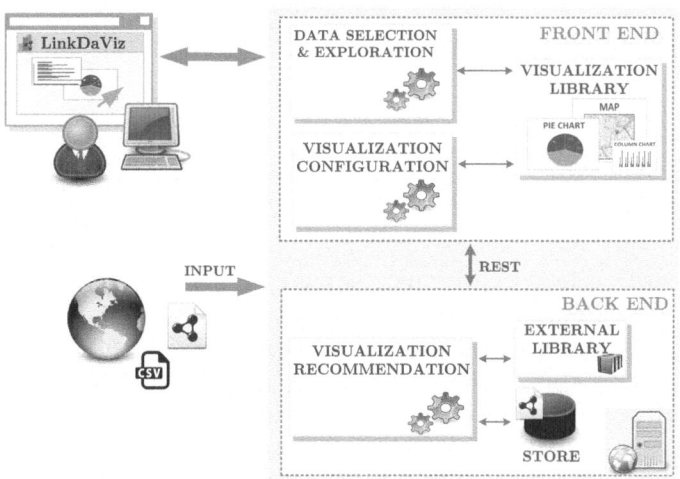

Fig. 5. Architecture of LinkDaViz.

---

[1] Publicly available at: http://eis.iai.uni-bonn.de/Projects/LinkDaViz.html
[2] http://emberjs.com/
[3] http://d3js.org/, http://dimplejs.org/
[4] http://leafletjs.com/

The backend is written in JavaScript and runs on *Node.js*[5], an open-source runtime environment for server-side applications, and consists of: *i)* a component for computing visualization recommendations and *ii)* a component managing the data being queried by the frontend through a REST API. The store contains datasets, the visualization ontology, from where the visualization metadata is extracted and the saved visualization configurations that can be reloaded for further customization.

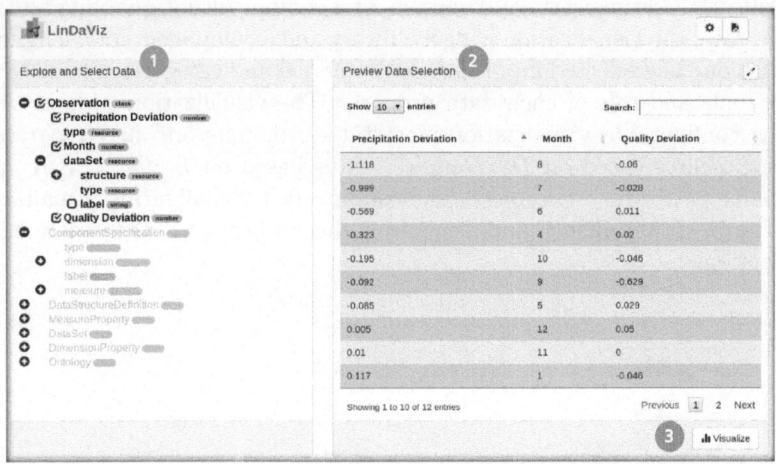

Fig. 6. LinkDaViz - select data: **1.** Browse and select data. **2.** Explore selection. **3.** Visualize selection.

Data Exploration and Selection. The component for data selection displayed in Figure 6 of the LinkDaViz UI consists of a tree-view of the input dataset with labeled nodes for browsing and selecting data (Figure 6 **(1)**) and a preview for exploring the selection (Figure 6 **(2)**). As described in subsection 3.2, the input dataset is modeled as a list of trees, with RDF classes as root nodes. Each tree consists of a set of inner nodes representing RDF object properties and leaf nodes representing RDF data properties. Data properties are labeled corresponding to the data type of their values (e.g. number, string, date, spatial) and object properties are labeled as resources. When selecting data properties, a preview is generated displaying the values of the data properties in a table. Following the selection step is the actual visualization of the selected data **(2)**.

Visualization Selection and Customization. The component for selecting and customizing visualizations of the LinkDaViz UI is depicted in (Figure 7) and consists of a list of visualization suggestions that are computed based on the dataset's content (Figure 7 **(4)**), a configuration component (Figure 7 **(5)**), the visualization (Figure 7 **(6)**) and consumption actions (export, save Figure 7

---

[5] https://nodejs.org/

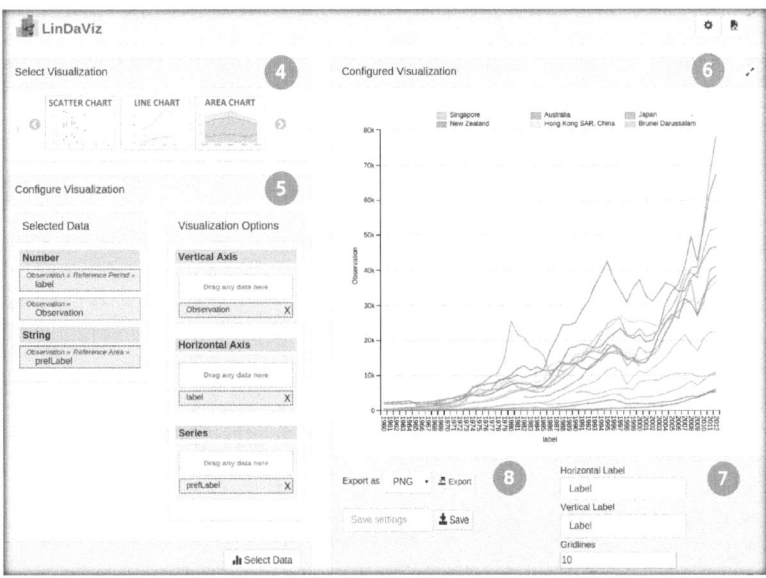

Fig. 7. LinkDaViz - visualize data: **4.** Select recommended visualization. **5.** Customize suggested configuration. **6.** Visualize data. **7.** Customize layout. **8.** Save or export visualization.

(**8**)) and tuning options (Figure 7 (**7**)). The configuration component contains an overview of the selected properties and the suggested mapping ("Visualization Options") for the selected visualization. The suggested mapping can be manually changed by dragging and dropping properties from the list of selected properties to the visualization options. The visualization's layout can be customized as well, for instance by adding labels to the axes or changing the number of grid lines. Finally, the visualization can be exported in different formats (e.g. PNG, SVG) and saved for later re-use.

5   Evaluation

In order to evaluate usability, scalability and effectiveness of the LinkDaViz tool, a comprehensive study has been conducted.

Setup. For the evaluation the application was deployed in Linux Virtual Machine on Intel Core i5 machine (2.5 GHz, 4GB RAM) and on an Amazon EC2 t2.micro instance (2.5 GHz, 1 GB RAM). The datasets used for evaluation contain statistical, temporal and geographical data and were collected mainly from the World Bank Linked Data project, Data.Gov and DataHub.

Methodology. In preparation of the user study, the participants and the evaluation criteria were identified, and a list of tasks to perform and a feedback questionnaire were created. Overall 20 participants of age range 20-30 took part

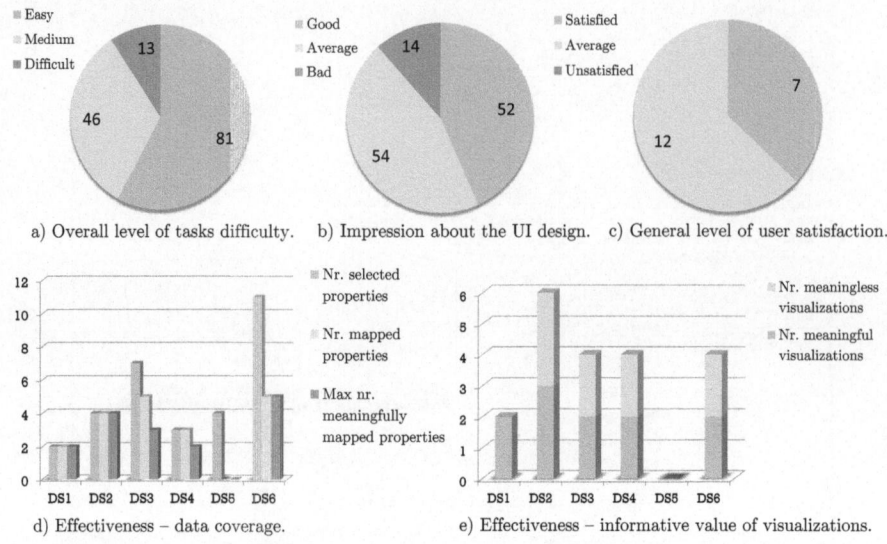

a) Overall level of tasks difficulty.   b) Impression about the UI design.   c) General level of user satisfaction.

d) Effectiveness – data coverage.   e) Effectiveness – informative value of visualizations.

Fig. 8. Evaluation Results of LinkDaViz.

in the evaluation, i.e. 15 males, 5 females, 17 students, 2 PhD students and one working professional. Seven tasks and corresponding questions were composed in order to evaluate the level of difficulty, the UI design, the effectiveness of the produced visualizations and the scalability of the recommendation engine. The tasks the users were asked to perform have been designed according to standard user evaluation protocols[9] and are the following: 1) Select a dataset, 2) Assign parameters of a visualization, 3) Visualize data, explore a chart, 4) Modify structural options of a chart, 5) Modify layout options of a chart, 6) Save a chart, 7) Visualize another slice of a dataset.

To evaluate effectiveness aspects of the recommendations, the number and quality of suggested visualizations were measured by exploring and estimating possible visualizations and configurations of visualizations for a particular dataset. The quality of recommendations was determined according to how much of the selected data could be visualized and on the meaningfulness of the suggested visualizations from the perspective of the evaluators.

Scalability was tested by producing visualizations for datasets of different sizes. The largest dataset consists of about 350 millions triples.

Results. In figure Figure 8a and Figure 8b the number of responses for each question regarding the level of difficulty and the UI design are summed up. From the 20 participants who took part in the evaluation, we collected 140 (Figure 8a) responses to the seven questions on difficulty and 120 (Figure 8b) responses to the six questions on the UI design. As Figure 8a indicates, the overall impression of performing the tasks was rated satisfactorily as average to good. The majority of the participants experienced little difficulties with the tasks given and considered the LinkDaViz UI as an effective and easy to use application for selecting data and configuring visualizations. The design of the UI was also rated average to good (Figure 8b). LinkDaViz can successfully produce previews and visualizations of RDF and CSV datasets in the majority of cases, depending on the quality (e.g. correct datatypes), nature and size of the selected data. The overall level of satisfaction (Figure 8c – one person didn't answer the question) and the quality of recommendations was rated positively. The quality varied with the number of selected data properties that could be automatically visualized (Figure 8d) and the meaningfulness of the suggestions (Figure 8e). Having conducted the effectiveness evaluation on six datasets (DS1 to DS6) collected from Data.Gov it should be noted that there is a negative impact on recommendations from the varying dataset quality (e.g. wrong datatypes, non-uniform properties, aggregated values represented like raw data). A visualization has been generated and displayed for almost every dataset in a reasonable time. However on a selection from a large, homogeneous dataset with more than 300 millions of triples no visualization could be produced due to the browsers' memory limit.

6   Conclusion and Future Work

In this paper we have introduced LinkDaViz, a novel visualization approach and software implementation which allows for automatic visualization of Linked Data. A formal description of the approach, the visualization components and the input data has been provided. Additionally, we have introduced a recommendation algorithm that automatically binds selected data properties to visualization options. The validity of our approach has been tested with a comprehensive evaluation of our LinkDaViz software tool. We conducted a user study to evaluate usability, effectiveness and scalability of the tool. The results of the evaluation are very encouraging, considering the complexity of the task of automating a typical visualization workflow.

The insight we gained through the evaluation is that we managed to develop an easy to follow workflow for creating visualizations for RDF data and that the suggested visualizations were indeed helpful for the participants. However, the meaningfulness of the recommendations varied depending on the selected subset of data and the data quality. One possible improvement would therefore be to provide assistance to the user not only in choosing and configuring visualizations but also in choosing a reasonable subset of data that can be visualized.

Acknowledgments. The research and implementation of this work has been conducted by the University of Bonn within the LinDA project, funded by the European Union's Seventh Framework Programme under grant agreement no 610565 and at Fraunhofer IAIS within the European Union's Horizon 2020 research and innovation programme under grant agreement no 644564 for the project BigDataEurope (http://www.big-data-europe.eu/).

References

1. Bikakis, N., Skourla, M., Papastefanatos, G.: rdf:Synopsviz - a framework for hierarchical linked data visual exploration and analysis. In: 11th Extended Semantic Web Conference (ESWC 2014) (2014)
2. Brunetti, J.M., Auer, S., García, R., Klímek, J., Nečaský, M.: Formal linked data visualization model. In: Proc. IIWAS, IIWAS 2013, pp. 309–318. ACM, NY (2013)
3. Burkard, R., Dell'Amico, M., Martello, S.: Assignment Problems, Revised Reprint: Other titles in applied mathematics. Society for Industrial and Applied Mathematics (SIAM) (2009)
4. Dadzie, A.S., Rowe, M.: Approaches to visualising linked data: A survey. Semantic Web 2(2), 89–124 (2011)
5. Höfler, P., Mutlu, B.: Code query wizard and vis wizard: Supporting exploration and analysis of linked data. ERCIM News (96) (2014)
6. Klíme, J., Helmich, J., Nečaský, M.: *Payola*: collaborative linked data analysis and visualization framework. In: Cimiano, P., Fernández, M., Lopez, V., Schlobach, S., Völker, J. (eds.) ESWC 2013. LNCS, vol. 7955, pp. 147–151. Springer, Heidelberg (2013)
7. Munkres, J.: Algorithms for the assignment and transportation problems. Journal of the Society for Industrial and Applied Mathematics 5(1), 32–38 (1957)
8. Mutlu, B., Hoefler, P., Sabol, V., Tschinkel, G., Granitzer, M.: Automated visualization support for linked research data. In: Lohmann, S. (ed.) CEUR Workshop Proceedings, vol. 1026, pp. 40–44. CEUR-WS.org (2013)
9. Nielsen, J., Landauer, T.K.: A mathematical model of the finding of usability problems. In: Proceedings of the INTERACT 1993 and CHI 1993 Conference on Human Factors in Computing Systems, pp. 206–213. ACM (1993)
10. Skjaeveland, M.G.: Sgvizler: a javascript wrapper for easy visualization of sparql result sets. In: Simperl, E., Norton, B., Mladenic, D., Della Valle, E., Fundulaki, I., Passant, A., Troncy, R. (eds.) The Semantic Web: ESWC 2012 Satellite Events, Lecture Notes in Computer Science, vol. 7540, pp. 361–365. Springer, Heidelberg (2015). http://dx.doi.org/10.1007/978-3-662-46641-4_27
11. Stevens, S.S.: On the theory of scales of measurement. Science 103, 677–680 (1946)
12. Stevens, S.S.: Measurement. In: Maranell, G.M. (ed.) Scaling; a Sourcebook for Behavioral Scientists. Aldine Publishing Company (1974)
13. Voigt, M., Pietschmann, S., Grammel, L., Meißner, K.: Context-aware recommendation of visualization components. In: 4th Int. Conf. on Information, Process, and Knowledge Management, eKNOW 2012, pp. 101–109 (2012)
14. Voigt, M., Pietschmann, S., Meißner, K.: A semantics-based, end-user-centered information visualization process for semantic web data. In: Semantic Models for Adaptive Interactive Systems, pp. 83–107. Springer (2013)

Facilitating Entity Navigation Through Top-K Link Patterns

Liang Zheng, Yuzhong Qu$^{(\boxtimes)}$, Jidong Jiang, and Gong Cheng

State Key Laboratory for Novel Software Technology, Nanjing University,
Nanjing 210023, People's Republic of China
{zhengliang,jdjiang}@smail.nju.edu.cn, {yzqu,gcheng}@nju.edu.cn

Abstract. Entity navigation over Linked Data often follows semantic links by using Linked Data browsers. With the increasing volume of Linked Data, the rich and diverse links make it difficult for users to traverse the link graph and find target entities. Besides, there is a necessity for navigation paradigm to take into account not only single-entity-oriented transition, but also entity-set-oriented transition. To facilitate entity navigation, we propose a novel concept called link pattern, and introduce link pattern lattice to organize semantic links when browsing an entity or a set of entities. Furthermore, to help users quickly find target entities, top-K link patterns are selected for entity navigation. The proposed approach is implemented in a prototype system and then compared with two Linked Data browsers via a user study. Experimental results show that our approach is effective.

Keywords: Entity navigation · Link pattern · Formal concept analysis · Link pattern selection

1 Introduction

With the advent of Linked Data, its navigational feature has been largely recognized during its use in practice. Just as traditional Web browsers allow users to navigate between HTML pages by following hypertext links, Linked Data browsers [1,8–11,15] allow users to navigate between entities by following semantic links. However, with the enrichment of available Linked Data on the Web, challenges in navigating the data space arise: large numbers of linked entities and high diversity of links among entities. For example, Steven Spielberg in DBpedia [2] is linked to 117 entities (e.g., Cincinnati, Los Angeles) through 51 semantic links (e.g., birthPlace, residence). Relying solely on link traversal, users would have to browse and choose among a potentially long list of semantic links, and synthesize information by themselves. This procedure is often time-consuming and error-prone.

Besides, there is a necessity for navigation paradigm to take into account not only single-entity-oriented transition, but also entity-set-oriented transition. Existing solutions allow users to navigate over Linked Data through common

© Springer International Publishing Switzerland 2015
M. Arenas et al. (Eds.): ISWC 2015, Part I, LNCS 9366, pp. 163–179, 2015.
DOI: 10.1007/978-3-319-25007-6_10

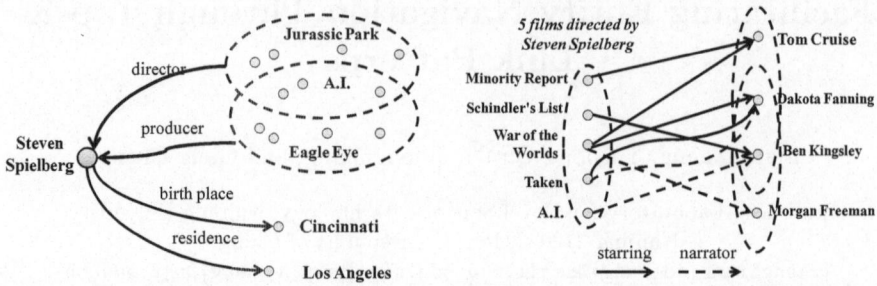

Fig. 1. The context of browsing an entity   **Fig. 2.** The context of browsing a set of entities

links [10,11]. Yet, there are many potential relationships between the current entity (entities) and its (their) related entities. As shown in Figure 1, `Steven Spielberg` is the producer and also the director of `A.I.`. As shown in Figure 2, `Tom Cruise` starred in 2 films directed by `Steven Spielberg`. Moreover, there is a hierarchical relationship among semantic links (e.g., both `residence` and `birthplace` are subproperties of `location`). These rich structural features could be leveraged to improve entity navigation.

In order to mitigate the effect of these problems and improve the efficiency of navigation, we propose a novel approach that facilitates link traversal and assists users' navigation. In our approach, a link pattern lattice is constructed to organize semantic links based on Formal Concept Analysis (FCA) [7], a methodology of data analysis and knowledge representation. Here, link pattern represents the rich semantic relationships between the current entity (entities) and its (their) related entities (e.g., "starred at least k films", "direct and also produce"). Further, there could be an inclusion relationship between link patterns. The link pattern lattice provides a visual navigation method to explore the information space [5,6]. However, users' direct interaction with the complex lattice could cause the problem of disorientation and cognitive overhead. To lighten users' navigational burden, we give a method to select top–K link patterns for entity navigation based on the Budgeted Maximum Coverage (BMC) model [12]. The contribution of this paper is summarized as follows.

- We present a novel way to organize semantic links. We propose a new notion of link pattern and give a way to construct the link pattern lattice in the context of entity browsing.
- We introduce a measure of the "goodness" of link pattern, and give a method to select top–K link patterns based on the Budgeted Maximum Coverage (BMC) model.
- We implement the proposed approach in a prototype system and compare it with two Linked Data browsers by conducting a user study. The experimental results demonstrate the effectiveness of our approach.

The remainder of this paper is structured as follows. Section 2 discusses related work. Section 3 introduces the notion of link pattern and a way to construct the link pattern lattice in the context of browsing entities. Section 4 describes an optimization method for link pattern selection. Our evaluation is reported in Section 5. Section 6 concludes this paper.

2   Related Work

Navigation as an important feature of Linked Data, has been supported by many Linked Data browsers. Tabulator [1] allows users to browse data by starting from a single resource and following links to other resources. It also allows users to select a resource for further exploration in a nest tree view. gFacet [10] is a tool that supports the exploration of the Web of data by combining graph-based visualization with faceted filtering functionalities. With gFacet it is possible to choose one class and then pivot to a related class keeping those filters for the instances of the second class connected to the filtered instances in the first class. OpenLink Faceted Search & Find Service[1], offers several paths of DBpedia data exploration, starting from Keyword, URI or Label. It represents metadata by an entity-attribute-value view. It also provides a facet filter view by selecting different attributes. Parallax [11] is one of the first browsers to offer pivoting (or set-oriented browsing) but it is originally tied to Freebase. It shows the set of resources, accompanied by a list of facets for filtering. It also provides a list of connections, showing those properties that can be used in a pivoting operation. VisiNav [9] is a system based on an interaction model designed to easily search and navigate large amounts of Web data. It provides four atomic operations over object structured datasets: keyword search, object focus, path traversal, and facet specification. Users incrementally assemble complex queries that yield sets of objects. Rhizomer [8] addresses the exploration of semantic data by applying the data analysis mantra of overview, zoom and filter. Users can interactively explore the data using facets. Moreover, facets also feature a pivoting operation. Visor [15] is a generic RDF data explorer that can work over SPARQL endpoints. In Visor, exploration starts by selecting a class of interest from the ontology. Then, users can pivot to related collections and continue browsing. Visor provides a hierarchical overview of the collections and also provides a spreadsheet requiring manual customization to filter the collection.

Whereas the above efforts mainly focus on providing the user with powerful interaction modes, we aim to appropriately organize and select links, which is complementary to all of them.

3   Link Pattern Lattice Construction

This section introduces link pattern lattice for organizing semantic links based on Formal Concept Analysis (FCA) [7]. First, we formally define the notion of link pattern in Section 3.1 and introduce FCA in Section 3.2. Then we construct link pattern lattice in our context in Section 3.3.

---

[1] http://dbpedia.org/fct/

3.1 Link Pattern

Let U be a set of URI named entities and L be a set of links including object properties, property chains and inverse of them. In the implementation of this study, we only consider those links that directly connect entities or indirectly connect entities through blank nodes. A link graph $T \subseteq U \times L \times U$ is a set of triples. There is a partial ordering $\preceq$ on L, which is deduced from rdfs:subPropertyOf relationship.

Definition 1 (Link Pattern with Minimum Number Restriction). *Let T be a link graph, k be a positive integer, $l \in L$. A link pattern of l with minimum k restriction, denoted by $LP((min\ k),\ l)$, is a function from 2^U to 2^U such that*
$$LP((min\ k),\ l)(S) = \{v \in U \mid |\{u \in S \mid (u, l, v) \in T\}| \geq k\}\ for\ S \subseteq U.$$

The link pattern $LP((min\ k),\ l)$ is proposed to express the degree of connection between current entities and target entities. For simplicity, we use $(min\ k)l$ to denote $LP((min\ k),\ l)$. Note that $(min\ 1)l$ represents the same meaning as the traditional link l. We abbreviate $(min\ 1)l$ to l.

In Figure 1, $E_1 = \{$Steven Spielberg$\}$. $director^{-1}(E_1) \supseteq \{$A.I., Jurassic Park$\}$.[2] $producer^{-1}(E_1) \supseteq \{$A.I., Eagle Eye$\}$. In Figure 2, $E_2 = \{$War of the Worlds, Taken, A.I., Minority Report, Schindler's List$\}$, $S=\{$War of the Worlds, Taken, A.I.$\} \subseteq E_2$, $narrator(S)=\{$Dakota Fanning, Ben Kingsley, Morgan Freeman$\}$. $((min\ 2)starring)(S) = \{$Dakota Fanning$\}$, which represents that Dakota Fanning starred at least 2 films in S.

Definition 2 (Conjunctive Link Pattern). *Given two link patterns LP_1 and LP_2, the conjunctive link pattern of LP_1 and LP_2, denoted by $LP_1 \wedge LP_2$, is a function from 2^U to 2^U such that*
$$(LP_1 \wedge LP_2)(S) = LP_1(S) \cap LP_2(S)\ for\ S \subseteq U.$$

In Figure 1, $(director^{-1} \wedge producer^{-1})(E_1) \supseteq \{$A.I.$\}$, which represents that Steven Spielberg is the producer and also the director of A.I.. In Figure 2, $(narrator \wedge ((min\ 2)starring))(S)=\{$Dakota Fanning$\}$, which represents Dakota Fanning narrated at least 1 film and also starred at least 2 films in S.

In this paper, a link pattern can be a link pattern with minimum number restriction or a conjunctive link pattern. Besides, link patterns with minimum number restriction can be called atomic link patterns.

Definition 3 (Sub-pattern Relationship). *Given two link patterns LP_1 and LP_2, LP_1 is called a sub-pattern of LP_2, denoted by $LP_1 \subseteq LP_2$, if $LP_1(S) \subseteq LP_2(S)$ holds for every subset S of U.*

We have the following proposition, the proof of which can be easily obtained from the definition of sub-pattern and the inference rule for rdfs:subPropertyOf.

---

[2] We use l^{-1} to denote the inverse of link l.

Proposition 1. *Let l, l_1, $l_2 \in L$, k, k_1, $k_2 \in Z^+$, and then we have*

1. *if $k_1 \leq k_2$, then $(min\ k_2)l \subseteq (min\ k_1)l$.*
2. *if $l_1 \preceq l_2$, then $(min\ k)l_1 \subseteq (min\ k)l_2$.*

3.2 Formal Concept Analysis

In FCA [7], there are three main concepts: formal context, formal concept and concept lattice.

Definition 4 (Formal Context K). *A formal context is a triple $K=(G, M, I)$, where G denotes a set of objects, M a set of attributes, and $I \subseteq G \times M$ a binary relation between G and M. The statement $(g, m) \in I$ is interpreted as "the object g has attribute m". The two derivation operators $(\cdot)'$ define a Galois connection between the powersets $(2^G, \subseteq)$ and $(2^M, \subseteq)$: $A' = \{m \in M \mid \forall\ g \in A : (g, m) \in I\}$ for $A \subseteq G$, and $B' = \{g \in G \mid \forall\ m \in B : (g, m) \in I\}$ for $B \subseteq M$.*

Definition 5 (Formal Concept c). *Given a formal context $K=(G, M, I)$ and $A \subseteq G$, $B \subseteq M$, a pair $c= (A, B)$ satisfying $A' = B$ and $B' = A$, is called a formal concept of K. A and B are called the extent and intent of c, respectively.*

A partial ordering $\preceq$ over the concepts C of K can be defined as follows: $(A_1, B_1) \preceq (A_2, B_2) \iff A_1 \subseteq A_2\ (\iff B_2 \subseteq B_1)$.

For two concepts c_1 and c_2, if $c_1 \preceq c_2$ and there is no concept c_3 with $c_3 \neq c_1$, $c_3 \neq c_2$, $c_1 \preceq c_3 \preceq c_2$, then c_1 is called a child of c_2, and c_2 is called a parent of c_1. This relationship is denoted by $c_1 \prec c_2$.

Definition 6 (Concept Lattice L). *With respect to a formal context K and the partial order $\prec$, the concepts in C constitute a lattice, called the concept lattice of K.*

3.3 Link Pattern Lattice Construction Using FCA

FCA is a mathematically well founded classification framework allowing to derive implicit relationships from a set of objects and their attributes. We construct link pattern lattice by using FCA. The construction process includes two steps: constructing a formal context K and generating a link pattern lattice of K.

Firstly, given a link graph $T \subseteq U \times L \times U$ and a set of entities $S \subseteq U$ being the focus, we consider the set of links $L' = \{l \in L | \exists u \in S, \exists v \in U, (u, l, v) \in T\}$. A formal context $K = (G, M, I)$ in FCA can be defined as follows: $G = \{v \in U | \exists u \in S, \exists l \in L, (u, l, v) \in T\}$ denotes the set of linked entities. M is a subset of atomic link patterns, i.e., the attributes in M take the form $(min\ k)l$. $I \subseteq G \times M$, $(v, (min\ k)l) \in I$ iff $v \in ((min\ k)l)(S)$, which means there are at least k entities in S having link l to v. The algorithm for constructing a formal context K is in Algorithm 1. Line 3 generates G and line 8-14 generate M and I.

Secondly, we choose a well-known lattice generation algorithm called Bordat [3], which produces both the concepts and the concept lattice. The worst-case running time of Bordat is $O(|G||M|^2|N|)$, where $|N|$ is the number of link patterns in the resulting lattice. We will show the running time on real-life data in our experiments.

With the following examples, we illustrate how to use FCA to construct link pattern lattice in two cases: single-entity-oriented and entity-set-oriented transitions.

Algorithm 1. Construct Formal Context

Input: T: a link graph; S: a set of entities
Output: K: a formal context

1 Initialize a formal context $K = (G, M, I)$, $G \leftarrow \emptyset$, $M \leftarrow \emptyset$, $I \leftarrow \emptyset$;
2 $L' \leftarrow \{l \in L | \exists u \in S, \exists v \in U, (u, l, v) \in T\}$;
3 $G \leftarrow \{v \in U | \exists u \in S, \exists l \in L, (u, l, v) \in T\}$;
4 **foreach** $l \in L'$ **do**
5 $\quad$ Find each sup-link l_{sup} of l;
6 $\quad$ **if** $l_{sup} \notin L'$ **then**
7 $\quad\quad$ $L' \leftarrow L' \cup \{l_{sup}\}$, $T \leftarrow T \cup \{(u, l_{sup}, v) | \exists u \in S, \exists v \in U, (u, l, v) \in T\}$;

8 **foreach** $l \in L'$ **do**
9 $\quad$ **foreach** $v \in G$ **do**
10 $\quad\quad$ $k = |\{u \in S | (u, l, v) \in T\}|$;
11 $\quad\quad$ **if** $k > 0$ **then**
12 $\quad\quad\quad$ **for** $i \leftarrow 1$ **to** k **do**
13 $\quad\quad\quad\quad$ $M \leftarrow M \cup \{(min\ i)l\}$;
14 $\quad\quad\quad\quad$ $I \leftarrow I \cup \{(v, (min\ i)l)\}$.

15 **return** K;

Single-Entity-Oriented. Suppose a user is viewing the RDF description of Steven Spielberg, as shown in Figure 1. In this case $E_1 = \{$Steven Spielberg$\}$ be the focus, the linked entity set $G = \{$A.I., Jurassic Park, Eagle Eye, Cincinnati, Los Angeles$\}$, and the semantic links $L' = \{director^{-1}, producer^{-1}, birthPlace, residence\}$. Moreover, there is a subLinkOf hierarchy among these links in Figure 3. The link $participator^{-1}$ and $location$ are added to L'.

For each link $l \in L'$, we obtain the link patterns of l with minimum k restriction. k is equal to 1 in the single-entity-oriented transition. The atomic link patterns $M = \{director^{-1}, producer^{-1}, participator^{-1}, birthPlace, residence, location\}$. The formal context K is shown in Table 1.

We have $\{director^{-1}, producer^{-1}, participator^{-1}\}' = \{$A.I.$\}$ and $\{$A.I.$\}' = \{director^{-1}, producer^{-1}, participator^{-1}\}$. $\{$A.I.$\}$ and $\{director^{-1}, producer^{-1}, participator^{-1}\}$ satisfy a Galois connection. According to Definition 5, $(\{$A.I.$\}, \{director^{-1}, producer^{-1}, participator^{-1}\})$ is a formal concept emerging from Table 1. Its intent $\{director^{-1}, producer^{-1}, participator^{-1}\}$ represents a conjunctive link pattern.

Figure 4 shows the link pattern lattice associated with Table 1. In the diagram, each node denotes a link pattern while edges reflect the partial ordering $\prec$ between link patterns.

Table 1. An example of formal context

	$director^{-1}$	$producer^{-1}$	$participator^{-1}$	$birthPlace$	$residence$	$location$
A.I.	×	×	×			
Jurassic Park	×		×			
Eagle Eye		×	×			
Cincinnati				×		×
Los Angeles					×	×

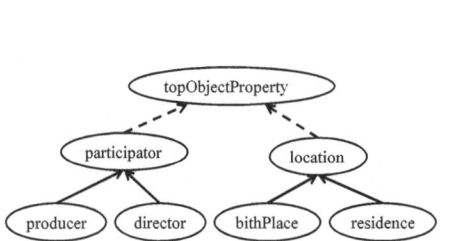
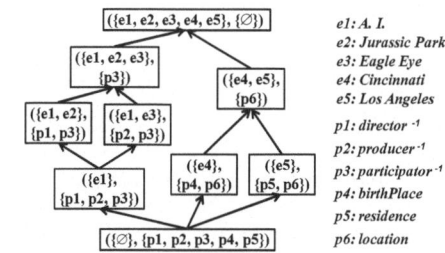

Fig. 3. An example of link hierarchy

Fig. 4. Link pattern lattice associated with Table 1.

Entity-Set-Oriented. Suppose the user explores the films directed by `Steven Spielberg` by following a `director` link, as shown in Figure 2. In this case $E_2 = \{$`War of the Worlds, Taken, A.I., Minority Report, Schindler's List`$\}$ be the focus, the semantic links $L' = \{$`starring, narrator`$\}$ and the linked entity set $G = \{$`Tom Cruise, Dakota Fanning, Ben Kingsley, Morgan Freeman`$\}$. Note that the atomic link patterns $M = \{starring, (min\ 2)starring, narrator\}$. The formal context K is shown in Table 2.

($\{$`Dakota Fanning, Ben Kingsley`$\}, \{starring, narrator\}$) is a formal concept emerging from Table 2. Its intent $\{starring, narrator\}$ represents a conjunctive link pattern. Besides, ($\{$`Dakota Fanning`$\}, \{starring, (min\ 2)starring, narrator\}$) is another concept of this context. Furthermore, we have ($\{$`Dakota Fanning`$\}, \{starring, (min\ 2)starring, narrator\}$) $\prec$ ($\{$`Dakota Fanning, Ben Kingsley`$\}, \{starring, narrator\}$). The link pattern lattice for Table 2 is shown in Figure 5.

4   Link Pattern Selection

A link pattern lattice provides a multi-granular, progressive navigation assistance. In some cases, the lattice may have a complex structure so that users feel disoriented and require several interactions to arrive at target entities.

For lightening users' burden, we give a method to select top–K link patterns from lattice to enable users to find target entities more quickly. Firstly, we introduce three metrics to measure the "goodness" of link patterns in Section 4.1. Then we select top–K link patterns that are as "good" as possible while being able to retrieve as many linked entities as possible in Section 4.2.

Table 2. An example of formal context

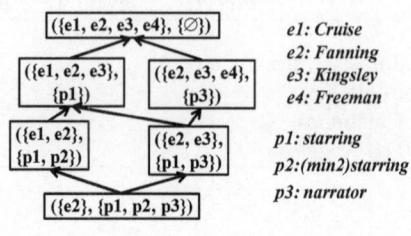

	starring	(min2)starring	narrator
Cruise	×	×	
Fanning	×	×	×
Kingsley	×		×
Freeman			×

e1: Cruise
e2: Fanning
e3: Kingsley
e4: Freeman

p1: starring
p2:(min2)starring
p3: narrator

Fig. 5. Link pattern lattice for Table 2.

4.1 Metrics of Link Pattern

Given a link pattern lattice LPL of a formal context $K = (G, M, I)$ and a link pattern c, the "goodness" of link pattern c can be defined from various perspectives. In this paper, we prefer to provide informative (measured by informativeness), understandable (measured by conciseness) and specific (measured by specificness) link patterns.

Informativeness. As to link patterns, the idea is that a link pattern having fewer reachable linked entities is more informative. We compute the self-information of the link pattern c using information theory [13],

$$info(c) = -\log pr(c),$$
$$pr(c) = \frac{|ext(c)|}{|G|}. \tag{1}$$

$ext(c)$ is the extent of c. G is the set of linked entities in K. Further, we normalize $info(c)$ into the range $[0, 1]$ as the *informativeness* of link pattern c:

$$info_K(c) = \frac{info(c)}{\log|G|}. \tag{2}$$

Conciseness. In practice, we use the label of the intent of link pattern c as a "road sign" in users' navigation (e.g., $director^{-1} \wedge producer^{-1} \wedge participator^{-1}$). The longer the lengths of intents become, involving many links at various levels of generality, the harder it becomes to understand what the link patterns mean or represent.

A concise link pattern having a shorter label is more understandable and preferable. So, we formalize the conciseness of link pattern c as follows:

$$conc(c) = a^{-(|inte(c)|-1)} \quad (a > 1).$$ (3)

$inte(c)$ is the intent of c and the value of $conc(c)$ is in the range $(0, 1]$.

Specificness. As shown in Figure 4, the link pattern lattice LPL provides a hierarchy among link patterns. The depth of link pattern in the hierarchy is useful. The larger the depth of link pattern is, the more specific the link pattern is. We measure the depth of link pattern c:

$$depth(c) = distance(a, c),$$ (4)

where $distance(a, c)$ is the length of a shortest path from a (the greatest element of LPL) to c. Further, we normalize $depth(c)$ into the range $[0, 1]$ as the *specificness* of link pattern c:

$$spec(c) = \frac{depth(c)}{D(c)},$$ (5)
$$D(c) = distance(a, c, b).$$

$distance(a, c, b)$ is the length of a shortest path from a, through c, to b (the least element of LPL).

4.2 Selecting Link Patterns

For diversity and coverage considerations, we aim to select top–K link patterns that are as informative, concise and specific as possible while being able to retrieve as many linked entities as possible.

Our problem can be formalized based on the Budgeted Maximum Coverage (BMC) model [12]. The BMC problem is defined as follows: Let $S = \{S_1, S_2, \ldots, S_m\}$ be a collection of sets defined over a domain of elements $X = \{x_1, x_2, \ldots, x_n\}$. Each set has a cost $\{c_i\}_{i=1}^m$ while each element has a weight $\{w_i\}_{i=1}^n$. The goal is to find a collection of sets $S' \subseteq S$, such that the total cost of S', denoted by $c(S')$, does not exceed a given budget B, while the total weight of elements covered by S', denoted by $w(S')$, is maximized. $c(S')$ and $w(S')$ are defined as follows:

$$c(S') = \sum_{S_i \in S'} c_i,$$ (6)

$$w(S') = \sum_{j=1}^{n} (w_j \cdot f(x_j, S')\}),$$ (7)

where

$$f(x_j, S') = \begin{cases} 1 & \text{if } x_j \text{ is covered by } S'. \\ 0 & \text{otherwise.} \end{cases}$$ (8)

In our context, each link pattern can be considered as a set $S_i \in S$ and all the linked entities as the elements X. The weight of each element is trivially set to 1. The cost of S_i is defined as follows:

$$c_i = \left(\frac{1}{e}\right)^{\sigma(S_i)}. \tag{9}$$

$\sigma(S_i)$ is a scoring function of link pattern S_i as follows:

$$\sigma(S_i) = \alpha_1 \cdot info_K(S_i) + \alpha_2 \cdot conc(S_i) + \alpha_3 \cdot spec(S_i), \tag{10}$$

where $\alpha_1, \alpha_2, \alpha_3 \in [0, 1]$ indicate the weights for each metric to be tuned empirically. According to Equation (9), the higher the score of a link pattern is, the less the cost is.

BMC is an NP-hard problem and several efficient approximation algorithms have been developed. By comparing the approximation ratio and the time complexity of these algorithms, we use the $\frac{1}{2} \cdot (1 - \frac{1}{e})$ approximation algorithm with time complexity $O(m^2 n)$ provided by [12] in our implementation.

5   Evaluation

In this section, we first present the frequency distribution of link patterns in two real-life datasets (Section 5.1). Then, we describe an overview of the prototype system (Section 5.2) and compare it with two Linked Data browsers by conducting a user study in section 5.3. Finally, we evaluate the performance of our approach by measuring the average execution time in section 5.4.

5.1   Data Sets

This section aims to show that *minimum number restriction* and *conjunctive* link patterns do exist widely in real-life data sets such as DBpedia[3] and Semantic Web Dog Food[4].

Data Collection. As to DBpedia, we used the DBpedia *mapping-based properties* dataset, excluding RDF triples containing literals. We selected 8 classes (i.e., Scientist, Artist, Athlete, City, River, Company, University, Film).

For each class, we firstly collected the top 1000 entities according to descending order of the number of their related entities (i.e., the degree of node in RDF graph). Secondly, we established 100 entity sets and each set included 10 entities by selecting at random from these 1000 entities. Finally, we calculated the percentage of entity sets having *minimum number restriction (k >1)* and *conjunctive* link patterns in these 100 entity sets.

As to Semantic Web Dog Food, we firstly selected 3 classes: Person (7,180 entities), Organization (1,965 entities) and Conference (20 entities). For the first two classes, we collected the top 100 entities (using the same method as above).

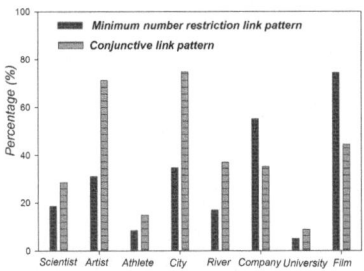

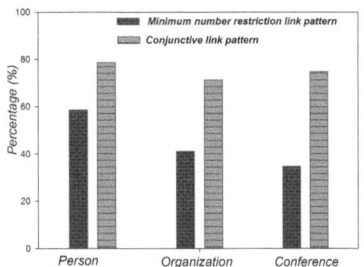

Fig. 6. Link patterns in DBpedia.   **Fig. 7.** Link patterns in Semantic Web Dog Food.

For Conference, we collected all the entities. Secondly, we established entity sets for each class. For Person and Organization, we established 10 entity sets and each set included 10 entities by selecting at random from these 100 entities. For Conference, we established 5 entity sets and each set included 4 entities by selecting at random from these 20 entities. The method calculating the frequency distribution of link patterns was the same as above.

Data Analysis. In Figure 6, *minimum number restriction* link patterns (e.g., $(min\ k)distributor$, $(min\ k)developer^{-1}$) are found in more than 50% of Film and Company entity sets. Artist and City have more *conjunctive* link patterns (e.g., $occupation \wedge foundedBy^{-1}$, $birthPlace \wedge residence$), which occupied 70% of entity sets.

In Figure 7, around 60% of entity sets of Person have *minimum number restriction* link patterns (e.g., $(min\ k)made$, $(min\ k)based\_near$). Every class has more *conjunctive* link patterns (e.g., $made \wedge author^{-1}$, $affiliation^{-1} \wedge member$).

In summary, we investigate entities having the largest number of linked entities in two datasets because the above link patterns are more likely to be observed there. As expected *minimum number restriction* and *conjunctive* link patterns exist widely in many classes, which can be used to improve entity navigation.

5.2   Overview of Prototype

We implemented our proposed approach as a navigation module (called "Link") in a Link Data browser, SView[5]. Figure 8 shows a screenshot of "Link" in SView.

Users can start browsing with an entity URI by entering into the input box (A). Navigation was provided in the "Link" panel. The left-hand side of the interface lists the label of link patterns (B). The right-hand side lists linked entities (C). Users can click the button "browse all" to explore all the linked entities (D). Also, users can choose some link patterns to filter the target entities (E).

---

[3] http://wiki.dbpedia.org/Downloads2014

[4] http://data.semanticweb.org/

[5] http://ws.nju.edu.cn/sview/

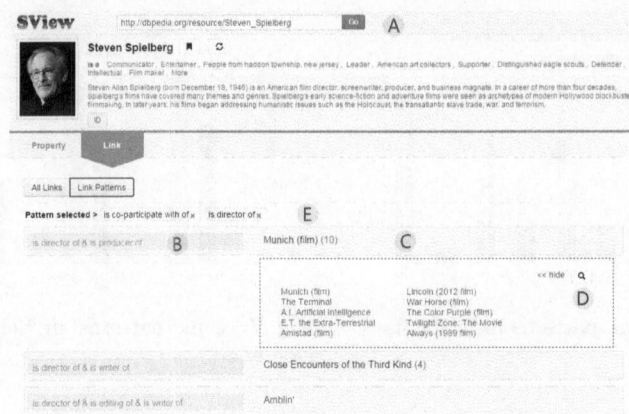

Fig. 8. A screenshot of "Link" in SView.

5.3   User Study

We conducted a user study to compare our approach with two Linked Data browsers (i.e., OpenLink Faceted Search & Find Service, Rhizomer[6]), and to evaluate the effectiveness of our approach.

Table 3. An example of navigation tasks about `Steven Spielberg`

	Tasks
G1	*E1* Explore the information related to `Steven Spielberg`.
	F1 Find the films directed and also produced by `Steven Spielberg`.
G2	*E2* Explore the information related to the films directed by `Steven Spielberg`.
	F2 Find the actors starred in at least 2 films directed by `Steven Spielberg`.

Participant Systems. As reviewed in the Related Work section, the only active tools capable of entity-set-oriented browsing are gFacet, Parallax, OpenLink Faceted Search & Find Service, Rhizomer and Visor. We did not include Visor and gFacet because their interfaces are based on graphs. We did not consider Parallax because it only tied to Freebase. OpenLink Faceted Search & Find Service and Rhizomer provide a user interface with HTML and components similar to those we propose.

Tasks. In a browsing scenario, navigation tasks can be divided into two types: *Explore* (a user has a fuzzy need) and *Find* (a user has a clear need) tasks [14, 16]. According to navigation paradigm, tasks can also be divided into two groups: single-entity-oriented (*G1*) and entity-set-oriented (*G2*) tasks.

---

[6] http://rhizomik.net/html/rhizomer/

We used 8 classes of entities from DBpedia dataset in section 5.1. For each class, we selected 10 entities from the top 1000 entities at random as the starting points of user navigation. For each starting point, we established 4 navigation tasks. The navigation tasks about `Steven Spielberg` is shown in Table 3.

Procedure. The subjects consisted of 24 students majoring in computer science who were familiar with the Web, but with no knowledge of our project. The evaluation was conducted in three phases.

Table 4. Navigation questionnaire

	Questions
Q1:	The number of navigation options (links) was overwhelming.
Q2:	The navigation options (links) were well organized.
Q3:	The navigation option (link) titles were understood well.
Q4:	The navigation options (links) were pleasantly surprising.
Q5:	It was easy to reorient myself in the navigation.

Table 5. Results of navigation questionnaire

	Response: Mean (SD)			$F(2,69)$	LSD post-hoc
	OpenLink	Rhizomer	SView	(p-value)	($p < 0.05$)
Q1:	3.919 (0.717)	3.75 (0.854)	2.667 (1.095)	21.643 (0.000)	OpenLink, Rhizomer > SView
Q2:	3.026 (1.052)	3.24 (1.014)	4.11 (0.887)	13.580 (0.000)	SView > OpenLink, Rhizomer
Q3:	3.833 (0.717)	4.00 (0.582)	2.583 (0.62)	9.658 (0.000)	Rhizomer, OpenLink > SView
Q4:	2.58 (0.793)	3.25 (1.055)	4.33 (0.778)	11.958 (0.000)	SView > OpenLink, Rhizomer
Q5:	3.917 (0.514)	3.667 (0.778)	3.5 (0.937)	11.367 (0.000)	OpenLink > Rhizomer, SView

First, the subjects learned how to use the given systems through a 20 min tutorial, and had additional 10 minutes for free use and questions. Second, the subjects used each of the three systems arranged in random order. For each system, the subjects were randomly assigned to one starting point, and required to complete 4 navigation tasks. Meanwhile, the starting points of user navigation among the three systems were different. The subjects were asked to complete all the tasks in 30 minutes. We recorded their answers, and the time they spent on each task.

With regard to each system, the subjects responded to the navigation questionnaire, as shown in Table 4. Then, for each system, the subjects responded to the widely-used system usability scale (SUS) questionnaire [4]. The questions in the two above questionnaires were responded by using a five-point Likert scale ranging from 1 (strongly disagree) to 5 (strongly agree). Finally, the subjects were asked to comment on the three systems.

Results and Discussion

User Experience. Navigation questionnaire Q1–Q5 captured subjects' navigation experience with different systems in Table 5. Repeated measures ANOVA revealed that the differences in subjects' mean ratings were all statistically significant ($p < 0.01$). LSD post-hoc tests ($p < 0.05$) revealed that, according to Q1, OpenLink and Rhizomer provided too many links compared with SView. According to Q2, SView provided a better organization of links than OpenLink and Rhizomer. According to Q3, OpenLink and Rhizomer helped subjects more easily understand the label of links. According to Q4, SView directly provided subjects with more interesting relationships among the entities. Finally, according to Q5, OpenLink and Rhizomer helped subjects keep track of browsing and provided easy rollback.

Table 6 summarizes SUS scores of different systems. Repeated measures ANOVA revealed that the difference in SUS score was statistically significant ($p < 0.05$). LSD post-hoc tests ($p < 0.05$) revealed that SView was more usable than OpenLink and Rhizomer.

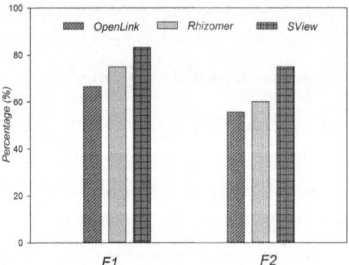

Fig. 9. Success rate of *Find* tasks.

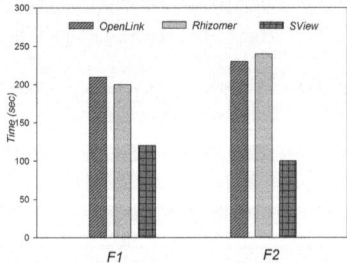

Fig. 10. Average consumption time of *Find* tasks.

Table 6. SUS scores

Mean (SD)			$F(2, 69)$	LSD post-hoc
OpenLink	Rhizomer	SView	(p-value)	($p < 0.05$)
59.62	67.31	75	10.195	SView > Rhizomer > OpenLink
(9.177)	(9.098)	(7.706)	(0.001)	

User Behavior. Figure 9 shows the success rate of *Find* tasks. In F1, using SView, subjects achieved the highest overall success rate. In F2, the situation was similar. Figure 10 shows the average time spent on *Find* tasks. According to F1 and F2, using SView, subjects required far less time to complete these tasks, because links were appropriately organized and selected.

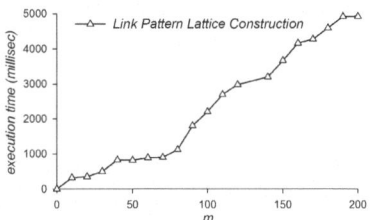
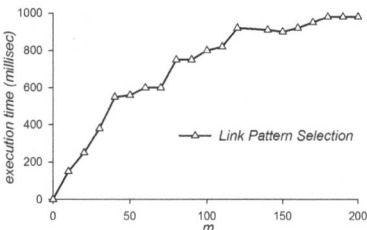

Fig. 11. Execution time of link pattern lattice construction.

Fig. 12. Execution time of link pattern selection.

User Feedback and Discussion. We summarized all the major comments that were made by at least five subjects. On OpenLink, 21 subjects (88%) said the large quantities of links often made it difficult to retrieve the target entities. 17 subjects (71%) said the browsing track assisted them to browse intermediate entities. On Rhizomer, 20 subjects (83%) said faceted navigation helped them filter out those entities that were not interesting. On SView, 22 subjects (92%) said recommended patterns provided a fast locating mechanism, but 6 subjects (25%) said it had some potential risks, such as target losses (i.e., not covering all the needed entities). 10 subjects (42%) said the diverse link patterns made users know more potential relationships among the entities, but 8 subjects (33%) said some link pattern labels were too long to be understood.

5.4   Performance Evaluation

We evaluated the performance of link pattern lattice construction and link pattern selection by measuring the average execution time for varying number of current entities denoted by m (m from 5 to 200). The two algorithms were implemented in Java and carried out on an Intel Xeon E3 3.2GHz CPU, Windows 7 with 10GB JVM.

As can be seen from Figure 11 and Figure 12, the two algorithms were reasonably fast in practice. When m increased, the curves of the two algorithms kept ascend slowly. In Figure 11, it took 2 seconds to construct a lattice for 80 current entities, and 5 seconds for 200 current entities.

6   Conclusion

In this paper, we propose a novel concept called link pattern, in particular link pattern with minimum number restriction as well as conjunctive link pattern. It enables a new way of semantic navigation over linked entities. We also describe how to generate link pattern lattice and how to select top-K link patterns in the context of entity browsing. The proposed approach is implemented in a prototype system. The evaluation results demonstrate that link patterns effectively make explicit complex relationships among entities, and help users discover target entities more quickly.

Currently, link patterns are generated based on the "local" context, i.e. the data about current entities being visited. It is interesting to consider a way to extract link patterns from the "global" context, i.e. the Web of Data. Another future work is to study "human factors" in the context of entity navigation. For example, users' preference on link patterns can be collected and then leveraged to select patterns more intelligently.

Acknowledgments. This work is supported by the 863 Program under Grant 2015AA015406, in part by the National Science Foundation of China under Grant Nos. 61170068, and in part by National Social Science Foundation of China under Grant 11AZD121 and JSNSF under Grant BK2012723. We are also grateful to all the participants in the experiments of this work.

References

1. Berners-lee, T., Chen, Y., Chilton, L., Connolly, D., Dhanaraj, R., Hollenbach, J., Lerer, A., Sheets, D.: Tabulator: exploring and analyzing linked data on the semantic web. In: 3rd International Semantic Web User Interaction Workshop (2006)
2. Bizer, C., Lehmann, J., Kobilarov, G., Auer, S., Becker, C., Cyganiak, R., Hellmann, S.: DBpedia-A crystallization point for the Web of Data. J. Web Sem. **7**(3), 154–165 (2009)
3. Bordat, J.P.: Calcul pratique du treillis de Galois dune correspondance. Math. Sci. Hum. **96**, 31–47 (1986)
4. Brooke, J.: SUS-A quick and dirty usability scale. Usability evaluation in industry **189**(194), 4–7 (1996)
5. Carpineto, C., Romano, G., Bordoni, F.U.: Exploiting the Potential of Concept Lattices for Information Retrieval with CREDO. J. UCS. **10**(8), 985–1013 (2004)
6. Ferre, S.: Camelis: a logical information system to organise and browse a collection of documents. International Journal of General Systems **38**(4), 379–403 (2009)
7. Ganter, B., Wille, R.: Formal Concept Analysis: Mathematical Foundations. Springer, Berlin (1999)
8. Garcia, R., Gimeno, J.M., Perdrix, F., et al.: Building a usable and accessible semantic web interaction platform. World Wide Web **13**(1–2), 143–167 (2010)
9. Harth, A.: VisiNav: A system for visual search and navigation on web data. J. Web Sem. **8**(4), 348–354 (2010)
10. Heim, P., Ertl, T., Ziegler, J.: Facet graphs: complex semantic querying made easy. In: Aroyo, L., Antoniou, G., Hyvönen, E., ten Teije, A., Stuckenschmidt, H., Cabral, L., Tudorache, T. (eds.) ESWC 2010. LNCS, vol. 6088, pp. 288–302. Springer, Heidelberg (2010)

11. Huynh, D.F., Karger, D.: Parallax and companion: set-based browsing for the data web. In: 18th International World Wide Web Conference. ACM, Madrid (2009)
12. Khuller, S., Moss, A., Naor, J.: The budgeted maximum coverage problem. Information Processing Letters **70**(1), 39–45 (1999)
13. Manning, C.D., Raghavan, P., Schütze, H.: Introduction to information retrieval. Cambridge University Press (2008)
14. Pandit, S., Olston, C.: Navigation aided retrieval. In: 16th International Conference on World Wide Web, pp. 391–400. ACM, New York (2007)
15. Popov, I.O., Schraefel, M.C., Hall, W., Shadbolt, N.: Connecting the dots: a multi-pivot approach to data exploration. In: Aroyo, L., Welty, C., Alani, H., Taylor, J., Bernstein, A., Kagal, L., Noy, N., Blomqvist, E. (eds.) ISWC 2011, Part I. LNCS, vol. 7031, pp. 553–568. Springer, Heidelberg (2011)
16. Wagner, A., Ladwig, G., Tran, T.: Browsing-oriented semantic faceted search. In: Hameurlain, A., Liddle, S.W., Schewe, K.-D., Zhou, X. (eds.) DEXA 2011, Part I. LNCS, vol. 6860, pp. 303–319. Springer, Heidelberg (2011)

Serving DBpedia with DOLCE – More than Just Adding a Cherry on Top

Heiko Paulheim[1]($\boxtimes$) and Aldo Gangemi[2,3]

[1] Research Group Data and Web Science, University of Mannheim,
Mannheim, Germany
heiko@informatik.uni-mannheim.de
[2] Université Paris 13 - Sorbonne Paris Cité - CNRS, Paris, France
[3] STLab, ISTC-CNR, Rome, Italy
aldo.gangemi@lipn.univ-paris13.fr

Abstract. Large knowledge bases, such as DBpedia, are most often created heuristically due to scalability issues. In the building process, both random as well as systematic errors may occur. In this paper, we focus on finding *systematic* errors, or *anti-patterns*, in DBpedia. We show that by aligning the DBpedia ontology to the foundational ontology DOLCE-Zero, and by combining reasoning and clustering of the reasoning results, errors affecting millions of statements can be identified at a minimal workload for the knowledge base designer.

Keywords: Data quality · Formal ontologies · Foundational ontologies · Anti-pattern · DBpedia · DOLCE

1 Introduction

For the creation of large-scale knowledge bases, like DBpedia [18], there is often a trade off between coverage and precision. They cannot be curated manually, but only created by applying heuristic methods. Since those heuristics are most often not 100% exact, the resulting knowledge bases are not free of errors.

In this paper, we concentrate on *DBpedia*, which is a large-scale, cross domain knowledge base created from Wikipedia. To that end, Wikipedia infoboxes are mapped to a central ontology in a crowd-sourced process. Those mappings are then used to extract the DBpedia knowledge base from Wikipedia dumps. In the past years, DBpedia has become one of the central hubs of the Linked Open Data (LOD) cloud [27], with many applications using DBpedia for various purposes.

Due to the importance of DBpedia both as a linking hub in the LOD cloud, as well as a knowledge base for various applications, many works have been proposed in the recent past which target the improvement of the data in DBpedia. However, most of those approaches target at identifying *individual* errors, i.e., statements which are likely to be wrong. In contrast, in this paper, we aim at the identification of *systematic* errors, such as shortcomings of the heuristics used, or wrong mappings. Systematic errors are sets of individual errors following a similar pattern and having a common root cause (e.g., a wrong mapping).

© Springer International Publishing Switzerland 2015
M. Arenas et al. (Eds.): ISWC 2015, Part I, LNCS 9366, pp. 180–196, 2015.
DOI: 10.1007/978-3-319-25007-6_11

Since DBpedia version 3.9, released in 2013, mappings of the DBpedia ontology to DOLCE-Zero [9,11], a subset of the modules of the formal ontology DOLCE, are included in the DBpedia ontology. We exploit those mappings to identify conflicting statements in DBpedia with the help of a reasoner, and use clustering to extract common patterns in the justifications. We find that in many cases, each cluster is related to a particular problem in the construction of the DBpedia knowledge base. While DOLCE has been used for improving several ontologies on the T-Box (i.e., terminological) level, this work is novel since it does not solely aim at improving the T-Box, but also the construction of the A-Box (assertional level) of a large-scale knowledge base.

The rest of this paper is structured as follows. In section 2, we review related works both w.r.t. debugging knowledge bases such as DBpedia, as well as the use of formal top level ontologies for improving such knowledge bases. We introduce our approach in section 3. An evaluation is carried out in section 4 by examining the results as well as quantifying the influence of DOLCE-Zero, and by analyzing the largest clusters identified and a sample from the long tail of non-clustered statements. We show that both views lead to the identification of a number of issues in DBpedia by inspecting only a very small fraction of selected statements. We conclude with a summary and an outlook on future work.

2   Related Work

In this paper, we target the identification of *systematic errors* in the construction of the large-scale knowledge base DBpedia. More specifically, we consider the identification of wrong relation assertions between two individuals.

There is a larger body of work which targets at finding errors in web knowledge bases such as DBpedia. The approaches vary both with respect to the methods employed as well as to the targeted type of assertions – i.e., identifying wrong type assertions, relational assertions, literals, etc.

Methods found in the literature range from statistical methods [24] and outlier detection [6,22,34] to using external methods, such as web search engines [17]. In addition, crowdsourcing [1] and games with a purpose [32] have been proposed as non-automatic means for identifying errors in knowledge bases.

In this paper, we propose the use of reasoning, in combination with further processing of the reasoning results by means of data mining. The DBpedia ontology – as many schemas used for providing Linked Open Data – is not very expressive, in particular with respect to the presence of disjointness axioms. Thus, there is a natural limitation for reasoning-based approaches. Hence, such approaches are often combined with ontology learning as a preprocessing step to enrich the ontology at hand [16,19,31]. In contrast to those approaches, we exploit the links to the foundational ontology DOLCE-Zero, and the high-level disjointness axioms defined therein.

This approach has been applied in the past, starting from the creation of the DOLCE foundational ontology in 2002 [10], and its use in the restructuring of WordNet [9,12]. Indeed, one of the main goals of upper level and foundational ontologies, jointly with meaning negotiation among ontology designers, and harmonization of ontologies, is that of "cleaning" a schema or a knowledge base by inducing inferences (which can produce inconsistencies, or not) due to the axioms defined on the classes and properties that are used as alignment targets of the knowledge base schema. Examples include: [26], which describes the detection of thousands of incoherences in a large collection of medical ontologies; [7], which uses a foundational ontology to detect incoherences in anti-money-laundering rules, as well as in suspicious financial transactions; [20], which uses foundational axioms to integrate and cleanup alternative service ontologies; [8], which also describes the detection of incoherences emerging from the formalization of a collection of thesauri and classification schemes in the fishery domain.

To our knowledge, foundational ontologies have never been used to detect inconsistencies in very large knowledge bases at the scale of millions of individuals and facts, although using this approach was actually suggested pretty soon [15]. More recently, an attempt [29] has been made in using a lightweight (non-foundational) upper ontology (UMBEL) to populate DBpedia 3.7 with disjointness axioms, and derive inconsistencies. However, only 55,829 inconsistencies are detected, from 5 logical-level types, with many of them due to a multi-hierarchical categorization of certain buildings in that version of DBpedia. To our knowledge, the latter is also the only approach that tries to target the identification of *systematic* errors, instead of individual ones.

3   Approach

We pursue a multi-stage process, as shown in Fig. 1. First, a reasoner is used to list all property assignment statements that are inconsistent with the ontology, along with their explanations. Then, those statements are clustered in order to isolate patterns in the inconsistent statements. The patterns are then examined manually to assess the inconsistencies identified.

While DBpedia contains type, relational, and literal assertions, we concentrate on identifying problems with relational assertions. The type assertions in DBpedia are mostly correct, but incomplete [23], there exists a reasonable amount of noise in the relational assertions. For example, Weaver et al. [33] determine the fraction of wrong relational assertions in Wikipedia links to be 2.8%, a number that can also serve as a rough estimate for DBpedia.

3.1   The Graph

The graph considered is constituted by the DBpedia 2014 ontology, mapping-based types, and mapping-based properties datasets.[1] The alignment to DOLCE-Zero (see below) is included in the ontology dataset (T-Box: the alignments of classes and properties), and in the mapping-based types dataset (A-Box: the

---

[1] http://wiki.dbpedia.org/Downloads2014. The namespaces used are:
   http://dbpedia.org/resource/, prefix=dbpedia,
   http://dbpedia.org/ontology/, prefix=dbo

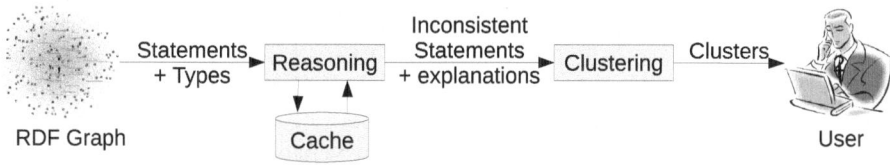

Fig. 1. The overall process. Statements from the DBpedia RDF graph are examined together with the subject's and object's types. The resulting inconsistent statements are clustered by similar explanations, and an expert user examines the clusters.

materialized types). The schema mapping has been defined by a DOLCE-Zero designer (one of the authors of this paper) at the time of the call for mappings (issued in 2014 by DBpedia maintainers); the mapping is relative to the DBpedia 3.9 ontology and dataset. The alignment has been created by carefully inspecting the T-Box axioms and a sample of the A-Box axioms for each class and property, in order to compare the wiki-based ontology development to the actual data models. The instance type materialization is based on the schema mapping.

For the 2014 release, the DBpedia maintainers have created the ontology dataset and the materialized instance mappings of DOLCE-Zero with reference to DBpedia 2014, with the mapping having been defined for the DBpedia 3.9 ontology. This results in a few issues. In particular, as new classes and properties have been added to the DBpedia 2014 version, some domain and range restriction axioms have changed, and some infobox mapping has changed as well, some of the alignments to DOLCE-Zero need to be revised, while some alignments are missing because of the new classes and properties. For this experiment, we have not revised the alignments, because the instance type materialization was still based on the 3.9 mapping in the DBpedia 2014 dataset.[2]

DOLCE-Zero consists of two OWL ontology modules derived from DOLCE [9] and the D&S [11] ontologies. The original design was made in the S5 modal logic [4] (DOLCE), and KIF [14] (D&S). DOLCE covers general distinctions concerning physical and social objects, events, abstractions, attributes, dimensional regions, as well as mereological (part), participation, inherence (attributive), and localization relations. In other words, DOLCE covers some of the core ontology design patterns that are typically assumed in the majority of conceptual schemata. D&S defines a vocabulary for roles, frames, concepts, and situations, which help representing many domains (e.g., biomedicine, law, business, organizations) that are often ambiguous in using words for expressing actual entities vs. concepts describing various collections of entities.In other words, D&S complements DOLCE with conceptual-level ontology design patterns.

The original DOLCE was hardly reusable on the Semantic Web, because of idiosyncratic terminological choices, and the strong expressivity of many of its axioms (n-ary relations, possible world and temporal indexing of relationships,

---

[2] Actually, our approach was capable of automatically discovering the places in which changes in the DBpedia ontology lead to invalid alignments (cf. Section 4), and led to fixes that will become part of the DBpedia 2015 version.

non-trivial first-order co-reference of variables). Therefore, the DOLCE designers decided soon to create a lighter version in OWL by relaxing n-ary relations, removing possible world and temporal indexing, and ignoring the most complex axioms. During the years, additional modules have been developed to cover e.g. WordNet's top level, as well as to link the light versions of DOLCE and D&S. Eventually, two modules have emerged as mostly useful to work with LOD:

- an OWL module called DOLCE+DnS Ultralight (DUL),[3] which contains a simplification of the original DOLCE axioms, with some additional concepts and relations, and the D&S vocabulary
- an upper level module, called DOLCE-Zero (D0)[4] that simplifies some of the distinctions in DUL, which has been created to optimize the alignment of WordNet used by the Tìpalo method for automatic typing of Wikipedia resources [13].

D0 is a small set of classes on top of DUL, which deal with ambiguity and completeness issues. Firstly, it introduces four "union classes" (d0#Characteristic, d0#Eventuality, d0#Activity, and d0#Location) that generalize some disjoint classes from DUL that are sometimes considered too "picky", e.g. qualities vs. dimensional regions, events vs. situations, actions vs. tasks, space regions vs. physical locations. In practice, those distinctions are seldom represented in lightweight ontologies and natural language lexicons, and often originate debatable inconsistencies. Secondly, D0 introduces three top-level classes that have never been clarified and eventually accepted in DOLCE: d0#CognitiveEntity, d0#System, and d0#Topic. Those classes are needed in order to align existing ontologies. The combination of DBpedia Ontology and D0 is coherent in itself with one exception: in DBpedia, the class dbo#Library is a case of metonymy, since is a subclass of both Building and Organization. However, the alignments are respectively to d0#PhysicalObject and to d0#SocialObject, which are disjoint classes.

3.2   Identifying Conflicting Statements

For each relation $r(s, o)$ that holds between a subject s and an object o, we collect all direct types of the subject and the object, i.e., $T_s = \{T | T(s)\}$, $T_o = \{T | T(o)\}$. Those statements – i.e., the relation as well as the type assertions – are presented to a reasoner, together with the DBpedia and D0 ontologies. Typically, a statement is detected as conflicted if the domain or range assignment of r contains a class which is disjoint with a class in T_s or T_o, respectively. Fig. 2 illustrates such an inconsistency.

Once a reasoner detects such an inconsistency for a statement, it can also deliver an *explanation*, i.e., the set of axioms that, together, are inconsistent. In the example in Fig. 2, it comprises the original relation assertion, the type assertion for the object, the property's range assertion, as well as all the subclass,

---

[3] http://www.ontologydesignpatterns.org/ont/dul/DUL.owl, prefix=dul
[4] http://www.ontologydesignpatterns.org/ont/dul/d0.owl, prefix=d0

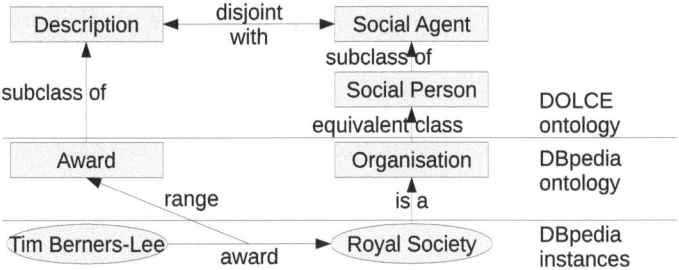

Fig. 2. Conflict detection example for the statement `dbpedia#Tim_Berners-Lee dbo#award dbpedia#Royal_Society`

equivalence, and disjointness assertions depicted in the figure. It is important to note that a detected inconsistency for a statement does not mean that the statement as such is wrong. It is rather the case that one of the axioms comprising the explanation (including the original statement) are wrong, which can also apply to a type assertion or any axiom in the DBpedia or D0 ontology.

Using a reasoner to check each and every statement in a large-scale dataset like DBpedia would lead to intractable runtimes. However, it is obvious that for two pairs of statements $r(s, o)$ and $r(s', o')$, the results of an inconsistency check are equivalent if $T_s = T_{s'}$ and $T_o = T_{o'}$. Hence, we can cache the reasoning results for a *characteristic signature* $\langle r, T_s, T_o \rangle$ and only invoke the reasoner for statements with a previously unseen characteristic signature.

3.3   Clustering Conflicts

The result of the previous step is a set of conflicting statements, where each statement has a set of axioms that lead to the conflict. In order to group similar conflicts, we use *clustering* and assign statements with similar axiom sets to the same cluster.

For determining the clusters, we represent each conflicting statement as a binary feature vector, where the features are the ontology axioms. As a distance function, we use the Manhattan distance between the feature vectors, i.e., the number of axioms by which the two explanations differ:

$$d(A_1, A_2) = |A_1 \cup A_2 - A_1 \cap A_2|, \tag{1}$$

where A_1 and A_2 are the axiom sets that lead to the inconsistency of two statements. Manhattan distance was chosen for simple computation and interpretability (i.e., a distance of n means that two explanations differ in n axioms).

As a clustering algorithm, we use DBSCAN [5]. That clustering algorithm forms clusters based on *density*, given two parameters ϵ and M. A cluster is formed around an instance if at least M instances are within a distance of ϵ of that instance. In our example, this means that clusters contain conflicting statements whose explanations do not differ by more than ϵ axioms. DBSCAN was used since (a) it does not require specifying the number of clusters upfront, (b) its efficiency, and (c) its capacity of isolating noise.

Instances which are not assigned to any cluster are marked as *noise*. These are conflicting statements whose explanation is not similar to that of at least M other statements. Hence, choosing the parameter M gives us control on the minimum frequency of a particular conflict to regard it as a *systematic* error.

4   Evaluation

We have evaluated our approach on DBpedia 2014, using the mapping-based types and properties datasets. We have run the conflicting statement detection and clustering once with, once without the D0 ontology. For reasoning, we used the HermiT reasoner [28], for clustering, we used a slightly modified version of the DBSCAN implementation in RapidMiner[5,6].

4.1   Basic Results

Without D0, a total of 97,749 statements (0.65% of all statements) was found to be inconsistent, with 630 different axioms involved in the corresponding explanations. With D0, this number increases to 3,654,255 statements (24.36% of all statements), with 1,467 axioms involved in the corresponding explanations.

As discussed above, we use caching of reasoner results. In total, the reasoner had to examine only 34,554 out of 15,001,543 statements, i.e., 0.03%. Computing the consistency and explanation of a statement took 2.6 seconds on average, which totals to 25h (i.e., without caching, the whole consistency checking step would take more than one year). The clustering took around five minutes. All computations were performed on a standard laptop.

We ran DBSCAN with $\epsilon = 2$ and $\epsilon = 4$, and used 5,10,25,50, and 100 as values for M. The cluster sizes and number of noise instances are depicted in Table 1. Although the absolute number of clusters when using D0 is only four times larger, while the total number of detected inconsistent statements is 37 times larger. The reason is that some of the clusters found when using D0 are quite large, i.e., the inconsistencies found affect a large number of statements. In fact, the largest 16 clusters are clusters that use D0 axioms in their explanations.

The values in the table also demonstrate the value of clustering: even if inspecting only a few hundred clusters (each presented as an example statement

---

[5] http://www.rapidminer.com

[6] The modification was made in order to make DBSCAN incorporate instance weights when counting instances. This allows us to reduce the dataset to only one instance per conflicting set of axioms, and set the number of statements exposing that conflict as the instance weight. With this modification, the dataset size to be processed in RapidMiner could be reduced by a factor larger than 1,000. The modification is contained in the *Mannheim RapidMiner Toolbox Extension*, available at https://marketplace.rapidminer.com/UpdateServer/faces/product_details. xhtml?productId=rmx_maratool

Table 1. Number of clusters and noise instances with and without D0 for DBSCAN different parameter settings of ϵ and M. #C denotes the number of clusters, $\varnothing$C denotes the average cluster size, and #N denotes the number of noise instances.

ϵ	M	without D0			with D0		
		#C	$\varnothing$C	#N	#C	$\varnothing$C	#N
2	5	218	447	355	915	3,992	1,835
4		182	536	264	745	4,903	1,390
2	10	180	540	614	681	5,361	3,392
4		151	644	474	565	6,463	2,574
2	25	129	747	1,406	457	7,981	6,746
4		108	894	1,160	380	9,602	5,454
2	50	98	972	2,529	338	10,779	10,958
4		84	1,139	2,075	288	12,658	8,709
2	100	68	1,370	4,623	254	14,321	16,797
4		62	1,519	3,570	219	16,624	13,537

and the corresponding explanation), a user can fix several million statements in DBpedia.

At a first manual inspection, we found out that the clusters with the larger ϵ value of 4 still looked rather coherent, i.e., the explanations are reasonably similar to group them together. Moreover, to keep the number of clusters tractable, we focus on the configuration with $\epsilon = 4$ and $M = 100$. Fig. 3 shows the distribution of clusters with this configuration.

4.2   Major Sources of Inconsistencies

Table 2 depicts the top 10 disjointness axioms, asserted classes, and asserted properties which occur in the inconsistencies identified by our approach. Again, the trend is confirmed that the absolute number of problems discovered when exploiting D0 is by several orders of magnitude larger than when relying only on the DBpedia ontology.

Furthermore, we can observe that some of the major problem sources, such as the modeling of species, career stations, and musical artists/bands (see below), are not captured without D0. This shows that in those areas, the formalization depth of the DBpedia ontology is rather low.

When using D0, seven out of the ten top 10 disjointness assertions are from the D0 ontology, while only three come from the DBpedia ontology. The fundamental distinction between social and physical objects is responsible for by far most of the inconsistencies detected.

It is further noteworthy that even for the disjointness axioms asserted in the DBpedia ontology, the number of conflicts detected when using D0 are higher in absolute numbers. For example, the disjointness between dbo#Person and dbo#Event is involved in over 10 times more inconsistencies when using D0. This is due to the fact that other assertions within D0, such as inverse properties, are also exploited by the reasoner.

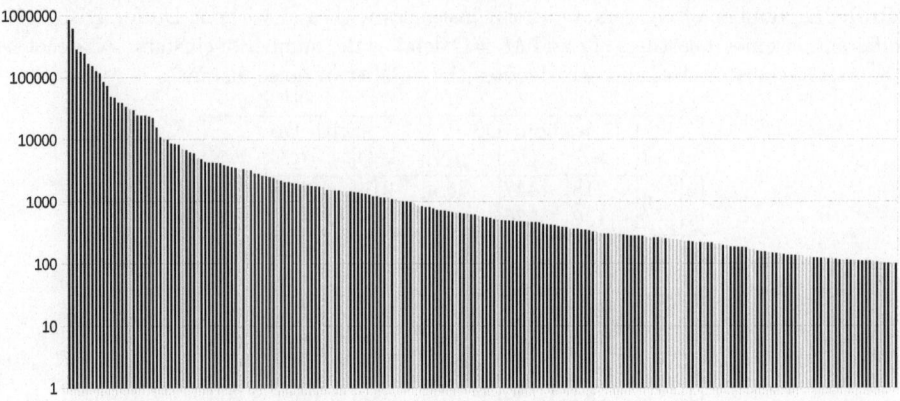

Fig. 3. Distribution of clusters and their sizes at $\epsilon = 4$ and $M = 100$ (note that the y axis uses a logarithmic scale). Black bars denote clusters of explanations using D0, grey bars represent clusters of explanations not using D0.

4.3 Evaluation of the Largest Clusters

The 40 largest clusters cover 3,497,068 inconsistent triples, corresponding to about 96% of all inconsistencies. 36 clusters use axioms from D0, i.e., only four would be found when considering the DBpedia ontology alone. We report here a classification of the 40 top clusters, according to the origin of the inconsistency, and the way(s) to fix it. Each category reveals an *anti-pattern*, i.e. a modeling solution used systematically, which produces unintended consequences.

Firstly, all the clusters contain an *inconsistency anti-pattern*: at least one domain or range restriction for a property is disjoint with at least one of the types declared for the subject or the object of an instance of that property. Formally, assuming the domain EA of explanation axioms, the domain $IA \subset EA$ of inconsistent A-Box axioms, the subsets $EA_{a1,...,an}$, $EA_{ai} \subset EA$ of explanation axioms for each inconsistent A-Box axiom $a_i \in IA$, with ρ being the object property from a_i, ϕ and ψ being domain and range classes for ρ, and χ, ξ being classes used as types of the individuals from a_i, the following description logic schema and data axiom templates are present in each cluster:

$$\rho \sqsubseteq \phi \times \psi \qquad (2)$$
$$\phi \setminus \chi \sqcup \psi \setminus \xi \qquad (3)$$
$$\rho(x,y) \wedge (\chi(x) \sqcup \xi(y)) \qquad (4)$$

Secondly, specific anti-patterns emerge from the analysis of the systematic errors for the top 40 clusters:

Overcommitment (19). A conflict arises between the schema emerging from data, and the schema from the ontology. In these cases, the ontology provides a typically reasonable intuition on how a certain property should be used, e.g., dbo#team is designed as a relation between agents and sports teams,

Table 2. Top 10 disjointness axioms, classes, and properties involved in the inconsistencies detected.

With DOLCE-Zero		Without DOLCE-Zero	
dul#PhysicalObject , dul#SocialObject	3,363,689	dbo#Agent , dbo#Place	60,120
dul#Event , dul#Object	174,917	dbo#Person , dbo#TimePeriod	31,330
dbo#Event , dbo#Person	65,649	dbo#Event , dbo#Person	4,443
dbo#Agent , dbo#Place	62,250	dbo#MeanOfTransp. , dbo#Person	1,521
dul#InformationObject , dul#SocialAgent	51,022	dbo#Building , dbo#Person	245
dbo#Person , dbo#TimePeriod	31,323	dbo#Activity , dbo#Person	34
dul#Abstract , dul#Object	27,663	dbo#Person , dbo#Plant	31
dul#InformationObject , dul#Situation	26,693	dbo#Person , dbo#Tower	14
dul#Situation , dul#SocialAgent	20,594	dbo#Mountain , dbo#Person	9
dul#Concept , dul#SocialAgent	12,498	dbo#Person , dbo#UnitOfWork	1
dbo#Species	1,273,521	dbo#TimePeriod	31,330
dbo#Person	1,182,729	dbo#Agent	28,827
dbo#CareerStation	621,575	dbo#Place	17,555
dbo#MusicalArtist	131,810	Wikidata#Q532	9,539
dbo#Event	124,757	dbo#Event	4,295
dbo#Organisation	63,725	dbo#Organisation	1,832
dbo#Band	53,448	dbo#Astronaut	1,488
dbo#Agent	36,472	dbo#Company	1,366
dbo#TelevisionShow	31,607	dbo#Region	640
dbo#TimePeriod	31,330	dbo#Broadcaster	263
dbo#team	1,520,216	dbo#team	39,065
dbo#family	335,398	dbo#birthPlace	10,285
dbo#order	278,229	dbo#district	7,167
dbo#currentMember	260,325	dbo#owner	4,569
dbo#kingdom	244,427	dbo#leaderName	3,414
dbo#phylum	200,431	dbo#province	3,267
dbo#genus	175,478	dbo#deathPlace	2,272
dbo#associatedMusicalArtist	97,243	dbo#location	1,766
dbo#battle	96,112	dbo#recordedIn	1,728
dbo#class	44,434	dbo#locationCity	1,612

but is often used in ways that conflicts arise with the basic intuition. For example dbo#team can be used as a relation between events and teams participating in that event. Since dul#Agent is disjoint with dul#Event, inconsistencies are detected. The restriction on the domain of dbo#team results therefore as an *overcommitment*: the interpretation of a property universe is too specific compared to actual usage. Other examples of overcommitment include instances for the properties dbo#associatedMusicalArtist, dbo#musicalBand, dbo#network, dbo#militaryBranch, etc.

Metonymy (11). A conflict arises between two disjoint – but related – interpretations of a same concept. An example appears with dbo#family, used in triples expressing relations between species. dbo#family has been aligned to the property dul#specializes, holding for instances of dul#Concept, but the class dbo#Species has been aligned to dul#Organism, because species in DBpedia include species as well as individual exemplars of a species (for example, famous race horses), i.e. dbo#Species is used metonymically in data. Since dul#Concept is disjoint with dul#Organism, inconsistencies are detected. The metonymy anti-pattern is difficult to resolve, because it is due to ambiguities that seem widespread in human language. Metonymy seems related to human propensity for an economy of means: an interesting cognitive experiment [25] proves the communicative function of ambiguity (cf. also [21] for a discussion). D0 tries to accommodate this "power of ambiguity" (cf. Section 3) to a certain extent, but relaxing all distinctions would prevent inconsistency checking in general. D0 relaxation has been limited to well known cases of metonymy, and the concept vs. organism metonymy for natural classifications was not considered.[7]

Misalignment (5). A conflict arises because a property (or a class) has been aligned to a wrong D0 entity, which causes inconsistencies in data classification. For example, the property dbo#commander has been aligned to dul#coparticipatesWith, but its usage in data is actually a case of dul#hasParticipant. dul#coparticipatesWith holds for instances of dul#Object only, but data include a 98% usage between dul#Event and dul#Object, and only 2% between dul#Object, therefore intended usage leans clearly towards the participation pattern.

Since the domain of dul#coparticipatesWith is dul#Object, and that of dul#hasParticipant is dul#Event (with dul#Object owl#disjointWith dul#Event), inconsistencies are detected. This anti-pattern suggests that DBpedia ontology choices proposed by the crowd, or by infobox reengineering, should also be made based on the actual resulting usage in data.

Version branching (3). A conflict arises between an alignment defined on a version, and a newer version. In these cases, the alignment provided for an older version, may become incoherent in case of a non-conservative change of the ontology in the newer version, e.g. dbo#team used to hold between career stations (professional situations of e.g. an athlete) and teams in DBPedia 3.9 ontology, but in DBPedia 2014 it holds between agents and sports teams. Since dul#Situation (aligning dbo#CareerStation), and dul#Person (aligning dbo#Athlete) are disjoint, inconsistencies are detected. This anti-pattern suggests that the design of new versions of DBpedia ontology should update the alignments to any change that has been made in the new version. Since this is an interaction problem, our clustering-based approach seems particularly appropriate to scale down the time needed to check all the interactions between the proposed changes in infobox reengineering, crowd modeling, and alignments.

Mistyping (1). A conflict arises between a type ϕ declared for some argument (subject or object) of an object property, and an expected type ψ expected for the universe of that property, when $\phi \setminus \psi$. This is typically due to systematic mistyping of individuals, and is not very frequent; an example is dbpedia#Alfonso_XII_of_Spain dbo#birthPlace dbpedia#Madrid, where dbpedia#Madrid is erroneously typed as dbo#Agent. Since dbo#Agent is disjoint with dbo#Place, which is expected in the range of dbo#birthPlace, inconsistencies are detected. Places being typed as agents occasionally occur in DBpedia, with dbpedia#Korea and dbpedia#New Brunswick being other prominent examples

---

[7] D0 was from WordNet requirements [13], and a new axiom – such as dbo#Species $\sqsubseteq$ dul#Concept $\sqcup$ dul#Organism – would be justified only if there is a substantial amount of individual exemplars (actual organisms) typed as species in DBpedia.

Table 3. Amount of clusters and inconsistencies found for each anti-pattern in the 40 top clusters, and the expected fix to resolve them.

anti-pattern	DO?	#clusters	#inco	%	fix type
Overcommitment	16 yes, 3 no	19	587962	.168	Schema restriction axioms
Metonymy	yes	11	1277977	.365	Schema or data refactoring
Misalignment	yes	5	133663	.038	Alignment tuning
Version branching	yes	3	1477296	.422	Alignment tuning, workflow change
Mistyping	no	1	10285	.003	Entity typing
Wrong taxonomy	yes	1	9885	.003	Schema taxonomical axioms

Wrong taxonomy (1). A conflict arises between a property or class restriction ϕ, and another restriction from a property or class ψ, where $\phi \equiv \psi$. For example, the inconsistency in triples like dbpedia#2002%E2%80%9303_Plymouth_ Argyle_F.C._season dbo#team dbpedia#Plymouth_Argyle_F.C. is due to the fact that the property dbo#team is owl#equivalentProperty dbo#club, but a specific domain is only stated for dbo#club (i.e. dbo#Athlete), while dbo#team is used in triples with subject of type dbo#SportsSeason, which is aligned to dul#Situation ⊔ dul#TimeInterval, which are both disjoint with dbo#Athlete.

Concerning possible fixes for the inconsistencies, solution patterns apply homogeneously for each of the anti-patterns. In particular, Overcommitment requires refactoring at the property restriction level, and need non-trivial design choices; Metonymy requires refactoring of both the ontology and the data, in order to partition the extension of a metonymical class or property; Misalignment requires tuning the alignments; Version branching requires tuning of the resulting misalignments, but in general a change in the ontology design workflow; Mistyping requires refactoring at the entity typing level; and finally, Wrong taxonomy needs to be solved at the schema level.

As a summary, Table 3 shows the amount of clusters and inconsistencies found for each anti-pattern, and the expected fix to resolve them.[8]

4.4   A Look at the Long Tail

In addition to the analysis of the top clusters, we also looked at the "long tail", i.e., the infrequent sources of inconsistencies which DBSCAN assigns to the *Noise* cluster. Out of those statements, we drew a random sample of 100 statements, and evaluated them by hand. From those 100 statements, 64 were actually erroneous, 30 were false negatives (i.e., statements which are actually correct), and the remaining six were unclear or questionable. The main sources for the 64 errors are as follows:

Link in longer text (23). If the value of an infobox key-value pair is a complex expression containing several links, all of them are extracted

---

[8] A detailed list of findings and proposed solutions is available at http://dws. informatik.uni-mannheim.de/en/research/dbpedia+dolce/

into a relational statement with the corresponding subject and predicate. However, this does not always make sense. One example is the statement `dbpedia#Cosmo_Cramer dbo#occupation dbpedia#Bagel`, which is extracted from the corresponding value *Bagel shop worker*, with *Bagel* linked to the corresponding Wikipedia page.

Wrong link (9). These are simply wrong links in the Wikipedia infobox. Following those links does not make sense to a human visitor of Wikipedia, since the link is completely wrong. One example is the statement `dbpedia#Stone_ (band) associatedMusicArtist dbpedia#Dementia`, where the object denotes the disease *dementia*, not the artist of the same name.

Redirect (7). Redirects are resolved when building DBpedia. This can result in nonsensical statements. One typical example is the statement `dbpedia#Ben_ Casey company dbpedia#Bing_Crosby`. Here, the original infobox value is `Bing_Crosby_Productions`, which would be the correct object for the statement. However, the production company has no Wikipedia page on its own, but the object is a redirect to the person *Bing Crosby*, which leads to the error.

Link/anchor text mismatch (6). This is a special case of wrong links – here, the anchor link would actually suggest a different link target. In contrast to wrong links as stated above, following the link in Wikipedia could actually make sense to a Wikipedia user, since there is related information on the website. One example is the statement `dbpedia#Deutschland_sucht_den_Super-star judge dbpedia#MIA.`, where the judge of the TV show is the singer of the band *MIA.*, not the band as such. Nevertheless, the page about the band contains information about the singer.

Metonymy (4). These are a special case of link/anchor mismatches, where the linked resource and the object which was actually meant share their surface form. One example is the statement `dbpedia#Human_Nature_(band) genre dbpedia#Motown`, where the object denotes the record label *Motown*. The term *Motown*, however, is often used as a genre name for the artists signed by the label.

Anchor link (4). When building DBpedia, URI fragments are removed from the link. However, they are used in Wikipedia to point to certain sections on a page, which, in total, is on a different, but related topic. Thus, removing the fragment can sometimes lead to wrong statements in DBpedia. One example is the statement `dbpedia#Pierre_Langlais battle dbpedia#First_Army_ (France)`, where the original link had a fragment pointing to the section on the page describing the actual battle.

Multiple Infoboxes (2). If a page contains multiple infoboxes, those can sometimes lead to wrong statements. One example observed is the Wikipedia page *Snooker World Rankings 1978/1979*, which contains infoboxes about individual players.

Unknown (9). In nine out of 64 cases, the authors of this paper could not find the reason for the error to come into existence.

It is noteworthy that in the long tail, i.e., the noise cluster, we could observe only those kinds of errors which are not specific to a certain class or property, but uniformly distributed across DBpedia classes and properties. This shows that the approach actually separates class-specific and class-independent problems, and assigns the latter to a separate cluster.

Furthermore, the analysis of the long tail has revealed four major sources of errors in DBpedia, which can be easily identified during the extraction phase and should obtain further attention in the future: links in longer texts, redirects, anchor links, and pages with multiple infoboxes. Given that the noise cluster contains 13,537 instances, these four sources account for an estimate of at least 4,800 wrong statements in total[9]. A possible treatment strategy could quarantine statements which have one of those characteristics, and treat them with special care, e.g., check them with a reasoner and/or statistical methods such as *SDValidate* [24].

5   Conclusion and Outlook

In this paper, we have shown how mappings to the foundational ontology DOLCE-Zero, which have been introduced in DBpedia from version 3.9 on, can be exploited for finding systematic errors in the construction of the DBpedia knowledge base. The combination of reasoning and clustering of the reasoner's explanations helps minimizing the human expert's workload: for the analysis of problems affecting millions of statements, no more than 140 statements (40 representative examples from the top clusters, plus 100 statements from the long tail) – i.e., 0.001% of DBpedia – have been inspected manually.

As a result of the analysis, some of the mappings used for creating DBpedia, as well as a number of assertions in the DBpedia ontology were directly changed. For problems that were not trivial to resolve, bug reports were filed. Furthermore, we have identified some areas where the construction of DBpedia requires additional attention, i.e., the extraction of relational statements from infobox values containing more text than just a plain link or literal, the handling of redirects, and the creation of relational statements from links containing an anchor fragment. Furthermore, our approach has revealed some non-optimal mappings between DBpedia and DOLCE-Zero, in particular where a) the DBpedia2014 ontology has used DBpedia 3.9 alignments, but the basic ontology had changed; and b) some properties are applied ambiguously, which should lead either to a change of the alignment, or of the DBpedia data or ontology.

So far, we have used a rather naive distance function for clustering the explanations, i.e., Manhattan distance on binary axiom occurrence vectors. More sophisticated similarity measures can be thought of, but are still subject to research [2].

The approach presented in this paper can be transferred to other datasets whose ontology is mapped to DOLCE-Zero. For the future, we are interested

---

[9] Since not all problematic statements rooted in one of those four problems lead to an inconsistency, we expect the number to be even higher.

in testing the approach also on other knowledge bases, such as YAGO [30] or NELL [3], and compare the findings. From such experiments, we expect further insights in the prevalent challenges for building large-scale knowledge bases.

Acknowledgments. The work presented in this paper was supported by RapidMiner in the course of the RapidMiner Academia program.

References

1. Acosta, M., Zaveri, A., Simperl, E., Kontokostas, D., Auer, S., Lehmann, J.: Crowd-sourcing linked data quality assessment. In: Alani, H., et al. (eds.) ISWC 2013, Part II. LNCS, vol. 8219, pp. 260–276. Springer, Heidelberg (2013)
2. Bail, S., Parsia, B., Sattler, U.: Declutter your justifications: determining similarity between OWL explanations. In: 1st International Workshop on Debugging Ontologies and Ontology Mappings, pp. 13–24 (2012)
3. Carlson, A., Betteridge, J., Wang, R.C., Hruschka Jr., E.R., Mitchell, T.M.: Coupled semi-supervised learning for information extraction. In: International Conference on Web Search and Data Mining, pp. 101–110. ACM (2010)
4. Chellas, B.F.: Modal logic: an introduction, vol. 316. Cambridge Univ Press (1980)
5. Ester, M., Kriegel, H.P., Sander, J., Xu, X.: A density-based algorithm for discovering clusters in large spatial databases with noise. Kdd **96**, 226–231 (1996)
6. Fleischhacker, D., Paulheim, H., Bryl, V., Völker, J., Bizer, C.: Detecting errors in numerical linked data using cross-checked outlier detection. In: Mika, P., et al. (eds.) ISWC 2014, Part I. LNCS, vol. 8796, pp. 357–372. Springer, Heidelberg (2014)
7. Gangemi, A., Pisanelli, D., Steve, G.: An ontological framework to represent norm dynamics. In: Proceedings of the 2001 Jurix Conference, Workshop on Legal Ontologies (2001)
8. Gangemi, A., Fisseha, F., Keizer, J., Lehmann, J., Liang, A., Pettman, I., Sini, M., Taconet, M.: A core ontology of fishery and its use in the fishery ontology service project. In: CEUR Proceedings, vol. 118 (2004)
9. Gangemi, A., Guarino, N., Masolo, C., Oltramari, A.: Sweetening WordNet with DOLCE. AI Magazine (Fall) (2003)
10. Gangemi, A., Guarino, N., Masolo, C., Oltramari, A., Schneider, L.: Sweetening ontologies with DOLCE. In: Gómez-Pérez, A., Benjamins, V.R. (eds.) EKAW 2002. LNCS (LNAI), vol. 2473, pp. 166–181. Springer, Heidelberg (2002)
11. Gangemi, A., Mika, P.: Understanding the semantic web through descriptions and situations. In: Meersman, R., Schmidt, D.C. (eds.) CoopIS 2003, DOA 2003, and ODBASE 2003. LNCS, vol. 2888, pp. 689–706. Springer, Heidelberg (2003)
12. Gangemi, A., Navigli, R., Velardi, P.: The OntoWordNet project: extension and axiomatization of conceptual relations in WordNet. In: Meersman, R., Schmidt, D.C. (eds.) CoopIS 2003, DOA 2003, and ODBASE 2003. LNCS, vol. 2888, pp. 820–838. Springer, Heidelberg (2003)
13. Gangemi, A., Nuzzolese, A.G., Presutti, V., Draicchio, F., Musetti, A., Ciancarini, P.: Automatic typing of DBpedia entities. In: Cudré-Mauroux, P., et al. (eds.) ISWC 2012, Part I. LNCS, vol. 7649, pp. 65–81. Springer, Heidelberg (2012)
14. Genesereth, M.R., Fikes, R.E.: Knowledge interchange format-version 3.0: reference manual. Tech. rep. (1992)

15. Jain, P., Hitzler, P., Yeh, P.Z., Verma, K., Sheth, A.P.: Linked data is merely more data. In: AAAI Spring Symposium: Linked Data Meets Artificial Intelligence, vol. 11 (2010)
16. Lehmann, J., Bühmann, L.: ORE - a tool for repairing and enriching knowledge bases. In: Patel-Schneider, P.F., Pan, Y., Hitzler, P., Mika, P., Zhang, L., Pan, J.Z., Horrocks, I., Glimm, B. (eds.) ISWC 2010, Part II. LNCS, vol. 6497, pp. 177–193. Springer, Heidelberg (2010)
17. Lehmann, J., Gerber, D., Morsey, M., Ngonga Ngomo, A.-C.: DeFacto - deep fact validation. In: Cudré-Mauroux, P., et al. (eds.) ISWC 2012, Part I. LNCS, vol. 7649, pp. 312–327. Springer, Heidelberg (2012)
18. Lehmann, J., Isele, R., Jakob, M., Jentzsch, A., Kontokostas, D., Mendes, P.N., Hellmann, S., Morsey, M., van Kleef, P., Auer, S., Bizer, C.: DBpedia - A Large-scale, Multilingual Knowledge Base Extracted from Wikipedia. Semantic Web Journal (2013)
19. Ma, Y., Gao, H., Wu, T., Qi, G.: Learning disjointness axioms with association rule mining and its application to inconsistency detection of linked data. In: Zhao, D., Du, J., Wang, H., Wang, P., Ji, D., Pan, J.Z. (eds.) CSWS 2014. CCIS, vol. 480, pp. 29–41. Springer, Heidelberg (2014)
20. Mika, P., Oberle, D., Gangemi, A., Sabou, M.: Foundations for service ontologies: aligning OWL-S to dolce. In: Staab, S., Patel-Schneider, P. (eds.) Proceedings of the World Wide Web Conference (WWW2004) (2004)
21. Nuzzolese, A.G., Gangemi, A., Presutti, V., Ciancarini, P.: Type inference through the analysis of wikipedia links. In: LDOW (2012)
22. Paulheim, H.: Identifying wrong links between datasets by multi-dimensional out-lier detection. In: International Workshop on Debugging Ontologies and Ontology Mappings (2014)
23. Paulheim, H., Bizer, C.: Type inference on noisy RDF data. In: Alani, H., et al. (eds.) ISWC 2013, Part I. LNCS, vol. 8218, pp. 510–525. Springer, Heidelberg (2013)
24. Paulheim, H., Bizer, C.: Improving the quality of linked data using statistical distributions. International Journal on Semantic Web and Information Systems (IJSWIS) 10(2), 63–86 (2014)
25. Piantadosi, S.T., Tily, H., Gibson, E.: The communicative function of ambiguity in language. Cognition 122(3), 280–291 (2012)
26. Pisanelli, D., Gangemi, A., Steve, G.: An Ontological Analysis of the UMLS Metathesaurus. J. of American Medical Informatics Association 5 (1998)
27. Schmachtenberg, M., Bizer, C., Paulheim, H.: Adoption of the linked data best practices in different topical domains. In: Mika, P., et al. (eds.) ISWC 2014, Part I. LNCS, vol. 8796, pp. 245–260. Springer, Heidelberg (2014)
28. Shearer, R., Motik, B., Horrocks, I.: Hermit: A highly-efficient OWL reasoner. In: OWLED, vol. 432 (2008)
29. Sheng, Z., Wang, X., Shi, H., Feng, Z.: Checking and handling inconsistency of DBpedia. In: Wang, F.L., Lei, J., Gong, Z., Luo, X. (eds.) WISM 2012. LNCS, vol. 7529, pp. 480–488. Springer, Heidelberg (2012)
30. Suchanek, F.M., Kasneci, G., Weikum, G.: Yago: a core of semantic knowledge. In: 16th International Conference on World Wide Web, pp. 697–706 (2007)
31. Töpper, G., Knuth, M., Sack, H.: DBpedia ontology enrichment for inconsistency detection. In: Proceedings of the 8th International Conference on Semantic Systems, pp. 33–40. ACM (2012)

32. Waitelonis, J., Ludwig, N., Knuth, M., Sack, H.: Whoknows? evaluating linked data heuristics with a quiz that cleans up dbpedia. Interactive Technology and Smart Education 8(4), 236–248 (2011)
33. Weaver, G., Strickland, B., Crane, G.: Quantifying the accuracy of relational statements in wikipedia: a methodology. JCDL 6, 358–358 (2006)
34. Wienand, D., Paulheim, H.: Detecting incorrect numerical data in DBpedia. In: Presutti, V., d'Amato, C., Gandon, F., d'Aquin, M., Staab, S., Tordai, A. (eds.) ESWC 2014. LNCS, vol. 8465, pp. 504–518. Springer, Heidelberg (2014)

Ontology-Based Data Access

Ontology-Based Integration of Cross-Linked Datasets

Diego Calvanese[1], Martin Giese[2], Dag Hovland[2], and Martin Rezk[1]([⊠])

[1] Free University of Bozen-Bolzano, Bolzano, Italy
mrezk@inf.unibz.it
[2] University of Oslo, Oslo, Norway

Abstract. In this paper we tackle the problem of answering SPARQL queries over *virtually integrated* databases. We assume that the entity resolution problem has already been solved and explicit information is available about which records in the different databases refer to the same real world entity. Surprisingly, to the best of our knowledge, there has been no attempt to extend the standard *Ontology-Based Data Access* (OBDA) setting to take into account these DB links for SPARQL query-answering and consistency checking. This is partly because the OWL built-in `owl:sameAs` property, the most natural representation of links between data sets, is not included in OWL 2 QL, the *de facto* ontology language for OBDA. We formally treat several fundamental questions in this context: how links over database identifiers can be represented in terms of `owl:sameAs` statements, how to recover rewritability of SPARQL into SQL (lost because of `owl:sameAs` statements), and how to check consistency. Moreover, we investigate how our solution can be made to scale up to large enterprise datasets. We have implemented the approach, and carried out an extensive set of experiments showing its scalability.

1 Introduction

Since the mid 2000s, *Ontology-Based Data Access* (OBDA) [9,14,15] has become a popular approach for *virtual* data integration [6]. In (virtual) OBDA, a conceptual layer is given in the form of (the intensional part of) an ontology (usually in OWL 2 QL) that defines a shared vocabulary, models the domain, hides the structure of the data sources, and can enrich incomplete data with background knowledge. The ontology is connected to the data sources through a declarative specification given in terms of mappings [4] that relate symbols in the ontology (classes and properties) to (SQL) views over data. The ontology and mappings together expose a virtual RDF graph, which can be queried using SPARQL queries, that are then translated into SQL queries over the data sources. In this setting, users no longer need an understanding of the data sources, the relation between them, or the encoding of the data.

One aspect of OBDA for data integration is less well studied however, namely the fact that in many cases, complementary information about the same entity is distributed over several data sources, and this entity is represented using

M. Arenas et al. (Eds.): ISWC 2015, Part I, LNCS 9366, pp. 199–216, 2015.
DOI: 10.1007/978-3-319-25007-6_12

different identifiers. The first important issue that comes up is that of *entity resolution*, which requires to understand which records actually represent the same real world entity. We do not deal with this problem here, and assume that this information is already available.

Traditional relational data integration techniques use extract, transform, load (ETL) processes to address this problem [6]. These techniques usually choose a single representation of the entity, merge the information available in all data sources, and then answer queries on the merged data. However, this approach of physically merging the data is not possible in many real world scenarios where one has no complete control over the data sources, so that they cannot be modified, and where the data cannot be moved due to freshness, privacy, or legal issues (see, e.g., Section 3).

An alternative that can be pursued in OBDA is to make use of mappings to *virtually merge* the data, by consistently generating only one URI per real world entity. Unfortunately, also this approach is not viable in general: 1. it does not scale well for several datasets, since it requires a central authority for defining URI schemas, which may have to be revised along with all mappings whenever a new source is added, and 2. it is crucial for the efficiency of OBDA that URIs be generated from the primary keys of the data sources, which will typically differ from source to source.

The approach we propose in this paper is based on the natural idea of representing the links between database records resulting from entity resolution in the form of *linking tables*, which are binary tables in *dedicated* data sources that simply maintain the information about pairs of records representing the same entity. This bring about several problems that need to be addressed: 1. links over database identifiers should be represented in terms of OWL owl:sameAs statements, which is the standard approach in semantic technologies for connecting entity identifiers; 2. the presence of owl:sameAs statements, which are inherently transitive, breaks rewritability of SPARQL queries into SQL queries over the sources, and one needs to understand whether rewritability can be recovered by imposing suitable restrictions on the linking mechanism; 3. a similar problem arises for checking consistency of the data sources with respect to the ontology, which is traditionally addressed through query answering; 4. since performance can be prohibitively affected by the presence of owl:sameAs, it becomes one of the key issues to address, so as to make the proposed approach scalable over large enterprise datasets.

In this paper we tackle the above issues in the setting where we are given an OWL 2 QL ontology that is mapped to a set of data sources, which are then extended with linking tables. Specifically, we provide the following contributions:

- We propose a mapping-based framework that carefully virtually constructs owl:sameAs statements from the linking tables, and deals with transitivity and symmetry, in such a way that performance is not compromised.
- We define a suitable set of restrictions on the linking mechanisms that ensures rewritability of SPARQL query answering, despite the presence of owl:sameAs statements.

- We develop a sound and complete SPARQL query translation technique, and show how to apply it also for consistency checking.
- We show how to optimize the translation so as to critically reduce the size of the produced SQL query.
- To empirically demonstrate scalability of our solution, we carry out an extensive set of experiments, both over a real enterprise cross-linked data set from the oil&gas industry, and in a controlled environment; this demonstrates the feasibility of our approach.

The structure of the paper is as follows: Section 2 briefly introduces the necessary background needed to understand this paper, and Section 3 describes our enterprise scenario. Section 4 provides a sound and complete SPARQL query translation technique for cross-linked datasets. Section 5 presents the main contribution of the paper, showing how to construct an OBDA setting over cross-linked datasets, and Section 6 presents our optimization technique. Section 7 presents an extensive experimental evaluation. Section 8 surveys related work, and Section 9 concludes the paper.

2   Preliminaries

Ontology Based Data Access. In the traditional OBDA setting $(\mathcal{T}, \mathcal{M}, D)$, the three main components are a set $\mathcal{T}$ of OWL 2 QL [12] axioms (called the TBox), a relational database D, and a set $\mathcal{M}$ of mappings. The OWL 2 QL profile of OWL 2 guarantees that queries formulated over $\mathcal{T}$ can be *rewritten* into SQL [2]. The mappings allow one to define how classes and properties in $\mathcal{T}$ should be populated with objects constructed from the data retrieved from D by means of SQL queries. Each mapping has one of the forms:

$$\text{Class(subject)} \leftarrow \text{sql}_{class} \qquad \text{Property(subject,object)} \leftarrow \text{sql}_{prop},$$

where sql_{class} and sql_{prop} respectively are a unary and binary SQL query over D. For both types of mappings we also use the equivalent notation $(s\ p\ o) \leftarrow \text{sql}$. Subjects and objects in RDF triples are resources (individuals or values) represented by URIs or literals. They are generated using templates in the mappings. For example, the URI template for the subject can take the form `<http://www.statoil.com/{id}>` where {id} is an attribute in some DB table, and it generates the URI `<http://www.statoil.com/25>` when {id} is instantiated as `"25"`. From $\mathcal{M}$ and D, one can derive a (*virtual*) RDF graph $G_{\mathcal{M},D}$, obtained by applying all mappings. Any RDF graph can be seen as a set of logical assertions. Thus, the Tbox together with $G_{\mathcal{M},D}$ constitutes an *ontology* $\mathcal{O} = (\mathcal{T}, G_{\mathcal{M},D})$.

To handle ontology-based integration of cross-linked datasets, we extend here the traditional OBDA setting with a fourth component $\mathcal{A}_S$ containing a set of statements of the form $\text{owl:sameAs}\ (o_1, o_2)$. Thus, in this paper, an OBDA setting is a tuple $(\mathcal{T}, \mathcal{M}, D, \mathcal{A}_S)$, and its corresponding *ontology* is the tuple $\mathcal{O} = (\mathcal{T}, G_{\mathcal{M},D} \cup \mathcal{A}_S)$. Unless stated differently, in the following we work with OBDA settings of this form.

Semantics: To interpret ontologies, we use the standard notions of first order interpretation, model, and satisfaction. That is, $\mathcal{O} \models A(\boldsymbol{v})$ iff for every model $\mathcal{I}$ of $\mathcal{O}$, we have that $\mathcal{I} \models A(\boldsymbol{v})$. Intuitively, adding an ontology $\mathcal{T}$ on top of an RDF graph G, *extends* G with extra triples inferred by $\mathcal{T}$. Formally, the RDF graph *(virtually)* exposed by the OBDA setting $((\mathcal{T}, \mathcal{M}, D, \mathcal{A}_S)$ is $G^{(\mathcal{T}, \mathcal{M}, D, \mathcal{A}_S)} = \{A(\boldsymbol{v}) \mid (\mathcal{T}, G_{\mathcal{M}, D} \cup \mathcal{A}_S) \models A(\boldsymbol{v})\}$.

SPARQL. SPARQL is a W3C standard language designed to query RDF graphs. Its vocabulary contains four pairwise disjoint and countably infinite sets of symbols: $\mathbf{I}$ for *IRIs*, $\mathbf{B}$ for *blank nodes*, $\mathbf{L}$ for *RDF literals*, and $\mathbf{V}$ for *variables*. The elements of $\mathbf{T} = \mathbf{I} \cup \mathbf{B} \cup \mathbf{L}$ are called *RDF terms*. A *triple pattern* is an element of $(\mathbf{T} \cup \mathbf{V}) \times (\mathbf{I} \cup \mathbf{V}) \times (\mathbf{T} \cup \mathbf{V})$. A *basic graph pattern* (*BGP*) is a finite set of triple patterns. Finally, a *graph pattern*, Q, is an expression defined by the grammar

$$Q ::= \text{BGP} \mid \text{FILTER}(P, F) \mid \text{UNION}(P_1, P_2) \mid \text{JOIN}(P_1, P_2) \mid \text{OPT}(P_1, P_2, F),$$

where F, is a *filter expression*. More details can be found in [3].

A *SPARQL query* (Q, V) is a graph pattern Q with a set of variables V which specifies the *answer variables*—the set of variables in Q whose values we are interested in. The values to variables are given by *solution mappings*, which are *partial* maps $s : \mathbf{V} \to \mathbf{T}$ with (possibly empty) domain $dom(s)$. Here, following [9,15], we use the set-based semantics for SPARQL (rather than the bag-based one, as in the specification).

The SPARQL algebra operators are used to evaluate the different fragments of the SPARQL query. Given an RDF graph G, the *answer to a graph pattern* Q *over* G is the set $[\![Q]\!]_G$ of solution mappings defined by induction using the SPARQL algebra operators and starting from the base case: triple patterns. Due to space limitation, and since the entailment regime only modifies the SPARQL semantics for triple patterns, here we only show the definition of for this basic case. We provide the complete definition in our technical report [3].

For a triple pattern B, $[\![B]\!]_G = \{s : var(B) \to \mathbf{T} \mid s(B) \subseteq G\}$ where $s(B)$ is the result of substituting each variable u in B by $s(u)$. This semantics is known as *simple entailment*. Given a set V of variables, the *answer to* (Q, V) *over* G is the restriction $[\![Q]\!]_{G|V}$ of the solution mappings in $[\![Q]\!]_G$ to the variables in V.

SPARQL Entailment Regime. We present now the standard W3C semantics for SPARQL queries over OWL 2 ontologies under different entailment regimes. We use here the entailment regimes only to reason about individuals and, unlike [9], we do not allow for variables in triple patterns ranging over class and property names. We leave the problem of extending our results to handle also this case for future work, but we do not expect this to present any major challenge.

We work with TBoxes expressed in the OWL 2 QL profile, which however may contain also owl:sameAs statements. Therefore, we consider two Direct Semantics entailment regimes for SPARQL queries, which differ in how they interpret `owl:sameAs`: the *DL entailment regime* (which defines $\models_{DL}$) interprets `owl:sameAs` internally, implicitly adding to the ontology $\mathcal{O}$ the axioms to handle equality, i.e., transitivity, symmetry, and reflexivity. Instead, the *QL entailment regime* (which defines $\models_{QL}$) interprets `owl:sameAs` as a standard object property, hence does not assign to it any special semantics.

Observe that a basic property of logical equality is that if a and b are equal, everything that holds for a should hold also for b, and viceversa. In the context of SPARQL, informally it means that given the answer $[\![B]\!]_{\mathcal{T},G\cup\mathcal{A}_s}$ to a triple pattern B, if the answer contains the solution mapping $s : v \mapsto o$ and $\mathcal{T} \models$ `owl:sameAs`(o, o'), then $[\![B]\!]_{\mathcal{T},G\cup\mathcal{A}_s}$ must also contain a solution mapping s' that coincides with s but $s' : v \mapsto o'$. Formally, the answer $[\![B]\!]_{\mathcal{T},G\cup\mathcal{A}_s}^{R}$ to a BGP B over an ontology $\mathcal{O}$ under entailment regime R is defined as follows:

$$[\![B]\!]_{\mathcal{O}}^{R} \;=\; \{s\colon var(B) \to \mathbf{T} \mid (\mathcal{O}) \models_R s(B)\},$$

Starting from the $[\![B]\!]_{\mathcal{O}}^{R}$ and applying the SPARQL operators in Q, we compute the set $[\![Q]\!]_{\mathcal{O}}^{R}$ of *solution mappings*.

3   Use Case and Motivating Example

In this section we briefly describe the real-world scenario we have examined at Statoil, and we illustrate the challenges it presents for OBDA with an example.

At Statoil, users access several databases on a daily basis, some of them are the Exploration and Production Data Store (EPDS), the Norwegian Petroleum Directorate (NPD) FactPages, and several OpenWorks databases. EPDS is a large Statoil-internal legacy SQL (Oracle 10g) database comprising over 1500 tables (some of them with up to 10 million tuples), 1600 views and 700 Gb of data. The NPD FactPages[1] is a dataset provided by the Norwegian government, and it contains information regarding the petroleum activities on the Norwegian continental shelf. OpenWorks Databases contain projects data produced by geoscientists at Statoil. The information in these databases overlap, and often they refer to the same entities (companies, wells, licenses) with different identifiers. In this use case the entity resolution problem has been solved since the links between records are available.

The users at Statoil need to query (and get an answer in reasonable time) the information about these objects without worrying about what is the particular identifier in each database. Thus, we assume that the SPARQL queries provided by the users *will not* contain `owl:sameAs` statements. The equality between identifiers should be handled *internally* by the OBDA system. To illustrate this we provide the following simplified example:

Example 1. Suppose we have the three datasets (from now on D_1, D_2, D_3) with wellbore[2] information, and a dataset D_4 with information about companies and

---

[1] http://factpages.npd.no/
[2] A wellbore is a hole drilled for the purpose of exploration or extraction of natural resources.

D_1		D_2			D_3		D_4	
id1	Name	id2	Name	Well	id3	AName	id4	LName
a1	'A'	b1	null	1	c3	'U1'	9	'Z1'
a2	'B'	b2	'C'	2	c4	'U2'	8	'Z2'
a3	'H'	b6	'B'	3	c5	'U6'	7	'Z3'

Fig. 1. Wellbore datasets D_1, D_2, D_3, and company dataset D_4

licenses, as illustrated in Figure 1. The wellbores in D_1, D_2, D_3 are linked, but companies in D_4 are not linked with the other datasets. These four datasources are integrated virtually by topping them with an ontology. The ontology contains the concept Wellbore and the properties hasName, hasAlternativeName and hasLicense.

The terms Wellbore and hasName are defined using D_1 and D_2. The property hasAlternativeName is defined using D_3. The property hasLicense is defined over the isolated dataset D_4. We assume that mappings for wellbores from D_i use URI templates uri_i. In addition, we know that the wellbores are cross-linked between datasets as follows: wellbores $a1$, $a2$ in D_1 are equal to $b2$, $b1$ in D_2 and $c3$, $c4$ in D_3, respectively. In addition, $a3$ is equal to $c5$. These links are represented at the ontology level by owl:sameAs statements of the form: owl:sameAs (uri1(a1),uri2(b2)), owl:sameAs (uri2(b2),uri3(c3)), etc.

Consider now a user looking for all the wellbores and their names. According to the SPARQL entailment regime, the system should return all the 12 combinations of equivalent ids and names ((uri1(a1),A), (uri2(b2),A), (uri3(c3),A), (uri1(a2),B), (uri2(b1),B), etc.) since all this tuples are entailed by the ontology and the data (c.f. Section 2). Note that no wellbores from D_4 are returned. □

The first issue in the context of OBDA is how to translate the user query into a query over the databases. Recall that owl:sameAs is not included in OWL QL, thus it is not handled by the current query translation and optimization techniques. If we solve the first issue by applying suitable constraints, we get into a second issue, how to minimize the negative impact on the query execution time when reasoning over cross-linked datasets.A third issue is how to check, for instance, whether hasName is a functional property considering the linked entities. A fourth issue is how to handle the multiplicity of equivalent answers required by the standard. For instance, in our example, in principle, it could be enough to pick individuals with template uri_1 as class representative, and return only those triples. In the next sections we will tackle all these issues in turn.

4   Handling owl:sameAs by SPARQL Query Rewriting

In this section we present the theoretical foundations for query answer over ontology-based integrated datasets. We also discuss how to perform consistency checking using this approach. We assume for now that the links are given in the form of `owl:sameAs` statements, and address later, in Section 5, the proper OBDA scenario, where links are not given between URIs, but between database records. Recall that `owl:sameAs` is not in the OWL 2 QL profile, and moreover, by adding the unrestricted use of `owl:sameAs` we lose first order rewritability [1], since one can encode reachability in undirected graphs. This implies that, if we allow for the unrestricted use of `owl:sameAs`, we cannot offer a sound and complete translation of SPARQL queries into SQL.[3]

We present here an approach, based on partial materialization of inference, that in principle allows us to exploit a relational engine for query answering in the presence of `owl:sameAs` statements. This approach, however, is not feasible in practice, and we will then show in Section 5 how to develop it into a practical solution. Our approach is based on the simple observation that we can expand the set $\mathcal{A}_S$ of `owl:sameAs` facts into the set $\mathcal{A}_S^*$ obtained from $\mathcal{A}_S$ by closing it under reflexivity, symmetry, and transitivity. Unlike other approaches based on (partial) materialization [8], we do not expand here also data triples (specifically, those in $G_{\mathcal{M},D}$), but instead rewrite the input SPARQL query to guarantee completeness of query answering. We assume that user queries in general will not contain `owl:sameAs` statements, and therefore, for simplicity of presentation, here we do not consider the case where they are present as input. However, our approach can be easily extended to deal also with `owl:sameAs` statements in user queries. Given a SPARQL query (Q, V) over $(\mathcal{T}, G \cup \mathcal{A}_S)$, we generate a new SPARQL query $(\varphi(Q), V)$ over $(\mathcal{T}, G \cup \mathcal{A}_S^*)$ that returns the same answers as (Q, V) over $(\mathcal{T}, G \cup \mathcal{A}_S)$. This approach is very similar to the singularisation technique in [11]. The translation $\varphi(\cdot)$ is defined as follows.

Definition 1. *Given a query* (Q, V)*, the query* $(\varphi(Q), V)$ *is obtained by replacing every triple pattern* t *in* Q *with* $\varphi(t)$*, where:*[4]

– $\varphi(\{\texttt{?v :P ?w}\}) = \{\texttt{?v owl:sameAs \_:a . \_:a :P \_:b . \_:b owl:sameAs ?w .}\}$
– $\varphi(\{\texttt{?v rdf:type :C}\}) = \{\texttt{?v owl:sameAs \_:a . \_:a rdf:type :C .}\}$

The following proposition states that answering SPARQL queries over a TBox $\mathcal{T}$ under the DL entailment regime can be reduced to answering SPARQL queries under the QL entailment regime (where `owl:sameAs` has no built-in semantics).

Proposition 1. *Given OBDA setting* $(\mathcal{T}, \mathcal{M}, D, \mathcal{A}_S)$ *and a query* (Q, V)*, we have that* $[\![Q]\!]^{DL}_{\mathcal{T}, G_{\mathcal{M},D} \cup \mathcal{A}_S}|_V = [\![\varphi(Q)]\!]^{QL}_{\mathcal{T}, G_{\mathcal{M},D} \cup \mathcal{A}_S^*}|_V.$

Consistency Check: Ontology languages, such as OWL 2 QL, allow for the specification of constraints on the data. If the data exposed by the database through the mappings does not satisfy these constraints, then we say that the ontology is *inconsistent with respect to the mappings and the data.* OBDA allows one to

---

[3] Using the linear recursion mechanism of SQL-99, a translation would be possible, but with a severe performance penalty for evaluating queries involving transitive closure.

[4] Recall that terms of the form _:x are blank nodes that, when occuring in a query, correspond to existential variables.

check two types of constraints: (i) *functionality* of properties (although it cannot be expressed in OWL 2 QL), which imposes that an individual is connected to at most one element; (ii) *disjointness* of classes/properties, which cannot have (pairs of) individuals in common. In OBDA, consistency checking can be reduced to query-answering [2]. This does not hold anymore in general, when considering cross-linked datasets (where UNA does not hold). For instance, suppose we want to check if the property :hasName in Example 1 is functional. Clearly without considering equality between datasets the property is functional, however, when we integrate the datasets, it is not anymore since we have in the graph (url1(a1) :hasName 'A') and (url2(b2) :hasName 'C') and (url1(a1) owl:sameAs url2(b2)). This implies that the wellbore url1(a1) has two names. Using the translation above we can extend the results in [2] for checking violations of class disjointness and of functionality of data and object properties, to account for owl:sameAs statements. For disjointness and functionality of data properties this is accomplished straightforwardly by the translation. Instead, for functionality of object properties, we need to modify the query used in [2] and explicitly incorporate the negation of owl:sameAs. For instance, to check if functionality of the object property :isRelatedTo *might be violated*, we can check if the following query returns a non-empty answer over $(\mathcal{T}, G \cup \mathcal{A}_S^*)$:

```
SELECT ?x ?y1 ?y2 ?y3 WHERE {
    ?x :isRelatedTo ?y1 .   ?x :isRelatedTo ?y2 .
    FILTER(?y1 != ?y2 AND NOT EXISTS {?y1 owl:sameAs ?y2} ) }
```

If the answer is non-empty, the returned elements might witness the violation of functionality. Notice that, because of the OWA if two elements are *not known* to be equal, in general we cannot infer that they are not equal, and hence functionality might still hold in some models. We refer to [3] for more details.

5   Handling Cross-Linked Datasets in Practice

We now deal with the proper case of querying cross-linked datasets, where we are given: *(a)* an OWL 2 QL TBox, *(b)* a collection of datasets, *(c)* a set of mappings, and *(d)* a set of *linking tables*[5] stating equality between records in different datasets that represent the same entity. For simplicity, we can think of each dataset as corresponding to a different data source, but datasets could be decoupled from the actual physical data sources. In

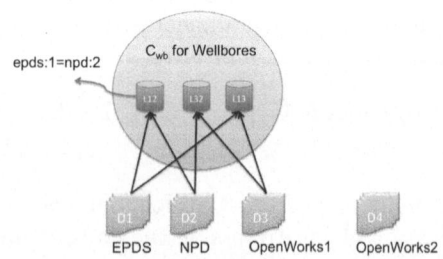

Fig. 2. Linking tables for the wellbores category

---

[5] Note that these tables could be available virtually, and hence retrieved through queries.

general, in different datasets, the same identifiers might be used to denote different objects, and the same objects might be denoted by different identifiers. Moreover, each dataset may contain data records belonging to different *pairwise disjoint* categories $C_1, \ldots, C_m$, for example wellbores, or company names. A category corresponds to a set of records that can be mapped to individuals in the ontology belonging to the same TBox class (different from owl:Thing), and that could, in principle, be joined. For instance, cats and men belong to the same class mammal, but a cat can never be joined with a man, hence cat and men constitute two different categories. We assume that in addition to the datasets $D_1, \ldots, D_n$, for each category C there is a database D^C containing the linking tables for the records in C. Specifically, we denote a linking table for datasets D_i, D_j and category C with $L_{ij}^C(id_i, id_j)$. A tuple r_1, r_2 in L_{ij}^C means that the record r_1 in D_i represents the same object as the record r_2 in D_j. Notice that, we do not assume that there is a linking table for each pair of datasets D_i, D_j for each category C. The concepts above are illustrated in Figure 2. Our aim is to efficiently answer user SPARQL queries in this setting.

The approach presented in the previous section is theoretical, and cannot be effectively applied in practice because: *(1)* it assumes that the links are given in the form of owl:sameAs statements whereas in practice, in an cross-linked setting, they will be given as tables (with the results of the entity resolution process); and *(2)* it requires pre-computing a large number of triples (namely $\mathcal{A}_S^*$) and materializing them into the ontology. Since these triples are not stored in the database, they cannot be efficiently retrieved using SQL. This negatively impacts the performance of query execution.

To tackle these problems, in this section we show how to: *(a)* expose, using mapping assertions that are *optimization-friendly*, the information in the tables expressing equality between DB records, as a set $\mathcal{A}_S$ of owl:sameAs statements; *(b)* extend the mappings so as to encode also transitivity and symmetry (but not reflexivity), and hence expose the symmetric transitive closure $\mathcal{A}_S^+$ of $\mathcal{A}_S$; *(c)* modify the query-rewriting algorithm (cf. Definition 1) so as to return sound and complete answers over the (virtual) ontology extended with $\mathcal{A}_S^+$. We detail now the above steps.

(a) Generating $\mathcal{A}_S$: We now present a set of constraints on the structure of the linking tables that are fully compatible with real-world requirements, and that allow us to process queries efficiently, as we will show below:

1. All the information about which objects of category C are linked in datasets D_i and D_j is contained in L_{ij}^C. Formally: If there are tables L_{ij}^C, L_{ik}^C and L_{kj}^C, then L_{ij}^C contains all the tuples in $\pi_{id_i, id_j}(L_{ik}^C \bowtie L_{kj}^C)$, when evaluated over D^C.
2. Linking tables cannot state equality between different elements in the same dataset[6]. Formally: There is no join of the form $L_{ik}^C \bowtie \cdots \bowtie L_{ni}^C$ such that

---

[6] Observe that this amounts to making the Unique Name Assumption for the objects retrieved by the mappings from one dataset

$L_{1,2}$ $L_{2,3}$ $L_{1,3}$

id1	id2
a1	b2
a2	b1

id2	id3
b1	c4
b2	c3

id1	id3
a1	c3
a2	c4
a3	c5

Fig. 3. Linking Tables

(o, o'), with $o \neq o'$, occurs in $\pi_{L^C_{ik}.id_i, L^C_{ni}.id_i}(L^C_{ik} \bowtie \cdots \bowtie L^C_{ni})$, when evaluated over D^C.

Example 2 (Categories). Consider Example 1. Here we consider only wellbores, therefore we have a single category C_{wb} with three linking tables $L^{C_{wb}}_{12}$, $L^{C_{wb}}_{23}$, and $L^{C_{wb}}_{13}$ as shown in Figure 3. From the constraints above we know that $\pi_{id_1, id_3}(L^{C_{wb}}_{12} \bowtie L^{C_{wb}}_{23})$ is contained in $L^{C_{wb}}_{13}$, when both are evaluated over $D^{C_{wb}}$. □

A key factor that affects performance of the overall OBDA system, is the form of the mappings, which includes the structure of the URI templates used to generate the URIs. Here, we discuss how the part of the mappings (including URI templates) that deal with linking tables should be designed, so this approach scales up. The SPARQL-to-SQL translation must add *all* the SQL queries defining owl:sameAs. However, as shown in Section 6, we exploit our URI design to (intuitively) remove as many owl:sameAs SQL definitions as possible before query execution.

We propose here to use a different URI template $uri_{C,D}$ for each pair constituted by a category C and a dataset D.[7] Observe that this design decision is quite natural, since objects belonging to different categories should not join, even if in some dataset they are identified in the same way. For example, wellbore n. 25 should not be confused with the employee whose id is 25.

Next we generate the set of equalities $\mathcal{A}_S$ extending the set of mappings $\mathcal{M}$, using a different URI template for each tuple (category C,dataset D). More precisely, to generate $\mathcal{A}_S$ out of the categories $C_1 \ldots C_n$, $\mathcal{M}$ is extended with mappings as follows. For each category C, and each linking table L^C_{ij} we extend $\mathcal{M}$ with:

$$uri_{C,D_i}(\{id_i\}) \text{ owl:sameAs } uri_{C,D_j}(\{id_j\}) \leftarrow select * from L^C_{ij} \quad (1)$$

When the category C is clear from the context we write uri_i to denote uri_{C,D_i}

Example 3 (Mappings). To generate the owl:sameAs statements from the tables in Example 2, we extend our set of mappings $\mathcal{M}$ with the following mappings (fragment):

---

[7] In the special case where there *are* several datasets that can be mapped to use common URIs, there is no need for linking tables or any of the techniques presented in this paper. We address the more general case, where this is not the case.

```
uri1({id1}) owl:sameAs uri2({id2}) ← SELECT * FROM L^C_{1,2}
uri2({id2}) owl:sameAs uri3({id3}) ← SELECT * FROM L^C_{2,3}
```

Observe that this also implies that to populate the concept Wellbore with elements from D_1, the mappings in $\mathcal{M}$ will have to use the URI template: uri1. □

Considering that the same URIs in different triples of the virtual RDF graph can be generated from different mapping assertions, we observe that the form of the templates in the mappings related to linking tables will affect also those in the remaining mapping assertions in the OBDA system.

(b) Approximating $\mathcal{A}_S^+$: To be able to rewrite SPARQL queries into SQL without adding $\mathcal{A}_S^*$ as facts in the ontology, (relying only on the databases), we embed the owl:sameAs axioms together with the axioms for symmetry and transitivity into the mappings, that is, extending the notion of $\mathcal{T}$-mappings [14] ($\mathcal{T}$ stands for terminology). Intuitively, $\mathcal{T}$-mappings embed the consequences from a OWL QL ontology into the mappings. This allow us to drop the implicit axioms for symmetry, and transitivity from the Tbox $\mathcal{T}$.

For each category C and for each set of non-empty tables $L^C_{i_1,i_2} L^C_{i_2,i_3} \dots L^C_{i_{n-1},i_n}$, if $L^C_{i_1,i_n}$ *does not exist*, we include the following transitivity mappings in $\mathcal{M}$:

$$t_1(\{id_1\}) \; \texttt{owl:sameAs} \; t_n(\{id_n\}) \leftarrow select * from \; L^C_{i_1,i_2} \bowtie \dots \bowtie L^C_{i_{n-1},i_n} \quad (2)$$

and for each of the owl:sameAs mapping described in (1) and (2) we include the following symmetry mappings in $\mathcal{M}$:

$$t_j(\{id_j\}) \; \texttt{owl:sameAs} \; t_i(\{id_i\}) \leftarrow select * from \; sql_{ij} \quad (3)$$

We call the resulting set of mappings $\mathcal{M}_S$

(c) Rewriting the query Q: Encoding reflexivity would be extremely detrimental for performance, not only by the large number of extra mappings we should consider but also because it would render the optimizations explained in the next sections ineffective. Intuitively, the reason for this is that while symmetry and transitivity affect only elements which are linked to other datasets, reflexivity affects *all* the objects in the OBDA setting. Thus, we would not be able to distinguish during the query transformation process, which classes and properties actually deal with linked objects (and should be rewritten) and which ones are not. Therefore, we modify the query-rewriting technique to keep soundness and completeness with respect to the DL entailment regime while evaluating the query under the QL entailment regime over $(\mathcal{T}, \mathcal{M}_S, D)$.

We modify the query translation as follows:

Definition 2 $((\varphi(Q), V))$. *Given a query (Q, V), the query $(\varphi(Q), V)$ is obtained by replacing every triple pattern t in Q with $\varphi(t)$, where: $\varphi(\{?v :P ?w\})$ is shown in Fig. 4 (A) and $\varphi(\{?v \; rdf:type :C\})$ is shown in Fig. 4 (B).*

```
{ ?v :P ?w . } UNION {              ?v rdf:type :C . UNION {
?v owl:sameAs _:z1 . _:z1 :P ?w .   ?v owl:sameAs [ rdf:type :C ] .
} UNION {                           }
?v :P _:z2 . _:z2 owl:sameAs ?w .
} UNION {
?v owl:sameAs _:a .
_:b owl:sameAs ?w . _:a :P _:b . }
```

(A)   (B)

Fig. 4. SPARQL translation to handle owl:sameAs without Reflexivity

Intuitively, following up our running example, the first BGP in Fig. 4 (A) gets all triples such as (uri1(a1), :hasName, A) that do not need equality reasoning. The second BGP, will get triples such as (uri1(a1), :hasName, C), that require owl:sameAs(uri1(a1),uri2(b2)). The two last BGPs are used *only* for object properties, and it tackles the cases where equality reasoning is needed for the object (?w).

Recall that we do not allow owl:sameAs in the user query language. Therefore the user will not be able to query $?x$ owl:sameAs$?x$. In principle, we could also move transitivity and symmetry to the query, but it will not reduce the SQL query rewriting.

Theorem 1. *Given OBDA setting* $(\mathcal{T}, \mathcal{A}_S, \mathcal{M}, D)$ *and a query* (Q, V), *we have that* $[\![Q]\!]^{DL}_{\mathcal{T},G_{\mathcal{M},D} \cup \mathcal{A}_S}|_V = [\![\varphi(Q)]\!]^{QL}_{\mathcal{T},G_{\mathcal{M}_S,D}}|_V$.

6   Optimization

The technique presented in Section 5 can cause excessive overhead on the query size and therefore on the query execution time, since it has to extend *every* triple pattern with owl:sameAs statements. In this section we show how to remove the owl:sameAs statements that do not contribute to the answer. For instance, in our running example the property hasLicense is defined over the companies in D_4, which are not linked with the other 3 databases. Thus, the owl:sameAs statements should not contribute to "populate" this property.

To translate SPARQL to SQL, in the literature [15] and in the implementation, we encode the SPARQL algebra tree as a logic program. Intuitively, each SPARQL operator is represented by a rule in the program as illustrated in Example 4. The translation algorithm employs a well-known process in Logic Programming called *partial evaluation* [10]. Intuitively, the partial evaluation of a SPARQL query Q (represented as a logic program) is another query Q', that represents the *partial execution* of Q. This process iterates over the structure of the query and *specializes* the query going from the highly abstract query to the concrete SQL query over the database. It starts by replacing the atoms that correspond to leaves in the algebra tree (triple patterns) with the union of *all* its definitions in the mappings, and then it iterates over remaining atoms trying to replace the atoms by their definitions. This procedure is done without executing any SQL query over the databases.

```
Select * WHERE {
?v :hasLicense ?w .
}
```

(A)

```
Select * WHERE {
{?v :hasLicense ?w .} UNION {
?v owl:sameAs [ :hasLicense :w ] . } }
```

(B)

Fig. 5. Optimizable Queries

We detect and remove `owl:sameAs` statements that do not contribute to the answer using this procedure. It is critical to notice that this optimization can be performed because we intentionally added two constraints: *(i)* we disallow mappings modeling reflexivity; and *(ii)* we force unique URIs for each pair of category/database. We illustrate this optimization in the following example.

Example 4 (Companies). Consider the query asking for the list of companies and licenses shown in Figure 5 (A). This query is translated into the query (fragment) shown in Figure 5 (B). Since we know that only wellbore are linked through the different datasets, it is clear that there is no need for `owl:sameAs` statements (nor unions) in this query. In the following, we show how the system *partially evaluates* the query to remove such pointless union. This translated query is represented as the following program encoding the SPARQL algebra tree:

$$
\begin{aligned}
&(1)\, \text{answer}(v,w) \leftarrow \textbf{union}(v,w) \\
&(2)\quad \textbf{union}(v,w) \leftarrow bgp_1(v,w) \\
&(3)\qquad bgp_1(v,w) \leftarrow \text{hasLicense}(v,w) \\
&(4)\quad \textbf{union}(v,w) \leftarrow bgp_2(v,w) \\
&(5)\qquad bgp_2(v,w) \leftarrow \text{owl:sameAs}(v,x),\ \text{hasLicense}(x,w)
\end{aligned}
$$

The next step is to replace the leaves of the SPARQL tree (the triple patterns `owl:sameAs` and `hasLicense`) with their definitions (fragment without including transitivity and symmetry):

$$
\begin{aligned}
&(6)\ \text{hasLicense}(\text{uri4}(v),\text{uri4}(w)) \leftarrow \text{sql}(v,w) \\
&(7)\ \text{owl:sameAs}(\text{uri1}(v),\text{uri2}(x)) \leftarrow \mathcal{T}_{12}(v,w) \\
&(8)\ \text{owl:sameAs}(\text{uri2}(v),\text{uri3}(x)) \leftarrow \mathcal{T}_{23}(v,w) \\
&(9)\ \text{owl:sameAs}(\text{uri1}(v),\text{uri3}(x)) \leftarrow \mathcal{T}_{13}(v,w)
\end{aligned}
$$

Thus, the system try to replace `hasLicense(x,w)` in (5) by its definition in (6), and analogously with `owl:sameAs` (5 by the union of 7-9) Using partial evaluation, the system will try to unify the head of (6) with `hasLicense` in (5). The result is:

$$(5')\, bgp_2(v, uri4(w)) \rightarrow \text{owl:sameAs}(v,uri4(x)),\ \text{sql}(uri4(x),uri4(w))$$

In the next step, the algorithm will try to unify the `owl:sameAs` in (5') with the head of at least one of the rules $(7),(8),(9)$ (if all matched, it would add the union of the tree). Given that the URI template (represented as a function) *uri*4 does not occur in any of the rules, the whole branch will be removed. The resulting program is:

```
(1) answer(v,w) ⟶ union(v,w)
(2)        union(v,w) ⟶ bgp₁(v,w)
(4)              bgp₁(v,w) → hasLicense(v,w)
(5)                    hasLicense(uri4(v),uri4(w)) ⟶ sql(v,w)
```

This query without `owl:sameAs` overhead is now ready to be translated into SQL.   □

This process will also take care of eliminating unnecessary SQL queries used to define `owl:sameAs`. For instance, if the user queries for wellbores, it will remove all the SQL queries used for linking company names. This is why we require a unique URI for each pair category/dataset.

7   Experiments

In this section we present a sets of experiments evaluating the performance of queries over crossed-linked datasets. We integrated EPDS and the NPD fact pages at Statoil extending the existing ontology and the set of mappings, and creating the linking tables. We ran 22 queries covering real information needs of end-users over this integrated OBDA setting. Since EPDS is a production server with confidential data, and its loads changes constantly, and in addition the OBDA setting is too complex to isolate different features of this approach, we also created a controlled OBDA environment in our own server to perform a careful study our technique. In addition, we exported the triples of this controlled environment and load them into the commercial triple store Stardog[8] (v3.0.1).

To perform the controlled experiments, we setup an OBDA cross-linked environment based on the Wisconsin Benchmark [5].[9] The Wisconsin benchmark was designed for the systematic evaluation of database performance with respect to different query characteristics. It comes with a schema that is designed so one can quickly understand the structure of each table and the distribution of each attribute value. This allows easy construction of queries that isolate the features that need to be tested. The schema can be used to instantiate multiple tables. These tables, which we now call "Wisconsin tables", contain 16 attributes, and a primary key.

Observe that *Ontop* does not perform SQL federation, therefore it usually relies on systems such as Teiid [10] or EXAREME [17] (a.k.a. ADP) to integrate multiple databases. These systems expose to *Ontop* a set of tables coming from the different databases. Thus, to mimic this scenario we created a single database with 10 tables: 4 Wisconsin tables, representing different datasets, and 6 linking tables. Each Wisconsin table contains 100M rows, the 6 tables occupied ca. 100GB of disk space, exposing +1.8B triples.

---

[8] http://stardog.com

[9] All the material to reproduce the experiments can be found online: https://github.com/ontop/ontop-examples/tree/master/iswc-crosslinked

[10] http://teiid.jboss.org

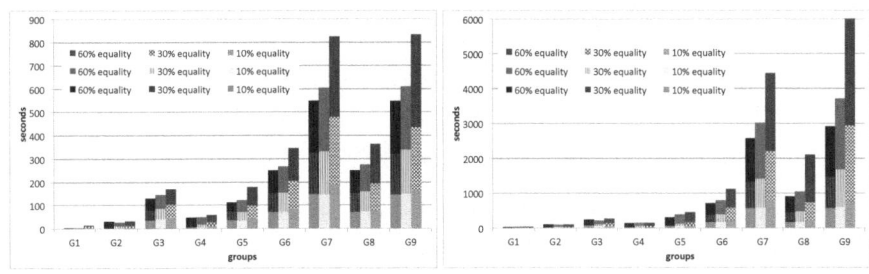

Fig. 6. Worst Execution Time including fetching time - 2 linked-DS (left) and 3 linked-DS (right)

The following experiments evaluate the overhead of equality reasoning when answering SPARQL queries. The variables we considered are: *(i)* Number of SPARQL joins (1-4); *(ii)* Number and type of properties (0-4 /data-object); *(iii)* Number of linked datasets (2-3); *(iv)* Selectivity of the query (0.001%, 0.01%, 0.1%); *(v)* Number of equal objects between datasets (10%,30%,60%). In total we ran 1332 queries. The SPARQL queries have the following template:

```
SELECT *  WHERE {
?x rdf:type :Class_i . // i =1..4
?x :DataProperty_{j-1} ?y1 . ?x :DataProperty_j ?y2 . // j =0..4
?x :ObjectProperty_{k-1} ?z1 . ?x :ObjectProperty_k ?z2 . // k =0..4
Filter( ?y < k% ) }
```

where a 0 or negative subindex means that the property is not present in the query. When we evaluated 2 datasets we included equalities between elements of the classes A_1 and A_2. When we evaluated 3 datasets the equality was between A_1, A_2 and A_4. The class A_3 and the properties S_3 and R_3 are isolated. We group the queries in 9 groups: (G1) No properties (c), (G2) 1 d. prop. 0 obj. prop. (1d), (G3) 0 d. prop. 1 obj. prop. (1o),..., (G9)2 d. prop. 2 obj. prop. (2d2o).

The average start-up time is ≈5 seconds. Observe that SPARQL engines based on materialization can take hours to start-up with OWL-DL ontologies [9]. The results are summarized in Figure 6. We show the *worst* execution time in each group including the time that it takes to fetch the results.

Discussion: The results confirm that reasoning over OBDA-based integrated data has a high cost, but this cost is not prohibitive. The execution times at Statoil range from 3.2 seconds to 12.8 minutes, with mean 53 secs, and median 8.6 secs. An overview of the execution times are shown in Fig. 7. The most complex query had 15 triple patterns, using object and data properties coming from both data sources.

In the controlled environment, in the 2 linked-datasets scenario, with 120M equal objects (60%), even in the worst case most of the queries run in ≈ 5min. The query that performs the worst in this setting, (4 joins, 2 data properties,

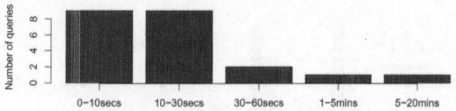

Fig. 7. Overview of query execution times for tests on EPDS at Statoil.

2 object properties, 10^5 selectivity) returns 480.000 results, and takes $\approx$ 13min. When we move to the 3 linked-datasets scenario, most executions (again worst time in every group) take around than 15min. In this case, the worst query in $G9$ takes around 1.5hs and returns 1.620.000 results. One can see that the number of linked datasets is the variable that impacts the most on the query performance. The second variable is the number of object properties since its translation is more complex than the one for data properties. The third variable, is the selectivity. It is worth noticing that these results measure an almost pathological case taking the system to its very limit. In practice, it is unlikely that 60% of the all the objects of a 300M integrated dataset will be equal and belong to the same category. Recall that if they are not in the same category, the optimization presented in Section 6 removes the unnecessary SQL subqueries. For instance, in the integration of EPDS and NPD there are less than 10.000 equal wellbores and there are millions of objects of different categories. Moreover, even 1.5hs is a reasonable time. Recall that Statoil users required weeks to get an answer for this sort of queries.

Because of the partial evaluation-based optimizations proposed in Section 6, with 2 datasets 30 out of 48 queries (52 out of 100 with 3 datasets) get optimized and executed in a few milliseconds. These queries are the ones that join elements in $A_{1,2,4}$ (3 datasets) with $A3$, S_3 and R_3 elements. Since there is no equality between these elements, neither through owl:sameAs, nor with standard equality, the SPARQL translation produces an empty SQL, and no SQL query gets executed returning automatically 0 answers.

To load the data into Stardog we used *Ontop* to materialize the triples. The materialization took 11hs, and it took another 4hs to load the triples into Stardog. The default semantics that Stardog gives to owl:sameAs is not compliant with the official OWL semantics since "Stardog designates one canonical individual for each owl:sameAs equivalence set"; however, one can force Stardog to consider all the URIs in the equivalence set. Our experiments show that Stardog does not behave according to the claimed semantics. Details can be found in [3].

8   Related Work

The treatment of owl:sameAs in reasoning and query evaluation has received considerable interest in recent years. After all, many data sources in the Linked Opend Data (LOD) cloud give owl:sameAs links to equivalent URIs, so it would be desirable to use them. Surprisingly, to the best of our knowledge, there has been no attempt to extend OBDA to take into account owl:sameAs. Next we discuss several approaches that handle owl:sameAs trough rewriting.

Balloon Fusion [16] is a line of work that attempts to make use of owl:sameAs information in the LOD cloud for query answering. The approach is similar to ours in that it is based on *rewriting a query* to take into account equality inferences, before executing it. The treatment of owl:sameAs is semantically very incomplete however, since the rewriting only applies to URIs stated explicitly in the query. No equality reasoning is applied to the *variables* in the query, which is a main point of our work.

The question of equality handling becomes quite different in nature in the context of a single data store that is already in triple format. Equality can then be handled essentially by rewriting equal URIs to one common representative. E.g. [13] report on doing this for an in-memory triple store, while simultaneously saturating the data with respect to a set of forward chaining inference rules. Observe that in many scenarios (such as the Statoil scenario discussed here) this approach is not possible, both due to the fact that the data should be moved from the original source, and because of the amount of data that should be loaded into memory. In a query rewriting, OBDA setting, this corresponds to the idea of making sure that mappings will map equivalent entities from several sources to the same URI – which is often not practical or even impossible.

Our approach is only valid when the links between records really mean semantic identity. When the links are uncertain, query answering then requires the use of probabilistic database methods, as discussed e.g. in [7] for a limited type of queries. Extending these methods to handle arbitrary SPARQL-style queries is not trivial.

9   Conclusions

In this paper we showed how to represent links over database as owl:sameAs statements, we propose a mapping-based framework that carefully constructs owl:sameAs statements to minimize the performance impact of equality reasoning. To recover rewritability of SPARQL into SQL we imposed a suitable set of restrictions on the linking mechanisms that are fully compatible with real world requirements, and together with the owl:sameAs-mappings make it possible to do the SPARQL-to-SQL translation. We showed how to answer SPARQL queries over crossed linked datasets using query transformation. and how to optimize the translation to improve the performance of the produced SQL query. To empirically support this claim, we provided an extensive set of experiments over real enterprise data, and also in a controlled environment.

Acknowledgments. This paper is supported by the EU under the large-scale integrating project (IP) Optique (Scalable End-user Access to Big Data), grant agreement n. FP7-318338.

References

1. Artale, A., Calvanese, D., Kontchakov, R., Zakharyaschev, M.: The DL-Lite family and relations. J. of Artificial Intelligence Research **36**, 1–69 (2009)
2. Calvanese, D., De Giacomo, G., Lembo, D., Lenzerini, M., Rosati, R.: Tractable reasoning and efficient query answering in description logics: The DL-Lite family. J. Autom. Reasoning **39**(3), 385–429 (2007)
3. Calvanese, D., Giese, M., Hovland, D., Rezk, M.: Ontology-based integration of cross-linked datasets (2015). http://www.inf.unibz.it/~mrezk/pdf/techRep-ISWC15.pdf (accessed April 30, 2015)
4. Das, S., Sundara, S., Cyganiak, R.: R2RML: RDB to RDF mapping language. W3C Recommendation, W3C (September 2012). http://www.w3.org/TR/r2rml/
5. DeWitt, D.J.: The wisconsin benchmark: past, present, and future. In: Gray, J. (ed.) The Benchmark Handbook. Morgan Kaufmann (1992)
6. Doan, A., Halevy, A.Y., Ives, Z.G.: Principles of Data Integration. Morgan Kaufmann (2012)
7. Ioannou, E., Nejdl, W., Niederée, C., Velegrakis, Y.: On-the-fly entity-aware query processing in the presence of linkage. PVLDB **3**(1), 429–438 (2010)
8. Kontchakov, R., Lutz, C., Toman, D., Wolter, F., Zakharyaschev, M.: The combined approach to ontology-based data access. In: Proc. of IJCAI 2011, pp. 2656–2661 (2011)
9. Kontchakov, R., Rezk, M., Rodríguez-Muro, M., Xiao, G., Zakharyaschev, M.: Answering SPARQL queries over databases under OWL 2 QL entailment regime. In: Mika, P., et al. (eds.) ISWC 2014, Part I. LNCS, vol. 8796, pp. 552–567. Springer, Heidelberg (2014)
10. Lloyd, J.W.: Foundations of Logic Programming, 2nd edn. Springer-Verlag New York Inc, Secaucus (1993)
11. Marnette, B.: Generalized schema-mappings: from termination to tractability. In: PODS 2009, pp. 13–22. ACM, New York (2009)
12. Motik, B., Cuenca Grau, B., Horrocks, I., Wu, Z., Fokoue, A., Lutz, C.: OWL 2 Web Ontology Language profiles, 2nd edn. W3C Recommendation, W3C (December 2012). http://www.w3.org/TR/owl2-profiles/
13. Motik, B., Nenov, Y., Piro, R.E.F., Horrocks, I.: Handling owl:sameAs via rewriting. In: Bonet, B., Koenig, S. (eds) Proc. 29th AAAI, pp. 231–237. AAAI Press (2015)
14. Rodríguez-Muro, M., Kontchakov, R., Zakharyaschev, M.: Ontology-based data access: *Ontop* of databases. In: Alani, H., et al. (eds.) ISWC 2013, Part I. LNCS, vol. 8218, pp. 558–573. Springer, Heidelberg (2013)
15. Rodriguez-Muro, M., Rezk, M.: Efficient SPARQL-to-SQL with R2RML mappings. J. of Web Semantics **33**, 141–169 (2015)
16. Schlegel, K., Stegmaier, F., Bayerl, S., Granitzer, M., Kosch, H.: Balloon fusion: SPARQL rewriting based on unified co-reference information. In: Proc. of the 30th Int. Conf. on Data Engineering Workshops (ICDE 2014), pp. 254–259. IEEE (2014)
17. Tsangaris, M.M., Kakaletris, G., Kllapi, H., Papanikos, G., Pentaris, F., Polydoras, P., Sitaridi, E., Stoumpos, V., Ioannidis, Y.E.: Dataflow processing and optimization on grid and cloud infrastructures. IEEE Bull. on Data Engineering **32**(1), 67–74 (2009)

Mapping Analysis in Ontology-Based Data Access: Algorithms and Complexity

Domenico Lembo[1][(✉)], Jose Mora[1], Riccardo Rosati[1], Domenico Fabio Savo[1],
and Evgenij Thorstensen[2]

[1] Sapienza Università di Roma, Rome, Italy
{lembo,mora,rosati,savo}@dis.uniroma1.it
[2] University of Oslo, Oslo, Norway
evgenit@ifi.uio.no

Abstract. Ontology-based data access (OBDA) is a recent paradigm
for accessing data sources through an ontology that acts as a conceptual, integrated view of the data, and declarative mappings that connect the ontology to the data sources. We study the formal analysis of
mappings in OBDA. Specifically, we focus on the problem of identifying mapping inconsistency and redundancy, two of the most important
anomalies for mappings in OBDA. We consider a wide range of ontology
languages that comprises OWL 2 and all its profiles, and examine mapping languages of different expressiveness over relational databases. We
provide algorithms and establish tight complexity bounds for the decision problems associated with mapping inconsistency and redundancy.
Our results prove that, in our general framework, such forms of mapping
analysis enjoy nice computational properties, in the sense that they are
not harder than standard reasoning tasks over the ontology or over the
relational database schema.

1 Introduction

Ontology-based data access (OBDA) [18] is a recent paradigm for accessing
data sources through an *ontology* (also called TBox) that acts as a conceptual,
integrated view of the data, and declarative *mappings* that connect the ontology
to the data sources. The framework of OBDA has received a lot of attention in
the last years: many theoretical studies have paved the way for the construction
of OBDA systems (e.g., [6,11,19] and the development of OBDA projects for
enterprise data management in various domains [2,15].

One important aspect in OBDA concerns the construction of a system specification, i.e., defining the ontology and the mappings over an existing set of
data sources. Mappings are indeed the most complex part of an OBDA specification, since they have to capture the semantics of the data sources and express
such semantics in terms of the ontology. More precisely, a mapping is a set
of assertions, each one associating a query $\phi(\boldsymbol{x})$ over the source schema with
a query $\psi(\boldsymbol{x})$ over the ontology. The intuitive meaning of a mapping assertion is that all the tuples satisfying the query $\phi(\boldsymbol{x})$ also satisfy the query

© Springer International Publishing Switzerland 2015
M. Arenas et al. (Eds.): ISWC 2015, Part I, LNCS 9366, pp. 217–234, 2015.
DOI: 10.1007/978-3-319-25007-6_13

$\psi(\boldsymbol{x})$. We write a mapping assertion as $\phi(\boldsymbol{x}) \rightsquigarrow \psi(\boldsymbol{x})$. As an example, consider $\mathsf{tabP}(x, y, z) \rightsquigarrow \mathsf{person}(x), \mathsf{name}(x, y)$, which maps the ontology predicates person and name to the database relation tabP, thus indicating how ontology instances can be constructed from the data retrieved at the sources.

The first experiences in the application of the OBDA framework in real-world scenarios (e.g., [2, 15]) have shown that the semantic distance between the conceptual and the data layer is often very large, because data sources are mostly application-oriented: this makes the definition, debugging, and maintenance of mappings a hard and complex task. Such experiences have clearly shown the need of tools for supporting the management of mappings.

However, no specific approach (with the exception of [17]) has explicitly dealt with the problem of mapping analysis in the context of OBDA. The work on *schema mappings in data exchange* has considered the problem of analyzing the formal properties of mappings, although in a different framework. Indeed, in data exchange the ontology is replaced by a relational schema, called target schema, possibly equipped with tuple-generating dependencies and equality-generating dependencies [3, 10]. Such kinds of dependencies are not able to capture arbitrary ontology languages, such as those considered in this paper. Also, in data exchange suitable conditions are imposed on the interaction among database dependencies to guarantee that *finite* instances for the target schema exist that are coherent with the database at the sources, the mapping, and the target dependencies. Such conditions are normally not imposed in OBDA, where the focus is not on moving data from the sources to the target, and indeed we do not adopt them. Among the works on data exchange, [12] is the closest to our approach: it proposes techniques for the optimization and normalization of schema mappings, in particular, finding a global, semantically equivalent transformation of a set of mappings that is optimal with respect to some minimality criterion.

In a recent paper [17], we started providing a theoretical basis for mapping management support in OBDA, focusing on the formal analysis of mappings in ontology-based data access. In particular, in that paper the two most important semantic anomalies of mappings have been analyzed: inconsistency and redundancy. Roughly speaking, an inconsistent mapping for an ontology and a source schema is a specification that gives rise to logical contradictions with the ontology and/or the source schema. Then, a mapping $\mathcal{M}$ is redundant with respect to an OBDA specification if adding $\mathcal{M}$ to the specification does not change its semantics. Verifying whether a mapping is affected by these anomalies is a crucial task in OBDA. A designer that is creating (or modifying) the mapping needs to know whether the new (or updated) mapping leads to an inconsistency. Given the complexity of the OBDA specification, this is very hard to check manually. Similarly, a redundant mapping is not wanted, since it is very difficult to maintain; furthermore, it may affect the performance of query answering [8].

The work presented in [17] has defined both a *local* notion of mapping inconsistency and redundancy, which focuses on single mapping assertions, and a *global* notion, where inconsistency and redundancy is considered with respect to a whole mapping specification (set of mapping assertions). In this paper, we study the computational properties of verifying both local and global mapping inconsistency and redundancy in an OBDA specification. We consider a wide range of ontology languages that comprises the description logics underlying OWL 2 and all its profiles (OWL 2 EL, OWL 2 QL, and OWL 2 RL),[1] and examine mapping languages of different expressiveness (the so-called GAV and GLAV mappings [9]) over sources corresponding to relational databases. We provide algorithms and establish tight complexity bounds for the decision problems associated with both local and global mapping inconsistency and mapping redundancy, for both GAV mappings and a large class of GLAV mappings, and for both combined complexity and TBox complexity (which only considers the size of the TBox).

The outcome of our analysis is twofold. First, in our framework, it is possible to define *general and modular techniques* that are able to reduce the analysis of mappings to the composition of standard reasoning tasks over the ontology (inconsistency and instance checking, query answering) and over the data sources (query answering and containment). This is a non-trivial result, because mappings are formulas combining both ontology and data source elements. Moreover, the above forms of mapping analysis enjoy *nice computational properties*, in the sense that they are not harder than the above mentioned standard reasoning tasks over the ontology and the data sources (see Figure 1 and Figure 2 at the end of the paper).

The above results allow us to conclude that, in our OBDA framework, the formal analysis of mappings is feasible, at least for ontology languages enjoying nice computational properties, as in the case of the three OWL 2 profiles.

The paper is organized as follows. In Section 2 we recall OBDA specifications and the formal notions of mapping inconsistency and redundancy in OBDA. In Section 3 we study the complexity of checking local and global mapping inconsistency, while in Section 4 we study the complexity of verifying local and global mapping redundancy. We conclude the paper in Section 5.

2   Preliminaries

In the following, we assume to have three pairwise disjoint, countably infinite alphabets: an alphabet Γ_T of ontology predicates, an alphabet Γ_S of source schema predicates, and an alphabet Γ_C of constants.

Source Schemas.   A source schema $\mathcal{S}$ is a relational schema containing relations in Γ_S, possibly equipped with integrity constraints (ICs). A *legal instance* D *for* $\mathcal{S}$ is a database for $\mathcal{S}$ (i.e., a finite set of ground atoms over $\mathcal{S}$ and the constants in Γ_C) that satisfies the ICs of $\mathcal{S}$. We denote by $Const(D)$ the set of constants occurring in D.

We consider *simple schemas*, i.e., relational schemas without ICs, and *FD schemas*, i.e., simple schemas with *functional dependencies* (FDs) [1]. We adopt standard notions for conjunctive queries (CQs) over relational schemas [1], and

---

[1] http://www.w3.org/TR/owl2-profiles/

by a CQ over a source schema $\mathcal{S}$ we mean a CQ over the alphabet of $\mathcal{S}$. With $\phi(\boldsymbol{x})$ we denote a CQ with free variables $\boldsymbol{x}$. The number of variables in $\boldsymbol{x}$ is the arity of the query. A Boolean CQ is a CQ without free variables. Given a CQ q over $\mathcal{S}$ and a legal instance D for $\mathcal{S}$, $eval(q, D)$ denotes the evaluation of q over D. Throughout the paper $\mathcal{S}$ will always denote a source schema.

Ontologies. We consider ontologies expressed in some Description Logic (DL) language $\mathcal{L}_{\mathcal{O}}$ and use standard DL notions [16]. In particular, a DL ontology $\mathcal{O}$ is pair $\langle \mathcal{T}, \mathcal{A} \rangle$, where $\mathcal{T}$ is the TBox and $\mathcal{A}$ is the ABox. $\mathcal{O}$, $\mathcal{T}$, and $\mathcal{A}$ will always have the same meaning in the paper. As in the W3C standard OWL, we do not interpret ontologies under the Unique Name Assumption. We denote with $Mod(\mathcal{O})$ the set of models of $\mathcal{O}$, and with $\mathcal{O} \models \alpha$ the fact that $\mathcal{O}$ entails a sentence α. Also, by *ontology inconsistency* we mean the task of deciding whether $Mod(\mathcal{O}) = \emptyset$, and by *instance checking* the task of deciding whether $\mathcal{O} \models \beta$, where β is a ground atom. By *CQs over* $\mathcal{O}$ we mean CQs over the alphabet of the TBox of $\mathcal{O}$, and by *CQ entailment* the task of checking whether $\mathcal{O} \models q$, where q is a Boolean CQ. In the following, we consider DLs that are the logical basis of the W3C standard OWL and of its profiles, i.e., $\mathcal{SROIQ}$ [14], which underpins OWL, $DL\text{-}Lite_R$ [5], which is the basis of OWL 2 QL, RL [16], a simplified version of OWL 2 RL, and $\mathcal{EL}_{\perp}$, a slight extension of the DL $\mathcal{EL}$ [4], which is the basis of OWL 2 EL.

Mappings. A *mapping assertion* m from a source schema $\mathcal{S}$ to a TBox $\mathcal{T}$ has the form $\phi(\boldsymbol{x}) \rightsquigarrow \psi(\boldsymbol{x})$, where $\phi(\boldsymbol{x})$, called the *body of* m, and $\psi(\boldsymbol{x})$, called the *head of* m, are queries over $\mathcal{S}$ and $\mathcal{T}$, respectively, both with free variables $\boldsymbol{x}$, which are called the *frontier variables*. The number of variables in $\boldsymbol{x}$ is the *arity* of the mapping assertion. Given a mapping assertion m, we also use $FR(m)$ do denote the frontier variables $\boldsymbol{x}$, $head(m)$ to denote the query $\psi(\boldsymbol{x})$, and $body(m)$ to denote the query $\phi(\boldsymbol{x})$. We also remark that queries used in our mappings, besides variables, may contain constants from Γ_C. A mapping $\mathcal{M}$ from $\mathcal{S}$ to $\mathcal{T}$ is a finite set of mapping assertions from $\mathcal{S}$ to $\mathcal{T}$. Hereinafter $\mathcal{M}$ will always denote a mapping.

In principle, $\phi(\boldsymbol{x})$ and $\psi(\boldsymbol{x})$ can be specified in generic query languages. The literature on data integration and OBDA has mainly considered $\phi(\boldsymbol{x})$ expressed in a (fragment of) first-order logic, and $\psi(\boldsymbol{x})$ expressed as a CQ [9,17,18]. In this paper, we focus on the notable cases in which $\phi(\boldsymbol{x})$ is a CQ over $\mathcal{S}$ and $\psi(\boldsymbol{x})$ is as follows:

- $\psi(\boldsymbol{x})$ is a CQ over $\mathcal{T}$. This is a powerful form of GLAV mapping [9], and is among the most expressive types of mappings studied in the literature. We refer to it simply as *GLAV*.
- $\psi(\boldsymbol{x})$ is a CQ with a bounded number of existential variables in the head. This is a practically relevant form of GLAV mappings, which we call $GLAV_{BE}$.
- $\psi(\boldsymbol{x})$ is a CQ without existential variables in the head. Such mappings are the most used in OBDA applications [2,13], and are a special case of the W3C standard R2RML mappings [7]. According to the data integration literature, we call them *GAV*.

We say that a mapping assertion m *is active on a source instance* D if $eval(body(m), D)$ is a non-empty set of tuples of constants. A mapping $\mathcal{M}$ is active on D if all its mapping assertions $m \in \mathcal{M}$ are active on D.

Without loss of generality, we assume that different mapping assertions use different variable symbols. A *freeze* of a set of atoms Γ is a set of ground atoms obtained from Γ by replacing every variable with a *fresh* distinct constant. In this paper, the freeze is always used in the context of a mapping $\mathcal{M}$, so it suffices to assume that fresh constants do not appear in $\mathcal{M}$. Different freezes of the same set of atoms are equal up to renaming of constants. Thus, in the following we assume, without loss of generality, that the freeze of a set of atoms Γ is unique and is obtained by replacing each variable occurrence x with a fresh constant c_x, and we denote it by $freeze(\Gamma)$.

Given a mapping assertion m of arity n and an n-tuple of constants $\boldsymbol{t}$, we denote by $m(\boldsymbol{t})$ the mapping assertion obtained by replacing $FR(m)$ in m with the constants in $\boldsymbol{t}$.

OBDA Specifications.   An OBDA specification is a triple $\mathcal{J} = \langle \mathcal{T}, \mathcal{S}, \mathcal{M} \rangle$. The semantics of $\mathcal{J}$ is given with respect to a database instance D legal for $\mathcal{S}$: a model for $\mathcal{J}$ w.r.t. D is a FOL interpretation $\mathcal{I}$ over the alphabet $\Gamma_\mathcal{T} \cup \Gamma_\mathcal{C}$ that satisfies both $\mathcal{T}$ and $\mathcal{M}$. Formally, we say that $\mathcal{I}$ satisfies the mapping $\mathcal{M}$ if for each assertion $m \in \mathcal{M}$ and each tuple of constants $\boldsymbol{t}$ such that $\boldsymbol{t} \in eval(body(m), D)$ we have that $\mathcal{I} \models head(m(\boldsymbol{t}))$. The set of models of $\mathcal{J}$ w.r.t. D is denoted with $Mod(\mathcal{J}, D)$. Also, we use $(\mathcal{J}, D)$ to denote $\mathcal{J}$ with source instance D, say that $(\mathcal{J}, D)$ *is inconsistent* if $Mod(\mathcal{J}, D) = \emptyset$, and denote with $(\mathcal{J}, D) \models \alpha$ the entailment of a sentence α by $(\mathcal{J}, D)$.

Example 1. We consider a source schema $\mathcal{S}$ where the `plants` relation contains data on extraction facilities, while the `eZones` relation contains data on the areas used for oil and gas extraction. Below, the underlined attributes represent the keys of the relations, which can be expressed by FDs.

$$\text{plants}(\underline{\text{id\_pl}}, \text{pl\_typ}, \text{id\_zn}) \qquad \text{eZones}(\underline{\text{id\_zn}}, \text{zn\_typ})$$

The following RL TBox models a very small portion of the domain of oil and gas production extracted from an ontology developed within the Optique EU project[2]. In particular, the TBox focuses on the facilities (concept Facility) used in the oil and gas extraction and on the geographical areas (concept Area) in which they are located (role locatedIn). Facilities that are located in a marine area (concept MarArea) are platforms (concept Platform).

$\mathcal{T} = \{$ Platform $\sqsubseteq$ Facility,   MarArea $\sqsubseteq$ Area, $\exists$locatedIn $\sqsubseteq$ Facility,
$\qquad \exists$locatedIn$^-$ $\sqsubseteq$ Area   Facility $\sqcap$ Area $\sqsubseteq$ $\bot$ $\exists$locatedIn.MarArea $\sqsubseteq$ Platform $\}$

An example of a GAV mapping $\mathcal{M}$ from $\mathcal{S}$ to $\mathcal{T}$ follows:

m_1 : $\text{plants}(x, y, z)$ $\rightsquigarrow$ Facility(x), locatedIn(x, z)
m_2 : $\text{plants}(x', \text{`pl'}, y')$ $\rightsquigarrow$ Platform(x')
m_3 : $\text{eZones}(z', \text{`mz'})$ $\rightsquigarrow$ MarArea(z').   ∎

――――――――――
[2] http://www.optique-project.eu/

Mapping Inconsistency and Redundancy. The following definitions are taken from [17].

In brief, a mapping assertion m from $\mathcal{S}$ to $\mathcal{T}$ is head-inconsistent or body-inconsistent if $head(m)$ or $body(m)$ have certainly an empty evaluation in every model for $\mathcal{T}$ or legal instance for $\mathcal{S}$, respectively.

Definition 1 (mapping head-inconsistency). *Let $\mathcal{T}$ be a TBox, $\mathcal{S}$ a source schema, and $m : \phi(\boldsymbol{x}) \rightsquigarrow \psi(\boldsymbol{x})$ a mapping assertion from $\mathcal{S}$ to $\mathcal{T}$. We say that m is head-inconsistent for $\mathcal{T}$ if $\mathcal{T} \models \forall\boldsymbol{x}.(\neg\psi(\boldsymbol{x}))$.*

Example 2. Let $\mathcal{T}$ and $\mathcal{S}$ be as in Example 1. Consider the following mapping assertion:

$m : \mathtt{plants}(x,\text{`pl'},z) \rightsquigarrow \mathsf{Platform}(x), \mathsf{MarArea}(x)$

Then, m is head-inconsistent for $\mathcal{T}$ since $\mathcal{T} \models \mathsf{Platform} \sqcap \mathsf{MarArea} \sqsubseteq \bot$.   ∎

Definition 2 (mapping body-inconsistency). *Let $\mathcal{T}$ be a TBox, $\mathcal{S}$ a source schema, and $m : \phi(\boldsymbol{x}) \rightsquigarrow \psi(\boldsymbol{x})$ a mapping assertion from $\mathcal{S}$ to $\mathcal{T}$. We say that m is body-inconsistent for $\mathcal{S}$ if $\mathcal{S} \models \forall\boldsymbol{x}.(\neg\phi(\boldsymbol{x}))$.*

Example 3. Let $\mathcal{T}$ and $\mathcal{S}$ be as in Example 1. Then, the following mapping assertion is body-inconsistent for $\mathcal{S}$.

$m : \mathtt{plants}(x,\text{`pl'},z), \mathtt{plants}(x,\text{`ref'},k) \rightsquigarrow \mathsf{Facility}(x)$ ∎

We extend the inconsistency notions to whole mapping assertions and whole mappings.

Definition 3 (local mapping inconsistency). *Let $\mathcal{T}$ be a TBox, $\mathcal{S}$ a source schema, and $m : \phi(\boldsymbol{x}) \rightsquigarrow \psi(\boldsymbol{x})$ a mapping assertion from $\mathcal{S}$ to $\mathcal{T}$. We say that m is inconsistent for $\langle\mathcal{T},\mathcal{S}\rangle$ if m is head-inconsistent for $\mathcal{T}$ or body-inconsistent for $\mathcal{S}$.*

Definition 4 (global mapping inconsistency). *Let $\mathcal{J} = \langle\mathcal{T},\mathcal{S},\mathcal{M}\rangle$ be an OBDA specification. We say that $\mathcal{M}$ is globally inconsistent for $\langle\mathcal{T},\mathcal{S}\rangle$ if there does not exist a source instance D legal for $\mathcal{S}$ such that $\mathcal{M}$ is active on D and $Mod(\mathcal{J},D) \neq \emptyset$.*

Intuitively, it is impossible to consistently activate all the assertions of a globally inconsistent mapping simultaneously.

Example 4. Let $\mathcal{J} = \langle\mathcal{T},\mathcal{S},\mathcal{M}\rangle$ be an OBDA specification where $\mathcal{T}$ and $\mathcal{S}$ are as in Example 1. Suppose that the mapping $\mathcal{M}$ contains the following mapping assertions:

$m_1 : \mathtt{plants}(x,y,z) \rightsquigarrow \mathsf{Area}(x)$
$m_2 : \mathtt{plants}(x',\text{`pl'},z') \rightsquigarrow \mathsf{Platform}(x'), \mathsf{locatedIn}(x',z')$

It is easy to see that $\mathcal{M}$ is globally inconsistent for $\langle \mathcal{T}, \mathcal{S} \rangle$, because $\mathcal{T} \models$ Platform$\sqcap$ Area $\sqsubseteq \bot$ and every activation of m_2 also activates m_1, thus implying Platform(x) and Area(x) for the same individual x.   ∎

Then, we recall the notion of global mapping redundancy.

Definition 5 (global mapping redundancy). *Let $\mathcal{J} = \langle \mathcal{T}, \mathcal{S}, \mathcal{M} \rangle$ be an OBDA specification and let $\mathcal{M}'$ be a mapping from $\mathcal{S}$ to $\mathcal{T}$. We say that $\mathcal{M}'$ is globally redundant for $\mathcal{J}$ if, for every source instance D that is legal for $\mathcal{S}$, $Mod(\langle \mathcal{T}, \mathcal{S}, \mathcal{M} \rangle, D) = Mod(\langle \mathcal{T}, \mathcal{S}, \mathcal{M} \cup \mathcal{M}' \rangle, D)$.*

Informally, a mapping $\mathcal{M}'$ is redundant for an OBDA specification $\mathcal{J}$ if adding $\mathcal{M}'$ to $\mathcal{J}$ produces a specification equivalent to $\mathcal{J}$.

Example 5. Let $\langle \mathcal{T}, \mathcal{S}, \mathcal{M} \rangle$ be an OBDA specification, where $\mathcal{T}$ and $\mathcal{S}$ are as in Example 1, and $\mathcal{M}$ is as follows:

m_1 : plants(x, y, z), eZones$(z, \text{'mz'})$ $\rightsquigarrow$ locatedIn(x, z)
m_2 : eZones$(x', \text{'mz'})$ $\rightsquigarrow$ MarArea(x')
m_3 : plants$(y', \text{'pl'}, z')$, eZones$(z', \text{'mz'})$ $\rightsquigarrow$ Platform(y')

Then, $\{m_3\}$ is globally redundant for $\langle \mathcal{T}, \mathcal{S}, \{m_1, m_2\} \rangle$.   ∎

Finally, *local mapping redundancy* is a special case of global mapping redundancy in which the mappings $\mathcal{M}$ and $\mathcal{M}'$ are both composed of a single assertion.

3   Complexity of Mapping Inconsistency

We now study local and global mapping inconsistency and show that, for every DL $\mathcal{L}_\mathcal{O}$, both problems have the same TBox complexity as ontology inconsistency in $\mathcal{L}_\mathcal{O}$. We also establish combined complexity results for the DLs considered in this paper.

We start with some auxiliary definitions.

Definition 6 (minimal instance activating a mapping). *Let $\mathcal{M}$ be a mapping and let $\mathcal{S}$ be a source schema. A minimal instance for $\mathcal{S}$ that activates $\mathcal{M}$ is a source instance D legal for $\mathcal{S}$ such that $\mathcal{M}$ is active on D and, for every source instance D' legal for $\mathcal{S}$ such that $\mathcal{M}$ is active on D', there exists a homomorphism h from $Const(D)$ to $Const(D')$ that maps constants occurring in $\mathcal{M}$ to themselves and is such that $h(D) \subseteq D'$, where $h(D) = \{r(h(c_1), \ldots, h(c_n)) \mid r(c_1, \ldots, c_n) \in D\}$.*

Given a GLAV mapping assertion m of arity n, we denote by $cvars(m)$ the sequence of frontier variables occurring together with an existential variable in an atom of the head of m. Moreover, given an n-tuple of constants $\boldsymbol{t}$, we denote by $cvars(m)[\boldsymbol{t}]$ the tuple of constants obtained from $cvars(m)$ by replacing each occurrence of a frontier variable with the corresponding constant of $\boldsymbol{t}$. For instance, if m is the assertion $\phi(x, w) \rightsquigarrow R(x, y), S(y, z), T(z, w), R(x, z), S(w, x)$, then $cvars(m)$ is the tuple of variables $\langle x, w, x \rangle$, and if $\boldsymbol{t} = \langle a, b \rangle$ then $cvars(m)[\boldsymbol{t}]$ is the tuple of constants $\langle a, b, a \rangle$.

Definition 7 (retrieved ABox). *Given a mapping $\mathcal{M}$ from $\mathcal{S}$ to $\mathcal{T}$ and an instance D legal for $\mathcal{S}$, the ABox retrieved by $\mathcal{M}$ from D, denoted by $Retr(\mathcal{M}, D)$, is the ABox defined as follows: $Retr(\mathcal{M}, D) = \{freezeH(head(m(\boldsymbol{t}))) \mid \boldsymbol{t} \in eval(body(m), D)\})$, where $freezeH(head(m(\boldsymbol{t})))$ is the set of atoms obtained from $head(m(\boldsymbol{t}))$ by replacing each occurrence of a (existential) variable x with the fresh constant $c_{x, cvars(m)[\boldsymbol{t}]}$.*

3.1   Local Mapping Inconsistency

We start from the following property (whose proof is trivial) for the problem of head inconsistency.

Lemma 1. *Let m be a GLAV mapping assertion, $\mathcal{T}$ a TBox, and let $\mathcal{A} = freeze(head(m))$. Then, m is head-inconsistent for $\mathcal{T}$ iff $\langle \mathcal{T}, \mathcal{A} \rangle$ is inconsistent.*

Conversely, inconsistency of an ontology $\langle \mathcal{T}, \mathcal{A} \rangle$ can be immediately reduced to head inconsistency, considering $\mathcal{T}$ as the TBox of the OBDA specification, and constructing a GAV mapping assertion m (with no frontier variables) whose head is the conjunction of the ABox assertions in $\mathcal{A}$. Consequently, the following property holds.

Lemma 2. *For both GAV and GLAV mappings and for every ontology language $\mathcal{L}_{\mathcal{O}}$, the combined (resp., TBox) complexity of mapping head inconsistency is the same as the combined (resp., TBox) complexity of ontology inconsistency in $\mathcal{L}_{\mathcal{O}}$.*

Now, from the definition of local mapping inconsistency, it follows that the TBox complexity of local mapping inconsistency is the same as the TBox complexity of mapping head inconsistency. Therefore:

Theorem 1. *For both GAV and GLAV mappings and for every ontology language $\mathcal{L}_{\mathcal{O}}$, the TBox complexity of local mapping inconsistency is the same as the TBox complexity of ontology inconsistency in $\mathcal{L}_{\mathcal{O}}$.*

The above theorem implies row 1 in Figure 1.

Moreover, from the definition of local mapping inconsistency, it follows that, for simple source schemas, local mapping inconsistency corresponds to mapping head inconsistency (since all mapping assertions are trivially body-consistent). Therefore:

Corollary 1. *For simple source schemas, for both GAV and GLAV mappings, and for every ontology language $\mathcal{L}_{\mathcal{O}}$, the combined complexity of local mapping inconsistency is the same as the combined complexity of ontology inconsistency in $\mathcal{L}_{\mathcal{O}}$.*

The above result is summarized in row 1 in Figure 2.

Then, we analyze the case of FD schemas. We start by defining the algorithm freezeFD$(\mathcal{M}, \mathcal{S})$, which takes as input a mapping $\mathcal{M}$ and a source schema $\mathcal{S}$, and applies the *chase* procedure [1] to the database instance $D =$

$\bigcup_{m \in \mathcal{M}} freeze(body(m))$ using the functional dependencies of $\mathcal{S}$, and considering the constants occurring in D but not occurring in $\mathcal{M}$ as unifiable terms (since they act as "soft constants" differently from the constants occurring in $\mathcal{M}$). Such a chase procedure runs in PTIME and may end up in two ways: (i) it fails, i.e., it derives that two constants occurring in $\mathcal{M}$ should be equal (which violates the Unique Name Assumption of databases); (ii) it returns a database D' that is obtained from D by unifying constants occurring in D but not occurring in $\mathcal{M}$ according to the equalities induced by the functional dependencies.

We are now able to show the following lemma.

Lemma 3. *Let $\mathcal{S}$ be a source schema and let $\mathcal{M}$ be a mapping. Deciding whether there exists a minimal instance D for $\mathcal{S}$ that activates $\mathcal{M}$, and computing such a D if it exists, can be done: (i) in linear time, if $\mathcal{S}$ is a simple schema; (ii) in PTIME, if $\mathcal{S}$ is an FD schema.*

Proof. The proof easily follows from the fact that the algorithm $\mathsf{freezeFD}(\mathcal{M}, \mathcal{S})$ runs in PTIME, and computes a minimal instance D for $\mathcal{S}$ that activates $\mathcal{M}$ iff such an instance exists. In particular, for property (i), it is easy to verify that, if $\mathcal{S}$ is a simple schema, then $\bigcup_{m \in \mathcal{M}} freeze(body(m))$ is a minimal instance for $\mathcal{S}$ that activates $\mathcal{M}$. For property (ii), in the case when $\mathcal{S}$ is an FD schema, if the algorithm $\mathsf{freezeFD}(\mathcal{M}, \mathcal{S})$ fails, then there exists no legal instance for $\mathcal{S}$ that activates $\mathcal{M}$; otherwise, the algorithm returns a database D' that corresponds to the application of the equalities induced by the functional dependencies over the constants occurring in D but not occurring in $\mathcal{M}$. Therefore, there exists a endomorphism h of the constants in D that is the identity for the constants of $\mathcal{M}$ and is such that $h(D) = D'$. Due to the property of the chase, it follows that such an instance D' is a minimal instance for $\mathcal{S}$ that activates $\mathcal{M}$. □

We can now prove the following property.

Theorem 2. *For both GAV and GLAV mappings, and for FD schemas, the combined complexity of local mapping inconsistency is PTIME-complete for DL-Lite$_R$, RL, and $\mathcal{EL}_\perp$, and is N2EXPTIME-complete for $\mathcal{SROIQ}$.*

Proof. To decide local mapping consistency of m, besides head inconsistency we also have to check body inconsistency of m. This corresponds to decide whether there exists a minimal instance for $\mathcal{S}$ that activates the mapping $\{m\}$. By Lemma 3, this can be done in PTIME in the case of FD schemas. Moreover, consistency of a database D with respect to an FD schema $\mathcal{S}$ can be immediately reduced to mapping body inconsistency, by creating a GAV mapping assertion whose body contains the conjunction of the facts in D. In the case of FD schemas, this provides a PTIME lower bound for body inconsistency, and hence for local mapping inconsistency. The lower bound in the case of $\mathcal{SROIQ}$ follows from the lower bound for head inconsistency. □

The above results are summarized in row 1 in Figure 2.

3.2   Global Mapping Inconsistency

To define a technique for global mapping inconsistency, we start by showing the following property.

Theorem 3. *Let* $\mathcal{J} = \langle \mathcal{T}, \mathcal{S}, \mathcal{M} \rangle$ *be an OBDA specification. Then,* $\mathcal{M}$ *is globally inconsistent for* $\langle \mathcal{T}, \mathcal{S} \rangle$ *iff either* freezeFD$(\mathcal{M}, \mathcal{S})$ *fails or the instance* D *returned by* freezeFD$(\mathcal{M}, \mathcal{S})$ *is such that* $(\mathcal{J}, D)$ *is inconsistent.*

Proof. The proof of the only-if part is trivial. For the if part, we will prove the contrapositive: If $\mathcal{M}$ is not globally inconsistent for $\langle \mathcal{T}, \mathcal{S} \rangle$, then freezeFD$(\mathcal{M}, \mathcal{S})$ returns an instance D such that $(\mathcal{J}, D)$ is consistent.

Let D' be a source instance legal for $\mathcal{S}$ such that $\mathcal{M}$ is active on D', and let $\mathcal{I}$ be a model of $(\mathcal{J}, D')$. Then, freezeFD$(\mathcal{M}, \mathcal{S})$ does not fail and returns an instance D. Since D is minimal, Definition 6 implies that there exists a homomorphism h from the constants of D to the constants of D' such that $h(D) \subseteq D'$. Now let $\mathcal{I}'$ be the interpretation obtained from $\mathcal{I}$ by changing the interpretation of constants as follows: If c occurs in D then $c^{\mathcal{I}'} = h(c)^{\mathcal{I}}$, otherwise $c^{\mathcal{I}'} = c^{\mathcal{I}}$. It is immediate to verify that $\mathcal{I}'$ is a model for $\mathcal{J}$ w.r.t. D.   □

The above theorem immediately implies the following algorithm for deciding the global inconsistency of a GLAV mapping $\mathcal{M}$ for a TBox $\mathcal{T}$ and a source schema $\mathcal{S}$.

Algorithm GlobalInconsistency:
Input: OBDA specification $\langle \mathcal{T}, \mathcal{S}, \mathcal{M} \rangle$
  if (a) algorithm freezeFD$(\mathcal{M}, \mathcal{S})$ fails
  then return true
  else
      let D be the instance returned by freezeFD$(\mathcal{M}, \mathcal{S})$;
      if (b) $(\langle \mathcal{T}, \mathcal{S}, \mathcal{M} \rangle, D)$ is inconsistent
      then return true **else** return false

The complexity of step (a) of the algorithm, i.e., deciding the existence and computing a minimal instance for $\mathcal{S}$ that activates $\mathcal{M}$, has been established by Lemma 3. It remains to analyze the complexity of checking inconsistency of $(\langle \mathcal{T}, \mathcal{S}, \mathcal{M} \rangle, D)$. To this aim, we present two techniques for deciding the inconsistency of $(\langle \mathcal{T}, \mathcal{S}, \mathcal{M} \rangle, D)$. First, we use the following property, whose proof easily follows from Definition 7.

Lemma 4. *For every model* $\mathcal{I}$ *of* $(\langle \mathcal{T}, \mathcal{S}, \mathcal{M} \rangle, D)$ *there exists a model* $\mathcal{I}'$ *of* $\langle \mathcal{T}, Retr(\mathcal{M}, D) \rangle$ *such that* $\mathcal{I}$ *and* $\mathcal{I}'$ *coincide except for the interpretation of the constants in* $Const(Retr(\mathcal{M}, D)) \setminus Const(D)$. *The converse also holds.*

From the above lemma, to decide inconsistency of $(\langle \mathcal{T}, \mathcal{S}, \mathcal{M} \rangle, D)$, we can compute the ABox $\mathcal{A} = Retr(\mathcal{M}, D)$ and then check inconsistency of $\langle \mathcal{T}, \mathcal{A} \rangle$.

Example 6. Let $\mathcal{J} = \langle \mathcal{T}, \mathcal{S}, \mathcal{M} \rangle$ be the OBDA specification of Example 4. We show how algorithm GlobalInconsistency runs on $\mathcal{J}$. First, the algorithm computes a minimal instance D for $\mathcal{S}$ by means of the algorithm freezeFD (cf. Lemma 3). In our example, this actually coincides with computing $freeze(body(m))$ for each mapping $m \in \mathcal{M}$. Hence, we have that $D = \{\text{plants}(c_x, c_y, c_z), \text{plants}(c_{x'}, \text{pl}, c_{z'})\}$. The second step consists in checking if $\langle \mathcal{J}, D \rangle$ is consistent. To this end, one can exploit Lemma 4 and: (i) compute the ABox $\mathcal{A} = Retr(\mathcal{M}, D)$, which is $\{\text{Area}(c_x), \text{Area}(c_{x'}), \text{Platform}(c_{x'}), \text{Platform}(c_x), \text{locatedIn}(c_{x'}, c_{z'}), \text{locatedIn}(c_x, c_z)\}$ and (ii) check the consistency of the ontology $\langle \mathcal{T}, \mathcal{A} \rangle$. Since, e.g., both $\text{Area}(c_{x'})$ and $\text{Platform}(c_{x'})$ belong to $\mathcal{A}$, and since $\mathcal{T} \models \text{Platform} \sqcap \text{Area} \sqsubseteq \bot$, the ontology $\langle \mathcal{T}, \mathcal{A} \rangle$ is inconsistent. Hence, the algorithm returns true. ∎

Now, observe that the cost of computing $Retr(\mathcal{M}, D)$ does not depend on the size of the TBox. This implies that, with respect to TBox complexity, the complexity of ontology inconsistency is an upper bound for global mapping inconsistency. Conversely, ontology inconsistency can be easily reduced to global mapping inconsistency, by creating a GAV mapping assertion (with no frontier variables) whose head is the conjunction of the ABox assertions in $\mathcal{A}$. Consequently:

Theorem 4. *For both simple and FD schemas, for both GAV and GLAV mappings, and for every ontology language $\mathcal{L}_\mathcal{O}$, the TBox complexity of global mapping inconsistency is the same as the TBox complexity of ontology inconsistency in $\mathcal{L}_\mathcal{O}$.*

The above theorem implies row 2 in Figure 1.

To establish combined complexity, we define a second way to decide inconsistency of $(\langle \mathcal{T}, \mathcal{S}, \mathcal{M} \rangle, D)$. We start from the following property.

Lemma 5. *Let $\mathcal{M}$ be a $GLAV_{BE}$ mapping, and let D be a source instance. Then, the size of $Retr(\mathcal{M}, D)$ is polynomial with respect to the size of $\mathcal{M}$ and D.*

Proof. When $\mathcal{M}$ is a GAV mapping, from Definition 7 it follows that the number of assertions in $Retr(\mathcal{M}, D)$ is bounded by $(n_c \cdot n_v) + (n_r \cdot n_v^2)$, where n_c is the number of concepts, n_r is the number of roles, and n_v is the number of constants occurring in D and $\mathcal{M}$. When $\mathcal{M}$ is a $GLAV_{BE}$ mapping, observe that, by Definition 7, the number of fresh constants n_f occurring in $Retr(\mathcal{M}, D)$ is not greater than $m \cdot k \cdot n^k$, where m is the number of mapping assertions in $\mathcal{M}$, n is the number of constants in D, and k is the maximum number of occurrences of existential variables in the head of a mapping assertion (observe that k is the maximum length of $cvars(m)$ in the definition of $Retr(\mathcal{M}, D)$). Since k is bounded in $GLAV_{BE}$ mappings, we derive that such a number of constants n_f is polynomially bounded. And since the number of assertions in $Retr(\mathcal{M}, D)$ is bounded by $(n_c \cdot n_w) + (n_r \cdot n_w^2)$, where n_c is the number of concepts, n_r is the number of roles, and $n_w = n_v + n_f$, the thesis follows. □

Notice that the above property does not hold for arbitrary GLAV mappings (for which $Retr(\mathcal{M}, D)$ may be of exponential size), so in the rest of this section we focus on GLAV$_{\mathrm{BE}}$ mappings. Notice also that the above lemma does not imply that for GLAV$_{\mathrm{BE}}$ mappings $Retr(\mathcal{M}, D)$ can be computed in polynomial time with respect to the size of $\mathcal{M}$ and D: conversely, it is immediate to verify that deciding whether an ABox assertion belongs to $Retr(\mathcal{M}, D)$ is an NP-hard problem.

From the above lemma and from Lemma 4, it follows that, in the case of GLAV$_{\mathrm{BE}}$ mappings, inconsistency of $(\langle \mathcal{T}, \mathcal{S}, \mathcal{M} \rangle, D)$ can be decided by checking the existence of a polynomial subset $\mathcal{A}'$ of $Retr(\mathcal{M}, D)$ such that $\langle \mathcal{T}, \mathcal{A}' \rangle$ is inconsistent.

Given a mapping assertion m, a *grounding for* m is the mapping assertion obtained from m by replacing every variable in m with a constant symbol. A grounding for a mapping $\mathcal{M}$ is a set $\{ m_g \mid \exists\ m \in \mathcal{M}\ \text{s.t. } m_g \text{ is a grounding for } m \}$. Now let D be a source instance. A grounding $\mathcal{G}$ for $\mathcal{M}$ is *generated by* D if, for every $m_g \in \mathcal{G}$, every atom in $body(m_g)$ occurs in D. Given a grounding $\mathcal{G}$ for $\mathcal{M}$, the *ABox induced by* $\mathcal{G}$, denoted as $\mathcal{A}(\mathcal{G})$, is defined as the set of atoms occurring in the heads of the mapping assertions of $\mathcal{G}$.

Lemma 6. *Let $\mathcal{M}$ be a GLAV$_{\mathrm{BE}}$ mapping and let D be a source instance. Then: (i) for every grounding $\mathcal{G}$ for $\mathcal{M}$ that is generated by D, if $\langle \mathcal{T}, \mathcal{A}(\mathcal{G}) \rangle$ is inconsistent, then $\langle \mathcal{T}, Retr(\mathcal{M}, D) \rangle$ is inconsistent; (ii) there exists a grounding $\mathcal{G}$ for $\mathcal{M}$ that is generated by D such that $\mathcal{G}$ has polynomial size with respect to $\mathcal{M}$ and D, and $\langle \mathcal{T}, \mathcal{A}(\mathcal{G}) \rangle$ is inconsistent iff $\langle \mathcal{T}, Retr(\mathcal{M}, D) \rangle$ is inconsistent.*

Proof. The proof of (i) follows from the fact that there exists a homomorphism h from $Const(\mathcal{A}(\mathcal{G})) \setminus Const(D)$ to $Const(Retr(\mathcal{M}, D))$ such that $h(\mathcal{A}(\mathcal{G})) \subseteq Retr(\mathcal{M}, D)$. Consequently, if $\mathcal{I}$ is a model for $\langle \mathcal{T}, Retr(\mathcal{M}, D) \rangle$, we can immediately derive a model $\mathcal{I}'$ for $\langle \mathcal{T}, \mathcal{A}(\mathcal{G}) \rangle \rangle$ from $\mathcal{I}$ by just changing the interpretation of the constants, defining $c^{\mathcal{I}'} = h(c)^{\mathcal{I}}$ for every $c \in Const(\mathcal{A}(\mathcal{G})) \setminus Const(D)$, and $c^{\mathcal{I}'} = c^{\mathcal{I}}$ otherwise. Then, the proof of (ii) easily follows from (i), Lemma 5 and the fact that, by definition of $Retr(\mathcal{M}, D)$, there exists a grounding $\mathcal{G}$ for $\mathcal{M}$ such that $\mathcal{A}(\mathcal{G})$ is equal to $Retr(\mathcal{M}, D)$. $\qquad\square$

Consequently, the following algorithm is able to decide inconsistency of $(\langle \mathcal{T}, \mathcal{S}, \mathcal{M} \rangle, D)$.

Algorithm OBDAInconsistency:
Input: OBDA specification $\langle \mathcal{T}, \mathcal{S}, \mathcal{M} \rangle$ with $\mathcal{M}$ GLAV$_{\mathrm{BE}}$ mapping, source instance D
   if there exists a polynomial grounding $\mathcal{G}$ for $\mathcal{M}$
   such that $\mathcal{G}$ is generated by D **and** the ontology $\langle \mathcal{T}, \mathcal{A}(\mathcal{G}) \rangle$ is inconsistent
   then return true **else** return false

We are now able to analyze the combined complexity of the algorithm GlobalInconsistency when step (b) is executed through the algorithm OBDAInconsistency. As shown by Lemma 3, step (a) can always be executed in polynomial time. Then, if the ontology inconsistency check is in PTIME, check (b) can be executed in nondeterministic polynomial time. Consequently, the algorithm GlobalInconsistency provides an NP upper bound for $DL\text{-}Lite_R$, RL, and $\mathcal{EL}_\perp$, while it provides a N2EXPTIME upper bound for $\mathcal{SROIQ}$.

Concerning the lower bounds, the one for $\mathcal{SROIQ}$ is trivial, while the NP bound for the other three cases can be proved by an easy reduction of conjunctive query containment in relational databases. Consequently:

Theorem 5. *For both simple and FD schemas, and for both GAV and $GLAV_{BE}$ mappings: (i) if the ontology language is $DL\text{-}Lite_R$, RL, or $\mathcal{EL}_\perp$, then the combined complexity of global mapping inconsistency is NP-complete; (ii) if the ontology language is $\mathcal{SROIQ}$, then the combined complexity of global mapping inconsistency is N2EXPTIME-complete.*

The above results are summarized in row 2 in Fig. 2.

4   Complexity of Mapping Redundancy

We now show that local and global mapping redundancy have the same TBox complexity as instance checking for GAV mappings and CQ entailment over an ontology for GLAV mappings. We also study the combined complexity for the DLs considered in this paper. We focus on the global case only, since as we said, the local redundancy is a special case of the global one. Also, observe that a mapping $\mathcal{M}'$ is globally redundant for an OBDA specification iff each subset of $\mathcal{M}'$ is redundant. We thus consider only the case in which $\mathcal{M}' = \{m\}$, and with a slight abuse of notation, we call such case global redundancy of a mapping assertion m for $\mathcal{J}$.

From now on, we do not consider the trivial case when m is body-inconsistent for $\mathcal{S}$. Under this assumption, a minimal instance for $\mathcal{S}$ that activates $\{m\}$ always exists (and the algorithm freezeFD does never fail for every mapping $\mathcal{M}$ and source schema $\mathcal{S}$ as input). We notice, however, that all the complexity results of this section also hold without this assumption.

Theorem 6. *Let $\mathcal{J} = \langle \mathcal{T}, \mathcal{S}, \mathcal{M} \rangle$ be an OBDA specification and m a mapping assertion. Then, m is globally redundant for $\mathcal{J}$ iff there exists a minimal instance D for $\mathcal{S}$ that activates $\{m\}$ such that $Mod(\mathcal{J}, D) = Mod(\langle \mathcal{T}, \mathcal{S}, \mathcal{M} \cup \{m\}\rangle, D)$.*

Proof (sketch). The proof of the only-if part is trivial. As for the if part, since a minimal instance has a homomorphism to every other instance, the fact that the models for a minimal instance are the same can be used to show that, for every legal instance D' for $\mathcal{S}$, a model for $(\langle \mathcal{T}, \mathcal{S}, \mathcal{M} \rangle, D')$ has to be a model for $(\langle \mathcal{T}, \mathcal{S}, \mathcal{M} \cup \{m\}\rangle, D')$ too.   □

Based on the above theorem, below we provide an algorithm that establishes whether m is globally redundant for $\mathcal{J}$ by checking whether a suitable Boolean CQ is entailed by $\mathcal{J}$ coupled with the minimal instance that activates $\{m\}$ returned by the algorithm freezeFD$(\mathcal{M}, \mathcal{S})$ (cf. Lemma 3). In the following, with a little abuse of notation, we denote with $freeze(FR(m))$ the tuple obtained by freezing the frontier variables of m.

Algorithm mapRedundancy:
Input: OBDA specification $\langle \mathcal{T}, \mathcal{S}, \mathcal{M} \rangle$, mapping assertion m
  (a) $D \leftarrow$ freezeFD$(\{m\}, \mathcal{S})$;
  let σ be the substitution derived by freezeFD$(\{m\}, \mathcal{S})$;
  $\mathbf{t}_F \leftarrow \sigma(\textit{freeze}(FR(m)))$;
  if (b) $(\mathcal{J}, D) \models \textit{head}(m(\mathbf{t}_F))$
  then return true **else** return false

In the algorithm, σ denotes the substitution of terms derived by the application of freezeFD$(\{m\}, \mathcal{S})$, i.e., $\sigma = \{x_1 \rightarrow y_1, \ldots, x_n \rightarrow y_n\}$ where each y_i is a constant (either fresh or non-fresh) and each x_i is a fresh constant in $\textit{freeze}(\textit{body}(m))$; σ is applied to the tuple obtained by freezing the frontier variables of m, in order to propagate the term substitutions derived by the chase to such a tuple. Notice that, for simple source schemas, σ is the identity and thus it has no effect. Finally, mapRedundancy verifies whether the Boolean query corresponding to the head of the mapping m whose frontier variables are substituted with $\mathbf{t}_F$ is entailed by $(\mathcal{J}, D)$.

The following theorem states that mapRedundancy is sound and complete with respect to the problem of establishing global mapping redundancy (termination of the algorithm is straightforward).

Theorem 7. *Let $\mathcal{J} = \langle \mathcal{T}, \mathcal{S}, \mathcal{M} \rangle$ be an OBDA specification and m a mapping assertion. Then, m is globally redundant for $\mathcal{J}$ iff mapRedundancy$(\mathcal{J}, m)$ returns true.*

As shown in Section 3, step (a) can be executed in polynomial time for both simple schemas and FD schemas. As for step (b), the first technique we present is tailored to establish TBox complexity of global mapping redundancy. We first give the following lemma.

Lemma 7. *Let $\mathcal{J} = \langle \mathcal{T}, \mathcal{S}, \mathcal{M} \rangle$ be and OBDA specification, D a minimal instance for $\mathcal{S}$ that activates $\mathcal{M}$, and q a Boolean CQ. Then, $(\mathcal{J}, D) \models q$ iff $\langle \mathcal{T}, \textit{Retr}(\mathcal{M}, D) \rangle \models q$.*

According to the above result, step (b) of mapRedundancy can be performed by first computing the ABox $\textit{Retr}(\mathcal{M}, D)$, and then checking whether $(\mathcal{T}, \textit{Retr}(\mathcal{M}, D)) \models \textit{head}(m(\sigma(\textit{freeze}(FR(m)))))$.

Example 7. Consider the OBDA specification $\mathcal{J} = \langle \mathcal{T}, \mathcal{S}, \mathcal{M} \rangle$, where $\mathcal{T}$ and $\mathcal{S}$ are as in Example 1, and $\mathcal{M}$ is as follows:

m_1 : $\texttt{plants}(x, y, z), \texttt{eZones}(z, \text{`mz'}) \quad \leadsto \quad \textsf{locatedIn}(x, z)$
m_2 : $\texttt{eZones}(x', \text{`mz'}) \qquad\qquad\qquad\quad \leadsto \quad \textsf{MarArea}(x')$

Moreover, consider the following mapping assertion:

m_3 : $\texttt{plants}(y', \text{`pl'}, z'), \texttt{eZones}(z', \text{`mz'}) \quad \leadsto \quad \textsf{Platform}(y')$.

The algorithm mapRedundancy first computes $D = \mathsf{freezeFD}(\{m\}, \mathcal{S}) = \{\mathsf{plants}(c_{y'}, \text{'pl'}, c_{z'}), \mathsf{eZones}(c_{z'}, \text{'mz'})\}$. Then, it produces the Boolean CQ $q_{m_3} = head(m(t_F)) = \mathsf{Platform}(c_{y'})$. To check whether $(\mathcal{J}, D) \models q_{m_3}$ the algorithm computes $Retr(\mathcal{M}, D) = \{\mathsf{locatedIn}(c_{y'}, c_{z'}), \mathsf{MarArea}(c_{z'})\}$. Since $\mathsf{locatedIn.MarArea} \sqsubseteq \mathsf{Platform} \in \mathcal{T}$, we have that $\langle \mathcal{T}, Retr(\mathcal{M}, D) \rangle \models q_{m_3}$, and thus mapRedundancy returns *true* (i.e., m_3 is globally redundant for $\mathcal{J}$). ∎

For TBox complexity, we notice that in mapRedundancy both step (a) and the size of $Retr(\mathcal{M}, D)$ do not depend on the TBox $\mathcal{T}$. In particular, we have that:

- In the case of GAV mappings, the check in step (b) corresponds to a linear number (in the size of $head(m)$) of instance checking tasks in the language $\mathcal{L}_{\mathcal{O}}$ used for $\mathcal{T}$.
- In the case of GLAV mappings, the check in step (b) corresponds to a single Boolean CQ entailment task in $\mathcal{L}_{\mathcal{O}}$.

Thus, mapRedundancy together with the techniques for step (a) and (b) discussed above allows us to obtain upper bounds for the TBox complexity of global mapping redundancy. More precisely, the complexity of instance checking in $\mathcal{L}_{\mathcal{O}}$ is an upper bound for GAV mappings, while the complexity of CQ entailment in $\mathcal{L}_{\mathcal{O}}$ is an upper bound for GLAV.

As for lower bounds, we notice that both instance checking and CQ entailment in $\mathcal{L}_{\mathcal{O}}$ can be easily reduced to *local* mapping redundancy for GAV and GLAV mappings, respectively, with a technique similar to the one we used for Lemma 2.

The following theorem sums up the above results.

Theorem 8. *For both simple and FD schemas, and for every ontology language $\mathcal{L}_{\mathcal{O}}$, the TBox complexity of both local and global mapping redundancy for GAV and GLAV mappings is the same as the TBox complexity of instance checking in $\mathcal{L}_{\mathcal{O}}$ and TBox complexity of CQ entailment in $\mathcal{L}_{\mathcal{O}}$, respectively.*

The above theorem implies rows 3 and 4 in Figure 1.

Similarly to the case of global mapping inconsistency, since executing step (b) by computing the retrieved ABox $Retr(\mathcal{M}, D)$ requires exponential time in combined complexity, to establish combined complexity of the overall problem we need to resort to a different strategy for step (b). To this aim, we exploit a property that generalizes Lemma 6 (which focuses on inconsistency) to query entailment. From this property, it follows that, for every CQ q that does not mention constants occurring in $Const(Retr(\mathcal{M}, D)) \setminus Const(D)$, and for every $\mathsf{GLAV_{BE}}$ mapping $\mathcal{M}$, $\langle \mathcal{T}, Retr(\mathcal{M}, D) \rangle \models q$ can be decided by checking the existence of a polynomial grounding $\mathcal{G}$ for $\mathcal{M}$ that is generated by D such that $\langle \mathcal{T}, \mathcal{A}(\mathcal{G}) \rangle \models q$. Therefore, the following algorithm for checking CQ entailment over an OBDA specification $\mathcal{J}$ and a source instance D follows.

task	GAV				GLAV			
	DL-$Lite_R$	RL	$\mathcal{EL}_\perp$	$\mathcal{SROIQ}$	DL-$Lite_R$	RL	$\mathcal{EL}_\perp$	$\mathcal{SROIQ}$
local inc.	=NLOGSPACE	=P	=P	=N2EXPTIME	=NLOGSPACE	=P	=P	=N2EXPTIME
global inc.	=NLOGSPACE	=P	=P	=N2EXPTIME	=NLOGSPACE	=P	=P	=N2EXPTIME
local red.	=NLOGSPACE	=P	=P	=N2EXPTIME	=NP	=NP	=NP	open
global red.	=NLOGSPACE	=P	=P	=N2EXPTIME	=NP	=NP	=NP	open

Fig. 1. TBox compl. of mapping inconsistency and redundancy (for both simple and FD schemas).

task	GAV				GLAV$_{BE}$			
	DL-$Lite_R$	RL	$\mathcal{EL}_\perp$	$\mathcal{SROIQ}$	DL-$Lite_R$	RL	$\mathcal{EL}_\perp$	$\mathcal{SROIQ}$
local inc.	=NLOGSPACE (SI) =P (FD)	=P	=P	=N2EXPTIME	=NLOGSPACE (SI)* =P (FD)*	=P*	=P*	=N2EXPTIME*
global inc.	=NP	=NP	=NP	=N2EXPTIME	=NP	=NP	=NP	=N2EXPTIME
local red.	=NP	=NP	=NP	=N2EXPTIME	=NP	=NP	=NP	open
global red.	=NP	=NP	=NP	=N2EXPTIME	=NP	=NP	=NP	open

Fig. 2. Combined compl. of mapping inconsistency and redundancy (SI = simple schemas, FD = FD schemas). * The result also holds for arbitrary GLAV mappings.

Algorithm CQEntailment:
Input: OBDA specification $\langle \mathcal{T}, \mathcal{S}, \mathcal{M} \rangle$ with $\mathcal{M}$ GLAV$_{BE}$ mapping, source instance D, CQ q
  if there exists a polynomial grounding $\mathcal{G}$ for $\mathcal{M}$
  such that $\mathcal{G}$ is generated by D **and** $\langle \mathcal{T}, \mathcal{A}(\mathcal{G}) \rangle \models q$
  then return true **else** return false

Then, in the case of GLAV$_{BE}$ mappings we can perform step (b) of mapRedundancy by executing CQEntailment$(\mathcal{J}, D, head(m(freeze(FR(m)))))$.

As for combined complexity, in the following we consider simple source schemas for the lower bounds and FD source schemas for the upper bounds. First, step (b) can be executed through the nondeterministic algorithm CQEntailment. Consequently, this algorithm provides an NP upper bound for the case of GLAV$_{BE}$ mappings if, for the ontology language $\mathcal{L}_\mathcal{O}$, CQ entailment is in NP, i.e., for DL-$Lite_R$, RL, and $\mathcal{EL}_\perp$. The matching NP lower bounds can be proved already for GAV mappings, by an easy reduction of conjunctive query containment in relational databases. In the case of $\mathcal{SROIQ}$, for GLAV$_{BE}$ mappings we are not able to even prove decidability of global mapping redundancy (since decidability of CQ entailment in this language is currently an open problem too), while for the GAV case we can easily derive a N2EXPTIME exact bound.

Theorem 9. *For both simple and FD source schemas, global and local mapping redundancy are: (i) NP-complete w.r.t. combined complexity for both GAV and GLAV$_{BE}$ mappings, in the case of DL-$Lite_R$, RL, or $\mathcal{EL}_\perp$; (ii) N2EXPTIME-complete w.r.t. combined complexity for GAV mappings, in the case of $\mathcal{SROIQ}$.*

The above theorem implies rows 3 and 4 in Figure 2.

5   Conclusions

The tables in Fig. 1 and Fig. 2 report the results presented in Sec. 3 and 4. These results clarify the complexity of the fundamental mapping analysis tasks studied in this paper.

The analysis presented in this paper can be extended in different directions. First, it would be interesting to establish tight combined complexity bounds for general GLAV mappings, and extend our study to other forms of mappings (beyond GLAV), admitting, for instance, forms of negation in the source queries. Then, it would be interesting to extend our analysis beyond the OWL framework, considering, e.g., DLs interpreted under the Unique Name Assumption, or languages of the Datalog+/- family. Finally, we believe that the problems and techniques studied in this paper may constitute the core of practical tools for the crucial task of constructing, debugging, and maintaining an OBDA specification. So, an important direction for future work is the implementation and practical evaluation of techniques for mapping analysis in OBDA.

Acknowledgments. This research has been partially supported by the EU under FP7 project Optique (n. FP7-318338), and by the RCN under project DOIL (n. 213115).

References

1. Abiteboul, S., Hull, R., Vianu, V.: Foundations of Databases. Addison Wesley Publ. Co. (1995)
2. Antonioli, N., Castanò, F., Coletta, S., Grossi, S., Lembo, D., Lenzerini, M., Poggi, A., Virardi, E., Castracane, P.: Ontology-based data management for the Italian public debt. In: Proc. of FOIS, pp. 372–385 (2014)
3. Arenas, M., Barceló, P., Libkin, L., Murlak, F.: Foundations of Data Exchange. Cambridge University Press (2014)
4. Baader, F., Brandt, S., Lutz, C.: Pushing the $\mathcal{EL}$ envelope. In: Proc. of IJCAI, pp. 364–369 (2005)
5. Calvanese, D., De Giacomo, G., Lembo, D., Lenzerini, M., Rosati, R.: Tractable reasoning and efficient query answering in description logics: The DL-Lite family. JAR **39**(3), 385–429 (2007)
6. Civili, C., Console, M., De Giacomo, G., Lembo, D., Lenzerini, M., Lepore, L., Mancini, R., Poggi, A., Rosati, R., Ruzzi, M., Santarelli, V., Savo, D.F.: MASTRO STUDIO: Managing ontology-based data access applications. PVLDB **6**, 1314–1317 (2013)
7. Das, S., Sundara, S., Cyganiak, R.: R2RML: RDB to RDF Mapping Language. W3C RDB2RDF Working Group, W3C recommendation (September 2012)
8. Di Pinto, F., Lembo, D., Lenzerini, M., Mancini, R., Poggi, A., Rosati, R., Ruzzi, M., Savo, D.F.: Optimizing query rewriting in ontology-based data access. In: Proc. of EDBT, pp. 561–572. ACM Press (2013)
9. Doan, A., Halevy, A.Y., Ives, Z.G.: Principles of Data Integration. Morgan Kaufmann (2012)
10. Fagin, R., Kolaitis, P.G., Miller, R.J., Popa, L.: Data exchange: Semantics and query answering. TCS **336**(1), 89–124 (2005)
11. Giese, M., Soylu, A., Vega-Gorgojo, G., Waaler, A., Haase, P., Jiménez-Ruiz, E., Lanti, D., Rezk, M., Xiao, G., Özçep, Ö.L., Rosati, R.: Optique: Zooming in on big data. IEEE Computer **48**(3), 60–67 (2015)
12. Gottlob, G., Pichler, R., Savenkov, V.: Normalization and optimization of schema mappings. VLDBJ **20**(2), 277–302 (2011)

13. Haase, P., et al.: Optique system: towards ontology and mapping management in OBDA solutions. In: Proc. of WoDOOM, pp. 21–32 (2013)
14. Horrocks, I., Kutz, O., Sattler, U.: The even more irresistible $\mathcal{SROIQ}$. In: Proc. of KR, pp. 57–67 (2006)
15. Kharlamov, E., et al.: Optique 1.0: Semantic access to big data: the case of norwegian petroleum directorate's factpages. In: Proc. of ISWC, pp. 65–68 (2013)
16. Kontchakov, R., Zakharyaschev, M.: An introduction to description logics and query rewriting. In: Koubarakis, M., Stamou, G., Stoilos, G., Horrocks, I., Kolaitis, P., Lausen, G., Weikum, G. (eds.) Reasoning Web. LNCS, vol. 8714, pp. 195–244. Springer, Heidelberg (2014)
17. Lembo, D., Mora, J., Rosati, R., Savo, D.F., Thorstensen, E.: Towards mapping analysis in ontology-based data access. In: Proc. of RR, pp. 108–123 (2014)
18. Poggi, A., Lembo, D., Calvanese, D., De Giacomo, G., Lenzerini, M., Rosati, R.: Linking data to ontologies. In: Spaccapietra, S. (ed.) Journal on Data Semantics X. LNCS, vol. 4900, pp. 133–173. Springer, Heidelberg (2008)
19. Rodríguez-Muro, M., Kontchakov, R., Zakharyaschev, M.: Ontology-based data access: *Ontop* of databases. In: Alani, H., et al. (eds.) ISWC 2013, Part I. LNCS, vol. 8218, pp. 558–573. Springer, Heidelberg (2013)

Ontology Alignment

Database Alignment

Towards Defeasible Mappings for Tractable Description Logics

Kunal Sengupta$^{(\boxtimes)}$ and Pascal Hitzler

Wright State University, Dayton, OH 45435, USA
{sengupta.4,pascal.hitzler}@wright.edu

Abstract. We present a novel approach to denote mappings between $\mathcal{EL}$-based ontologies which are defeasible in the sense that such a mapping only applies to individuals if this does not cause an inconsistency. This provides the advantage of handling exceptions automatically and thereby avoiding logical inconsistencies that may be caused due to the traditional type of mappings. We consider the case where mappings from many possibly heterogeneous ontologies are one-way links towards an overarching ontology. Questions can then be asked in terms of the concepts in the overarching ontology. We provide the formal semantics for the defeasible mappings and show that reasoning under such a setting is decidable even when the defeasible axioms apply to unknowns. Furthermore, we show that this semantics actually is strongly related to the idea of answer sets for logic programs.

1 Introduction

Description logic (DL) based knowledge representation is gaining in popularity and with that the number of domain ontologies is also on the rise. Especially in the medical domain, tractable fragments of DLs are heavily used. For example, SNOMED CT is a medical ontology which consists of more than 300,000 concepts, and which can be described in the description logic $\mathcal{EL}$ [1]. Smaller fragments of DLs are especially interesting for application scenarios where fast and efficient reasoning may be critical.

In this paper, we provide a formal framework for dealing with defeasible reasoning for smaller fragments of DLs, especially in the context of ontology alignment. In particular we consider a language $\mathcal{ER}_{\perp,\mathcal{O}}$ which allows for conjunction, existentials, role chains, disjointness of concepts and ABox statements and provide a semantics for one-way (defeasible) alignments from terms in several ontologies to one overarching ontology such that queries can be asked in terms of this overarching ontology, while answers may contain instances from several lower level ontologies. For defeasibility we take motivation from default logic [21] and define the semantics along similar lines. It turns out that combining DLs with default-like semantics is not very straightforward as unrestricted default applications may result in undecidability [2,23]. Previously, decidability was usually obtained for such logics by restricting defeasibility to known individuals, i.e. to a finite set of entities. In this paper, we show that the combination

© Springer International Publishing Switzerland 2015
M. Arenas et al. (Eds.): ISWC 2015, Part I, LNCS 9366, pp. 237–252, 2015.
DOI: 10.1007/978-3-319-25007-6_14

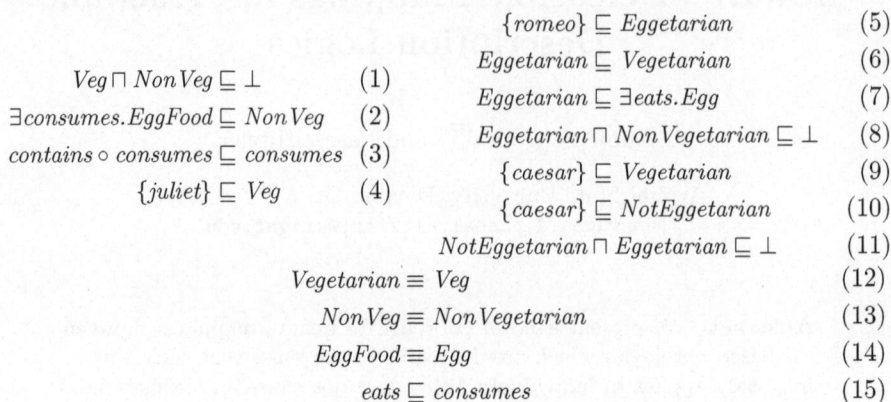

$$\{romeo\} \sqsubseteq Eggetarian \tag{5}$$

$$Eggetarian \sqsubseteq Vegetarian \tag{6}$$

$$Veg \sqcap NonVeg \sqsubseteq \bot \tag{1}$$

$$Eggetarian \sqsubseteq \exists eats.Egg \tag{7}$$

$$\exists consumes.EggFood \sqsubseteq NonVeg \tag{2}$$

$$Eggetarian \sqcap NonVegetarian \sqsubseteq \bot \tag{8}$$

$$contains \circ consumes \sqsubseteq consumes \tag{3}$$

$$\{caesar\} \sqsubseteq Vegetarian \tag{9}$$

$$\{juliet\} \sqsubseteq Veg \tag{4}$$

$$\{caesar\} \sqsubseteq NotEggetarian \tag{10}$$

$$NotEggetarian \sqcap Eggetarian \sqsubseteq \bot \tag{11}$$

$$Vegetarian \equiv Veg \tag{12}$$

$$NonVeg \equiv NonVegetarian \tag{13}$$

$$EggFood \equiv Egg \tag{14}$$

$$eats \sqsubseteq consumes \tag{15}$$

Fig. 1. Example mapping with selected axioms.

of defeasible mappings with DLs presented here is decidable even without this type of restriction. Decidability in our setting results from our restriction to a tractable language in the $\mathcal{EL}$ family, together with the avoidance of recursion through the defeasible axioms resulting from our specific, but practically important application scenario, namely the one-way alignment of ontologies.

Indeed, similar concepts appear in several ontologies from heterogeneous domains, but these concepts may slightly differ semantically. The motivation of using defeasible axioms as alignments stems from the need to handle such heterogeneity among various data models. As we discuss in our previous work [23], DL axioms are semantically too rigid to be able to deal with alignments in such heterogeneous settings, in particular in the light of the fact that ontology alignment systems mostly rely on string similarity matching [7]. For example, the concept that represents those human beings who consume only vegetarian food may be part of two different domain ontologies but the notion of what vegetarian food means might slightly differ depending on the context, e.g. in some places eggs might be part of a typical vegetarian diet while in others this may not be so. Aligning these different world views appropriately cannot be done by simply mapping the respective concepts representing a "vegetarian person" in different ontologies, as claiming that they were equivalent may lead to inconsistencies.

For example consider the axioms in Figure 1 (see section 2 for explanations of the notation). Axioms 1–4 represent one ontology and axioms 5–11 another ontology. An alignment system may give alignments similar to axioms 12–15. Since *romeo* is an *Eggetarian* (axiom 5) he is also a *Vegetarian* (axiom 6). And since every *Vegetarian* is also a *Veg* as per the mapping axiom 12, *romeo* is a *Veg*. From axioms 5, 7, 14, 15 and 2 we obtain that *romeo* is also a *NonVeg*. But *Veg* and *NonVeg* are disjoint classes, so this results in an inconsistency. But applying the same rules to *caesar* does not cause an inconsistency. The usual process of repairing alignments like this is to remove mappings that cause the inconsistency [13]. But we would then lose the conclusion that *caesar* is also a *Veg*. If we replace the mapping axioms with defeasible axioms as introduced below, then we could achieve this outcome where we carry over the similarities while respecting the differences.

The paper is organized as follows. In section 2, we set the preliminaries by describing the language $\mathcal{ER}_{\perp,\mathcal{O}}$. The context of ontology mappings as well as the syntax and the semantics of defeasible mapping axioms along with the discussion on decidability is presented in section 3. Section 4 contains a description of the relation of the semantics of this approach with that of answer set programming for logic programs. Finally we discuss related work in section 5 and provide closing remarks in section 6.

2   The Description Logic $\mathcal{ER}_{\perp,\mathcal{O}}$

We consider the DL $\mathcal{ER}_{\perp,\mathcal{O}}$ (see [1] for further background). Let N_C be a set of *atomic concepts* (or *atomic classes*), let N_R be a set of *roles* and let N_I be a set of *individuals*, which contains an element $\iota_{R,D}$ for each pair $(R, D) \in N_R \times N_C$. These $\iota_{R,D}$ are called *auxilliary* individuals. *Complex class expressions* (short, *complex classes*) in $\mathcal{ER}_{\perp,\mathcal{O}}$ are defined using the grammar
$$C ::= A \mid \top \mid \perp \mid C_1 \sqcap C_2 \mid \exists R.C \mid \{a\},$$
where $A \in N_C$, $R \in N_R$ and C_1, C_2, C are complex class expressions. Furthermore, a *nominal class* (short, *nominal*) is represented as $\{a\}$, where $a \in N_I$. A *TBox* in $\mathcal{ER}_{\perp,\mathcal{O}}$ is a set of *general class inclusion* (*GCI*) axioms of the form $C \sqsubseteq D$, where C and D are complex classes. $C \equiv D$ abbreviates two GCIs $C \sqsubseteq D$ and $D \sqsubseteq C$. An *RBox* in $\mathcal{ER}_{\perp,\mathcal{O}}$ is a set of *role inclusion* (*RI*) axioms of the form $R_1 \circ \cdots \circ R_n \sqsubseteq R$, where $R_1, \ldots, R_n, R \in N_R$. An *ABox* in $\mathcal{ER}_{\perp,\mathcal{O}}$ is a set of GCIs of the form $\{a\} \sqsubseteq C$ and $\{a\} \sqsubseteq \exists R.\{b\}$ where $\{a\}, \{b\}$ are nominals and C is a complex class.

An $\mathcal{ER}_{\perp,\mathcal{O}}$ *knowledge base* or *ontology* is a set of TBox, RBox and ABox statements which furthermore satisfy the condition that nominals occur only in ABox statements. This condition is a restriction of $\mathcal{ER}_{\perp,\mathcal{O}}$ as compared to, e.g., the allowed use of nominals in OWL 2 EL: While we allow for a full ABox, the TBox remains free of nominals. In particular, axioms such as $A \sqsubseteq \exists R.\{a\}$, with A an atomic or complex class other than a nominal, are not allowed.

An *initial* $\mathcal{ER}_{\perp,\mathcal{O}}$ knowledge base is an $\mathcal{ER}_{\perp,\mathcal{O}}$ knowledge base which does not contain any auxiliary individuals.

Example 1. The following is an example of an (initial) $\mathcal{ER}_{\perp,\mathcal{O}}$ knowledge base.

$$Bird \sqsubseteq Fly$$
$$Penguin \sqsubseteq Bird$$

$$Penguin \sqcap Fly \sqsubseteq \perp$$
$$\{tom\} \sqsubseteq \exists hasPet.Penguin$$

Table 1. Semantics of the language $\mathcal{ER}_{\perp,\mathcal{O}}$

Concept	Semantics
$\top$	$\Delta^{\mathcal{I}}$
$\perp$	$\emptyset$
$\{a\}$	$\{a^{\mathcal{I}}\}$
$C \sqcap D$	$C^{\mathcal{I}} \cap D^{\mathcal{I}}$
$C \sqsubseteq D$	$C^{\mathcal{I}} \subseteq D^{\mathcal{I}}$
$\exists R.D$	$\{x \mid \text{there exists some } y \text{ with } (x,y) \in R^{\mathcal{I}} \text{ and } y \in D^{\mathcal{I}}\}$
$R_1 \circ R_2$	$R_1^{\mathcal{I}} \circ R_2^{\mathcal{I}}$
$\{a\}$	$\{a^{\mathcal{I}}\}$

Next, we describe the semantics of the language $\mathcal{ER}_{\perp,\mathcal{O}}$ using the notion of interpretation. An *interpretation* $\mathcal{I}$ of an $\mathcal{ER}_{\perp,\mathcal{O}}$ knowledge base KB is a pair $(\Delta^{\mathcal{I}}, \cdot^{\mathcal{I}})$ where $\Delta^{\mathcal{I}}$ is a non-empty set of elements called the *domain of interpretation* and $\cdot^{\mathcal{I}}$ is the *interpretation function* that maps every individual in KB to an element of $\Delta^{\mathcal{I}}$, every concept in KB to a subset of $\Delta^{\mathcal{I}}$, and every role to a subset of $\Delta^{\mathcal{I}} \times \Delta^{\mathcal{I}}$. Concept expressions are interepreted as shown in Table 1. An interpretation $\mathcal{I}$ is a *model* of an $\mathcal{ER}_{\perp,\mathcal{O}}$ knowledge base KB if it satisfies all the TBox, RBox and ABox axioms such that if $C \sqsubseteq D$ then $C^{\mathcal{I}} \subseteq D^{\mathcal{I}}$, if $R \sqsubseteq S$ the $R^{\mathcal{I}} \sqsubseteq S^{\mathcal{I}}$, and $\{a\} \sqsubseteq C$ then $a^{\mathcal{I}} \in C^{\mathcal{I}}$ respectively.

It is well-known that any such knowledge base can be cast into normal form, as follows.

Definition 1. *An initial* $\mathcal{ER}_{\perp,\mathcal{O}}$ *knowledge base is in normal form if it contains axioms of only the following forms, where* $C, C_1, C_2, D \in N_C$, $R, R_1, R_2 \in N_R$ *and* $a, b \in N_I$

$$C \sqsubseteq D \qquad\qquad C_1 \sqcap C_2 \sqsubseteq D \qquad\qquad R_1 \circ R_2 \sqsubseteq R$$
$$\exists R.C \sqsubseteq D \qquad\qquad C_1 \sqcap C_2 \sqsubseteq \perp \qquad\qquad \{a\} \sqsubseteq C$$
$$C \sqsubseteq \exists R.D \qquad\qquad R_1 \sqsubseteq R \qquad\qquad \{a\} \sqsubseteq \exists R.\{b\}$$

Theorem 1. *For every initial* $\mathcal{ER}_{\perp,\mathcal{O}}$ *knowledge base* KB *there exists a knowledge base* KB' *in normal form such that* $KB \models \bar{A} \sqsubseteq B$ *if and only if* $KB' \models \bar{A} \sqsubseteq B$, *where* $\bar{A}$ *is a class name or a nominal and* B *is a class name occurring in* KB.

Definition 2. *Given an initial* $\mathcal{ER}_{\perp,\mathcal{O}}$ *knowledge base* KB *in normal form, we define the following:*

1. *Completion: the completion* $comp(KB)$ *of* KB *is obtained from* KB *by exhaustively applying the completion rules from Figure 2.*
2. *Clash: a completion* $comp(KB)$ *of* KB *contains a clash if* $\{a\} \sqsubseteq \perp \in comp(KB)$, *for some nominal class* $\{a\}$.

It is easily verified that repeated applications of completion rules on an initial $\mathcal{ER}_{\perp,\mathcal{O}}$ knowledge base produces only axioms which are also in normal form, with one exception: Axioms of the form $\{a\} \sqsubseteq \exists R.D$, with $R \in N_R$ and $D \in N_C$, can also appear.

$$\bar{A} \sqsubseteq C, C \sqsubseteq D \mapsto \bar{A} \sqsubseteq D \tag{16}$$

$$\bar{A} \sqsubseteq C_1, \bar{A} \sqsubseteq C_2, C_1 \sqcap C_2 \sqsubseteq D \mapsto \bar{A} \sqsubseteq D \tag{17}$$

$$\bar{A} \sqsubseteq C, C \sqsubseteq \exists R.D \mapsto \bar{A} \sqsubseteq \exists R.D \tag{18}$$

$$\bar{A} \sqsubseteq \exists R.\bar{B}, \bar{B} \sqsubseteq C, \exists R.C \sqsubseteq D \mapsto \bar{A} \sqsubseteq D \tag{19}$$

$$\bar{C} \sqsubseteq \exists R.\bar{D}, \bar{D} \sqsubseteq \bot \mapsto \bar{C} \sqsubseteq \bot \tag{20}$$

$$\bar{A} \sqsubseteq \exists R.\bar{B}, R \sqsubseteq S \mapsto \bar{A} \sqsubseteq \exists S.\bar{B} \tag{21}$$

$$\bar{A} \sqsubseteq \exists R_1.\bar{B}, \bar{B} \sqsubseteq \exists R_2.\bar{C}, R_1 \circ R_2 \sqsubseteq R \mapsto \bar{A} \sqsubseteq \exists R.\bar{C} \tag{22}$$

Fig. 2. $\mathcal{ER}_{\bot,\mathcal{O}}$ completion rules. New axioms resulting from the rules are added to the existing axioms in *KB*. Symbols of the form $\bar{A}$ can be either a class name or a nominal class. We initialize comp(*KB*) with *KB* and $C \sqsubseteq C, \bot \sqsubseteq C, \bot \sqsubseteq \bot$ for all named classes $C \in N_C$.

It is straightforward to show that *comp(KB)* is well-defined and that the completion process has a polynomial time complexity. This and the soundness and completeness results below are adapted from [1]. Since the proofs are relevant to understanding the discussions in this paper, we include them in the appendix of the technical report [22] available online.

Theorem 2. *(soundness and completeness) Let KB be an initial $\mathcal{ER}_{\bot,\mathcal{O}}$ knowledge base in normal form. Then every model of KB is a model of comp(KB). Furthermore, if comp(KB) contains a clash then KB is inconsistent.*

Conversely, if A is an atomic class or a nominal and B is an atomic class such that $KB \models A \sqsubseteq B$, then $A \sqsubseteq B \in comp(KB)$. Furthermore, if KB is inconsistent then comp(KB) contains a clash.

Note now that the $\mathcal{ER}_{\bot,\mathcal{O}}$ knowledge base given in Example 1 is inconsistent.

Central to the proof of Theorem 2 is the following construction, which we will also use later in this paper.

Given an $\mathcal{ER}_{\bot,\mathcal{O}}$ knowledge base *KB*, let $\mathcal{I} = \mathcal{I}(KB)$ be defined as the following interpretation of *comp(KB)*.

$$\Delta^{\mathcal{I}} = \{x_{\{a\}}, x_C \mid C \text{ is a class name in } KB \text{ and } a \text{ is an individual in } KB\}$$

$$A^{\mathcal{I}} = \begin{cases} \emptyset, & \text{if } A \sqsubseteq \bot \in comp(KB) \\ \{x_C \mid C \sqsubseteq A \in comp(KB)\} \cup \{x_{\{a\}} \mid \{a\} \sqsubseteq A \in comp(KB)\}, \\ & \text{if } A \sqsubseteq \bot \notin comp(KB) \end{cases}$$

$$\{a\}^{\mathcal{I}} = \begin{cases} \emptyset, & \text{if } \{a\} \sqsubseteq \bot \in comp(KB) \\ \{x_{\{a\}}\}, & \text{if } \{a\} \sqsubseteq \bot \notin comp(KB) \end{cases}$$

$$R^{\mathcal{I}} = \{(x_C, x_D) \mid C \sqsubseteq \exists R.D \in comp(KB)\} \cup$$
$$\{(x_{\{a\}}, x_D) \mid \{a\} \sqsubseteq \exists R.D \in comp(KB)\} \cup$$
$$\{(x_{\{a\}}, x_{\{b\}}) \mid \{a\} \sqsubseteq \exists R.\{b\} \in comp(KB)\}$$

The proof of Theorem 2 shows that $\mathcal{I}$ is a model of both $comp(KB)$ and KB.

3   Mapping Ontologies with $\mathcal{ER}_{\perp,\mathcal{O}}$-Defaults

We consider a rather specific but fundamentally important scenario, namely the integration of ontology-based information by means of an overarching ontology, as laid out and applied e.g. in [14,20] – see also the discussion of this in [23]. One of the central issues related to this type of information integration is how to obtain the mappings of the to-be-integrated ontologies to the overarching ontology, as the manual creation of these mappings is very costly for large ontologies.

However, methods for the automated creation of such mappings – commonly refered to as *ontology alignment* – are still rather crude [7,12], and are therefore prone to lead to inconsistencies of the integrated ontologies, as discussed in section 1. In order to deal with this, we introduce a defeasible mechanism to deal with such mappings. For simplicity of presentation we consider only two ontologies, with one taking the role of the overarching ontology. The other ontology can be considered the disjoint union of the ontologies which are to be integrated.

The following notion is going to be central.

Definition 3. *(defeasible axiom) A* defeasible axiom *is of the form* $C \sqsubseteq_d D$ *or* $R \sqsubseteq_d S$, *where* C, D *are class names and* R, S *are roles.*

Intuitively speaking, our intention with defeasible axioms is the following: It shall function just like a class inclusion axiom, unless it causes an inconsistency, in which case it should not apply to individuals causing this inconsistency. In a sense, such defeasible axioms act as a type of semantic debugging of mappings: The semantics itself encodes the removal of inconsistencies. More specifically speaking, given a defeasible axiom $C \sqsubseteq_d D$, instances of C will also be instances of D, except those instances of C which cause an inconsistency when also an instance of D. Such Cs are usually known as exceptions. Of course this intuitive understanding of defeasible axioms is not entirely straightforward to cast into a formal semantics.[1] We will give such a formal semantics in section 3.1 below.

Definition 4. *(mappings) Let* $\mathcal{O}_1, \mathcal{O}_2$ *be two consistent* $\mathcal{ER}_{\perp,\mathcal{O}}$ *knowledge bases. A (*defeasible*) mapping* from $\mathcal{O}1$ to $\mathcal{O}2$ *is a defeasible axiom with the left-hand side of the axiom a concept or role from* $\mathcal{O}_1$, *and the right-hand side a concept or role from* $\mathcal{O}_2$.

Note that here we restrict the mappings to axioms involving roles and atomic classes. However, we do so without loss of generality as $C \sqsubseteq_d D$, for complex classes C, D, can be replaced by adding the axiom $C \sqsubseteq A$ to $\mathcal{O}1$ and the axiom $B \sqsubseteq D$ to $\mathcal{O}2$, where A and B are new concept names, and replacing $C \sqsubseteq_d D$ in δ by $A \sqsubseteq_d B$. Similarly, our approach encompasses the specific case of *ontology population*, where $\mathcal{O}1$ is empty and all mappings are of the form $\{a\} \sqsubseteq_d C$.

---

[1] Different ways how to do this lead to different non-monotonic logics. This is a well-studied subfield of artificial intelligence, from which we take inspiration.

Definition 5. *(mapped-tuple) Let $\mathcal{O}_1, \mathcal{O}_2$ be two ontologies in $\mathcal{ER}_{\perp,\mathcal{O}}$ with δ the set of defeasible mappings from $\mathcal{O}_1$ to $\mathcal{O}_2$. Then the tuple $(\mathcal{O}_1, \mathcal{O}_2, \delta)$ is called a mapped-tuple.*

3.1 Semantics and Decidability

Given a mapped-tuple $(\mathcal{O}_1, \mathcal{O}_2, \delta)$, we define the formal semantics of the mappings following our intuitive reading as discussed above. Informally speaking, the semantics of $C \sqsubseteq_d D$ is similar to that of normal defaults as in Reiter's default logic [21]: if x is in C, then it can be assumed that x is also in D, unless it causes an inconsistency with respect to the current knowledge.

We define the semantics formally as follows. For each mapping axiom $C \sqsubseteq_d D$ in δ we define a set Cand that represents the set of axioms that could be possibly added to the completion of $\mathcal{O}_2$ as a result of the mapping axiom.

$$\mathsf{Cand}(C \sqsubseteq_d D) = \{\{a\} \sqsubseteq D \mid \{a\} \sqsubseteq C \in comp(\mathcal{O}_1)\} \tag{23}$$

Furthermore, we define the set Cand^n as the power set of Cand for each mapping axiom.

$$\mathsf{Cand}^n(C \sqsubseteq_d D) = \{X \mid X \subseteq \mathsf{Cand}(C \sqsubseteq_d D)\} \tag{24}$$

Similarly, we define the corresponding sets $\mathsf{Cand}_\mathcal{R}$ and $\mathsf{Cand}^n_\mathcal{R}$ for mapping axioms involving roles.

$$\mathsf{Cand}_\mathcal{R}(R \sqsubseteq_d S) = \{\{a\} \sqsubseteq \exists S.\{b\} \mid \{a\} \sqsubseteq \exists R.\{b\} \in comp(\mathcal{O}_1)\} \tag{25}$$

$$\mathsf{Cand}^n_\mathcal{R}(R \sqsubseteq_d S) = \{X \mid X \subseteq \mathsf{Cand}_\mathcal{R}(R \sqsubseteq_d S)\} \tag{26}$$

Note that a and b may be auxiliary individuals.

Definition 6. *(mapped ontology) Let $(\mathcal{O}_1, \mathcal{O}_2, \delta)$ be a mapped-tuple. Define selections and the corresponding mapped ontology as follows:*

(i) *For each mapping axiom of the form $C \sqsubseteq_d D \in \delta$, a selection for $C \sqsubseteq_d D$ is any $\Sigma_{C \sqsubseteq_d D} \subseteq \mathsf{Cand}^n(C \sqsubseteq_d D)$.*

(ii) *For each mapping axiom of the form $R \sqsubseteq_d S \in \delta$, a selection for $R \sqsubseteq_d S$ is any $\Sigma_{R \sqsubseteq_d S} \subseteq \mathsf{Cand}^n_\mathcal{R}(R \sqsubseteq_d S)$*

(iii) *Given selections for all mappings $\mu \in \delta$, we use Σ to denote their union $\Sigma = \bigcup_{\mu \in \delta} \Sigma_\mu$, and call Σ a selection for the given mapped-tuple.*

(iv) *$\mathcal{O}_2^\Sigma = comp(\mathcal{O}_2) \cup \bigcup_{X \in \Sigma} X$ is then called a mapped ontology.*

Note that each mapped-tuple $(\mathcal{O}_1, \mathcal{O}_2, \delta)$ can give rise to only a finite number of corresponding mapped ontologies, and the number is bounded by $|\mathsf{Cand}^n(C \sqsubseteq_d D)|^{|\delta_1|} \times |\mathsf{Cand}^n_\mathcal{R}(R \sqsubseteq_d S)|^{|\delta_2|}$, where δ_1 (respectively, δ_2) is the set of class (respectively, role) mappings contained in δ.

Definition 7. *(preferred mapping) Let $(\mathcal{O}_1, \mathcal{O}_2, \delta)$ be a mapped-tuple. Then for any two mapped ontologies $\mathcal{O}_2^{\Sigma^i}, \mathcal{O}_2^{\Sigma^j}$ we say $\mathcal{O}_2^{\Sigma^i} \succ \mathcal{O}_2^{\Sigma^j}$ or $\mathcal{O}_2^{\Sigma^i}$ is preferred over $\mathcal{O}_2^{\Sigma^j}$, if all of the following hold.*

- $\Sigma_\mu^i \supseteq \Sigma_\mu^j$, for all $\mu \in \delta$
- $\Sigma_\mu^i \supset \Sigma_\mu^j$, for some $\mu \in \delta$

Note that μ can be of the form $C \sqsubseteq_d D$ or $R \sqsubseteq_d S$.

The notion of preferred mapping is used to identify the individuals to which the defeasible axioms maximally apply.

Definition 8. *(mapped completion and mapped entailment) Given a mapped-tuple $(\mathcal{O}_1, \mathcal{O}_2, \delta)$, let $\mathcal{O}_2^\Sigma$ be a mapped ontology obtained from some selection Σ. Then the completion $comp(\mathcal{O}_2^\Sigma)$ obtained by exhaustively applying the rules in Figure 2 is said to be a* mapped completion *of $(\mathcal{O}_1, \mathcal{O}_2, \delta)$ if $\mathcal{O}_2^\Sigma$ is consistent and there is no consistent mapped ontology $\mathcal{O}_2^{\Sigma^i}$ such that $\mathcal{O}_2^{\Sigma^i} \succ \mathcal{O}_2^\Sigma$ holds.*

Furthermore, let α an axiom of the form $\{a\} \sqsubseteq \{b\}$ or $\{a\} \sqsubseteq \exists R.\{b\}$. Then α is entailed *by $(\mathcal{O}_1, \mathcal{O}_2, \delta)$, written $(\mathcal{O}_1, \mathcal{O}_2, \delta) \models_d \alpha$, if $\alpha \in comp(\mathcal{O}_2^\Sigma)$ for each mapped completion $\mathcal{O}_2^\Sigma$ of $(\mathcal{O}_1, \mathcal{O}_2, \delta)$.*

Lemma 1. *A mapped-tuple $(\mathcal{O}_1, \mathcal{O}_2, \delta)$ always has a mapped completion.*

Proof. There are two conditions for obtaining a mapped completion $comp(\mathcal{O}_2^\Sigma)$: (1) $\mathcal{O}_2^\Sigma$ is consistent, and (2) $\mathcal{O}_2^\Sigma$ is maximal with respect to $\succ$. It is clear that there is at least one Σ such that $\mathcal{O}_2^\Sigma$ is consistent, namely $\Sigma = \emptyset$. If this is the only Σ producing a consistent mapped ontology, then $comp(\mathcal{O}_2^\Sigma)$ is the corresponding mapped completion. Now let $\mathcal{S}$ be the set of all selections which produce a consistent mapped ontology. We already know that $\mathcal{S}$ is finite, and so the set of corresponding consistent mapped ontologies is also finite, and therefore contains maximal elements with respect to the preference relation $\prec$. Each of these maximal elements is then a mapped completion of $(\mathcal{O}_1, \mathcal{O}_2, \delta)$.

Theorem 3. *The problem of entailment checking for a mapped-tuple $(\mathcal{O}_1, \mathcal{O}_2, \delta)$ is decidable.*

Proof. In order to check entailment, it suffices to obtain all the possible mapped completions as per definition 8. Since there is only a finite number of possible selections for $(\mathcal{O}_1, \mathcal{O}_2, \delta)$, then as argued in the proof of Lemma 1 there is only a finite number of corresponding mapped ontologies, and furthermore we know that exhaustive application of the completion rules terminates. Hence the task is decidable. □

3.2   Applying Defeasible Mappings to Unknowns

So far we have defined the semantics of defeasible mappings and a way to derive entailments. Using these mappings, queries can be asked in terms of concepts of the ontology which is being mapped to.

For instance let the ontology $\mathcal{O}_1$ have axioms

$$\{john\} \sqsubseteq USCitizen \qquad\qquad \{john\} \sqsubseteq Traveler$$
$$USCitizen \sqsubseteq \exists hasPassport.USPassport,$$

let the ontology $\mathcal{O}_2$ have axioms

$$Tourist \sqsubseteq \exists hasPP.Passport$$
$$\exists hasPP.AmericanPassport \sqsubseteq EuVisaNotRequired,$$

and let δ consist of the mappings

$$Traveler \sqsubseteq_d Tourist \qquad\qquad hasPassport \sqsubseteq_d hasPP$$
$$USPassport \sqsubseteq_d AmericanPassport.$$

We can then ask questions in terms of the concepts and roles of $\mathcal{O}_2$ like "list all the tourists," i.e., all instances that belong to the class $Tourist$, and we would get the answer $john$. But if we look carefully, we would also expect $john$ as an instance of the class $EuVisaNotRequired$.

However, as per the semantics we have defined in the previous section, we would not be able to derive this conclusion. This is because the defeasible mappings do not apply to unknowns. In this case the unknown in question is $john$'s $USPassport$. We address this issue by modifying the semantics in order to apply the mappings to unknowns as well.

First of all, recall that the set N_I already contains the auxiliary individuals ι_{RC} for every $R \in N_R$ and $C \in N_C$ – we have not yet made use of them, but we will do so now. In fact, we now modify the completion rules in Figure 2 by adding two additional rules as follows, and where $a \in N_I$, i.e. a may also be an auxiliary individual.

$$\{a\} \sqsubseteq \exists R.D \mapsto \{a\} \sqsubseteq \exists R.\{\iota_{RD}\} \tag{27}$$
$$\{a\} \sqsubseteq \exists R.D \mapsto \{\iota_{RD}\} \sqsubseteq D \tag{28}$$

Furthermore, we retain all the definitions from section 3.1 starting from Cand, $\mathsf{Cand}_\mathcal{R}$ but using the completion $comp_u(\mathcal{O}_1)$ obtained by applying the completion rules in Figure 2 in conjunction with the new rules when producing selections. We still use $comp$, the previous version without the new rules, for all other steps.

Returning to the example above, $comp_u(\mathcal{O}_1)$ now becomes

$$\{john\} \sqsubseteq USCitizen \qquad\qquad \{john\} \sqsubseteq Traveler$$
$$USCitizen \sqsubseteq \exists hasPassport.USPassport \qquad \{\iota_{hpp,usp}\} \sqsubseteq USPassport$$
$$\{john\} \sqsubseteq \exists hasPassport.\{\iota_{hpp,usp}\},$$

and from the mappings we obtain

$$\mathcal{O}_2^\Sigma = comp(\mathcal{O}_2) \cup \{ \quad \{john\} \sqsubseteq Tourist, \quad \{john\} \sqsubseteq \exists hasPP.\{\iota_{hpp,usp}\},$$
$$\{\iota_{hpp,usp}\} \sqsubseteq AmericanPassport\} \quad \}.$$

Note, that this $\mathcal{O}_2^\Sigma$ is the only maximal mapped ontology. When we apply the completion rules of Figure 2 on $\mathcal{O}_2^\Sigma$, rule 19 will produce the axiom $\{john\} \sqsubseteq EuVisaNotRequired$.

We now show that, under this new version, default mappings behave just as ordinary mappings provided no inconsistencies arise. This is of course exactly what we would like to obtain, i.e., the new semantics is conservative in this respect and "kicks in" only if needed due to inconsistencies.

Theorem 4. *Let $(\mathcal{O}_1, \mathcal{O}_2, \delta)$ be a mapped-tuple such that for any selection Σ, $\mathcal{O}_2^{\Sigma}$ is consistent. Let α be an $\mathcal{ER}_{\perp, \mathcal{O}}$ axiom of the form $\{a\} \sqsubseteq C$ or $\{a\} \sqsubseteq \exists R.\{b\}$, where a, b are named individuals from $\mathcal{O}_1$ and C, R are class names, respectively role names, from $\mathcal{O}_2$. Then $(\mathcal{O}_1, \mathcal{O}_2, \delta) \models \alpha$ if and only if $\mathcal{O}_1 \cup \mathcal{O}_2 \cup \bar{\delta} \models \alpha$, where $\bar{\delta}$ is exactly the same as δ but with all $\sqsubseteq_d$ replaced by $\sqsubseteq$.*

Proof. In this case there is only one relevant selection Σ, namely the full selection, since for every possible Σ, $\mathcal{O}_2^{\Sigma}$ is consistent.

Consider an interpretation $\mathcal{I} = \mathcal{I}(\mathcal{O}_2^{\Sigma})$ of $\mathcal{O}_2^{\Sigma}$, defined as at the end of Section 2, and recall that $\mathcal{I} \models \mathcal{O}_2^{\Sigma}$.

Let $\mathcal{I}'$ be an interpretation of $\mathcal{O}_1 \cup \mathcal{O}_2^{\Sigma}$ which extends $\mathcal{I}$ such that $\Delta^{\mathcal{I}'} = \Delta^{\mathcal{I}} \cup \{x_C \mid C \in N_C^{\mathcal{O}_1}\}$, and for all $C \in N_C^{\mathcal{O}_1}$ and $R \in N_R^{\mathcal{O}_1}$, $C^{\mathcal{I}'}$ and $D^{\mathcal{I}'}$ are constructed from $comp_u(\mathcal{O}_1)$ exactly as it is done for $\mathcal{I}$ from $comp(\mathcal{O}_2^{\Sigma})$. Then clearly $\mathcal{I}' \models \mathcal{O}_2^{\Sigma} \cup \mathcal{O}_1$. Furthermore, axioms of the form $\{a\} \sqsubseteq C$, $\{a\} \sqsubseteq \exists R.\{b\}$ where $a, b \in N_I^{\mathcal{O}_1}, C \in N_C^{\mathcal{O}_2}$ and $R \in N_R^{\mathcal{O}_2}$ are only produced from the axioms of $\mathcal{O}_2^{\Sigma}$.

Moreover, $\mathcal{I}' \models \mathcal{O}_1 \cup \mathcal{O}_2 \cup \bar{\delta}$ holds. To prove this it suffices to show that $\mathcal{I}'$ satisfies all axioms $C \sqsubseteq D \in \bar{\delta}$ and $R \sqsubseteq S \in \bar{\delta}$ since we already know that $\mathcal{I}' \models \mathcal{O}_1 \cup \mathcal{O}_2$. And indeed, for every axiom $C \sqsubseteq D \in \bar{\delta}$ (which also means $C \sqsubseteq_d D \in \delta$), we know that if $\{a\} \sqsubseteq C \in comp_u(\mathcal{O}_1)$ then $\{a\} \sqsubseteq D \in \mathcal{O}_2^{\Sigma}$. Hence, by definition of $\mathcal{I}'$, $a \in C^{\mathcal{I}'} \cap D^{\mathcal{I}'}$. Similarly, for every axiom $R \sqsubseteq S \in \bar{\delta}$, we know that whenever $\{a\} \sqsubseteq \exists R.\{b\} \in comp_u(\mathcal{O}_1)$, we have $\{a\} \sqsubseteq \exists S.\{b\} \in \mathcal{O}_2^{\Sigma}$, and by definition of $\mathcal{I}'$, we obtain $(a, b) \in R^{\mathcal{I}'}, S^{\mathcal{I}'}$.

So now, in particular, if $\mathcal{O}_1 \cup \mathcal{O}_2 \cup \bar{\delta} \models \alpha$ then $\mathcal{I}' \models \alpha$, and therefore $\mathcal{I} \models \alpha$, since α does not contain any class or role names from $\mathcal{O}_1$. By definition of $\mathcal{I}$, we then obtain $\alpha \in comp(\mathcal{O}_2^{\Sigma})$ and consequently $(\mathcal{O}_1, \mathcal{O}_2, \delta) \models \alpha$ as required.

Conversely, consider an interpretation $\mathcal{I} = \mathcal{I}(\overline{\mathcal{O}})$ of $\overline{\mathcal{O}} = \mathcal{O}_1 \cup \mathcal{O}_2 \cup \bar{\delta}$ obtained as defined at the end of Section 2, and recall that $\mathcal{I} \models \overline{\mathcal{O}}$.

Now consider $\mathcal{O}' = comp_u(\mathcal{O}_1) \cup comp(\mathcal{O}_2) \cup \delta \cup \Sigma$ and note that $\mathcal{O}_2^{\Sigma} = comp(\mathcal{O}_2) \cup \Sigma \subseteq \mathcal{O}'$ and also that $\overline{\mathcal{O}} \subseteq \mathcal{O}'$. Let $\mathcal{I}' = \mathcal{I}(\mathcal{O}')$ be obtained as defined at the end of Section 2, and recall that $\mathcal{I}' \models \mathcal{O}'$. By construction, we also obtain $\mathcal{I}' \models \mathcal{O}_2^{\Sigma}$ and also that $\mathcal{I}'$ and $\mathcal{I}$ coincide on the signature of $\overline{\mathcal{O}}$.

So now, in particular, if $(\mathcal{O}_1, \mathcal{O}_2, \delta) \models \alpha$, for α as in the statement of the theorem, then $\mathcal{I}' \models \alpha$, and therefore $\mathcal{I} \models \alpha$, and by definition of $\mathcal{I}$ we obtain $\alpha \in comp(\mathcal{O}_1 \cup \mathcal{O}_2 \cup \bar{\delta})$. Consequently, $\mathcal{O}_1 \cup \mathcal{O}_2 \cup \bar{\delta} \models \alpha$ as required. $\square$

4   Relationship with Answer sets

The above semantics is inspired by Reiter's default logic, as already mentioned. Formally, we show that it is very closely related with the prominent answer set semantics from logic programming, which in turn has a well-established relationship to Reiter's default logic. We first recall the definition of answer sets from [10], see [11] for exhaustive background reading.

Definition 9. *(answer sets) An extended program is a logic program that contains rules of the form $L_0 \leftarrow L_1, \ldots, L_m, not\ L_{m+1}, \ldots, not\ L_n$ where $0 \leq m \leq n$*

Table 2. Rewriting of axioms to rules

	Axiom	Rule
1	$C \sqsubseteq D$	$D(x) \leftarrow C(x)$
2	$C \sqsubseteq \bot$	$\neg C(x) \leftarrow C(x)$
3	$\exists R.C \sqsubseteq D$	$D(x) \leftarrow R(x,y) \land C(y)$
4	$C_1 \sqcap C_2 \sqsubseteq D$	$D(x) \leftarrow C_1(x) \land C_2(x)$
5	$C_1 \sqcap C_2 \sqsubseteq \bot$	$\neg C_2(x) \leftarrow C_1(x), \neg C_1(x) \leftarrow C_2(x)$
6	$R_1 \sqsubseteq R$	$R(x,y) \leftarrow R_1(x,y)$
7	$R_1 \circ R_2 \sqsubseteq R$	$R(x,z) \leftarrow R_1(x,y) \land R_2(y,z)$
8	$\{a\} \sqsubseteq C$	$C(a) \leftarrow$
9	$\{a\} \sqsubseteq \exists R.\{b\}$	$R(a,b) \leftarrow$

and each L_i is a literal A or $\neg A$. $\neg$ denotes so-called classical negation, *as opposed to* not *which denotes* default negation.

For Π an extended program that contains no variables and does not contain not *, let Lit be the set of ground literals in the language of Π. The* answer set $\alpha(\Pi)$ *of Π is the smallest subset S of Lit such that*

1. *for any rule $L_0 \leftarrow L_1, \ldots, L_m \in \Pi$, if $L_1, \ldots L_2 \in S$, then $L_0 \in S$, and*
2. *if S contains a pair of complementary literals, then $S = Lit$.*

For Π a (general) extended program and Lit the set of all literals in the language of Π, define Π^S, for a set $S \subseteq Lit$, as the extended program obtained by deleting, from Π,

1. *each rule that has some* not L *in its body with $L \in S$, and*
2. *all expressions of the form* not L *in the bodies of the remaining rules.*

Finally, S is an answer set *of Π if $S = \alpha(\Pi^S)$.*

Let $(\mathcal{O}_1, \mathcal{O}_2, \delta)$ be a mapped-tuple. We now define an extended program $\Pi(\mathcal{O}_1, \mathcal{O}_2, \delta)$ as follows. For every axiom of the form $C \sqsubseteq_d D \in \delta$ and for all $\{a\} \sqsubseteq C \in comp(\mathcal{O}_1)$, we add rules of the following form to $\Pi(\mathcal{O}_1, \mathcal{O}_2, \delta)$.

$$C(a) \leftarrow \tag{29}$$

$$D(a) \leftarrow C(a), not \; \neg D(a) \tag{30}$$

For mapping axioms of the form $R \sqsubseteq_d S \in \delta$, we add the following rules.

$$R(a,b) \leftarrow \tag{31}$$

$$S(a,b) \leftarrow R(a,b), not \; \neg S(a,b) \tag{32}$$

Furthermore, we add to $\Pi(\mathcal{O}_1, \mathcal{O}_2, \delta)$ all possible groundings of the rules obtained by rewriting $comp(\mathcal{O}_2)$ as per the rules in Table 2, using all the individuals that occur in $\mathcal{O}_1, \mathcal{O}_2$.

It should be noted that we do not provide a transformation for axioms of the form $C \sqsubseteq \exists R.D$ in Table 2. This is because for representing defeasible axioms in logic programs we need the classical negation [10] and to represent axioms with existentials on the right hand side we require existential rules. Although

$$\{a\} \sqsubseteq C \quad (33) \qquad C \sqsubseteq_d D \quad (35) \qquad \begin{aligned} D \sqcap E \sqsubseteq \bot \quad &(37) \\ D \sqsubseteq F \quad &(38) \end{aligned}$$
$$\{a\} \sqsubseteq B \quad (34) \qquad B \sqsubseteq_d E \quad (36) \qquad \qquad E \sqsubseteq F \quad (39)$$

Fig. 3. Example mapping

a stable model semantics for existential rules has been defined in [17], it is not defined for extended programs with classical negation. Furthermore, it is not straightforward to extend the approach from [17] to extended programs. So we restrict ourselves to showing that our reduction works for the case when axioms of the form $C \sqsubseteq \exists R.D$ are not present. This is sufficient to show that our approach aligns well with the answer set semantics.

Example 2. Consider the axioms listed in Figure 3 where axioms 33, and 34 are from $\mathcal{O}_1$, axioms 37, 38, and 39 are from $\mathcal{O}_2$ and the axioms 35, and 36 represent the set δ of defeasible mappings. The corresponding extended program $\Pi(\mathcal{O}_1, \mathcal{O}_2, \delta)$ is as follows.

$$C(a) \leftarrow \qquad D(a) \leftarrow C(a) \wedge \text{not } \neg D(a) \qquad \neg E(a) \leftarrow D(a) \qquad F(a) \leftarrow D(a)$$
$$B(a) \leftarrow \qquad E(a) \leftarrow B(a) \wedge \text{not } \neg E(a) \qquad \neg D(a) \leftarrow E(a) \qquad F(a) \leftarrow E(a)$$

Note there are two answer sets, $S_1 = \{C(a), B(a), D(a), \neg E(a), F(a)\}$ and $S_2 = \{C(a), B(a), E(a), \neg B(a), F(a)\}$, for $\Pi(\mathcal{O}_1, \mathcal{O}_2, \delta)$.

Definition 10. *Let $\mathcal{O}_2^{\Sigma}$ be a mapped ontology for $(\mathcal{O}_1, \mathcal{O}_2, \delta)$, and let $comp(\mathcal{O}_2^{\Sigma})$ be a corresponding mapped completion. Then we define the mapped answer set $S(\mathcal{O}_2^{\Sigma})$ to be the following set.*

$\{C(a) \mid C \sqsubseteq_d D \in \delta \text{ and } \{a\} \sqsubseteq C \in comp(\mathcal{O}_1)\} \cup$
$\{R(a,b) \mid R \sqsubseteq_d S \in \delta \text{ and } \{a\} \sqsubseteq \exists R.\{b\} \in comp(\mathcal{O}_1) \cup$
$\{C(a) \mid \{a\} \sqsubseteq C \in comp(\mathcal{O}_2^{\Sigma})\} \cup$
$\{\neg D(a) \mid C \sqsubseteq_d D \in \delta, \{a\} \sqsubseteq C \in comp(\mathcal{O}_1) \text{ and } \{a\} \sqsubseteq D \notin comp(\mathcal{O}_2^{\Sigma})\} \cup$
$\{R(a,b) \mid \{a\} \sqsubseteq \exists R.\{b\} \in comp(\mathcal{O}_2^{\Sigma})\} \cup$
$\{\neg S(a,b) \mid R \sqsubseteq_d S \in \delta, \{a\} \sqsubseteq \exists R.\{b\} \in comp(\mathcal{O}_1) \text{ and } \{a\} \sqsubseteq \exists S.\{b\} \notin comp(\mathcal{O}_2^{\Sigma})\}$

Lemma 2. *Let $\mathcal{O}_2^{\Sigma}$ be a mapped ontology for $(\mathcal{O}_1, \mathcal{O}_2, \delta)$, and let $comp(\mathcal{O}_2^{\Sigma})$ be a corresponding mapped completion. Then the mapped answer set $S(\mathcal{O}_2^{\Sigma})$ is an answer set of $\Pi(\mathcal{O}_1, \mathcal{O}_2, \delta)$.*

The proofs of this lemma and the next have been omitted due to space restrictions. They can be found in the appendix of the technical report [22].

Lemma 3. *Let $(\mathcal{O}_1, \mathcal{O}_2, \delta)$ be a mapped-tuple and let S be an answer set of $\Pi(\mathcal{O}_1, \mathcal{O}_2, \delta) = \overline{\Pi}$. Then $S = S(\mathcal{O}_2^{\Sigma})$ for some mapped ontology $\mathcal{O}_2^{\Sigma}$ of $(\mathcal{O}_1, \mathcal{O}_2, \delta)$.*

The following theorem is a now direct consequence of Lemmas 2 and 3.

Theorem 5. *Let $(\mathcal{O}_1, \mathcal{O}_2, \delta)$ be a mapped-tuple. Then $(\mathcal{O}_1, \mathcal{O}_2, \delta) \models_d \{a\} \sqsubseteq C$ if, and only if, $\Pi(\mathcal{O}_1, \mathcal{O}_2, \delta) \models_S C(a)$, where $\models_S$ represents stable model entailment.*

5   Related Work

This work is relevant to at least two areas of work, (1) advancing the use of non-monotonic logics in description logics, and especially in the $\mathcal{EL}$ family, and (2) providing a robust mapping language.

We introduced the use of defeasible semantics to denote mappings in [23], but therein we had to impose a rather significant restriction that exceptions to the default rules may occur only in the known individuals, a restriction which we could completely lift with the approach and setting described in the earlier sections of this work. Our approach provides a significant result over [23] because (1) It is not straight forward to obtain this result, (2) this approach can be applied to any logic in the EL family without any change in the semantics, (3) It removes the 20 year old road block in the research area of defaults and description logics due to the results from [2], and (4) all of the previously known decidability results of defaults + dl combinations placed a some sort of restriction on the applicability of defaults to the individuals: [2], [23] where [23] improved the results from [2] but by placing a different restriction on applicability of defaults to unknowns. Furthermore, the mapping scenario presented in this paper is also a practical approach to querying heterogeneous datasets using our approach towards a mapping language. It is also established in this paper that the approach here is closer to Reiter's semantics than in [23] by showing the similarity with ASP semantics.

With respect to repairing ontology alignments there are approaches like [1, 16,19]. The work in [19] is specifically close in spirit to our approach, though we provide a much more detailed semantic treatment which is closely related to Reiter's defaults and answer set programming. Furthermore, we also include defeasible axioms for roles and obtain a mild tractability result. Our approach also forms a basis for a mapping language rather than focusing on the repairing of ontology alignments.

In terms of integration of non-monotonic logics with DLs, recent work [4–6] has been proposed in integrating the semantics of rational closure and KLM style semantics to DLs. These are alternative semantics to defaults and thus give a different perspective for apply defeasible logic to DLs. A plethora of other proposals have been made for the integration of non-monotonic logics with DLs, and we refer the reader to [15] which provides pointers to most of the prominent relevant work.

Similar in spirit to our approach, though on a different logic, is also [3].

6   Conclusion

In this paper we provide an extension for the description logic $\mathcal{ER}_{\bot,\mathcal{O}}$ with the ability to have defeasible mappings between ontologies. This work should be easily extendable to other logics in the $\mathcal{EL}$ family, provided soundness and completeness proofs can be obtained for the base logic along similar lines. We show a reduction from our semantics of defeasible mappings to that of answer set programming. This shows that the approach outlined here is very close to the original notion of defaults. Furthermore, the application of defaults is not limited to named individuals but also applies to unknowns that are implicitly referred to in the knowledge base due to existentials.

Of course, our resulting logic appears to be no longer tractable. However, it should be remarked that the application of a monotonic semantics is completely impossible in the context of inconsistencies coming from the mappings, and repair approaches currently require human intervention and are generally employed at the level of axioms, rather than individuals. Some form of paraconsistent reasoning [18] may be a more efficient contender, but then paraconsistent approaches such as [18] tend to miss many desired consequences.

As a part of future work we consider a smart algorithmization for entailment checking that would perform with reasonable efficiency. One possible approach would be to find a method to generate rules that act as templates which could be used to check which selections used to create the mapped ontologies would lead to inconsistencies without actually running the completion algorithm on the mapped ontologies. We also plan to implement the algorithm and perform a detailed evaluation of its performance with respect to time when compared to the monotonic extensions and also with respect to the quality of entailments obtained by defeasible mappings compared to traditional alignments produced by automatic alignment systems. We could make use of data made available by the ontology alignment evaluation initiative [8,9]. Good results would lead to a solid framework towards a robust mapping language for tractable ontology languages.

Acknowledgments. This work was supported by the National Science Foundation under award 1017225 "III: Small: TROn—Tractable Reasoning with Ontologies" and award 1440202 "EarthCube Building Blocks: Collaborative Proposal: GeoLink—Leveraging Semantics and Linked Data for Data Sharing and Discovery in the Geosciences." The authors also thank an anonymous reviewer of a previous version of this paper for detecting a flaw in our initial semantics, which has now been removed.

References

1. Baader, F., Brandt, S., Lutz, C.: Pushing the EL envelope. In: Kaelbling, L.P., Saffiotti, A. (eds.) IJCAI 2005, Proceedings of the Nineteenth International Joint Conference on Artificial Intelligence, Edinburgh, Scotland, UK, July 30–August 5, pp. 364–369 (2005)
2. Baader, F., Hollunder, B.: Embedding defaults into terminological knowledge representation formalisms. Journal Automed Reasoning **14**(1), 149–180 (1995)

3. Bozzato, L., Eiter, T., Serafini, L.: Contextualized knowledge repositories with justifiable exceptions. In: Bienvenu, M., Ortiz, M., Rosati, R., Simkus, M. (eds.) Informal Proceedings of the 27th International Workshop on Description Logics, Vienna, Austria, July 17–20, 2014. CEUR Workshop Proceedings, vol. 1193, pp. 112–123. CEUR-WS.org (2014)
4. Casini, G., Meyer, T., Moodley, K., Nortjé, R.: Relevant closure: a new form of defeasible reasoning for description logics. In: Fermé, E., Leite, J. (eds.) JELIA 2014. LNCS, vol. 8761, pp. 92–106. Springer, Heidelberg (2014)
5. Casini, G., Meyer, T., Moodley, K., Varzinczak, I.J.: Towards practical defeasible reasoning for description logics. In: Eiter, T., Glimm, B., Kazakov, Y., Krötzsch, M. (eds.) Informal Proceedings of the 26th International Workshop on Description Logics, Ulm, Germany, July 23–26, vol. 1014, pp. 587–599. CEUR-WS.org (2013)
6. Casini, G., Meyer, T., Varzinczak, I.J., Moodley, K.: Nonmonotonic reasoning in description logics: rational closure for the abox. In: Eiter, T., Glimm, B., Kazakov, Y., Krötzsch, M. (eds.) Informal Proceedings of the 26th International Workshop on Description Logics, Ulm, Germany, July 23–26. CEUR Workshop Proceedings, vol. 1014, pp. 600–615. CEUR-WS.org (2013)
7. Cheatham, M., Hitzler, P.: String similarity metrics for ontology alignment. In: Alani, H., et al. (eds.) ISWC 2013, Part II. LNCS, vol. 8219, pp. 294–309. Springer, Heidelberg (2013)
8. Dragisic, Z., Eckert, K., Euzenat, J., Faria, D., Ferrara, A., Granada, R., Ivanova, V., Jiménez-Ruiz, E., Kempf, A.O., Lambrix, P., Montanelli, S., Paulheim, H., Ritze, D., Shvaiko, P., Solimando, A., dos Santos, C.T., Zamazal, O., Grau, B.C.: Results of the ontology alignment evaluation initiative 2014. In: Shvaiko, P., Euzenat, J., Mao, M., Jiménez-Ruiz, E., Li, J., Ngonga, A. (eds.) Proceedings of the 9th International Workshop on Ontology Matching Collocated with the 13th International Semantic Web Conference (ISWC 2014), Riva del Garda, Trentino, Italy, October 20, pp. 61–104 (2014)
9. Euzenat, J., Meilicke, C., Stuckenschmidt, H., Shvaiko, P., dos Santos, C.T.: Ontology alignment evaluation initiative: Six years of experience. Journal Data Semantics 15, 158–192 (2011)
10. Gelfond, M., Lifschitz, V.: Classical negation in logic programs and disjunctive databases. New Generation Computing 9(3/4), 365–386 (1991)
11. Hitzler, P., Seda, A.K.: Mathematical Aspects of Logic Programming Semantics. Chapman and Hall/CRC studies in informatics series, CRC Press (2011)
12. Jain, P., Hitzler, P., Yeh, P.Z., Verma, K., Sheth, A.P.: Linked Data is merely more data. In: Linked Data Meets Artificial Intelligence, Papers from the 2010 AAAI Spring Symposium, Technical Report SS-10-07, Stanford, California, USA, March 22–24. AAAI (2010)
13. Jiménez-Ruiz, E., Meilicke, C., Grau, B.C., Horrocks, I.: Evaluating mapping repair systems with large biomedical ontologies. In: Eiter, T., Glimm, B., Kazakov, Y., Krötzsch, M. (eds.) Informal Proceedings of the 26th International Workshop on Description Logics, Ulm, Germany, July 23–26. CEUR Workshop Proceedings, vol. 1014, pp. 246–257 (2013)
14. Joshi, A.K., Jain, P., Hitzler, P., Yeh, P.Z., Verma, K., Sheth, A.P., Damova, M.: Alignment-based querying of linked open data. In: Meersman, R., et al. (eds.) OTM 2012, Part II. LNCS, vol. 7566, pp. 807–824. Springer, Heidelberg (2012)

15. Knorr, M., Hitzler, P., Maier, F.: Reconciling OWL and non-monotonic rules for the semantic web. In: Raedt, L.D., Bessière, C., Dubois, D., Doherty, P., Frasconi, P., Heintz, F., Lucas, P.J.F. (eds.) ECAI 2012–20th European Conference on Artificial Intelligence. Including Prestigious Applications of Artificial Intelligence (PAIS 2012) System Demonstrations Track, Montpellier, France, August 27–31. Frontiers in Artificial Intelligence and Applications, vol. 242, pp. 474–479. IOS Press (2012)
16. Lambrix, P., Wei-Kleiner, F., Dragisic, Z., Ivanova, V.: Repairing missing is-a structure in ontologies is an abductive reasoning problem. In: Lambrix, P., Qi, G., Horridge, M., Parsia, B. (eds.) Proceedings of the Second International Workshop on Debugging Ontologies and Ontology Mappings, Montpellier, France, May 27, vol. 999, pp. 33–44. CEUR-WS.org (2013)
17. Magka, D., Krötzsch, M., Horrocks, I.: Computing stable models for nonmonotonic existential rules. In: Rossi, F. (ed.) IJCAI 2013, Proceedings of the 23rd International Joint Conference on Artificial Intelligence, Beijing, China, August 3–9. IJCAI/AAAI (2013)
18. Maier, F., Ma, Y., Hitzler, P.: Paraconsistent OWL and related logics. Semantic Web 4(4), 395–427 (2013)
19. Meilicke, C., Stuckenschmidt, H., Tamilin, A.: Repairing ontology mappings. In: Holte, R.C., Howe, A. (eds.) Proceedings of the Twenty-Second AAAI Conference on Artificial Intelligence, Vancouver, British Columbia, Canada, July 22–26, pp. 1408–1413 (2007)
20. Oberle, D., Ankolekar, A., Hitzler, P., Cimiano, P., Sintek, M., Kiesel, M., Mougouie, B., Baumann, S., Vembu, S., Romanelli, M., Buitelaar, P., Engel, R., Sonntag, D., Reithinger, N., Loos, B., Porzel, R., Zorn, H.P., Micelli, V., Schmidt, C., Weiten, M., Burkhardt, F., Zhou, J.: DOLCE ergo SUMO: on foundational and domain models in the SmartWeb Integrated Ontology (SWIntO). Journal on Web Semantics 5(3), 156–174 (2007)
21. Reiter, R.: A logic for default reasoning. Artificial Intelligence 13(1–2), 81–132 (1980)
22. Sengupta, K., Hitzler, P.: Technical report: Towards defeasible mappings for tractable description logics. Tech. rep., Data Semantics Lab, Wright State University (2015). http://pascal-hitzler.de/pub/2015-ER-mappings.pdf
23. Sengupta, K., Hitzler, P., Janowicz, K.: Revisiting default description logics – and their role in aligning ontologies. In: Supnithi, T., Yamaguchi, T., Pan, J.Z., Wuwongse, V., Buranarach, M. (eds.) JIST 2014. LNCS, vol. 8943, pp. 3–18. Springer, Heidelberg (2015)

An Algebra of Qualitative Taxonomical Relations for Ontology Alignments

Armen Inants[(✉)] and Jérôme Euzenat

Inria, Univ. Grenoble Alpes, Grenoble, France
{Armen.Inants,Jerome.Euzenat}@inria.fr

Abstract. Algebras of relations were shown useful in managing ontology alignments. They make it possible to aggregate alignments disjunctively or conjunctively and to propagate alignments within a network of ontologies. The previously considered algebra of relations contains taxonomical relations between classes. However, compositional inference using this algebra is sound only if we assume that classes which occur in alignments have nonempty extensions. Moreover, this algebra covers relations only between classes. Here we introduce a new algebra of relations, which, first, solves the limitation of the previous one, and second, incorporates all qualitative taxonomical relations that occur between individuals and concepts, including the relations "is a" and "is not". We prove that this algebra is coherent with respect to the simple semantics of alignments.

Keywords: Relation algebra · Ontology alignment · Network of ontologies

1 Introduction

The heterogeneity of ontologies on the semantic web requires finding correspondences between them in order to achieve semantic interoperability. The operation of finding correspondences is called ontology matching and its result is a set of correspondences called an alignment [6]. Alignments are used for importing data from one ontology to another or for translating queries.

In previous work [5], we put forward a framework for manipulating alignments based on algebras of relations. This allows for merging alignments conjunctively or disjunctively, amalgamate alignments with relations of different granularity and compose alignments.

The general approach was illustrated in [5] on a particular algebra $\mathbb{A}5$. It is generated by 5 atoms: $=, >, <, \emptyset, \bot$, which stand for "equivalent to", "more/less general than", "partially overlaps with" and "disjoint with" respectively. The composition table of $\mathbb{A}5$ is given in Table 1. It was shown that an algebra of relations induces composition, union, intersection and conversion operations on alignments.

This may be particularly useful as a fast way to reason about alignments without resorting to full reasoning. For instance, this may be used for generating new alignments from existing ones or for checking the unsatisfiability of a network of ontologies.

© Springer International Publishing Switzerland 2015
M. Arenas et al. (Eds.): ISWC 2015, Part I, LNCS 9366, pp. 253–268, 2015.
DOI: 10.1007/978-3-319-25007-6_15

Example 1. For instance, in Figure 1, there are two correspondences: "$\mathcal{O}_2$:Serial writer is subsumed by $\mathcal{O}_1$:Successful creator" and "$\mathcal{O}_2$:Serial writer is equivalent to $\mathcal{O}_3$:Popular writer". Subsumption and equivalence are encoded in $\mathbb{A}5$ as $\{=,<\}$ and $\{=\}$ respectively. By composing these relations we infer a correspondence between $\mathcal{O}_1$:Successful creator and $\mathcal{O}_3$:Popular writer:

$$\left(\text{Successful creator},\ \text{Serial writer},\ \{=\}\right) * \left(\text{Serial writer},\ \text{Popular writer},\ \{=,<\}\right)$$
$$= \left(\text{Successful creator},\ \text{Popular writer},\ \{=\} * \{=,<\}\right)$$
$$= \left(\text{Successful creator},\ \text{Popular writer},\ (= * =) \cup (= * <)\right)$$
$$= \left(\text{Successful creator},\ \text{Popular writer},\ \{=\} \cup \{<\}\right)$$
$$= \left(\text{Successful creator},\ \text{Popular writer},\ \{=,<\}\right)$$

However, the algebra of relations $\mathbb{A}5$ suffers from two problems:

1. $\mathbb{A}5$ covers relations only between classes. This leaves out of scope the relations owl:sameAs (noted $=$), owl:differentFrom (noted $\neq$), which are defined between instances, and the instance-class relation rdf:type ($\in$). Compositional reasoning with these relations may be used for debugging link sets as shown by Example 1.

Example 2. In Figure 1, composing $\{<,=\} * \{=\} * \{\perp\}$ is equivalent to $\{\perp\}$, i.e., "Mystery novelist" and "Academic" are disjoint classes. This leaves aside further relation composition. Indeed, one would like that $\{\in\}*\{\perp\}*\{\ni\}$ actually yields $\{\neq\}$, i.e., "Amanda Cross" is different from "Carolyn Gold Heilbrun". This would be very useful for debugging data sets since the actual relation between these individuals is $\{=\}$ so the intersection of these relations is empty revealing unsatisfiability.

However, this requires to compose class relations ($\perp$) and individual-class relations ($\in$). Moreover, this composition yields an individual relation ($\neq$).

To make this work within the considered framework, one needs an algebra incorporating all these relations. This would allow for encoding such RDF triples as correspondences and use them for the refinement and evolution of alignments.

2. The algebraic calculus that $\mathbb{A}5$ induces on alignments does not allow for distinguishing between unsatisfiability and incoherence of alignments. An alignment

Table 1. Composition table of $\mathbb{A}5$.

$*$	$=$	$>$	$<$	$\lozenge$	$\perp$
$=$	$=$	$>$	$<$	$\lozenge$	$\perp$
$>$	$>$	$>$	$=><\lozenge$	$>\lozenge$	$>\lozenge\perp$
$<$	$<$	$=><\lozenge\perp$	$<$	$<\lozenge\perp$	$\perp$
$\lozenge$	$\lozenge$	$>\lozenge\perp$	$<\lozenge$	$=><\lozenge\perp$	$>\lozenge\perp$
$\perp$	$\perp$	$\perp$	$<\lozenge\perp$	$<\lozenge\perp$	$=><\lozenge\perp$

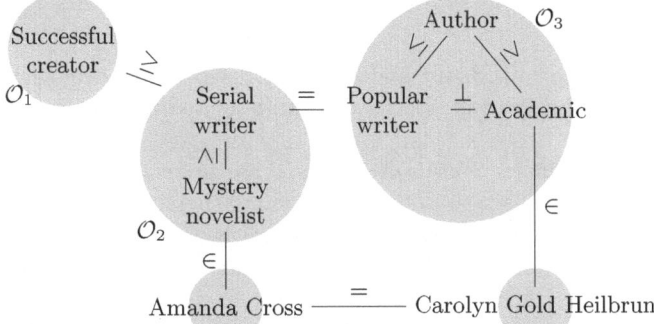

Fig. 1. An example of unsatisfiability in a linked data sets that can be detected through simple composition of relations across ontologies, data, links and correspondences.

is satisfiable if it has a model, and coherent, if it does not force incoherence on any of its entities. If, by applying algebraic reasoning on alignments, we deduce a correspondence $(C, D, \varnothing)$, then it means that the alignments are algebraically inconsistent. However, algebraic inconsistency does not imply unsatisfiability, as one would expect. This is illustrated in Example 3.

Example 3. Consider an alignment $\mathcal{A}$ with two correspondences between the same pair of entities: $\mu = (\mathsf{C}, \mathsf{D}, \{\bot\})$ and $v = (\mathsf{C}, \mathsf{D}, \{<, =\})$. Their conjunction is equal to $(\mathsf{C}, \mathsf{D}, \varnothing)$:

$$\mu \wedge v = (\mathsf{C}, \mathsf{D}, \{\bot\}) \wedge (\mathsf{C}, \mathsf{D}, \{<, =\}) = (\mathsf{C}, \mathsf{D}, \{\bot\} \cap \{=, <\}) = (\mathsf{C}, \mathsf{D}, \varnothing).$$

This means that $\mathcal{A}$ is algebraically inconsistent. But $\mathcal{A}$ has models, thus it is not unsatisfiable. Indeed, if C is interpreted as the empty set, then, whatever the interpretation of D, both μ and v are satisfied by this interpretation. However, $\mathcal{A}$ is incoherent, since it does not allow the class C to have instances.

In this paper, we introduce a new algebra of relations $\mathbb{A}16$, which solves these limitations of $\mathbb{A}5$. $\mathbb{A}16$ incorporates the relations "same as" (owl:sameAs), "different from" (owl:differentFrom), "is a" (rdf:type), "is not", "equivalent to" (owl:equivalentClass), "subsumed by" (rdfs:subClassOf), "disjoint with" (owl:disjointWith), "partially overlaps with" in compliance with OWL semantics. The calculus that $\mathbb{A}16$ induces on alignments allows to differenciate between unsatisfiability and incoherence of alignments.

The paper is structured as follows. In Section 2, we discuss the related work. Section 3 covers some preliminaries, including networks of ontologies and algebras of relations. In Section 4, we build the algebra $\mathbb{A}16$ and establish its soundness with respect to the direct semantics of alignments. In Section 5, we discuss some changes that $\mathbb{A}16$ brings to the calculus of alignments.

2   Related Work

This paper is related to formal frameworks for distributed ontologies on the one hand, and to the theory of qualitative calculi on the other hand.

Languages for distributed ontologies. There are several languages that allow for expressing relations across ontologies. Among them are Distributed Description Logics (DDL) [3], ε-connections [12], Package-based Description Logics (P-DL) [2], Integrated Distributed Description Logics (IDDL) [19] and Distributed Ontology Language (DOL) [14].

Mappings between ontologies in DDL assert relations from the perspective of the target ontology. Mappings between concepts are expressed as *bridge rules*, and those between individuals as *individual correspondences*. The key feature of DDL reasoning is subsumption propagation from one ontology to another. Subsumption is not transitive in DDL, thus cannot be propagated by composition. ε-connections are a framework for modular ontologies. Connection between ontological modules are established with *links*, which act as inter-ontology properties. A distinctive feature of ε-connections is that each ontology module is supposed to model a portion of the domain that is complementary and non-overlapping with respect to the other ontology modules. As the domains of ontologies in an ε-connection system must be disjoint, it is not possible to have a concept in some ontology module that has subconcepts or instances in another ontology. *Ontology importing*, which is implemented in P-DL, allows for reusing concepts, relations and individuals defined in one ontology inside another ontology. *Alignments* in IDDL constitute a separate layer and can be regarded independently from ontologies. This makes possible to reason about alignments alone, considering them as first class citizens. Some comparative analysis of DDL, ε-connections, P-DL and IDDL can be found in [10, 20].

An algebraic calculus of alignments is not intended as a proof theory for a particular semantics of alignments. It is a framework, which allows to use custom algebras of relations for inducing operations on alignments. In this paper, we limit ourselves with taxonomical relations between classes and instances. We design the algebra of taxonomical relations to be sound with respect to the OWL semantics of relations [7]. In principle, algebras of ontology alignment relations can be designed in compliance with other semantics as well, e.g., with the integrated semantics used in IDDL.

Qualitative calculi. Algebras of relations have been used in knowledge representation and reasoning, particularly in the spatio-temporal domain, since the pioneering work of Allen [1]. Allen considered the universe of time intervals, formalized as pairs of real-valued endpoints, and defined 13 binary relations on that universe. Between any two time intervals one and only one out of the 13 base relations holds. This important property allows to factorize the infinite Boolean algebra of binary relations over the universe into a finite Boolean algebra of (qualitative) relations of interest. Moreover, these 13 base relations and their arbitrary unions are closed under composition and converse. This allowed Allen to induce composition and converse on the Boolean algebra of relation symbols, yielding an algebra called the *interval algebra*.

Allen put forward an algorithm for reasoning over relations between time intervals based on constraint propagation. This algorithm decides the satisfiability of a network of temporal constraints, consisting of variables ranging over the universe of time intervals, and binary constraints on variables expressed by elements of the interval algebra.

The interval algebra is an instance of Tarski's relation algebra [18]. [13] defined a class of *qualitative binary constraint satisfaction problems* (QBCSP), which is a class of binary constraint satisfaction problems abstracted to relation algebras. They generalized the *constraint propagation* algorithm of Allen to an arbitrary relation algebra. Reasoning with relation algebras is studied in [4,9].

Meanwhile, calculi similar to Allen's were developed in both temporal and spatial domains. Among them are two variants of the *Region Connection Calculus*: RCC5 and RCC8. In order to study the properties of RCC5, RCC8 and many other calculi existing by that time within a single framework, Ligozat and Renz [15] proposed a formal definition of the implicit concept of a qualitative calculus. In the framework of Ligozat and Renz, a qualitative calculus arises from a partition scheme over some universe. Such calculi can have a weaker algebraic structure than relation algebras: they can be non-associative.

The development of this paper was initially based on the framework of Ligozat and Renz. However, the algebra $\mathbb{A}16$ that we construct does not arise from a partition scheme, but from a more general construct which we call a general partition scheme. We extend the result of Ligozat and Renz to general partition schemes.

3 Preliminaries

3.1 Networks of Ontologies

Here we give a logical account of networks of ontologies in the sense of [6].

Definition 1 (Correspondence). *Given two ontologies $\mathcal{O}$ and $\mathcal{O}'$, with associated entity languages $Ent(\mathcal{O})$ and $Ent(\mathcal{O}')$, and a set of alignment relations* **R**, *a correspondence is a triple (e, e', r), such that $e \in Ent(\mathcal{O})$, $e' \in Ent(\mathcal{O}')$ and $r \in \mathbf{R}$.*

A correspondence (e, e', r) is an assertion that a certain pragmatic relation denoted by the symbol r holds between the entities e and e'.

The entities can be restricted to a particular kind of terms of the ontology language based on the ontology vocabulary, e.g., named entities. The entity language can also be an extension of the ontology language. For instance, it can be a query language, such as SPARQL [8], adding operations for manipulating ontology entities that are not available in the ontology language itself, like concatenating strings or joining relations. The developments of this paper are independent of the chosen entity language.

An important component of a correspondence is the relation that holds between the entities. We fix a set of relations $\mathbf{R}$ that is used for expressing the relations between the entities. The set $\mathbf{R}$ can contain relation symbols like =, which is used by matching algorithms, or IRIs like http://www.w3.org/2004/02/skos/extensions#broaderPartitive. Relations from ontology languages, such as owl:sameAs, owl.differentFrom, owl:equivalentClass, owl:disjointWith, rdfs:subClassOf or rdf:type, can also be used.

An alignment is defined as a set of correspondences.

Definition 2 (Alignment). *Given two ontologies $\mathcal{O}$ and $\mathcal{O}'$, an alignment is a set of correspondences between pairs of entities belonging to $Ent(\mathcal{O})$ and $Ent(\mathcal{O}')$ respectively.*

Definition 3 (Network of ontologies). *A network of ontologies (Ω, Λ) is made up of a set Ω of ontologies and a set Λ of alignments between these ontologies. We denote by $\Lambda(\mathcal{O}, \mathcal{O}')$ the set of alignments in Λ between $\mathcal{O}$ and $\mathcal{O}'$.*

A correspondence is interpreted with respect to three features: a pair of models from each ontology and a semantic structure, denoted as Δ. The class of models of an ontology $\mathcal{O}$ is denoted as $\mathcal{M}(\mathcal{O})$.

Definition 4 (Satisfied correspondence). *A correspondence $\mu = (e, e', r)$ is satisfied by two models m, m' of $\mathcal{O}, \mathcal{O}'$ for some semantic structure Δ if and only if $(m(e), m'(e')) \in r^{\Delta}$, such that r^{Δ} provides the interpretation of the relation r in the structure. This is denoted by $m, m' \models_{\Delta} \mu$.*

Three different kinds of semantic structures are outlined in [21]: simple, contextualized and integrated. Let us fix two ontologies $\mathcal{O}_1$ and $\mathcal{O}_2$ and their models m_1 and m_2 with domains of interpretation D_1 and D_2 respectively. An integrated semantic structure consists of functions ε_i from the local domains D_i ($i = 1, 2$) to a global domain D. A simple semantic structure is a particular case of integrated structure: when $D = \cup_i D_i$ and ε_i are canonical embeddings of D_i into D. Contextualized semantics is given by a family of binary relations r_{ij} ($i = 1, 2$) between the local domains D_i and D_j.

Below is an example of how relation symbols are interpreted with respect to each semantics. As an example consider the semantics of the relation symbol $\sqsubseteq$ depending on Δ.

$$\sqsubseteq^{simple(\Delta)} = \{(X, Y)\ :\ X \subseteq D_1, Y \subseteq D_2 \text{ and } X \subseteq Y\}$$
$$\sqsubseteq^{integrated(\Delta)} = \{(X, Y)\ :\ X \subseteq D_1, Y \subseteq D_2 \text{ and } \varepsilon_1(X) \subseteq \varepsilon_2(Y)\}$$
$$\sqsubseteq^{contextual(\Delta)} = \{(X, Y)\ :\ X \subseteq D_1, Y \subseteq D_2 \text{ and } r_{12}(X) \subseteq Y\}$$

If Δ is simple, then $\sqsubseteq^{\Delta}$ depends only on D_1 and D_2. In this case the semantics of $\sqsubseteq$ corresponds to the interpretation of rdfs:subClassOf if we consider $\mathcal{O}_1$ and $\mathcal{O}_2$ as one large ontology. Likewise, the simple semantics of relation symbols $\bot$ (disjointness) and = (equivalence) corresponds to owl:disjointWith and owl:equivalentClass.

Definition 5 (Models of alignments). *Given two ontologies $\mathcal{O}$ and $\mathcal{O}'$ and an alignment A between these ontologies, a model of this alignment is a triple (m, m', Δ) with $m \in \mathcal{M}(\mathcal{O})$, $m' \in \mathcal{M}(\mathcal{O}')$, and Δ a semantic structure, such that $\forall \mu \in A$, $m, m' \models_\Delta \mu$ (denoted by $m, m' \models_\Delta A$).*

An alignment is said to be *satisfiable* if it has a model. An alignment is said to be *coherent* if, for any of its class entities, it has a model that makes this class non empty.

3.2   Algebraic Calculus of Ontology Alignments

It was shown that algebras of relations are useful for managing ontologies [5]. The adopted algebraic formalism is Tarskian relation algebras.

Definition 6 (Relation algebra). *A relation algebra is an algebra*

$$\mathbb{A} = (A, +, \cdot, -, 0, 1, ;, \smile, 1'), \tag{3.1}$$

with binary operations $+$ (Boolean sum), $\cdot$ (Boolean product) and $;$ (composition, or relative product), unary operations $-$ (complement) and $\smile$ (converse), and constants $0, 1, 1' \in A$ called zero, unit and identity respectively, such that

1) *the reduct $(A, +, \cdot, -, 0, 1)$ is a Boolean algebra,*
2) *identity: $1'; x = x; 1' = x$, for all $x \in A$,*
3) *Peircean law: $(x; y) \cdot z = 0 \Leftrightarrow (x^\smile; z) \cdot y = 0 \Leftrightarrow x \cdot (z; y^\smile) = 0$, for all $x, y, z \in A$,*
4) *associativity: $(x; y); z = x; (y; z)$, for all $x, y, z \in A$.*

We will denote by $\mathbb{A}$ both the algebra and its carrier set. The class of relation algebras is denoted as RA. In the sequel, by "algebra of relations" we will imply an instance of RA, if not stated otherwise.

Consider an algebra of relations $\mathbb{A}$. The approach put forward in [5] is that we allow any element of $\mathbb{A}$ to be used in a correspondence. In other words, referring to the previous subsection, we take $\mathbf{R} = \mathbb{A}$.

Each alignment may be normalized through *norm* to contain exactly one correspondence between any two entities. $\mathbb{A}$ induces the following operations on alignments:

$$\mathcal{A} \wedge \mathcal{A}' = norm(\mathcal{A} \cup \mathcal{A}') \tag{3.2}$$

$$\mathcal{A} \vee \mathcal{A}' = \{(e, e', r + r') \ : \ (e, e', r) \in norm(\mathcal{A}) \wedge (e, e', r') \in norm(\mathcal{A}')\} \tag{3.3}$$

$$\mathcal{A}^\smile = \{(e', e, r^\smile) \ : \ (e, e', r) \in \mathcal{A}\} \tag{3.4}$$

If there exists an alignment between ontology $\mathcal{O}$ and ontology $\mathcal{O}'$, and another alignment between $\mathcal{O}'$ and a third ontology $\mathcal{O}''$, we would like to find which correspondences hold between $\mathcal{O}$ and $\mathcal{O}''$. The operation that returns this set of correspondences is called composition.

$$\mathcal{A} \circ \mathcal{A}' = norm(\{(e, e'', r; s) \ : \ \exists \ (e, e', r) \in \mathcal{A} \text{ and } \exists \ (e', e'', s) \in \mathcal{A}'\}) \tag{3.5}$$

We can regard a network of ontologies as a directed graph, with ontologies being vertices and alignments being edges. Moreover, one can assume that there is at most one alignment between any pair of ontologies in the network. A *closure* of a network of ontologies can be computed by applying a path-consistency algorithm, e.g., PC2 [16], which in essence is an iterative application of

$$\mathcal{A}_{\mathcal{O}_i,\mathcal{O}_j} \leftarrow \mathcal{A}_{\mathcal{O}_i,\mathcal{O}_j} \wedge (\mathcal{A}_{\mathcal{O}_i,\mathcal{O}_k} \circ \mathcal{A}_{\mathcal{O}_k,\mathcal{O}_j}), \tag{3.6}$$

for every triple $(\mathcal{O}_i, \mathcal{O}_j, \mathcal{O}_k)$ of ontologies in Λ, until a fixed point is reached.

3.3   Algebras of JEPD Binary Relations

In general terms, a connection between an algebra of relations and some domain of knowledge is given by specifying a *universe* of objects and a set of *base relations*. For example, the universe of Allen's interval algebra is the set of time intervals encoded as pairs of real numbers (x, y), where $x > y$, whereas base relations are defined by certain conditions on the endpoints of two intervals. Here we give an account of algebras that arise from a set of jointly exhaustive and pairwise disjoint (JEPD) binary relations.

A *binary relation* over a nonempty set $\mathcal{U}$ is a subset of the Cartesian product $\mathcal{U} \times \mathcal{U}$. The *converse* (also called inverse) of a binary relation R is a relation symmetric to R, defined as $R^{-1} = \{(x, y) : (y, x) \in R\}$. The relation $Id_{\mathcal{U}} = \{(x, y) \in \mathcal{U} \times \mathcal{U} : x = y\}$ is called the *identity* over $\mathcal{U}$. *Composition* of binary relations R and S is defined as $R \circ S = \{(x, y) \in \mathcal{U} \times \mathcal{U} : \exists z \in \mathcal{U}$ such that $(x, z) \in R$ and $(z, y) \in S\}$. The *field* of a binary relation R is defined as $Fd(R) = \{x \in \mathcal{U} : \exists y, (x, y) \in R$ or $(y, x) \in R\}$.

A set $\mathcal{P}$ of binary relations over $\mathcal{U}$ is called *jointly exhaustive and pairwise disjoint*, if $\cup_{R \in \mathcal{P}} R = \mathcal{U} \times \mathcal{U}$ and $R \cap R' = \varnothing$ for each $R \neq R' \in \mathcal{P}$. Such $\mathcal{P}$ is called a *partition* of $\mathcal{U} \times \mathcal{U}$. We will assume $\mathcal{P}$ to be finite. Relations in $\mathcal{P}$ are called *base relations*. We call an arbitrary union of base relations a $\mathcal{P}$-*relation*. $\mathcal{P}$-relations form a subalgebra of the Boolean algebra $\mathcal{U} \times \mathcal{U}$, in which the base relations are atoms. If a $\mathcal{P}$-relation is a union of two or more base relations, it is called a *disjunctive relation*. Each $\mathcal{P}$-relation is identified by the set of constituting base relations, thus there is a one-to-one correspondence between the set of $\mathcal{P}$-relations and the powerset $2^{\mathcal{P}}$. In the sequel a set of base relations $\{R_1, \ldots, R_n\} \subseteq \mathcal{P}$ will denote their union.

Generally speaking, composition of $\mathcal{P}$-relations may not be a $\mathcal{P}$-relation. In other words, $\circ$ may not be closed on the set of $\mathcal{P}$-relations. One can approximate the composition by a so-called *weak composition* $\diamond$, defined as the least $\mathcal{P}$-relation which contains the composition. Weak composition is a binary operation on $\mathcal{P}$-relations ($\diamond : 2^{\mathcal{P}} \times 2^{\mathcal{P}} \to 2^{\mathcal{P}}$).

A *partition scheme* is a pair $(\mathcal{U}, \mathcal{P})$, where $\mathcal{U}$ is a nonempty set and $\mathcal{P} = (R_i)_{i \in I}$ is a partition of $\mathcal{U} \times \mathcal{U}$, which is closed under converse and contains the identity over $\mathcal{U}$. Given a partition scheme, both weak composition and converse become operations on the Boolean algebra $2^{\mathcal{P}}$. The algebra

$$\mathbb{A}_{\mathcal{P}} = (2^{\mathcal{P}}, \cup, \cap, -_{\mathcal{U} \times \mathcal{U}}, \varnothing, \mathcal{P}, \diamond, ^{-1}, Id_{\mathcal{U}}) \tag{3.7}$$

is said to be generated by $\mathcal{P}$.

Proposition 1 (Ligozat and Renz [15]). *If $(\mathcal{U}, \mathcal{P})$ is a partition scheme, then $\mathbb{A}_\mathcal{P}$ satisfies all axioms of RA, except, possibly, the associativity axiom.*

An algebra of relations which satisfies all axioms of RA except possibly the associativity axiom is called a *non-associative algebra* [17]. The class of non-associative algebras NA is broader than RA. Assume $\mathbb{A} = (A, +, \cdot, -, 0, 1, ;, \breve{\ }, 1') \in$ NA, $x \le y$ is used as a shortcut for $x + y = y$. By $At(\mathbb{A})$ we denote the set of atoms of the Boolean reduct of $\mathbb{A}$.

Any finite non-associative algebra $\mathbb{A}$ is fully specified by its *atom structure*. The atom structure of an algebra $\mathbb{A}$ consists of the set of atoms $At(\mathbb{A})$, the set of identity atoms $At(1') \subseteq At(\mathbb{A})$, the converse restricted to atoms $\breve{\ } : At(\mathbb{A}) \to At(\mathbb{A})$ and the composition restricted to atoms, which is a function $CT : At(\mathbb{A}) \times At(\mathbb{A}) \to 2^{At(\mathbb{A})}$ defined by $z \in CT(x, y)$ iff $x; y \le z$. CT is usually specified by a *composition table*. The triples (x, y, z), where x, y and z are atoms and which satisfy $x; y \le z$ are called *consistent scenarios*. In order to find the consistent scenarios of $\mathbb{A}_\mathcal{P}$, one has to find all triples (R_i, R_j, R_k) of base relations, for which $\exists x, y, z$, such that $(x, y) \in R_i$, $(y, z) \in R_j$ and $(x, z) \in R_k$.

A non-associative algebra is said to be *integral* if the composition of any non-zero elements, i.e., those different from 0, is non-zero. A finite $\mathbb{A}_\mathcal{P}$ is integral iff the composition of any two base relations is not equal to the empty set.

4   An Algebra of Qualitative Taxonomical Relations

In this section, we define an algebra, which contains the relations "equivalent to", "subsumed by", "disjoint with", "same as", "different from", "is a" and "is not". We call an ontology alignment relation *taxonomical*, if it is associated with some set-theoretic relation (predicate) R. For instance, subsumption $\sqsubseteq$ is associated with the set-theoretic inclusion $\subseteq$. A taxonomical relation holds between two ontological entities iff the relation R holds between the interpretations of these entities. A set-theoretic relation R is said to be *qualitative*, if, for any pair of sets (x, y), xRy is characterized by 3 parameters: whether each of the sets $x \cap y$, $x \backslash y$, $y \backslash x$ is empty or not.

All relations listed above are taxonomical and qualitative (if interpreted with the simple semantics of alignments). The simple semantics of alignments assumes a common domain of interpretation for all ontologies in a network. Given an arbitrary infinite domain D, the relations "same as" and "different from" correspond to binary relations $=$ and $\neq$ on D, "equivalent to", "subsumed by" and "disjoint with" correspond to binary relations $\equiv$, $\subseteq$ and $\perp$ on 2^D, and finally "is a" and "is not" correspond to $\in$ and $\notin$ on $D \times 2^D$. Thus, the binary relations $=, \neq, \equiv, \subseteq, \perp, \in$ and $\notin$ are defined on the set $D \cup 2^D$, which we will call a universe and denote as $\mathcal{U}^{(D)}$. We will refer to the elements of D as *individuals*, and to the elements of 2^D as *sets*.

The relations

$$\mathbf{G} = \{=, \neq, \equiv, \subseteq, \supseteq, \perp, \in, \notin, \ni, \not\ni\}, \tag{4.1}$$

where $\supseteq = \subseteq^{-1}$, $\ni = \in^{-1}$ and $\not\ni = \notin^{-1}$, are not JEPD. What is the minimal partition $\mathcal{P}$ of $\mathcal{U}^{(D)} \times \mathcal{U}^{(D)}$ that has relations in $\mathbf{G}$ as $\mathcal{P}$-relations? Since $\mathcal{U}^{(D)} \times \mathcal{U}^{(D)}$

is a Boolean algebra, the question is to find its subalgebra generated by $\mathbf{G}$. Atoms of the sought-after subalgebra are nonempty intersections of generators (the elements of $\mathbf{G}$ in our case) and their complements. This yields a partition $\mathcal{P}^{14}$ with 14 base relations, which are defined below:

$$
\begin{aligned}
&=_n (\alpha, \beta) \text{ iff } \alpha, \beta \text{ are nonempty sets and } \alpha = \beta \\
&< (\alpha, \beta) \text{ iff } \alpha, \beta \text{ are nonempty sets and } \alpha \subset \beta \\
&> (\alpha, \beta) \text{ iff } \alpha, \beta \text{ are nonempty sets and } \alpha \supset \beta \\
&\langle\!\rangle (\alpha, \beta) \text{ iff } \alpha, \beta \text{ are sets and } \alpha \backslash \beta, \ \alpha \cap \beta, \ \beta \backslash \alpha \neq \varnothing \\
&\| (\alpha, \beta) \text{ iff } \alpha, \beta \text{ are nonempty sets and } \alpha \cap \beta = \varnothing \\
&EN(\alpha, \beta) \text{ iff } \alpha = \varnothing, \ \beta \text{ is a nonempty set} \\
&NE(\alpha, \beta) \text{ iff } \alpha \text{ is a nonempty set and } \beta = \varnothing \\
&=_e (\alpha, \beta) \text{ iff } \alpha = \beta = \varnothing \\
&\in (\alpha, \beta) \text{ iff } \alpha \text{ is an individual}, \beta \text{ is a set and } \alpha \in \beta \\
&\ni (\alpha, \beta) \text{ iff } \alpha \text{ is a set}, \beta \text{ is an individual and } \alpha \ni \beta \\
&\notin (\alpha, \beta) \text{ iff } \alpha \text{ is an individual}, \beta \text{ is a set and } \alpha \notin \beta \\
&\not\ni (\alpha, \beta) \text{ iff } \alpha \text{ is a set}, \beta \text{ is an individual and } \alpha \not\ni \beta \\
&=_i (\alpha, \beta) \text{ iff } \alpha, \beta \text{ are individuals and } \alpha = \beta \\
&\neq_i (\alpha, \beta) \text{ iff } \alpha, \beta \text{ are individuals and } \alpha \neq \beta
\end{aligned}
$$

The relation $\perp$, for instance, is equal to the $\mathcal{P}^{14}$-relation $\{\|, EN, NE, =_e\}$. $\mathcal{P}^{14}$ is closed under converse, but the identity relation $Id_{\mathcal{U}^{(D)}}$ does not belong to $\mathcal{P}^{14}$. It is a disjunctive $\mathcal{P}^{14}$-relation with three *identity atoms*: $=_n$, $=_e$ and $=_i$. Therefore, $(\mathcal{U}^{(D)}, \mathcal{P}^{14})$ is not a partition scheme. Below we define a broader class of partitions that includes $\mathcal{P}^{14}$.

Definition 7 (General partition scheme). *Let $\mathcal{P} = (R_i)_{i \in I}$ be a partition of $\mathcal{U} \times \mathcal{U}$. $(\mathcal{U}, \mathcal{P})$ is called a* general partition scheme *if $\mathcal{P}$ is closed under converse $^{-1}$ and the identity $Id_{\mathcal{U}}$ is a $\mathcal{P}$-relation (possibly disjunctive).*

The following proposition ensures that the algebra $\mathbb{A}_{\mathcal{P}^{14}}$ (or simply $\mathbb{A}14$) generated by $\mathcal{P}^{14}$ is a non-associative algebra.

Proposition 2. *Let $\mathcal{P} = (R_i)_{i \in I}$ be a partition of $\mathcal{U} \times \mathcal{U}$, such that it is closed under converse and the identity $Id_{\mathcal{U}}$ is a $\mathcal{P}$-relation (possibly disjunctive). Then the algebra $\mathbb{A}_{\mathcal{P}}$ generated by $\mathcal{P}$ is a non-associative algebra.*

Proof. $Id_{\mathcal{U}} \diamond R_i = Id_{\mathcal{U}} \circ R_i = R_i = R_i \circ Id_{\mathcal{U}} = R_i \diamond Id_{\mathcal{U}}$. *The Peircean law follows from the fact that $R_i \diamond R_j \cap R_k = \varnothing$ iff $R_i \circ R_j \cap R_k = \varnothing$ [see 15, Lemma2].*

The composition table of $\mathbb{A}14$ is given in Table 2. The presence of empty cells in the composition table means that the algebra $\mathbb{A}14$ is nonintegral.

$\mathbb{A}14$ is not associative. For instance,

$$
=_e \diamond (1 \diamond 1) \ = \ (=_e \diamond 1) \ = \ \{EN, =_e, \not\ni\},
$$

Table 2. Composition table of A14.

$\diamond$	$=_n$	$\wedge$	$\vee$	$\propto$	$=$	EN	NE	$=_e$	$\supset$	$\not\supset$	$\in$	$\notin$	$=_i$	$\neq_i$
$=_n$	$=_n$	$\vee$	$\wedge$	$\propto$	$=$		NE							
$\vee$	$\vee$	$=_n \vee {<}\diamond\|$	$\vee\wedge\propto$	$\vee\propto{<}\diamond\|$	$\propto$	EN	NE							
$\wedge$	$\wedge$	$\wedge$	$=_n \wedge {<}\diamond\|$	$\wedge\propto{<}\diamond\|$	$\propto{<}\diamond\|$	EN	NE							
$\propto$	$\propto$	$\wedge\propto{<}\diamond\|$	$\propto{<}\diamond\|$	$=_n\vee{<}\diamond\|$	$\propto{<}\diamond\|$	EN	NE							
$=$	$=$	$=$	$=$	$\propto{<}\diamond\|$	$=$	EN	NE							
NE	NE	NE	$=_n{><}\diamond\|$	$=_n{><}\diamond\|$	$=_n{><}\diamond\|$		NE	$=_e$	$\not\supset$	$\not\supset$	$\notin$	$\notin$	$\neq_i$	$\neq_i$
EN	EN	EN	EN	EN	EN	EN		$=_e$	$\not\supset$		$\notin$	$\notin$		
$=_e$	$=_e$				$=_e$		$=_e$	$=_e$	$\not\supset$		$\notin$		$=_i\neq_i$	
$\in$	$\in$	$\notin$	$\in$	$\notin$	$\in\notin$	$\notin$	$\notin$		$=_i\neq_i$	$\neq_i$				
$\notin$	$\notin$	$\notin$	$\notin$	$\notin$	$\in\notin$	$\notin$	$\notin$		$\neq_i$	$=_i\neq_i$				
$\supset$	$\supset$						$\supset$		$=_n{><}\diamond$	$\supset$	$\supset\not\supset$				
$\not\supset$	$\not\supset$						$\not\supset$		${<}\diamond\|$ EN	$=_n{><}\diamond\|$ EN NE	$=_e$	$\not\supset$	$\not\supset$		
$=_i$	$=_i$								$\supset$	$\not\supset$	$\in$	$\notin$	$=_i$	$\neq_i$
$\neq_i$	$\neq_i$								$\supset\not\supset$	$\not\supset$	$\in\notin$	$\notin$	$\neq_i$	$=_i\neq_i$

Table 3. Composition tables of $\mathbb{A}16$.

$\diamond$	$=_n$	$>$	$<$	$⌀$	$\|$	$\ni$	$\not\ni_{ni}$	NE
$=_n$	$=_n$	$>$	$<$	$⌀$	$\|$	$\ni$	$\not\ni_{ni}$	NE
$<$	$<$	$=_n{>}{<}⌀\|$	$<$	$<⌀\|$	$\|$	$\ni\not\ni_{ni}$	$\not\ni_{ni}$	NE
$>$	$>$	$>$	$=_n{>}{<}⌀$	$>⌀$	$>⌀\|$	$\ni$	$\ni\not\ni_{ni}$	NE
$⌀$	$⌀$	$>⌀\|$	$<⌀$	$=_n{>}{<}⌀\|$	$>⌀\|$	$\ni\not\ni_{ni}$	$\ni\not\ni_{ni}$	NE
$\|$	$\|$	$\|$	$<⌀\|$	$<⌀\|$	$=_n{>}{<}⌀\|$	$\not\ni_{ni}$	$\ni\not\ni_{ni}$	NE
$\in$	$\in$	$\in\not\in_{in}$	$\in$	$\in\not\in_{in}$	$\not\in_{in}$	$=_i\neq_i$	$\neq_i$	IE
$\not\in_{in}$	$\not\in_{in}$	$\not\in_{in}$	$\in\not\in_{in}$	$\in\not\in_{in}$	$\in\not\in_{in}$	$\neq_i$	$=_i\neq_i$	IE
EN	EN	EN	EN	EN	EN	EI	EI	$=_e$

$\diamond$	$=_i$	$\neq_i$	$\in$	$\not\in_{in}$	IE
$=_i$	$=_i$	$\neq_i$	$\in$	$\not\in_{in}$	IE
$\neq_i$	$\neq_i$	$=_i\neq_i$	$\in\not\in_{in}$	$\in\not\in_{in}$	IE
$\ni$	$\ni$	$\ni\not\ni_{ni}$	$=_n{>}{<}⌀$	$>⌀\|$	NE
$\not\ni_{ni}$	$\not\ni_{ni}$	$\ni\not\ni_{ni}$	$<⌀\|$	$=_n{>}{<}⌀\|$	NE
EI	EI	EI	EN	EN	$=_e$

$\diamond$	$=_e$	EN	EI
$=_e$	$=_e$	EN	EI
NE	NE	$=_n{>}{<}⌀\|$	$\ni\not\ni_{ni}$
IE	IE	$\in\not\in_{in}$	$=_i\neq_i$

whereas

$$(=_e \diamond 1) \diamond 1 = \{EN, =_e, \not\ni\} \diamond 1 = \{=_n, >, <, ⌀, \|, =_e\ EN, NE, \ni, \not\ni\}.$$

How to refine the partition $\mathcal{P}^{14}$ so that it generates an associative algebra, i.e., a relation algebra? The following proposition defines a condition, which a sought-for refined partition scheme must satisfy.

Proposition 3. *Let $(\mathcal{U}, \mathcal{P})$ be a general partition scheme. If the algebra $\mathbb{A}_\mathcal{P}$ is associative, then for any base relation $R \in \mathcal{P}$ there exist identity atoms $Id_i, Id_j \in \mathcal{P}$ such that $R \subseteq Fd(Id_i) \times Fd(Id_j)$.*

Proof. From Theorem 3.5 [17] it follows that if $\mathbb{A} \in RA$, then $x; x^\smile \cdot 1', x^\smile; x \cdot 1' \in At(\mathbb{A})$ for all $x \in At(\mathbb{A})$. Applied to $\mathbb{A}_\mathcal{P}$ we obtain that $(\forall R \in \mathcal{P})$ $(\exists Id_i, Id_j \in \mathcal{P})$ $(R \diamond R^{-1}) \cap Id_\mathcal{U} = Id_i$ and $(R^{-1} \diamond R) \cap Id_\mathcal{U} = Id_j$. $(\forall (x,y) \in R)$ $(x,x) \in (R \diamond R^{-1}) \cap Id_\mathcal{U}$ and $(y,y) \in (R^{-1} \diamond R) \cap Id_\mathcal{U}$, hence $x \in Fd(Id_i)$ and $y \in Fd(Id_j)$. Therefore, $(x,y) \in Fd(Id_i) \times Fd(Id_j)$, from which follows that $R \subseteq Fd(Id_i) \times Fd(Id_j)$.

The fields of the identity atoms $=_n$, $=_e$ and $=_i$ are:

$$Fd(=_n) = 2^D \backslash \{\varnothing\}, \qquad Fd(=_e) = \{\varnothing\}, \qquad Fd(=_i) = D.$$

Proposition 3 contains a necessary condition for a general partition scheme to generate a relation algebra. The fact that the algebra generated by $\mathcal{P}^{14}$ is not associative implies that $\mathcal{P}^{14}$ violates this condition. More concretely, this condition fails on the base relations $\not\in$ and $\not\ni$. Indeed, $\not\in$ is contained in $D \times 2^D$, but it is contained in neither $D \times (2^D \backslash \{\varnothing\})$ nor $D \times \{\varnothing\}$. The necessary refinement of $\mathcal{P}^{14}$ is the following: $\not\in$ splits into $\not\in_{in}$ and IE, likewise $\not\ni$ splits into $\not\ni_{ni}$ and EI. We denote the refined partition as $\mathcal{P}^{16}$. The refined base relations are:

$$\not\in_{in} (\alpha, \beta) \text{ iff } \alpha \text{ is an individual, } \beta \text{ is a nonempty set and } \alpha \not\in \beta$$
$$IE(\alpha, \beta) \text{ iff } \alpha \text{ is an individual, } \beta = \varnothing$$
$$\not\ni_{ni} (\alpha, \beta) \text{ iff } \alpha \text{ is a nonempty set, } \beta \text{ is an individual and } \alpha \not\ni \beta$$
$$EI(\alpha, \beta) \text{ iff } \beta \text{ is an individual, } \alpha = \varnothing$$

Weak composition of the algebra $\mathbb{A}16$, which is generated by $\mathcal{P}^{16}$, is specified in Table 3. It is given by three composition tables. If the composition of two relations is not given by either table, then it is equal to zero.

Proposition 4. $\mathbb{A}16$ *is a relation algebra.*

Proof. Associativity can be checked manually, whereas satisfiability of the remaining axioms of RA follows from Proposition 2.

5   The Calculus of Alignments Revisited

The calculus of alignments defined in [5] assumes that all ontology alignment relations are elements of an algebra of relations, and vice versa. However, this scheme does not work with $\mathbb{A}16$. In $\mathbb{A}16$, not all relations are meaningful enough to be used in alignments. Here we consider the set of base relations independently from the algebra $\mathbb{A}16$.

Let $\mathbf{R}$ be the set of base ontology alignment relations (relation symbols):

$$\mathbf{R} = \{\equiv, \sqsubset, \sqsupset, \lozenge, \perp, \in, \not\in, \ni, \not\ni, =, \neq\}. \tag{5.1}$$

$\mathbf{R}$ is so to speak an interface for the algebra $\mathbb{A}16$. Ontology alignment relations are then refined as disjunctions of symbols in $\mathbf{R}$, denoted as $\mathbf{R}^\vee$. The relations $\equiv \vee \sqsubset$ and $\equiv \vee \sqsupset$ are abbreviated as $\sqsubseteq$ and $\sqsupseteq$ respectively.

We distinguish between two kinds of atoms in $\mathbb{A}16$: coherent and incoherent.

$$At_{coh}(\mathbb{A}16) = \{=_n, <, >, \lozenge, \|, \in, \not\in_{in}, \ni, \not\ni_{ni}, =_i, \neq_i\} \tag{5.2}$$
$$At_{incoh}(\mathbb{A}16) = \{=_e, EN, NE, EI, IE\} \tag{5.3}$$

Coherent atoms correspond to base ontology alignment relations. A relation $r \in \mathbb{A}16$ is said coherent if all its atoms are coherent. $Coherent(r)$ denotes the set of coherent atoms in r, and $Coherent(\mathbb{A})$, the set of coherent relations in $\mathbb{A}$.

We further define a function ϕ from $\mathbf{R}$ to $\mathbb{A}16$ (given in Table 4). This function is naturally extended on $\mathbf{R}^\vee$, so that $\phi(r \vee s) = \phi(r) \cup \phi(s)$. Coherent relations of

Table 4. The function ϕ from ontology alignment relations $\mathbf{R}^\vee$ to the algebra $\mathbb{A}16$.

Base OA relation r	Synonyms	$\phi(r)$
$\equiv$	owl:equivalentClass	$=_n, =_e$
$\sqsubseteq$	less general than	$<, EN$
$\sqsupseteq$	more general than	$>, NE$
$\between$	partially overlaps with	$\between$
$\perp$	owl:disjointWith	$\parallel, =_e, EN, NE$
$\in$	is a, rdf:type	$\in$
$\notin$	is not	$\notin_{in}, IE$
$\ni$		$\ni$
$\not\ni$		$\not\ni_{ni}, EI$
$=$	owl:sameAs	$=_i$
$\neq$	owl:differentFrom	$\neq_i$

$\mathbb{A}16$ are in a one-to-one correspondence with ontology alignment relations. This is given by a function η:

$$\eta : Coherent(\mathbb{A}16) \to \mathbf{R}^\vee. \tag{5.4}$$

The operations on alignments with relations from $\mathbb{A}16$ are defined in the same way as in Section 3.2. The difference is that we add a correspondence interpretation level. Let $\mu = (e,\ e',\ r)$ be a correspondence, in which $r \in \mathbb{A}16$.

- If $r = \varnothing$, then μ is *inconsistent*.
- If r contains only incoherent atoms $(Coherent(r) = \varnothing)$, then μ is *incoherent*.
- In all other cases r is interpreted as $\eta(Coherent(r)) \in \mathbf{R}^\vee$.

For instance, assume that we want to compose the correspondences $\mu = (e,\ e',\ \perp)$ and $\upsilon = (e',\ e'',\ \sqsubseteq)$. In $\mathbb{A}5$ the relations $\perp$ and $\sqsubseteq$ are considered as shortcuts for the elements $\{\perp\}$ and $\{<,=\}$ respectively. Thus,

$$\mu \circ \upsilon = (e,\ e',\ \{\perp\}) \circ (e',\ e'',\ \{<,=\})$$
$$= (e,\ e'',\ \{\perp\} \circ \{<,=\}) = (e,\ e'',\ \{<, \between, \perp\}).$$

To compose the correspondences with $\mathbb{A}16$, we first get the elements which correspond to $\perp$ and $\sqsubseteq$ (using the function ϕ) and then compose them:

$$(e,\ e',\ \{\parallel, =_e, EN, NE\}) \circ (e',\ e'',\ \{=_n, <, =_e, EN\})$$
$$= (e,\ e',\ \{\parallel, =_e, EN, NE\}) \circ \{=_n, <, =_e, EN\})$$
$$= (e,\ e'',\ \{=, >, <, \between, \parallel, =_e, EN, NE\}).$$

Finally, $\mu \circ \upsilon = (e,\ e'',\ \eta(Coherent(\{=_n, >, <, \between, \parallel, =_e, EN, NE\})))$

$$= (e,\ e'',\ \equiv \vee \sqsubseteq \vee \sqsupseteq \vee \between \vee \perp).$$

This means that we have not deduced anything useful between e and e''. Indeed, if e' is interpreted as an empty set, then for any interpretation of e and e'' the correspondences μ and v will hold. But if we add one more correspondence, which guarantees that e' is not empty, e.g., $\left(e''', \ e', \ \in\right)$ or $\left(e''', \ e', \ \sqsubseteq\right)$, then, by computing the algebraic closure of these three correspondences, we would deduce $\left(e, \ e'', \ \sqsubseteq \vee \between \vee \perp\right)$.

6   Discussion and Future Work

The algebra that we introduced in this paper, $\mathbb{A}16$, covers all qualitative relations between ontology entities from the taxonomy perspective. It is better than $\mathbb{A}5$, which we considered in previous work, in two ways:

– $\mathbb{A}16$ combines class-level and instance-level relations within a single algebra,
– the calculus that it induces on alignments allows to tell between unsatisfiability and incoherence of alignments.

Here are some issues that should be worth of consideration.

Non-taxonomical relations. Algebras of relations for ontology alignment are not limited to taxonomical relations. For example, one may build an algebra of relations from biomedical ontologies like SNOMED CT or NDF-RT, using relations like snomed:hasActiveIngredient or ndfrt:mayTreat. Such an algebra can have, for example, a composition rule hasActiveIngredient ∘ mayTreat = mayTreat.

Algebraic formalism. The algebra considered is this paper satisfies the axioms of RA. But weaker structures can be used as algebras of ontology alignment relations, e.g., non-associative algebras [17], or Boolean algebras with operators [11].

Non-simple semantics of alignments. Here we adopted the simple semantics of alignments. However, algebraic calculi can potentially be adopted to other semantics as well, like the integrated semantics, which is more tolerant to heterogeneity.

Acknowledgments. This research has been partially supported by the join NSFC-ANR Lindicle project (12-IS01-0002) in cooperation with Tsinghua university.

References

1. Allen, J.F.: Maintaining Knowledge About Temporal Intervals. Communications of the ACM **26**(11), 832–843 (1983)
2. Bao, J., Caragea, D., Honavar, V.G.: On the Semantics of linking and importing in modular ontologies. In: Cruz, I., Decker, S., Allemang, D., Preist, C., Schwabe, D., Mika, P., Uschold, M., Aroyo, L.M. (eds.) ISWC 2006. LNCS, vol. 4273, pp. 72–86. Springer, Heidelberg (2006)
3. Borgida, A., Serani, L.: Distributed description logics: assimilating information from peer sources. Journal of Data Semantics **1**, 153–184 (2003)
4. Düntsch, I.: Relation algebras and their application in temporal and spatial reasoning. Articial Intelligence Review **23**(4), 315–357 (2005)

5. Euzenat, J.: Algebras of ontology alignment relations. In: Sheth, A.P., Staab, S., Dean, M., Paolucci, M., Maynard, D., Finin, T., Thirunarayan, K. (eds.) ISWC 2008. LNCS, vol. 5318, pp. 387–402. Springer, Heidelberg (2008)
6. Euzenat, J., Shvaiko, P.: Ontology Matching, 2nd edn. Springer, Heidelberg (2013)
7. Grau, B.C., Patel-Schneider, P., Motik, B.: OWL 2 Web Ontology Lan- guage Direct Semantics, 2nd edn. W3C Recommendation. W3C, December 2012. http://www.w3.org/TR/2012/REC-owl2-direct-semantics-20121211/
8. Harris, S., Seaborne, A., Prud'hommeaux, E.: SPARQL 1.1 Query Language (2013). W3C Recommendation (2013)
9. Hirsch, R.: Expressive Power and Complexity in Algebraic Logic. J. Log. Comput. **7**(3), 309–351 (1997)
10. Homola, M.: Semantic Investigations in Distributed Ontologies. PhD thesis. Bratislava, Slovakia: Comenius University (2010)
11. Jónsson, B., Tarski, A.: Boolean algebras with operators. Part II. American Journal of Mathematics **74**, 127–162 (1952)
12. Kutz, O., Lutz, C., Wolter, F., Zakharyaschev, M.: E-connections of abstract description systems. Artif. Intell. **156**(1), 1–73 (2004)
13. Ladkin, P., Maddux, R.D.: On binary constraint problems. Journal of the ACM (JACM) **41**(3), 435–469 (1994)
14. Lange, C., Mossakowski, T., Kutz, O., Galinski, C., Grüninger, M., Vale, D.C.: The distributed ontology language (DOL): use cases, syntax, and extensibility. In: Proc. of TKE 2012 (2012)
15. Ligozat, G., Renz, J.: What is a qualitative calculus? a general framework. In: Zhang, C., W. Guesgen, H., Yeap, W.-K. (eds.) PRICAI 2004. LNCS (LNAI), vol. 3157, pp. 53–64. Springer, Heidelberg (2004)
16. Mackworth, A.K., Freuder, E.C.: The Complexity of Some Polynomial Network Consistency Algorithms for Constraint Satisfaction Problems. Artif. Intell. **25**(1), 65–74 (1985)
17. Maddux, R.D.: Some Varieties Containing Relation Algebras. Trans. Amer. Math. Soc. **272**, 501–526 (1982)
18. Tarski, A.: On the Calculus of Relations. J. Symb. Log. **6**(3), 73–89 (1941)
19. Zimmermann, A.: Integrated distributed description logics. In: Proc. of DL 2007, pp. 507–514 (2007)
20. Zimmermann, A.: Logical formalisms for agreement technologies. In: Ossowski, S. (ed.) Agreement Technologies. Law, Governance and Technology Series, vol. 8, pp. 69–82. Springer, Netherlands (2013)
21. Zimmermann, A., Euzenat, J.: Three semantics for distributed systems and their relations with alignment composition. In: Cruz, I., Decker, S., Allemang, D., Preist, C., Schwabe, D., Mika, P., Uschold, M., Aroyo, L.M. (eds.) ISWC 2006. LNCS, vol. 4273, pp. 16–29. Springer, Heidelberg (2006)

CogMap: A Cognitive Support Approach to Property and Instance Alignment

Jan Nößner, David Martin, Peter Z. Yeh, and Peter F. Patel-Schneider$^{(\boxtimes)}$

AI Research Group, Nuance Communications, Sunnyvale, CA 94085, USA
jan.noessner@gmail.com,
{david.martin,peter.yeh,peter.patel-schneider}@nuance.com

Abstract. The iterative user interaction approach for data integration proposed by Falconer and Noy can be generalized to consider interactions between integration tools (generators) that generate potential schema mappings and users or analysis tools (analyzers) that select the best mapping. Each such selection then provides high-confidence guidance for the next iteration of the integration tool. We have implemented this generalized approach in CogMap, a matching system for both property and instance alignments between heterogeneous data. The generator in CogMap uses the instance alignment from the previous iteration to create high-quality property alignments and presents these alignments and their consequences to the analyzer. Our experiments show that multiple iterations as well as the interplay between instance and property alignment serve to improve the final alignments.

1 Introduction

In recent years, companies have spent more and more effort in building knowledge graphs based on light-weight ontologies, which incorporate data from multiple heterogeneous sources (which we will henceforth call "information stores"). A key challenge of these efforts is determining the best alignment of the schema of a new store to the ontology of the knowledge graph, while minimizing the "manual" analytical effort required of a human knowledge engineer.

Most of the current ontology alignment systems, such as those evaluated recently in the annual ontology alignment evaluation initiative [1], have several limitations. Most of these alignment algorithms solve one integration problem (deriving a mapping between two ontologies) using a fully-automated, "one-shot" approach. Thus, they are often not able to improve by iterating over previous alignments. Partly for this reason, the results of fully automated algorithms are often error prone [32] and cannot be reliably used for high-quality data integration.

Currently much information to be integrated is obtained from non-ontological sources such as relational databases or XML documents. Classical ontology alignment systems are often not able to process this data [1]. To address this need, systems like OntoDB [20] and standards like D2RQ [3] have emerged. However,

© Springer International Publishing Switzerland 2015
M. Arenas et al. (Eds.): ISWC 2015, Part I, LNCS 9366, pp. 269–285, 2015.
DOI: 10.1007/978-3-319-25007-6_16

these solutions do not include semi-automated alignment algorithms which take instance information into account.

Our approach, implemented in the CogMap system, follows a cognitively-inspired, iterative approach. With multiple iterations the system is able to improve over time, since it builds on the results of previous iterations (or, in the case of the first iteration, seed queries given by the user). At each iteration, the results are augmented with new information that has been verified by a user or automated verification capability.

CogMap uses instance information to perform property alignment. While most state-of-the-art schema alignment algorithms do not take instance information into account, focusing exclusively on the alignment of classes and properties and mainly considering their labels or structural information [7,29], using instance matching has attended more and more attention over the last years [16].

CogMap explores instances by not only focusing on data properties but also taking object properties into account. In the case of databases, it follows foreign keys; with RDF information stores it explores sub-tags. To the best of our knowledge, there exists no other approach which explores the space of potential mappings between information stores as we do.

CogMap is not restricted to the alignment of information based on formal ontologies. It also supports relational databases and XML documents, which can serve either as the source or the target of an alignment. In addition, CogMap allows support for other data formats to be added in a modular fashion.

2   Related Work

Many schema alignment systems have been developed in ontology matching. The development of these systems has largely been driven by the available benchmark datasets of the ontology alignment evaluation initiative. An overview of the current systems and their evaluation is given by Grau et al. [14]. The most important datasets, however, cover only a small problem space.

Although most ontology matching systems ignore instances, there exists a strand of literature which combines schema alignment and instance alignment [16]. Bilke and Naumann [2] developed an approach that first aligns instances and uses this information for schema alignment. Their evaluation is based on artificially populated data whereas we employ real-world data information stores like FREEBASE and DBPEDIA. Bilke et al. [1,26], Thor et al. [34], Gal [12], and Leme et al. [24] use instances to align schema and resolve conflicts. Another fully automated system that integrates both schema and instance alignment is PARIS [33]. Its algorithms are, however, resource intensive, in some cases taking days to produce a solution. In contrast, the CogMap algorithms are much less resource intensive and can be run on a typical desktop computer. Wang et al. investigates the problem of having only a few non-overlapping instances by approaching the mapping problem as a classification problem. However, this approach is limited to mapping concepts and ignores properties. Duan et al. [5] use hashing techniques to speed up instance-based matching. Nunes et al. [30]

present an instance-based algorithm for complex data property matching. A prominent example is the system RIMOM, which dynamically combines several alignment strategies including instance alignment [25]. Due to its recent excellent achievements at the ontology alignment evaluation initiative, we chose this system for our evaluation.

To the best to our knowledge, none of these approaches is exploring object properties with an iterative cognitive support approach. QUICKMIG [4] is a migration tool for database systems which follows a semi-automated approach. However, it considers only exact value matches and their results are not used to improve the ongoing iterations.

A smaller number of systems utilize learning. A prominent example is SILK [17–19] which learns expressive linking rules by using genetic programming. However, its target user is a technical expert who can, e.g., analyse complex matching trees while CoGMAP focuses on domain experts by hiding technical complexity. LIMES [27] focuses on runtime improvements by using the triangle inequality. However, it does not allow a user-centric iterative approach. Furthermore, neither system is able to map data properties to object properties, which is required by the real-world datasets we examined. (See the algorithm section for details.)

Recently, the ontology alignment evaluation initiative initiated an interactive track which simulates interactive matching [31], where a human expert is involved to validate mappings found by the matching system. The client was modified to allow interactive matchers to ask an oracle, which emulates a perfect user. The interactive matcher can present a correspondence to the oracle, which then tells the user whether the correspondence is right or wrong. However, the initiative uses a dataset which does not contain any instance data and thus is not suitable for evaluating our approach. The two most successful participating systems 2014 were AML[11] with respect to gained f-measure due to the interactive approach and LOGMAP [22] with respect to efficiency (number of interactions required). We have included both systems in our evaluation.

Tools have been developed to support the alignment of databases to ontologies. One example is ONTOP (ontop.inf.unibz.it), which provides a PROTÉGÉ plug-in to facilitate the creation of integration rules. ONTOP focuses on fast execution of already existing data integration rules, but not on the (semi-)automated construction of them. Furthermore, its target ontology is assumed to be small and to contain only schema information but no instance information. There have also been attempts to build graphical tools for supporting the user in data integration. KARMA [23], for example, loads data from different information stores and uses instance information for schema alignment. However, its approach is different from our algorithm. KARMA learns the general structure of fields based on previous alignments made whereas COGMAP operates on instance information. Two disadvantages of KARMA's approach are that it generally assumes that fields (e.g., ids) have similar structures in different datasets and its algorithms require a large amount of training data.

3   The Cognitive Support Approach

Researchers in ontology and schema matching have recently recognized the need for various types of cognitive support in aligning complex conceptual models [8,10]. Most approaches are based on advanced visualization of the models to be integrated and the mappings created by the user [13]. While the appropriate use of visualizations is known to be a key aspect for successful manual data integration, visualizations quickly reach their limits in the presence of very complex or very large models.

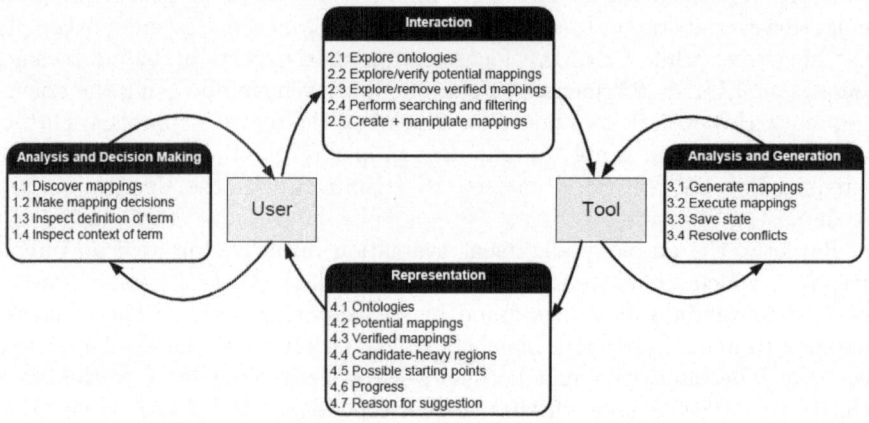

Fig. 1. The cognitive support model for data integration by Falconer [9].

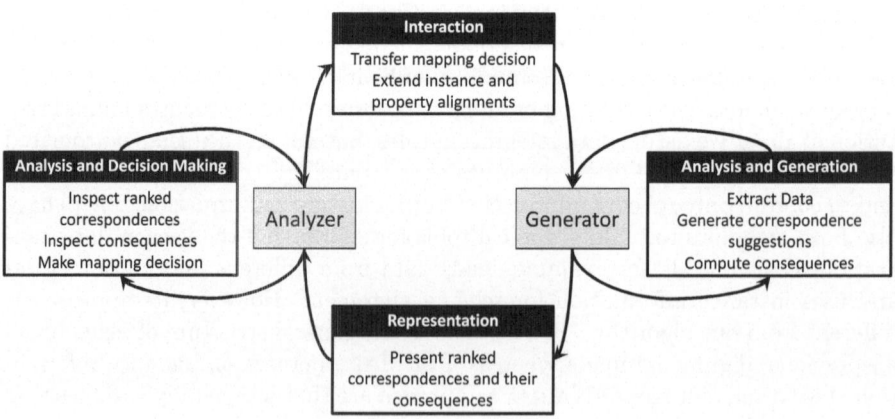

Fig. 2. Modified cognitive support Model as implemented in CogMap.

As a result, recent work has tried to go beyond pure visualization support to include cognitively efficient interaction strategies to support the user [9]. Falconer [8] proposed an interactive strategy for data integration where the integration task is distributed between the user and the tool (Figure 1). The MappingAssistant [32] project used a modified cognitive support model for data integration, focusing on detecting and correcting incorrect data integration rules.

In our implementation of the cognitive support model, which we call CogMap, we go one step further and allow the "user" to be either a human user or an intelligent automated agent. Thus, in our implementation of the cognitive support model (Figure 2), we distinguish between an *analyzer* and a *generator*, instead of a user and a tool.[1]

In each iteration, CogMap extracts data based on the results of previous iterations (or, in the first iteration, based on given seed queries), generates property correspondence suggestions, and computes the consequences for the top suggestions. These consequences are the instances that would be aligned if the analyzer selects (verifies) this property correspondence. Next, CogMap sends the ranked correspondences and their consequences to the analyzer. The analyzer then inspects this information and selects a correspondence. The selected property correspondence, and the resulting instance alignment, are added to the evolving results sets, which allows the system to improve its suggestions in subsequent iterations. The algorithm terminates when no properties remain to generate new correspondences, or no correspondence is selected by the analyzer.

CogMap is designed to cope with many different types of data stores, in many different formats. We currently have implemented support for RDF accessed via SPARQL, relational databases, and general XML based files. This list is easily extended by implementing our `Connector` interface.

4   Algorithm

The primary focus of the CogMap algorithm (Algorithm 1) is to construct property correspondences and instance alignments. An alignment (or mapping) consists of a set of correspondences. According to Euzenat *et al.* [6], a correspondence is a 4-tuple $\langle e_s, e_t, r, c \rangle$, where e_s and e_t are source and target entities, r is a semantic relation, and c is a confidence value (usually, $c \in [0, 1]$). Like most ontology alignment systems [1], we focus on equivalent relations $\langle e_s, e_t, \equiv, c \rangle$.

The algorithm can be split into three phases. The *data extraction* (lines 4-6) and *data exploration* (lines 13-16) phases are only executed in the first iteration ($i = 0$). The *alignment generation and selection* (lines 7-12) phase is repeated until no more correspondences are found. This phase includes the decision making of the analyzer. The following subsections will explain the phases in more depth.

---

[1] As stated, the analyzer can be a human. As this paper is about the effectiveness of the overall approach, we only use simple agents. Sophisticated automated agents or humans can utilize world knowledge or judgements to select bettter alignments instead of just picking the highest-scoring ones.

4.1 Data Extraction and Exploration

We adapt the terms data property, object property, and instances from the semantic web literature, extending them to databases and XML documents in an obvious fashion. For example, instances include database rows and XML nodes.

In the *data extraction* phase, we extract all data property names and their corresponding values for M instances into a source table T_s and a target table T_t (line 5). The left block (2nd column) of Table 1 illustrates the general form of T_s and T_t after extraction.

In the *data exploration* phase, we explore the search space by following object properties. In other words, for each object property op of an instance i, we examine the object which is the value of that property. Then, for each data

---

Algorithm 1 High-level algorithm of CogMap.

Input: S_s, S_t: Seed queries for source and target
Input: M: number of extracted instances of each information store (default: 5000)
Input: k: number of suggestions (default: 5)
Output: $\mathcal{X}, \mathcal{Y}$: Set of user-verified property correspondences and instance correspondences

GETALIGNMENTS
1: $\mathcal{X}, \mathcal{Y} \leftarrow \emptyset$
2: $i \leftarrow 0$
3: **repeat**
        ▷ *Data Extraction*
4:      **if** i=0 **then**
5:          $T_s, T_t \leftarrow$ Extract M instances and their data properties and values based on seeds S_s and S_t.
6:      **end if**
        ▷ *Alignment Generation and Selection*
7:      $X_i \leftarrow$ Compute top-k property correspondence suggestions based on T_s, T_t and $\mathcal{Y}$ (if not empty).
8:      **for every** $x \in X_i$ **do**
9:          $Y_x \leftarrow$ Compute instance alignment consequences for x based on T_s, T_t and $\mathcal{Y}$ (if not empty).
10:     **end for**
11:     Analyzer selects the optimal $x \in X_i$ based on X_i and $\{Y_x | \ x \in X_i\}$.
12:     add x to $\mathcal{X}$, $\mathcal{Y} \leftarrow Y_x$.
        ▷ *Data Exploration*
13:     **if** i=0 **then**
14:         $I_s, I_t \leftarrow$ Extract source and target instance sets from instance alignment $\mathcal{Y}$.
15:         $T_s, T_t \leftarrow$ Extend tables by following the object-property assertions of I_s and I_t.
16:     **end if**
17:     $i \leftarrow i + 1$
18: **until** No more suggestions found

Table 1. General form of source and target table. Initially, the direct data properties and the corresponding data are imported (left block). Second, and subsequent, steps further explore the data by including object properties (right blocks). (dp=data property, op= object property, i = instance, and v = value).

	dp_1	$\cdots$	dp_n	$dp_{1,a}$	$\cdots$	$dp_{n,a}$	op_b
					op_a		
i_1	$v_{1,1}$	$\cdots$	$v_{1,n}$	$v_{1,1,a}$	$\cdots$	$v_{1,n,a}$	$\cdots$
$\cdots$	$\cdots$	$\cdots$	$\cdots$	$\cdots$	$\cdots$	$\cdots$	$\cdots$
i_m	$v_{m,1}$	$\cdots$	$v_{m,n}$	$v_{m,1,a}$	$\cdots$	$v_{m,n,a}$	$\cdots$

property of that object, we add its value to the row for i. Thus, the right blocks of Table 1 ($op_a, op_b, \cdots$) are added during this phase. The reason this exploration happens at the end of the first iteration ($i = 0$, line 13-16) is that there may exist many object properties to follow. This often leads to a large amount of data. Thus, the idea is to restrict the exploration to the smaller instance sets I_s and I_t. These instance sets are extracted from the first instance alignment $\mathcal{Y}$ (line 15) such that $I_s = \{e_s | \langle e_s, e_t, \equiv, c \rangle \in \mathcal{Y}\}$ and $I_t = \{e_t | \langle e_s, e_t, \equiv, c \rangle \in \mathcal{Y}\}$. Then, CogMap only follows the object properties for the instance sets I_s and I_t which are usually much smaller.

For RDF repositories we utilize SPARQL queries to access data. We do not rely on the completeness of domain and range restrictions for extracting properties, since they are often poorly defined (e.g., in DBpedia). Instead we take the distinct set of all properties of the relevant instances (those retrieved by S for extraction or those identified as values of object properties for expansion) as the relevant data properties. For relational data extraction, we just add the limit M to the seed SQL query S, execute the query, and store the result in table T. For exploration, we follow the foreign keys according to the definitions in the database schema. For XML files, we extract every attribute and every direct child node that has a primitive value from the initial XPath expression S. We store both attribute and child node values as data properties in Table 1. For the exploration phase, we inspect the children x of all non-primitive nodes. From these nodes, we again store the values of every attribute and every direct child node that has primitive values.

For some properties, a given instance may have multiple values. For simplicity, we consider only single values in this presentation. In practice, we have found the concatenation of multiple values to be effective. More sophisticated strategies will be developed in future work. On the other hand, there may exist properties and/or instances which have almost no assertions, especially in large RDF knowledge bases and XML documents. To ensure the effectiveness of the approach, those assertions might need to be ignored. To cope with that issue, CogMap has an optional parameter ϕ to filter instances and data properties with sparse value assertions.

4.2   Alignment Generation and Selection

The goal of CogMap is to establish instance correspondences and correspondences between data and object properties. In doing so, the space of ontology elements (in RDF stores) or schema elements (in relational and XML stores) that CogMap considers is constrained by the seed information S. In addition, instance alignments are constrained by the domains and ranges of property alignments. For example, if we align a property e_s =id to a property e_t =movieName, then the resulting instance alignment is bounded by S_s =movie and S_t =film as domains. Thus, there is no need to consider possible correspondences involving other instances in the information stores.

In addition to the standard data-property to data-property, object-property to object-property, and instance to instance correspondences, we also support object- and data-property to data-property correspondences (Example: e_t = film/country/./name/ and e_s = movie/language).

Line 7 of Algorithm 1 first computes the top-k property correspondence suggestions X_i. In the first iteration ($i = 0$), CogMap uses all available instance data since no instance alignment exists yet ($\mathcal{Y} = \emptyset$). For computational reasons,

Table 2. Selected implemented components.

Aggregators		
Unions or joins of sets of correspondences. Average, maximum, or multiples of confidence values if correspondences share the same source entity e_s and target entity e_t.		
Name	**Description**	**Filters**
TopKFilter	Returns the top-k correspondences with the highest confidence value c.	
OneToOneFilter	Returns a functional one-to-one alignment. We implemented a greedy strategy. First, it orders the correspondences in descending order. Then, it traverses through the list and drops all correspondences whose entities e_s or e_t have been already matched.	
Name	**Description**	**Property Matchers**
PropertyNameMatcher	Matches properties according to their name.	
ValueLengthMatcher	Matches properties p_1 and p_2 with close average value	
DistinctValueMatcher	length / close percentages of distinct row entries l_1 and l_2. The similarity is computed with $Min(l_1, l_2)/(Max(l_1, l_2))$.	
InstanceBasedMatcher	If instance alignments $\mathcal{Y} = \emptyset$, we align properties by concatenating all values of all instances for each property and compute the string similarity. If $\mathcal{Y} \neq \emptyset$, we compute the property similarities for every instance pair in $\mathcal{Y}$ separately and average over the results.	
Instance Matchers		
Align instances by concatenating every value for every property and computing their string similarity. If a specific property p is given, consider only values of that property. If an instance alignment $\mathcal{Y}$ is given, traverse through that alignment and update the similarities based on the string values of all the given property value(s).		

we use an implicit cutoff at this initial stage. In the following iterations, we can improve the suggestions by considering the instance correspondences from the previous iteration and comparing the property values only for the instance pairs in $\mathcal{Y}$. In these iterations, we do not apply any threshold but rank the correspondences at the end.

Then, we compute the consequences Y_x for the top-k suggestions X_i (line 8-10). That is, for each of those suggested property correspondences, we compute the instance alignment that will result if this correspondence is selected by the analyzer. Initially ($i = 0$), all source instances are compared against all target instances. In following iterations the instance alignment $\mathcal{Y}$ from the previous iteration is used to compute the new alignment. The threshold applied for the instance alignment equals the confidence value c of $\langle e_1, e_2, \equiv, c \rangle \in X_i$.

The value of k is relatively unimportant here. As long as a correct correspondence is in the top-k suggestions, the results of the approach will not be significantly affected. We have found that $k = 5$ is generally adequate to achieve this condition, and results in a reasonable load on human analysts. In an automated setting it would be easy to use a larger k, which might produce slightly better results at the price of of somewhat longer run times (to score the extra suggestions).

Finally, the analyzer selects the optimal $x \in X_i$ based on the suggestions X_i and the consequences $\{Y_x | \ x \in X_i\}$. As noted above, this selection can either be made by a human user or by an automated selection function that takes the confidence value and the suggestions into account. In this paper, we use only a simple automated agent that selects the best-scoring alignment. Employing humans or more-sophisticated agents would presumably produce better results, but then any advantage of the approach might only come from the intelligence in the human or agent—using a simple agent means that the benefits come from the overall alignment philosophy. (We plan to address elsewhere the user interface issues associated with supporting selections by a human.) After selection of x, we update the seed property alignment $\mathcal{X}$ and the seed instance alignment $\mathcal{Y}$ for the next iteration.

CoGMAP supports many different components to match instances and properties. Every `Filter`, `Aggregator`, and `Matcher` is a component. Each component has an `execute()` method, which returns a set of alignments.

The components are organized as a tree. The `Matchers` form the leaves. They take a source table T_s, a target table T_t, a set of previously verified property alignments $\mathcal{X}$ and a set of instance alignments $\mathcal{Y}$ from the previous iteration as input. An `Aggregator` executes every component in the list `cs` and aggregate the results. It might, for example, just take the maximum confidence value c of all correspondences with equal entities e_s and e_t. A `Filter` reduces the size of the alignment of its component after executing it. A simple filter might, for example, only return the correspondences for which confidence values c are above a certain threshold.

Table 2 lists a selection of implemented components and a short explanation of their functionality. CoGMAP incorporates mechanisms to deal with different

Table 3. Benchmark Statistics.

	Benchmark (1)		Benchmark (2)	
	DBPEDIA	EPG	FREEBASE	FANDANGO
	People	Cast	Film	Movie
Format	RDF	RDB	RDF	XML
Data Properties	6	18	233	26
Object Properties	0	10	234	14
Instances	1,045,474	6,857	247,608	100,959

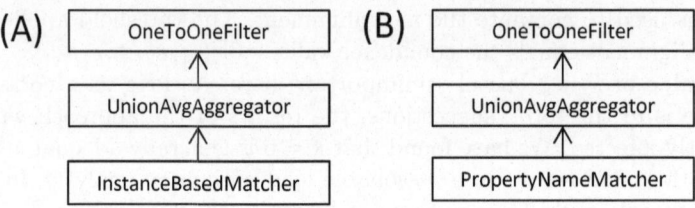

Fig. 3. Experiment Configurations.

date and number formats, which are omitted here for brevity, and easy interfaces to facilitate new component development. Figure 3 provides example trees built from these components.

5   Evaluation

We have selected two natural alignment tasks using real-world data, assessed the performance of COGMAP on them benchmarks, and compared its performance with that of AML, LOGMAP, and RIMOM.

5.1   Benchmarks

The first benchmark aligns all people from DBPEDIA in FOAF format (wiki. dbpedia.org/Downloads39#persondata) with cast information of all programs playing on TV in the U.S. over a two week window from a commercial Electronic Program Guide (EPG) database. The second benchmark aligns FREEBASE films (www.freebase.com/film/film) with movie data from FANDANGO (www. fandango.com). Table 3 provides details on the number of instances and properties of each benchmark.

We designed and selected these benchmarks because existing state-of-the-art ontology alignment benchmarks, e.g., in the Ontology Alignment Evaluation Intiative campaigns[2], lack sufficient instance data, which are required by

---

CogMap. Because of the size of these benchmarks, it was not possible to prepare in advance an official gold-standard. Instead, a human judge was employed to grade the correctness of the alignment results, which we discuss below.

5.2   Experiment Setup

We used the following experiment setup to answer three key questions:

- What is the impact of implementing a cognitive support model for alignment?
- What is the impact of using instance data for alignment?
- How general is our solution?

We first setup our solution, CogMap, using configuration (A) in Figure 3. A description of each component used in configuration (A) can be found in Table 2. CogMap analyzes the property correspondences, and selects the one with the highest confidence value to iterate on (see lines 11 and 12 of Algorithm 1).

We then created two variants of CogMap to answer the first two experimental questions above. We first created a variant—called InstMap—by ablating the cognitive support model used by CogMap. InstMap still uses instance data but does not iterate on the results to further improve alignment.

We also created a second variant—called Baseline—by ablating both the cognitive support model and the use of instance data. Baseline performs alignment using a property name matcher, but the other configuration components are the same (see configuration (B) in Figure 3).

Moreover, we selected three state-of-the-art ontology alignment systems [15] to compare CogMap against, in order to assess its practical impact. The three systems are AML [11], LogMap [22], and RiMOM [25]. AML is focused on computational efficiency and designed to handle very large ontologies. It is the leading system in the conference and anatomy tracks of the 2014 ontology alignment evaluation, in terms of f-measure. LogMap provides a scalable logical ontology alignment framework. RiMOM automatically combines multiple alignment strategies with the goal of finding the optimal alignment results. We selected these systems because they are the most established systems in the 2014 ontology alignment evaluation, and an executable version is available to the public.

Finally, we applied all systems above to both Benchmarks 1 and 2 to assess their generality, and hence answer the third experimental question. Unless otherwise noted, we set the number of instances to use from each benchmark to $M = 5000$, and the fraction of non-null values required for each property to $\phi = 0.1$. We also converted each benchmark into the RDF OWL syntax because many of the ontology matching systems compared cannot directly consume databases or XML files.

All experiments were run on a desktop PC with 4GB of RAM and an Intel i5 duo-core processor. We used Fast-Join [37] as the underlying matching algorithm for instances. Fast-Join combines both token-based similarity (Jaccard,

Table 4. Benchmark 1 results.

	Baseline	AML	LogMap	RiMOM	InstMap	CogMap
$nDCG@3$	0.38	0.76	0.38	0.38	0.76	1.00
$nDCG@6$	0.35	0.51	0.25	0.48	0.74	0.89
$P@3$	0.33	0.67	0.33	0.33	0.67	1.00
$P@6$	0.33	0.33	0.17	0.50	0.67	0.83
Runtime in sec	0.4	2.7	9.1	5.8	1.9	3.0

Cosine, or Dice) and string edit distance. Moreover, it is currently the fastest matching algorithm (see [21]), by implementing efficient pruning and hashing techniques, with soundness and completeness guarantees. This efficiency is required because of our large benchmarks, which make it infeasible to compare every source instance with every target instance.

The output of each system was graded by a human judge familiar with the data sources in each benchmark[3] using the metrics of *Precision at n (P@n)* and the *normalized (logarithmic) Discounted Cumulative Gain at n (nDCG@n)* [38] where n denotes that the top-n results. Precision P is defined as:

$$P = \frac{|\text{correct correspondences}|}{|\text{retrieved correspondences}|}$$

and $nDCG$ is defined as:

$$nDCG = \frac{rel_1 + \sum_{i=2}^{n} \frac{rel_i}{log_2 i}}{(1 + \sum_{i=2}^{n} \frac{1}{log_2 i})}$$

where rel_i is 1 if the correspondence at position i is correct and 0 else. $nDCG@n$ gives more weight to correct correspondences that are ranked higher.

5.3   Results and Discussions

Tables 4 and 5 show the results for benchmarks 1 and 2, respectively. From these results, we observed that CogMap outperformed InstMap in most cases. We attribute this improvement to the only difference between the two systems: CogMap uses a cognitive support model while InstMap does not. Hence, the use of a cognitive support model has a positive impact on alignment results.

We also observed that InstMap outperformed Baseline in all cases. We attribute this improvement to the only difference between the two systems: the use of instance data. For example, Baseline could not correctly align the following data properties in benchmark 1 by matching just the names of these properties.

```
first_name ⇔ givenName
last_name ⇔ surName
full_name ⇔ name
```

---

[3] Determining the correctness of the correspondences produced by each system was simple for the human judge. We thus believe that the use of a human judge in this manner did not introduce any biases and did not affect the comparison.

Table 5. Benchmark 2 results.

	Baseline	AML	LogMap	RiMOM	InstMap	CogMap
$nDCG@3$	0.38	0.76	0.38	0.38	1.00	1.00
$nDCG@6$	0.25	0.60	0.49	0.38	0.90	1.00
$nDCG@9$	0.20	0.68	0.39	0.30	0.79	1.00
$nDCG@12$	0.17	0.68	0.38	0.25	0.69	0.85
$P@3$	0.33	0.67	0.33	0.33	1.00	1.00
$P@6$	0.17	0.50	0.50	0.33	0.83	1.00
$P@9$	0.11	0.67	0.33	0.22	0.67	1.00
$P@12$	0.08	0.67	0.33	0.17	0.50	0.75
Runtime in sec	2.6	7.0	21.7	33.2	20.5	29.1

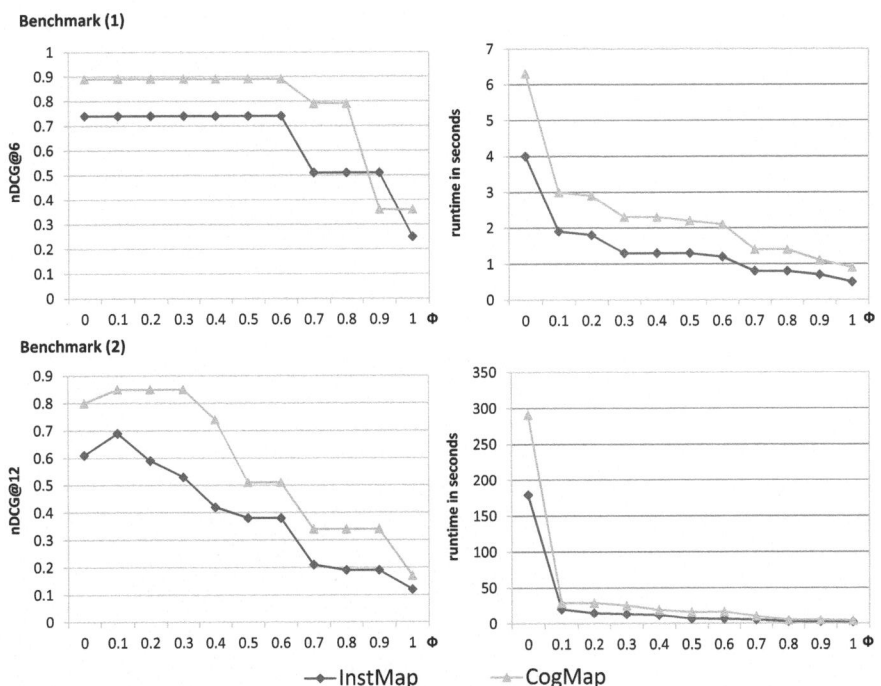

Fig. 4. Results for varying ϕ (number of non-null values) for CogMap and InstMap for both benchmarks. For high ϕ, $nDGC$ and runtime decrease because fewer alignment candidates remain.

However, InstMap correctly found these alignments because of the overlap between the instances of these properties. Hence, these results show that the use of instance data also has a positive impact on performance.

Finally, we observed that CogMap out performed all three state-of-the-art ontology matching systems compared, i.e. AML, LogMap, and RiMOM. We attribute this improvement to the following factors:

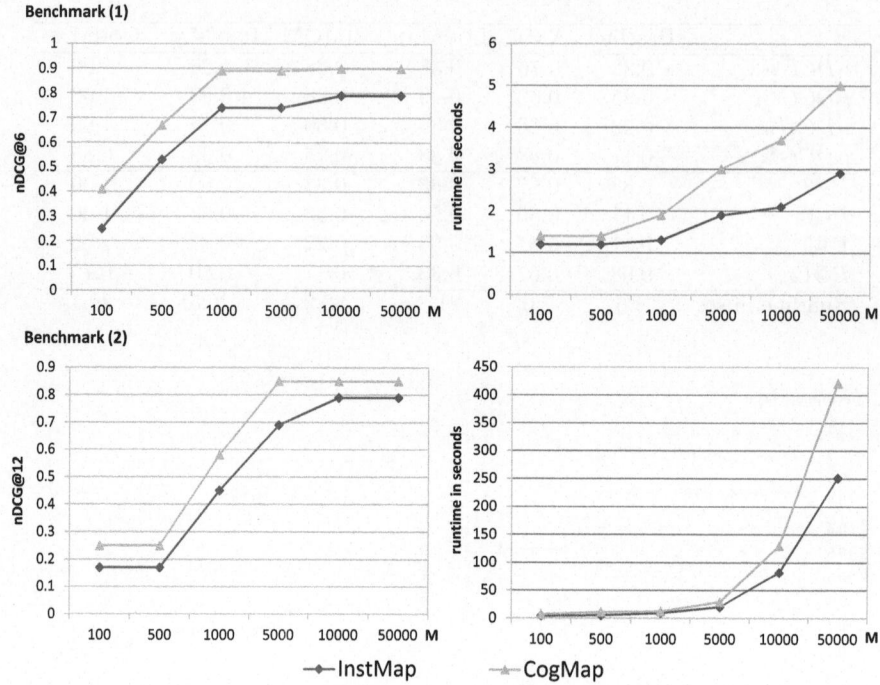

Fig. 5. Results for varying M (number of instances) for COGMAP and INSTMAP for both benchmarks. The more instances included, the higher the overlap and hence better results ($nDCG$).

- COGMAP uses instance data for alignment.
- COGMAP uses an iterative cognitive model for alignment.
- COGMAP can ignore rarely used properties by using the ϕ parameter.

Given the different characteristics of these two benchmark, the results above suggest the general utility of an alignment system like COGMAP that combines a cognitive support model with the use of instance data. Moreover, the additional computation does not contribute to a significant increase in runtime. Across both benchmarks, COGMAP had comparable (or better) runtime than the other state-of-the-art systems compared.

Figures 4 and 5 show the impact of varying ϕ (the fraction of non-null values required for each property) and M (the number of instances used) for COGMAP and INSTMAP on both benchmarks. These results demonstrate the relative robustness of COGMAP to these parameter settings compared to INSTMAP, and further demonstrate the positive impact of using a cognitive support model. For example, we observed on both benchmarks that the performance of COGMAP only became negatively impacted for larger values of ϕ, which was in contrast to INSTMAP. Similarly, the performance of COGMAP increased at a faster rate compared to INSTMAP as M was increased, and plateaued sooner than INSTMAP.

6   Conclusion and Future Work

This paper presents a cognitive based approach for aligning properties by taking instance information into account. The approach is implemented in the system CoGMAP which iteratively suggests property correspondences and their consequences in terms of instance alignments. In each round, the system is able to improve these alignments based on the user verifications of the previous round. Experiments show that the cognitive based approach outperforms both a baseline approach and the purely instance-based approach.

Currently, the system is restricted to aligning instances and properties. In future work, we will enable class alignments and complex matchings [36]. These complex matchings will be described using the R2RML standard (www.w3.org/ TR/r2rml).

We will extend exploration of the knowledge sources. First, we will integrate object properties that are more than one hop away. This will require efficient pruning techniques to avoid an intolerable blowup of both data size and processing requirements. Second, we will use the organization of the knowledge structure (ontologies and schemas, when they are specified) to widen the search space by, e.g., exploring the data of the superclasses.

The knowledge structures will also help to improve the alignment itself by including ideas from [28,29]). Additionally, tree structure learning algorithms, inspired by [35], will be used to learn the optimal composition of matching trees.

Finally, we plan to explore the possibility of integration into KARMA [23], which we believe would provide a suitable graphical user interface.

References

1. Bilke, A., Bleiholder, J., Naumann, F., Böhm, C., Draba, K., Weis, M.: Automatic data fusion with hummer. In: Proceedings of the 31st International Conference on Very Large Data Bases, pp. 1251–1254. VLDB Endowment (2005)
2. Bilke, A., Naumann, F.: Schema matching using duplicates. In: Proceedings of the 21st International Conference on Data Engineering, ICDE 2005, pp. 69–80. IEEE (2005)
3. Bizer, C., Seaborne, A.: D2RQ-treating non-RDF databases as virtual RDF graphs. In: Proceedings of the 3rd International Semantic Web Conference (ISWC 2004), vol. 2004 (2004)
4. Drumm, C., Schmitt, M., Do, H.-H., Rahm, E.: Quickmig: automatic schema matching for data migration projects. In: Proceedings of the Sixteenth ACM Conference on Information and Knowledge Management, pp. 107–116. ACM (2007)
5. Duan, S., Fokoue, A., Hassanzadeh, O., Kementsietsidis, A., Srinivas, K., Ward, M.J.: Instance-based matching of large ontologies using locality-sensitive hashing. In: Cudré-Mauroux, P., Heflin, J., Sirin, E., Tudorache, T., Euzenat, J., Hauswirth, M., Parreira, J.X., Hendler, J., Schreiber, G., Bernstein, A., Blomqvist, E. (eds.) ISWC 2012, Part I. LNCS, vol. 7649, pp. 49–64. Springer, Heidelberg (2012)
6. Euzenat, J., Shvaiko, P., et al.: Ontology matching, vol. 18. Springer (2007)
7. Euzenat, J., Valtchev, P., et al.: Similarity-based ontology alignment in owl-lite. In: ECAI, vol. 16, p. 333 (2004)

8. Falconer, S.: Cognitive support for semi-automatic ontology mapping. Ph.D. Thesis, University of Victoria (2009)
9. Falconer, S., Noy, N.: Interactive techniques to support ontology matching. Schema Matching and Mapping, pp. 29–51 (2011)
10. Falconer, S.M., Storey, M.-A.D.: A cognitive support framework for ontology mapping. In: Aberer, K., Choi, K.-S., Noy, N., Allemang, D., Lee, K.-I., Nixon, L.J.B., Golbeck, J., Mika, P., Maynard, D., Mizoguchi, R., Schreiber, G., Cudré-Mauroux, P. (eds.) ASWC 2007 and ISWC 2007. LNCS, vol. 4825, pp. 114–127. Springer, Heidelberg (2007)
11. Faria, D., Pesquita, C., Santos, E., Palmonari, M., Cruz, I.F., Couto, F.M.: The agreementmakerlight ontology matching system. In: Meersman, R., Panetto, H., Dillon, T., Eder, J., Bellahsene, Z., Ritter, N., De Leenheer, P., Dou, D. (eds.) ODBASE 2013. LNCS, vol. 8185, pp. 527–541. Springer, Heidelberg (2013)
12. Gal, A.: Interpreting similarity measures: bridging the gap between schema matching and data integration. In: IEEE 24th International Conference on Data Engineering Workshop, ICDEW 2008, pp. 278–285. IEEE (2008)
13. Granitzer, M., Sabol, V., Onn, K.W., Lukose, D., Tochtermann, K.: Ontology alignment - a survey with focus on visually supported semi-automatic techniques. Future Internet 2(3), 238–258 (2010)
14. Grau, B.C., Dragisic, Z., Eckert, K., Euzenat, J., Ferrara, A., Granada, R. Ivanova, V., Jiménez-Ruiz, E., Kempf, A.O., Lambrix, P., et al.: Results of the ontology alignment evaluation initiative 2013. In: Proc. 8th ISWC Workshop on Ontology Matching (OM), pp. 61–100 (2013)
15. Grau, B.C., Dragisic, Z., Eckert, K., Euzenat, J., Ferrara, A., Granada, R., Ivanova, V., Jiménez-Ruiz, E., Kempf, A.O., Lambrix, P., et al.: Results of the ontology alignment evaluation initiative 2014. In: Proc. 8th ISWC Workshop on Ontology Matching (OM), pp. 61–100 (2013)
16. Isaac, A., Van Der Meij, L., Schlobach, S.: An empirical study of instance-based ontology matching. The Semantic Web. LNCS, vol. 4825, pp. 253–266. Springer, Heidelberg (2007)
17. Isele, R., Bizer, C.: Learning linkage rules using genetic programming. In: Proceedings of the Sixth International Workshop on Ontology Matching, pp. 13–24 (2011)
18. Isele, R., Bizer, C.: Learning expressive linkage rules using genetic programming. Proceedings of the VLDB Endowment 5(11), 1638–1649 (2012)
19. Isele, R., Bizer, C.: Active learning of expressive linkage rules using genetic programming. Web Semantics: Science, Services and Agents on the World Wide Web 23, 2–15 (2013)
20. Jean, S., Dehainsala, H., Xuan, D.N., Pierra, G., Bellatreche, L., Aït-ameur, Y.: OntoDB: it is time to embed your domain ontology in your database. In: Kotagiri, R., Radha Krishna, P., Mohania, M., Nantajeewarawat, E. (eds.) DASFAA 2007. LNCS, vol. 4443, pp. 1119–1122. Springer, Heidelberg (2007)
21. Jiang, Y., Li, G., Feng, J., Li, W.-S.: String similarity joins: An experimental evaluation. Proceedings of the VLDB Endowment 7(8) (2014)
22. Jiménez-Ruiz, E., Cuenca Grau, B.: LogMap: logic-based and scalable ontology matching. In: Aroyo, L., Welty, C., Alani, H., Taylor, J., Bernstein, A., Kagal, L., Noy, N., Blomqvist, E. (eds.) ISWC 2011, Part I. LNCS, vol. 7031, pp. 273–288. Springer, Heidelberg (2011)

23. Knoblock, C.A., Szekely, P., Ambite, J.L., Goel, A., Gupta, S., Lerman, K., Muslea, M., Taheriyan, M., Mallick, P.: Semi-automatically mapping structured sources into the semantic web. In: Simperl, E., Cimiano, P., Polleres, A., Corcho, O., Presutti, V. (eds.) ESWC 2012. LNCS, vol. 7295, pp. 375–390. Springer, Heidelberg (2012)

24. Leme, L.A.P.P., Casanova, M.A., Breitman, K.K., Furtado, A.L.: Instance-based OWL schema matching. In: Filipe, J., Cordeiro, J. (eds.) Enterprise Information Systems. LNBIP, vol. 24, pp. 14–26. Springer, Heidelberg (2009)

25. Li, J., Tang, J., Li, Y., Luo, Q.: Rimom: A dynamic multistrategy ontology alignment framework. IEEE Transactions on Knowledge and Data Engineering **21**(8), 1218–1232 (2009)

26. Naumann, F., Bilke, A., Bleiholder, J., Weis, M.: Data fusion in three steps: Resolving schema, tuple, and value inconsistencies. IEEE Data Eng. Bull. **29**(2), 21–31 (2006)

27. Ngomo, A.-C.N., Auer, S.: Limes-a time-efficient approach for large-scale link discovery on the web of data. Integration **15**, 3 (2011)

28. Niepert, M., Noessner, J., Meilicke, C., Stuckenschmidt, H.: Probabilistic-logical web data integration. In: Polleres, A., d'Amato, C., Arenas, M., Handschuh, S., Kroner, P., Ossowski, S., Patel-Schneider, P. (eds.) Reasoning Web 2011. LNCS, vol. 6848, pp. 504–533. Springer, Heidelberg (2011)

29. Noessner, J., Niepert, M., Meilicke, C., Stuckenschmidt, H.: Leveraging terminological structure for object reconciliation. In: Aroyo, L., Antoniou, G., Hyvönen, E., ten Teije, A., Stuckenschmidt, H., Cabral, L., Tudorache, T. (eds.) ESWC 2010, Part II. LNCS, vol. 6089, pp. 334–348. Springer, Heidelberg (2010)

30. Pereira Nunes, B., Mera, A., Casanova, M.A., Fetahu, B., P. Paes Leme, L.A., Dietze, S.: Complex matching of RDF datatype properties. In: Decker, H., Lhotská, L., Link, S., Basl, J., Tjoa, A.M. (eds.) DEXA 2013, Part I. LNCS, vol. 8055, pp. 195–208. Springer, Heidelberg (2013)

31. Paulheim, H., Hertling, S., Ritze, D.: Towards evaluating interactive ontology matching tools. In: Cimiano, P., Corcho, O., Presutti, V., Hollink, L., Rudolph, S. (eds.) ESWC 2013. LNCS, vol. 7882, pp. 31–45. Springer, Heidelberg (2013)

32. Stuckenschmidt, H., Noessner, J., Fallahi, F.: User-centric data integration with the mappingassistant. In: Cordeiro, J., Maciaszek, L.A., Filipe, J. (eds.) ICEIS 2012. LNBIP, vol. 141, pp. 323–339. Springer, Heidelberg (2013)

33. Suchanek, F.M., Abiteboul, S., Senellart, P.: Paris: Probabilistic alignment of relations, instances, and schema. Proceedings of the VLDB Endowment **5**(3), 157–168 (2011)

34. Thor, A., Kirsten, T., Rahm, E.: Instance-based matching of hierarchical ontologies. In: BTW, vol. 103, pp. 436–448 (2007)

35. Volz, J., Bizer, C., Gaedke, M., Kobilarov, G.: Silk-a link discovery framework for the web of data. LDOW **538** (2009)

36. Walshe, B., Brennan, R., O'Sullivan, D.: A comparison of complex correspondence detection techniques. In: OM (2012)

37. Wang, J., Li, G., Fe, J.: Fast-join: an efficient method for fuzzy token matching based string similarity join. In: 2011 IEEE 27th International Conference on Data Engineering (ICDE), pp. 458–469. IEEE (2011)

38. Wang, Y., Liwei, W., Li, Y., He, D., Chen, W., Liu, T.-Y.: A theoretical analysis of NDCG ranking measures. In: 26th Annual Conference on Learning Theory (2013)

Effective Online Knowledge Graph Fusion

Haofen Wang[1]([✉]), Zhijia Fang[1], Le Zhang[1], Jeff Z. Pan[2], and Tong Ruan[1]

[1] East China University of Science and Technology, Shanghai 200237, China
whfcarter@ecust.edu.cn
[2] University of Aberdeen, Aberdeen, UK

Abstract. Recently, Web search engines have empowered their search with knowledge graphs to satisfy increasing demands of complex information needs about entities. Each engine offers an online knowledge graph service to display highly relevant information about the query entity in form of a structured summary called *knowledge card*. The cards from different engines might be complementary. Therefore, it is necessary to fuse knowledge cards from these engines to get a comprehensive view. Such a problem can be considered as a new branch of ontology alignment, which is actually an on-the-fly online data fusion based on the users' needs. In this paper, we present the first effort to work on knowledge cards fusion. We propose a novel probabilistic scoring algorithm for card disambiguation to select the most likely entity a card should refer to. We then design a learning-based method to align properties from cards representing the same entity. Finally, we perform value deduplication to group equivalent values of the aligned properties as value clusters. The experimental results show that our approach outperforms the state of the art ontology alignment algorithms in terms of precision and recall.

1 Introduction

With the prevalence of entity search [1], a large portion of Web queries are to search entity related information. To support the ever growing information needs, search engines leverage public available knowledge bases such as Wikipedia and Freebase to build their own knowledge graphs. When submitting a query to Google (Bing or Yahoo!), the engine will provide a structured summary called *knowledge card* describing attributes of the given entity and relations with other entities. Such a card can be regarded as a query-based online form of the knowledge graph. Since a query might be ambiguous, it could return several cards corresponding to different real-world entities. Google returns three cards for the query "Fox" while Bing returns two more different cards. Even though the two cards represent the same entity, some property may just appear in one card. For example, only Google gives an attribute named "Daily sleep" in the card describing "Fox (animal)". So it is necessary to fuse knowledge cards from various search engines automatically to provide a more comprehensive summary with

---

This work was partially supported by the National Science Foundation of China (project No: 61402173), the Fundamental Research Funds for the Central Universities (Grant No: 22A201514045) and the EC MSC K-Drive project (286348).

© Springer International Publishing Switzerland 2015
M. Arenas et al. (Eds.): ISWC 2015, Part I, LNCS 9366, pp. 286–302, 2015.
DOI: 10.1007/978-3-319-25007-6_17

all important facts for a given entity. Also, search engines usually update their contents quickly so that the fused cards always contain up-to-date information.

Knowledge cards fusion can be regarded as an ontology alignment task. Different from traditional ontology alignment, cards are fused online when a query is submitted. Actually, it is a new branch of ontology alignment considering that input ontologies (i.e., cards) might be lack of schema-level information like concepts and domains or ranges of properties. Further, each input ontology (or a card) only contains a limited number of attribute value pairs. Instances might be expressed as string values in a card. Equivalent numeric values might use different units. Therefore, sophisticated ontology alignment algorithms working for large ontologies with rich information cannot be directly applied.

In this paper, we present the first effort to work on fusing knowledge cards from various search engines automatically. More specifically, we introduce an integrated approach with the following contributions. (1) We propose a novel *probabilistic scoring* method for knowledge card disambiguation. Two widely used measures namely the *commonness* score and the *relatedness* score in entity linking are combined to find the most likely Wikipedia entity a card should refer to. Therefore, different cards representing the same entity can be merged as aligned instances. (2) We design a *learning-based* method with four novel features to predict property alignments. The features include the property similarity and different aspects of similarities between values of two properties. In this way, we not only consider the similarity between two properties but also leverage their *context-based similarities*. (3) We normalize values of a same unit type and complete links for values representing same entities in a pre-processing step. As a result, equivalent values using different expressions are normalized into a same value or linked to a same entity. Both *data and unit normalization* and *missing link completion* can further increase the coverage of property alignment. Moreover, it helps group equivalent values of aligned properties into value clusters during value deduplication. (4) We carried out comprehensive experiments to test the effectiveness of card disambiguation, property alignment, and value deduplication on knowledge cards collected from a number of real entity queries. Furthermore, we convert the cards into ontologies and feed them into several state of the art ontology alignment tools. Our approach outperforms these tools in terms of precision and recall for both instance alignment and property alignment. The rest is organized as follows. Section 2 gives a brief overview. Section 3 introduces the approach details. Section 4 shows the experiment results. Section 5 lists the related work and Section 6 concludes the paper.

2   Approach Overview

2.1   Problem Definition

Input: Given an entity query, a search engine (e.g., Google) may return zero to several knowledge cards. Search on a specific KB like Freebase or Wikidata can also be regarded as a special case of search engine. Each card c describes one real-world entity e with a label on top. The card can also contain several attribute

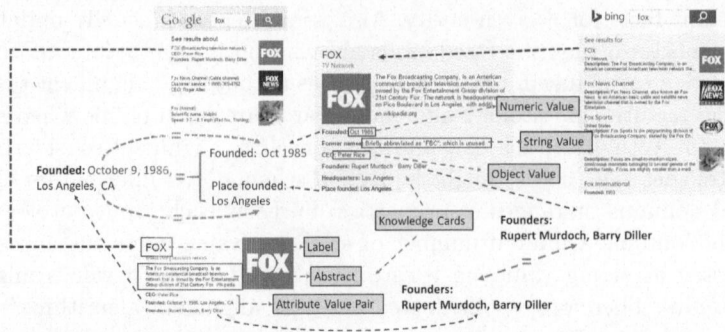

Fig. 1. Knowledge cards from Google and Bing when searching "fox"

value pairs $AVP_c=\{avp_1,avp_2,\ldots,avp_m\}$ in which each pair is composed of a property p and a set of corresponding values $V_{p,c}=\{v_1,v_2,\ldots,v_k\}$. Among them, if v links to a knowledge card representing another entity, we call v an *object* value. Otherwise, if a value v represents some numeric value of a data type like length, currency, or date, it is called a *numeric* value. The remaining values are *string* values. Besides, a short abstract might be provided to describe the card.

Output: One or more merged knowledge cards $\{c_{m1},c_{m2},\ldots,c_{mi}\}$ are returned. Each c_{mi} corresponds to a set of cards representing the same entity from different engines (e.g., c_{gi}). Here, c_{gi} can be a card returned by Google. In c_{mi}, each avp_{mi} becomes a cluster of the original avps. More precisely, equivalent properties $\{p_1,p_2,\ldots,p_j\}$ are aligned together to constitute a merged property p_{mi} of avp_{mi}. Furthermore, the value sets of these properties are grouped into a merged value set V_m. Each member of V_m is a value cluster containing equivalent values of aligned properties from different cards.

Taking "fox" as an example query, Figure 1 shows a list of possible knowledge cards returned by each engine. It also shows the details of two cards from Google and Bing respectively. The figure illustrates the label, the abstract, attribute value pairs as well as properties and different types of values in these pairs of an individual card. Since these two cards represent the same entity, they can be merged together. Here, we show two aligned pair examples: one is a one-to-one mapping between two "Founders" properties and their values, while the other is a one-to-many mapping which will be explained later.

2.2 Challenges

In order to fuse knowledge cards from various search engines for an entity query effectively, we face several challenges which are listed as follows.

Ambiguous cards from a same Query: Since an input query can be ambiguous, it may returned several knowledge cards. As shown in Figure 1, Google returns three different cards and Bing returns five cards. In addition, a card representing the same entity "Fox Broadcasting Company" may have a different label "FOX

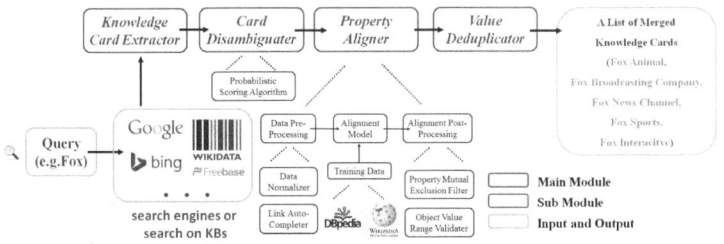

Fig. 2. Overall workflow of our approach to fuse knowledge cards

(Broadcasting television network)". How to merge cards into different entities correctly is challenging. It can also be treated as an instance alignment task.

Same value but Different Expressions: Even two cards are merged correctly, they might have equivalent properties or values with different expressions. For example, a card "Inception (2010)" returned by Bing has a property named "Estimated budget" while the corresponding card from Yahoo! describes the same meaning by using "Budget". Furthermore, one value is expressed as "$160 million USD" while the value of the "Budget" property is "$160,000,000". The similar situation also occurs when expressing other kinds of values.

One to Many Mappings: A property of one card can be aligned with one or several properties of another card. As shown in Figure 1, the property "Founded" of the card "FOX (Broadcasting television network)" introduces the founded date and the founded place of the company. It should be aligned with two properties "Founded" and "Place founded" of the card "Fox Broadcasting Company" from Bing. In most cases, the labels of properties to be aligned are not the same, sometimes even totally different. Moreover, these properties may share very few values in common. The above two factors make property alignment difficult.

2.3   Workflow

As shown in Figure 2, there are three main components, namely *Card Disambiguater*, *Property Aligner*, and *Value Deduplicator*, to fuse knowledge cards. When submitting a query, knowledge cards along with other related data are first fetched from the search engines through the *Knowledge Card Extractor*. Then the *Card Disambiguater* identifies corresponding entities in Wikipedia for these cards based on a probabilistic scoring algorithm. In this way, we can merge cards if they represent the same entity. Before aligning properties of these merged cards, the *Property Aligner* performs a pre-processing step for data normalization and link completion. In the following step, we design a learning-based method to predict whether two properties can be aligned. In particular, mappings from Wikipedia infobox properties to ontology properties in DBpedia are used as training data to learn the prediction model. In order to further increase the accuracy, post-processings including *Property Mutual Exclusion Filter* and

Object Value Range Validator are carried out. Finally, the *Value Deduplicator* groups equivalent values of aligned properties into value clusters.

3   Approach Details

3.1   Card Disambiguation

Card disambiguation can be treated as an *entity linking* problem, i.e. linking a mention found in text to entities defined in a target KB. Due to the wide coverage of Wikipedia, it is selected as our KB. There are about 4.8M entities in Wikipedia and it's continuously growing. A sizable entities can be dealt with in this step. We use the card label as a mention m for disambiguation. Then we adopt $commonness(m, e) = \frac{|L_{m,e}|}{\sum_{e'} |L_{m,e'}|}$ as commonness score [14] to measure the strength m links to a Wikipedia entity e. Here $|L_{m,e}|$ is the number of links in Wikipedia with the target e and the anchor text m.

Since the card label might be ambiguous, m can refer to several entities E_m. In order to determine the most likely entity the card should correspond to, we additionally consider the object values of the card as its context. If an entity is tightly connected with the corresponding entities of these object values, it has a high possibility to be the target of the card. For this purpose, we adopt $relatedness(e, v) = 1 - \frac{\log(1+\max(|L_e|,|L_{e_v}|))-\log(1+|L_e \cap L_{e_v}|)}{\log(|WP|)-\log(1+\min(|L_e|,|L_{e_v}|))}$ as the relatedness score [15] to measure how close an entity $e \in E_m$ is to an object value v. Here $|L_e|$ ($|L_{e_v}|$) is the number of links with the target e (or the corresponding entity e_v of v) respectively, $L_e \cap L_{e_v}$ is the intersection of links with the target e and e_v, and $|WP|$ is the total number of Wikipedia entities.

We further adopt $relatedness(e, V_o) = 1 - \prod_{v \in V_o}(1 - relatedness(e, v))$ to measure the relatedness between e and a set of object values V_o in the card. $relatedness(e, V_o)$ is indeed the probabilistic sum of all relatedness scores between e and each object value in V_o. We use $\hat{e} = \arg\max_e(commonness(m, e) \times relatedness(e, V_o))$ as the final score of a possible entity. Finally, the entity with the highest score greater than a threshold is selected as the disambiguation result of the card. Note that if a possible entity of the card does not co-occur with any corresponding entities, the final score is degraded to its commonness score.

For any $v \in V_o$, in order to get the corresponding Wikipedia entity, we can leverage object values in the card v links to and use the same formula to disambiguate v first. After we get the most likely entity e_v it refers to, we can get the relatedness score for $relatedness(e, v)$. So it is a recursive process. In our implementation, we simply choose the maximal relatedness score between a possible entity of v and e for $relatedness(e, v)$ as an approximation.

3.2   Aligning Properties Between Cards

Pre-processing. The focus of this step is to normalize values of different types. More specifically, for a string value, it is lowercased. If it contains any delimiter, the value is segmented into different parts by the delimiter and it will be normalized by lowercasing all its characters. A numeric value belongs to a particular type and is often associated with some unit. For instance, a currency "$160 million USD" from Bing is expressed as "$160,000,000" in Yahoo!. Since value expressions vary a lot from one unit to another, we need prepare specific normalization rules for each unit. According to the unit distribution statistics reported in Section 4.3, by considering only several units such as date time, currency, length and weight, we can deal with a large proportion of numeric values in knowledge cards. For an object value, we try to add a missing link to the correspding Wikipedia entity. The link completion process is same as that of card disambiguation introduced in Section 3.1.

Learning-Based Property Alignment. In this sub-section, we introduce the details of our learning-based method to check whether a property pair can be aligned. If one property is aligned with two or more properties from a second card, we will consider it as a one-to-many mapping. In particular, we design four novel features to constitute the learning model. Besides one property-related feature, we also consider several value-related features because values of a property can be regarded as its context to help predict property alignments.

- *Property Similarity* (PS). It measures the similarity between two properties p_1 and p_2. We consider two kinds of similarities: the lexical similarity (sim_{ls}) and the semantic similarity (sim_{ss}). The former works well if the property labels (l_{p_1} and l_{p_2} for p_1 and p_2 respectively) are close in their lexical forms. The latter can be a complementary to discover semantically similar properties in different expressions. So we first use $sim_{ls}(p_1, p_2) = w \times \frac{|substr(l_{p_1}, l_{p_2})|}{\min(|l_{p_1}|, |l_{p_2}|)}$ to calculate the PS value for p_1 and p_2. If the value is below a threshold, $sim_{ss}(p_1, p_2)$ is further used as the value. $|s|$ is the length of a string s, $substr(s_1, s_2)$ returns the longest substring of s_1 and s_2, and w is a weight. We set $w = 1$ if two strings are equal. If s_1 is a prefix or a suffix of s_2, w is set to 0.8. While s_1 is a substring (except prefix or suffix) of s_2, w is 0.6. Otherwise, $w = 0.4$. The reason to set different weights is because we assign different priorities to exact match, prefix or suffix, substring, and overlap. For sim_{ss}, we adopt the WUP measure [20] $sim_{ss}(p_1, p_2) = \frac{2 \times depth(LCA(s_{p_1}, s_{p_2}))}{depth(s_{p_1}) + depth(s_{p_2})}$ to calculate the relatedness by considering the depths of the two synsets and the depth of their lowest common ancestor (LCA) in WordNet. s_{p_i} is the most likely synset of p_i in the WordNet taxonomy.
- *Value Overlap Ratio* (VOR). If two properties do not have any value of the same type (i.e., string, numeric, and object), they are unlikely to be aligned. Let T_p be the value type set of a property p. For instance, if p has one numeric value and two object values in a card, $T_p = \{n, o\}$. The larger overlap T_{p_1} and T_{p_2} have, the higher coherence two properties achieve. We use the Jaccard similarity $VOR(p_1, p_2) = \frac{|T_{p_1} \cap T_{p_2}|}{|T_{p_1} \cup T_{p_2}|}$ to calculate the overlap.
- *Value Match Ratio* (VMR). It further considers the match ratio of value pairs of a property pair. The higher the match ratio, the more chance the pair can be aligned. We use the equation $VMR(p_1, p_2) = \frac{|MP_{(p_1, p_2)}|}{|CP_{(p_1, p_2)}|}$ to measure this

similarity. A value pair is a *match pair* if the two values are of the same type and their similarity is above a matching threshold. $MP_{(p_1,p_2)}$ is the set of match pairs of the pair (p_1,p_2) and $CP_{(p_1,p_2)}$ is the set of candidate value pairs. For example, if p_1 has one numeric value and one object value while p_2 has only one numeric value, then $CP_{(p_1,p_2)} = 1$. If the two values are dissimilar, then no match pair is found and $VMR(p_1,p_2) = 0$.

In order to get match pairs, we define a similarity measure for each specific value type. For string values, we use the same similarity measure used for property similarity. For the numeric ones, we used $sim_n(n_1,n_2) = 1 - \frac{dist(abs(n_1),abs(n_2))}{NormFactor}$ to calculate the similarity between n_1 and n_2.

Here $abs(n)$ returns the absolute value of n, $dist$ is the absolute difference between n_1 and n_2, and a $NormFactor$ is an normalization factor which picks the larger absolute value in general. Numeric values of the *date* type are special as each value contains three parts namely *year*, *month*, and *day*. Sometimes some date value (e.g., 2010-7) is even incomplete. Given a *date* type value pair with incomplete parts, we only focus on the common parts both values have during comparison. For a pair 2010-7-1 and 2011-6, the *day* part is ignored. Going back to Equation of $sim_n(n_1,n_2)$, we use 360 (counting 30 days per month) for $NormFactor$ instead. Taking the above value pair as the example, their distance is 330 and the similarity is 1/12 accordingly.

For object values, we choose the ESA (Explicit Semantic Analysis) [6] measure to compute their similarities. ESA computes semantic relatedness of natural language texts of arbitrary lengths. It represents the meaning of texts using relevant Wikipedia entity pages in form of concept vectors. It has been proved effectively for textual entailment and query expansion. Here, the similarity $sim_o(o_1,o_2)$ between two objects o_1 and o_2 of a pair is calculated by using the equation $sim_o(o_1,o_2) = \frac{\sum_{wc} wc(o_1) \cdot wc(o_2)}{\sqrt{\sum_{wc} wc(o_1)^2 \cdot \sum_{wc} wc(o_2)^2}}$.

It is actually the cosine similarity between concept vectors $wc(o_1)$ and $wc(o_2)$.

– *Value Similarity Variance* (VSV). It measures the similarity distribution of match pairs. The smaller the VSV, the more match pairs have high similarities, which indicates that the property pair is more likely to be aligned. We adopt the equation $VSV(p_1,p_2) = \frac{\sum(1-sim)^2}{|MP_{(p_1,p_2)}|}$ where sim is the similarity score (ranging from 0 to 1) of a match pair.

Post-processing. To increase the precision of property alignment, we design two heuristic rules to filter out as many false positives as possible.

– *Property mutual exclusion filtering.* Since a knowledge card only contains a limited number of highly selected properties, it is unlikely to display redundant properties. Thus properties in a card can be assumed to be distinct safely. That is, a property is disjoint with any other property in the same card. Based on this premise, given an aligned property pair predicted by the learning model, if one property happens to be in the disjoint set of another property, the aligned pair should be filtered out.

- *Object value range validation.* If two properties can be aligned, their ranges should be compatible. In another word, the categories of their corresponding values cannot be disjoint. According to this principle, for any object value pair of two aligned properties, if their categories are disjoint, the property alignment should be removed. More precisely, for each object value, we use the categories of the corresponding Wikipedia entity. If the two category sets have no overlap, we think the categories of the value pair are disjoint.

3.3   Value Deduplication for Aligned Properites

After properties are aligned, values of these aligned properties should be deduplicated so that equivalent ones in different expressions are grouped together into value clusters. Here, we introduce a simple but effective method. As mentioned in Section 3.2, numeric values of the same unit type are normalized. Also, string values are lowercased and segmented into parts as new string values by predefined delimiters. For object values, links to their corresponding Wikipedia entities are completed. The above processing steps ease the deduplication of these values. That is, if two object values link to the same Wikipedia entity, they are merged together. For the two normalized numeric values or string values, we compare their similarity with the corresponding matching threshold to check whether the two values can be deduplicated.

4   Experiment

4.1   Experiment Setup

We selected a set of queries and submitted them to three search engines to collect knowledge cards to be fused. A query is chosen if at least two engines return knowledge cards for it. Secondly, a portion of selected queries should be ambiguous so that some engine will return several possible cards. Third, the returned cards should have different numbers of attribute value pairs (AVPs). We tried different titles of Wikipedia entity pages as well as disambiguation pages, and finally selected 26,583 different entity queries in total. Among these queries, about one fifth are ambiguous. Furthermore, We find that more than half of the cards are medium rich (includes AVPs ranging from 3 to 5), 19% are poor (fewer than 2 AVPs), and 24 percent are rich (more than 6 AVPs). We further randomly chose 154 queries from the above query set. The subset of queries conform the same richness distribution and have the similar percent of ambiguous queries. As a result, 464 knowledge cards are collected and manually labeled as ground truths to evaluate the performance of card disambiguation and property alignment. We downloaded mapping-based properties under DBpedia 2014 downloads[1] to collect

---

[1] http://wiki.dbpedia.org/Downloads2014

Wikipedia infobox properties and the corresponding ontology properties in DBpedia ontology. Due to the large community of DBpedia, the collected mappings can be assumed to be of high quality. While it is impossible for these mappings to be 100 percent correct, they can still be used to train a robust learning model for property alignment. These cards are also converted to ontologies as inputs of several ontology alignment tools. We finally compare the alignment performance of these tools with that of ours. All the data can be downloaded via the following link[2] for the purpose of experiment reproductivity. For more experiment details, you can refer to our technical report[3].

4.2   Card Disambiguation Evaluation

We compare our disambiguation method with two baselines in terms of accuracy and coverage. One baseline only considers the commonness score and the other uses the relatedness score. Here, coverage means the fraction of cards that have been disambiguated w.r.t. all cards while accuracy is the fraction of cards that are disambiguated correctly. The threshold is 0.01 to filter entities of low scores.

Figure 3 shows the comparison results. Using commonness score only can deal with the largest number of cards but achieves the lowest accuracy. In most cases, the card label is an anchor text linking to some Wikipedia entities so it can always return some entities as the disambiguation result. But the label is usually ambiguous and can refer to several entities. So using the label alone cannot distinguish among these possible entities. On the other hand, when considering the relatedness score only, the coverage becomes slightly lower but the accuracy increases significantly. This indicates that using object values in the card as its context can actually help filter unlikely entities the card might refer to. However, if two possible entities have similar relatedness scores, this baseline cannot decide which one to choose. For these cases, the commonness score might help. Therefore, our algorithm combines the strengths of both baselines. As a result, it gets 100 percent accuracy with very high coverage.

4.3   Unit Distribution Statistics

The same numeric values can be expressed differently using different units of the same type and should be normalized in a same unit, which has a positive impact on property alignment and value deduplication. It is impossible to enumerate all of them so we aim to prepare normalization rules for as few unit types as possible while still covering a sizeable cases. Since Wikipedia has a wide coverage and is an important source to build knowledge graphs, we can assume real data has the similar unit distribution. Thus, we collected 104,101 numeric values with units from Wikipedia infoboxes to analyze unit distributions. Statistically these units fall into nine types (i.e., currency, time, length, velocity, voltage, electric current, frequency, mass and area) and occupy almost 90 percent.

---

[2] http://kcf.hiekn.com/download/experiment.tar.gz
[3] http://kcf.hiekn.com/download/tr.pdf

4.4   Property Alignment Performance

In this section, we first discuss how to tune different parameters for the learning-based alignment on DBpedia mappings. Then we apply the learned model to aligning properties of real world knowledge cards.

Alignment Performance on DBpedia Mappings. The DBpedia mappings dataset contains mappings from Wikipedia infobox properties to ontology properties in DBpedia. According to these mappings, we can get a large number of Wikipedia infobox property pairs in which each pair maps to the same ontology property. These pairs are used as positive examples for training a learning-based alignment model. The negative examples are those property pairs which have large values for any of the above introduced features but have not been declared to map to a same ontology property. We then discuss parameter tuning to learn a best alginment model without overfitting.

First, we determine matching thresholds for string, numeric and object values respectively to verfiy whether a pair of values of the same type can match. Changing thresholds will impact the MVR value of each property pair to be aligned. Instead of training another model to predict the most suitable thresholds, we analyze the precision distribution by setting different thresholds and pick the one achieving the highest precision. More precisely, we randomly select 200 value pairs for each type (i.e., numeric, string, or object) from positive and negative examples equally. Then we calculate the similarity of each value pair accordingly. Given a threshold, if the corresponding property pair is aligned having its similarity greater than or equal the threshold, or the property pair cannot be aligned and the similarity is below the threshold, we mark the value pair "T" (indicating a true positive or true negative). Otherwise, we mark it "F". The whole process is repeated ten times. Then we get the average precision under this threshold by calculating the proportion of the number of "T"s to the total number (i.e., 200). The thresholds range from 0 to 1 and the step is 0.1. When the string threshold is 0.2, we get the highest precision. Similarly, we set the thresholds for numeric and object values as 0.8 and 0.5 respectively.

Second, we try to find an empirical value of the minimal size of training data to learn an "approximately best" alignment model. Here, we use Logistic Regression, one of the most widely used learning algorithms, to learn a model and test the performance of property alignment under different sizes of training data. More specifically, we randomly selected 200, 600, 2,000, 6,000, and 10,000 labeled property pairs from positive and negative examples equally. 5-fold cross validation is performed during model training. When adding the training data size from 200 to 6,000, the alignment performance improves significantly. But when we further increase the size to 10,000, the performance is almost unchanging. So we set 6,000 as the empirical training data size for further model selection.

We then use different learning algorithms to train various models. The alignment performance under these models are compared. Here, we choose Logistic Regression (LR), SVM, Decision Tree (DT), and Random Forest (RF) to compare. All the parameters are set as the ones used in the previous step. The learned

RF model achieves the best F1-Measure. Since we have a post-processing step to filter out incorrect alignment candidates, we should pay more attention to recall. In this case, the selected model also has the best coverage.

Finally, we study the contributions of different features. Here, we choose five groups of feature combinations, namely all our features (All), all features except property similarity (All-PS), all features except value overlap ratio (All-VOR), all features except value match ratio (All-VMR), and all features except value similarity variance (All-VSV). The same training data is used to learn five different random forest models.

The model using all features performs best. The F1-Measure scores of other models decrease to a certain extent, which indicates all features have some positive impacts to boost the performance of property alignment. Moreover, when removing property similarity from the feature set, the learned model has the lowest performance. This means that the property similarity feature is a key factor to judge if a property pair can be aligned.

Alignment Performance on Real Data. From 464 knowledge cards, we randomly selected 3,487 attribute value pairs and asked students to manually label whether two properties in each pair can be aligned. As a result, 480 pairs are positive and 3,007 are negative. We applied the best model trained on DBpedia mappings to predict alignments on the above pairs. Moreover, we have two extensions. One considers pre-processing and the other further adds a post-processing step. Precision, recall, and F1-Measure are used for effectiveness study.

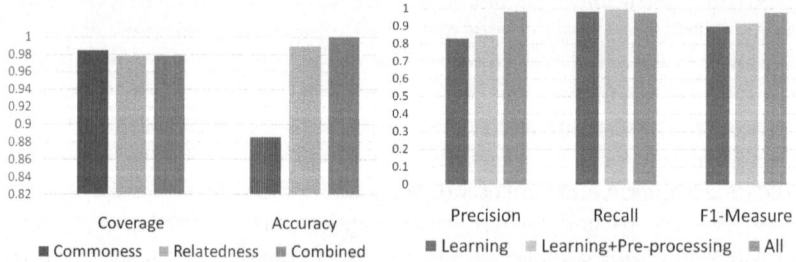

Fig. 3. Card disambiguation results   **Fig. 4.** Property alignment results

Figure 4 shows the alignment performance based on three methods. If an entity cannot refer to any Wikipedia entity, property alignment can still be executed. We get acceptable results without pre-processing. The model especially with pre-processing can actually predict aligned property pairs with a relatively high precision (more than 0.8) and almost perfect recall. Furthermore, after post-processing, the precision increases significantly at the expense of a slight drop of recall. This shows the effectiveness of post-processing used in post-processing. Regarding recall decrease, there exist two possible reasons. One is two similar

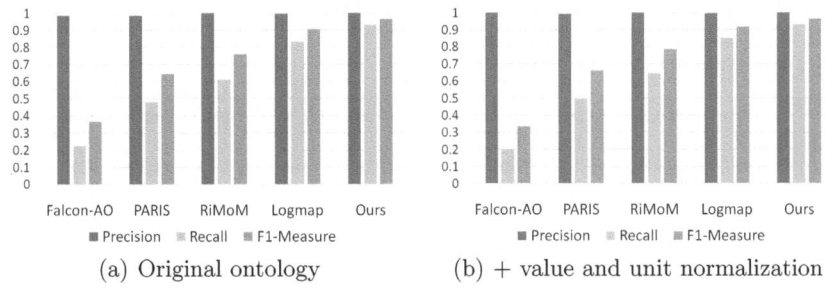

(a) Original ontology   (b) + value and unit normalization

Fig. 5. Performance comparison of instance alignment

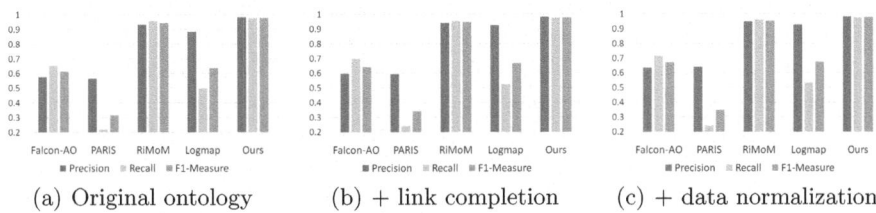

(a) Original ontology   (b) + link completion   (c) + data normalization

Fig. 6. Performance comparison of property alignment

object values are categorized into different types. The other is the disjoint sets are too tight so that the mutual exclusion filter kicks out some similar properties.

4.5 Effectiveness of Value Deduplication

Through deduplication, values associated with the same aligned property are clustered into different groups within an attribute value pair in a fused card. Our experiments were carried out on the aligned attribute value pairs in the previous section (where 480 pairs are collected). As a result, we receive 1,431 value clusters which consist of at least one value. It is important to verify both precision and recall of this step. We manually labeled the correct clusters in which all the related candidate values are clustered correctly. Statistically, the recall of this step reaches 73.17% while precision is 98.9%. Due to the preprocessing, we have normalized both object values and numeric values so that values with same expressions can be easily deduplicated. However, there still left a certain amount of values which are not clustered. After analyzing bad cases, we find that some values may be originally out-of-date or inaccurate. For instance, a knowledge card of Arrian who is a Greek historian is presented by all the three search engines. Google and Bing show his death date as 175 AD while the same property is displayed as 160 AD in the Yahoo!'s card. Since the similarity between these two dates is below the threshold, they are clustered in two groups, which reduces the recall. On the other hand, some related values are not clustered correctly due to the failure in link completion. Considering two equivalent object values, if one has completed the link while the other does not, such a case will fail and reduce the recall.

4.6   Performance Comparison with Ontology Alignment Tools

Actually, card disambiguation and value deduplication can be treated as instance alignment tasks. So we compare our approach with the state of the art ontology matching tools for both instance alignment and property alignment. Here, we selected RiMoM [12], Logmap [11], Falcon-AO [10], and PARIS [19] as the tools for alignment performance comparison. The former two are among the top-3 tools of the OAEI champaign[4] in recent three years. The latter two also support both alignment tasks and have been widely used in practical applications.

We convert cards returned by one engine for a query into an ontology in the OWL format. Each card is treated as an instance with several attribute value pairs. Both object values and numeric values are treated as instances as well. For each numeric value, it is represented as an instance of a certain unit type (a concept defined in the unitontology[5]). The string values are treated as literals. If a property is associated with instances as its values, it is an *ObjectProperty*. Otherwise, it is a *DatatypeProperty*. Considering that there may be more than one kind of values in one property of a card, we divide this property into several ones in which each new property is associated with either instances or literals. A label is provided for each instance or property. Together with another ontology returned by a different engine for the same query, the above tools can be executed to get alignment results for instances and property pairs between two ontologies.

Here, we collected 204 cards from Google and 130 cards from Bing for all 154 queries used in previous experiments. Among 204 cards, there exist 848 properties with 1,377 values in all. Similarly, 610 properties with 913 values are found in 130 cards. We asked four students to manually label alignment ground truths. As a result, we totally get 596 instance alignments in which 108 are card pairs referring to the same entities and 488 are value pairs with two equivalent object values or numeric values. We also get 427 aligned property pairs.

Instance Alignment. We record the precision, recall, and F1-measure of instance alignment run by each tool based on the above introduced ontologies as inputs. As shown in Figure 5(a), our approach not only achieves the best accuracy, but also the highest coverage. Among the selected tools, Logmap performs best especially in terms of recall. This is because Logmap can identify equivalent values of some particular unit type with the help of a Hermit reasoner. For instance, Logmap can align 105.3 mi^2 with 105.30 sq miles while the other tools fail. Given an alignment returned by our approach (one value is 0.056-0.11kg and the other value is 0.12-0.24lb), none of the tools are able to find out this alignment. This shows that Logmap might be able to deal with abbreviations or alias of some units, but unit conversion is still out of its ability scope.

---

[4] http://oaei.ontologymatching.org/
[5] https://code.google.com/p/unit-ontology/

Besides the original ontologies, we further add our pre-processing results to enrich these ontologies. As a result, the enriched ontologies contain normalized values and units, which are of higher quality with more unified vocabularies. When using the enriched ontologies as inputs of these tools, almost all tools have performance increases in terms of recall (shown in Figure 5(b)). This indicates that these tools do not complete missing links of object values, which can actually reduce the ambiguities, and thus have positive impacts on instance alignments.

Property Alignment. Similarly, during property alignment, we not only use the original ontologies as inputs for these tools, but also feed them with two enriched version of ontologies. One enrichment is to add the card links to the original ontologies. Another is to further add our pre-processing results (i.e., value and unit normalization) similar to the enrichment made for instance alignment.

Figure 6(a), Figure 6(b), and Figure 6(c) show the property alignment performance comparison results of these tools and our approach based on original ontologies and two versions of enrichments respectively. From these figures, we can find that all tools are benefited from the two versions of enriched ontologies and gain precision and recall improvements. Our approach gets the best performance again. Among these tools, RiMoM is the best. The performance gap between RiMoM and ours mainly lies on dealing with one-to-many property alignments. For example, Both "Born" with two object values "July 18, 1918", "Mvezo, South Africa" and "Died" with two object values "December 5, 2013", "Houghton Estate, Johannesburg, South Africa" of a card should be aligned with the property "Lived" (who has an object value named "Jul 18, 1918 - Dec 05, 2013 (age 95)" from another card about Nelson Mandela. But RiMoM fails to find such an aligned property pair. Moreover, a small number of bad cases happen when one property has multiple values while the other with the same property name only has one value to be aligned. For example, a property named "Previous offices" with one value "Representative (NY 9th District) 1993-1999" cannot be aligned with the property of the same name with multiple values "Representative NY 9th District (1993 - 1999)", and "Representative NY 10th District (1983 - 1993)". Instead, we are able to solve the above bad cases of RiMoM thanks for our learning-based property alignment method.

5   Related Work

There are three lines of research related to our work. They are entity search, Web data fusion, and ontology alignment in the following subsections respectively.

5.1   Entity Search

Entity search has attracted more and more attentions from both academia and industry. Jeffrey Pound et al. [16] provided a solid framework for ad-hoc object retrieval. Jeffrey Dalton et al. [4] developed a method for coreference aware retrieval over a collection of objects containing a large degree of duplication.

Roi Blanco et al. [2] proposed a content-based recommendation algorithm to provide a list of related entities for an input entity query. Roi Blanco et al. [3] presented an evaluation framework for repeatable and reliable semantic search evaluation. All these work focus on entity retrieval and ranking.

More recently, Daniel M. Herzig et al. [9] proposed different language models to tackle vocabulary and structure mismatches among different data sources for heterogenous entity retrieval. In [8], he further proposed a novel method for on-the-fly entity consolidation during federated entity search. The above two works consider instance alignment only during the query time. Thus, there is no existing research work on fusing knowledge cards from various search engines for an entity query.

5.2 Web Data Fusion

Essentially, knowledge cards fusion is a kind of data fusion considering both property alignment and instance alignment.

Xuan Liu et al. [13] proposed SOLARIS which starts with returning answers from the first probed source and refreshes the answers as it probes more sources. While it considers online data fusion, it expands to more sources iteratively. Different from it, we extract knowledge cards from multiple search engines (sources) at the same time before further fusion. D.Rinser et al. [17] leverages the inter-language links to identify equivalent entities. In our work, the link-completer plays the same role but uses a different method. R.Gupta et al. [7] focuses on creating a rich-attribute ontology by extracting attributes from query-stream and plain-text while our work invests heavily in ontology alignment.

More recently, Stefanidis et al. [18] described some efficient block-based entity resolution on the Web of data. All the above two work are about entity matching without considering property or class alignment, which are necessary in knowledge cards fusion.

5.3 Ontology Alignment

The closest work to ours is ontology alignment. PARIS [19], Falcon-AO [10], RiMOM [12], and Logmap [11] are ontology matching tools for the automatic alignment of entities, properties and classes from multiple ontologies. These tools get satisfactory results in the recent OAEI campaigns. They are selected to compare with our approach on alignment performance of knowledge cards fusion. Different from traditional ontology alignment settings, in our problem, schema-level information such as domains and ranges of properties are not provided. Sometimes, links to some object values are missing. Lack of such ontological knowledge, these tools fail to return important instance alignments or property alignments. Thus knowledge cards fusion can be seen as a new branch of ontology alignment task requiring new methods to deal with the above challenges.

6   Conclusion and Future Work

In this paper, we presented the first effort to work on fusing knowledge cards from various search engines. We proposed a probabilistic scoring method for card disambiguation. A learning-based method is then applied to align properties coming from different cards. Finally, we deduplicate the values of aligned properties and group these values into clusters. Knowledge cards fusion is actually a kind of online data fusion task involving both instance alignment and property alignment. Compared with several state of the art ontology alignment tools, our approach achieves better accuracy and wider coverage. As for future work, we plan to handle inconsistent [5] cards and to design ranking functions to rank values, attribute value pairs, and cards respectively so that we can return the most relevant fused cards with highly informative information for entity search.

References

1. Balog, K., Meij, E., de Rijke, M.: Entity search: building bridges between two worlds. In: Proceedings of the 3rd Semsearch Workshop, p. 9 (2010)
2. Blanco, R., Cambazoglu, B.B., Mika, P., Torzec, N.: Entity recommendations in web search. In: Alani, H., et al. (eds.) ISWC 2013, Part II. LNCS, vol. 8219, pp. 33–48. Springer, Heidelberg (2013)
3. Blanco, R., Halpin, H., Herzig, D.M., Mika, P., Pound, J., Thompson, H.S., Tran, T.: Repeatable and reliable semantic search evaluation. Web Semantics: Science, Services and Agents on the World Wide Web **21**, 14–29 (2013)
4. Dalton, J., Blanco, R., Mika, P.: Coreference aware web object retrieval. In: Proceedings of the 20th ACM CIKM, pp. 211–220 (2011)
5. Flouris, G., Huang, Z., Pan, J.Z., Plexousakis, D., Wache, H.: Inconsistencies, negations and changes in ontologies. In: Proceedings of AAAI, pp. 1295–1300 (2006)
6. Gabrilovich, E., Markovitch, S.: Computing semantic relatedness using wikipedia-based explicit semantic analysis. In: Proceedings of the 20th IJCAI, pp. 6–12 (2007)
7. Gupta, R., Halevy, A., Wang, X., Whang, S.E., Wu, F.: Biperpedia: An ontology for search applications. Proceedings of the VLDB Endowment **7**(7), 505–516 (2014)
8. Herzig, D.M., Mika, P., Blanco, R., Tran, T.: Federated entity search using on-the-fly consolidation. In: Alani, H., et al. (eds.) ISWC 2013, Part I. LNCS, vol. 8218, pp. 167–183. Springer, Heidelberg (2013)
9. Herzig, D.M., Tran, T.: Heterogeneous web data search using relevance-based on the fly data integration. In: Proceedings of the 21st WWW, pp. 141–150 (2012)
10. Hu, W., Qu, Y., Cheng, G.: Matching large ontologies: A divide-and-conquer approach. Data & Knowledge Engineering **67**(1), 140–160 (2008)
11. Jiménez-Ruiz, E., Grau, B.C., Zhou, Y.: Logmap 2.0: towards logic-based, scalable and interactive ontology matching. In: Ontology Matching, pp. 45–46 (2011)
12. Li, Y., Li, J.Z., Zhang, D., Tang, J.: Result of ontology alignment with RiMOM at OAEI 2006. In: Ontology Matching, p. 181 (2006)
13. Liu, X., Dong, X.L., Ooi, B.C., Srivastava, D.: Online data fusion. Proceedings of the VLDB Endowment **4**(11) (2011)

14. Medelyan, O., Witten, I.H., Milne, D.: Topic indexing with wikipedia. In: Proceedings of the AAAI WikiAI workshop, pp. 19–24 (2008)
15. Milne, D., Witten, I.H.: Learning to link with wikipedia. In: Proceedings of the 17th ACM CIKM, pp. 509–518 (2008)
16. Pound, J., Mika, P., Zaragoza, H.: Ad-hoc object retrieval in the web of data. In: Proceedings of the 19th WWW, pp. 771–780 (2010)
17. Rinser, D., Lange, D., Naumann, F.: Cross-lingual entity matching and infobox alignment in wikipedia. Information Systems **38**(6), 887–907 (2013)
18. Stefanidis, K., Efthymiou, V., Herschel, M., Christophides, V.: Entity resolution in the web of data. In: WWW (Companion Volume), pp. 203–204 (2014)
19. Suchanek, F.M., Abiteboul, S., Senellart, P.: PARIS: Probabilistic Alignment of Relations, Instances, and Schema. PVLDB **5**(3), 157–168 (2011)
20. Wu, Z., Palmer, M.: Verbs semantics and lexical selection. In: Proceedings of the 32nd ACL, pp. 133–138 (1994)

Reasoning

Reasoning

Adding *DL-Lite* TBoxes to Proper Knowledge Bases

Giuseppe De Giacomo[1]($\boxtimes$) and Hector Levesque[2]

[1] Sapienza Università di Roma, Rome, Italy
degiacomo@dis.uniroma1.it
[2] University of Toronto, Toronto, Canada
hector@cs.toronto.edu

Abstract. Levesque's proper knowledge bases (proper KBs) correspond to infinite sets of ground positive and negative facts, with the notable property that for FOL formulas in a certain normal form, which includes conjunctive queries and positive queries possibly extended with a controlled form of negation, entailment reduces to formula evaluation. However proper KBs represent extensional knowledge only. In description logic terms, they correspond to ABoxes. In this paper, we augment them with *DL-Lite* TBoxes, expressing intensional knowledge (i.e., the ontology of the domain). *DL-Lite* has the notable property that conjunctive query answering over TBoxes and standard description logic ABoxes is reducible to formula evaluation over the ABox only. Here, we investigate whether such a property extends to ABoxes consisting of proper KBs. Specifically, we consider two *DL-Lite* variants: $DL\text{-}Lite_{rdfs}$, roughly corresponding to RDFS, and $DL\text{-}Lite_{core}$, roughly corresponding to OWL 2 QL. We show that when a $DL\text{-}Lite_{rdfs}$ TBox is coupled with a proper KB, the TBox can be compiled away, reducing query answering to evaluation on the proper KB alone. But this reduction is no longer possible when we associate proper KBs with $DL\text{-}Lite_{core}$ TBoxes. Indeed, we show that in the latter case, query answering even for conjunctive queries becomes coNP-hard in data complexity.

1 Introduction

Many applications involving knowledge representation require an *open-world* setting, with *incomplete information* on their domain of interest [2,7,15,16]. In such conditions, querying a knowledge base is typically based on *logical inference*, which is generally computationally infeasible. Indeed, the most successful applications of logics in Computer Science, namely relational databases [1] and model checking [5] assume complete information, and are based on the *evaluation* of logical formulas over a finite model. In particular, evaluating a FOL formula against a database requires only a simple recursive procedure and is indeed sub-polynomial (AC^0) in data complexity (i.e., in the computational complexity measured over the size of the database only). A natural question is whether there are interesting cases in which logical inference, required to deal with incomplete information, can be compiled into formula evaluation and hence

© Springer International Publishing Switzerland 2015
M. Arenas et al. (Eds.): ISWC 2015, Part I, LNCS 9366, pp. 305–321, 2015.
DOI: 10.1007/978-3-319-25007-6_18

retain the deductive efficiency of database retrieval without requiring complete knowledge, as with databases.

Based on this idea, Levesque [17] proposes the notion of a *proper knowledge base* (proper KB), where incomplete knowledge amounts to a possibly infinite set of positive or negative ground facts (without disjunctions or existentials), which allow for selectively making open and close world assumption on (possibly part of the extension of) single predicates. For this kind of KB he devises a reasoning procedure based on formula *evaluation* that essentially has the efficiency of first-order logic evaluation over a finite model (AC^0 in data complexity). This evaluation procedure is logically sound, and also complete when the formula is in a special normal form, called $\mathcal{NF}$. This class of formula notably includes conjunctive queries and positive queries, possibly extended with a controlled form of negation. Proper KBs are further investigated in [12,18,19].

Compiling logical inference into evaluation is also at the base of one of the most fruitful developments in description logics (DLs) [3] in the last decade, the introduction of so called ontology-based query answering systems and the *DL-Lite* family [9,10]. These logics are designed for retaining the data complexity of FOL evaluation, while being able to capture most constructs used in UML Class Diagrams or Entity Relationship Diagrams [6]. They generalize W3C RDF Schema (RDFS) [8,14], and are at the base of the OWL 2 QL profile of the W3C standard OWL 2 [20].

DLs consider knowledge divided into intensional knowledge and extensional knowledge. Intensional knowledge is expressed as a *TBox*, i.e., a finite set of universal logical assertions describing the domain of interest in terms of classes (called *concepts*), which are unary predicates, and relationships between classes (called *roles*), which are binary predicates. Extensional knowledge is expressed as an *ABox*, which consist of a finite set of positive facts involving concepts and roles of the TBox. (Open-world semantics is assumed.) Often the TBox is used to capture the ontology of the domain, while the ABox is used to capture contingent knowledge on individuals belonging to the domain. The main reasoning task of interest for the logics in the *DL-Lite* family is *query answering*, that is, computing substitutions for the open variables in the query for which the resulting formulas are logically entailed by the TBox and the ABox. The queries typically considered are conjunctive queries and the union of conjunctive queries. The first are FOL formulas where only conjunction and existential quantification is allowed, while the second include also disjunction (but, no forms of negation, nor universal quantification). The key feature of the DLs belonging to the *DL-Lite* family is the so-called *first-order* rewritability: query answering for a query Q can be performed in a sound and complete way by compiling away the TBox into a new FOL query $Q_\mathcal{T}$ that can be evaluated over the ABox, considered as a database. As the result, query answering in *DL-Lite* is AC^0 in data complexity like formula evaluation in a relational DB.

In this paper, we consider knowledge bases constituted by a TBox expressed in variants of *DL-Lite* and an ABox consisting of a Levesque's proper KB. In particular we consider two members of the *DL-Lite* family: *DL-Lite$_{rdfs}$*, which roughly correspond to RDFS [14], and *DL-Lite$_{core}$*, which roughly correspond to OWL 2 QL [9,10]. The latter is actually the simplest *DL-Lite* that includes assertions of the form $A \sqsubseteq \exists R$.

We show that in the case of proper KBs extended with $DL\text{-}Lite_{rdfs}$ TBoxes, we can compile away the TBox retaining soundness and completeness of reasoning, so that when the resulting query is in $\mathcal{NF}$, the proper KB evaluation procedure is both sound and complete. (In particular, for conjunctive queries and union of conjunctive queries, this is always be the case.) This theoretical result has an immediate practical impact: it is possible to build effective ontology-based query aswering systems where: *(i)* RDFS is used to express the ontology of the domain (considering that $DL\text{-}Lite_{rdfs}$ captures the description logic fragment of RDFS, i.e., the fragment obtained by dropping RDFS meta-modeling features); *(ii)* proper KBs are used to express extensional knowledge in a very rich way, and *(iii)* SPARQL is used as a concrete query language for expressing ($\mathcal{NF}$) first-order queries [21].

Then we turn to $DL\text{-}Lite_{core}$ and show that, in this case, it is not possible to reduce query answering to FOL query evaluation. We do so by proving that even for conjunctive queries, any sound and complete procedure must be *coNP*-hard, and hence, the proper KB evaluation procedure remains sound but must necessarily be incomplete. This has the practical impact of ruling out the possibility of building sound, complete and computationally tractable ontology-based query answering systems that adopt OWL 2 QL as the ontology language.[1]

The rest of the paper is organized as follows. In Sections 2 and 3, we review proper KBs and *DL-Lite*. In Section 4, we show soundness and completeness results for TBoxes in $DL\text{-}Lite_{rdfs}$. In Section 5, we show that moving to TBoxes in $DL\text{-}Lite_{core}$, we lose the required computational tractability. Finally in Section 6, we draw some conclusions and discuss future work. An appendix with the detailed proof of the result in Section 4 completes the paper.

2   Proper Knowledge Bases

Standard Names. We use an ordinary first-order logical language $\mathcal{L}$ with an infinite supply of predicate symbols (including $=$), an infinite supply of constants, called *standard names* (which we write as $^\#1, ^\#2, ^\#3, \ldots$), and no other function or constant symbols. We denote the set of standard names by $\mathcal{N}$. We use the notation α_n^x to mean the result of replacing every free occurrence of variable x in formula α by standard name n. We adopt the usual Tarski semantics for $\mathcal{L}$, with $\models$ understood as normal logical entailment. However, we make the *unique name assumption* for the standard names. This means that we implicitly assume a theory of equality $\mathcal{E}$ formed by the usual axioms of equality (reflexivity, symmetry, transitivity, and substitution of equals for equals) together with $\{\, n \neq n' \mid n$ and n' are distinct standard names $\}$. A *knowledge base* (KB) $\mathcal{K}$ consists of a finite set of sentences (closed formulas) belonging to $\mathcal{L}$. To $\mathcal{K}$ we will always implicitly add the equality theory $\mathcal{E}$. The (implicit) adoption of $\mathcal{E}$ implies that

---

[1] In fact, our infeasibility result applies also to $\mathcal{EL}$, and hence rules out also OWL 2 EL [4,20].

$\mathcal{K}$ has a model iff it has a *standard* model, that is, one where $=$ is interpreted as identity and the domain is isomorphic to the set of standard names. Hence, w.l.o.g., we can make *domain closure assumption*: we can assume that the only objects in the domain of interpretation are the standard names. A key property of adopting standard names is the following.

Theorem 1. *[17] Suppose that $\mathcal{K}$ is a KB (including $\mathcal{E}$) and α a possibly open formula in $\mathcal{L}$. Let H be the set formed by all the (finitely many) standard names that appear in $\mathcal{K}$ or α and at least one other not occurring in $\mathcal{K}$ and α. Then*

$$\mathcal{K} \models \forall x.\alpha \ \ \textit{iff} \ \ \mathcal{K} \models \alpha_n^x \ \textit{for every } n \in H.$$

This means that we can determine whether $\forall x.\alpha$ is entailed by checking whether a finite set of instances of α are entailed.

Proper KBs. Following [17], a *proper knowledge base* $\mathcal{A}$ is a finite collection of sentences of $\mathcal{L}$ of the form

$$\forall \boldsymbol{x}.(e \supset \varrho),$$

where

- e is an *equality formula*, i.e., a quantifier-free formula whose only predicate is equality, and free variables are among $\boldsymbol{x}$,
- ϱ is $P(\boldsymbol{x})$ or $\neg P(\boldsymbol{x})$, for some predicate P of arity $|\boldsymbol{x}|$ in $\mathcal{L}$,
- "$\supset$" is the usual material implication connective.

Proper KBs are required to be *consistent* (under the implicit equality theory for standard names $\mathcal{E}$). A proper KB can be seen as a finite representation for a possibly infinite consistent set of ground literals $\{ \varrho\theta \mid \mathcal{A} \models \varrho\theta \}$, where θ is a substitution of free variables by standard names, and $\varrho\theta$ denotes ϱ after the substitution.

Proper KBs can play the role of ABoxes typical of description logics (cf. 3), since they express extensional knowledge as ABox do. Though, they generalize ABoxes in several ways as exemplified below.

Using proper KBs, we can encode finite sets of positive facts (i.e., standard ABoxes), saying that objects or tuples belong to predicates, but also we can encode negative facts saying that objects or tuples do *not* belong to predicates. Indeed any *finite* set of ground literals can be reformulated as a proper KB, by simply rewriting any ground literal $\varrho\theta$ in the set as $\forall \boldsymbol{x}.(\boldsymbol{x} = \boldsymbol{x}\theta \supset \varrho)$.

We can make the close-world assumption (like in databases) on selected predicates, using assertions $\{\forall x.(e(x) \supset P(x)), \forall x.(\neg e(x) \supset \neg P(x))\}$. For example, the following proper KB

$$\{\forall x.\, (x = {}^{\#}2 \vee x = {}^{\#}3 \vee x = {}^{\#}5 \supset P(x)), \ \forall x.\, (x \neq {}^{\#}2 \wedge x \neq {}^{\#}3 \wedge x \neq {}^{\#}5 \supset \neg P(x))\}$$

makes the closed-world assumption on P, saying that the extension of P is exactly $\{{}^{\#}2, {}^{\#}3, {}^{\#}5\}$. This capability can be used, e.g., to describe an authoritative source, which contains exactly all the data about the predicate P.

We can leave the status of some predicate open for some objects only. For example we can write

$$\forall x.(x \neq {}^{\#}0 \wedge \cdots \wedge x \neq {}^{\#}9 \supset \neg P(x))$$

saying that only ${}^{\#}0, \ldots, {}^{\#}9$ may belong to P, without saying which. This can be used to circumscribe the presence of objects in certain data sources. Similarly we can write

$$\forall x.(x \neq {}^{\#}0 \wedge x \neq {}^{\#}1 \supset \neg R({}^{\#}100, x)) \tag{1}$$

saying that the object ${}^{\#}100$ is *not* linked through R to any object different from ${}^{\#}0$ and ${}^{\#}1$, leaving open whether $R({}^{\#}100, {}^{\#}0)$ or $R({}^{\#}100, {}^{\#}1)$ holds. More generally, proper KBs can capture quite advanced forms of partial knowledge on the extension of data sources.

Reasoning with Proper KBs. The reasoning task of interest for proper KBs is query answering. In particular, as in [17], here we focus implicitly on boolean queries only. A (boolean) query Q is a sentence, i.e., a closed formula, in $\mathcal{L}$. Answering Q over a proper KB $\mathcal{A}$ consists in checking the entailment

$$\mathcal{A} \models Q.$$

It is in general *undecidable* to determine whether or not $\mathcal{A} \models Q$. (Consider the case $\mathcal{A} = \emptyset$, where we still need to determine whether an arbitrary first order formula is valid.) As an alternative, Levesque [17] proposes a *limited reasoning procedure V* analogous to the *evaluation* function used for databases under the closed-world assumption, which, however, may return 1 (known to be true), 0 (known to be false), or $\frac{1}{2}$ (unknown). Given a proper KB $\mathcal{A}$ and a query Q, the evaluation procedure $V[\mathcal{A}, Q]$ is defined as follows:

1. (Ground atomic fact) if $Q = \varrho\theta$ then

$$V[\mathcal{A}, \varrho\theta] = \begin{cases} 1 \text{ if there is a } \forall \boldsymbol{x}.(e \supset \varrho) \in \mathcal{A} \text{ s.t. } \mathcal{E} \models e\theta \\ 0 \text{ if there is a } \forall \boldsymbol{x}.(e \supset \overline{\varrho}) \in \mathcal{A} \text{ s.t. } \mathcal{E} \models e\theta \\ \frac{1}{2} \text{ otherwise} \end{cases}$$

   where $\overline{\varrho}$ denotes the result of adding or removing negation from ϱ.

2. (Ground equality atom) if $Q = (n = n')$ then

$$V[\mathcal{A}, (n = n')] = \begin{cases} 1 \text{ if } n \text{ and } n' \text{ are the same standard name} \\ 0 \text{ otherwise} \end{cases}$$

3. (Negation) if $Q = \neg\alpha$ then

$$V[\mathcal{A}, \neg\alpha] = 1 - V[\mathcal{A}, \alpha]$$

4. (Disjunction) if $Q = \alpha \vee \beta$ then

$$V[\mathcal{A}, (\alpha \vee \beta)] = \max\{V[\mathcal{A}, \alpha], V[\mathcal{A}, \beta]\}$$

5. (Conjunction) if $Q = \alpha \wedge \beta$ then

$$V[\mathcal{A}, (\alpha \wedge \beta)] = \min \{V[\mathcal{A}, \alpha], V[\mathcal{A}, \beta]\}$$

6. (Existential quantification) if $Q = \exists x.\alpha$ then

$$V[\mathcal{A}, \exists x.\alpha] = \max_{n \in H} V[\mathcal{A}, \alpha_n^x]$$

where H is the set of standard names appearing in $\mathcal{A}$ or α plus a new one.

7. (Universal quantification) if $Q = \forall x.\alpha$ then

$$V[\mathcal{A}, \forall x.\alpha] = \min_{n \in H} V[\mathcal{A}, \alpha_n^x]$$

where again H is the set of standard names appearing in $\mathcal{A}$ or α plus a new one.

Notice that as expected we have that

$$V[\mathcal{A}, \alpha \wedge \beta] = V[\mathcal{A}, \neg(\neg\alpha \vee \neg\beta)], \qquad V[\mathcal{A}, \forall x.\alpha] = V[\mathcal{A}, \neg\exists x.\neg\alpha].$$

The evaluation procedure V *is tractable* in a very strong sense. Analogously to database evaluation, is is easy to see that $V[\mathcal{A}, Q]$ can be computed in AC^0 in data complexity, i.e., in the number of standard names mentioned in $\mathcal{A}$ and Q. From a more practical point of view we have:

1. If e is a ground equality formula, then $\mathcal{E} \models e$ iff $V[\emptyset, e] = 1$ and can be determined in time linear in $|e|$.
2. $V[\mathcal{A}, \varrho\theta]$ can be determined in time linear in $|\mathcal{A}|$: scan $\mathcal{A}$ for $\forall \boldsymbol{x}.(e \supset \varrho)$ or $\forall \boldsymbol{x}.(e \supset \overline{\varrho})$ and check if $\mathcal{E} \models e\theta$.
3. Overall, computing $V[\mathcal{A}, Q]$ can be made as efficient as database retrieval [19].

The procedure V is always *logically sound*:

Theorem 2. *[17] For any proper KB $\mathcal{A}$ and any query Q in $\mathcal{L}$, we have:*

- *if $V[\mathcal{A}, Q] = 1$ then $\mathcal{A} \models Q$;*
- *if $V[\mathcal{A}, Q] = 0$ then $\mathcal{A} \models \neg Q$.*

However V *is not (and cannot be) logically complete* in general. For example: $\mathcal{E} \models (p \vee \neg p)$ but $V[\emptyset, (p \vee \neg p)] = \frac{1}{2}$.

In [17] completeness is shown for a semantically defined sublanguage of $\mathcal{L}$, called $\mathcal{NF}$, for "normal form". We say that a set of sentences S is *logically separable* iff for every consistent set of ground literals L, if $L \cup S$ has no standard model, then for some $\alpha \in S$, $L \cup \{\alpha\}$ has no standard model. Then $\mathcal{NF} \subseteq \mathcal{L}$ is defined as the least set such that: (i) if α is a ground atom or equality formula, then $\alpha \in \mathcal{NF}$; (ii) if $\alpha \in \mathcal{NF}$, then $\neg\alpha \in \mathcal{NF}$; (iii) if $S \subseteq \mathcal{NF}$, S is logically separable, and S is finite, then $\bigwedge S \in \mathcal{NF}$; (iv) if $S \subseteq \mathcal{NF}$, S is logically separable, and $S = \{\alpha_n^x \mid n \text{ is a standard name }\}$, then $\forall x.\alpha \in \mathcal{NF}$.

Theorem 3. *[17] For any proper KB $\mathcal{A}$ and any Q in $\mathcal{NF}$, we have:*

- *if $\mathcal{A} \models Q$ then $V[\mathcal{A}, Q] = 1$;*
- *if $\mathcal{A} \models \neg Q$ then $V[\mathcal{A}, Q] = 0$.*

Unfortunately $\mathcal{NF}$ is a semantical condition and checking if a formula is in $\mathcal{NF}$ is itself undecidable. However an interesting sufficient syntactic condition for belonging to $\mathcal{NF}$ is the following: we say two literals are *conflict-free* iff either they have the same polarity, or they use different predicates, or they use different standard names at some argument position.

Theorem 4. *[17] Let Q be a query in $\mathcal{L}$, if all pairs of literals in Q are conflict-free, then Q in $\mathcal{NF}$.*

Notably all *positive queries* (i.e., without $\neg$ and $\forall$), hence including *conjunctive queries* (i.e., using only $\wedge$ and $\exists$) and *union of conjunctive queries* (i.e., disjunctions of conjunctive queries), are conflict-free.

3   *DL-Lite$_{rdfs}$* and *DL-Lite$_{core}$*

Description logics (DLs) [3] describe the domain of interest in terms of individuals denoting objects, concepts, denoting sets of objects, and roles, denoting binary relations between objects. In DLs, starting from *concepts names* (denoted by A) and *roles names* (denoted by R), we can construct complex *concepts C, D* and *roles ρ, τ* by inductively applying suitable constructors that depend on the DL in question.

A DL knowledge base $\mathcal{K}$ consists of a TBox $\mathcal{T}$, expressing intensional knowledge, and an ABox $\mathcal{A}$, expressing extensional knowledge. *TBox $\mathcal{T}$* is constituted by a finite set of *concept and role inclusions* of the form

$$C \sqsubseteq D, \qquad \rho \sqsubseteq \tau$$

where the form of concepts C, D and roles ρ, τ depend on the specific DL. We allow inclusions to be cyclic, which is required in virtually all ontology-based and conceptual modeling applications[2]. A standard DL *ABox $\mathcal{A}$* consists of a finite set of positive ground literals involving concepts and roles of the TBox.

In this paper, we consider *DL-Lite$_{core}$*, the simplest language of the *DL-Lite* family [9,10]. A *TBox* in *DL-Lite$_{core}$* is a finite set of *inclusion assertions* of the form:

$$C \sqsubseteq D, \qquad C \sqsubseteq \neg D$$

where concepts C, D and roles ρ, τ are defined by the following syntax:

$$C, D ::= A \mid \exists \rho \qquad \rho ::= R \mid R^-$$

where $\exists \rho$ is the projection of binary role ρ on the first component and R^- is the *inverse* of role R. TBoxes expressed in *DL-Lite$_{core}$* capture a core fragment of

---

[2] When a TBox is acyclic, it can be treated as a set of abbreviations and eliminated w.l.o.g.

UML class diagrams: isa between classes ($A \sqsubseteq B$, A and B are concepts names), typing of roles ($\exists R \sqsubseteq A$, $\exists R^- \sqsubseteq B$), disjointness between classes ($A \sqsubseteq \neg B$), and mandatory participation of instances of a class to roles ($A \sqsubseteq \exists R$ or $B \sqsubseteq \exists R^-$), see [9]. *DL-Lite$_{core}$* roughly corresponds to OWL 2 QL profile [20], where we disallow the use of inclusion assertion on roles $\rho \sqsubseteq \tau$.

Besides *DL-Lite$_{core}$*, we consider also *DL-Lite$_{rdfs}$*, which is obtained from *DL-Lite$_{core}$* by dropping the possibility of using $\exists \rho$ on the right-hand side of inclusion assertions, but including *inclusion assertions on roles* of the form:

$$\rho \sqsubseteq \tau$$

with $\rho, \tau ::= R \mid R^-$. Hence, we loose the possibility of expressing mandatory participation, but we gain the possibility of expressing "subproperties" through isa's on roles, thus capturing RDFS [8] (without meta-level assertions), interpreted according to the *extensional semantics* [14].

We give the semantics of *DL-Lite$_{core}$* and *DL-Lite$_{rdfs}$* by exhibiting the FOL formula corresponding to each concept and role expression. In particular, if t and t' are terms, then $\rho[t, t']$ is the first-order formula defined by

$$R[t, t'] = R(t, t')$$
$$R^-[t, t'] = R(t', t).$$

Similarly, $C[t]$ is the first-order formula defined by (below z stands for any variable such that $z \neq t$):

$$A[t] = A(t)$$
$$\exists \rho[t] = \exists z.\rho[t, z]$$
$$\neg A[t] = \neg A(t)$$
$$\neg \exists \rho[t] = \forall z.\neg \rho[t, z].$$

Assertions of the form $C \sqsubseteq D$ and of the form $\rho \sqsubseteq \tau$ correspond, respectively, to

$$\forall x.(C[x] \supset D[x]) \qquad \forall x, y.(\rho[x, y] \supset \tau[x, y])$$

Typically in *DL-Lite*, we are interested in query answering, where queries are conjunctive queries or union of conjunctive queries. These are possibly open formulas expressed in terms of the concepts (unary predicates) and roles (binary predicate) of $\mathcal{T}$ and $\mathcal{A}$. When such formulas are closed we call such queries boolean. In particular, in this paper, we focus on *boolean queries* only. Given a TBox $\mathcal{T}$ and ABox $\mathcal{A}$, and a (boolean) query Q we are interested in checking whether

$$\mathcal{T} \cup \mathcal{A} \models Q$$

Notably the *DL-Lite* variants enjoy the *first-order rewritability* property, which in our setting says that for every conjunctive query or union of conjunctive queries Q:

$$\mathcal{T} \cup \mathcal{A} \models Q \text{ iff } \mathcal{A} \models Q_{\mathcal{T}}$$

where $Q_{\mathcal{T}}$ is a union of conjunctive query obtained by *rewriting Q using $\mathcal{T}$*, e.g., by the reformulation algorithm in [9], so as to "compile away" the TBox $\mathcal{T}$, and evaluate $Q_{\mathcal{T}}$ over the ABox $\mathcal{A}$ only, considered as a database (with complete information, i.e., closed world assumption). As a result, query evaluation in *DL-Lite* is AC^0 in data complexity, i.e., in the size of the ABox.

4   Proper KBs with *DL-Lite*$_{rdfs}$ TBoxes

The question that this paper addresses is whether something analogous to *DL-Lite* first-order rewritability holds also in the case of ABoxes consisting of proper KBs.

More precisely let's consider KBs formed by a *DL-Lite*$_{rdfs}$ TBox $\mathcal{T}$ and an ABox $\mathcal{A}$ constituted by an proper KB over the unary and binary predicates forming the alphabet of the TBox. We restrict our attentions to proper KBs $\mathcal{A}$ that are *consistent* with the TBox $\mathcal{T}$, i.e., that $\mathcal{A} \not\models \neg \mathcal{T}$ where $\neg \mathcal{T}$ denotes the negation of the conjunction of all assertions in the TBox $\mathcal{T}$. On such KBs, we consider boolean queries Q, i.e., first-order sentences, and we are interested in query answering, i.e., checking whether:

$$\mathcal{T} \cup \mathcal{A} \models Q$$

In particular, we want to study whether there exists another FOL query $Q_{\mathcal{T}}$ such that

$$\mathcal{T} \cup \mathcal{A} \models Q \text{ iff } \mathcal{A} \models Q_{\mathcal{T}}$$

That is, we want to compile away the TBox and obtain another query $Q_{\mathcal{T}}$ to ask over the proper KB $\mathcal{A}$ alone. Notice that, differently from the case of standard *DL-Lite*, $\mathcal{A}$ cannot be seen as a database, since it still includes incomplete information and the close world assumption cannot be made. However if we can reduce $\mathcal{T} \cup \mathcal{A} \models Q$ to $\mathcal{A} \models Q_{\mathcal{T}}$, we can then use the evaluation procedure V to compute $V[\mathcal{A}, Q_{\mathcal{T}}]$, which is always sound and complete for queries in $\mathcal{NF}$. Indeed we are also interested in sufficient conditions for completeness. We show below that when $\mathcal{T}$ is a *DL-Lite*$_{rdfs}$ TBox, $Q_{\mathcal{T}}$ can always be obtained. Moreover there are interesting class of queries Q (including conjunctive queries, and union of conjunctive queries) for which the evaluation procedure V applied to $Q_{\mathcal{T}}$ is indeed complete.

Without loss of generality we assume the query Q to be in negation normal form (NNF), i.e., with negation appearing only in literals. We use the following notation: $\overline{C}$ denotes the concept that results from adding or removing a negation from C, and ρ^- denotes the role that results from adding or removing a superscript minus from ρ.

Next we define two crucial relations $\sqsubseteq_{\mathbf{R}}$ and $\sqsubseteq_{\mathbf{c}}$ denoting the chain of "asserted" inclusions among concepts and roles respectively.

– The $\sqsubseteq_{\mathbf{R}}$ relation holding between pairs of roles is the reflexive transitive closure of the relation

$$\{ (\rho, \tau) \mid \rho \sqsubseteq \tau \in \mathcal{T} \quad \text{or} \quad \rho^- \sqsubseteq \tau^- \in \mathcal{T} \ \}.$$

– The $\sqsubseteq_{\mathbf{c}}$ relation holding between pairs of concept is the reflexive transitive closure of the relation

$$\{ (C, D) \mid C \sqsubseteq D \in \mathcal{T} \quad \text{or} \quad \overline{D} \sqsubseteq \overline{C} \in \mathcal{T} \quad \text{or}$$
$$C = \exists \rho, \ D = \exists \tau, \ \rho \sqsubseteq_{\mathbf{R}} \tau \ \}.$$

Note that, if $C \sqsubseteq_{\mathbf{c}} D$ then $\mathcal{T} \models \forall x.(C[x] \supset D[x])$ and similarly, if $\rho \sqsubseteq_{\mathbf{R}} \tau$ then $\mathcal{T} \models \forall x, y.(\rho[x,y] \supset \tau[x,y])$.

With these two relations at hand, we can define the rewriting $Q_{\mathcal{T}}$ of a query Q wrt a $DL\text{-}Lite_{rdfs}$ TBox $\mathcal{T}$.

Definition 1 (Rewriting). *Let $\mathcal{T}$ be a $DL\text{-}Lite_{rdfs}$ TBox and query Q in NNF, we define the* rewriting $Q_{\mathcal{T}}$ *of Q wrt $\mathcal{T}$ to be Q with every positive $A(t)$ replaced by*

$$\bigvee_{C \sqsubseteq_{\mathbf{c}} A} C[t],$$

every $\neg A(t)$ replaced by

$$\bigvee_{A \sqsubseteq_{\mathbf{c}} D} \overline{D}[t],$$

every positive $R(t, t')$ replaced by

$$\bigvee_{\rho \sqsubseteq_{\mathbf{R}} R} \rho[t, t'],$$

and every $\neg R(t, t')$ replaced by

$$\bigvee_{R \sqsubseteq_{\mathbf{R}} \tau} \neg\tau[t, t'] \vee \bigvee_{\exists R \sqsubseteq_{\mathbf{c}} D} \overline{D}[t] \vee \bigvee_{\exists R^{-} \sqsubseteq_{\mathbf{c}} D} \overline{D}[t'].$$

As we show below, the resulting formula enjoys the desired property: it is the result of compiling away the TBox from Q.

Theorem 5. *Let $\mathcal{T}$ be a $DL\text{-}Lite_{rdfs}$ TBox, $\mathcal{A}$ be a proper KB consistent with $\mathcal{T}$, Q a boolean query in NNF, and $Q_{\mathcal{T}}$ its rewriting defined as above. Then*

$$\mathcal{T} \cup \mathcal{A} \models Q \quad \text{iff} \quad \mathcal{A} \models Q_{\mathcal{T}}$$

Proof. The proof requires extra machinery and has been moved to the appendix. □

In general, Theorem 5 does not induce an analogue of "first-order rewritability", in the sense that $Q_{\mathcal{T}}$ cannot be "evaluated" over the ABox $\mathcal{A}$. However, if $Q_{\mathcal{T}}$ is $\mathcal{NF}$, then it does, since the evaluation procedure V becomes sound and complete and hence it becomes sufficient to check whether $V[\mathcal{A}, Q_{\mathcal{T}}]$ to know whether $\mathcal{A} \models Q_{\mathcal{T}}$. Unfortunately checking whether $Q_{\mathcal{T}}$ is in $\mathcal{NF}$ is in general undecidable. However we can polynomially check $Q_{\mathcal{T}}$ for conflict-freeness. We can exploit this for giving a nice sufficient condition for the completeness of V.

Definition 2 (Conflict-free for a TBox). *Let $\mathcal{T}$ be a $DL\text{-}Lite_{rdfs}$ TBox, Q a boolean query in NNF and $Q_{\mathcal{T}}$ its rewriting defined as above. Q is* conflict-free *for a TBox $\mathcal{T}$ iff $Q_{\mathcal{T}}$ is conflict-free.*

Note that *positive queries* are always conflict free for $DL\text{-}Lite_{rdfs}$ TBoxes, including *conjunctive queries* and *union of conjunctive queries*. For example, if Q is a conjunctive query then $Q_{\mathcal{T}}$ is equivalent to a union of conjunctive queries, and hence is conflict-free.

For conflict free queries, we can exploit Theorem 5 and the soundness and completenes results for V to get:

Theorem 6. *Let $\mathcal{T}$ be a DL-Lite$_{rdfs}$ TBox, $\mathcal{A}$ be a proper KB consistent with $\mathcal{T}$, Q a boolean query in NNF , and $Q_{\mathcal{T}}$ its rewriting defined as above. If Q is conflict-free for $\mathcal{T}$, we have:*

- $\mathcal{T} \cup \mathcal{A} \models Q$ *iff* $V[\mathcal{A}, Q_{\mathcal{T}}] = 1;$
- $\mathcal{T} \cup \mathcal{A} \models \neg Q$ *iff* $V[\mathcal{A}, Q_{\mathcal{T}}] = 0.$

Hence, for queries that are conflict-free for the TBox, query answering reduces to evaluation and is indeed AC^0 in data complexity (i.e., in the number of standard names occurring in the ABox and in the query).

5   Proper KBs with *DL-Lite$_{core}$* TBoxes

Next we investigate KBs formed by a $DL\text{-}Lite_{core}$ TBox $\mathcal{T}$ and an ABox $\mathcal{A}$ formed as a proper KB. Unfortunately in this case we have a negative result: query answering by evaluation is in general unachievable even for queries consisting of boolean conjunctive queries. Indeed, if query aswering by evaluation were possible the data complexity of query answering would be AC^0. However we show that, even with a TBox consisting of a single assertion of the form $A \sqsubseteq \exists R$, conjunctive query answering in proper KBs is *coNP*-hard in data complexity, since proper KB assertions like (1) in Section 2 force reasoning by cases on the data.

Theorem 7. *Conjunctive query answering in proper KBs with TBoxes including assertions of the form*

$$A \sqsubseteq \exists R$$

is coNP-hard with respect to data complexity.

Proof. The proof is based on a reduction from $2 + 2$-CNF unsatisfiability, which is shown to be *coNP*-complete in [13]. A $2 + 2$-CNF formula is a CNF formula in which each clause has exactly four literals: two positive ones and two negative ones.

Given a 2+2-CNF formula $F = c_1 \wedge \cdots \wedge c_n$, where $c_i = \ell_{1+}^i \vee \ell_{2+}^i \vee \neg \ell_{1-}^i \vee \neg \ell_{2-}^i$, we associate with it the knowledge base $\mathcal{K} = \langle \mathcal{T}, \mathcal{A} \rangle$. The alphabet of $\mathcal{K}$ includes one concept A and five roles P_1, P_2, N_1, N_2 and R with the following intuitive meaning:

- concept $A(x)$ denotes that x is an atomic proposition;
- role $P_1(x, y)$ (resp. $P_2(x, y)$) denotes that the atomic proposition y is in first (resp. second) positive position of the clause x;

- role $N_1(x, y)$ (resp. $N_2(x, y)$) denotes that the atomic proposition y is in first (resp. second) negative position of the clause x;
- role $R(x, y)$ denotes that the truth value y is assigned to the atomic proposition x.

The TBox $\mathcal{T}$ is simply:

$$A \sqsubseteq \exists R$$

The ABox $\mathcal{A}$ is formed by the proper KR equivalent to the following atomic assertions (see examples in Section 2 for hints on how to represent these finitely using equality):

$$A(\ell_{1+}^1), A(\ell_{2+}^1), A(\ell_{1-}^1), A(\ell_{2-}^1),$$
$$\ldots$$
$$A(\ell_{1+}^n), A(\ell_{2+}^n), A(\ell_{1-}^n), A(\ell_{2-}^n),$$

$$P_1(c_1, \ell_{1+}^1), P_2(c_1, \ell_{2+}^1), N_1(c_1, \ell_{1-}^1), N_2(c_1, \ell_{2-}^1),$$
$$\ldots$$
$$P_1(c_n, \ell_{1+}^n), P_2(c_n, \ell_{2+}^n), N_1(c_n, \ell_{1-}^n), N_2(c_n, \ell_{2-}^n)$$

$$\neg R(\ell_{1+}^1, {}^\#2), \neg R(\ell_{1+}^1, {}^\#3), \neg R(\ell_{1+}^1, {}^\#4), \cdots$$
$$\neg R(\ell_{2+}^1, {}^\#2), \neg R(\ell_{2+}^1, {}^\#3), \neg R(\ell_{2+}^1, {}^\#4), \cdots$$
$$\neg R(\ell_{1-}^1, {}^\#2), \neg R(\ell_{1-}^1, {}^\#3), \neg R(\ell_{1-}^1, {}^\#4), \cdots$$
$$\neg R(\ell_{2-}^1, {}^\#2), \neg R(\ell_{2-}^1, {}^\#3), \neg R(\ell_{2-}^1, {}^\#4), \cdots$$
$$\ldots$$
$$\neg R(\ell_{1+}^n, {}^\#2), \neg R(\ell_{1+}^n, {}^\#3), \neg R(\ell_{1+}^n, {}^\#4), \cdots$$
$$\neg R(\ell_{2+}^n, {}^\#2), \neg R(\ell_{2+}^n, {}^\#3), \neg R(\ell_{2+}^n, {}^\#4), \cdots$$
$$\neg R(\ell_{1-}^n, {}^\#2), \neg R(\ell_{1-}^n, {}^\#3), \neg R(\ell_{1-}^n, {}^\#4), \cdots$$
$$\neg R(\ell_{2-}^n, {}^\#2), \neg R(\ell_{2-}^n, {}^\#3), \neg R(\ell_{2-}^n, {}^\#4), \cdots$$

where, $c_1, \ldots, c_n$ and $\ell_{1+}^1, \ell_{2+}^1, \ell_{1-}^1, \ell_{2-}^1, \ldots, \ell_{1+}^n, \ell_{2+}^n, \ell_{1-}^n, \ell_{2-}^n$ are standard names chosen to be different from each other. The standard names ${}^\#0$ and ${}^\#1$ are used to represent the truth values *true* and *false* respectively. Intuitively the binary predicates P_1 P_2, N_1, N_2 associate to clauses c_i their four atomic propositions $\ell_{1+}^i, \ell_{2+}^i, \ell_{1-}^i, \ell_{2-}^i$ in their respective first/second, positive/negative position. The binary predicate R associates truth values to atomic propositions, which given the infinite set of assertions of the from $\neg R(\ell, k)$ can only be either ${}^\#0$ or ${}^\#1$ for the atomic propositions mentioned in the clauses.

Finally, we consider the following boolean conjunctive query:

$$Q = \exists x, y_{1+}, y_{2+}, y_{1-}, y_{2-}.$$
$$(P_1(x, y_{1+}) \wedge R(y_{1+}, {}^\#0) \wedge P_2(x, y_{2+}) \wedge R(y_{2+}, {}^\#0) \wedge$$
$$N_1(x, y_{1-}) \wedge R(y_{1-}, {}^\#1) \wedge N_2(x, y_{2-}) \wedge R(y_{2-}, {}^\#1))$$

Intuitively query Q checks if it is possible to assign the "wrong" truth value to all propositions $y_{1+}, y_{2+}, y_{1-}, y_{2-}$ of some clause x. More precisely, checking whether $\mathcal{T} \cup \mathcal{A} \models Q$ (i.e., whether the query is certainly true in $\mathcal{T} \cup \mathcal{A}$) corresponds to checking whether in every truth assignment for the formula F there exists a clause whose positive atomic propositions are interpreted as false and whose negative atomic propositions are interpreted as true, i.e., a clause that is not satisfied. Next we show that the formula F is unsatisfiable if and only if $\mathcal{T} \cup \mathcal{A} \models Q$.

"$\Rightarrow$" Towards contradiction, suppose that the formula F is unsatisfiable but $\mathcal{T} \cup \mathcal{A} \not\models Q$. Then there exists a model $\mathcal{M}$ such that $\mathcal{M} \models \mathcal{T} \cup \mathcal{A}$, but $\mathcal{M} \not\models Q$. Notice that the given the assertions in $\mathcal{A}$ the only way not to satisfy Q is that for each $i = 1, \ldots, n$, we have that either $\neg R(\ell_{1+}^i, {}^\#0)$ or $\neg R(\ell_{2+}^i, {}^\#0)$ or $\neg R(\ell_{1-}^i, {}^\#1)$ or $\neg R(\ell_{2-}^i, {}^\#1)$. On the other hand for each such ℓ^i, by the TBox assertion $A \sqsubseteq \exists R$, there must exists some v such that $R(\ell^i, v)$, and because of the infinite assertions on $\neg R(\ell^i, {}^\#2)$, $\neg R(\ell^i, {}^\#3)$, $\neg R(\ell^i, {}^\#4)$, ... it must be the case that $v = {}^\#0$ or $v = {}^\#1$. So we have that for each clause c_i we must have that $R(\ell_{1+}^i, {}^\#1)$ or $R(\ell_{2+}^i, {}^\#1)$ or $R(\ell_{1-}^i, {}^\#0)$ or $R(\ell_{2-}^i, {}^\#0)$. But this would imply that the set of clauses F is indeed satisfiable, contradicting the hypotesis.

"$\Leftarrow$" Towards contradiction, suppose that $\mathcal{T} \cup \mathcal{A} \models Q$ but the formula F is satisfied by some truth assignment ϱ to its atomic propositions. Then, let $\mathcal{M}_\varrho$ be the interpretation for $\mathcal{T} \cup \mathcal{A}$ defined as follows:

$$A^{\mathcal{M}_\varrho} = \{\ell \mid \ell \text{ is an atomic proposition in } F\}$$
$$P_1^{\mathcal{M}_\varrho} = \{(c_i, \ell_{1+}^i) \mid \text{in } F, \ell_{1+}^i \text{ is the first positive atomic proposition of } c_i\}$$
$$P_2^{\mathcal{M}_\varrho} = \{(c_i, \ell_{2+}^i) \mid \text{in } F, \ell_{2+}^i \text{ is the second positive atomic proposition of } c_i\}$$
$$N_1^{\mathcal{M}_\varrho} = \{(c_i, \ell_{1-}^i) \mid \text{in } F, \ell_{1-}^i \text{ is the first negative atomic proposition of } c_i\}$$
$$N_2^{\mathcal{M}_\varrho} = \{(c_i, \ell_{2-}^i) \mid \text{in } F, \ell_{2-}^i \text{ is the second negative atomic proposition of } c_i\}$$
$$R^{\mathcal{M}_\varrho} = \{(\ell, v) \mid \varrho(\ell) = v\}$$

It is easy to see that $\mathcal{M}_\varrho$ is a model of $\mathcal{T} \cup \mathcal{A}$. On the other hand, since F is satisfiable, for every clause in F there exists a positive atomic proposition interpreted as *true* or a negative atomic proposition interpreted as *false*. It follows that for every (standard name corresponding to) a clause c_i, either P_1 or P_2 relates c_i to a atomic proposition ℓ such that $(\ell, {}^\#1) \in R$ and $(\ell, {}^\#0) \notin R$, or either N_1 or N_2 relates c_i to a to a atomic proposition ℓ such that $(\ell, {}^\#0) \in R$ and $(\ell, {}^\#1) \notin R$. Hence Q evaluates to *false* in $\mathcal{M}_\varrho$, and therefore $\mathcal{T} \cup \mathcal{A} \not\models Q$, contradicting the hypothesis. $\square$

This theorem rules out *DL-Lite$_{core}$* and virtually all variants of *DL-Lite*, which allow for expressing $A \sqsubseteq \exists R$, including the two most prominent ones: *DL-Lite$_R$*, directly corresponding to OWL 2 QL [20], and *DL-Lite$_\mathcal{A}$*, often used in ontology-based data access applications [11]. For the same reason, it also rules out the whole $\mathcal{EL}$ family [4].

6   Conclusion

In this paper we have shown that is it feasible to extend Levesque's proper KBs with TBoxes expressed in *DL-Lite$_{rdfs}$* while retaining the ability to reason by evaluating formulas for first-order queries of certain forms and hence solve query answering in AC^0 in data complexity as for standard database query evaluation. This result is of practical interest considering that *DL-Lite$_{rdfs}$* captures the description logic fragment of RDFS (i.e., dropping meta-modeling features) and that SPARQL can be used as a concrete query language for expressing first-order queries over RDFS [21].

We also showed that this result cannot be generalized to TBoxes expressed in OWL 2 QL or any *DL-Lite* variant that allows for assertions of the form $A \sqsubseteq \exists R$ [9,10], including *DL-Lite$_{core}$*, since when combined with the power of proper KBs, reasoning by cases become necessary (query answering becomes *coNP*-hard). In fact, the result applies also to the DL $\mathcal{EL}$ [4] and hence to OWL 2 EL [20] as well.

Our result on proper KBs with *DL-Lite$_{rdfs}$* TBoxes could be slightly generalized. In particular, it would be interesting to extend the TBox language, e.g., to deal with assertions of the form $\rho \sqsubseteq \neg \tau$ to express disjoint extension of roles, and getting closer to OWL 2 QL [9,20], or to by considering n-ary roles [10]. Also, the language of proper KBs themselves can be extended, e.g., to deal with unknown individuals, i.e., *nulls*, as in [12]. We leave these extensions for future studies.

A   Appendix

In this appendix we prove Theorem 5. As ABox $\mathcal{A}$ we consider any set (possibly infinite) of assertions of the form $A(n)$, $R(n,m)$ and $\neg A(n)$, $\neg R(n,m)$, where n and m are standard names. Notice that these ABoxes are more general then proper KBs (which indeed correspond to *certain* ABoxes of this form). The TBox $\mathcal{T}$ is a standard *DL-Lite$_{rdfs}$* TBox. We assume $\mathcal{A}$ to be consistent with $\mathcal{T}$ (i.e., $\mathcal{A} \not\models \neg \mathcal{T}$.) We use the following notation. If $\mathcal{M}$ is a logical interpretation, then the extension of a concept C and a role ρ are respectively:

$$C^{\mathcal{M}} = \{n \mid \mathcal{M} \models C[n]\}, \qquad \rho^{\mathcal{M}} = \{(n,n') \mid \mathcal{M} \models \rho[n,n']\}.$$

Note that for any C, $\overline{C}^{\mathcal{M}} = \overline{C^{\mathcal{M}}}$. For any concept C and role ρ, we define

$$MIN(C) = \{n \mid \mathcal{A} \models C[n]\}, \qquad MIN(\rho) = \{(n,m) \mid \mathcal{A} \models \rho[n,m]\}.$$

Note that for any $\mathcal{M}$ such that $\mathcal{M} \models \mathcal{A}$, $MIN(C) \subseteq C^{\mathcal{M}}$ and $MIN(\rho) \subseteq \rho^{\mathcal{M}}$. For any $\mathcal{M}$ and C, we define

$$\mathcal{F}(C) = \bigcup_{D \sqsubseteq_c C} \mathcal{E}(D) \quad \text{where} \quad \mathcal{E}(C) = MIN(C) \cup \bigcap_{C \sqsubseteq_c D} D^{\mathcal{M}}.$$

Note that for any C, $MIN(C) \subseteq \mathcal{E}(C) \subseteq \mathcal{F}(C)$.

Lemma 1. *If $\mathcal{M} \models \mathcal{A}$ then $\mathcal{F}(C) \cap \mathcal{F}(\overline{C}) = \emptyset$.*

Proof. Suppose not. Then there is $n \in \mathcal{F}(C)$ and $n \in \mathcal{F}(\overline{C})$. Then for some $D \sqsubseteq_c C$, $n \in \mathcal{E}(D)$ and for some $D' \sqsubseteq_c \overline{C}$, $n \in \mathcal{E}(D')$. Since we have $D \sqsubseteq_c C$ and $C \sqsubseteq_c \overline{D'}$ (which is contrapositive of $D' \sqsubseteq_c \overline{C}$), we also have $D \sqsubseteq_c \overline{D'}$.

Now consider the cases for $n \in \mathcal{E}(D)$. If $n \in MIN(D)$, then $\mathcal{A} \models D[n]$. Since $\mathcal{A} \not\models \neg \mathcal{T}$, $\mathcal{A} \not\models D'[n]$ and so $n \notin MIN(D')$. Moreover, since $\mathcal{M} \models \mathcal{A}$ it follows $n \in D^{\mathcal{M}}$, and hence $n \notin D'^{\mathcal{M}}$. Since by definition $D' \sqsubseteq_c D'$, we get $n \notin \bigcap_{D' \sqsubseteq_c E} E^{\mathcal{M}}$. This contradicts $n \in \mathcal{E}(D')$.

On the other hand, if $n \in \bigcap_{D \sqsubseteq_C E} E^{\mathcal{M}}$, then $n \in \overline{D'}^{\mathcal{M}}$, so $n \notin D'^{\mathcal{M}}$. Since $\mathcal{M} \models \mathcal{A}$, $n \notin MIN(D')$. Moreover $n \notin \bigcap_{D' \sqsubseteq_C E} E^{\mathcal{M}}$, since $D' \sqsubseteq_C D'$. This again contradicts $n \in \mathcal{E}(D')$. $\qquad\square$

For any $\mathcal{M}$ and ρ, we define

$$\mathcal{G}(\rho) = \bigcup_{\tau \sqsubseteq_R \rho} \mathcal{H}(\tau) \quad \text{where} \quad \mathcal{H}(\rho) = MIN(\rho) \cup [(\mathcal{E}(\exists\rho) \times \mathcal{E}(\exists\rho^-)) \cap \bigcap_{\rho \sqsubseteq_R \tau} \tau^{\mathcal{M}}].$$

Lemma 2. $\mathcal{G}(\rho) \subseteq \mathcal{F}(\exists\rho) \times \mathcal{F}(\exists\rho^-)$.

Proof. We prove it for $\rho = R$. (The case of R^- is analogous.) If $(n, m) \in \mathcal{G}(R)$ then for some $\rho \sqsubseteq_R R$, $(n, m) \in \mathcal{H}(\rho)$. There are two cases: if $(n, m) \in MIN(\rho)$, then $n \in MIN(\exists\rho)$ and then $m \in MIN(\exists\rho^-)$, in which case, $n \in \mathcal{E}(\exists\rho)$ and $m \in \mathcal{E}(\exists\rho^-)$; if $(n, m) \in (\mathcal{E}(\exists\rho \times \mathcal{E}(\exists\rho^-))$, then again $n \in \mathcal{E}(\exists\rho)$ and $m \in \mathcal{E}(\exists\rho^-)$. Since $\rho \sqsubseteq_R R$, $\exists\rho \sqsubseteq_C \exists R$ and $\exists\rho^- \sqsubseteq_C \exists R^-$. It follows that $n \in \mathcal{F}(\exists R)$ and $m \in \mathcal{F}(\exists R^-)$. $\qquad\square$

Given a logical interpretation $\mathcal{M}$, we define a related one $\mathcal{M}^*$ by $A^{\mathcal{M}^*} = \mathcal{F}(A)$ and $R^{\mathcal{M}^*} = \mathcal{G}(R)$.

Lemma 3. *If* $\mathcal{M} \models \mathcal{A}$ *then* $\mathcal{M}^* \models \mathcal{T}$.

Proof. First suppose $C \sqsubseteq D \in \mathcal{T}$. Note that if $C \sqsubseteq_C D$, then $\{E \mid E \sqsubseteq_C C\} \subseteq \{E \mid E \sqsubseteq_C D\}$, and so $\mathcal{F}(C) \subseteq \mathcal{F}(D)$. Because of the restriction on the TBOX language, $C = A$ or $C = \exists\rho$. In the case of A, we have $A^{\mathcal{M}^*} = \mathcal{F}(A)$; in the case of $\exists\rho$, we have $\exists\rho^{\mathcal{M}^*} \subseteq \mathcal{F}(\exists\rho)$ by Lemma 2. In both cases, $C^{\mathcal{M}^*} \subseteq \mathcal{F}(C)$. Similarly, because of the language restriction, $D = A$ or $D = \neg A$, and so either way $\mathcal{F}(D) \subseteq D^{\mathcal{M}^*}$ (since $\mathcal{F}(\neg A) \subseteq \overline{\mathcal{F}(A)}$ by Lemma 1). It then follows that $C^{\mathcal{M}^*} \subseteq \mathcal{F}(C) \subseteq \mathcal{F}(D) \subseteq D^{\mathcal{M}^*}$.

Now suppose $\rho \sqsubseteq \tau \in \mathcal{T}$. As above, we have that if $\rho \sqsubseteq_R \tau$, then $\{\rho' \mid \rho' \sqsubseteq_R \rho\} \subseteq \{\tau' \mid \tau' \sqsubseteq_R \tau\}$, and so $\mathcal{G}(\rho) \subseteq \mathcal{G}(\tau)$. It follows that $\rho^{\mathcal{M}^*} = \mathcal{G}(\rho) \subseteq \mathcal{G}(\tau) = \tau^{\mathcal{M}^*}$. $\qquad\square$

Lemma 4. *If* $\mathcal{M} \models \mathcal{A}$ *then* $\mathcal{M}^* \models \mathcal{A}$.

Proof. We consider the four cases of assertions in $\mathcal{A}$.

Suppose $A(n) \in \mathcal{A}$. Then $n \in MIN(A)$, so $n \in \mathcal{E}(A) \subseteq \mathcal{F}(A)$. Therefore, $\mathcal{M}^* \models A(n)$.

Suppose $\neg A(n) \in \mathcal{A}$. Then $n \in MIN(\neg A)$ and $n \notin A^{\mathcal{M}}$. Now suppose that $D \sqsubseteq_C A$ for some D. Then $n \notin MIN(D)$ since otherwise $\mathcal{A} \models \neg\mathcal{T}$. Since $n \notin A^{\mathcal{M}}$, $n \notin \mathcal{E}(D)$. Since this holds for any $D \sqsubseteq_C A$, $n \notin \mathcal{F}(A)$ and hence $\mathcal{M}^* \models \neg A(n)$.

Suppose $R(n, m) \in \mathcal{A}$. Then $(n, m) \in MIN(R)$, so $(n, m) \in \mathcal{H}(R) \subseteq \mathcal{G}(R)$. Therefore, $\mathcal{M}^* \models R(n, m)$.

Finally, suppose $\neg R(n, m) \in \mathcal{A}$. Then $(n, m) \notin R^{\mathcal{M}}$. Now suppose that $\tau \sqsubseteq_R R$ for some τ. Then $(n, m) \notin MIN(\tau)$ since otherwise $\mathcal{A} \models \neg\mathcal{T}$. Since $(n, m) \notin R^{\mathcal{M}}$, $(n, m) \notin \mathcal{H}(\tau)$. Since this holds for any $\tau \sqsubseteq_R R$, $(n, m) \notin \mathcal{G}(R)$ and hence $\mathcal{M}^* \models \neg R(n, m)$. $\qquad\square$

Lemma 5. $\mathcal{T} \models (Q_{\mathcal{T}} \supset Q)$.

Proof. Assume that $\mathcal{M} \models \mathcal{T}$ and prove by induction on $|Q|$ that if $\mathcal{M} \models Q_{\mathcal{T}}$ then $\mathcal{M} \models Q$. Here are the base cases only.

Suppose $Q = A(n)$ and $\mathcal{M} \models Q_{\mathcal{T}}$. So for some $C \sqsubseteq_{\mathbf{c}} A$, $\mathcal{M} \models C[n]$. Since $\mathcal{M} \models \mathcal{T}$, $\mathcal{M} \models A(n)$.

Suppose $Q = \neg A(n)$ and $\mathcal{M} \models Q_{\mathcal{T}}$. So for some $A \sqsubseteq_{\mathbf{c}} D$, $\mathcal{M} \models \neg D[n]$. Since $\mathcal{M} \models \mathcal{T}$, $\mathcal{M} \models \neg A(n)$.

Suppose $Q = R(n, m)$ and $\mathcal{M} \models Q_{\mathcal{T}}$. So for some $\rho \sqsubseteq_{\mathbf{R}} R$, $\mathcal{M} \models \rho[n, m]$. Since $\mathcal{M} \models \mathcal{T}$, $\mathcal{M} \models R(n, m)$.

Suppose $Q = \neg R(n, m)$ and $\mathcal{M} \models Q_{\mathcal{T}}$. So one of the following: for some $R \sqsubseteq_{\mathbf{R}} \tau$, $\mathcal{M} \models \neg \tau[n, m]$ or for some $\exists R \sqsubseteq_{\mathbf{c}} D$, $\mathcal{M} \models \neg D[n]$ or for some $\exists R^- \sqsubseteq_{\mathbf{c}} D$, $\mathcal{M} \models \neg D[m]$. In all cases, since $\mathcal{M} \models \mathcal{T}$, $\mathcal{M} \models \neg R(n, m)$.   □

Lemma 6. *If* $\mathcal{M} \models \mathcal{A}$ *and* $\mathcal{M}^* \models Q$, *then* $\mathcal{M} \models Q_{\mathcal{T}}$.

Proof. The proof is by induction on $|Q|$. Here are the base cases only.

Suppose $\mathcal{M}^* \models A(n)$. So for some $C \sqsubseteq_{\mathbf{c}} A$, $n \in \mathcal{E}(C)$. There are two cases: $n \in MIN(C)$ or $n \in C^{\mathcal{M}}$. Either way, since $\mathcal{M} \models \mathcal{A}$, $\mathcal{M} \models C[n]$. So $\mathcal{M} \models Q_{\mathcal{T}}$.

Suppose $\mathcal{M}^* \models \neg A(n)$. So for every $C \sqsubseteq_{\mathbf{c}} A$, $n \notin \mathcal{E}(C)$ and so $n \notin \mathcal{E}(A)$. So for some $A \sqsubseteq_{\mathbf{c}} D$, $n \notin D^{\mathcal{M}}$, and thus $\mathcal{M} \models \overline{D}[n]$. Therefore $\mathcal{M} \models Q_{\mathcal{T}}$.

Suppose $\mathcal{M}^* \models R(n, m)$. So for some $\rho \sqsubseteq_{\mathbf{R}} R$, $(n, m) \in \mathcal{H}(\rho)$. There are two cases: $(n, m) \in MIN(\rho)$ or $(n, m) \in \rho^{\mathcal{M}}$. Either way, since $\mathcal{M} \models \mathcal{A}$, $\mathcal{M} \models \rho[n, m]$. So $\mathcal{M} \models Q_{\mathcal{T}}$.

Suppose $\mathcal{M}^* \models \neg R(n, m)$. So for every $\rho \sqsubseteq_{\mathbf{R}} R$, $(n, m) \notin \mathcal{H}(\rho)$ and so $(n, m) \notin \mathcal{H}(R)$. Then $(n, m) \notin R^{\mathcal{M}} \cap (\mathcal{E}(\exists R) \times \mathcal{E}(\exists R^-))$. There are three cases: $(n, m) \notin R^{\mathcal{M}}$, in which case for some $R \sqsubseteq_{\mathbf{R}} \tau$, $\mathcal{M} \models \neg \tau[n, m]$, namely $\tau = R$; or $n \notin \mathcal{E}(\exists R)$ in which case for some $\exists R \sqsubseteq_{\mathbf{c}} D$, $n \notin D^{\mathcal{M}}$, and so $\mathcal{M} \models \overline{D}[n]$; or $m \notin \mathcal{E}(\exists R^-)$ in which case for some $\exists R^- \sqsubseteq_{\mathbf{c}} D$, $m \notin D^{\mathcal{M}}$, and so $\mathcal{M} \models \overline{D}[m]$. In all cases, $\mathcal{M} \models Q_{\mathcal{T}}$.   □

Finally we are ready to prove the main claim.

Main Claim. $\mathcal{T} \cup \mathcal{A} \models Q$ *iff* $\mathcal{A} \models Q_{\mathcal{T}}$.

Proof. ($\Leftarrow$) Suppose $\mathcal{A} \models Q_{\mathcal{T}}$. Let $\mathcal{M}$ be any logical interpretation such that $\mathcal{M} \models \mathcal{T} \cup \mathcal{A}$. Since, $\mathcal{M} \models \mathcal{A}$ and $\mathcal{A} \models Q_{\mathcal{T}}$, $\mathcal{M} \models Q_{\mathcal{T}}$. Since $\mathcal{M} \models \mathcal{T}$, $\mathcal{M} \models Q$ by Lemma 5. Therefore, $\mathcal{T} \cup \mathcal{A} \models Q$.

($\Rightarrow$) Suppose $\mathcal{A} \not\models Q_{\mathcal{T}}$. Then, there is an $\mathcal{M}$ such that $\mathcal{M} \models \mathcal{A}$ and $\mathcal{M} \not\models Q_{\mathcal{T}}$. By Lemma 3, $\mathcal{M}^* \models \mathcal{T}$. By Lemma 4, $\mathcal{M}^* \models \mathcal{A}$. By Lemma 6, $\mathcal{M}^* \not\models Q$. Therefore, $\mathcal{T} \cup \mathcal{A} \not\models Q$.   □

Acknowledgments. This research has been partially supported by the EU IP project n. FP7-318338 Optique (*Scalable End-user Access to Big Data*).

References

1. Abiteboul, S., Hull, R., Vianu, V.: Foundations of Databases. Addison Wesley (1995)
2. Allemang, D., Hendler, J.: Semantic Web for the Working Ontologist: Effective Modeling in RDFS and OWL. Morgan Kaufmann (2008)
3. Baader, F., Calvanese, D., McGuinness, D., Nardi, D., Patel-Schneider, P.F. (eds.): The Description Logic Handbook: Theory, Implementation and Applications. Cambridge University Press (2003)
4. Baader, F., Brandt, S., Lutz, C.: Pushing the $\mathcal{EL}$ envelope, pp. 364–369 (2005)
5. Baier, C., Katoen, J.P.: Principles of model checking. MIT Press (2008)
6. Berardi, D., Calvanese, D., De Giacomo, G.: Reasoning on UML class diagrams. Artif. Intell. **168**(1–2), 70–118 (2005)
7. Brachman, R., Levesque, H.: Knowledge Representation and Reasoning. Morgan Kaufmann (2004)
8. Brickley, D., Guha, R., McBride, B.: RDF Schema 1.1. W3C Recommendation. World Wide Web Consortium, February 2014. http://www.w3.org/TR/rdf-schema/
9. Calvanese, D., De Giacomo, G., Lembo, D., Lenzerini, M., Rosati, R.: Tractable reasoning and efficient query answering in description logics: The DL-Lite family. J. Autom. Reasoning **39**(3), 385–429 (2007)
10. Calvanese, D., De Giacomo, G., Lembo, D., Lenzerini, M., Rosati, R.: Data complexity of query answering in description logics. Artif. Intell. **195**, 335–360 (2013)
11. Calvanese, D., De Giacomo, G., Lembo, D., Lenzerini, M., Rosati, R., Ruzzi, M.: Using OWL in data integration. In: Semantic Web Information Management - A Model-Based Perspective, pp. 397–424. Springer (2009)
12. De Giacomo, G., Lespérance, Y., Levesque, H.J.: Efficient reasoning in proper knowledge bases with unknown individuals. In: Proc. of IJCAI 2011, pp. 827–832 (2011)
13. Donini, F.M., Lenzerini, M., Nardi, D., Schaerf, A.: Deduction in concept languages: from subsumption to instance checking. J. of Logic and Computation **4**(4), 423–452 (1994)
14. Franconi, E., Gutierrez, C., Mosca, A., Pirrò, G., Rosati, R.: The logic of extensional RDFS. In: Alani, H., et al. (eds.) ISWC 2013, Part I. LNCS, vol. 8218, pp. 101–116. Springer, Heidelberg (2013)
15. Lenzerini, M.: Data integration: a theoretical perspective. In: Proceedings of the Twenty-first ACM SIGACT-SIGMOD-SIGART Symposium on Principles of Database Systems, June 3–5, Madison, Wisconsin, USA, pp. 233–246 (2002)
16. Lenzerini, M.: Ontology-based data management. In: Proceedings of the 6th Alberto Mendelzon International Workshop on Foundations of Data Management, Ouro Preto, Brazil, June 27–30, pp. 12–15 (2012)
17. Levesque, H.J.: A completeness result for reasoning with incomplete first-order knowledge bases. In: KR, pp. 14–23 (1998)
18. Liu, Y.: Tractable Reasonng in Incomplete First-Order Knowledge Bases. Ph.D. thesis, Department of Computer Science, University of Toronto (2006)
19. Liu, Y., Levesque, H.J.: A tractability result for reasoning with incomplete first-order knowledge bases. In: IJCAI, pp. 83–88 (2003)
20. W3C: OWL 2 web ontology language primer, 2nd edn. Tech. rep., W3C Recommendation, December 11, 2012
21. W3C: SPARQL 1.1 overview. Tech. rep., W3C Recommendation March 21, 2013

R2O2: An Efficient Ranking-Based Reasoner for OWL Ontologies

Yong-Bin Kang[1], Shonali Krishnaswamy[2], and Yuan-Fang Li[1 (✉)]

[1] Faculty of IT, Monash University, Melbourne, Australia
{yongbin.kang,yuanfang.li}@monash.edu
[2] Institute for Infocomm Research, A*STAR, Singapore, Singapore
spkrishna@i2r.a-star.edu.sg

Abstract. It has been shown, both theoretically and empirically, that performing core reasoning tasks on large and expressive ontologies in OWL 1 and OWL 2 is time-consuming and resource-intensive. Moreover, due to the different reasoning algorithms and optimisation techniques employed, each reasoner may be efficient for ontologies with different characteristics. In this paper, we present R2O2, a *meta-reasoner* that automatically combines, ranks and selects from a number of state-of-the-art OWL 2 DL reasoners to achieve high efficiency, making use of performance prediction models and ranking models. Our comprehensive evaluation on a large ontology corpus shows that R2O2 significantly and consistently outperforms 6 state-of-the-art OWL 2 DL reasoners on average performance, with an average speedup of up to 14x. R2O2 also shows a 1.4x speedup over Konclude, the current dominant OWL 2 DL reasoner.

1 Introduction

Core reasoning services such as consistency checking and classification are at the heart of ontology-based applications. For expressive description logics (DLs), such reasoning services have a very high worst-case complexity. For instance, satisfiability checking for $\mathcal{SROIQ}$, the description logic underpinning OWL 2 DL, has worst-case complexity of 2NExpTime-complete [4]. Recent work has also demonstrated empirically [5,11,15] that large and complex ontologies indeed pose a real computational challenge even for state-of-the-art reasoners.

In the past decade, highly optimised ontology reasoners such as FaCT++ [25], HermiT [8] and Konclude [22] have been developed that are capable of reasoning about highly expressive DLs. They implement different reasoning algorithms and employ different sets of preprocessing and optimisation techniques. As a result, they are optimised for certain, but not all ontologies. Dramatic differences in reasoning time among reasoners, sometimes by up to four orders of magnitude, have been observed for some ontologies [5]. Such disparities can cause significant and unnecessary loss in productivity for developers and users of ontologies.

The *robustness* of ontology reasoners was recently investigated [10], with a particular focus on reasoning efficiency. It was observed that given a corpus of

© Springer International Publishing Switzerland 2015
M. Arenas et al. (Eds.): ISWC 2015, Part I, LNCS 9366, pp. 322–338, 2015.
DOI: 10.1007/978-3-319-25007-6_19

ontologies and a number of state-of-the-art reasoners, it is highly likely that one of the reasoners performs sufficiently well on any given ontology in the corpus. However, this *virtual best reasoner* is only found *a posteriori*, and the paper did not discuss how the best reasoner may be selected automatically. It only stated that this task is not straightforward.

The prediction of ontology reasoning performance was recently studied [15, 17], where a prediction model, either a classifier or a regression model, is trained for a given reasoner to make predictions on reasoning time (discretised or actual) of a given ontology. High prediction accuracy is achieved for some state-of-the-art reasoners. These prediction models enable efficient and accurate estimation of a reasoner's performance on an ontology. However, it was not discussed how these models can be used to improve reasoning efficiency.

Portfolio-based algorithm selection methods [13] have been successfully applied to SAT and constraint satisfaction problems. The portfolio SAT solver SATvilla has consistently outperformed single SAT solvers in many SAT competitions [30]. Compared to SAT, ontology languages are more expressive with the inclusion of many more language constructs. As a result, it is more challenging to accurately characterising ontology complexity. Moreover, the performance of a portfolio-based algorithm heavily depends on the accuracy of performance prediction models, and this dependency makes it difficult to further improve its efficiency.

Recently we conducted a preliminary study [14] on constructing a portfolio-based OWL reasoner from six reasoners: FaCT++, HermiT, JFact, MORe, Pellet and TrOWL. This preliminary study made use of classifiers that predict discretised reasoning time. Evaluation shows that, for average performance, it outperforms all of the component reasoners. However, due to increasing sizes of the bins (discretised reasoning time), a best reasoner may not be identified. Moreover, Konclude, a dominant OWL 2 DL reasoner was not included in the study, making its results less significant.

The above work motivates and enables us to propose R$_2$O$_2$, a *meta-reasoner* that combines reasoners with their respective prediction models, and aims at determining the most efficient reasoner for a given ontology. It achieves this by (1) training *prediction models* for predicting actual reasoning time for all reasoners, (2) learning *ranking models* (simply *rankers*) that automatically and efficiently rank the reasoners according to their predicted reasoning performance, and (3) selecting a possible best reasoner given the outputs of the rankers.

Our main contribution is the proposal of a novel meta-reasoner, R$_2$O$_2$, that automatically and efficiently combines, ranks and selects OWL reasoners with the aim of determining the most efficient reasoner for a given ontology. We conducted a comprehensive evaluation on more than 2,000 ontologies and six state-of-the-art OWL 2 DL reasoners, including Konclude, the current dominant reasoner. The evaluation shows that, for average performance over a large ontology corpus, R$_2$O$_2$ significantly and consistently outperforms all six reasoners, achieving an average speedup of up to 14x, and a 1.4x speedup over Konclude.

R_2O_2 also outperforms the traditional portfolio-based approach (that does not perform ranking) with a 1.5x speedup.

2   The Meta-reasoner R_2O_2

R_2O_2 is a supervised meta-reasoner that utilises the state-of-the-art performance prediction models of different reasoners and ranking models (or rankers). R_2O_2 encompasses a number of component reasoners and operates in two phases: offline training and online reasoning. During the training phase, R_2O_2 trains rankers that rank component reasoners on their predicted reasoning time data generated by performance prediction models for these reasoners. After training is completed, R_2O_2 makes predictions of the most efficient reasoners for unseen ontologies, and carries out actual reasoning.

More specifically, the training phase of R_2O_2 is divided into two steps:

1. Given a set of training ontologies, each represented by values of *ontology metrics*, and actual reasoning time for a set of reasoners on each ontology, the performance prediction model of each reasoner is built, following the methodology in [17]. That is, we build a Random Forest-based regression model for each reasoner with the metrics as features (see Section 2.2).

2. Given another set of training ontologies (distinct from the ones used in the first step), we generate a *ranking matrix* where each row represents the values of ontology metrics and a ranking of the reasoners where the ranking is made according to their *predicted* reasoning time. Rankers are then trained on this ranking matrix to learn how the characteristics of an ontology represented by its metrics can be optimally mapped to relative ordering of the predicted performance of reasoners (see Section 2.3).

In the reasoning phase, given an unknown ontology, R_2O_2 makes performance predictions for all the component reasoners. R_2O_2 then ranks the reasoners according to their predicted reasoning time. The rankings recommended by the trained rankers are averaged across all the rankers to determine a unique rank for each reasoner. The highest ranked reasoner will be eventually chosen to perform the reasoning task for the ontology (see Section 2.4).

In the reasoning phase, in our context, R_2O_2's main difference from the traditional portfolio-based approach (denoted PR) in the spirit of SATzilla [31] is that PR always selects the most efficient reasoner for any given ontology according to predicted reasoning time of all component reasoners. That is, given a new ontology, PR computes its ontology metrics, estimates the predicted reasoning time of each component reasoner using the corresponding prediction model, and recommends the reasoner predicted to be the fastest. In contrast, R_2O_2 uses a best possible reasoner by recommending the top ranked reasoner from an aggregation of the rankings of component reasoners, according to their predicted reasoning time, estimated by the trained rankers. Our evaluation shows that R_2O_2 highly and consistently outperforms PR.

Learning rankers from preferences has recently received much attention in the machine learning community [6]. Contrary to the *classification* problems, in the ranking matrix, a training example (i.e. an ontology) is not assigned a single label, but a set of preferences of multiple labels representing reasoners, where one is preferred over another according to their predicted reasoning performance (i.e., the more efficient a reasoner is, the higher its rank is). Once a ranker is learned, our goal is to use it in predicting the most likely relative ordering (i.e., ranking) of all reasoners under consideration for unknown ontologies represented by their ontology metrics.

In our approach, the learning of our rankers is based on *preference learning* [6], which is concerned with the acquisition of preference models from data. In general, the goal of preference learning is to learn preference orders (i.e. rankings) of all possible labels (i.e. performance prediction models) from a training example (i.e. ranking matrix) and predict an ordering (i.e. ranking) to an unseen instance (i.e. ontology).

In the rest of this section, we describe how R$_2$O$_2$ is built in more detail.

2.1 Notation Definition

The following notations will be used in the paper:

- Let $R = \{r_1, \ldots, r_n\}$ be a set of n reasoners.
- Let $\hat{R} = \{\hat{r}_1, \ldots, \hat{r}_n\}$ be a set of n performance prediction models such that for each reasoner $r_i \in R$, $\hat{r}_i \in \hat{R}$ predicts the actual reasoning time of r_i on a given ontology, i.e., $\hat{r}_i$ estimates the performance of r_i.
- Let $RM = \{rm_1, \ldots, rm_m\}$ be a set of m rankers. Each ranker produces a ranking of the reasoners based on their predicted reasoning performance for a given ontology. Specifically, a ranker rm is a function that, given an ontology o and a set of reasoners R, $rm(o, R)$ produces an ordering, a *permutation*, of R.
- Let $OM = \{om_1, \ldots, om_q\}$ be a set of q ontology metrics.
- Given a reasoner r (resp. a performance prediction model $\hat{r}$) and on ontology o, let $RT(r, o)$ (resp. $RT(\hat{r}, o)$) represent the actual (resp. predicted) reasoning time of r on o.
- Let $O \subseteq \mathcal{O} = \{o_1, \ldots, o_p\}$ be a set of p ontologies that can be reasoned about by at least one reasoner in R, i.e., for each $o \in O$, there is at least one reasoner in R that can successfully complete the reasoning task (e.g., classification) without any errors and within the specified time limit. Note that O includes those ontologies that timeout for *some* reasoners. Let $O_c \subseteq O$ be the set of common ontologies that can be reasoned about by all reasoners in R (no errors and no timeout). Note that O_c also includes those ontologies that timeout for some reasoners. Two disjoint subsets O_r and O_t are drawn from O_c, for training the rankers and testing R$_2$O$_2$, respectively. Furthermore, for each reasoner r_i, let set $O_{p_i} \subseteq O \setminus (O_r \cup O_t)$ represent a separate subset of ontologies that r_i can successfully reason about, without timing out. O_{p_i} is used for training the performance prediction model $\hat{r}_i$ for reasoner r_i.

2.2   Building Performance Prediction Models

For each reasoner $r_i \in R$, we train a Random Forest-based prediction model, a *regression model*, $\hat{r}_i \in \hat{R}$ on the training data O_{p_i} with the aim of estimating the *actual*, but not discretised, reasoning time of r_i. Ontology metrics [17] are collected for ontologies in O and used as features to train prediction models in $\hat{R}$.

The produced prediction models in $\hat{R}$ will be used for generating a *ranking matrix* to train the rankers in RM. R^2 (i.e. the coefficient of determination) is widely used to assess the quality of regression models. In our context, R^2 indicates how well each prediction model $\hat{r}$ approximates the actual reasoning time of the corresponding reasoner r. It is possible that two different reasoners are predicted to have the same reasoning time on a given ontology. R^2 is used for *tie-breaking* purposes in R_2O_2, which will be explained in Section 2.4.

2.3   Generating the Ranking Matrix and Training Rankers

Once the performance prediction models in $\hat{R}$ are built, a *ranking matrix* is constructed for training the rankers in RM.

Recall that $O_r \subseteq O_c$ is the set of common ontologies for training rankers. Initially, we build a $|O_r| \times (q + n)$ data matrix $\mathbf{M_d}$ (recall that $|OM| = q$, $|R| = |\hat{R}| = n$), where row i represents $o_i \in O_r$ and is constructed as:

$$\underbrace{(om_{i,1}, \ldots, om_{i,q})}_{\text{ontology metrics}}, \underbrace{(RT(\hat{r}_1, o_i), \ldots, RT(\hat{r}_n, o_i))}_{\text{predicted reasoning time}} \tag{1}$$

where $om_{i,j}$ is the value of the j-th ontology metric om_j of ontology o_i, and $RT(\hat{r}_s, o_i)$ denotes the reasoning time predicted by the prediction model $\hat{r}_s$ for ontology o_i.

Based on the data matrix $\mathbf{M_d}$, we build the corresponding $|O_r| \times (q + n)$ ranking matrix $\mathbf{M_r}$, where row i is represented as:

$$\underbrace{(om_{i,1}, \ldots, om_{i,q})}_{\text{ontology metrics}}, (\underbrace{\pi(\hat{r}_1, o_i), \ldots, \pi(\hat{r}_n, o_i)}_{\text{ranking of prediction models}}) \tag{2}$$

where $\pi(\hat{r}_s, o_i)$ denotes the *rank* of the prediction model $\hat{r}_s$ (hence the corresponding reasoner r_s) on ontology o_i, determined by $RT(\hat{r}_s, o_i)$. In the ranking matrix $\mathbf{M_r}$, the more efficient a performance prediction model is, the higher ranked it is (the smaller the ranking number is).

For example, suppose that there are 3 reasoners $\{r_1, r_2, r_3\}$, and thus 3 performance prediction models $\{\hat{r}_1, \hat{r}_2, \hat{r}_3\}$. Given an ontology o_i, suppose that the predicted reasoning time for o_i estimated by the models is 100s, 90s, and 10s respectively, i.e., $(RT(\hat{r}_1, o_i), RT(\hat{r}_2, o_i), RT(\hat{r}_3, o_i)) = (100s, 90s, 10s)$. Thus, the ranking of the prediction models is $(\pi(\hat{r}_1, o_i), \pi(\hat{r}_2, o_i), \pi(\hat{r}_3, o_i)) = (3, 2, 1)$. If the estimated reasoning time is $(10s, 10s, 100s)$ instead, the ranking produced will be $(1, 1, 3)$.

To recommend the most likely best reasoner, we note that our goal is not to predict the absolute expected reasoning time of any component reasoner, but rather the relative performance of the reasoners. Therefore, we generate a ranking matrix using ontology metrics and the rankings of the reasoners on the training data O_r to train rankers.

Once the ranking matrix $\mathbf{M_r}$ is generated, each ranker $rm_i \in RM$ is trained on $\mathbf{M_r}$. In our context, the problem of learning a ranker is to induce a ranking function f that can order n performance prediction models $\hat{r}_1, \ldots, \hat{r}_n \in \hat{R}$. That is, $rm_i \in RM$ takes as input an ontology and a set of reasoners R, and produces as output a permutation π of R. The interpretation of this permutation is that $\hat{r}_i$ is preferred to (more efficient than) $\hat{r}_j$ whenever $RT(\hat{r}_i, o) < RT(\hat{r}_j, o)$ for a given o. These function $rm_i \in RM$ are then used to estimate the rankings of the performance prediction models for unknown ontologies.

Different ranking models that use different ranking measure to evaluate the performance of the learned rankers [6]. Thus, the maximisation of the ranking measure will lead to the maximisation of a ranker's performance. Normalised Discounted Cumulative Gain (NDCG) and Mean Average Precision (MAP) have often been used to measure ranking performance [3].

Five ranking models are included: *k-NN* (the nearest neighbor-based approach), *RPC* (the pairwise binary classification approach), *BinaryART* (the ranking tree-based approach), *ARTForests* (the ranking forest-based approach), and *RegRanker* (the regression-based approach). Readers interested in the details of the rankers are referred to [23].

In this work, we apply *rank average*, a widely-used rank aggregation method from a number of state-of-the-art rankers to induce the final ranking function f. Experimentally we also observe that aggregation of such rankings usually leads to better and more stable ranking performance.

2.4   Invoking the Meta-reasoner R$_2$O$_2$

Once the rankers in RM are trained, for an unknown ontology, R$_2$O$_2$ combines the rankings estimated by different trained rankers in RM to produce a final ranking, and selects the best reasoner based on it, as given in Algorithm 1. A detailed description is provided below.

1. Given an unknown ontology o_t, R$_2$O$_2$ first calculates its values of ontology metrics in OM (line 1).
2. Initialise a variable *ranking* as a sequence of 0's, where the length of *ranking* is $|\hat{R}| = n$. Intuitively, *ranking* keeps a merged ranking list of n prediction models produced by the trained rankers in RM. For instance, for $n = 3$ prediction models (reasoners) $\hat{R} = \{\hat{r}_1, \hat{r}_2, \hat{r}_3\}$ with $RT(\hat{r}_1) < RT(\hat{r}_2) < RT(\hat{r}_3)$, *ranking* stores their current ranking, and is a permutation of $(1, 2, 3)$ (line 2).
3. For each ranker $rm_i \in RM$, R$_2$O$_2$ finds and merges the ranking of n prediction models. The merge operation is implemented as a pointwise summation of rankings produced by all rankers. For example, if $n = 3$ and

---

Algorithm 1. Predict the most efficient reasoner in R_2O_2.

Input: o_t a test ontology, $RM = \{rm_1, \ldots, rm_m\}$ the learned rankers,
   and $\Omega = \{R^2(\hat{r}_1), \ldots, R^2(\hat{r}_n)\}$ the R^2 values of prediction models in $\hat{R}$

Output: The most efficient reasoner r_{best} for ontology o_t

1 $om_t \leftarrow generateOntologyMetrics(o_t)$
2 $ranking \leftarrow (0, \ldots, 0)$
3 **foreach** $rm_i \in RM$ **do**
4 $\quad$ $ranking_i \leftarrow recommendRanking(rm_i, om_t)$
5 $\quad$ $ranking \leftarrow mergeRanking(ranking, ranking_i)$

6 **foreach** $\hat{r}_j \in \hat{R}$ **do**
7 $\quad$ $\pi(\hat{r}_j, o_t) \leftarrow averageRanking(ranking, |RM|, \hat{r}_j)$

8 $r_{bestCandidate} \leftarrow \arg\min_{\hat{r}_j \in \hat{R}} \pi(\hat{r}_j, o_t)$

9 **if** $(|r_{bestCandidate}| \geq 2)$ **then**
10 $\quad$ $r_{best} \leftarrow tieBreaking(r_{bestCandidate}, \Omega)$
11 **else**
12 $\quad$ $r_{best} \leftarrow r_{bestCandidate}$

13 **return** r_{best}

$ranking = (1, 1, 3)$ and a new ranking $(1, 2, 3)$ is produced by a ranker, then $ranking$ is merged as $(1, 1, 3) + (1, 2, 3) = (2, 3, 6)$ (lines 3-5).

4. For each prediction model $\hat{r}_j \in \hat{R}$, R_2O_2 computes its average ranking from the variable $ranking$ over $|RM|$ (lines 6-7). Then, R_2O_2 selects the prediction model(s) ($r_{bestCandidate}$) whose rank is the minimum. If only one top-ranked prediction model $\hat{r}_k \in \hat{R}$ is selected, the corresponding reasoner $r_k \in R$ is chosen to perform the reasoning task for o_t (line 12).

However, if two or more prediction models are selected, a tie-breaking method is applied to select one of them (line 10). This method takes into consideration the R^2 values of the prediction models that are described from Section 2.2. Our tie-breaking finds the best possible prediction model $\hat{r}_k$ by identifying the prediction model that is the most accurate:

$$\hat{r}_k = \arg\max_{\hat{r}_i \in \hat{R}} R^2(\hat{r}_i), \tag{3}$$

where we choose $\hat{r}_i$ that maximises its R^2 value $R^2(\hat{r}_i)$ (the higher the better). Finally, R_2O_2 determines $r_k \in R$ as $\hat{r}_{best}$, and invokes it to perform reasoning for the ontology o_t.

3 Evaluation

3.1 Data Collection

For this work, we collected ontologies from the ORE 2014 reasoner competition [1], comprising a total of 16,555 ontologies.[1] In our evaluation, we randomly choose 25% of the ORE 2014 dataset by splitting it into four groups by percentiles of file size; and randomly sampling from within these groups. This is to ensure that files of different sizes are sufficiently represented. As a result, 4,138 ontologies were eventually used in our evaluation.

Six state-of-the art OWL 2 DL reasoners that participated in ORE 2014 reasoner competition are used as component reasoners for R_2O_2: FaCT++ [25], HermiT [8], JFact,[2] Konclude [22], MORe [20] (with HermiT as the underlying OWL 2 DL reasoner), and TrOWL [24].[3] The versions of the reasoners are the same as those in ORE 2014. The competition framework is adapted to invoke the reasoners and to record their runtime.

The reasoning time (for consistency checking and classification) of each reasoner is measured for each ontology in the dataset on a high-performance server running OS Linux 2.6.18 and Java 1.6 on two dual-core AMD Opteron 2218 processors each at 2.6GHz, with a maximum of 10GB memory allocated to the reasoner. A timeout of one hour wall-time is imposed on each (reasoner, ontology) pair.

Of the 4,138 ontologies, 2,847 ontologies (which we denote by O in Section 2.1) are successfully reasoned by at least one reasoner (without errors and within the one-hour time limit). In O, 2,407 ontologies are successfully reasoned by all the six component reasoners, while the others encountered processing errors by at least one reasoner. These 2,407 common ontologies constitute the dataset O_c.

A 10-fold cross validation is employed to adequately assess the performance of R_2O_2. In each fold, O is split according to Section 2.1. In the experiment, each of O_{p_i}, O_r and O_t is approximately 40%, 50% and 10% of the size of O respectively. The performance evaluation results presented in the rest of this section is the average across the 10 folds.[4]

Note that TrOWL is an approximate reasoner, hence it is sound but incomplete. All the other five reasoners are sound and complete. As an approximate reasoner, TrOWL gains efficiency by sacrificing completeness. This results in significant performance gain, as can be seen in Table 1. Hence, to assess the impact of TrOWL's inclusion on R_2O_2's performance, we conduct two sets of experiments, one with TrOWL included and one without.

---

[1] http://www.easychair.org/smart-program/VSL2014/ORE-index.html

[2] http://jfact.sourceforge.net

[3] The Chainsaw reasoner [26] (an OWL 2 DL reasoner that participated in ORE 2014) is excluded due to reasoning errors in an excessive number of ontologies.

[4] Data associated with the evaluation can be found at http://www.csse.monash.edu.au/~yli/r2o2/.

3.2   Training R_2O_2

Training the Prediction Models. Using the 91 ontology metrics proposed previously [17,32] and dataset O_p, a performance prediction model is trained for each reasoner. Specifically, one Random Forest-based *regression model* (i.e., those in $\hat{R}$) is trained for each of the six reasoners (i.e., those in R). All the regression models in $\hat{R}$ are shown to be highly accurate, achieving high R^2 values that range from 0.73 (Konclude) to 0.91 (TrOWL).

Training the Ranking Models. Using the predicted reasoning time of the ontologies in O_r obtained from $\hat{R}$ as features, we trained five rankers (i.e., those in RM) specified in Section 2.2. The performance of each ranker is evaluated in terms of *precision at 1* (P@1). For a ranker, P@1 measures the proportion of the prediction model correctly ranked as the fastest. All rankers show high performance, achieving a P@1 between 88.7% and 90.6%.

3.3   Performance Evaluation of R_2O_2

We also employ P@1 as a performance metric for evaluating R_2O_2. For R_2O_2, P@1 measures the proportion of the component reasoner selected being the most efficient. We choose P@1 as we are only interested in evaluating how accurately R_2O_2 is able to recommend the single most efficient component reasoner, but not its ability to generate a total ranked list of the reasoners.

Besides the six component reasoners, we also compare R_2O_2 against a Portfolio-based reasoner (denoted PR) in the spirit of SATzilla [30] as well as the *virtual best reasoner* (denoted VBR), which always selects the most efficient component reasoner for any given ontology.

Table 1 and Table 2 show and compare the performance of R_2O_2 against all the other reasoners, across the 10 folds. TrOWL is in incomplete reasoner, and it gains efficiency by ignoring/approximating certain difficult language constructs. Two sets of experiments were conducted to assess the impact on performance of including TrOWL as a component reasoner in R_2O_2, one with TrOWL (Table 1) and one without (Table 2). For each reasoner r, three values are presented: (1) the average reasoning time per ontology (the lower the better), (2) the percentage of r being the most efficient (P@1, the higher the better), and (3) the average number of ontologies timed out on r (the lower the better) per fold. For R_2O_2, average ranking time per ontology is 0.03ms, trivial compared to reasoning time. For (1) and (2) above, the rank of each reasoner is also presented (the lower the better). As can be seen, in both experiments, R_2O_2 is the closest to VBR, and is more efficient than other reasoners with a speedup of up to 14x. It can also be observed that R_2O_2 times out on the smallest number of ontologies, which shows that R_2O_2 is not only efficient, its performance is also stable (less fluctuations).

It can be observed that Konclude dominates the other component reasoners, with a significantly faster reasoning time and a much larger percentage of being the fastest. However, R_2O_2 outperforms Konclude in both experiments, with a speedup of 1.48x and 1.46x respectively. This attests to the effectiveness of

Table 1. Performance comparison, with TrOWL included as a component reasoner, between reasoners for O_t on: (1) average reasoning time per ontology (in seconds) for O_t, (2) average percentage of ontology being the fatest (P@1), and (3) average number of timeout ontologies per fold. The best performance values (lower is better) are typeset in **bold**. For comparison purposes, performance figures for the virtual best reasoner (VBR) are also shown.

Reasoner	Runtime in seconds (rank)	% P@1 (rank)	No. timeout
FaCT++	108.05 (7)	5.49 (4)	6.4
HermiT	75.31 (6)	0.00 (8)	3.9
JFact	239.93 (8)	0.07 (7)	12.4
Konclude	26.00 (4)	90.85 (2)	1.5
MORe	39.01 (5)	2.32 (5)	2.2
TrOWL	21.50 (2)	1.37 (6)	**0.8**
PR	24.24 (3)	90.00 (3)	1.5
R$_2$O$_2$	**17.52 (1)**	**91.30 (1)**	1.0
VBR	2.94 (–)	–	0.0

Table 2. Performance comparison, excluding TrOWL, between reasoners for O_t on: (1) average reasoning time per ontology (in seconds) for O_t, (2) average percentage of ontology being the fatest (P@1), and (3) average number of timeout ontologies per fold. The best performance values (lower is better) are typeset in **bold**. For comparison purposes, performance figures for the virtual best reasoner (VBR) are also shown.

Reasoner	Runtime in seconds (rank)	% P@1 (rank)	No. timeout
FaCT++	116.32 (6)	6.16 (4)	6.9
HermiT	79.39 (5)	0.11 (7)	4.1
JFact	234.4 (7)	0.14 (6)	13.2
Konclude	24.01 (2)	91.76 (2)	1.5
MORe	48.78 (4)	2.29 (5)	3.0
PR	24.36 (3)	90.53 (3)	1.5
R$_2$O$_2$	**16.46 (1)**	**92.25 (1)**	0.9
VBR	7.52 (–)	–	0.3

R$_2$O$_2$'s approach: the combination of accurate performance prediction models and rankers successfully identifies the rare cases when another reasoner is faster than Konclude, and improves overall reasoning performance.

The evaluation also demonstrates the performance disparity among the reasoners. For example, JFact has the largest average runtime. However, it is the fastest for a small portion of ontologies, hence contributing to meta-reasoning. On the other hand, HermiT has a much smaller average runtime, but with less contribution to meta-reasoning. Moreover, even with a dominant reasoner such as Konclude, the other reasoners do outperform it sometimes (approximately 10%), and the performance of R$_2$O$_2$ as well as VBR validates the value of meta-reasoning: that the combination of reasoners indeed improves reasoning performance.

The effect of TrOWL is a little surprising. The performance of both PR and R_2O_2 remain relatively unchanged with or without the inclusion of TrOWL. However, VBR is significantly faster when TrOWL is included than when it is not, and it does not timeout on any ontology. It seems to suggest that TrOWL indeed reduces reasoning time for some hard ontologies. Further investigation is required to study the impact on reasoning performance and completeness.

To better assess reasoning performance, Figure 1 below shows a boxplot depicting the distributions of reasoning performance of the nine reasoners (including TrOWL and VBR). In a boxplot, the box itself contains the middle 50% of the values, the median (resp. mean) is represented by the horizontal bar (resp. '+') inside the box. The upper (resp. lower) whisker extends to the highest (resp. lowest) value within the upper (resp. lower) quartile. The reasoning time of all ontologies (across 10 folds) are also shown as dots in the plot to show their distributions. As can be seen, besides VBR, R_2O_2 has the lowest mean as well as median values, demonstrating its efficiency as well as stability.

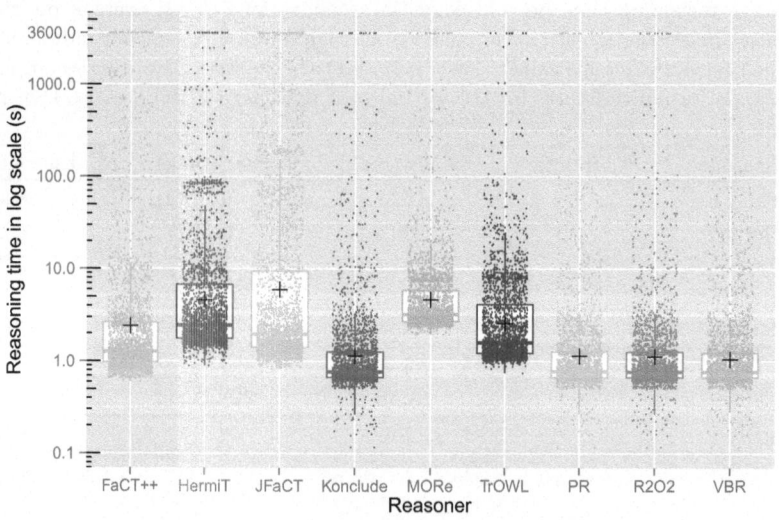

Fig. 1. A boxplot of the distributions of actual reasoning time (log-transformed) for the nine reasoners.

From Table 1 above, among the component reasoners, it seems that Konclude and TrOWL dominate the other component reasoners, as they are the fastest component reasoners and faster than the others by a large margin. It seems to make intuitive sense that they are the most efficient for most ontologies, and that R_2O_2 (and VBR) selects these two reasoners most of the time as the most efficient reasoner. However, this is not the case, as can be seen in Table 3 below. To better understand the reasoner selection based on performance, we discretise ontology reasoning time (in seconds) into four bins: 'A' (0, 1), 'B' [1, 10), 'C' [10, 100), and 'D' [100, 3,600]; and partition ontologies into these bins by their reasoning time by VBR. For brevity reasons only the figures for the experiment that includes TrOWL are shown. Note that in the training of R$_2$O$_2$, *actual*, but not discretised, reasoning is predicted.

Table 3. The percentage of each component reasoner being the most efficient reasoner (P@1=1) for each bin as well as for all the ontologies in O_t. The highest percentage in each bin is typeset in **bold**.

Reasoner	A	B	C	D	All
FaCT++	3.79	8.52	9.35	**50.00**	5.49
HermiT	0	0	0	0	0
JFaCT	0	0.25	0	0	0.07
Konclude	**96.21**	**86.22**	37.38	0.00	**90.85**
MORe	0.00	1.25	**48.60**	40.00	2.32
TrOWL	0.00	4.14	4.67	10.00	1.37

Table 3 shows the percentage each component reasoner being the most efficient (P@1=1) for ontologies in each bin and overall. A number of interesting observations can be made.

- Even though Konclude is the most efficient among the six reasoners, as can be seen in Table 1, Konclude does not dominate the other reasoners in bins 'C' and 'D', the bins for most difficult ontologies. Furthermore, even though Konclude has the fastest average runtime and overall P@1 value, it is not the fastest for any of the hardest ontologies (bin 'D').
- Even FaCT++ is only the fastest with a very small percentage overall (P@1=5.49%), it is the fastest for half of the most difficult ontologies (bin 'D').
- MORe has an even smaller percentage of being the fastest overall (P@1=2.32%), it is the fastest for 40% of the most difficult ontologies (bin 'D'). It is also the dominate reasoner for bin 'C'.

4   Related Work

Boolean satisfiability checking, or SAT, is a well-known and widely studied NP-complete decision problem. Many theoretical advances and practically useful heuristics have been developed over the past decades. However, it is recently recognised that the *empirical hardness* of NP-complete problems such as SAT [19, 28] is still not well understood, and that theoretical, worst-case complexity analysis does not always provide useful insights on hardness of real-world problem instances. Hence, more research is needed to understand the sources of instance hardness and reasons why certain optimisations are effective while others are not, given a specific problem instance.

Ontology reasoning tasks such as consistency checking is a type of hard decision problems that may go beyond NP-hard. For very expressive DLs, ontology reasoning has a very high worst-case complexity of 2NExpTime-complete [4]. The research community has recognised the importance of empirical studies given the rapid development in ontology reasoning optimisation.

Ontology reasoners have been repeatedly benchmarked over the years [2,5,7, 16]. It is observed from these benchmarking efforts that different reasoners have different levels of support, robustness and efficiency for ontologies with different features (e.g., language constructs used and their interactions), confirming the need for further investigation of sources of instance hardness.

Recently, the OWL Reasoner Evaluation (ORE) workshop series began an OWL reasoner competition [1,9] on a number of reasoning tasks (consistency checking, classification, and realisation) and for different profiles of the OWL language (OWL 2 DL and EL). The recent reasoner Konclude [22] is a novel parallellised OWL 2 DL reasoner. It is very efficient, significantly outperforming other reasoners in the latest ORE 2014 competition, winning 5 of the 6 categories. As part of the competition, the ontology corpus and the competition framework have been made publicly available, making it easy to reuse the data and to reproduce the results.

The empirical *robustness* of OWL reasoners was investigated [10]. A reasoner is said to be *successful* for a given ontology if it successfully loads the ontology and performs reasoning within a specified timeout cutoff (e.g., two hours). A reasoner is *robust* if it is successful for at least 90% of a given corpus. Experiments on 4 OWL reasoners and three corpora of ontologies revealed that the *best combo*, the virtual best reasoner (or the meta-reasoner), is "extremely robust over all corpora" [10], achieving an overall robustness of over 98% for all three corpora. However, such a meta-reasoner was only identified manually and *post festum*.

Inspired by the success of empirical software engineering research, we proposed a number of metrics to measure the design complexity of ontologies [32]. These metrics measure various aspects of complexity: overall complexity of the ontology, complexity of classes and properties, as well as those characterising complex class and property expressions.

We studied the problem of estimating ontology reasoning time by applying machine learning techniques to building classifiers [15] and regression models [17] to estimate (discretised or actual) reasoning time of a given (ontology, reasoner) pair. High accuracy was achieved in both approaches, which were used to identify important features that affect performance the most, and to identify performance hotspots efficiently. An ontology is represented by a number of syntactic and structural metrics that are efficient to calculate. These metrics are used as features to train classifiers and regression models, one for each reasoner.

A different, *local*, reasoning performance prediction method was proposed in [21]. It decomposes an ontology into smaller subsets with increasing sizes, and then extrapolates their performance to the entire ontology. The local approach does not require a corpus, but instead does require repeated reasoner invocations over ontology subsets. Using the k-NN classifier as a baseline, it was observed that using only one metric, number of axioms, the local approach achieves comparable classification performance with [15]. The local prediction approach can be regarded as an *online* prediction approach as it needs to invoke reasoners on the subsets of growing sizes, whereas [15,17] as well as this work are *offline*.

Understanding empirical hardness of ontologies has also garnered attention in recent years. The identification of sources of ontologies in terms of *performance hotspots* was investigated [11,17], where hotspots are found in a number of hard biomedical ontologies. The removal of such hotspots dramatically reduces the reasoning time of the remaining ontology. However, as a result, reasoning soundness and completeness cannot be guaranteed.

Portfolio-based algorithm selection [13] has been successfully applied to combinatorial optimisation and constraint satisfaction problems. SATzilla [30], for instance, a portfolio SAT solver, has demonstrated higher efficiency over single solvers. Compared to ontology languages OWL and OWL 2, k-SAT instances are described by a simpler language, whereas OWL and OWL 2 contain many more language constructs (various class expressions, property expressions and axioms). The richness of the ontology languages make it difficult to define features to sufficiently describe characteristics of ontologies. Moreover, SATzilla does not employ a ranking component but solely relies on prediction models. Evaluation in Section 3 above shows that R$_2$O$_2$ outperforms a SATzilla-style portfolio reasoner, demonstrating the advantages of integrating a ranking component.

Recently, preference learning [6] has been shown to be effective for developing meta-learners with an aim to predicting the most efficient algorithm from a few promising ones on different types of datasets such as those represented using meta-features [23] and data streams [27]. In these studies, preference learning has been demonstrated to significantly reduce optimisation time needed for choosing a best model on a given dataset.

Often, ranking algorithms in preference learning use machine learning approaches by analysing the association information between characteristics of a given dataset (in our context, ontology metrics) and the relative performance of the available algorithms. Such ranking algorithms include the algorithms proposed in [23] such as the nearest neighbour-based approach, the pairwise binary classification approach, the regression-based approach, the ranking tree-based approach and the ranking forest-based approach. Also, the learning-to-rank approach [29] and the label ranking approach [12] have been shown to be used for preference learning. In R$_2$O$_2$, we utilise some of the ranking algorithms introduced in [23] to predict the most efficient reasoners for a set of new ontologies. The incorporation of such a ranking component demonstrably improves reasoning efficiency.

5   Conclusions

In this paper, we present R_2O_2, a novel meta-reasoner that combines component reasoners in an efficient way, by automatically selecting the reasoner that is most likely the most efficient for any given ontology. A key novel feature of our approach is the incorporation of reasoner ranking to determine the best component reasoner according to their predicted reasoning time. Another important feature is the use of prediction models for ontology reasoners for estimating reasoning time. The performance of R_2O_2 is further improved by the incorporation of the *second-order* prediction (ranking), as compared to the traditional portfolio-based meta-reasoning approach.

Our comprehensive, large-scale evaluation involving more than 4,000 ontologies and 6 state-of-the-art OWL 2 DL reasoners—including the currently dominant reasoner Konclude—demonstrates the superiority of our meta-reasoner, in both efficiency and stability. A speedup of up to 14x is achieved, with a 1.4x speedup over Konclude. We show that R_2O_2 achieves significant efficiency improvements over the 6 component reasoners, as well as a SATzilla-style portfolio reasoner with a 1.5x speedup.

In future we will investigate novel prediction models and ranking models to further improve their accuracy, as well as the performance of R_2O_2. We will study the effectiveness of incorporting additional efficient reasoners such as ELK [18] that provide efficient reasoning support of less expressive DLs. Moreover, we will also investigate sources of instance hardness by studying similarity of ontologies that have similar performance for a given reasoner.

Acknowledgments. We thank Andreas Steigmiller for his kind and timely assistance in helping us set up the ORE 2014 reasoner competition framework in our evaluation.

References

1. Bail, S., Glimm, B., Jiménez-Ruiz, E., Matentzoglu, N., Parsia, B., Steigmiller, A.: Summary ore 2014 competition. In: Proceedings of the 3rd International Workshop on OWL Reasoner Evaluation (ORE 2014), vol. 1207, pp. iv–vii. CEUR Workshop Proceedings (2014)
2. Bock, J., Haase, P., Ji, Q., Volz, R.: Benchmarking OWL reasoners. In: ARea2008 - Workshop on Advancing Reasoning on the Web: Scalability and Commonsense, June 2008
3. Chen, W., Liu, T.-Y., Lan, Y., Ma, Z., Li, H.: Ranking measures and loss functions in learning to rank. In: 23rd Annual Conference on Neural Information Processing Systems (NIPS 2009), pp. 315–323. Curran Associates Inc. (2009)
4. Grau, B.C., Horrocks, I., Motik, B., Parsia, B., Patel-Schneider, P., Sattler, U.: OWL 2: The next step for OWL. Journal of Web Semantics: Science, Services and Agents on the World Wide Web **6**, 309–322 (2008)
5. Dentler, K., Cornet, R., ten Teije, A., de Keizer, N.: Comparison of reasoners for large ontologies in the OWL 2 EL profile. Semantic Web Journal **2**(2), 71–87 (2011)
6. Fründkranz, J., Hüllermeier, E.: Preference Learning, 1st edn. Springer-Verlag New York Inc., New York (2010)

7. Gardiner, T., Tsarkov, D., Horrocks, I.: Framework for an automated comparison of description logic reasoners. In: Cruz, I., Decker, S., Allemang, D., Preist, C., Schwabe, D., Mika, P., Uschold, M., Aroyo, L.M. (eds.) ISWC 2006. LNCS, vol. 4273, pp. 654–667. Springer, Heidelberg (2006)
8. Glimm, B., Horrocks, I., Motik, B., Stoilos, G., Wang, Z.: Hermit: An owl 2 reasoner. J. Autom. Reason. **53**(3), 245–269 (2014)
9. Gonçalves, R.S., Bail, S., Jiménez-Ruiz, E., Matentzoglu, N., Parsia, B., Glimm, B., Kazakov, Y.: OWL reasoner evaluation (ORE) workshop 2013 results: short report. In: 2nd International Workshop on OWL Reasoner Evaluation (ORE-2013), vol. 1015, pp. 1–18. CEUR Workshop Proceedings (2013)
10. Gonçalves, R.S., Matentzoglu, N., Parsia, B., Sattler, U.: The empirical robustness of description logic classification. In: Description Logics, vol. 1014, pp. 197–208. CEUR Workshop Proceedings (2013)
11. Gonçalves, R.S., Parsia, B., Sattler, U.: Performance heterogeneity and approximate reasoning in description logic ontologies. In: Cudré-Mauroux, P., et al. (eds.) ISWC 2012, Part I. LNCS, vol. 7649, pp. 82–98. Springer, Heidelberg (2012)
12. Hüllermeier, E., Fürnkranz, J., Cheng, W., Brinker, K.: Label ranking by learning pairwise preferences. Artif. Intell. **172**(16–17), 1897–1916 (2008)
13. Hutter, F., Xu, L., Hoos, H.H., Leyton-Brown, K.: Algorithm runtime prediction: Methods & evaluation. Artif. Intell. **206**, 79–111 (2014)
14. Kang, Y.-B., Krishnaswamy, S., Li, Y.-F.: A meta-reasoner to rule them all: Automated selection of OWL reasoners based on efficiency. In: 23rd ACM International Conference on Conference on Information and Knowledge Management (CIKM 2014), New York, NY, USA, pp. 1935–1938. ACM (2014)
15. Kang, Y.-B., Li, Y.-F., Krishnaswamy, S.: Predicting reasoning performance using ontology metrics. In: Cudré-Mauroux, P., et al. (eds.) ISWC 2012, Part I. LNCS, vol. 7649, pp. 198–214. Springer, Heidelberg (2012)
16. Kang, Y.-B., Li, Y.-F., Krishnaswamy, S.: A rigorous characterization of reasoning performance - a tale of four reasoners. In: Proceedings of the 1st International Workshop on OWL Reasoner Evaluation (ORE-2012), June 2012
17. Kang, Y.-B., Pan, J.Z., Krishnaswamy, S., Sawangphol, W., Li, Y.-F.: How long will it take? accurate prediction of ontology reasoning performance. In: AAAI, pp. 80–86. AAAI Press (2014)
18. Kazakov, Y., Krötzsch, M., Simancik, F.: The incredible ELK - from polynomial procedures to efficient reasoning with $\mathcal{EL}$ ontologies. J. Autom. Reasoning **53**(1), 1–61 (2014)
19. Leyton-Brown, K., Hoos, H.H., Hutter, F., Xu, L.: Understanding the empirical hardness of NP-complete problems. Commun. ACM **57**(5), 98–107 (2014)
20. Romero, A.A., Grau, B.C., Horrocks, I.: MORe: modular combination of OWL reasoners for ontology classification. In: Cudré-Mauroux, P., et al. (eds.) ISWC 2012, Part I. LNCS, vol. 7649, pp. 1–16. Springer, Heidelberg (2012)
21. Sazonau, V., Sattler, U., Brown, G.: Predicting OWL reasoners: locally or globally? In: 27th International Workshop on Description Logics, vol. 1193, pp. 713–724. CEUR Workshop Proceedings (2014)
22. Steigmiller, A., Liebig, T., Glimm, B.: Konclude: System description. J. Web Sem. **27**, 78–85 (2014)
23. Sun, Q., Pfahringer, B.: Pairwise meta-rules for better meta-learning-based algorithm ranking. Machine Learning **93**(1), 141–161 (2013)

24. Thomas, E., Pan, J.Z., Ren, Y.: TrOWL: tractable OWL 2 reasoning infrastructure. In: Aroyo, L., Antoniou, G., Hyvönen, E., ten Teije, A., Stuckenschmidt, H., Cabral, L., Tudorache, T. (eds.) ESWC 2010, Part II. LNCS, vol. 6089, pp. 431–435. Springer, Heidelberg (2010)
25. Tsarkov, D., Horrocks, I.: FaCT + + description logic reasoner: system description. In: Furbach, U., Shankar, N. (eds.) IJCAR 2006. LNCS (LNAI), vol. 4130, pp. 292–297. Springer, Heidelberg (2006)
26. Tsarkov, D., Palmisano, I.: Chainsaw: a metareasoner for large ontologies. In: 1st International Workshop on OWL Reasoner Evaluation (ORE-2012), vol. 858. CEUR Workshop Proceedings (2012)
27. van Rijn, J.N., Holmes, G., Pfahringer, B., Vanschoren, J.: Algorithm selection on data streams. In: Džeroski, S., Panov, P., Kocev, D., Todorovski, L. (eds.) DS 2014. LNCS, vol. 8777, pp. 325–336. Springer, Heidelberg (2014)
28. Vardi, M.Y.: Boolean satisfiability: Theory and engineering. Commun. ACM **57**(3), 5 (2014)
29. Xu, J., Li, H.: Adarank: a boosting algorithm for information retrieval. In: 30th International ACM Conference on Research and Development in Information Retrieval, SIGIR 2007, New York, NY, USA, pp. 391–398. ACM (2007)
30. Xu, L., Hutter, F., Hoos, H.H., Leyton-Brown, K.: SATzilla-07: the design and analysis of an algorithm portfolio for SAT. In: Bessière, C. (ed.) CP 2007. LNCS, vol. 4741, pp. 712–727. Springer, Heidelberg (2007)
31. Xu, L., Hutter, F., Hoos, H.H., Leyton-Brown, K.: SATzilla: Portfolio-based algorithm selection for SAT. J. Artif. Int. Res. **32**(1), 565–606 (2008)
32. Zhang, H., Li, Y.-F., Tan, H.B.K.: Measuring design complexity of Semantic Web ontologies. Journal of Systems and Software **83**(5), 803–814 (2010)

Rewriting-Based Instance Retrieval for Negated Concepts in Description Logic Ontologies

Jianfeng Du[1]([✉]) and Jeff Z. Pan[2]

[1] Guangdong University of Foreign Studies, Guangzhou 510006, China
jfdu@gdufs.edu.cn
[2] The University of Aberdeen, Aberdeen AB24 3UE, UK

Abstract. Instance retrieval computes all instances of a given concept in a consistent description logic (DL) ontology. Although it is a popular task for ontology reasoning, there is no scalable method for instance retrieval for negated concepts by now. This paper studies a new approach to instance retrieval for negated concepts based on query rewriting. A class of DL ontologies called the *inconsistency-based first-order rewritable* (*IFO-rewritable*) class is identified. This class guarantees that instance retrieval for an atomic negation can be reduced to answering a disjunction of conjunctive queries (CQs) over the ABox. The IFO-rewritable class is more expressive than the first-order rewritable class which guarantees that answering a CQ is reducible to answering a disjunction of CQs over the ABox regardless of the TBox. Two sufficient conditions are proposed to detect IFO-rewritable ontologies that are not first-order rewritable. A rewriting-based method for retrieving instances of a negated concept is proposed for IFO-rewritable ontologies. Preliminary experimental results on retrieving instances of all atomic negations show that this method is significantly more efficient than existing methods implemented in state-of-the-art DL systems.

1 Introduction

Description logics (DLs) [2] are popular knowledge representation languages underpinning the Web Ontology Language (OWL). A DL ontology consists of a TBox and an ABox, where the TBox describes relations between concepts and roles, and the ABox describes instances of concepts and roles. DLs enable a number of tasks for ontology reasoning based on the classical first-order semantics. Among these tasks, instance retrieval is a popular one which computes all individuals in a consistent DL ontology that are instances of a given concept.

Most studies on instance retrieval focus on atomic concepts, namely concept names. It is well-known that instance retrieval for atomic concepts is tractable for those DLs that underpin the three profiles QL, EL and RL of OWL 2, the newest version of OWL. There have also been optimization and approximation techniques proposed for instance retrieval in expressive DLs [13,17,21]. However, to the best of our knowledge, there is seldom any dedicated study on instance retrieval for negated concepts. A negated concept is of the form $\neg C$ where C is

© Springer International Publishing Switzerland 2015
M. Arenas et al. (Eds.): ISWC 2015, Part I, LNCS 9366, pp. 339–355, 2015.
DOI: 10.1007/978-3-319-25007-6_20

a DL concept without the negation symbol ¬. In the reality, it is often required to compute instances of a negated concept. For example, one may often raise questions like the following ones upon a DL ontology describing people in universities: Who is not an undergraduate? Who does not have a friend who is a professor? Who does not get a PhD degree from a Chinese university?

According to the semantics of DLs, the set of instances of a negated concept $\neg C$ cannot be returned as the set of those instances explicitly declared in the given ontology, nor the complement set of the set of instances of C. A common sound and complete method for instance retrieval for $\neg C$ is to reduce the problem to instance retrieval for P_C, where P_C is a fresh atomic concept, by adding an axiom $\neg C \sqsubseteq P_C$ to the TBox. This method is commonly implemented in state-of-the-art DL systems. However, the added axiom $\neg C \sqsubseteq P_C$ introduces concept disjunctions and cannot be expressed in DLs that guarantee tractable instance retrieval. To guarantee tractability, one may apply another method which retrieves all instances of $\neg C$ by checking if $\{C(a)\}$ is consistent with the given ontology for every individual a in the ontology. However, this method is hardly scalable for large DL ontologies with many individuals.

Inspired by the successful query rewriting approach to ontology reasoning (see e.g. [5,7]), we solve the problem of instance retrieval for negated concepts from a new perspective, i.e., by query rewriting. There are some challenges in making use of query rewriting. First of all, existing query rewriting methods are designed for conjunctive queries (CQs) but not for negated concepts. It requires us to establish a connection between negated concepts and CQs. More importantly, it is required that the applicable DLs be as expressive as possible.

In this paper we tackle all the above challenges and make the following contributions. Firstly, we identify a class of DL ontologies, called the *inconsistency-based first-order rewritable* (*IFO-rewritable*) class, which guarantees that instance retrieval for an atomic negation is reducible to answering a disjunction of CQs over the ABox. The class is characterized by an *inconsistency-rewritten set* of Boolean conjunctive queries (BCQs) whose size is finite and independent of the ABox. From an inconsistency-rewritten set S of BCQs for an atomic concept A, we can extract a disjunction of CQs $Q_D(x)$ in time linear in the size of S such that the set of instances of $\neg A$ is the set of answers of $Q_D(x)$ in the ABox.

Secondly, we show that the IFO-rewritable class is more expressive than the first-order rewritable class, where the latter is commonly used in query rewriting and guarantees that answering a CQ is reducible to answering a disjunction of CQs over the ABox. We propose two sufficient conditions for detecting IFO-rewritable ontologies that are not first-order rewritable. One condition relies on extracting first-order rewritable subsets of the given ontology and can be checked regardless of the ABox in time polynomial in the size of the TBox. The other condition is applicable to the DL $\mathcal{ELR}_\perp$ and can be checked in time polynomial in the size of the ABox by considering certain subgraphs of the ABox graph.

Finally, we conduct experiments on large first-order rewritable ontologies to demonstrate the advantages of exploiting inconsistency-rewritten sets of BCQs to retrieve instances of atomic negations. We compare this proposed method with the two aforementioned methods for instance retrieval for atomic negations. Experimental results obtained by several state-of-the-art DL systems show that the proposed method is significantly more efficient than the two aforementioned methods in retrieving instances of all atomic negations. Moreover, among all compared methods only the proposed one is scalable for large ontologies with tens of millions of assertions. All proofs are available at http://www.dataminingcenter.net/rebsir/ISWC15-full.pdf.

2   Preliminaries

We assume that the reader is familiar with DLs [2]. A DL ontology consists of a TBox and an ABox, where the TBox is a finite set of axioms on relations between concepts and roles, and the ABox is a finite set of assertions declaring instances of concepts and roles. In this work we only consider *normalized* ABoxes. An ABox is said to be *normalized* if it consists of *basic assertions* that are concept assertions of the form $A(a)$ or role assertions of the form $r(a,b)$, where A is an atomic concept, r is an atomic role, and a and b are individuals. Other concept assertions and role assertions can be normalized to basic ones in a standard way. For a normalized ABox $\mathcal{A}$, let $\mathsf{Ind}(\mathcal{A})$ denote the set of individuals appearing $\mathcal{A}$ and $\mathsf{Cn}(\mathcal{A})$ the set of atomic concepts appearing in $\mathcal{A}$.

The semantics of DLs coincides with the classical first-order semantics. A DL ontology $\mathcal{O}$ is said to be *consistent*, denoted by $\mathcal{O} \not\models \bot$, if it has at least one model, otherwise *inconsistent*, denoted by $\mathcal{O} \models \bot$. An ABox $\mathcal{A}$ is said to be *consistent with* a TBox $\mathcal{T}$ if $\mathcal{T} \cup \mathcal{A}$ is consistent. An individual a is said to be an *instance* of a concept C in $\mathcal{O}$ if the concept assertion $C(a)$ is satisfied by all models of $\mathcal{O}$, denoted by $\mathcal{O} \models C(a)$. The problem of *instance retrieval* for C in $\mathcal{O}$ is to compute the set of instances of C in $\mathcal{O}$.

A *conjunctive query* (CQ) $Q(\boldsymbol{x})$ is a formula of the form $\exists \boldsymbol{y}\, \phi(\boldsymbol{x}, \boldsymbol{y})$, where $\phi(\boldsymbol{x}, \boldsymbol{y})$ is a conjunction of atoms over atomic concepts, atomic roles and the (in)equality predicate, $\boldsymbol{x}$ are *answer variables*, and $\boldsymbol{y}$ are *quantified variables*. A CQ without answer variables is called a *Boolean conjunctive query* (BCQ). Here a BCQ is written and treated as a set of atoms. For example, the BCQ $\exists x\, A(x) \wedge B(x)$ is written as $\{A(x), B(x)\}$. A *disjunction* of CQs, also called a *union* of CQs or a *UCQ* in the literature, is a formula of the form $Q_1(\boldsymbol{x}) \vee \ldots \vee Q_n(\boldsymbol{x})$ where $n \geq 1$ and $Q_1(\boldsymbol{x}), \ldots, Q_n(\boldsymbol{x})$ are CQs. We say a disjunction of BCQs Q_D is *entailed by* $\mathcal{O}$, denoted by $\mathcal{O} \models Q_D$, if Q_D is satisfied by all models of $\mathcal{O}$. A tuple $\boldsymbol{t}$ of individuals is called an *answer* to a disjunction of CQs $Q_D(\boldsymbol{x})$ in an ontology $\mathcal{O}$ if $\mathcal{O} \models Q_D(\boldsymbol{t})$, where $Q_D(\boldsymbol{t})$ is a disjunction of BCQs obtained from $Q(\boldsymbol{x})$ by replacing variables in $\boldsymbol{x}$ with corresponding individuals in $\boldsymbol{t}$. The set of answers to $Q_D(\boldsymbol{x})$ in $\mathcal{O}$ is denoted by $\mathsf{ans}(\mathcal{O}, Q_D(\boldsymbol{x}))$. For a disjunction of BCQs Q_D, $\mathsf{ans}(\mathcal{O}, Q_D) = \{\langle\rangle\}$ if $\mathcal{O} \models Q_D$, or $\mathsf{ans}(\mathcal{O}, Q_D) = \emptyset$ otherwise.

Datalog$^{\pm}$ [4] is highly related to DLs. It extends datalog with existential rules, which are formulae of the form $\forall \boldsymbol{x} \forall \boldsymbol{y}\, \phi(\boldsymbol{x}, \boldsymbol{y}) \rightarrow \exists \boldsymbol{z}\, \varphi(\boldsymbol{x}, \boldsymbol{z})$, where $\phi(\boldsymbol{x}, \boldsymbol{y})$ and $\varphi(\boldsymbol{x}, \boldsymbol{z})$ are conjunctions of atoms (often treated as sets of atoms), and $\boldsymbol{x}$,

y and z are pairwise disjoint sets of variables. The part of R at left-hand side of $\rightarrow$ is the *body* of R, whereas the part of R at right-hand side of $\rightarrow$ is the *head* of R. An existential rule R is called an *equality generating dependency* (*EGD*) if the head of R is of the form $x_1 = x_2$ where x_1 and x_2 are different variables appearing in the body of R; called a *constraint* if the head of R is empty; otherwise, called a *tuple generating dependency* (*TGD*). A TGD is said to be *linear* if its body contains a single atom; *multi-linear* if all atoms in its body have the same variables. A linear TGD is also a multi-linear TGD.

A datalog$^\pm$ program is a finite set of existential rules, amounting to the conjunction of all existential rules in it. Since existential rules are formulae in first-order logic with equality, a TBox expressed in some DLs can be translated to a datalog$^\pm$ program. It follows that an ontology expressed in some DLs can be translated to the union of a datalog$^\pm$ program and a normalized ABox. We call such an ontology *datalog$^\pm$-translatable*. For a datalog$^\pm$-translatable ontology with TBox $\mathcal{T}$, throughout this paper we use $\mathcal{S}_{\mathcal{T}}^D$ to denote the set of TGDs translated from $\mathcal{T}$, $\mathcal{S}_{\mathcal{T}}^C$ to denote the set of constraints translated from $\mathcal{T}$, and $\mathcal{S}_{\mathcal{T}}^E$ to denote the set of EGDs translated from $\mathcal{T}$. Since datalog$^\pm$ works with the *unique name assumption*, this assumption is also adopted in an arbitrary datalog$^\pm$-translatable ontology, which means that all individuals appearing in the ontology are interpreted as different in any model of the ontology.

By $|S|$ we denote the cardinality of a set S. A *substitution* for a first-order entity (such as atom, formula, etc.) E is a mapping from variables in E to individuals or variables; it is *ground* if it maps variables in E to individuals only.

We recall the notions of first-order rewritability and separability in the context of DLs [4]. A set $\mathcal{S}^D$ of TGDs is said to be *first-order rewritable* if, for every conjunctive query $Q(\boldsymbol{x})$, there exists a finite disjunction of conjunctive queries $Q_D(\boldsymbol{x})$ such that $\mathsf{ans}(\mathcal{S}^D \cup \mathcal{A}, Q(\boldsymbol{x})) = \mathsf{ans}(\mathcal{A}, Q_D(\boldsymbol{x}))$ for all ABoxes $\mathcal{A}$. It has been shown [4] that a set $\mathcal{S}^D$ of TGDs is first-order rewritable if all TGDs in $\mathcal{S}^D$ are multi-linear. A set $\mathcal{S}^E$ of EGDs is said to be *separable* from a set $\mathcal{S}^D$ of TGDs if the following holds for every ABox $\mathcal{A}$: if there exists an EGD $\forall \boldsymbol{x}\, \phi(\boldsymbol{x}) \rightarrow x_1 = x_2$ in $\mathcal{S}^E$ and a ground substitution σ for $\boldsymbol{x}$ such that $\mathcal{S}^D \cup \mathcal{A} \models \phi(\boldsymbol{x}\sigma)$ and $x_1\sigma \neq x_2\sigma$, then there is a ground substitution θ for $\boldsymbol{x}$ such that $\mathcal{A} \models \phi(\boldsymbol{x}\theta)$ and $x_1\theta \neq x_2\theta$; otherwise, $\mathcal{S}^D \cup \mathcal{S}^E \cup \mathcal{A} \models Q$ if and only if $\mathcal{S}^D \cup \mathcal{A} \models Q$ for all BCQs Q. It has been shown [4] that deciding if $\mathcal{S}^D \cup \mathcal{S}^C \cup \mathcal{S}^E \cup \mathcal{A} \models Q$ for a first-order rewritable set $\mathcal{S}^D$ of TGDs, a set $\mathcal{S}^C$ of constraints, a set $\mathcal{S}^E$ of EGDs separable from $\mathcal{S}^D$, an ABox $\mathcal{A}$ and a BCQ Q is in AC^0 in *data complexity*, the complexity measured in the size of $\mathcal{A}$ only.

3 Rewriting-Based Instance Retrieval

Query rewriting is an efficient and scalable approach to reasoning over ontologies that are expressed in lightweight DLs and have large ABoxes. The idea is to rewrite a given CQ into a disjunction of CQs or a datalog program such that the given CQ can be answering by evaluating the rewriting result over the ABox only. Query rewriting has been implemented in modern DL systems such as

Rapid [7] and MASTRO [5]. To enable query rewriting for all CQs, we require that the back-end ontology be *first-order rewritable* based on the first-order rewritable class of TGDs. We call a DL ontology $\mathcal{O}$ with TBox $\mathcal{T}$ *first-order rewritable* if it is a datalog$^\pm$-translatable ontology such that $\mathcal{S}_\mathcal{T}^D$ is first-order rewritable, $\mathcal{S}_\mathcal{T}^E$ is separable from $\mathcal{S}_\mathcal{T}^D$ and $\mathcal{S}_\mathcal{T}^C$ can be arbitrary. It has been shown [4] that most DLs in the DL-Lite family [6], such as DL-Lite$_X$ and DL-Lite$_{X,\sqcap}$ for $X \in \{\mathcal{F}, \mathcal{R}, \mathcal{A}\}$, express first-order rewritable ontologies, where DL-Lite$_\mathcal{R}$ underpins the QL profile of OWL 2.

Inspired by the exciting progress on query rewriting, we intend to solve the problem of instance retrieval for negated concepts by exploiting query rewriting. As mentioned in Section 1, there are challenges in making use of query rewriting, including the establishment of a bridge from negated concepts to CQs and the guarantee of the expressivity for applicable DLs. To tackle these challenges, we start with the study on instance retrieval for atomic negations.

Given a consistent DL ontology $\mathcal{O}$ with ABox $\mathcal{A}$ and an atomic negation $\neg A$, the basic idea for instance retrieval for $\neg A$ in $\mathcal{O}$ is to compute a disjunction of CQs $Q_D(x)$ such that the set of answers to $Q_D(x)$ in $\mathcal{A}$ amounts to the set of instances of $\neg A$ in $\mathcal{O}$. To compute $Q_D(x)$, we first compute a set $\mathcal{S}$ of BCQs, each of which is entailed by $\mathcal{A} \cup \{A(a)\}$ for some instance a of $\neg A$ in $\mathcal{O}$, and then construct $Q_D(x)$ from $\mathcal{S}$. We call the set of BCQs computed in the first step an *inconsistency-rewritten set*, which is formally defined below.

Definition 1. *Given an atomic concept A and a consistent DL ontology $\mathcal{O}$ with ABox $\mathcal{A}$, a set $\mathcal{S}$ of BCQs is called an* inconsistency-rewritten set *for A in $\mathcal{O}$ if $\mathcal{S}$ has a finite size that is independent of the size of $\mathcal{A}$, $\mathcal{A} \not\models \bigvee \mathcal{S}$, and for all individuals a in $\mathcal{O}$, $\mathcal{O} \cup \{A(a)\} \models \perp$ if and only if $\mathcal{A} \cup \{A(a)\} \models \bigvee \mathcal{S}$. $\mathcal{O}$ is said to be* inconsistency-based first-order rewritable *(simply IFO-rewritable) for A, if there is an inconsistency-rewritten set of BCQs for A in $\mathcal{O}$.*

The IFO-rewritable class is characterized by inconsistency-rewritten sets of BCQs. Note that all BCQs considered in this paper do not contain individuals. After an inconsistency-rewritten set $\mathcal{S}$ of BCQs for A is computed, the set of instances of $\neg A$ in an IFO-rewritable ontology $\mathcal{O}$ for A can be computed as the set of answers to a disjunction of CQs $Q_D(x)$ in the ABox $\mathcal{A}$ of $\mathcal{O}$, where $Q_D(x)$ is extracted from $\mathcal{S}$ by separating an atom over A from the other atoms in every BCQ in $\mathcal{S}$. We introduce some notations to explain this method. Given a set $\mathcal{S}$ of BCQs and an atomic concept A, we call the set of BCQs in $\mathcal{S}$ that contain at least one atom over A the *A-projection* of $\mathcal{S}$, denoted by $\mathcal{S}|_A$. For a BCQ Q that has some atoms over A, we call a pair $\langle A(t), Q' \rangle$ for t a variable an *A-bipartition* of Q if $Q' \cup \{A(t)\} = Q$ and $A(t) \notin Q'$. By bipart(Q, A) we denote the set of A-bipartitions of Q. Let $\varrho_{\mathcal{S},A}(z) = \bigvee\{Q'[t/z] \mid Q \in \mathcal{S}|_A, \langle A(t), Q' \rangle \in \text{bipart}(Q, A)\}$, where $Q'[t/z]$ denotes the CQ obtained from Q' by renaming t to z, and z does not occur in $\mathcal{S}$ and is the unique answer variable in $Q'[t/z]$. The following theorem shows a method for extracting a disjunction of CQs from an inconsistency-rewritten set of BCQs.

Theorem 1. *Let A be an atomic concept, $\mathcal{O}$ an IFO-rewritable ontology for A with TBox $\mathcal{T}$ and ABox $\mathcal{A}$, and $\mathcal{S}$ an inconsistency-rewritten set of BCQs for A in $\mathcal{O}$. Then the set of instances of $\neg A$ in $\mathcal{O}$ is $\mathsf{ans}(\mathcal{A}, \varrho_{\mathcal{S},A}(z))$.*

Note that the disjunction of CQs computed by the above method is independent of the size of the ABox. It follows that checking an instance of a given atomic negation in an IFO-rewritable ontology can be done in AC^0 in data complexity.

Example 1. This example illustrates how to retrieve instances of an atomic negation $\neg A$ in an IFO-rewritable ontology for A after an inconsistency-rewritten set of BCQs for A is computed. Let $\mathcal{O}$ be a consistent DL ontology with TBox $\mathcal{T}$ and ABox $\mathcal{A}$. The TBox $\mathcal{T}$ consists of the following three axioms.

$$\mathsf{Husband} \sqsubseteq \exists \mathsf{marries}.\mathsf{Woman} \qquad \top \sqsubseteq_{\leq 1} \mathsf{marries}.\top \qquad \exists \mathsf{marries}.\mathsf{Woman} \sqsubseteq \neg \mathsf{Woman}$$

The ABox $\mathcal{A}$ consists of the following four assertions.

$$\mathsf{marries}(\mathsf{Tom}, \mathsf{Ann}) \qquad \mathsf{Woman}(\mathsf{Ann}) \qquad \mathsf{marries}(\mathsf{Aba}, \mathsf{Bob}) \qquad \mathsf{Woman}(\mathsf{Aba})$$

Consider computing all instances of $\neg\mathsf{Woman}$ in $\mathcal{O}$. By Definition 1 it can be checked that $\mathcal{S} = \{Q_1, Q_2, Q_3\}$ is an inconsistency-rewritten set of BCQs for Woman in $\mathcal{O}$, where $Q_1 = \{\mathsf{marries}(x, y), \mathsf{Woman}(y), \mathsf{Woman}(x)\}$, $Q_2 = \{\mathsf{Husband}(x), \mathsf{Woman}(x)\}$, and $Q_3 = \{\mathsf{marries}(x, y_1), \mathsf{marries}(x, y_2), y_1 \neq y_2\}$. We have $\mathcal{S}|_{\mathsf{Woman}} = \{Q_1, Q_2\}$. The disjunction of CQs extracted from $\mathcal{S}|_{\mathsf{Woman}}$ is $\varrho_{\mathcal{S},\mathsf{Woman}}(z) = (\exists y\, \mathsf{marries}(z, y) \wedge \mathsf{Woman}(y)) \vee (\exists x\, \mathsf{marries}(x, z) \wedge \mathsf{Woman}(x)) \vee \mathsf{Husband}(z)$. The set of answers to $\varrho_{\mathcal{S},\mathsf{Woman}}(z)$ in $\mathcal{A}$ is $\mathcal{S} = \{\mathsf{Tom}, \mathsf{Bob}\}$, which is the set of instances of $\neg\mathsf{Woman}$ in $\mathcal{O}$ by Theorem 1.

By $\rho(R)$ we denote the BCQ $\exists \boldsymbol{x}\, \phi(\boldsymbol{x})$ if R is a constraint $\forall \boldsymbol{x}\, \phi(\boldsymbol{x}) \rightarrow$, or the BCQ $\exists \boldsymbol{x}\, \phi(\boldsymbol{x}) \wedge x_1 \neq x_2$ if R is an EGD $\forall \boldsymbol{x}\, \phi(\boldsymbol{x}) \rightarrow x_1 = x_2$. For a first-order rewritable set $\mathcal{S}$ of TGDs and a BCQ Q, by $\gamma(Q, \mathcal{S})$ we denote a set $\mathcal{S}_Q$ of BCQs such that $\mathcal{S} \cup \mathcal{A} \models Q$ if and only if $\mathcal{A} \models \bigvee \mathcal{S}_Q$ for all ABoxes $\mathcal{A}$. The following theorem shows that a consistent first-order rewritable ontology is an IFO-rewritable ontology for an arbitrary atomic concept in the ontology.

Theorem 2. *Let $\mathcal{O}$ be a consistent first-order rewritable ontology with TBox $\mathcal{T}$. Then $\bigcup \{\gamma(\rho(R), \mathcal{S}_{\mathcal{T}}^D) \mid R \in \mathcal{S}_{\mathcal{T}}^C\} \cup \{\rho(R) \mid R \in \mathcal{S}_{\mathcal{T}}^E\}$ is an inconsistency-rewritten set of BCQs for an arbitrary atomic concept in $\mathcal{O}$.*

Example 2. This example illustrates how to compute an inconsistency-rewritten set of BCQs from the ontology $\mathcal{O}$ given in Example 1, which is also a first-order rewritable ontology. According to Theorem 2, we first translate $\mathcal{T}$ to the union of a set $\mathcal{S}_{\mathcal{T}}^D$ of TGDs, a set $\mathcal{S}_{\mathcal{T}}^C$ of constraints and a set $\mathcal{S}_{\mathcal{T}}^E$ of EGDs, where

$$\mathcal{S}_{\mathcal{T}}^D = \{\forall x\, \mathsf{Husband}(x) \rightarrow \exists y\, \mathsf{marries}(x, y) \wedge \mathsf{Woman}(y)\},$$
$$\mathcal{S}_{\mathcal{T}}^C = \{\forall x, y\, \mathsf{marries}(x, y) \wedge \mathsf{Woman}(y) \wedge \mathsf{Woman}(x) \rightarrow\},$$
$$\mathcal{S}_{\mathcal{T}}^E = \{\forall x, y_1, y_2\, \mathsf{marries}(x, y_1) \wedge \mathsf{marries}(x, y_2) \rightarrow y_1 = y_2\}.$$

$\mathcal{S}_T^D$ contains a linear TGD and is first-order rewritable. $\mathcal{S}_T^E$ is separable from $\mathcal{S}_T^D$. Now, we compute $\gamma(\rho(R), \mathcal{S}_T^D)$ for all $R \in \mathcal{S}_T^C$ by a query rewriting method such as the one implemented in Rapid [7], yielding $Q_1 = \{\mathsf{marries}(x,y), \mathsf{Woman}(y), \mathsf{Woman}(x)\}$ and $Q_2 = \{\mathsf{Husband}(x), \mathsf{Woman}(x)\}$. We compute $\rho(R)$ for all $R \in \mathcal{S}_T^E$, yielding $Q_3 = \{\mathsf{marries}(x, y_1), \mathsf{marries}(x, y_2), y_1 \neq y_2\}$. Eventually, we obtain an inconsistency-rewritten set of BCQs for an arbitrary atomic concept in $\mathcal{O}$, which is $\mathcal{S} = \{Q_1, Q_2, Q_3\}$.

The expressivity of the IFO-rewritable class is actually higher than that of the first-order rewritable class. In the following, we present two sufficient conditions for detecting IFO-rewritable ontologies that are not first-order rewritable.

A Condition Based on Reachability from Constraints and EGDs. To facilitate finding inconsistency-responsible subsets of a consistent DL ontology $\mathcal{O}$, we restrict $\mathcal{O}$ to be a datalog$^\pm$-translatable ontology. In such an ontology, the inconsistencies are caused by constraints or EGDs translated from the TBox and inconsistency-responsible subsets of the TBox can be found by backward traversal from constraints or EGDs. To explain the method for backward traversal from constraints or EGDs, we introduce the notion of *triggering* below.

Definition 2. *Given a set $\mathcal{S}$ of TGDs, we say a predicate P triggers another predicate P' in $\mathcal{S}$ if either there is a TGD $R \in \mathcal{S}$ such that P appears in the body of R and P' appears in the head of R, or there exists a predicate P'' such that P triggers P'' and P'' triggers P' in $\mathcal{S}$. Moreover, we say a predicate P triggers a constraint or an EGD R in $\mathcal{S}$ if P triggers at least one predicate appearing in the body of R in $\mathcal{S}$; we say a TGD $R \in \mathcal{S}$ triggers a constraint or an EGD R' in $\mathcal{S}$ if there is a predicate appearing in the head of R triggers R' in $\mathcal{S}$.*

For a constraint or an EGD R and a set $\mathcal{S}$ of TGDs, by $\mathsf{trg}(R, \mathcal{S})$ we denote the set of TGDs in $\mathcal{S}$ that trigger R in $\mathcal{S}$. Then $\mathsf{trg}(R, \mathcal{S})$ is essentially the unique maximal subset of $\mathcal{S}$ that can be backward traversed from R. By considering $\mathsf{trg}(R, \mathcal{S})$ for all constraints or EGDs R rather than the original TBox, we can obtain a condition for detecting IFO-rewritable ontologies that are not first-order rewritable. The following theorem shows this condition and the corresponding method for computing an inconsistency-rewritten set of BCQs, where $\mathsf{pred}(\mathcal{S})$ denotes the set of predicates appearing in a set $\mathcal{S}$ of existential rules.

Theorem 3. *Let $\mathcal{O}$ be a consistent datalog$^\pm$-translatable ontology with TBox $\mathcal{T}$, and A an atomic concept in $\mathcal{O}$. If for all $R \in \mathcal{S}_T^C$, $A \notin \mathsf{pred}(\mathsf{trg}(R, \mathcal{S}_T^D) \cup \{R\})$ or $\mathsf{trg}(R, \mathcal{S}_T^D)$ is first-order rewritable, and for all $R \in \mathcal{S}_T^E$, $A \notin \mathsf{pred}(\mathsf{trg}(R, \mathcal{S}_T^D) \cup \{R\})$ or $\{R\}$ is separable from $\mathsf{trg}(R, \mathcal{S}_T^D)$, then $\bigcup\{\gamma(\rho(R), \mathsf{trg}(R, \mathcal{S}_T^D)) \mid R \in \mathcal{S}_T^C, A \in \mathsf{pred}(\mathsf{trg}(R, \mathcal{S}_T^D))\} \cup \{\rho(R) \mid R \in \mathcal{S}_T^E, A \in \mathsf{pred}(\mathsf{trg}(R, \mathcal{S}_T^D))\}$ is an inconsistency-rewritten set of BCQs for A in $\mathcal{O}$.*

The condition given in the above theorem can be checked regardless of the ABox in time polynomial in the size of the TBox, because computing $\mathsf{trg}(R, \mathcal{S}_T^D)$ can be done in time polynomial in the size of $\mathcal{S}_T^D$ for every constraint or EGD R. The following example shows a datalog$^\pm$-translatable ontology that satisfies this condition for some atomic concept but is not first-order rewritable.

Example 3. Let $\mathcal{O}$ be a consistent datalog$^{\pm}$-translatable ontology whose TBox $\mathcal{T}$ consists of the following three axioms.

$$\exists r.A \sqsubseteq A \qquad A \sqcap B \sqsubseteq \bot \qquad B \sqcap C \sqsubseteq \bot$$

Consider computing an inconsistency-rewritten set of BCQs for C in $\mathcal{O}$ by the method in Theorem 3. We first translate $\mathcal{T}$ to the union of a set $\mathcal{S}_{\mathcal{T}}^D$ of TGDs, a set $\mathcal{S}_{\mathcal{T}}^C$ of constraints and a set $\mathcal{S}_{\mathcal{T}}^E$ of EGDs, where $\mathcal{S}_{\mathcal{T}}^D = \{\forall x, y\, r(x,y) \wedge A(y) \rightarrow A(x)\}$, $\mathcal{S}_{\mathcal{T}}^C = \{R_1 : \forall x\, A(x) \wedge B(x) \rightarrow, R_2 : \forall x\, B(x) \wedge C(x) \rightarrow\}$, and $\mathcal{S}_{\mathcal{T}}^E = \emptyset$. Since the CQ $A(x)$ cannot be rewritten to a finite disjunction of CQs $Q_D(x)$ such that $\mathsf{ans}(\mathcal{S}_{\mathcal{T}}^D \cup \mathcal{A}, A(x)) = \mathsf{ans}(\mathcal{S}, Q_D(x))$ for all ABoxes $\mathcal{A}$, $\mathcal{S}_{\mathcal{T}}^D$ is not first-order rewritable, and nor is $\mathcal{O}$. But we can show that $\mathcal{O}$ is IFO-rewritable for C. Since $\mathsf{trg}(R_1, \mathcal{S}_{\mathcal{T}}^D) = \mathcal{S}_{\mathcal{T}}^D$ and $\mathsf{trg}(R_2, \mathcal{S}_{\mathcal{T}}^D) = \emptyset$, we have $C \notin \mathsf{pred}(\mathsf{trg}(R_1, \mathcal{S}_{\mathcal{T}}^D) \cup \{R_1\})$ and $C \in \mathsf{pred}(\mathsf{trg}(R_2, \mathcal{S}_{\mathcal{T}}^D) \cup \{R_2\})$. Moreover, since $\mathsf{trg}(R_2, \mathcal{S}_{\mathcal{T}}^D)$ is empty, it is clearly first-order rewritable. Hence an inconsistency-rewritten set of BCQs for C in $\mathcal{O}$ is $\gamma(\rho(R_2), \mathsf{trg}(R_2, \mathcal{S}_{\mathcal{T}}^D)) = \{\rho(R_2)\}$, where $\rho(R_2) = \{B(x), C(x)\}$.

A Condition Based on Rooted Subgraphs of the ABox Graph. Let $\mathcal{O}$ be a consistent DL ontology with TBox $\mathcal{T}$ and ABox $\mathcal{A}$, and A an atomic concept. Another condition for guaranteeing the existence of an inconsistency-rewritten set of BCQs for A in $\mathcal{O}$ is that, there is a set $\mathcal{S}$ of small subsets of $\mathcal{A}$ such that the number of assertions in any $S \in \mathcal{S}$ is not greater than a given threshold n and every instance a of $\neg A$ in $\mathcal{O}$ is also an instance of $\neg A$ in $\mathcal{T} \cup S$ for some $S \in \mathcal{S}$. The validness of this condition can be shown as follows. Let $\mathcal{S}_A = \{S_a \cup \{A(a)\} \mid \mathcal{O} \models \neg A(a)\}$ where S_a is an element in $\mathcal{S}$ such that $\mathcal{T} \cup S_a \models \neg A(a)$, then $\mathcal{A} \not\models \bigvee \mathcal{S}_A$, and for all individuals a in $\mathcal{O}$, $\mathcal{O} \cup \{A(a)\} \models \bot$ if and only if $\mathcal{A} \cup \{A(a)\} \models \bigvee \mathcal{S}_A$. By $\mathsf{lift}(S)$ we denote the set of atoms obtained from a set S of assertions by replacing different individuals in S with different variables. Let $\mathcal{S}_A' = \{\mathsf{lift}(S) \mid S \in \mathcal{S}_A\}$, then the size of $\mathcal{S}_A'$ is independent of the size of $\mathcal{A}$ and at most polynomial in the size of $\mathcal{T}$ with an exponent not greater than $n+1$. If $\mathcal{T} \cup S \models \bot$ implies $\mathcal{T} \cup \mathsf{lift}(S)\theta \models \bot$ for all ground substitutions θ for $\mathsf{lift}(S)$, $\mathcal{S}_A'$ will be an inconsistency-rewritten set of BCQs for A.

To satisfy the above condition as possible, we restrict $\mathcal{O}$ to be an $\mathcal{ELR}_{\bot}$ ontology made up of an $\mathcal{ELR}_{\bot}$ TBox and a normalized ABox. An $\mathcal{ELR}_{\bot}$ TBox consists of role inclusions of the form $r_1 \circ \ldots \circ r_k \sqsubseteq s$ and concept inclusions of the form $C \sqsubseteq D$, where $k \geq 1$, $r_1, \ldots, r_k$, s are atomic roles, and C and D are $\mathcal{EL}_{\bot}$ concepts recursively constructed by $\bot$, $\top$, atomic concepts, existential restrictions $\exists s.C$ and concept conjunctions $C \sqcap D$. The above condition requires computing small ABox subsets preserving instances of $\neg A$ in the ontology. In an $\mathcal{ELR}_{\bot}$ ontology, these ABox subsets can be treated as *maximal rooted subgraphs* of the *ABox graph*. Before showing this result, we formally provide the related notions below.

Definition 3. *The* ABox graph *of a normalized ABox $\mathcal{A}$, denoted by $\mathcal{G}(\mathcal{A})$, is a graph $G = (V, E, L)$ where $V = \mathsf{Ind}(\mathcal{A})$ is a set of vertexes, $E = \{(a, b, r) \mid r(a, b) \in \mathcal{A}\}$ is a set of labeled edges, and $L : \mathsf{Ind}(\mathcal{A}) \mapsto 2^{\mathsf{Cn}(\mathcal{A})}$ is a label function such that $L(a) = \{A \mid A(a) \in \mathcal{A}\}$ for all $a \in V$. We say a graph $G' = (V', E', L')$*

is a subgraph of $G = (V, E, L)$, wirtten $G' \subseteq G$, if $V' \subseteq V$, $E' \subseteq E$ and for all $a \in V'$, $L'(a) \subseteq L(a)$. We say an individual a has a path to another individual b in $G = (V, E, L)$, if there is a sequence of labeled edges (a, a_1, r_0), (a_1, a_2, r_1), $\ldots$, (a_n, b, r_n) in E. A root a of a graph $G = (V, E, L)$ is an individual in V such that for all individuals b other than a in V, a has a path to b in G. A rooted subgraph G' of G is a subgraph of G that has at least one root; it is maximal if there is no rooted subgraph G'' of G such that $G' \subseteq G''$ and $G'' \not\subseteq G'$.

Every normalized ABox has a one-to-one mapping to its ABox graph. By $\mathcal{G}^-(G)$ we denote the unique ABox mapped from an ABox graph $G = (V, E, L)$, i.e., $\mathcal{G}^-(G) = \{A(a) \mid a \in V, A \in L(a)\} \cup \{r(a, b) \mid (a, b, v) \in E\}$.

Example 4. Suppose an ABox $\mathcal{A}$ consists of the following $5+m$ assertions.

$$r(a_1, a_2) \quad r(a_2, a_1) \quad r(a_1, b) \quad r(a_2, b) \quad A(b) \quad r(c_1, b) \quad \ldots \quad r(c_m, b)$$

The ABox graph $\mathcal{G}(\mathcal{A})$ of $\mathcal{A}$ is shown below. We can see that $\mathcal{G}(\{r(a_1, a_2)$, $r(a_2, a_1)$, $r(a_1, b)$, $r(a_2, b)$, $A(b)\})$ is a maximal rooted subgraph of $\mathcal{G}(\mathcal{A})$ which has two roots a_1 and a_2; moreover, for all $1 \leq i \leq m$, $\mathcal{G}(\{r(c_i, b), A(b)\})$ is also a maximal rooted subgraph of $\mathcal{G}(\mathcal{A})$ with the unique root c_i.

In general, all maximal rooted subgraphs of an ABox graph can be retrieved in time polynomial in the size of the ABox, by first identifying all roots of maximal rooted subgraphs and then computing all *full subgraphs* led by these roots. A *full subgraph* of $G = (V, E, L)$ led by an individual a is a subgraph $G' = (V', E', L')$ of G such that $V' = \{a\} \cup \{b \mid a$ has a path to b in $G\}$, $E' = \{(b, c, r) \in E \mid b \in V', c \in V'\}$ and $L'(b) = L(b)$ for all $b \in V'$. There is a unique full subgraph led by a certain individual. The roots of maximal rooted subgraphs are identified as those individuals a having paths to any individual that has paths to a in the ABox graph. The maximal rooted subgraph in which a is a root can be defined as the full subgraph led by a. The following theorem shows the correctness of this method for computing all maximal rooted subgraphs.

Theorem 4. *Let $G = (V, E, L)$ be an ABox graph and a an individual in V. Then (1) if a is a root of some maximal rooted subgraph of G, then a has paths to any individual that has paths to a in G; (2) if a has paths to any individual that has paths to a in G, then the full subgraph of G led by a is a maximal rooted subgraph of G in which a is a root.*

The following lemma shows that the required set of ABox subsets that preserves all instances of $\neg A$ in an $\mathcal{ELR}_\perp$ ontology can be defined as the set of $\mathcal{G}^-(G)$ for G a maximal rooted subgraph of the ABox graph.

Algorithm. ComputeInconsistencyRewrittenSet($\mathcal{T}$, $\mathcal{A}$, A)
Input: An $\mathcal{ELR}_\perp$ ontology with TBox $\mathcal{T}$ and ABox $\mathcal{A}$, and an atomic concept A.
Output: An inconsistency-rewritten set of BCQs for A in $\mathcal{T} \cup \mathcal{A}$.
1: $\mathcal{S}_Q \leftarrow \emptyset$;
2: **for** each G in NonIsomorphicMRS($\mathcal{G}(\mathcal{A})$) and each individual a in G **do**
3: $\quad$ **if** $A(a) \notin \mathcal{A}$ and there is no $Q \in \mathcal{S}_Q$ and ground substitution θ for Q such that
$Q\theta \subseteq \mathcal{G}^-(G) \cup \{A(a)\}$ **then**
4: $\quad\quad$ **if** $\mathcal{T} \cup \mathcal{G}^-(G) \models \neg A(a)$ **then**
5: $\quad\quad\quad$ $Q \leftarrow \mathsf{lift}(\mathcal{G}^-(G) \cup \{A(a)\})$; // *replace diff. individuals with diff. variables*
6: $\quad\quad\quad$ **for** each $Q' \in \mathcal{S}_Q$ such that $Q\theta \subseteq Q'$ for some substitution θ for Q **do**
7: $\quad\quad\quad\quad$ $\mathcal{S}_Q \leftarrow \mathcal{S}_Q \setminus \{Q'\}$;
8: $\quad\quad\quad$ $\mathcal{S}_Q \leftarrow \mathcal{S}_Q \cup \{Q\}$;
9: **return** $\mathcal{S}_Q$;

Fig. 1. The algorithm for computing an inconsistency-rewritten set of BCQs

Lemma 1. *Given an atomic concept A and a consistent $\mathcal{ELR}_\perp$ ontology $\mathcal{O}$ with TBox $\mathcal{T}$ and ABox $\mathcal{A}$, if a is an instance of $\neg A$ in $\mathcal{O}$, then there is a maximal rooted subgraph G of $\mathcal{G}(\mathcal{A})$ such that $\mathcal{T} \cup \mathcal{G}^-(G) \models \neg A(a)$.*

By the above lemma, we can use an integer threshold n to determine (in PTIME in data complexity) if a consistent $\mathcal{ELR}_\perp$ ontology has an inconsistency-rewritten set of BCQs for an arbitrary atomic concept. That is, if the number of assertions in any maximal rooted subgraph of the ABox graph is not greater than n, then we can find an inconsistency-rewritten set of BCQs for a given atomic concept by the algorithm shown in Fig. 1.

The resulting set $\mathcal{S}_Q$ of the algorithm ComputeInconsistencyRewrittenSet($\mathcal{T}$, $\mathcal{A}$, A) only keeps the most general BCQs, where a set of atoms (or BCQ) Q is said to be *more general* than another set of atoms (or BCQ) Q' if there is a substitution θ for Q such that $Q\theta \subseteq Q'$. To avoid generating equivalent BCQs up to renaming of variables, the algorithm only handles non-isomorphic subgraphs of $\mathcal{G}(\mathcal{A})$, where two subgraphs G_1 and G_2 are said to be *isomorphic* if $\mathsf{lift}(\mathcal{G}^-(G_1))$ and $\mathsf{lift}(\mathcal{G}^-(G_2))$ are equivalent up to renaming of variables. In the algorithm, NonIsomorphicMRS($\mathcal{G}(\mathcal{A})$) denotes the set of non-isomorphic maximal rooted subgraphs of $\mathcal{G}(\mathcal{A})$, i.e., any two subgraphs in this set are not isomorphic. The cardinality of this set is at most polynomial in the size of $\mathcal{T}$ with an exponent not greater than n. The algorithm handles all subgraphs G in NonIsomorphicMRS($\mathcal{G}(\mathcal{A})$) and all individuals a in G to construct $\mathcal{S}_Q$. In case $A(a) \in \mathcal{A}$, since $\mathcal{T} \cup \mathcal{A}$ is consistent and $\mathcal{G}^-(G) \cup \{A(a)\} \subseteq \mathcal{A}$, $\mathcal{T} \cup \mathcal{G}^-(G) \cup \{A(a)\}$ is also consistent, i.e., $\mathcal{T} \cup \mathcal{G}^-(G) \not\models \neg A(a)$. In case there is some $Q \in \mathcal{S}_Q$ that is more general than $\mathcal{G}^-(G) \cup \{A(a)\}$, since no individual occurs in Q, the BCQ $\mathsf{lift}(\mathcal{G}^-(G) \cup \{A(a)\})$ is less general than Q and thus is not added to $\mathcal{S}_Q$. In other cases (lines 4–8), if and only if $\mathcal{T} \cup \mathcal{G}^-(G) \models \neg A(a)$, all BCQs that are less general than $\mathsf{lift}(\mathcal{G}^-(G) \cup \{A(a)\})$ are removed from $\mathcal{S}_Q$, making $\mathcal{S}_Q$ contain only the most general BCQs; moreover, $\mathsf{lift}(\mathcal{G}^-(G) \cup \{A(a)\})$ is added to $\mathcal{S}_Q$.

The algorithm first computes $\texttt{NonIsomorphicMRS}(\mathcal{G}(\mathcal{A}))$ regardless of $\mathcal{T}$ in time polynomial in the size of $\mathcal{A}$, and then computes $\mathcal{S}_Q$ from $\texttt{NonIsomorphic-}$ $\texttt{MRS}(\mathcal{G}(\mathcal{A}))$ regardless of $\mathcal{A}$ in time polynomial in the size of $\mathcal{T}$. The correctness follows from Lemma 1 and the following lemma, as shown in Theorem 5.

Lemma 2. *For an $\mathcal{ELR}_\perp$ TBox $\mathcal{T}$ and a set S of assertions such that $\mathcal{T} \cup S$ is inconsistent, $\mathcal{T} \cup \mathsf{lift}(S)\,\theta$ is inconsistent for all ground substitutions θ for $\mathsf{lift}(S)$.*

Theorem 5. *Given an atomic concept A and a consistent $\mathcal{ELR}_\perp$ ontology $\mathcal{O}$ with TBox $\mathcal{T}$ and ABox $\mathcal{A}$, $\texttt{ComputeInconsistencyRewrittenSet}(\mathcal{T},\ \mathcal{A},\ A)$ returns an inconsistency-rewritten set $\mathcal{S}_Q$ of BCQs for A in $\mathcal{O}$, when $|\mathcal{G}^-(G)|$ is not greater than a fixed constant n for all maximal rooted subgraphs G of $\mathcal{G}(\mathcal{A})$.*

Example 5. Consider the ontology $\mathcal{O}$ given by Example 3 where its ABox $\mathcal{A}$ is given by Example 4. $\mathcal{O}$ is a consistent $\mathcal{ELR}_\perp$ ontology, but it is not first-order rewritable. Suppose the threshold n is 5. We show that there is an inconsistency-rewritten set of BCQs for B in $\mathcal{O}$. The maximal rooted subgraphs of $\mathcal{G}(\mathcal{A})$ given in Example 4 are $G_0, G_1, \ldots, G_m$, where $\mathcal{G}^-(G_0) = \{r(a_1, a_2), r(a_2, a_1), r(a_1, b),$ $r(a_2, b), A(b)\}$ and $\mathcal{G}^-(G_i) = \{r(c_i, b), A(b)\}$ for all $1 \le i \le m$. Since $|\mathcal{G}^-(G_i)| \le$ n for all $0 \le i \le m$, we call $\texttt{ComputeInconsistencyRewrittenSet}(\mathcal{T}, \mathcal{A}, B)$. Initially, we have $\texttt{NonIsomorphicMRS}(\mathcal{G}(\mathcal{A})) = \{G_0, G_1\}$ and set $\mathcal{S}_Q = \emptyset$. For $\mathcal{G}^-(G_0)$ and a_1, since $B(a_1) \notin \mathcal{A}$, $\mathcal{S}_Q = \emptyset$ and $\mathcal{T} \cup \mathcal{G}^-(G_0) \models \neg B(a_1)$, we add $Q_1 = \{r(x, y), r(y, x), r(x, z), r(y, z), A(z), B(x)\}$ to $\mathcal{S}_Q$. For $\mathcal{G}^-(G_0)$ and a_2, since $Q_1 \cdot \{x/a_2, y/a_1, z/b\} = \mathcal{G}^-(G_0) \cup \{B(a_2)\}$, a_2 is not handled. For $\mathcal{G}^-(G_0)$ and b, since $B(a_1) \notin \mathcal{A}$, $\mathcal{T} \cup \mathcal{G}^-(G_0) \models \neg B(b)$ and Q_1 is not more general than $\mathcal{G}^-(G_0) \cup \{B(b)\}$, we add $Q_2 = \{r(x, y), r(y, x), r(x, z), r(y, z), A(z), B(z)\}$ to $\mathcal{S}_Q$. For $\mathcal{G}^-(G_1)$ and c_1, since $B(c_1) \notin \mathcal{A}$ and $\mathcal{T} \cup \mathcal{G}^-(G_1) \models \neg B(c_1)$, we add $Q_3 = \{r(x, y), A(y), B(x)\}$ to $\mathcal{S}_Q$; moreover, since Q_3 is more general than Q_1, we remove Q_1 from $\mathcal{S}_Q$. For $\mathcal{G}^-(G_1)$ and b, since $B(b) \notin \mathcal{A}$ and $\mathcal{T} \cup \mathcal{G}^-(G_1) \models \neg B(b)$, we add $Q_4 = \{r(x, y), A(y), B(y)\}$ to $\mathcal{S}_Q$; moreover, since Q_4 is more general than Q_2, we remove Q_2 from $\mathcal{S}_Q$. Finally we get $\mathcal{S}_Q = \{Q_3, Q_4\}$, which is an inconsistency-rewritten set of BCQs for B in $\mathcal{O}$.

The DL $\mathcal{ELR}_\perp$ is a core of the EL profile of OWL 2, roughly corresponding to this profile without range restrictions and nominals. However, extending the algorithm in Fig. 1 to deal with range restrictions or nominals is hard or even impossible. On the one hand, applying the algorithm to $\mathcal{ELR}_\perp$ plus range restrictions or inverse roles is incorrect since Lemma 1 does not hold. For example, consider a consistent ontology $\mathcal{O}$ with TBox $\mathcal{T} = \{\exists r.A \sqcap B \sqsubseteq \perp,$ $\exists s^-.\top \sqsubseteq A\}$ and ABox $\mathcal{A} = \{r(a, b), s(c, b)\}$, where $s^-.\top \sqsubseteq A$ says that the range of s is A. It can be seen that a is an instance of $\neg B$ in $\mathcal{O}$, but it is not an instance of $\neg B$ in either $\mathcal{T} \cup \mathcal{G}^-(G_1)$ or $\mathcal{T} \cup \mathcal{G}^-(G_2)$, where $G_1 = \mathcal{G}(\{r(a, b)\})$ and $G_2 = \mathcal{G}(\{s(c, b)\})$ are the two maximal rooted subgraphs of $\mathcal{G}(\mathcal{A})$. To handle range restrictions or inverse roles, we need to consider maximal connected components of $\mathcal{G}(\mathcal{A})$ in which all edges are treated as undirected, but the sizes of these components can easily be greater than a given threshold. On the other hand, applying the algorithm to $\mathcal{ELR}_\perp$ plus nominals is incorrect since Lemma 2 does not hold. For example, consider a TBox $\mathcal{T} = \{\exists r.\{b\} \sqsubseteq \bot\}$ and a set of assertions $S = \{r(a, b)\}$. It can be seen that $\mathcal{T} \cup S$ is inconsistent, but since $\mathsf{lift}(S) = \{r(x, y)\}$, $\mathcal{T} \cup \mathsf{lift}(S)\,\theta = \mathcal{T} \cup \{r(a, a)\}$ is consistent for $\theta = \{x/a, y/a\}$. To extend the algorithm to handle nominals, we need to keep individuals in the resulting set of BCQs. But then it is hard to guarantee that the resulting set is an inconsistency-rewritten set since its size may depend on the size of the ABox.

Handling General Negated Concepts. The proposed method for instance retrieval for atomic negations can be extended to handle general negated concepts $\neg C$. It can be seen that the set of instances of $\neg C$ in a DL ontology $\mathcal{O}$ amounts to the set of instances of $\neg P_C$ in $\mathcal{O} \cup \{P_C \sqsubseteq C\}$, where P_C is a fresh atomic concept not in $\mathcal{O}$. Therefore, the proposed method still works for retrieving instances of $\neg C$ as long as $\mathcal{O} \cup \{P_C \sqsubseteq C\}$ is an IFO-rewritable ontology for P_C.

4   Experimental Evaluation

The goal of our preliminary experiments is to verify if the proposed method is significantly more efficient and scalable than existing methods in retrieving instances of all atomic negations. We focused on first-order rewritable ontologies and implemented the method in JAVA (based on Theorems 1&2), using the query-rewriting system Rapid [7] to compute inconsistency-rewritten sets and using the database system MySQL to store and access ABoxes. We call the implemented system *REwriting-Based System for Instance Retrieval* (*REBSIR*).

We collected two groups of ontologies, where one group was from the Lehigh University Benchmark (LUBM) [11] and the other from DBPedia (version 2014)[1] [3]. Since Rapid cannot handle axioms about concrete roles (i.e. datatype properties), we removed axioms about concrete roles from both the LUBM TBox and the DBPedia TBox, rendering them first-order rewritable. In addition, since there is no constraint translated from the LUBM TBox and none of the atomic negations has instances in LUBM ontologies, we added disjointness axioms to the LUBM TBox for every two sibling atomic concepts in the concept hierarchy such that they have no common instances in any original LUBM ontology. At last we obtained five consistent ontologies named LUBMdn ($n = 1, 5, 10, 50, 100$) for the first group, where n is the number of universities. For the second group, we dumped basic assertions about atomic concepts and abstract roles (i.e. object properties) in the DBPedia TBox from DBPedia-as-Tables[2] to construct the ABox. Since the downloaded DBPedia TBox and DBPedia-as-Tables were generated separately, our constructed ABox was inconsistent with the TBox. To restore consistency, we first computed all minimal conflicts (i.e. minimal subsets of the ABox that are inconsistent with the TBox) by using the rewriting-based method proposed in [8], then removed from the ABox a small hitting set S for the set of minimal conflicts. S was iteratively computed by, in each iteration, adding

---

[1] http://downloads.dbpedia.org/2014/dbpedia_2014.owl.bz2
[2] http://web.informatik.uni-mannheim.de/DBpediaAsTables/

Table 1. The statistics about test ontologies

Ontology	#C	#R	#TA	#AA	#I
LUBMd1–LUBMd100	43	25	158	100,543–13,824,437	17,174–2,179,766
DBPedia1%–DBPedia100%	811	1,309	3,679	141,039–14,164,192	116,683–3,695,525

Note: #C/#R/#TA/#AA/#I is the number of atomic concepts/abstract roles/
TBox axioms/ABox assertions/individuals.

Table 2. The number of timeout cases (* for running out of memory)

System	LUBMd1	LUBMd5	LUBMd10	DBPedia1%	DBPedia5%	DBPedia10%
FaCT++	0	21	19	0	1	1
KAON2	0	0	0	63	400	734
Pellet	12	12	43	0	0	*811
HermiT	36	38	38	811	811	811

to S an assertion that locates in the most minimal conflicts without any element in S. Finally, we kept $n\%$ of assertions in the modified ABox and obtained five consistent ontologies named DBPedia$n\%$, where $n = 1, 5, 10, 50, 100$. The statistics about all test ontologies are summarized in Table 1.[3]

We first compared the proposed method with the common method implemented in most state-of-the-art DL systems. For every atomic negation $\neg A$, the common method first adds a new axiom $\neg A \sqsubseteq P_A$ to the TBox and then retrieves instances of P_A, where P_A is a fresh atomic concept. Since the performance of the common method may vary with different DL systems, we compared REB-SIR with FaCT++ (version 1.6.3) [19], KAON2 (version 2008-06-29) [14], Pellet (version 2.3.1) [18] and HermiT (version 1.3.8) [9]. We set a time limit of five minutes for retrieving instances of a single atomic negation. All experiments were conducted on a laptop with Intel Dual-Core 2.60GHz CPU and 8GB RAM, running Windows 7 with the maximum Java heap size set to 8GB.

For the LUBMd (resp. DBPedia) TBox, REBSIR computes an inconsistency-rewritten set made up of 3,178 (resp. 865,437) BCQs in 200 milliseconds (resp. 65 seconds). This computation is done once before retrieving instances of any atomic negation in a test ontology.

All compared systems except REBSIR run out of memory for LUBMd50, LUBMd100, DBPedia50% and DBPedia100%, and sometimes exceed the time limit of five minutes for other ontologies. Table 2 reports the number of time-out cases. REBSIR has no timeout cases, thus it does not appear in the table. Figure 2 shows the comparison results on the average execution time (in milliseconds) for retrieving instances of an atomic negation. The displayed execution time for REBSIR includes the equally shared time for computing the inconsistency-rewritten set, while the execution time for other systems excludes

---

[3] All test ontologies and compared systems including REBSIR and others are available at http://www.dataminingcenter.net/rebsir/.

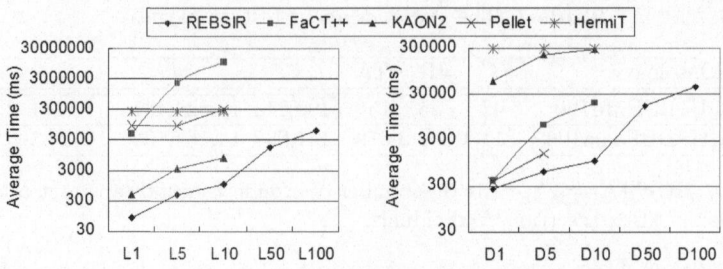

Note: Ln and Dn are respectively short for LUBMdn and DBPedia$n$%. The average execution time is not shown if the system runs out of memory in a test ontology.

Fig. 2. The average execution time for retrieving instances of an atomic negation

the time for loading the test ontology. Moreover, for all compared systems except FaCT++, the execution time in a timeout case is approximated as five minutes since these systems are forced to stop handling the current atomic negation and start handling the next atomic negation once timeout occurs.

As can be seen in Fig. 2, FaCT++ works much better on DBPedia$n$% than on LUBMdn. Pellet also works better on DBPedia$n$% than on LUBMdn, except that for DBPedia10% it runs out of memory. KAON2 works much better on LUBMdn than on DBPedia$n$%, possibly because the resolution-based method used in KAON2 works worse with more axioms in the TBox. HermiT works sightly better on LUBMdn than on DBPedia$n$%. It cannot finish within the time limit for any atomic negation in any DBPedia ontology. Our system REBSIR is the best among all compared systems. It is significantly more efficient than other compared systems and scales to tens of millions of assertions. In particular, it only spends one minute or so on average to retrieve instances of an atomic negation in the two largest ontologies that have more than ten million assertions.

We also compared the proposed method with the consistency checking (CC-) based method under the same test environment. For retrieving instances of an atomic negation $\neg A$ in a consistent ontology $\mathcal{O}$, the CC-based method retrieves the set S of instances of A in $\mathcal{O}$, and then for every individual a occurring in $\mathcal{O}$ but not in S, checks if $\mathcal{O} \cup \{A(a)\} \models \bot$ to determine instances of $\neg A$ in $\mathcal{O}$. We implemented the CC-based method in the state-of-the-art DL system ELK (version 0.4.1) [15], which is highly optimized for DLs in the $\mathcal{EL}$ family [1]. We removed axioms that are not supported by ELK from LUBMdn and kept DBPedia$n$% intact. In this experiment, REBSIR has a similar performance on the modified test ontologies, but ELK (with the default four workers) cannot finish retrieving instances of any atomic negation in any test ontology within the time limit. Although ELK is highly efficient in performing a consistency check, it fails to perform tens of thousands of consistency checks within the time limit and is impractical for instance retrieval for negated concepts.

5   Related Work

In DL systems, instance retrieval for a concept C is often reduced to instance retrieval for an atomic concept P_C by adding $C \sqsubseteq P_C$ to the TBox and then solved by certain reasoning methods. Tableau-based methods [2] are common reasoning methods implemented in state-of-the-art DL systems such as FaCT++ [19], Pellet [18] and HermiT [9]. In [13] existing optimization techniques are summarized and some new optimization techniques are proposed for instance retrieval inside tableau-based methods. In [21] a filter-and-refine paradigm is proposed for optimizing instance retrieval inside tableau-based methods. It first computes obvious non-instances and obvious instances and then performs instance checking for remaining candidate instances. We do not explicitly compare the above optimization techniques with our proposed method because these techniques have at least partially been implemented in most DL systems. For reasoning in expressive DLs, resolution-based methods [14] are another popular paradigm, implemented in a modern DL system KAON2. Our experimental results have shown that our proposed method is more efficient and scalable than both tableau-based and resolution-based methods in retrieving instances of all atomic negations.

Instance retrieval is also related to conjunctive query answering (CQA). There are three efficient approaches to CQA. The first approach is query rewriting, which has been adapted in this work. The second approach is materialization, implemented in scalable DL systems such as WebPIE [20]. It computes an ABox completion containing all ABox consequences wrt the TBox so that subsequent reasoning can be performed in the ABox completion only. The last approach (see e.g. [16]) is a combination of query rewriting and materialization, which first approximates an ABox completion, then rewrites the given query to another one so as to filter out incorrect answers. Except for a query rewriting method proposed in [10], all the above approaches are only applicable to Horn fragments of DLs and cannot be applied to instance retrieval for negated concepts due to the necessity of adding non-Horn features (i.e. concept disjunctions) to the given ontology. The method proposed in [10], however, involves a rather complicated step for transforming disjunctive datalog to datalog and has no evaluation result by now. Recently, a hybrid approach to CQA is proposed in [22]. It first computes a lower bound and an upper bound of the set of answers, then computes answers between the two bounds. Similarly, it needs to add non-Horn features to the ontology before applied to instance retrieval for negated concept, making the complexity beyond PTIME in data complexity. In [12] the CQA problem extended by negative atoms is studied for two simple DLs in the DL-Lite family. However, the study [12] focuses on the computational complexity and does not provide practical solutions to the extended CQA problem.

6   Conclusion and Future Work

In this paper we have studied a new approach to instance retrieval for negated concepts based on query rewriting. We identified the class of IFO-rewritable ontologies which guarantees that instance retrieval for an atomic negation can be reduced to answering a disjunction of CQs over the ABox. To show that the IFO-rewritable class is more expressive than the first-order rewritable class, we presented two sufficient conditions for detecting IFO-rewritable ontologies that are not first-order rewritable. An IFO-rewritable ontology $\mathcal{O}$ for an atomic concept A is characterized by an inconsistency-rewritten set of BCQs for A, which witnesses the inconsistency of $\mathcal{O} \cup \{A(a)\}$ for all instances a of $\neg A$ in $\mathcal{O}$. We empirically showed that using inconsistency-rewritten sets makes instance retrieval for all atomic negations more efficient and scalable than existing methods.

For future work, we plan to conduct extensive experiments on more IFO-rewritable ontologies. Moreover, we plan to develop incremental methods for computing inconsistency-rewritten sets. Finally, we intend to discover more sufficient conditions for detecting IFO-rewritable ontologies. In particular, we plan to relax the second sufficient condition from $\mathcal{ELR}_\perp$ to more expressive DLs by considering concept disjunctions and cardinality restrictions.

Acknowledgments. This work is partly supported by NSFC (61375056), Guang-dong Natural Science Foundation (S2013010012928) and the EC MSC K-Drive project (286348).

References

1. Baader, F., Brandt, S., Lutz, C.: Pushing the EL envelope. In: IJCAI, pp. 364–369 (2005)
2. Baader, F., Calvanese, D., McGuinness, D.L., Nardi, D., Patel-Schneider, P.F. (eds.): The Description Logic Handbook: Theory, Implementation, and Applications. Cambridge University Press (2003)
3. Bizer, C., Lehmann, J., Kobilarov, G., Auer, S., Becker, C., Cyganiak, R., Hellmann, S.: DBpedia - A crystallization point for the web of data. J. Web Sem. **7**(3), 154–165 (2009)
4. Calì, A., Gottlob, G., Lukasiewicz, T.: A general datalog-based framework for tractable query answering over ontologies. J. Web Sem. **14**, 57–83 (2012)
5. Calvanese, D., De Giacomo, G., Lembo, D., Lenzerini, M., Poggi, A., Rodriguez-Muro, M., Rosati, R., Ruzzi, M., Savo, D.F.: The MASTRO system for ontology-based data access. Semantic Web **2**(1), 43–53 (2011)
6. Calvanese, D., Giacomo, G., Lembo, D., Lenzerini, M., Rosati, R.: Tractable reasoning and efficient query answering in description logics: The DL-Lite family. J. Autom. Reasoning **39**(3), 385–429 (2007)
7. Chortaras, A., Trivela, D., Stamou, G.: Optimized query rewriting for OWL 2 QL. In: Bjørner, N., Sofronie-Stokkermans, V. (eds.) CADE 2011. LNCS, vol. 6803, pp. 192–206. Springer, Heidelberg (2011)
8. Du, J., Wang, K., Shen, Y.: Towards tractable and practical ABox abduction over inconsistent description logic ontologies. In: AAAI, pp. 1489–1495 (2015)

9. Glimm, B., Horrocks, I., Motik, B., Stoilos, G., Wang, Z.: HermiT: An OWL 2 reasoner. J. Autom. Reasoning **53**(3), 245–269 (2014)
10. Grau, B.C., Motik, B., Stoilos, G., Horrocks, I.: Computing datalog rewritings beyond horn ontologies. In: IJCAI, pp. 832–838 (2013)
11. Guo, Y., Pan, Z., Heflin, J.: LUBM: A benchmark for OWL knowledge base systems. J. Web Sem. **3**(2–3), 158–182 (2005)
12. Gutiérrez-Basulto, V., Ibañez-García, Y., Kontchakov, R., Kostylev, E.V.: Conjunctive queries with negation over DL-Lite: a closer look. In: Faber, W., Lembo, D. (eds.) RR 2013. LNCS, vol. 7994, pp. 109–122. Springer, Heidelberg (2013)
13. Haarslev, V., Möller, R.: On the scalability of description logic instance retrieval. J. Autom. Reasoning **41**(2), 99–142 (2008)
14. Hustadt, U., Motik, B., Sattler, U.: Reasoning in description logics by a reduction to disjunctive datalog. J. Autom. Reasoning **39**(3), 351–384 (2007)
15. Kazakov, Y., Krötzsch, M., Simancik, F.: The incredible ELK - from polynomial procedures to efficient reasoning with $\mathcal{EL}$ ontologies. J. Autom. Reasoning **53**(1), 1–61 (2014)
16. Lutz, C., Toman, D., Wolter, F.: Conjunctive query answering in the description logic EL using a relational database system. In: IJCAI, pp. 2070–2075 (2009)
17. Pan, J.Z., Ren, Y., Jekjantuk, N., Garcia, J.: Reasoning the FMA ontologies with TrOWL. In: ORE, pp. 107–113 (2013)
18. Sirin, E., Parsia, B., Grau, B.C., Kalyanpur, A., Katz, Y.: Pellet: A practical OWL-DL reasoner. J. Web Sem. **5**(2), 51–53 (2007)
19. Tsarkov, D., Horrocks, I.: FaCT++ description logic reasoner: system description. In: Furbach, U., Shankar, N. (eds.) IJCAR 2006. LNCS (LNAI), vol. 4130, pp. 292–297. Springer, Heidelberg (2006)
20. Urbani, J., Kotoulas, S., Maassen, J., van Harmelen, F., Bal, H.E.: WebPIE: A web-scale parallel inference engine using mapreduce. J. Web Sem. **10**, 59–75 (2012)
21. Wandelt, S., Möller, R., Wessel, M.: Towards scalable instance retrieval over ontologies. Int. J. Software and Informatics **4**(3), 201–218 (2010)
22. Zhou, Y., Nenov, Y., Grau, B.C., Horrocks, I.: Pay-as-you-go OWL query answering using a triple store. In: AAAI, pp. 1142–1148 (2014)

Optimizing the Computation of Overriding

Piero A. Bonatti, Iliana M. Petrova, and Luigi Sauro$^{(\boxtimes)}$

Dip. Ing. Elet. e Tecnologie dell'Informazione,
Università di Napoli Federico II, Naples, Italy
luigi.sauro74@gmail.com

Abstract. We introduce optimization techniques for reasoning in $\mathcal{DL}^{N}$ – a recently introduced family of nonmonotonic description logics whose characterizing features appear well-suited to model the examples naturally arising in biomedical domains and semantic web access control policies. Such optimizations are validated experimentally on large KBs with more than 30K axioms. Speedups exceed 1 order of magnitude. For the first time, response times compatible with real-time reasoning are obtained with nonmonotonic KBs of this size.

1 Introduction

Recently, a new family of nonmonotonic Description Logics (DLs), called $\mathcal{DL}^{N}$, has been introduced [8]. It supports *normality concepts* NC to denote the normal/standard/ prototypical instances of a concept C, and prioritized *defeasible inclusions* (DIs) $C \sqsubseteq_n D$ with the following meaning: *"by default, the instances of C satisfy D, unless stated otherwise"*, that is, unless some higher priority axioms entail $C \sqcap \neg D$; in that case, $C \sqsubseteq_n D$ is *overridden*. The normal/standard/prototypical instances of C are required to satisfy all the DIs that are not overridden in C.

Given the negligible number of applications based on nonmonotonic logics deployed so far, $\mathcal{DL}^{N}$ has been designed to address real-world problems and concrete knowledge engineering needs. In this regard, the literature provides clear and articulated discussions of how nonmonotonic reasoning can be of help in important contexts related to the semantic web, such as biomedical ontologies [25, 28] (with several applications, such as literature search) and (semantic web) policy formulation [29]. These and other applications are extensively discussed in [8].

The distinguishing features in $\mathcal{DL}^{N}$'s design are: (*i*) $\mathcal{DL}^{N}$ adopts the simplest possible criterion for overriding, that is, inconsistency with higher priority axioms; (*ii*) all the normal instances of a concept C conform to the same set of default properties, also called *prototype* in the following; (*iii*) the conflicts between DIs that cannot be resolved with priorities are regarded as knowledge representation errors and are to be fixed by the knowledge engineer (typically, by adding specific DIs). No traditional nonmonotonic logic satisfies (*i*), and very few satisfy (*ii*) or (*iii*). $\mathcal{DL}^{N}$ behaves very well on application examples due to the following consequences of (*i*)–(*iii*) (a comparison with other nonmonotonic DLs with respect to these features is summarized in Table 1):

© Springer International Publishing Switzerland 2015
M. Arenas et al. (Eds.): ISWC 2015, Part I, LNCS 9366, pp. 356–372, 2015.
DOI: 10.1007/978-3-319-25007-6_21

No inheritance blocking: In several nonmonotonic logics a concept with exceptional properties inherits *none* of the default properties of its superclasses. This undesirable phenomenon is known as *inheritance blocking*.

No undesired closed-world assumption (CWA) effects: In some nonmonotonic DLs, an exceptional concept is shrinked to the individuals that explicitly belong to it, if any; hence, it may become inconsistent.

Control on role ranges: Unlike most nonmonotonic DLs, $\mathcal{DL}^N$ axioms can specify whether a role should range only over normal individuals or not.

Detect inconsistent prototypes: $\mathcal{DL}^N$ facilitates the identification of all conflicts that cannot be resolved with priorities (via consistency checks over normality concepts), because their correct resolution is application dependent and should require human intervention (cf. [8, Sec. 1] and Example 1 below).

Tractability: $\mathcal{DL}^N$ is currently the only nonmonotonic DL known to preserve the tractability of all low-complexity DLs, including $\mathcal{EL}^{++}$ and *DL-lite* (that underly the OWL2-EL and OWL2-QL profiles). This opens the way to processing very large nonmonotonic KBs within these fragments.

Table 1. Partial comparison with other nonmonotonic DLs, cf.[8], where CIRC, DEF, AEL, TYP, RAT, PR stand, respectively, for Circumscribed DLs, Default DLs, Autoepistemic DLs, DLs with Typicality, DLs with Rational Closure, and Probabilistic DLs.

Features	CIRC [5,6]	DEF [1,2]	AEL [13]	TYP [17,18]	RAT [10,11] [12]	PR [22]	$\mathcal{DL}^N$
no inheritance blocking	✓	✓	✓		✓	✓	✓
no CWA effects		✓	✓		✓	✓	✓
fine-grained control on role ranges				sometimes			✓
detects inconsistent prototypes				sometimes		✓	✓
preserves tractability							✓(*)

(*) It holds for subsumption, assertion checking, concept consistency, KB consistency.

The performance of $\mathcal{DL}^N$ inference has been experimentally analyzed on large KBs (with more than 20K concept names and over 30K inclusions). The results are promising; still, as defeasible inclusions approach 25% of the KB, query response time slows down enough to call for improvements. In this paper, we study two optimization techniques to improve $\mathcal{DL}^N$ query response time:

1. Many of the axioms in a large KB are expected to be irrelevant to the given query. We investigate the use of *module extractors* [24,27] to focus reasoning on relevant axioms only. The approach is not trivial (module extractors are unsound for most nonmonotonic logics, including circumscription, default and autoepistemic logics) and requires an articulated correctness proof.
2. We introduce a new algorithm for query answering, that is expected to exploit incremental reasoners at their best. Incremental reasoning is crucial as $\mathcal{DL}^N$'s reasoning method iterates consistency tests on a set of KBs with large intersections. While the assertion of new axioms is processed very

efficiently, the computational cost of axiom deletion is generally not negligible. We introduce an *optimistic reasoning method* that is expected to reduce the number of deletions.

Both optimizations are validated experimentally. Speedups exceed 1 order of magnitude. To the best of our knowledge, this is the first time that response times compatible with real-time reasoning are obtained with nonmonotonic KBs of this size.

The paper is organized as follows: Sec. 2 provides the basics of $\mathcal{DL}^N$ and illustrates its inferences with examples. Sections 3 and 4 introduce the two optimization methods, respectively, and prove their correctness. Their experimental assessment is in Sec. 5. Proofs have been omitted due to space limitations. They can be found in [7], together with further explanations and examples. We assume the reader to be familiar with description logics, see [15] for all details. The code and test suites are available at: http://goo.gl/KnMO9l.

2   Preliminaries

Let $\mathcal{DL}$ be any classical description logic language (see [15] for definitions), and let $\mathcal{DL}^N$ be the extension of $\mathcal{DL}$ with a new concept name NC for each $\mathcal{DL}$ concept C. The new concepts are called *normality concepts*.

A $\mathcal{DL}^N$ *knowledge base* is a disjoint union $\mathcal{KB} = \mathcal{S} \cup \mathcal{D}$ where $\mathcal{S}$ is a finite set of $\mathcal{DL}^N$ inclusions and assertions (called *strong* or classical axioms) and $\mathcal{D}$ is a finite set of *defeasible inclusions* (DIs, for short) that are expressions $C \sqsubseteq_n D$ where C is a $\mathcal{DL}$ concept and D a $\mathcal{DL}^N$ concept. If $\delta = (C \sqsubseteq_n D)$, then $\mathsf{pre}(\delta)$ and $\mathsf{con}(\delta)$ denote C and D, respectively. Informally speaking, the set of DIs satisfied by all the instances of a normality concept NC constitute the *prototype* associated to C.

DIs are prioritized by a strict partial order $\prec$. If $\delta_1 \prec \delta_2$, then δ_1 has higher priority than δ_2. $\mathcal{DL}^N$ solves automatically only the conflicts that can be settled using $\prec$; any other conflict shall be resolved by the knowledge engineer (typically by adding suitable DIs). Two priority relations have been investigated so far. Both are based on *specificity*: the specific default properties of a concept C have higher priority than the more generic properties of its superconcepts (i.e. those that subsume C). The priority relation used in most of [8]'s examples identifies those superconcepts with strong axioms only:

$$\delta_1 \prec \delta_2 \text{ iff } \mathsf{pre}(\delta_1) \sqsubseteq_{\mathcal{S}} \mathsf{pre}(\delta_2) \text{ and } \mathsf{pre}(\delta_2) \not\sqsubseteq_{\mathcal{S}} \mathsf{pre}(\delta_1).^{[1]} \tag{1}$$

The second priority relation investigated in [8] is

$$\delta_1 \prec \delta_2 \text{ iff } rank(\delta_1) > rank(\delta_2), \tag{2}$$

where $rank(\cdot)$ is shown in Algorithm 1 and corresponds to the ranking function of rational closure [11,12]. This relation uses also DIs to determine superconcepts,

---

[1] As usual, $C \sqsubseteq_{\mathcal{S}} D$ means that $\mathcal{S} \models C \sqsubseteq D$.

Algorithm 1. Ranking function

Input: Ontology $\mathcal{KB} = \mathcal{S} \cup \mathcal{D}$
Output: the function $rank(\cdot)$

1 $i := -1;$ $\mathcal{E}_0 := \{C \sqsubseteq D \mid C \sqsubseteq_n D \in \mathcal{D}\}$
2 **repeat**
3 $\quad$ $i := i + 1$
4 $\quad$ $\mathcal{E}_{i+1} := \{C \sqsubseteq D \in \mathcal{E}_i \mid \mathcal{S} \cup \mathcal{E}_i \models C \sqsubseteq \bot\}$
5 $\quad$ **forall** $C \sqsubseteq_n D$ s.t. $C \sqsubseteq D \in \mathcal{E}_i \setminus \mathcal{E}_{i+1}$ **do**
6 $\quad$ $\quad$ $\lfloor$ assign $rank(C \sqsubseteq_n D) := i$
7 **until** $\mathcal{E}_{i+1} = \mathcal{E}_i$
8 **forall** $C \sqsubseteq_n D \in \mathcal{E}_{i+1}$ **do** assign $rank(C \sqsubseteq_n D) := \infty$
9 **return** $rank(\cdot)$

---

so (roughly speaking) a DI $C \sqsubseteq_n D$—besides defining a default property for C—gives the specific default properties of C higher priority than those of D. The advantage of this priority relation is that it resolves more conflicts than (1); the main advantage of (1) is predictability; e.g. the effects of adding default properties to an existing, classical KB are more predictable, as the hierarchy used for determining specificity and resolving conflicts is the original, validated one, and is not affected by the new DIs (see also the related discussion in [3,4], that adopt (1)).

The expression $\mathcal{KB} \mathrel{\rlap{\sim}{\succ}} \alpha$ means that α is a $\mathcal{DL}^N$ consequence of $\mathcal{KB}$. Due to space limitations, we do not report the model-theoretic definition of $\mathrel{\rlap{\sim}{\succ}}$ and present only its reduction to classical reasoning [8]. For all subsumptions and assertions α, $\mathcal{KB} \mathrel{\rlap{\sim}{\succ}} \alpha$ holds iff $\mathcal{KB}^{\Sigma} \models \alpha$, where Σ is the set of normality concepts that explicitly occur in $\mathcal{KB} \cup \{\alpha\}$, and $\mathcal{KB}^{\Sigma}$ is a classical knowledge base obtained as follows (recall that $\mathcal{KB} = \mathcal{S} \cup \mathcal{D}$):

First, for all DIs $\delta \in \mathcal{D}$ and all $NC \in \Sigma$, let:

$$\delta^{NC} = \left(NC \sqcap \mathsf{pre}(\delta) \sqsubseteq \mathsf{con}(\delta)\right). \tag{3}$$

The informal meaning of δ^{NC} is: "NC's instances satisfy δ".

Second, let $\mathcal{S}' \downarrow_{\prec\delta}$ denote the result of removing from the axiom set $\mathcal{S}'$ all the δ_0^{NC} such that $\delta_0 \not\prec \delta$:

$$\mathcal{S}' \downarrow_{\prec\delta} = \mathcal{S}' \setminus \{\delta_0^{NC} \mid NC \in \Sigma \wedge \delta_0 \not\prec \delta\}.$$

Third, let $\delta_1, \ldots, \delta_{|\mathcal{D}|}$ be any *linearization* of $(\mathcal{D}, \prec)$.[2]

Finally, let $\mathcal{KB}^{\Sigma} = \mathcal{KB}_{|\mathcal{D}|}^{\Sigma}$, where the sequence $\mathcal{KB}_i^{\Sigma}$ $(i = 1, 2, \ldots, |\mathcal{D}|)$ is inductively defined as follows:

$$\mathcal{KB}_0^{\Sigma} = \mathcal{S} \cup \{NC \sqsubseteq C \mid NC \in \Sigma\} \tag{4}$$

$$\mathcal{KB}_i^{\Sigma} = \mathcal{KB}_{i-1}^{\Sigma} \cup \{\delta_i^{NC} \mid \delta_i \in \mathcal{KB}, NC \in \Sigma, \text{ and}$$

$$\mathcal{KB}_{i-1}^{\Sigma} \downarrow_{\prec\delta_i} \cup \{\delta_i^{NC}\} \not\models NC \sqsubseteq \bot\}. \tag{5}$$

---

[2] That is, $\{\delta_1, \ldots, \delta_{|\mathcal{D}|}\} = \mathcal{D}$ and for all $i, j = 1, \ldots, |\mathcal{D}|$, if $\delta_i \prec \delta_j$ then $i < j$.

In other words, the above sequence starts with $\mathcal{KB}$'s strong axioms extended with the inclusions $NC \sqsubseteq C$, then processes the DIs δ_i in non-increasing priority order. If δ_i can be consistently added to C's prototype, given all higher priority DIs selected so far (which is verified by checking that $NC \not\sqsubseteq \bot$ in line (5)), then its translation δ_i^{NC} is included in $\mathcal{KB}^\Sigma$ (i.e. δ_i enters C's prototype), otherwise δ_i is discarded, and we say that δ_i is *overridden in* NC.

2.1   Examples

We start with a brief discussion of $\mathcal{DL}^N$'s conflict handling. Most other logics silently neutralize the conflicts between nonmonotonic axioms with the same (or incomparable) priorities by computing the inferences that are invariant across all possible ways of resolving the conflict. A knowledge engineer might solve it in favor of *some* of its possible resolutions, instead; however, if the logic silently neutralizes the conflict, then missing knowledge may remain undetected and unfixed. This approach may cause serious problems in the policy domain:

Example 1. Suppose that project coordinators are both administrative staff and research staff. By default, administrative staff are allowed to sign payments, while research staff are not. A conflict arises since both of these default policies apply to project coordinators. Formally, $\mathcal{KB}$ can be formalized with:

$$\text{Admin} \sqsubseteq_n \exists\text{has\_right.Sign} \quad (6)$$
$$\text{Research} \sqsubseteq_n \neg\exists\text{has\_right.Sign} \quad (7)$$

$$\text{PrjCrd} \sqsubseteq \text{Admin} \sqcap \text{Research} \quad (8)$$

Leaving the conflict unresolved may cause a variety of security problems. If project coordinators should *not* sign payments, and the default policy is *open* (authorizations are granted by default), then failing to infer $\neg\exists\text{has\_right.Sign}$ would improperly authorize the signing operation. Conversely, if the authorization is to be granted, then failing to prove $\exists\text{has\_right.Sign}$ causes a *denial of service* (the user is unable to complete a legal operation). To prevent these problems, $\mathcal{DL}^N$ makes the conflict visible by inferring $\mathcal{KB} \models N\,\text{PrjCrd} \sqsubseteq \bot$ (showing that PrjCrd's prototype is inconsistent). This can be proved by checking that $\mathcal{KB}^\Sigma \models N\,\text{PrjCrd} \sqsubseteq \bot$, where $\Sigma = \{N\,\text{PrjCrd}\}$. Then $\mathcal{KB}^\Sigma$ consists of (8), $N\,\text{PrjCrd} \sqsubseteq \text{PrjCrd}$, and the translation of (6) *and* (7) (none overrides the other because none is more specific under any of the two priorities):

$$N\,\text{PrjCrd} \sqcap \text{Admin} \sqsubseteq \exists\text{has\_right.Sign},$$
$$N\,\text{PrjCrd} \sqcap \text{Research} \sqsubseteq \neg\exists\text{has\_right.Sign}. \qquad \square$$

Here is another application example from the semantic policy domain, showing $\mathcal{DL}^N$'s behavior on multiple exception levels.

Example 2. We are going to axiomatize the following natural language policy: *"In general, users cannot access confidential files; Staff can read confidential files; Blacklisted users are not granted any access. This directive cannot be overridden."* Note that each of the above directives contradicts (and is supposed to override) its predecessor in some particular case. Authorizations can be reified as objects with attributes *subject* (the access requestor), *target* (the file to be accessed), and *privilege* (such as *read* and *write*). Then the above policy can be encoded as follows:

$$\text{Staff} \sqsubseteq \text{User} \tag{9}$$
$$\text{Blklst} \sqsubseteq \text{Staff} \tag{10}$$
$$\text{UserReqst} \sqsubseteq_n \neg\exists\text{privilege} \tag{11}$$
$$\text{StaffReqst} \sqsubseteq_n \exists\text{privilege.Read} \tag{12}$$
$$\text{BlkReq} \sqsubseteq \neg\exists\text{privilege} \tag{13}$$

where $\text{BlkReq} \doteq \exists\text{subj.Blklst}$, $\text{StaffReqst} \doteq \exists\text{subj.Staff}$, and $\text{UserReqst} \doteq \exists\text{subj.User}$. By (9), both the specifity relations (1) and (2) yield $(12) \prec (11)$, that is, (12) has higher priority than (11). Let $\Sigma = \{\text{NStaffReqst}\}$; (12) overrides (11) in NStaffReqst (under (1) as well as (2)), so $\mathcal{KB}^\Sigma$ consists of: (9), (10), (13), plus

$$\text{NStaffReqst} \sqsubseteq \text{StaffReqst}$$
$$\text{NStaffReqst} \sqcap \text{StaffReqst} \sqsubseteq \quad \exists\text{privilege.Read}$$

Consequently, $\mathcal{KB} \mathrel{\vert\!\approx} \text{NStaffReqst} \sqsubseteq \exists\text{privilege.Read}$. Similarly, it can be verified that:

1. Normally, access requests involving confidential files are rejected, if they come from generic users: $\mathcal{KB} \mathrel{\vert\!\approx} \text{NUserReqst} \sqsubseteq \neg\exists\text{privilege}$;
2. Blacklisted users cannot do anything by (13), so, in particular: $\mathcal{KB} \mathrel{\vert\!\approx} \text{NBlkReq} \sqsubseteq \neg\exists\text{privilege}$. $\qquad\square$

Some application examples from the biomedical domain can be found in [8] (see Examples 3, 4, 10, 12, and the drug contraindication example in Appendix C). Like the above examples, they are all correctly solved by $\mathcal{DL}^\text{N}$ with both priority notions. Applicative examples hardly exhibit the complicated networks of dependencies between conflicting defaults that occur in artificial examples. Nonetheless, we briefly discuss the artificial examples, too, as a means of comparing $\mathcal{DL}^\text{N}$ with other logics such as [5,12,26].

In several cases, e.g. examples B.4 and B.5 in [26], $\mathcal{DL}^\text{N}$ agrees with [5,12,26] under both priority relations. Due to space limitations, we illustrate only B.4.

Example 3 (Juvenile offender). Let $\mathcal{KB}$ consist of axioms (14)–(18) where J, G, M, P abbreviate JuvenileOffender, GuiltyOfCrime, IsMinor and ToBePunished, respectively.

$$J \sqsubseteq G \tag{14} \qquad\qquad J \sqsubseteq G \tag{19}$$
$$J \sqsubseteq M \tag{15} \qquad\qquad J \sqsubseteq M \tag{20}$$
$$M \sqcap G \sqsubseteq_n \neg P \tag{16} \qquad\qquad NJ \sqsubseteq J \tag{21}$$
$$M \sqsubseteq_n \neg P \tag{17} \qquad\qquad NJ \sqcap M \sqcap G \sqsubseteq \neg P \tag{22}$$
$$G \sqsubseteq_n P \tag{18} \qquad\qquad NJ \sqcap M \sqsubseteq \neg P \tag{23}$$

On one hand, criminals have to be punished and, on the other hand, minors cannot be punished. So, what about juvenile offenders? The defeasible inclusion (16) breaks the tie in favor of their being underage, hence not punishable. By setting $\Sigma = \{NJ\}$, priorities (1) and (2) both return axioms (19)–(23) as $\mathcal{KB}^{\Sigma}$. Then, clearly, $\mathcal{KB}^{\Sigma} \models NJ \sqsubseteq \neg P$ which is $\mathcal{DL}^N$'s analogue of the inferences of [5,12,26].

In other cases (e.g. example B.1 in [26]) $\mathcal{DL}^N$ finds the same conflicts as [5,12,26]. However, $\mathcal{DL}^N$'s semantics signals these conflicts to the knowledge engineer whereas in [5,12,26] they are silently neutralized.

Example 4 (Double Diamond). Let $\mathcal{KB}$ be the following set of axioms:

$$A \sqsubseteq_n T \qquad (24)$$
$$A \sqsubseteq_n P \qquad (25)$$
$$T \sqsubseteq_n S \qquad (26)$$
$$P \sqsubseteq_n \neg S \qquad (27)$$

$$S \sqsubseteq_n R \qquad (28)$$
$$P \sqsubseteq_n Q \qquad (29)$$
$$Q \sqsubseteq_n \neg R \qquad (30)$$

DIs (26) and (27) have incomparable priority under (1) and (2). Consequently, it is easy to see that $NA \sqsubseteq S$ and $NA \sqsubseteq \neg S$ are both implied by $\mathcal{KB}^{\Sigma}$ and hence the knowledge engineer is warned that NA is inconsistent. The same conflict is silently neutralized in [5,12,26] (A's instances are subsumed by neither S nor $\neg S$ and no inconsistency arises). Similarly for the incomparable DIs (28) and (30) and the related conflict.

The third category of examples (e.g. B.2 and B.3 in [26]) presents a more variegated behavior. In particular, [12] and $\mathcal{DL}^N$ with priority (2) solve all conflicts and infer the same consequences; [26] solves only some conflicts; [5] is not able to solve any conflict and yet it does not raise any inconsistency warning; $\mathcal{DL}^N$ with priority (1) cannot solve the conflicts but raises an inconsistency warning. Here, for the sake of simplicity, we discuss in detail a shorter example which has all relevant ingredients.

Example 5. Let $\mathcal{KB}$ be the following defeasible knowledge base:

$$A \sqsubseteq_n B \quad (31) \qquad\qquad A \sqsubseteq_n C \quad (32) \qquad\qquad B \sqsubseteq_n \neg C \quad (33)$$

According to priority (1) all DIs are incomparable. Therefore, $\mathcal{DL}^N$ warns (by inferring $NA \sqsubseteq \bot$) that the conflict between $NA \sqsubseteq C$ and $NA \sqsubseteq \neg C$ cannot be solved. Note that [5] adopts priority (1), too, however according to circumscription, any interpretation where A's instances are either in $\neg C \sqcap B$ or in C is a model, so A is satisfiable (the conflict is silently neutralized). Under priority (2), instead, axiom (31) gives (31) and (32) higher priority than (33). Consequently, $NA \sqsubseteq C$ prevails over $NA \sqsubseteq \neg C$. In this case, $\mathcal{DL}^N$ and rational closure infer the same consequences.

3   Relevance and Modularity

The naive construction of $\mathcal{KB}^{\Sigma}$ must process all the axioms in $\mathcal{KB}_{all}^{\Sigma} = \mathcal{KB}_0^{\Sigma} \cup \{\delta^{NC} \mid \delta \in \mathcal{D}, \ NC \in \Sigma\}$. Here we optimize $\mathcal{DL}^{N}$ inference by quickly discarding some of the irrelevant axioms in $\mathcal{KB}_{all}^{\Sigma}$ using modularization techniques.

Roughly speaking, the problem of module extraction can be expressed as follows: given a reference vocabulary Sig, a module is a (possibly minimal) subset $\mathcal{M} \subseteq \mathcal{KB}$ that is relevant for Sig in the sense that it preserves the consequences of $\mathcal{KB}$ that contain only terms in Sig.

The interest in module extraction techniques is motivated by several ontology engineering needs. We are interested in modularization as an optimization technique for querying large ontologies: the query is evaluated on a (hopefully much smaller) module of the ontology that preserves the query result (as well as any inference whose signature is contained in the query's signature).

However, the problem of deciding whether two knowledge bases entail the same axioms over a given signature is usually harder than standard reasoning tasks. Consequently deciding whether $\mathcal{KB}'$ is a module of $\mathcal{KB}$ (for Sig) is computationally expensive in general. For example, $DL\text{--}Lite_{horn}$ complexity grows from PTIME to coNP-TIME-complete [21]; for $\mathcal{ALC}$, complexity is one exponential harder [16], while for $\mathcal{ALCQIO}$ the problem becomes even undecidable [23].

In order to achieve a practical solution, a syntactic approximation has been adopted in [19,27]. The corrisponding algorithm $\top\bot^*\text{-}\mathrm{Mod}(Sig, \mathcal{KB})$ is defined in [27, Def. 4] and reported in Algorithm 2 below. It is based on the property of $\bot$-locality and $\top$-locality of single axioms (line 15). An axiom is local w.r.t. Sig if the substitution of all non-Sig terms with $\bot$ (resp. $\top$) turns it into a tautology.

The module extractor identifies a subset $\mathcal{M} \subseteq \mathcal{KB}$ of the knowledge base and a signature Sig (containing all symbols of interest) such that all axioms in $\mathcal{KB} \setminus \mathcal{M}$ are local w.r.t. Sig. This guarantees that every model of $\mathcal{M}$ can be extended to a model of $\mathcal{KB}$ by setting each non-Sig term to either $\bot$ or $\top$. In turn, this property guarantees that any query whose signature is contained in Sig has the same answer in $\mathcal{M}$ and $\mathcal{KB}$.

The function $x\text{-}\mathrm{Mod}(Sig, \mathcal{KB})$ (lines 9-19), where x stands for $\top$ or $\bot$, describes the procedure for constructing modules of a knowledge base $\mathcal{KB}$ for each notion of locality. Starting with an empty set of axioms (line 11), iteratively, the axioms α that are non-local are added to the module (line 16) and, in order to preserve soundness, the signature against which locality is checked is extended with the terms in α (line 15). Iteration stops when a fixpoint is reached.

Modules based on a single syntactic locality can be further shrinked by iteratively nesting $\top$-extraction into $\bot$-extraction, thus obtaining $\top\bot^*\text{-}\mathrm{Mod}(Sig, \mathcal{KB})$ modules (lines 1-8).

The notions of module and locality must be extended to handle DIs, before we can apply them to $\mathcal{DL}^{N}$. Definition 1 generalizes the substitutions operated by the module extraction algorithm, abstracting away procedural details. As in [27], both $\widetilde{X}$ and $\mathrm{sig}(X)$ denote the signature of X.

---

[2] For efficiency, this test is approximated by a matching with a small set of templates.

Algorithm 2. $\top\!\perp^*$-Mod$(Sig, \mathcal{KB})$

Input: Ontology $\mathcal{KB}$,   signature Sig
Output: $\top\!\perp^*$-module $\mathcal{M}$ of $\mathcal{KB}$ w.r.t. Sig

```
// main
```
1 **begin**
2 | $\mathcal{M} := \mathcal{KB}$
3 | **repeat**
4 | | $\mathcal{M}' := \mathcal{M}$
5 | | $\mathcal{M} := \top\text{-Mod}(\perp\text{-Mod}(\mathcal{M}, Sig), Sig)$
6 | **until** $\mathcal{M} \neq \mathcal{M}'$
7 | **return** $\mathcal{M}$
8 **end**

9 **function** x-Mod$(\mathcal{KB}, Sig)$ // $x \in \{\perp, \top\}$
10 **begin**
11 | $\mathcal{M} := \emptyset$, $\mathcal{T} := \mathcal{KB}$
12 | **repeat**
13 | | changed = false
14 | | **forall** $\alpha \in \mathcal{T}$ **do**
15 | | | **if** α *is not x-local w.r.t. $Sig \cup \widetilde{\mathcal{M}}$* **then**
16 | | | | $\mathcal{M} := \mathcal{M} \cup \{\alpha\}$
17 | | | | $\mathcal{T} := \mathcal{T} \setminus \{\alpha\}$
18 | | | | changed = true
19 | | **until** changed = false
20 | **return** $\mathcal{M}$
21 **end**

Definition 1. *(Module, locality)* *A* $\top\!\perp^*$-substitution *for $\mathcal{KB}$ and a signature Sig is a substitution σ over $\widetilde{\mathcal{KB}} \setminus Sig$ that maps each concept name on $\top$ or $\perp$, and every role name on the universal role or the empty role. A strong axiom α is σ-local iff $\sigma(\alpha)$ is a tautology. A DI $C \sqsubseteq_n D$ is σ-local iff $C \sqsubseteq D$ is σ-local. A set of axioms is σ-local if all of its members are. We say that an axiom α is $\top$-local (resp. $\perp$-local) if α is σ-local where the substitution σ uniformly maps concept names to $\top$ (resp. $\perp$).*

A (syntactic) module *of $\mathcal{KB}$ with respect to Sig is a set $\mathcal{M} \subseteq \mathcal{KB}$ such that $\mathcal{KB} \setminus \mathcal{M}$ is σ-local for some $\top\!\perp^*$-substitution σ for $\mathcal{KB}$ and $\widetilde{\mathcal{M}} \cup Sig$.*

Let $\text{Mod}_{\text{DI}}(Sig, \mathcal{KB})$ be the variant of $\top\!\perp^*$-Mod$(Sig, \mathcal{KB})$ where the test in line 2 is replaced with (the complement of) the $\top$ or $\perp$-locality condition of Def. 1 (that covers DIs, too). Using the original correctness argument for $\top\!\perp^*$-Mod$(Sig, \mathcal{KB})$ cf. [19, Prop.42], it is easy to see that $\text{Mod}_{\text{DI}}(Sig, \mathcal{KB})$ returns a syntactic module of $\mathcal{KB}$ w.r.t. Sig according to Def. 1. If $\mathcal{KB}$ contains no DIs (i.e. it is classical), then Def. 1 is essentially a rephrasing of standard syntactic notions of modules and locality,[3] so

---

[3] Informally, $\top\!\perp^*$-Mod's greedy strategy tends to find small Def. 1's modules.

for all queries α such that $\widetilde{\alpha} \subseteq Sig$, $\mathcal{M} \models \alpha$ iff $\mathcal{KB} \models \alpha$. (34)

However, proving that $\top\bot^*\text{-Mod}_{\mathrm{DI}}(Sig, \mathcal{KB})$ is correct for *full* $\mathcal{DL}^{\mathrm{N}}$ is far from obvious: removing axioms from $\mathcal{KB}$ using module extractors is incorrect under most nonmonotonic semantics (including circumscription, default logic and autoepistemic logic). The reason is that nonmonotonic inferences are more powerful than classical inferences, and the syntactic locality criterions illustrated above fail to capture some of the dependencies between different symbols.

Example 6. Given the knowledge base $\{\top \sqsubseteq A \sqcup B\}$ and $Sig = \{A\}$, the module extractor returns an empty module (because by setting $B = \top$ the only axiom in the KB becomes a tautology). The circumscription of this KB, assuming that both A and B are minimized, does not entail $A \sqsubseteq \bot$, while the circumscription of the empty module entails it.

Now we illustrate the correct way of applying $\top\bot^*\text{-Mod}_{\mathrm{DI}}$ to a $\mathcal{DL}^{\mathrm{N}}$ $\mathcal{KB} = \mathcal{S} \cup \mathcal{D}$ and a query α (subsumption or assertion). Let Σ be the union of $\widetilde{\alpha}$ and the set of normality concepts occurring in $\mathcal{KB}$. Let

$$\mathcal{M}_0 = \mathrm{Mod}_{\mathrm{DI}}(\Sigma, \mathcal{KB} \cup \mathrm{N}\Sigma),$$

where $\mathrm{N}\Sigma$ abbreviates $\{NC \sqsubseteq C \mid NC \in \Sigma\}$.

Example 7. Let $\mathcal{KB}$ be the knowledge base:

$A \sqsubseteq B$	(35)	$B \sqcap C \sqsubseteq A$	(37)
$A \sqsubseteq_n D \sqcap E$	(36)	$F \sqsubseteq_n A$	(38)

and α the query $NA \sqsubseteq D$. $\mathcal{M}_0$ is calculated as follows: first, since no normality concept occurs in $\mathcal{KB}$, Σ is equal to the signature $\widetilde{\alpha} = \{NA, D\}$.

Algorithm 2 calls first the function $\bot\text{-Mod}(\mathcal{KB} \cup \mathrm{N}\Sigma, \Sigma)$. Notice that by replacing C and F with $\bot$, axioms (37) and (38) become tautologies. Consequently, it is easy to see that the returned knowledge base is $\mathcal{KB}' = \{(35), (36), NA \sqsubseteq A\}$.

Then, $\top\text{-Mod}$ is called on $\mathcal{KB}'$ and Σ. Now, replacing B with $\top$ makes $A \sqsubseteq B$ a tautology, so the resulting knowledge base is $\mathcal{KB}'' = \{(36), NA \sqsubseteq A\}$. It is easy to see that a fix point is reached and hence $\mathcal{KB}''$ is returned.

We shall prove that $(\mathcal{KB} \cap \mathcal{M}_0)^\Sigma$ can be used in place of $\mathcal{KB}^\Sigma$ to answer query α. This saves the cost of processing $\mathcal{KB}_{all}^\Sigma \setminus \mathcal{M}$, where

$$\mathcal{M} = (\mathcal{KB}_0^\Sigma \cap \mathcal{M}_0) \cup \{\delta^{NC} \mid \delta \in \mathcal{D} \cap \mathcal{M}_0, NC \in \Sigma\}.$$

Note that $\mathcal{KB}_{all}^\Sigma \setminus \mathcal{M}$ is usually even larger than $\mathcal{KB} \setminus \mathcal{M}_0$ because for each DI $\delta \notin \mathcal{M}_0$, all its translations δ^{NC} ($NC \in \Sigma$) are removed from $\mathcal{M}$.

Lemma 1. *$\mathcal{M}$ is a module of $\mathcal{KB}_{all}^\Sigma$ w.r.t. Σ.*

Lemma 2. *If $\mathcal{M}$ is a module of $\mathcal{KB}$ w.r.t. a signature Sig and $\mathcal{KB}' \subseteq \mathcal{KB}$, then $\mathcal{KB}' \cap \mathcal{M}$ is a module of $\mathcal{KB}'$ w.r.t. Sig.*

The relationship between $(\mathcal{KB} \cap \mathcal{M}_0)^{\Sigma}$ and $\mathcal{KB}^{\Sigma}$ is:

Lemma 3. $\mathcal{KB}^{\Sigma} \cap \mathcal{M} \subseteq (\mathcal{KB} \cap \mathcal{M}_0)^{\Sigma} \subseteq \mathcal{KB}^{\Sigma}$.

As a consequence, the modularized construction is correct:

Theorem 1. $(\mathcal{KB} \cap \mathcal{M}_0)^{\Sigma} \models \alpha$ iff $\mathcal{KB}^{\Sigma} \models \alpha$.

Proof. By Lemmas 1 and 2, and (34), $\mathcal{KB}^{\Sigma} \models \alpha$ iff $\mathcal{KB}^{\Sigma} \cap \mathcal{M} \models \alpha$. The Theorem then follows by Lemma 3.   □

4   Optimistic Computation

The construction of $\mathcal{KB}^{\Sigma}$ repeats the concept consistency check (5) over a sequence of knowledge bases $(\mathcal{KB}_{i-1}^{\Sigma} \downarrow_{\prec \delta_i} \cup \{\delta_i^{NC}\})$ that share a (possibly large) common part $\mathcal{KB}_0^{\Sigma}$, so incremental reasoning mechanisms help by avoiding multiple computations of the consequences of $\mathcal{KB}_0^{\Sigma}$. On the contrary, the set of δ_j^{NC} may change significantly at each step due to the filtering $\downarrow_{\prec \delta_i}$. This operation requires many axiom deletions, which as already highlighted in [20], are less efficient than monotonically increasing changes. The optimistic algorithm introduced here (Algorithm 3) computes a knowledge base $\mathcal{KB}^{*}$ equivalent to $\mathcal{KB}^{\Sigma}$ in a way that tends to reduce the number of deletions, as it will be assessed in Sec. 5.

Phase 1 optimistically assumes that the DIs with the same priority as δ_i^{NC} do not contribute to entailing $NC \sqsubseteq \bot$ in (5), so they are not filtered with $\downarrow_{\delta_i}$ in line 3. Phase 2 checks whether the DIs discarded during Phase 1 are actually overridden by applying $\downarrow_{\delta_i}$ (lines 14 and 21). DIs are processed in non-increasing priority order as much as possible (cf. line 19) so as to exploit monotonic incremental classifications.

The following theorem shows the correctness of Alghorithm 3 in case the normality concepts do not occur in $\mathcal{KB}$, but only in the queries. We call such knowledge bases *N-free*. It is worth noting that the optimistic method is not generally correct when $\mathcal{KB}$ is not N-free and $|\Sigma| > 1$, yet it may still be applicable after the module extractor if the latter removes all normality concepts from $\mathcal{KB}$.

Theorem 2. *If $\mathcal{KB}$ is N-free, then Algorithm 3's output is equivalent to $\mathcal{KB}^{\Sigma}$.*

5   Experimental Assessment

Currently there are no "real" KBs encoded in a nonmonotonic DL, because standard DL technology does not support nonmonotonic reasoning. The nonmonotonic KBs encoded in the hybrid rule+DL system DLV-Hex [14] are not suited to our purposes because they do not feature default inheritance due to a restriction of the language: DL predicates cannot occur in rule heads, so rules cannot be used for encoding default inheritance. Consequently, synthetic test cases are the only choice for evaluating our algorithms. We start with the two

---

Algorithm 3. Optimistic-Method

Input: $\mathcal{KB} = \mathcal{S} \cup \mathcal{D}$, Σ
Output: a knowledge base $\mathcal{KB}^*$ such that $\mathcal{KB}^* \equiv \mathcal{KB}^\Sigma$

```
// Phase 1
```
1   compute a linearization $\delta_1, \ldots, \delta_{|\mathcal{D}|}$ of $\mathcal{D}$
2   $\Pi := \emptyset$ `// ` Π ` collects the prototypes`
3   $\Delta := \emptyset$ `// ordered list of all discarded ` δ_i^{NC}
4   **for** $i = 1, 2, \ldots, |\mathcal{D}|$ **do**
5   **for** $NC \in \Sigma$ **do**
6         $\Pi' := \Pi \cup \{\delta_i^{NC}\}$
7   **if** $\mathcal{KB}_0^\Sigma \cup \Pi' \not\models NC \sqsubseteq \bot$ **then**
8            $\Pi := \Pi'$
9   **else**
10   append δ_i^{NC} to Δ

```
// Phase 2
```
11   $\mathcal{KB}^* = \mathcal{KB}_0^\Sigma \cup \Pi$
12   **while** $\Delta \neq \emptyset$ **do**
13   extract from Δ its first element δ_i^{NC}
14   **if** $(\mathcal{KB}_0^\Sigma \cup \Pi) \downarrow_{\prec \delta_i} \cup \{\delta_i^{NC}\} \not\models NC \sqsubseteq \bot$ **then**
15         $\mathcal{KB}^* := \mathcal{KB}^* \cup \{NC \sqsubseteq \bot\}$
16   extract all δ_k^{NE} with $E = C$ from Δ
17   **else**
        `// ` δ_i^{NC} ` is actually overridden`
18         $\delta := \delta_i$
19   **while** Δ *contains some* δ_j^{ND} *such that* $\delta \prec \delta_j$ **do**
20   extract from Δ the first such δ_j^{ND}
21   **if** $(\mathcal{KB}_0^\Sigma \cup \Pi) \downarrow_{\prec \delta_j} \cup \{\delta_j^{ND}\} \not\models ND \sqsubseteq \bot$ **then**
22               $\mathcal{KB}^* := \mathcal{KB}^* \cup \{ND \sqsubseteq \bot\}$
23   extract all δ_k^{NE} with $E = D$ from Δ
24               $\delta := \delta_j$

---

test suites introduced in [8] as they have been proved to be nontrivial w.r.t. a number of structural parameters, including nonclassical features like exception levels and the amount of overriding. The two test suites are obtained by modifying the popular Gene Ontology (GO)[4], which contains 20465 atomic concepts and 28896 concept inclusions. In one test suite, randomly selected axioms of GO are turned into DIs, while in the second suite random synthetic DIs are injected in GO. The amount of strong axioms transformed into DIs is controlled by *CI-to-DI-rate*, expressed as the percentage of transformed axioms w.r.t. |GO| while the amount of additional synthetic DIs is controlled by *Synthetic-DI-rate*, i.e. the ratio $|\mathcal{D}|/|\text{GO}|$. The number of conflicts between DIs can be increased by adding

---

[4] http://www.geneontology.org

an amount of random disjointness axioms specified by parameter DA-$rate$ (see [8] for further details).

The experiments were performed on an Intel Core i7 2,5GHz laptop with 16 GB RAM and OS X 10.10.1, using Java 1.7 configured with 8 GB RAM and 3 GB stack space. Each reported value is the average execution time over ten nonmonotonic ontologies and fifty queries on each ontology. For each parameter setting, we report the execution time of: (i) the naive $\mathcal{DL}^{N}$ reasoner of [8]; (ii) the optimistic method introduced in Sec. 4 (Opt); (iii) the module extraction method of Sec. 3 (Mod) using the module extraction facility of the OWLAPI; (iv) the sequential execution of Mod and Opt, i.e. Algorithm 3 is applied to $\mathcal{KB} \cap \mathcal{M}_0$. This combined method is correct by Theorem 2 and Theorem 1.

Table 2. Impact of $|\mathcal{D}|$ on performance (sec) – DA rate = 15% – priority (1)

CI-to-DI	naive	opt	mod	mod+opt	Synth DIs	naive	opt	mod	mod+opt
05%	12.91	05.93	00.30	00.25	05%	11.64	06.94	0.41	0.42
10%	22.37	11.13	00.32	00.27	10%	21.66	11.21	0.62	0.67
15%	31.50	15.90	00.37	00.32	15%	32.80	14.90	1.11	1.64
20%	42.97	20.67	00.40	00.33	20%	41.51	18.82	2.01	1.42
25%	55.22	25.17	00.44	00.36	25%	51.85	22.33	3.05	2.09

Table 2 shows the impact of the number of DIs on response time for the two test suites, as DI rate ranges from 5% to 25%. The methods Mod and Mod+Opt are slightly less effective in the second suite probably because random defaults connect unrelated parts of the ontology, thereby hindering module extraction. In both suites, Opt's speedup factor (w.r.t. the naive method) is about two, while on average Mod is approximately 87 times faster in the first test suite (max. speedup 125), and 28 times faster in the second (max. speedup 35). On average, the combined method yields a further 13% improvement over Mod alone; the maximum reduction is 31% (2nd suite, Synthetic-DI-rate=25%, DA-rate=15%). The additional conflicts induced by injected disjointness axioms have moderate effects on response time (cf. Table 3). Mod+Opt's average response time across both test suites is 0.7 sec., and the longest Mod+Opt response time has been 2.09 sec. As a term of comparison, a single classification of the original GO takes approximately 0.4 seconds.

Table 4 is the analogue of Table 2 given priority (2). With respect to priority (1), the computation time for $\mathcal{KB}^{\Sigma}$ and query answering in the first test suite grows faster for the naive algorithm, while there are smaller differences for the optimized approaches (the reponse times of the combined approach are almost identical). In the second test suite, the performance of the naive algorithms decreases less dramatically, while the optimized methods seem slightly less effective than in the first test suite. In all cases, the speedups of Mod and Mod-Opt remain well above one order of magnitude. The performance as DAs grow has similar features (see Table 5).

Table 3. Impact of DAs on performance (sec) – DI rate = 15% – priority (1)

Test suite 1 (CI-to-DI)					Test suite 2 (Synth. DIs)			
DA	naive	opt	mod	mod+opt	DA	naive	opt	mod	mod+opt
05%	29.88	13.21	0.36	0.31	05%	28.20	12.63	0.99	0.84
10%	32.96	14.08	0.37	0.32	10%	30.18	13.68	1.04	0.97
15%	31.50	15.90	0.37	0.32	15%	32.80	14.90	1.11	1.06
20%	34.23	16.23	0.39	0.33	20%	35.68	16.29	1.18	1.10
25%	36.47	17.80	0.40	0.34	25%	37.46	17.02	1.25	1.15
30%	37.71	18.09	0.40	0.34	30%	38.37	18.79	1.36	1.23

Table 4. Impact of $|\mathcal{D}|$ on performance (sec) – DA rate = 15% – priority (2)

CI-to-DI	naive	opt	mod	mod+opt	Synth DIs	naive	opt	mod	mod+opt
05%	22.01	05.74	00.30	00.25	05%	12.76	07.21	0.45	0.46
10%	52.82	11.48	00.32	00.28	10%	23.72	14.44	0.81	0.86
15%	81.84	16.56	00.34	00.31	15%	34.53	17.05	1.57	1.21
20%	133.62	20.51	00.38	00.33	20%	44.92	21.77	2.67	1.96
25%	193.27	26.42	00.41	00.36	25%	55.92	25.77	3.87	2.46

Table 5. Impact of DAs on performance (sec) – DI rate = 15% – priority (2)

Test suite 1 (CI-to-DI)					Test suite 2 (Synth. DIs)			
DA	naive	opt	mod	mod+opt	DA	naive	opt	mod	mod+opt
05%	84.53	15.02	0.34	0.29	05%	29.55	14.93	1.28	1.07
10%	90.38	16.12	0.35	0.30	10%	30.81	15.82	1.41	1.15
15%	91.84	16.56	0.35	0.31	15%	34.54	17.05	1.57	1.21
20%	92.93	16.67	0.36	0.31	20%	36.79	16.93	1.62	1.27
25%	93.54	17.76	0.37	0.32	25%	40.86	17.90	1.78	1.36
30%	96.37	19.49	0.38	0.33	30%	43.35	18.74	1.79	1.34

The above test sets are N-free. We carried out a new set of experiments by randomly introducing normality concepts in DIs, within the scope of quantifiers.[5] Specifically, $\exists R.C$ is transformed into $\exists R.N\,C$. The response times of the naive algorithm and Mod[6] under priority (1) are listed in Table 6 for increasing values of $|\Sigma|$ (that is directly related to the amount of normality concepts occurring in $\mathcal{KB}$). We estimate that the values of $|\Sigma|$ considered here are larger than what should be expected in practice, given the specific role of explicit normality concepts, cf. footnote 5. Such values are also much larger than in N-free

---

[5] So far, all the application examples that are not N-free satisfy this restriction, as apparently the only purpose of explicit normality concepts is restricting default role ranges to normal individuals, cf. Ex. 12 and the nomonotonic design pattern in [8, Sec. 3.3].

[6] In this setting Opt and Mod+Opt are not applicable, in general.

Table 6. Impact of normal roles values (sec) – DI rate = 25% DA rate = 15%

$|\Sigma|$	50	100	150	200	250
		Test suite 1			
naive	1794.37	>30 min.	>30 min.	>30 min.	>30 min.
mod	2.31	7.26	14.77	25.32	39.22
		Test suite 2			
naive	>30 min.	>30 min.	>30 min.	>30 min.	>30 min.
mod	103.4	211.5	327.4	459.2	586.7

experiments, where $|\Sigma|$ is bounded by the query size. Response times increase accordingly. In most cases, the naive algorithm exceeded the timeout. In the first test suite, Mod remains well below 1 minute; in the second suite it ranges between 100 seconds and 10 minutes. The reason of the higher computation times in the second suite is that the extracted modules are significantly larger, probably due to the random dependencies between concept names introduced by fully synthetic DIs.

6   Conclusions

The module-based and optimistic optimizations introduced here are sound and complete, where the later applies only if the knowledge base is N-free. In our experiments, the combined method (when applicable) and the module-based method make $\mathcal{DL}^N$ reasoning at least one order of magnitude faster (and up to ~780 times faster in some case). In most cases, optimized reasoning is compatible with real time $\mathcal{DL}^N$ reasoning. This is the first time such performance is reached over nonmonotonic KBs of this size: more than 20K concept names and over 30K inclusions.[7] Our approach brings technology closer to practical nonmonotonic reasoning with very large KBs. Only the random dependencies introduced by synthetic DIs, combined with numerous restrictions of role ranges to normal individuals, can raise response time over 40 seconds; in most of the other cases, computation time remains below 2 seconds.

We are currently exploring a more aggressive module extraction approach, capable of eliminating some of the normality concepts in Σ and related axioms. Besides improving performance over non-N-free KBs, a more powerful module extractor might enable the application of the combined Mod+Opt method to non-N-free $\mathcal{DL}^N$ knowledge bases, by removing all normality concepts from $\mathcal{KB}$ before Opt is applied.

We are also planning to adopt a different module extractor [24] that is promising to be faster than the OWLAPI implementation.

Last but not least, we are progressively extending the set of experiments by covering the missing cases and by widening the benchmark set, using real ontologies different from GO as well as thoroughly synthetic ontologies.

---

[7] Good results have been obtained also for KBs with ~5200 inclusions under rational closure semantics [9,10].

Acknowledgments. The authors would like to thank the reviewers for their valuable comments and suggestions. This work has been partially supported by the PRIN project Security Horizons.

References

1. Baader, F., Hollunder, B.: Embedding defaults into terminological knowledge representation formalisms. J. Autom. Reasoning **14**(1), 149–180 (1995)
2. Baader, F., Hollunder, B.: Priorities on defaults with prerequisites, and their application in treating specificity in terminological default logic. J. Autom. Reasoning **15**(1), 41–68 (1995)
3. Bonatti, P.A., Faella, M., Sauro, L.: $\mathcal{EL}$ with default attributes and overriding. In: Patel-Schneider, P.F., Pan, Y., Hitzler, P., Mika, P., Zhang, L., Pan, J.Z., Horrocks, I., Glimm, B. (eds.) ISWC 2010, Part I. LNCS, vol. 6496, pp. 64–79. Springer, Heidelberg (2010)
4. Bonatti, P.A., Faella, M., Sauro, L.: Adding default attributes to EL++. In: Burgard, W., Roth, D. (eds.) AAAI. AAAI Press (2011)
5. Bonatti, P.A., Faella, M., Sauro, L.: Defeasible inclusions in low-complexity DLs. J. Artif. Intell. Res. (JAIR) **42**, 719–764 (2011)
6. Bonatti, P.A., Lutz, C., Wolter, F.: The complexity of circumscription in DLs. J. Artif. Intell. Res. (JAIR) **35**, 717–773 (2009)
7. Bonatti, P.A., Petrova, I.M., Sauro, L.: Optimizing the computation of overriding. ArXiv e-prints, July 2015
8. Bonatti, P.A., Petrova, I.M., Sauro, L.: A new semantics for overriding in description logics. Artif. Intell. **222**, 1–48 (2015). http://www.sciencedirect.com/science/article/pii/S0004370215000028
9. Casini, G., Meyer, T., Moodley, K., Nortjé, R.: Relevant closure: a new form of defeasible reasoning for description logics. In: Fermé, E., Leite, J. (eds.) JELIA 2014. LNCS, vol. 8761, pp. 92–106. Springer, Heidelberg (2014)
10. Casini, G., Meyer, T., Moodley, K., Varzinczak, I.J.: Towards practical defeasible reasoning for description logics. In: Eiter, T., Glimm, B., Kazakov, Y., Krötzsch, M. (eds.) Description Logics. CEUR Workshop Proceedings, vol. 1014, pp. 587–599. CEUR-WS.org (2013)
11. Casini, G., Straccia, U.: Rational closure for defeasible description logics. In: Janhunen, T., Niemelä, I. (eds.) JELIA 2010. LNCS, vol. 6341, pp. 77–90. Springer, Heidelberg (2010)
12. Casini, G., Straccia, U.: Defeasible inheritance-based description logics. J. Artif. Intell. Res. (JAIR) **48**, 415–473 (2013)
13. Donini, F.M., Nardi, D., Rosati, R.: Description logics of minimal knowledge and negation as failure. ACM Trans. Comput. Log. **3**(2), 177–225 (2002)
14. Drabent, W., Eiter, T., Ianni, G., Krennwallner, T., Lukasiewicz, T., Małuszyński, J.: Hybrid reasoning with rules and ontologies. In: Bry, F., Małuszyński, J. (eds.) Semantic Techniques for the Web. LNCS, vol. 5500, pp. 1–49. Springer, Heidelberg (2009)
15. Baader, F., Calvanese, D., Mcguinness D., Nardi, D., Patel Schneider, P.: The description logic handbook, theory, implementation, and applications (2nd edition). In: The Description Logic Handbook, pp. 555–555. Cambridge University Press, Cambridge (2010)

16. Ghilardi, S., Lutz, C., Wolter, F.: Did I damage my ontology? a case for conservative extensions in description logics. In: Doherty, P., Mylopoulos, J., Welty, C. (eds.) Proceedings of the Tenth International Conference on Principles of Knowledge Representation and Reasoning (KR 2006), pp. 187–197. AAAI Press (2006)

17. Giordano, L., Gliozzi, V., Olivetti, N., Pozzato, G.L.: A non-monotonic description logic for reasoning about typicality. Artif. Intell. **195**, 165–202 (2013)

18. Giordano, L., Olivetti, N., Gliozzi, V., Pozzato, G.L.: ALC + T: a preferential extension of description logics. Fundam. Inform. **96**(3), 341–372 (2009)

19. Grau, B.C., Horrocks, I., Kazakov, Y., Sattler, U.: Modular reuse of ontologies: Theory and practice. J. Artif. Intell. Res. (JAIR) **31**, 273–318 (2008)

20. Kazakov, Y., Klinov, P.: Incremental reasoning in EL+ without bookkeeping. In: Description Logics, pp. 294–315 (2013)

21. Kontchakov, R., Wolter, F., Zakharyaschev, M.: Can you tell the difference between dl-lite ontologies? In Brewka, G., Lang, J. (eds.) Principles of Knowledge Representation and Reasoning: Proceedings of the Eleventh International Conference, KR 2008, Sydney, Australia, 16–19 September 2008, pp. 285–295. AAAI Press (2008)

22. Lukasiewicz, T.: Expressive probabilistic description logics. Artif. Intell. **172**(6–7), 852–883 (2008)

23. Lutz, C., Walther, D., Wolter, F.: Conservative extensions in expressive description logics. In: Veloso, M.M. (ed.) Proceedings of the 20th International Joint Conference on Artificial Intelligence, IJCAI 2007, Hyderabad, India, 6–12 January 2007, pp. 453–458 (2007)

24. Martin-Recuerda, F., Walther, D.: Axiom dependency hypergraphs for fast modularisation and atomic decomposition. In: Bienvenu, M., Ortiz, M., Rosati, R., Simkus, M. (eds.) Proceedings of the 27th International Workshop on Description Logics (DL 2014). CEUR Workshop Proceedings, vol. 1193, pp. 299–310 (2014)

25. Rector, A.L.: Defaults, context, and knowledge: Alternatives for OWL-indexed knowledge bases. In: Pacific Symposium on Biocomputing, pp. 226–237. World Scientific (2004)

26. Sandewall, E.: Defeasible inheritance with doubt index and its axiomatic characterization. Artif. Intell. **174**(18), 1431–1459 (2010)

27. Sattler, U., Schneider, T., Zakharyaschev, M.: Which kind of module should I extract? In: Grau, B.C., Horrocks, I., Motik, B., Sattler, U. (eds.) Proceedings of the 22nd International Workshop on Description Logics (DL 2009), Oxford, UK, 27–30 July 2009, vol. 477. CEUR Workshop Proceedings. CEUR-WS.org (2009)

28. Stevens, R., Aranguren, M.E., Wolstencroft, K., Sattler, U., Drummond, N., Horridge, M., Rector, A.L.: Using OWL to model biological knowledge. Int. J. Man Mach. Stud. **65**(7), 583–594 (2007)

29. Woo, T.Y.C., Lam, S.S.: Authorizations in distributed systems: A new approach. J. Comput. Secur. **2**(2–3), 107–136 (1993)

Instance Matching, Entity Resolution and Topic Generation

LANCE: Piercing to the Heart of Instance Matching Tools

Tzanina Saveta[1]($\boxtimes$), Evangelia Daskalaki[1], Giorgos Flouris[1], Irini Fundulaki[1],
Melanie Herschel[2], and Axel-Cyrille Ngonga Ngomo[3]

[1] Institute of Computer Science-FORTH, Heraklion, Greece
jsaveta@ics.forth.gr
[2] IPVS - University of Stuttgart, Stuttgart, Germany
[3] IFI/AKSW, University of Leipzig, Leipzig, Germany

Abstract. One of the main challenges in the Data Web is the identification of instances that refer to the same real-world entity. Choosing the right framework for this purpose remains tedious, as current
instance matching benchmarks fail to provide end users and developers with the necessary insights pertaining to how current frameworks
behave when dealing with real data. In this paper, we present LANCE,
a domain-independent instance matching benchmark generator which
focuses on benchmarking instance matching systems for Linked Data.
LANCE is the first Linked Data benchmark generator to support complex
semantics-aware test cases that take into account expressive OWL constructs, in addition to the standard test cases related to structure and
value transformations. LANCE supports the definition of matching tasks
with varying degrees of difficulty and produces a weighted gold standard,
which allows a more fine-grained analysis of the performance of instance
matching tools. It can accept *any* linked dataset and its accompanying
schema as input to produce a target dataset implementing test cases
of varying levels of difficulty. We provide a comparative analysis with
LANCE benchmarks to assess and identify the capabilities of state of the
art instance matching systems as well as an evaluation to demonstrate
the scalability of LANCE's test case generator.

1 Introduction

Instance matching (IM), refers to the problem of identifying instances that
describe the *same real-world object* (alternative names include entity resolution [1], duplicate detection [2], record linkage [3] and object identification in the
context of databases [4]). With the increasing adoption of Semantic Web Technologies and the publication of large interrelated RDF datasets and ontologies
that form the Linked Data Cloud,[1] it is crucial to develop IM techniques adapted
to this setting that is characterized by an unprecedented number of sources across

---

This work was partially supported by the EU FP7 projects LDBC (FP7-ICT-2011-8
#317548) and H2020 PARTHENOS (#654119).
[1] http://linkeddata.org/

M. Arenas et al. (Eds.): ISWC 2015, Part I, LNCS 9366, pp. 375–391, 2015.
DOI: 10.1007/978-3-319-25007-6_22

which to detect matches, a high degree of heterogeneity both at the schema and at the instance level, and rich semantics that accompany schemas defined in terms of expressive languages such as OWL, OWL 2, and RDFS. For such data, many IM techniques have recently been proposed (e.g., [5,6], survey in [7]).

Clearly, the large variety of IM techniques requires their comparative evaluation to determine which technique is best suited for a given application. Performing such an assessment generally requires *well-defined and widely accepted benchmarks* to determine the weak and strong points of the methods or systems and to motivate the development of better systems in order to overcome identified weak points. Hence, suited benchmarks help push the limit of existing systems, advancing both research and technology. A number of benchmarks have already been proposed, both for relational and XML data [8] and, more recently, for RDF data, the type of data prevalent in the Web of Data [9–12].

This paper presents the *Linked Data Instance Matching Benchmark Generator*[2] (LANCE), a novel IM *benchmark generator* for assessing IM techniques for RDF data with an associated schema. The main features of LANCE are:

Wider Set of Test Cases. LANCE supports a set of *test cases* based on *transformations* that distinguish different types of matching entities. Similarly to existing IM benchmarks, LANCE supports the *value-based* (typos, date/number formats, etc.) and *structure-based* (deletion of properties, aggregations, splits, etc.) test cases. LANCE is the *first benchmark generator* to support *explicitly* advanced *semantics-aware* test cases that go beyond the standard RDFS constructs. These test cases test the use of RDFS/OWL semantics to identify matches, and include tests involving *instance (in)equality*, class and property *equivalence* and *disjointness, property constraints*, as well as *complex class definitions*. LANCE also supports *simple combination (SC)* test cases (implemented using the aforementioned transformations applied on different triples pertaining to the same instance), as well as *complex combination (CC)* test cases (implemented by combinations of individual transformations on the same triple).

Similarity Score and Fine-Grained Evaluation Metrics. LANCE provides an enriched, *weighted gold standard* and related evaluation metrics, which allow a more fine-grained analysis of the performance of systems for tests with varying difficulty. In particular, the ground truth (or gold standard, i.e., pairs consisting of an entity in the source dataset and its matching entity in the target dataset) is enriched with annotations specific to the test case that generated each pair, i.e., the type of test case it represents, the property on which a transformation was applied, and a *similarity score* (or *weight*) that essentially quantifies the difficulty of finding a particular match. This detailed information, which is not provided by previous benchmarks, allows LANCE to adopt more detailed views and evaluation metrics to assess the completeness, soundness, and overall matching quality of an IM system. In particular, LANCE uses the *average similarity score* of the gold standard in combination with the *standard deviation* of the weight of each pair from the average score in order to asses the benchmark's level of difficulty.

---

[2] http://www.ics.forth.gr/isl/lance

This fine-grained analysis allows LANCE users to more easily identify the reasons underlying the obtained performance results, and thereby supports IM systems' debugging and extension.

High Level of Customization and Scalability Testing. LANCE provides the ability to build a benchmark on top of any dataset, thereby allowing the implementation of diverse test cases for different domains, dataset sizes and morphology. This makes LANCE highly customizable and domain-independent. Perhaps more importantly, this feature allows also systematic scalability testing of IM systems, a feature which is not available in most state-of-the-art IM benchmarks.

The rest of the paper is structured as follows: in Section 2, we discuss related work; Section 3 describes the different components of our benchmark generator; Section 4 demonstrates the suitability of our benchmark generator in assessing and identifying the capabilities of an IM system; Section 5 concludes the paper.

2   Related Work

Several benchmarks have been proposed for testing the performance of IM systems for Linked Data. These benchmarks were the first to consider structure-based test cases, as previous benchmarks for relational and XML data primarily focused on value-based ones. A summary of the benchmarks relevant for LANCE is shown in Table 1; a more complete survey can be found in [13].

Our approach is based on the test cases proposed by our previous work SPIMBENCH [12] but unlike SPIMBENCH, LANCE is a domain-independent benchmark generator.

Table 1. IM benchmark summary showing dataset size (VOL), supported test cases (value-based (VAL), structure-based (STR), semantics-aware (SEM)) and support for multilinguality (ML). A star (*) indicates a benchmark proposed by OAEI [9].

Benchmark	VOL	VAL	STR	SEM	ML
Synthetic IM benchmarks					
IIMB (2009) [14]*	2K	√	√	ltd	
IIMB (2010) [15]*	14K	√	√	ltd	
PR (2010) [16]*	9K	√	√		
IIMB (2011) [17]*	4K	√	√	ltd	
Sandbox (2012) [18]*	4K	√			
IIMB (2012) [18]*	2K	√	√	ltd	
RDFT (2013) [19]*	4K	√	√		√
ID-REC (2014) [20]*	3K	√			
ONTOBI (2010) [10]	14K	√	√	ltd	√
LANCE (2015)	√	√	√	√	√
Real IM benchmarks					
ARS (2009) [14]*	1M	√	√		
DI (2010) [15]*	6K	√	√		
DI (2011) [17]*	N/A	√	√		

OAEI. The most important initiative regarding IM benchmarks is the *Ontology Alignment Evaluation Initiative (OAEI)* [9] that organizes a related annual track since 2009. OAEI proposes benchmarks based on both real and synthetic datasets. Synthetic datasets are mostly small (up to a few thousand instances) but allow a more accurate evaluation of the matching quality of IM systems, since they provide an accurate gold standard that is automatically constructed. Real datasets are much larger (millions of instances) and allow evaluating the scalability of IM frameworks; nevertheless, the provided gold standard is error-prone, as it is practically infeasible to identify the complete and correct set of matches either manually (ARS [14]) or semi-automatically (DI 2010 [15], DI 2011 [17]). Thus, evaluating the ability of IM methods to scale comes at the price of a less accurate evaluation of matching quality. LANCE avoids this trade-off, as it generates the datasets along with the gold standard containing the matched instances. Most OAEI benchmarks consider both value-based and structure-based test cases (see Table 1). The support for semantics-aware test cases is limited to the IIMB benchmarks: IIMB 2009 considered only simple features such as class hierarchies and the OWL sameAs, whereas later versions used the SWING benchmark data generator [21] to support more complex cases, but still in a limited fashion compared to LANCE. Multilinguality (an important feature in practice) supported by LANCE, is considered by RDFT [19] only.

ONTOBI. ONTOBI is a synthetic IM benchmark that uses the DBpedia ontology (v.3.4) to propose 16 different test cases that include spelling mistakes, suppressed comments, change in date and number formats, deleted data types, language modifications, random names changes, synonym-based changes, disjunct dataset and flattening/expansion of the structure. ONTOBI is a domain-specific benchmark that supports mainly value and structure based test cases, as well as a limited amount of semantics-aware ones. It considers larger datasets than OAEI, but still in the range of a few thousand triples.

SWING. The SWING benchmark data generator [21] provides a general framework for creating IM benchmarks; it supports various test cases based on value and structure transformations at the instance level. The semantics-aware test cases are built upon class and property subsumption hierarchies, class disjointness and inverse properties. LANCE builds on SWING to implement most of the value-based test cases, but is also applying some novel value-based transformations, as well as a richer set of structure-based and semantics-aware test cases. SWING generates an artificial benchmark (without size limitations) and the corresponding gold standard, based on a given schema, thus allowing the creation of domain-independent benchmarks suitable for both scalability and matching quality evaluation. However, unlike LANCE, SWING does not support weighted gold standards and thus provides less insights for developers to debug or improve their IM system.

3   LANCE

3.1   Transformation-Based Test Cases

In LANCE we propose a set of *value-based*, *structure-based*, and *semantics-aware* test cases. The former two are implemented using *transformations* as proposed in Ferrara et. al [21] on *data* and *object type* properties respectively; the last refers to the use of a subset of OWL *semantic* constructs. Value and structure-based test cases are produced by applying the appropriate transformation(s) on a *source* instance to obtain a *target* instance. The same principle holds in the case of semantics-aware test cases, with the difference that appropriate instance-level triples are constructed and added in the target dataset to consider the respective OWL constructs. This pair of instances is then used as input for the instance matching system (along with the gold standard) to test its performance.

Value-based Test Cases refer to scenarios implemented using *transformations* on *instance data type properties* that consider mainly typographical errors and the use of different data formats. In LANCE we extended the transformations of SWING [21], by adding antonyms, country abbreviations and multilinguality.

Table 2. LANCE value-based transformations

VT1	Blank char. Addition/Deletion
VT2	Random char. Addition/Deletion/Modification
VT3	Token Addition/Deletion/Shuffle
VT4	Date Formats
VT5	Country & Simple Abbreviations
VT6	Synonym/Antonym
VT7	Stem of a Word
VT8	Multilinguality

Table 2 presents the transformations implemented in LANCE. Each transformation takes as input a *data type property* and a *severity* that determines how severe this modification is. Transformations VT1-VT3 can be perceived as different cases of *misspellings*. VT4 addresses the use of different date formats; Abbreviations are addressed by VT5: LANCE supports abbreviations that are very common in texts (such as "United States of America" vs "USA"), as well as those of SWING. VT6 refers to the use of synonyms and antonyms taken from Wordnet[3]. Stemming is applied using transformation VT7. LANCE also supports *multilinguality* (transformation VT8) from English to 64 languages.

Structure-Based Test Cases are based on transformations applied on *object and data type* properties of instances such as *splitting, aggregation, deletion* and *addition*. Splitting refers to expanding properties whereas aggregation refers to merging a number of properties to a single one. In addition to property aggregation we support all the structure-based transformations that are proposed and implemented in SWING. These transformations are a superset of those considered in other IM benchmarks (see Section 2).

Semantics-Aware Test Cases are primarily used to examine if the matching systems take into consideration OWL and OWL 2 axioms to discover matches between instances that can be found only when considering schema information. The axioms that we consider in LANCE are:

- *class* and *property equivalence* (`equivalentClass`, `equivalentProperty`)
- *instance (in)equality* (`sameAs`, `differentFrom`)

---

[3] http://wordnet.princeton.edu/

Table 3. Semantics-aware test cases

	SOURCE DATASET	TARGET DATASET	SCHEMA TRIPLES	GS
ltSubC	$(u_1, \mathtt{rdf:type}, C_1)$	$(u_1', \mathtt{rdf:type}, C_1')$	$(C_1, \mathtt{subClassOf}, C_1')$	(u_1, u_1')
ltEqC	$(u_1, \mathtt{rdf:type}, C_1)$	$(u_1', \mathtt{rdf:type}, C_1')$	$(C_1, \mathtt{equivalentClass}, C_1')$	(u_1, u_1')
ltSameAs1	$(u_1, \mathtt{rdf:type}, C_1)$ $(u_2, \mathtt{rdf:type}, C_1)$	$(u_1', \mathtt{rdf:type}, C_1)$ $(u_2', \mathtt{rdf:type}, C_1)$ $(u_1', \mathtt{sameAs}, u_2')$		(u_1, u_1') (u_1, u_2') (u_2, u_2') (u_2, u_1')
ltDiff	$(u_1, \mathtt{rdf:type}, C_1)$	$(u_1', \mathtt{rdf:type}, C_1)$ $(u_1'', \mathtt{rdf:type}, C_1)$ $(u_1', \mathtt{differentFrom}, u_1'')$		(u_1, u_1')
ltDisjC	$(u_1, \mathtt{rdf:type}, C_1)$	$(u_1', \mathtt{rdf:type}, C_1')$	$(C_1, \mathtt{disjointWith}, C_1')$	—
ltFuncP	(u_1, p_1, o_1)	(u_1, p_1, o_1')	$(p_1, \mathtt{rdf:type}$ $\mathtt{FunctionalProperty})$	(o_1, o_1')
ltInvFuncP	(u_1, p_1, o_1)	(o_1, p_1, u_1')	$(p_1, \mathtt{rdf:type},$ $\mathtt{InverseFunctionalProperty})$	(u_1, u_1')
ltUnionOf	$(u_1, \mathtt{rdf:type}, C_1)$	$(u_1', \mathtt{rdf:type}, C_1')$	$(C_1', \mathtt{unionOf}, \{C_1, C_2, \ldots\})$	(u_1, u_1')
ltIntersect1	$(u_1, \mathtt{rdf:type}, C_1)$	$(u_1', \mathtt{rdf:type}, C_1')$	$(C_1, \mathtt{intersectionOf}, S)$ $(C_1', \mathtt{intersectionOf}, S)$	(u_1, u_1')
ltIntersect2	$(u_1, \mathtt{rdf:type}, C_1)$	$(u_1', \mathtt{rdf:type}, C_1')$	$(C_1, \mathtt{intersectionOf}, S)$ $(C_1', \mathtt{intersectionOf}, S')$ $S' \subset S$	(u_1, u_1')

- *class* and *property disjointness* (`disjointWith`, `AllDisjointClasses`, `property-DisjointWith`, `AllDisjointProperties`)
- *class* and *property* hierarchies (`subClassOf`, `subPropertyOf`)
- *property constraints* (`FunctionalProperty`, `InverseFunctionalProperty`)
- *complex class definitions* (`unionOf`, `intersectionOf`)

Table 3 shows some of these semantics-aware test cases: column SCHEMA TRIPLES refers to *schema triples* that the instance matcher under test should take into consideration when performing the matching tasks and GS shows the pairs of matches (ui, ui') that will be included in the gold standard. In all the tables we write ui to refer interchangeably to an RDF instance and its URI. The rules in Table 3 should not be viewed as inference rules, but as *hints* for a system to derive that a match holds.

Class Hierarchy & Equivalence: test cases **ltSubC**, **ltEqC** shown in Table 3 consider the `subClassOf` and `equivalentClass` constructs respectively. Given a source URI u_1, instance of class C_1, we create target URI u_1', instance of class C_1' by copying all the properties of u_1 (except `rdf:type` triples) to create u_1'. For **ltSubC**, C_1 is a subclass of C_1' (schema triple $(C_1$, `subClassOf`, $C_1')$) and u_1 and u_1' are considered as *matches* in the gold standard since they are of similar type due to the `subClassOf` semantics that specify that a class contains all instances of its subclasses. For **ltEqC**, C_1 and C_1' are equivalent classes (schema triple $(C_1$, `equivalentClass`, $C_1'))$, so the two instances are considered matches since they are of the same type due to the semantics of class equivalence, according to which two equivalent classes have the same set of instances.

The rationale for properties is exactly the same since subPropertyOf and equivalentProperty axioms have similar semantics as their class counterparts. Test cases for subClassOf and subPropertyOf hierarchies are supported by the IM benchmarks that provide a limited support for this type of tests [10,14,15,17,18].

Instance (in)equality: test case **ltSameAs1** shown in Table 3 is a complex test for OWL construct sameAs; for this case we consider two source URIs u_1 and u_2 instances of the same class C_1; for u_1 and u_2, we create target instances u'_1 and u'_2. These are added in the target dataset along with triple (u'_1, sameAs, u'_2). A matcher that understands the semantics of sameAs should report all possible four matches between instances u_1, u'_1, u_2 and u'_2, otherwise it will report matches (u_1, u'_1) and (u_2, u'_2). OWL construct differentFrom is used to explicitly state that two resources refer to different real world objects. Test case **ltDiff** shown in Table 3 follows the same lines as the test case for sameAs construct: for a source instance u_1, we create two target instances u'_1 and u''_1 by copying all the properties of u_1 (including the rdf:type property). Target instance u''_1 is obtained by applying additional value and structure transformations to u'_1. Triple $(u'_1, \text{differentFrom}, u''_1)$ is also added in the target dataset. If the matcher does not take under consideration the differentFrom construct it should produce a match between instances u_1 and u''_1 when it should not, since there is an *explicit* statement that these two instances refer to a different real world object (u_1, differentFrom, u''_1). Note that for all the test cases concerning sameAs and differentFrom OWL constructs, we assume that the source and target instances are of the same *type* (i.e., belong to the same class).

Class Disjointness: test case **ltDisjC** shown in Table 3 addresses class disjointness. To implement this test we produce target instance u'_1 from source instance u_1 as discussed before; these are instances of two *disjoint* classes C_1 and C'_1 - schema triple $(C_1, \text{disjointWith}, C'_1)$ - respectively. In this case, the matcher should not return any match since according to the OWL semantics, two disjoint classes *cannot* share the same set of instances. Disjointness of properties follows the same rationale as disjointness of classes. Test cases for AllDisjointClasses and AllDisjointProperties follow the same principles for disjointWith and propertyDisjointWith respectively.

Functional & Inverse Functional Properties: A functional property is a property that can have only one (unique) value y for each instance x. Inverse functional properties are useful to denote values that uniquely identify an entity. Note that, due to the fact that the semantics of OWL do not include the Unique Name Assumption, inverse functional properties should not be viewed as integrity constraints, because they cannot directly (by themselves) lead to contradictions. Instead, they force us to assume (infer) that certain individuals are the same as declared by the OWL semantics. **ltFuncP** test case shown in Table 3 considers FunctionalProperty: for a source instance u_1, subject of triple (u_1, p_1, o_1) with p_1 being a functional property (schema triple $(p_1, \text{rdf:type}, \text{FunctionalProperty})$) we produce a triple (u_1, p_1, o'_1) in the target dataset, where o'_1 is obtained by applying a set of value and structure based transformations. If the matcher takes into consideration the fact that p_1 is a functional property, then it should produce a match between instances o_1 and o'_1 since according to the semantics of FunctionalProperty if a property p is declared as functional, then an instance u cannot have two properties p with different values. The same rationale is followed for **ltInvFuncP** test case that addresses InverseFunctionalProperty.

Complex Class Definitions: LANCE supports test cases for the unionOf and intersectionOf constructs shown in Table 3. As with all OWL constructs, the semantics of unionOf are intentional: unionOf implies a subsumption relationship between the constituents of the union, and the union itself. Therefore, if a class A is defined as a union of A_1, A_2, ..., A_k then all instances that are known to be instances of any $A_i,...,A_k$ will also be instances of their union. In **ltUnionOf** we assume that C'_1 is defined as a union of a set of classes $C_1, C_2, ... C_k$. For this test, we create for u_1 instance of class C_1 in the source dataset, u'_1 instance of class C'_1 in the target dataset. According to the unionOf semantics, u'_1 is an instance of class C'_1, and hence we go back to the subClassOf test case. Hence, we add (u_1, u'_1) as matched instances in the gold standard.

Similar to unionOf, intersectionOf semantics are also intentional: if a class A is defined as an intersection of A_1, A_2, ..., A_k then A contains exactly those instances that are common to all classes. In addition, A is defined as the subclass of A_1, A_2, ... A_k. In **ltIntersect1**, u_1 is an instance of class C_1 in the source dataset and u'_1 is an instance of class C'_1 in the target dataset. C_1 and C'_1 are defined as the intersection of the *same* set of classes S. In that case, u_1 and u'_1 have the same type, and we include pair (u_1, u'_1) in the gold standard. In **ltIntersect2**, classes C_1 and C'_1 are defined as the intersection of two different sets of classes S and S', the latter being a subset of the former. Instances u_1 and u'_1 are again reported as matches in the gold standard since they have the same type (through the semantics of intersectionOf).

Simple and Complex Combination Test Cases. In LANCE we consider combinations of the aforementioned test cases. We distinguish between *simple combination (SC)* test cases based on value, structure based and semantics-aware test cases, applied on different triples pertaining to one class instance. For example, for an instance u_1, we can perform a value-based transformation on its triple (u_1, p_1, o_1) where p_1 is a data type property and a structure-based transformation on its triple (u_1, p_2, o_2). We also consider *complex combination (CC)* test cases that are based on combinations of test cases applied to a *single* triple along with a transformation applied to the class of the instance. For instance, when a semantics-aware test case is considered, then for a triple (u_1, p_1, o_1) we can produce a triple (u_1, p'_1, o'_1) where p_1 is a subproperty of p'_1 and o'_1 is obtained by applying a value transformation on o_1.

3.2 Weighted Gold Standard

In the following, we present the weighted gold standard generated by LANCE. We begin by presenting how we store the transformations that were used to generate a target instance u'_i based on a source instance u_i. Thereafter, we present our approach to computing similarity scores for each pair (u_i, u'_i).

Computing the Similarity Scores. To improve the debugging of instance matching tools and algorithms, we assign a similarity score (weight) to each pair of instances that should be matched. In essence, the weight of a match (u_i, u'_i) quantifies how similar the source and target instances are. We adopt an information-theoretical approach to compute the weight w of (u_i, u'_i) by measuring the information loss that results from applying transformations to the source data to generate the target data. The basic idea behind our approach is to apply a multi-relational learning (MRL) approach $\mathcal{L}$ to the input knowledge base K and the transformed knowledge base K'. By comparing the description of u_i in $\mathcal{L}(K)$ and u'_i in $\mathcal{L}(K')$, we should then be able to quantify how much information was lost through the transformation of K to K'. We implement this insight in the current version of LANCE by using RESCAL [22,23] as MRL approach.

The idea behind RESCAL is that each RDF graph K can be represented as a tensor $\mathcal{T}$ of order 3 and dimensions $|R| \times |R| \times |P|$, where R is the set of all RDF resources, P is the set of all RDF properties and $\mathcal{T}(i,j,k) = 1$ iff $< u_i, p_k, u_j > \in K$. Let $\mathcal{T}(\cdot,\cdot,k)$ be the kth $|R| \times |R|$-matrix that makes up $\mathcal{T}$, i.e., the matrix that is such that $\mathcal{T}(\cdot,\cdot,k)_{ij} = 1$ iff $< u_i, p_k, u_j > \in K$. RESCAL approximates the matrix A which minimizes the error $||\mathcal{T}(\cdot,\cdot,k) - X_k A X_k^\top||_F^2$ over all $\mathcal{T}(\cdot,\cdot,k)$ simultaneously. Based on A and the X_k matrices, we can approximate the whole of $\mathcal{T}$ to a tensor $\tilde{\mathcal{T}}$ with $\tilde{\mathcal{T}}(\cdot,\cdot,k) = X_k A X_k^\top$. As shown in previous work [23], each matrix $\tilde{\mathcal{T}}(i,\cdot,\cdot)$ contains all predicted relations of the resource u_i. Hence, it can be regarded as a complete description of u_i. The similarity in information content of u_i and u'_i can thus be computed by using the squared cosine of the angle between the matrices $\tilde{\mathcal{T}}(i,\cdot,\cdot)$, $\tilde{\mathcal{T}}'(i,\cdot,\cdot)$, where $\tilde{\mathcal{T}}'(i,\cdot,\cdot)$ is the tensor that results from applying the transformations above to the input (K):

$$cos^2(\tilde{\mathcal{T}}(i,\cdot,\cdot), \tilde{\mathcal{T}}'(i,\cdot,\cdot)) = \frac{\sum_{jk} \tilde{\mathcal{T}}(i,j,k)\tilde{\mathcal{T}}'(i,j,k)}{||\tilde{\mathcal{T}}(i,\cdot,\cdot)||_F^2 ||\tilde{\mathcal{T}}'(i,\cdot,\cdot)||_F^2}. \tag{1}$$

A squared cosine value close to 1 suggests that u_i and u'_i contain similar information and that the information loss due to the transformation was small. Hence, it should be easier for an instance matching framework to detect this match than a match with a smaller squared cosine similarity.

On the hardware used for our evaluation of LANCE (see Section 4), RESCAL's performance grew linearly with the size of the benchmark. In particular, the approach required approximately 6 minutes to compute $\tilde{\mathcal{T}}$ for 10^4 triples. While the corresponding waiting times are acceptable for up to medium-sized datasets (i.e., data sets in orders of magnitude up to 10^5 triples), they are too large to be used when generating large benchmarks with more than 10^6 triples. We thus extended the approach above to be used on larger data sets by using sampling.

The idea behind our sampling approach is to partition the input knowledge base K into n partitions $K_1 \ldots K_n$ of the same size and run the approach above on user-selected partitions. Now for each pair of resources (u_i, u'_i) from the gold standard that belongs to the user-chosen partitions, we can compute a weight where instance u_i, and its transformed instance u_i are stored in partitions K_i (input knowledge base) and K_i' (transformed knowledge base). In addition, we know how many transformations of which type were used to generate u_i' out of u_i. Based on this information, we can compute how much each transformation contributes to the information loss that occurs when generating u_i out of u_i' by solving the corresponding linear regression problem. Note that the matrices generated when applying our approach are commonly degenerate and that we thus use a numerical solver based on gradient descent to detect an approximate solution.

3.3 Metrics

The performance metric(s) in a benchmark determine the *effectiveness* and *efficiency* of the IM systems and tools. Traditionally, IM benchmarks focus on the quality of the output in terms of standard metrics such as *precision, recall* and *f-measure* [24]. In LANCE, opportunities for more sophisticated metrics arise due to the use of a *weighted gold standard*, which records, for each match, the *similarity* (or *weight*) of its source and target instances that is in the range $0 \ldots 1$, and essentially quantifies the *difficulty* for an IM system to find this match.

In particular, a weight close to 1 means that the two instances are similar i.e., practically no transformations were applied to the source instances in order to generate the target instance; this match can be discovered relatively "easily" by an IM system and is hence considered a *low-difficulty* match. On the other hand, a weight close to 0 means that the target instance was obtained by applying complex transformations such as changing the topology of the graph through semantics-aware test cases (i.e., changing the class type of an instance), together with structure-based ones. This is a *difficult match* to discover for an IM system, since it needs to use effective similarity algorithms and be aware of possibly complex constraints or lower the employed threshold consequently affecting negatively precision.

In particular, by knowing the similarities of the matched instances recorded in the gold standard of a LANCE benchmark (say w_i), we can compute its *average similarity score* and the *standard deviation of its similarities*. These two numbers describe the average "difficulty" of the matched instances (i.e., of the test cases implemented in the benchmark) and the spread of the similarity scores (difficulty) in their range $(0 \ldots 1)$.

A benchmark with a *high average similarity score* contains matched instances that are easier to find (easier cases have weights close to 1); a benchmark with a high standard deviation means that the weights are spread out from the average, so there is a larger variety of weights in the gold standard. The formulas are:

$$\mu = \tfrac{1}{N} \textstyle\sum_{i=1}^{N} w_i \qquad\qquad \sigma = \tfrac{1}{N} \textstyle\sum_{i=1}^{N} (w_i - \mu)^2$$

In a similar fashion, we can compute the average and standard deviation of the *true positives* of a tested IM system (returned matches that are also in the gold standard). By comparing these numbers with the corresponding numbers for the benchmark, we can get a more fine-grained understanding of the system's effectiveness. In particular, comparing the averages, we can determine whether the IM system was able to find the easier or the more difficult matches; comparing the standard deviations gives an indication of whether the system is good for a specific range of transformations (as indicated by a deviation that is smaller than the benchmark's standard deviation) or for many different ones.

4   Evaluation

Applicability and Scalability. Our evaluation focused on demonstrating the capability of our benchmark generator in assessing and identifying the strengths and weaknesses of instance matching systems. For this purpose, we evaluated LogMap Version 2.4 [25] using the MoRe [26] reasoner, OtO [27] and LIMES [6] running the EAGLE [28] algorithm (Section 4.1). We chose these tools because they are prototypical working instances of existing IM systems[4]. LogMap considers both schema and instance level matching; hence it should perform well on all variations of the benchmark. OtO on the other hand, needs to be configured manually to implement instance matching tasks, so we assume that it will perform well on tasks with value transformations. The same holds for EAGLE, which can learn specifications and focuses on instance matching tasks only; we expect EAGLE to have a hard time at finding matches when faced with semantic transformations. We also report on the *scalability* aspect of LANCE (Section 4.1). The purpose of this experiment is to show that LANCE can be used for source datasets of arbitrary size and can generate target datasets that implement a large number of test cases without any additional processing overhead.

Datasets. We used as source datasets those generated by LDBC's[5] SPIMBEN-CH [12]. Nevertheless, various data generators can be used in order to produce the *source* datasets. Indicatively we name Berlin SPARQL Benchmark (BSBM) [31], the DBpedia SPARQL Benchmark [32] and UOBM [33]. Due to space constraints we only present results achieved when using SPIMBENCH datasets. We produced two datasets, one with 10K triples and around 500 instances, and a larger one with 50K triples and around 2500 instances. All experiments were conducted on an Intel(R) Core(TM) 2 Duo CPU E8400 @3.00GHz with 8G of main memory running Windows 7 (64-bit).

Implementation of LANCE. LANCE[6] is a highly configurable instance matching benchmark generator for Linked Data that consists of two components : (i) an

---

[4] Attempts to evaluate LANCE benchmarks with systems such as RiMOM-IM [29], COMA++ [30] and CODI [17] were not successful. We were not able to work with RiMOM-IM due to incomplete information regarding the use of the system; COMA++ supports instance-based ontology matching but does not aim for instance matching per se. Finally CODI is no longer supported by the development team.

[5] LDBC Semantic Publishing Benchmark: http://ldbcouncil.org/developer/spb

[6] The code of LANCE is available at https://github.com/jsaveta/Lance

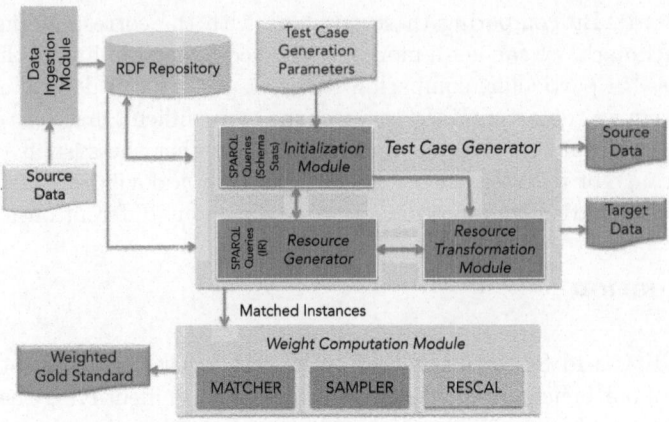

Fig. 1. LANCE System Architecture

RDF repository that stores the *source datasets* and (ii) a *test case generator* (see Figure 1). The test case generator takes as input a *source* dataset and produces a *target* dataset that implements various *test cases* according to the specified configuration parameters to be used for testing instance matching tools. It consists of the *Initialization, Resource Generator* and the *Resource Transformation* modules. The first reads the test case generation parameters and retrieves by means of SPARQL queries the schema information (e.g., schema classes and properties) from the RDF repository that will be used for producing the target dataset. The *Resource Generator* uses this input to retrieve instances of those schema constructs from the RDF repository and passes those (along with the configuration parameters) to the *Resource Transformation Module*. The latter returns for a source instance u_i the transformed instance u'_i and stores this in the target dataset; this module is also responsible in producing an entry in the gold standard. Once LANCE has performed all the requested transformations, the *Weight Computation Module* calculates the similarity scores of the produced matches as discussed in Section 3.2. The configuration parameters specify the part of the schema and data to consider when producing the different test cases as well as the the percentage and the type of transformations to consider. More specifically, parameters for *value-based* test cases specify the kind and severity of transformation to be applied; for *structure* and *semantics-aware* test cases the parameters specify the type of transformation to be considered. The idea behind configuration parameters is to allow one to tune the benchmark generator into producing benchmarks of varying degrees of difficulty which test different aspects of an instance matching tool. LANCE is implemented in Java and in the current version we use OWLIM Version 2.7.3. as our RDF repository.

4.1   Experimental Results

Applicability of LANCE. In order to show that LANCE is well suited to identify strong and weak points of state-of-the-art IM systems, we provided the tools at hand with difficult tasks and allowed the whole of the source dataset to be transformed so as to obtain the target dataset. Figure 2 reports the results for the different types of test cases and for datasets up to 10K and 50K triples. In all cases, we measured recall, precision, f-measure along with the *similarity score* and *standard deviation* we introduced in Section 3.3.

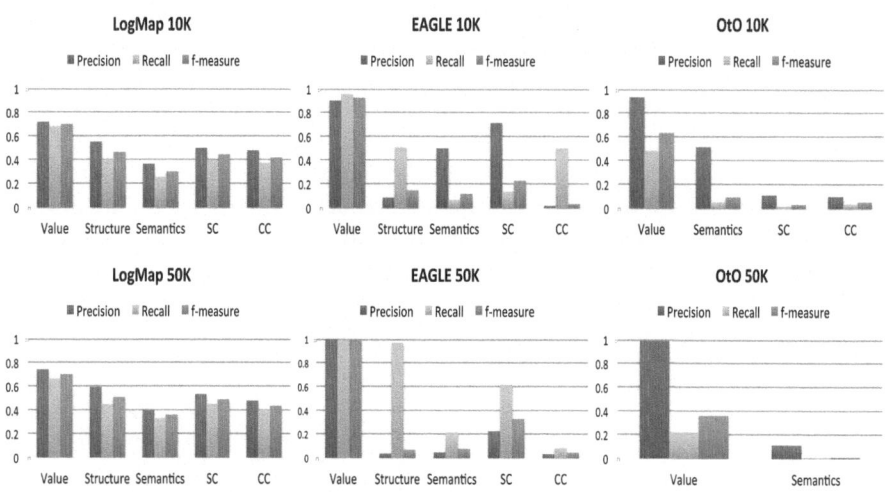

Fig. 2. Applicability experiments for LogMap, EAGLE and OtO

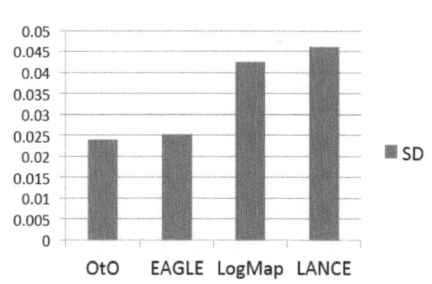

Fig. 3. Standard Deviation for LogMap, EAGLE, OtO, for 10K and semantics-aware test cases. The standard deviation of the gold standard is also shown (column LANCE).

As expected, LogMap responds well to the value-based test cases having a high precision and recall (close to 0.75) but its performance degrades when the instances are involved in semantics-aware test cases with precision and recall (below 0.4). Still, the large number of transformations applied to the source dataset to generate the target dataset suggest that LogMap does indeed perform sufficiently well when faced with semantics-aware transformations. OtO gives very good precision results for the value-based test cases but faces many issues concerning all the others as in some cases is not able to find any match (recall is below 0.1). EAGLE also reacts as expected. The algorithm performs well when faced with syntactic transformations. Increasing changes to the topology of the underlying RDF graphs (the case of semantics-aware test cases) leads to a degradation of the performance of the algorithm. The performance of EAGLE is not consistent since it is non-deterministic and uses unsupervised learning. We ran EAGLE thrice for both datasets. The similarity scores as well as the standard deviation of the results returned by the instance matching systems provide insights on the ability of the systems to address the challenges proposed by LANCE benchmarks. Figures 3 and 4 give the standard deviation and similarity scores for all three systems and for the semantics-aware test cases in the case of the 10K triples dataset. They also show the corresponding quantities for the benchmark itself for comparison. We can see that LogMap reports scores and standard deviation close to the ones given by LANCE verifying that it can address the "difficult" test cases. EAGLE and OtO report lower similarity scores and standard deviation, meaning that they cannot address the challenges imposed by the, harder, semantics-aware test cases. In summary, we conclude that LANCE is able to determine the capabilities of the IM systems and also reflect the difficulty of the test cases through the *weighted gold standard*.

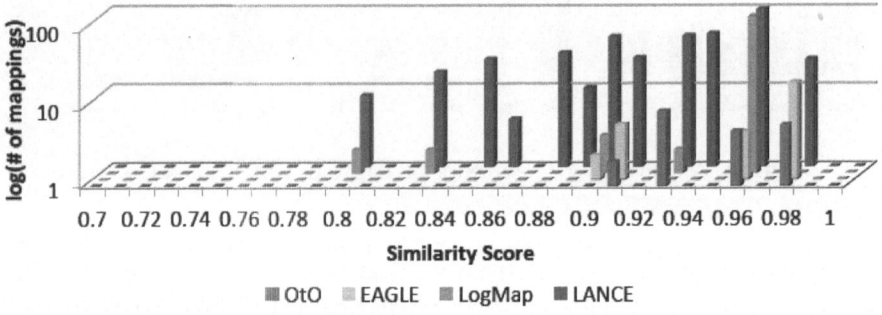

Fig. 4. Similarity score distribution for LogMap, EAGLE, OtO, for 10K and semantics-aware test cases. The similarity score of the benchmark is also shown (column LANCE).

Scalability. We also studied the scalability of the test case generator by measuring the runtime required by our framework to generate the *target* datasets for all different test cases, for various dataset sizes and percentages of source instances to be transformed. This time also includes the time required to retrieve the source instances from the RDF repository as previously discussed. We observe that the time for the data transformation is linear to the dataset size.

5   Conclusions

This paper presents LANCE, an instance matching benchmark generator focusing on benchmarking instance matching systems for Linked Data. LANCE is a domain-independent, highly modular and configurable generator that can accept as input *any* linked dataset and its accompanying schema to produce a target dataset implementing matching tasks of varying levels of difficulty. LANCE is the first Linked Data benchmark generator to support complex *semantics-aware* test cases that take into account expressive OWL constructs, in addition to the standard test cases related to structure and value transformations. The former type is largely absent in previous efforts. LANCE also produces a provably correct gold standard that allows a more fine-grained analysis of the performance of instance matching tools. This is in contrast to other benchmarks which are either based on manually generated gold standards, or based on gold standards produced semi-automatically (and are thus limited by the quality of the used approach, often producing inaccurate gold standards). Moreover, LANCE proposes the use of a *weighted gold standard* which records the similarity between a pair of matched instances as well as information on the type of transformation that was used to produce said match. This motivates the developers of IM systems to try benchmarks of varying levels of difficulty, and helps them identify the weak points of their systems, explain benchmark performance and more easily debug them. In the future, we plan to extend LANCE to work with spatial and streaming data; we also intend to work with datasets that include *blank nodes* thereby creating more challenging tasks for instance matching tools. Last, we plan to evaluate the frequency of appearance of the various types of transformations in existing datasets that would help us create realistic test cases.

References

1. Bhattacharya, I., Getoor, L.: Entity resolution in graphs. Mining Graph Data. Wiley and Sons (2006)
2. Elmagarmid, A.K., Ipeirotis, P.G., et al.: Duplicate Record Detection: A Survey. TKDE **19**(1) (2007)
3. Li, C., Jin, L., et al.: Supporting efficient record linkage for large data sets using mapping techniques. In: WWW (2006)
4. Noessner, J., Niepert, M., Meilicke, C., Stuckenschmidt, H.: Leveraging terminological structure for object reconciliation. In: Aroyo, L., Antoniou, G., Hyvönen, E., ten Teije, A., Stuckenschmidt, H., Cabral, L., Tudorache, T. (eds.) ESWC 2010. LNCS, vol. 6089, pp. 334–348. Springer, Heidelberg (2010)
5. Isele, R., Jentzsch, A., et al.: Silk server - adding missing links while consuming linked data. In: COLD (2010)
6. Ngonga Ngomo, A.-C., Auer, S.: LIMES - a time-efficient approach for large-scale link discovery on the web of data. IJCAI (2011)
7. Stefanidis, K., Efthymiou, V., et al.: Entity resolution in the web of data. In: WWW, Companion Volume (2014)

8. Weis, M., Naumann, F., et al.: A duplicate detection benchmark for XML and relational data. In: IQIS (2006)
9. Ontology Alignment Evaluation Initiative. http://oaei.ontologymatching.org/
10. Zaiss, K., Conrad, S., et al.: A benchmark for testing instance-based ontology matching methods. In: KMIS (2010)
11. Alexe, B., Tan, W.-C., et al.: STBenchmark: towards a benchmark for mapping systems. In: PVLDB (2008)
12. Saveta, T., Daskalaki, E., et al.: Pushing the limits of instance matching systems: a semantics-aware benchmark for linked data. In: WWW, Companion Volume (2015)
13. Daskalaki, E., Fundulaki, I., et al.: Instance matching benchmarks for linked data. In: ISWC (Tutorial) (2014)
14. Euzenat, J., Ferrara, A., et al.: Results of the ontology alignment evaluation initiative 2009. In: ISWC Workshop on Ontology Matching (OM) (2009)
15. Euzenat, J.: Results of the ontology alignment evaluation initiative. In: OM (2010)
16. OAEI Instance Matching (2010). http://oaei.ontologymatching.org/2010
17. Euzenat, J., et. al.: Final results of the ontology alignment evaluation initiative 2011. In: OM (2011)
18. Aguirre, J.L., et. al.: Results of the ontology alignment evaluation initiative 2012. In: OM (2012)
19. Dragisic, Z., Eckert, K., et al.: Results of the ontology alignment evaluation initiative 2013. In: OM (2013)
20. Dragisic, Z., Eckert, K., et al.: Results of the ontology alignment evaluation initiative 2014. In: OM (2014)
21. Ferrara, A., Montanelli, S., Noessner, J., Stuckenschmidt, H.: Benchmarking matching applications on the semantic web. In: Antoniou, G., Grobelnik, M., Simperl, E., Parsia, B., Plexousakis, D., De Leenheer, P., Pan, J. (eds.) ESWC 2011, Part II. LNCS, vol. 6644, pp. 108–122. Springer, Heidelberg (2011)
22. Krompass, D., Nickel, M., et al.: Non-negative tensor factorization with RESCAL. In: TML (2013)
23. Nickel, M., Tresp, V., et al.: Factorizing YAGO: scalable machine learning for linked data. In: WWW (2012)
24. Goutte, C., Gaussier, É.: A probabilistic interpretation of precision, recall and F-score, with implication for evaluation. In: Losada, D.E., Fernández-Luna, J.M. (eds.) ECIR 2005. LNCS, vol. 3408, pp. 345–359. Springer, Heidelberg (2005)
25. Jiménez-Ruiz, E., Cuenca Grau, B.: LogMap: logic-based and scalable ontology matching. In: Aroyo, L., Welty, C., Alani, H., Taylor, J., Bernstein, A., Kagal, L., Noy, N., Blomqvist, E. (eds.) ISWC 2011, Part I. LNCS, vol. 7031, pp. 273–288. Springer, Heidelberg (2011)
26. Romero, A.A., Grau, B.C., et al.: MORe: a modular OWL reasoner for ontology classification. In: ORE, pp. 61–67 (2013)
27. Daskalaki, E., Plexousakis, D.: OtO matching system: a multi-strategy approach to instance matching. In: Ralyté, J., Franch, X., Brinkkemper, S., Wrycza, S. (eds.) CAiSE 2012. LNCS, vol. 7328, pp. 286–300. Springer, Heidelberg (2012)
28. Ngomo, A.-C.N., Lyko, K.: EAGLE: efficient active learning of link specifications using genetic programming. In: Simperl, E., Cimiano, P., Polleres, A., Corcho, O., Presutti, V. (eds.) ESWC 2012. LNCS, vol. 7295, pp. 149–163. Springer, Heidelberg (2012)
29. Li, J., Tang, J., et al.: Rimom: A dynamic multistrategy ontology alignment framework. TKDE 21(8) (2009)

30. Massmann, S., Raunich, S., et al.: Evolution of the COMA match system. Ontology Matching **49** (2011)

31. Bizer, C., Schultz, A.: The Berlin SPARQL Benchmark. IJSWIS **5**(2) (2009)

32. Morsey, M., Lehmann, J., Auer, S., Ngonga Ngomo, A.-C.: DBpedia SPARQL benchmark – performance assessment with real queries on real data. In: Aroyo, L., Welty, C., Alani, H., Taylor, J., Bernstein, A., Kagal, L., Noy, N., Blomqvist, E. (eds.) ISWC 2011, Part I. LNCS, vol. 7031, pp. 454–469. Springer, Heidelberg (2011)

33. Ma, L., Yang, Y., Qiu, Z., Xie, G., Pan, Y., Liu, S.: Towards a complete OWL ontology benchmark. In: Sure, Y., Domingue, J. (eds.) ESWC 2006. LNCS, vol. 4011, pp. 125–139. Springer, Heidelberg (2006)

Decision-Making Bias in Instance Matching Model Selection

Mayank Kejriwal$^{(\boxtimes)}$ and Daniel P. Miranker

University of Texas at Austin, Austin, USA
{kejriwal,miranker}@cs.utexas.edu

Abstract. Instance matching has emerged as an important problem in the Semantic Web, with machine learning methods proving especially effective. To enhance performance, task-specific knowledge is typically used to introduce bias in the model selection problem. Such biases tend to be exploited by practitioners in a piecemeal fashion. This paper introduces a framework where the model selection design process is represented as a factor graph. Nodes in this bipartite graphical model represent opportunities for explicitly introducing bias. The graph is first used to unify and visualize common biases in the design of existing instance matchers. As a direct application, we then use the graph to hypothesize about potential unexploited biases. The hypotheses are evaluated by training 1032 neural networks on three instance matching tasks on Microsoft Azure's cloud-based platform. An analysis over 25 GB of experimental data indicates that the proposed biases can improve efficiency by over 65% over a baseline configuration, with effectiveness improving by a smaller margin. The findings lead to a promising set of four recommendations that can be integrated into existing supervised instance matchers.

Keywords: Instance matching · Model selection · Decision-making bias

1 Introduction

With its growing cross-domain collection of ontologies and instances, the Semantic Web has evolved into a diverse information space [21], [15]. Its growth has motivated researchers to investigate high-quality and automated solutions to the *instance matching* problem, which concerns identifying pairs of instances that refer to the same underlying entity [14].

Given their robust generalization properties, machine learning methods have come to dominate instance matching [17], [2], [19]. Once a machine learning model (e.g. a neural network) is trained on *labeled* data, *unseen* data is classified, and **:sameAs**-like links are forged between equivalent instances [21].

Designing a full instance matching system requires a practitioner to make decisions with respect to the *model selection* problem. For example, a practitioner must decide on a sampling strategy for acquiring labeled data, craft functions for converting raw labeled data into feature vectors, decide on a classifier and

© Springer International Publishing Switzerland 2015
M. Arenas et al. (Eds.): ISWC 2015, Part I, LNCS 9366, pp. 392–407, 2015.
DOI: 10.1007/978-3-319-25007-6_23

hyperparameter optimization strategy (for tuning the classifier), and partition the labeled data into training and validation sets. In order to keep the model selection process *tractable*, it is necessary to base some of these decisions on *task-specific* knowledge. For example, certain features, such as phonetic and string-similarity features, are known to be especially effective for instance matching tasks that involve names and misspellings [4]. As another example, the real-world observation that class distribution in the instance matching problem often exhibits *data skew* (Section 3) influences *sampling* decisions (Section 4.1).

Given the challenging nature of instance matching in the Semantic Web, systems have become steadily more complex as practitioners have exploited task-specific knowledge as *piecemeal heuristics* to improve overall system performance [12], [17], [19]. These heuristics inevitably *bias* both the design and performance of any system that relies on them. For example, recent studies of *dataset bias* in the computer vision community show that systems that exhibit superior performance on one set of benchmarks may not necessarily be superior on a different dataset [20]. The reason was that, whether consciously or subconsciously, system designers used their knowledge of the task and the dataset to bias model selection decisions. Understanding such *decision-making biases* is a crucial step for subsequent research to reproduce and improve complex models, as well as to adapt them to novel situations without repeating the entire design process.

This paper attempts to achieve this goal by explicitly *modeling* decision-making bias in instance matching model selection as a bipartite undirected graphical model called a *factor graph* [10], with factor nodes representing bias opportunities. Several common decision-making biases in existing instance matching designs are explained and *visualized* by using this model. As a direct *application* of this visualization, we use the model to derive *new* opportunities for decision-making bias that, to the best of our knowledge, are not utilized by the majority of instance matchers. We empirically evaluate the proposed biases by training 1032 neural networks on Microsoft Azure's cloud-based platform using labeled data from three challenging instance matching benchmarks.

Evaluations on the test data lead to a set of four general recommendations that could potentially be used to improve existing supervised machine learning-based instance matchers both in terms of effectiveness and efficiency. Specifically, the analysis shows that (1) proportionate allocation stratified sampling [13] is a better sampling strategy for labeled data than a balanced (and traditionally more favored) approach, that (2) the training and validation sets should be as equal-sized as possible, that, (3) despite much lower efficiency, a hyperparameter optimizer based on grid search is no more effective than a random search conducted around reasonably set default hyperparameter values, and that, (4) under reasonable supervision assumptions, a setting that *favors* validation over training leads to run-time reductions of almost 70%, with a relatively smaller loss in effectiveness. Together, the last two recommendations are shown to lead to *efficiency* savings of over 65% with a small *increase* in *effectiveness* as well.

To enable repeatability, we provide screenshots of the employed experimental template, which may be run in a browser on a free MS Azure subscription.

For further analysis, all 25 GB of structured experimental data are exposed on a high-availability server via a public URL.

2   Related Work

In the general Artificial Intelligence community, *instance matching* is a 50-year old problem that continues to be actively researched, with a good survey of frameworks provided by Köpcke and Rahm [11]. Examples of some Semantic Web instance matching systems are Silk, RDF-AI and Limes [21], [18] [14]. Recent years have seen a proliferation of sophisticated machine learning approaches for improving instance matching performance, with Soru and Ngomo providing a comparative evaluation of various supervised classifiers [19], and Köpcke et al. providing a comparative evaluation of various competing systems that have emerged as popular choices for practitioners [12]. The latter work, in particular, showed that most systems only succeeded in certain settings, with hand-crafted features and with non-trivial amounts of training data [12]. In a similar manner, other systems have made expert-guided decisions on model and feature selection, an example being the random forest-based system of Rong et al. [17]. Instead of developing another instance matcher that competes with existing systems, the goal of this work is to model the myriad model selection decisions made by instance matching practitioners using a unified framework.

There are two important lines of prior research that come closest to this goal. The first line of research concerns knowledge-guided model *construction* in the context of *expert systems* [5]. In contrast, this work considers knowledge-guided model *selection* decisions in a machine learning-based instance matching context. A second, more recent line of research, attempts to unify various applications of *Statistical Relational Learning* (SRL) using Markov Logic [7]. This paper takes a complementary approach by restricting the application (e.g. instance matching) but not restricting the learning technique (e.g. SRL). Instead, we investigate and exploit the decision-making biases that go into the design of a generic machine learning-based instance matcher.

Much of the discourse on machine learning models in this paper is derived from classic material, Bishop's text being the primary reference [3]. Rojas' text is used for a more detailed discourse on neural networks [16]. Factor graphs, a special class of probabilistic graphical models central to the developments herein, are detailed in the text by Koller and Friedman [10].

3   Preliminaries

In the Semantic Web, link discovery is the problem of locating pairs of instances that satisfy a hidden *specification function* [14]. Without loss of generality, the specification function is often assumed to be that of *equivalence*, in which case the problem is referred to as *instance matching* [11]. Forging such *:sameAs*-like links between entities is important for maintaining connectivity in Linked Open Data per the *fourth* Linked Data principle [21].

Before the emergence of the RDF data model, it was often the case in the Relational Database literature that *schema matching* and *record linkage* tasks were considered orthogonal components of the broader data integration application [11]. The dominance of the RDF data model in the Semantic Web enables practitioners in the related sub-areas of ontology matching and instance matching to *cross-fertilize* their research, a manifestation of which is the annual Ontology Alignment Evaluation Initiative[1]. Although this paper primarily covers instance matching, an evaluation task in Section 5 also involves ontology matching.

An important issue that affects real-world instance matching problem instances is *data skew* [15]. Consider two RDF datasets G_A and G_B with respective sets of instances E_A and E_B. A naïve instance matcher attempts to classify the full Cartesian product space $E_A \times E_B$, a process that is time-prohibitive even for moderate datasets. Under reasonable assumptions, the number of true positives is $O(min(|E_A|, |E_B|))$ and is far outnumbered by the number of true negatives (a *quadratic* function) [4], [15]. One common technique that reduces this skew before further processing is *blocking* [15], [14]. A blocking algorithm clusters instances into blocks, based on a heuristic function. Instances sharing a block are paired and become candidates for further evaluation. Although the size of the candidate set is small relative to the Cartesian product, the skew is not completely eliminated and is still quite considerable (Section 5).

This paper assumes that the specification function is unknown but that it can be approximated through training a *machine learning classifier*. A typical machine learning-based instance matcher works as follows. First, a candidate set of instance pairs is generated through blocking, as described above [15]. Next, each pair is converted to a *feature vector* [4]. The choice of features is important, and guided by knowledge of the task [12]. Thus, it is a source of decision-making bias in the model selection design process, as described in the next section. A set of *labeled* feature vectors is split into *training* and *validation* sets and respectively used to train and tune the classifier, which is then used to label *unseen* instance pairs (the *test* data). The choice of classifier, the number of labeled samples on which the classifier is trained, the hyperparameter tuning strategy and the proportion of positively and negatively labeled samples are all issues that are crucial to the design and complexity of the final instance matcher. A framework for this decision-making process is subsequently presented.

4   Decision-Making Bias in Model Selection

Before a machine learning classifier can be trained on labeled data, the *model selection* problem must be solved. For instance, a practitioner must craft the features that should be extracted from the data, and decide on hyperparameter optimization and sampling strategies. Usually, there are many choices at each step of the decision process, including default options (e.g. bag-of-words features for text representations [19], and random search for hyperparameter optimization [1]) derived from a survey of existing instance matchers.

---

[1] http://oaei.ontologymatching.org/

Empirical evidence indicates that this passive effort is typically insufficient, with non-trivial tasks demanding considerable model selection effort [12]. We also note that this decision-making process is not restricted to the *machine learning* component of model selection, but is an integral design component of any non-trivial system that *models* some phenomenon and is required to be empirically testable[2].

In this broader model selection process, *decision-making bias* arises because it is infeasible to consider all points in the design space, even when certain aspects of the model are fixed (e.g. restricting the instance matcher to only use machine learning). The decisions are typically justified through a variety of means, most notably early experimental findings or a study of existing systems [12], [4]. As briefly illustrated in Section 2, recent instance matchers have become steadily more complex in an effort to outperform the state-of-the-art. With added complexity, it becomes important to *model* the set of (possibly interlinked) decisions in order to reproduce (and improve upon) the system.

Figure 1 illustrates a possible framework for this process, namely a bipartite undirected graphical model, or a *factor graph* [10]. In the figure, oval nodes represent sets of objects, with shaded nodes representing sets provided to a practitioner *a priori*[3]. As in traditional factor graphs, the square nodes (labeled *Nodes 1-4*) represent points of *interaction* between their neighboring decision nodes [10]. Described below, these nodes can also be used to exercise prior task-specific knowledge to bias certain decisions towards a model selection outcome that is expected to be empirically favorable.

4.1   Node 1: Decision-Making Bias in Sampling Strategy

In a supervised setting, data has to be collected and labeled in order to train (and *tune*) the machine learning classifier. Intuitively, the more labeled data is collected, the better the performance of the classifier. Labeling data can be a costly endeavor. The level of supervision, expressed as a percentage of the labeled instances to the total instances, depends directly on the allocated *labeling budget*. Once the level of supervision is determined (e.g. 50%), a practitioner has to pick an appropriate *sampling strategy*. With *simple random sampling*, an instance from the data pool is chosen (for labeling) with uniform probability till the budget is exhausted. Data skew can be problematic for this default strategy, since under moderate budgets, the probability of under-sampling true positives is high.

The risk of under-representing true positives in the labeled set can be mitigated by randomly sampling $q/2$ instances from each of the two classes, with q the total number of labelings allowed by the budget. This technique, which is a variant of *stratified sampling*, was designed by statisticians to reduce the variance caused by simple random sampling in skewed datasets [13].

---

[2] In the context of instance matching, for example, the choice of machine learning is itself a model selection decision, since it indicates that we *model* the *unknown* link specification function (see Section 3) using a trainable classifier.

[3] Thus, these nodes represent the fixed aspects of the model, or the *design constraints*, described in the previous paragraph.

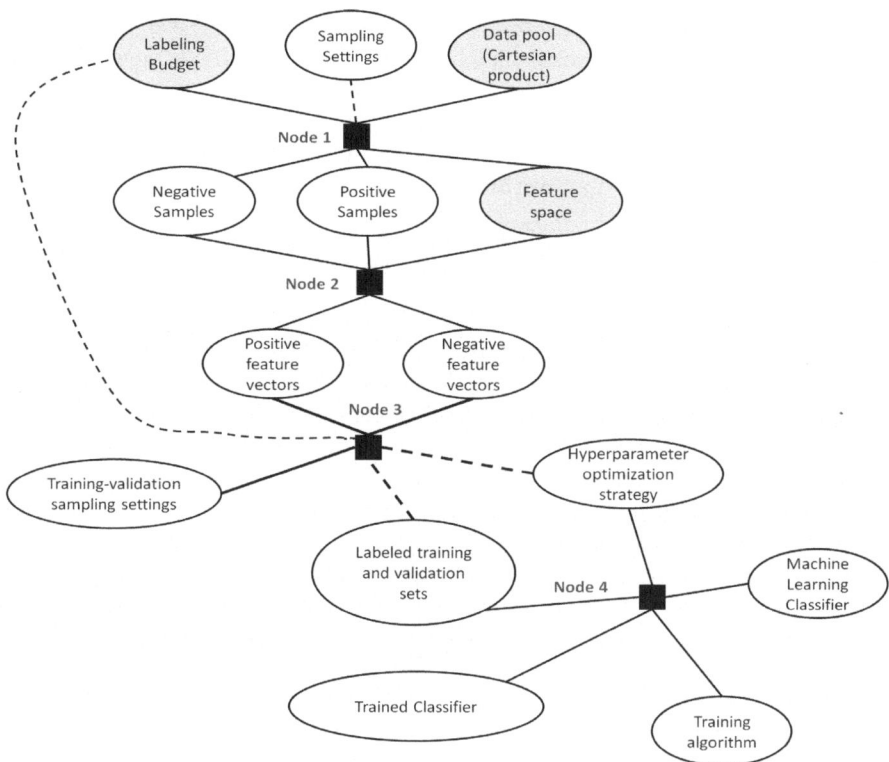

Fig. 1. A factor graph representing the model selection process. The oval nodes represent generic sets of objects (the concrete results of design decisions) while the square nodes represent opportunities for decision-making bias based on exploiting task-specific knowledge. Shaded nodes represent sets provided *a priori* (and are hence, *design constraints*) and the dashed lines indicate specific influences studied in this work.

Existing stratified sampling strategies used in several instance matchers attempt an approximate *balancing* strategy in order to *eliminate* the skew from the labeled set [12]. This violates a key assumption of predominant machine learning theory, namely that the labeled data has (at least approximately) the same distribution as the unlabeled test data [3]. In keeping with machine learning norm, the authors hypothesize that skew should *not* be eliminated in the labeled set for good empirical performance on test data. In other words, the domain expert should use her knowledge of data skew to perform *proportionate allocation* stratified sampling [13]. For example, if the domain expert estimates, *a priori* or through experience and an educated guess, that 90% of the data pool is negatively labeled, she should use this estimate to sample $0.9q$ and $0.1q$ instances from the negative and positive pools respectively. We empirically comment on this hypothesis in Section 5. In Figure 1, this influence is noted through the dashed line incident on Node 1. We note that decision-making bias arises in the choice of sampling strategy because of knowledge of the task. If, for some reason, the practitioner suspects that her data does not exhibit skew, the bias should be in the opposite direction. A third alternative is that nothing can be said about the data with reasonable probability. In this case, it is dangerous to introduce any bias at all in the choice of sampling strategy; a better approach is to model the data distribution through additional analysis.

4.2   Node 2: Decision-Making Bias in Feature Crafting

In many instance matching tasks, special features can be devised (or chosen from a *global* feature space, as illustrated in Figure 1) to maximize performance. Traditionally, string similarity and token similarity features such as *Levenstein* and *tf-idf* have been popular; other practitioners have followed suit with phonetic and numeric functions as well [4], [17]. Crafting features for a machine learning problem using knowledge of the underlying task is by no means unique to instance matching, but also arises in other tasks such as speech recognition and computer vision [3]. Research on this issue in recent years have led to the emergence of deep learning techniques for automatically devising high-level features [8], but to the best of our knowledge, deep learning has not been applied to instance matching. Thus, decision-making bias in crafting features remains important in current instance matchers. For example, Soru and Ngomo favor token-based features in their evaluations [19], while Rong et al. devise special features individually for short text, descriptions and dates [17]. We do not study this bias further in this paper, but leave an extensive treatment for future work.

4.3   Node 3: Decision-Making Bias in Training-Validation Strategy

The labeled sets of feature vectors need to be split up into *training* and *validation* sets, which are both assumed to have the same proportion of positive and negative samples. A practitioner is typically expected to provide a sampling parameter that determines the ratio[4] of the size of the training set to the labeled set. In the literature, authors have experimented with several ratios, the most common being 50% and 90% (with the other 50% and 10% used for validation) [2], [19]. Once the sampling (and splitting) process is complete, a *hyperparameter optimization strategy* must also be chosen, in order to minimize chances of *overfitting* [3]. In principal, the validation set can be used to provide an unbiased estimate of classifier error [3]. Thus, the chosen optimizer makes hyperparameter assignments so as to maximize *validation* set performance [1].

   Two extreme (and common) cases of hyperparameter optimization strategies are *random search* and *grid search* strategies [1]. In a random search, the optimizer randomly tests s different hyperparameter settings before selecting the best one, s being a user-defined parameter. A grid search, which can be performed at arbitrarily fine levels of granularity, exhaustively searches through combinations of hyperparameter value assignments.

---

[4] If the training ratio is r, the validation ratio is automatically $1 - r$.

We argue that there is scope for introducing decision-making bias by exploiting information about the *level of supervision* (or indirectly, the labeling budget). This hypothesis is indicated by the dashed lines in Figure 1 incident on Node 3. The rationale behind the hypothesis is as follows. First, the training time for most machine learning models depends directly on the size of the training set [3]. Thus, if the level of supervision is low, training times are also expected to be low. Thus, expensive grid search can potentially compensate for the adverse effects of low supervision. The level of supervision can also be used to inform the training-validation ratio under the assumption that both parameter and hyperparameter optimization (controlled by the training and validation sets respectively) exhibit *diminishing* returns with more labeled data. The choice of ratio is important under efficiency considerations, as making the validation set larger allows the training time to be reduced, along with better hyperparameter optimization. In principle, this form of bias can be used for more efficient training, without significantly sacrificing performance (and possibly improving it), as empirically investigated in Section 5.

4.4   Node 4: Decision-Making Bias in Classification

Node 4 offers additional potential for decision-making bias that involves choosing an appropriate machine learning classifier based on task-specific information. As one example, boosted multi-layer perceptrons were recently investigated for *minimally supervised* instance matching tasks (with extremely low labeling budgets) [9]. Similarly, logistic regression models were empirically demonstrated to be suitable for *noisy* instance matching tasks [19]. The takeaway is that, if the characteristics of the dataset are known, prior experience can be used to inform the choice of classifier. Conversely, if nothing is known about the data with reasonable certainty, a caveat similar to the one presented in Section 4.1 applies. A practitioner may be forced to investigate several classifiers and training algorithms (e.g. through pilot experiments) before selecting one.

4.5   Undirected vs. Directed Graphical Representation

There are two reasons why the model selection process in Figure 1 is framed as an *undirected* graphical model rather than a *directed* model (e.g. a *Bayes Network* [10]). First, decision making processes are typically *iterative* in real-world operational settings, and not necessarily *causal* as directed edges in a Bayes Network would seem to indicate. In a 'first pass', for example, a practitioner may choose default settings to get an initial feel for system performance on a specific instance matching task. If the task is inherently less challenging than presupposed[5], the default settings may be adopted with minor changes. For more challenging cases, an iterative trial-and-error model selection process may be necessary for good performance.

---

[5] Two concrete examples are the OAEI benchmarks *Restaurants* and *Persons 1*, which have yielded 90%+ f-scores in several Semantic Web evaluations [19], [9].

A second reason for choosing a factor graph is its bipartite nature. Crucially, the graph allows us to distinguish between decision nodes and object nodes and captures the *mutual influence* exerted by various components of the model selection process on each other. The graph can also serve as a visual tool and be crafted in as much detail as warranted by the practitioner and the task. These advantages allow us to detect potential beneficial sources of decision-making bias (or lack thereof). The dashed edges in Figure 1 are examples of bias that the graph allowed us to detect and exploit. To the best of our knowledge, these biases have not been exploited in recent instance matchers. For example, we are unaware of any instance matcher that has explicitly used the labeling budget to inform training-validation ratios.

The factor graph may also be useful where several (possibly conflicting) sources of decision-making bias are involved in the design of the instance matcher. This scenario can occur because of differences in opinion (among collaborators) about dataset characteristics, different practical experiences or simply a lack of evidence. The factor graph is useful in this scenario because, by definition, factors are used to model probability distributions over neighboring object nodes. In principal, this is similar to the framework used by Domingos and Richardson whereby Markov logic was used to unify various applications of Statistical Relational Learning [7]. Although not explored here, the *probabilistic* study of decision-making bias is the natural next step for attempting to *explain* the bias and is left for future work.

4.6   The Cost of Decision-Making Bias

Throughout this paper, the assumption is that introducing decision-making bias into the model selection process is *beneficial* to actual system performance, that is, reduces the *variance* of prediction. We note that the concept of both introducing and penalizing *statistical bias* in model selection to reduce variance is well established [3]. The *Occam's razor* principle essentially states that, all else equal, simple hypotheses are *inherently* more superior than complex hypotheses [3]. The *no free lunch* theorem of Wolpert and Macready disproves this superiority in the mathematical sense [22]; in this framework, simplicity itself is a form of decision-making bias that makes model selection tractable.

In the present context, this finding has an intuitive takeaway, namely that each decision-making bias introduced into the system implies a *cost*. The reason is that biases are introduced precisely because a practitioner has task-dependent knowledge; the more the system is tuned for the specific task, the less applicable it will be to other tasks. In the longer run, this may be undesirable if instance matching tasks of many different flavors are involved, and a single system is expected to service them over a long horizon. With respect to the current state of the research, this is also problematic; if researchers exhibited significant decision-making bias in their design, their system may not perform as expected beyond the datasets in their experimental design. The computer vision community has already begun addressing this issue as *dataset bias* [20]. Given the complexity of

Table 1. Test suite details. The second column only includes true negatives and positives in the *candidate set* (see Section 5.1). Mean sparsity (with resp. standard deviations in paranthesis) is the average percentage of features set to 0 in an arbitrary feature vector in the true negatives/positives in the candidate set. A *skew* of y% at x% (with x=10/50/90%) indicates that y% of the negative pool equals x% of the positive pool. Exact numbers may vary slightly due to rounding error

Dataset Name	True Negatives/Positives	Mean Negatives/Positives Sparsity	Skew at 10%/50%/90%
Amazon-Google Products (AGP)	95,889/1300	67.64%/55.68% (7.66%/9.14%)	0.14%/0.68%/1.22%
Abt-Buy (AB)	40,917/1097	63.06%/58.00% (12.27%/12.20%)	0.27%/1.34%/2.41%
Film (F)	53,070/412	88.12%/80.79% (4.85%/6.96%)	0.078%/0.39%/0.70%

recent instance matchers in the Semantic Web (see Section 2), we believe that costs introduced by decision-making bias are worth investigating.

5 Experiments

5.1 Test Suite: Preparation and Statistics

The proposed biases are tested on three instance matching benchmarks. Two benchmarks, *Amazon-GoogleProducts* and *Abt-Buy* are public e-commerce datasets evaluated by Köpcke et al. on state-of-the-art approaches [12]. As the authors of that evaluation noted, these are difficult test cases in that the best supervised performance (in terms of f-scores; see Section 5.2) achieved on them was well below 70% [12]. The third test case concerns real-world *film* data from IMDB, but with artificial *semantic noise* injected into the data using an established Semantic Web generator [6]. The final test case involves both instance and ontology matching and has been used in OAEI evaluations.

We do not consider other OAEI benchmarks like *Persons* and *Restaurants* (see footnote 5) in these evaluations. The main reason is that even simple systems have performed well on these test cases, leaving little room for more improvement. A second reason is that the datasets used in our evaluations have also been used in at least three recent evaluations [12], [19], [9]. Because performance on them continues to be poor, they present interesting challenges for modern matchers. Finally, the most recent OAEI instance matching benchmarks do not have publicly accessible ground-truths at the time of writing.

As performing classification on all $O(n^2)$ instance pairs (with n being the number of instances) is infeasible, *blocking* techniques are used to heuristically generate a smaller *candidate set* of instance pairs that does *not* exclude the true positives [14], [4]. Instance pairs not in the candidate set are automatically classified as negatives. In this paper, we use a recently proposed unsupervised method called *Attribute Clustering* to generate a high-performing candidate set

[15]. Algorithm parameters are adjusted to ensure that all true positives in the ground-truth are included. Table 1 summarizes test suite details; note that the candidate set is still skewed, but less so (by over three orders of magnitude) than the space of all $O(n^2)$ pairs.

Once generated, all instance pairs in the candidate set are converted into binary feature vectors. Specifically, for every pair of matching attributes in every instance pair (or *properties* in RDF terminology), 28 features are generated, including phonetic, numeric and string comparison features. This feature set is used because of good performance in prior work[6] and shown to exhibit high performance [4]. In pilot experiments, the features were also found to work well in binary rather than real-valued form, possibly because of reduced classifier overfitting due to sparsity. As another advantage, sparsity is also known to lead to faster training convergence [16], [3]. Complete details on feature generation are provided on the project website (footnote 11).

5.2   Methodology

All experiments were run on Microsoft Azure's cloud-based machine learning studio[7] on a free preview subscription. At the time of experimentation, Microsoft was the only cloud vendor that offered a full suite of easy-to-deploy machine learning facilities. Since that time, some other vendors have released similar products, most notably Amazon. We leave repeating the experiments herein on alternate cloud vendors for future work. In all experiments, the classifier is fixed as a fully-connected, two-class neural network with a single hidden layer comprising 100 sigmoid units to guarantee sufficient expressivity [16]. The backpropagation algorithm is used for training the network, with five algorithm parameters[8] constituting the hyperparameters that need optimizing. Since the feature set is also fixed, the experimental goal is to test newly proposed biases.

To this end, four *categorical* variables are introduced to investigate the dashed influences in Figure 1, namely *Skew* ={*True, False*}, *Hyper* ={*Random Search, Grid Search*}, *Level-of-Supervision* ={*10%, 50%, 90%*}, *Training-ratio*= {*90%, 50%, 10%*}. *Skew* relates to Node 1 decision-making bias, with a *True* value indicating that complete data skew is maintained in the labeled set. A *False* value indicates instead that equal *numbers* are maintained (called the *balanced* approach; see Section 4.1). *Hyper* refers to the two hyperparameter optimization strategies employed in this work. Specifically, *Random Search* explores ten randomly chosen hyperparameter vectors in an attempt to improve upon the *default* hyperparameter settings in their *neighborhood*. *Grid Search* performs a full hyperparameter sweep at a pre-defined granularity[9]. *Level-of-Supervision* or

---

[6] This is an example of Node 2 decision-making bias (Section 4.2).

[7] Accessed at https://studio.azureml.net/.

[8] The learning rate, number of learning iterations, initial learning weights diameter, momentum and normalizer type.

[9] Based on the observed data, the MS Azure grid search setting divides the hyperparameter space into roughly 20-30 grid cells.

LoS refers to the quantity $|LabeledDataPool|/|DataPool|$; note that both negatively and positively labeled samples are included in the numerator, with *Skew* determining the relative proportion. *Training-ratio* is the ratio r in footnote 6.

For each test case and *joint* assignment to the four categorical variables, a model selection framework of the form in Figure 1 can be fully *instantiated*, with the end result being an instance matcher. This model is tested on the portion of the data pool that was not sampled and included in the labeled set. We measure instance matching performance using *precision* and *recall* metrics. Let the set of samples labeled as positives by the classifier be denoted as P, with $RP \subseteq P$ being the true positives retrieved by the classifier. Let TP denote the set of all true positives. The ratios $|RP|/|P|$ and $|RP|/|TP|$ respectively quantify precision and recall . Their harmonic mean, or *f-score*, illustrates their tradeoff and is a measure of system *effectiveness* [19].

To measure system *efficiency*, we record and add the run-times of both hyperparameter optimization and classifier training. The Microsoft Azure platform allows the experimenter to record fine-grained run-times of read and write times as well. These are not included herein as they are subject to data-center variance. Note that the actual optimization and classifier training takes place on a *single* node (attested to by the MS Azure documentation), and is not subject to such variance. Thus, the reported run-times are expected to be *low-variance proxies* for true model selection time.

Ten random trials are conducted for each dataset and joint categorical assignment, with the random number generator provided by Microsoft Azure. In total, almost[10] $3 \times 2 \times 2 \times 3 \times 3 \times 10 = 1080$ model selection experiments were conducted to investigate the biases. All 25 GB of experimental data, structured in directories and spreadsheets, have been made available on a high-availability server[11], together with screenshots of the experimental template that was used and all experimental data.

5.3 Results and Analysis

The subsequent analysis focuses is on the data tabulated in Table 2, with *Skew=True*. We comment on the *Skew=False* case, but due to space constraints, reproduce the full table for *Skew=False* only on the project website.

A cursory count of the bold (or *better*) f-score values in the two *Hyper* columns of Table 2 shows that, on 17/27 cases, *Grid Search* outperforms *Random Search* as a hyperparameter optimization strategy. This is expected (since *Grid Search* explores more hyperparameter space) and is closer to the empirical norm in the literature [12]. A more informed analysis indicates that *Random Search* also has its merits. The *mean difference* in f-scores between *Grid Search* and *Random Search* is 0.99%, which is not statistically significant from 0 at the 95%

---

[10] The actual number was 1032. In the final phase of the experimental runs, 48 trials on the *Film* dataset did not terminate due to subscription exhaustion.

[11] The project website is accessed at https://sites.google.com/a/utexas.edu/mayank-kejriwal/projects/semantics-and-model-selection

Table 2. Mean results (over 10 random trials/cell) on described metrics (Section 5.2) for the three test cases (Table 1) and with *Skew=True*. The bold lines separate (from top to bottom) results for *Training-ratio=90%, 50%* and *10%* respectively. Bold values indicate better performance across the two *Hyper* columns, and shaded cells indicate best values across the three *Training-ratio* segments

Test	LoS	Hyper=Random Search				Hyper=Grid Search			
		Precision	Recall	F-score	Run-time	Precision	Recall	F-score	Run-time
AGP	10%	**54.13%**	25.77%	34.89%	14.16s	48.62%	**33.08%**	**39.37%**	26.02s
AGP	50%	**61.51%**	28.77%	**39.20%**	1m 0.47s	54.76%	**29.23%**	38.11%	1m 50.70s
AGP	90%	**73.27%**	27.69%	40.22%	1m 31.93s	65.67%	**33.85%**	**44.67%**	3m 8.97s
AB	10%	70.00%	6.38%	11.70%	7.80s	**72.90%**	**7.90%**	**14.26%**	13.10s
AB	50%	**71.90%**	**20.07%**	**31.38%**	25.01s	63.10%	19.34%	29.61%	44.99s
AB	90%	**91.67%**	20.00%	32.84%	36.81s	85.19%	**20.91%**	**33.58%**	1m 18.35s
F	10%	68.46%	**57.48%**	63.99%	56.72s	**86.20%**	51.35%	**64.36%**	57.85s
F	50%	**83.59%**	**79.13%**	**81.30%**	2m 1.34s	83.42%	78.16%	80.70%	3m 53.09s
F	90%	74.07%	**97.56%**	**84.21%**	3m 29.42s	**76.09%**	85.37%	80.46%	6m 49.84s
AGP	10%	45.47%	**35.64%**	**39.96%**	10.16s	**49.46%**	31.28%	38.33%	17.88s
AGP	50%	55.50%	34.92%	42.87%	32.02s	**57.87%**	**35.08%**	**43.68%**	1m 8.56s
AGP	90%	**66.67%**	36.92%	47.53%	54.73s	62.79%	**41.54%**	**50.00%**	1m 57.03s
AB	10%	**52.10%**	16.31%	24.85%	6.31s	48.23%	**24.82%**	**32.78%**	22.72s
AB	50%	67.77%	14.96%	24.51%	14.93s	67.77%	14.96%	24.51%	31.64s
AB	90%	**76.32%**	26.36%	**39.19%**	23.00s	63.83%	**27.27%**	38.22%	45.24s
F	10%	79.93%	57.95%	67.19%	18.32s	**80.00%**	**62.53%**	**70.20%**	35.97s
F	50%	**85.85%**	85.44%	85.65%	1m 10.78s	85.51%	**85.92%**	**85.71%**	2m 24.32s
F	90%	73.59%	95.12%	82.98%	2m 3.22s	**74.07%**	**97.56%**	**84.21%**	6m 9.18s
AGP	10%	39.88%	**40.94%**	**40.41%**	5.71s	**44.93%**	34.44%	38.99%	8.49s
AGP	50%	**54.02%**	21.69%	30.96%	11.43s	48.06%	**28.62%**	**35.87%**	20.15s
AGP	90%	58.33%	32.31%	41.58%	16.95s	**64.18%**	**33.08%**	**43.66%**	32.02s
AB	10%	0%	0%	0%	4.84s	0%	0%	0%	5.68s
AB	50%	**63.72%**	**13.14%**	**21.79%**	6.92s	62.62%	12.23%	20.46%	10.46s
AB	90%	**68.97%**	18.18%	28.78%	8.85s	60.00%	**19.09%**	**28.97%**	14.86s
F	10%	**75.00%**	32.35%	45.20%	8.38s	74.47%	**32.86%**	**45.60%**	14.07s
F	50%	**84.08%**	64.08%	72.73%	22.57s	82.08%	**68.93%**	**74.93%**	44.91s
F	90%	77.55%	92.68%	84.44%	35.34s	**78.00%**	**95.12%**	**85.71%**	1m 14.33s

confidence level[12] (c.l.). When contrasted with the (statistically significant at the 99% c.l.) average percentage *increase* of 93.44% in run-time of *Grid Search* over *Random Search*, the latter is clearly a better choice.

In terms of run-time, two definitive observations can be derived from Table 2. First, when comparing a row across *LoS* settings, the run-time declines (as *LoS* declines), albeit not proportionally. This is again expected, since the

---

[12] Significance levels were tested using the Student's t-test for sample means.

backpropagation algorithm does not typically[13] run in linear time in the training set size [16]. Similarly, when comparing across table segments (different values of *Training-ratio*) run-time also declines. The latter observation is interesting because the same amount of labeled data is used for a fixed *LoS*; the change is merely in the relative proportion allocated to training versus validation.

Quantitatively, the average percentage *reduction* in run-time when comparing *Training-ratios* of 90% against 50% (with mean taken at all values of *LoS* and *Hyper* in Table 2) is 30.83%, which is statistically significant at the 99% c.l., while the average f-score *increases* by 4.08% (not statistically significant from 0 at the 95% c.l.). The difference is more dramatic when performing the same comparison but with *Hyper=Grid Search* at *Training-ratio=90%* and *Hyper=Random Search* at *Training-ratio=50%*. The average run-time for this case reduces by 66.70%, while the average f-score *increases* by 11.98%. Although the f-score increase is not significant (even at 95% c.l.), the run-time reduction is significant at the 99% level.To the best of our knowledge, the only (Relational Database) data matcher that has used a *Training-ratio* of 50% is MARLIN, which continues to outperform many systems [2], [12]. Systems can improve efficiency and (potentially) effectiveness by using this *combined* bias (that is, favoring *Hyper=Random Search* and *Training-ratio=50%* over alternate options).

As another example of how Figure 1 can favorably inform the model selection process, consider system performance at *LoS* values of *50%* and *90%*, and with *Training-ratio=10%*. While system performance at *Training-ratio=10%* degrades significantly[14] at *LoS=10%*, with AB achieving 0% f-score, the loss is less drastic at other *LoS* values. At *LoS=50%* and *90%*, the average percentage reductions in f-score (compared to the best f-score achieved by the other two *Training-ratio* settings) are 21.56% and 18.99%, with average run-times decreasing by 70.16% and 67.59% respectively. Although there is a cost[15] (in lost f-score performance) to using *Training-ratio=10%*, a practitioner constrained by *efficiency* (e.g. in *real-time* applications) should consider this bias.

The analysis is concluded with a brief note on the *Skew=False* setting. The broad conclusions noted above were also found to hold for this setting; a comparison *between* the two settings found that *Skew=False* performed much worse overall than *Skew=True*, with the average f-score reducing by 58.27% and 63.71% across the *Hyper=Random Search* and *Grid Search* settings respectively. These values are statistically significant at the 99% level. This confirms machine learning theory [3], in that the training set should be as *representative* of the full skewed distribution as possible. Traditional systems tended to (approximately) favor the balancing (i.e. *Skew=False*) heuristic [12].

---

[13] Empirically, that is. A closed-form formula is not known [16].

[14] The exception is AGP, which achieves its best f-score performance (40.41%) at *Training-ratio=90%* when *LoS=10%*.

[15] Even with only six sample (mean) data point comparisons for the two *LoS* settings described, the f-score reductions *are* significant at the 95% level but not the 99% level. Both run-time reductions are significant at the 99% level.

Standard deviations on all effectiveness metrics across each set of trial runs were observed to be very low (in many cases 0), an advantage of cloud-based experimentation in obtaining reliable estimates. Run-time standard deviations were also extremely low ($<< 5\%$ on average). The last point justifies the chosen proxy for true model selection run-time in Section 5.2.

6   Summary and Future Work

This paper studies the application of decision-making bias to the instance matching model selection problem. First, the model selection design process is presented as a factor graph, with one class of nodes representing opportunities for bias. Existing decision-making biases in the instance matching literature are explicitly cast as special fragments of this model. These biases, and their mutual influences on each other, can then be visualized or further analyzed by a practitioner to understand the full extent of their design decisions.

As one form of analysis, we show that the model can be used to hypothesize about unexploited potential biases. Four specific recommendations were derived from the analysis. First, a practitioner should not artificially balance the labeled data but maintain skew through proportionate allocation stratified sampling (*Skew=True*). Secondly, good results are achieved, on average, when the training and validation ratios are equal (*Training-ratio=50%*). Third, the mean difference in effectiveness (i.e. f-scores) is not significant when a more expensive hyperparameter optimization strategy (*Hyper=Grid Search*) is preferred over simple random search in the neighborhood of default hyperparameter values (*Hyper=Random Search*), despite considerably increased run-times. Together, the last two prescriptions can be used to achieve a run-time reduction of over 65%, along with a slight increase in effectiveness.

Future work will study decision-making bias on a more theoretical foundation, and use the factor graphs for probabilistically reasoning about multiple sources of bias, as explained in Section 4.5. Also interesting is the issue of whether the proposed model can be applied to applications other than instance matching.

Acknowledgments. The authors thank Microsoft Research for providing infrastructure support. The authors were also supported by a US National Science Foundation grant.

References

1. Bergstra, J., Bengio, Y.: Random search for hyper-parameter optimization. The Journal of Machine Learning Research **13**(1), 281–305 (2012)
2. Bilenko, M., Mooney, R.J.: Adaptive duplicate detection using learnable string similarity measures. In: Proceedings of the Ninth ACM SIGKDD International Conference on Knowledge Discovery and Data Mining, pp. 39–48. ACM (2003)
3. Bishop, C.M., et al.: Pattern Recognition and Machine Learning, vol. 4. Springer, New York (2006)

4. Christen, P.: Data Matching: Concepts and Techniques for Record Linkage, Entity Resolution, and Duplicate Detection. Springer, Heidelberg (2012)
5. Clancey, W.J.: Model construction operators. Artificial Intelligence **53**(1), 1–115 (1992)
6. Daskalaki, E.: Instance matching benchmarks for linked data
7. Domingos, P., Richardson, M.: 1 markov logic: A unifying framework for statistical relational learning. In: Statistical Relational Learning, p. 339 (2007)
8. Hinton, G., Osindero, S., Teh, Y.-W.: A fast learning algorithm for deep belief nets. Neural Computation **18**(7), 1527–1554 (2006)
9. Kejriwal, M., Miranker, D.P.: Semi-supervised instance matching using boosted classifiers. In: Gandon, F., Sabou, M., Sack, H., d'Amato, C., Cudré-Mauroux, P., Zimmermann, A. (eds.) ESWC 2015. LNCS, vol. 9088, pp. 388–402. Springer, Heidelberg (2015)
10. Koller, D., Friedman, N.: Probabilistic Graphical Models: Principles and Techniques. MIT Press, Cambridge (2009)
11. Köpcke, H., Rahm, E.: Frameworks for entity matching: A comparison. Data & Knowledge Engineering **69**(2), 197–210 (2010)
12. Köpcke, H., Thor, A., Rahm, E.: Evaluation of entity resolution approaches on real-world match problems. Proceedings of the VLDB Endowment **3**(1–2), 484–493 (2010)
13. Neyman, J.: On the two different aspects of the representative method: the method of stratified sampling and the method of purposive selection. Journal of the Royal Statistical Society, 558–625 (1934)
14. Ngomo, A.-C.N.: A time-efficient hybrid approach to link discovery. In: Ontology Matching, p. 1 (2011)
15. Papadakis, G., Ioannou, E., Niederée, C., Fankhauser, P.: Efficient entity resolution for large heterogeneous information spaces. In: Proceedings of the Fourth ACM International Conference on Web Search and Data Mining, pp. 535–544. ACM (2011)
16. Rojas, R.: Neural Networks: A Systematic Introduction. Springer, Heidelberg (1996)
17. Rong, S., Niu, X., Xiang, E.W., Wang, H., Yang, Q., Yu, Y.: A machine learning approach for instance matching based on similarity metrics. In: Cudré-Mauroux, P., et al. (eds.) ISWC 2012, Part I. LNCS, vol. 7649, pp. 460–475. Springer, Heidelberg (2012)
18. Scharffe, F., Liu, Y., Zhou, C.: Rdf-ai: an architecture for rdf datasets matching, fusion and interlink. In: Proc. IJCAI 2009 Workshop on Identity, Reference, and Knowledge Representation (IR-KR), Pasadena, CA US (2009)
19. Soru, T., Ngomo, A.-C.N.: A comparison of supervised learning classifiers for link discovery. In: Proceedings of the 10th International Conference on Semantic Systems, pp. 41–44. ACM (2014)
20. Torralba, A., Efros, A., et al.: Unbiased look at dataset bias. In: 2011 IEEE Conference on Computer Vision and Pattern Recognition (CVPR), pp. 1521–1528. IEEE (2011)
21. Volz, J., Bizer, C., Gaedke, M., Kobilarov, G.: Discovering and maintaining links on the web of data. In: Bernstein, A., Karger, D.R., Heath, T., Feigenbaum, L., Maynard, D., Motta, E., Thirunarayan, K. (eds.) ISWC 2009. LNCS, vol. 5823, pp. 650–665. Springer, Heidelberg (2009)
22. Wolpert, D.H., Macready, W.G.: No free lunch theorems for optimization. IEEE Transactions on Evolutionary Computation **1**(1), 67–82 (1997)

Klink-2: Integrating Multiple Web Sources to Generate Semantic Topic Networks

Francesco Osborne[✉] and Enrico Motta

Knowledge Media Institute, The Open University, Milton Keynes MK7 6AA, UK
{francesco.osborne,enrico.motta}@open.ac.uk

Abstract. The amount of scholarly data available on the web is steadily increasing, enabling different types of analytics which can provide important insights into the research activity. In order to make sense of and explore this large-scale body of knowledge we need an accurate, comprehensive and up-to-date ontology of research topics. Unfortunately, human crafted classifications do not satisfy these criteria, as they evolve too slowly and tend to be too coarse-grained. Current automated methods for generating ontologies of research areas also present a number of limitations, such as: i) they do not consider the rich amount of indirect statistical and semantic relationships, which can help to understand the relation between two topics – e.g., the fact that two research areas are associated with a similar set of venues or technologies; ii) they do not distinguish between different kinds of hierarchical relationships; and iii) they are not able to handle effectively ambiguous topics characterized by a noisy set of relationships. In this paper we present Klink-2, a novel approach which improves on our earlier work on automatic generation of semantic topic networks and addresses the aforementioned limitations by taking advantage of a variety of knowledge sources available on the web. In particular, Klink-2 analyses networks of research entities (including papers, authors, venues, and technologies) to infer three kinds of semantic relationships between topics. It also identifies ambiguous keywords (e.g., "ontology") and separates them into the appropriate distinct topics – e.g., "ontology/philosophy" vs. "ontology/semantic web". Our experimental evaluation shows that the ability of Klink-2 to integrate a high number of data sources and to generate topics with accurate contextual meaning yields significant improvements over other algorithms in terms of both precision and recall.

Keywords: Scholarly data · Ontology learning · Bibliographic data · Scholarly ontologies · Data mining

1 Introduction

The amount of scholarly data available on the web is steadily increasing, enabling different types of analytics which can provide important insights into the research activity. Increasingly, Semantic Web standards are being used to represent this complex data and, as a result, we have seen the emergence of a number of bibliographic

© Springer International Publishing Switzerland 2015
M. Arenas et al. (Eds.): ISWC 2015, Part I, LNCS 9366, pp. 408–424, 2015.
DOI: 10.1007/978-3-319-25007-6_24

repositories in the Linked Data Cloud [1, 2, 3] and a variety of ontologies to describe scholarly data, including SWRC[1], BIBO[2], BiDO[3], AKT[4] and FABIO[5]. The semantic enhancement of scholarly articles, known as *semantic publishing* [4], is also becoming an important topic, attracting the interest of major publishers and leading to the formation of new communities (e.g., FORCE11[6]), workshops (e.g., Linked Science at ISWC, Sepublica at ESWC, SAVE-SD at WWW), and challenges (e.g., the ESWC Semantic Publishing Challenge[7]).

Indeed, today's scientific knowledge is so vast that scientists necessarily tend to specialize in relatively narrow fields, thus potentially missing important links across different fields and/or ending up reinventing solutions already available in other domains. However, there is growing consensus that semantic technologies can help to overcome this problem by improving our ability to discover, query, explore, annotate and visualize research information on the web [4, 5, 6, 7, 8, 9, 10]. Nonetheless, we still face some important technical challenges before this vision can be realized. These crucially include the problem of identifying and modelling the various relationships that exist between components of the research environment. While this task is relatively easy when describing the relationships between real world entities, such as authors and organizations, it becomes much harder when taking in consideration abstract concepts, such as the notion of *research topic*. For example, while it is easy to retrieve all the co-authors of Enrico Motta, it is much more difficult to identify all the papers of Enrico Motta which are relevant to research on the Semantic Web or one of its sub-areas. For this reason many popular systems for the exploration of research data, such as Google Scholar[8], Microsoft Academic Search[9] and Scopus[10], sidestep the challenge of identifying research topics and linking them to other relevant research entities, and simply use keywords as proxy. Unfortunately, this purely syntactic solution is unsatisfactory, as it fails i) to distinguish research topics from other keywords which can be used to annotate papers; ii) to deal with situations where multiple labels exist for the same research area; iii) to deal with the fact that a keyword may denote different topics depending on the context, and iv) to model and take advantage of the semantic relationships that hold between research areas, treating them instead as lists of unstructured keywords.

The traditional way to address the problem of identifying and structuring research topics has been to adopt human-crafted taxonomies, such as the ACM Computing Classification System[11]. Unfortunately, as we discussed in [11], this solution also presents a number of problems. First, building a large taxonomy of research areas requires a large number of experts and is an expensive and lengthy process.

---

[1] http://ontoware.org/swrc/

[2] http://bibliontology.com.

[3] http://purl.org/spar/bido

[4] http://www.aktors.org/publications/ontology

[5] http://purl.org/spar/fabio

[6] https://www.force11.org

[7] https://github.com/ceurws/lod/wiki/SemPub2015

[8] https://scholar.google.com

[9] http://academic.research.microsoft.com/

[10] http://www.scopus.com/

[11] http://www.acm.org/about/class/2012

For example, the 2012 version of ACM taxonomy was finalized fourteen years after the previous version. Hence, by the time these taxonomies are released they tend to be already obsolete, especially in fields such as Computer Science, where the most interesting topics are the newly emerging ones. Moreover, these taxonomies are very coarse-grained and usually represent wide categories of approaches, rather then the fine-grained topics addressed by researchers. For example, in the ACM Classification, the Semantic Web area is characterized as "Semantic web description languages" and has only two sub-areas: "OWL" and "RDF". Finally, these taxonomies are ambiguous, since the semantics of their links is not specified.

For these reasons, it is our view that building large-scale and timely taxonomies of research topics is a task that needs to be tackled through automatic methods and in 2012 we developed Klink [11], an algorithm which takes as input large amounts of scholarly metadata and automatically generates an OWL ontology containing all the research areas mined from the input data and their semantic relationships. This approach was demonstrated to work very well in comparison with the state of art and the ontology produced by Klink has been used to provide a comprehensive semantic topic network for Rexplore [5], a novel system which integrates semantic technologies, statistical analysis and visual analytics to provide effective support for making sense of scholarly data. In particular, the ontology generated by Klink enhances semantically a variety of data mining and information extraction techniques, and improves search and visual analytics. A variation of Klink was also used in the field of recommender systems to improve significantly the performance of a state of the art content-based recommender [12].

However, both Klink and similar solutions – e.g., [8, 13, 14], suffer from a number of limitations. First, they only consider the graph of co-occurrences between keywords [11] and/or direct semantic relationships [12], thus ignoring relevant indirect statistical and semantic relationships – e.g., the situation where two topics are related to the same conferences or associated to the same standards, knowledge which can improve the robustness and the performance of a solution, especially in the presence of noisy data. Moreover, they fail to deal with keywords which can denote different topics depending on the context in which they are used – e.g., "java" can be a programming language, but also an Indonesian island.

To address these problems we have developed Klink-2, an evolution of the Klink algorithm that addresses these limitations and provides a much better performance than Klink. Klink-2 introduces a number of new features, including:

- The ability to take as input any kind of statistical or semantic relationship between scholarly keywords and other entities – e.g., authors, organizations, venues and others.
- The ability to handle ambiguous keywords characterized by a noisy set of relationships – e.g., "java", by splitting them into multiple topics and labeling them correctly with their highest level super topic – e.g., "java (programming)" and "java (Indonesia)".
- The ability to scale up to large interdisciplinary ontologies, by being able to generate the topic ontology incrementally on different runs, rather than having to process all the data at the same time.

In the rest of the paper we will describe Klink-2 in detail, illustrating the main features of the algorithm and analyzing its performance in comparison to a number of alternative algorithms. In particular, we will show that the ability of Klink-2 to integrate a high number of data sources and to generate topics with accurate contextual meaning yields significant improvements over the other tested algorithms in terms of both precision and recall.

2   The Klink-2 Algorithm

2.1   Data Model

Many classifications of research areas simply take in consideration a single hierarchical relation, for example the 2012 ACM Classification uses *skos:narrower* to build a taxonomy of topics in computer science. However, as we discussed in [11], this is a limited solution and therefore our model[12], which builds on the BIBO ontology[13], uses a richer set of relationships:

1) *skos:broaderGeneric*. This is used when we have solid evidence that a topic is a sub-area of another one – e.g., "linked data" is a sub-area of "sematic web".

2) *contributesTo* (sub-property of *skos:related*). This indicates that while a topic, *x*, is not a sub-area of another one, *y*, its research outputs contribute to research in *y* to the extent that, for the purposes of querying and exploration, it is useful to consider *x* as 'under' *y*. For example, research on "ontology" contributes to research on "semantic web".

3) *relatedEquivalent* (sub-property of *skos:related*). This indicates that two topics can be treated as equivalent for the purpose of exploring research data – e.g., "ontology mapping" and "ontology matching".

Skos:broaderGeneric and *relatedEquivalent* are necessary to build a taxonomy of topics and to handle different labels for the same research areas, while *contributesTo* provides an additional relationship that can be used to assist the user in browsing research topics [5] and analyzing research data –e.g., for identifying topic-based research communities [10].

2.2   Overview of Klink-2

Klink-2 takes as input a set of scholarly keywords and their relationships with a variety of entities, including research papers, venues, authors, and organizations. The output is a populated OWL ontology describing the semantic relationships between the research topics identified from the set of keywords and the other data provided as input. This semantic network can then be used for improving the processes of searching and performing analytics on scholarly data [3, 5, 6, 7]. As in the case of the Klink algorithm, Klink-2 generates an ontology of research topics linked by the three relationships introduced above. To support those scenarios where we simply wish to gen-

---

[12] http://kmi.open.ac.uk/technologies/rexplore/ontologies/BiboExtension.owl
[13] http://purl.org/ontology/bibo/

erate the topic network relevant to a specific area – e.g., "Semantic Web", Klink-2 can also start from some given seed topics and expand this initial set by inferring their semantic connections with other topics, which in turn become the new seeds. The user can define a number of levels of recursion after which this process will stop.

The relationships taken as input can be either statistical, such as the number of citations received by the papers tagged with keyword k in venue v, or semantic, such as the *dbpedia-owl:field* relation used in DBpedia for associating fields to researchers. The former can be derived from article metadata, while the latter can be queried via SPARQL from the Linked Data Cloud or other RDF datasets.

While Klink-2 has been designed to generate ontologies of research topics, it can actually be applied to other domains. For example, we have previously shown that Klink could be used to generate ontologies for recommender systems in the gastronomic domain [12].

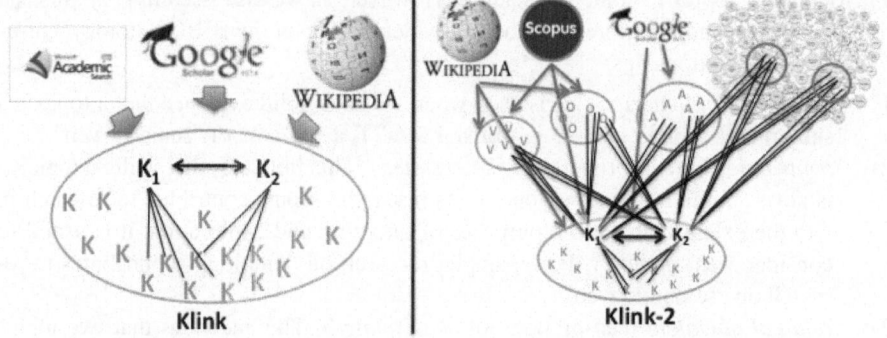

Fig. 1. Relationships used for inferring the topic ontology in Klink and Klink-2.

```
function Klink-2 (keywords, input_rel) returns (owl) {
split_merge=true;
   while (some keywords yet to process) {
     foreach k in keywords {
       keywords2 = getRelatedKeywords(k, input_rel);
         foreach k2 in keywords2 {
             rel = inferRelationships(k,k2, input_rel, rel); }
     }
     rel = fixLoops(rel);
     if (split_merge) keywords = splitAmbiguosKeywords(keywords, rel);
     else keywords = mergeSimilarKeywords(keywords, rel);
     split_merge = ¬ split_merge;
   }
keywords= filterNotAcademicKeywords(keywords, input_rel, rel);
return generateSemanticRelationships(keywords, rel);
}
```

Algorithm 1. The Klink-2 algorithm

Figure 1 shows the difference between Klink and Klink-2 in terms of relationships processed to create the topic network. Klink integrates a number of external sources, but only in order to produce an unbiased co-occurrence graph, which is the only knowledge used by the inference process. Klink-2 can instead exploit multiple relationships and thus take advantage of the rich network of interconnections between the different types of research entities, including papers, authors, venues, and technologies.

The Klink-2 algorithm is structured as follows:

1. Each pair of keywords whose number of common relationships with other scholarly entities is higher than a threshold is analyzed to check whether a hierarchical relationship between the components of the pair can be inferred. If this is the case, *skos:broaderGeneric* and *contributesTo* relationships are derived.
2. Each keyword is analyzed in order to detect possible multiple meanings associated to it. The keywords that seem ambiguous are split into multiple topics with unique meaning, which are then compared to the other keywords, possibly inferring new relationships.
3. The keywords which appear to be very similar are merged together and the *relatedEquivalent* semantic relationships are inferred. As in the previous case, the aggregated keywords are then compared to the already computed ones.
4. Step 2 and 3 are repeated until no new keywords are split or aggregated. Then Klink-2 filters out the keywords that do not represent research areas, fixes the loops in the topic network, and generates the triples describing the semantic relationships between topics.

In what follows we will describe the different phases of the algorithm. We will discuss only briefly the steps already present in the original Klink algorithm – e.g., filtering out keywords which do not denote research areas, to focus instead on the novel solutions.

2.3 Inferring Semantic Relationships

Klink-2 examines each pair of keywords which share a minimum number of relationships to the same scholarly entities and infers the semantic relationships discussed in Section 2.1 by means of three metrics: i) $H_R(x, y)$, which uses a semantic variation of the subsumption method to estimate whether a hierarchical relationship exists between two topics; ii) $T_R(x, y)$, which uses temporal information also to estimate whether a hierarchical relationship exists between two topics; and iii) $S_R(x, y)$, which estimates the similarity between two topics. The first two are used as statistical indicators to detect *skos:broaderGeneric* and *contributesTo* relationships, while the other is used to infer *relatedEquivalent* relationships.

These metrics are computed for each semantic or statistical relation R linking keywords x and y to a set of entities. The keywords (e.g., "semantic web") are mapped to entities (e.g., *dbpedia:Semantic_Web*) by using DBpedia spotlight[14]. Of course, the

---

[14] spotlight.dbpedia.org

selected relationships should have a minimum degree of quality and number of linked entities to be analyzed statistically. Hence, in some cases, it can be convenient to aggregate a number of similar semantic relations. For example, DBpedia uses a variety of different relations to connect topics to prominent authors in a discipline, such as *dbpprop:field, dbpprop:fields, dbpedia-owl:knownFor*. We can thus consider these relations as equivalent for our purposes, so as to improve the number of linked entities and the robustness of the statistical inferences.

2.3.1   Hierarchical Relationship Indicators

A classical way to infer a hierarchical relationship between two entities, which can occur in a set of documents, is the subsumption method [13]. According to this approach, term x subsumes term y if $P(x|y) \geq \alpha$ and $P(y|x) < 1$, with α usually set to 0.8. The original Klink improved on this method by considering the similarity between the distributions of co-occurring keywords as well as their string similarity. Klink-2 generalizes this approach by taking also in consideration the relationships linking keywords x and y to common entities. It does it by computing the conditional probability that an entity e linked to x by relation R will also be linked to y by the same relation. For example, a relationship between "semantic web" and "linked data" can also be inferred by the probability that an author working in one of these topics would also work in the other, or that a tool used in one of these topics would be used in the other. Hence, for every relation R, Klink-2 computes two statistical indicators ($H_R(x, y)$ and $T_R(x, y)$) that are used to detect a hierarchical relationship and then establish its nature.

Our approach distinguishes two classes of relations: quantified and unquantified ones. An unquantified relation is a triple in the form of *rel(t, e)* linking a topic t to an entity e. For instance, this could be a triple of the form *isAbout(p, t)* from the SWRC ontology, which states that a publication p is about topic t. A quantified relation is a quadruple in the form of *rel(t, e, q)*, where q quantifies numerically the intensity of the relationship. For example, *haveCitationInTopic(a,* t, 25) points to the fact that author a has 25 citations in topic t. The former are usually queried directly from RDF repositories, while the latter are inferred from metadata.

Using these input data we compute the statistical indicator $H_R(x, y)$ between keywords x and y for relation R with the following formula:

$$H_R(x, y) = \left(\frac{I_R(x,y)}{I_R(x,x)} - \frac{I_R(y,x)}{I_R(y,y)}\right) \cdot c_R(x, y) \cdot n(x, y) \qquad (1)$$

The first factor gives the direction of the possible hierarchical relationship, while the others give the intensity. $\frac{I_R(x,y)}{I_R(x,x)}$ is the conditional probability that an element associated with keyword x will be associated also with keyword y. If R is an unquantified relation, $I_R(x, y)$ is simply the number of elements associated with both x and y according to relation R. For example, in the case of *isAbout(p, x)*, $I_R(x, y)$ is equal to the number of co-occurrences between x and y, while $I_R(x, x)$ and $I_R(y, y)$ indicate the total number of publications in x and y. If R is a quantified relation, we should also take into account the intensity of the relationship. In this case, $I_R(x, y)$ is computed as the summation of the minimum values quantifying the two relationships connecting

x and y with e. For example, in the case of the relationship *haveCitationInTopic(a,x,c)*, $I_R(x,y)$ is the sum of the minimum numbers of citations in x and y received by each author, while $I_R(x,x)$ and $I_R(y,y)$ are respectively the sum of the total number of citations in x and in y received by all authors.

$c_R(x,y)$ measures the semantic similarity of x and y and is computed as the cosine similarity between the two vectors in which each index represents the keyword k, which has in common with x and/or y a set of instantiations of a relation, say R, with the same scholarly entities, with the values equal to $I_R(k,x)$ for x and $I_R(k,y)$ for y.

Finally $n_R(x,y)$ defines the string similarity between two keywords. It is computed as the linear combination of a number of string metrics based on the longest common sub-string, the percentage of identical words, the number of characters in common, the presence of acronyms, and so on.

When $H_R(x,y) \geq t_R$ we infer that, according to relation R, x is a candidate to becoming a sub-area of y, while when $H_R(x,y) \leq -t_R$, x is a candidate to becoming a super-area of y. The value of t_R can be set manually by analyzing the trade-off between precision and recall or alternatively it can be estimated by running the algorithm on training data and using the Nelder-Mead algorithm [12] to choose the thresholds which maximize the performances (usually in term of F-measure).

It is interesting to note that the formula used by the original Klink algorithm [11] can be considered (except for the improved $n_R(x,y)$ component) as a $H_R(x,y)$ indicator, using as relation *isAbout(p,x)*.

In many cases, it is also useful to consider the diachronic component of the relationships between two keywords, e.g. how their relationship evolved in time. For example, in the case of *isAbout(p,x)*, it can be argued that after some time certain topics may stop to co-occur simply because their association has become implicit.

This may cause a statistical indicator, which does not consider the diachronically dimension, to miss some important semantic relationships. Moreover the temporal dimension is useful to understand better the nature of the relationship linking two topics. The fact that the relationship was strong when one of the topics was young may point to the fact that this topic actually derived from the other and thus is truly one of its sub-areas. For this reason, Klink-2 computes also $T_R(x,y)$, a temporal version of $H_R(x,y)$, which gives more weight to the information associated with the first years of x. This is calculated using a variation of formula (1) in which $I_R(x,y)$ is computed by weighting the number and intensity of the relationships in each year according to the distance from the debut of x. The weight is computed as *w(year, x)=* *(year - debut(x) +1)* $^{-\gamma}$, with $\gamma > 0$ ($\gamma = 2$ in the prototype).

2.3.2   Inferring Hierarchical Semantic Relationships

A hierarchical relationship between two topics (represented by the keywords) is inferred when a sufficient number of indicators, i.e., a number above a given threshold, agree on the direction of the relationship. The precise threshold depends on the desired precision/recall trade-off. In some rare cases the situation may arises where indicators provide conflicting information – i.e., both $x > y$ and $y > x$ are suggested. In such a case we compute the difference between the two groups and go for a 'majority vote', assuming the difference is higher than the given threshold.

The nature of the inferred relationship is assessed by Klink-2 using a rule-based approach. This method takes into consideration a variety of factors, including the number of publications associated to x and y, the number of entities related to them, their debut years (i.e., the years in which the keywords first appeared), and the prevalence of $T_R(x, y)$ indicators versus $H_R(x, y)$ ones. If x is older, associated with more entities and there is a prevalence of $T_R(x, y)$ indicators, Klink-2 will infer a *skos:broaderGeneric* relationship. If these conditions do not apply, it will infer a *contributesTo* relationship. If the choice is unclear, it will be conservative and generate a *contributesTo* relationship since it provides a less risky assumption. A *skos:broaderGeneric(x,y)* relationship is transitive and implies that every publication tagged with x should also be tagged with y. Hence it is important to minimize as much as possible errors with the derivation of *skos:broaderGeneric* relationships, which will adversely affect the exploration of the scholarly data.

At the end of each main analysis loop, Klink-2 will also run the `fixLoops()` procedure, which detects loops in the graph of *skos:broaderGeneric* relationships and breaks them by eliminating the relationships with weaker statistical indicators.

2.3.3 Inferring RelatedEquivalent Relationships

Klink-2 uses the $S_R(x, y)$ similarity metric to infer *relatedEquivalent* relationships. We compute $S_R(x, y)$ by normalizing $c_R(x, y)$ with respect to the similarity between the super-areas and the siblings of x and y, according to the previously inferred hierarchical relationships. For this reason the *relatedEquivalent* relationships start to be inferred only after the first loop. The rationale is that for considering two elements in a taxonomy near enough to be merged they must be not only similar in absolute terms, but also more similar to each other than their super areas and siblings are to each other. Hence, we adopt the following formula:

$$S_R(x, y) = \frac{c_R(x,y)}{max\left(c_R^{super}(x,y), c_R^{sib}(x,y)\right)+1} \tag{2}$$

This formula is an evolution of the one used in Klink and proved to work better both on scholarly domains and on other domains [12]. Each pair of keywords which receives enough positive indicators is then linked by a similarity link. These pairs are then given in input to a bottom-up single-linkage hierarchical clustering algorithm [14], labeled in the pseudocode as `mergeSimilarKeywords()`, which uses as distance criterion a linear combination of the $S_R(x, y)$ indicators. For each pair of keywords clustered together, Klink-2 infers a *relatedEquivalent* relationship. The keywords in the cluster are then merged by aggregating all their relationships and will be re-analyzed in the next loop to infer additional relationships

2.4   Handling Ambiguous Keywords

The assumption that each keyword can be mapped to only one topic is unsafe, even when we consider keywords which were directly associated to a paper by the authors themselves. Our analysis on a subset of the Scopus dataset revealed mainly three categories of ambiguous keywords:

1. Terms which happen to have two or more different meanings, e.g., "java", the programming language, and "java", the island.
2. Vague terms, with meaning that can change according to the paper they are associated to – e.g., "mapping".
3. Terms that used to have a unique meaning, but are now used in specialized ways by different research communities – e.g. "ontology".

The first case is the most trivial, but also the one that may yield the biggest mistakes. For example, the original version of Klink, when processing a mixed database of life science and computer science, would infer that "owl" is both a sub-area of "semantics" and of "birds". The second case is partially addressed by the original Klink by excluding from the process the generic terms that co-occur significantly with a very high number of uncorrelated keywords. However, this quick solution may lose potentially interesting pieces of information. For example, we may assume with a good degree of confidence that the keyword "mapping", when combined with "ontology" and "interoperability", acquires an accurate meaning that is useful to capture. The third category is subtler, but can still yield a number of problems both for users, who may want to query the data using only the meanings more commonly used in their research community, and for algorithms that rely on statistical inferences. For example, "ontology" is used by most philosophers with the original meaning of study of the nature of being, while computer scientists usually refer to it as a practical tool for modeling a domain.

The ambiguous keywords are usually associated with a noisy set of relationships, which hinders the statistical inference process discussed in section 2.3. For this reason, Klink-2 addresses these cases by detecting the ambiguous terms and splitting them in multiple distinct topics. Differently from the disambiguation of probabilistic topic models [15, 16, 17], this process is driven by both pre-existing and inferred semantic relationships.

```
function splitAmbiguosKeywords(keywords, rel) returns (keywords) {
  foreach k in keywords {
    related_keywords = getRelatedKeywords(keywords, rel);
    clusters = quickHierarchicalClustering(related_keywords, rel);
    if ( count(clusters) > 1) {
      clusters2 = intersectBasedClustering(related_keywords, rel);
      if ( count(clusters2) > 1) {
        keywords = split(k, clusters2, keywords, rel); }
    }
  }
return keywords;
}
```

Algorithm 2. Detecting and splitting ambiguous keywords.

The first step is to quickly detect that a keyword x is probably ambiguous and thus a valid candidate to be analyzed more in depth. Since Klink-2 aims to be a scalable method, able to process a very large number of keywords, this first phase should be as quick as possible. To this purpose, we first select the keywords which share with x a minimum number of relationships to the same entities. We then run a hierarchical bottom-up clustering algorithm on this set of keywords, using as initial distance a linear combination of the $S_R(x, y)$ indicators. At each iteration of the algorithm, the distances between the new cluster n and each other cluster c is quickly updated by computing the weighted average of the distances between the merged elements and c, using as weight the number of papers associated with each keyword. If the algorithm yields more than one cluster, Klink-2 estimates that the analyzed keyword is connected to two or more distinct groups of keywords and thus may be ambiguous. For example, the keywords associated to 'owl' would be grouped in two clusters, one including terms such as 'RDF and 'semantic web' and the other including terms such as 'raptores' and 'barn owl'. However, it would be careless to directly generate new topics from this result, since a keyword may actually be associated with different groups of keywords without necessary being ambiguous. For this reason we run a slower and more accurate clusterization algorithm only on the keywords that yielded more than one cluster in the first phase. This method, `intersectBasedClustering()`, assigns to each cluster a pseudo-keyword, whose relationships are recomputed by considering only the entities that are connected both with the potential ambiguous keyword and at least one of the other keywords occurring in the cluster, which thus act as disambiguators. For example, in the case of "owl", the *isAbout* relation will be recomputed by considering only the publications tagged by the intersection of "owl" and a number of keywords associated to the general meaning of either "semantics" or "birds". The clustering process is then restarted and, at each iteration, the distances between clusters are re-calculated by updating the pseudo-keywords. If the process yields more than one cluster, the original keyword is used to produce as many topics as the resulting number of clusters. This is done by inserting the pseudo-keywords associated with the final clusters in the set of keywords to analyze, after labeling them accordingly to the most important high-level topics in the cluster. The related higher-level keyword used in the label is the member of the cluster with the highest harmonic mean between the number of co-occurrences with the original keyword and its total number of associated publications. For example, "owl" may be split into two different pseudo-keywords: *"owl (semantics)"* and *"owl (birds)"*. These keywords will be associated with the set of disambiguated relationships re-computed during the clustering process and will be compared with the other keywords for inferring new relationships.

In some cases, it would be inconvenient for the algorithm to return all the possible meanings of a keyword. For example, a researcher interested in the Semantic Web would just want the algorithm to automatically assign to "owl" the meaning of "owl (semantics)", without actually producing a second topic related to birds. For this reason, the approach can also be run in *contextual mode*. In this modality, Klink-2 will only keep the disambiguated keyword that is more similar to the input keywords, according to the cosine distance of the associated keyword distributions. Hence, if the input keywords were about the Semantic Web, "owl" will automatically take the correct contextual meaning and have its relationships disambiguated by using keywords about "semantics".

The threshold to stop the clustering process can be set to a high value, so to address only the first two categories of ambiguous keywords, or can be relaxed to tackle also the third one. While the second solution may produce an excessively fine-grained set of topics, it will also reduce the noise in the data and foster the quality of the relationships, by mapping each topic to a very accurate and unique meaning.

2.5   Triple Generation

Klink-2 exits the main loop when it has no more keywords to analyze. It then filters the keywords considered "not academic" or "too generic" according to a number of heuristics, such as the profile of distribution of their co-occurrences or their absence from relevant academic sources – this process is fully described in [11]. While the first version of Klink used to filter the keywords before analyzing them, Klink-2 does it afterwards. This is because the ability to process ambiguous keywords can actually generate usable topics from many of the keywords that the original version would have discarded. In this phase, Klink-2 also deletes the redundant relationships which would be entailed by other relationships. Finally, Klink-2 generates the triples describing the research topics and their relationships. The output can be used to create a new OWL knowledge base or can be added to an existing one. In the latter case Klink-2 will check the relationships for inconsistencies and loops and may delete some of them. Being able to build an ontology iteratively on different runs is indeed very useful to address scalability, since the algorithm will not be forced to load the full graph of all existing keywords, but can run on different sub-taxonomies, which are then merged.

3   Evaluation

We tested our approach on the keywords of a dataset extracted from Scopus, consisting of 16 million publications about computer science and life sciences. Additional knowledge about these keywords and their relationships was extracted from DBpedia, Google Scholar and Wikipedia. We evaluated our method by testing a number of alternative algorithms for their ability of building an ontology about the Semantic Web and related areas. To this end, we adopted as gold standard the ontology used in [11], after updating it by i) mapping some of the terms in the ontology to keywords used by Scopus (e.g., "linked datum"), which were not present in the data used in the 2012 evaluation, and ii) adding 30 new topics co-occurring with "Semantic Web" and "Semantics" in the Scopus database. The new version of the ontology was validated and corrected by three external domain experts with publications in ISWC and ESWC conferences. The resulting gold standard[15] includes 88 topics linked by 133 semantic relationships (263 when taking in consideration also the subsumption relationships that can be derived from transitive relations).

---

[15] The gold standard and the data generated in the evaluation are publicly available at http://kmi.open.ac.uk/technologies/rexplore/iswc2015/.

We tested four different methods:

1)   the classic subsumption method [8, 13], mentioned in section 2.3.1 (labelled **S**);

2)   the original Klink algorithm, as described in [11] (labelled **K**);

3)   a first version of Klink-2, with the ability of integrating multiple relationships, but not addressing ambiguous keywords (labelled **KR**);

4)   the final version of Klink-2, with also the ability to detect and split ambiguous keywords in contextual mode (labelled **K2**);

The co-occurrence graph derived from Scopus was enriched by exploiting the co-occurrences on Google Scholar and Wikipedia, as described in [11]. **KR** and **K2** used six statistical relationships computed on the Scopus dataset, i.e. the number of associated publications/citations for publications, authors and venues. These methods also queried a variety of semantic relationships from DBpedia, such as *foaf:primaryTopic*, *dbpprop:discipline*, *dcterms:subject*, *dbpprop:domain*, *dbpprop:field*, *dbpedia-owl:knownFor* and so on. The thresholds for **S**, **K**, **KR** and **K2** were set to maximize the F-measure on the topic taxonomy used by Rexplore [5], and originally generated from the Microsoft Academic Search dataset. The minimum number of indicators used by **KR** and **K2** for inferring semantic relationships was empirically set to 2.

Table 1. F-measure, precision and recall of the four approaches.

	S	K	KR	K2
F-measure	49.01%	78.05%	82.73%	**85.88%**
Precision	40.86%	83.84%	82.58%	**86.21%**
Recall	61.22%	73.00%	82.89%	**85.55%**

The ontologies generated by **S**, **K**, **KR** and **K2** were compared with the gold standard by computing recall, precision and F-measure of the inferred semantic relationships. Table 1 shows the metrics relative to the four approaches. The statistical significance between the approaches was assessed by arranging data in cross-correlation tables analyzed with the chi-square test (with Yates' correction for 2x2 tables). All outcomes of **K, KR** and **K2** are significantly superior to those of **S** ($p < 0.0001$), confirming the results presented in [11]. The F-measure increases from **K** (78%) to **KR** (83%), to **K2** (86%), with a significant difference between **K2** and **K** ($p=0.001$). The precision is essentially similar for **K** and **KR,** improving slightly for **K2** ($p=0.51$). However, the recall increases notably from **K** (73%) to **KR** (83%) to **K2** (86%) with differences which are significant for **KR** versus **K** ($p=0.008$) and even more so for **K2** versus **K** ($p=0.0005$).

Hence, the results indicate that allowing the approach to take into account multiple relationships has an important impact on the recall of semantic relationships. Moreover, the technique to address ambiguous keywords discussed in section 2.4 yields a significant improvement in both precision and recall.

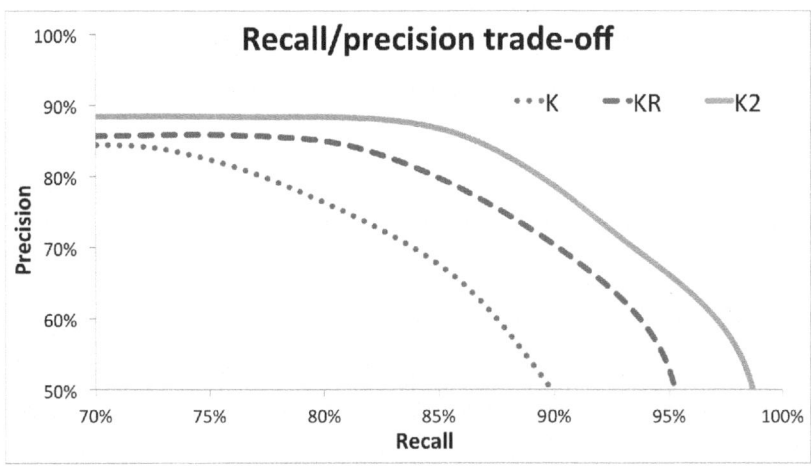

Fig. 2. Recall/precision trade off.

In many scenarios, the users may want to optimize the approach so that it yields either a high recall or a high precision, depending on the context. For example, if humans will validate and correct the generated semantic relationships, e.g., by using crowdsourcing ontology verification [18, 19], it may be more important to have a high recall. On the contrary, if this step is not carried out and the ontology is used by automatic methods, precision is usually more important.

We explored the recall/precision trade-off of **K**, **KR** and **K2** by running the algorithms with different thresholds modulated by a factor ranging from 0.25 to 3, to obtain an increasingly stricter inference process. Figure 3 shows the precision of the algorithms as a function of the recall. **K2** clearly outperforms again the other two algorithms by yielding a higher precision over the whole recall range (p=0.005 with non-parametric Wilcoxon's test), especially in the highest recall region. For example, when a recall of 90% is required, **K** yields a precision of 50%, **KR** of 73% and **K2** of 80%: hence, Klink-2 allows also a greater flexibility in choosing the recall/precision trade-off tailored to the user needs. Taking in consideration a high number of relationships obviously requires more time. The topics of the gold standard were analyzed in about 4 seconds (average on the various runs) by **S**, in 7 by **K**, in 36 by **KR** and in 45 by **K2**. However, since this kind of algorithm does not usually run in real time (e.g., Rexplore updates its ontology every three months), an increment in running time is a low price to pay for significantly better performances.

4   Related Work

Ontologies of research topics can be helpful for exploring and making sense of academic data in a variety of ways. For example, they can enhance semantically many information extraction techniques, such as trend detection [6] and community detection [7, 10]. They also make it possible to improve search results and their presentation, e.g., by supporting semantic faceted search [20].

There are a variety of approaches for learning taxonomies or ontologies, including natural language processing [21], clustering techniques [22], statistical methods [13], and methods based on spreading activation [19]. Text2Onto [21] is a popular system for learning ontologies, which represents the learned ontological structures in a probabilistic ontology model and uses natural language processing techniques. The Lexico-Syntactic Pattern Extraction (LSPE) approach [23] exploits linguistic patterns, e.g., "such as…" and "and other…", to discover relationships between terms. However, these approaches are based on the analysis of textual documents, while Klink-2 focuses instead on metadata, statistics and semantic relationships, since its scope is a large-scale analysis of research data.

The *TaxGen* framework [14] creates taxonomies from a set of documents by means of a hierarchical agglomerative clustering algorithm and text mining techniques. Klink-2 also adopts a clusterization algorithm for inferring the *relatedEquivalent* relationship and handling ambiguous keywords.

A very popular statistical approach is the subsumption method [13], which computes the conditional probability for a keyword to be associated with another in order to infer hierarchical relationships, as discussed in section 2.2. The same idea is extended in the GrowBag algorithm [8], which enriches the original model by using second order co-occurrences made explicit by a biased *PageRank* algorithm. The original Klink algorithm [11] also used statistical methods on the co-occurrence graph, while Klink-2 goes a step further by allowing the use of semantic or statistical relationships from multiple sources. The use of multiple sources for this task was also strongly advocated by Wohlgenannt et al [19], who proposed a framework for inferring lightweight ontologies which first build a semantic network through co-occurrence analysis, trigger phrase analysis, and disambiguation techniques, and then uses spread activation to find candidate concepts. Klink-2 does a similar co-occurrence analysis, but also uses indirect relationships and generates novel topics derived from the combination of different keywords. Similarly to the approach of Wohlgenannt et al, Klink-UM [12], a variation of Klink designed to generate lightweight ontologies for recommender systems, adopts spreading activation for tailoring semantic relationships to user needs.

Klink-2 is able to manage ambiguous keywords by generating multiple topics with a unique meaning, according to the semantic context. This is conceptually similar to the disambiguation performed by probabilistic topics models which detect latent topics by exploiting Probabilistic Latent Semantic Indexing (pLSI) [15] or Latent Dirichlet Allocation [16]. For example the Author-Conference-Topic (ACT) model [17] treats authors as probability distributions over topics, conferences and journals. Differently from them, our approach uses explicit semantic relationships, rather than latent semantic, to drive the generation of unambiguous topics. These topics are accurately described by a number of semantic relationships and not simply as term distributions.

Methods for automatically learning ontologies can be complementary to crowdsourcing ontology verification [18, 19], a process in which a large number of workers solve micro-tasks for validating and correcting semantic relationships.

As mentioned in the introduction, Klink-2 is currently integrated in the Rexplore system [5], and is used to semantically enhance a number of algorithms for exploring research data. Nowadays we have several interesting tools which exploit semantic technologies to make sense of research. The Saffron system [9], which builds on the Semantic Web Dog Food Corpus [1], allows for advanced expert search and estimates the strength of an author/topic relationship by analyzing co-occurrences on the Web. Arnetminer [17] also provides support for expert search and a variety of analytics on research topics. RKBExplorer [3] is an application that generates comprehensive visualizations of the research environment from a number of heterogeneous data sources. Klink-2 can benefit these systems by generating an accurate, large-scale and up-to-date topic network.

5   Conclusions

We presented Klink-2, a novel approach to generate semantic topic networks which can integrate a number of web sources and exploit multiple semantic and statistical relationships. The output can be useful to a vast number of tools as it can be used to provide a semantic structure to support the identification, search, exploration and visualization of research data. The evaluation shows that Klink-2 performs significantly better than alternative solutions. In particular, Klink-2 is able to yield a good precision (80%) even when a very high recall (90%) is needed.

Our approach opens up many interesting directions of work. On the research side, we plan to investigate diachronically the shift in meaning of scholarly keywords to better characterize the evolution of research areas. We also want to exploit natural language processing techniques to augment our semantic model with additional entities (e.g., methods, tools, and standards) which can be extracted from the text of scientific publications. Finally, on the technology transfer side, we are currently collaborating with two major academic publishers, who are looking to deploy Klink-2 in their organizations, thus providing a strong semantic topic structure to support classification, search and exploration in their digital libraries.

Acknowledgements. We would like to thank Elsevier BV and Springer DE for providing us with access to their large repositories of scholarly data.

References

1. Moller, K., Heath, T., Handschuh, S., Domingue, J.: Recipes for semantic web dog food — the ESWC and ISWC metadata projects. In: 6th International Semantic Web Conference, November 11–15, 2007, Busan, South Korea (2007)
2. Latif, A., Afzal, M.T., Helic, D., Tochtermann, K., Maurer, H.: Discovery and construction of authors' profile from linked data (A case study for Open Digital Journal). In: WWW 2010 Workshop on Linked Data on the Web (LDOW 2010). CEUR-WS, vol. 628, Raleigh, North Carolina, USA (2010)
3. Glaser, H., Millard, I.: Knowledge-enabled research support: RKBExplorer.com. In: Proceedings of Web Science 2009, Athens, Greece (2009)
4. Peroni, S., Shotton, D.: FaBiO and CiTO: ontologies for describing bibliographic resources and citations. Journal of Web Semantics **17**, 33–43 (2012)

5. Osborne, F., Motta, E., Mulholland, P.: Exploring scholarly data with rexplore. In: Alani, H., et al. (eds.) ISWC 2013, Part I. LNCS, vol. 8218, pp. 460–477. Springer, Heidelberg (2013)
6. Decker, S.L., Aleman-Meza, B., Cameron, D., Arpinar, I.B.: Detection of bursty and emerging trends towards identification of researchers at the early stage of trends (Doctoral dissertation, University of Georgia) (2007)
7. Erétéo, G., Gandon, F., Buffa, M.: SemTagP: semantic community detection in folksonomies. In: 2011 IEEE/WIC/ACM International Conference on Web Intelligence and Intelligent Agent Technology (WI-IAT), vol. 1, pp. 324–331. IEEE (2011)
8. Diederich, J., Balke, W., Thaden, U.: Demonstrating the semantic GrowBag: automatically creating topic facets for FacetedDBLP. In: JCDL 2007, NY, USA (2007)
9. Monaghan, F., Bordea, G., Samp, K., Buitelaar, P.: Exploring your research: sprinkling some saffron on semantic web dog food. In: Semantic Web Challenge at the International Semantic Web Conference (2010)
10. Osborne, F., Scavo, G., Motta, E.: Identifying diachronic topic-based research communities by clustering shared research trajectories. In: Presutti, V., d'Amato, C., Gandon, F., d'Aquin, M., Staab, S., Tordai, A. (eds.) ESWC 2014. LNCS, vol. 8465, pp. 114–129. Springer, Heidelberg (2014)
11. Osborne, F., Motta, E.: Mining semantic relations between research areas. In: Cudré-Mauroux, P., et al. (eds.) ISWC 2012, Part I. LNCS, vol. 7649, pp. 410–426. Springer, Heidelberg (2012)
12. Osborne, F., Motta, E.: Inferring semantic relations by user feedback. In: Janowicz, K., Schlobach, S., Lambrix, P., Hyvönen, E. (eds.) EKAW 2014. LNCS, vol. 8876, pp. 339–355. Springer, Heidelberg (2014)
13. Sanderson, M., Croft, B.: Deriving concept hierarchies from text. In: Proceedings of the SIGIR Conference, pp. 206–213 (1999)
14. Müller, A., Dorre, J.: The TaxGen framework: automating the generation of a taxonomy for a large document collection. In: Proceedings of the 32nd Hawaii International Conference on System Sciences, vol. 2, pp. 20–34 (1999)
15. Hofmann, T.: Probabilistic latent semantic indexing. In: the 22nd Conference on Research and Development in Information Retrieval, pp. 50–57, Berkeley, CA (1999)
16. Blei, D.M., Ng, A.Y., Jordan, M.I.: Latent Dirichlet allocation. Journal of Machine Learning Research 3, 993–1033 (2003)
17. Tang, J., Zhang, J., Yao, L., Li, J., Zhang, L., Su, Z.: Arnetminer: extraction and mining of academic social networks. In Proceedings of the 14th ACM International Conference on Knowledge Discovery and Data Mining, pp. 990–998. ACM (2008)
18. Mortensen, J.M., Alexander, P.R., Musen, M.A., Noy, N.F.: Crowdsourcing ontology verification. In: The Semantic Web–ISWC 2013, pp. 448–455 (2013)
19. Wohlgenannt, G., Weichselbraun, A., Scharl, A., Sabou, M.: Dynamic integration of multiple evidence sources for ontology learning. Journal of Information and Data Management 3(3), 243 (2012)
20. Suominen, O, Viljanen, K., Hyvänen, E.: User-centric faceted search for semantic portals. In: 4th European Conference on the Semantic Web (ESWC 2007), pp. 356–370 (2007)
21. Cimiano, P., Völker, J.: Text2Onto. In: Montoyo, A., Muñoz, R., Métais, E. (eds.) NLDB 2005. LNCS, vol. 3513, pp. 227–238. Springer, Heidelberg (2005)
22. Assadi, H.: Construction of a regional ontology from text and its use within a documentary system. In: Guarino, N. (ed.) Proceedings of FOIS 1998 Formal Ontology in Information Systems, pp. 236–249, Trento, Italy (1999)
23. Hearst, M.: Automated discovery of WordNet relations. In: Fellbaum, C. (ed.) WordNet: An Electronic Lexical Database, pp. 131–153. MIT Press (1998)

TabEL: Entity Linking in Web Tables

Chandra Sekhar Bhagavatula$^{(\boxtimes)}$, Thanapon Noraset, and Doug Downey

Northwestern University, Evanston, IL 60201, USA
{csbhagav,nor.thanapon}@u.northwestern.edu, ddowney@eecs.northwestern.edu

Abstract. Web tables form a valuable source of relational data. The Web contains an estimated 154 million HTML tables of relational data, with Wikipedia alone containing 1.6 million high-quality tables. Extracting the semantics of Web tables to produce machine-understandable knowledge has become an active area of research.

A key step in extracting the semantics of Web content is *entity linking* (EL): the task of mapping a phrase in text to its referent entity in a knowledge base (KB). In this paper we present *TabEL*, a new EL system for Web tables. *TabEL* differs from previous work by weakening the assumption that the semantics of a table can be mapped to pre-defined types and relations found in the target KB. Instead, *TabEL* enforces soft constraints in the form of a graphical model that assigns higher likelihood to sets of entities that tend to co-occur in Wikipedia documents and tables. In experiments, *TabEL* significantly reduces error when compared to current state-of-the-art table EL systems, including a 75% error reduction on Wikipedia tables and a 60% error reduction on Web tables. We also make our parsed Wikipedia table corpus and test datasets publicly available for future work.

Keywords: Web tables · Entity linking · Named entity disambiguation · Graphical models

1 Introduction

Web tables, or HTML tables on the Web, are a valuable source of relational data and an important input for information extraction (IE) systems. It is estimated that out of a total of 14.1 billion tables on the Web, 154 million tables contain relational data [1] and Wikipedia alone is the source of nearly 1.6 million relational tables. Unlike text, a single relational table contains a high-quality set of relation instances, along with associated metadata (in the form of column headers). The wealth and utility of relational tables on the Web has made *semantic interpretation* of tables, i.e. the task of converting Web tables into machine-understandable knowledge, an active area of research [2–12].

A key step in extracting the semantics of Web content is entity linking (EL): the task of mapping phrases of text to their referent entities in a given Knowledge Base (KB). For example, in Table 1, the EL task is to link "Chicago" in the second

© Springer International Publishing Switzerland 2015
M. Arenas et al. (Eds.): ISWC 2015, Part I, LNCS 9366, pp. 425–441, 2015.
DOI: 10.1007/978-3-319-25007-6_25

column to its corresponding entity Chicago (the city) in a KB, e.g. YAGO [13].[1] Polysemy of phrases is the main challenge for EL systems. An EL system must disambiguate each given phrase utilizing clues from surrounding content, called the *context* of the phrase. In Table 1, the phrase "New York" occurs multiple times, but it is evident from context that it refers to the city in the second column and to the state in the third column.

We present *TabEL*, a system that performs the *Entity Linking* task on phrases in cells of Web tables. Existing table semantic interpretation systems typically employ graphical models to jointly model three semantic interpretation tasks: *entity linking*, *column type identification* and *relation extraction* from tables (detailed in Section 2) [4,6,7,12]. Such joint models are based on a strong assumption that the column types and relations expressed in a table can be mapped to pre-defined types and relations in the target KB. While the type and relation information conveyed by the structure

Table 1. Table containin g a list of tallest buildings in the U.S. and the city and state that they are located in. Underlines represent an existing reference to an entity in a KB.

Building Name	City	State
One WTC	New York	New York
Willis Tower	Chicago	Illinois
⋮	⋮	⋮
MetLife Tower	New York	New York

of tables are valuable clues for the EL task, relying on a strict mapping into a KB is prone to errors as KBs can be incomplete or noisy.

In this paper, we investigate an alternative to the strict mapping into a KB. *TabEL* incorporates type and relation information through a graphical model of soft constraints. The constraints encode a preference for sets of referent entities that are "coherent", in that pairs of entities in the set tend to co-occur in Wikipedia documents and tables. Although our graphical model is densely connected (see Section 3), we show in experiments that we can tractably arrive at disambiguations using the Iterative Classification Algorithm (ICA) [14]. In experiments, we show that *TabEL* is more accurate than previous work, reducing error over the benchmark system [4] by ∼60% on Web tables. *TabEL* performs particularly well on Wikipedia tables and reduces error over previous work by ∼75%. In ablation studies, we analyze the impact of *TabEL*'s components on accuracy and demonstrate that our features result in an improvement of ∼12% over a system that chooses the most usual meaning of a phrase as its referent entity.

Finally, we release our table corpus containing more than 1.6 million tables from Wikipedia. We also make datasets of entity-annotated Wikipedia and Web tables publicly available for future table EL systems.[2]

---

[1] https://gate.d5.mpi-inf.mpg.de/webyagospotlx/Browser?entityIn=%3C
Chicago%3E

[2] http://websail-fe.cs.northwestern.edu/TabEL/

2   Preliminaries

The general task of semantic interpretation of tables takes as input a table and a reference Knowledge Base (KB), and typically includes the following sub-tasks:

1. *Entity linking* (EL): the task of finding phrases of text, called *mentions*, in cells and associating each with its referent entity
2. *Column type identification*: the task of associating a column in a table with the KB type of entities it contains
3. *Relation extraction*: the task of associating a pair of columns in a table with the KB relation that holds between each pair of entities in a given row of the columns

The referent entities, types and relations are all grounded in the given KB. As a concrete example, given Table 1 and the YAGO [13] KB, the entity linking task would include linking "Chicago" to the entity Chicago in the KB.[3] Type identification would include associating the second column to the City type in the KB.[4] The relation extraction task would include identifying the relation isLocatedIn between entities Willis_Tower and Chicago.[5]

In this paper, we focus on just the first semantic interpretation task, entity linking. We now formally define the EL task for tables. We also introduce notation that will be used in the rest of this paper.

Formal Definition

A *potential mention* is a phrase in text whose referent entity in the given KB is unknown. We denote a potential mention for a phrase s as $m_{s,?}$ (where ? denotes an unknown entity). An *annotated mention*, on the other hand, is a phrase whose referent entity is known and is denoted by $m_{s,e}$, where s is the phrase of text whose referent entity is e.

A *table* from the Web is represented as a matrix, T, of cells containing r rows and c columns. Tables that use row- and column-spans can be easily normalized into an $r \times c$ matrix by duplicating cells. $T[i, j]$ represents the cell in the ith row and j^{th} column of T.

Task: Given a table T and a KB $\mathcal{K}$ of entities, the *entity linking* task is to identify and link each potential mention in cells of T to its referent entity $e \in \mathcal{K}$.

3   System Description

Given a table T and a KB $\mathcal{K}$, *TabEL* performs the EL task in three steps:

1. *mention identification:* identifies each potential mention, $m_{s,?}$, in cells of T

---

[3] https://gate.d5.mpi-inf.mpg.de/webyagospotlx/Browser? entityIn=%3CChicago%3E

[4] https://gate.d5.mpi-inf.mpg.de/webyagospotlx/Browser?entity=%3Cwordnet_city_108524735%3E

[5] https://gate.d5.mpi-inf.mpg.de/webyagospotlx/WebInterface? L01=%3CWillis_Tower%3E\&L0R=%3CisLocatedIn%3E&L02=%3CChicago%3E

2. *entity candidate generation:* for each potential mention $m_{s,?}$, identifies a set of candidate entities, $\mathcal{C}(m_{s,?})$ - a subset of entities in $\mathcal{K}$ that are possible referents of $m_{s,?}$
3. *disambiguation:* for each potential mention $m_{s,?}$, chooses an entity $e \in \mathcal{C}(m_{s,?})$ (its candidate set), as the referent entity of $m_{s,?}$, based on its context.

TabEL uses a supervised learning approach, and uses annotated mentions in tables to train its components. Like most EL systems, *TabEL* also relies on a prior estimate that a given string s refers to a particular entity e, i.e. $P(e|s)$. As in previous work [15], we estimate this distribution $P(e|s)$ from hyperlinks on the Web and in Wikipedia, as described in Section 4.

While we use YAGO as our knowledge base in our experiments, our approach is general and can use any KB, given some labeled examples for that KB and a suitable entity-similarity measure that we use in our system.

3.1 Mention Identification

The first step for any EL system is to find potential mentions that can be linked to their referent entities in $\mathcal{K}$. Given the text content, t_q, of each cell of the input table, *TabEL* identifies as a potential mention the longest phrase, s of t_q that has non-zero probability in $P(e|s)$ for some e. If the length of s is less than the length of t_q, *TabEL* finds the longest phrase starting after s and so on. For example, for a cell with text "Barack Obama & Mitt Romney", *TabEL* finds two potential mentions: one for "Barack Obama" and one for "Mitt Romney".

3.2 Candidate Generation

For each potential mention, $m_{s,?}$, *TabEL* sets the set of candidate entities $\mathcal{C}(m_{s,?})$ for the mention to be all those e for which $P(e|s)$ has non-zero probability, i.e. $\mathcal{C}(m_{s,?}) = \{e | P(e|s) > 0\}$. For example, the candidate entity set for the phrase "Chicago" would contain the entities Chicago, Chicago_Bulls, Chicago_(1927_film), etc.

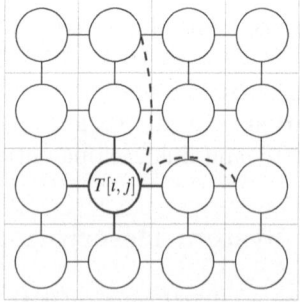

Fig. 1. Graphical Model used for disambiguation. Circles represent variables and edges represent their dependencies. For brevity, we show non-adjacent dependencies only for the cell $T[i;j]$

3.3 Disambiguation

Our disambiguation technique is based on the assumption that entities in a given row or column tend to be related. As we show in our experiments, when disambiguating multiple cells of a table, we can achieve higher accuracy by preferring sets of disambiguations that are coherent (i.e. sets composed of related entities). To exploit this fact, we utilize a collective classification technique in which soft constraints encourage disambiguations of mentions in the same row and column to be related to one another. The disambiguations in a given table are optimized jointly, to arrive at a globally coherent set of entities.

In the disambiguation step, an EL system needs to choose an entity from the candidate set $\mathcal{C}(m_{s,?})$ as the referent entity of a given mention $m_{s,?}$. We represent a table, T, as a graphical model in which each potential mention is associated with a discrete random variable, whose possible values are its candidate entities. Each variable has a direct dependency with all other variables in its row and column. The model can be drawn as a Markov Network, shown in Figure 1, in which each row (and each column) forms a fully-interconnected clique.

Our graphical model is much more densely connected than the models used in previous work on this task [4,7]. However, we find that an iterative, approximate inference approach is tractable for the model. *TabEL* uses the Iterative Classification Algorithm (ICA) [14] to collectively disambiguate all mentions in a given table. ICA is an iterative inference method which greedily re-assigns each variable to its maximum-likelihood value, conditioned on the current values of other variables. In each iteration, we compute the maximum-likelihood value for each variable using a trained *local classifier*, $\mathcal{M}_{LR}$, which takes the form of a logistic-regression-based ranking model. Algorithm 1 shows how ICA performs iterative inference over the graphical model to find a high-likelihood set of referent entities for all mentions in a given test table. The method initializes each mention with an entity using $\mathcal{M}_{LR}$ (lines 2 to 4) and then iteratively re-computes features and assignments (lines 6 to 18) until there is no change in assignment for any mention or the maximum iteration limit is reached.

$\mathcal{M}_{LR}$ ranks the candidate entities for a given mention, based on a set of features computed from the current settings of the other variables. The local model $\mathcal{M}_{LR}$ is trained in advance on a set of annotated mentions. $\mathcal{M}_{LR}$ utilizes the following groups of features:

Prior probability features, $P(e|s)$ are estimated from hyperlinks on the Web and in Wikipedia. For example, the phrase "Chicago" appears 16,884 times as an anchor text in Wikipedia. It links to one of 289 distinct pages including the city, the movie, the music band etc. But the string "Chicago" most likely refers to the city ($P(\texttt{Chicago\_City}\,|\,\textit{"Chicago"}) = 0.80$). For each distinct source of hyperlinks, we compute features for both case-sensitive and case-insensitive matching of the phrase. In addition, we include the averages of case-sensitive and case-insensitive probability estimates across all sources.

Semantic relatedness (SR) features are used to measure the coherence between a candidate entity and other entities in the table. *TabEL* has three SR based features: average SR between a candidate entity and all entities in the mention's 1) row, 2) column, and 3) context i.e. row and column.

In *TabEL*, we use SR defined between a pair of Wikipedia pages based on their in-link and out-link overlap. We use the SR implementation from Hecht et al. [16]. This is a modified version of Milne-Witten Semantic Relatedness measure [17] in which the links in the first paragraph of a Wikipedia page are considered more important than other links when calculating relatedness.

Algorithm 1. ICA for Disambiguation in *TabEL*

1: **function** *TabEL*-ICA($\mathcal{M}_{LR}$, T, maxIter)   ▷ $\mathcal{M}_{LR}$: Local Disambiguation Model
                                                                  ▷ T: Input Table
                                         ▷ maxIter: Maximum number of inference iterations
2:     **for all** $m_{s,?} \in T$ **do**
3:         $m_{s,?} \leftarrow m_{s,e_0}$ ▷ where $e_0 \leftarrow \mathcal{M}_{LR}(\mathcal{C}(m_{s,?}))$
4:     **end for**
5:     $k \leftarrow 1$
6:     **do**
7:         **for all** $m_{s,?} \in T$ **do**
8:             ▷ Re-calculate features according to current assignment to other variables
9:             $reCalculateFeatures(m_{s,?})$
10:        **end for**
11:        $hasChange \leftarrow False$
12:        **for all** $m_{s,?} \in T$ **do**
13:            $m_{s,e_{k-1}} \leftarrow m_{s,e_k}$ ▷ Re-assign value. $e_k \leftarrow \mathcal{M}_{LR}(\mathcal{C}(m_{s,e_{k-1}}))$
14:            **if** $e_{k-1} == e_k$ **then**
15:                $hasChange \leftarrow True$
16:            **end if**
17:        **end for**
18:     **while** $hasChange$ AND $k < maxIter$
19: **end function**

The average SR value between a candidate entity and entities in a mention's context is an important feature for the EL task in tables, as shown by our experiments in Section 5. In the special case of applying *TabEL* to Wikipedia tables, we also include a feature for relatedness between the candidate entity and the Wikipedia page containing the table.

Mention-Entity Similarity features capture the similarity between the *context* of a potential mention and the *context-representation* of each of its candidate entities. We define the context of a mention as the contents of the cells in its row and column. The context-representation of an entity is the aggregation of the contexts in which it occurs in the training data.

For example, $m_{Chicago,?}$ is a potential mention in the cell $T[2,2]$ in Table 1. The highlighted column is referred to as the column context of the mention, denoted by $\mathcal{X}^C(T[2,2])$. Similarly, the highlighted row is referred to as the row-context and denoted by $\mathcal{X}^R(T[2,2])$. Consider the entity New_York_City in $T[1,2]$ in Table 1. Its context contains entities Chicago, One_World_Trade_Center, MetLife_Tower etc. To construct a context-representation for New_York_City, we aggregate the contexts of all mentions in our table corpus that link to New_York_City.

In general, the row and column contexts of a mention in cell $T[i,j]$ are given by:

$$\mathcal{X}^R(T[i,j]) = T[i,\cdot] \setminus T[i,j]$$
$$\mathcal{X}^C(T[i,j]) = T[\cdot,j] \setminus T[i,j]$$

where T[i,·] refers to the cells in the ith row and T[·, j] refers to cells in the jth column. $\mathcal{X}^R_W(T[i,j])$ denotes a multiset of word tokens found in $\mathcal{X}^R(T[i,j])$.

$\mathcal{X}_E^R(T[i,j])$ denotes a multiset of entities found in $\mathcal{X}^R(T[i,j])$. Similarly, we define $\mathcal{X}_W^C(T[i,j])$ and $\mathcal{X}_E^C(T[i,j])$ to denote multisets of word tokens and entities found in $\mathcal{X}^C(T[i,j])$.

The context-representation of an entity can be derived from a corpus of tables, $\mathcal{T}$ with annotated mentions. We define two kinds of context-representations for an entity: 1) word-context-representation, $\mathcal{R}_W(e)$ is an aggregation of words and their frequencies from the contexts of all cells in $\mathcal{T}$ which contain a reference to e. 2) entity-context-representation $\mathcal{R}_E(e)$ is a similar aggregation of entities and their frequencies. Formally,

$$\mathcal{R}_W(e) = \biguplus_{T \in \mathcal{T}} \left(\mathcal{X}_W^R(T[i,j]) \uplus \mathcal{X}_W^C(T[i,j]) \right)$$

$$\mathcal{R}_E(e) = \biguplus_{T \in \mathcal{T}} \left(\mathcal{X}_E^R(T[i,j]) \uplus \mathcal{X}_E^C(T[i,j]) \right)$$

where, $m_{\cdot,e} \in \mathrm{T}[i,j]$, i.e. the cell $T[i,j]$ contains a mention whose target entity is e and $\uplus$ denotes a multiset union.

TabEL uses the following six features based on similarity between a mention's contexts and a candidate entity's context-representations.

Text-context similarity features   **Entity-context similarity features**

$$S_C\left(\mathcal{X}_W(T[i,j]), \mathcal{R}_W(e_c)\right) \qquad S_C\left(\mathcal{X}_E(T[i,j]), \mathcal{R}_E(e_c)\right)$$

$$S_C\left(\mathcal{X}_W^R(T[i,j]), \mathcal{R}_W(e_c)\right) \qquad S_C\left(\mathcal{X}_E^R(T[i,j]), \mathcal{R}_E(e_c)\right)$$

$$S_C\left(\mathcal{X}_W^C(T[i,j]), \mathcal{R}_W(e_c)\right) \qquad S_C\left(\mathcal{X}_E^C(T[i,j]), \mathcal{R}_E(e_c)\right)$$

where, S_C denotes cosine similarity between the two multisets. We weight the multiplicity of the words and entities in these multisets by their Residual IDF (r-idf) values [18], which we pre-computed for our corpus.

Existing Link features are related to mentions that are already linked to their referent entity in the input table. We include two boolean features in our system. The first feature captures whether there is an existing mention in the context of $m_{s,?}$ with the same surface s that links to the candidate entity. The second feature captures whether the candidate is linked from a surface s' different from s in the input table.

Surface features are related to the phrase, s of the potential mention $m_{s,?}$. We have two boolean features. The first feature is true if s is the only text content in its cell, false otherwise. The second feature is true if s exactly matches the name of an entity in the input KB, $\mathcal{K}$.

4   Implementation

Table Corpus: Our dataset of tables $\mathcal{T}$ has 1.6 million Wikipedia tables. We extracted all HTML tables from Wikipedia which had the class attribute "wikitable" (used to easily identify data tables) from the November 2013 XML dump of English Wikipedia using the Sweble parser [19].[6] As described in Section 2, all HTML tables are represented as an $r \times c$ matrix of cells. Tables in $\mathcal{T}$ contain ~ 30 million hyperlinks in all. 75% of these hyperlinks are used to build other resources described below. The other 25% are exclusively used for training, validation and testing of the local disambiguation model $\mathcal{M}_{LR}$, described in Section 3.3.

Knowledge Base of Entities: We use YAGO, which contains more than 2.8 million entities, as our reference KB, $\mathcal{K}$. *TabEL* links mentions to one of these 2.8 million entities in $\mathcal{K}$. YAGO contains a bi-directional mapping between Wikipedia pages and its entities. We exploit this mapping to identify the YAGO entity of the targets of hyperlinks in $\mathcal{T}$.

Source of Annotated Mentions: As mentioned in Section 3, we utilize a dataset of annotated mentions to train the $\mathcal{M}_{LR}$ model and to construct context representations described in Section 3.3. As explained above, pages on Wikipedia can be easily mapped to entities in the YAGO knowledge base. Thus, annotated mentions can be obtained from hyperlinks on the Web and Wikipedia by considering the anchor text as the phrase and the link target as its referent entity in the KB, $\mathcal{K}$.

To reliably estimate the probability that a surface s refers to an entity e, we use hyperlinks from both the Web and Wikipedia. The Google Cross-Lingual Dictionary for English Wikipedia Concepts described by Spitkovsky et al.[20] contains a dataset of all hyperlinks on the Web which link to a page in Wikipedia. We augmented this with hyperlinks obtained from Wikipedia. We mined over 100 million hyperlinks from the Web and Wikipedia and obtained a large dataset of annotated mentions. With the availability of high quality resources such as the Google Cross-Lingual Dictionary, EL systems that rely *only* on prior probability, $P(e|s)$, can still perform very well. We include a system, $TabEL_{prior}$ in our experiments which disambiguates a potential mention by choosing the most frequently linked entity, for a given phrase, as its referent entity.

5   Experiments

In this section, we evaluate the accuracy of *TabEL* and compare with previous work on both (i) Web tables and (ii) Wikipedia tables. In an ablation study we evaluate the utility of each group of features employed in *TabEL*, and establish the importance of features that are based on entity co-occurrence. We show the effectiveness of the collective inference method, ICA, in improving the accuracy of *TabEL*.

Evaluation Metric: *TabEL* performs disambiguation on all test mentions and always chooses an entity that exists in the given KB. Thus, following previous work on table EL, we use accuracy as our main metric for evaluation and

---

[6] http://dumps.wikimedia.org/enwiki/20131104/

comparison with other table EL systems. We define accuracy as the fraction of test set mentions that an EL system links correctly. For comparison with text EL systems, we use the macro-averaged precision, recall and F1 metrics, which are popularly used for the text EL task.

5.1 Web Tables

To evaluate the performance of *TabEL* on Web tables, we use the WEB_MANUAL dataset from previous work by Limaye et al. [4], both with and without corrections as described below. The WEB_MANUAL dataset consists of more than 9,000 test mentions from 428 tables from the Web. Using methods from Gupta et al. [21], this dataset was originally created (in [4]) by finding Web tables similar to a seed set of 36 non-infobox tables from Wikipedia. Out of the 9,036 test mentions in the WEB_MANUAL dataset, we found that around 5% of the gold annotations were erroneous. Mulwad et al. [7] have also noted errors in the gold annotations of this dataset, but left corrections to future work. We re-labeled these erroneous mentions and created a new dataset, WEB_MANUAL-FIXED, of Web tables with corrected annotations.

Table 2. Accuracy comparison between previous work and *TabEL* on Web and Wikipedia tables datasets

Dataset	Limaye et al. [4]	$TabEL_{prior}$	$TabEL$
WEB_MANUAL	81.37	84.41	**89.41**
WEB_MANUAL- FIXED	-	87.56	**92.94**
WIKI_LINKS	84.28	91.27	**97.16**
WIKI_LINKS- RANDOM	-	87.83	**96.17**

Table 2 shows the accuracy of $TabEL_{prior}$ and *TabEL* on the fixed dataset, WEB_MANUAL-FIXED. For completion and comparison with previous work, we also show the accuracy of our system on the original WEB_MANUAL dataset. *TabEL* outperforms previous work on the WEB_MANUAL dataset and $TabEL_{prior}$ on the WEB_MANUAL-FIXED dataset. A list of errors we found in the gold annotations in WEB_MANUAL and the re-annotated dataset WEB_MANUAL-FIXED are available on our project web page.

5.2 Wikipedia Tables

In Table 2 we show the performance of *TabEL* on two datasets derived from Wikipedia. We adopted the WIKI_LINKS dataset from previous work by Limaye et al. [4], which consists of more than 140,000 test mentions from around 3,000 tables from Wikipedia. *TabEL* outperforms previous work by reducing the error on the WIKI_LINKS dataset by more than 75%.

We evaluate on a second dataset, WIKI_LINKS-RANDOM, of Wikipedia tables in an attempt to provide a more comprehensive measure of performance. The WIKI_LINKS dataset, from Limaye et. al [4], was originally constructed by choosing Wikipedia tables which contained links in at least 90% of their cells. We believe that this dataset is possibly biased as the high density of links in the tables suggests that the tables are important and probably contain commonly known entities in their cells. This bias is evident from the contrast in performance of $TabEL_{prior}$ on the WIKI_LINKS and WIKI_LINKS-RANDOM datasets. The $TabEL_{prior}$ system, which selects the most common referent entity for a given text mention, performs much better on WIKI_LINKS compared to WIKI_LINKS-RANDOM. Thus, we created the WIKI_LINKS-RANDOM dataset containing randomly selected Wikipedia tables, irrespective of the density of existing links in the tables. WIKI_LINKS-RANDOM consists of around 50,000 test mentions from around 3000 tables randomly drawn from Wikipedia. Each existing link in a table is used as a test mention, with its target entity treated as a gold annotation.

Table 2 shows that $TabEL$ achieves very high accuracy on both WIKI_LINKS and WIKI_LINKS-RANDOM datasets. Performing table EL on Wikipedia tables at high level of accuracy is important as many systems utilize links in Wikipedia tables to create RDF triples or to support table search systems (see Section 7).

5.3   Disambiguating Missing Wikipedia Links

An interesting variation of the EL task for tables is to identify and disambiguate unlinked mentions to entities in a Wikipedia table - while *retaining* existing links, unlike the experiments above in Section 5.2 in which all existing links were removed. To evaluate $TabEL$ on this task, we created a dataset, TABEL_35K, containing 35,000 randomly selected annotated mentions in Wikipedia. These mentions are not used in estimating prior probabilities and in building context representations. $TabEL$ performs particularly well on this task and its accuracy on this dataset is 98.38%, while the accuracy of $TabEL_{prior}$ is 88.13%. Interestingly, we found that 16% of the errors made by $TabEL$ on this dataset are actually not errors in $TabEL$, but instead errors in the hyperlinks within Wikipedia. Another 22% of the errors are cases for which both the gold annotation and $TabEL$'s annotation can be considered correct for the mention. Details of all errors made by $TabEL$ on this dataset can be found linked from our project page.

5.4   Comparison with other Table EL Systems

Zhang et al. [12] introduced a table EL system that jointly performs the three semantic interpretation tasks. Direct comparison with this system is difficult as this work presented results on the EL task on the union of WEB_MANUAL and WIKI_LINKS datasets and used the F1 metric. Compared to 83.7 F1 in this work, $TabEL$ achieves F1 of 96.92. This is equal to the accuracy of our system on the union of WEB_MANUAL and WIKI_LINKS as $TabEL$ does not ignore any test mention.

5.5   Comparison With Text EL System

EL techniques for free-text input are well established [15, 22–29] and it can be argued that they can be applied to tabular data as well. Here, we evaluate the performance of many existing text EL systems on the WEB-MANUAL-FIXED dataset and show that *TabEL* outperforms all text EL systems on the table EL task. Our results show that the table EL task is better addressed by systems like *TabEL* that are specifically designed to handle tabular data.

Table 3. Macro-averaged precision, recall and F1 score comparison with six text-EL systems on WEB-MANUAL-FIXED dataset. GERBIL link for results: http://gerbil.aksw.org/gerbil/experiment?id=201507180000

	AGDISTIS [29]	Babelfy [30]	Dbpedia Spotlight [28]	KEA [31]	NERD-ML [32]	WAT [33]	*TabEL*
Macro-Precision	0.7773	0.9464	0.8248	0.9209	0.7611	0.9490	**0.9855**
Macro-Recall	0.3587	0.3431	0.1086	0.369	0.6907	0.3442	**0.9237**
Macro-F1	0.3835	0.3663	0.1637	0.4008	0.697	0.3695	**0.9237**

We used the GERBIL framework [34] to compare against text EL systems. Each table in the test dataset is converted into text format with their mentions identified and given to the GERBIL framework as input. Table 3 shows the macro-averaged precision, recall and F1 scores of *TabEL* compared with six other text EL systems. *TabEL* significantly outperforms all text EL systems on precision, recall and F1.

5.6   Ablation Study

We performed an ablation study on the TABEL-35K dataset to evaluate the effectiveness of each group of features used in $\mathcal{M}_{LR}$. Table 4 shows the groups of features in descending order of the percentage increase in error when that feature group is removed from $\mathcal{M}_{LR}$. All feature groups included in $\mathcal{M}_{LR}$ have a positive effect on the system, with the SR group of features being the most valuable of all. Context-based features also have a high impact on the accuracy of the overall system.

6   Analysis

In our experiments above, we show that *TabEL* consistently outperforms previous state-of-the-art systems. One reason for this is that joint approaches, such as the one in [4], make the *common most-specific type (CMST) assumption*: that all else being equal, an EL system should prefer to link mentions within a column to entities sharing a common most-specific type grounded in a KB. In principle, this assumption could be leveraged to prefer disambiguations that resulted in column entities sharing the same data type, and thereby improve accuracy. However, this assumption is often violated in practice because existing KBs, in which the types are grounded, are incomplete and noisy. In fact, when mapped to types in the DBpedia ontology, we find that only 24.3% of the columns from Wikipedia tables satisfy the *CMST* assumption. Further, when a CMST does exist for a column, it is often not specific enough to aid EL: over 50% of the entities in a column remain ambiguous even after restricting entities to the column's CMST. As a result, rather than restricting EL targets based on strict types in a KB, we use a weaker type constraint encoded by features based on entity co-occurrence statistics, i.e. SR and entity context similarity features. At the same time, rather than using a joint model to solve the EL and type identification tasks together, our system solves the EL task for tables in isolation. This allows *TabEL* to sidestep the risks of making the CMST assumption. It has also been found in previous work by Venetis et al. [10] that solving the table column type-identification task in isolation yields better performance than an approach that tackles the three table semantic interpretation tasks jointly.

6.1   Effectiveness of ICA

Table 3 shows the number of iterations it took ICA to converge and the improvement of accuracy due to inference performed in multiple iterations on two test datasets. Results show that collective inference is useful for this task.

6.2   Analysis of Entity Prevalence Bias

The EL task is known to be easy for prominent entities and particularly difficult for the long-tail of less common entities. Here, we analyze the distribution of prominence of entities in Wikipedia tables and show that our system performs equally well even for the long tail of less prominent entities. On the other hand, accuracy of the $TabEL_{prior}$ system is low for less prominent entities and high for common entities.

We use the number of in-links to an entity in Wikipedia is an indicator of its prominence. Figure 2 (a) shows a histogram of the number of in-links (in log-scale) of the target entity of mentions in the TABEL_35K dataset. Interestingly, the number of in-links of mention targets is log-normally distributed. The estimated normal distribution fit is also shown.

We divide the TABEL_35K dataset into 5 bins at equal intervals of in-link

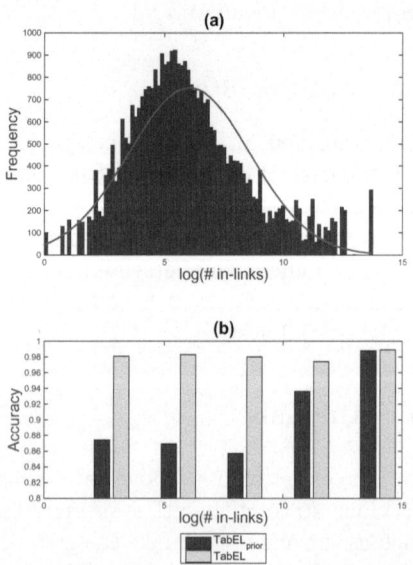

Fig. 2. (a) Histogram of in-link counts (in log-scale) of targets of mentions in Wikipedia tables. A normal distribution fit is shown in red (b) Variation of *TabEL* performance as number of in-links of the target entity varies.

counts (in log scale). Figure 2 (b) shows how the performance of *TabEL* varies as the number of in-links of a mention's target varies. The accuracy of our system remains nearly the same across these bins.

6.3   Run Time Analysis

To estimate the scalability of our system, we measured the time taken to disambiguate mentions in each dataset. Table 4 shows the disambiguation time per-table and the number of iterations for collective inference in to converge. Limaye et. al. [4] reported a disambiguation time of 0.7 s / table.

Table 4. Per-table disambiguation time and number of inference iterations of *TabEL* on different datasets

Dataset	Average Time (s/table)	No. of iterations
WEB_MANUAL- FIXED	1.12	6
WIKI_LINKS- RANDOM	2.32	18
WIKI_LINKS	31.9	27

The WIKI_LINKS dataset is densely populated with mentions, hence the higher run-time. There are many parameters, such as number of candidates, maximum number of inference iterations, convergence criteria, that can be tuned to further improve the disambiguation time of our system.

Table 5. Effect of varying the maximum number of candidates on *TabEL*'s accuracy on the TABEL_35K dataset

Max No. of Candidates	Average No. of Candidates	*TabEL* Accuracy
5	1.68	0.73
10	2.32	0.83
15	2.97	0.90
20	3.54	0.94
25	4.04	0.96
40	7.18	0.98

One possible optimization for *TabEL* is the number of entities in the candidate set. We vary a global parameter to threshold the number of candidates for each mention and analyze its effect on the accuracy of *TabEL* on the TABEL_35K dataset. We find that changing this parameter from 5 to 20 results in a considerable jump in accuracy. Increasing this threshold further gives diminishing returns. Table 5 shows these results along with the average number of candidates per mention as this threshold is varied.

7   Previous Work

Cafarella et al. [1] pioneered the work on Web tables and found that there are 154 million tables on the Web that contain relational data. Since then, various efforts have been made to extract semantics from Web tables. Muñoz et al. [5,35] described an approach that relies on existing links to convert Wikipedia tables to RDF triples. They use facts from an existing knowledge base (KB) like DBpedia, in order to find existing relations in pairs of columns in tables, and then extract new relations for entities in corresponding columns. Sekhavat et al. [36] proposed a probabilistic approach to augment a KB with facts from tabular data using a Web text corpus and natural language patterns associated with relations in the KB. These methods of RDF extraction which rely on existing links in tables can benefit significantly from our system *TabEL*, which achieves better precision than previous work on the entity linking task on Web tables and performs especially well on Wikipedia tables.

Syed et al. [9] describe methods to automatically infer a partial semantic model of Web tables using Wikitology [37], a topic ontology built using Wikipedia's articles and associated pages. Their system tackles all three tasks of semantic interpretation of tables. Mulwad et al. [6,7] also jointly model entity linking, column type identification and relation extraction using a graphical model. The closest previous work for our system is by Limaye et al. [4] and Zhang et al. [12]. Both their systems jointly model the entity linking, column class identification and relation extraction tasks for Web tables. As argued in Section 1, owing to heavy reliance on the correctness and completeness of a KB, joint models run the risk of negatively affecting performance on entity linking. Venetis et al. [10] have shown that a system built to handle only the type identification task performs better than the joint model in [4] on this task. In *TabEL*, we focus on the individual task of *entity linking*, and show EL can be similarly improved by solving it in isolation, rather than through a joint approach.

Finally, previous work has studied applications built upon extracted Web tables. Table augmentation has been studied by Das et al.[38], Gupta et al.[21], Fan et al.[39] and our previous work [40]. Das et al.[38] and our previous work [40] also studied *table search*, the task of returning a list of tables for a given text query ranked by their relevance to a text query. All these systems utilize existing entity references in tables in different ways, and adding more links to tables using *TabEL* may improve the accuracy of the applications.

8   Conclusion and Future Work

In this paper, we described our table entity linking system *TabEL*. *TabEL* uses a collective classification technique to collectively disambiguate all mentions in a given table. Instead of using a strict mapping of types and relations into a reference Knowledge Base, *TabEL* uses soft constraints in its graphical model to sidestep errors introduced by an incomplete or noisy KB and outperforms previous work on multiple datasets. We also showed that *TabEL* performs equally well even for the long tail of infrequently-mentioned entities – for which the EL task is particularly hard. Ablation studies demonstrate the effectiveness of our Semantic Relatedness features.

We made our table corpus containing 1.6 million Wikipedia tables publicly available along with annotated datasets which can be used by future table-EL systems for comparison.

In future work, we plan to integrate *TabEL* with systems that identify column types and relations between columns of a table to convert table data into machine-understandable formats like RDF. Finally, we plan to release our code in future.

Acknowledgments. This research was supported in part by NSF grant IIS-1351029 and the Allen Institute for Artificial Intelligence.

References

1. Cafarella, M.J., Halevy, A., Wang, D.Z., Wu, E., Zhang, Y.: Webtables: exploring the power of tables on the web. Proceedings of the VLDB Endowment **1**(1), 538–549 (2008)
2. Buche, P., Dibie-Barthelemy, J., Ibanescu, L., Soler, L.: Fuzzy web data tables integration guided by an ontological and terminological resource. IEEE Transactions on Knowledge and Data Engineering **25**(4), 805–819 (2013)
3. Hignette, G., Buche, P., Dibie-Barthélemy, J., Haemmerlé, O.: Fuzzy annotation of web data tables driven by a domain ontology. In: Aroyo, L., Traverso, P., Ciravegna, F., Cimiano, P., Heath, T., Hyvönen, E., Mizoguchi, R., Oren, E., Sabou, M., Simperl, E. (eds.) ESWC 2009. LNCS, vol. 5554, pp. 638–653. Springer, Heidelberg (2009)
4. Limaye, G., Sarawagi, S., Chakrabarti, S.: Annotating and searching web tables using entities, types and relationships. Proceedings of the VLDB, 1338–1347 (2010)
5. Munoz, E., Hogan, A., Mileo, A.: Triplifying wikipedia's tables. In: LD4IE@ISWC (2013)
6. Mulwad, V., Finin, T., Joshi, A.: Automatically generating government linked data from tables. In: Working Notes of AAAI Fall Symposium on Open Government Knowledge: AI Opportunities and Challenges, vol. 4 (2011)
7. Mulwad, V., Finin, T., Joshi, A.: Semantic message passing for generating linked data from tables. In: Alani, H., Kagal, L., Fokoue, A., Groth, P., Biemann, C., Parreira, J.X., Aroyo, L., Noy, N., Welty, C., Janowicz, K. (eds.) ISWC 2013, Part I. LNCS, vol. 8218, pp. 363–378. Springer, Heidelberg (2013)
8. Mulwad, V., Finin, T., Syed, Z., Joshi, A.: T2ld: Interpreting and representing tables as linked data. In: 9th International Semantic Web Conference, ISWC 2010, p. 25. Citeseer (2010)
9. Syed, Z., Finin, T., Mulwad, V., Joshi, A.: Exploiting a web of semantic data for interpreting tables. In: Proceedings of the Second Web Science Conference (2010)
10. Venetis, P., Halevy, A., Madhavan, J., Paşca, M., Shen, W., Fei, W., Miao, G., Chung, W.: Recovering semantics of tables on the web. Proceedings of the VLDB Endowment **4**(9), 528–538 (2011)
11. Wang, J., Wang, H., Wang, Z., Zhu, K.Q.: Understanding tables on the web. In: Atzeni, P., Cheung, D., Ram, S. (eds.) ER 2012 Main Conference 2012. LNCS, vol. 7532, pp. 141–155. Springer, Heidelberg (2012)
12. Zhang, Z.: Start small, build complete: effective and efficient semantic table interpretation using tableminer. The Semantic Web Journal, Under Transparent Review (2014)

13. Suchanek, F.M., Kasneci, G., Weikum, G.: Yago: a core of semantic knowledge. In: 16th International World Wide Web Conference (WWW 2007). ACM Press, New York (2007)

14. Qing, L., Getoor, L.: Link-based classification. In: ICML, vol. 3, pp. 496–503 (2003)

15. Hoffart, J., Yosef, M.A., Bordino, I., Fürstenau, H., Pinkal, M., Spaniol, M., Taneva, B., Thater, S., Weikum, G.: Robust disambiguation of named entities in text. In: Proceedings of the Conference on Empirical Methods in Natural Language Processing, pp. 782–792. Association for Computational Linguistics (2011)

16. Hecht, B., Carton, S.H., Quaderi, M., Schöning, J., Raubal, M., Gergle, D., Downey, D.: Explanatory semantic relatedness and explicit spatialization for exploratory search. In: Proceedings of the 35th International ACM SIGIR Conference on Research and Development in Information Retrieval, pp. 415–424. ACM (2012)

17. Witten, I., Milne, D.: An effective, low-cost measure of semantic relatedness obtained from wikipedia links. In: Proceeding of AAAI Workshop on Wikipedia and Artificial Intelligence: an Evolving Synergy, Chicago, USA, pp. 25–30. AAAI Press (2008)

18. Church, K.W.: One term or two? In: Proceedings of the 18th Annual International ACM SIGIR Conference on Research and Development in Information Retrieval, pp. 310–318. ACM (1995)

19. Dohrn, H., Riehle, D.: Design and implementation of the sweble wikitext parser: unlocking the structured data of wikipedia. In: Proceedings of the 7th International Symposium on Wikis and Open Collaboration, pp. 72–81. ACM (2011)

20. Spitkovsky, V.I., Chang, A.X.: A cross-lingual dictionary for english wikipedia concepts. In LREC, pp. 3168–3175 (2012)

21. Gupta, R., Sarawagi, S.: Answering table augmentation queries from unstructured lists on the web. Proceedings of the VLDB Endowment 2(1), 289–300 (2009)

22. Bunescu, R.C., Pasca, M.: Using encyclopedic knowledge for named entity disambiguation. In: EACL, vol. 6, pp. 9–16 (2006)

23. Cheng, X., Roth, D.: Relational inference for wikification. Urbana 51, 61801 (2013)

24. Moro, A., Raganato, A., Navigli, R.: Entity linking meets word sense disambiguation: A unified approach. Transactions of the Association for Computational Linguistics 2 (2014)

25. Ling, X., Singh, S., Weld, D.S.: Context representation for named entity linking. In: Proceedings of the 3rd Pacific Northwest Regional NLP Workshop (NW-NLP 2014) (2014)

26. Noraset, T., Bhagavatula, C., Downey, D.: Websail wikifier at ERD 2014. In: Proceedings of the First International Workshop on Entity Recognition & Disambiguation, pp. 119–124. ACM (2014)

27. Cucerzan, S.: Large-scale named entity disambiguation based on wikipedia data. In EMNLP-CoNLL, vol. 7, pp. 708–716. Citeseer (2007)

28. Mendes, P.N., Jakob, M., García-Silva, A., Bizer, C.: Dbpedia spotlight: shedding light on the web of documents. In: Proceedings of the 7th International Conference on Semantic Systems, pp. 1–8. ACM (2011)

29. Usbeck, R., Ngonga Ngomo, A.-C., Röder, M., Gerber, D., Coelho, S.A., Auer, S., Both, A.: AGDISTIS - graph-based disambiguation of named entities using linked data. In: Mika, P., Tudorache, T., Bernstein, A., Welty, C., Knoblock, C., Vrandečić, D., Groth, P., Noy, N., Janowicz, K., Goble, C. (eds.) ISWC 2014, Part I. LNCS, vol. 8796, pp. 457–471. Springer, Heidelberg (2014)

30. Moro, A., Cecconi, F., Navigli, R.: Multilingual word sense disambiguation and entity linking for everybody. In: Proc. of ISWC (P&D), pp. 25–28 (2014)

31. Steinmetz, N., Sack, H.: Semantic multimedia information retrieval based on contextual descriptions. In: Cimiano, P., Corcho, O., Presutti, V., Hollink, L., Rudolph, S. (eds.) ESWC 2013. LNCS, vol. 7882, pp. 382–396. Springer, Heidelberg (2013)

32. Van Erp, M., Rizzo, G., Troncy, R.: Learning with the web: spotting named entities on the intersection of nerd and machine learning. In: # MSM, pp. 27–30. Citeseer (2013)

33. Ferragina, P., Scaiella, U.: Fast and accurate annotation of short texts with wikipedia pages. arXiv preprint arXiv:1006.3498 (2010)

34. Usbeck, R., Röder, M., Ngonga-Ngomo, A.C., Baron, C., Both, A., Brümmer, M., Ceccarelli, D., Cornolti, M., Cherix, D., Eickmann, B., et al.: Gerbil-general entity annotation benchmark framework. In: 24th World Wide Web Conference (WWW) (2015)

35. Muñoz, E., Hogan, A., Mileo, A.: Using linked data to mine rdf from wikipedia's tables. In: Proceedings of the 7th ACM International Conference on Web Search and Data Mining, pp. 533–542. ACM (2014)

36. Sekhavat, Y.A., di Paolo, F., Barbosa, D., Merialdo, P.: Knowledge base augmentation using tabular data. In: Linked Data on the Web at WWW 2014 (2014)

37. Syed, Z.S., Finin, T., Joshi, A.: Wikitology: using wikipedia as an ontology. In: Proceeding of the Second International Conference on Weblogs and Social Media (2008)

38. Sarma, A.D., Fang, L., Gupta, N., Halevy, A., Lee, H., Wu, F., Xin, R., Yu, C.: Finding related tables. In: Proceedings of the 2012 ACM SIGMOD International Conference on Management of Data, pp. 817–828. ACM (2012)

39. Fan, J., Lu, M., Ooi, B.C., Tan, W.-C., Zhang, M.: A hybrid machine-crowdsourcing system for matching web tables. In: 2014 IEEE 30th International Conference on Data Engineering (ICDE), pp. 976–987. IEEE (2014)

40. Bhagavatula, C.S., Noraset, T., Downey, D.: Methods for exploring and mining tables on wikipedia. In: Proceedings of the ACM SIGKDD Workshop on Interactive Data Exploration and Analytics, pp. 18–26. ACM (2013)

Path-Based Semantic Relatedness on Linked Data and Its Use to Word and Entity Disambiguation

Ioana Hulpuş[(⊠)], Narumol Prangnawarat, and Conor Hayes

Insight Centre for Data Analytics, National University of Ireland,
Galway (NUIG), Galway, Ireland
{ioana.hulpus,narumol.prangnawarat,conor.hayes}@insight-centre.org

Abstract. Semantic relatedness and disambiguation are fundamental problems for linking text documents to the Web of Data. There are many approaches dealing with both problems but most of them rely on word or concept distribution over Wikipedia. They are therefore not applicable to concepts that do not have a rich textual description. In this paper, we show that semantic relatedness can also be accurately computed by analysing only the graph structure of the knowledge base. In addition, we propose a joint approach to entity and word-sense disambiguation that makes use of graph-based relatedness. As opposed to the majority of state-of-the-art systems that target mainly named entities, we use our approach to disambiguate both entities and common nouns. In our experiments, we first validate our relatedness measure on multiple knowledge bases and ground truth datasets and show that it performs better than related state-of-the-art graph based measures. Afterwards, we evaluate the disambiguation algorithm and show that it also achieves superior disambiguation accuracy with respect to alternative state-of-the-art graph-based algorithms.

1 Introduction

With the advancements in Linked Data, more and more graph-based (i.e. RDF) structured knowledge bases become available. Still, most of the digital content we produce as a society is in text format. Linking unstructured text to structured data is fundamental for leveraging the benefits of the vast amounts of knowledge (in text as well as in structured format) available.

In this paper, we tackle two strongly interdependent problems, semantic relatedness and disambiguation. The aim of semantic relatedness is to weight the semantic associations between pairs of concepts. The aim of entity and word-sense disambiguation, is to link strings in the text to the corresponding concepts in external knowledge bases (KBs). These problems are fundamental for the integrationn text and structured data. The most important cue for disambiguation is the semantic relatedness between the concepts mentioned in a particular context (i.e., text), therefore the two problems are highly interdependent.

© Springer International Publishing Switzerland 2015
M. Arenas et al. (Eds.): ISWC 2015, Part I, LNCS 9366, pp. 442–457, 2015.
DOI: 10.1007/978-3-319-25007-6_26

With respect to these two problems, with the exception of some very recent approaches, most systems use distributional semantics techniques and traditionally require detailed textual description of concepts. Furthermore, since the relatedness is distilled from vast amount of text documents, these approaches do not have the capability of extracting the explicit relations between concepts.

These limitations can be overcome by using knowledge-based systems. While the idea of using structured knowledge for assessing semantic relatedness can be tracked back more than fifty years, research is still needed in order to understand how the relatively new, very broad KBs like DBpedia, Freebase, YAGO, can be most effectively used. In this paper, we first introduce a novel graph-based relatedness measure that uses the paths in the KB in order to score the association between pairs of concepts. Afterwards, we propose a joint disambiguation approach that can use any path-based pairwise relatedness. Our experiments for assessing the quality of our relatedness measure show higher positive correlations to human judgements than the current state of the art. Similarly, our experiments for assessing the quality of disambiguation show that graph-based joint disambiguation produces superior results as compared to very recent alternative graph-based approaches.

1.1   Related Work on Semantic Relatedness

Semantic relatedness of entities has been heavily researched over the past couple of decades. Two main directions can be identified. The first one, which we call *corpus-based*, models entities as multi-dimensional vectors that are computed based on distributional semantics techniques [4,9]. The *de facto* standard corpus is Wikipedia. The second direction, which we call *structure-based* or *graph-based* and which makes the focus of this paper, relies on a graph structured KB. Approaches of this type have been very prolific since the publication of Word-Net [29,30]. However, most WordNet based semantic relatedness measures rely on hierarchical relations (isA, broaderOf). The problem with such measures is that they cannot exploit other semantically rich properties of concepts in more complex KBs.

Other structure-based approaches use the network of Wikipedia pages formed by their hyperlink connections [7,18,24]. Their drawback is that they require pages that contain hyperlinks to the targeted concepts, or that the concepts themselves have corresponding pages. Furthermore, the hyperlinks do not provide any semantics to the relation between the source and target concepts.

Recent approaches that are motivated by Linked Data make use of the different types of relations that exist in structured KBs (i.e., DBpedia). Some of them suffer from the drawback of requiring domain adaptation, and focus on manually selected types of concepts and relations [15,20]. Other measures are very restrictive, computing semantic similarity between either neighbouring concepts, or concepts connected through a single intermediate node by the same relation type [23].

The approach that is most related to ours is the very recent work of Schumacher and Ponzetto [27]. Like us, the authors automatically weight relations in the knowledge graph and use them to compute relatedness between concepts that are not directly connected. However, their weighting scheme considers information theoretic global measures for the relationship type and object, while our measures are local, specific to the targeted pair and therefore less computationally demanding. Furthermore, our local measures have the added advantage of requiring very little update overhead when the background KB changes, while the global ones require the update of all scores. In our work, we have compared all our methods to their approach and we report our findings in the Evaluation section of this paper.

We evaluate our approach with both DBpedia and Freebase, from three perspectives: (1) named entity (NE) relatedness; (2) common noun similarity; and (3)common noun relatedness. Our extensive evaluation sheds light not only on our measures, but also on the general use of path-based relatedness measures on the used knowledge graphs.

1.2   Related Work on Entity and Word-Sense Disambiguation

An important class of related methods to disambiguation is formed by the *centrality-based* approaches. For each ambiguous word, the selected sense is the one that has the highest graph centrality with respect to the candidate senses of the other words in context. They have mostly been used on WordNet [2,17,21]. A very recent centrality-based approach is AGDISTIS [32]. To the best of our knowledge, it is the only previous approach that achieves entity disambiguation by using only DBpedia knowledge. After finding the candidate sets for all the ambiguous named entities, AGDISTIS extracts a subgraph of DBpedia that contains all the candidate senses of all the targeted entities as well as their n-hop neighbours and the relations between them. Then, the HITS algorithm is run over the extracted subgraph and for each targeted entity, DBpedia concept that has the highest authority score is selected. All these *centrality-based* suffer from the drawback that the selection of the senses of entities and words is "infested" by the wrong candidate senses.

Another important research direction related to ours uses graph-based relatedness measures on a semantic network that is built on-the-fly on top of the words that make the definitions that describe the candidate senses [6,11,28]. A similar dependence to the text that describes senses is noticed in most of the other systems [5,8,16] that link to DBpedia, as they apply their algorithms on Wikipedia text. In this paper, we research novel graph-based methods that do not require textual description of senses.

2   Path-Based Relatedness Measures on Knowledge Graphs

2.1   Preliminaries

In this section, we define and formalise the main concepts we refer to in this paper. By *knowledge graph* we refer to any graph used to represent knowledge about concepts and relations between them. A knowledge graph can be seen as a *property graph*, a graph whose nodes and edges have properties. Also, knowledge graphs are a superset of *multigraphs* because they can contain multiple edges between the same pair of nodes. An RDF KB is in this case also a knowledge graph. Given a triple of the form $< s, p, o >$, the predicate p and object o resources become nodes in the graph connected by an edge of type p.

Definition 1. *We define a **knowledge graph** as a directed graph $G(V, E, \mathcal{T}, \tau)$, where V represents the set of all vertices, E represents the set of all edges (that we also call relations), connecting vertices in V, $\mathcal{T}$ is the set of edge types, and $\tau : E \to \mathcal{T}$ is a function that maps every edge in E to a type in $\mathcal{T}$.*

Although the edges are directed, we consider that the reverse relations also hold and can be traversed. The assumption behind this decision is that all semantic relations can be considered to have a semantically sound inverse relation. We use $E^{\mp}$ to denote the set of edges in the graph united with the set of their reversed edges, and $\mathcal{T}^{\mp}$ to denote the set of relationship types united to the set of their reversed types.

Definition 2. *A **path** $\mathcal{P}$ through the knowledge graph $G(V, E, \mathcal{T}, \tau)$ is a sequence of nodes and relations $n_1 \xrightarrow{\tau_1} n_2 \xrightarrow{\tau_2} ..., \xrightarrow{\tau_{K-1}} n_K$ such that for every two consecutive nodes in the sequence, n_{k-1}, n_k, there exists an edge $e \in E^{\mp}$ of type $\tau_{k-1} \in \mathcal{T}^{\mp}$.*

Using these definitions, we now introduce the path-based relatedness measures that we analyse in this paper. We start with a baseline measure inspired from social network analysis and afterwards we describe in detail the measure that makes the main contribution of this paper.

2.2 Baseline - Katz Relatedness

The length of the shortest path between two nodes is a common way of measuring proximity between nodes in a graph. However, it lacks the ability to discriminate between the relatedness of many node pairs, for example, a node will be considered of equal relatedness to all its 2-hop neighbours. To better differentiate, other methods make use of more and longer paths than just the shortest. Here, we adapt Katz's [13] centrality measure that is commonly used in social network analysis. This centrality measure has inspired another previously proposed semantic relatedness measure [22]. The idea is that the effectiveness of a link between two nodes is governed by a known, constant probability, α. In case of a path made up of k nodes, the probability of the path is α^k. We use this idea in a relatedness measure, where the relatedness between two nodes is the accumulated score over the top-k shortest paths between them.

$$rel^{(k)}_{Katz}(x, y) = \frac{\sum\limits_{p \in SP^{(k)}_{xy}} \alpha^{length(p)}}{k} \tag{1}$$

where $SP^{(k)}_{xy}$ is the set of the top-k shortest paths between concepts x and y.

2.3   Exclusivity-Based Relatedness

The rationale behind the previous relatedness measure is that the more and shorter relation paths between two nodes, the higher their relatedness. However, it has been long known that not all direct relationships weight the same. Manual assignment of weights based on relationship type is infeasible, given the great amount of relationship types in knowledge graphs (almost 14000 in Freebase and more than 1100 in DBpedia). Therefore, we must devise automatic ways of assessing the importance of individual direct relations.

At the core of our next suggested measure, is one main rationale: a relation between two concepts is stronger if each of the concepts is related through the same type of relation to fewer other concepts. We name this property of relations *exclusivity* and we formalise it in the following.

Definition 3. *Given an edge e of type τ between two adjacent nodes x and y, directed from x to y, we define the **exclusivity** of edge e as the probability that, if we randomly select an edge e′ out of the set of all edges of type τ that exit node x and all edges of type τ entering node y, that edge e′ is edge e. Formally,*

$$exclusivity(x \xrightarrow{\tau} y) = \frac{1}{|x \xrightarrow{\tau} *| + |* \xrightarrow{\tau} y| - 1};$$ (2)

where $|x \xrightarrow{\tau} *|$ denotes the number of relations of type $\tau \in T$ that exit node x, and $|* \xrightarrow{\tau} y|$ denotes the number of relations of type $\tau \in T$ that enter node y.

1 is subtracted from the denominator because the relation $x \xrightarrow{\tau} y$ is otherwise counted twice, once for the relations of x and once for the relations of y. As of Formula 2, the exclusivity score of a relation lies inside the $(0, 1]$ interval, with value 1 being obtained when the targeted relation is the only relation of its type for both x and y.

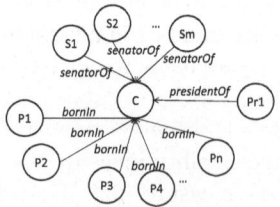

Fig. 1. Example exclusivity

Example 1. Let us look at the toy example in Figure 1, where we consider node C a country and all the other nodes, people. The exclusivity of the *bornIn* relations is $1/n$, for the *senatorOf* relations it is $1/m$, and for the *presidentOf* relation exclusivity is 1. Naturally, n would be much higher than m, giving the *bornIn* relation a smaller exclusivity than the *senatorOf* and *presidentOf* relations.

Since the exclusivity is computed for each individual relation, the *bornIn* relations to a small country will have a higher exclusivity than the *bornIn* relations to a bigger country. Extrapolating this measure to nodes that are not directly connected, people born in the same small country will be more related to each other than people born in a bigger country, and senators of a country will be more related to each other than random citizens born in the country.

An important property of our exclusivity property of relations is **symmetry**: $exclusivity(x \xrightarrow{\tau} y) = exclusivity(y \xrightarrow{\bar{\tau}} x)$. Symmetry of exclusivity is crucial for consistency with our assumption that relations in the knowledge graph can be traversed in both directions.

Given a path through G, $\mathcal{P} = n_1 \xrightarrow{\tau_1} n_2 \xrightarrow{\tau_2}, ..., n_K$, with $\tau_i \in \mathcal{T}^{\mp}$ its weight can be computed by Formula 3.

$$weight(\mathcal{P}) = \frac{1}{\sum_i 1/exclusivity(n_i \xrightarrow{\tau_i} n_{i+1})}; \tag{3}$$

Then, given two nodes x and y we compute their relatedness as the sum of the path weights of the top-k paths with highest weight between them. In order to give preference to shorter paths, we introduce a constant length decay factor, $\alpha \in (0, 1]$. When $\alpha = 1$ longer paths are not penalised.

$$rel_{Excl}^{(k)}(x, y) = \sum_{\mathcal{P}_i \in P_{xy}^{(k)}} \alpha^{length(\mathcal{P}_i)} weight(\mathcal{P}_i); \tag{4}$$

This being the exclusivity based relatedness measure, we now move on to the problem of word-sense disambiguation and our proposed solution.

3   Joint Disambiguation on Knowledge Graphs

Joint disambiguation approaches treat disambiguation as a combinatorial optimisation problem. Given multiple ambiguous words, the correct senses for all words are selected simultaneously, by maximising a function of relatedness between the selected senses. Therefore, this methodology avoids the influence that wrong senses might have on the final solution. Having a context of n words, with each word w_i having m_i possible senses, a solution R contains n senses, one sense for each word. There are $\prod_{i \in [1,n]} m_i$ solutions. We denote the set of all solutions as **R**. A solution R^* is chosen that has the highest *coherence*. The most common way of computing the coherence of a solution R is by summing up all the pairwise relatedness scores of the senses in R, as shown in Formula (5). In this approach, the disambiguated sense s_w^* of word w is the sense of w that belongs to solution R^* as shown in Formula (6):

$$R^* = \arg\max_{R \in \mathbf{R}} \sum_{s \in R} \sum_{\substack{s' \in R; \\ s' \neq s}} rel(s, s'); \tag{5}$$

$$s_w^* = R^*[w]; \tag{6}$$

In Formula (5), the $rel(s, s')$ factor represents any pairwise relatedness measure. What sets graph-based joint disambiguation apart from other methods of joint disambiguation, is that $rel(s, s')$ is a graph-based measure. This problem is equivalent to the problem of finding the clique with the maximum sum of edge weights which is an NP-hard problem. We solve it by using the branch-and-bound algorithm wrapped in an approximate search routine. For complete details about the algorithm we refer to Hulpuş [10], page 114. However, any maximum edge weight clique finding algorithm can be used instead.

3.1   Kan-Dis: The Knowledge Graph Based Disambiguation System

In order to evaluate the joint disambiguation with DBpedia, we implemented a system whose disambiguation process is illustrated in Figure 2.

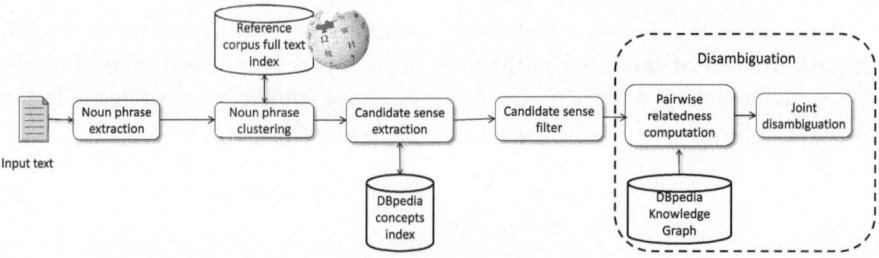

Fig. 2. Disambiguation process with Kan-Dis

We are only interested in disambiguating the nouns and noun-phrases of the document. We extract them by using the Stanford CoreNLP toolkit[1]. After the noun-phrases are extracted, the possible senses of the noun-phrases are retrieved from a Lucene Index[2] where we have indexed all DBpedia concepts based on their names.

In order to form groups of words to be simultaneously disambiguated (disambiguation context), we cluster the noun-phrases based on their co-occurrence in a reference corpus (i.e., Wikipedia). We experimented with two clustering algorithms: Louvain, which is a modularity-based community finding algorithm and hierarchical clustering with various linkage types and dendrogram cutting thresholds. The relatedness measures are computed between all pairs of candidates for the noun-phrases in each cluster. These relatedness scores are then sent to the joint disambiguation algorithm. The last two steps are part of the joint disambiguation algorithm, and they can be replaced with any other disambiguation algorithm.

---

[1] http://nlp.stanford.edu/software/corenlp.shtml
[2] http://lucene.apache.org/core/

4   Experiments and Results

We have described our relatedness measures and how we plan to use it for disambiguation. In the following, we detail the experiments we made to validate our hypothesis that our exclusivity based measure for relatedness correlates with human assessments. Afterwards we detail our experiments that show that path-based joint disambiguation outperforms centrality based disambiguation.

4.1   Evaluation of Relatedness Measures

We now present the experiments we carried out in order to verify the suitability of the proposed measures for assessing semantic relatedness. We follow the most established methodology for validating semantic relatedness measures, which consists of computing the correlation between human assessed scores and the proposed automatic measures. Our main hypothesis is that the exclusivity-based measure of relatedness will improve over the baseline and show high positive correlation to human assessments.

Ground-Truth Datasets. We experiment with five of the most commonly used datasets:

R&G [26] is one of the oldest and most used datasets that contain human assessment of word **similarity**. It contains 65 pairs of words together with the overall assessment of humans, gathered from 51 subjects. The users were requested to judge the "similarity of meaning" on a scale from 0.0 to 4.0, where a high score means high similarity.

WordSim353 [1,3] contains 353 pairs of words assessed on a scale from 0 to 10 by 13 to 16 human users. Agirre et al [1] split the dataset through another user study in two overlapping parts

> **WS353-Sim** - containing 203 pairs that the users considered suitable for similarity computation;
>
> **WS353-Rel** - containing 252 pairs that the users considered suitable for relatedness computation;

R122 [31] is more recent and was created specifically for measuring **relatedness** [31] . It contains 122 pairs of words, scored within a range from 0.0 (completely unrelated) to 4.0 (very strongly related), each pair being evaluated by 14 to 22 annotators out of a total of 92 participants.

KORE [9] has also been created for measuring **relatedness**, but between NEs. It consists of 21 main entities, whose relatedness to other 20 entities each has been manually assessed, leading to 420 entity pairs.

Except for the last dataset, all others contain pairs of words rather than DBpedia concepts. Table 1 shows the exact number of pairs of words that we could directly and unambiguously link to concepts from DBpedia and Freebase.

Table 1. Number of concept pairs per ground truth dataset

Dataset	R&G	WS353-Sim	R-122	WS353-Rel	KORE
#pairs	38	139	93	168	419

Knowledge Bases. In order to verify the generalisability of our measures, we evaluate them with both DBpedia and Freebase. All reported experiments were run on DBpedia 2014 version[3], and Freebase dump[4] from 18th January 2015. We remove from the graph of DBpedia the so-called stopURIs [12,27]. Regarding Freebase, we remove all edges with an exclusivity score lower than 10^{-7} as they bring no impact on our measures due to their very small contribution, but they dramatically impact the performance of graph traversal algorithms. Table 2 shows the sizes of the resulting knowledge graphs.

Table 2. Number of elements in the knowledge bases

KB	#nodes	#relationships	#relationship types
DBpedia	7,514,827	35,762,630	1,198
Freebase	41,527,432	253,813,430	13,991

Regarding the DBpedia graph, we experiment with two settings:

- the full graph: DBpedia Full;
- the categories and types graph: DBpedia Categories;

In the case of the latter, we restrict the graph traversals to the relationships: *rdf:type, dcterms:subject, skos:broaderOf, skos:narrowerOf, rdfs:subClassOf.* We expect that the aforementioned properties are mostly useful in assessing similarity of concepts. We similarly expect that the full set of properties is most useful when assessing relatedness.

Compared Methods. We report our results on the methods described in Section 2. We have experimented with various values for the α parameter for both Katz relatedness and exclusivity based relatedness. In the following, we report the values obtained with $\alpha \in \{0.25, 0.5\}$ for Katz relatedness, and with $\alpha \in \{0.25, 0.5, 0.75, 1\}$ for exclusivity-based methods. We have also experimented with different k (1 to 20) values for the top-k paths in Katz as well as the exclusivity based methods. We report our results for top-1, top-5 and top-10 paths.

For comparison to related work, we have also implemented the *combIC* measure of Schuhmacher & Ponzetto [27]

---

[3] http://wiki.dbpedia.org/Downloads2014

[4] https://developers.google.com/freebase/data

Results. Tables 3, 4, and 5 show the Spearman correlations obtained. In Table 3, we show the results on the datasets assessed for semantic similarity of common nouns and noun-phrases.

Table 3. Spearman correlations with ground truth on common nouns similarity datasets: R&G and WS353-Sim.

Dataset	Method	DBpedia CAT			DBpedia Full			Freebase		
		top-1	top-5	top-10	top-1	top-5	top-10	top-1	top-5	top-10
R & G	Katz $\alpha = 0.25$	**0.79**	0.78	0.79	0.71	0.67	0.64	0.45	0.41	0.51
	Katz $\alpha = 0.5$	**0.79**	0.78	0.79	0.71	0.67	0.63	0.45	0.41	0.20
	Katz $\alpha = 0.75$	**0.79**	0.78	0.78	0.71	0.67	0.61	0.45	0.41	0.11
	ER $\alpha = 0.25$	**0.79**	**0.81**	0.81	**0.72**	0.73	0.73	**0.67**	**0.66**	**0.67**
	ER $\alpha = 0.5$	0.78	**0.82**	**0.81**	0.66	0.73	0.73	**0.67**	**0.66**	**0.67**
	ER $\alpha = 0.75$	0.76	0.79	**0.81**	0.66	**0.75**	**0.75**	**0.67**	**0.66**	**0.67**
	ER $\alpha = 1$	0.76	0.79	**0.81**	0.66	0.72	0.74	0.61	0.60	0.61
	CombIC	0.74			0.57			0.59		
WS 353-Sim	Katz $\alpha = 0.25$	0.74	0.75	0.75	0.69	0.66	0.64	0.29	0.30	0.33
	Katz $\alpha = 0.5$	0.74	0.75	0.74	0.69	0.65	0.61	0.29	0.30	0.20
	Katz $\alpha = 0.75$	0.74	0.74	0.72	0.69	0.64	0.58	0.29	0.29	0.17
	ER $\alpha = 0.25$	**0.77**	**0.78**	**0.78**	0.68	**0.67**	**0.66**	0.58	0.57	0.57
	ER $\alpha = 0.5$	0.76	0.77	0.77	0.63	0.64	0.63	**0.59**	**0.59**	**0.59**
	ER $\alpha = 0.75$	0.71	0.73	0.73	0.59	0.61	0.61	**0.59**	**0.59**	**0.59**
	ER $\alpha = 1$	0.63	0.68	0.69	0.54	0.57	0.58	**0.59**	**0.59**	**0.59**
	CombIC	0.72	–	–	0.59	–	–	0.40	–	–

We notice that all measures have very high correlation with human assessment of similarity, when used on the DBpedia Categories. Our Exclusivity based relatedness performs best, reaching 0.82 correlation with the R&G dataset for $\alpha = 0.5$ and when top-5 paths are used. For comparison, *CombIC* reaches 0.74 in the same setup. *ER* also performs better than *Katz* and this is visible especially on the Freebase corpus.

Table 4 presents the results on the datasets assessed for semantic relatedness of common nouns and noun-phrases. We notice that overall, the results are much lower than for the similarity datasets (Table 3). No method correlates more than 0.57 with human assessment. Most likely, the cause of this poor assessment of noun relatedness has to do with the type of knowledge within the analysed KBs. They contain encyclopedic knowledge rather than common sense knowledge. For example, humans assess relatedness of concepts in pairs *(caffeine, headache)* and *(game, victory)* as moderately to strongly related but the KBs do not have any path shorter than 6 between them.

Nevertheless, *ER* performs much better than both *CombIC* and *Katz*. *ER* with $\alpha = 0.25$ produces the best results on the noun relatedness datasets, which means that the smaller the influence of the longer paths, the better. We also notice that all measures perform extremely poorly when used on Freebase. This indicates that Freebase's graph structure connects in a less meaningful way the concepts referred to by common nouns, than DBpedia.

Table 5 shows the results obtained on the KORE dataset, which contains pairs of NEs assessed for semantic relatedness. On this dataset, the first thing to notice is that all measures perform very bad on DBpedia Categories, but very

Table 4. Spearman correlations to ground truth on common nouns relatedness datasets: R-122 and WS353-Rel

Dataset	Method	DBpedia CAT			DBpedia Full			Freebase		
		top-1	top-5	top-10	top-1	top-5	top-10	top-1	top-5	top-10
R 122	Katz $\alpha = 0.25$	0.56	0.54	0.52	0.46	0.45	0.44	0.17	0.15	0.15
	Katz $\alpha = 0.5$	0.56	0.52	0.50	0.46	0.43	0.40	0.17	0.15	0.15
	Katz $\alpha = 0.75$	0.56	0.50	0.49	0.46	0.41	0.40	0.17	0.15	0.15
	ER $\alpha = 0.25$	**0.57**	**0.57**	**0.55**	**0.56**	**0.55**	**0.54**	**0.33**	**0.32**	**0.32**
	ER $\alpha = 0.5$	0.56	0.55	0.53	0.53	0.52	0.51	0.32	**0.32**	0.31
	ER $\alpha = 0.75$	0.52	0.53	0.50	0.50	0.49	0.48	**0.33**	**0.32**	0.31
	ER $\alpha = 1$	0.46	0.49	0.46	0.49	0.47	0.45	**0.33**	**0.32**	0.31
	CombIC	0.53	-	-	0.41	-	-	0.20	-	-
WS 353-Rel	Katz $\alpha = 0.25$	0.44	0.44	0.44	0.45	0.40	0.38	0.14	0.16	0.20
	Katz $\alpha = 0.5$	0.44	0.44	0.44	0.45	0.40	0.38	0.14	0.16	0.21
	Katz $\alpha = 0.75$	0.44	0.44	0.44	0.45	0.40	0.38	0.14	0.16	0.22
	ER $\alpha = 0.25$	**0.48**	**0.48**	0.47	**0.47**	**0.46**	**0.46**	**0.35**	**0.35**	**0.35**
	ER $\alpha = 0.5$	0.47	**0.48**	**0.48**	0.44	0.44	0.45	**0.35**	**0.35**	**0.35**
	ER $\alpha = 0.75$	0.47	**0.48**	0.47	0.42	0.43	0.44	**0.35**	0.34	0.34
	ER $\alpha = 1$	0.46	0.47	0.47	0.40	0.41	0.42	0.34	0.33	0.34
	CombIC	0.45	-	-	0.42	-	-	0.14	-	-

well on Freebase. This indicates that Freebase's structure has a focus on named entities. On this dataset as well, *ER* outperforms both other methods, but from a smaller distance than on the other datasets.

The results clearly show that the exclusivity-based measure we introduce in this paper outperforms the Katz relatedness as well as the *CombIC* measure [27]. The measure that overall obtains the highest results is exclusivity based relatedness, with the α parameter set to 0.25 (ER 0.25). These results show that our graph-proximity measures are able to accurately capture semantic relatedness and similarity on both DBpedia and Freebase. We also notice the trend that the lower α values lead to better performance. This indicates that the lower the influence of longer paths, the better.

Table 5. Spearman correlations to ground truth on NE relatedness dataset KORE

	KORE								
	DBpedia CAT			DBpedia Full			Freebase		
	top-1	top-5	top-10	top-1	top-5	top-10	top-1	top-5	top-10
Katz $\alpha = 0.25$	0.31	0.33	0.32	0.56	0.53	0.49	0.57	0.58	0.57
Katz $\alpha = 0.5$	0.31	0.33	0.32	0.57	0.50	0.48	0.57	0.58	0.56
Katz $\alpha = 0.75$	0.31	0.32	0.32	0.56	0.48	0.46	0.57	0.58	0.55
ER $\alpha = 0.25$	**0.35**	**0.35**	**0.35**	**0.62**	0.62	0.62	**0.64**	**0.64**	**0.64**
ER $\alpha = 0.5$	**0.35**	**0.35**	**0.35**	**0.62**	**0.63**	**0.63**	0.63	0.63	0.63
ER $\alpha = 0.75$	**0.35**	**0.35**	0.34	0.60	0.61	0.61	0.60	0.61	0.61
ER $\alpha = 1$	0.34	0.34	0.34	0.60	0.61	0.61	0.60	0.60	0.61
CombIC	0.33	-	-	0.60	-	-	0.61	-	-

4.2 Evaluation of Joint Disambiguation with DBpedia

We now present the experiments we carried out in order to evaluate the proposed approach to disambiguation. Our hypothesis is that joint disambiguation approaches perform better than the graph centrality based approaches.

Evaluated Methods. In order to test our hypothesis, we implement Kan-Dis introduced earlier. We use it with three settings:

Joint ER implements joint disambiguation with our Relation Exclusivity based relatedness measure, with $\alpha = 0.25$ and top-5 most relevant paths.

Joint CombIC implements joint disambiguation with *CombIC* [27] relatedness measure;

HITS Authority implements the HITS centrality based disambiguation algorithm used by AGDISTIS [32].

Ground Truth Datasets. We are using five commonly used datasets of texts that have been manually annotated by humans:

NYT10 dataset consists of ten excerpts from news articles published by New York Times [16]. Each text has all the meaning bearing phrases annotated with *at most one* DBpedia resource.

Aquaint50 dataset contains 50 documents from the AQUAINT corpus, that were used by Milne and Witten [19]. They have been linked and disambiguated to Wikipedia articles by their system, and the results were evaluated using Amazon Mechanical Turk[5].

IITB dataset contains 103 manually annotated documents. It has been published by Kulkarni et al [14].

RSS500 [25] dataset contains 500 manually annotated sentences mainly from news documents, automatically scrapped from RSS feeds.

Reuters-21578 [25] dataset contains 145 news randomly sampled from Reuters-21578 news articles dataset. The sampled news items were manually annotated with the linked named entities by domain experts.

Each of these datasets was produced with a particular purpose. NYT10 and IITB try to link as many meaning bearing words as possible. The other three focus on named entities only. Some datasets link every mention of a concept, while others link only the first occurrence. To deal with these differences, we use various performance measures, as follows.

Performance Measures. In order to understand the performance of the relatedness measures and the joint disambiguation algorithm, we evaluate them under two tests.

The first test is an *annotation test* and consists of the traditional information retrieval evaluation measures, precision and recall. This test is highly influenced by the noun-phrase extraction phase. In case our text analysis component extracts different noun-phrases than the ground truth, it is penalised. Similarly, if the ground truth targets only named entities, the precision of our systems is penalised, since we target both named entities and common nouns. As we consider noun-phrase extraction a complementary problem to word-sense disambiguation, we reduce its influence by devising the so-called *disambiguation test*.

---

[5] https://www.mturk.com

The Noun-Phrase Disambiguation Test The second test is a "disambiguation test" as it verifies to what extent a noun-phrase whose corresponding DBpedia concept is set by humans is linked and disambiguated by the system to the same DBpedia concept. It computes the *disambiguation accuracy* measure (denoted by Acc) by dividing the number of correctly linked noun phrases that are both annotated in the ground truth and extracted by the system, to the total number of noun-phrases both annotated by humans and extracted by the system. As such, as opposed to the "annotation test", the results obtained at the "disambiguation test" cancel out the impact of the noun phrase extraction. Furthermore, since many entities are not ambiguous in DBpedia, we also report a variation of this measure, in which we compute the disambiguation accuracy only on the entities and words that have more than one candidate sense (denoted by $Acc^{>1}$).

Results. Table 6 shows the results achieved by the evaluated algorithms. It is easily noticeable that joint disambiguation performs generally better than the centrality based one, especially when used with $CombIC$ relatedness. On both hierarchical and Louvain clustering, joint disambiguation with $CombIC$ achieves best precision. With respect to recall, $HITSAuthority$ used by AGDISTIS tends to perform better. The most relevant performance measure for our setup are the accuracies Acc and $Acc^{>1}$. The accuracy of 0.916 achieved by joint disambiguation with $CombIC$ on the Reuters dataset means that out of the noun phrases that are annotated in the dataset and extracted by Kan_Dis, 91.6% are linked to the correct DBpedia concept. The 0.727 $Acc^{>1}$ score means that out of the noun-phrases that are annotated in the ground truth dataset, were extracted by Kan_Dis, and have more than one disambiguation candidate, 72% were disambiguated to the correct DBpedia concept. The $Acc^{>1}$ scores of joint disambiguation with $CombIC$ are with 0.1 higher than those of $HITSAuthority$ in average.

Regarding the datasets, there is a noticeable decrease of precision for the datasets that only annotate named entities (AQUAINT, RSS500, Reuters). This is because Kan_Dis links and disambiguates both common nouns and named entities. Therefore, in order to get an idea of its performance, the Acc and $Acc^{>1}$ measures are the most conclusive. We notice that on $RSS500$ the accuracies of all the methods are very poor. This is due to the fact that $RSS500$ contains single sentences, therefore there might be not sufficient context for achieving correct disambiguation.

The disambiguation context produced with hierarchical clustering leads to higher precision but lower recall than Louvain clustering. This is due to the used dendrogram cutting threshold that we use (0.8) with hierarchical clustering and that leads to smaller clusters than the Louvain clusters. Small clusters tend to be cleaner, therefore the disambiguation accuracy improves. However, the small clusters have less disambiguation cues, and lead to more words not being disambiguated, producing lower recall.

Table 6. Disambiguation results: P - precision; R - recall; Acc- linking accuracy, $Acc^{>1}$ - disambiguation accuracy for words with more than 1 candidate. Joint ER uses decay 0.25 and top 5 paths.

Dataset	Method	Hierarchical					Louvain				
		P	R	F	Acc	$Acc^{>1}$	P	R	F	Acc	$Acc^{>1}$
NYT10	HITS Authority	0.567	**0.584**	0.572	0.834	0.658	0.576	0.593	0.581	0.851	0.693
	Joint ER	0.607	0.573	0.585	**0.919**	**0.842**	0.586	0.590	0.585	0.885	0.79
	Joint CombIC	**0.613**	0.568	**0.586**	0.912	0.82	**0.595**	**0.601**	**0.595**	**0.892**	**0.802**
IITB	HITS Authority	0.417	**0.435**	0.420	0.761	0.591	0.417	0.436	0.421	0.760	0.587
	Joint ER	0.437	0.432	0.429	0.775	0.653	0.429	**0.437**	0.428	0.780	0.626
	Joint CombIC	**0.472**	0.413	**0.435**	**0.813**	**0.717**	**0.446**	0.428	**0.431**	**0.802**	**0.710**
AQUAINT	HITS Authority	0.247	**0.583**	0.341	0.801	0.594	0.247	0.582	0.340	0.800	0.589
	Joint ER	0.257	0.563	0.346	0.809	0.638	0.250	0.574	0.341	0.816	0.688
	Joint CombIC	**0.264**	0.564	**0.353**	**0.824**	**0.708**	**0.256**	**0.583**	**0.348**	**0.831**	**0.733**
RSS500	HITS Authority	0.171	**0.543**	0.238	0.760	**0.315**	0.171	**0.543**	0.238	0.760	0.315
	Joint ER	0.190	0.524	0.252	0.784	0.224	0.174	0.540	0.240	0.763	0.307
	Joint CombIC	**0.194**	0.524	**0.256**	**0.789**	0.241	**0.176**	0.540	**0.242**	**0.768**	**0.321**
REUTERS	HITS Authority	0.152	**0.700**	0.235	0.894	0.704	0.152	**0.701**	0.235	0.894	0.704
	Joint ER	0.156	0.653	0.237	0.906	0.652	0.153	0.692	0.236	0.892	0.638
	Joint CombIC	**0.162**	0.633	**0.241**	**0.929**	**0.727**	**0.159**	0.676	**0.241**	**0.906**	**0.729**

5   Conclusion and Future Work

In this paper, we have proposed a novel measure for assessing strength of relations in knowledge graphs, called relation exclusivity. We used this measure for computing semantic relatedness as well as similarity. Besides, we also proposed an entity and word-sense disambiguation pipeline Kan_Dis that uses the proposed relatedness measures. We analysed our approach from different perspectives, on five ground truth datasets, and three knowledge graphs. We showed that when used with full DBpedia or Freebase it achieves better results than state-of-the-art approaches.

With respect to our disambiguation approach, we focused specifically on graph-based algorithms. We implemented algorithms from the related work and used them in the same experimental setup with ours, in order to obtain a conclusive comparison. We then showed that joint path-based disambiguation achieves better performance than the graph centrality based approach.

An interesting outcome of our experiments is that while $CombIC$ achieved much worse performance when evaluated against human assessment of relatedness, it achieved the best disambiguation capability. This indicates that for disambiguation, measures must have additional properties than correlation to human assessment of relatedness. One such property might be the scale of the resulted scores. We plan to investigate this in future work.

A very interesting future research path is that of extraction of relevant relation paths between given concepts. We plan to investigate and formally evaluate if the paths deemed relevant by our measure are indeed relevant to humans.

Acknowledgments. This work was supported by Science Foundation Ireland (SFI) under Grant No. 12/RC/2289 (Insight Centre for Data Analytics).

References

1. Agirre, E., Alfonseca, E., Hall, K., Kravalova, J., Paşca, M., Soroa, A.: A study on similarity and relatedness using distributional and wordnet-based approaches. In: NAACL 2009, pp. 19–27. ACL (2009)
2. Agirre, E., Soroa, A.: Personalizing pagerank for word sense disambiguation. In: Proc. 12th Conf. of the European Chapter of the Association for Computational Linguistics (2009)
3. Finkelstein, L., Gabrilovich, E., Matias, Y., Rivlin, E., Solan, Z., Wolfman, G., Ruppin, E.: Placing search in context: The concept revisited. ACM Trans. Inf. Syst. **20**(1), 116–131 (2002). http://doi.acm.org/10.1145/503104.503110
4. Gabrilovich, E., Markovitch, S.: Computing semantic relatedness using wikipedia-based explicit semantic analysis. In: IJCAI 2007, pp. 1606–1611. Morgan Kaufmann Publishers Inc., San Francisco (2007)
5. Garcia, A., Szomszor, M., Alani, H., Corcho, O.: Preliminary results in tag disambiguation using dbpedia. In: Knowledge Capture (K-Cap 2009) - 1st International Workshop on Collective Knowledge Capturing and Representation (2009)
6. Gentile, A.L., Zhang, Z., Xia, L., Iria, J.: Semantic relatedness approach for named entity disambiguation. In: Agosti, M., Esposito, F., Thanos, C. (eds.) IRCDL 2010. CCIS, vol. 91, pp. 137–148. Springer, Heidelberg (2010)
7. Grieser, K., Baldwin, T., Bohnert, F., Sonenberg, L.: Using ontological and document similarity to estimate museum exhibit relatedness. ACM Journal of Computing and Cultural Heritage **3**(3), 1–20 (2011)
8. Hakimov, S., Oto, S.A., Dogdu, E.: Named entity recognition and disambiguation using linked data and graph-based centrality scoring. In: Proceedings of the 4th International Workshop on Semantic Web Information Management, SWIM 2012, pp. 4:1–4:7. ACM, New York (2012)
9. Hoffart, J., Seufert, S., Nguyen, D.B., Theobald, M., Weikum, G.: Kore: keyphrase overlap relatedness for entity disambiguation. In: CIKM 2012, pp. 545–554. ACM (2012)
10. Hulpuş, I.: Semantic Network Analysis for Topic Linking and Labelling. Ph.D. thesis, National University of Ireland, Galway (2014)
11. Hulpuş, I., Hayes, C., Karnstedt, M., Greene, D.: An eigenvalue-based measure for word-sense disambiguation. In: FLAIRS 2012 (2012)
12. Hulpuş, I., Hayes, C., Karnstedt, M., Greene, D.: Unsupervised graph-based topic labelling using dbpedia. In: WSDM, pp. 465–474. ACM, New York (2013)
13. Katz, L.: A new status index derived from sociometric analysis. Psychometrika **18**(1), 39–43 (1953)
14. Kulkarni, S., Singh, A., Ramakrishnan, G., Chakrabarti, S.: Collective annotation of wikipedia entities in web text. In: Proceedings of the 15th ACM SIGKDD International Conference on Knowledge Discovery and Data Mining, KDD 2009, pp. 457–466. ACM, New York (2009)
15. Leal, J.P., Rodrigues, V., Queirs, R.: Computing semantic relatedness using dbpedia. In: Simes, A., Queirs, R., da Cruz, D.C. (eds.) SLATE. OASICS, vol. 21, pp. 133–147 (2012)
16. Mendes, P.N., Jakob, M., García-Silva, A., Bizer, C.: DBpedia spotlight: shedding light on the web of documents. In: I-Semantics 2011, pp. 1–8 (2011)
17. Mihalcea, R., Tarau, P., Figa, E.: Pagerank on semantic networks, with application to word sense disambiguation. In: Proceedings of the 20th International Conference on Computational Linguistics, COLING 2004. ACL (2004)

18. Milne, D., Witten, I.H.: An effective, low-cost measure of semantic relatedness obtained from wikipedia links. In: Proceedings of AAAI 2008 (2008)
19. Milne, D., Witten, I.H.: Learning to link with wikipedia. In: Proceedings of the 17th ACM CIKM, CIKM 2008, pp. 509–518. ACM (2008)
20. Mirizzi, R., Di Noia, T., Ragone, A., Ostuni, V.C., Di Sciascio, E.: Movie recommendation with dbpedia. In: CEUR Workshop Proceedings, vol. 835 (2012)
21. Navigli, R., Lapata, M.: Graph connectivity measures for unsupervised word sense disambiguation. In: Proceedings of the 20th International Joint Conference on Artifical Intelligence, IJCAI 2007, pp. 1683–1688 (2007)
22. Pereira Nunes, B., Dietze, S., Casanova, M.A., Kawase, R., Fetahu, B., Nejdl, W.: Combining a co-occurrence-based and a semantic measure for entity linking. In: Cimiano, P., Corcho, O., Presutti, V., Hollink, L., Rudolph, S. (eds.) ESWC 2013. LNCS, vol. 7882, pp. 548–562. Springer, Heidelberg (2013)
23. Passant, A.: Measuring semantic distance on linking data and using it for resources recommendations. In: Linked Data Meets Artificial Intelligence, Papers from the 2010 AAAI Spring Symposium, Stanford, California, USA (2010)
24. Ratinov, L., Roth, D., Downey, D., Anderson, M.: Local and global algorithms for disambiguation to wikipedia. In: HLT 2011, pp. 1375–1384. Association for Computational Linguistics (2011)
25. Röder, M., Usbeck, R., Hellmann, S., Gerber, D., Both, A.: N3 - a collection of datasets for named entity recognition and disambiguation in the nlp interchange format. In: The 9th edition of LREC, May 26–31, Reykjavik, Iceland (2014)
26. Rubenstein, H., Goodenough, J.B.: Contextual correlates of synonymy. Commun. ACM **8**(10), 627–633 (1965). http://doi.acm.org/10.1145/365628.365657
27. Schuhmacher, M., Ponzetto, S.P.: Knowledge-based graph document modeling. In: Proceedings of the 7th ACM WSDM, WSDM 2014, pp. 543–552. ACM (2014)
28. Sinha, R., Mihalcea, R.: Unsupervised graph-based word sense disambiguation using measures of word semantic similarity. In: Proc. International Conference on Semantic Computing, pp. 363–369. IEEE Computer Society (2007)
29. St-Onge, D.: Detecting and Correcting Malapropisms with Lexical Chains. Master's thesis, University of Toronto (1995)
30. Sussna, M.: Word sense disambiguation for free-text indexing using a massive semantic network. In: Proceedings of the second CIKM, CIKM 1993, pp. 67–74. ACM, New York (1993)
31. Szumlanski, S.R., Gomez, F., Sims, V.K.: A new set of norms for semantic relatedness measures. In: ACL (2), pp. 890–895 (2013)
32. Usbeck, R., Ngonga Ngomo, A.-C., Röder, M., Gerber, D., Coelho, S.A., Auer, S., Both, A.: AGDISTIS - graph-based disambiguation of named entities using linked data. In: Mika, P., Tudorache, T., Bernstein, A., Welty, C., Knoblock, C., Vrandečić, D., Groth, P., Noy, N., Janowicz, K., Goble, C. (eds.) ISWC 2014, Part I. LNCS, vol. 8796, pp. 457–471. Springer, Heidelberg (2014)

SANAPHOR: Ontology-Based Coreference Resolution

Roman Prokofyev[1]([✉]), Alberto Tonon[1], Michael Luggen[1], Loic Vouilloz[2],
Djellel Eddine Difallah[1], and Philippe Cudré-Mauroux[1]

[1] eXascale Infolab, University of Fribourg, Fribourg, Switzerland
{roman.prokofyev,alberto.tonon,michael.luggen,djelleleddine.difallah,
philippe.cudre-mauroux}@unifr.ch
[2] Linguistics Department, University of Fribourg, Fribourg, Switzerland
loic.vouilloz@unifr.ch

Abstract. We tackle the problem of resolving coreferences in textual
content by leveraging Semantic Web techniques. Specifically, we focus
on noun phrases that coreference identifiable entities that appear in the
text; the challenge in this context is to improve the coreference resolution
by leveraging potential semantic annotations that can be added to the
identified mentions. Our system, SANAPHOR, first applies state-of-the-art
techniques to extract entities, noun phrases, and candidate coreferences.
Then, we propose an approach to type noun phrases using an inverted
index built on top of a Knowledge Graph (e.g., DBpedia). Finally, we use
the semantic relatedness of the introduced types to improve the state-
of-the-art techniques by splitting and merging coreference clusters. We
evaluate SANAPHOR on CoNLL datasets, and show how our techniques
consistently improve the state of the art in coreference resolution.

1 Introduction

Natural language understanding is often referred to as an *AI-complete* task,
meaning that it belongs to the class of the most difficult problems in Artificial
Intelligence, which would require machines to become as intelligent as people
prior to being solved. While perfect natural language understanding is still out
of reach, recent advances in machine learning, entity linking, and relationship
mining are closing the gap between humans and machines when it comes to
processing natural language. Semantic technologies have played a key role in
those developments, by providing mechanisms to classify, describe, and interre-
late entities using machine-processable languages.

Less attention has however been given to the problem of leveraging Semantic
Web techniques and knowledge bases to find all expressions referring to the same
entity in a text, i.e., *coreference resolution*. While a flurry of previous contributions have proposed techniques to resolve coreferences (see the Related Work
section below), the extent to which semantic technologies can be leveraged in
this context remains unclear. In this paper, we investigate this question and

© Springer International Publishing Switzerland 2015
M. Arenas et al. (Eds.): ISWC 2015, Part I, LNCS 9366, pp. 458–473, 2015.
DOI: 10.1007/978-3-319-25007-6_27

introduce SANAPHOR, a new system focusing on the last stage of a typical coreference resolution pipeline and improving the quality of the coreference clusters by exploiting semantic entities and fine-grained types to split or merge coreference clusters.

The following piece of text, for example, motivates our approach:

"Laiwu City of Shandong Province has established a cell structure cultivation center ... currently Shangong has established ten agricultural development and model zones similar to that of Laiwu City."

With purely syntactic and grammatical approaches, it is easy to get confused between the name of the province and the name of the city, since they initially appear together. In fact, Stanford Coref will put occurrences of both the province and the city into one coreference cluster. Access to external knowledge such as ontologies or knowledge bases is key in this context.

In the following, we add a semantic layer on top of the prominent Stanford Coref pipeline[1] to tackle such cases. Throughout our process, we leverage a number of state-of-the-art Semantic Web techniques ranging from entity linking to type ranking. We concentrate on type-based coreferences, excluding part-of-speeches that do not bare self-contained semantics (e.g. determiners, pronouns etc).

In summary, the contributions of this work are:

- A new system that adds a semantic layer to the state-of-the-art Stanford Coref pipeline.
- A novel NLP technique that leverages the semantic web to better resolve coreferences.
- An empirical evaluation of our system on standard datasets showing that our techniques consistently improve on the state-of-the-art approach by tackling those cases where semantic annotations can be beneficial.

The rest of this paper is structured as follows: in the rest of this section we define the concepts of coreference and anaphora by presenting several examples; in Section 2 we discuss related work in Semantic Web technologies and on coreference resolution systems; Section 3 describes the architecture of the system we propose; finally, Sections 4 and 5 describe the experimental evaluation of SANAPHOR and conclude the paper.

1.1   Preliminaries

We start below by introducing the terminology used throughout the rest of this paper. Some of the linguistic units appearing in textual contents have the function of representing physical or conceptual objects. Linguists often call such units *referring expressions*, while the objects are called *referents* and the relations that unite a referring expression and its referent are called *references*. In the following example: *So Jesus said again, "I assure you, I am the gate for the sheep. All those who came before me were thieves and robbers. [...] I have other sheep too. They are not in this flock here."* the referring expressions are:

---

[1] http://nlp.stanford.edu/projects/coref.shtml

- Noun Phrases (NPs) and pronouns referring to people (e.g. *Jesus* ; *all those who came before me*), things (*the gate*), classes (*sheep*; *they*) or that designate interlocutors (*I*; *you*)
- clauses, that names facts (*I am the gate for the sheep*; *I have other sheep too*; *they are not in this flock here*)
- the adverb *here* that designates a location.

In order to satisfy cohesion [14], the same object is often recalled throughout the text repeatedly so that it can be enriched with new attributes.

In this context, linguists often distinguish *coreference* from *anaphora*. The difference between the two concepts is subtle and is explained in the following. We have a *coreference* every time two (possibly different) referring expressions denote *the same referent*, that is, the same entity. For example, in the sentence *Abraham Lincoln, the first president of the USA, died in 1865.*, "Abraham Lincoln" and "the first president of the USA" refer to the same entity, thus, they co-refer. We have an *anaphora* every time the reference of an expression $E2$, called *anaphoric expression*, is function of a previous expression $E1$, called *antecedent*, so that one needs $E1$ to interpret $E2$. For example, in the sentence *I like dragons! Those animals are really cute!* "those animals" is an anaphoric expression and the reader needs to know that it refers to "dragons" (the antecedent) in order to understand the sentence. Finally, the two concepts can be combined:

- The sentence *You have a cat? I don't like them.* is a case of anaphora without coreference since the pronoun *them* needs the antecedent *a cat* to be interpreted (it is the anaphoric), but the two references do not designate the same object (*a cat* = an individual / *them* = the entire species).
- The sentence about Abraham Lincoln we presented before is an example of coreference without anaphora, since if we remove "Abraham Lincoln" one can still understand the sentence.
- The sentence *The dragon is coming. It is going to burn the city!* is an example of anaphora and coreference since one needs an antecedent to resolve "It", and both "It" and "the dragon" refer to the same entity.

In this paper we show how entity types can be used in order to resolve the two last cases.

2   Related Work

2.1   Named Entity Recognition

Named entity recognition (NER) refers to the task of correctly identifying words or phrases in textual documents that represent entities such as people, organizations, locations, etc. During the last decades, NER has been widely studied and the best NER approaches nowadays produce near-human recognition accuracy for generic domains such as news articles. Several prominent NER systems employ supervised learning methods based on maximum entropy [4] and conditional random fields [8], or fuse the results of other systems using a supervised classifier [33].

2.2   Entity Linking

Entity linking is the task of associating a textual mention of an entity to its corresponding entry in a knowledge base. It can be divided into three subtasks: mention detection, link generation, and disambiguation [21]. One of the main issues that needs to be tackled when doing entity linking is the ambiguity of the textual representation of the entity given as input. For example, the mention "Michael Jordan" can be linked to both Michael Jordan the basketball player and Michael Jordan the well-known machine learning professor. Much work has been done on entity linking. Recently, Houlsby and Ciaramita dealt with ambiguities by using a variant of LDA in which each topic is a Wikipedia article (that is, an entity) [17]. Cheng and Roth used Integer Linear Programming to combine relational analysis of entities in the text, features extracted from external sources and statistics on the text [6].

In the context of this paper, both NER and Entity Linking are prerequisites for coreference resolution as we take advantage of external knowledge to improve the resolution of coreferences and hence must first identify and link as many entity mentions as possible to their counterparts in the knowledge base. Since, however, those two tasks are not the focus of this work, we decided to use in this paper the TRank pipeline because of its simplicity and its good performance in practice on our dataset (see Section 4).

2.3   Entity Types

Knowing the types of a certain entity is valuable information that can be used in a variety of tasks. Much work has been done on extracting entity types both from text and from semi-structured data. In this context, Gangemi *et al.* [9] exploit the textual description of Wikipedia entities to extract entity types, Nakashole *et al.* [24] designed a probabilistic model to extract the types out of knowledge base entities, and Paulheim and Bizer [28] worked on adding missing type statements by exploiting statistical distributions of types as subjects and objects of properties. Much effort has been put also on ranking entity types in several contexts. TRank [38] is a system for ranking entity types given the textual context in which they appear. Tylenda *et al.* [39] select the most relevant types to summarize entities. In this paper we leverage entity types as evidences for deciding if, given a piece of text, different entity mentions refer to the same entity or not.

2.4   Coreference and Anaphora

According to Ng [25], practically all coreference and anaphora resolution systems are instantiations of a seven-step generic algorithm[2]:

---

[2] Note that steps 3, 5 and 6 can be absent in a coreference or anaphora resolution algorithm. Moreover, existing algorithms differ in the way these seven steps are implemented

1. Identification of referring expressions: This first step is mostly to identify all of the pronouns and noun phrases in the text. Clauses and adverbs can also be spotted.

2. Characterization of referring expressions: This second step consists of determining and computing the information regarding referring expressions that might be relevant to its linking to another expression in the text. Most approaches rely on some preprocessing modules (e.g. part-of-speech tagging, parsing, named entity recognizer,...) to perform this step ; however, they differ in the level of sophistication of the extracted information, ranging from knowledge-rich to knowledge-poor (see below).

3. Anaphoricity determination: Involves distinguishing anaphoric expressions, that should have an antecedent, from non-anaphoric expressions, that should not. Thus, this step is always performed as part of anaphora resolution, but not always for coreference resolution (see 1.1).

4. Generation of antecedent candidates: This fourth step identifies a set of potential antecedents, named *candidates*, that linearly precedes the anaphoric expression in the text.

5. Filtering: This step involves removing from the set some unlikely candidates based on ensemble of hard constraints, for example morphologic, syntactic and semantic constraints.

6. Scoring/Ranking: The aim of this step, that is optional, is to rank remaining candidates according to an ensemble of soft constraints, also called *preferences*, that often depend on psycholinguistic and discourse principles (especially *focus* [34], *centering* [12] or *accessibility* [1]).

7. Searching/Clustering: Finally, the goal of this last step is to select an antecedent for a given anaphoric expression from the set of candidates returned by the fifth and/or the sixth steps. If step 6 has been performed, then *searching* becomes the task of selecting the highest-ranking element in the candidate list; otherwise, the "best" expression is selected as the antecedent in accordance with criteria specified by the resolution algorithm. In the case of coreference resolution, this process corresponds to applying a single-link clustering algorithm to each anaphoric expression to cluster the referring expressions in the document and generate a partition.

Although this generic algorithm characterizes most of the resolution pipelines, research on coreference and anaphora resolution in computational linguistics has been proceeding in many different directions for the last 30 years. Nevertheless, it is possible to identify important trends [7,25,27]. In the context of this paper, two trends are of particular significance and are presented below.

First, coreference and anaphora resolution systems can be classified with respect to the types of knowledge sources they leverage. One typically differentiates *Knowledge-rich* systems from *knowledge-lean systems*. Early anaphora resolution systems [11,35] as well as more recent ones [5,13,26,29,37,40] are knowledge-rich systems that rely on domain informations (such as FrameNet, WordNet, Wikipedia, Yago, etc.), semantic and discourse analysis, and sophisticated inference mechanisms (induction for example). Knowledge-lean systems

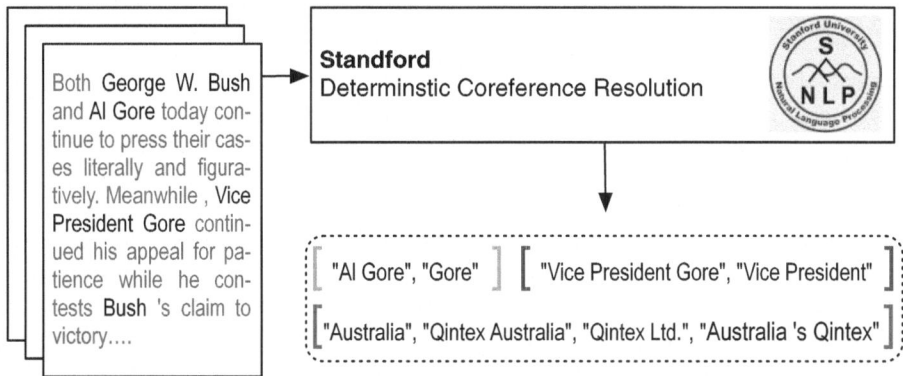

Fig. 1. The `Stanford Coref` system takes plain text as an input and outputs clusters (`[]`) of mentions (`""`) which are potentially coreferenced.

instead rely only on morphological and possibly syntactic information [3,18,19, 23], and reach high performance without semantic and world knowledge. Our system belongs to the first category, using YAGO and DBpedia.

Early coreference and anaphora resolution systems also differ from more recent ones by the fact that they adopt *knowledge-based approaches*, in which the rulesets used in *filtering* and *scoring/ranking* (see steps 5 and 6 above) are based on a set of hand-coded heuristics that specify whether two referring expressions can or cannot have any coreferential/anaphoric relationship [12,16]. Actually, these approaches are often called *linguistic approaches* as they are based on linguistic theories. In contrast, *corpus-based approaches* acquire knowledge using a learning algorithm and training data, i.e., a corpus annotated with coreference and anaphora information in *filtering* and *scoring/ranking* [10,15,36]. Again, our own system belongs to the first category.

3 System Architecture

In this section, we describe the overall architecture of SANAPHOR and provide details on each of its components.

3.1 System Input

Starting from the `Stanford Coref` framework [19] (Figure 1), which covers the steps 1-7 described in Section 2.4, we obtain for each document (e.g., a news article) a set of clusters containing textual mentions. The clusters are non-overlapping and contain potentially coreference mentions. In addition, `Stanford Coref` associates a headword to each mention (especially for long mentions) when possible.

3.2   System Overview

Many potential improvements are conceivable throughout the generic pipeline introduced in Section 2.4. In that context, our efforts first focused on improving coreference resolution using semantic word and phrase similarities based on Word Vectors [22]. However, word vectors did not work well in our experiments. For example, the vector of the word "shepherd" was very close to the vector of "sheep", which is reasonable, but does not work well for the coreference resolution task, since these two words often appear in one document. Motivated by the results analysis presented above, SANAPHOR focuses instead on splitting and merging of candidate clusters (see Step 7 in Section 2.4) using semantic information, as it is (in our opinion) the most susceptible to benefit from a tight integration of semantic technologies.

Figures 2 and 3 give an overview of our system, illustrating the preprocessing steps and the splitting/merging steps respectively. SANAPHOR receives as input the clusters of coreferences generated by Stanford Coref. Each cluster is a set of mentions extracted from the original text. Each mention comes in the form of

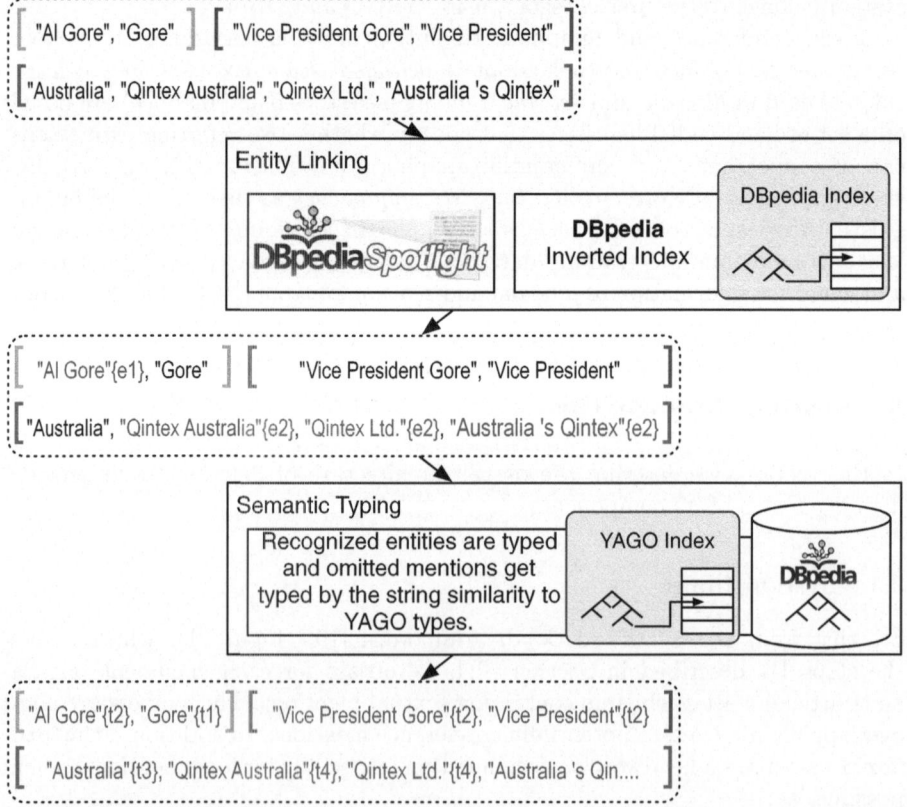

Fig. 2. The pre-processing steps of SANAPHOR annotating semantics to the mentions.

a string and, potentially, an associated headword (the most salient word in the mention). The mentions can be either Named Entities, pronouns, or determiners, as identified and clustered by `Stanford Coref`. Our system then takes those clusters and proceeds in two successive steps I) Preprocessing, where we leverage linked data to represent named entities with their semantic counterparts (either Entities or Types) whenever possible; II) Cluster Optimization, where using annotations obtained from the preprocessing step we derive a strategy for splitting clusters containing unrelated mentions, or, conversely for merging mentions that semantically should belong together.

We describe in more detail the functionalities provided by those components in the following, starting with the semantic annotation pipeline and then moving to cluster management methods.

3.3   Semantic Annotation

Entity Linking. The goal of the Entity Linking component is to link entity mentions to DBpedia entries. We exploit an inverted index associating DBpedia

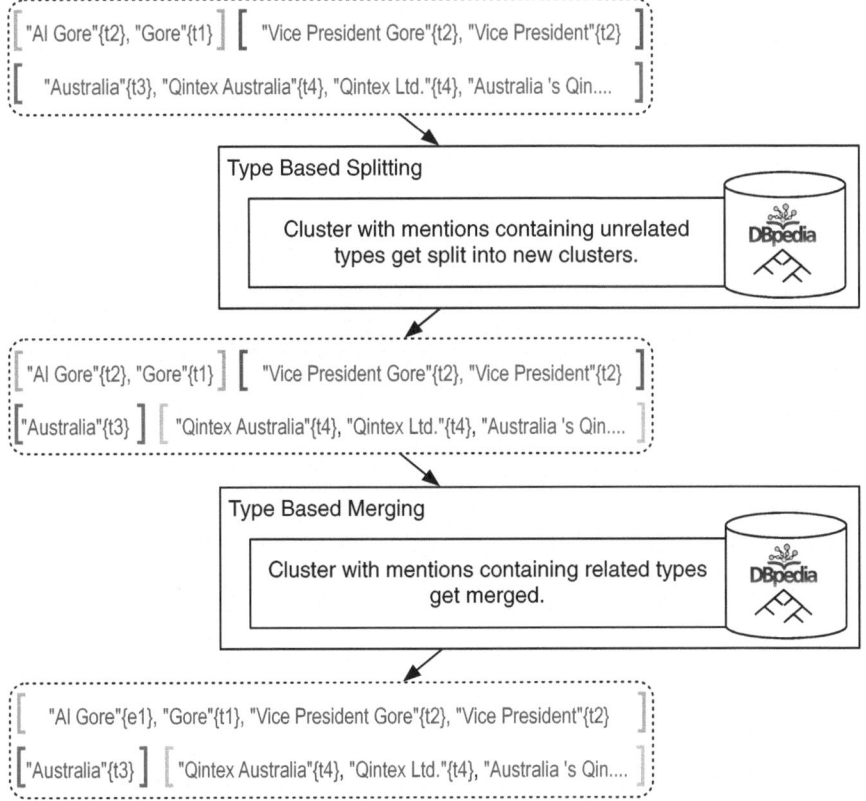

Fig. 3. The final type-based splitting and merging of the clusters in `SANAPHOR`.

labels to entity URIs. In order to generate high-quality links, we decided to only link mentions that exactly match DBpedia labels[3]. Entities with multiple aliases are handled by using Wikipedia redirection links and, in order to foster precision, by discarding URIs that link to ambiguous entities (i.e., entities having a `wikiPageDisambiguates` property).

Semantic Typing. The next step in our preprocessing pipeline is assigning *Types* to mentions appearing in the text. In this context, we use the YAGO ontology as a target database. We created an inverted index of the types obtained from the YAGO ontology[4] and performed a string matching between every mention and the inverted index. For example, a noun phrase "rock singer" is typed as Wikicategory_American_Rock_Singers . For the mentions linked in the previous step, we employ the mappings between DBPedia and YAGO ontologies provided by TRank Hierarchy [38] to map DBPedia types to YAGO ones.

We chose to optimize our preprocessing steps for precision rather then recall, since the subsequent steps rely on precise linking to be effective at improving the mention clusters. As a result, we do not annotate labels that refer to multiple entity types.

3.4   Cluster Management

Splitting Coreference Clusters. The first task SANAPHOR undertakes to optimize the clusters of mentions is to split clusters containing mentions of different types. This step tackles cases where Stanford Coref was not able to deal with ambiguity in the text, for example for the following cases: "Aspen"(the Colorado city) and "Aspen"(the tree), which can be wrongly interpreted as referring to the same referent, thus producing a series of incorrect coreferences. Instead, SANAPHOR leverages the output of the entity linking process to resolve the ambiguity of the mentions: since during the linking phase the two mentions will probably be associated to different entities, the system can decide to split them into separate clusters.

The result of the semantic annotation phase is a series of sets $\{\mathcal{S}_0, \ldots, \mathcal{S}_n\}$, one per coreference cluster, containing entities $e \in \mathcal{E}$ and/or fined-grained semantic types $t \in \mathcal{T}$ attached to each mention $m \in \mathcal{M}$. The splitting process examines all pairs of mentions $\{m_i, m_j\}$ in a given cluster, and decides whether or not to split the cluster depending on the potential entities $\{e_i, e_j\}$ and types $\{t_i, t_j\}$ attached to the mentions. Formally, we split a cluster whenever, $\forall \{m_i, m_j\} \in S$:

- $\exists \{e_i, e_j\} \mid e_i \neq e_j$ or
- $\exists \{t_i, t_j\} \mid t_i \nleq t_j$ (where $\nleq$ stands for equivalence or subsumption relation w.r.t. the type hierarchy of the ontology), or

---

[3] We have also tried more complex methods that take context into account, such as *DBPedia Spotlight*, but they lead to less precise linkings and worse overall results.

[4] http://www.mpi-inf.mpg.de/departments/databases-and-information-systems/ research/yago-naga/yago/downloads/

– $\exists\{e_i, t_j\} \mid T(e_i) \not\leq t_j$ (where $T(e_i)$ stands for the type of e_i according to the ontology).

Since a coreference cluster might also contain non-annotated mentions, we need a way to properly assign them to the split clusters. In order to do this, we first identify the words that belong exclusively to one of the mentions m_i or m_j. We assign all other mentions to one of the new clusters based on the overlap of their words with the exclusive words of each new cluster.

However, these steps alone do not systematically result in a substantial performance increase due to many possible reductions of the original mention. For example, a text might contain "Aspen Airways" first and then have the word "Aspen" to refer to the airline, which our method might incorrectly link to a city or a tree type. To overcome this problem, we introduce a simple heuristic that ignores entity linkings of the mentions whose words represent a complete subset of any other mention in the same cluster.

Merging Coreference Clusters. The second task that we are tackling in the context of cluster management is merging, that is, joining pairs of sets $\{S_i, S_j\}$ that contain similar entities or types. For instance, consider the mention "Hosni Mubarak", the former president of Egypt, which can also be referred to as "President Mubarak" in a news article. In such a case, `Stanford Coref` might assign those two mentions to two different clusters. Thus, starting from entity and type linking as before, we propose to merge clusters, each of which contains at least one mention that refers to the same entity. Formally, two sets $\{S_i, S_j\}$ corresponding to two clusters are merged whenever:

– $\exists (e_i \in S_i \wedge e_j \in S_j) \mid e_i \equiv e_j$ or
– $\exists (e_i \in S_i \wedge t_j \in S_j) \mid T(e_i) \leq t_j$ and when the condition just above does not apply.

We note that in this step we do not use any heuristic to pre-filter the clusters.

Our system, `SANAPHOR`, is available as an open-source[5] extension to `Stanford Coref`. The pipeline allows to use different entity and type linkers for future experiments.

4   Experimental Evaluation

4.1   Datasets

We evaluate our system on standard datasets from the CoNLL-2012 Shared Task on Coreference Resolution [30] distributed as a part of the OntoNotes 5 dataset[6]. We use only the English part of the dataset which consists of over one million words from newswire, magazine articles, broadcast news, broadcast

---

[5] http:///github.com/xi-lab/sanaphor
[6] https://catalog.ldc.upenn.edu/LDC2013T19

conversations, web data, telephone conversations and English translation of the New Testament.

The English dataset is split into three: development, training and test sub-collections. The development dataset is intended to be analyzed during the development of the coreference resolution system in order to build intuitions and tune the system. The training dataset is designed to be used in the supervised training phase, while the final results have to be reported on the test dataset. In the following sections, we analyze results and we design our methods based on the development collection and report the final results based on the test collection. Since our system improves on the Stanford Coreference Resolution System, which already includes supervised models, we do not directly use the training sub-collection in our pipeline.

4.2 Metrics

Many metrics have been proposed to evaluate the performance of coreference resolution systems, from early metrics like MUC [41], to the most recent metric proposed—BLANC [32].

As a final evaluation metric, we use the most recently proposed BLANC, which addresses the drawbacks of previously proposed metrics such as MUC, B-cubed [2], or CEAF [20], as it neither ignores singleton mentions nor does it inflate the final score in their presence.

In addition, we use a pairwise metric based on the *Rand Index* [31] to evaluate the performance of the individual parts of our system in isolation.

4.3 Analysis of the Results of Stanford Coreference Resolution System

We start by analyzing the results of the Stanford Coref on the development dataset in the context of two possible error classes: 1) mentions that were put into one cluster, but that in fact belong to different clusters, 2) mentions that refer to the same thing, but that were put into different clusters. Additionally, since we focus on noun-phrase mentions, we want to see how many noun-only clusters exist in the dataset in order to estimate the effect of a possible improvement.

Overall, the Stanford Coref system creates 5078 coreference clusters, out of which 270 clusters need to be merged and 77 "has-to-be-merged" clusters are noun-only. The total number of clusters that should be split is 118, out of which 52 are noun-only.

As we can observe, the total amount of potential split and merge clusters account for approximately 8% of total data, which can result in a significant performance improvement for coreference resolution (for which even small improvements are considered as important given the maturity of the tools developed over more than 30 years).

In the following, we report results for the different steps in our pipeline on the test dataset.

Table 1. Cluster linking distributions for all the clusters and for noun-only clusters

	0 Links	1 Distinct Link	2 Distinct Links	3 Distinct Links
All Clusters	4175	849	49	5
Noun-Only Clusters	1208	502	33	2

4.4 Preprocessing Results

The main innovation of SANAPHOR is the semantic layer that enhances classic coreference clustering, hence we focus on evaluating clusters that contain at least one entity (or one type) at the output of our preprocessing steps. The overall recall of our approach is therefore bound by the number of clusters that were identified as containing linked entities and/or types.

In total, we linked 2607 mentions out of 9664 noun phrase mentions (i.e., mentions that have nouns as headwords) extracted by Stanford Coref from the **CoNLL dev dataset**. Out of these 9664 mentions, 4384 were recognized by Stanford Coref as entities. Table 1 summarizes the distribution of clusters and the links obtained using our preprocessing step.

For evaluation purposes, we consider only clusters that contain at least one link. Moreover, we make the following distinction of clusters for evaluation purposes:

- **All Linked Clusters.** That is, clusters that contain at least one linked mention, or
- **Noun-Only Linked Clusters.** These are clusters which contain at least one linked mention, headwords, but have no pronouns nor determiners.

We make this distinction in order to evaluate whether considering clusters with pronouns and determiners (which bare little semantic information) affects the overall results.

4.5 Cluster Optimization Results

Now, we turn our attention to the evaluation of the effectiveness of our cluster optimization methods (splitting and merging). The following experiments are performed on the CoNLL test dataset. We compute Precision, Recall and F1 metrics for the clusters on which we operate. Since we are evaluating clusters, we use the pairwise definition of the metrics (see Section 4.2).

We distinguish the results for both the split and merge operations as compared to the ground-truth. For instance, for all the clusters generated by each system, we perform pairwise comparisons of all mentions in the clusters and evaluate whether the two mentions were correctly separated (in case of a split) or put together (in case of a merge).

Table 2 summarizes the results of our evaluation. As can be seen, SANAPHOR outperforms Stanford Coref in both the split and merge tasks for both All and Noun-Only clusters. Moreover, we notice that the absolute increase in F1 score

Table 2. Results of the evaluation of the cluster optimization step (split and merge).

		SANAPHOR			Stanford Coref		
		P(%)	R(%)	F1(%)	P(%)	R(%)	F1(%)
Split	All Clusters	82.56	90.27	**86.25**	71.39	100.00	83.31
	Noun-Only Clusters	78.99	90.38	**84.30**	58.43	100.00	73.76
Merge	All Clusters	94.58	100.00	**97.21**	96.65	55.10	70.18
	Noun-Only Clusters	76.92	100.00	**86.96**	85.00	56.67	68.00

for the split task is greater for the Noun-Only case (+10.54% vs +2.94%). This results from the fact that All Clusters also contain non-noun mentions, such as pronouns, which we don't directly tackle in this work but have to be assigned to one of the splits nevertheless. Our approach in that context is to keep the non-noun mentions with the first noun-mention in the cluster, which seems to be suboptimal for this case.

For the merge task, the difference between All and Noun-Only clusters is much smaller (+27.03% for the All Clusters vs +18.96% for the Noun-Only case). In this case, non-noun words do not have any effect, since we merge clusters and also include all other mentions.

4.6   End-to-End Performance

Finally, and in addition to the previous results that reflect the effectiveness of SANAPHOR on relevant clusters, we evaluate the impact of our approach on the end-to-end coreference resolution pipeline using the CoNLL test collection. In that context, we use the Precision, Recall and F1 scores of the BLANC metric (Section 4.3). Our system consistently outperforms the Stanford Coref baseline in both Precision (60.63% vs 60.61%), Recall (55.16% vs 55.07%) and F1 values (57.11% vs 57.04%). The reason behind the limited improvement on the overall dataset is imputable to the recall we achieve during the linking step (see Section 4.4) and to the limited number of cases in which a split or a merge is required (8% of the total data).

To further elaborate on the significance of our results, we also ran our SANAPHOR pipeline on the data where we annotated all entities with the "gold" (i.e., ground-truth) URLs. This corresponds to the optimal case where the system is able to link all possible entities correctly. The performance of Stanford Coref for such a best-case scenario is 57.17% in terms of F1, which is comparable to the performance of our entity linking method, thus confirming the validity of our approach.

5   Conclusions

In this paper, we tackled the problem of coreference resolution by leveraging semantic information contained in large-scale knowledge bases. Our open-source system, SANAPHOR, focuses on the last stage of a typical coreference resolution pipeline (*searching and clustering*) and improves the quality of the coreference clusters by exploiting semantic entities and fine-grained types to split or merge the clusters. Our empirical evaluation on a standard dataset showed that our techniques consistently improve on the state-of-the-art approach by tackling those cases where semantic annotations can be beneficial.

Our approach can be extended in a number of ways. One of the limitations of SANAPHOR affecting its recall is due to the potential lack of information being available in the knowledge base. In that sense, techniques that take advantage of a series of knowledge bases (e.g., based on federated queries), that identify missing entities in the knowledge base or that dynamically enrich the knowledge base could be developed. Another interesting extension would be to bring more structure to the coreference clusters, for example by introducing semantic links between the candidates in order to foster more elaborate post-processing at the merging step.

Acknowledgments. This work was supported by the Swiss National Science Foundation under grant number PP00P2 153023, and by the Haslerstiftung in the context of the Smart World 11005 (Mem0r1es) project.

References

1. Ariel, M.: Accessing noun-phrase antecedents. Routledge (2014)
2. Bagga, A., Baldwin, B.: Algorithms for scoring coreference chains. In: The first International Conference on Language Resources and Evaluation Workshop on Linguistics Coreference, vol. 1, pp. 563–566. Citeseer (1998)
3. Baldwin, B.: Cogniac: high precision coreference with limited knowledge and linguistic resources. In: Proceedings of a Workshop on Operational Factors in Practical, Robust Anaphora Resolution for Unrestricted Texts, pp. 38–45. Association for Computational Linguistics (1997)
4. Borthwick, A., Sterling, J., Agichtein, E., Grishman, R.: Exploiting diverse knowledge sources via maximum entropy in named entity recognition. In: Sixth Workshop on Very Large Corpora (1998)
5. Bryl, V., Giuliano, C., Serafini, L., Tymoshenko, K.: Using background knowledge to support coreference resolution. In: ECAI, vol. 10, pp. 759–764 (2010)
6. Cheng, X., Roth, D.: Relational inference for wikification. In: Empirical Methods in Natural Language Processing, pp. 1787–1796 (2013)
7. Elango, P.: Coreference resolution: A survey. Technical report, University of Wisconsin, Madison (2005)
8. Finkel, J.R., Grenager, T., Manning, C.: Incorporating non-local information into information extraction systems by gibbs sampling. In: Proceedings of the 43rd Annual Meeting on Association for Computational Linguistics, ACL 2005, Stroudsburg, PA, USA, pp. 363–370. Association for Computational Linguistics (2005)
9. Gangemi, A., Nuzzolese, A.G., Presutti, V., Draicchio, F., Musetti, A., Ciancarini, P.: Automatic typing of DBpedia entities. In: Cudré-Mauroux, P., Heflin, J., Sirin, E., Tudorache, T., Euzenat, J., Hauswirth, M., Parreira, J.X., Hendler, J., Schreiber, G., Bernstein, A., Blomqvist, E. (eds.) ISWC 2012, Part I. LNCS, vol. 7649, pp. 65–81. Springer, Heidelberg (2012)

10. Ge, N., Hale, J., Charniak, E.: A statistical approach to anaphora resolution. In: Proceedings of the Sixth Workshop on Very Large Corpora, vol. 71 (1998)
11. Grosz, B.J., et al.: The representation and use of focus in a system for understanding dialogs. In: IJCAI, vol. 67, pp. 76 (1977)
12. Grosz, B.J., Weinstein, S., Joshi, A.K.: Centering: A framework for modeling the local coherence of discourse. Computational Linguistics **21**(2), 203–225 (1995)
13. Haghighi, A., Klein, D.: Simple coreference resolution with rich syntactic and semantic features. In: Proceedings of the 2009 Conference on Empirical Methods in Natural Language Processing: Volume 3, EMNLP 2009, Stroudsburg, PA, USA, vol. 3, pp. 1152–1161. Association for Computational Linguistics (2009)
14. Halliday, M.A.K., Hasan, R.: Cohesion in English. Longman, London (1976)
15. Harabagiu, S.M., Bunescu, R.C., Maiorano, S.J.: Text and knowledge mining for coreference resolution. In: Proceedings of the second meeting of the North American Chapter of the Association for Computational Linguistics on Language Technologies, pp. 1–8. Association for Computational Linguistics (2001)
16. Hobbs, J.: Resolving pronoun references. In: Readings in Natural Language Processing, pp. 339–352. Morgan Kaufmann Publishers Inc. (1986)
17. Ciaramita, M., Houlsby, N.: A scalable gibbs sampler for probabilistic entity linking. In: de Rijke, M., Kenter, T., de Vries, A.P., Zhai, C.X., de Jong, F., Radinsky, K., Hofmann, K. (eds.) ECIR 2014. LNCS, vol. 8416, pp. 335–346. Springer, Heidelberg (2014)
18. Lappin, S., Leass, H.J.: An algorithm for pronominal anaphora resolution. Computational Linguistics **20**(4), 535–561 (1994)
19. Lee, H., Peirsman, Y., Chang, A., Chambers, N., Surdeanu, M., Jurafsky, D.: Stanford's multi-pass sieve coreference resolution system at the conll-2011 shared task. In: Proceedings of the Fifteenth Conference on Computational Natural Language Learning: Shared Task, pp. 28–34. Association for Computational Linguistics (2011)
20. Luo, X.: On coreference resolution performance metrics. In: Proceedings of the conference on Human Language Technology and Empirical Methods in Natural Language Processing, pp. 25–32. Association for Computational Linguistics (2005)
21. Meij, E., Balog, K., Odijk, D.: Entity linking and retrieval. In: Proceedings of the 36th International ACM SIGIR Conference on Research and Development in Information Retrieval, SIGIR 2013, pp. 1127–1127. ACM, New York (2013)
22. Mikolov, T., Sutskever, I., Chen, K., Corrado, G.S., Dean, J.: Distributed representations of words and phrases and their compositionality. In: Advances in Neural Information Processing Systems, pp. 3111–3119 (2013)
23. Mitkov, R.: Robust pronoun resolution with limited knowledge. In: Proceedings of the 36th Annual Meeting of the Association for Computational Linguistics and 17th International Conference on Computational Linguistics, vol. 2, pp. 869–875. Association for Computational Linguistics (1998)
24. Nakashole, N., Tylenda, T., Weikum, G.: Fine-grained semantic typing of emerging entities. In: ACL (1), pp. 1488–1497 (2013)
25. Ng, V.: Machine learning for coreference resolution: Recent successes and future challenges. Technical report, Cornell University (2003)
26. Ng, V.: Semantic class induction and coreference resolution. In: AcL, pp. 536–543 (2007)
27. Ng, V.: Supervised noun phrase coreference research: the first fifteen years. In: Proceedings of the 48th annual meeting of the association for Computational Linguistics, pp. 1396–1411. Association for Computational Linguistics (2010)

28. Paulheim, H., Bizer, C.: Improving the Quality of Linked Data Using Statistical Distributions. Int. J. Semantic Web Inf. Syst. **10**(2), 63–86 (2014)
29. Ponzetto, S.P., Strube, M.: Exploiting semantic role labeling, wordnet and wikipedia for coreference resolution. In: Proceedings of the main conference on Human Language Technology Conference of the North American Chapter of the Association of Computational Linguistics, pp. 192–199. Association for Computational Linguistics (2006)
30. Pradhan, S., Moschitti, A., Xue, N., Uryupina, O., Zhang, Y.: Conll-2012 shared task: modeling multilingual unrestricted coreference in ontonotes. In: Joint Conference on EMNLP and CoNLL - Shared Task, CoNLL 2012, Stroudsburg, PA, USA, pp. 1–40. Association for Computational Linguistics (2012)
31. Rand, W.M.: Objective criteria for the evaluation of clustering methods. Journal of the American Statistical Association **66**(336), 846–850 (1971)
32. Recasens, M., Hovy, E.: Blanc: Implementing the rand index for coreference evaluation. Nat. Lang. Eng. **17**(4), 485–510 (2011)
33. Rizzo, G., Troncy, R.: NERD : a framework for evaluating named entity recognition tools in the web of data. In: Proceedings of the 11th Interational Semantic Web Conference ISWC 2011, pp. 1–4 (2011)
34. Sidner, C.: Focusing in the comprehension of definite anaphora. In: Readings in Natural Language Processing, pp. 363–394. Morgan Kaufmann Publishers Inc. (1986)
35. Sidner, C.L.: Towards a computational theory of definite anaphora comprehension in english discourse. Technical report, DTIC Document (1979)
36. Soon, W.M., Ng, H.T., Lim, D.C.Y.: A machine learning approach to coreference resolution of noun phrases. Computational Linguistics **27**(4), 521–544 (2001)
37. Strube, M., Ponzetto, S.P.: Wikirelate! computing semantic relatedness using wikipedia. In: AAAI, vol. 6, pp. 1419–1424 (2006)
38. Tonon, A., Catasta, M., Demartini, G., Cudré-Mauroux, P., Aberer, K.: *TRank*: ranking entity types using the web of data. In: Alani, H., et al. (eds.) ISWC 2013, Part I. LNCS, vol. 8218, pp. 640–656. Springer, Heidelberg (2013)
39. Tylenda, T., Sozio, M., Weikum, G.: Einstein: physicist or vegetarian? summarizing semantic type graphs for knowledge discovery. In: Proceedings of the 20th International Conference Companion on World Wide Web, WWW 2011, pp. 273–276. ACM, New York (2011)
40. Uryupina, O., Poesio, M., Giuliano, C., Tymoshenko, K.: Disambiguation and filtering methods in using web knowledge for coreference resolution. In: FLAIRS Conference, pp. 317–322 (2011)
41. Van Deemter, K., Kibble, R.: On coreferring: Coreference in muc and related annotation schemes. Computational Linguistics **26**(4), 629–637 (2000)

Improving Entity Retrieval on Structured Data

Besnik Fetahu$^{(\boxtimes)}$, Ujwal Gadiraju, and Stefan Dietze

L3S Research Center, Leibniz Universität Hannover, Hannover, Germany
{fetahu,gadiraju,dietze}@L3S.de

Abstract. The increasing amount of data on the Web, in particular of Linked Data, has led to a diverse landscape of datasets, which make entity retrieval a challenging task. Explicit cross-dataset links, for instance to indicate co-references or related entities can significantly improve entity retrieval. However, only a small fraction of entities are interlinked through explicit statements. In this paper, we propose a two-fold entity retrieval approach. In a first, offline preprocessing step, we cluster entities based on the *x–means* and *spectral* clustering algorithms. In the second step, we propose an optimized retrieval model which takes advantage of our precomputed clusters. For a given set of entities retrieved by the BM25F retrieval approach and a given user query, we further expand the result set with relevant entities by considering features of the queries, entities and the precomputed clusters. Finally, we re-rank the expanded result set with respect to the relevance to the query. We perform a thorough experimental evaluation on the Billions Triple Challenge (BTC12) dataset. The proposed approach shows significant improvements compared to the baseline and state of the art approaches.

1 Introduction

The emergence of the Web of Data, particularly supported through W3C standards such as RDF and the Linked Data principles [2], has led to a wide range of semi-structured RDF data being available on the Web. Data is spread across datasets, complemented through a growing amount of entities as part of structured annotations of Web documents, using RDFa or Microformats. Recent studies have shown that approximately 26% of pages already contain structured annotations [19].

Web data forms a highly heterogeneous knowledge-graph spanning an estimated 100 billion triples [17], with a wide variety of languages, schemas, domains and topics [7]. Even though a large number of entities and concepts are highly overlapping, that is they represent the same or related concepts, explicit links are still limited and often concentrated within large established knowledge graphs, like DBpedia [1].

The entity-centric nature of the Web of data has led to a shift towards tasks related to entity and object retrieval [3,21] or entity-driven text summarization [6]. Major search engine providers such as Google and Yahoo! already exploit

© Springer International Publishing Switzerland 2015
M. Arenas et al. (Eds.): ISWC 2015, Part I, LNCS 9366, pp. 474–491, 2015.
DOI: 10.1007/978-3-319-25007-6_28

such data to facilitate semantic search using knowledge graphs, or as part of similar efforts such as the *EntityCube-Renlifang* project at Microsoft Research [14]. In such scenarios, data is aggregated from a range of sources calling for efficient means to search and retrieve entities in large data graphs. Specifically, *entity retrieval* (also known as Ad-Hoc Object retrieval) [17,21] aims at retrieving relevant entities given a user query. The result is a ranked list of entities [3]. By simply applying standard keyword search algorithms, like the BM25F, promising results can be achieved. A common practice is to construct indexes over the textual descriptions (*literals*) of entities.

In most cases, queries are entity centric. However, there are a large number of queries that are also topic-based, e.g. 'U.S. Presidents'. Therefore, approaches like [21] have proposed retrieval techniques that make use of the explicit links between entities in the WoD for results or query expansion. For instance, following owl:sameAs or rdfs:seeAlso predicates from dbp:Barack_Obama, one can retrieve co-references or highly related entities. However, considering the size of the WoD such statements are very sparse (see Figure 1a).

In this work, we propose a method for improving entity retrieval results in two aspects. We improve the task by *expanding* and *re-ranking* the result set from a baseline retrieval model (BM25F). Sparsity of explicit links is addressed through clustering of entities based on their similarity, using a combination of lexical and structural features. Consequently, we expand the result set with additional entities from the *cluster space* (clusters with which the baseline entities are associated), retrieved from the baseline.

For the expanded result set, there is a need for re-ranking. The re-ranking considers the similarity of entities to the user query, and their relevance likelihood based on the corresponding entity type, defined as *query type affinity*. We empirically model the query type affinity between the entity type in a query (e.g. 'Barack Obama' isA Person) and the entity types in the result set (see Section 3.2).

In terms of *scalability* and *efficiency*, the clustering process is carried out offline, where we *bucket* entities of particular types together before clustering. This improves the efficiency by reducing the run-time of the clustering algorithms (Section 4.2 and 7.3). The entity retrieval, expansion and re-ranking on the other hand are performed online and the computational overhead is negligible (Section 5 and 7.3).

Our experimental evaluation is carried out on the BTC12 dataset [19], and using the SemSearch[1] query dataset. The individual steps in our approach are evaluated through a reliable crowdsourced evaluation approach. The results show that the proposed approach outperforms existing basslines for the entity retrieval task.

The main contributions of our work are as follows: (a) an entity retrieval model combining keyword search and entity clustering, and (b) an entity ranking model considering the query type affinity w.r.t the set of relevant entity types.

---

[1] http://km.aifb.kit.edu/ws/semsearch10/

2   Related Work

A large portion of queries issued in Web search engines target entities or contain semantic resources (such as types, relations and attributes) [17] as a primary intent. Consequently, the identification of entity-centric queries has become of particular concern for commercial search engines serving as a means to narrow the search space and to provide contextual query results [12]. Thus, the traditional task of Ad-hoc Document Retrieval (ADR) [11] is moving towards an entity retrieval task [17]. Hence, instead of top–k document retrieval that match a keyword query, the task and therefore the results are increasingly becoming entity-centric.

Following this direction, Tonon et al. [21] proposed a hybrid approach based on query expansion and relevance feedback techniques on top of the BM25 ranking function to build an entity retrieval framework. In contrast to this work, we use the state-of-the-art BM25F [5,20] to assign varying degrees of importance to different parts of a document. Further, through an offline pre-processing step we are able to infer links between similar entities for the retrieval process. This is particularly important when considering datasets that have less links between entities, a significant feature of the work by Tonon et al [21]. Another advantage of adopting BM25F is penalising documents/entities, consisting of long textual literals, in the final ranking [10]. Sindice [15] is another approach focusing on indexing RDF documents. It supports data discovery and integration by taking advantage of DBpedia entities as a source to actively index resources. The process performed by Sindice plays a key role in centralising disparate data sources on the Web. The adoption of entities and foremost entity types (topics) is also supported by [3] in the recommendation of entities in Web search. Our approach can benefit Sindice by indexing documents following a topic-based fashion.

Zhiltsov and Agichtein [23] propose a learning to rank approach, where they model the relations between entities through a various set of features, such as language models and other query related features (e.g query length). Finally, through tensor matrix factorisation they find latent similarities between entities, later used in their learning to rank model. One major disadvantage of this approach is that it is supervised, hence, unlikely to perform reasonably well on ad-hoc entity search tasks.

3   Approach and Overview

In this section, we motivate and define our work in the context of the addressed challenge, and provide an overview of our approach.

3.1   Preliminaries

The *entity retrieval (ER) task*, also known as ad-hoc object retrieval, is concerned with retrieving a top–k ranked set of entities from dataset for a given a user query q. User queries are typically entity centric. A *dataset* in our case is a set of triples $\langle s, p, o \rangle$, where s is the *subject* (the URI of an entity), p is the *predicate*, and o is the *object* (a URI or a literal). An *entity* profile of e is the set of triples sharing the same subject URI s. The *type* of an entity is determined by the object of the triple $t_e = \langle s, \text{rdf:type}, o \rangle$. Additionally, we define the *query type* t_q, corresponding to the entity type in q, e.g. *'Barack Obama'*, hence t_q hasType Person.

3.2 Motivation: Result Set Expansion and Query Affinity in Entity Retrieval

Recent studies [21] have shown that *explicit similarity statements*, which indicate some form of similarity or equivalence between entities, for instance through predicates such as owl:sameAs, are useful for improving entity retrieval results as retrieved through approaches like BM25F, i.e. improving significantly on standard precision/recall metrics. However, such explicit similarity statements usually are sparse and often focused towards a few well established datasets like DBpedia, Freebase etc. One main reason is that these datasets represent known, and well structured graphs, which show a comparably high proportion of such dedicated similarity statements, in turn linking similar entities within and beyond their original namespace.

In Figure 1a we show the total amount of explicit similarity statements (on the x–axis) that interlink entities in the BTC12 dataset. Referring to [21], here we specifically consider triples of the form $\langle e, p, e' \rangle$ where the predicate $p \in \{\text{owl:sameAs}, \text{skos:related}, \text{dbp:wikiPageExternalLink},$ $\text{dbp:wikiPageDisambiguates}, \text{dbp:synonym}\}$. These are plotted against the total number of *object properties* (y–axis), where each point in the plot represents a graph in the BTC12 collection. From the figure, it is obvious that the number of explicit similarity statements is very sparse, considering the size of the dataset.

Nonetheless, missing links between entities can be partially remedied by computing their pair-wise similarity, thereby complementing statements like owl:sameAs or skos:related. Given the semi-structured nature of RDF data, graph-based and lexical features can be exploited for similarity computation. Particularly, lexical features derived from literals provided by predicates such as *rdfs:label* or *rdfs:description* are prevalent in LOD. Our analysis on the BTC12 dataset reveals that a large portion of entities (around 90%) have an average literal length of 50 characters.

Furthermore, while the query type usually is not considered in state of the art ER methods, we investigated its correlation with the corresponding entity types from the query result set. We refer to a ground truth[2] using the BTC10 dataset. We focus only on relevant entities for q. We analyze the *query type affinity* of the result sets by assessing the likelihood of an entity in the results to be of the same type as the query type. Figure 1b shows the query type affinity. On the x-axis we show the query type, whereas on the y-axis the corresponding relevant

---

[2] http://km.aifb.uni-karlsruhe.de/ws/semsearch10/Files/assess

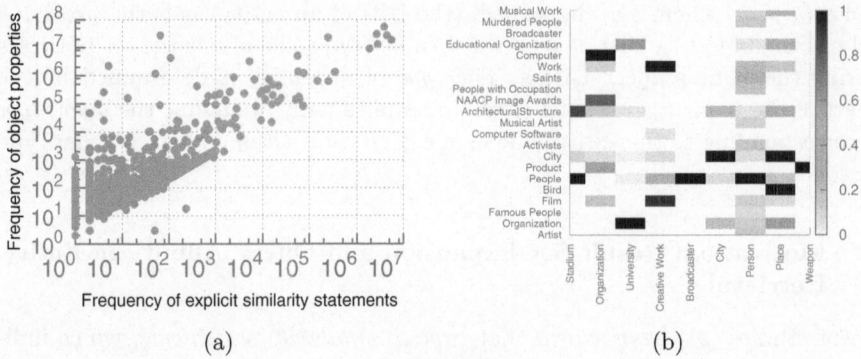

(a)   (b)

Fig. 1. (a) Number of explicit similarity statements in contrast to the frequency of object property statements overall, shown for all data graphs. (b) Query type affinity shows the query type and the corresponding entity types from the retrieved and relevant entities.

entity types are shown. Figure 1b shows that most queries have high affinity with a specific entity type, with the difference being the query type Person, where relevant entities have a wider range of types.

Our work exploits such *query type affinity* to improve the ranking of entities for a query q (see Section 5). Based on these observations, we argue that (a) *entity clustering* can remedy the lack of existing linking statements and (b) entity *re-ranking* considering the *query type affinity* are likely to improve the entity retrieval task.

3.3   Approach Overview

In this work we propose a novel approach for the *entity retrieval* task which builds on the observations described earlier. Figure 2 shows an overview of the proposed approach. The individual steps are outlined below and described in detail in Section 4 and 5. We distinguish between two main steps: (I) *offline pre-processing*, including step I.a and I.b in the following overview, and (II) *online entity retrieval*, covered by steps II.a to II.c.

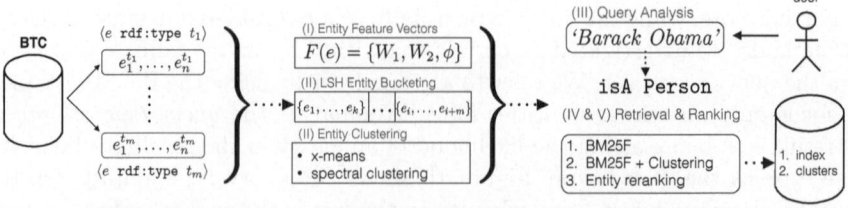

Fig. 2. Overview of the *entity retrieval* approach.

I.a Entity Feature Vectors: We construct the entity feature vector as follows: $F(e) = \{\mathbf{W}_1(e), \mathbf{W}_2(e), \phi\}$, where $\mathbf{W}_1(e)$ and $\mathbf{W}_2(e)$ represent the *unigrams* and *bigrams* extracted from literals of e, and ϕ represents the structural features.

I.b Entity Bucketing & Clustering: is used to compute implicit relationships between entities emerging from their feature vectors. For the sake of efficiency, before we proceed with entity clustering, we exploit the locality-sensitive hashing (LSH) algorithm for bucketing.

II.a Query Analysis: As part of the retrieval task, we initially analyse the given user queries q. From the query terms, which typically represent named entities, we determine the type of the named entity, e.g. 'Location' in order to support the query type affinity-based reranking at a later stage.

II.b Entity Retrieval: In the retrieval process, we rely on a combination of standard IR approaches, like BM25F and further expand the result set with entities showing a high similarity according to the computed clusters.

II.c Entity Ranking. In the final step, we rank the expanded entity result set for q, taking into account similarity to the query and the modelled query type affinity.

4   Data Pre-processing and Entity Clustering

In this section, we describe the offline pre-processing to cluster entities and remedy the sparsity of explicit entity links.

4.1   Entity Feature Vectors

Entity similarity is measured based on a set of structural and lexical features, denoted by the *entity feature vector* $F(e)$. The features for clustering are described below.

Lexical Features: We consider a weighted set of *unigrams* and *bigrams* for an entity e, by extracting all textual literals used to describe e denoted as $\mathbf{W}_1(e)$ and $\mathbf{W}_2(e)$. The weights are computed using the standard *tf–idf* metric. Lexical features represent core features when considering the entity retrieval task, more so for the clustering process. A high lexical similarity between an entity pair is a good indicator for expanding the result set from the corresponding cluster space.

Structural Features: The feature set $\phi(e)$ considers the set of all object properties that describe e. The range of values for the structural features is $\phi(o, e) \rightarrow [0, 1]$, i.e., to indicate if a object value is present in e. **Feature Space:** To reduce the feature space, we filter out items from the lexical and structural features that occur with low frequency across entities and presumably, have a very low impact on the clustering process due to their scanty occurrence.

4.2   Entity Bucketing and Clustering

Entity Bucketing. In this step we *bucket* entities of a given *entity type* by computing their *MinHash* signature, which is used thereafter by the LSH algorithm [18]. This step is necessary as the number of entities is very large. In this way we reduce the number of pair-wise comparisons for the entity clustering, and limit it to only the set of entities within a bucket. Depending on the *clustering algorithm*, the impact of bucketing on the clustering scalability varies. Since the LSH algorithm itself has linear complexity, bucketing entities presents a scalable approach considering the size of datasets in our experimental evaluation. A detailed analysis is presented in Section 7.

Entity Clustering. Based on the computed feature vectors, we perform entity clustering for the individual entity types and the computed LSH buckets. Taking into account scalability aspects of such a clustering process we consider mainly two clustering approaches: (i) *X–means* and (ii) *Spectral Clustering*. In both approaches we use Euclidean distance as the similarity metric. The dimensions of the Euclidean distance are the feature items in $F(\cdot)$. The similarity metric is formally defined in Equation 1.

$$d(e, e') = \sqrt{\sum \left(\mathbf{F}(e) - \mathbf{F}(e') \right)^2} \tag{1}$$

where the sum aggregates over the union of feature items from $\mathbf{F}(e), \mathbf{F}(e')$. The outcome of this process is a set of clusters $\mathbf{C} = \{C_1, \ldots, C_n\}$. The clustering process represents a core part of our approach from which we expand the entity results set for a given query, beyond the entities that are retrieved by a baseline as a starting point. The way the clusters are computed has an impact on the entity retrieval task, thus we present a thorough evaluation of cluster configurations in Section 7.1.

X–means. To cluster entities bucketed together through the LSH algorithm and of specific entity types, we adopt an extended version of *k-means* clustering, presented by Pelleg et al. which estimates the number of clusters efficiently [16]. *X–means* overcomes two major drawbacks of the standard *k-means* clustering algorithm; (i) computational scalability, and (ii) the requirement to provide the number of clusters k beforehand. It extends the *k–means* algorithm, such that a user only specifies a range $[K_{min}, K_{max}]$ in which the number of clusters, K, may reasonably lie in. The bounds for K in our case are set to $[2, 50]$ clusters.

Spectral Clustering. In order to proceed with the *spectral clustering* process, we first construct the adjacency matrix $\mathbf{A}$. The adjacency matrix corresponds to the similarity between entity pairs $d(e, e')$ of a given entity type and bucket. Next, from $\mathbf{A}$ we compute the unnormalised graph Laplacian [22] as defined in Equation 2:

$$\mathbf{L} = diag(\mathbf{A}) - \mathbf{A} \tag{2}$$

where, $diag(\mathbf{A})$ corresponds to the diagonal matrix, i.e., $diag(\mathbf{A})_{i,i} = \mathbf{A}_{i,j}$ for $i = j$.

From matrix **L** we are particularly interested in specific properties, which we use for *clustering* and which are extracted from the *eigenvectors* and *eigenvalues* by performing a singular value decomposition on **L**. The eigenvectors correspond to a square matrix $n \times n$, where each row represents the projected entity into a n-dimensional space. Eigenvectors are later used to cluster entities using standard k–*means* algorithm.

However, an important aspect that has impact on the clustering accuracy, is the number of dimensions considered for the k–*means* and the k itself. We adopt a heuristic proposed in [22]. The number of dimensions that are used in the clustering step corresponds to the first spike in the eigenvalue distribution. In addition, this heuristic is also used to determine the number k for the clustering step.

5   Entity Retrieval - Expansion and Reranking

In this section, we describe the online process of entity retrieval, including the process of *expansion* and *re-ranking* of the query result set.

5.1   Query-Biased Results Expansion

Having obtained an initial result set $E_b = \{e_1, \ldots, e_k\}$ through a state of the art ER method (BM25f), the next step deals with expanding the result set for a given user query. From entities in E_b, we extract their corresponding set of clusters **C** as computed in the pre-processing stage. The result set is expanded with entities belonging to the clusters in **C**. We denote the entities extracted from the clusters with E_c.

There are several precautions that need to be taken into account in this step. We define two threshold parameters for expanding the result set. The first parameter, *cluster size*, defines a threshold with respect to the number of entities belonging to a cluster. If the number is above a specific threshold, we do not take into account entities from that cluster. The underlying rationale is that clusters with a large number of entities tend to be generic and less homogeneous, i.e. they tend to be a weak indicator of similarity. The second parameter deals with the *number of entities* with which we expand the result set for a given entity cluster. The entities are considered based on their distance to the entity e_b. We experimentally validate the two parameters in Section 7.

The *fit* of expanded entities $e_c \in E_c$ concerns their similarity to query q and the similarity to e_b, which serves as the starting point for the expansion of e_c. We measure the *query-biased* entity similarity in Equation 3, where the first component of the equation measures the *string* distance of e_c to q, that is $\varphi(q, e_c)$. Furthermore, this is done relative to entity e_b, such that if the e_b is more similar to q, $\varphi(q, e_b) < \varphi(q, e_c)$ the similarity score will be increased, hence, the expanded entity e_c will be penalized later on in the ranking (note that we measure distance, therefore, the lower the $sim(q, e)$ score the more similar an entity is to q).

The second component represents the actual distance score $d(e_b, e_c)$.

$$sim(q, e_c) = \lambda \frac{\varphi(q, e_c)}{\varphi(q, e_b)} + (1 - \lambda)d(e_b, e_c) \tag{3}$$

We set the parameter $\lambda = 0.5$, such that entities are scored equally with respect to their match to query q and the distance between entities, based on our baseline approach. The main outcome of this step is to identify possibly relevant entities that have been missed by the scoring function of BM25F. Such entities could be suggested as relevant from the extensive clustering approaches that consider the structural and lexical similarity.

5.2   Query Analysis for Re-ranking

Following the motivation example in Figure 1b, an important factor on the re-ranking of the result set is the *query type affinity*. It models the relevance likelihood of a given entity type t_e for a specific query type t_q. We give priority to entities that are most likely to be relevant to the the given query type t_q and are least likely to be relevant for other query types t'_q. The probability distribution is modeled empirically based on a previous dataset, BTC10. The score γ, we assign to any entity coming from the expanded result set is computed as in Equation 4.

$$\gamma(t_e, t_q) = \frac{p(t_e|t_q)}{\sum\limits_{t'_q \neq t_q} \left(1 - p(t_e|t'_q)\right)} \tag{4}$$

An additional factor we use in the re-ranking process is the *context score*. To better understand the query intent, we decompose a query q into its *named entities* and additional *contextual terms*. An example is the query $q = \{\text{'harry potter movie'}\}$ from our query set, in which case the contextual terms would be *'movie'* and the named entity *'Harry Potter'* respectively. In case of ambiguous queries, the contextual terms can further help to determine the query intent. The *context score* (see Equation 5) indicates the relevance of entity e to the contextual terms Cx of the query q. For entities with a high number of textual literals, we focus on the main literals like *labels, name* etc.

$$context(q, e) = \frac{1}{|Cx|} \sum_{c_x \in Cx} \mathbb{1}_{e \text{ has } c_x} \tag{5}$$

5.3   Top–k Ranking Model

The final step in our entity retrieval approach, re-ranks the expanded entity result set for a query q. The result set is the union of entities $\mathbf{E} = \mathbf{E}_b \cup \mathbf{E}_c$. In the case of entities retrieved through the baseline approach $e \in \mathbf{E}_b$, we simply re-use the original score, but normalize the values between $[0, 1]$. For entities from E_c we normalize the similarity score relative to the rank of entity e_b (the position of e_b in the result set) which was used to suggest e_c. This boosts entities which are the result of expanding top-ranked entities.

$$rank\_score(e) = \begin{cases} \frac{sim(q,e)}{rank(e_b)} & \text{if } e \in E_c \\ bm25f(q, e) & \text{otherwise} \end{cases} \tag{6}$$

The final ranking score $\alpha(e, t_q)$, for entity e and query type t_q assigns higher rank score in case the entity has high similarity with q and its type has high relevance likelihood of being relevant for query type t_q. Finally, depending on the query set, in case q contains contextual terms we can add $context(q, e)$ by controlling the weight of λ (in this case $\lambda = 0.5$).

$$\alpha(e, t_q) = \lambda\,(rank\_score(e) * \gamma(t_e, t_q)) + (1 - \lambda) * context(q, e) \qquad (7)$$

The score α is computed for all entities in **E**. In this way based on observations of similar cases in previous datasets, like the BTC10 we are able to rank higher entities of certain types for specific queries.

6 Experimental Setup

Here we describe our experimental setup, specifically the datasets, baselines and the ground truth. The setup and evaluation data are available for download[3].

6.1 Evaluation Data

Dataset. In our experimental setup we use the BTC12 dataset [9]. It represents one of the largest periodic crawls of Linked Data, also containing well-known knowledge bases like Freebase and DBpedia. The overall statistics of the data are: (i) 1.4 billion triples, (ii) 107,967 graphs, (iii) 3,321 entity types, and (iv) 454 million entities.

Entity Clusters. The statistics for the generated clusters are as follows: the average number of entities fed into the *LSH* bucketing algorithm is 77,485, whereas the average number of entities fed into *x–means* and *spectral* is 400. The number of generated entity buckets by LSH is 20,2009, while the number of clusters for *x–means* and *spectral* is 13 and 38, with an average of 10 and 20 entities per cluster respectively.

Query Dataset. To evaluate our retrieval approach we use the *SemSearch*[4] query set from 2010 with 92 queries. The SemSearch query set is a standard collection for evaluating entity retrieval tasks.

6.2 Baseline and State of the Art

Baseline. We distinguish between two cases for the original BM25F baseline: (i) $\mathbf{B_t}$ and (ii) $\mathbf{B_b}$. In the first case, we use the *title* or *label* of an entity as a query field, whereas in the second case we use the full *body* of an entity (consisting of all textual literals). The scoring of the fields is performed similar as in [5].

State of the Art. We consider the approach proposed in [21] as the state-of-the-art. Similar to their experimental setup, we analyze two cases: (i) $\mathbf{S1}$ and (ii)

---

[3] http://l3s.de/~fetahu/iswc2015/

[4] http://km.aifb.kit.edu/ws/semsearch10/

S2. S1 expands the entity set from the baseline approach with directly connected entities, and **S2** expands with entities up to the second hop. For further details we refer the reader to [21]. In our experiments, we found that the **S2** did not result in any significant change in performance when compared to **S1**, and we therefore do not report further on **S2**.

Our Approaches. We analyze two entity retrieval techniques from our approach. The first is based on the *x–means* clustering approach, which we denote by **XM**. The second technique is based on *spectral* clustering and is denoted by **SP**. In both cases, we only expand the result set with entities coming from clusters with a total of ten entities associated with a cluster (see Section 5.1), and finally add only the most relevant entity based on the $sim(q, e_c)$ score.

BTC Indexes. For the baseline, we generate a Lucene index, where we index entity profiles on two fields `title` and `body` (consisting of all the textual literals of an entity). The second index is an RDF index over the BTC dataset with support for SPARQL queries, for which we use the RDF3X tool [13]. The first index is used for the baseline approach, while the second for the state of the art approach.

6.3   Ground Truth for Evaluation of Entity Retrieval

For each query in the *SemSearch2010* query set, we first establish the ground truth through crowdsourcing. Crowdsourced evaluation campaigns for the task of ad-hoc object retrieval have been shown to be reliable [4,8]. For each of the 92 queries, we pool the top 50 entities retrieved by the various methods, resulting in the top-k pooled entities corresponding to the query. By doing so we generate 4,600 query-entity pairs.

We deploy atomic tasks in order to acquire relevance labels from the crowd for each query-entity pair. We follow the key prescriptions for task design and deployment that emerged from the work of Blanco et al. [4] to build a ground truth. Workers are asked to assess the relevance of each retrieved entity to the corresponding query on a 5-point Likert-type scale[5].

We collect 5 judgements from different workers for each pair to ensure reliable relevance assessments and discernible agreement between workers. This results in a total of 23,000 judgements. The final relevance of an entity is considered to be the aggregated relevance score over the 5 judgements. We assess and compare the performance of the different methods by relying on the ground truth thus generated (see Section 7).

6.4   Evaluation Metrics

Evaluation metrics assess the clustering accuracy and the retrieval performance.

Cluster Accuracy. As an initial evaluation, we assess the quality of our clusters. From a set of entities belonging to the same cluster, the accuracy is measured

---

[5] *1:Not Relevant, 2:Slightly Relevant, 3:Moderately Relevant, 4:Fairly Relevant and 5:Highly Relevant.*

as the ratio of entities that *belong together* over the total number of entities in a cluster, where assessments are obtained through crowdsourcing (see Section 7).

Precision. P@k measures the precision at rank k, in our case $k = \{1, \ldots, 10\}$. It is measured as the ratio of retrieved and relevant entities up to rank k over the total number of entities retrieved up to rank k.

Recall. R@k is measured as the ratio of retrieved and relevant entities up to rank k over the total number of relevant entities up to rank k. The total number of relevant entities for a query is determined by the relevance judgements on a large pool of entities.

Mean Average Precision. MAP provides an overall precision of a retrieval approach across all considered ranks.

Normalized Discounted Cumulative Gain. It takes into account the ranking of entities generated using one of the retrieval approaches and compares it against the ideal ranking in the *ground truth*.

$$nDCG@k = \frac{DCG@k}{iDCG@k} \quad DCG@k = rel_1 + \sum_{i=2}^{k} \frac{rel_i}{log_2 i}$$

where $DCG@k$ represents the discounted cumulative gain at rank k, and $iDCG@k$ is the ideal $DCG@k$ computed from the *ground truth*.

7   Evaluation and Discussion

In this section we report evaluation results of the two main steps in our approach. We first evaluate the quality of the pre-processing step, i.e., the clustering results for the *x–means* and *spectral* clustering algorithms. Next, we present the findings from our rigorous evaluation of the entity retrieval task.

7.1   Cluster Accuracy Evaluation

Considering the large number of clusters that are produced in the pre-processing step for a given *type* and *bucket*, evaluating the accuracy and quality of all clusters is infeasible. We randomly select 10 entity types and 10 buckets, resulting in 100 clusters for evaluation, where for each cluster we randomly select a maximum of 10 entities.

To evaluate the *cluster accuracy*, we deploy atomic microtasks modeled such that a worker is presented with sets of 10 entities belonging to a cluster, along with a description of the entity in the form of the entity profile. The task of the worker is to pick the odd entities out (if any). We gather 5 judgments from different workers for each cluster. By enforcing restrictions available on the Crowd-Flower platform, and following state of the art task design recommendations, we ensure that we receive judgments from the best workers (workers with high reputation as indicated by CrowdFlower).

Figure 3b presents our findings for the evaluation of the clustering process. We note that for *x–means* and *spectral* clustering approaches, nearly 35% and 38% of the clusters are judged to be perfect respectively (i.e., the entities within the cluster were all found to belong together). 39% of the clusters corresponding to *spectral* clustering and 40% of the clusters corresponding to *x-means*, have an accuracy of 80%. Considering its multidimensional representation of the entities, *spectral* clustering has higher accuracy and it does not have clusters below 70% accuracy. The lowest accuracy of 70% for *spectral* clustering implies that in each cluster there were only 3 entities that did not belong to the cluster. The implications of an accurate clustering process become clearer in the next section, where we assess the accuracy of finding relevant entities in the generated entity clusters.

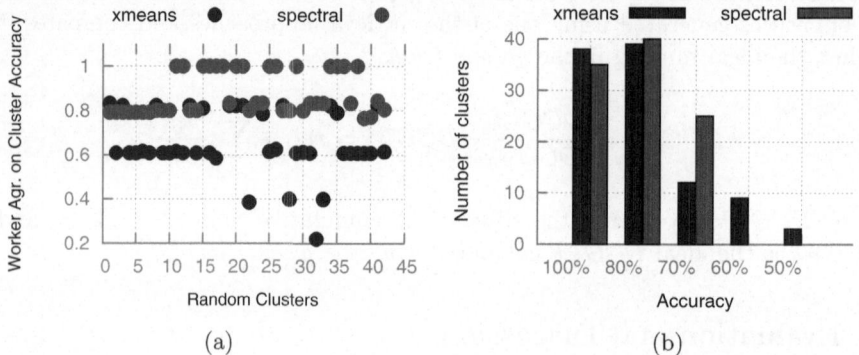

Fig. 3. (a) Worker agreement on cluster accuracy for *spectral* and *x–means* clustering. (b) Cluster accuracy for the *spectral* and *x–means* clustering approaches.

Figure 3a presents the pairwise agreement between workers on the quality of each cluster. In case of the *spectral* clustering, we observe a high inter-worker agreement of 0.75 as per Krippendorf's Alpha. We observe a moderate inter-worker agreement of 0.6 as per Krippendorf's Alpha on the clusters resulting from *x–means*.

7.2 Entity Retrieval Evaluation

Figure 4a presents a detailed comparison between the $P@k$ for the different methods. The proposed approaches outperform the baseline and state of the art at all ranks. The precision is highest at $P@1 = 0.6$ whereas for the later ranks it stabilizes at 0.4. In contrast to our approach, the performance of the baseline and the state of the art is more uniform, and is around $P@k = 0.25$. The best overall performing approach is the retrieval approach based on spectral clustering SP. Table 1 shows the details about the performance of the respective approaches as measured for our evaluation metrics.

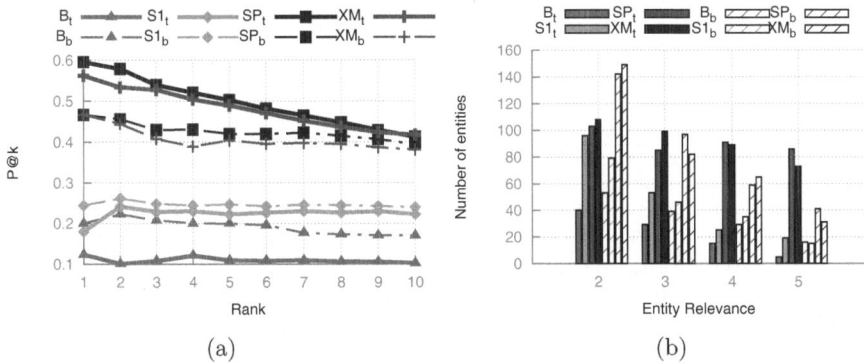

Fig. 4. (a) P@k for the different entity retrieval approaches under comparison. (b) The relevant entity frequency based on their graded relevance (from *2-Slightly Relevant* to *5-Highly Relevant*) for the different methods.

An interesting observation is that for our approaches the best performance is achieved when querying for the field *title*. In the case of the baseline, the best performance is achieved when querying for the field *body* (B_b) while the same is inconclusive in case of the state-of-the-art methods ($S1_t$ and $S1_b$). We achieve a significantly higher retrieval performance when using the title field. This can be explained by the fact that entities that match a query on their *title* field when compared to those that match a query on their *body* field, have a higher likelihood of being an exact match.

The high gain in performance through our methods (SP and XM) stems mainly from the two steps in our approach. The first step expands the result set with relevant entities as shown in Figure 4b. The figure shows the number of relevant entities corresponding to the different grading scales as described in Section 7.1. In all cases we note that our methods find more relevant entities. The second step which re-ranks the expanded result set helps in reducing the number of *'non-relevant'* entities. We find that $S1_t$ has a 14% decrease of non-relevant entities, whereas SP_t and XM_t depict a 35% decrease, respectively. In second case where we query the *body* field, the number of *'non-relevant'* entities for $S1_b$ decreases by about 13%, while SP_b and XM_b depict a 24% decrease.

We additionally analyze the performance of the entity retrieval approaches through the $NDCG@k$ metric. Figure 5 shows the NDCG scores. Similar to our findings for $P@k$ presented in Table 1, our approaches perform best for the query field *title* and significantly outperform the approaches under comparison.

Next, we present observations concerning the different *query types* and the entity result set expansion (see Section 5.1) parameters. In Figure 6a we show the improvement we gain in terms of MAP for the different *query types*. We observe that there is quite a variance for the different query types, however, in nearly all cases, the biggest improvement is achieved through the SP approach. Interestingly for the query type *'Creative Work'* the state of the art is nearly as good as the XM approach, whereas in the case of *'Weapon'* the baseline

Table 1. Performance of the different entity retrieval approaches. In all cases our approaches are significantly better in terms of P/R ($p < 0.05$ measured for *t-test*) compared to *baseline* and *state of the art*. There is no significant difference between SP and XM approaches.

	B_t	B_b	$S1_t$	$S1_b$	SP_t	SP_b	XM_t	XM_b
P@10	0.103	0.170	0.222	0.240	0.413	0.394	**0.417**	0.381
R@10	0.052	0.089	0.112	0.118	0.206	**0.219**	0.216	0.215
MAP	0.110	0.191	0.224	0.246	**0.497**	0.426	0.482	0.407
$Avg(R)$	0.031	0.058	0.063	0.074	0.132	**0.133**	0.131	0.130

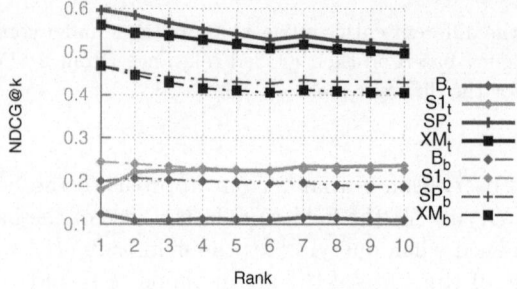

Fig. 5. NDCG@k for $B1$, $S1$ and SP, XM

performs best. One possible explanation for this is that in the case of *'Creative Work'* the explicit entity similarity statements are abundant.

Addressing the case of optimizing our retrieval approaches, SP and XM, we experimentally show the impact that the expansion of the result set has on the measured performance metrics. Here, we show the impact on the *average NDCG* score. Figure 6b shows the performance at average NDCG for the varying *cluster size* and *number of entities* added (result set expansion) for every entity in E_b. The best performance is achieved for a rather smaller *cluster size* ranging between 5 and 10 entities per cluster. Regarding the number of entities with which the result set is expanded for every e_b, the best performance is achieved by expanding with one entity per cluster. The increase in cluster size and number of entities attributes to a decrease in performance.

7.3   Discussion

Scalability. In the pre-processing stage we introduced the clustering approaches, which first bucket entities together based on the LSH algorithm. This particular step significantly improves the *scalability* of such an offline step. If considering the *x-means* algorithm, under the simplistic assumption that it represents the original *k-means* for which the complexity is $\mathcal{O}(n^{dk+1}log(n))$ (we assume the number of dimensions for the Euclidean space is fixed) for a fixed number of

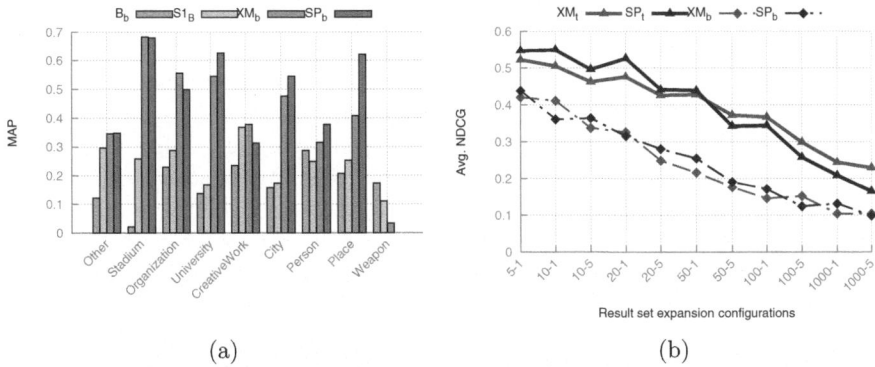

(a)   (b)

Fig. 6. (a) The aggregated MAP for different query types and for the different retrieval approaches (note, we show the results for field *body* where baseline performs best). (b) The various configurations for the number of expanded entities for SP and XM.

clusters and dimensions. Now, clustering without the bucketing step, we would have around $n = 77,485$ entities for clustering with an average of $k = 13$ clusters. Hence, $\mathcal{O}(77485^{d \cdot 13+1} log(77485)) > \mathcal{O}(400^{d \cdot 13+1} log(400))$, where after bucketing we have on average $n = 400$. Thus, we see a significant decrease in the runtime (while the complexity in theory remains of the same magnitude). For the case of *spectral* clustering this is even more evident, where for the adjacency matrix we consider $n(n-1)/2$ entity pairs, and its singular value decomposition (dependent on the algorithm used) is cubical in terms of big-O notation.

Crowdsourced Evaluation: Precautions. In order to ensure that we acquire reliable responses from the crowd workers, we take several precautions while designing the tasks for the evaluation of clusters, as well as establishing the ground-truth for the retrieval of entities. We provide clear instructions and examples to avoid misinterpretations in the relevance scoring, leading to a bias in the judgements. We compensate workers with monetary incentives that are proportionate to their contribution. In addition, we use *gold standard questions* as recommended by previous works to curtail malicious activity.

Caveats and Limitations. Considering the optimization of the pre-processing step, the process scales well even for large datasets like the BTC. The retrieval task itself is an online process with no complex approaches and hence the corresponding computational overhead is negligible for the user. We acknowledge the need to re-cluster entities periodically in order to maintain a persistently good entity retrieval performance. However, we believe that this is a relatively minor overhead, when compared to the improvement in performance that it brings about, and given the fact that it is an offline process which can be scaled using parallel infrastructure.

8   Conclusions and Future Work

In this work, we presented an approach to improve the performance of entity retrieval on structured data. Building on existing state of the art methods, we follow an approach consisting of offline preprocessing clustering, and online retrieval, results expansion and reranking. Preprocessing exploits $x-means$ and *spectral* clustering algorithms using lexical as well as structural features. The clustering process was carried out on a large set of entities (over 450 million). The evaluation of the clustering process shows that over 80% of clusters have an accuracy of more than 80%. As part of the online entity retrieval, for a given a starting result set of entities as retrieved by the baseline approach BM25F we further expand the result set with relevant entities. Additionally, we propose an entity ranking model that takes into account the query type affinity. Finally, we carry out an extensive evaluation of the retrieval process using the SemSearch and the BTC12 datasets. The results show that our methods outperform the baseline and state of the art approaches. In terms of standard IR metrics, our method in combination with one of the clustering approaches, e.g. SP_t improves over $S1_t$ with $\Delta P@10 = +0.19$, $\Delta MAP = +0.273$ and $\Delta R@10 = +0.1$.

Acknowledgments. This work is partly funded by the EU under FP7 project DURAARK (grant no. 600908) and ERC Advanced Grant ALEXANDRIA (grant no. 339233).

References

1. Auer, S., Bizer, C., Kobilarov, G., Lehmann, J., Cyganiak, R., Ives, Z.G.: DBpedia: a nucleus for a web of open data. In: Aberer, K., Choi, K.-S., Noy, N., Allemang, D., Lee, K.-I., Nixon, L.J.B., Golbeck, J., Mika, P., Maynard, D., Mizoguchi, R., Schreiber, G., Cudré-Mauroux, P. (eds.) ASWC 2007 and ISWC 2007. LNCS, vol. 4825, pp. 722–735. Springer, Heidelberg (2007)
2. Bizer, C., Heath, T., Berners-Lee, T.: Linked data - the story so far. Int. J. Semantic Web Inf. Syst. **5**(3), 1–22 (2009)
3. Blanco, R., Cambazoglu, B.B., Mika, P., Torzec, N.: Entity recommendations in web search. In: Alani, H., Kagal, L., Fokoue, A., Groth, P., Biemann, C., Parreira, J.X., Aroyo, L., Noy, N., Welty, C., Janowicz, K. (eds.) ISWC 2013, Part II. LNCS, vol. 8219, pp. 33–48. Springer, Heidelberg (2013)
4. Blanco, R., Halpin, H., Herzig, D.M., Mika, P., Pound, J., Thompson, H.S., Tran, D.T.: Repeatable and reliable search system evaluation using crowdsourcing. In: Proceeding of the 34th ACM SIGIR, pp. 923–932 (2011)
5. Blanco, R., Mika, P., Vigna, S.: Effective and efficient entity search in RDF data. In: Aroyo, L., Welty, C., Alani, H., Taylor, J., Bernstein, A., Kagal, L., Noy, N., Blomqvist, E. (eds.) ISWC 2011, Part I. LNCS, vol. 7031, pp. 83–97. Springer, Heidelberg (2011)
6. Demartini, G., Missen, M.M.S., Blanco, R., Zaragoza, H.: Entity summarization of news articles. In: Proceeding of the 33rd ACM SIGIR, pp. 795–796 (2010)

7. Guéret, C., Groth, P., Stadler, C., Lehmann, J.: Assessing linked data mappings using network measures. In: Simperl, E., Cimiano, P., Polleres, A., Corcho, O., Presutti, V. (eds.) ESWC 2012. LNCS, vol. 7295, pp. 87–102. Springer, Heidelberg (2012)

8. Halpin, H., Herzig, D.M., Mika, P., Blanco, R., Pound, J., Thompson, H.S., Duc, T.T.: Evaluating ad-hoc object retrieval. In: Proceedings of the IWEST (2010)

9. Harth, A.: Billion Triples Challenge data set (2012). Downloaded from http://km. aifb.kit.edu/projects/btc-2012/

10. Lv, Y. Zhai, C.: When documents are very long, bm25 fails! In: Proceedings of 34th ACM SIGIR, pp. 1103–1104. ACM, New York (2011)

11. Manning, C.D., Raghavan, P., Schütze, H.: Introduction to Information Retrieval. Cambridge University Press, New York (2008)

12. Mika, P., Meij, E., Zaragoza, H.: Investigating the semantic gap through query log analysis. In: Bernstein, A., Karger, D.R., Heath, T., Feigenbaum, L., Maynard, D., Motta, E., Thirunarayan, K. (eds.) ISWC 2009. LNCS, vol. 5823, pp. 441–455. Springer, Heidelberg (2009)

13. Neumann, T., Weikum, G.: Rdf-3x: A risc-style engine for rdf. Proc. VLDB Endow. 1(1), 647–659 (2008)

14. Nie, Z., Ma, Y., Shi, S., Wen, J.-R., Ma, W.-Y.: Web object retrieval. In: Proceedings of the 16th WWW, pp. 81–90 (2007)

15. Oren, E., Delbru, R., Catasta, M., Cyganiak, R., Stenzhorn, H., Tummarello, G.: Sindice.com: a document-oriented lookup index for open linked data. IJMSO 3(1), 37–52 (2008)

16. Pelleg, D., Moore, A.W., et al.: X-means: Extending k-means with efficient estimation of the number of clusters. In: ICML, pp. 727–734 (2000)

17. Pound, J., Mika, P., Zaragoza, H.: Ad-hoc object retrieval in the web of data. In: Proceedings of the 19th WWW, pp. 771–780 (2010)

18. Rajaraman, A., Ullman, J.D.: Mining of massive datasets. Cambridge University Press (2011)

19. Meusel, R., Petrovski, P., Bizer, C.: The webdatacommons microdata, rdfa and microformat dataset series. In: Mika, P., Tudorache, T., Bernstein, A., Welty, C., Knoblock, C., Vrandečić, D., Groth, P., Noy, N., Janowicz, K., Goble, C. (eds.) ISWC 2014, Part I. LNCS, vol. 8796, pp. 277–292. Springer, Heidelberg (2014)

20. Robertson, S., Zaragoza, H.: The probabilistic relevance framework: Bm25 and beyond. Found. Trends Inf. Retr. 3(4), 333–389 (2009)

21. Tonon, A., Demartini, G., Cudré-Mauroux, P.: Combining inverted indices and structured search for ad-hoc object retrieval. In: Proceedings of the 35th ACM SIGIR, pp. 125–134 (2012)

22. von Luxburg, U.: A tutorial on spectral clustering. Statistics and Computing 17(4), 395–416 (2007)

23. Zhiltsov, N., Agichtein, E.: Improving entity search over linked data by modeling latent semantics. In: Proceedings of the 22nd ACM CIKM, pp. 1253–1256 (2013)

RDF Data Dynamics

A Flexible Framework for Understanding the Dynamics of Evolving RDF Datasets

Yannis Roussakis[1](✉), Ioannis Chrysakis[1], Kostas Stefanidis[1],
Giorgos Flouris[1], and Yannis Stavrakas[2]

[1] Institute of Computer Science, FORTH, Heraklion, Greece
{rousakis,hrysakis,kstef,fgeo}@ics.forth.gr
[2] Institute for the Management of Information Systems, ATHENA, Athens, Greece
yannis@imis.athena-innovation.gr

Abstract. The dynamic nature of Web data gives rise to a multitude of problems related to the description and analysis of the evolution of RDF datasets, which are important to a large number of users and domains, such as, the curators of biological information where changes are constant and interrelated. In this paper, we propose a framework that enables identifying, analysing and understanding these dynamics. Our approach is flexible enough to capture the peculiarities and needs of different applications on dynamic data, while being formally robust due to the satisfaction of the completeness and unambiguity properties. In addition, our framework allows the persistent representation of the detected changes between versions, in a manner that enables easy and efficient navigation among versions, automated processing and analysis of changes, cross-snapshot queries (spanning across different versions), as well as queries involving both changes and data. Our work is evaluated using real Linked Open Data, and exhibits good scalability properties.

1 Introduction

With the growing complexity of the Web, we face a completely different way of creating, disseminating and consuming big volumes of information. The recent explosion of the Data Web and the associated Linked Open Data (LOD) initiative has led several large-scale corporate, government, or even user-generated data from different domains (e.g., DBpedia, Freebase, YAGO) to be published online and become available to a wide spectrum of users [22]. Dynamicity is an indispensable part of LOD; LOD datasets are constantly evolving for several reasons, such as the inclusion of new experimental evidence or observations, or the correction of erroneous conceptualizations [23]. Understanding this evolution by finding and analysing the differences (*deltas*) between datasets has been proved to play a crucial role in various curation tasks, like the synchronization of autonomously developed dataset versions [3], the visualization of the evolution history of a dataset [13], and the synchronization of interconnected LOD datasets [15]. Deltas are also necessary in certain applications that require access to previous versions of a dataset to support historical or cross-snapshot queries

© Springer International Publishing Switzerland 2015
M. Arenas et al. (Eds.): ISWC 2015, Part I, LNCS 9366, pp. 495–512, 2015.
DOI: 10.1007/978-3-319-25007-6_29

[21], in order to review past states of the dataset, understand the evolution process (e.g., to identify trends in the domain of interest), or detect the source of errors in the current modelling. Unfortunately, it is often difficult, or even infeasible, for curators or editors to accurately record such deltas; studies have shown that manually created deltas are often incomplete or erroneous, even for centrally curated datasets [15]. In addition, such a recording would require a closed and controlled system, and is thus, not suitable for the chaotic nature of the Web.

To study the dynamics of LOD, we propose a framework for *detecting and analysing changes and the evolution history of LOD datasets.* This would allow remote users of a dataset to identify changes, even if they have no access to the actual change process. Apart from identifying the change, we focus on empowering users to perform sophisticated analysis on the evolution data, so as to understand how datasets (or parts of them) evolve, and how this evolution is related to the data itself. For instance, one could be interested in specific types of evolution, e.g., transfers of soccer players, along a certain timeframe, e.g., DBpedia versions v3.7-v3.9, with emphasis on specific parts of the data, e.g., only for strikers being transferred to Spanish teams. This motivating example is further discussed in Section 2, where we give an informal description of our framework. We restrict ourselves to RDF[1] datasets, which is the de facto standard for representing knowledge in LOD. Analysis of the evolution history is based on SPARQL [18], a W3C standard for querying RDF datasets. Details on RDF and SPARQL appear in Section 3.

Regarding change detection, our framework acknowledges that there is no one-size-fits-all solution, and that different uses (or users) of the data may require a different set of changes being reported, since the importance and frequency of changes vary in different application domains. For this reason, our framework supports both *simple* and *complex* changes. Simple changes are meant to capture fine-grained types of evolution. They are defined at *design time* and should meet the formal requirements of *completeness* and *unambiguity*, which guarantee that the detection process is well-behaved [15]. Complex changes are meant to capture more coarse-grained, or specialized, changes that are useful for the application at hand; this allows a customized behaviour of the change detection process, depending on the actual needs of the application. Complex changes are totally dynamic, and *defined at run-time*, greatly enhancing the flexibility of our approach. More details on the definition of changes are given in Section 4.

To support the flexibility required by complex changes, our detection process is based on SPARQL queries (one per defined change) that are provided to the algorithm as configuration parameters; as a result, the core detection algorithm is agnostic to the set of simple or complex changes used, thereby allowing new changes to be easily defined. Furthermore, to support sophisticated analysis of the evolution process, we propose an *ontology of changes*, which allows the persistent representation of the detected changes, in a manner that permits easy and efficient navigation among versions, analysis of the deltas, cross-snapshot

---

[1] http://www.w3.org/RDF/

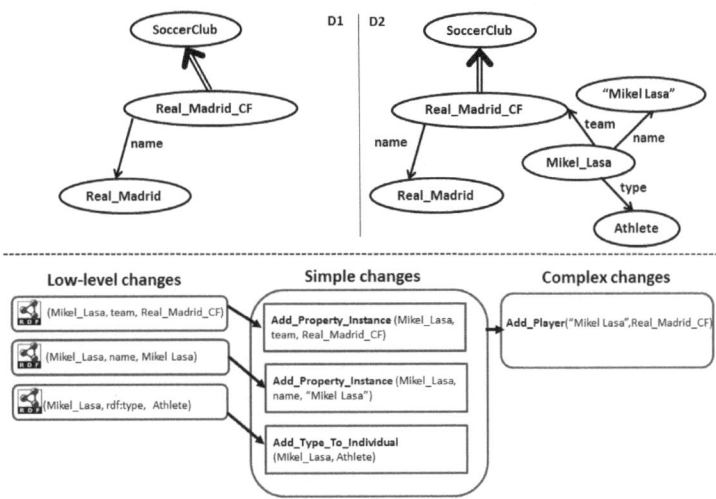

Fig. 1. Motivating Example

or historical queries, and the raising of changes as first class citizens. This, in a multi-version repository, allows queries that refer uniformly to both the data and its evolution. This framework provides a generic basis for analyzing the dynamics of LOD datasets, and is described in Section 5.

In our experimental evaluation (Section 6), we used 3 real RDF datasets of different sizes to study the number of simple and complex changes that usually occur in real-world settings, and provide an analysis of their types. Moreover, we report the evaluation results of the efficiency of our change detection process and quantify the effect of the size of the compared versions and the number of detected changes in the performance of the algorithm. To our knowledge, this is the first time that change detection has been evaluated for datasets of this size.

2   Motivating Example

In our work, we provide a change recognition method, which, given two dataset versions $\mathcal{D}_{old}$, $\mathcal{D}_{new}$, produces their *delta* (Δ), i.e., a formal description of the changes that were made to get $\mathcal{D}_{new}$ from $\mathcal{D}_{old}$. The naive approach is to express the delta with low-level changes (consisting of triple additions and deletions). Our approach builds two more layers on top of low level changes, each adding a semantically richer change vocabulary.

Low-level changes are easy to define and detect, and have several nice properties [24]. For example, assume two DBpedia versions of a partial ontology with information about football teams (Figure 1 (top)), in which the RDF class of Real_Madrid_CF is subclass of SoccerClub. Commonly, change detection compares the current with the previous dataset version and returns the low-level delta containing the added triples: (Mikel_Lasa, team, Real_Madrid_CF),

(Mikel_ Lasa, name, Mikel Lasa), (Mikel_Lasa, type, Athlete). Clearly, the representation of changes at the level of (added/deleted) triples, leads to a syntactic delta, which does not properly capture the intent behind a change and generates results that are not intuitive enough for the human user. What we would like to report is: Add_Player("Mikel Lasa", Real_Madrid_CF), which corresponds to the actual essence of the change.

In order to achieve this, we need an intermediary level of changes, called *simple changes*. Simple changes are fine-grained, predefined and domain-agnostic changes. In our example, the low-level changes found as added triples, reflect three simple changes, namely, two Add_Property_Instance changes, for the property:team and property:name, and one Add_Type_To_Individual change, for denoting the type of athlete (Figure 1). Interestingly, a simple change can group a set of different low-level changes.

However, it is still not easy for the user who is not domain expert and familiar with the notion of triples to define simple changes. To address this problem, changes of coarser granularity are needed. The main idea is to group simple changes into *complex* ones, that are data model agnostic and carry domain-specific semantics, thereby making the description of the evolution (delta) more human-understandable and concise. In our example, the three simple changes can be grouped under one complex, called Add_Player. The change's definition includes two arguments: Add_Player("Mikel Lasa", Real_Madrid_CF). Such a complex change consumes the corresponding simple changes, thus, there is no need for further reporting them.

In a nutshell, complex changes are user-defined, custom changes, which intend to capture changes from the application perspective. Different applications are expected to use different sets of complex changes. Complex changes are defined at a semantic level, and may be used to capture coarse grained changes that happen often; or changes that the curator wants to highlight because they are somehow useful or interesting for a specific domain or application; or changes that indicate an abnormal situation or type of evolution. Thus, complex changes build upon simple ones because, intuitively, complex changes are much easier to be defined on top of simple changes.

On the other hand, complex changes, being coarse-grained, cannot capture all evolution aspects; moreover, it would be unrealistic to assume that complex changes would be defined in a way that captures all possible evolution types. Thus, simple changes are necessary as a "default" set of changes for describing evolution types that are not interesting, common, or coarse-grained enough to be expressed using complex changes.

3   Preliminaries

We consider two disjoint sets $\mathbb{U}$, $\mathbb{L}$, denoting the *URIs* and *literals* (we ignore here blank nodes that can be avoided when data are published according to the LOD paradigm); the set $\mathbb{T} = \mathbb{U} \times \mathbb{U} \times (\mathbb{U} \cup \mathbb{L})$ is the set of all *RDF triples*. A *version* $\mathcal{D}_i$ is a set of RDF triples ($\mathcal{D}_i \subseteq \mathbb{T}$); a *dataset* $\mathcal{D}$ is a sequence of versions $\mathcal{D} = \langle \mathcal{D}_1, \ldots, \mathcal{D}_n \rangle$.

SPARQL 1.1 [18] is the official W3C recommendation language for querying RDF graphs. The building block of a SPARQL statement is a *triple pattern tp* that is like an RDF triple, but may contain *variables* (prefixed with character ?); variables are taken from an infinite set of variables $\mathbb{V}$, disjoint from the sets $\mathbb{U}$, $\mathbb{L}$, so the set of triple patterns is: $\mathbb{TP} = (\mathbb{U} \cup \mathbb{V}) \times (\mathbb{U} \cup \mathbb{V}) \times (\mathbb{U} \cup \mathbb{L} \cup \mathbb{V})$. SPARQL triple patterns can be combined into *graph patterns gp*, using operators like *join* ("."), *optional* (**OPTIONAL**) and *union* (**UNION**) [1] and may also include *conditions* (using **FILTER**). In this work, we are only interested in SELECT SPARQL queries, which are of the form: "*SELECT* $v_1, \ldots, v_n$ *WHERE gp*", where $n > 0$, $v_i \in \mathbb{V}$ and gp is a graph pattern.

Evaluation of SPARQL queries is based on *mappings*, which are partial functions $\mu : \mathbb{V} \mapsto \mathbb{U} \cup \mathbb{L}$ that associate variables with URIs or literals (abusing notation, $\mu(tp)$ is used to denote the result of replacing the variables in tp with their assigned values according to μ). Then, the evaluation of a SPARQL triple pattern tp on a dataset $\mathcal{D}$ returns a set of mappings (denoted by $[[tp]]^{\mathcal{D}}$), such that, $\mu(tp) \in \mathcal{D}$ for $\mu \in [[tp]]^{\mathcal{D}}$. This idea is extended to graph patterns by considering the semantics of the various operators (e.g., $[[tp_1 \; UNION \; tp_2]]^{\mathcal{D}} = [[tp_1]]^{\mathcal{D}} \cup [[tp_2]]^{\mathcal{D}}$). Given a SPARQL query "*SELECT* $v_1, \ldots, v_n$ *WHERE gp*", its result when applied on $\mathcal{D}$ is $(\mu(v_1), \ldots, \mu(v_n))$ for $\mu \in [[gp]]^{\mathcal{D}}$. For the precise semantics and further details on the evaluation of SPARQL queries, the reader is referred to [1, 16].

4 Semantics

4.1 Language of Changes

We assume a set $\mathcal{L} = \{c_1, \ldots, c_n\}$ of *changes*, which is disjoint from $\mathbb{V}, \mathbb{U}, \mathbb{L}$. The set $\mathcal{L}$ is called a *language of changes* and is partitioned into the set of *simple changes* (denoted by $\mathcal{L}^s$) and the set of complex changes (denoted by $\mathcal{L}^c$). Each change has a certain arity (e.g., Add_Player has two arguments); given a change c, a *change specification* is an expression of the form $c(p_1, \ldots, p_n)$, where n is the arity of c, and $p_1, \ldots, p_n \in \mathbb{V}$.

As was made obvious in Section 2, the detection semantics of a change specification are determined by the changes that it *consumes* and the related conditions. Formally:

Definition 1. *Given a simple change* $c \in \mathcal{L}^s$, *and its change specification* $c(p_1, \ldots, p_n)$, *the detection semantics of* $c(p_1, \ldots, p_n)$ *is defined as a tuple* $\langle \delta, \phi_{old}, \phi_{new} \rangle$ *where:*

- δ *determines the consumed changes of* c *and is a pair* $\delta = (\delta^+, \delta^-)$, *where* δ^+, δ^- *are sets of triple patterns (corresponding to the added/deleted triples respectively).*
- ϕ_{old}, ϕ_{new} *are graph patterns, called the conditions for* $\mathcal{D}_{old}$, $\mathcal{D}_{new}$, *respectively.*

Definition 2. *Given a complex change* $c \in \mathcal{L}^c$, *and its change specification* $c(p_1, \ldots, p_n)$, *the detection semantics of* $c(p_1, \ldots, p_n)$ *is defined as a tuple* $\langle \delta, \phi_{old}, \phi_{new} \rangle$ *where:*

- δ *determines the consumed changes of* c *and is a set of change specifications from* $\mathcal{L}^s$, *i.e.,* $\delta = \{c_1(p_1^1, \ldots, p_{n1}^1), \ldots, c_m(p_1^m, \ldots, p_{n\,m}^m)\}$ *where* $\{c_1, \ldots, c_m\} \subseteq \mathcal{L}^s$.
- ϕ_{old}, ϕ_{new} *are graph patterns, called the conditions for* $\mathcal{D}_{old}, \mathcal{D}_{new}$, *respectively.*

In our running example, the detection semantics of Add_Property_Instance (Mikel_Lasa,team, Real_Madrid_CF) are: $\delta^+ = \{(Mikel\_Lasa, team, Real\_Madrid\_CF)\}$, $\delta^- = \emptyset$, $\phi_{old} = $ " ", $\phi_{new} = $ " ". Additionally, the detection semantics of Add_Player("Mikel Lasa", Real_Madrid_CF) are: Add_Property_Instance(Mikel_Lasa, team, Real_ Madrid_ CF), Add_Property_Instance(Mikel_Lasa, name, "Mikel Lasa"), Add_Type_To_Individual (Mikel_Lasa, Athlete).

The structure of the above definitions determines the SPARQL to be used for detection (see Subsection 5.2, and [20]). Any actual detection will give specific values (URIs or literals) to the variables appearing in a change specification. For example, when Add_Property_Instance is detected, the returned result should specify the subject and object of the instance added to the property; essentially, this corresponds to an association of the three variables (parameters) of Add_Property_Instance to specific URIs/literals. Formally, for a change c, a *change instantiation* is an expression of the form $c(x_1, \ldots, x_n)$, where n is the arity of c, and $x_1, \ldots, x_n \in \mathbb{U} \cup \mathbb{L}$.

4.2 Detection Semantics

Simple changes. For simple changes, a *detectable change instantiation* corresponds to a certain assignment of the variables in δ^+, δ^-, ϕ_{old}, ϕ_{new}, such that the conditions (ϕ_{old}, ϕ_{new}) are true in the underlying datasets, and the triples in δ^+, δ^- have been added/deleted, respectively, from $\mathcal{D}_{old}$ to get $\mathcal{D}_{new}$. Formally:

Definition 3. *A change instantiation* $c(x_1, \ldots, x_n)$ *of a simple change specification* $c(p_1, \ldots, p_n)$ *is detectable for the pair* $\mathcal{D}_{old}, \mathcal{D}_{new}$ *iff there is a* $\mu \in [[\phi_{old}]]^{\mathcal{D}_{old}} \cap [[\phi_{new}]]^{\mathcal{D}_{new}}$ *such that for all* $tp \in \delta^+$: $\mu(tp) \in \mathcal{D}_{new} \setminus \mathcal{D}_{old}$ *and for all* $tp \in \delta^-$: $\mu(tp) \in \mathcal{D}_{old} \setminus \mathcal{D}_{new}$ *and for all* i: $\mu(p_i) = x_i$.

Simple changes must satisfy the properties of completeness and unambiguity; this guarantees that the detection process exhibits a sound and deterministic behaviour [15]. Essentially, what we need to show is that each change that the dataset underwent is properly captured by one, and only one, simple change. Formally:

Definition 4. *A detectable change instantiation* $c(x_1, \ldots, x_n)$ *of a simple change specification* $c(p_1, \ldots, p_n)$ *consumes* $t \in \mathcal{D}_{new} \setminus \mathcal{D}_{old}$ *(respectively,* $t \in \mathcal{D}_{old} \setminus \mathcal{D}_{new}$) *iff there is a* $\mu \in [[\phi_{old}]]^{\mathcal{D}_{old}} \cap [[\phi_{new}]]^{\mathcal{D}_{new}}$ *and a* $tp \in \delta^+$ *(respectively,* $tp \in \delta^-$) *such that* $\mu(tp) = t$ *and for all* i: $\mu(p_i) = x_i$.

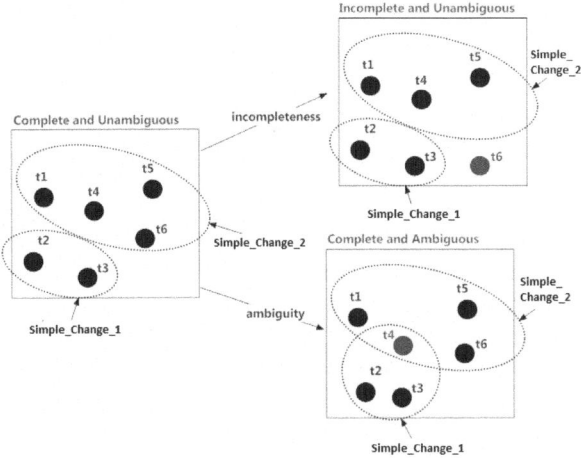

Fig. 2. Visualization of Completeness and Unambiguity

The concept of consumption represents the fact that low-level changes are "assigned" to simple ones, essentially allowing a grouping (partitioning) of low-level changes into simple ones. To fulfil its purpose, this "partitioning" should be perfect, as dictated by the properties of completeness and unambiguity. Formally:

Definition 5. *A set of simple changes C is called complete iff for any pair of versions $\mathcal{D}_{old}$, $\mathcal{D}_{new}$ and for all $t \in (\mathcal{D}_{new} \setminus \mathcal{D}_{old}) \cup (\mathcal{D}_{old} \setminus \mathcal{D}_{new})$, there is a detectable instantiation $c(x_1, \ldots, x_n)$ of some $c \in C$ such that $c(x_1, \ldots, x_n)$ consumes t.*

Definition 6. *A set of simple changes C is called unambiguous iff for any pair of versions $\mathcal{D}_{old}$, $\mathcal{D}_{new}$ and for all $t \in (\mathcal{D}_{new} \setminus \mathcal{D}_{old}) \cup (\mathcal{D}_{old} \setminus \mathcal{D}_{new})$, if $c, c' \in C$ and $c(x_1, \ldots, x_n), c'(x'_1, \ldots, x'_m)$ are detectable and consume t, then $c(x_1, \ldots, x_n) = c'(x'_1, \ldots, x'_m)$.*

In a nutshell, completeness guarantees that all low level changes are associated with at least one simple change, thereby making the reported delta complete (i.e., not missing any change); unambiguity guarantees that no race conditions will emerge between simple changes attempting to consume the same low level change (see Figure 2 for a visualization of the notions of completeness and unambiguity). The combination of these two properties guarantees that the delta is produced in a complete and deterministic manner. Regarding the simple changes, $\mathcal{L}^s$, used in this work (for a complete list, see [20]), the following holds:

Proposition 1. *The simple changes in $\mathcal{L}^s$ [20] are complete and unambiguous.*

Complex Changes. As complex changes can be freely defined by the user, it would be unrealistic to assume that they will have any quality guarantees, such as completeness or unambiguity. As a consequence, the detection process may lead to non-deterministic consumption of simple changes and conflicts; to avoid this, complex changes are associated with a *priority level*, which is used to resolve such conflicts.

The detection for complex changes is defined on top of simple ones. A complex change is detectable if its conditions are true for some assignment, while at the same time the corresponding simple changes in δ are detectable. However, this naive definition could lead to problems, as it could happen that the same detectable simple change instantiation is simultaneously contributing in the detection of two (or more) complex changes. Such a case would lead to undesirable race conditions, so we define a total order (called *priority*, and denoted by $<$) over $\mathcal{L}^c$, which helps disambiguate these cases. This leads to the following definitions:

Definition 7. *A complex change instantiation $c(x_1, \ldots, x_n)$ is initially detectable for the pair $\mathcal{D}_{old}$, $\mathcal{D}_{new}$ iff there is a $\mu \in [[\phi_{old}]]^{\mathcal{D}_{old}} \cap [[\phi_{new}]]^{\mathcal{D}_{new}}$ such that $c'(\mu(p'_1), \ldots, \mu(p'_m))$ is detectable for all $c'(p'_1, \ldots, p'_m) \in \delta$, and $\mu(p'_i) = x_i$ for $i = 1, \ldots, n$.*

Definition 8. *An initially detectable complex change instantiation $c(x_1, \ldots, x_n)$ consumes a simple change instantiation $c'(x'_1, \ldots, x'_m)$ iff $c'(p'_1, \ldots, p'_m) \in \delta$ and there is a $\mu \in [[\phi_{old}]]^{\mathcal{D}_{old}} \cap [[\phi_{new}]]^{\mathcal{D}_{new}}$ such that for all i, $\mu(p_i) = x_i, \mu(p'_i) = x'_i$.*

Definition 9. *A complex change instantiation $c(x_1, \ldots, x_n)$ is detectable for the pair $\mathcal{D}_{old}, \mathcal{D}_{new}$ iff it is initially detectable for the pair $\mathcal{D}_{old}, \mathcal{D}_{new}$ and there is no initially detectable change instantiation $c'(x'_1, \ldots, x'_m)$ such that $c < c'$ and c, c' have at least one consumed simple change instantiation in common.*

5   Change Detection for Evolution Analysis

5.1   Representing Detected Changes

We treat detected changes (i.e., change instantiations) as first-class citizens in order to be able to perform queries analysing the evolution of datasets. Further, we are interested in performing combined queries, in which both the datasets and the changes should be considered to get an answer. To achieve this, the representation of the changes that are detected on the data cannot be separated from the data itself.

For example, consider the following query: "return all the left backs born before 1980, which were transferred to Athletic Bilbao between versions $\mathcal{D}_{old}$ and $\mathcal{D}_{new}$ and used to play for Real Madrid CF in any version". Such a query requires access to the changes (to identify transfers to Athletic Bilbao), and to the data (to identify which of those transfers were related to left backs born before 1980); in addition, it requires access to all previous versions (cross-snapshot query) to determine whether any of the potential results (players) used to play for Real Madrid CF in any version.

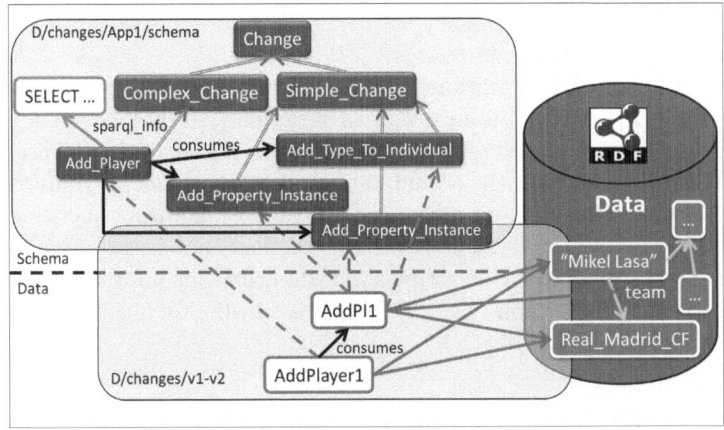

Fig. 3. The Ontology of Changes

To answer such queries, the repository should include all versions, as well as their changes. We opt to store the changes in a structured form; their representation should include connections with the actual entities (e.g., teams or players) and the versions that they refer to. This can be achieved by representing changes as RDF entities, with connections to the actual data and versions, so that a detectable change can be associated with the corresponding data entities that it refers to.

In particular, we propose the use of an adequate schema (that we call the *ontology of changes*) for storing the detected changes, thereby allowing a supervisory look of the detected changes and their association with the entities they refer to in the actual datasets, facilitating the formulation and the answering of queries that refer to both the data and their evolution (see Figure 3). In a nutshell, the schema in our representation describes the change specifications and detection semantics, whereas the detected changes (change instantiations) are classified as instances under this schema. More specifically, at schema level, we introduce one class for each simple and complex change $c \in \mathcal{L}$. Each such class c is subsumed by one of the main classes "Simple_Change" or "Complex_Change", indicating the type of c. Each change is also associated with its user-defined name, a number of properties (one per parameter), and the names of these parameters (not shown in Figure 3 to avoid cluttering the image).

For complex changes, we also store information regarding the changes being consumed by each complex change, as well as the SPARQL query used for its detection, which is automatically generated at change definition time; this is done for efficiency, to avoid having to generate this query in every run of the detection process. Note that the information related to complex changes is generated on the fly at change creation time (in contrast to simple changes, which are built in the ontology at design time). All schema information is stored in a dataset-specific named graph ("D/changes/App1/schema", for a dataset D and a related application App1); this is necessary because each different application may adopt a different set of complex changes.

At instance level, we introduce one individual for each detectable change instantiation $c(x_1, \ldots, x_n)$ in each pair of versions (AddPI1 and AddPlayer1). This individual is associated with the values of its parameters, which are essentially URIs or literals from the actual dataset versions. This provides the "link" between the change repository and the data, thereby allowing queries involving both the changes and the data. In addition, complex changes are connected with their consumed simple ones. The triples that describe this information are stored in an adequate named graph (e.g., "D/changes/v1-v2", for the changes detected between v1, v2 of the dataset D).

5.2 Change Detection Process and Storage

To detect simple and complex changes, we rely on plain SPARQL queries, which are generated from the information drawn from the detection semantics of the corresponding changes (Definition 1 and 2). For simple changes, this information is known at design time, so the query is loaded from a configuration file, whereas for complex changes, the corresponding query is generated once at change-creation time (run-time) and is loaded from the ontology of changes (see Figure 3). For examples of such queries, see [20]. The results of the generated queries determine the change instantiations that are detectable; these results determine the actual triples to be inserted in the ontology of changes.

The SPARQL queries used for detecting a simple change are SELECT queries, whose returned values are the values of the change instantiation; thus, for each variable in the change specification, we put one variable in the SELECT clause. Then, the WHERE clause of the query includes the triple patterns that should (or should not) be found in each of the versions in order for a change instantiation to be detectable; more specifically, the triple patterns in δ^+ must be found in $\mathcal{D}_{new}$ but not in $\mathcal{D}_{old}$, the triple patterns in δ^- must be found in $\mathcal{D}_{old}$ but not in $\mathcal{D}_{new}$, and the graph patterns in ϕ_{old}, ϕ_{new} should be applied in $\mathcal{D}_{old}, \mathcal{D}_{new}$, respectively.

The generation of the SPARQL queries for the complex changes follows a similar pattern. The main difference is that complex changes check the existence of simple changes in the ontology of changes, rather than triples in the two versions (as is the case with simple changes detection); therefore, complex changes should be detected after the detection of simple changes and their storage in the ontology. Note also that the considered simple changes should not have been marked as "consumed" by other detectable changes of a higher priority; thus, it is important for queries associated with complex changes to be executed in a particular order, as implied by their priority.

Following detection, the information about the detectable (simple or complex) change instantiations is stored in the ontology of changes along with any new consumptions of simple changes. To do so, we process each result row to create the corresponding triple blocks, as specified in Section 5.1. This is done as a separate process that first stores the triple blocks in a file (on disk) and subsequently uploads them in the triple store (in our implementation, we use Virtuoso[2] and its bulk loading process for triple ingestion). Note that the detection and storing of changes could be done in one step, if one used an adequately defined SPARQL INSERT statement[3] that identified the detectable change instantiations, created the corresponding triple blocks and inserted them in the ontology using a single statement. However, this approach turned out to be slower by 1 to 2 orders of magnitude, partly because it does not exploit bulk updates based on multiple threads, and also because bulk loading is much faster.

6   Experimental Evaluation

Our evaluation focuses on identifying the number and type of simple and complex changes that usually occur in real-world settings, study the performance of our change detection process and quantify the effect of different parameters in the performance of the algorithm. Our experiments are based on the changes defined in [20].

Setting. For the management of linked data (e.g., storage of datasets and query execution), we worked with a scalable triple store, namely the open source version of Virtuoso Universal Server[4], v7.10.3209 (note that, our work is not bounded to any specific infrastructure or triple-store). Virtuoso is hosted on a machine which uses an Intel Xeon E5-2630 at 2.30GHz, with 384GB of RAM running Debian Linux wheezy version, with Linux kernel 3.16.4. The system uses 7TB RAID-5 HDD configurations. From the total amount of memory, we dedicated 64GB for Virtuoso and 5GB for the implemented application. Moreover, taking into account that CPU provides 12 cores with 2 threads each, we decided to use a multi-threaded implementation; specifically, we noticed that the use of 8 threads during the creation of the RDF triples along with the ingestion process gave us optimal results for our setting. This was one more reason to select Virtuoso for our implementation, as it allows the concurrent use of multiple threads during ingestion. To eliminate the effects of hot/cold starts, cached OS information etc., each change detection process was executed 10 times and the average times were considered.

For our experimental evaluation, we used 3 real RDF datasets of different sizes: a subset of the English DBpedia[4] (consisting of article categories, instance types, labels and mapping-based properties), and the FMA[5] and EFO[6] datasets. Table 1 summarizes the sizes of the evaluated versions of these datasets. To evaluate the performance of the complex change detection process, we created 3 sets of complex changes, one for each dataset. To do this, we exploit domain

---

[2] http://virtuoso.openlinksw.com

[3] http://www.w3.org/TR/2013/REC-sparql11-update-20130321/

[4] http://dbpedia.org

[5] http://sig.biostr.washington.edu/projects/fm/AboutFM.html

[6] http://www.ebi.ac.uk/efo/

Table 1. Evaluated Datasets: Versions and Sizes

	DBpedia			FMA			EFO						
Version	v3.7	v3.8	v3.9	v1.4	v3.0	v3.1	v2.44	v2.45	v2.46	v2.47	v2.48	v2.49	v2.50
# Triples	49M	63M	68M	1.51M	1.67M	1.71M	0.38M	0.38M	0.39M	0.39M	0.4M	0.4M	0.42M

Table 2. Sets of Complex Changes for DBpedia, FMA and EFO

DBpedia	FMA	EFO
Add_Subject (1)	Add_Concept (1)	Add_Definition (1)
Delete_Subject (1)	Delete_Concept (1)	Add_Synonym (1)
Add_Thing (1)	Add_Restriction (1)	Delete_Definition (1)
Delete_Thing (1)	Delete_Restriction (1)	Delete_Synonym (1)
Add_Athlete (1)	Add_Synonym (1)	Mark_as_Obsolete (2)
Update_Label (2)	Update_Comment (2)	Update_Comment (2)
Add_Place (2)	Update_Domain (2)	Update_Domain (2)
Delete_Place (2)	Update_Range (2)	Update_Label (2)
Add_Person (3)	Add_Observation (3)	Update_Range (2)
Delete_Person (3)	Delete_Observation (3)	Update_Property (4)

experts knowledge[7], so as to have sets of changes that reflect real-users needs and show similar characteristics, namely (i) same number of complex changes in the sets and (ii) very close numbers of simple changes consumed by the complex changes in the sets. Table 2 presents the particular complex changes used for each dataset along with the number of simple changes consumed (for the definition of the changes, see [20]).

For DBpedia and FMA, let DBp1, DBp2 and FMA1, FMA2 stand for the pairs of versions (v3.7, v3.8), (v3.8, v3.9), and (v1.4, v3.0), (v3.0, v3.1), respectively. Similarly, we denote with EFO1 the pair of versions (v2.44, v2.45) of the EFO dataset, with EFO2 the pair of versions (v2.49, v2.50), and so forth. To our knowledge, this is the first time that change detection has been evaluated for datasets of this size.

Detected Simple Changes. Figure 4 summarizes the number and type of simple changes that appear in the evaluated datasets. We note the large number of changes which occurred during DBpedia evolution compared to the FMA and EFO datasets, due mostly to its bigger size. However, even if the versions sizes of FMA are much smaller than DBpedia (Table 1), there are cases in which the number of changes between two FMA versions are of the same order of magnitude compared to the number of changes between two DBpedia versions (e.g., Add_Property_Instance). This is explained by the fact that FMA contains experimental biological results and measurements that change over time, thus new versions are vastly different from previous ones. Moreover, observe that the majority of changes (in all datasets except EFO) are applied to the data level (e.g., Add_Property_Instance), whereas in EFO, we have also changes which

---

[7] http://www.ebi.ac.uk/

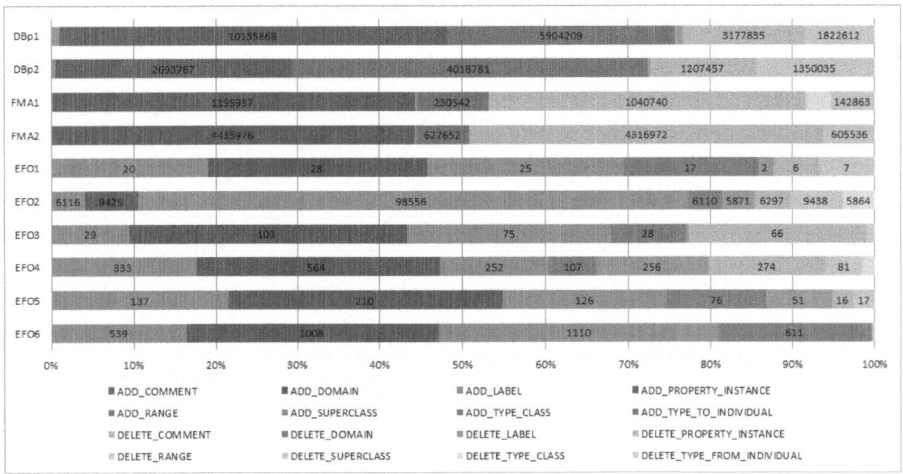

Fig. 4. Detected Simple Changes

are applied to the schema (we notice a big number of Add_Superclass changes, expressing a modification on the hierarchy of the EFO schema).

Performance of Simple Change Detection. Table 3 reports on the performance of the detection process for the employed datasets. We split the results in two parts, namely triple creation and triple ingestion; the former includes the execution of the SPARQL queries for detection and the identification of the triples to be inserted in the ontology of changes, whereas the latter is the actual enrichment of the ontology of changes. Our main conclusion is that the number of simple changes is a more crucial factor for performance than the sizes of the compared versions. This observation is more clear in the DBpedia dataset, where the evolution between v3.7 and v3.8 produces about twice the number of changes than the evolution between v3.8 and v3.9; despite the fact that in the second case, we compare larger dataset versions (Table 1), the execution time in the former case is almost twice as large. Note that this conclusion holds for both triple creation and ingestion. Overall, our approach is about 1 order of magnitude faster compared to the most relevant approach, presented in [15]. To show this, we performed an additional experiment with the largest dataset used in [15], namely the GO[8] dataset (versions v22-09-2009 and v20-04-2010) with about 0.2M triples per version. In this experiment, our approach needs 1,52 sec, while [15] requires 33,13 sec.

Detected Complex Changes. Figure 5 summarizes the number of complex changes per type for the evaluated datasets. Clearly, the size of the datasets determines the number of the complex changes occurred during the datasets evolution; abstractly speaking, the bigger the dataset (see Table 1), the more the changes. From Figure 5, we can identify the particular types of complex

---

[8] http://geneontology.org

Table 3. Performance of Simple Change Detection

Versions Pairs	# Simple Changes	# Ingested Triples	Triple Creation (sec)	Triple Ingestion (sec)	Duration (sec)
DBp1	20.7M	74.8M	412	143	555
DBp2	9.3M	32M	235	73	308
FMA1	2.7M	8.8M	113	12	125
FMA2	2.5M	9.7M	140	12	152
EFO1	0.1K	0.3K	0.33	0.11	0.44
EFO2	59K	180K	0.9	1.63	2.53
EFO3	0.3K	1K	0.22	0.79	1.01
EFO4	1.9K	6.4K	0.64	0.33	0.97
EFO5	0.6K	2K	0.57	0.2	0.77
EFO6	2.8K	8.9K	0.47	0.39	0.86

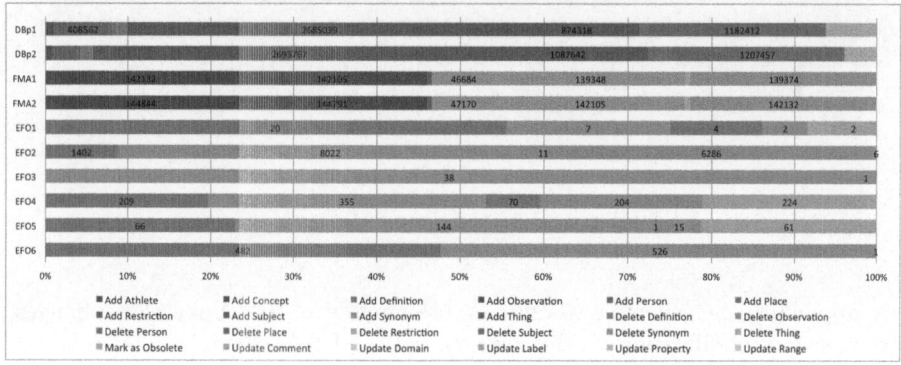

Fig. 5. Detected Complex Changes

changes that are the most popular ones. Specifically, in DBpedia, changes like Add_Subject, Add_Thing and Add_Person are very common (on average, there are 2.7M, 1M and 0.5M changes, respectively). In FMA, we observe a big number of Add_Concept, Delete_Concept, Add_Observation, Delete_Observation and Add_Synonym changes with about 140K, 140K, 140K, 140K, 46K changes, respectively. EFO is the smallest dataset with the smaller number of changes; for example, we count about 7K, 7K and 1.5K Add_Synonym, Delete_Synonym and Add_Definition changes. In overall, the majority of complex changes are applied to the data level.

Performance of Complex Change Detection. Table 4 reports on the performance of the complex change detection process for the employed RDF datasets. Again, we provide execution times for both the triple creation, i.e., for the execution of the SPARQL queries for detecting the triples to be inserted in the ontology of changes, and the triple ingestion, i.e., for the actual enrichment of the ontology of changes. Moreover, we show the size, in number of triples, of the ontology of changes per dataset; the ontology of changes, as produced after identifying the simple changes, is used for searching for complex changes, instead of the actual datasets versions. The bigger the size of the ontology of changes, the higher the execution time (for both triple creation and ingestion). Given that, typically, the ontologies of changes contain much fewer triples than the datasets versions, searching for complex changes needs much less time, compared to the

Table 4. Performance of Complex Change Detection

Versions Pairs	# Complex Changes	Ontology of Changes Size	# Ingested Triples	Triple Creation (sec)	Triple Ingestion (sec)	Duration (sec)
DBp1	5.79M	74.8M	100.2M	136.5	52.8	189.3
DBp2	5.67M	32M	53.6M	130.7	48	178.7
FMA1	616.4K	8.8M	13.6M	20.93	19.65	40.58
FMA2	627.8K	9.7M	13.1M	20.84	19.23	40.07
EFO1	36	0.3K	0.5K	0.79	0.04	0.83
EFO2	15.7M	180K	243.6K	1.17	0.93	2.1
EFO3	39	1K	1.2K	0.08	0.02	0.1
EFO4	1M	6.4K	11.1K	0.35	0.21	0.56
EFO5	287	2K	3.4K	0.57	0.06	0.63
EFO6	1M	8.9K	14.3K	0.44	0.07	0.51

time required for searching simple changes. The reported small execution times are affected as well by the smaller number of complex changes identified, compared to the number of the identified simple changes. Finally, note that here we follow a multi-threaded implementation only for triple ingestion. Due to the fact that unambiguity does not hold for complex changes, we cannot perform triple creation in parallel.

7   Related Work

In general, approaches for change detection can be classified into low-level and high-level ones, based on the types of changes they support. Low-level change detection approaches report simple add/delete operations, which are not concise or intuitive enough to human users, while focusing on machine readability. [4] discusses a low-level detection approach for propositional Knowledge Bases (KBs), which can be easily extended to apply to KBs represented under any classical knowledge representation formalism. This work presents a number of desirable formal properties for change detection languages, like delta uniqueness and reversibility of changes. Similar properties appear in [24], where a low-level change detection formalism for RDFS datasets is presented. [10] describes a low-level change detection approach for the Description Logic $\mathcal{EL}$; the focus is on a concept-based description of changes, and the returned delta is a set of concepts whose position in the class hierarchy changed. [11] presents a low-level change detection approach for DL-Lite ontologies, which focuses on a semantical description of the changes. Recently, [8] introduces a scalable approach for reasoning-aware low-level change detection that uses an RDBMS, while [12] supports change detection between RDF datasets containing blank nodes. All these works result in non-concise, low-level deltas, which are difficult for a human to understand.

High-level change detection approaches provide more human-readable deltas. Although there is no agreed-upon list of changes necessary for any given context, various high-level operations, along with the intuition behind them, have been proposed. Specifically, [9,14] describes a fixed-point algorithm for detecting changes, implemented in PromptDiff. The algorithm incorporates heuristic-based matchers to detect changes between two versions, thus introducing uncertainty in the results. [17] proposes the Change Definition Language (CDL) as a means to define high-level changes. A change is defined and detected using temporal queries over a version log that contains recordings of the applied low-level changes. The version log must be updated whenever a change occurs; this overrules the use of this approach in non-curated or distributed environments. In general, these approaches do not present formal semantics of high-level operations, or of the corresponding detection process; thus, no useful formal properties can be guaranteed.

The most relevant work appears in [15], where an approach for detecting high-level changes appears. In that work, unlike our approach, a fixed set of high-level changes is proposed, without providing facilities related to representing the detected changes and answering cross-snapshot queries, or queries accessing both the changes and the data; as such, it only partly addresses the problem of analyzing datasets' dynamics. Interestingly, we experience significantly improved performance and scalability (see Section 6). In [2] the authors focus on formally defining high-level changes as sequences of triples, but do not describe a detection process or a specific language of changes, while [6] proposes an interesting high-level change detection algorithm that takes into account the semantics of OWL. Using a layered approach designed for OWL as well, [7] focuses on representing changes only at schema level.

The idea of using SPARQL query templates to identify evolution patterns is also used in [19]; however, this paper aims to identify problems caused during ontology evolution, rather than analyse the evolution and report or represent changes. A complementary to ours work is presented in [5]; it defines a SPARQL-like language for expressing complex changes and querying the ontology of changes in a user-friendly manner. On the contrary, our work provides the semantics of the created complex changes, and the changes ontology, upon which the evolution analysis will be made.

8   Conclusions

The dynamicity of LOD datasets makes the automatic identification of deltas between versions increasingly important for several reasons, such as storing and communication efficiency, visualization and documentation of deltas, efficient synchronization and study of the dataset evolution history. In this paper, we proposed an approach to cope with the dynamicity of Web datasets via the management of changes between versions. We advocated in favour of a flexible, extendible and triple-store independent approach, which prescribes (i) the definition of custom, application-specific changes, and their management (definition, storage, detection) in a manner that ensures the satisfaction of formal properties, like completeness and unambiguity, (ii) the flexibility and customization of the considered changes, via complex changes that can be defined at run-time, and (iii) the easy configuration of a scalable detection mechanism, via a generic algorithm that builds upon SPARQL queries easily generated from the changes' definitions.

An important feature of our work, in which we handle real datasets snapshots, is the ability to perform sophisticated analysis on top of the detected changes, via the representation of the detected changes in an ontology and their treatment as first-class citizens. This allows queries spanning multiple versions of the data (cross-snapshot), as well as queries involving both the evolution history and the data.

Acknowledgments. This work was partially supported by the EU FP7 projects DIACHRON (#601043) and IdeaGarden (#318552).

References

1. Arenas, M., Gutierrez, C., Pérez, J.: On the semantics of SPARQL. In: Semantic Web Information Management - A Model-Based Perspective. Springer (2009)
2. Auer, S., Herre, H.: A versioning and evolution framework for RDF knowledge bases. In: Virbitskaite, I., Voronkov, A. (eds.) PSI 2006. LNCS, vol. 4378, pp. 55–69. Springer, Heidelberg (2007)
3. Cloran, R., Irvin, B.: Transmitting RDF graph deltas for a cheaper semantic web. In: SATNAC (2005)
4. Franconi, E., Meyer, T., Varzinczak, I.: Semantic diff as the basis for knowledge base versioning. In: NMR (2010)
5. Galani, T., Stavrakas, Y., Papastefanatos, G., Flouris, G.: Supporting complex changes in RDF(S) knowledge bases. In: MEPDaW-15 (2015)
6. Gröner, G., Silva Parreiras, F., Staab, S.: Semantic recognition of ontology refactoring. In: Patel-Schneider, P.F., Pan, Y., Hitzler, P., Mika, P., Zhang, L., Pan, J.Z., Horrocks, I., Glimm, B. (eds.) ISWC 2010, Part I. LNCS, vol. 6496, pp. 273–288. Springer, Heidelberg (2010)
7. Hartmann, J., Palma, R., Sure, Y., Haase, P., Suarez-Figueroa, M.C.: OMV ontology metadata vocabulary. In: Ontology Patterns for the Semantic Web Workshop (2005)
8. Im, D.-H., Lee, S.-W., Kim, H.-J.: Backward inference and pruning for RDF change detection using RDBMS. J. Information Science **39**(2), 238–255 (2013)
9. Klein, M., Proefschrift, A., Christiaan, M., Klein, A., Akkermans, J.M.: Change management for distributed ontologies. Technical report, VU University Amsterdam (2004)
10. Konev, B., Walther, D., Wolter, F.: The logical difference problem for description logic terminologies. In: Armando, A., Baumgartner, P., Dowek, G. (eds.) IJCAR 2008. LNCS (LNAI), vol. 5195, pp. 259–274. Springer, Heidelberg (2008)
11. Kontchakov, R., Wolter, F., Zakharyaschev, M.: Can you tell the difference between DL-lite ontologies? In: KR (2008)
12. Lee, D.-H., Im, D.-H., Kim, H.-J.: A change detection technique for RDF documents containing nested blank nodes. In: PSI (2007)
13. Noy, N.F., Chugh, A., Liu, W., Musen, M.A.: A framework for ontology evolution in collaborative environments. In: Cruz, I., Decker, S., Allemang, D., Preist, C., Schwabe, D., Mika, P., Uschold, M., Aroyo, L.M. (eds.) ISWC 2006. LNCS, vol. 4273, pp. 544–558. Springer, Heidelberg (2006)
14. Noy, N.F., Musen, M.A.: Promptdiff: a fixed-point algorithm for comparing ontology versions. In: AI (2002)

15. Papavasileiou, V., Flouris, G., Fundulaki, I., Kotzinos, D., Christophides, V.: High-level change detection in RDF(S) KBs. ACM Trans. Database Syst., **38**(1) (2013)
16. Pérez, J., Arenas, M., Gutierrez, C.: Semantics and complexity of SPARQL. In: Cruz, I., Decker, S., Allemang, D., Preist, C., Schwabe, D., Mika, P., Uschold, M., Aroyo, L.M. (eds.) ISWC 2006. LNCS, vol. 4273, pp. 30–43. Springer, Heidelberg (2006)
17. Plessers, P., De Troyer, O., Casteleyn, S.: Understanding ontology evolution: A change detection approach. Web Semant. **5**(1), 39–49 (2007)
18. Prud'hommeaux, E., Harris, S., Seaborne, A.: SPARQL 1.1 Query Language. Technical report, W3C (2013)
19. Rieß, C., Heino, N., Tramp, S., Auer, S.: EvoPat – pattern-based evolution and refactoring of RDF knowledge bases. In: Patel-Schneider, P.F., Pan, Y., Hitzler, P., Mika, P., Zhang, L., Pan, J.Z., Horrocks, I., Glimm, B. (eds.) ISWC 2010, Part I. LNCS, vol. 6496, pp. 647–662. Springer, Heidelberg (2010)
20. Roussakis, Y., Chrysakis, I., Stefanidis, K., Flouris, G.: A flexible framework for understanding the dynamics of evolving RDF sdatasets: Extended version. Technical Report TR-456, FORTH-ICS, July 2015
21. Stefanidis, K., Chrysakis, I., Flouris, G.: On designing archiving policies for evolving rdf datasets on the web. In: Yu, E., Dobbie, G., Jarke, M., Purao, S. (eds.) ER 2014. LNCS, vol. 8824, pp. 43–56. Springer, Heidelberg (2014)
22. Stefanidis, K., Efthymiou, V., Herchel, M., Christophides, V.: Entity resolution in the web of data. In: WWW (2014)
23. Umbrich, J., Hausenblas, M., Hogan, A., Polleres, A., Decker, S.: Towards dataset dynamics: change frequency of linked open data sources. In: LDOW (2010)
24. Zeginis, D., Tzitzikas, Y., Christophides, V.: On computing deltas of RDF/S knowledge bases. ACM Trans. Web **5**(3), 14:1–14:36 (2011)

Interest-Based RDF Update Propagation

Kemele M. Endris$^{(\boxtimes)}$, Sidra Faisal, Fabrizio Orlandi,
Sören Auer, and Simon Scerri

University of Bonn & Fraunhofer IAIS, Bonn, Germany
{endris,faisals,orlandi}@cs.uni-bonn.de

Abstract. Many LOD datasets, such as DBpedia and LinkedGeoData, are voluminous and process large amounts of requests from diverse applications. Many data products and services rely on full or partial local LOD replications to ensure faster querying and processing. Given the evolving nature of the original and authoritative datasets, to ensure consistent and up-to-date replicas frequent replacements are required at a great cost. In this paper, we introduce an approach for interest-based RDF update propagation, which propagates only interesting parts of updates from the source to the target dataset. Effectively, this enables remote applications to 'subscribe' to relevant datasets and consistently reflect the necessary changes locally without the need to frequently replace the entire dataset (or a relevant subset). Our approach is based on a formal definition for graph-pattern-based interest expressions that is used to filter interesting parts of updates from the source. We implement the approach in the iRap framework and perform a comprehensive evaluation based on DBpedia Live updates, to confirm the validity and value of our approach.

Keywords: Change propagation · Dataset dynamics · Linked data · Replication

1 Introduction

In recent years, there has been an increasing number of structured data published on the Web as Linked Open Data (LOD). As of 2014, the size of the LOD cloud consisted of more than 1.000 published datasets comprising almost 100 Billion triples[1]. Many of these datasets are huge and process large amount of requests from diverse applications. Providing services on top of these datasets is becoming a challenge due to the lack of service levels regarding the availability of datasets [11] and restrictions imposed by the publisher on the type of query forms and number of results[2]. Replication of Linked Data datasets enhances flexibility of information sharing and integration infrastructures. Since hosting a replica of large datasets is costly, organizations might want to host only a relevant subset

---

[1] http://linkeddatacatalog.dws.informatik.uni-mannheim.de/state/

[2] https://lists.w3.org/Archives/Public/public-lod/2011Aug/0028.html

© Springer International Publishing Switzerland 2015
M. Arenas et al. (Eds.): ISWC 2015, Part I, LNCS 9366, pp. 513–529, 2015.
DOI: 10.1007/978-3-319-25007-6_30

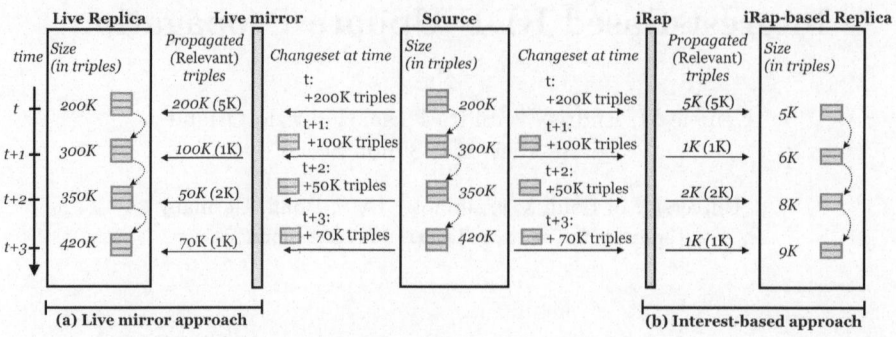

Fig. 1. Changeset propagation approaches: left part (a) – Live mirror approach; right part (b)– Interest-based approach

of the data, for example, using approaches such as *RDFSlice* [4]. However, due to the evolving nature of these datasets, maintaining a consistent and up-to-date replica of the relevant data is a major challenge. Resources in a dataset might be added, updated, or removed. Applications consuming these datasets should be capable of dealing with such updates to keep their local copies consistent.

Typically, dataset mirror applications propagate updates published by the source dataset to a target dataset (replica). For instance, the *DBpedia Live mirror tool*[3] propagates all changes to a target dataset, so that at any point of time the target dataset contains the same triples as the DBpedia Live dataset. However, for example, an application interested in athletes uses only 268,773 out of 4,584,616 instances of the English DBpedia 2014 dataset[4]. In this paper, we present an approach for interest-based update propagation, which is based on the specification of data interests by a target application. Based on such interest expressions all updates are evaluated and only those changes satisfying target applications' interest are shipped to the target dataset. An interest-based update propagation could significantly reduce the amount of data to be shipped and managed at the application side and thus lower the barrier for the deployment of Linked Data applications. We provide a thorough formalization of our approach.

Figure 1 shows the propagation of unfiltered data from a source to a target, referred to as *Live Replica* (part *(a)* on the left). This approach propagates all the updates irrespective of the relevance or usefulness of the data. Whereas, using iRap (interest-based RDF update propagation) framework the source-to-target data propagation (*iRap-based Replica* in Figure 1 part *(b)* on the right) is filtered. With this interest-based approach only relevant data is being transfered. Our evaluation shows, that the data required to be transfered and handled by applications can be reduced by several orders of magnitude thus substantially lowering the Linked Data re-use barrier.

---

[3] https://github.com/dbpedia/dbpedia-live-mirror
[4] http://wiki.dbpedia.org/services-resources/datasets/dataset-statistics

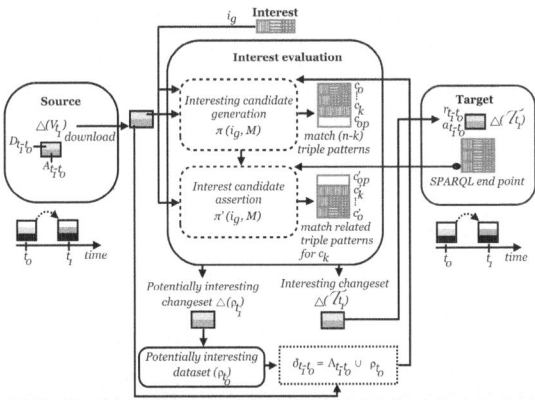

Fig. 2. Formalization overview of the interest-based RDF update propagation.

The article is structured as follows: section 2 extensively describes the formalization for our framework. section 3 and section 4 discusses the implementation and evaluation of the iRap framework in detail. section 5 describes the related work. Finally, section 6 concludes and proposes directions for future work.

2   Formalization of Interest-Based RDF Updates

Figure 2 illustrates the overall interest-based RDF Update Propagation approach; summarizing the concepts defined through the formalization. Interest evaluation takes place over the input set of deleted ($D_{t_1-t_0}$) and added ($At_1 - t_0$) triples from the source dataset (V_{t_1}) in between time interval (t_0, t_1). Since updates do not only contain interesting and uninteresting parts, but also triples which can become interesting along with subsequent updates. We have to compute and store these sets of *potentially interesting triples* (see Definition 8) and take them in subsequent update assessments into account.

For our formalization we will use the standard notations **I**, **B**, **L** and *Var* for the disjoint sets of all IRIs, blank nodes, literals (typed and untyped) and variables respectively. An *RDF graph* V is a finite set of RDF triples, i.e, $V \subset$ (**I**∪**B**) × **I** × (**I**∪**B**∪**L**). In this paper we use the terms RDF graph, *RDF dataset*, and *dataset* interchangeably. An *evolving dataset* V^g is a dataset identified using the persistent IRI g whose content changes over time. V_t^g denotes a specific revision of V^g at a particular time t. For simplicity, we will just refer to V_t instead of V_t^g.

Definition 1 (BGP). *A SPARQL basic graph pattern (BGP) expression is defined recursively as follows:*

1. *a triple pattern tp $\in$ (**I**∪ **B**∪ Var) × (**I**∪ Var) × (**I**∪ **B**∪ **L**∪ Var) is a BGP*
2. *the expression (P1 AND P2) is a BGP, where P1 and P2 are themselves BGPs*

3. *the expression (P FILTER E) is a BGP, where P is a BGP and E is a SPARQL filter expression that evaluates to boolean value.*

Definition 2 (Non-disjoint BGP). *A non-disjoint BGP is a BGP that represents a connected graph.*

An optional graph pattern (OGP) is syntactically specified with the OPTIONAL keyword applied to a graph pattern. A set of triple patterns in a BGP must match for there to be a solution whereas triple patterns in OGP may extend the solution but their non-binding nature means that they cannot reject it [1].

Definition 3 (Partial Matches). *Partial matches are a set of triples that does not fully match the BGP but matches at least one triple pattern in BGP or OGP of a query.*

Triples added to, and removed from, an evolving dataset within a time-frame are called *changeset* for a dataset within that time-frame.

Definition 4 (Changeset). *Let V_{t_1} be an evolving dataset at time t_1. A changeset $\Delta(V_{t_1})$, between V_{t_0} and V_{t_1}, where $t_0 < t_1$, is defined as:*

$$\Delta(V_{t_1}) = \langle D_{t_1-t_0}, A_{t_1-t_0} \rangle$$

where: $D_{t_1-t_0}$ is a set of removed triples from V_{t_0} between time-points t_0 and t_1, and $A_{t_1-t_0}$ is a set of added triples to V_{t_0} between time-points t_0 and t_1.

Changesets can be computed using the difference between two versions of the RDF dataset. The result of this computation gives the removed triples, $D_{t_1-t_0} = V_0 \setminus V_1$, and added triples, $A_{t_1-t_0} = V_1 \setminus V_0$, between given dataset revisions V_{t_0} and V_{t_1}. Datasets can be accompanied with a tool that publishes changesets at real-time, so that users can download these changesets and synchronize their local replicas. For instance, DBpedia publishes updates in a public changesets folder (http://live.dbpedia.org/changesets/).

Example 1. Let us assume two files (Listing 1.1 and Listing 1.2) are being published by the DBpedia Live extractor for the changes made on Feb 06, 2015 between 05:00 PM (t_0) and 05:02 PM (t_1). A changeset $\Delta(V_{t_1})$ for the DBpedia Live dataset between t_0 and t_1, contains $D_{05:02-05:00} = 000001.removed.nt$ and $A_{05:02-05:00} = 000001.added.nt$.
    That is, $\Delta(V_{05:02}) = \langle 000001.removed.nt,\ 000001.added.nt \rangle$.

Definition 5 (Changeset Propagation). *A changeset propagation is a function v that transforms a given dataset V_{t_0} to a new dataset V_{t_1} by applying a changeset, $\Delta(V_{t_1})$. That is: $v(V_{t_0}, \Delta(V_{t_1})) = (V_{t_0} \setminus D_{t_1-t_0}) \cup A_{t_1-t_0} = V_{t_1}$*

The changeset propagation function v, for example, deletes the triples in 000001.removed.nt from the target dataset and then inserts all triples from 000001.added.nt. This order of operation (deleted first) ensures that inserted triples are not removed again immediately. If an organization maintaining a replica wants to host only a subset of the original dataset, it needs to obtain

```
dbr:Marcel              dbp:goals    1 .
dbr:Marcel              dbo:team     dbr:FNFT .
dbr:Tim%02              foaf:name
                             "Tim Berners-Lee" .
dbr:Cristiano_Ronaldo dbo:goals    96 .
```

Listing (1.1) File 000001.removed.nt

```
dbr:Cristiano_Ronaldo  dbo:goals 216 .
dbr:Barack_Obama       foaf:name "Barack Obama" .
dbr:Barack_Obama       foaf:homepage
                         "http://www.barackobama.com/" .
dbr:Rio_Ferdinand      a         foaf:Person .
dbr:Rio_Ferdinand      a         dbo:Athlete .
dbr:Rio_Ferdinand      dbp:goals 2 .
dbr:Arvid_Smit         a         dbo:Athlete .
```

Listing (1.2) File 000001.added.nt

Fig. 3. Changeset files published by DBpedia Live extractor

only relevant updates for this subset. For that purpose, we specify *interests* to subscribe to 'interesting' changes only. During interest registration, an organization provides information about the source dataset to synchronize with, a target dataset endpoint that supports SPARQL Update to propagate interesting changes, and an interest query to select relevant parts of a changeset.

Definition 6 (Interest Expression). *An interest expression over an evolving dataset, V_t, is defined as: $i_g = \langle \tau, b, op \rangle$ where g is an IRI identifying an evolving RDF dataset V_t, τ is an IRI identifying the target dataset endpoint, b is a non-disjoint BGP, and op is an optional graph pattern (OGP) connected to b.*

Example 2. An interest expression for a list of an athlete with information about goals scored, and optionally their homepage, is expressed as follows:
- g = *http://live.dbpedia.org/changesets*
- τ = *http://localhost:3030/target/sparql*
- b = { ?a a dbo:Athlete . ?a dbp:goals ?goals . }
- op = { ?a foaf:homepage ?page . }

The equivalent interest expression SPARQL query will be:

```
SELECT * WHERE { ?a a dbo:Athlete . ?a dbp:goals ?goals . OPTIONAL { ?a foaf:homepage ?page . } }
```

In order to initialize a local data store, i.e., the target dataset, SPARQL CONSTRUCT queries can be used by employing the interest expression's BGPs to extract and load a subset of the source dataset. Then interest expressions are registered with our iRap framework to retrieve interesting updates from the source dataset. iRap evaluates interest expressions over changesets being published along with the source dataset. Without a restriction of generality, we assume interest expressions here to be static for the lifetime of a target dataset, since an evolution of interest expressions can be simulated by removal and addition. The result of executing an interest evaluation for an interest expression against a changeset are three sets or triples: *1. interesting, 2. potentially interesting, and 3. uninteresting* triples.

Definition 7 (Interesting Triples). *Interesting triples are all triples comprised in full matches of the BGP and possibly OGP of an interest expression, i_g, against the sets of added or deleted triples of a changeset. Interesting triples originating from the first element (i.e., removed triples $(D_{t_1-t_0})$) of a changeset, $\Delta(V_{t_1})$, are called interesting-removed triples. Interesting triples originating from the second element (i.e., added triples $(A_{t_1-t_0})$) of a changeset, $\Delta(V_{t_1})$, are called interesting-added triples.*

In addition to parts of an changeset for which the 'interestingness' can be immediately decided, there might also be parts, which are *potentially interesting* since, i) the missing parts to render them as interesting are already contained in the target knowledge base or ii) they will be propagated in subsequent updates.

Definition 8 (Potentially Interesting Triples). *Potentially interesting triples are triples comprised in partial matches of the BGP or in OGP of interest expression, i_g:*

- *Potentially interesting triples originating from the first element (i.e., removed triples $(D_{t_1-t_0})$) of a changeset $\Delta(V_{t_1})$, are called potentially interesting-removed triples.*
- *Potentially interesting triples originating from the second element (i.e., added triples $(A_{t_1-t_0})$) of a changeset, $\Delta(V_{t_1})$, are called potentially interesting-added triples.*

Potentially interesting triples can become interesting if triples missing in the changeset, but required for a full BGP match, are found in the target dataset or in subsequent changesets. Finally, there are triples in the changeset that are neither interesting nor potentially interesting.

Definition 9 (Uninteresting Triples). *Uninteresting triples are triples that do not match any triple pattern in a BGP or OGP of any interest expression, i_g, against the sets of added or deleted triples of a changeset.*

Uninteresting triples are not interesting at the moment and can never become interesting with subsequent changesets. iRap uses an interest query to select candidate triples from a changeset and to assert from a target dataset. These candidates are retrieved in decreasing order of number of matching BGP triple patterns of interest expressions and triples that match any part of optional graph patterns.

Definition 10 (Interest Candidate Generation). *An interest candidate generation is the extraction of matching triples from a changeset for a non-disjoint combination of triple patterns in BGP of an interest expression, i_g. The result of this extraction is an $(n+1)$-tuple with decreasing order of matching:*

$$\pi(i_g, M) = \langle c_0, c_1, ..., c_{n-1}, c_{op} \rangle$$

where:

- *M is a set of removed (respectively added) triples in a changeset,*
- *n is the number of triple patterns in the BGP of interest expression, i_g,*
- *c_k is a set of candidate triples in M that match $n - k$ ($0 \le k < n$) triple patterns of the BGP of the interest expression, i_g, and*
- *c_{op} is a set of candidate triples in M that match at least one triple pattern in the OGP of interest expression, i_g, but none of the triple patterns in the BGP.*

Example 3. An interest candidate generation for the interest expression i_g from Example 2 over the changeset from Example 1 gives the following result:

1. $\pi(i_g, D_{05:02-05:00}) = \langle c_0, c_1, c_{op} \rangle$ where:
   $c_0 = \emptyset$
   c_1 = dbr:Marcel dbp:goals 1. dbr:Cristiano_Ronaldo dbo:goals 96.
   $c_{op} = \emptyset$
2. $\pi(i_g, A_{05:02-05:00}) = \langle c_0, c_1, c_{op} \rangle$ where:
   c_0 = dbr:Rio_Ferdinand a dbo:Athlete . dbr:Rio_Ferdinand dbp:goals 10.
   c_1 = dbr:Cristiano_Ronaldo dbp:goals 216 . dbr:Arvid_Smit a dbo:Athlete.
   c_{op} = dbr:Barack_Obama foaf:homepage "http://www.barackobama.com".

Now an interest candidate assertion verifies candidate triples with respect to all triple patterns in the BGP of an interest expression.

Definition 11 (Interest Candidate Assertion). *The candidate assertion function extracts missing triples for the candidate, c_i of $\pi(i_g, M)$ of an interest expression i_g from the target dataset, τ_{t_0}:*

$$\pi'(i_g, M) = \langle c'_{op}, c'_{n-1}, ..., c'_1, c'_0 \rangle$$

where:

- *M is a set of removed (respectively added) triples in a changeset,*
- *n is the number of triple patterns in the BGP of interest expression, i_g,*
- *c'_{op} is a set of triples from target dataset, τ, that matches the missing optional graph patterns for candidate c_0, of $\pi(i_g, M)$,*
- *c'_k is a set of triples from target dataset, τ, that matches the missing triple patterns for candidate c_{n-k}, where $0 < k < n$, of $\pi(i_g, M)$, and*
- *c'_0 is a set of triples from target dataset, τ, that matches all triple patterns in BGP of interest expression for candidate c_{op}, of $\pi(i_g, M)$.*

Example 4. Let the target dataset, τ_{t_0}, at time t_0 contains the following triples:

```
#Target dataset at time t0 = 05:00 PM Feb 06, 2015
dbr:Marcel               a            dbo:Athlete .
dbr:Marcel               dbp:goals    1 .
dbr:Cristiano_Ronaldo    a            dbo:Athlete .
dbr:Cristiano_Ronaldo    dbo:goals    96 .
dbr:Cristiano_Ronaldo    foaf:homepage "http://cristianoronaldo.com" .
```

An interest candidate assertion for interest candidates generated in Example 3 yields the following result:

1. $\pi'(i_g, D_{05:02-05:00}) = \langle c'_{op}, c'_1, c'_0 \rangle$ where:
   $c'_{op} = \emptyset$
   $c'_1 = $ dbr:Marcel a dbo:Athlete .
       dbr:Cristiano_Ronaldo a dbo:Athlete .
       dbr:Cristiano_Ronaldo foaf:homepage "http://cristianoronaldo.com" .
   $c'_0 = \emptyset$
2. $\pi'(i_g, A_{05:02-05:00}) = \langle c'_{op}, c'_1, c'_0 \rangle$ where:
   $c'_{op} = \emptyset$
   $c'_1 = $ dbr:Cristiano_Ronaldo a dbo:Athlete .
       dbr:Cristiano_Ronaldo foaf:homepage "http://cristianoronaldo.com" .
   $c'_0 = \emptyset$

The interest evaluation over a changeset $\Delta(V_{t_1})$ is performed in two steps. First, interest expressions are evaluated against removed triples of a changeset as $d(i_g, D_{t_1-t_0})$, see Definition 12. Second, interest expressions are evaluated against added triples of a changeset as $\alpha(i_g, A_{t_1-t_0})$, see Definition 13. During interest evaluation, added triples are combined with potentially interesting triples from previous changesets (i.e., $I_{t_1-t_0} = A_{t_1-t_0} \cup \rho_{t_0}$) to check their potential promotion to interesting triples.

Definition 12 (Interest Evaluation over Deleted Triples). *Interest evaluation over deleted triples is a function, $d(i_g, D_{t_1-t_0})$, that returns a 3-element tuple[5]:*

$$d(i_g, D_{t_1-t_0}) = \pi(i_g, D_{t_1-t_0}) \; \cup^* \; \pi'(i_g, D_{t_1-t_0}) = \langle r_{t_1-t_0}, r_{i(t_1-t_0)}, r'_{t_1-t_0} \rangle$$

where:
- $\pi(i_g, D_{t_1-t_0})$ *is an interest candidate generation against deleted triples,*
- $\pi'(i_g, D_{t_1-t_0})$ *is an interest candidate assertion against deleted triples,*
- $r_{t_1-t_0} = \{c_0 \cup c_k \cup c_{op} | \; c_0, c_k, c_{op} \in \pi(i_g, D_{t_1-t_0}) \text{ and } \exists c'_{n-k}, c'_0 \in \pi'(i_g, D_{t_1-t_0})\}$ *is the set of interesting removed triples, i.e., no longer interesting,*
- $r_{i(t_1-t_0)} = \{c_k \cup c_{op} | c_k, c_{op} \in \pi(i_g, D_{t_1-t_0}) \text{ and } \nexists c'_{n-k}, c'_0 \in \pi'(i_g, D_{t_1-t_0})\}$ *is the set of potentially interesting removed triples (existing only in removed triples of a changeset) and*
- $r'_{t_1-t_0} = \{c'_0 \cup c'_k \cup c'_{op} | c'_0, c'_k, c'_{op} \in \pi'(i_g, D_{t_1-t_0}) \text{ and } \exists c_{op}, c_{n-k}, c_0 \in \pi(i_g, D_{t_1-t_0})\}$ *is the set of triples that become potentially interesting after removing $r_{t_1-t_0}$.*

Example 5. An interest evaluation over deleted triples in our running example (using the results of Example 3 and Example 4, respectively) is as follows:

$$d(i_g, D_{05:02-05:00}) = \pi(i_g, D_{05:02-05:00}) \; \cup^* \; \pi'(i_g, D_{05:02-05:00})$$
$$= \langle r_{05:02-05:00}, r_{i(05:02-05:00)}, r'_{05:02-05:00} \rangle$$

---

[5] Note: $\cup^*$ indicates that after the component-wise union of the two sets the results are combined to three categories of the resulting 3-tuple, namely, (i) elements from left that have matching right elements, (ii) elements from left that do not have matching right elements, and (iii) element from right that have a match left.

1. $r_{05:02-05:00} = c_1$ (in Example 3)

```
dbr:Marcel              dbp:goals    1 .
dbr:Cristiano_Ronaldo   dbo:goals    96 .
```

2. $r_{i(05:02-05:00)} = \emptyset$ (Since all the potentially interesting removed triples of c_1 in Example 3 becomes interesting and no other triples in c_op)

3. $r'_{05:02-05:00} = c'_1$

```
dbr:Marcel              a               dbo:Athlete .
dbr:Cristiano_Ronaldo   a               dbo:Athlete .
dbr:Cristiano_Ronaldo   foaf:homepage   "http://cristianoronaldo.com" .
```

Definition 13 (Interest Evaluation over Added Triples). *Interest evaluation over added triples is a function, $\alpha(i_g, A_{t_1-t_0})$, that returns 3 element tuple as:*

$$\alpha(i_g, A_{t_1-t_0}) = \pi(i_g, I_{t_1-t_0}) \cup^* \pi'(i_g, I_{t_1-t_0}) = \langle a_{t_1-t_0}, a_{i(t_1-t_0)}, a'_{t_1-t_0} \rangle$$

where:

- $I_{t_1-t_0} = A_{t_1-t_0} \cup \rho_{t_0}$ *is a set of added triples and potentially interesting triples dataset,*
- $\pi(i_g, I_{t_1-t_0})$ *is an interest candidate generation over $I_{t_1-t_0}$,*
- $\pi'(i_g, I_{t_1-t_0})$ *is an interest candidate assertion over $I_{t_1-t_0}$,*
- $a_{t_1-t_0} = \{c_0 \cup c_k \cup c_{op} | c_0, c_k, c_{op} \in \pi(i_g, I_{t_1-t_0})$ *and* $\exists c'_{n-k}, c'_0 \in \pi'(i_g, I_{t_1-t_0})\}$ *is the set of interesting added triples,*
- $a_{i(t_1-t_0)} = \{c_k \cup c_{op} | c_k, c_{op} \in \pi(i_g, I_{t_1-t_0})$ *and* $\nexists c'_{n-k}, c'_0 \in \pi'(i_g, I_{t_1-t_0})\}$ *is the set of potentially interesting added triples that do not have related triples in target dataset, and*
- $a'_{t_1-t_0} = \{c'_0 \cup c'_k \cup c'_{op} | c'_0, c'_k, c'_{op} \in \pi'(i_g, I_{t_1-t_0})$ *and* $\exists c_{op}, c_{n-k}, c_0 \in \pi(i_g, I_{t_1-t_0})$ *respectively*$\}$ *is the set of triples from target dataset that are related to $a_{i(t_1-t_0)}$.*

Example 6. An interest evaluation over added triples in our running example (using the results of Example 3 and Example 4, respectively) is as follows:

$$\alpha(i_g, A_{05:02-05:00}) = \pi(i_g, I_{05:02-05:00}) \cup^* \pi'(i_g, I_{05:02-05:00})$$
$$= \langle a_{05:02-05:00}, a_{i(05:02-05:00)}, a'_{05:02-05:00} \rangle$$

1. $a_{05:02-05:00} = c_1 \cup c'_1 \cup c_0$

```
dbr:Cristiano_Ronaldo   dbo:goals       216 .
dbr:Cristiano_Ronaldo   a               dbo:Athlete .
dbr:Cristiano_Ronaldo   foaf:homepage   "http://cristianoronaldo.com" .
dbr:Rio_Ferdinand       a               dbo:Athlete .
dbr:Rio_Ferdinand       dbp:goals       10 .
```

2. $a_{i(05:02-05:00)} =$

```
dbr:Arvid_Smit      a               dbo:Athlete .
dbr:Barack_Obama    foaf:homepage   "http://www.barackobama.com" .
```

3. $a'_{05:02-05:00} = \emptyset$

Now, we will use the results from Definition 12 and Definition 13 to compute interesting and potentially interesting changesets.

Definition 14 (Interest Evaluation). *An interest evaluation over a change-set $\Delta(V_{t_1})$ at time t_1 is a function $e(i_g, \Delta(V_{t_1}))$ that combines the results from an interest evaluation over deleted triples, $d(i_g, D_{t_1-t_0})$, and an interest evaluation over added triples, $\alpha(i_g, I_{t_1-t_0})$, to return an interesting changeset and potentially interesting changeset as follows:*

$$e(i_g, \Delta(V_{t_1})) = d(i_g, D_{t_1-t_0}) \ \chi \ \ \alpha(i_g, I_{t_1-t_0}) = \langle \Delta(\tau_{t_1}), \Delta(\rho_{t_1}) \rangle$$

where i_g is an interest expression over an evolving dataset, $\Delta(\tau_{t_1})$ is an interesting changeset (see Definition 15), and $\Delta(\rho_{t_1})$ is potentially interesting changeset (see Definition 16).

Definition 15 (Interesting Changeset). *Let τ_{t_0} be a target dataset at time t_0. An interesting changeset, $\Delta(\tau_{t_1})$, for τ_{t_0} at time t_1 is defined as:*

$$\Delta(\tau_{t_1}) = \langle [r_{t_1-t_0} \cup r'_{t_1-t_0}], \ a_{t_1-t_0} \rangle$$

where:
- *$r_{t_1-t_0}$ is the set of interesting removed triples, interesting removed optional triples and potentially interesting removed triples with match found in target dataset during candidate generation, $\pi(i_g, D_{t_1-t_0})$,*
- *$r'_{t_1-t_0}$ is the set of triples from target dataset that are related to potentially interesting removed triples computed by $\pi'(i_g, D_{t_1-t_0})$, and*
- *$a_{t_1-t_0}$ is the set of interesting added triples, interesting optional triples and potentially interesting added triples with match found in target dataset during candidate generation, $\pi(i_g, A_{t_1-t_0})$.*

Example 7. An interesting changeset for our running example is as follows: $\Delta(\tau_{05:02}) = \langle (r_{05:02-05:00} \cup r'_{05:02-05:00}), \ a_{05:02-05:00} \rangle$
1. interesting removed triples $-(r_{05:02-05:00} \cup r'_{05:02-05:00})$:

```
dbr:Marcel              a            dbo:Athlete .
dbr:Marcel              dbp:goals    1 .
dbr:Cristiano_Ronaldo   dbo:goals    96 .
dbr:Cristiano_Ronaldo   a            dbo:Athlete .
dbr:Cristiano_Ronaldo   foaf:homepage   "http://cristianoronaldo.com" .
```

2. interesting added triples $- a_{05:02-05:00}$:

```
dbr:Cristiano_Ronaldo   dbo:goals     216 .
dbr:Cristiano_Ronaldo   a             dbo:Athlete .
dbr:Cristiano_Ronaldo   foaf:homepage   "http://cristianoronaldo.com" .
dbr:Rio_Ferdinand       a             dbo:Athlete .
dbr:Rio_Ferdinand       dbp:goals     10 .
```

Triples that were interesting will be downgraded to potentially interesting and stored in ρ_{t_1}, if deletion involves triples matching at least one triple pattern from interest expression BGP.

Definition 16 (Potentially Interesting Changeset). *Let ρ_{t_0} be a potentially interesting dataset for interest expression i_g at time t_0. A changeset, $\Delta(\rho_{t_1})$, for ρ_{t_0} at time t_1 is defined as:*

$$\Delta(\rho_{t_1}) = \left\langle r_{i(t_1-t_0)}, \left(a_{i(t_1-t_0)} \cup r'_{t_1-t_0}\right)\right\rangle$$

where:

- $r_{i(t_1-t_0)}$ *is a set of potentially interesting removed triples,*
- $a_{i(t_1-t_0)}$ *is a set of potentially interesting added triples computed on added triples of a changeset and related triples extracted from target while removing potentially interesting removed triples, and*
- $r'_{t_1-t_0}$ *is the set of triples from target dataset that are related to potentially interesting removed triples computed by $\pi'(i_g, D_{t_1-t_0})$.*

Example 8. Potentially interesting changeset for our running example is as follows: $\Delta(\rho_{05:02}) = \left\langle r_{i(05:02-05:00)}, \left(a_{i(05:02-05:00)} \cup r'_{05:02-05:00}\right)\right\rangle$
1. Potentially interesting removed triples $- r_{i(05:02-05:00)} = \emptyset$
2. Potentially interesting added triples $- \left(a_{i(05:02-05:00)} \cup r'_{05:02-05:00}\right)$

```
dbr:Arvid_Smit      a              dbo:Athlete .
dbr:Barack_Obama    foaf:homepage  "http://www.barackobama.com" .
dbr:Marcel          a              dbo:Athlete .
```

Note: since all triples in $r'_{05:02-05:00}$ are added back to target dataset, they are no longer stored in the potentially interesting dataset.

Definition 17 (Interesting Update Propagation). *An interesting changeset propagation is an update operation that transforms the target dataset τ_{t_0} to the new dataset τ_{t_1} and ρ_{t_0} to new dataset ρ_{t_1} by applying the result of interest evaluation, $e(i_g, \Delta(V_{t_1}))$. That is:*

$$\Upsilon(i_g, \Delta(V_{t_1})) = \upsilon(\tau_{t_0}, \Delta(\tau_{t_1})) \wedge \upsilon(\rho_{t_0}, \Delta(\rho_{t_1})) = \tau_{t_1} \wedge \rho_{t_1}$$

- $\Delta(V_{t_1})$ *is a changeset at time t_1,*
- $\upsilon(\tau_{t_0}, \Delta(\tau_{t_1})) = \left(\tau_{t_0} \backslash [r_{t_1-t_0} \cup r'_{t_1-t_0}]\right) \cup a_{t_1-t_0}$ *is changeset propagation of interesting changeset, and*
- $\upsilon(\rho_{t_0}, \Delta(\rho_{t_1})) = \left(\rho_{t_0} \backslash r_{i(t_1-t_0)}\right) \cup \left(a_{i(t_1-t_0)} \cup r'_{t_1-t_0}\right)$ *is changeset propagation of potentially interesting changeset.*

Example 9. Propagation of an interesting changeset of Example 7 to the target dataset, τ_{t_0} and potentially interesting changeset of Example 8 to the potentially interesting datasetρ_{t_0} transforms the datasets to:

More details on the formalization and implementation of the approach can be found here: http://eis.iai.uni-bonn.de/Projects/iRap.html.

3 iRap RDF Update Propagation Framework

In this section we describe the architecture of our interest-based update propagation framework, iRap, and its implementation. iRap was implemented in Java

```
dbr:Cristiano_Ronaldo  dbo:goals      216 .
dbr:Cristiano_Ronaldo  a              dbo:Athlete .
dbr:Cristiano_Ronaldo  foaf:homepage
                       "http://cristianoronaldo.com" .
dbr:Rio_Ferdinand      a              dbo:Athlete .
dbr:Rio_Ferdinand      dbp:goals      10 .
```

Listing (1.3) Resulting target dataset (τ_{t_1})

```
dbr:Arvid_Smit     a              dbo:Athlete .
dbr:Barack_Obama   foaf:homepage
                   "http://www.barackobama.com" .
dbr:Marcel         a              dbo:Athlete .
```

Listing (1.4) Potentially interesting dataset after change propagation (ρ_{t_1})

Fig. 4. State of τ_{t_1} and ρ_{t_1} after propagation

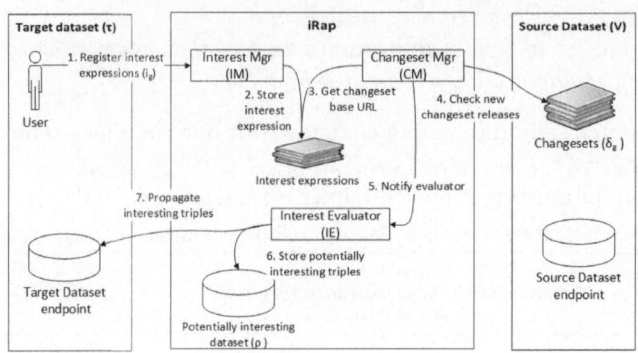

Fig. 5. Architecture of the iRap interest-based RDF update propagation framework.

using Jena-ARQ. It is available as open-source and consists of three modules: (1) *Interest Manager* (IM), (2) *Changeset Manager* (CM) and (3) *Interest Evaluator* (IE), each of which can be extended to accommodate new or improved functionality.

Changeset evaluation starts after a user registers an interest expression using the IM service, as shown in Figure 5. The CM module fetches a list of changeset folders from interest expressions and regularly (configurable) checks for new changesets. After downloading and decompressing new changesets, the CM notifies the IE, which then imports a list of interest expressions registered for this particular changeset through the IM and initiates the evaluation. Resulting interesting triples are propagated to the target dataset whereas potentially interesting triples are stored in the potentially interesting dataset (ρ). After all interest expressions have been evaluated over the changeset, the IE notifies the CM to clean the downloaded files.

4   Evaluation

To evaluate the proposed approach, we performed experiments on the iRap framework using changesets published by DBpedia and compared the results with the DBpedia Live Mirror tool. The comparison considers two cases: using iRap to update a previously-established local replica of i) an entire remote

Table 1. Distribution of DBpedia Live changesets published October 01-15, 2014.

Date	Oct 01	Oct 02	Oct 03	Oct 04-12	Oct 13	Oct 14	Oct 15
Total Changesets	0	1,621	1,755	0	5,352	751	2,578

```
CONSTRUCT WHERE {
    ?footballer  a        dbo:SoccerPlayer .
    ?footballer  foaf:name    ?name.
    ?footballer  dbo:team     ?team .
    ?team        rdfs:label   ?teamName.
}
```

Listing (1.5) I_1 – Football interest query

```
CONSTRUCT WHERE {
    ?location  a            ?type .
    ?location  wgs:long     ?long .
    ?location  wgs:lat      ?lat .
    ?location  rdfs:label   ?label .
    ?location  dbo:abstract ?abstract .
    OPTIONAL { ?location dcterms:subject ?subject }
}
```

Listing (1.6) I_2 – Location interest query

dataset ii) a subset of a remote dataset. These two cases simulate two ways in which iRap can be used: i) using interest-based changeset propagation for future updates of a local copy of a large dataset or ii) starting with a new subset of the large dataset.

Experimental Setting. In order to test our approach we used the DBpedia dump[6] of September 30, 2014 for the initial setup of the target datasets for two different application domains, namely, *Location and Football* datasets. Changesets published between October 01 and October 15, 2014 were used for evaluation (see Table 1). Changesets are not sequential with modified date but with extraction from DBpedia Live, as discussed in the DBpedia mailing list. Initially we set up two Jena TDB datasets for each target dataset from the DBpedia dump. We loaded all triples from the dump to the Location dataset, whereas for the Football dataset we only loaded a slice corresponding to interesting triples matching Listing 1.5.

Initially, the Location dataset contains all triples from DBpedia yielding a total of 3 billion triples, whereas the Football dataset contains only 265,622 triples. A total of 12,057 changesets (pairs of removed and added .nt.gz files) have been published in the evaluation timeframe.

The evaluation comprises two interest expressions, I_1 and I_2. I_1 comprises a non-disjoint BGP containing 4 triple patterns with a maximum of two variables per triple pattern (object-subject join), Listing 1.5. I_2 comprises a non-disjoint BGP containing 5 triple patterns with a maximum of two variables per triple pattern (subject-subject joins) and one an OGP containing one triple pattern, Listing 1.6.

We set up two target datasets and potentially interesting dataset using Jena TDB and jena-fuseki for each dataset. The potentially interesting dataset stores potentially interesting triples for each interest expression within a named graph. All experiments were carried out on a 64-bit machine with Windows 7, Intel(R) Core i7-4770 CPU, 16GB RAM and 1TB HD.

---

[6] http://live.dbpedia.org/dumps/dbpedia_2014_09_30_00_00.fixed.ttl.gz

Table 2. Comparison of results for Football App

Day	Total Removed	Interesting Removed	Total Added	Interesting Added	Potentially Interesting	Elapsed (in minutes)
1	1,895,179	9,065	2,051,976	184	169,554	15.18
2	1,748,511	4,865	2,384,232	155	168,856	20.85
3	1,716	0	10,728,855	45,429	684,491	69.86
4	449	0	1,522,939	7,970	97,300	10.17
5	1,677	0	5,234,788	19,598	333,232	60.06

Table 3. Comparison of results for Location App

Day	Total Removed	Interesting Removed	Total Added	Interesting Added	Potentially Interesting	Elapsed (in minutes)
1	1,895,179	77,377	2,051,976	7,093	430376	166.59
2	1,748,511	82,461	2,384,232	7,301	509,972	242.62
3	1,716	0	10,728,855	259,587	2,002,271	417.87
4	449	0	1,522,939	27,292	280,718	64.41
5	1,677	0	5,234,788	100,073	972,284	176.78

Evaluation Results and Discussion. Figure 7 summarizes our experimental results for two target datasets shows the growth of the potentially interesting dataset. Results of the interest evaluation for the Football dataset are presented in Table 2. From the overall changesets considered for this evaluation, in Table 1, only 0.38% of the removed and 0.335% of the added triples were identified as interesting for the Football dataset. The average changeset publication interval was 18.81s and average time required for a changeset evaluation is 0.87s. This shows that iRap efficiently performs changeset propagations way before the next changeset is published.

Results of the interest evaluation for the Location dataset are shown in Table 3. From the overall changesets considered for this evaluation, in Table 1, only 4.38% of the removed and 1.81% of the added triples were interesting for the Location dataset. The average time spent for a changeset evaluation is 5.31s. The interest evaluation for the Location dataset takes longer than Football dataset, because of the number of triples in the target dataset was the full DBpedia. Figure 7a shows the number of triples published per day and the number of interesting triples and potentially interesting triples found from interest evaluation for Football dataset. Figure 7b shows the dataset growth comparison between iRap and a full mirror approach. As the figure clearly shows, iRap managed datasets are almost two orders of magnitude smaller and grow much slower than with a mirror approach. Note that the growth for each datasets is calculated by subtracting the number of removed triples from and adding the number of added triples to the total number of triples in the dataset.

We observed a logarithmic growth of the potentially interesting dataset for Location and Football datasets. This is due to the number of variables used in triple patterns, and the number and type of triple patterns in interest expression. For example, the Football dataset interest query contains the common predicates foaf:name and rdfs:label which are used in almost all resources and thus result in many potentially interesting triples. Again, the average processing time per changeset is always way below the average time between two changesets. The

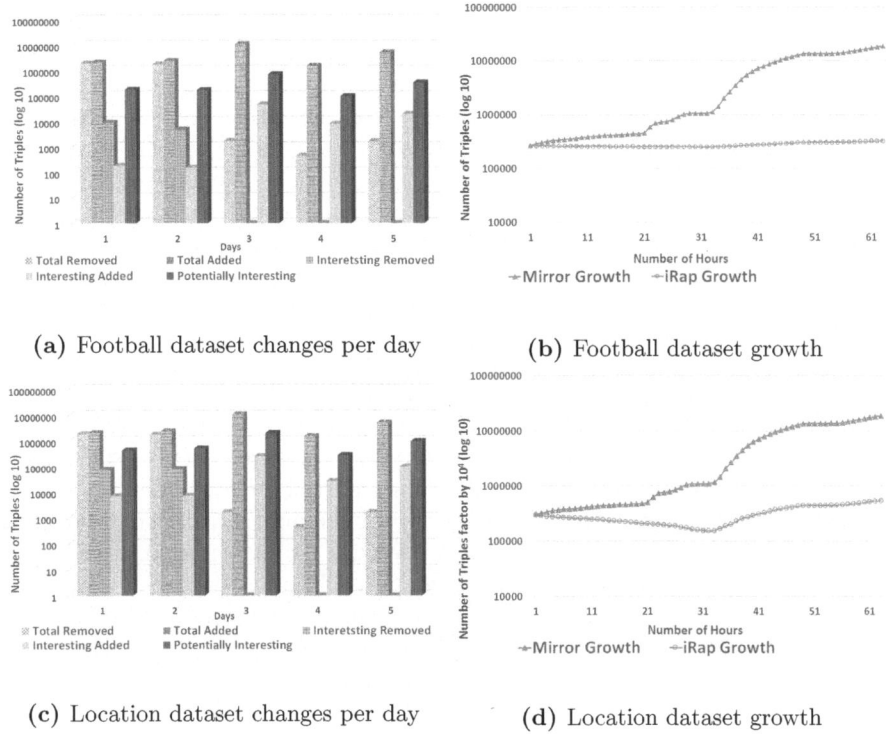

(a) Football dataset changes per day

(b) Football dataset growth

(c) Location dataset changes per day

(d) Location dataset growth

Fig. 7. Evaluation results

correctness of the resulting triples from the first changesets, for Football dataset interest expression, was checked by manual inspection.

5   Related Work

Most related work on dataset change detection and propagation focuses on distributed publish/subscribe systems [3,7], resource link maintenance [8,10], target synchronization [5], partial replicas [9], data-shipping [12], lazy updates [2], and real-time update notification [6,10]. In [7], the authors propose a peer-to-peer publish/subscribe system for events described in RDF. By avoiding the use of multiple indexes for the same publication they manage to reduce storage space. Similarly, [3] provide an implementation with publish/subscribe capabilities in an RDF-based peer-to-peer system to manage digital resources. As for resource link maintenance, *DSNotify* [8] offers a change-detection framework to detect and fix broken links between resources in two datasets while, *Semantic Pingback* [10] proposes a notification system for the creation of new links between Web resources. To note that this approach is suitable for relatively static resources, i.e. RDF documents or RDFa annotated Web pages. In contrast, *SparqlPuSH* [6] offers a real-time notification framework for data updates in a

RDF store using a semantic *PubSubHubbub*-based protocol (PuSH). SparqlPuSH allows users to subscribe for changes updates of a subset of content in a RDF store using SPARQL. However, notification and broadcasting are only available as RSS and Atom feeds. As regards target synchronization, *RDFSync* [5] performs update synchronization by merging source and target graphs to get the updated target RDF graph. Alternatively, [9] has designed an approach to replicate, modify, and write-back parts of an RDF graph on devices with low computing power. In distributed databases, where data is replicated on different sites, Lazy update protocols [2] disseminate updates to replicas to ensure consistency. These protocols guarantee serializable execution as well as high performance.

6 Conclusion and Future Work

In this paper we presented a novel approach for interest-based RDF update propagation that can consistently maintain a full or partial replication of large LOD datasets. We have demonstrated the validity of the approach through detailed formalizations and their application in a reference implementation of the iRap Framework. A thorough evaluation of the approach indicates that our method can significantly cut down on both the size of the data updates required to consistently maintain a localized dataset replication up-to-date, as well as the speed by which such updates can take place. Future work will focus on extending the iRap Framework with a publish/subscribe distributed architecture. The framework will be improved also from the usability point of view, including a user interface and making the initial generation of RDF slices easier and more efficient. An extensive evaluation of scalability and performance of the framework will be performed and a benchmark dataset for future reference will be made available to the research community.

Acknowledgments. This work is supported by LinDA project, funded by the European Union's Seventh Framework Programme for research, technological development and demonstration under grant agreement number 610565.

References

1. SPARQL 1.1 Query Language (2013).
   http://www.w3.org/TR/2013/REC-sparql11-query-20130321/
2. Breitbart, Y., Komondoor, R., Rastogi, R., Seshadri, S., Silberschatz, A.: Update propagation protocols for replicated databates. ACM SIGMOD Record 28 (1999)
3. Chirita, P.-A., Idreos, S., Koubarakis, M., Nejdl, W.: Publish/subscribe for RDF-based P2P networks. In: Bussler, C.J., Davies, J., Fensel, D., Studer, R. (eds.) ESWS 2004. LNCS, vol. 3053, pp. 182–197. Springer, Heidelberg (2004)
4. Marx, E., Shekarpour, S., Auer, S., Ngomo, A.N.: Large-scale RDF dataset slicing. In: 2013 IEEE Seventh International Conference on Semantic Computing, Irvine, CA, USA, pp. 228–235, 16–18 September 2013

5. Tummarello, G., Morbidoni, C., Bachmann-Gmür, R., Erling, O.: RDFSync: efficient remote synchronization of RDF models. In: Aberer, K., Choi, K.-S., Noy, N., Allemang, D., Lee, K.-I., Nixon, L.J.B., Golbeck, J., Mika, P., Maynard, D., Mizoguchi, R., Schreiber, G., Cudré-Mauroux, P. (eds.) ASWC 2007 and ISWC 2007. LNCS, vol. 4825, pp. 537–551. Springer, Heidelberg (2007)
6. Passant, A., Mendes, P.: sparqlPuSH: Proactive notification of data updates in RDF stores using PubSubHubbub. In: Scripting for the Semantic Web Workshop (SFSW2010) (2010)
7. Pellegrino, L., Huet, F., Baude, F., Alshabani, A.: A distributed publish/subscribe system for RDF data. In: Hameurlain, A., Rahayu, W., Taniar, D. (eds.) Globe 2013. LNCS, vol. 8059, pp. 39–50. Springer, Heidelberg (2013)
8. Popitsch, N., Haslhofer, B.: Dsnotify - a solution for event detection and link maintenance in dynamic datasets. J. Web Sem. **9**(3), 266–283 (2011)
9. Schandl, B.: Replication and versioning of partial RDF graphs. In: Aroyo, L., Antoniou, G., Hyvönen, E., ten Teije, A., Stuckenschmidt, H., Cabral, L., Tudorache, T. (eds.) ESWC 2010, Part I. LNCS, vol. 6088, pp. 31–45. Springer, Heidelberg (2010)
10. Tramp, S., Frischmuth, P., Ermilov, T., Auer, S.: Weaving a social data web with semantic pingback. In: Cimiano, P., Pinto, H.S. (eds.) EKAW 2010. LNCS, vol. 6317, pp. 135–149. Springer, Heidelberg (2010)
11. Verborgh, R., Hartig, O., De Meester, B., Haesendonck, G., De Vocht, L., Vander Sande, M., Cyganiak, R., Colpaert, P., Mannens, E., Van de Walle, R.: Querying datasets on the web with high availability. In: Mika, P., Tudorache, T., Bernstein, A., Welty, C., Knoblock, C., Vrandečić, D., Groth, P., Noy, N., Janowicz, K., Goble, C. (eds.) ISWC 2014, Part I. LNCS, vol. 8796, pp. 180–196. Springer, Heidelberg (2014)
12. Voruganti, K., Özsu, M.T., Unrau, R.C.: An adaptive data-shipping architecture for client caching data management systems. Distributed and Parallel Databases **15**(2), 137–177 (2004)

Ontology Extraction and Generation

General Terminology Induction in OWL

Viachaslau Sazonau[✉], Uli Sattler, and Gavin Brown

The University of Manchester, Oxford Road, Manchester M13 9PL, UK
{sazonauv,sattler,gbrown}@cs.manchester.ac.uk

Abstract. Automated acquisition, or learning, of ontologies has attracted research attention because it can help ontology engineers build ontologies and give domain experts new insights into their data. However, existing approaches to ontology learning are considerably limited, e.g. focus on learning descriptions for given classes, require intense supervision and human involvement, make assumptions about data, do not fully respect background knowledge. We investigate the problem of general terminology induction, i.e. learning sets of general class inclusions, GCIs, from data and background knowledge. We introduce measures that evaluate logical and statistical quality of a set of GCIs. We present methods to compute these measures and an anytime algorithm that induces sets of GCIs. Our experiments show that we can acquire interesting sets of GCIs and provide insights into the structure of the search space.

1 Introduction

An ontology is a machine-processable representation of knowledge about a domain of interest. Ontologies are encoded in formal languages, such as the Web Ontology Language [8], OWL, underpinned by expressive Description Logics, DLs [1]. OWL ontologies are widely-used to represent and share knowledge in application areas such as medicine, biology, astronomy, defence and others.[1] An ontology can contain data and background knowledge (terminology) where both may be incomplete. One might benefit from finding informative correlations in their data taking background knowledge into account. Those correlations may suggest new axioms for the background knowledge or start new inquiries about the data.

However, the problem of terminology induction is generally hard. Firstly, an ideal solution should represent a coherent, self-contained, expert-level modelling. Due to high expressivity of OWL and its Open World Assumption (OWA), the search space can be vast or even infinite depending on the language chosen. Secondly, as usual, the quality of the result depends on the quality of the data which can be incorrect, noisy or insufficient. Ideally, new knowledge should respect the existing knowledge along with the data in order to be maximally informative and avoid contradictions.

Thus, some restrictions and assumptions that simplify the problem are necessary. Another consequence is that any induced knowledge is hypothetical only

---

[1] http://bioportal.bioontology.org/

M. Arenas et al. (Eds.): ISWC 2015, Part I, LNCS 9366, pp. 533–550, 2015.
DOI: 10.1007/978-3-319-25007-6_31

and requires a domain expert judgement. The contributions of this paper are as follows.

- We state the problem of general terminology induction, i.e. learning sets, called *hypotheses*, of general class inclusions, GCIs, from data (ABox) and background knowledge (TBox).
- We view the problem as multi-objective and define quality criteria for a hypothesis: readability, logical quality, and statistical quality. We define quality measures for a hypothesis that respect the OWA, interactions between axioms in the hypothesis, and interaction of the hypothesis with the background knowledge.
- We have designed and implemented methods to compute the quality measures.
- We have designed, implemented and evaluated an anytime algorithm for general terminology induction. We have gained insights into the structure of the search space and developed heuristics to find out promising hypotheses. The experiments show that we can indeed learn interesting hypotheses.

2   Preliminaries

We assume the reader to be familiar with DLs [1] and OWL [8]. The following nomenclature is used throughout this paper. $\mathcal{O} = \mathcal{T} \cup \mathcal{A}$ is an ontology where $\mathcal{T}$, $\mathcal{A}$ are TBox and ABox, respectively. N_C, N_R, N_I are disjoint and countably infinite sets of class, property, and individual names, respectively. Σ is a signature, $\widetilde{\mathcal{T}}, \widetilde{\mathcal{A}}, \widetilde{\mathcal{O}}$ are signatures of $\mathcal{T}, \mathcal{A}, \mathcal{O}$, respectively. $ind(\mathcal{O}) = N_I \cap \widetilde{\mathcal{O}}$ is a set of individual names occurring in $\mathcal{O}$. α is a general class inclusion, GCI, also called *axiom*. A, B, X, Y are atomic classes (class names), C, D are complex classes (class expressions), R is a property, a, b, c, d are individuals. $mod(\mathcal{O}, \Sigma)$ is a module [5] of an ontology $\mathcal{O}$ given a signature Σ. $\mathbb{C}$ is a set of (possibly complex) classes. H is a hypothesis, $\mathbb{H}$ is a set of hypotheses. In the following, ABox and TBox are called *data* and *background knowledge*, respectively.

3   Related Work

Ontology learning approaches can be characterised along several dimensions. The first one is a type of the data source, e.g. texts, RDF(S), an oracle (a domain expert), positive and negative examples for a class along with the ABox. The second one is a type of the output knowledge, e.g. class descriptions, class inclusions, and its expressivity. The third dimension is methods used: natural language processing, machine learning, association rules mining, oracle queries, Formal Concept Analysis (FCA), least common subsumer (LCS) computation, etc. The fourth dimension is semantics used that can differ from the OWL semantics, e.g. the Closed World Assumption (CWA). One more characteristic is appreciation of available background knowledge. Finally, the degree of domain expert involvement into the learning process greatly varies across approaches. A survey can be found in [12].

We concentrate on learning from instance-level data, i.e. both class and property assertions. Among the approaches aimed at this type of input data are class description learning, CDL [3,6,11], knowledge base completion, KBC [2], association rules mining, ARM [17].

The main method of CDL is machine learning, in particular, Inductive Logic Programming, ILP [13]. The goal is to find a "good" description (class expression) of a given class name from a set of positive and negative examples [11] for it, i.e. learning is *supervised*. The class description must cover all positive and none of the negative examples. Learning is essentially a search in the space of class expressions guided by refinement operators and heuristics. The background knowledge can be used to optimize the search by exploiting the classification hierarchy. To supervise learning, a domain expert has to provide additional information in form of positive and negative examples for a given class, which can be difficult. As a consequence, there are techniques to sample examples from data. In particular, instances of the class are taken as its positive examples and the CWA is made to obtain its negative examples. However, this way can cause problems [10]. Another method of CDL is finding the least common subsumer (LCS) [3]. LCS is computed from the most specific class (MSC) of each instance of a target class. The method, however, is only applicable to weakly expressive languages.

KBC is based on Formal Concept Analysis (FCA) [7]. It is aimed at acquiring (in some sense) complete knowledge bases, in contrast to CDL. KBC requires to define a set of class expressions in advance which can be hard. The degree of domain expert involvement is high as the expert judges axioms and has to supply a counterexample in the case of rejection. One more limitation is that standard FCA can only be applied under the CWA and the OWA of OWL requires modifications of FCA [2].

ARM is yet another approach to ontology learning [17]. Association rules are mined from transaction tables where columns are predefined class expressions which, similarly to the case of KBC, can be difficult to define in advance. In contrast to KBC, ARM, however, permits acquiring axioms that have counterexamples. In contrast to CDL, ARM induces class inclusions and demands neither positive nor negative examples. The approach focuses on weakly expressive languages. Among other restrictions are its CWA and little appreciation of interaction between induced axioms and the background knowledge, as well as mutual interactions between induced axioms, since they are acquired independently.

Thus, ontology learning approaches simplify the problem in different aspects. As a result, there is no approach that has all following capabilities: learns sets of GCIs, appreciates interactions between axioms within the set and interactions of the set with the background knowledge, uses standard OWL semantics, requires no supervision, does not demand frequent human interventions.

4   Settings and Assumptions

This paper is aimed at addressing the problem of inducing general terminological knowledge from data and background knowledge which together constitute the input ontology. New knowledge is acquired in form of *hypotheses*. A hypothesis is a set of axioms which does not contradict the input ontology, i.e. *consistent* with it, and carries new information, i.e. *informative* for it.

Definition 1. *(Hypothesis) An axiom α is informative for an ontology $\mathcal{O}$ if $\mathcal{O} \nvDash \alpha$. A set H of axioms (GCIs) is called a hypothesis for an ontology $\mathcal{O}$ if H is consistent with $\mathcal{O}$, i.e. $\mathcal{O} \cup H \nvDash \top \sqsubseteq \bot$, and each $\alpha \in H$ is informative for $\mathcal{O}$.*

A hypothesis is evaluated by *quality criteria*: *readability, statistical quality*, and *logical quality*. Clearly, a hypothesis can be better on one criterion and worse on another. Therefore, we view terminology induction as a multi-objective problem where objectives are *quality measures* corresponding to the quality criteria. Hypotheses are presented to a domain expert who accepts some of them and rejects others. In order to suggest, or *recommend*, good hypotheses first, a preference relation based on quality measures is imposed on the set of hypotheses. In this paper, we apply the following *settings*.

(i) We use OWL and its standard semantics.
  (a) We allow for the usual OWA, i.e. for an instance a and a class C it is possible that $\mathcal{O} \nvDash C(a)$ and $\mathcal{O} \nvDash (\neg C)(a)$. As a consequence, data can be regarded as just "incomplete".
  (b) Data normally consists of both class and property assertions, e.g. people with family relations, proteins with interactions between them.
  (c) We consider any logic for which subsumption, $\mathcal{O} \vDash C \sqsubseteq D$, and instance checking, $\mathcal{O} \vDash C(a)$, are decidable. We use OWL ontologies and reasoners.
(ii) Any input ontology $\mathcal{O}$ is consistent, i.e. data contains no noise which causes inconsistency.
(iii) Learning is *unsupervised*, i.e. no additional information is required in form of positive or negative examples.
(iv) A set $\mathbb{C}$ of target (possibly complex) classes is fixed and finite.

The goal of induction is finding good hypotheses over classes $\mathbb{C}$, or $\mathbb{C}$-*hypotheses*. In the following, we only consider $\mathbb{C}$-hypotheses and omit $\mathbb{C}$ from the name. We also define $\mathbb{C}^- := \mathbb{C} \cup \{\neg C \mid C \in \mathbb{C}\}$.

Definition 2. *($\mathbb{C}$-Hypothesis) Given an ontology $\mathcal{O}$, a hypothesis H for $\mathcal{O}$ is called a $\mathbb{C}$-hypothesis if $\alpha \in H$ implies $\alpha = C \sqsubseteq D$, where $C, D \in \mathbb{C}^-$.*

It makes sense to establish a correspondence, sufficient for the task at hand, between an ontology $\mathcal{O}$ and classes $\mathbb{C}$, which we call *projection*.

Definition 3. *(Projection) A projection π of an ontology $\mathcal{O}$ to $\mathbb{C}$ is*

$$\pi(\mathcal{O}, \mathbb{C}) := \{D(a) \mid \mathcal{O} \vDash D(a) \wedge D \in \mathbb{C}^- \wedge a \in ind(\mathcal{O})\}.$$

Thus, a projection is a set of positive and negative class assertions over classes $\mathbb{C}$ entailed by $\mathcal{O}$. A projection can be viewed as a table where rows are labelled with individuals $ind(\mathcal{O})$ and columns are labelled with classes $\mathbb{C}$. Each cell with indices a, C can contain one of three possible values: "1" if $\mathcal{O} \models C(a)$, "0" if $\mathcal{O} \models \neg C(a)$, "?" if $\mathcal{O} \nvDash C(a)$ and $\mathcal{O} \nvDash \neg C(a)$. Although there are similarities with a transaction table of ARM, our table view is imaginary only and it permits question marks. We will use the table view for better presentation of examples, see Example 1 and Table 1.

Example 1. Given $\mathbb{C} = \{A, B, \exists R.B\}$, $\mathcal{T} = \emptyset$,

$$\mathcal{A} = \{A(a_1), A(a_2), A(a_3), A(a_4), (\neg A)(b), (\neg A)(c), B(c)$$
$$R(a_1, b), R(a_2, b), R(a_3, b), R(a_4, c)\}.$$

We use the projection to evaluate how well a hypothesis fits the *known* data assuming it is correct on the *unknown* data. Indeed, due to the OWA, a hypothesis can make *assumptions* on the unknown data by turning question marks into ones or zeros. If a hypothesis makes too many assumptions, it may be too "strong", e.g. $H = \{\top \sqsubseteq \sqcap_{C \in \mathbb{C}} C\}$. Therefore, it is necessary to evaluate how "brave" a hypothesis is.

Table 1

	A	B	$\exists R.B$
a_1	1	?	?
a_2	1	?	?
a_3	1	?	?
a_4	1	?	1
b	0	?	?
c	0	1	?

Definition 4. *(Assumption) An* assumption *of a hypothesis H in an ontology $\mathcal{O}$ given $\mathbb{C}$ is*

$$\psi(H, \mathcal{O}, \mathbb{C}) := \{D(a) \mid \mathcal{O} \nvDash D(a) \wedge \mathcal{O} \cup H \models D(a) \wedge D \in \mathbb{C}^- \wedge a \in ind(\mathcal{O})\}.$$

As a consequence, $\psi(H, \mathcal{O}, \mathbb{C}) \cap \pi(\mathcal{O}, \mathbb{C}) = \emptyset$ for any hypothesis H. Requiring $\mathcal{O} \nvDash (\neg D)(a)$ in Definition 4 is not necessary because if $\mathcal{O} \models (\neg D)(a)$ then H is not a hypothesis due its inconsistency with $\mathcal{O}$. Hypotheses making fewer assumptions are preferred according to Occam's razor.

One can think of suggesting hypotheses as single axioms. However, this approach ignores interactions between axioms that can influence the quality of the hypothesis. Two axioms, which are logically "good" individually, do not necessarily create a logically "good" hypothesis. For example, a hypothesis can become *redundant*, e.g. $H = \{A \sqsubseteq B, \neg B \sqsubseteq \neg A\}$, see Section 5.2. In fact, a set of two logically "good" axioms is not necessarily a hypothesis. For example, given that $\{A \sqsubseteq B\}$ and $\{B \sqsubseteq C\}$ are hypotheses for $\mathcal{O}$, a set $\{A \sqsubseteq B, B \sqsubseteq C\}$ is not a hypothesis for $\mathcal{O}$ if $\mathcal{O} \models (A \sqcap \neg C)(a)$. Similar to logical quality, two axioms which are statistically "good" individually may not create a "good" hypothesis which is discussed below, see Section 5.3.

5 Quality Criteria and Measures for a Hypothesis

5.1 Syntactic Length as a Readability Measure

Readability is the ease with which a hypothesis can be read and understood by a human. One of possible measures of readability is the usual *syntactic length* of a hypothesis.

Definition 5. *(Syntactic Length) Let* A, C, D *be (possibly complex) classes,* $A \in N_C$ *a class name,* $R \in N_R$ *a property name,* $a \in N_I$ *an individual name. The syntactic length of a GCI is defined as follows:* $|C \sqsubseteq D| := |C| + |D|$, *where* $|\top| = |\bot| = |A| := 1$, $|\neg C| := 1 + |C|$, $|C \sqcap D| = |C \sqcup D| := 1 + |C| + |D|$, $|\exists R.C| = |\forall R.C| := 1 + |C|$, $| \geq nR.C| = | \leq nR.C| := 1 + n + |C|$. *The syntactic length of a hypothesis* H *is* $|H| := \sum_{\alpha \in H} |\alpha|$.

5.2   Logical Quality

Logical quality evaluates logical properties of a hypothesis: *logical strength* and *redundancy*. Logical strength is commonly called generality in machine learning.

Definition 6. *(Logical Strength) A hypothesis* H *is* weaker *(more general) than another hypothesis* H' *if* $H' \models H$ *and* $H \nvDash H'$.

A hypothesis can contain axioms which are superfluous, or *redundant*, within the hypothesis, even if those axioms are informative. For example, axiom $A \sqsubseteq C$ is redundant in hypothesis $\{A \sqsubseteq B, B \sqsubseteq C, A \sqsubseteq C\}$ and axiom $\neg B \sqsubseteq \neg A$ is redundant in hypothesis $\{A \sqsubseteq B, \neg B \sqsubseteq \neg A\}$. Axioms can also have *redundant parts*. For example, D is a redundant part of axiom $A \sqsubseteq C \sqcap D$ in hypothesis $\{A \sqsubseteq B \sqcap D, A \sqsubseteq C \sqcap D\}$.

Definition 7. *(Redundancy) A hypothesis* H *is* redundant *if there exists a hypothesis* H' *such that* $H' \equiv H$ *and* $|H'| < |H|$. *Otherwise,* H *is* non-redundant.

Lemma 1. *If a hypothesis* H *is non-redundant, then* $|H| = min\{|H'| \mid H' \equiv H\}$.

We define the logical strength and redundancy of a hypothesis H regardless of $\mathcal{O}$. The reason is that an axiom $\alpha \in H$, which is informative for $\mathcal{O}$ and non-redundant in H, can be interesting, even if it is not informative for $\mathcal{O} \cup H \backslash \{\alpha\}$. Such axiom reveals yet only implicit (and possibly unknown) relation between classes. Additionally, the search for good hypotheses would require entailment checking $\mathcal{O} \cup H \models H'$ which could make it infeasible for hard ontologies.

5.3   Statistical Quality

Statistical quality criteria are aimed at selecting hypotheses that best represent data given background knowledge. In order to comply with the standard OWL semantics and its OWA, we consider the statistical quality of a hypothesis as two-fold. Firstly, hypotheses differently fit data along with background knowledge. Secondly, hypotheses make different number of assumptions in data given background knowledge, i.e. some hypotheses are more cautious than others. Statistically better hypotheses have greater *fitness* and lower *braveness*.

Fitness and Braveness. In order to evaluate the statistical quality of a hypothesis, we exploit the idea that axioms can encode regularities in the data. Those regularities can be used to "compress" the data, i.e. to present it in a shorter way. This is the fundamental principle of the *minimum description length induction* [4,16]. According to it, the better a hypothesis fits the data, the shorter description of the data it provides.

A standard way of measuring the description length is using syntactic measures. However, syntactic measures do not respect logical interactions of a hypothesis with data and background knowledge. Therefore, we introduce a semantic measure of the description length. We define fitness and braveness of a hypothesis as follows.

Definition 8. *(Description Length, Fitness, Braveness) The description length of an ABox $\mathcal{B}$ given an ontology $\mathcal{O} = \mathcal{T} \cup \mathcal{A}$ is*

$$minSize(\mathcal{B}, \mathcal{O}) := min\{|\mathcal{B}'| \mid \mathcal{B}' \cup \mathcal{O} \equiv \mathcal{B} \cup \mathcal{O}\}.$$

Given an ontology $\mathcal{O}$, a set $\mathbb{C}$ of classes, and a hypothesis H, let $\pi := \pi(\mathcal{O}, \mathbb{C})$ and $\psi := \psi(H, \mathcal{O}, \mathbb{C})$. Then

(i) fitness *of H is $fit(H, \mathcal{O}, \mathbb{C}) := |\pi| - minSize(\pi, \mathcal{T} \cup H)$,*
(ii) braveness *of H is $bra(H, \mathcal{O}, \mathbb{C}) := minSize(\psi, \mathcal{O})$.*

As a consequence of Definition 8, all semantically equivalent hypotheses have the same fitness and the same braveness which is stated by Lemma 2.

Lemma 2. *Given an ontology $\mathcal{O}$, a set $\mathbb{C}$ of classes, and two hypotheses H_1, H_2, if $H_1 \equiv H_2$ then $fit(H_1, \mathcal{O}, \mathbb{C}) = fit(H_2, \mathcal{O}, \mathbb{C})$ and $bra(H_1, \mathcal{O}, \mathbb{C}) = bra(H_2, \mathcal{O}, \mathbb{C})$.*

Fitness of a hypothesis indicates how well the projection can be shrunk using the hypothesis and background knowledge, i.e. a better shrinkage corresponds to a better fitness. Braveness of a hypothesis measures how many assumptions it makes in the data given the background knowledge. Respecting Occam's razor, hypotheses of lower braveness (or more cautious) are preferred, see Example 2.

Table 2

	A	B
a	1	1
b	1	?

Example 2. The projection π is given by Table 2, $\mathcal{T} = \emptyset$. For $H_1 = \{A \sqsubseteq B\}$ $fit(H_1, \mathcal{O}, \mathbb{C}) = |B(a)| = 1$, $bra(H_1, \mathcal{O}, \mathbb{C}) = |B(b)| = 1$. For $H_2 = \{B \sqsubseteq A\}$ $fit(H_2, \mathcal{O}, \mathbb{C}) = |B(a)| = 1$, $bra(H_2, \mathcal{O}, \mathbb{C}) = 0$. Hence, H_2 is statistically better than H_1.

Two axioms which are statistically "good" individually may or may not create a "good" hypothesis, see Example 3.

Table 3

	A	B	C
a	?	?	1
b	1	1	1
c	1	1	1

Example 3. The projection is given by Table 3, $\mathcal{T} = \emptyset$. Hypotheses $H_1 = \{A \sqsubseteq B\}$, $H_2 = \{B \sqsubseteq C\}$, $H_3 = \{A \sqsubseteq C\}$ are individually statistically confident: $fit(H_1, \mathcal{O}, \mathbb{C}) =$

$fit(H_2, \mathcal{O}, \mathbb{C}) = fit(H_3, \mathcal{O}, \mathbb{C}) = 2$. However, hypothesis $H_{23} = H_2 \cup H_3$ has the same fitness as H_2, H_3: $fit(H_{23}, \mathcal{O}, \mathbb{C}) = 2$. On the other hand, hypothesis $H_{12} = H_1 \cup H_2$ has the fitness twice as big as one of H_1, H_2: $fit(H_{12}, \mathcal{O}, \mathbb{C}) = 4$.

In addition, axioms in the hypothesis can enforce each other, see Example 4.

Example 4. The projection is given by Table 4, $\mathcal{T} = \{B \sqsubseteq C\}$. Hypotheses $H_1 = \{A \sqsubseteq B\}$, $H_2 = \{C \sqsubseteq D\}$ individually have zero fitness. So, the fitness of collective hypothesis $H_{12} = H_1 \cup H_2$ is greater than the total fitness of H_1 and H_2: $fit(H_{12}, \mathcal{O}, \mathbb{C}) = 3$.

Although projection simplifies induction, we may lose some information, in particular, relations between individuals. The latter can result in the overestimation of hypothesis's assumption. In Example 1 let hypothesis $H = \{\neg A \sqsubseteq B\}$, then $\psi(H, \mathcal{O}, \mathbb{C}) = \{B(b), (\exists R.B)(a_1), (\exists R.B)(a_2), (\exists R.B)(a_3)\}$.

Table 4

	A	B	C	D
a	1	?	?	1
b	1	?	?	1
c	1	?	?	1

However, $(\exists R.B)(a_1), (\exists R.B)(a_2), (\exists R.B)(a_3)$ are, in fact, the consequences of $B(b)$ and should not be counted. Braveness correctly handles this: $bra(H, \mathcal{O}, \mathbb{C}) = |\{B(b)\}| = 1$. Illusive assumptions can also be forced by background knowledge and braveness handles this as well, see Example 5.

Example 5. The projection π is given by Table 5, $\mathcal{T} = \{B \sqcap C \sqsubseteq D\}$ and $H = \{A \sqsubseteq B, B \sqsubseteq D\}$. The assumption of H is $\psi(H, \mathcal{O}, \mathbb{C}) = \{B(a), B(b), D(a), D(b)\}$ and the braveness is $bra(H, \mathcal{O}, \mathbb{C}) = |\{B(a), B(b)\}| = 2$.

As a consequence of Definition 8, fitness and braveness are semantically sound and syntax independent measures of the statistical quality of a hypothesis. They take into account both the interaction of a hypothesis with the background knowledge and interactions between axioms within the hypothesis. The

Table 5

	A	B	C	D
a	1	?	1	?
b	1	?	1	?

measures respect the standard OWL semantics, in particular, they deal with its OWA and, consequently, with incomplete data. Finally, they demand no supervision, such as positive or negative examples, and no additional information besides the input ontology.

Computing Fitness and Braveness. Computing fitness and braveness requires finding the size of the minimal projection and assumption, respectively. These may not be unique. All minimal subsets can be found using a hitting set tree algorithm [14]. However, this may require an exponential number of reasoner updates which is computationally expensive given that the fitness and braveness are computed for each hypothesis.

Fortunately, there is a more efficient way to compute the fitness and braveness of a hypothesis avoiding reasoner updates. The idea is to introduce into $\mathcal{O}$ fresh names for classes from $\mathbb{C}^-$, i.e. $\mathcal{O}_X = \mathcal{O} \cup \{X_C \equiv C \mid C \in \mathbb{C}^-\}$, and exploit the inferred class hierarchy of $\mathcal{O}_X$. The function $minSizeUp(\mathcal{B}, \mathcal{O}_X)$ computes an upper bound of the description length $minSize(\mathcal{B}, \mathcal{O})$, which is used for calculating fitness and braveness (see Definition 8):

$minSizeUp(\mathcal{B}, \mathcal{O}_X) := |\mathcal{B}| - |redun(\mathcal{B}, \mathcal{O}_X)|$, where

$\quad redun(\mathcal{B}, \mathcal{O}_X) := \{D(a) \in \mathcal{B} \mid$ there is $C \in \widetilde{\mathcal{O}}_X$ s.t. either

$\qquad$ (i) $\mathcal{O}_X \models C \sqsubseteq D \wedge \mathcal{O}_X \not\models D \sqsubseteq C \wedge (\mathcal{O}_X \models C(a) \vee C(a) \in \mathcal{B})$ or

$\qquad$ (ii) $\mathcal{O}_X \models C \equiv D \wedge D \neq unique(D, \mathcal{O}_X)\}$, where

$\qquad unique$ is a function s.t. $unique(D, \mathcal{O}_X) = D'$ implies $\mathcal{O}_X \models D' \equiv D$.

$minSizeUp(\mathcal{B}, \mathcal{O}_X)$ is based on detecting redundancy of $\mathcal{B}$ given $\mathcal{O}_X$, $redun(\mathcal{B}, \mathcal{O}_X)$, which is the set of those class assertions that can be "easily" inferred from $\mathcal{B} \cup \mathcal{O}_X$ after full classification of $\mathcal{O}_X$. This avoids costly reasoner updates: a reasoner can be executed just once for each hypothesis to classify classes and individuals. However, $minSizeUp(\mathcal{B}, \mathcal{O}_X)$ can overestimate $minSize(\mathcal{B}, \mathcal{O})$ if some redundancy is missed by it. Hence, fitness can be underestimated and braveness can be overestimated, i.e. we may label a hypothesis worse than it is.

6   General Terminology Induction

According to Definition 1, we only consider hypotheses which are logically sound, i.e. informative and consistent with the background knowledge and data. The goal of the induction is finding among those hypotheses ones which have maximal fitness and minimal braveness, or better represent the data.

We impose a readability constraint on a hypothesis: it must not exceed a given syntactic length. The logical weakness of a hypothesis is reflected by its braveness: weaker hypotheses have a lower braveness and are preferred (respecting their fitness) according to Occam's razor. A redundant hypothesis has the same fitness and braveness as its non-redundant counterpart but a greater length that might be occupied by better axioms. We state the problem of general terminology induction in OWL as follows.

Definition 9. *(General Terminology Induction) Given an ontology $\mathcal{O}$ and a set $\mathbb{C}$ of classes, the problem of* general terminology induction *is to find all best hypotheses which do not exceed length ℓ.*

Thus, as in ILP, we view induction as search in the space of hypotheses restricted by a language bias, determined by $\mathbb{C}$ and ℓ in our case. We regard the process of constructing hypotheses as being equivalent to ranking them in a justified way which is based on fitness and braveness.

6.1   Dominance and Anytime Algorithm

So far, the comparison of hypotheses and terms "better", "best" have not been fully defined. We now define an order on hypotheses via *dominance*.

Definition 10. *(Dominance) Given an ontology $\mathcal{O}$ and a set $\mathbb{C}$ of classes, a hypothesis H dominates a hypothesis H', written $H' \prec H$, if $\widetilde{H} = \widetilde{H}'$ and either*

(i) $fit(H, \mathcal{O}, \mathbb{C}) > fit(H', \mathcal{O}, \mathbb{C}) \wedge bra(H, \mathcal{O}, \mathbb{C}) \leq bra(H', \mathcal{O}, \mathbb{C})$, *or*
(ii) $fit(H, \mathcal{O}, \mathbb{C}) \geq fit(H', \mathcal{O}, \mathbb{C}) \wedge bra(H, \mathcal{O}, \mathbb{C}) < bra(H', \mathcal{O}, \mathbb{C})$.

By Definition 10 dominance $\prec$ is a strict partial order, i.e. two different hypotheses may be incomparable. *Best* hypotheses are those which are dominated by no other hypotheses. Definition 10 considers only two competitive objectives: fitness and braveness. In addition, we compare hypotheses only if they have the same signature because otherwise interesting hypotheses could be discarded.

The size of the search space depends on $\mathbb{C}$ and ℓ. It varies from $2 \cdot |\mathbb{C}|^2$ (if a hypothesis is restricted to be a single axiom) to $2^{|\mathbb{C}|^2}$ (if a hypothesis is permitted to include all possible axioms). Consequently, the explicit enumeration can be infeasible. We employ an *anytime algorithm*, Algorithm 1, that attempts to explore promising regions of the search space first.

Algorithm 1. $induceHypotheses(\mathcal{O}, \mathbb{C}, \ell, stop)$

1: **inputs**
2:    $\mathcal{O}$: an ontology
3:    $\mathbb{C}$: a set of concepts
4:    ℓ: maximal syntactic length of a hypothesis
5:    *stop*: termination criteria
6: **outputs**
7:    $\mathbb{H}_{best}$: best hypotheses
8: **do**
9:    $\mathcal{O}_X = \mathcal{O} \cup \{X_C \equiv C \mid C \in \mathbb{C}\}$
10:    classify $\mathcal{O}_X$ and compute the projection
11:    $\mathbb{H}_{init} \leftarrow \{\{C \sqsubseteq D\} \mid \{C \sqsubseteq D\}$ is a hypothesis $\wedge C, D \in \mathbb{C}^-\}$
12:    $\mathbb{H} \leftarrow \mathbb{H}_{init}, \mathbb{H}_{best} \leftarrow \emptyset$
13:    **while** $\mathbb{H} \neq \emptyset$ and *stop* is not satisfied **do**
14:        $H \leftarrow choose(\mathbb{H}, \mathcal{O}_X)$
15:        $\mathbb{H} \leftarrow \mathbb{H} \backslash \{H\}$
16:        classify $\mathcal{O}_X \cup H$ and compute the assumption of H
17:        compute fitness and braveness of H using $minSizeUp$
18:        $\mathbb{H}_{best} \leftarrow \mathbb{H}_{best} \cup \{H\}$
19:        **if** H is not complete   **then**   % extensions are possible
20:            $\mathbb{H}_{ext} \leftarrow \{H \cup H' \mid H' \in \mathbb{H}_{init} \wedge |H \cup H'| \leq \ell \wedge H \cup H' \notin \mathbb{H} \cup \mathbb{H}_{best}\}$
21:            $\mathbb{H} \leftarrow \mathbb{H} \cup \mathbb{H}_{ext}$ % add all direct extensions of H
22:        **end if**
23:    **end while**
24:    remove dominated hypotheses from $\mathbb{H}_{best}$
25:    **return** $\mathbb{H}_{best}$

The longer Algorithm 1 runs, the better hypotheses it returns. It can be interrupted at any point which is specified by the termination criteria *stop*, e.g. a timeout, maximal number of iterations, quality threshold, etc. The algorithm processes the whole search space if *stop* does not prevent it from doing so.

The function $choose(\mathbb{H}, \mathcal{O})$ determines which regions of the search space are explored first. Various heuristics can be applied to guide the search. We use the following heuristic for $choose(\mathbb{H}, \mathcal{O})$: select $H \in \mathbb{H}$ with maximal

$$q(H, \mathcal{O}) := \frac{1}{|\widetilde{H}|} \cdot \sum\nolimits_{\alpha := C \sqsubseteq D \ \in \ H} (sup(\alpha, \mathcal{O}) - \rho \cdot [cov(\alpha, \mathcal{O}) - sup(\alpha, \mathcal{O})]),$$

where $sup(\alpha, \mathcal{O}) := |ins(C \sqcap D, \mathcal{O})|$ is support of α,

$cov(\alpha, \mathcal{O}) := |ins(C, \mathcal{O})|$ is coverage of α,

$ins(C, \mathcal{O}) := \{a \in ind(\mathcal{O}) \mid \mathcal{O} \models C(a)\}$ are instances of C,

$\rho \in (0, \infty)$ is a predefined penalty of "unsupported" coverage.

The heuristic chooses hypotheses that have smaller signatures and consist of axioms with larger support and smaller unsupported coverage. More importantly, it forces Algorithm 1 to firstly explore hypotheses with connected axioms (due to $1/|\widetilde{H}|$) of higher independent statistical quality. The higher the penalty ρ is, the more likely it is for cautious hypotheses to be evaluated first. If Algorithm 1 enumerates the full search space, then the heuristic does not affect the outcome. Only in this case Algorithm 1 is guaranteed to be complete.

Although a reasoner is updated just once per hypothesis, computing the fitness and braveness can still be expensive if the ontology is computationally hard. This can result in a small number of evaluated hypotheses once the termination criteria *stop* are satisfied. Incremental reasoners, such as FaCT++ [15], can improve the performance if a hypothesis is not big. Hence, besides readability and size of the search space, the length of a hypothesis may affect the performance of computing its fitness and braveness.

6.2   Choice of Classes

So far, we have assumed that a set $\mathbb{C}$ of interesting classes is known. For example, it can be defined by a domain expert. Unfortunately, this can be a difficult problem on its own. There are several possibilities to automate the choice of target classes. First, one can extract all subclasses, including complex ones, occurring in the ontology $\mathcal{O}$. These are suitable candidates because they are explicitly asserted in the ontology which implies that a domain expert is more likely to find them sensible and interesting.

However, an ontology can have poor terminological knowledge, in particular, it can contain mostly atomic classes. In this case, classes $\mathbb{C}$ can be generated from some signature $\Sigma \subseteq \widetilde{\mathcal{O}}$ using a target *class language*, see Example 6.

Example 6. The signature is $\Sigma = \{A_1, A_2, R_1, R_2\}$ and target class language is $G = \{X \mid X \in \Sigma\} \cup \{X \sqcap Y \mid X, Y \in \Sigma\} \cup \{\exists R.X \mid X \in \Sigma\}$ (OWL's structural equivalence is employed to avoid duplicates). Then, the set of classes is generated as follows: $\mathbb{C} := \{A_1, A_2, A_1 \sqcap A_2, \exists R_1.A_1, \exists R_1.A_2, \exists R_2.A_1, \exists R_2.A_2\}$.

If the ontology signature is large and our class language is expressive, the produced set of class expressions can be vast. One way to deal with the problem is to determine unpromising classes in $\mathbb{C}$ and discard them. Another way is to select a signature of interest $\Sigma \subset \mathcal{O}$ of manageable size and construct classes $\mathbb{C}$ from it using a language G. Σ can be specified by a domain expert which may be hard due to the lack of knowledge, large ontology signature, etc. Alternatively, Σ can be selected automatically.

Since we run our experiments on OWL ontologies which we are not familiar with and do not have access to domain experts, we select a signature Σ of an ontology $\mathcal{O}$ with respect to $\mathcal{A}$ using the modular structure of the ontology as follows: $\Sigma := \widetilde{M}$, where $M = module(\mathcal{T}, \widetilde{\mathcal{A}})$ (we use $\top\bot$-modules [5]).

This approach yields class and property names that are logically connected with $\mathcal{A}$ and discards logically disconnected ones (those can be numerous). We construct classes $\mathbb{C}$ from Σ using a language G. Finally, we discard classes from $\mathbb{C}$ that have no instances.

7   Implementation and Evaluation

7.1   Implementation

Tools and Hardware. All algorithms are implemented in Java 7 using OWL API (3.5.0). We use the OWL 2 DL reasoner FaCT++ (1.6.3) [15] which supports incremental reasoning. The experiments are executed on the following machine: Linux Ubuntu 14.04.2 LTS (64 bit), Intel Core i5-3470 3.20 GHz, 8 GB RAM.

7.2   Evaluation

Evaluation Goals. By Definition 9, the solution of the general terminology induction problem is a set of hypotheses. It depends on the following parameters: an ontology $\mathcal{O}$, a set $\mathbb{C}$ of classes, and a maximal length ℓ. The evaluation aim is to empirically assess the influence of these parameters on the solution. More specifically, the experiments are aimed at answering the following questions.

Q1 Where are we likely to find good hypotheses: in more expressive languages for $\mathbb{C}$ or bigger values of ℓ?
Q2 How does expressivity of the language and maximal length of a hypothesis influence the performance of computing the fitness and braveness?
Q3 Can we acquire hypotheses that seem plausible, so that we can use them to enrich our background knowledge, or that tell us interesting information about our data?

Choice of Ontologies. We conduct the empirical evaluation on a corpus of ontologies selected from related work [6,10] including DL-Learner datasets,[2] Protégé OWL,[3] and TONES[4] repositories. The Kinship ontology is obtained

---

[2] https://github.com/AKSW/DL-Learner
[3] http://protegewiki.stanford.edu/index.php/Protege_Ontology_Library
[4] http://owl.cs.manchester.ac.uk/repository/

from UCI Machine Learning Repository.[5] We have selected the ontologies based on the following criteria. Firstly, data contains both class and property assertions, at least 15 individuals. Secondly, ontology classification takes less 10 minutes. Thirdly, we are sufficiently confident that we understand the topic of the ontology. The corpus is available online.[6]

Table 6 describes the corpus where we use the following metrics. $|ind(\mathcal{A})|$, CA, RA are numbers of individuals, concept and property assertions in the ABox, respectively. $degree(\mathcal{A})$, $conn(\mathcal{A})$ are the average degree and average number of individuals in a connected component, respectively. $|\widetilde{\mathcal{A}}|$, $|\widetilde{\mathcal{T}}|$ are sizes of the ABox and TBox signature. $Jac(\widetilde{\mathcal{A}}, \widetilde{\mathcal{T}})$ is the Jaccard index of ABox and TBox signatures, $open(\mathcal{A}, \mathcal{T})$ is the average number of question marks per individual-class name pair.

Table 6. Ontologies and their metrics

	DL	$|ind(\mathcal{A})|$	CA	RA	$degree(\mathcal{A})$	$conn(\mathcal{A})$	$|\widetilde{\mathcal{A}}|$	$|\widetilde{\mathcal{T}}|$	$Jac(\widetilde{\mathcal{A}}, \widetilde{\mathcal{T}})$	$open(\mathcal{A}, \mathcal{T})$
Alzheimer	$\mathcal{AL}$	150	106	854	5.7	150	40	0	0	0.96
Arch	$\mathcal{ALC}$	19	26	26	1.4	3.8	10	13	0.77	0.53
BasicFamily	$\mathcal{ALI}$	31	50	95	3.1	10.3	6	6	1	0.67
Carcinogenesis	$\mathcal{ALC}(\mathcal{D})$	22372	22372	40666	1.8	65.8	113	146	0.77	0.65
Cinema	$\mathcal{ALCOF}$	45	45	76	1.7	45	7	37	0.19	0.88
Earthrealm	$\mathcal{SHOIN}(\mathcal{D})$	171	179	203	1.2	7.4	23	2482	0.01	0.89
Economy	$\mathcal{ALCH}(\mathcal{D})$	482	649	555	1.2	5.3	29	380	0.04	0.94
Financial	$\mathcal{ALCOIF}$	17941	17941	47248	2.6	8970.5	52	76	0.68	0.54
GeoSkills	$\mathcal{ALCHOIN}(\mathcal{D})$	2592	4681	3896	1.5	13.9	569	618	0.90	0.69
Heart	$\mathcal{AL}(\mathcal{D})$	280	275	1080	3.9	280	9	11	0.82	0.90
Kinship	$\mathcal{ALI}$	24	116	40	1.7	12	18	4	0.16	0.81
KRK	$\mathcal{SHI}$	420	525	1508	3.6	4	25	40	0.55	0.65
Mammographic	$\mathcal{AL}(\mathcal{D})$	975	975	2883	3.0	975	18	22	0.82	0.97
MDM073	$\mathcal{ALCHOF}(\mathcal{D})$	112	130	169	1.5	2.0	82	215	0.38	0.51
Mutagenesis	$\mathcal{AL}(\mathcal{D})$	14145	14145	26533	1.9	61.5	60	91	0.66	0.99
NTN	$\mathcal{SHOIN}(\mathcal{D})$	724	724	1636	2.3	2.8	64	78	0.82	0.96
Suramin	$\mathcal{AL}(\mathcal{D})$	2979	2979	6008	2.0	175.2	20	49	0.41	0.97

Evaluation Setup. To answer the raised questions, we set up the following experimental pipeline. Given an ontology $\mathcal{O}$, for each combination of a class language G and maximal length ℓ we run Algorithm 1 with the timeout $stop$ set to 10 minutes. Once Algorithm 1 terminates, we record the fitness and braveness of each hypothesis in the output set. We also record the average hypothesis evaluation time which comprises computing the fitness and braveness. Finally, we store all hypotheses if their number is less than 100 and only 100 hypotheses of maximal $q(H, \mathcal{O})$ otherwise.

---

[5] https://archive.ics.uci.edu/ml/datasets/Kinship
[6] http://www.cs.man.ac.uk/~sazonauv/tbox_induction/corpus/

We choose maximal length ℓ from $\{2, 4, 6, 8, 10\}$. In order to generate classes $\mathbb{C}$, we use the process described in Section 6.2. The signature is $\Sigma := \widetilde{M}$, where $M = module(\mathcal{T}, \widetilde{\mathcal{A}})$. We investigate 5 class languages G_i, such that $G_i \subseteq G_{i+1}$ (duplicates are avoided by the means of OWL's structural equivalence):

$G_1 := \{X \mid X \in \Sigma\};$
$G_2 := G_1 \cup \{X_M \mid X_M \text{ is a possibly complex subclass in } M\};$
$G_3 := G_2 \cup \{X \sqcap Y \mid X, Y \in \Sigma\};$
$G_4 := G_3 \cup \{\exists R.X \mid X, R \in \Sigma\};$
$G_5 := G_4 \cup \{X \sqcap \exists R.Y \mid X, Y, R \in \Sigma\}.$

7.3   Results

Dependence of fitness and braveness on language and length is shown on Figure 1. For each ontology the experiment is executed as described above. The values obtained are normalised, i.e. divided by the maximal value. Then, the values are aggregated across the corpus and the average value is reported per cell.

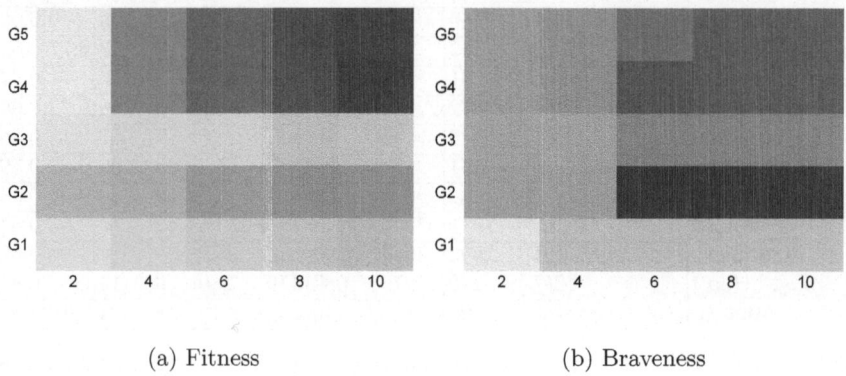

(a) Fitness   (b) Braveness

Fig. 1. Dependence of fitness (a) and braveness (b) on language expressivity and maximal length: darker colours reflect greater numbers

Our first observation is that some languages and lengths result in no hypotheses induced which happens if a class language is not expressive enough or hypothesis length is too low. We aggregate and average only over non-empty values. An expected observation is that increasing expressivity is useless if an ontology is poor, e.g. contains few relations in the data and axioms in the background knowledge. On the other hand, if an ontology is rich, increasing expressivity may or may not be fruitful.

Figure 1 shows that increasing length always results in hypotheses of higher fitness and mostly, but not always, of higher braveness since added axioms may make no assumptions or repeat the assumptions already made. Increasing expressivity also generally leads to higher fitness and higher braveness. However, the changes are not as gradual as for length, in particular, braveness seems irregular.

Interestingly, we observe that G_2 consistently outperforms G_3 in fitness, despite $G_2 \subseteq G_3$, which can be explained as follows. On the one hand, the search space considerably increases from G_2 to G_3. On the other hand, G_3 appears to be less fruitful than G_2 (compare to G_4 and G_5). As a result, it becomes harder to find equally good hypotheses in the same time. Thus, the answer to Q2 is that increasing expressivity and length promises better fitness but commonly worse braveness.

We also observe that the average hypothesis evaluation time does not vary widely. Thus, the answer to Q2 is that performance does not degrade significantly for higher expressivity and length. The performance of evaluating a hypothesis is as follows: less than 0.1 second for 8 ontologies, from 0.1 to 1 second for 4 ontologies, from 1 to 10 seconds for 4 ontologies, and around 15 seconds for 1 ontology. The results can be found online.[7]

Table 7. Examples of hypotheses induced within 10 minutes

Ontology	Examples of hypotheses
Alzheimer	$Drug \sqsubseteq \exists getsReplacedBy.Substituent$
	$Substituent \sqsubseteq \exists hasPolatisation.Polar$
	$\exists hasPolatisation.Polar \sqsubseteq \exists isHAcceptor.HAcceptor$
Arch	$construction \sqsubseteq \exists hasPillar.pillar$
	$\exists hasParallelpipe.wedge \sqsubseteq \exists hasPillar.freeStandingPillar$
	$\exists touches.pillar \sqsubseteq \exists leftof.pillar$
BasicFamily	$\exists hasChild.Person \sqsubseteq Person$
	$\exists hasParent.Person \sqsubseteq Person$
	$\exists hasParent.Female \sqsubseteq \exists hasParent.Male$
Cinema	$Movie \sqsubseteq \exists hasForActor.Actor$
	$Movie \sqsubseteq \exists hasForGenre.Genre$
	$\exists hasForActor.\{Eastwood\} \sqsubseteq \exists hasForGenre.\{Western\}$
	$\exists hasForDirector.\{Burton\} \sqsubseteq \exists hasForActor.\{Depp\}$
Earthrealm	$\exists hasDefaultUnit.BaseUnit \sqsubseteq \exists hasDefaultUnit.ComplexUnit$
	$\exists hasDefaultUnit.\{second\} \sqsubseteq TimeRelatedQuantity$
	$\exists hasDefaultUnit.\{meterPerSecond\} \sqsubseteq DrySeasonDuration$
Economy	$Nation \equiv IndependentState$
	$\exists economyType.EconomicDevelopmentLevel$
	$\sqsubseteq \exists economyType.IMFDevelopmentLevel$
Financial	$Account \sqsubseteq \exists hasStatementIssuanceFrequency.Monthly$
	$\exists isOwnerOf.Account \sqsubseteq Client$
Mammographic	$\exists hasMargin.spiculated \sqsubseteq \exists hasShape.irregular$
	$\exists hasShape.irregular \sqsubseteq \exists hasDensity.low$
Mutagenesis	$Compound \sqsubseteq \exists hasBond.Bond1$
	$\exists inBond.Hydrogen3 \sqsubseteq Bond1$
	$\exists inBond.Oxygen40 \sqsubseteq \exists inBond.Nitrogen38$
NTN	$Man \equiv \forall spouseOf.Woman$
	$\exists knows.Man \sqsubseteq Man$
	$\exists relativeOf.Man \sqsubseteq Man$

In order to answer Q3, we act as domain experts and eyeball the induced hypotheses. We aim at finding plausible and interesting hypotheses. Some results

---

[7] http://www.cs.man.ac.uk/~sazonauv/tbox_induction/results/

are shown in Table 7. Firstly, we observe that induced hypotheses can, in fact, enrich the background knowledge, see Table 7. If the background knowledge is poor, as in **BasicFamily** and **Cinema**, or even absent, as in **Alzheimer**, hypotheses seem to be a good starting point for modellers. If the background knowledge is incomplete, hypotheses appear to be interesting missing bits, e.g. for **Economy**, **Financial**, **NTN**, and **Mutagenesis**.

Secondly, we observe that hypotheses can reveal interesting relations in our data. This can expose new knowledge about the domain and help to understand the data. For example, hypotheses discover relations between particular actors, directors, and movie genres from **Cinema**. Another example is **Mammographic** where we can learn relations between diagnostic observations, e.g. having irregular shape implies having lower density. Such hypotheses can potentially inform doctors of yet unknown relations in their data, facilitate future research in the domain, and lead to data improvements, e.g. a supplement of images of tumours that have irregular shape and high density.

Thirdly, hypotheses can contain "strange" axioms which may help us highlight, on the one hand, odd or erroneous modelling and, on the other hand, inaccurate or abnormal data. We observe this for **Arch** inducing $\exists touches.pillar \sqsubseteq \exists leftof.pillar$ (why is there nothing to the right?) and for **Earthrealm** inducing $\exists hasDefaultUnit.\{meterPerSecond\} \sqsubseteq DrySeasonDuration$ (wrong unit?). Thus, we can answer Q3 positively.

Although we use different settings and the goal of induction is different, we make some comparison of our results with related work. In particular, we consider the supervised CDL and its implementation DL-Learner [11]. Given a set of positive and negative examples for a target class *construction* in **Arch**, it searches for definition *construction* $\equiv \exists hasPillar.(freeStandingPillar \sqcap \exists leftof.\exists supports.\top)$. As Table 7 shows, our approach induces a weaker definition of *construction* along with some related knowledge. For **Cinema** we observe that descriptions of different movie types are induced, e.g. *EastwoodMovie* $\sqsubseteq \exists hasForActor.\{Eastwood\}$, *EastwoodMovie* $\sqsubseteq \exists hasForGenre.\{Western\}$. For **NTN** the definition $Man \equiv \forall spouseOf.Woman$ is induced. Thus, although our approach is unsupervised, it shows the potential to learn class definitions.

8 Discussion and Future Work

The evaluation shows that our approach is able to induce interesting hypotheses. On the one hand, they can potentially be helpful to build and improve the background knowledge. On the other hand, hypotheses seemingly discover new knowledge about the domain and help us understand the data. Interestingly, they may help us identify modelling errors and data flaws.

Although the search space is vast, general terminology induction is feasible. It is encouraging given that statistically and logically sound measures are used to evaluate a hypothesis and this requires reasoning. We observe that larger and more expressive hypotheses are generally better and still feasible.

As for future work, we will investigate more informed ways of constructing a set of promising initial classes, e.g. using techniques from CDL, along with new algorithms and heuristics for search space exploration. We will also attempt to extend the methodology to deal with noisy data that causes inconsistency, e.g. using techniques from [9]. We plan to investigate learning property hierarchies.

We intend to go beyond the corpus and carry out case studies with domain experts to evaluate our approach in more detail. We also consider other scenarios, e.g. how acceptance or rejection of a hypothesis affects other hypotheses, how hypotheses can be used for predicting class memberships of individuals, terminology abduction and "what if" analysis of data under the OWA.

References

1. Baader, F., Calvanese, D., McGuinness, D., Nardi, D., Patel-Schneider, P.F. (eds.): The Description Logic Handbook: Theory, Implementation, and Applications. Cambridge University Press (2003)
2. Baader, F., Ganter, B., Sertkaya, B., Sattler, U.: Completing description logic knowledge bases using formal concept analysis. In: Proceedings of the 20th International Joint Conference on Artifical Intelligence, IJCAI 2007, pp. 230–235. Morgan Kaufmann Publishers Inc., San Francisco (2007)
3. Baader, F., Sertkaya, B., Turhan, A.Y.: Computing the least common subsumer w.r.t. a background terminology. Journal of Applied Logic 5(3), 392–420 (2007)
4. Conklin, D., Witten, I.H.: Complexity-based induction. Machine Learning 16(3), 203–225 (1994)
5. Grau, B.C., Horrocks, I., Kazakov, Y., Sattler, U.: Modular reuse of ontologies: Theory and practice. Journal of Artificial Intelligence Research, 273–318 (2008)
6. Fanizzi, N., d'Amato, C., Esposito, F.: DL-FOIL concept learning in description logics. In: Železný, F., Lavrač, N. (eds.) ILP 2008. LNCS (LNAI), vol. 5194, pp. 107–121. Springer, Heidelberg (2008)
7. Ganter, B., Wille, R.: Formal Concept Analysis, vol. 284. Springer, Heidelberg (1999)
8. Grau, B.C., Horrocks, I., Motik, B., Parsia, B., Patel-Schneider, P., Sattler, U.: OWL 2: The next step for OWL. Web Semantics 6(4), 309–322 (2008)
9. Haase, P., Stojanovic, L.: Consistent evolution of OWL ontologies. In: Gómez-Pérez, A., Euzenat, J. (eds.) ESWC 2005. LNCS, vol. 3532, pp. 182–197. Springer, Heidelberg (2005)
10. Lehmann, J., Auer, S., Bühmann, L., Tramp, S.: Class expression learning for ontology engineering. Web Semantics 9(1), 71–81 (2011)
11. Lehmann, J., Hitzler, P.: Concept learning in Description Logics using refinement operators. Machine Learning 78(1–2), 203–250 (2010)
12. Lehmann, J., Völker, J. (eds.): Perspectives On Ontology Learning, Studies in the Semantic Web, vol. 18. IOS Press (2014)
13. Muggleton, S.: Inductive logic programming. New Generation Computing 8(4), 295–318 (1991)
14. Reiter, R.: A theory of diagnosis from first principles. Artificial Intelligence 32(1), 57–95 (1987)
15. Tsarkov, D., Horrocks, I.: FaCT++ description logic reasoner: system description. In: Furbach, U., Shankar, N. (eds.) IJCAR 2006. LNCS (LNAI), vol. 4130, pp. 292–297. Springer, Heidelberg (2006)

16. Vitányi, P.M., Li, M.: Minimum description length induction, bayesianism, and kolmogorov complexity. IEEE Transactions on Information Theory **46**(2), 446–464 (2000)
17. Völker, J., Niepert, M.: Statistical schema induction. In: Antoniou, G., Grobelnik, M., Simperl, E., Parsia, B., Plexousakis, D., De Leenheer, P., Pan, J. (eds.) ESWC 2011, Part I. LNCS, vol. 6643, pp. 124–138. Springer, Heidelberg (2011)

Understanding How Users Edit Ontologies: Comparing Hypotheses About Four Real-World Projects

Simon Walk[1]([⊠]), Philipp Singer[2], Lisette Espín Noboa[2], Tania Tudorache[3], Mark A. Musen[3], and Markus Strohmaier[2,4]

[1] Graz University of Technology, Graz, Austria
simon.walk@tugraz.at
[2] GESIS - Leibniz Institute for the Social Sciences, Cologne, Germany
{philipp.singer,Lisette.Noboa}@gesis.org
[3] Stanford Center for Biomedical Informatics Research, Stanford, CA, USA
{Tudorache,Musen}@stanford.edu
[4] University of Koblenz-Landau, Mainz, Germany
Markus.Strohmaier@gesis.org, Strohmaier@uni-koblenz.de

Abstract. Ontologies are complex intellectual artifacts and creating them requires significant expertise and effort. While existing ontology-editing tools and methodologies propose ways of building ontologies in a normative way, empirical investigations of how experts *actually* construct ontologies "in the wild" are rare. Yet, understanding actual user behavior can play an important role in the design of effective tool support. Although previous empirical investigations have produced a series of interesting insights, they were exploratory in nature and aimed at gauging the problem space only. In this work, we aim to advance the state of knowledge in this domain by systematically defining and comparing a set of hypotheses about how users edit ontologies. Towards that end, we study the user editing trails of four real-world ontology-engineering projects. Using a coherent research framework, called HypTrails, we derive formal definitions of hypotheses from the literature, and systematically compare them with each other. Our findings suggest that the *hierarchical structure* of an ontology exercises the strongest influence on user editing behavior, followed by the *entity similarity*, and the *semantic distance* of classes in the ontology. Moreover, these findings are strikingly consistent across all ontology-engineering projects in our study, with only minor exceptions for one of the smaller datasets. We believe that our results are important for ontology tools builders and for project managers, who can potentially leverage this information to create user interfaces and processes that better support the observed editing patterns of users.

1 Introduction

Large real-world ontologies are intellectual artifacts that are inherently complex and hard to build. Most such ontologies are found in the biomedical domain. For

© Springer International Publishing Switzerland 2015
M. Arenas et al. (Eds.): ISWC 2015, Part I, LNCS 9366, pp. 551–568, 2015.
DOI: 10.1007/978-3-319-25007-6_32

example, SNOMED-CT,[1] a comprehensive clinical health terminology, has over 300,000 classes, the National Cancer Institute Thesaurus (NCIT)[2] has more than 100,000 classes, and the 11th revision of the International Classification of Diseases (ICD-11)[3] has over 50,000 classes. The development of such large ontologies usually takes place in distributed teams, and requires a significant effort both in the ontological modeling and coordination of the entire process.

One of the biggest challenges in developing large real-world ontologies is proper tool support. While existing ontology-editing tools and methodologies prescribe certain ways of building ontologies, there is very little research on how users actually use these tools. Empirical analyses of how users develop ontologies "in the wild" are very rare. We address this gap with this paper, by aiming to broaden our understanding of editing behaviors in large ontology-engineering projects. It is the ultimate vision of our work to lay a more solid foundation for creating tools that better support ontology authors based on their actual authoring behavior.

We define a *sequential edit trail* as a chronologically sorted list of all actions a user takes while editing an ontology. We derive such editing trails from the change logs recorded by the ontology-editing tools. In previous work, we have conducted exploratory empirical analyses of various types of edit trails in several ontology-engineering projects [21,22], and we have discussed our findings and potential implications [23]. In these works, we have been able to explore different editing patterns and potential explanations via manual inspection and qualitative interpretation. For example, we have speculated that users edit ontologies in a top-down fashion or that users navigate along similar concepts. However, it is still unclear how such hypotheses can best be expressed formally, or how they can be systematically compared with each other in order to explain the production of edit trails, and hence an ontology, at hand.

Thus, in this paper, we systematically investigate previous, mostly exploratory, results using HypTrails [11]—a generic methodology for comparing hypotheses about human trails in ontology-engineering projects. This allows us to (i) formally define, (ii) systematically study, and (iii) rank different hypotheses about ontology-editing behavior within a coherent research framework. By using HypTrails, we approach this problem by modeling edit trails as first-order Markov chains (see Section 3.2) and hypotheses as priors. From our analyses, we find that the *hierarchical structure* of an ontology exercises the strongest influence on observed user behaviors, followed by the *similarity* of entities, and the *distance* of classes in the ontology. These findings are strikingly consistent across the four real-world ontology-engineering projects used in our study, with only minor exceptions for one of the smaller datasets. We believe that our results are important for ontology tools builders and for project managers, who can potentially leverage this information to create user interfaces and processes that better support the observed editing patterns of users.

---

[1] http://www.ihtsdo.org/snomed-ct

[2] http://ncit.nci.nih.gov

[3] http://who.int/classifications/icd/revision/en/

The main research contributions of this work are:

- A formal way to define hypotheses about how users edit an ontology (e.g., top-down vs. bottom-up editing strategies).
- A detailed systematic comparison of such hypotheses across four real-world ontology-engineering projects.
- A ranking of all investigated hypotheses according to their relative plausibility for each dataset by adopting a coherent research approach.

The remainder of the paper is structured as follows: In Section 2, we discuss the related work. The methodology and datasets are described in Section 3, followed by a detailed formal description of all investigated hypotheses in Section 4. We present the results of our analysis in Section 5, discuss implications and limitations of our findings in Section 6 and conclude our work and discuss opportunities for future work in Section 7.

2   Related Work

The related work relevant for this paper is covered by two different research fields: *Human Trails on the Web* and *Analysis of Ontology Editing Behavior*.

2.1   Human Trails on the Web

Previous research has studied human trails on the Web in various settings. Modeling trails has received a lot of attention [3,12], as well as the detection of regularities, patterns and strategies in trails of interest [6,25]. Most prominently, researchers have focused on studying human navigational trails on the Web—capturing the subsequent websites that humans navigate to [6,12,25]. This research on navigational trails has inspired other works in the effort to improve the Web, e.g., better website design (usability) [4], identifying related links [18] or constructing an e-learning Semantic Web [2]. Researchers have also investigated other kinds of human trails, e.g., search trails [13,26], diffusion trails [1] or song listening trails [11]. Our work directly connects to these studies as we are interested in shedding more light on the production of human trails on the Web; however, in our case, we look at human edit trails in ontology-engineering projects by using the approach presented in [11].

2.2   Analysis of Ontology Editing Behavior

In this line of research, a large part of the literature has focused on analyzing the editing behavior or identifying editing patterns in collaborative ontology-engineering. To perform these types of analyses, researchers have used the change logs recorded by the different ontology-editing environments, similar to our approach.

Strohmaier et al. [14] conducted an empirical analysis to investigate the hidden social dynamics that take place when editors develop an ontology, and provided new metrics to quantify various aspects of the engineering processes. Falconer et al. [5] did a change-log analysis of different ontology-engineering projects, showing that contributors exhibit specific roles, which can be used to group and classify these users. Pesquita and Couto [9] analyzed the influence of the location and specific structural features to determine if and where the next change will be conducted in the Gene Ontology[4]. The work by Wang et al. [24] presents an analysis of user editing patterns derived from change logs of several real-world ontology-engineering projects utilizing association-rule mining. The results suggest that users tend to edit in a vertical way, i.e., users edit the same properties for different classes in a sequential way. Rospocher et al [10] analyzed the change logs for two different Web-based collaborative ontology-editing tools and found similar collaboration and editing patterns. For example, they found that users tend to edit in the local neighborhood of an entity. Van Laere et al. [19] analyzed behavior-based user profiles in collaborative ontology-engineering projects using K-means clustering to group similar users.

In contrast to our previous research [21–23], this work represents a systematic and comparative study of different hypotheses in a coherent mathematical research framework, whereas our previous analyses have mostly been exploratory. We can thereby—for the first time—make relative, empirically grounded statements about the plausibility of different hypotheses given data.

3   Materials and Methodology

We present the four datasets used in our research (Section 3.1), and the HypTrails framework (Section 3.2) that forms the basis of the methodology used in this work.

3.1   Datasets

We used the change logs of four real-world ontology-engineering projects to conduct the analyses presented in this work. These projects use WebProtégé [17] as the editing platform, a Web-based generic ontology-editing tool, which records a log of all changes performed by each user. Each change record stores metadata about the change, such as the user who performed the change, a textual description of the change, the timestamp, and the entity on which the change occurred.

To extract the editing trails from the change logs, we performed a preprocessing step in which we merged consecutive changes on the same entity by the same user (i.e., *self-loops*) into one change. Such changes occurred when users would edit different properties of the same entity. For the purpose of this work, we have not been interested in such changes, but rather in the ones which occurred on different entities. Further, we have limited all our analyses on *isA* relationships and removed equivalence links. However, multiple *isA* inheritances have been kept "as-is". We provide a brief description of the four datasets used in our research below.

---

[4] http://www.geneontology.org

The International Classification of Diseases (ICD),[5] developed by the World Health Organization (WHO), is the international standard for diagnostic classification used to encode information relevant to epidemiology, health management, and clinical use in over one hundred United Nations countries. WHO regularly publishes new revisions of the classifications. The 11th revision of the classification, **ICD-11**,[6] is currently in progress, and is planned to be finalized in 2017. In contrast to previous revisions, ICD-11 is developed as a rich OWL ontology [16]. Over 100 domain experts are using a customized version of WebProtégé to author the ontology collaboratively.

The International Classification of Traditional Medicine (ICTM)[7] is a WHO-led project that aimed to produce an international standard terminology and classification for diagnoses and interventions in Traditional Medicine. ICTM was developed collaboratively as an OWL ontology with the goal to unify the knowledge from the traditional medicine practices from China, Japan and Korea. Its content is authored in 4 languages: English, Chinese, Japanese and Korean. More than 20 domain experts from the three countries developed ICTM using a customized version of WebProtégé. The development of ICTM ended in 2012.

The Biomedical Resource Ontology (BRO)   [15] was developed as part of the Biositemaps project. Biositemaps is a mechanism for researchers working in biomedicine to publish metadata about biomedical data, tools, and services. Applications can then aggregate this information for tasks such as semantic search. BRO is the enabling technology used in Biositemaps; a controlled terminology for describing the resource types, areas of research, and activity of a biomedical related resource. A small group of editors authored BRO using WebProtégé to modify the ontology and to carry out discussions.

The Ontology for Parasite Lifecycle (OPL) models the life cycle of the *T.cruzi*, a protozoan parasite, which is responsible for a number of human diseases [8]. OPL uses expressive OWL (SHOIF) to represent its knowledge base, and extends several other OWL ontologies. Several users from different institutions collaborate on OPL development using WebProtégé as a collaborative platform.

Table 1 provides some characteristics about each of the datasets used in our analysis. The average trail length ranges from 1, 637.13 transitions for ICD-11 to 136.60 transitions for BRO. Trails refer to the number of different human edit trails per dataset, where each trail represents a chronologically ordered list of all the classes a user has edited. Users with less than 2 distinct changes have been removed from our analysis.

---

[5] http://who.int/classifications/icd/en/
[6] http://who.int/classifications/icd/ICDRevision/
[7] http://who.int/mediacentre/news/notes/2010/trad_medicine_20101207/en/

Table 1. Characteristics of the four datasets.

	ICD-11	ICTM	BRO	OPL
Classes	48, 771	1, 506	528	393
Changes	439, 229	67, 522	2, 507	1, 993
Users	109	27	5	3
Trails	102	26	5	3
Avrg. trail length	1, 637.13	673.54	136.60	152.00
Transitions	361, 491	66, 708	2, 388	2, 668
Self-Loops	194, 504	49, 196	1, 705	2, 212
First change	18.11.2009	02.02.2011	12.02.2010	09.06.2011
Last change	29.08.2013	17.7.2013	06.03.2010	23.09.2011
Period (ca.)	4 years	2.5 years	1 month	3 months

3.2 Methodology

By and large, HypTrails [11] is an approach that allows us to compare hypotheses about human trails. In our case, we are interested in studying: (i) the human edit trails in ontology-engineering projects, and (ii) the relative plausibility of hypotheses about the production of these trails that have been manifested in previous studies. In Section 1, we used the hypothesis that users edit ontologies in a top-down manner as an example. Using HypTrails, we are able to compare this hypothesis to other such hypotheses, and determine which one is more plausible to describe the production of the corresponding editing trails, and hence the ontology at hand. Section 4 provides a formal description of all hypotheses that we have compared as part of this research. Figure 1 shows a graphical representation of the editing patterns represented by each hypothesis. Next, we introduce the core concepts of HypTrails; for a more thorough introduction please refer to [11].

Technically, HypTrails models trails with first-order Markov chain models, and compares hypotheses using Bayesian inference, and more specifically, the *marginal likelihood* which can also be referred to as the *evidence* (we use both terms throughout this work synonymously). The marginal likelihood $P(H|D)$ describes the probability of a hypothesis H (e.g., uniform hypothesis) given the data (trails). For expressing generic hypotheses and being able to compare them, HypTrails uses the sensitivity of the marginal likelihood on the prior. Thus, hypotheses are expresses as different priors—in case of a Markov chain model the conjugate prior is the *Dirichlet distribution*. The hyperparameters of Dirichlet distributions can be interpreted as *pseudo counts*. Thus, simply put, higher pseudo counts refer to higher beliefs in corresponding transition for a given hypothesis.

Consequently, we have to provide HypTrails with matrices that capture our generic hypotheses and corresponding beliefs in transitions (see Section 4). Based on these matrices, HypTrails internally elicits proper Dirichlet priors for given hypotheses by setting the pseudo counts accordingly, based on a parameter k which steers the total number of pseudo counts assigned. Basically, the higher we set k, the stronger we believe in a given hypothesis. Analogously, this means that with higher k, we expect to see less transitions contradicting the corresponding hypothesis (e.g., only transitions from higher level classes to lower level classes in the top-down hypothesis). For fairness, we always want to compare hypotheses with each other for the same values of k.

Finally, by using different priors for different hypotheses, we get different marginal likelihoods when combined with empirical trail data. Based on these evidences, we can compare the relative plausibility of hypotheses—higher evidences indicate higher plausibility. In theory, we need to further calculate *Bayes factors* [7] between the marginal likelihoods of two hypotheses, so that we would be able to judge the strength of the evidence for one hypothesis over the other. However, as all Bayes factors are decisive, we resort from presenting them individually throughout this paper. Thus, we can produce a partial ordering of hypotheses based on their relative plausibility by ranking their marginal likelihoods from largest to smallest for single values of k.

4 Hypotheses

HypTrails allows us to compare hypotheses about the production of human edit trails in ontology-engineering projects, and helps us to understand how an ontology is produced in an ontology-development tool. Hypotheses are *beliefs about transitions* (see Figures 1(a)–1(h)) opposed to actual empirical transitional observations (see Figure 1(i)). With HypTrails, we express these transitional beliefs as our assumptions about Markov chain transitions. In detail, we specify hypotheses as matrices that reflect our assumptions about transitions between states where higher values correspond to higher beliefs.

Thus, for each hypothesis, we need to specify the *hypothesis matrix* Q with elements $q_{i,j}$ that represent the belief in the transition between states s_i and s_j. A *state* corresponds to a class in the ontology that users are editing. A *transition* between states s_i and s_j corresponds to a two sequential user edit: first of the class represented by s_i, and then of the class represented by s_j. In order to express our hypotheses as beliefs in Markov transitions, and to have a better interpretation capability, we directly set $q_{i,j}$ as row probabilities $P(s_j|s_i)$. Thus, for each row i of Q it holds that $\sum_j q_{i,j} = 1$.

For example, Figure 1(e) depicts the *hierarchy-based hypothesis*, which postulates the belief that users are likelier to edit classes along the hierarchical (isA) structure of the ontology and the shortest distance. In this example, if a user has just previously changed class C, this hypothesis believes that the user is most likely to change class A (the *parent*) or G (the *child*) next. Classes B and D are both *siblings* (and two steps away) of C, which is why this hypothesis expresses a smaller belief in these transitions. Other hierarchical transitions, *ancestors*, *descendants* and *cousins*, follow analogously with less belief (i.e., lower proability; not depicted in Figure 1(e)).

Figure 2 shows an exemplary illustration of the transition graph and the corresponding matrix for the *top-down* hypothesis, which believes that users

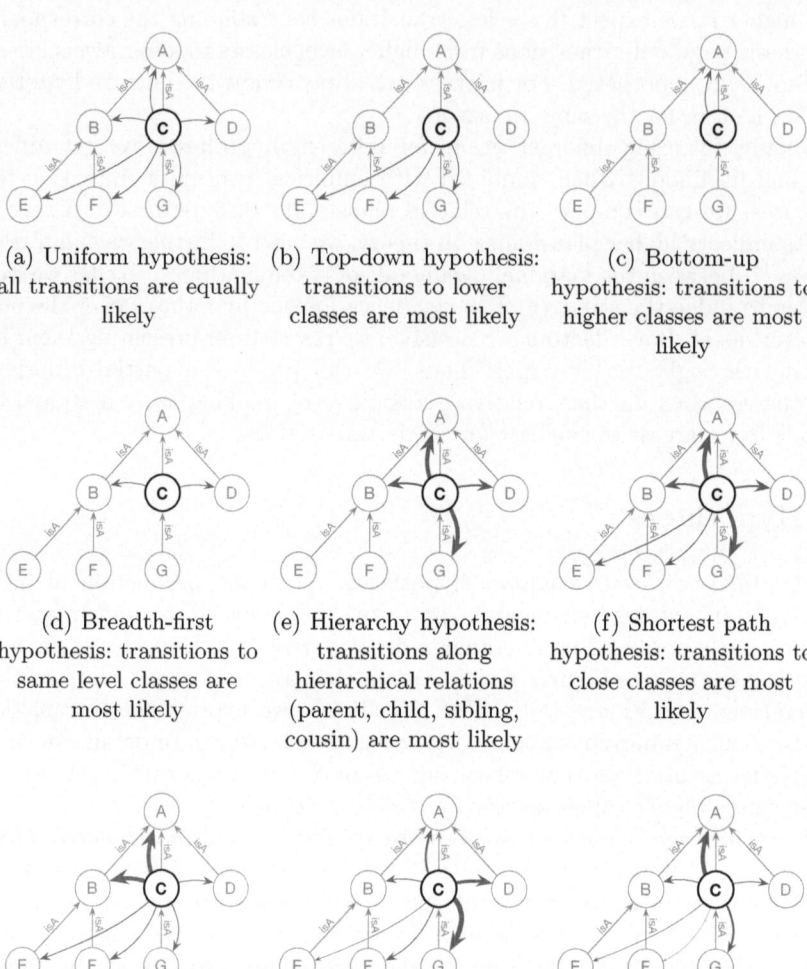

(a) Uniform hypothesis: all transitions are equally likely

(b) Top-down hypothesis: transitions to lower classes are most likely

(c) Bottom-up hypothesis: transitions to higher classes are most likely

(d) Breadth-first hypothesis: transitions to same level classes are most likely

(e) Hierarchy hypothesis: transitions along hierarchical relations (parent, child, sibling, cousin) are most likely

(f) Shortest path hypothesis: transitions to close classes are most likely

(g) Connectivity hypothesis: transitions to popular classes are most likely

(h) Similarity hypothesis: transitions to similar (title and definition) classes are most likely

(i) Empirical transitions: obtained from real world data

Fig. 1. Sample-Hypotheses. This figure depicts eight hypotheses about how humans consecutively edit classes in ontology-engineering projects derived from our previous research (a-h), as well as empirical observations (i). The curved arrows represent transitions we believe in for a given hypothesis (a-h), or observed transition probabilities from data (i). The thicker an arrow, the higher our belief in the corresponding transition for a given hypothesis (a-h), or the higher the number of transitions we observed in the data (i). For simplicity, we always only visualize the transitions for class C; all other classes follow analogously.

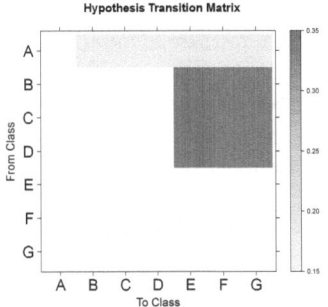

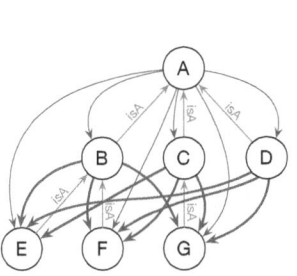

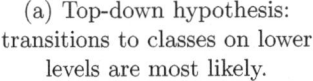

(a) Top-down hypothesis: transitions to classes on lower levels are most likely.

(b) Hypothesis matrix: the transition matrix representing the top-down hypothesis.

Fig. 2. Top-down hypothesis. This figure depicts (a) the top-down hypothesis and (b) its corresponding hypothesis matrix Q that is generated from its formal definition. Darker transitions between classes represent a strong belief in these transitions, while white transitions represent a disbelief in a transition. Note that the matrix is normalized per row, hence the sum of all beliefs for each row is 1.

consecutively edit classes at deeper levels in the hierarchy. In this example, our state space consists of seven classes $S = \{A, B, C, D, E, F, G\}$. The beliefs in the transitions between states are shown in Figure 2(a). As this hypothesis has stronger beliefs in top-down transitions, the graph and matrix will only contain beliefs in transitions from higher-level classes to lower-level classes, such as, from C to E, F and G. Figure 2(b) shows the corresponding representation of the beliefs in the hypothesis matrix. For example, for the row corresponding to the transitions from class C, we may set $q_{C,E} = 1/3$, $q_{C,F} = 1/3$ and $q_{C,G} = 1/3$. For all other classes, we can proceed analogously.

In the remainder of this section, we thoroughly describe the hypotheses used in this research, and provide formal descriptions of how we built the corresponding hypothesis matrices Q. Note that for each hypothesis and equation, we always calculate $q_{i,j}$, for all i and j. We set the diagonal of each hypothesis matrix Q to 0 as we do not consider self-loops in our data. As it is not always possible to express our beliefs with direct probabilities, we additionally normalize each row of Q using the ℓ_1-norm.

Figure 1 shows a graphical representation of the hypotheses investigated in our research. The *top-down, bottom-up, breadth-first* and *hierarchy hypotheses* resulted as part of our prior research from a manual inspection of Markov chains of different orders [21–23]. Additionally, we are also considering the *shortest path, connectivity,* and *similarity* hypotheses to also investigate further "strategies" of how users edit an ontology that could provide plausible explanations for the underlying data.

Uniform Hypothesis. This hypothesis believes that each transition from one state to any other state is equally likely (cf. Figure 1(a)). Thus, it assumes that humans edit ontologies at random. We can see this hypothesis as a baseline. If other hypotheses are not more plausible than this uniform one, we cannot expect them to provide good explanations about the production of the trails (and the ontology) at hand. The elements of matrix Q for this hypothesis are defined as follows:

$$q_{i,j} = \frac{1}{|S - 1|} \tag{1}$$

Top-down Hypothesis. For the top-down hypothesis, we express the belief that classes that are deeper in the hierarchy (further away from the root class) than the previously edited class, are likelier to be changed next. For expressing this hypothesis, we measure the depth level of each class (the distance to the root); classes deeper in the hierarchy have larger depth levels. In this hypothesis, we have stronger beliefs in transitions to classes that have a *larger depth level* than the current class (cf. Figure 1(b)). We express this hypothesis according to the following definition with $depth_i$ and $depth_j$ representing the depth-levels of the corresponding classes s_i and s_j.

$$q_{i,j} = \begin{cases} 1, & \text{if } depth_i < depth_j, \\ 0, & \text{otherwise.} \end{cases} \tag{2}$$

Bottom-up Hypothesis. Analogously to the top-down hypothesis, this hypothesis believes that classes that are closer to the root class (i.e., they have lower depth levels) than the previously edited class, are likelier to be changed next (cf. Figure 1(c)).

$$q_{i,j} = \begin{cases} 1, & \text{if } depth_i > depth_j, \\ 0, & \text{otherwise.} \end{cases} \tag{3}$$

Breadth-first Hypothesis. Similar to the top-down and bottom-up hypotheses, we express the belief that classes are likelier to be changed next, if they are on the same depth levels (cf. Figure 1(d)).

$$q_{i,j} = \begin{cases} 1, & \text{if } depth_i = depth_j, \\ 0, & \text{otherwise.} \end{cases} \tag{4}$$

Shortest Path Hypothesis. With this hypothesis, we express the belief that users consecutively edit classes in an ontology that are close to each other in the class hierarchy (cf. Figure 1(f)). In detail, we look at the shortest path distances $d(i, j)$ between pairs of classes—the shorter the distance, the stronger we believe in the corresponding transition. To invert the shortest path length, we subtract it from the diameter $\max_{x,y}(d(x,y))$ of the whole hierarchy.

$$q_{i,j} = \max_{x,y}(d(x,y)) - d(i,j) \tag{5}$$

Hierarchy Hypothesis. The hierarchy hypothesis represents our belief that users edit classes along the hierarchical structure of the ontology (i.e., *isA* links). In particular, the next edit operation is likelier to occur on close relatives than on relatives that are further away (cf. Figure 1(e)). This hypothesis has the following weight initialization of our belief matrix:

$$q_{i,j} = \begin{cases} 4, & \text{if } d(i,j) = 1 \text{ and } depth_i \neq depth_j, \\ 3, & \text{if } d(i,j) = 2 \text{ and } depth_i = depth_j \text{ and } check\_siblings(i,j) > 0, \\ 2, & \text{if } d(i,j) = 4 \text{ and } depth_i = depth_j \text{ and } check\_cousins(i,j) > 0, \\ 1, & \text{if } sp(i,j) = |depth_i - depth_j|, \\ 0, & \text{otherwise.} \end{cases} \tag{6}$$

Where $sp(i,j)$ is the shortest path between pairs (i,j). It holds that $check\_siblings(i,j) = |parents(i) \cap parents(j)|$ and $check\_cousins(i,j) = |grandparents(i) \cap grandparents(j)|$. Hence, both functions are larger than zero, if classes i and j share at least one parent or grandparent, respectively.

Connectivity Hypothesis. In this hypothesis, we believe that the next edit operation will likelier occur on a class that is better connected in the class hierarchy. We define the *connectivity level* of a class as the number of *isA* relationships a class has to and from other classes. We represent the connectivity level of class j as k_j. The higher the connectivity level of a class, the higher our belief in a given transition (cf. Figure 1(g)). Note that for this hypothesis, each row of Q is the same—it can be seen as a zero-order Markov chain hypothesis that is weighted by the connectivity of nodes.

$$q_{i,j} = k_j \tag{7}$$

Similarity Hypothesis. In this hypothesis, we believe that transitions between similar classes are likelier to occur than between less similar classes (cf. Figure 1(h)). To calculate the similarity between classes i and j, we first generate *tf-idf* vectors, v_i and v_j, consisting of the values of the annotation properties corresponding to the label of a class, and the textual definition. Using these *tf-idf* vectors, we compute the cosine similarity between classes.

$$q_{i,j} = cos\_sim(v_i, v_j) \tag{8}$$

$cos\_sim(v_i, v_j)$ is the cosine similarity between the *tf-idf* vectors of the property values corresponding to the labels and textual definitions of classes i and j.

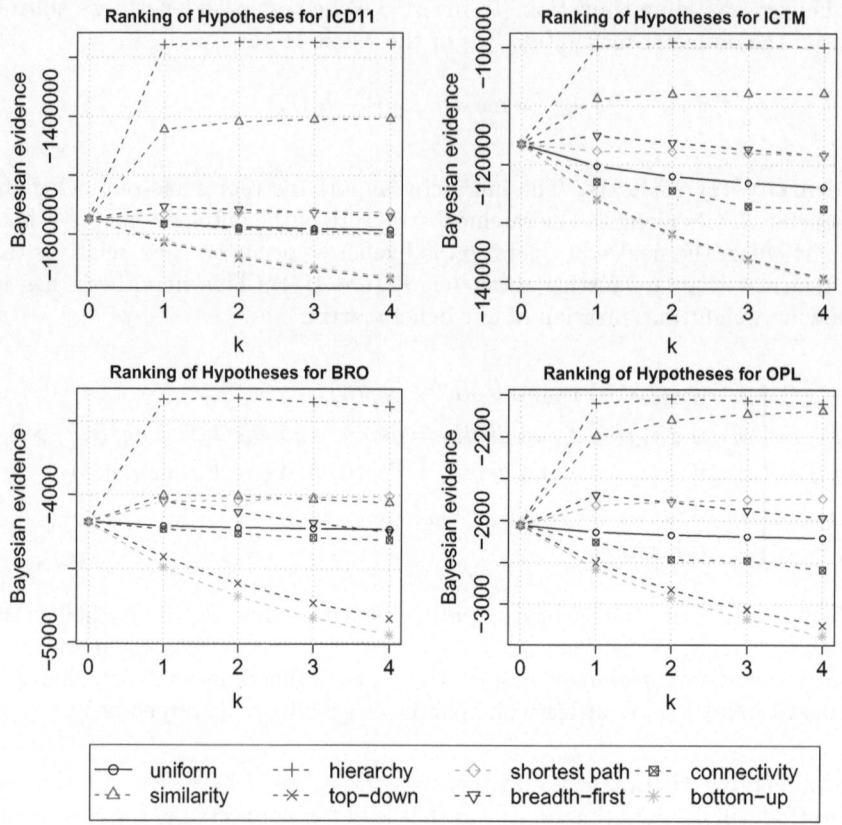

Fig. 3. Hypotheses ranking. Results for comparing hypotheses for the four datasets using HypTrails. The x-axes represent the hypothesis weighting factor k representing the "strength" of our belief in a hypothesis. In general, the stronger we believe in a hypothesis (i.e., the higher we set k), the less we expect to see transitions opposing the parametric beliefs of the corresponding hypothesis. The y-axes depict the Bayesian evidences. The higher the evidence for a given hypothesis, the better it is suited for describing the production of the extracted human edit trails (see Section 3).

5   Results

By applying HypTrails, we are able to gain insights into the relative plausibility of the hypotheses of interest based on the empirical data at hand. We illustrate the results in Figure 3. As mentioned in Section 3, we can compare the plausibility of hypotheses by comparing their marginal likelihoods—the higher, the more plausible. The hypothesis weighting factor k describes the "strength" of our belief in a given hypothesis; for fairness, we compare the plausibility of hypotheses by comparing their Bayesian evidences for the same values of k. For tractability, we report and interpret results for $0 <= k <= 4$; for higher values of k the results might slightly vary. Next, we highlight the main results for each ontology-engineering project (see Table 2 for a comparison of all hypotheses and datasets). We thoroughly discuss the results in Section 6.

International Classification of Diseases (ICD-11). The results for ICD-11, our biggest dataset, are depicted in the top-left part of Figure 3. The top-down and bottom-up hypotheses indicate lower evidences than the uniform hypothesis, suggesting that users are likelier to randomly change classes in the ontology than strictly follow a top-down or bottom-up approach. The connectivity hypothesis starts out to be nearly as plausible as the uniform hypothesis, but looses in Bayesian evidence faster with increasing k. The breadth-first and shortest-path hypotheses indicate higher evidences than the uniform hypothesis for our $k > 0$ at interest and thus, seem to be plausible explanations for the creation of the given human edit trails. Clearly, for ICD-11, the hierarchy hypothesis represents the most plausible explanation for the production of the trails, and thus the ontology at hand, followed by the similarity hypothesis.

International Classification of Traditional Medicine (ICTM). Similarly to ICD-11, the top-down, bottom-up and connectivity hypotheses exhibit lower evidences than the uniform hypothesis for all analyzed values of $k > 0$ (see top-right part of Figure 3). According to our experiments, the most plausible hypothesis for explaining the production of the edit trails of ICTM is the hierarchy hypothesis as it exhibits the highest Bayesian evidences for all $k > 0$. Further, the similarity hypothesis, as well as the breadth-first and shortest path hypotheses, are also better suited for describing the production of the human edit trails in ontology-engineering projects than the uniform hypothesis. For $k > 2$, we can also observe that the shortest-path hypothesis is increasing in plausibility and takes over the breadth-first hypothesis at $k = 4$.

Table 2. Results. The table depicts the relative ranking of each hypothesis for the corresponding datasets at $k = 4$. The best performing hypotheses are highlighted bold-face. If a hypothesis is less likely to explain the production of the corresponding edit trails than the uniform hypothesis, we have marked them with "-" for the corresponding dataset.

	ICD-11	ICTM	BRO	OPL
Hierarchy Hypothesis	**1**	**1**	**1**	**1**
Similarity Hypothesis	2	2	3	2
Shortest Path Hypothesis	3	3	2	3
Breadth-First Hypothesis	4	4	-	4
Uniform Hypothesis	5	5	4	5
Connectivity Hypothesis	-	-	-	-
Bottom-Up Hypothesis	-	-	-	-
Top-Down Hypothesis	-	-	-	-

Biomedical Resource Ontology (BRO). For BRO, the hypothesis with the highest Bayesian evidences for $k > 0$ is, again, the hierarchy hypothesis. Similarly to ICTM, the connectivity, top-down and bottom-up hypotheses are less plausible for explaining the production of the human edit trails in ontology-engineering projects than the uniform hypothesis. In contrast to ICD-11 and ICTM, the similarity hypothesis is less likely to be a plausible explanation for the trails than the shortest path hypotheses. Further, the shortest path hypothesis gains evidence with growing k, while the breadth-first hypothesis drops below the uniform hypothesis at $k = 4$.

Ontology for Parasite Lifecycle (OPL). Similarly to all other projects, the most plausible hypothesis for explaining the production of the trails at hand for OPL is the hierarchy hypothesis, followed by the similarity hypothesis (especially for higher k). The top-down, bottom-up and connectivity hypotheses are again, less plausible than the uniform hypothesis at $k > 0$. Analogously to ICTM, the breadth-first and shortest path hypotheses are more plausible for explaining the creation of the human edit trails than the uniform hypothesis, and switch ranks with growing k.

6   Discussions

The results of comparing the different hypotheses for the four datasets with HypTrails are surprisingly consistent. In all of the four ontology-engineering projects, the hierarchy hypothesis represents the most plausible hypothesis to explain the production of the human edit trails in ontology-engineering projects, and therefore the corresponding ontology at hand. The similarity hypothesis is the second most plausible hypothesis for explaining the production of the human edit trails in ontology-engineering projects for ICD-11, ICTM and OPL (at $k = 4$). The reason for the high Bayesian evidences of the similarity hypothesis is most probably due to the fact that (semantically) similar classes are usually grouped into the same parts of an ontology, hence the similarity calculations are likely to reflect our beliefs of the hierarchy hypothesis. For example, in a biomedical ontology, similar classes are grouped together as siblings or cousins, sharing at least one common parent or grandparent among them. Hence, additional adaptions to further distinguish the similarity hypothesis from the hierarchy hypothesis are warranted. In particular, we plan on investigating correlation between the similarity of classes and existing hierarchical links in future work.

In Walk et al. [23], we have been arguing that users are editing the ontology in a combined top-down and breadth-first fashion. The results of our analysis confirm the results from our exploratory analysis. In particular, the hierarchy hypothesis emphasizes transitions along top-down and breadth-first hierarchical relations (i.e., children, siblings and cousins opposed to uncles and aunts). This finding is also supported by the empirical research conducted by Vigo et al. [20], which shows that the class hierarchy is the central focus of user activity in an ontology-editing session. Users spend more than 45% of their time navigating or editing the class hierarchy, which serves as an index and external memory of the ontology. The authors have identified the class hierarchy as the central component of the user interface, which also explains very well our findings.

Thus, these observations reinforce our initial belief that the ontological hierarchy influences the selection of which class to edit next. Among other potential scenarios, this information can be leveraged by ontology-engineering tools creators to minimize the efforts required by users to create new, or edit existing content in an ontology. For example, ontology-editing tools may visually highlight the corresponding classes in the user interface, and provide keyboard shortcuts that allow for quicker and more productive editing sessions. Vigo et al. [20] also make the recommendation to place editing features close to the class hierarchy to better support the users in their editing patterns.

In our investigations, we have also identified hypotheses that were weak, and potentially not useful for the purpose of improving the user interface or editing process: the top-down, bottom-up and connectivity hypotheses are less plausible than the uniform hypothesis, meaning that randomly selecting classes to work on is likelier to produce the corresponding edit trails than specifically editing highly connected classes, or editing classes in a top-down or bottom-up fashion.

Our study also has limitations, for example, all investigated ontologies are authored with the same tool, WebProtégé (or its customizations), which may biases some of our findings. However, we believe that the bias is attenuated by the fact that the projects are completely different efforts by different teams, and they also use different customizations of the user interface. Furthermore, Rospocher et al. [10], who have analyzed the change logs of two different ontology-editing platforms (WebProtégé and a Wiki system), have come to the conclusion that users tend to edit around the hierarchy, indifferent of the tool that they used. One difficulty in overcoming this limitation is the fact that obtaining change logs for real-world projects from different platforms is almost impossible. Another limitation is the fact that HypTrails focuses on comparing the relative plausibility of hypotheses. Hence, we can say that the hierarchy hypothesis is the most plausible one for explaining the production of the edit trails at hand. However, we do not know if another hypothesis, other than the ones compared, is more plausible than the hierarchy hypothesis. For example, calculating the actual transition probabilities directly from the trails yields highest Bayesian evidences. However, understanding and interpreting this empirical "hypothesis" is very hard. Also, to be able to conduct an analysis using HypTrails, we need to have detailed change-tracking information, which WebProtégé provides, but might not be as easily obtained for other projects and tools.

7   Conclusions

In this paper, we have formally defined several hypotheses of how users edit an ontology, and systematically investigated, analyzed, and ranked these hypotheses according to their relative plausibility for describing edit trails of four real-world ontology-engineering projects using HypTrails, a coherent research approach.

We have found that the hierarchical structure of an ontology exercises the strongest influence on the observed user behavior, followed by the similarity of concepts. These findings are remarkably consistent across four different real-world projects, with some minor exception for the BRO dataset. We have also discussed how these findings may be used to improve ontology-editing tools. We think that our findings represent an advancement of the empirical research on how ontologies are created, which is a field that has been chronically lacking in our community.

We believe that the insights, uncovered in this paper, into how users *actually* edit real-world ontologies, represent a great opportunity for ontology-tools builders and for project managers, who can potentially leverage this information to create user interfaces and processes that better support the editing patterns of the users.

For future work, we plan to extend our set of formally defined hypotheses by including theories on how users edit properties (current work only considers class-based trails) and include different types of relationships for the analyses presented in this paper. In particular, studying individual (clustered) user behavior to automatically detect subsets of users that behave differently to other subsets of users represents a very promising opportunity for future work. On the longer term, we would like to create a recommendation module for ontology-editing tools, which would be informed by the editing patterns that we identify through our empirical research. We believe that the recommendation module and an adapted user interface will vastly improve the editing experience of the users.

Acknowledgments. This work is supported in part by grants GM086587 and GM103316 from NIH, and grant STR1191/2-1 from the German Research Foundation (DFG).

References

1. An, J., Quercia, D., Crowcroft, J.: Partisan sharing: facebook evidence and societal consequences. In: Conference on Online Social Networks, pp. 13–24. ACM (2014)
2. Beydoun, G.: Formal concept analysis for an e-learning semantic web. Expert Systems with Applications **36**(8), 10952–10961 (2009)
3. Borges, J., Levene, M.: Evaluating Variable-Length Markov Chain Models for Analysis of User Web Navigation Sessions. IEEE Transactions on Knowledge and Data Engineering **19**(4), 441–452 (2007). http://dx.doi.org/10.1109/TKDE.2007.1012
4. Chi, E.H., Pirolli, P., Pitkow, J.: The scent of a site: a system for analyzing and predicting information scent, usage, and usability of a web site. In: Proceedings of the SIGCHI Conference on Human Factors in Computing Systems, pp. 161–168. ACM (2000)
5. Falconer, S.M., Tudorache, T., Noy, N.F.: An analysis of collaborative patterns in large-scale ontology development projects. In: K-CAP, pp. 25–32. ACM (2011)
6. Huberman, B.A., Pirolli, P.L.T., Pitkow, J.E., Lukose, R.M.: Strong Regularities in World Wide Web Surfing. Science **280**(5360), 95–97 (1998). http://www.sciencemag.org/content/280/5360/95.abstract

7. Kass, R.E., Raftery, A.E.: Bayes factors. Journal of the American Statistical Association **90**(430), 773–795 (1995)
8. Parikh, P., Zheng, J., Logan-Klumpler, F.J., Stoeckert Jr., C.J., Louis, C., Topalis, P., Protasio, A.V., Sheth, A.P., Carrington, M., Berriman, M., et al.: The Ontology for Parasite Lifecycle (OPL): towards a consistent vocabulary of lifecycle stages in parasitic organisms. J. Biomedical Semantics **3**, 5 (2012)
9. Pesquita, C., Couto, F.M.: Predicting the Extension of Biomedical Ontologies. PLoS Comput. Biol. **8**(9), e1002630 (2012)
10. Rospocher, M., Tudorache, T., Musen, M.A.: Investigating collaboration dynamics in different ontology development environments. In: Buchmann, R., Kifor, C.V., Yu, J. (eds.) KSEM 2014. LNCS, vol. 8793, pp. 302–313. Springer, Heidelberg (2014)
11. Singer, P., Helic, D., Hotho, A., Strohmaier, M.: HypTrails: a bayesian approach for comparing hypotheses about human trails on the web. In: International Conference on World Wide Web (2015)
12. Singer, P., Helic, D., Taraghi, B., Strohmaier, M.: Detecting Memory and Structure in Human Navigation Patterns Using Markov Chain Models of Varying Order. PloS one **9**(7), e102070 (2014)
13. Singla, A., White, R., Huang, J.: Studying trailfinding algorithms for enhanced web search. In: Proceedings of the 33rd International ACM SIGIR Conference on Research and Development in Information Retrieval, pp. 443–450. ACM (2010)
14. Strohmaier, M., Walk, S., Pöschko, J., Lamprecht, D., Tudorache, T., Nyulas, C., Musen, M.A., Noy, N.F.: How Ontologies are Made: Studying the Hidden Social Dynamics Behind Collaborative Ontology Engineering Projects. Web Semantics: Science, Services and Agents on the World Wide Web **20** (2013)
15. Tenenbaum, J.D., Whetzel, P.L., Anderson, K., Borromeo, C.D., Dinov, I.D., Gabriel, D., Kirschner, B.A., Mirel, B., Morris, T.D., Noy, N.F., Nyulas, C., Rubenson, D., Saxman, P.R., Singh, H., Whelan, N., Wright, Z., Athey, B.D., Becich, M.J., Ginsburg, G.S., Musen, M.A., Smith, K.A., Tarantal, A.F., Rubin, D.L., Lyster, P.: The Biomedical Resource Ontology (BRO) to enable resource discovery in clinical and translational research. Journal of Biomedical Informatics **44**(1), 137–145 (2011)
16. Tudorache, T., Falconer, S., Nyulas, C., Noy, N.F., Musen, M.A.: Will semantic web technologies work for the development of ICD-11? In: Patel-Schneider, P.F., Pan, Y., Hitzler, P., Mika, P., Zhang, L., Pan, J.Z., Horrocks, I., Glimm, B. (eds.) ISWC 2010, Part II. LNCS, vol. 6497, pp. 257–272. Springer, Heidelberg (2010)
17. Tudorache, T., Nyulas, C., Noy, N.F., Musen, M.A.: WebProtégé: A Distributed Ontology Editor and Knowledge Acquisition Tool for the Web. Semantic Web Journal, 11–165 (2011)
18. Tufts, P.: Use of web usage trail data to identify related links. US Patent 6, 691, 163, February 10, 2004. https://www.google.com/patents/US6691163
19. Van Laere, S., Buyl, R., Nyssen, M.: A method for detecting behavior-based user profiles in collaborative ontology engineering. In: Meersman, R., Panetto, H., Dillon, T., Missikoff, M., Liu, L., Pastor, O., Cuzzocrea, A., Sellis, T. (eds.) OTM 2014. LNCS, vol. 8841, pp. 657–673. Springer, Heidelberg (2014)
20. Vigo, M., Jay, C., Stevens, R.: Constructing conceptual knowledge artefacts: activity patterns in the ontology authoring process. In: Proceedings of the 33rd Annual ACM Conference on Human Factors in Computing Systems, CHI 2015, Seoul, Republic of Korea, pp. 3385–3394 (2015)

21. Walk, S., Singer, P., Strohmaier, M.: Sequential action patterns in collaborative ontology-engineering projects: a case-study in the biomedical domain. In: Proceedings of the 23rd ACM International Conference on Conference on Information and Knowledge Managemen, pp. 1349–1358. ACM (2014)

22. Walk, S., Singer, P., Strohmaier, M., Helic, D., Noy, N.F., Musen, M.A.: Sequential Usage Patterns in Collaborative Ontology-Engineering Projects (2014). arXiv preprint arXiv:1403.1070

23. Walk, S., Singer, P., Strohmaier, M., Tudorache, T., Musen, M.A., Noy, N.F.: Discovering beaten paths in collaborative ontology-engineering projects using markov chains. Journal of Biomedical Informatics **51**, 254–271 (2014)

24. Wang, H., Tudorache, T., Dou, D., Noy, N.F., Musen, M.A.: Analysis of user editing patterns in ontology development projects. In: Meersman, R., Panetto, H., Dillon, T., Eder, J., Bellahsene, Z., Ritter, N., De Leenheer, P., Dou, D. (eds.) ODBASE 2013. LNCS, vol. 8185, pp. 470–487. Springer, Heidelberg (2013)

25. West, R., Leskovec, J.: Human wayfinding in information networks. In: International Conference on World Wide Web, pp. 619–628. ACM (2012). http://doi.acm.org/10.1145/2187836.2187920

26. White, R.W., Huang, J.: Assessing the scenic route: measuring the value of search trails in web logs. In: Conference on Research and Development in Information Retrieval, pp. 587–594. ACM (2010)

Next Step for NoHR: OWL 2 QL

Nuno Costa, Matthias Knorr$^{(\boxtimes)}$, and João Leite

NOVA LINCS, Departamento de Informática, Faculdade de Ciências E Tecnologia,
Universidade Nova de Lisboa, Caparica, Portugal
mkn@fct.unl.pt

Abstract. The Protégé plug-in NoHR allows the user to combine an OWL 2 EL ontology with a set of non-monotonic (logic programming) rules – suitable, e.g., to express defaults and exceptions – and query the combined knowledge base (KB). The formal approach realized in NoHR is polynomial (w.r.t. data complexity) and it has been shown that even very large health care ontologies, such as SNOMED CT, can be handled. As each of the tractable OWL profiles is motivated by different application cases, extending the tool to the other profiles is of particular interest, also because these preserve the polynomial data complexity of the combined formalism. Yet, a straightforward adaptation of the existing approach to OWL 2 QL turns out to not be viable. In this paper, we provide the non-trivial solution for the extension of NoHR to OWL 2 QL by directly translating the ontology into rules without any prior classification. We have implemented our approach and our evaluation shows encouraging results.

1 Introduction

NoHR[1] is a plug-in for the ontology editor Protégé[2] that allows its users to query combinations of $\mathcal{EL}_\bot^+$ ontologies and non-monotonic rules in a top-down manner.

Its motivation stems from the fact that many ontologies, such as the very large health care ontologies widely used in the area of medicine, e.g., SNOMED CT,[3] are expressed in OWL 2 EL, one of the OWL 2 profiles [24], and its underlying description logic (DL) $\mathcal{EL}^{++}$ [4]. Yet, due to their monotonic semantics, i.e., previously drawn conclusions persist when new additional information is adopted, DL-based ontology languages [3] are not suitable to model defaults and exceptions with a closed-world view, a frequently requested feature, e.g., when matching patient records to clinical trial criteria [26].

Among the plethora of approaches for extending DLs with non-monotonic features and deal with this problem (c.f. related work in [9,25]), NoHR builds on (Hybrid) MKNF KBs [25], which are based on the logic of minimal knowledge and negation as failure (MKNF) [23], under their well-founded semantics [18],

---

[1] http://centria.di.fct.unl.pt/nohr/
[2] http://protege.stanford.edu
[3] http://www.ihtsdo.org/snomed-ct/

© Springer International Publishing Switzerland 2015
M. Arenas et al. (Eds.): ISWC 2015, Part I, LNCS 9366, pp. 569–586, 2015.
DOI: 10.1007/978-3-319-25007-6_33

a formalism that combines DLs and non-monotonic rules as known from Logic Programming.

This choice is motivated, on the one hand, by the fact that non-monotonic logic programming rules are one of the most well-studied formalisms that admit expressing defaults, exceptions, and also integrity constraints in a declarative way, and are part of RIF [17], the other expressive language for the Semantic Web whose standardization is driven by the W3C.[4] On the other hand, MKNF KBs provide a very general and flexible framework for combining DL ontologies and non-monotonic rules (see [25]). In addition, [18], which is a variant of [25] based on the well-founded semantics [10] for logic programs, has a (lower) polynomial data complexity and is amenable for applying top-down query procedures, such as $\mathbf{SLG}(\mathcal{O})$ [1], to answer queries based only on the information relevant for the query, i.e., without computing the entire model.

NoHR is thus applicable to combinations of non-monotonic rules and OWL 2 EL ontologies. However, other applications (see, e.g., [6,27]) require ontologies using DL constructors which are not covered by OWL 2 EL, such as concept and role negation or role inverses – adding these to OWL 2 EL would raise its polynomial complexity [4].

OWL 2 QL and the *DL-Lite* family [2,5] to which the DL underneath OWL 2 QL belongs, $DL\text{-}Lite_R$, is suitable in these cases and has recently drawn a lot of attention in research and in applications. Even though a simple language at first glance, it is expressive enough to capture basic ontology languages, conceptual data models, e.g., Entity-Relationship, and object-oriented formalisms, e.g., basic UML class diagrams. Reasoning focuses on answering queries by rewriting the initial query, with the help of the ontology, into a set of queries that can be answered using an industry-strength SQL engine over the data. This yields that query answering in OWL 2 QL is in LOGSPACE (more precisely AC^0), but also links directly to applications in ontology-based data access (OBDA) [6,20]. Altogether, OWL 2 QL is naturally tailored towards huge datasets.

To also provide such OWL 2 QL based applications with the additional expressive power obtained from combining DL ontologies with non-monotonic rules, in this paper, we extend NoHR to deal with the OWL 2 QL profile. Whereas, at first sight, this could seem like a routine exercise, to the best of our knowledge, there is currently no dedicated open-source OWL 2 QL classifier with OWL API available that also classifies negative concepts (similar to the NI-closure in [5], but whose direct adaptation would potentially introduce a huge number of additional axioms). Thus, since we cannot simply replace the reasoner ELK [16], used currently in NoHR for $\mathcal{EL}$, with a correspondent for $DL\text{-}Lite_R$, we translate the ontology directly into rules. This introduces some non-trivial problems such as the need to capture unsatisfiable concepts and roles, and irreflexive roles (covered in [5] also by the NI-closure). We solve this problem by introducing an extension of the graph, used e.g., for classification in OWL QL [22], to negative axioms, which is already a contribution in its own right. The resulting translation is implemented as a module of NoHR, and its performance evaluated. Our main contributions are:

---

[4] http://www.w3.org

- A procedure for translating *DL-Lite$_R$* ontologies into rules which allows answering queries over MKNF KBs combining such ontologies and non-monotonic rules;
- A substantial extension of the Protégé plug-in NoHR to include OWL 2 QL ontologies, beyond *DL-Lite$_R$* via normalizations, including optimizations on the number of created rules and the use of tabling in the top-down query engine XSB;[5]
- An evaluation of our extension that shows that NoHR for OWL 2 QL maintains all positive evaluation results of the OWL 2 EL version [13], and is even faster during pre-processing, as no classification is necessary, in exchange for a slightly longer average response time during querying.

The remainder of the paper is structured as follows. In Sect. 2, we briefly recall *DL-Lite$_R$* and MKNF KBs as a tight combination of the former DL and non-monotonic rules, followed, in Sect. 3, by the translation of *DL-Lite$_R$* ontologies into rules. In Sect. 4, we discuss the changes made in the implementation for OWL 2 QL including optimizations, and evaluate it in Sect. 5, before we conclude in Sect. 6.

2 Preliminaries

2.1 *DL-Lite$_R$*

The description logic underlying OWL QL is *DL-Lite$_R$*, one language of the *DL-Lite* family [2,5], which we recall following the presentation in [19].

The syntax of *DL-Lite$_R$* is based on three disjoint sets of *individual names* N_I, *concept names* N_C, and *role names* N_R. *Complex concepts* and *roles* can be formed according to the following grammar

$$B \to A \mid \exists Q \qquad C \to B \mid \neg B \qquad Q \to P \mid P^- \qquad R \to Q \mid \neg Q$$

where $A \in N_C$ is a concept name, $P \in N_R$ a role name, and P^- its inverse. We also call B a *basic concept*, Q a *basic relation*, C a *general concept* and R a *general role*.

A *DL-Lite$_R$* knowledge base $\mathcal{O} = (\mathcal{T}, \mathcal{A})$ consists of a TBox $\mathcal{T}$ and an ABox $\mathcal{A}$. The TBox contains *general inclusion axioms (GCI)* of the form $B \sqsubseteq C$ and *role inclusion axioms* (RI) of the form $Q \sqsubseteq R$, with B, C, Q, and R defined as above. We term *positive inclusion axioms* all GCIs and RIs in $\mathcal{O}$ such that C is a basic concept and R is a basic relation, respectively, and all other GCIs and RIs *negative inclusion axioms*. We also assume that Q^- denotes the role P if $Q = P^-$, and P^- if $Q = P$. The ABox contains assertions of the form $A(a)$ and $P(a,b)$ where $A \in N_C$, $P \in N_R$, and $a,b \in N_I$. Assertions $C(a)$ for general concepts C can be included by $A \sqsubseteq C$ and $A(a)$ for a new concept name A.

---

[5] http://xsb.sourceforge.net

The semantics of $DL\text{-}Lite_R$ is based on *interpretations* $\mathcal{I} = (\Delta^{\mathcal{I}}, \cdot^{\mathcal{I}})$ consisting of a nonempty interpretation domain $\Delta^{\mathcal{I}}$ and an interpretation function $\cdot^{\mathcal{I}}$ that assigns to each individual a a distinct[6] element $a^{\mathcal{I}}$ of $\Delta^{\mathcal{I}}$, to each concept name A a subset $A^{\mathcal{I}}$, and to each role name P a binary relation $P^{\mathcal{I}}$ over $\mathcal{I}$. This can be extended as usual:

$$(P^-)^{\mathcal{I}} = \{(i_2, i_1) \mid (i_1, i_2) \in P^{\mathcal{I}}\} \qquad (\neg B)^{\mathcal{I}} = \Delta^{\mathcal{I}} \setminus B^{\mathcal{I}}$$

$$(\exists Q)^{\mathcal{I}} = \{i \mid (i, i') \in Q^{\mathcal{I}}\} \qquad (\neg Q)^{\mathcal{I}} = \Delta^{\mathcal{I}} \times \Delta^{\mathcal{I}} \setminus Q^{\mathcal{I}}$$

An interpretation $\mathcal{I}$ is a *model of GCI* $B \sqsubseteq C$ and *of RI* $Q \sqsubseteq R$ if $B^{\mathcal{I}} \subseteq C^{\mathcal{I}}$ and $Q^{\mathcal{I}} \subseteq R^{\mathcal{I}}$ respectively. $\mathcal{I}$ is also a *model of an assertion* $A(a)$ $(P(a,b))$ if $a^{\mathcal{I}} \in A^{\mathcal{I}}$ $((a^{\mathcal{I}}, b^{\mathcal{I}}) \in P^{\mathcal{I}})$. Given an axiom/assertion α we denote by $\mathcal{I} \models \alpha$ that $\mathcal{I}$ is a model of α. A *model* of a $DL\text{-}Lite_R$ KB $\mathcal{O} = (\mathcal{T}, \mathcal{A})$ is an interpretation $\mathcal{I}$ such that $\mathcal{I} \models \alpha$ holds for all $\alpha \in \mathcal{T} \cup \mathcal{A}$, and $\mathcal{O}$ is *satisfiable* if it has at least one model, and *unsatisfiable* otherwise. Also, $\mathcal{O}$ *entails* axiom α, written $\mathcal{O} \models \alpha$, if every model of $\mathcal{O}$ satisfies α.

2.2 MKNF Knowledge Bases

MKNF knowledge bases (KBs) build on the logic of minimal knowledge and negation as failure (MKNF) [23]. Two main different semantics have been defined [18,25], and we focus on the well-founded version [18], due to its lower computational complexity and amenability to top-down querying without computing the entire model. Here, we only point out important notions following [13], and refer to [18] and [1] for the details.

We start by recalling MKNF knowledge bases as presented in [1] to combine an ontology and a set of non-monotonic rules (similar to a normal logic program).

Definition 1. *Let $\mathcal{O}$ be an ontology. A function-free first-order atom $P(t_1, \ldots, t_n)$ s.t. P occurs in $\mathcal{O}$ is called* DL-atom; *otherwise* non-DL-atom. *A rule r is of the form*

$$H \leftarrow A_1, \ldots, A_n, \textbf{not } B_1, \ldots, \textbf{not } B_m. \tag{1}$$

where the head *of r, H, and all A_i with $1 \leq i \leq n$ and B_j with $1 \leq j \leq m$ in the* body *of r are atoms. A program $\mathcal{P}$ is a finite set of rules, and an MKNF knowledge base $\mathcal{K}$ is a pair $(\mathcal{O}, \mathcal{P})$. A rule r is* DL-safe *if all its variables occur in at least one non-DL-atom A_i with $1 \leq i \leq n$, and $\mathcal{K}$ is* DL-safe *if all its rules are DL-safe.*

DL-safety ensures decidability of reasoning with MKNF knowledge bases and can be achieved by introducing a new predicate o, adding $o(i)$ to $\mathcal{P}$ for all constants i appearing in $\mathcal{K}$ and, for each rule $r \in \mathcal{P}$, adding $o(X)$ for each variable X appearing in r to the body of r. Therefore, we only consider DL-safe MKNF knowledge bases.

---

[6] Hence, the unique name assumption is applied and, as shown in [2], dropping it would increase significantly the computational complexity of $DL\text{-}Lite_R$.

Example 2. Consider the following MKNF knowledge base $\mathcal{K}$ for recommending CDs, adapted from [18] (with some modifications). We denote DL-atoms and constants with upper-case names and non-DL-atoms and variables with lower-case names.[7]

$$\exists HasArtist^- \sqsubseteq Artist \qquad\qquad Piece \sqsubseteq \exists HasArtist$$

$$\exists HasComposed^- \sqsubseteq Piece \qquad\qquad Artist \sqsubseteq \neg Piece$$

$$HasComposed^- \sqsubseteq HasArtist$$

$$recommend(x) \leftarrow Piece(x), \textbf{not } owns(x), \textbf{not } lowEval(x), interesting(x).$$

$$interesting(x) \leftarrow Piece(x), \textbf{not } owns(x), Piece(y), owns(y),$$
$$Artist(z), HasArtist(y, z), HasArtist(x, z).$$

$owns(Summertime).$ $\qquad\qquad\qquad$ $HasArtist(Summertime, Gershwin).$

$Piece(Summertime).$ $\qquad\qquad\qquad$ $HasComposed(Gershwin, RhapsodyInBlue).$

This example shows that we can seamlessly express defaults and exceptions, such as recommending pieces as long as they are not owned or having a low evaluation, and at the same time taxonomic/ontological knowledge including information over unknown individuals, such as every piece having at least one artist without having to specify whom, but also features of $DL\text{-}Lite_R$, such as domain and range restrictions (of roles).

The semantics of MKNF knowledge bases $\mathcal{K}$ is usually given by a translation π into an MKNF formula $\pi(\mathcal{K})$, i.e., a formula over first-order logic extended with two modal operators $\mathbf{K}$ and $\textbf{not}$. Namely, every rule of the form (1) is translated into a rule of the form $\mathbf{K}H \leftarrow \mathbf{K}A_1, \ldots, \mathbf{K}A_n, \textbf{not } B_1, \ldots, \textbf{not } B_m$, and $\pi(\mathcal{P})$ is the conjunction of the translations of its rules, and $\pi(\mathcal{K}) = \mathbf{K}\pi(\mathcal{O}) \wedge \pi(\mathcal{P})$ where $\pi(\mathcal{O})$ is the first-order translation of $\mathcal{O}$. Reasoning with such MKNF formulas is then commonly achieved using a partition of *modal atoms*, i.e., all expressions of the form $\mathbf{K}\varphi$ for each $\mathbf{K}\varphi$ or $\textbf{not } \varphi$ occurring in $\pi(\mathcal{K})$. For [18], such a partition assigns *true*, *false*, or *undefined* to (modal) atoms, and can be effectively computed in polynomial time. If $\mathcal{K}$ is *MKNF-consistent*, then this partition does correspond to the unique model of $\mathcal{K}$ [18], and, like in [1], we call the partition the *well-founded MKNF model* $\mathsf{M}_{\mathsf{wf}}(\mathcal{K})$. Here, $\mathcal{K}$ may indeed not be MKNF-consistent if the ontology alone is unsatisfiable, or by the combination of appropriate axioms in $\mathcal{O}$ and rules in $\mathcal{P}$, e.g., axiom $A \sqsubseteq \neg B$ in $\mathcal{O}$, and facts $A(a)$ and $B(a)$ in $\mathcal{P}$. Strictly speaking, unlike [13], we do not have to make assumptions on the satisfiability of $\mathcal{O}$ as we are not going to use a classifier when processing $DL\text{-}Lite_R$ ontologies. Still, for the technical results established in Sec. 3, we will rely on satisfiability since we are able to entail everything from an unsatisfiable $\mathcal{O}$, whereas the translation into rules defined in Sec. 3 would

---

[7] To ease readability, we omit the auxiliary atoms that ensure DL-safety and leave them implicit. Also, whenever the body of a rule is empty, we dub it a *fact* and omit the $\leftarrow$ occasionally.

not permit that. This is why, in the following, we assume that $\mathcal{O}$ occurring in $\mathcal{K}$ is satisfiable, which does not truly constitute a restriction as we can always turn the ABox into rules without any effect on $\mathsf{M_{wf}}(\mathcal{K})$. An alternative approach would be to use one of the paraconsistent semantics for MKNF knowledge bases [15], but this is outside the scope of this paper, and an issue for future work, as no paraconsistent correspondence to the querying procedure $\mathbf{SLG}(\mathcal{O})$ used here currently exists.

2.3   Querying in MKNF Knowledge Bases

In [1], a procedure, called $\mathbf{SLG}(\mathcal{O})$, is defined for querying MKNF knowledge bases under the well-founded MKNF semantics. This procedure extends SLG resolution with tabling [7] with an *oracle* to $\mathcal{O}$ that handles ground queries to the DL-part of $\mathcal{K}$ by returning (possibly empty) sets of atoms that, together with $\mathcal{O}$ and information already proven true, allows us to derive the queried atom. We refer to [1] for the full account of $\mathbf{SLG}(\mathcal{O})$, and only recall a few crucial notions necessary in the following.

$\mathbf{SLG}(\mathcal{O})$ is based on creating top-down derivation trees with the aim of answering *(DL-safe) conjunctive queries* $Q = q(\boldsymbol{X}) \leftarrow A_1, \ldots, A_n, \mathbf{not}\ B_1, \ldots, \mathbf{not}\ B_m$, where each variable in Q occurs in at least one non-DL atom in Q, and where $\boldsymbol{X}$ is the (possibly empty) set of requested variables appearing in the body.

In general, the computation of $\mathsf{M_{wf}}(\mathcal{K})$ uses two different versions of $\mathcal{K}$ in parallel to guarantee that a) coherence is ensured, i.e., if $\neg P(a)$ is derivable, then $\mathbf{not}\ P(a)$ has to be true as well (cf. also [18]), and b) MKNF-consistency of $\mathcal{K}$ can be verified. For a top-down approach this is impractical, so, instead, a doubled MKNF knowledge base $\mathcal{K}^d = (\mathcal{O}, \mathcal{O}^d, \mathcal{P}^d)$ is defined in which a copy of $\mathcal{O}$ with new doubled predicates is added, and two rules occur in $\mathcal{P}^d$ for each rule in $\mathcal{P}$, intertwining original and doubled predicates (see Def. 3.1 in [1]). It is shown that an atom A is true in $\mathsf{M_{wf}}(\mathcal{K})$ iff A is true in $\mathsf{M_{wf}}(\mathcal{K}^d)$ and A is false in $\mathsf{M_{wf}}(\mathcal{K})$ iff A^d is false in $\mathsf{M_{wf}}(\mathcal{K}^d)$. Note that $\mathcal{K}^d$ is necessary in general, but we can use $\mathcal{K}$ here if it contains no negative inclusion axioms.

In [1], the notion of oracle is defined to handle ground queries to the ontology, but before we recall that notion, we use an example to illustrate the idea.

Example 3. Recall $\mathcal{K}$ in Ex. 2. As this suffices for our purposes, we omit $\mathcal{K}^d$ and restrict ourselves to $\mathcal{K}$ here. Consider query $q = recommend(Summertime)$. There is a matching rule head in $\mathcal{K}$, and, by instantiating the rule body with $x = Summertime$, we obtain a new set of queries. The first one, $Piece(Summertime)$, can be answered by means of the rule with matching head. The second, $\mathbf{not}\ owns(Summertime)$, is handled by querying for $owns(Summertime)$, for which also exists a corresponding rule, which means that $\mathbf{not}\ owns(Summertime)$ fails, so q is false.

Consider $q_1 = recommend(RhapsodyInBlue)$. We can use the same rule with matching rule head and, again, obtain four new instantiated queries from the rule body. Now, $Piece(RhapsodyInBlue)$ cannot be derived from the rules, but we can query the ontology and the oracle will return, e.g., a query *HasComposed*(x_1, *RhapsodyInBlue*) that if proven true can be added to $\mathcal{O}$, which would allow us to derive the queried goal. Because of the fact *HasComposed*(*Gershwin*, *RhapsodyInBlue*), this query succeeds, and so does *Piece*(*RhapsodyInBlue*). Subsequently, neither *owns*(*RhapsodyInBlue*) nor *lowEval*(*RhapsodyInBlue*) can be proven, so both fail, and their (default) negated queries succeed. For the remaining new query *interesting*(*RhapsodyInBlue*), the second rule head matches, which creates a further set of subgoals. The first two have just been answered, so have the next two with $y = Summertime$ for q, and it can be verified that the remaining also follow from the interplay of $\mathcal{O}$ and $\mathcal{P}$ in $\mathcal{K}$. Thus, q_1 succeeds.

We recall the notions of a complete and a (correct) partial oracle from [1].

Definition 4. *Let* $\mathcal{K}^d = (\mathcal{O}, \mathcal{O}^d, \mathcal{P}^d)$ *be a doubled MKNF KB,* $\mathcal{I}$ *a set of ground atoms (already proven to be true),* S *a ground query, and* $\mathcal{L}$ *a set of ground atoms such that each* $L \in \mathcal{L}$ *is unifiable with at least one rule head in* $\mathcal{P}^d$. *The complete oracle for* $\mathcal{O}$, *denoted* $compT_{\mathcal{O}}$, *is defined by* $compT_{\mathcal{O}}(\mathcal{I}, S, \mathcal{L})$ *iff* $\mathcal{O} \cup \mathcal{I} \cup \mathcal{L} \models S$ *or* $\mathcal{O}^d \cup \mathcal{I} \cup \mathcal{L} \models S$. *A* partial oracle *for* $\mathcal{O}$, *denoted* $pT_{\mathcal{O}}$, *is a relation* $pT_{\mathcal{O}}(\mathcal{I}, S, \mathcal{L})$ *such that if* $pT_{\mathcal{O}}(\mathcal{I}, S, \mathcal{L})$, *then* $\mathcal{O} \cup \mathcal{I} \cup \mathcal{L} \models S$ *or* $\mathcal{O}^d \cup \mathcal{I} \cup \mathcal{L} \models S$ *for consistent* $\mathcal{O} \cup \mathcal{I} \cup \mathcal{L}$ *and* $\mathcal{O}^d \cup \mathcal{I} \cup \mathcal{L}$, *respectively.*

A partial oracle $pT_{\mathcal{O}}$ *is* correct *w.r.t.* $compT_{\mathcal{O}}$ *iff, for all MKNF-consistent* $\mathcal{K}^d$, *replacing* $compT_{\mathcal{O}}$ *in* **SLG**($\mathcal{O}$) *with* $pT_{\mathcal{O}}$ *succeeds for exactly the same set of queries.*

Partial oracles may avoid returning unnecessary answers $\mathcal{L}$, such as non-minimal answers or those that try to derive an MKNF-inconsistency even though $\mathcal{K}^d$ is MKNF-consistent. Also, correctness of partial oracles is only defined w.r.t MKNF-consistent $\mathcal{K}$. The rationale is that, when querying top-down, we want to avoid checking whether the entire KB $\mathcal{K}^d$ is MKNF-consistent. This leads to para-consistent derivations if $\mathcal{K}^d$ is not MKNF-consistent, e.g., some atom P is true, yet P^d is false, while other independent atoms are evaluated as if $\mathcal{K}^d$ was MKNF-consistent (see [1]).

3   Translating the Ontology into Rules

As argued for the case of $\mathcal{EL}_{\perp}^+$ [13], axioms with $\exists$ on the right-hand side, e.g., *Piece* $\sqsubseteq \exists HasArtist$, cannot be translated straightforwardly into rules, nor do they directly contribute to the result when querying for ground instances, e.g., of *HasArtist*(x, y). Still, such axioms may contribute to derivations within $\mathcal{O}$, which is why, in [13], classification using the dedicated and highly efficient $\mathcal{EL}$ reasoner ELK [16] is first applied to derive implicit consequences. These, together with all axioms in $\mathcal{O}$, are then translated into rules, now discarding certain axioms with $\exists$ on the right-hand side.

Since, to the best of our knowledge, no dedicated and open-source OWL 2 QL classifier with OWL API that also classifies negative concepts is currently available, we translate the ontology directly into rules. This also simplifies and shortens the preprocessing phase and avoids a priori-classification, but requires some non-trivial considerations to ensure that no derivations are lost in the process, which we now explain.

Essentially, axioms, such as *Piece* $\sqsubseteq$ $\exists HasArtist$, cannot be translated into a rule $HasArtist(x, y) \leftarrow Piece(x)$ using a universal variable y, as this would allow us to derive $HasArtist(x, y)$ for any $Piece(x)$ and y, which is clearly not what the axiom expresses. Using a new constant c instead of y would not be correct either, as querying for $HasArtist(x, y)$ would return $HasArtist(x, c)$ for any $Piece(x)$ for the same c. Therefore, we proceed differently by introducing new auxiliary predicates that intuitively represent the domain and range of roles. For our example, this will yield the rule $DHasArtist(x) \leftarrow Piece(x)$ where $DHasArtist$ stands for the domain of $HasArtist$ (and $RHasArtist$ its range). Using such auxiliary predicates also means that we have to make sure that, e.g., $HasArtist(Summertime, Gershwin)$ allows us to derive $DHasArtist(Summertime)$, which can be achieved via an additional rule $DHasArtist(x) \leftarrow HasArtist(x, y)$. Moreover, for $HasComposed^- \sqsubseteq HasArtist$, it does not suffice to translate the axiom to $HasArtist(x, y) \leftarrow HasComposed(y, x)$, but also link the new auxiliary predicates for both roles, through the addition of the rules $DHasArtist(x) \leftarrow RHasComposed(x)$ and $RHasArtist(x) \leftarrow DHasComposed(x)$.

We now formalize this translation, and start by introducing notation on how to translate general concepts and roles. For that purpose, we formally introduce for each role $P \in \mathsf{N_R}$ auxiliary predicates DP and RP with the intuition of representing the domain and range of P. Also, similar to previous work in [1,13], we use special atoms $NH(t_i)$ in $\mathbf{SLG}(\mathcal{O})$ that represent a query $\neg H(t_i)$ to the oracle. These are, of course, only relevant if $\mathcal{O}$ contains negative inclusion axioms.

Definition 5. *Let C be a concept, R a role, x and y variables, and v a new (anonymous) variable (disjoint from x and y). We define $tr(C, x)$ and $tr(R, x, y)$ as follows:*

$$tr(C, x) = \begin{cases} A(x) & if\ C = A \\ DP(x) & if\ C = \exists P \\ RP(x) & if\ C = \exists P^- \\ NA(x) & if\ C = \neg A \\ tr(\neg Q, x, v) & if\ C = \neg \exists Q \end{cases} \quad tr(R, x, y) = \begin{cases} P(x, y) & if\ R = P \\ P(y, x) & if\ R = P^- \\ NP(x, y) & if\ C = \neg P \\ NP(y, x) & if\ C = \neg P^- \end{cases}$$

We obtain $tr^d(C, x)$ and $tr^d(Q, x, y)$ from $tr(C, x)$ and $tr(Q, x, y)$ by substituting all predicates P in $tr(C, x)$ and $tr(Q, x, y)$ with P^d, respectively.

This way, $tr(C, x)$ and $tr(R, x, y)$ handle both positive and negative inclusions and no additional case distinction is necessary.

Before we present the actual translation, we need to introduce one central notion, namely a graph to represent the axioms in a given TBox $\mathcal{T}$ as well as the implicitly derivable axioms, which will be necessary for defining the translation itself, but also turn out useful when establishing the correctness of the translation. Graphs have been used for classification in OWL QL (of positive inclusion

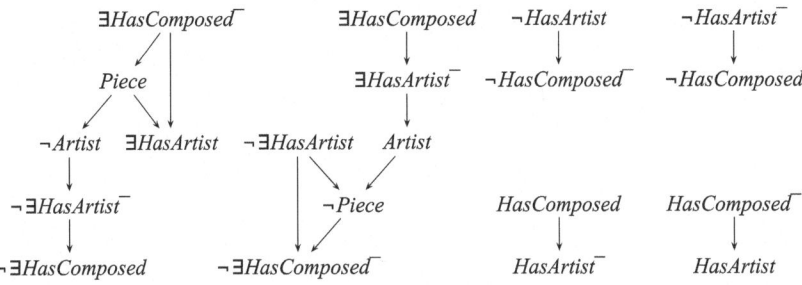

Fig. 1. The digraph $\mathcal{G}_{\mathcal{T}}$ for Example 2

axioms) [22], and we extend the notion here to also take negative inclusion axioms into account. We thus introduce the digraph (directed graph) of $\mathcal{T}$ as follows.

Definition 6. *Let $\mathcal{T}$ be a DL-Lite$_R$ TBox. The* digraph *of $\mathcal{T}$, $\mathcal{G}_{\mathcal{T}} = \langle \mathcal{V}, \mathcal{E} \rangle$, is constructively defined as follows.*

1. *If $A \in \mathsf{N}_C$, then A and $\neg A$ are in $\mathcal{V}$;*
2. *If $R \in \mathsf{N}_R$, then P, $\exists P$, $\exists P^-$, $\neg P$, $\neg \exists P$, and $\neg P^-$ are in $\mathcal{V}$;*
3. *If $B_1 \sqsubseteq B_2 \in \mathcal{T}$, then the edges (B_1, B_2) and $(\neg B_2, \neg B_1)$ are in $\mathcal{E}$;*
4. *If $Q_1 \sqsubseteq Q_2 \in \mathcal{T}$, then the edges (Q_1, Q_2), (Q_1^-, Q_2^-), $(\exists Q_1, \exists Q_2)$, $(\exists Q_1^-, \exists Q_2^-)$, $(\neg Q_2, \neg Q_1)$, $(\neg Q_2^-, \neg Q_1^-)$, $(\neg \exists Q_2, \neg \exists Q_1)$ e $(\neg \exists Q_2^-, \neg \exists Q_1^-)$ are in $\mathcal{E}$;*
5. *If $B_1 \sqsubseteq \neg B_2 \in \mathcal{T}$, then the edges $(B_1, \neg B_2)$ and $(B_2, \neg B_1)$ are in $\mathcal{E}$;*
6. *If $Q_1 \sqsubseteq \neg Q_2 \in \mathcal{T}$, then the edges $(Q_1, \neg Q_2)$, $(Q_2^-, \neg Q_1^-)$, $(\exists Q_1, \neg \exists Q_2)$, $(\exists Q_2, \neg \exists Q_1)$, $(\exists Q_1^-, \neg \exists Q_2^-)$ and $(\exists Q_2^-, \neg \exists Q_1^-)$ are in $\mathcal{E}$.*

Basically, each possible general concept and general role over N_C and N_R is a node in $\mathcal{G}_{\mathcal{T}}$, and the directed edges represent logical implications that follow from the axioms. Namely, for items 3. and 5., the subset inclusion itself and its contrapositive are in $\mathcal{E}$, and this is similar for items 4. and 6., only that the additional combinations due to inverses, $\exists$, and $\neg$ have to be taken into account. In this sense, the graph can be understood as capturing all subset inclusions (explicit and implicit) in $\mathcal{O}$, i.e., whenever there is a path from concept C_1 to concept C_2 and from role R_1 to role R_2, then $C_1 \sqsubseteq C_2$ and $R_1 \sqsubseteq R_2$ hold respectively. An Example of such a digraph is given in Fig. 1 for the TBox $\mathcal{T}$ from Example 2.

One observation w.r.t. Fig. 1, is that $\exists HasComposed \sqsubseteq \neg \exists HasComposed^-$, i.e., *HasComposed* is irreflexive. Even though this does not entail any assertion, knowing that $\forall x. \neg HasComposed(x, x)$ does hold should be captured in the translation. We introduce $\Psi(\mathcal{T})$, the set of irreflexive roles in $\mathcal{T}$, to be able to ensure exactly that.

Definition 7. *Let $\mathcal{T}$ be a DL-Lite$_R$ TBox and $\mathcal{G}_{\mathcal{T}}$ its digraph. We define $\Psi(\mathcal{T})$ as the smallest set of all $P \in \mathsf{N}_R$ that satisfy at least one of the following conditions:*

1. *For some $B_1 \sqsubseteq \neg B_2 \in \mathcal{T}$, there exist paths from $\exists P$ to B_1 and from $\exists P^-$ to B_2;*
2. *For some $B_1 \sqsubseteq \neg B_2 \in \mathcal{T}$, there exist paths from $\exists P^-$ to B_1 and from $\exists P$ to B_2;*
3. *For some $Q_1 \sqsubseteq \neg Q_2 \in \mathcal{T}$, there exist paths from P to Q_1 and from P^- to Q_2;*
4. *For some $Q_1 \sqsubseteq \neg Q_2 \in \mathcal{T}$, there exist paths from P^- to Q_1 and from P to Q_2.*

This notion builds on $\mathcal{G}_{\mathcal{T}}$, which is also required for detecting a further set of derivations. Imagine we would (wrongfully) add *Artist* $\sqsubseteq \exists HasComposed^-$ to $\mathcal{O}$ in Example 2. Then there would be a path from *Artist* to both *Piece* and $\neg Piece$, i.e., the concept *Artist* would be unsatisfiable. Note that independently of whether the MKNF KB is MKNF-inconsistent or not, we need to make sure that all unsatisfiable concepts and roles are determined, so we introduce $\Omega(\mathcal{T})$, quite similar in spirit to $\Psi(\mathcal{T})$.

Definition 8. *Let $\mathcal{T}$ be a DL-Lite$_R$ TBox and $\mathcal{G}_{\mathcal{T}}$ its digraph. We define $\Omega(\mathcal{T})$ as the smallest set of all $A \in \mathsf{N_C}$ such that, for some $B_1 \sqsubseteq \neg B_2 \in \mathcal{T}$, there exist paths from A to both B_1 and B_2, and all $P \in \mathsf{N_R}$ that satisfy at least one of the following conditions:*

1. *For some $B_1 \sqsubseteq \neg B_2 \in \mathcal{T}$, there exist paths from $\exists P$ to both B_1 and B_2;*
2. *For some $B_1 \sqsubseteq \neg B_2 \in \mathcal{T}$, there exist paths from $\exists P^-$ to both B_1 and B_2;*
3. *For some $Q_1 \sqsubseteq \neg Q_2 \in \mathcal{T}$, there exist paths from P to both Q_1 and Q_2;*
4. *For some $Q_1 \sqsubseteq \neg Q_2 \in \mathcal{T}$, there exist paths from P^- to both Q_1 and Q_2.*

With all pieces in place, we can introduce the translation of a *DL-Lite$_R$* ontology.

Definition 9. *Let $\mathcal{O}$ be a DL-Lite$_R$ ontology. We define $\mathcal{P}_{\mathcal{O}}^d$ from $\mathcal{O}$, where B_1, B_2 are basic concepts, Q_1, Q_2 basic roles, x, y variables, and a, b individuals, as the smallest set containing:*

(e) *for every $P \in \mathsf{N_R}$:*

$$DP(x) \leftarrow P(x, y). \qquad\qquad DP^d(x) \leftarrow P^d(x, y).$$
$$RP(y) \leftarrow P(x, y). \qquad\qquad RP^d(y) \leftarrow P^d(x, y).$$

(a1) *for every $A(a) \in \mathcal{O}$:*

$$A(a) \leftarrow . \qquad\qquad A^d(a) \leftarrow \mathbf{not}\ NA(a).$$

(a2) *for every $P(a, b) \in \mathcal{O}$:*

$$P(a, b) \leftarrow . \qquad\qquad P^d(a, b) \leftarrow \mathbf{not}\ NP(a, b).$$

(s1) *for every $B_1 \sqsubseteq B_2 \in \mathcal{O}$:*

$$tr(B_2, x) \leftarrow tr(B_1, x). \qquad tr^d(B_2, x) \leftarrow tr^d(B_1, x), \mathbf{not}\ tr(\neg B_2, x).$$
$$tr(\neg B_1, x) \leftarrow tr(\neg B_2, x).$$

(s2) *for every $Q_1 \sqsubseteq Q_2 \in \mathcal{O}$:*

$$tr(Q_2, x, y) \leftarrow tr(Q_1, x, y). \qquad tr^d(Q_2, x, y) \leftarrow tr^d(Q_1, x, y), \mathbf{not}\ tr(\neg Q_2, x, y).$$
$$tr(\exists Q_2, x) \leftarrow tr(\exists Q_1, x). \qquad tr^d(\exists Q_2, x) \leftarrow tr^d(\exists Q_1, x), \mathbf{not}\ tr(\neg \exists Q_2, x).$$
$$tr(\exists Q_2^-, x) \leftarrow tr(\exists Q_1^-, x). \qquad tr^d(\exists Q_2^-, x) \leftarrow tr^d(\exists Q_1^-, x), \mathbf{not}\ tr(\neg \exists Q_2^-, x).$$
$$tr(\neg Q_1, x, y) \leftarrow tr(\neg Q_2, x, y).$$

(n1) *for every $B_1 \sqsubseteq \neg B_2 \in \mathcal{O}$:*

$$tr(\neg B_1, x) \leftarrow tr(B_2, x). \qquad tr(\neg B_2, x) \leftarrow tr(B_1, x).$$

(n2) *for every $Q_1 \sqsubseteq \neg Q_2 \in \mathcal{O}$:*

$$tr(\neg Q_2, x, y) \leftarrow tr(Q_1, x, y). \qquad tr(\neg Q_1, x, y) \leftarrow tr(Q_2, x, y).$$

(i1) *for every* $A \in \Omega(\mathcal{T})$: $NA(x) \leftarrow .$
(i2) *for every* $P \in \Omega(\mathcal{T})$: $NP(x,y) \leftarrow .$
(ir) *for every* $P \in \Psi(\mathcal{T})$: $NP(x,x) \leftarrow .$

Item **(e)** ensures that the domain and range of roles is correctly encoded, items **(a1)** and **(a2)** translate the ABox, items **(s1)** and **(s2)** the positive inclusions, items **(n1)** and **(n2)** the negative inclusions, and items **(i1)**, **(i2)**, and **(ir)** introduce the rules representing unsatisfiable concepts and unsatisfiable and irreflexive roles. Note, that $\mathcal{P}_{\mathcal{O}}^d$ contains the rule representation for both $\mathcal{O}$ and $\mathcal{O}^d$, which is why items **(e)**–**(s2)** contain doubled rules. Of course, if $\mathcal{O}$ does not contain negative inclusion axioms, then we can skip all these, as well as items **(n1)**–**(ir)** which will not contribute anything anyway in this case. The additional default atoms are added to the doubled rules to be in line with the idea of the doubling of rules in [1]: whenever, e.g., $A(x)$ is "classically false" for some x, i.e., $NA(x)$ holds, then we make sure that $A^d(x)$ is derivable as false for that same x from the rules, but not necessarily $A(x)$, thus allowing to detect potential MKNF-inconsistencies. That is also the reason why neither **(n1)**–**(ir)** nor the contrapositives in **(s1)** and **(s2)** do produce the doubled counterparts: atoms based on predicates of the forms NC^d or NR^d are not used anywhere. Finally, the doubled rules in **(e)** do not contain the default negated atom as this case does really just associate domain and range to a role assertion, either present in the ABox or derived elsewhere. Additionally, predicates NDP or NRP are not used anywhere, so such default negated atoms would be of no impact anyway.

We can establish three correspondences between entailment from satisfiable $\mathcal{O}$ and the program resulting from the translation $\mathcal{P}_{\mathcal{O}}^d$. First, we consider positive atoms.

Lemma 10. *Let $\mathcal{O}$ be a DL-Lite$_R$ ontology, A a unary and R a binary predicate:*

- $\mathcal{O} \models A(a)$ *iff* $\mathcal{P}_{\mathcal{O}}^d \models A(a)$ *and* $\mathcal{O} \models R(a,b)$ *iff* $\mathcal{P}_{\mathcal{O}}^d \models R(a,b)$.

A similar property holds for (classically) negated atoms.

Lemma 11. *Let $\mathcal{O}$ be a DL-Lite$_R$ ontology, A a unary and R a binary predicate:*

- $\mathcal{O} \models \neg A(a)$ *iff* $\mathcal{P}_{\mathcal{O}}^d \models NA(a)$ *and* $\mathcal{O} \models \neg R(a,b)$ *iff* $\mathcal{P}_{\mathcal{O}}^d \models NR(a,b)$.

We can also show the correspondent to Lemma 10 for the doubled predicates.

Lemma 12. *Let $\mathcal{O}$ be a DL-Lite$_R$ ontology, A a unary and R a binary predicate:*

- $\mathcal{O}^d \models A^d(a)$ *iff* $\mathcal{P}_{\mathcal{O}}^d \models A^d(a)$ *and* $\mathcal{O}^d \models R^d(a,b)$ *iff* $\mathcal{P}_{\mathcal{O}}^d \models R^d(a,b)$.

Thus, we can define a correct partial oracle based on $\mathcal{P}_{\mathcal{O}}^d$.

Theorem 13. *Let $\mathcal{K}^d = (\mathcal{O}, \mathcal{O}^d, \mathcal{P}^d)$ be a doubled MKNF KB and $pT_{\mathcal{O}}^{QL}$ a partial QL oracle such that $pT_{\mathcal{O}}^{QL}(\mathcal{I}, S, \mathcal{L})$ iff $\mathcal{P}_{\mathcal{O}}^d \cup \mathcal{I} \cup \mathcal{L} \models S$. Then $pT_{\mathcal{O}}^{QL}$ is a correct partial oracle w.r.t. $compT_{\mathcal{O}}$.*

Instead of coupling two rule reasoners that interact with each other using an oracle, we can integrate both into one rule reasoner. The resulting approach is polynomial w.r.t. data complexity (as in [1,13], but not in AC^0 any longer as for OWL 2 QL alone).

Theorem 14. *Let* $\mathcal{K} = (\mathcal{O}, \mathcal{P})$ *be an MKNF KB with* $\mathcal{O}$ *in DL-Lite$_R$. An* **SLG**$(\mathcal{O})$ *evaluation of a query in* $\mathcal{K}_{QL} = (\emptyset, (\mathcal{P}^d \cup \mathcal{P}^d_{\mathcal{O}}))$ *is decidable with data complexity in* PTime*.*

4   System Description

In this section, we briefly describe the changes to the architecture of our plug-in and discuss some optimizations implemented w.r.t. the translation described in Sec. 3.

To allow the usage of OWL QL ontologies, changes were essentially made in the translator. Since NoHR now supports two OWL profiles a switch was introduced that checks the profile of the loaded/edited ontology. Whenever it belongs to OWL EL, NoHR behaves as described in [13], i.e., the reasoner ELK is used to classify the ontology and return the inferred axioms to translator, which are then translated. Otherwise, we treat $\mathcal{O}$ of the hybrid KB based on the translation described in Sec. 3 for OWL QL.

Notably, in Sec. 3, we only considered *DL-Lite$_R$*, while OWL QL includes a number of additional constructs which often can be expressed in *DL-Lite$_R$*. To account for that, we first normalize such expressions to axioms in *DL-Lite$_R$*. This includes ignoring certain expressions, most of which do not contribute to derivations, e.g., SubClassOf(B owl:Thing), while others make the ontology unsatisfiable, such as ClassAssertion(owl:Nothing a), although, as mentioned before, with no effect when querying the translated rules.

Subsequently, the graph is constructed, for determining unsatisfiable concepts and unsatisfiable and irreflexive roles, after which the translation is performed, which includes a number of optimizations. First, whenever there are no negative inclusions, the doubled rules are omitted in the cases (e)–(s2) of Def. 9. Additionally, case (e) is limited to those rules whose heads appear in the body of another rule. Both steps reduce the overall number of rules created during the translation.

The second group of optimizations is related to tabling in XSB, which contributes to help answering queries very efficiently in a top-down manner, and avoid infinite loops while querying. However, simply declaring all predicates to be tabled is very memory-consuming, so we reduced the number of tabled predicates without affecting loop detection. For example, only predicates that appear in any rule head and under negation in any rule body need to be tabled. In addition, rules with an empty body (facts) can be ignored in the previous criterion, as these will never cause infinite loops.

	q2	q3	q4	q5	q6	q7	q8	q9	q10	q13	q14
NoHR 1	5	5	20	200	1543	124	4538	324	4	2	1328
Pellet 1	24	15	17	14	33	13	67	104	14	13	30
NoHR 9	606	14	191	5745	58150	1455	54435	32525	18	8	67516
Pellet 9	148	108	96	96	358	102	123	524	99	97	177
NoHR 20	3602	29	308	5158	109898	3891	119744	90314	43	19	127772
Pellet 20	427	477	246	247	726	249	265	1329	249	249	469

Fig. 2. Query response times for NoHR and Pellet

5   Evaluation

In this section, we evaluate our system and show that a) our system scales reasonably well for OWL query answering (only being considerably slower for memory-intensive cases), b) preprocessing is even faster when compared to NoHR's previous version using a classifier (for EL), which was already capable of preprocessing large ontologies in a short period of time, c) querying scales well, even for over a million facts/assertions in the ABox, despite being slightly slower on average in comparison to EL, and d) adding rules scales linearly for pre-processing and querying, even for an ontology with many negative inclusions.

All tests were performed on a MacBook Pro (Retina, 13-inch, Early 2015) under OS X Yosemite 10.10.4 with 2.9 GHz Intel Core i5 processor and 16 GB of 1867 MHz DDR 3 memory. We ran all tests with a terminal version of NoHR with max. 8 GB of RAM allocated to Java 8 and we used XSB 3.6.0 for querying with the remaining RAM. Test results are averages over 5 runs.

We considered LUBM[8] [12], a standard benchmark for evaluating queries over a large data set. The benchmark's ontology contains 43 classes, 25 object and 7 data properties and 243 axioms, and it comes with a data generator and 14 queries q_1–q_{14}. First, to test general scalability, we utilized the material[9] in [21], that provides data instances of $LUBM_n$ for $n = 1, 9, 20$, where n specifies the number of universities and where LUBM is slightly simplified to fall completely into the QL profile. For our test, we focused on the provided material for Pellet,[10] as it worked correctly right away. Regarding pre-processing we observe that NoHR is slightly slower than Pellet (with the factor varying between 1.6 and 6.2), mainly due to the time of additionally loading the file in XSB, a step not necessary for Pellet. The results of answering queries q_2–q_{10}, q_{13}, and q_{14} can be found in Fig. 2.[11] We observe that NoHR is faster for some queries (q_3, q_{10}, q_{13} – up to factor 16), and slower for others, either below factor 15 (q_2, q_4, q_7), or with a significant difference (the remainder). The latter occurs due to the huge amount of data being stored in XSB's tables in the query process, ultimately

---

[8] http://swat.cse.lehigh.edu/projects/lubm/

[9] https://github.com/ontop/iswc2014-benchmark

[10] https://github.com/complexible/pellet

[11] q_1 is flawed for Pellet and the other two queries have been omitted here, as the restriction to QL cancels the OWL reasoning capability intended to be tested (transitivity and realization).

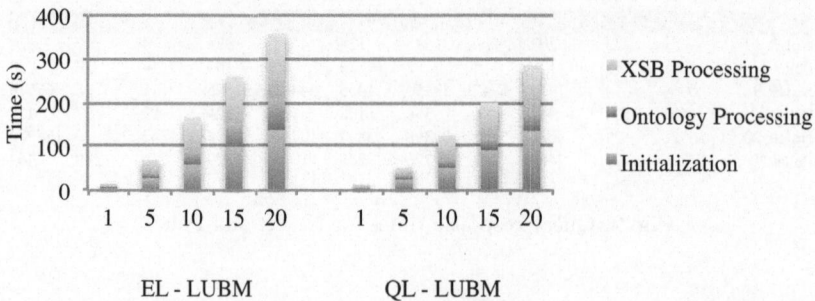

Fig. 3. Preprocessing time for LUBM for the two translation modes

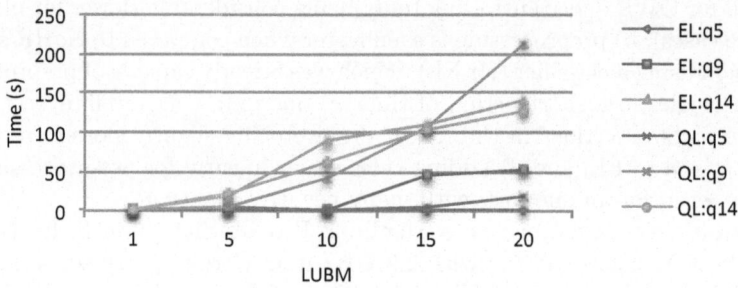

Fig. 4. Query time for three LUBM queries

intended for handling non-monotonic rules that are not even part of Pellet. Yet, at the same time, tabling enables NoHR to be faster, namely, when an already computed result can simply be looked up (see the test below on LIPID for further details).

Next, with the aim of comparing our new approach, based on a direct translation, with the one using a classifier (for OWL EL), we created instances of $LUBM_n$ with $n = 1, 5, 10, 15, 20$ using the provided generator, and a restricted version of LUBM which fits both OWL EL and QL (thus rendering q_{13} meaningless, but now permitting q_1 in exchange), with the number of assertions ranging from roughly 100,000 to over 2,700,000. We performed pre-processing and the results for both kinds of translators (EL and QL) can be found in Fig. 3. Note that "Initialization" includes loading the ontology and for EL also classifying it, "Ontology Processing" includes the actual translation, and "XSB Processing" the writing of the rule file and loading it in XSB. We observe that QL is considerably faster, indeed up to 80s for $LUBM_{20}$, which is to a considerable extent due to avoiding classification and a smaller rule file being created. Besides that, the preprocessing time increases linearly, and the overall time for preprocessing is acceptable in our opinion as this is only done once before querying.

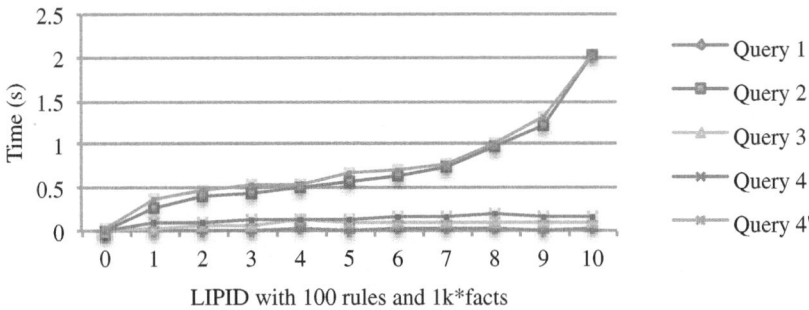

Fig. 5. Query time for LIPID

We also queried in XSB for both versions, EL and QL. Some representative results are shown in Fig. 4. Basically, for queries q_1–q_5, q_7 and q_{10} the response time is below 18s, often strictly below 1s, in general slightly in favor of the EL version (up to factor 8). For the other queries, response time increases more significantly with huge amounts of data, divided into those slightly in favor of QL (q_6, q_8, q_{14}, with a factor below 2, but up to 20s in absolute value), and those in favor of EL (q_9, up to factor 4 and 150s in absolute value). In all cases, the response time grows linearly w.r.t. the increasing size of data, and querying in QL is slightly slower on average. Here, EL compensates for the longer preprocessing, and it thus seems that deciding which of the two forms of translations performs better depends on the kind (and number) of queries we pose.

Finally, with the aim of also testing a more expressive OWL 2 QL ontology, we used the LIPID ontology,[12] which has, besides 749 subclass axioms, $1,486$ class disjointness axioms and 20 inverse object properties in combination with non-monotonic rules. The latter were created by means of the rule generator previously used in [13], containing a fixed number of 100 rules and a number of facts increasing in steps of 1k, also introducing some new predicates not present in the ontology itself. We performed the preprocessing step and observed only small effects due to the increasing amount of rules. The time for processing the ontology was naturally stable for all steps, and overall processing time was between 1.4 and 3.3s. Notably, the considerable amount of negative inclusions had no significant impact on time, e.g., when constructing the graph. Then, we posed four simple queries (Query1–4), namely Acyl_Ester_Chain(X), Lipid(X), Organic_Group(X), and Entity(X) to the resulting rule sets in XSB, with the position in the concept hierarchy varying from the lowest level (Query 1) to the topmost below ⊤ (Query 4) with 715 subclasses. The results are shown in Fig. 5. As we can see, the response time is very reasonable, from well below 1s to at most 2.2s. We also posed Query 4 without posing the three previous queries beforehand. The result is also included in Fig. 5 as Query 4', and it shows the speed-up that tabling of prior query results for subclasses has on the response

---

[12] http://bioonto.dcs.aber.ac.uk/ql-ont/

time of Query 4 (up to factor 11.5). Overall, the results somehow also show the effect of the arbitrary rules in raising the time for query answering, since they introduce additional non-hierarchical (positive and negative) links within the ontology. We conclude with noting that performance tests of querying (non-monotonic) rules and ontologies would considerably benefit from real datasets, but, unfortunately, to the best of our knowledge, none are currently available.

6   Conclusions

We have extended NoHR, the Protégé plug-in that allows to query non-monotonic rules and ontologies in OWL 2 EL, to also admit ontologies in OWL 2 QL. While the principal architecture of the tool remains the same, the crucial module that translates the ontology into rules with the help of a classifier simply cannot be reused, which is why we introduced a novel direct translation for OWL 2 QL ontologies to cover this profile. We have implemented this translation and discussed optimizations. The evaluation shows that it maintains all positive evaluation results of the OWL 2 EL version [13], and is even faster during pre-processing, as no classification is necessary, in exchange for an on average slightly longer response time during querying.

Besides the OWL 2 EL profile supported by NoHR, and compared to in Sect. 5, also [11,19] both build on the well-founded MKNF semantics [18]. While [11] uses the non-standard CDF framework integrated in XSB, which complicates compatibility to standard OWL tools based on the OWL API, [19] presents an OWL 2 QL oracle based on common rewritings in the underlying DL $DL\text{-}Lite_R$ [2], but would require constant interaction between a rule reasoner and a DL reasoner, which is why we believe it is ultimately less efficient than our approach. Two related tools are DReW [29] and HD Rules [8], but both are based on different base formalisms to combine ontologies and non-monotonic rules w.r.t. the way information can flow between its two components and how flexible the language is [9,25], which considerably complicates comparison.

For future work, the extension to OWL 2 RL seems an obvious next step, but developing an alternative for OWL 2 QL using the classifier integrated in ontop [21] or even the general reasoner Konclude [28], could shed more light on whether classification or direct translation fares better for proper OWL 2 QL ontologies. The efficiency of the latter reasoner also motivates looking into non-polynomial DLs, with possible influences from recent work on rewriting disjunctive datalog programs [14]. Using a relational database for the data as in OBDA would also be interesting, yet this would require non-trivial theoretical work on rewriting queries including non-monotonic rules. Finally, we may extend NoHR for OWL 2 QL (and EL) to the paraconsistent semantics [15] that would provide true support to the paraconsistent behavior already observed .

Acknowledgments. This work was partially supported by Fundação para a Ciência e a Tecnologia (FCT) under project PTDC/EIA-CCO/121823/2010, strategic project PEst/UID/CEC/04516/2013, and grant SFRH/BPD/86970/2012 (M. Knorr).

References

1. Alferes, J.J., Knorr, M., Swift, T.: Query-driven procedures for hybrid MKNF knowledge bases. ACM Trans. Comput. Log. **14**(2), 1–43 (2013)
2. Artale, A., Calvanese, D., Kontchakov, R., Zakharyaschev, M.: The *DL-Lite* family and relations. J. Artif. Intell. Res. (JAIR) **36**, 1–69 (2009)
3. Baader, F., Calvanese, D., McGuinness, D.L., Nardi, D., Patel-Schneider, P.F. (eds.): The Description Logic Handbook: Theory, Implementation, and Applications, 3rd edn. Cambridge University Press (2010)
4. Baader, F., Brandt, S., Lutz, C.: Pushing the $\mathcal{EL}$ envelope. In: Kaelbling, L.P., Saffiotti, A. (eds.) Procs. of IJCAI, pp. 364–369. Professional Book Center (2005)
5. Calvanese, D., de Giacomo, G., Lembo, D., Lenzerini, M., Rosati, R.: Tractable reasoning and efficient query answering in description logics: The *DL-Lite* family. Journal of Automated Reasoning **39**(3), 385–429 (2007)
6. Calvanese, D., De Giacomo, G., Lembo, D., Lenzerini, M., Poggi, A., Rodriguez-Muro, M., Rosati, R., Ruzzi, M., Savo, D.F.: The MASTRO system for ontology-based data access. Semantic Web **2**(1), 43–53 (2011)
7. Chen, W., Warren, D.S.: Tabled Evaluation with Delaying for General Logic Programs. J. ACM **43**(1), 20–74 (1996)
8. Drabent, W., Henriksson, J., Maluszynski, J.: Hd-rules: a hybrid system interfacing prolog with dl-reasoners. In: Polleres, A., et al. (eds.) Procs. of ALPSWS. CEUR-WS.org (2007)
9. Eiter, T., Ianni, G., Lukasiewicz, T., Schindlauer, R., Tompits, H.: Combining answer set programming with description logics for the semantic web. Artif. Intell. **172**(12–13), 1495–1539 (2008)
10. Gelder, A.V., Ross, K.A., Schlipf, J.S.: The well-founded semantics for general logic programs. J. ACM **38**(3), 620–650 (1991)
11. Gomes, A.S., Alferes, J.J., Swift, T.: Implementing query answering for hybrid MKNF knowledge bases. In: Carro, M., Peña, R. (eds.) PADL 2010. LNCS, vol. 5937, pp. 25–39. Springer, Heidelberg (2010)
12. Guo, Y., Pan, Z., Heflin, J.: LUBM: A benchmark for OWL knowledge base systems. J. Web Sem. **3**(2–3), 158–182 (2005)
13. Ivanov, V., Knorr, M., Leite, J.: A query tool for $\mathcal{EL}$ with non-monotonic rules. In: Alani, H., Kagal, L., Fokoue, A., Groth, P., Biemann, C., Parreira, J.X., Aroyo, L., Noy, N., Welty, C., Janowicz, K. (eds.) ISWC 2013, Part I. LNCS, vol. 8218, pp. 216–231. Springer, Heidelberg (2013)
14. Kaminski, M., Nenov, Y., Grau, B.C.: Datalog rewritability of disjunctive datalog programs and its applications to ontology reasoning. In: Brodley, C.E., Stone, P. (eds.) Procs. of AAAI, pp. 1077–1083. AAAI Press (2014)
15. Kaminski, T., Knorr, M., Leite, J.: Efficient paraconsistent reasoning with ontologies and rules. In: Yang, Q., Wooldridge, M. (eds.) Procs. of IJCAI. IJCAI/AAAI (2015)
16. Kazakov, Y., Krötzsch, M., Simančík, F.: The incredible ELK: From polynomial procedures to efficient reasoning with $\mathcal{EL}$ ontologies. Journal of Automated Reasoning **53**, 1–61 (2013)
17. Kifer, M., Boley, H. (eds.): RIF Overview (Second Edition). W3C Working Group Note 5 February 2013 (2013). http://www.w3.org/TR/rif-overview/
18. Knorr, M., Alferes, J.J., Hitzler, P.: Local closed world reasoning with description logics under the well-founded semantics. Artif. Intell. **175**(9–10), 1528–1554 (2011)

19. Knorr, M., Alferes, J.J.: Querying OWL 2 QL and non-monotonic rules. In: Aroyo, L., Welty, C., Alani, H., Taylor, J., Bernstein, A., Kagal, L., Noy, N., Blomqvist, E. (eds.) ISWC 2011, Part I. LNCS, vol. 7031, pp. 338–353. Springer, Heidelberg (2011)

20. Kontchakov, R., Lutz, C., Toman, D., Wolter, F., Zakharyaschev, M.: The combined approach to ontology-based data access. In: Walsh, T. (ed.) Procs. of IJCAI, pp. 2656–2661. IJCAI/AAAI (2011)

21. Kontchakov, R., Rezk, M., Rodríguez-Muro, M., Xiao, G., Zakharyaschev, M.: Answering SPARQL queries over databases under OWL 2 QL entailment regime. In: Mika, P., Tudorache, T., Bernstein, A., Welty, C., Knoblock, C., Vrandečić, D., Groth, P., Noy, N., Janowicz, K., Goble, C. (eds.) ISWC 2014, Part I. LNCS, vol. 8796, pp. 552–567. Springer, Heidelberg (2014)

22. Lembo, D., Santarelli, V., Savo, D.F.: Graph-based ontology classification in OWL 2 QL. In: Cimiano, P., Corcho, O., Presutti, V., Hollink, L., Rudolph, S. (eds.) ESWC 2013. LNCS, vol. 7882, pp. 320–334. Springer, Heidelberg (2013)

23. Lifschitz, V.: Nonmonotonic databases and epistemic queries. In: Mylopoulos, J., Reiter, R. (eds.) Procs. of IJCAI, pp. 381–386. Morgan Kaufmann (1991)

24. Motik, B., Cuenca Grau, B., Horrocks, I., Wu, Z., Fokoue, A., Lutz, C. (eds.): OWL 2 Web Ontology Language: Profiles (Second Edition). W3C Recommendation 11 December 2012 (2012). http://www.w3.org/TR/owl2-profiles/

25. Motik, B., Rosati, R.: Reconciling description logics and rules. J. ACM **57**(5), 93–154 (2010)

26. Patel, C., Cimino, J., Dolby, J., Fokoue, A., Kalyanpur, A., Kershenbaum, A., Ma, L., Schonberg, E., Srinivas, K.: Matching patient records to clinical trials using ontologies. In: Aberer, K., Choi, K.-S., Noy, N., Allemang, D., Lee, K.-I., Nixon, L.J.B., Golbeck, J., Mika, P., Maynard, D., Mizoguchi, R., Schreiber, G., Cudré-Mauroux, P. (eds.) ASWC 2007 and ISWC 2007. LNCS, vol. 4825, pp. 816–829. Springer, Heidelberg (2007)

27. Savo, D.F., Lembo, D., Lenzerini, M., Poggi, A., Rodriguez-Muro, M., Romagnoli, V., Ruzzi, M., Stella, G.: Mastro at work: experiences on ontology-based data access. In: Haarslev, V., et al. (eds.) Procs. of DL. CEUR Workshop Proceedings, vol. 573. CEUR-WS.org (2010)

28. Steigmiller, A., Liebig, T., Glimm, B.: Konclude: System description. J. Web Sem. **27**, 78–85 (2014)

29. Xiao, G., Eiter, T., Heymans, S.: The DReW system for nonmonotonic dl-programs. In: Li, J., et al. (eds.) SWWS 2012. Springer Proceedings in Complexity. Springer (2013)

Concept Forgetting in $\mathcal{ALCOI}$-Ontologies Using an Ackermann Approach

Yizheng Zhao[(⊠)] and Renate A. Schmidt

The University of Manchester, Manchester, UK
yizheng.zhao@student.manchester.ac.uk

Abstract. We present a method for forgetting concept symbols in ontologies specified in the description logic $\mathcal{ALCOI}$. The method is an adaptation and improvement of a second-order quantifier elimination method developed for modal logics and used for computing correspondence properties for modal axioms. It follows an approach exploiting a result of Ackermann adapted to description logics. An important feature inherited from the modal approach is that the inference rules are guided by an ordering compatible with the elimination order of the concept symbols. This provides more control over the inference process and reduces non-determinism, resulting in a smaller search space. The method is extended with a new case splitting inference rule, and several simplification rules. Compared to related forgetting and uniform interpolation methods for description logics, the method can handle inverse roles, nominals and ABoxes. Compared to the modal approach on which it is based, it is more efficient in time and improves the success rates. The method has been implemented in Java using the OWL API. Experimental results show that the order in which the concept symbols are eliminated significantly affects the success rate and efficiency.

1 Introduction

Ontology-based technologies provide novel ways of building knowledge processing systems and play an important role in many different areas, both in research projects but also in industry applications. Big ontologies contain large numbers of symbols and knowledge modelled in them is rich and inevitably heterogeneous. There are thus situations, where it is useful to be able to restrict the ontology to a subset of the signature and *forget* those symbols that do not belong to the subset, for example, when an ontology needs to be analysed by an ontology engineer to gain an understanding of the information represented in it. Other examples are scenarios where ontologies are located at separate remote sites and information is exchanged via agents. Since the vocabularies known to the agents at the different sites will vary, communication between the agents needs to be limited to using the common language to avoid ambiguity and confusion caused by mismatches between the vocabularies of the different agents. At this point, it would be beneficial if the signature symbols in one ontology that are not known to the other agents can be eliminated without losing information

© Springer International Publishing Switzerland 2015
M. Arenas et al. (Eds.): ISWC 2015, Part I, LNCS 9366, pp. 587–602, 2015.
DOI: 10.1007/978-3-319-25007-6_34

required for the communication. In other words, signature symbols belonging to only one of the ontologies are forgotten, and communication is confined to information expressed in the shared language of the agents' ontologies. Another use of forgetting is restricting the vocabulary of an ontology to more general concept symbols, and forgetting those that are more specific, to create a summary of the ontology [29]. Situations where ontologies are published, shared, or disseminated, but some sensitive parts described in terms of particular signature symbols need to be kept confidential or unseen to the receiver, are some other potential applications of forgetting [4]. This is relevant for medical and military uses, and uses in industry to ensure proprietary information can be kept hidden.

The contribution of this paper is the presentation of a method for forgetting concept symbols in ontologies specified in the description logic $\mathcal{ALCOI}$. $\mathcal{ALCOI}$ extends the description logic $\mathcal{ALC}$ with nominals and inverse roles. Forgetting concept symbols for $\mathcal{ALCOI}$ is a topic where no method is available yet, but a number of related methods exist. Forgetting can be viewed as the problem that is dual to uniform interpolation. A lot of recent work has been focussed on uniform interpolation of mainly TBoxes represented in several description logics, ranging from ones with more limited expressivity, such as DL-Lite [31] and $\mathcal{EL}$ [20,22] and $\mathcal{EL}$-extensions [11], to more expressive ones, such as $\mathcal{ALC}$ [13,14,19,21,30], $\mathcal{ALCH}$ [12], $\mathcal{SIF}$ [17] and $\mathcal{SHQ}$ [15].

Forgetting can also be viewed as a second-order quantification problem, which is the view we take in this paper. In second-order quantifier elimination, the aim is to eliminate existentially quantified predicate symbols in order to translate second-order formulae into equivalent formulae in first-order logic [3,5–8,23,24, 26,28]. In uniform interpolation the aim is to eliminate symbols too, though it is not required that the result is logically equivalent to the corresponding formula in second-order logic, only that all important consequences are preserved.

Our method is adapted from a method, called MSQEL, designed for modal logic to compute first-order frame correspondence properties for modal axioms and rules [26]. The adaptation exploits the close relationship between description logics and modal logics [25]. Our method contributes three novel aspects. It is the first method for forgetting concept symbols from ontologies specified in the description logic $\mathcal{ALCOI}$. It inherits from MSQEL the consideration of elimination orders, which has been shown to improve the success rate and make it succeed on a wider range for problems in the modal logic corresponding to $\mathcal{ALCOI}$ [26]. The success rate and its scope is further improved by the incorporation of a new case splitting rule and generalised simplification rules. Results of an empirical evaluation show better success rates and performance for these techniques.

The rest of the paper is organised as follows. Section 2 defines basic notions of the problem of concept forgetting, including the syntax and semantics of $\mathcal{ALCOI}$-ontologies, the language that our proposed method is aimed for. A formal definition of concept forgetting for $\mathcal{ALCOI}$-ontologies follows in Section 3. Section 4 sketches the general method to forget selected concept symbols, and correctness and termination results are stated. The forgetting calculus is introduced in

Section 5, where all the inference rules and two important simplification rules are presented. Section 6 describes a heuristic method for calculating good forgetting orders of the concept symbols that need to be eliminated. Results of an empirical evaluation of the method are presented in Section 7. A brief chronological overview of the most related work on forgetting and second-order quantifier elimination is given in Section 8. We conclude in Section 9 with a summary of the work and an outline of directions of future work.

2   Definition of $\mathcal{ALCOI}$ and Other Basic Notions

The basic syntactic elements in the language of $\mathcal{ALCOI}$ are the *atomic concepts*, *atomic roles*, and *nominals*. Together they form the *signature* of the language of $\mathcal{ALCOI}$. Let N_C and N_R be the set of atomic concepts and the set of atomic roles, respectively, and let N_O be the set of nominals. $\mathcal{ALCOI}$-concepts have one of these forms:

$$a \mid \bot \mid \top \mid A \mid \neg C \mid C \sqcup D \mid C \sqcap D \mid \exists R.C \mid \exists R^-.C \mid \forall R.C \mid \forall R^-.C,$$

where $a \in N_O$, $A \in N_C$, $R \in N_R$, and C and D are arbitrary $\mathcal{ALCOI}$-concepts. R^- denotes the inverse of the role R. By definition, $R^{--} := R$.

An ontology usually consists of two parts, namely a TBox and an ABox. A TBox contains a set of axioms of the form $C \sqsubseteq D$ or $C \equiv D$, where C and D are concepts. A concept definition $C \equiv D$ can be expressed by two general inclusion axioms $C \sqsubseteq D$ and $D \sqsubseteq C$. In $\mathcal{ALCOI}$, ABox axioms can be expressed as inclusions in the TBox: a concept assertion $C(a)$ can be expressed as $a \sqsubseteq C$, and a role assertion $R(a, b)$ as $a \sqsubseteq \exists R.b$. In our considerations $\mathcal{ALCOI}$-ontologies are therefore assumed to contain TBox axioms only.

We define an interpretation $\mathcal{I}$ for $\mathcal{ALCOI}$ over the signature (N_C, N_R, N_O) as a pair $\langle \Delta^{\mathcal{I}}, \cdot^{\mathcal{I}} \rangle$, where $\Delta^{\mathcal{I}}$ is a non-empty set that represents the interpretation domain, and $\cdot^{\mathcal{I}}$ is the interpretation function that assigns to every nominal $a \in N_O$ a singleton set $a^{\mathcal{I}} \subseteq \Delta^{\mathcal{I}}$; to every concept symbol $A \in N_C$ a subset $A^{\mathcal{I}}$ of $\Delta^{\mathcal{I}}$; and to every role symbol $R \in N_R$ a subset $R^{\mathcal{I}}$ of $\Delta^{\mathcal{I}} \times \Delta^{\mathcal{I}}$. We specify the semantics of $\mathcal{ALCOI}$-concepts by extending the interpretation function to the following:

$$\top^{\mathcal{I}} = \Delta^{\mathcal{I}} \qquad (\neg C)^{\mathcal{I}} = \Delta^{\mathcal{I}} \backslash C^{\mathcal{I}} \qquad (C \sqcup D)^{\mathcal{I}} = C^{\mathcal{I}} \cup D^{\mathcal{I}}$$
$$(\forall R.C)^{\mathcal{I}} = \{x \in \Delta^{\mathcal{I}} \mid \forall y.(x, y) \in R^{\mathcal{I}} \rightarrow y \in C^{\mathcal{I}}\}$$
$$(\exists R.C)^{\mathcal{I}} = \{x \in \Delta^{\mathcal{I}} \mid \exists y.(x, y) \in R^{\mathcal{I}} \wedge y \in C^{\mathcal{I}}\}$$
$$(R^-)^{\mathcal{I}} = \{(y, x) \in \Delta^{\mathcal{I}} \times \Delta^{\mathcal{I}} \mid (x, y) \in R^{\mathcal{I}}\}$$

The semantics of the TBox-axioms is defined as follows: an interpretation $\mathcal{I}$ *satisfies* $C \sqsubseteq D$ iff $C^{\mathcal{I}} \subseteq D^{\mathcal{I}}$, and $\mathcal{I}$ *satisfies* $C \equiv D$ iff $C^{\mathcal{I}} \equiv D^{\mathcal{I}}$. If $\mathcal{O}$ is a set of TBox axioms, $\mathcal{I}$ is a *model* of $\mathcal{O}$ iff it satisfies every axiom in $\mathcal{O}$, denoted by $\mathcal{I} \models \mathcal{O}$.

In the rest of the paper, we also need the following notions. A *clause* is a disjunction of $\mathcal{ALCOI}$-concepts. Clauses in our calculus are interpreted as globally true, i.e., an interpretation $\mathcal{I}$ satisfies a clause C iff $C^{\mathcal{I}} = \Delta^{\mathcal{I}}$.

By definition $\sim C = D$, if $C = \neg D$, else $\sim C = \neg D$. The $\sim$ operator helps avoid sequences of negations.

By R^{σ}, we denote the composition of a sequence of roles and by $R^{\sigma,-}$ we denote the composition of the sequence of inverses of the roles in R^{σ} with the order in the sequence reversed.

Let A be a concept symbol and let $\mathcal{I}$ and $\mathcal{I}'$ be interpretations. We say $\mathcal{I}$ and $\mathcal{I}'$ are *equivalent up to A*, or *A-equivalent*, if $\mathcal{I}$ and $\mathcal{I}'$ coincide but differ possibly in the valuation assigned to A. This means their domains coincide, i.e., $\Delta^{\mathcal{I}} = \Delta^{\mathcal{I}'}$, and for each symbol s in the signature, except for A, $s^{\mathcal{I}} = s^{\mathcal{I}'}$. More generally, suppose $\Sigma = \{A_1, \ldots, A_m\} \subseteq N_C$, $\mathcal{I}$ and $\mathcal{I}'$ are *equivalent up to Σ*, or *Σ-equivalent*, if $\mathcal{I}$ and $\mathcal{I}'$ are the same but differ possibly in the valuations assigned to the concept symbols in Σ.

3 Forgetting as Second-Order Quantifier Elimination

We are interested in forgetting concept symbols in axioms of an ontology $\mathcal{O}$ of TBox axioms. Let $\mathrm{sig}(\mathcal{O})$ denote the signature of $\mathcal{O}$.

Definition 1. *Let $\mathcal{O}$ and $\mathcal{O}'$ be $\mathcal{ALCOI}$-ontologies and let $\Sigma = \{A_1, \ldots, A_m\}$ be a set of concept symbols. $\mathcal{O}'$ is the* result of forgetting the symbols in Σ from $\mathcal{O}$, *if (i) $\mathrm{sig}(\mathcal{O}') \subseteq \mathrm{sig}(\mathcal{O}) \backslash \Sigma$ and (ii) for any interpretation $\mathcal{I}$,*

$$\mathcal{I} \models \mathcal{O} \quad \text{iff} \quad \mathcal{I}' \models \mathcal{O}' \quad \text{for some interpretation } \mathcal{I}' \ \Sigma\text{-equivalent to } \mathcal{I}.$$

The symbols in Σ are the symbols to be forgotten. We refer to them as the non-base symbols *and the symbols in $\mathrm{sig}(\mathcal{O}) \backslash \Sigma$ as the* base symbols. *The result of forgetting a concept symbol A from $\mathcal{O}$ is the result of forgetting $\{A\}$ from $\mathcal{O}$.*

Intuitively, the definition says that the forgetting result $\mathcal{O}'$ is equivalent to the given ontology up to the symbols in Σ, for which the truth assignments can be arbitrary. The result of forgetting a symbol A from an ontology $\mathcal{O}$ can be represented as $\exists X \, \mathcal{O}_X^A$ in the extension of the language with existentially quantified concept variables. $\mathcal{O}_X^A$ is our notation for substituting every occurrence of A is $\mathcal{O}$ by X. In general, in the target language which extends the (source) language of the logic under consideration with existential quantification of predicate symbols, the result of forgetting always exists. The challenge of forgetting, as a computational problem, is to find an ontology $\mathcal{O}'$ in the source language (without second-order quantification) that is equivalent to $\exists X \, \mathcal{O}_X^A$ (where $\mathcal{O}$ is expressed in the source language). Finding such an ontology $\mathcal{O}'$ that is equivalent to $\exists X \, \mathcal{O}_X^A$ is an instance of the *second-order quantifier elimination problem*. Forgetting a concept symbol A is thus the problem of eliminating the existential quantifier $\exists X$ from $\exists X \, \mathcal{O}_X^A$. In the following, we slightly informally say the aim is to eliminate the symbol A from $\mathcal{O}$. For this we apply second-order quantifier

---

1. Transform ontology $\mathcal{O}$ to clausal representation, $N := \mathrm{clause}(\mathcal{O})$.
2. Process every concept symbol A in Σ and check the frequency of the different polarities of A to generate the ordering $\succ$.
3. Guided by $\succ$, apply the DsQEL to produce the ontology $\mathcal{O}'$ (with clauses interpreted in the obvious way as inclusions).
4. Apply simplification rules to $\mathcal{O}'$, if needed, and return the resultant ontology. If it contains only the symbols in $\mathrm{sig}(\mathcal{O}')\backslash\Sigma$ the method was successful.

Fig. 1. The phases in the basic DsQEL routine

elimination techniques [8] to the axioms of $\mathcal{O}$ in order to forget A (the non-base symbol). In particular, we are going to exploit an adaptation of a result of Ackermann [1], which is known as *Ackermann's Lemma* in the literature.

Theorem 1 (Ackermann's Lemma for $\mathcal{ALCOI}$). *Let $\mathcal{O}$ be an $\mathcal{ALCOI}$-ontology, let C be a concept expression and suppose the concept symbol A does not occur in C. Let $\mathcal{I}$ be an arbitrary $\mathcal{ALCOI}$-interpretation. (i) If A occurs only positively in $\mathcal{O}$, then $\mathcal{I} \models \mathcal{O}_C^A$ iff for some interpretation $\mathcal{I}'$ A-equivalent to $\mathcal{I}$, $\mathcal{I}' \models A \sqsubseteq C$, $\mathcal{O}$. (ii) If A occurs only negatively in $\mathcal{O}$ then $\mathcal{I} \models \mathcal{O}_C^A$ iff for some interpretation $\mathcal{I}'$ A-equivalent to $\mathcal{I}$, $\mathcal{I}' \models C \sqsubseteq A$, $\mathcal{O}$.*

4   The DSQEL Forgetting Method

Our forgetting method is called DsQEL, which is short for Description logics Second-order Quantifier ELimination.

Figure 1 outlines the basic routine of the DsQEL method to forget concept symbols in $\mathcal{ALCOI}$-ontologies. Once receiving the input ontology $\mathcal{O}$ and a set Σ of concept symbols to forget, the method proceeds as follows. In *Phase 1*, a preprocessing step is performed to transform the axioms into a set N of clauses. This is done by replacing all inclusions $C \sqsubseteq D$ by $\neg C \sqcup D$, and all equivalences $C \equiv D$ by $\neg C \sqcup D$ and $\neg D \sqcup C$. Inexpensive equivalence-preserving syntactic simplification rules are also applied in this phase to simplify clauses. For example, $C \sqcup (C \sqcap D)$ is simplified to C. *Phase 2* counts the number of positive and negative occurrences of each concept symbol in Σ. Using these counts a *forgetting order* $\succ$ is defined on the symbols in Σ. This ordering determines the order in which the symbols in Σ are eliminated in the next phase. *Phase 3* applies the DsQEL calculus described in the next section to the non-base symbols in Σ one by one, starting with the symbol A largest in the forgetting order $\succ$. To forget A the inference rules of the DsQEL calculus are applied to the axioms containing A. Then the next largest non-base symbol is eliminated, and so on.

Forgetting a concept symbol may lead to a change of the polarities of the occurrences of the remaining Σ-symbols, and a new elimination order may have to be computed based on the refreshed polarity counts, before the forgetting method continues. This means Phase 2 and Phase 3 will be executed alternately and repeatedly with recomputed forgetting orders. If the largest current concept symbol to be eliminated could not be completely eliminated by DSQEL, then a different ordering not attempted before will be used. In the case that all possible orderings have been tried and every attempt to eliminate all non-base symbols using DSQEL is not successful, the method returns failure, because it was unable to solve the problem. On the other hand, when after a call of DSQEL the set returned does not contain any non-base symbols, then this is the result of forgetting Σ from $\mathcal{O}$.

Phase 4 subsequently applies further simplification rules and transforms the resulting axioms to simpler representations.

Different forgetting orders of concept symbols applied may lead to different but equivalent results. The intermediary results as well as the final result can be viewed (when the remaining non-base symbols are existentially quantified) as equivalent representations of $\exists \Sigma \mathcal{O}$.

What is returned by the algorithm, if it terminates successfully, is a (possibly empty) ontology with all occurrences of the non-base symbols eliminated, i.e., the ontology returned is specified in terms of only the symbols in $\mathrm{sig}(\mathcal{O}) \backslash \Sigma$.

There are situations where our method does not succeed, for instance, when no forgetting result finitely expressible in $\mathcal{ALCOI}$ exists. This means the method is not complete, but since no complete method can exist for forgetting, as considered in this paper with the target language being $\mathcal{ALCOI}$, this is to be expected. Concept forgetting is already not always computable for the description logic $\mathcal{EL}$ [10]. We also note that when concept symbols cannot be eliminated by our method this does not necessarily mean that they are ineliminable. It might be the case that they are eliminable, but simply our method is unable to find a solution.

We can show DSQEL algorithm is correct and is guaranteed to terminate. This follows as an adaptation of the correctness and termination results for the MSQEL procedure proved in [26], since the calculus given in the next section is correct and terminates, and all adaptations of MSQEL to DSQEL preserve logical equivalence.

5   The DSQEL Forgetting Calculus

The order in which the non-base symbols are eliminated is determined by the forgetting order $\succ$ computed in Phase 2 of the DSQEL algorithm. (Formally, $\succ$ may be any irreflexive, transitive relation on the non-base symbols to be eliminated; no additional conditions need to be imposed.) We say a concept symbol A is *strictly maximal* with respect to a concept C if for any concept symbol B ($\neq A$) in C, $A \succ B$.

A concept C is *positive* (*negative*) wrt. a concept symbol A iff all occurrences of A in C are *positive* (*negative*). A set N of concepts is *positive* (*negative*) with respect to a concept symbol A iff all occurrences of A in N are *positive* (*negative*).

The Ackermann rule and the Purify rule, given in Figure 2, are the *forgetting rules* in the DSQEL calculus, which will lead to the elimination of a non-base

Ackermann:

$$\frac{N, C_1 \sqcup A, \ldots, C_n \sqcup A}{(N^A_{\sim C_1 \sqcup \ldots \sqcup \sim C_n})^{\neg\neg C_1, \ldots, \neg\neg C_n}_{C_1, \ldots, C_n}}$$

provided:
    (i) A is a non-base symbol,
    (ii) A does not occur in any of the C_i,
    (iii) A is strictly maximal wrt. each C_i, and
    (iv) N is negative wrt. A.

Purify:

$$\frac{N}{(N^A_{\neg\top})^{\neg\neg\top}_{\top}}$$

provided:
    (i) A is a non-base symbol in N, and
    (ii) N is negative wrt. A.

Fig. 2. The forgetting rules

concept symbol. Both of them have to meet particular requirements on the form of the concepts to which they apply. N is a set of $\mathcal{ALCOI}$-clauses, and by N^D_C, we mean the set obtained from N by substituting the expression C for all occurrences of D in N, where C and D are both $\mathcal{ALCOI}$-concepts. Like all other inference rules in the DSQEL calculus, the Ackermann rule is restricted by a set of side-conditions. The side-conditions of the Ackermann rule require that A must be a non-base symbol and does not occur in $C_1, \ldots, C_n$, no non-base symbol occurring in C_i ($1 \leq i \leq n$) is larger than A under the ordering $\succ$, and every occurrence of A in N must be negative. The Purify rule can be seen as a special case of the Ackermann rule, since it eliminates the non-base symbols that occur only negatively, that is, when there are no positive occurrences of A.

The rules in Figures 3 and 4 are used to rewrite the clauses so they can be transformed into a form where either the Ackermann rule or the Purify rule is applicable. To apply the Ackermann or Purify rule, the clauses need to be in A-reduced form, where A is the largest non-base symbol. We say a clause is in *A-reduced form* if it is either negative in A or it has the form $A \sqcup C$, where C does not include any occurrences of A. A set of clauses is in *A-reduced form* if every clause is in A reduced form.

A set of clauses is transformed into A-reduced form, by repeatedly applying the Surfacing rule, the Skolemization rule, the Clausify rule and the Case Splitting rule to clauses containing positive occurrences of A that are not already in A-reduced form.

The Surfacing rule equivalently transforms a clause where the largest non-base symbol occurs positively below a universal restriction operator so that these occurrences pass up to levels closer to the top level of the clause. The Skolemization rule rewrites the existential expression in a clause of the form $\neg a \sqcup \neg \forall R^\sigma . C$, where a is a nominal. The implicit existential quantifier in $\neg \forall R^\sigma . C$ is Skolemized by introducing a new Skolem constant (nominal) b. The Clausify rule transforms a concept of the form $C \sqcup \neg (D_1 \sqcup \ldots \sqcup D_n)$ into a set of clauses. The Sign Switch-

Surfacing:
$$\frac{N, C \sqcup \forall R^\sigma.D}{N, (\forall R^{\sigma,-}.C) \sqcup D}$$

provided: (i) A is the largest non-base symbol in $C \sqcup \forall R^\sigma.D$,
(ii) A does not occur in C, and
(iii) A occurs positively in $\forall R^\sigma.D$.

Skolemization:
$$\frac{N, \neg a \sqcup \neg \forall R^\sigma.C}{N, \neg a \sqcup \neg \forall R^\sigma.\neg b, \neg b \sqcup {\sim}C}$$

provided: (i) A is the largest non-base symbol in $\neg a \sqcup \neg \forall R^\sigma.C$,
(ii) A occurs positively in $\neg \forall R^\sigma.C$, and
(iii) b is a new nominal.

Clausify:
$$\frac{N, C \sqcup \neg(D_1 \sqcup \ldots \sqcup D_n)}{N, C \sqcup {\sim}D_1, \ldots, C \sqcup {\sim}D_n}$$

provided: (i) A is the largest non-base symbol in $C \sqcup \neg(D_1 \sqcup \ldots \sqcup D_n)$, and
(ii) A occurs positively in $D_1 \sqcup \ldots \sqcup D_n$.

Sign Switching:
$$\frac{N}{(N^A_{\neg A})^{\neg\neg A}_A}$$

provided: (i) N is closed wrt. the other rules,
(ii) A is the largest non-base symbol in N, and
(iii) Sign switching wrt. A has not been performed before.

Fig. 3. The rewriting rules

ing rule is used to switch the polarity of a non-base symbol. It is applicable only when no other rules in the calculus are applicable wrt. this non-base symbol and the Sign Switching rule has not been performed for this non-base symbol before.

A novel aspect of the DSQEL calculus is the *Case Splitting* rule given in Figure 4. It splits a clause of the form $\neg a \sqcup C_1 \sqcup \ldots \sqcup C_n$ into smaller subclauses $\neg a \sqcup C_1, \ldots, \neg a \sqcup C_n$. A single clause $\neg a \sqcup C_i$, together with N, forms a *case*. The original clause means that a belongs to at least one of the disjuncts C_i ($1 \leq i \leq n$). The benefits of the Case Splitting rule are twofold. On the one hand, it makes up for a limitation of the Skolemization rule, because it splits a disjunction with more than two disjuncts into several smaller cases, which the Skolemization rule is then able to handle. On the other hand, our tests show that it reduces the search space and increases the success rate, because the transformation to A-reduced form is easier in the cases, in which the clauses are smaller.

As the purpose of the rewriting rules is finding A-reduced forms and letting the two forgetting rules become applicable, it is not difficult to see that the rewriting rules, excluding the Sign Switching rule, should be performed before the forgetting rules. The Sign Switching rule is the exception because, as men-

Case Splitting:	$$\frac{N, \neg a \sqcup C_1 \sqcup \ldots \sqcup C_n}{N, \neg a \sqcup C_1 \mid \ldots \mid N, \neg a \sqcup C_n}$$

provided: (i) A is the largest non-base symbol in $\neg a \sqcup C_1 \sqcup \ldots \sqcup C_n$, and
(ii) A occurs positively in $C_1 \sqcup \ldots \sqcup C_n$.

Fig. 4. The Case Splitting rule

Condensing I:	$$\frac{N\left[C \sqcup \forall R^{\sigma_1}.\forall R^{\sigma_1,-}.\ldots.\forall R^{\sigma_n}.\forall R^{\sigma_n,-}.(C \sqcup D)\right]}{N\left[C \sqcup D \sqcup \forall R^{\sigma_1}.\bot\right]}$$

provided: (i) C and D are arbitrary concepts, and
(ii) $\sigma_i \leq \sigma_1$ for $1 \leq i \leq n$.

$$\frac{N\left[C \sqcup \forall R^{\sigma_1}.\forall R^{\sigma_1,-}.\ldots.\forall R^{\sigma_n}.\forall R^{\sigma_n,-}.(C \sqcup D)\right]}{N\left[C \sqcup D \sqcup \forall R^{\sigma_n}.\bot\right]}$$

provided: (i) C and D are arbitrary concepts, and
(ii) $\sigma_i \leq \sigma_n$ for $1 \leq i \leq n$.

Fig. 5. Sample simplification rule

tioned earlier in this section, it is performed only when no other inference rules are applicable. Reruns of the rewriting rules, except for Sign Switching, are required since once a rule is applied, another rule that was previously unable to be applied may become applicable now. The rerun will continue until the clauses are not changed by any of the Clausify rule, the Surfacing rule, or the Skolemization rule. If either of the two forgetting rules becomes applicable, they are immediately applied.

We also introduced several simplification rules to transform more expressions so that inference rules become applicable, and in order to keep expressions in simpler forms for efficiency. Most importantly, they lead to success of forgetting in more cases. Figure 5 displays two cases of the simplification rules, called Condensing I, with which clauses of a particular pattern can be simplified, which other forgetting and second-order quantifier elimination methods cannot handle. The rules have the form $N[C]/N[D]$ and have the effect of replacing an occurrence of a subexpression C in some clause in N by the expression D.

6   Calculating the Forgetting Order

In a forgetting problem, the forgetting order is the order in which the non-base symbols are forgotten. Given n non-base symbols, in the worst case there are $n!$ possible orderings for the forgetting procedure to follow. Selecting a good forgetting order is important for the efficiency of the forgetting method and the success rate (when a timeout is used). This is best illustrated with an example.

We first show that the forgetting order matters. Consider the following ontology in clause form and suppose the forgetting order is $A \succ B$.

$$\star 1. \ (\forall R^-.\neg a) \sqcup (\neg \forall R.A) \sqcup B$$
$$2. \ (\forall R^-.\forall R^-.\neg a) \sqcup (\forall R.A) \sqcup \neg B$$
$$3. \ (\forall R^-.\neg a) \sqcup \neg \forall R.\forall R.\neg A$$

Since A is the largest non-base symbol the initial aim is to bring the clauses into A-reduced form and then eliminate A with one of the forgetting rules. The starred clause (Clause 1) is negative wrt. the current non-base symbol A; all others contain positive occurrences of A. At this point, no rules in the DSQEL calculus (excluding the Sign Switching rule) can be applied to transform Clause 3 to reduced form wrt. A. The Sign Switching rule is unable to change the situation either in this case. However, changing the forgetting order to $B \succ A$ opens a survival window for the problem.

Assume now the forgetting order is $B \succ A$,

$$1. \ (\forall R^-.\neg a) \sqcup (\neg \forall R.A) \sqcup B$$
$$\star 2. \ (\forall R^-.\forall R^-.\neg a) \sqcup (\forall R.A) \sqcup \neg B$$
$$3. \ (\forall R^-.\neg a) \sqcup \neg \forall R.\forall R.\neg A$$

The aim is to eliminate B first. Clause 2 is negative wrt. B and Clause 1 has a positive occurrence of B. Applying the Ackermann rule to Clauses 1 and 2 leads to Clause 4, which proves to be a tautology and thus can be deleted.

$$4. \ (\forall R^-.\forall R^-.\neg a) \sqcup \underline{(\forall R.A)} \sqcup (\forall R^-.\neg a) \sqcup \underline{(\neg \forall R.A)} \quad \text{1 into 2, Acker.}$$
$$5. \ (\forall R^-.\neg a) \sqcup \neg \forall R.\forall R.\bot \qquad\qquad\qquad\qquad \text{3, Sign Sw. \& Purify}$$

What remains is Clause 3, from which A can be forgotten by applying the Sign Switching and Purify rules, which produces Clause 5. The method terminates successfully, returning $\neg a \sqcup \forall R.\neg \forall R.\forall R.\bot$ after simplifying Clause 5.

A good forgetting order allows non-base symbols to be forgotten as quickly as possible, however it does not generally guarantee success of the procedure. In this case, another ordering will be used, and the success of forgetting will be pursued until all possible orderings have been attempted.

Our implementation of the DSQEL calculus involves a heuristic method to calculate forgetting orders with increased chances of quick and successful elimination of the non-base symbols. The method exploits polarity counts of the non-base symbols. Given n non-base symbols, we first count the number of positive and negative occurrences of each symbol and represent the results as pairs. We then choose the smaller value of each pair as their *actual counts*. These actual counts are sorted into ascending order, which is then taken as the forgetting order to be used. If the actual counts of some of the non-base symbols

Table 1. Results of polarity counting for each non-base symbol

Non-Base Symbol	A_1	A_2	A_3	A_4	A_5	A_6
No. of Positive Occurrences	6	3	**2**	**0**	**2**	1
No. of Negative Occurrences	**1**	**2**	3	8	4	1

are identical, we compare the counts for their opposite polarity. If these are the same, the positive counts have higher priority than the negative ones. Generally, symbols with lower counts are selected to be forgotten before symbols with higher counts. Note that if we fail to forget a symbol in an ordering, we simply go to the next symbol. Once a symbol has been forgotten, the forgetting order will be recomputed since the forgetting of a non-base symbol might affect the occurrences of the remaining non-base symbols. The reason why counting is not conducted wrt. a particular polarity (either positive or negative) of the non-base symbols, is the Sign Switching rule, with which we can change the polarity of the occurrences of a particular non-base symbol.

We use an example to illustrate the operation of this heuristic method. Suppose the frequency analysis of the polarity counting reveals the pairs as listed in Table 1. The numbers in bold indicate the smaller values of each pair, i.e., the actual counts. Thus the forgetting order $\succ$ calculated is $A_4 \succ A_6 \succ A_1 \succ A_3 \succ A_2 \succ A_5$.

In the previous example the frequency analysis computes the order $B \succ A$, which immediately leads to success, without requiring another round.

7   Empirical Results

We implemented our forgetting method in Java using the OWL API, fully realising every aspect of the inference rules and the simplification rules in DsQEL. An important part of the implementation is the calculation of the forgetting order of the non-base symbols based on a frequency analysis as described in the previous section. In order to evaluate how the DsQEL method behaves on real-life ontologies, we tested the system on a set of ontologies from the NCBO BioPortal,[1] a large repository of biomedical ontologies. The experiments were run on a machine with an Intel® Core™ i7-4790 processor, and four cores running at up to 3.60 GHz and 8 GB of DDR3-1600 MHz RAM.

Since DsQEL handles expressivity as far as $\mathcal{ALCOI}$, the ontologies for our evaluation were restricted to their $\mathcal{ALCOI}$-fragments, and axioms outside of the scope of $\mathcal{ALCOI}$ were dropped from the ontologies. Consequently, we used 292 ontologies from the repository for our evaluation. We ran the experiments on each ontology 100 times and averaged the results to explore how forgetting was influenced by the number of the concept symbols in an ontology. A timeout of 1000 seconds was used.

To fit with possible needs in applications, we conducted experiments where 10%, 30%, and 50% of the concept symbols in the ontologies were forgotten.

---

[1] http://bioportal.bioontology.org/

Table 2. Forgetting 10%, 30%, and 50% of the concept symbols in ontologies

Input		Experiment		Results		
Axioms Avg.	Symbols Avg.	%	Analysis	Timeouts	Duration Avg.	Success Rate
1407	876	10%	✗	3.8%	4.509 sec.	90.1%
			✓	1.7%	2.404 sec.	97.6%
		30%	✗	7.5%	8.562 sec.	88.4%
			✓	2.2%	2.753 sec.	95.5%
		50%	✗	13.4%	15.068 sec.	85.3%
			✓	3.1%	3.004 sec.	94.9%
1407	876	Average	✗	8.2%	9.380 sec.	87.9%
			✓	2.3%	2.720 sec.	96.0%

The DSQEL algorithm processed each non-base symbol and counted the number of their positive and negative occurrences. Based on these counts, a forgetting order was generated by the heuristic algorithm. In order to see how the forgetting order affected the performance of the method, we ran two sets of experiments, where we omitted the frequency analysis for determining the forgetting order for one set, and applied the analysis to the other set. Without the frequency analysis, the symbols were forgotten in the order as returned by an OWL API function that gets all concept symbols in the ontology.

The evaluation results obtained from 10%, 30%, 50% of the concept symbols in the ontologies, without and with the frequency analysis for determining the forgetting order, are shown in Table 2. It can be seen that, the frequency analysis led to a decrease in the average duration of the runs of every experiment, which means that it took less time to complete the same task than when the frequency analysis was not performed. It is evident from the last two rows in the table that basing the forgetting order to the frequency analysis has brought a positive effect on the overall success rate (increase by 8.1%) and the number of timeouts (decrease by 5.9%).

To show the difficulty of the forgetting problem, and how well our method behaves, we considered the extreme scenario of forgetting all concept symbols from each ontology. In this case, the selected ontologies (which were the same as used in the previous experiment) were divided first into three groups and each of them contained the ontologies with the numbers of concept symbols ranging from 1 to 1000, from 1001 to 4000, and more than 4000, respectively, in order to explore how forgetting was influenced by the number of the concept symbols that the ontologies contained. The other specifications remained the same, unless otherwise stated.

The results of the evaluation with and without the frequency analysis are shown in Tables 3 and 4, respectively. As with the results of the previous evaluation, the analysis of the forgetting order made a significant difference to the overall success rate (increase by 13.7%) and the number of timeouts (decrease by 14%). What can also be observed is that for smaller ontologies with fewer concept symbols, there were fewer timeouts and the success rate of the method was higher.

Table 3. Forgetting all concept symbols with frequency analysis

Input			Results		
Corpora	Axioms Avg.	Concept Symbols	Timeouts	Duration Avg.	Success Rate
1 – 1000	652	258	1.3%	0.869 sec.	96.4%
1001 – 4000	3091	2021	3.8%	9.148 sec.	92.5%
≥ 4001	6506	6048	13.3%	29.898 sec.	86.7%
Total	1407	876	2.4%	4.352 sec.	95.2%

Table 4. Forgetting all concept symbols without frequency analysis

Input			Results		
Corpora	Axioms Avg.	Concept Symbols	Timeouts	Duration Avg.	Success Rate
1 – 1000	652	258	9.8%	4.589 sec.	87.9%
1001 – 4000	3091	2021	28.3%	51.400 sec.	67.9%
≥ 4001	6506	6048	60.0%	224.133 sec.	40.0%
Total	1407	876	16.4%	24.363 sec.	81.5%

Evaluations of more aspects are being conducted at the moment. These evaluations are focussed on measuring the difference that case splitting and simplification make to the behaviour of the DSQEL calculus, and how our method compares to the related methods of SCAN [7], DLS [5], DLS* [6], SQEMA [3], MSQEL [26], and LETHE [16] in terms of success rate and efficiency (duration and number of timeouts).

8   Related Work

Probably the most important early work on the elimination of second-order quantifiers is that of Ackermann [1] in the nineteen-thirties and forties. Only in 1992, the first practical algorithm, called SCAN, was developed by Gabbay and Ohlbach [7]. SCAN is a resolution-based second-order quantifier elimination algorithm and can be used to forget predicate symbols from first-order logic formulae [24]. It has been shown that the SCAN algorithm is complete and terminates for modal axioms belonging to the famous Sahlqvist class [9]. In 1994, the hierarchical theorem proving method was developed by Bachmair et al. [2] and it has been shown that it can be used to solve second-order quantification problems. Around the same time, in 1995, Szałas [27] described a different algorithm for the second-order quantifier elimination problem, which exploits Ackermann's Lemma. The method was further extended to the DLS algorithm by Doherty et al. [5]. DLS uses a generalised version of Ackermann's Lemma and allows the elimination of existential second-order quantifiers from second-order formulae, for obtaining corresponding first-order equivalents. Nonnengart and Szałas [23] generalised the main result underlying the DLS algorithm to include fixpoints. Based on this work, Doherty et al. [6] proposed the DLS* algorithm, which attempts the derivation of either an equivalent first-order formula or a fixpoint formula from the original formula. DLS and DLS* are Ackermann-based second-order quantifier elimination methods. Ackermann-based second-order quantifier elimination was first applied to description logics in [28] by Szałas, where description logics were extended by a form of second-order quantification over concepts. More recently, Conradie et al. [3] introduced the SQEMA algorithm, which is also an Ackermann-based method but for modal logic formulae. It is specialised to find correspondences between modal formulae and hybrid modal logic formulae (and first-order formulae). Schmidt [26] has extended SQEMA and developed MSQEL as a refinement, with the use of elimination orders, and the presentation of second-order quantifier elimination as an abstract calculus, as key novelties.

Investigation of forgetting as uniform interpolation in more expressive description logics was started in [29] and [21]. The first approach to compute uniform interpolations for $\mathcal{ALC}$-TBoxes was presented in [29]. It is a tableau-based approach, where a disjunctive normal form is required for the representation of the TBox-axioms and the uniform interpolants are incrementally approximated. It was shown in [21] that deciding the existence of uniform interpolants that can be finitely represented in $\mathcal{ALC}$ without fixpoints is 2EXPTIME-complete and in the worst case, the size of uniform interpolants is triple exponential wrt. the size of the original TBox. The first goal-oriented method based on resolution was presented in [19] for computing uniform interpolants of $\mathcal{ALC}$-TBoxes, where experimental results show the practicality for real-life ontologies. Koopmann and Schmidt presented another resolution-based method exploiting structural transformation to compute uniform interpolants of $\mathcal{ALC}$-TBoxes, which uses fixpoint operators to make uniform interpolants finitely representable [14]. The method has been further extended to handle $\mathcal{ALCH}$ [12], $\mathcal{SIF}$ [17], $\mathcal{SHQ}$ [15], and $\mathcal{ALC}$ with ABoxes [18].

9   Conclusion and Future Work

We have presented a second-order quantifier elimination method, called DSQEL, for forgetting concept symbols in ontologies specified in the description logic $\mathcal{ALCOI}$. It is adapted from MSQEL, an Ackermann-based second-order quantifier elimination method for a multi-modal tense logic with second-order quantification. The method is enhanced with new inference and simplification rules. The adaptation was motivated for the purpose of applying second-order quantifier elimination techniques to the area of knowledge representation, where description logics provide important logical formalisms.

We have implemented a prototype system of our forgetting method, fully realising the DSQEL calculus. The evaluation results have confirmed that the success of a forgetting problem is highly dependent on, apart from the calculus itself, the non-base symbols Σ to be forgotten, and the forgetting order which the method follows. Overall, the results showed promising and very good success rates for concept symbol forgetting for our method.

Optimisations to both the calculus and the implementation are underway. One optimisation being investigated is the incorporation of more simplification rules in order to increase the efficiency and success rate further. We are also currently working on finding better heuristics for computing better forgetting orders of the non-base symbols.

Extending the method to handle ontologies going expressively further than $\mathcal{ALCOI}$ is a direction of ongoing research. To explore how forgetting of role symbols can be incorporated into our method is also of interest.

References

1. Ackermann, W.: Untersuchungen über das Eliminationsproblem der mathematischen Logik. Mathematische Annalen **110**(1), 390–413 (1935)
2. Bachmair, L., Ganzinger, H., Waldmann, U.: Refutational theorem proving for hierarchic first-order theories. Applicable Algebra in Engineering, Communication and Computing **5**(3–4), 193–212 (1994)
3. Conradie, W., Goranko, V., Vakarelov, D.: Algorithmic correspondence and completeness in modal logic. I. The core algorithm SQEMA. Logical Methods in Computer Science **2**(1) (2006)
4. Grau, B.C., Motik, B.: Reasoning over ontologies with hidden content: The importby-query approach. Journal of Artificial Intelligence Research **45**, 197–255 (2012)
5. Doherty, P., Łukaszewicz, W., Szałas, A.: Computing circumscription revisited: A reduction algorithm. Journal of Automated Reasoning **18**(3), 297–336 (1997)
6. Doherty, P., Łukaszewicz, W., Szałas, A.: General domain circumscription and its effective reductions. Fundamenta Informaticae **36**(1), 23–55 (1998)
7. Gabbay, D.M., Ohlbach, H.J.: Quantifier elimination in second-order predicate logic. In: Principles of Knowledge Representation and Reasoning (KR92), pp. 425–435. Morgan Kaufmann (1992)
8. Gabbay, D.M., Schmidt, R.A., Szałas, A.: Second Order Quantifier Elimination: Foundations, Computational Aspects and Applications. College Publications (2008)
9. Goranko, V., Hustadt, U., Schmidt, R.A., Vakarelov, D.: SCAN is complete for all Sahlqvist formulae. In: Berghammer, R., Möller, B., Struth, G. (eds.) RelMiCS 2003. LNCS, vol. 3051, pp. 149–162. Springer, Heidelberg (2004)
10. Konev, B., Lutz, C., Walther, D., Wolter, F.: Model-theoretic inseparability and modularity of description logic ontologies. Artificial Intelligence **203**, 66–103 (2013)
11. Konev, B., Walther, D., Wolter, F.: Forgetting and uniform interpolation in extensions of the description logic $\mathcal{EL}$. In: Proceedings of the 22nd International Workshop on Description Logics (DL 2009). CEUR Workshop Proceedings, vol. 477. CEUR-WS.org (2009)
12. Koopmann, P., Schmidt, R.A.: Forgetting concept and role symbols in $\mathcal{ALCH}$-ontologies. In: McMillan, K., Middeldorp, A., Voronkov, A. (eds.) LPAR 2013. LNCS, vol. 8312, pp. 552–567. Springer, Heidelberg (2013)
13. Koopmann, P., Schmidt, R.A.: Implementation and evaluation of forgetting in ALC-ontologies. In: Proceedings of the 7th International Workshop on Modular Ontologies (WoMo 2013). CEUR Workshop Proceedings, vol. 1081, pp. 1–12. CEUR-WS.org (2013)
14. Koopmann, P., Schmidt, R.A.: Uniform interpolation of $\mathcal{ALC}$-ontologies using fixpoints. In: Fontaine, P., Ringeissen, C., Schmidt, R.A. (eds.) FroCoS 2013. LNCS, vol. 8152, pp. 87–102. Springer, Heidelberg (2013)

15. Koopmann, P., Schmidt, R.A.: Count and forget: uniform interpolation of $\mathcal{SHQ}$-ontologies. In: Demri, S., Kapur, D., Weidenbach, C. (eds.) IJCAR 2014. LNCS, vol. 8562, pp. 434–448. Springer, Heidelberg (2014)

16. Koopmann, P., Schmidt, R.A.: LETHE: A saturation-based tool for non-classical reasoning (2015). Manuscript, submitted

17. Koopmann, P., Schmidt, R.A.: Saturated-based forgetting in the description logic SIF. In: Proceedings of the 28th International Workshop on Description Logics (DL 2015). CEUR Workshop Proceedings, vol. 1350. CEUR-WS.org (2015)

18. Koopmann, P., Schmidt, R.A.: Uniform interpolation and forgetting for $\mathcal{ALC}$-ontologies with ABoxes. In: Proceedings of the Twenty-Ninth AAAI Conference on Artificial Intelligence, pp. 175–181. AAAI Press (2015)

19. Ludwig, M., Konev, B.: Towards practical uniform interpolation and forgetting for $\mathcal{ALC}$ TBoxes. In: Proceedings of the 26th International Workshop on Description Logics (DL 2013). CEUR Workshop Proceedings, vol. 1014, pp. 377–389. CEUR-WS.org (2013)

20. Lutz, C., Seylan, I., Wolter, F.: An automata-theoretic approach to uniform interpolation and approximation in the description logic $\mathcal{EL}$. In: Principles of Knowledge Representation and Reasoning: KR 2012, pp. 286–297. AAAI Press (2012)

21. Lutz, C., Wolter, F.: Foundations for uniform interpolation and forgetting in expressive description logics. In: Proceedings of IJCAI 2011, pp. 989–995. IJCAI/AAAI (2011)

22. Nikitina, N.: Forgetting in general $\mathcal{EL}$ terminologies. In: Proceedings of the 24th International Workshop on Description Logics (DL 2011). CEUR Workshop Proceedings, vol. 745. CEUR-WS.org (2011)

23. Nonnengart, A., Szałas, A.: A fixpoint approach to second-order quantifier elimination with applications to correspondence theory. In: Orlowska, E. (ed.) Logic at Work: Essays Dedicated to the Memory of Helena Rasiowa, pp. 307–328. Springer (1999)

24. Ohlbach, H.J.: SCAN–elimination of predicate quantifiers. In: McRobbie, M.A., Slaney, J.K. (eds.) CADE 1996. LNCS, vol. 1104, pp. 161–165. Springer, Heidelberg (1996)

25. Schild, K.: A correspondence theory for terminological logics: preliminary report. In: Proceedings of IJCAI 1991, pp. 466–471. Morgan Kaufmann (1991)

26. Schmidt, R.A.: The Ackermann approach for modal logic, correspondence theory and second-order reduction. Journal of Applied Logic **10**(1), 52–74 (2012)

27. Szałas, A.: On the correspondence between modal and classical logic: An automated approach. Journal of Logic and Computation **3**, 605–620 (1993)

28. Szałas, A.: Second-order reasoning in description logics. Journal of Applied Non-Classical Logics **16**(3–4), 517–530 (2006)

29. Wang, K., Wang, Z., Topor, R., Pan, J.Z., Antoniou, G.: Concept and role forgetting in $\mathcal{ALC}$ ontologies. In: Bernstein, A., Karger, D.R., Heath, T., Feigenbaum, L., Maynard, D., Motta, E., Thirunarayan, K. (eds.) ISWC 2009. LNCS, vol. 5823, pp. 666–681. Springer, Heidelberg (2009)

30. Wang, K., Wang, Z., Topor, R., Pan, J.Z., Antoniou, G.: Eliminating concepts and roles from ontologies in expressive description logics. Computational Intelligence **30**(2), 205–232 (2014)

31. Wang, Z., Wang, K., Topor, R., Pan, J.Z.: Forgetting concepts in DL-Lite. In: Bechhofer, S., Hauswirth, M., Hoffmann, J., Koubarakis, M. (eds.) ESWC 2008. LNCS, vol. 5021, pp. 245–257. Springer, Heidelberg (2008)

Knowledge Graphs and Scientific Data Publication

Content-Based Recommendations via DBpedia and Freebase: A Case Study in the Music Domain

Phuong T. Nguyen, Paolo Tomeo,
Tommaso Di Noia(✉), and Eugenio Di Sciascio

SisInf Lab, Polytechnic University of Bari, Via Orabona 4, 70125 Bari, Italy
{phuong.nguyen,paolo.tomeo,tommaso.dinoia,eugenio.disciascio}@poliba.it

Abstract. The Web of Data has been introduced as a novel scheme for imposing structured data on the Web. This renders data easily understandable by human beings and seamlessly processable by machines at the same time. The recent boom in Linked Data facilitates a new stream of data-intensive applications that leverage the knowledge available in semantic datasets such as DBpedia and Freebase. These latter are well known encyclopedic collections of data that can be used to feed a content-based recommender system. In this paper we investigate how the choice of one of the two datasets may influence the performance of a recommendation engine not only in terms of precision of the results but also in terms of their diversity and novelty. We tested four different recommendation approaches exploiting both DBpedia and Freebase in the music domain.

Keywords: Linked open data · Quality assessment · Semantic similarity · Content-based recommender systems

1 Introduction

The Linked Open Data cloud has been launched in an effort to transform structured data into first class citizens in the Web thus moving it towards the so called Web of Data. The data published as Linked Data (LD) by means of RDF covers a wide range of knowledge, including life science, environment, industry, entertainment, to name a few. The new data platform paves the way for several fresh applications but the proliferation of LD is overshadowed by the fact that the quality of the newly uploaded data is yet to be thoroughly verified [22] and that the selection of the dataset may heavily influence the performance of an LD-based tool. Among all possible data intensive applications, recommender systems are gaining momentum to potentially profiting from the knowledge encoded in LD datasets. As background data is of crucial importance to recommender systems, one should consider the suitability of a dataset when designing a recommender system since it may depend on the type of tasks as well as the recommendation algorithm. A reasonable combination of the underlying

© Springer International Publishing Switzerland 2015
M. Arenas et al. (Eds.): ISWC 2015, Part I, LNCS 9366, pp. 605–621, 2015.
DOI: 10.1007/978-3-319-25007-6_35

data and recommendation approach might contribute towards a great difference in performance. This motivates us to perform an investigation on the adequacy of a dataset when adopting a recommendation strategy. In this paper we evaluate the fitness for use of LD sources to feed a pure content-based recommender system [7] and in particular we examine the suitability of two encyclopedic data sources namely DBpedia[1] and Freebase[2] for musical artists recommendation tasks. As the input for the calculation we exploit similarity values computed by four different feature-based semantic similarity metrics. The values are used to find similarities between items and eventually to produce the final recommendation list. Our experimental evaluations are conducted by using the well-known dataset Last.fm for musical artists recommendation[3]. To study the fitness for use of the data sources to recommendation tasks, we conducted an offline evaluation and we analyzed three different dimensions: *Accuracy*, *Sales Diversity*, and *Novelty*. Various indicators are employed to analyze the recommendations pertaining to these characteristics.

The main contributions of the paper can be summarized as follows:

– evaluating the fitness for use of DBpedia and Freebase as input for content-based recommendation tasks in the music domain by means of various quality dimensions and quality indicators;
– providing an evaluation of the performance for four semantic similarity metrics, with regard to recommendation tasks, on the aforementioned encyclopedic datasets.

The remainder of the paper is organized as follows. In Section 2 we summarize the main characteristics of the semantic similarity metrics used in the evaluation while in Section 3 our evaluation methodology is presented. The experimental settings and their outcomes are elaborated in Section 4. Section 5 brings in an overview of related work on recommender systems adopting LD. Finally, Section 6 sketches out future work and concludes the paper.

2   Feature-Based Semantic Similarity Measurement

Information resources in the Web of Data are semantically represented using RDF graphs. To evaluate the similarity between two resources, characteristics like nodes, links, and the mutual relationships are incorporated into calculation. Among others, feature-based semantic similarity metrics quantify similarity between resources in an RDF graph as a measure of commonality and distinction of their hallmarks. The work by Tversky in [1] sheds light on feature-based similarity. It aims at overcoming the major disadvantages of the approaches that compute similarity by measuring distance between points in a space. The work suggests representing objects as a set of common and distinctive features and the similarity of two objects is performed by matching their corresponding collections

---

[1] http://dbpedia.org
[2] http://www.freebase.com/
[3] http://ir.ii.uam.es/hetrec2011/datasets.html

of features. The features of an object can be represented in one of the following forms: binary values, nominal values, ordinal values, and cardinal values. Measuring similarity using features is based on the premise that the more common features two objects hold, the more similar they are. Bearing on this principle, feature-based semantic similarity metrics first attempt to characterize resources in an RDF graph as feature sets and then perform similarity calculation on them. In the following sub-sections we briefly recall the feature-based metrics for computing similarity being exploited in our evaluation. The four metrics have been chosen as representative of the feature-based similarity class since they consider different aspects of the underlying semantic graph for characterizing resources and computing similarity.

GbkSim. The authors in [3] propose a solution to compute similarity by means of a graph-based kernel. By *GbkSim*[4] an abstract walker is sent to explore the RDF graph to a specific depth d, en route it collects nodes and edges. The features of a resource α are represented as a vector: $\overrightarrow{a} = (w_{r_1}, w_{r_2}, .., w_{r_n})$. Each element of the vector corresponds to the weight of a resource in the feature set. The weight for resource r_i is calculated as $w_{r_i} = \sum_{m=1}^{d} \gamma_m \cdot c_{\hat{P}^m(\alpha), r_i}$; in which the coefficient γ_m is experimentally selected upon calculation; $c_{\hat{P}^m(\alpha), r_i}$ is the number of edges that connect α to node r_i and it is calculated as: $c_{\hat{P}^m(\alpha), r_i} = |\{(r_i, r_j) | (r_i, r_j) \in \hat{P}^m(\alpha)\}|$; $\hat{P}^m(\alpha)$ is the set of edges collected at depth m. The similarity between two resources α and β is computed as the product of their corresponding feature vectors $\overrightarrow{a} = \{a_i\}_{i=1,...,n}$ and $\overrightarrow{b} = \{b_i\}_{i=1,...,n}$:

$$GbkSim(\alpha, \beta) = \frac{\sum_{i=1}^{n} a_i \times b_i}{\sqrt{\sum_{i=1}^{n} (a_i)^2} \times \sqrt{\sum_{i=1}^{n} (b_i)^2}} \tag{1}$$

VsmSim. In [2] an approach to characterize entities and compute similarity is introduced and evaluated. By *VsmSim*, two entities are supposed to be similar if: (i) There exist direct links between them; (ii) They point to the same object with the same property; (iii) They are pointed by the same subject with the same property. The features of a movie α corresponding to property p are the nodes connected to α through p and represented using the Vector Space Model: $\overrightarrow{a_p} = (w_{r_1,p}, w_{r_2,p}, .., w_{r_n,p})$; in which $w_{r_i,p}$ is the weight of movie r_i wrt. property p, it is computed as the `tf-idf` value of the movie: $w_{r_i,p} = f_{r_i,p} * log(\frac{M}{a_{r_i,p}})$; where $f_{r_i,p}$ is the number of occurrence of movie r_i; M is the number of movies in the collection; $a_{r_i,p}$ is the number of movies pointing to a_{r_i} via p. The similarity related to p is obtained by calculating the cosine similarity of the vectors $\overrightarrow{a_p} = \{a_{i,p}\}_{i=1,..,n}$ and $\overrightarrow{b_p} = \{b_{i,p}\}_{i=1,..,n}$:

$$VsmSim_p(\alpha, \beta) = \frac{\sum_{i=1}^{n} a_{i,p} \times b_{i,p}}{\sqrt{\sum_{i=1}^{n} (a_{i,p})^2} \times \sqrt{\sum_{i=1}^{n} (b_{i,p})^2}}$$

---

[4] For a clear presentation, in the scope of this paper we assign a name for the metrics that have not been named originally.

Given a set P of properties, the final similarity value can be computed as the (weighted) mean of the values computed for each property p

$$VsmSim(\alpha, \beta) = \frac{\sum_{p \in P} \omega_p VsmSim_p(\alpha, \beta)}{|P|} \tag{2}$$

with ω_p being weights computed via a genetic algorithm.

FuzzySim. In an attempt to incorporate the human judgment of similarity, a similarity metric, *FuzzySim* is presented in [4]. Properties are considered as features and intuitively classified into groups in descending order according to their level of importance $(g_1, g_2, .., g_n)$. The similarity value between two resources α and β on group g_i is defined as: $S_i(\alpha, \beta) = \frac{f_i(\alpha, \beta)}{f_i(\alpha)}$; where $f_i(\alpha, \beta)$ is the set of features pertaining to property group g_i that α and β have in common; $f_i(\alpha)$ is the set of features of α wrt. g_i. The membership degree of the similarity value corresponding to g_i is: $\mu(S_i) = (S_i)^{i-r(g_i,c)}$; where $r(g_i, c)$ is the ratio of the number of properties for set g_i wrt. the total number of properties. The weight $\varphi_j(m)$ for the jth element of the property set is given by: $\varphi_j(m) = \sqrt{\frac{\sum_{k=1}^{j} m_k}{\sum_{k=1}^{n} m_k}} - \sqrt{\frac{\sum_{k=1}^{j-1} m_k}{\sum_{k=1}^{n} m_k}}$ in which $m = (\mu(b_1), \mu(b_1), .., \mu(b_n))$ is the ascending sorted membership vector of $(S_1, S_2, .., S_n)$. The similarity between α and β is computed by means of a fuzzy function:

$$FuzzySim(\alpha, \beta) = aggr(S_1, S_2, ..., S_n) = \sum_{j=1}^{n} b_j.\varphi_j(m) \tag{3}$$

Jaccard. For comparison, we use the Jaccard's index to compute similarity between feature sets. The features of a resource are modeled as a set of nodes in its surroundings. For two resources α and β, two abstract walkers are deployed to traverse the graph at a specific depth to acquire features. At each depth, a walker collects nodes, after visiting depth d, the walkers return the set of nodes $N_d(\alpha)$ and $N_d(\beta)$. The metric calculates the similarity between two resources using the Jaccard's index:

$$Jaccard(\alpha, \beta) = \frac{|N_d(\alpha) \bigcap N_d(\beta)|}{|N_d(\alpha) \bigcup N_d(\beta)|} \tag{4}$$

3   Assessment Methodology

Data extracted from LD might be suitable for certain purposes but not for every purpose [22]. The quality of a piece of data is heavily dependent on the usage as well as the tasks performed on it [23]. For measuring the *fitness for use* of a dataset, a set of *quality dimensions* needs to be identified [23]. Scoring functions can be used to calculate an assessment score from the related *quality indicators* as a gauge of how well suitable the data for a particular purpose is. In the scope

Table 1. Formulas used to evaluate the quality of recommendations. rel_k is 1 if the k-th item in the list is relevant for the user u, otherwise it is 0. $test(u)$ represents the set of relevant items in the test set for the user u. Since the rating scale in the Last.fm dataset is from 1 to 5, we consider the ratings 4 and 5 as relevant. I is the whole item set; $TopN(u)$ is the set of the N items recommended to u; $rec(i)$ represents the number of users who received the recommendation of the item i; $total$ is the overall number of recommendations across all users. To compute the Gini coefficient, set I must be indexed in ascending order wrt. the number of recommendations $(rec(i))$.

Accuracy	Sales Diversity	Novelty
$P@N(u) = \frac{\sum_{k=1}^{N} rel_k}{N}$ $R@N(u) = \frac{\sum_{k=1}^{N} rel_k}{|test(u)|}$	$coverage = \frac{|\bigcup_{u \in U} TopN(u)|}{|I|}$ $entropy = -\sum_{i \in I} \left(\frac{rec(i)}{total} \right) ln \left(\frac{rec(i)}{total} \right)$ $gini = 2 \sum_{i \in I} \left[\left(\frac{|I|+1-i}{|I|+1} \right) \left(\frac{rec(i)}{total} \right) \right]$	$\%Long\text{-}tail = \frac{\sum_{i \in Long\text{-}tail} rec(i)}{total}$

of this paper, we work with a specific use case, LD for the music domain used as input for recommendation tasks. Recommender systems are built to suggest things that are of interest to a user, e.g. books, movies, songs [2]. To be able to provide users with meaningful recommendations, recommender systems may enrich their background data by exploiting external sources. In this sense, the quality of the input data plays a key role in producing adequate recommendations. As seen in Section 5, most of the approaches to recommendation built on top of LD datasets exploits DBpedia. To our knowledge, an analysis on the influence of the underlying dataset for the quality of recommendation results has not been performed yet. Having this observation in mind, we compared recommendation results by using two of the richest encyclopedic LD sources. Data retrieved from both DBpedia and Freebase[5] is then used for computing similarity between resources employing the aforementioned similarity metrics. Afterwards, the computed similarity values are fed into a content-based recommender system to produce the final recommendations. For judging data quality, we take into account the quality dimensions of *Accuracy*, *Sales Diversity*, and *Novelty* in a top-N recommendation task. Recently, accuracy has been recognized to be not sufficient to evaluate a recommender system. *Sales Diversity* represents an important quality dimension for both business and user perspective, since improving the coverage of the items catalog and of the distributions of the items across the users may increase the sales and the user satisfaction [21]. *Novelty* measures the ability of the system to foster discovery in the recommendation workflow [25]. The formulas used to evaluate the quality dimensions are formally described in Table 1 and more discursively below.

(i) Considering only the top N results, for measuring *Accuracy* we use precision P@N (the fraction of the top-N recommended items being relevant to the user u) and recall R@N (the fraction of relevant items from the test set appearing in the N predicted items).

---

[5] We used the RDF version Freebase released as baseKB available at http://basekb.com/.

(ii) To measure *Sales Diversity*, we consider catalog coverage [19] (the percentage of items in the catalog that have ever been recommended to users), and Entropy and Gini coefficient [20,21] (for the distribution of recommended items). The latter are useful to analyze the concentration degree of items across the recommendations. The scale for Gini coefficient is reversed, thereby forcing small values to represent low distributional equity and large values to represent higher equity.

(iii) One metric is chosen to measure the *Novelty* of the recommendations: the percentage of long-tail items among the recommendations across all users [20], considering the 80 percent of less rated items in the training set as *Long-tail* items.

For our experiments, we re-used the setup adopted in [6]. Specifically, we have implemented a content-based recommender system using a k-nearest neighbors algorithm. It selects the k most similar entities β, called neighbors, to a given item α using a similarity function $sim(\alpha, \beta)$. The score P for a given user-item pair (u, α) is computed using a weighted sum, where the weights are the similarities between the items. The formula takes into account the neighbors of α belonging to the user profile $profile(u)$ and the relative scores $r(u, \beta)$ assigned by the user u.

$$P(u, \alpha) = \frac{\sum_{\beta \in neighbors(\alpha) \cap profile(u)} sim(\alpha, \beta) \cdot r(u, \beta)}{\sum_{\beta \in neighbors(\alpha) \cap profile(u)} sim(\alpha, \beta)}$$

The function $sim(\alpha, \beta)$ was computed using the similarity metrics shown in the previous section and k was fixed at 20. We selected the well-known dataset Last.fm hetrec-2011. In order to compare the two LD datasets in an ordinary situation, we downsized the number of artists and bands to the 1000 most popular ones and, after that reduction, we removed the cold users, i.e. those having the number of ratings below the average of all users. The reason behind this choice was to reduce as much as possible the well known negative effect on the computation of the recommendation list due to users with a low number of ratings. After that, we used the holdout method to split the dataset into training set and test set. We built the training set by using, for each user, the first 80% of the her ratings and the remaining 20% to build the test set. Therefore, the first 80% of the ratings of each user represents her profile. One of our mapping datasets[6] was utilized to associate each item with its counterpart in DBpedia [24]. By using owl:sameAs links we were then able to retrieve Freebase mappings from the DBpedia ones.

4   Experimental Results

Feature sets are a prerequisite in similarity calculation for feature-based similarity metrics. It is, therefore, necessary to build a set of features for each resource.

---

[6] http://sisinflab.poliba.it/semanticweb/lod/recsys/datasets/

Table 2. The set of properties used for collecting feature sets from DBpedia.

Outbound		Inbound	
rdf:type	dbo:associatedAct	dbo:previousWork	dbo:producer
owl:sameAs	dbo:influenced	dbo:subsequentWork	dbo:artist
dbo:instrument	dbo:influencedBy	dbo:knownFor	dbo:writer
dbo:writer	dbo:bandMember	dbo:award	dbo:associatedBand
dcterms:subject	dbo:formerBandMember	dbo:album	dbo:associatedMusicalArtist
dbo:associatedBand	dbo:currentMember	dbo:notableWork	dbo:musicalArtist
dbo:associatedMusicalArtist	dbo:pastMember	dbo:lastAppearance	dbo:musicalBand
dbo:background	dbo:occupation	dbo:basedOn	dbo:musicComposer
dbo:genre	dbo:birthPlace	dbo:starring	dbo:bandMember
		dbo:series	dbo:formerBandMember
		dbo:openingFilm	dbo:starring
		dbo:related	dbo:composer

In an LD setting, building the the set of features goes through the selection of a set of RDF properties considered as relevant for the domain. For DBpedia, the top 20% most popular properties of the DBpedia ontology used in the musical domain apart from dbo:wikiPageWikiLink have been chosen, plus owl:sameAs, rdf:type and the dcterms:subject property that connects resources to categories. Table 2 shows the selected list of properties. Similarly, for Freebase we selected the set of 20% most popular properties connecting to resources whose type is either basekb:music.musical_group[7] or basekb:music.artist[8]. This results in 288 outgoing and 220 incoming properties. The set of properties is not listed here due to space limitations. An RDF graph consists of a huge number of edges and nodes, spreading out on numerous layers of predicates. It is certainly impractical to address all nodes and edges in it. Therefore, we collected a set of features by expanding the graph using the selected set of properties up to a limited depth. Considering a pair of resources that are involved in the similarity calculation, a neighborhood graph was built by expanding from each resource using the selected set of properties. For each resource, depending on the type of experiments, features can be collected in one or two levels of edges. Furthermore, also depending on the purpose of measurement, an extension can either be done using only outbound edges or using both inbound and outbound edges.

In order to investigate the effect of the selection of feature sets on the outcome, we carried out experiments using independent settings. First, we considered different levels of depth and then in each setting, the selection of properties for collecting a set of features. Two independent similarity calculations have been performed: similarity computed with one-hop features and similarity computed with two-hop features. The experimental results are clarified in the following sub-sections.

One-hop Features. Experiments were conducted in accordance with two separate configurations:

Configuration 1. Both inbound and outbound properties are used to build the set of features of a resource.

---

[7] http://rdf.basekb.com/ns/music.musical_group
[8] http://rdf.basekb.com/ns/music.artist

Table 3. Comparison of results for the four algorithms with Top-10, Top-20, Top-30 between DBpedia and Freebase using both inbound and outbound properties. The name in a cell indicates the dataset that obtains the best result. With largest Top-N the differences between DBpedia and Freebase are similar to the Top-30 results, therefore they are omitted due to space limitations.

		Precision	Recall	Coverage	Entropy	Gini	%Long-tail
	Top-10	Freebase	Freebase	Freebase	DBpedia	DBpedia	DBpedia
GbkSim	Top-20	Freebase	Freebase	Freebase	DBpedia	DBpedia	DBpedia
	Top-30	Freebase	Freebase	Freebase	DBpedia	DBpedia	DBpedia
	Top-10	Freebase	Freebase	Freebase	DBpedia	DBpedia	DBpedia
VsmSim	Top-20	Freebase	DBpedia	DBpedia	DBpedia	DBpedia	DBpedia
	Top-30	Freebase	DBpedia	DBpedia	DBpedia	DBpedia	DBpedia
	Top-10	Freebase	Freebase	Freebase	DBpedia	DBpedia	DBpedia
FuzzySim	Top-20	Freebase	Freebase	Freebase	DBpedia	DBpedia	DBpedia
	Top-30	Freebase	Freebase	Freebase	DBpedia	DBpedia	DBpedia
	Top-10	Freebase	Freebase	Freebase	Freebase	Freebase	DBpedia
Jaccard	Top-20	Freebase	Freebase	Freebase	Freebase	DBpedia	DBpedia
	Top-30	Freebase	Freebase	Freebase	Freebase	Freebase	DBpedia

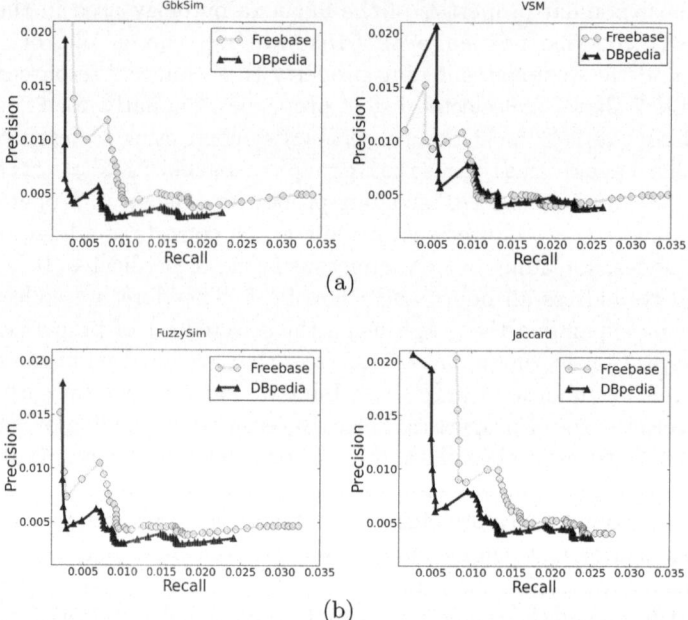

Fig. 1. Recommedation using similarity values computed on one-hop features: Precision - Recall curves obtained by varying the length of the recommendations list from 1 to 50, with 20 neighbors. Inbound and outbound links are used in combination.

Accuracy. Figure 1 shows the precision and recall values for all metrics. Generally, recommendations computed using data extracted from Freebase have a better precision-recall balance and higher recall values. This holds for all similarity metrics except for *VsmSim*. Using the latter, generally there is an overlap among the values, but still Freebase helps achieve the highest recall values. Table 3 displays the quality indicators for all the metrics on both datasets

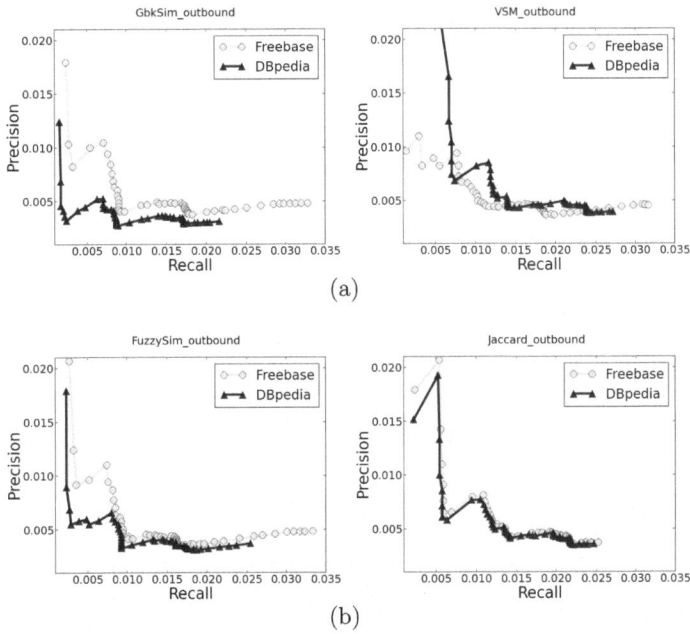

Fig. 2. Recommedation using similarity values computed on one-hop features: Precision - Recall curves obtained by varying the length of the recommendations list from 1 to 50, with 20 neighbors. Only outbound links are used.

considering Top-10, Top-20 and Top-30. Those results demonstrate that Freebase dataset brings the highest accuracy for all the similarity metrics, except for *VsmSim* as mentioned before. However, the differences between the two datasets often have a marginal significance, whereas the charts in Figure 1 show a more complete and general view in term of accuracy.

Sales Diversity. As shown in Table 3, using Freebase data always produces better coverage. In terms of distribution (Entropy and Gini), generally using data from DBpedia obtains better values compared to Freebase. However, those results are not easily comparable because the DBpedia coverage values are too low. By recommending very few items, it is much more likely to obtain a good distribution; whereas, by recommending more items, many of these may be suggested few times (even just once). This is confirmed by the fact that the entropy values are closer than the Gini values between DBpedia and Freebase, considering that Gini index is more sensible to the inequality and Entropy to the distribution among the recommendations.

Novelty. In terms of percentage of long-tail items, DBpedia contributes to a better novelty compared to Freebase in almost every configuration. This means that using DBpedia tends to suggest a smaller subset of items, but these do not necessarily belong to the most popular ones. In contrast, Freebase can help cover more items but generally with a slightly larger popularity bias.

Configuration 2. *Only outbound properties are used to build the set of features of a resource.*

Figure 2 shows the accuracy obtained by the recommendations computed using similarity results in this setting. A noteworthy observation is that, for all similarity metrics, the accuracy of the recommendations calculated by using data from DBpedia is analogous to the accuracy obtained by using data from Freebase. We also observed the same trend for all metrics by other quality dimensions (Sales Diversity and Novelty). Thus, the corresponding quality indicators are not depicted due to space limitations. Compared with Configuration 1, we come to the conclusion that the utilization of both inbound and outbound properties for computing semantic similarity contributes towards an improvement in the recommendation results.

Table 4. Comparison of results for the four algorithms with Top-10, Top-20, Top-30 between DBpedia and Freebase with exploration up to two hops using both inbound and outbound properties. The name in a cell indicates the dataset that obtains the best result.

		Precision	Recall	Coverage	Entropy	Gini	%Long-tail
GbkSim	Top-10	Freebase	Freebase	Freebase	Freebase	DBpedia	DBpedia
	Top-20	Freebase	Freebase	Freebase	DBpedia	DBpedia	DBpedia
	Top-30	Freebase	Freebase	Freebase	DBpedia	DBpedia	DBpedia
VsmSim	Top-10	DBpedia	DBpedia	Freebase	Freebase	Freebase	DBpedia
	Top-20	DBpedia	DBpedia	Freebase	DBpedia	DBpedia	DBpedia
	Top-30	DBpedia	DBpedia	Freebase	Freebase	DBpedia	DBpedia
FuzzySim	Top-10	Freebase	Freebase	Freebase	Freebase	DBpedia	DBpedia
	Top-20	Freebase	Freebase	Freebase	DBpedia	DBpedia	DBpedia
	Top-30	Freebase	Freebase	Freebase	Freebase	DBpedia	DBpedia
Jaccard	Top-10	Freebase	Freebase	Freebase	DBpedia	DBpedia	Freebase
	Top-20	Freebase	Freebase	Freebase	DBpedia	DBpedia	DBpedia
	Top-30	Freebase	Freebase	Freebase	DBpedia	DBpedia	DBpedia

Two-hop Features. We studied the influence of exploration depth for collecting features over the recommendation outcomes. Hence, the same experimental procedures were replicated with depth $d = 2$ and the results obtained are as follows:

Configuration 1.*Both inbound and outbound properties are used*

The accuracy values for all metrics using 2 hops are depicted in Figure 3. Similar to the experiments performed using one-hop features, we witnessed the same pattern of the quality indicators for this experimental setting. Using the Freebase dataset to produce recommendations yields a better precision-recall balance as well as higher recall values. For both *VsmSim* and *Jaccard*, similarity values on the DBpedia dataset help produce the best recommendations in terms of accuracy; meanwhile similarity values computed by *Jaccard* on the Freebase dataset contribute to a better precision-recall balance. Considering Top-10, Top-20 and Top-30, the corresponding quality indicators for all the metrics are shown in Table 4. Once again, apart from *VsmSim*, recommendation with the Freebase dataset using other similarity metrics still brings the highest accuracy.

Configuration 2.*Only outbound properties are used*

For this experimental setting, by all metrics we also obtained comparable results using similarity values calculated from Configuration 2 for one-hop features. Figure 4 depicts the precision-recall balance for all similarity metrics. The

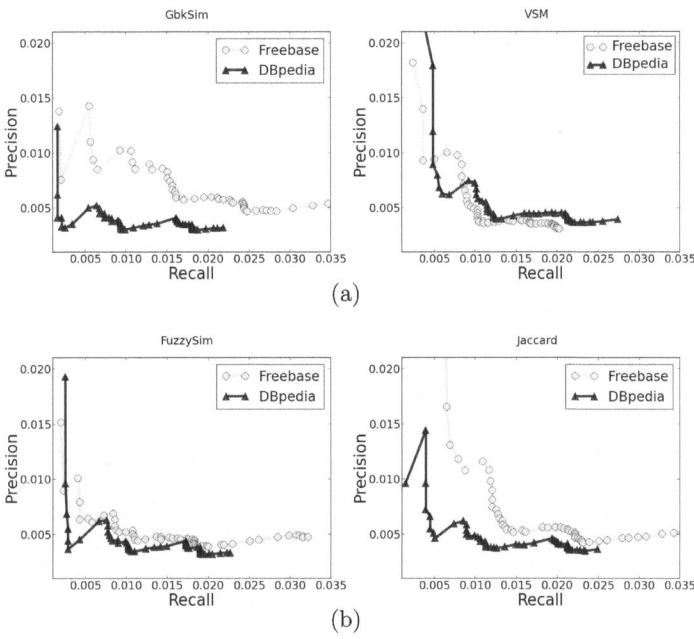

Fig. 3. Recommedation using similarity values computed on two-hop features: Precision - Recall curves obtained by varying the length of the recommendations list from 1 to 50, with 20 neighbors. Inbound and outbound links are used in combination.

results obtained using DBpedia show no substantial difference compared to the results with considering also inbound properties. While the results for Freebase show an overall strong decrease both in terms of precision-recall balance and recall values, demonstrating that the inbound properties in Freebase dataset play an important role, as already seen for one-hop configuration. This decrease is particularly evident using *GbkSim* and *Jaccard*.

It can be seen that, the outcomes of the recommendations on two-hop features confirm the experimental results for recommendation using one-hop features.

Comparison between using One-hop and Two-hop Features. We carried out a comparative analysis between using one-hop and two-hop features. As a matter of fact, the exploration of the graph comes at a price and sometime it might not be necessary. Using DBpedia with inbound and outbound properties, there are no relevant differences expanding the features up to two hops. Considering Figures 1 and 3, with respect to Freebase with inbound and outbound properties, *GbkSim* metric with two-hop features obtains better results in terms of precision with respect to one-hop configuration. In terms of recall, using the *Jaccard* metric with two-hop features obtains better results with respect to one-hop configuration. Conversely, the recall values using *VsmSim* decrease with two-hop instead one-hop features. There are no substantial differences in

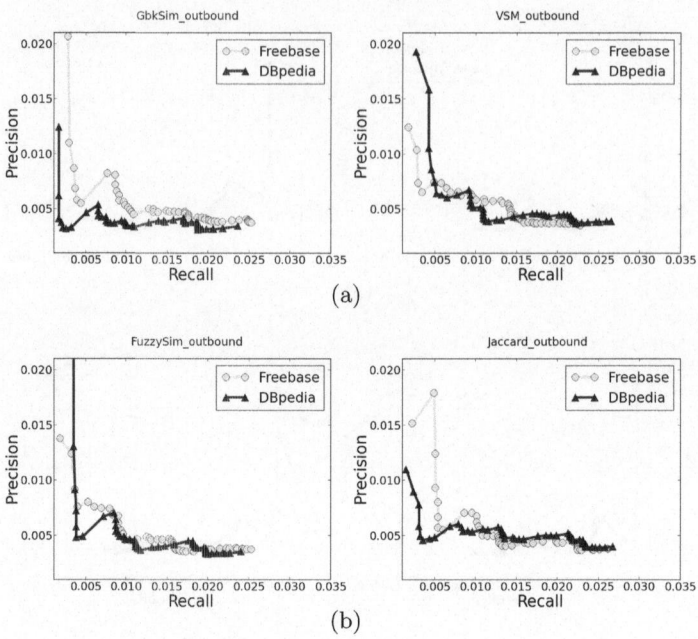

Fig. 4. Recommedation using similarity values computed on two-hop features: Precision - Recall curves obtained by varying the length of the recommendations list from 1 to 50, with 20 neighbors. Only outbound links are used.

the case of *FuzzySim*. Table 5 shows the gains and losses obtained expanding the features up to two hops with Top-10, Top-20 and Top-30, confirming what has been said so far. Considering the Sales Diversity measure, using DBpedia we obtain better results with two-hop features using all the similarity metrics. Using Freebase gains better results with two-hop features using *Jaccard* and *VsmSim*. However, Freebase always overcomes DBpedia. It is worth noticing that the recommendation distribution (Entropy and Gini measures) achieves substantial improvements with two-hop features for each configuration. Instead, when only outbound properties are used, the performances by utilizing DBpedia are slightly lower expanding the features up to two hops, especially in terms of precision with *VsmSim* and *FuzzySim*. With respect to Freebase, the recall decreases especially with *GbkSim* and *FuzzySim*. The adoption of Freebase instead of DBpedia shows its benefits when used in conjunction with *GbkSim*, when two-hop features are considered. The other similarity metrics – even though they are relatively simple – do not exhibit that considerable improvements to justify the increased computational effort needed to further explore the semantic graph of one more hop.

Table 5. Gains and losses obtained using two-hop features respect to one-hop ones using both inbound and outbound properties. The symbol + indicates a gain, − a loss while ∼ a negligible variation.

			Precision	Recall	Coverage	Entropy	Gini	%Long-tail
GbkSim	Top-10	Freebase	+	+	−	+	+	−
		DBpedia	−	−	+	−	−	−
	Top-20	Freebase	+	+	−	+	+	+
		DBpedia	+	+	+	+	+	∼
	Top-30	Freebase	+	+	−	+	+	∼
		DBpedia	+	+	+	∼	+	−
VsmSim	Top-10	Freebase	−	−	+	+	+	−
		DBpedia	−	−	+	+	+	−
	Top-20	Freebase	−	−	+	+	+	−
		DBpedia	−	−	+	+	+	−
	Top-30	Freebase	−	−	+	+	+	−
		DBpedia	−	−	+	+	−	−
FuzzySim	Top-10	Freebase	−	−	−	+	+	−
		DBpedia	+	+	+	−	∼	∼
	Top-20	Freebase	+	+	∼	+	+	−
		DBpedia	+	+	+	∼	+	+
	Top-30	Freebase	+	+	−	+	+	−
		DBpedia	+	+	+	+	+	∼
Jaccard	Top-10	Freebase	−	−	+	+	∼	+
		DBpedia	−	−	+	+	+	−
	Top-20	Freebase	−	−	+	−	−	−
		DBpedia	−	−	+	+	+	−
	Top-30	Freebase	∼	∼	+	−	−	−
		DBpedia	−	−	+	+	+	∼

4.1 Discussion

In this section we discuss the general trends emerging from Table 3, 4 and 5.

By looking at Table 3 and Table 4, an interesting question arises: *why Freebase seems to facilitate better accuracy and catalog coverage while DBpedia helps obtain superior novelty and aggregate diversity*[9]?

As for accuracy, we assume that in Freebase, at least for our target domain, items considered as similar by users are actually connected by relevant properties with each other. This reflects the strong crowd-sourced nature of Freebase and also means that, in this case, Freebase is richer than DBpedia in terms of encoded knowledge. Both data sources are derived from Wikipedia, however Freebase can be flexibly edited by user communities who utilize numerous sources for encoding metadata. Thus, each Freebase topic consists of an expansion of the original Wikipedia topic, which is not the case in DBpedia. Especially for domains being managed by Google, Freebase has a higher topic coverage than DBpedia [26]. Moreover, the social nature of Freebase also implies that items resulting popular among the users are also "popular" in the underlying graph. This means that they are richer in terms of related data and are more connected to other entities. This also explains both the higher value of precision and recall and the lower values of novelty when using Freebase. Indeed, on the one side we know that computing recommendations based on items popularity results in good predictions for the end users [5]; on the other side, as with Freebase we concentrate more on popular items we have lower results when evaluating novelty (long-tail) compared to DBpedia. Regarding the differences between Coverage and aggregate diversity (*Entropy* and *Gini* index) a possible explanation is due to the very low values of catalog coverage when using

---

[9] A further and more detailed investigation is needed for *VsmSim*.

DBpedia. Since there are less recommended items from the catalog, they have a higher probability to be better distributed across the users.

The results summarized in Table 5 show other interesting trends when exploring the underlying graph to compute recommendation. We see that values for novelty tend to decrease when we move from a one-hop to a two-hop exploration while this is not the case for catalog coverage and aggregate diversity. Possible explanations for these behaviors are: (i) popular items get more connected when exploring the graph thus obtaining better similarity results. This justifies the novelty decrease; (ii) the increasing in the number of connections also reflects in the selection of more items (better coverage) even if the new items are selected mostly among the popular ones; (iii) finally, as we have better similarity values due to better overlaps among items descriptions, we gain in aggregate diversity as a better similarity values means a better chance to be recommended.

5   Related Work

To the best of our knowledge, none of the existing work has conducted a comprehensive evaluation on the fitness for use of datasets in combination with different recommendation strategies. Some studies partly address the issue in different settings. In this section we review the most notable work on this topic.

Leveraging LD sources like DBpedia for recommendation tasks appears to be highly beneficial as demonstrated by numerous applications. One of the first approaches that exploits Linked Data for building recommender systems is [9]. The authors of [8] present a knowledge-based framework leveraging DBpedia for computing cross-domain recommendations. A graph-based recommendation approach utilizing model- and memory-based link prediction methods is presented in [10]. LD datasets are exploited in [11] for personalized exploratory search using a spreading activation method for finding semantic relatedness between items belonging to different domains. For recommending movies, a content-based system exploiting data extracted from DBpedia has been proposed in [2] based on the adaptation of Vector Space Model to semantic networks. In [24] a hybrid algorithm - named *Sprank* - is proposed to compute *top-N* item recommendations from implicit feedback. Path-based features are extracted from DBpedia to detect subtle relationships among items in semantic graphs. Afterwards, recommendations are produced by incorporating ontological knowledge with collaborative user preferences. The proposed algorithm gains good accuracy, especially in conditions of higher data sparseness. A work that can be considered as a base for our paper is [6]. Two semantic similarity metrics, *SimRank* and *Personalized PageRank* are used to compute similarity between resources in RDF graphs. There, exploiting semantic similarity in producing input for a content-based recommender system has proven to bring benefits. A full SPARQL-based recommendation engine named RecSPARQL is presented in [12]. The proposed tool extends the syntax and semantics of SPARQL to enable a generic and flexible way for collaborative filtering and content-based recommendations over arbitrary RDF graphs. The authors of [13] propose an approach for topic suggestions based on some proximity measures defined on the top of the DBpedia graph.

In [14] the authors present an event recommendation system based on LD and user diversity. A semantic-aware extension of the SVD++ model, named SemanticSVD++, is presented in [15]. It incorporates semantic categories of items into the model. The model is able also to consider the evolution over time of user's preferences. In [16] the authors improve their previous work for dealing with cold-start items by introducing a vertex kernel for getting knowledge about the unrated semantic categories starting from those categories which are known. Another interesting direction about the usage of LD for content-based RSs is explored in [17] where the authors present Contextual eVSM, a content-based context-aware recommendation framework that adopts a semantic representation based on distributional models and entity linking techniques. In particular entity linking is used to detect entities in free text and map them to LD.

Finally, in [18] the authors propose the usage of recommendation techniques for providing personalized access to LD. The proposed method is a user-user collaborative filtering recommender wherein the similarity between the users takes into account the commonalities and informativeness of the resources instead of treating resources as plain identifiers.

6   Conclusion

In this paper we analyze the fitness for use of two LD encyclopedic datasets, namely DBpedia and Freebase, to cope with recommendation tasks in the music domain. Similarity values computed on data retrieved from DBpedia and Freebase were used to feed a content-based recommender system to produce recommendation lists. To further study the influence of the selection of features on the recommendations, we performed experiments using (i) four different feature-based similarity values, (ii) two levels of depth in the graph exploration and (iii) different property sets for gathering features from RDF graphs. We executed a series of experiments on the Last.fm dataset thus comparing the recommendation results measuring their performances in terms of accuracy, catalog coverage, distribution and novelty. For most of the experimental settings, we saw that exploiting Freebase obtains better accuracy and catalog coverage. Whereas, the dataset from DBpedia generally fosters the novelty of recommendations. Regarding the distribution, at first glance using the DBpedia dataset appears to perform better, but a careful analysis shows that the results are somehow comparable. For all settings, the selection of both inbound and outbound links for computing similarity makes a difference to the overall performance. Indeed, it is worth noticing that considering links as undirected has a positive impact in the performance of the recommendation engine. We also saw that Freebase obtains improvements using *GbkSim* expanding the features up to two hops. Although Freebase will be retired at the end of June 2015 as a standalone project, all its data will flow into the Wikidata project thus becoming its stable nucleus. Hence, we are confident that the results presented in this paper will be useful also in the light of a comparison with the upcoming edition of Wikidata. In conclusion, we confirm that encyclopedic LD datasets are an interesting source of data to build content-based recommender systems, but the choice of the right dataset might affect the performance of the system with regards to some evaluation dimensions such as accuracy, novelty and diversity of results.

Acknowledgments. The authors acknowledge partial support of PON01_03113 ERMES, PON02_00563_3470993 Vincente and PON02_00563_3446857 KHIRA.

References

1. Tversky, A.: Features of similarity. Psychological Review **84**(4), 327–352 (1977)
2. Di Noia, T., Mirizzi, R., Ostuni, V.C., Romito, D., Zanker, M.: Linked open data to support content-based recommender systems. In: Proc. of I-SEMANTICS 2012, pp. 1–8 (2012)
3. Ostuni, V.C., Di Noia, T., Mirizzi, R., Di Sciascio, E.: A linked data recommender system using a neighborhood-based graph Kernel. In: Hepp, M., Hoffner, Y. (eds.) EC-Web 2014. LNBIP, vol. 188, pp. 89–100. Springer, Heidelberg (2014)
4. Zadeh, P.D.H., Reformat, M.Z.: Fuzzy semantic similarity in linked data using the OWA operator. In: Annual Meeting of the North American Fuzzy Inf. Proc. Society (2012)
5. Cremonesi, P., Koren, Y., Turrin, R.: Performance of recommender algorithms on top-n recommendation tasks. In: Proc. of RecSys10. pp. 39–46 (2010)
6. Nguyen, P.T., Tomeo, P., Di Noia, T., Di Sciascio, E.: An evaluation of SimRank and personalized PageRank to build a recommender system for the web of data. In: 7th International Workshop on Web Intelligence & Communities. ACM (2015)
7. Lops, P., Des Gemmi, M., Semeraro, G.: Recommender Systems Handbook, pp. 73–105. Springer, Heidelberg (2011)
8. Fernández-Tobías, I., Cantador, I., Kaminskas, M., Ricci., F.: A generic semantic-based framework for cross-domain recommendation. In: Proc. of HetRec 2011, pp. 25–32 (2011)
9. Heitmann, B., Hayes., C.: Using linked data to build open, collaborative recommender systems. In: AAAI Spring Symposium: Linked Data Meets Artificial Intelligence (2010)
10. Lommatzsch, A., Plumbaum, T., Albayrak., S.: A linked dataverse knows better: boosting recommendation quality using semantic knowledge. In: Proc. of SEMAPRO 2011, pp. 97–103 (2011)
11. Marie, N., Corby, O., Gandon, F., Ribière., M.: Composite interests' exploration thanks to on-the-fly linked data spreading activation. In: Proc. of HT 2013 (2013)
12. Ayala, V.A.A., Przyjaciel-Zablocki, M., Hornung, T., Schätzle, A., Lausen., G.: Extending sparql for recommendations. In: Proc. of SWIM 2014 (2014)
13. Stankovic, M., Breitfuss, W., Laublet., P.: Linked-data based suggestion of relevant topics. In: Proc. of I-Semantics 2011, pp. 49–55 (2011)
14. Khrouf, H., and Troncy., R.: Hybrid event recommendation using linked data and user diversity. In: Proc. of RecSys 2013, pp. 185–192 (2013)
15. Rowe, M.: SemanticSVD++: incorporating semantic taste evolution for predicting ratings. In: Proc. of 2014 IEEE/WIC/ACM WI 2014 (2014)
16. Rowe, M.: Transferring semantic categories with vertex Kernels: recommendations with SemanticSVD++. In: Mika, P., Tudorache, T., Bernstein, A., Welty, C., Knoblock, C., Vrandečić, D., Groth, P., Noy, N., Janowicz, K., Goble, C. (eds.) ISWC 2014, Part I. LNCS, vol. 8796, pp. 341–356. Springer, Heidelberg (2014)

17. Musto, C., Semeraro, G., Lops, P., de Gemmis, M.: Combining distributional semantics and entity linking for context-aware content-based recommendation. In: Dimitrova, V., Kuflik, T., Chin, D., Ricci, F., Dolog, P., Houben, G.-J. (eds.) UMAP 2014. LNCS, vol. 8538, pp. 381–392. Springer, Heidelberg (2014)
18. Dojchinovski, M., Vitvar, T.: Personalised Access to Linked Data. In: Janowicz, K., Schlobach, S., Lambrix, P., Hyvönen, E. (eds.) EKAW 2014. LNCS, vol. 8876, pp. 121–136. Springer, Heidelberg (2014)
19. Ge, M., Delgado-Battenfeld, C., Jannach, D.: Beyond accuracy: evaluating recommender systems by coverage and serendipity. In: Proc. of RecSys 2010, pp. 257–260, ACM (2010)
20. Adomavicius, G., Kwon, Y.: Improving Aggregate Recommendation Diversity Using Ranking-Based Techniques. IEEE TKDE **24**(5), 896–911 (2012)
21. Vargas, S., Castells, P.: Improving sales diversity by recommending users to items. In: Proc. of RecSys 2014, pp. 145–152 (2014)
22. Knuth, M., Kontokostas, D., Sack, H.: Linked data quality: identifying and tackling the key challenges. In: Proc. of LDQ@SEMANTiCS (2014)
23. Mendes, P.N., Mühleisen, H., Bizer, C.: Sieve: linked data quality assessment and fusion. In: Proc. of EDBT-ICDT 2012, pp. 116–123. ACM (2012)
24. Ostuni, V.C., Di Noia, T., Di Sciascio, E., Mirizzi, R.: Top-N recommendations from implicit feedback leveraging linked open data. In: Proc. of RecSys 2013 (2013)
25. Celma, O., Herrera, P.: A new approach to evaluating novel recommendations. In: Proc. RecSys 2008. ACM (2008)
26. Lehmann, J., et al.: DBpedia - A large-scale, multilingual knowledge base extracted from Wikipedia. Journal of Semantic Web **6**, 167–195 (2015)

Explaining and Suggesting Relatedness in Knowledge Graphs

Giuseppe Pirrò[✉]

Institute for High Performance Computing and Networking,
Italian National Research Council (ICAR-CNR), Rende, CS, Italy
pirro@icar.cnr.it

Abstract. Knowledge graphs (KGs) are a key ingredient for searching, browsing and knowledge discovery activities. Motivated by the need to harness knowledge available in a variety of KGs, we face the following two problems. First, given a pair of entities defined in some KG, find an explanation of their relatedness. We formalize the notion of relatedness explanation and introduce different criteria to build explanations based on information-theory, diversity and their combinations. Second, given a pair of entities, find other (pairs of) entities sharing a similar relatedness perspective. We describe an implementation of our ideas in a tool, called RECAP, which is based on RDF and SPARQL. We provide an evaluation of RECAP and a comparison with related systems on real-world data.

1 Introduction

Knowledge Graphs (KGs) maintaining structured data about entities are becoming a common support for browsing, searching and knowledge discovery activities. Search engines like Google, Yahoo! and Bing complement search results with facts about entities in their KGs. An even large number and variety of KGs, based on the Resource Description Framework (RDF) data format, stem from the Linked Open Data project [8]. Fig. 1 (a) shows information provided by the Google KG when giving the entity F. Lang as input; it reports some facts about the director along with relationships with other entities. Fig. 1 (b) and Fig. 1 (c) show information, encoded in RDF, about F. Lang taken from DBpedia and LinkedMDB, respectively. Note that the Google KG suggests entities like T. von Harbou as related to F. Lang with a short comment saying that T. von Harbou was F. Lang's former spouse. However, what is the mechanism behind this suggestion? What is the relationship between F. Lang and other entities like H. Hitchcock? KGs like DBpedia and LinkedMDB fail short when it comes to both explain the relatedness between an arbitrary pair of entities and suggest related

---

Part of this work was done while the author was working at the WeST institute, University of Koblenz-Landau, Germany. This work was partially supported by the EU Framework Programme for Research and Innovation under grant agreement no. 611242 (SENSE4US) and by the Cyber Security Technological District financed by the Italian Ministry of Education, University and Research.

M. Arenas et al. (Eds.): ISWC 2015, Part I, LNCS 9366, pp. 622–639, 2015.
DOI: 10.1007/978-3-319-25007-6_36

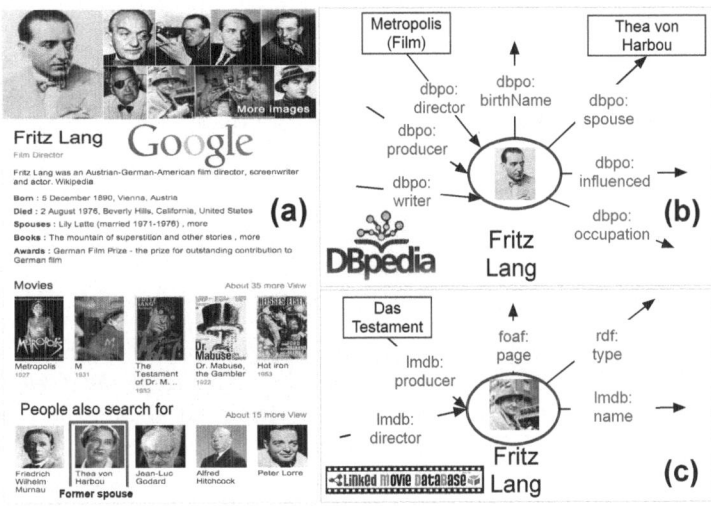

Fig. 1. F. Lang in the Google KG (a), DBpedia (b), and LinkedMDB (c).

entities. We contend that the usage of a standard data format (i.e., RDF) and the availability of a standard querying infrastructure (i.e., SPARQL endpoints) open new perspectives toward explaining relatedness and querying KGs by using pairs of entities as input.

The first problem that we face concerns how to build relatedness explanations. This has applications in several areas including: terrorist networks, to uncover the connections between two suspected terrorists [20]; co-author networks, to discover interlinks between researchers [5,6]; generic exploratory search. The need for relatedness explanations also emerged in the context of the SENSE4US FP7 project[1], which aims at creating a toolkit to support information gathering, analysis and policy modeling. Here, relatedness explanations are useful to investigate and show topic connectivity[2], thus enabling to find out previously unknown information that is of relevance, understand how it is of relevance, and navigate it.

Although the problem of finding connectivity structures between entities has been studied (e.g., [3,19]), existing approaches do not offer comprehensive mechanisms for building different types of relatedness explanations and controlling the amount of information to be included. Moreover, these approaches miss the possibility to query KGs.

The second problem that we tackle concerns querying KGs. KGs behind search engines (e.g., Google) provide limited querying capabilities, typically accepting one entity as input. KGs based on RDF (e.g., DBpedia) provide rich querying capabilities but require familiarity with languages like SPARQL [7]

---

[1] http://www.sense4us.eu
[2] A module of the SENSE4US toolkit extracts topics from policy documents.

and the underlying data/schema [10]. Our strategy recalls the query by example approach; given a pair of entities as input, we leverage their relatedness explanation to learn a query pattern, which is used to identify other (pairs of) related entities. Our approach goes beyond existing entity suggestion mechanisms mainly based on the syntactic analysis of query logs and pages [13]. We now provide an example about the two main challenges faced in this paper, that is, *how to build relatedness explanations* and *how to query KGs by giving entities as input*.

1.1   Overview of the Approach

Syd is fond of science-fiction films; he has heard about two German directors named Fritz Lang and Thea von Harbou and is interested in their relatedness.

By giving F. Lang and T. von Harbou as input to RECAP, the tool implementing our framework, Syd gets the explanation in Fig. 2 (a). This explanation is more informative than the short comment (i.e., former spouse) provided by the Google KG and *combines* information from Freebase and DBpedia. The explanation includes the top-20 most informative paths (out of 240) at max. distance 2; informativeness is defined in terms of edge labels occurrences. RECAP allows to generate different types of explanations (Fig. 2 (b)) and also provides information about nodes/edges (Fig. 2 (c)).

RECAP goes beyond related approaches (e.g., REX [4], Explass [2]) that provide visual information about connectivity as it allows to build different types of explanations (e.g., graphs, sets of paths), thus controlling the amount of information visualized. RECAP has the advantage of not requiring any data preprocessing; information is obtained by querying (remote) SPARQL endpoints. Moreover,

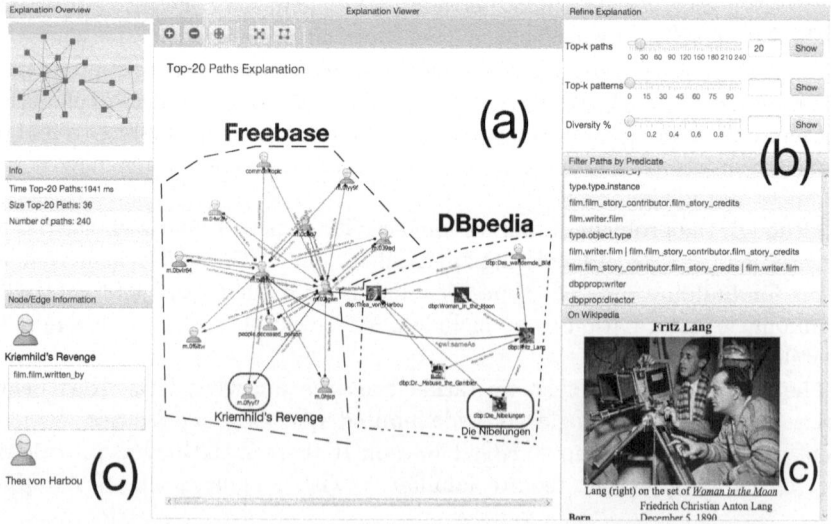

Fig. 2. The explanation perspective of the RECAP tool.

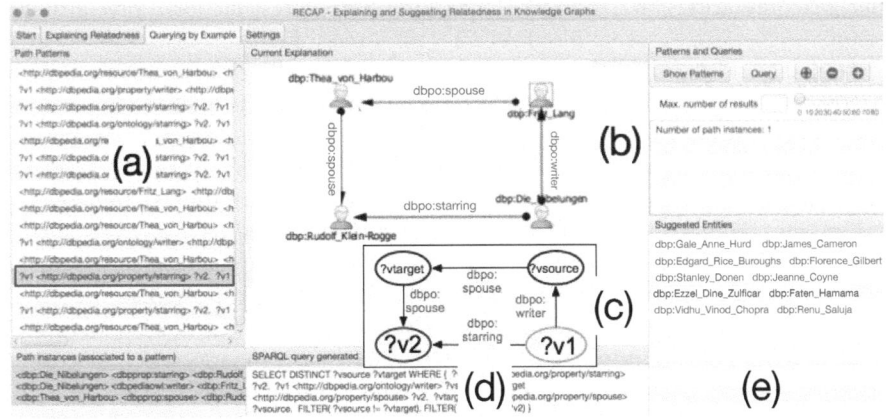

Fig. 3. The querying perspective of RECAP. Path patterns (a), explanation (b), query pattern (c), SPARQL query (d), and suggested entities (e) ranked by popularity (PageRank [17] in this case).

RECAP can combine information from multiple KGs. In the previous example, the combination of Freebase and DBpedia allowed to discover an additional episode of *Die Nibelungen* series (missing in DBpedia), that is, *Kriemhild's Revenge*, co-written by F. Lang and T. von Harbou. Last but not least, RECAP also allows to query KGs by using pairs of entities as input.

Given a pair of entities, RECAP finds other (pairs of) related entities by learning a SPARQL query from their relatedness explanation. By continuing our example, suppose that *Syd gives the pair (F. Lang, T. von Harbou) as input to RECAP with the aim to discover other entities.* Fig 3 (b) shows one possible explanation that RECAP uses to learn a SPARQL query. The explanation merges paths conforming to the pattern in Fig 3 (a). Fig 3 (c) abstracts the explanation by replacing nodes with variables.

The SPARQL query generated (shown in Fig 3 (d)) allows to find pairs of related entities that can be locally ranked. The top-5 pairs of entities found by RECAP, and ranked by their popularity, are show in Fig. 3 (e). As an example, for the pair (Gale Ann Hurd, James Cameron) we can reconstruct a similar pattern as that shown in Fig. 3 (b): J. Cameron was married with G. A. Hurd, he wrote the movie The Terminator where L. Hamilton (also married to J. Cameron) starred.

1.2 Related Work

There is solid body of work about *(i)* finding structures (e.g., paths, subgraphs) connecting entities [3,9,12,12,15,19]; *(ii)* learning relationships between entities; *(iii)* discovering and/or visualizing connectivity information between entities [2,4,9]. Differently from *(i)*, RECAP focuses on the problem of providing concise explanations by leveraging path informativeness and/or a diversity criterion. As for *(ii)*, systems like PATTY [16] mainly focus on learning semantic relationships. RECAP has a different departure point; it explains relatedness in the form of graphs that can be dynamically configured to include the desired amount of information. As for *(iii)*, Table 1 compares RECAP with related systems in terms of: KG supported (**KG**), output (**O**), filtering capabilities (**F**), querying capabilities (**Q**), requirement of local data (**L**). RECAP differs from related systems in the following main respects: as for **KG**, RECAP is *KG-independent*; it only requires the availability of a (remote) query endpoint. Moreover, RECAP can combine information from *multiple* KGs. As for **O** and **F**, RECAP focuses on building *different types* of explanations in the form of graphs or (sets of) paths by leveraging *informativeness* (to estimate the relative importance of edges), *diversity* (to include rare edges) and their combinations. Moreover, RECAP is the only approach that can be used to query KGs (**Q**). As for **L**, *neither* does RECAP assume *local availability* of data *nor* any data *preprocessing*. A more detailed comparison between RECAP and related systems on real data is discussed in Section 4.

Table 1. Comparison of RECAP with closely related systems.

System	KG	O	F	Q	L
REX [4]	Yahoo!	Graph	No	No	Yes
RelFinder [9]	DBpedia	Graph	No	No	Yes
Explass [2]	DBpedia	Paths	Yes (only paths)	No	Yes
RECAP	Any	Graph/Paths	Yes (paths and graphs)	Yes	No

1.3 Contributions and Outline

The framework that we are going to introduce poses several challenges, among which: *(i)* how to capture the notion of relatedness explanation between entities? we leverage informativeness of paths and a diversity criterion to construct different types of explanations; *(ii)* how to query KGs? we isolate the structure of an explanation to learn a SPARQL query; *(iii)* how to make RECAP readily available? We use RDF, the SPARQL query language, and SPARQL endpoints. The contributions of this paper are as follows: *(i)* a framework for building relatedness explanations; *(ii)* different path ranking strategies; *(iii)* a mechanism to query KGs by giving entity pairs as input; *(iv)* a KG-agnostic implementation of our framework; *(v)* an extensive experimental evaluation.

The remainder of the paper is organized as follows. Section 2 introduces the problem and gives some background. Section 3 presents the explanation framework. Section 4 discusses an evaluation of the performance of RECAP and a comparison with related work. We draw some conclusions and sketch future work in Section 5.

2   Problem Formalization

Motivation. The goal of this paper is to facilitate the discovery and explanation of knowledge in knowledge graphs. Part of this research was motivated by the SENSE4US project where explanations are a useful support to discover connectivity between topics emerging from policy documents.

Input. We consider as input a pair (w_s, w_t) of entities defined in some knowledge graph G. We focus on RDF knowledge bases $K = \langle G, O, A \rangle$ where G is a knowledge graph (KG), O is an ontology/schema, and A is a query endpoint.

Assumptions. The framework that we are going to introduce works on top existing knowledge bases. Our approach has to be flexible enough to be applied to different KGs as dictated by the SENSE4US project, which considers a variety of KGs in the LOD cloud. Hence, we consider the access to knowledge bases via the query endpoint A. Neither this requires local availability of the data (e.g., local copies) nor any complex data processing infrastructure from the user side. The computations are reduced to the evaluation of a set of queries against A plus some local refinement.

Desired Output. Given $K = \langle G, O, A \rangle$ and a pair of entities $(w_s, w_t) \in G$, the output can be of two different types. It can be an explanation $G_e(w_s, w_t) \subseteq G$. To produce the graph G_e, our explanation algorithm only considers nodes/edges in the set of paths between w_s and w_t. Given a set of paths, we define different mechanisms to rank/select paths to be included in G_e.

When focusing on querying KGs, the output is a set of (pairs of) entities. We isolate the structure of an explanation into an explanation pattern. Given a graph G_e, representing an explanation, an explanation pattern considers a graph G_e^v where nodes in G_e are replaced with variables. G_e^v is used to generate a SPARQL query that is evaluated against A. Results of such query can be locally ranked (e.g., via PageRank [17]).

Basic Definitions and Background. We now define what a knowledge graph (KG) is and outline the fragment of the query language supporting the implementation of our framework. Although there are several KGs today available (e.g., Yahoo!, Google) we will focus on those encoded in RDF[3]. The choice of RDF is merely practical; data in RDF is widely and openly accessible on the Web for querying via SPARQL [7]. Let $\mathcal{U}$ (URIs) and $\mathcal{L}$ (literals) be countably disjoint infinite sets. An RDF *triple* is a tuple of the form $\mathcal{U} \times \mathcal{U} \times (\mathcal{U} \cup \mathcal{L})$ whose elements are referred to as *subject*, *predicate* and *object*, respectively. As we are interested in discovering explanations in terms of nodes and edges carrying semantic meaning for the user, we do not consider blank nodes.

Definition 1 (Knowledge Graph). Given a set T of RDF triples, a KG is a multigraph $G = \langle V, \mathcal{E} \rangle$ where $V = \{s \mid (s, p, o) \in T\} \cup \{o \mid (s, p, o) \in T\}$ and $\mathcal{E} = \{(s, p, o) \in T\}$.

---

[3] A list is available at http://lod-cloud.net

For the purposes of this paper, we will consider the most basic form of SPARQL queries, that is, Basic Graph Patterns (BGPs). We shall also make usage of the COUNT aggregate operator. Let $\mathcal{V}$ be a set of SPARQL variables, that is, strings starting with the ? symbol, $\mathcal{U}$ a set of URIs and $\mathcal{L}$ a set of literals. A *triple pattern* is a triple of the form $(\mathcal{U} \cup \mathcal{L} \cup \mathcal{V}) \times (\mathcal{U} \cup \mathcal{V}) \times (\mathcal{U} \cup \mathcal{L} \cup \mathcal{V})$. BGPs are sets of triple patterns that can be combined via algebraic operators; we will make usage of the *join* operator (represented by the symbol . in the SPARQL syntax).

3 The RECAP Approach

We see an explanation as a concise representation of the relatedness between entities in terms of edges (carrying a semantic meaning via RDF predicates) and other entities. As graphs are a natural and flexible way to represent and visualize information about interlinked entities in a variety of scenarios, we represent explanations as graphs.

Definition 2 (Explanation). Given a knowledge base $K = \langle G, O, A \rangle$ and a pair of entities (w_s, w_t) where $w_s, w_t \in G$, an explanation is a tuple of the form $E = (w_s, w_t, G_e)$, where $w_s, w_t \in G_e$, $G_e \subseteq G$, and G_e is connected.

The above definition is very general; it only states that two entities are connected via nodes and edges in a graph G_e, which is a subgraph of the knowledge graph G and has an arbitrary structure. The challenging aspect is how to uncover the structure of G_e by accessing G only via queries against the endpoint A. To tackle this challenge we shall characterize the desired properties of G_e. Consider the explanation shown in Fig. 4 (a); G_e contains two types of nodes: nodes such as n_1, n_3, n_4 that do belong to some path between w_s and w_t and other nodes such as n_2 that do not.

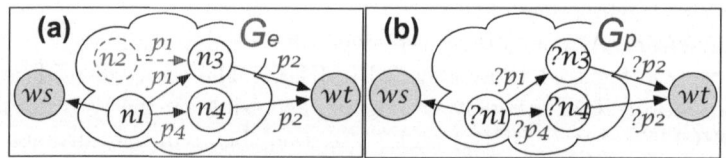

Fig. 4. An explanation (a) and a pattern graph (b).

Although the edge (n_2, p_1, n_3) can contribute to better characterize n_3, it is in a sense non-necessary as it does not directly contribute to explain how w_s and w_t are related. Hence, we introduce the notion of necessary edge.

Definition 3 (Necessary Edge). An edge $(n_i, p_k, n_j) \in G$ is necessary for an explanation $E = (w_s, w_t, G_e)$ if it is in a simple path (no node repetitions) between w_s and w_t.

The necessary edge property enables to refine the notion of explanation into that of minimal explanation.

Definition 4 (Minimal Explanation). Given $K=\langle G, O, A \rangle$ and a pair of entities (w_s, w_t) where $w_s, w_t \in G$, a minimal explanation is an explanation $E=(w_s, w_t, G_e)$ where G_e is obtained as the merge of all simple paths between w_s and w_t.

Minimal explanations enable to focus only on nodes and edges that are in some path between w_s and w_t thus preserving connectivity information only. The challenge is now how to retrieve minimal explanations.

Consider the explanation shown in Fig. 4 (a) (ignoring the dashed node and edge). G_e could be retrieved by matching the pattern graph G_p in Fig. 4 (b) (nodes and edges are query variables) against G. If the structure of G_p were available, one could find G_e. Unfortunately such structure, that is, the right way of joining query variables representing nodes and edges in G_p is unknown before knowing G_e. As the building blocks of minimal explanations are paths between w_s and w_t, finding these paths is crucial.

Generally speaking, paths between entities can have an arbitrary length; in practice it has been shown that for KGs like Facebook the average distance between entities is bound by a value $k \leq 5$ [21]. Considering paths of length k is also in line with the goal of providing explanations of manageable size that can be visualized/interpreted by users. Finally, related approaches like Explass [2] and REX [4] also considered bounded-length paths. Fig. 5 summarizes the explanation algorithm.

Algorithm 1: Building Relatedness Explanations

    Input: A pair (w_s, w_t) of entities, an integer k, the address of a query endpoint A
    Output: A graph G_e representing an explanation

(1) *Find paths*: we describe in Section 3.1 an approach based on SPARQL queries against A to retrieve paths between w_s and w_t of length k.

(2) *Rank paths*: We describe in Section 3.2 different mechanisms to rank paths by considering informativeness and diversity.

(3) *Select and merge top-m paths:* we discuss in Section 3.3 different ways of selecting ranked paths to build an explanation.

Fig. 5. An overview of the relatedness explanation algorithm.

3.1 Finding Paths Between Entities

We now describe the structure of queries used to retrieve paths via the endpoint A.

Definition 5 (*k*-**connectivity Pattern**). Given $K=\langle G,O,A\rangle$, a pair of entities (w_s, w_t) where $w_s, w_t \in G$ and an integer k, a k-connectivity pattern is a tuple $\Pi=\langle w_s, w_t, \mathcal{Q}, k\rangle$ where $\mathcal{Q}$ is a set of SPARQL queries composed by joining k triple patterns.

Note that SPARQL 1.1 supports property paths (PPs) [7], that is, a way for discovering routes between nodes in an RDF graph. However, since variables *cannot* be used as part of the path specification itself, PPs are not suitable for our purpose; we need information about all path elements (i.e., nodes and edges) to build explanations.

Example 6 (**Example of *k*-connectivity Pattern**). The 2-connectivity pattern between F. Lang (:FL) and T. von Harbou (:TvH) contains the following set of queries $\mathcal{Q}$:

```
SELECT DISTINCT * WHERE{:FL ?p1 ?n1. ?n1 ?p2 :TvH}
SELECT DISTINCT * WHERE{:FL ?p1 ?n1. :TvH ?p2 ?n1}
SELECT DISTINCT * WHERE{?n1 ?p1 :FL. :TvH ?p2 ?n1}
SELECT DISTINCT * WHERE{?n1 ?p1 :FL. ?n1 ?p2 :TvH}
```

Definition 7 (**Path**). Given $K=\langle G,O,A\rangle$ and a k-connectivity pattern $\Pi=\langle w_s, w_t, \mathcal{Q}, k\rangle$, a path π is a set of edges: $\pi(w_s, w_t)=w_s \overset{p_1}{-} n_1 \overset{p_2}{-} n_2 \overset{p_3}{-} n_3..n_q \overset{p_k}{-} w_t$, $n_i \in G \; \forall i \in [1,q]$, $p_j \in G \; \forall j \in [1,k]$ and $- \in \{\leftarrow, \rightarrow\}$.

3.2 Ranking Paths

The number of paths connecting two entities w_s and w_t can be large. Considering the merge of all paths, as done in minimal explanations (see Definition 4), can be an obstacle toward concise explanations. Therefore, we introduce different criteria to rank paths, a subset of which (e.g., top-m) can be merged to form an explanation.

Ranking By Path Informativeness
The first approach to estimate the informativeness of a path connecting a pair of entities $(w_s, w_t) \in G$ leverages the informativeness of its constituent RDF predicates [18].

Definition 8 (**Predicate Frequency Inverse Triple Frequency**). Given a knowledge graph $G=\langle V,\mathcal{E}\rangle$, an entity $w \in G$ and a predicate p appearing in some triple involving w, the incoming $\mathtt{pf}_i^w(p)$ and outgoing $\mathtt{pf}_o^w(p)$ predicate frequency are shown in equation (1) and equation (2), respectively. The Inverse Triple Frequency of p ($\mathtt{itf}(p)$) and the $\mathtt{pfitf}$ are shown in equation (3) and equation (4), respectively.

$$\mathtt{pf}_i^w(p,G) = \frac{|\mathcal{E}_i(w)|_{\pi(p)}}{|\mathcal{E}_i(w)|} \quad (1) \qquad \mathtt{pf}_o^w(p,G) = \frac{|\mathcal{E}_o(w)|_{\pi(p)}}{|\mathcal{E}_o(w)|} \quad (2)$$

$$\mathtt{itf}(p,G) = log\frac{|\mathcal{E}|}{|\mathcal{E}|_{\pi(p)}} \quad (3) \qquad \mathtt{pfitf}_x(p,G) = \mathtt{pf}_x \times \mathtt{itf} \quad (4)$$

where $|\mathcal{E}_i(w)|_{\pi(p)}$ (resp., $|\mathcal{E}_o(w)|_{\pi(p)}$) is the number of triples in G where the predicate p is incoming (resp., outgoing) in w, $|\mathcal{E}_i(w)|$ (resp., $|\mathcal{E}_o(w)|$) is the

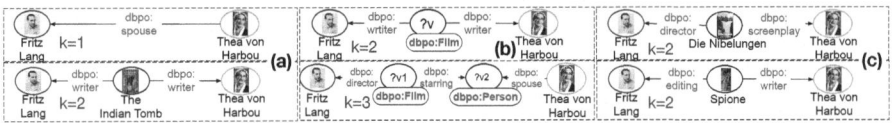

Fig. 6. Ranking: (a) *most* informative paths; (b) *most* informative patterns; (c) most *diverse* paths.

total number of incoming (resp., outgoing) triples including w. $|\mathcal{E}|_{\pi(p)}$ is the number of triples including p. In equation (4), $\texttt{pfitf}_x(p, G)$ can use $\texttt{pf}_i^w(p, G)$ or $\texttt{pf}_o^w(p, G)$.

Definition 9 (Path Informativeness). Let $\pi(w_s, w_t) = w_s \xrightarrow{p} w_t$ be a path between w_s and w_t in G of length $k=1$. The informativeness of π is defined as:

$$I(\pi, G) = [\texttt{pfitf}_o^{w_s}(p, G) + \texttt{pfitf}_i^{w_t}(p, G)]/2 \tag{5}$$

The informativeness of the path $\pi(w_s, w_t) = w_s \xleftarrow{p} w_t$ can be obtained by considering p as an incoming edge to w_s. For paths having length $k > 1$, we have:

$$I(\pi, G) = \frac{I(\pi(w_s, w_1), G) + \dots + I(\pi(w_k, w_t), G)}{k} \tag{6}$$

Ranking by Pattern Informativeness

We now introduce informativeness based on path patterns. A path pattern generalizes a path by replacing nodes with variables.

Definition 10 (Path Pattern). Given a path $\pi(w_s, w_t) = w_s \overset{p_1}{-} n_1 \overset{p_2}{-} n_2 .. n_q \overset{p_q}{-} w_t$, a path pattern is an expression of the form $\overline{\pi}(w_s, w_t) = w_s \overset{p_1}{-} ?v_1 \overset{p_2}{-} ?v_2 .. ?v_q \overset{p_q}{-} w_t$, where $?v_i$ $i \in \{1, 2, ...q\}$ are variables and $q \leq k$.

As an example, the path in the bottom-part of Fig. 6 (a) is abstracted in the pattern in the top-part of Fig. 6 (b). The usage of variables in place of intermediate entities enables to represent in a more concise way information about a *set of paths*. The pattern in the top-part of Fig. 6 (b) enables to capture the fact that F. Lang and T. von Harbou have co-written 11 movies (bindings of the variable ?v) according to DBpedia. Information in the ontology O (when available) can help to more precisely characterize the nature of intermediate entities by considering their $\texttt{rdf:type}$ (Fig. 6 (b)). RECAP includes a pattern-based exploration of the connectivity between w_s and w_t along with the possibility to generate explanations including all paths matching a pattern (see Fig. 3 (a)).

Definition 11 (Path pattern informativeness). Let $P_{\overline{\pi}}$ be the set of patterns obtained from a set of paths P_π. The informativeness of a path pattern $\overline{\pi} \in P_{\overline{\pi}}$ is:

$$I(\overline{\pi}, G) = log \frac{|P_{\overline{\pi}}|}{|(\overline{\pi}, G)|} \tag{7}$$

where $\mid P_{\overline{\pi}} \mid$ is the number of patterns and $\mid (\overline{\pi}, G) \mid$ is the number of paths sharing $\overline{\pi}$ in G.

Ranking By Path Diversity

The most informative paths of length $k=2$ between F. Lang and T. von Harbour often include predicates related to the fact that they have co-written movies (e.g., The Indian Tomb and Metropolis); this will potentially discard other predicates appearing in paths with low informativeness. To cope with this aspect, we introduce path diversity.

Definition 12 (Path Diversity). Given a source entity $w_s \in G$, a target entity $w_t \in G$ and two paths $\pi_1(w_s, w_t)$ and $\pi_2(w_s, w_t)$ we define path diversity as:

$$\delta(\pi_1, \pi_2) = \frac{|\texttt{Labels}(\pi_1) \cap \texttt{Labels}(\pi_2)|}{|\texttt{Labels}(\pi_1) \cup \texttt{Labels}(\pi_2)|} \tag{8}$$

where $\texttt{Labels}(\pi)$ denotes the set of labels (RDF predicates) in a path. Fig. 6 (c) shows the two most diverse paths at distance 2 between F. Lang and T. von Harbou. As it can be observed, the predicate `dbpo:screenplay` is included; such predicate is never present in the top-10 most informative paths.

3.3 Selecting and Merging Paths

The last step of the explanation algorithm concerns path selection. Table 2 describes different strategies that given a value m, select a subset (but $E^{\cup}$) of paths (patterns) according to one of the three approaches described in Section 3.2. Moreover, two strategies combine path (pattern) informativeness and diversity. The strategy in the last line of Table 2 does not merge paths and is used by RECAP to enable pattern-based explorations of the relatedness between w_s and w_t. We discuss an evaluation of the different strategies in Section 4.

Table 2. Path selection/merging strategies.

Symbol	Meaning
$E^{\cup}$	Merge all of paths
E_m^{π}	Merge the *top-m* most informative paths
$E_m^{\overline{\pi}}$	Merge paths belonging to the *top-m* most informative path *patterns*
E^{δ}	Merge paths whose value of diversity falls in $[(max-r),max]$ where max is the max diversity and r is a % value.
$E^{\pi,\delta}$	Merge the results of E_m^{π} and E^{δ}
$E^{\overline{\pi},\delta}$	Merge the results of $E_m^{\overline{\pi}}$ and E^{δ}
$\mathcal{P}$	Set of all paths (no merge)

3.4   Querying KGs by Example

We now describe the second building block of our framework, that is, an algorithm (shown in Fig.7) to query KGs by giving a pair of entities as input. In what follows we outline the steps, but (1), of Algorithm 2 after introducing explanation patterns.

Algorithm 2: Knowledge Graph Querying

> **Input:** A pair (w_s, w_t) of entities, an integer k, the address of a query endpoint A
>
> **Output:** A set of ranked (pairs of) entities
>
> **(1)** *Find an explanation* $E=(w_s, w_t, G_e)$ between w_s and w_t by using Algorithm 1.
>
> **(2)** *Build* the entity query pattern Q_e.
>
> **(3)** Query the KG with Q_e (via A) and get a set of (pairs of) entities.
>
> **(4)** Rank the answers to Q_e.

Fig. 7. An overview of the query answering algorithm.

Definition 13 (Explanation   Pattern).   Given   an   explanation $E=$ $\langle w_s, w_t, G_e \rangle$, an explanation pattern is a tuple $\overline{E}=\langle ?w_s, ?w_t, G_e^v \rangle$ where $G_e^v=\{\mathrm{TP}_1, \mathrm{TP}_2, ..., \mathrm{TP}_k\}$ is a query graph and $\mathrm{TP}_i=(\mathcal{U} \cup \mathcal{L} \cup \mathcal{V}) \times \mathcal{U} \times (\mathcal{U} \cup \mathcal{L} \cup \mathcal{V}), 1 < i < k$, is a triple pattern not containing variables in predicate position. Moreover, for $i > 1$ $|\mathrm{var}(\mathrm{TP}_i) \cap \mathrm{var}(\mathrm{TP}_{i-1})| = 1$.

In the above definition, G_e^v is the query graph obtained from G_e by replacing *all nodes* into an explanation with query variables. Basically, an explanation pattern generalizes the structure of an explanation by keeping edge labels only. Explanation patterns are used to generate entity query patterns.

Definition 14 (Entity Query Pattern). An entity query pattern is a SPARQL query of the form: SELECT DISTINCT ?ws ?wt WHERE{TP1. TP2. TPk.}

In the above definition, TPi, $i \in [1, k]$ are triple patterns in G_e^v and ?ws and ?wt are variables used in lieu of the entities in input. Query patterns are *automatically derived*; our algorithm neither requires familiarity with SPARQL nor with the underlying data/schema. The evaluation of a query pattern returns a set of pairs of entities.

Ranking of Results

Our approach for querying KG learns an entity query pattern Q_e from a relatedness explanation. Since the evaluation of Q_e can return a large number of results, our algorithm includes a ranking component. The problem of ranking results of SPARQL queries has been already studied (e.g., [1,14]) and is not the main purpose of the present paper.

Inspired by the Google KG, we consider a simple result ranking mechanism based on the popularity of entities; specifically, we leverage the PageRank [17] algorithm. Given a pair of entities (w_1, w_2) returned when evaluating Q_e (obtained from step (3) Algorithm 2), we estimate their popularity as $(PR(w_1) + PR(w_2))/2$, where $PR(w_i)$ is the PageRank value of the entity i. We leave as a future work the investigation of more sophisticated result-ranking mechanisms.

4   Implementation and Evaluation

We have implemented our ideas in the RECAP tool, which uses JavaFX[4] for the GUI and the Jena[5] framework to handle RDF data and SPARQL queries.

4.1   Evaluating the Explanation Generation Component

We start by discussing the evaluation of the explanation component of RECAP.

Experimental setting. We considered two KGs: DBpedia (DB)[6] and Freebase[7] (FB). We adopt the dataset of 26 pairs used to evaluate Explass [2] and set k≤4 as done in Explass. We use as reference graph for the computation of informativeness scores (see Def. 8 and Def. 11) the graph obtained by merging all paths. Experiments have been performed on a MacBook Pro with a 2.8 GHz i7 CPU and 16GBs RAM.

Experiment 1: Performance Evaluation: we investigate the performance of RECAP for *increasing values* of k[8] in terms of: (i) *obtaining paths*; (ii) *computing explanations*. Results that follow are the average of 5 runs. Fig. 8 (a) and (b) show the running times. Clearly, the higher k the higher the running time for path retrieval. The multi-thread implementation of RECAP allows to keep the time for finding paths on average around 6.4 secs for DB and 12 secs for FB when $k \leq 4$. When executing the queries *sequentially* (results are not reported for sake of space) the running times can be up to 30 times higher. We observed in another experiment on DB (not reported for sake of space) that local data reduces the running times by ~60% on average. However, this has the disadvantage that both a local processing infrastructure and local data are required.

Running times on DB for generating the different types of explanations described in lines 1-4 of Table 2 are shown in Figs. 9 (a). We report results on DB as this KG has been used in the (qualitative) comparison of RECAP with related approaches (see Section 4.1). Nevertheless, we report results on the combination DB-FB in Fig. 9 (b).

Generally speaking, $E^\cup$ explanations can be generated very fast; here, no path ranking/filtering is performed. However, $E^\cup$ can be very big, which makes

---

[4] http://docs.oracle.com/javafx/
[5] https://jena.apache.org/
[6] http://dbpedia.org/snorql
[7] http://lod.openlinksw.com/sparql
[8] In particular, for each k, all paths of length $\leq k$ are generated

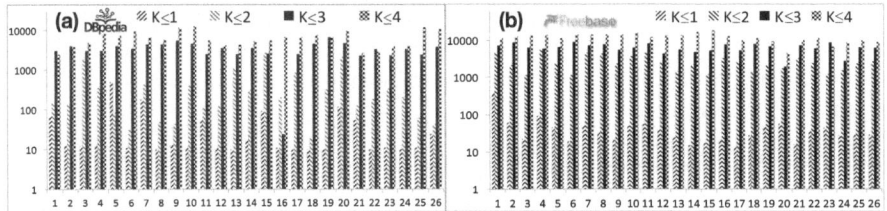

Fig. 8. Path retrieval in DB (a) and FB (b). Y-axis: time(ms) in log-scale; X-axis: entity pair.

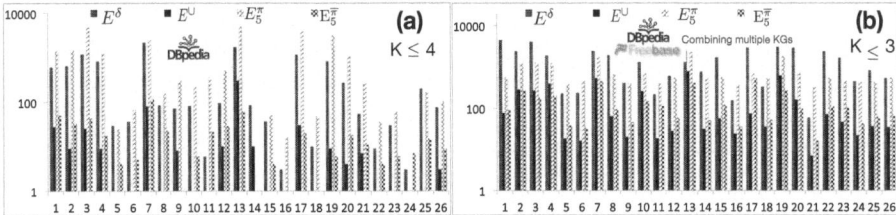

Fig. 9. Explanations in DB (a) and DB/FB (b). Y-axis: time(ms) in log-scale; X-axis: entity pair.

the interpretation by users difficult, as we will discuss in Experiment 2. E^δ explanations that use diversity (we considered $r=25\%$) are more expensive as they require the computation of distances between paths, for which RECAP leverages a multi-thread approach. Explanations based on path informativeness E_m^π (we considered $m=5$) require to compute pfitf scores; RECAP computes these scores in parallel and using the merge of all paths as reference graph thus not performing any remote query. Explanations based on pattern informativeness $E_m^{\overline{\pi}}$ (we considered $m=5$) are less expensive since they do not analyze the informativeness of all edges in a path. The most expensive explanations (not reported here for sake of space) are those combining path/pattern informativeness and diversity requiring $\sim$6 secs for $k\leq4$. When compared to related system (see Section 4.1), RECAP has been judged the fastest system in the overall task of generating different types of relatedness explanation. In terms of size (results not reported for sake of space), $E^\cup$ are the biggest one; their size can include up to 4000 paths ($k\leq4$) for pair 12 (C. Bale, C. Nolan) in FB.

Explanations of type E_5^π are smaller; the typical size is $\sim$8 nodes and $\sim$7 edges. $E_5^{\overline{\pi}}$ have variable size as it depends on the number of paths for each of the top-5 most informative patterns. In general these are bigger than E_5^π explanations ($\sim$15 nodes and $\sim$12 edges). Note that $E_5^{\overline{\pi}}$ explanations enable to focus on specific aspects as they include all the instantiations of each of the top-5 most informative path patterns. The sizes of E^δ are in the same order of magnitude as $E_5^{\overline{\pi}}$; however E^δ explanations guarantee to also include rare edges potentially discarded by path or pattern informativeness. The typical size of an explanation combining (top-5) path/pattern informativeness and diversity (r=25%) is ~20 nodes and ~15 edges. The possibility, featured by RECAP, to decide the amount of information to be included into an explanation is crucial toward understanding relatedness.

Experiment 2: Interpreting Explanations: This experiment aims at: *(i)* investigating whether RECAP *provides useful explanations to the user*; *(ii)* comparing RECAP against two related systems online available[9], that is, Explass [2][10] and RelFinder [9][11]. We used DB for the comparison as Explass and RelFinder only work on this KG.

Setting. Twenty participants were assigned each six random pairs among the 26 entity pairs. They were shown how the three systems work and asked to use each system (with no other support) in order to understand the relatedness between entities in a pair. Following the methodology in [2] participants were given a set of six questions; the response to each question was given with an agreement value from 1 (min) to 5 (max). Q6 was not considered in [2]; we included it to understand how users perceive the performance of the systems in terms of running time. Results are reported in Table 3.

Table 3. Questions/responses: means (standard deviation).

Question	RECAP	RelFinder	Explass
Q1: Information overview	4.55(0.65)	3.05(0.77)	3.82(0.75)
Q2: Easiness in finding information	4.45(0.55)	4.05(0.63)	3.85(0.67)
Q3: Easiness in comparing/synthesizing info	4.62(0.62)	3.10(0.82)	4.06(0.61)
Q4: Comprehensive support	4.81(0.73)	3.42(0.77)	4.15(0.79)
Q5: Sufficient support to the task	4.67(0.81)	3.28(0.86)	4.23(0.83
Q6: Running time	4.82(0.48)	4.12(0.72)	3.18(0.52)

According to questions Q1-Q5, users perceived RECAP and Explass as better supports to the explanation task. Users reported that RelFinder does not allow the flexible creation of explanation (e.g., by grouping paths into patterns), which makes it hard to control the amount of information shown. In general, RECAP was judged to be a more comprehensive solution; it provides both a graph-based and pattern-based exploration of results and several ways of controlling the amount of information to be shown. While RECAP and RelFinder quickly provide information immediately after retrieving paths, Explass requires a much longer time. On Q6 Explass was judged to be the less compelling system. RECAP was judged higher than the other two systems in all questions via LSD post-hoc tests ($p < 0.05$). The inter-annotator agreement was of 0.85.

Combining multiple KGs. We tested RECAP on the *combination* of DB and FB (see Fig. 9 (d)). Starting from DB, for the source/target entities we looked at

---

[9] REX [4] is not available for public usage

[10] http://ws.nju.edu.cn/explass/

[11] http://www.visualdataweb.org/relfinder/relfinder.php

`owl:sameAs` links to the corresponding FB entities. We then merged the set of paths from each KG by using `owl:sameAs` links. Users (∼75%) perceived the combination of multiple KGs as very useful toward more comprehensive explanations. This is especially true when KGs cover the same domain with different levels of detail (FB was judged more comprehensive than DB). The combination also produces graphs of bigger size. Indeed, the functionality of RECAP allowing to filter information to be included into an explanation was judged very useful (participants thought $E^{\cup}$ were too big when k≥ 3).

4.2   Evaluating the Querying Component

We now discuss the evaluation of the querying component of RECAP.

Experimental setting. We used the dataset of 18 pairs defined by Jayaram et al. [11] and considered DBpedia as KG. In order to rank query results, we compute PageRank values for the latest version of DBpedia and stored them in a local Lucene[12] index.

Table 4. Accuracy of RECAP (m=10).   **Table 5.** Accuracy of RECAP (m=15).

Pair	P@m	nDCG	Pair	P@m	nDCG	Pair	P@m	nDCG	Pair	P@m	nDCG
P_1	0.91	0.94	P_{10}	0.87	0.91	P_1	0.78	0.82	P_{10}	0.81	0.83
P_2	0.82	0.92	P_{11}	0.75	0.78	P_2	0.78	0.79	P_{11}	0.72	0.74
P_3	0.73	0.87	P_{12}	0.72	0.78	P_3	0.71	0.72	P_{12}	0.65	0.71
P_4	0.67	0.72	P_{13}	0.81	0.89	P_4	0.62	0.68	P_{13}	0.71	0.74
P_5	0.74	0.83	P_{14}	0.82	0.85	P_5	0.68	0.73	P_{14}	0.68	0.71
P_6	0.82	0.85	P_{15}	0.84	0.86	P_6	0.64	0.72	P_{15}	0.70	0.71
P_7	0.72	0.81	P_{16}	0.78	0.84	P_7	0.62	0.71	P_{16}	0.68	0.72
P_8	0.69	0.77	P_{17}	0.62	0.72	P_8	0.61	0.68	P_{17}	0.62	0.67
P_9	0.81	0.85	P_{18}	0.79	0.82	P_9	0.78	0.81	P_{18}	0.67	0.74

Evaluation Metrics. The aim of this experiment is to measure how precise are the results returned by RECAP as compared to a gold-standard. We measure the accuracy on a query by considering: **(i)** Precision-at-m (P@m): the percentage of the top-m results in the ground truth; **(ii)** Normalized Discounted Cumulative Gain (nDCG): the cumulative gain of the top-m results is $DCGm=rel_1+\sum_{1=2}^{m}\frac{rel_i}{log_2(i)}$; it penalizes the results if the ground truth result is ranked low. DCG_m is normalized by $IDCG_m$, the cumulative gain for an ideal ranking of the top-m results. Thus $nDCGm=\frac{DCG_m}{IDCG_m}$.

We report results for m=10 (in Table 4) and m=15 (in Table 5) that consider top-10 and top-15 entity pairs, respectively. We use E_{10}^{π} (top-10 most informative paths) explanations, at step (1) of Algorithm 2, to generate entity query patterns.

As it can be observed, the usage of PageRank scores, as a mechanism to weight the importance of query results, brings acceptable performance. In the

---

[12] https://lucene.apache.org/

majority of the 18 pairs, the P@10 score is above 0.75. In some cases like P_1 (i.e., Nike, Tiger Woods) RECAP was able to identify almost all the other entities (in the gold standard), among which M. Jordan, and K. Bryant (also sponsored by Nike). When the value of m increases performance decreases. However, usually providing top-10 results[13] is an acceptable compromise. Note that the nDCG is in most of the cases above 0.7; in this measure, the DCG emphasizes pairs of entities that appear early in the set of results. We leave as a future work the investigation of more sophisticated ranking mechanisms.

In terms of running time, the overhead introduced (besides explanation generation) by Algorithm 2 consists in the access to the Lucene index to retrieve PageRank scores and the computation of their average value. Typically, the overall running time for path finding, explanation generation and result ranking is ~10 secs.

5   Concluding Remarks and Future Work

We have introduced a framework to generate different types of relatedness explanations, possibly including information from multiple KGs. Our work is motived by the SENSE4US FP7 project, where there is the need to find topic connectivity information.

We have faced another important problem: querying KGs by using entities as input. As of today, either KGs provide limited querying capabilities (e.g., by accepting one entity as input) or require familiarity with languages such as SPARQL besides the underlying schema/data. We have shown how the usage of the relatedness explanation between a pair of entities can help in learning SPARQL queries to find other pairs of related entities. We plan to investigate optimization mechanisms to reduce the running time for path finding. One approach could be to leverage the ontology O to generate candidate queries according to paths between entities at the schema level, rank these queries, and check the most promising.

References

1. Anyanwu, K., Maduko, A., Sheth, A.: SemRank: ranking complex relationship search results on the semantic web. In: WWW, pp. 117–127 (2005)
2. Cheng, G., Zhang, Y., Qu, Y.: Explass: exploring associations between entities via top-k ontological patterns and facets. In: Mika, p, et al. (eds.) ISWC 2014, Part II. LNCS, vol. 8797, pp. 422–437. Springer, Heidelberg (2014)
3. Faloutsos, C., McCurley, K.S., Tomkins, A.: Fast discovery of connection subgraphs. In: SIGKDD, pp. 118–127. ACM (2004)
4. Fang, L., Sarma, A.D., Yu, C., Bohannon, P.: REX: explaining relationships between entity pairs. VLDB 5(3), 241–252 (2011)
5. Fionda, V., Gutierrez, C., Pirrò, G.: Knowledge maps of web graphs. In: KR (2014)

---

[13] Search engines usually provide top-10 results per page.

6. Fionda, V., Pirrò, G., Gutierrez, C.: NautiLOD: A Formal Language for the Web of Data Graph. ACM Transactions on the Web (TWEB) **9**(1) (2015)
7. Harris, S., Seaborne, A.: SPARQL 1.1 Query Language W3C Recommendation (2013)
8. Heath, T., Bizer, C.: Linked Data: Evolving the Web into a Global Data Space, 1st edn. Morgan & Claypool (2011)
9. Heim, P., Lohmann, S., Stegemann, T.: Interactive relationship discovery via the semantic web. In: Aroyo, L., Antoniou, G., Hyvönen, E., ten Teije, A., Stuckenschmidt, H., Cabral, L., Tudorache, T. (eds.) ESWC 2010, Part I. LNCS, vol. 6088, pp. 303–317. Springer, Heidelberg (2010)
10. Jagadish, H., Chapman, A., Elkiss, A., Jayapandian, M., Li, Y., Nandi, A., Yu, C.: Making database systems usable. In: Int. Conf. on Management of Data, pp. 13–24. ACM (2007)
11. Jayaram, N., Gupta, M., Khan, A., Li, C., Yan, X., Elmasri, R.: GQBE: querying knowledge graphs by example entity tuples. In: ICDE, pp. 1250–1253. IEEE (2014)
12. Kasneci, G., Elbassuoni, S., Weikum, G.: Ming: mining informative entity relationship subgraphs. In: CIKM, pp. 1653–1656. ACM (2009)
13. Luo, G., Tang, C., Tian, Y.-L.: Answering relationship queries on the web. In: WWW, pp. 561–570. ACM (2007)
14. Magliacane, S., Bozzon, A., Della Valle, E.: Efficient execution of top-K SPARQL queries. In: Cudré-Mauroux, p, et al. (eds.) ISWC 2012, Part I. LNCS, vol. 7649, pp. 344–360. Springer, Heidelberg (2012)
15. Mendes, P.N., Kapanipathi, P., Cameron, D., Sheth, A.P.: Dynamic associative relationships on the linked open data web. In: Web Science Conference (2010)
16. Nakashole, N., Weikum, G., Suchanek, F.: Discovering and exploring relations on the web. VLDB **5**(12), 1982–1985 (2012)
17. Page, L., Brin, S., Motwani, R., Winograd, T.: The PageRank Citation Ranking: Bringing Order to the Web (1999)
18. Pirrò, G.: REWOrD: semantic relatedness in the web of data. In: 26th Conference on Artificial Intelligence (AAAI) (2012)
19. Ramakrishnan, C., Milnor, W.H., Perry, M., Sheth, A.P.: Discovering informative connection subgraphs in multi-relational graphs. SIGKDD Newsletter **7**(2), 56–63 (2005)
20. Sheth, A., Aleman-Meza, B., Arpinar, I.B., Bertram, C., Warke, Y., Ramakrishanan, C., Halaschek, C., Anyanwu, K., Avant, D., Arpinar, F.S., et al.: Semantic Association Identification and Knowledge Discovery for National Security Applications. Journal of Database Management **16**(1), 33–53 (2005)
21. Ugander, J., Karrer, B., Backstrom, L., Marlow, C.: The Anatomy of the Facebook Social Graph. arXiv preprint arXiv:1111.4503 (2011)

Type-Constrained Representation Learning in Knowledge Graphs

Denis Krompaß[1,2(✉)], Stephan Baier[1], and Volker Tresp[1,2]

[1] Siemens AG Corporate Technology, Munich, Germany
{Denis.Krompass,Volker.Tresp}@siemens.com
[2] Ludwig Maximilian University, 80538 Munich, Germany
Stephan.Baier@campus.lmu.de

Abstract. Large knowledge graphs increasingly add value to various applications that require machines to recognize and understand queries and their semantics, as in search or question answering systems. Latent variable models have increasingly gained attention for the statistical modeling of knowledge graphs, showing promising results in tasks related to knowledge graph completion and cleaning. Besides storing facts about the world, schema-based knowledge graphs are backed by rich semantic descriptions of entities and relation-types that allow machines to understand the notion of things and their semantic relationships. In this work, we study how type-constraints can generally support the statistical modeling with latent variable models. More precisely, we integrated prior knowledge in form of type-constraints in various state of the art latent variable approaches. Our experimental results show that prior knowledge on relation-types significantly improves these models up to 77% in link-prediction tasks. The achieved improvements are especially prominent when a low model complexity is enforced, a crucial requirement when these models are applied to very large datasets. Unfortunately, type-constraints are neither always available nor always complete e.g., they can become fuzzy when entities lack proper typing. We show that in these cases, it can be beneficial to apply a local closed-world assumption that approximates the semantics of relation-types based on observations made in the data.

Keywords: Knowledge graph · Representation learning · Latent variable models · Type-constraints · Local closed-world assumption · Link-prediction

1 Introduction

Knowledge graphs (KGs), i.e., graph-based knowledge-bases, have proven to be sources of valuable information that have become important for various applications like web-search or question answering. Whereas, KGs were initially driven by academic efforts which resulted in KGs like Freebase [4], DBpedia [3], Nell [6] or YAGO [9], more recently commercial applications have evolved; a significant

M. Arenas et al. (Eds.): ISWC 2015, Part I, LNCS 9366, pp. 640–655, 2015.
DOI: 10.1007/978-3-319-25007-6_37

commercial application is the Freebase powered Google Knowledge Graph that supports Google's web search and the smart assistant Google Now, or Microsoft's Satori that supports Bing and Cortana. A related activity is the linked open data initiative which interlinks data sources using the W3C Resource Description Framework (RDF) [13] and thus also generates a huge KG accessible via querying [2].

Even though these graphs have reached an impressive size, containing billions of facts about the world, they are not error-free and far from complete. In Freebase and DBpedia for example a vast amount of persons (71% in Freebase [8] and 66% in DBpedia) are missing a place of birth. In DBpedia 58% of the scientists do not have a fact that describes what they are known for. Supporting KG cleaning, completion and construction via machine learning is one of the core challenges. In this context, Representation Learning in form of latent variable methods has successfully been applied to KG data [5,7,10,19,20]. These models learn latent embeddings for entities and relation-types from the data that can then be used as representations of their semantics. It is highly desirable that these embeddings are meaningful in low dimensional latent spaces, because a higher dimensionality leads to a higher model complexities which can cause unacceptable runtime performances and high memory loads. Latent variable models have recently been exploited for generating priors for facts in the context of automatic graph-based knowledge-base construction [8]. It has also been shown that these models can be interpreted as a compressed probabilistic knowledge representation, which allows complex querying over all possible triples and their uncertainties, resulting in a probabilistically ranked list of query answers [11].

In addition to the stored facts, schema-based KGs also provide rich descriptions of the semantics of entities and relation-types such as class hierarchies of entities and type-constraints for relation-types which define the semantic role of relations. This curated prior knowledge on relation-types provides valuable information to machines, e.g. that the `marriedTo` relation-type should relate only instances of the class `Person`. In recent work [7,10], it has been shown that RESCAL, a much studied latent variable approach, benefits greatly from prior knowledge about the semantics of relation-types. In this work we will study the impact of prior knowledge about the semantics of relation-types in the state of the art representative latent variable models TransE [5], RESCAL [18] and the multiway neural network approach used in the Google Knowledge Vault project [8]. These models are very different in the way they model KGs, and therefore they are especially well suited for drawing conclusions on the general value of prior knowledge about relation-types for the statistical modeling of KGs with latent variable models.

Additionally, we address the issue that type-constraints can also suffer from incompleteness, e.g. `rdfs:domain` or `rdfs:range` concepts are absent in the schema or the entities miss proper typing even after materialization. Here, we study the local closed-world assumption as proposed in prior work [10] that approximates the semantics of relation-types based on observed triples. We provide empirical proof that this prior assumption on relation-types generally improves link-prediction quality in case proper type-constraints are absent.

This paper is structured as follows: In the next section we motivate our model selection and briefly review RESCAL, TransE and the multiway neural network approach of [8]. The integration of type-constraints and local closed-world assumptions into these models will be covered in Section 3. In Section 4, we will motivate and describe our experimental setup before we discuss our results in Section 5. We provide related work in Section 6 and conclude in Section 7.

2   Latent Variable Models for Knowledge Graph Modeling

In this work, we want to study the general value of prior knowledge about the semantics of relation-types for the statistical modeling of KGs with latent variable models. For this reason, we have to consider a representative set of latent variable models that covers the currently most promising research activities in this field. We selected RESCAL [18], TransE [5] and the multiway neural network approach pursued in the Google?s Knowledge Vault project [8] (denoted as mwNN) for a number of reasons:

- To the best of our knowledge, these latent variable models are the only ones which have been applied to large KGs with more than 1 million entities, thereby proving their scalability [5,7,8,10,19].
- All of these models have been published at well respected conferences and are the basis for the most recent research activities in the field of statistical modeling of KGs (see Section 6).
- These models are very diverse, meaning they are very different in the way they model KGs, thereby covering a wide range of possible ways a KG can be statistically modeled; the RESCAL tensor-factorization is a bilinear model, where the distance-based TransE models triples as linear translations and the mwNN exploits non-linear interactions of latent embeddings in its neural network layers.

2.1   Notation

In this work, $\underline{\mathbf{X}}$ will denote a three-way tensor, where $\mathbf{X}_k$ represents the k-th frontal slice of the tensor $\underline{\mathbf{X}}$. Further $\hat{\mathbf{X}}_k$ will denote the frontal-slice $\mathbf{X}_k$ where only subject entities (rows) and object entities (columns) are included that agree with the domain and range constraints of relation-type k. $\mathbf{X}$ or $\mathbf{A}$ denote matrices and $\mathbf{x}_i$ is the i-th column vector of $\mathbf{X}$. A single entry of $\underline{\mathbf{X}}$ will be denoted as $x_{i,j,k}$. Additionally we use $\mathbf{X}_{[\mathbf{z},:]}$ to illustrate the indexing of multiple rows from the matrix $\mathbf{X}$, where $\mathbf{z}$ is a vector of indices and ":" the colon operator, generally used when indexing arrays. Further (s,p,o) will denote a triple with subject entity s, object entity o and predicate relation-type p, where the entities s and o represent nodes in the KG that are linked by the predicate relation-type p. The entities belong to the set of all observed entities $\mathcal{E}$ in the data.

2.2   RESCAL

RESCAL [18] is a three-way tensor factorization method that has been shown to lead to very good results in various canonical relational learning tasks like link-prediction, entity resolution and collective classification [19]. In RESCAL, triples are represented in an adjacency tensor $\underline{\mathbf{X}}$ of shape $n \times n \times m$, where n is the amount of observed entities in the data and m is the amount of relation-types. Each of the m frontal slices $\mathbf{X}_k$ of $\underline{\mathbf{X}}$ represents an adjacency matrix for all entities in the dataset with respect to the k-th relation-type. Given an adjacency tensor $\underline{\mathbf{X}}$, RESCAL computes a rank d factorization, where each entity is represented via a d-dimensional vector that is stored in the factor matrix $\mathbf{A} \in \mathbb{R}^{n \times d}$ and each relation-type is represented via a frontal slice $\mathbf{R}_k \in \mathbb{R}^{d \times d}$ of the core tensor $\underline{\mathbf{R}}$ which encodes the asymmetric interactions between subject and object entities. The embeddings are learned by minimizing the regularized least-squares function

$$\mathcal{L}_{RESCAL} = \sum_k^m \|\mathbf{X}_k - \mathbf{A}\mathbf{R}_k\mathbf{A}^T\|_F^2 + \lambda_A \|\mathbf{A}\|_F^2 + \lambda_R \sum_k^m \|\mathbf{R}_k\|_F^2 , \qquad (1)$$

where $\lambda_A \geq 0$ and $\lambda_R \geq 0$ are hyper-parameters and $\|\cdot\|_F$ is the Frobenius norm. The cost function can be minimized via very efficient Alternating Least-Squares (ALS) that effectively exploits data sparsity [18] and closed-form solutions. During factorization, RESCAL finds a unique latent representation for each entity that is shared between all relation-types in the dataset.

RESCAL's confidence $\theta_{s,p,o}$ for a triple (s,p,o) is computed through reconstruction by the vector-matrix-vector product

$$\theta_{s,p,o} = \mathbf{a}_s^T \mathbf{R}_p \mathbf{a}_o \qquad (2)$$

from the latent representations of the subject and object entities $\mathbf{a}_s$ and $\mathbf{a}_o$, respectively and the latent representation of the predicate relation-type $\mathbf{R}_p$.

2.3   Translational Embeddings Model

TransE [5] is a distance-based model that models relationships of entities as translations in the embedding space. The approach assumes for a true fact that a relation-type specific translation function exists that is able to map (or translate) the latent vector representation of the subject entity to the latent representation the object entity. The fact confidence is expressed by the similarity of the translation of the subject embedding to the object embedding.

In case of TransE, the translation function is defined by a simple addition of the latent vector representations of the subject entity $\mathbf{a}_s$ and the predicate relation-type $\mathbf{r}_p$. The similarity of the translation and the object embedding is measured by the L_1 or L_2 distance. TransE's confidence $\theta_{s,p,o}$ in a triple (s,p,o) is derived by

$$\theta_{s,p,o} = -\delta(\mathbf{a}_s + \mathbf{r}_p, \mathbf{a}_o), \qquad (3)$$

where δ is the L_1 or the $L2$ distance and $\mathbf{a}_o$ the latent embedding for the object entity. The embeddings are learned by minimizing the max-margin-based ranking cost function

$$\mathcal{L}_{TransE} = \sum_{(s,p,o)\in T} \max\{0, \gamma + \theta_{s',p,o} - \theta_{s,p,o}\} + \max\{0, \gamma + \theta_{s,p,o'} - \theta_{s,p,o}\}$$
$$\text{with} \quad \{s', o'\} \in \mathcal{E} \tag{4}$$

on a set of observed training triples T through Stochastic Gradient Descent (SGD), where $\gamma > 0$. The "corrupted" entities s' and o' are drawn from the set of all observed entities $\mathcal{E}$ where the ranking loss function enforces that the confidence in the corrupted triples ($\theta_{s',p,o}$ or $\theta_{s,p,o'}$) is lower than in the true triple by a certain margin. During training, it is enforced that the latent embeddings of entities have an L_2 norm of one after each SGD iteration.

2.4   Knowledge Vault Neural Network

In the Google Knowledge Vault project [8] a multiway neural network (mwNN) for predicting prior probabilities for triples from existing KG data was proposed to support triple extraction from unstructured web documents. The confidence value $\theta_{s,p,o}$ for a target triple (s, p, o) is predicted by

$$\theta_{s,p,o} = \sigma(\beta^T \phi(\mathbf{W}[\mathbf{a}_s, \mathbf{r}_p, \mathbf{a}_o])), \tag{5}$$

where $\phi()$ is a nonlinear function like e.g. $tanh$, $\mathbf{a}_s$ and $\mathbf{a}_o$ describe the latent embeddings for the subject and object entities and $\mathbf{r}_p$ is the latent embedding vector for the predicate relation-type p. $[\mathbf{a}_s, \mathbf{r}_p, \mathbf{a}_o] \in \mathbb{R}^{3d\times 1}$ is a column vector that stacks the three embeddings on top of each other. $\mathbf{W}$ and β are neural network weights and $\sigma()$ denotes the logistic function. The model is trained by minimizing the Bernoulli cost-function

$$\mathcal{L}_{mwNN} = -\sum_{(s,p,o)\in T} \log \theta_{s,p,o} - \sum_{o'\in\mathcal{E}}^{c} \log(1 - \theta_{s,p,o'}) \tag{6}$$

through SGD, where c denotes the number of object-corrupted triples sampled under a local closed-world assumption as defined by [8]. Note that corrupted are treated as negative evidence in this model.

3   Prior Knowledge on Relation-Type Semantics

Generally, entities in KGs like DBpedia, Freebase or YAGO are assigned to one or multiple predefined classes (or types) that are organized in an often hierarchical ontology. These assignments represent for example the knowledge that the entity Albert Einstein is a person and therefore allow a semantic description of the entities contained in the KG. This organization of entities in semantically meaningful classes permits a semantic definition of relation-types. The RDF-Schema, which provides schema information for RDF, offers among others the concepts `rdfs:domain` and `rdfs:range` for this purpose. These concepts are used to represent type-constraints on relation-types by defining the classes or types of entities which they should relate, where the *domain* covers the subject entity classes and the *range* the object entity classes in a RDF-Triple. This can be interpreted as an explicit definition of the semantics of a relation, for example by defining that the relation-type `marriedTo` should only relate instances of the class `Person` with each other. Recently [7] and [10] showed independently that including knowledge about these domain and range constraints into RESCAL's ALS optimization scheme resulted in better latent representations of entities and relation-types that lead to a significantly improved link-prediction quality at a much lower model complexity (lower rank) when applied to KGs like DBpedia or Nell. The need of a less complex model significantly decreases model training-time especially for larger datasets.

In the following, we denote $\mathbf{domain}_k$ as the ordered indices of all entities that agree with the domain constraints of relation-type k. Accordingly, $\mathbf{range}_k$ denotes these indices for the range constraints of relation-type k.

3.1   Type-Constrained Alternating Least-Squares

In RESCAL, the integration of typed relations in the ALS optimization procedure is achieved by indexing only those latent embeddings of entities for each relation-type that agree with the `rdfs:domain` and `rdfs:range` constraints. In addition, only the subgraph (encoded by the sparse adjacency matrix $\hat{\mathbf{X}}_k$) that is defined with respect to the constraints is considered in the equation

$$\mathcal{L}_{RESCAL}^{TC} = \sum_k \|\hat{\mathbf{X}}_k - \mathbf{A}_{[\mathbf{domain}_k,:]}\mathbf{R}_k\mathbf{A}_{[\mathbf{range}_k,:]}^T\|_F^2$$
$$+\lambda_A\|\mathbf{A}\|_F^2 + \lambda_R \sum_k \|\mathbf{R}_k\|_F^2, \tag{7}$$

where $\mathbf{A}$ contains the latent embeddings for the entities and $\mathbf{R}_k$ the embedding for the relation-type k. For each relation-type k the latent embeddings matrix $\mathbf{A}$ is indexed by the corresponding domain and range constraints, thereby excluding all entities that disagree with the type-constraints. Note that if the adjacency matrix $\hat{\mathbf{X}}_k$ of the subgraph defined by relation-type k and its type-constraints has the shape $n_k \times m_k$, then $\mathbf{A}_{[\mathbf{domain}_k,:]}$ is of shape $n_k \times d$, and $\mathbf{A}_{[\mathbf{range}_k,:]}$ of shape $m_k \times d$ where d is the dimension of the latent embeddings (or rank of the factorization).

3.2   Type-Constrained Stochastic Gradient Descent

In contrast to RESCAL, TransE and mwNN are both optimized through mini-batch Stochastic Gradient Descent (SGD), where a small batch of randomly sampled triples is used in each iteration of the optimization to drive the model parameters to a local minimum. Generally, KG data does not explicitly contain negative evidence, i.e. false triples [1], and is generated in this algorithms through corruption of observed triples (see Section 2.3 and 2.4). In the original algorithms of TransE and mwNN the corruption of triples is not restricted and can therefore lead to the generation of triples that violate the semantics of relation-types. For integrating knowledge about type-constraints into the SGD optimization scheme of these models, we have to make sure that none of the corrupted triples violates the type-constraints of the corresponding relation-types. For TransE we update Equation 4 and get

$$\mathcal{L}^{TC}_{TransE} = \sum_{(s,p,o)\in T} \sum_{(s',p,o')\in T'} [\gamma + \theta_{s',p,o} - \theta_{s,p,o}]_+ + [\gamma + \theta_{s,p,o'} - \theta_{s,p,o}]_+$$

$$\text{with} \quad s' \in \mathcal{E}_{[\mathbf{domain}_p]} \subseteq \mathcal{E}, \ o' \in \mathcal{E}_{[\mathbf{range}_p]} \subseteq \mathcal{E}, \tag{8}$$

where, in difference to Equation 4, we enforce by $s' \in \mathcal{E}_{[\mathbf{domain}_p]} \subseteq \mathcal{E}$ that the subject entities are only corrupted through the subset of entities that belong to the domain and by $o' \in \mathcal{E}_{[\mathbf{range}_p]} \subseteq \mathcal{E}$ that the corrupted object entities are sampled from the subset of entities that belong to the range of predicate relation-type p. For mwNN we corrupt only the object entities through sampling from the subset of entities $o' \in \mathcal{E}_{[\mathbf{range}_p]} \subseteq \mathcal{E}$ that belong to the range of the predicate relation-type p and get accordingly

$$\mathcal{L}^{TC}_{mwNN} = -\sum_{(s,p,o)\in T} \log \theta_{s,p,o} - \sum_{o'\in \mathcal{E}_{[\mathbf{range}_p]}\subseteq \mathcal{E}}^{c} \log(1 - \theta_{s,p,o'}). \tag{9}$$

3.3 Local Closed-World Assumptions

Type-constraints as given by KGs tremendously reduce the possible worlds of the statistically modeled KGs, but like the rest of the data represented by the KG, they can also suffer from incompleteness and inconsistency of the data. Even after materialization, entities and relation-types might miss complete typing leading to fuzzy type-constraints. Increased fuzziness of proper typing can in turn lead to disagreements of true facts and present type-constraints in the KG. For relation-types where these kind of inconsistencies are quite frequent we cannot simply apply the given type-constraints without the risk of loosing true triples. On the other hand, if the domain and range constraints themselves are missing (e.g. in schema-less KGs) we might consider many triples that do not have any semantic meaning.

We argue that in these cases a local closed-world assumption (LCWA) can be applied which approximates the domain and range constraints of the targeted relation-type not on class level, but on instance level based solely on observed triples. Given all observed triples, under this LCWA the domain of a relation-type k consists of all entities that are related by the relation-type k as subject.

---

[1] There are of course undetected false triples included in graph which are assumed to be true.

The range is accordingly defined, but contains all the entities related as object by relation-type k. Of course, this approach can exclude entities from the domain or range constraints that agree with the type-constraints given by the RDFS-Schema concepts `rdfs:domain` and `rdfs:range`, thereby ignoring them during model training when exploiting the LCWA (only for the target relation-type). On the other hand, nothing is known about these entities (in object or subject role) with respect to the target relation-type and therefore treating them as missing can be a valid assumption. In case of the ALS optimized RESCAL we reduce the size and sparsity of the data by this approach, which has a positive effect on model training compared to the alternative, a closed-world assumption that considers all entities to be part of the domain and range of the target relation-type [10]. For the SGD optimized TransE and mwNN models also a positive effect on the learned factors is expected since the corruption of triples will be based on entities from which we can expect that they do not disagree to the semantics of the corresponding relation-type.

4   Experimental Setup

[2]As stated before, we explore in our experiments the importance of prior knowledge about the semantics of relation-types for latent variable models. We consider two settings. In the first setting, we assume that curated type-constraints extracted from the KG's schema are available. In the second setting, we explore the local closed-world assumption (see Section 3.3). Our experimental setup covers three important aspects which will enable us to make generalizing conclusions about the importance of such prior knowledge when applying latent variable models to KGs:

- We test various representative latent variable models that cover the diversity of these models in the domain. As motivated in the introduction of Section 2, we belief that RESCAL, TransE and mwNN are especially well suited for this task.
- We test these models at reasonable low complexity levels, meaning that we enforce low dimensional latent embeddings, which simulates their application to very large datasets where high dimensional embeddings are intractable. In [8] for example, a latent embedding length $d = 60$ (see Section 2.4) was used.
- We extracted diverse datasets from instances of the Linked-Open Data Cloud, namely Freebase, YAGO and DBpedia, because it is expected that the value of prior knowledge about relation-type semantics is also dependent on the particular dataset the models are applied to. From these KGs we constructed datasets that will be used as representatives for general purpose KGs that cover a wide range of relation-types from a diverse set of domains, domain focused KGs with a small amount of entity classes and relation-types and high quality KGs.

---

[2] Code and datasets will be available from http://www.dbs.ifi.lmu.de/~krompass/

Table 1. Datasets used in the experiments.

Dataset	Source	Entities	Relation-Types	Triples
DBpedia-Music	DBpedia 2014	321,950	15	981,383
Freebase-150k	Freebase RDF-Dump	151,146	285	1,047,844
YAGOc-195k	YAGO2-Core	195,639	32	1,343,684

In the remainder of this section we will give details on the extracted datasets and the evaluation, implementation and training of RESCAL, TransE and mwNN.

4.1 Datasets

Below, we describe how we extracted the different datasets from Freebase, DBpedia and YAGO. In Table 1 some details about the size of these datasets are given. In our experiments, the Freebase-150k dataset will simulate a general purpose KG, the DBpedia-Music dataset a domain specific KG and the YAGOc-195k dataset a high quality KG.

Freebase-150k. The Freebase KG includes triples extracted from Wikipedia Infoboxes, MusicBrainz [21], WordNet [15] and many more. From the current materialized Freebase RDF-dump[3], we extracted entity-types, type-constraints and all triples that involved entities (*Topics*) with more than 100 relations to other topics. Subsequently, we discarded the triples of relation-types with incomplete type-constraints or which occurred in less than 100 triples. Additionally, we discarded all triples that involved entities that are not an instance of any class covered by the remaining type-constraints. The entities involved in type-constraint violating triples were added to the subset of entities that agree with the type-constraints since we assumed that they only miss proper typing.

DBpedia-Music. For the DBpedia-Music datasets, we extracted triples and types from 15 pre-selected object-properties regarding the music domain of DBpedia [4]; musicalBand, musicalArtist, musicBy, musicSubgenre, derivative, stylisticOrigin, associatedBand, associatedMusicalArtist, recordedIn, musicFusionGenre, musicComposer, artist, bandMember, formerBandMember, genre, where genre has been extracted to include only those entities that were covered by the other object-properties to restrict it to musical genres. We extracted the type-constraints from the DBpedia OWL-Ontology and for entities that occurred less than two times we discarded all triples. In case types for entities or type-constraints were absent we assigned them to owl#Thing. Remaining disagreements between triples and type-constraints were resolved as in case of the Freebase-150k dataset.

---

[3] https://developers.google.com/freebase/data

[4] http://wiki.dbpedia.org/Downloads2014, canonicalized datasets: mapping-based-properties(cleaned), mapping-based-types and heuristics.

YAGOc-195k. YAGO (Yet Another Great Ontology) is an automatically generated high quality KG that combines the information richness of Wikipedia Infoboxes and its category system with the clean taxonomy of WordNet. We extracted entitiy types, type-constraints[5] and all triples that involved entities with more than 5 and relation-types that were involved in more than 100 relations from the YAGO-core dataset[6]. We only included entities that share the types used in the `rdfs:domain` and `rdfs:range` triples.

4.2 Evaluation Procedure

We evaluate RESCAL, TransE and mwNN on link prediction tasks, where we delete triples from the datasets and try to re-predict them without considering them during model training. For model training and evaluation we split the triples of the datasets into three sets, where 20% of the triples were taken as holdout set, 10% as validation set for hyper-parameter tuning and the remaining 70% served as training set[7]. In case of the validation and holdout set, we sampled 10 times as many negative triples for evaluation, where the negative triples were drawn such that they did not violate the given domain and range constraints of the KG. Also, the negative evidence of the holdout and validation set are not overlapping. In KG data, we are generally dealing with a strongly skewed ratio of observed and unobserved triples, through this sampling we try to mimic this effect to some extend since it is intractable to sample all unobserved triples. In case of the LCWA, the domain and range constraints are always derived from the training set. After deriving the best hyper-parameter settings for all models, we trained all models with these settings using both, the training and the validation set to predict the holdout set (20% of triples). We report the Area Under Precision Recall Curve (AUPRC) for all models. In addition, we provide the Area Under Receiver Operating Characteristic Curve (AUROC), because it is widely used in this problem even though it is not well suited for evaluation in these tasks due to the imbalance of (assumed) false and true triples.[8] The discussions and conclusions will be primarily based on the AUPRC results.

4.3 Implementation and Model Training Details

All models were implemented in Python using in part Theano [1]. For TransE we exploited the code provided by the authors [9] as a basis to implement a type-constraints supporting version of TransE, but we replaced large parts of the original code to allow a significantly faster training.[10] We made sure that our

---

[5] yagoSchema and yagoTransitiveType.

[6] http://www.mpi-inf.mpg.de/departments/databases-and-information-systems/research/yago-naga/yago/downloads/

[7] Additional 5% of the training set were used for early stopping.

[8] AUROC considers the false-positive rate which relies on the amount of true-negatives that is generally high in these kind of datasets resulting in misleadingly high scores.

[9] https://github.com/glorotxa/SME

[10] Mainly caused by the ranking function used for calculating the validation error but also the consideration of trivial zero gradients during the SGD-updates.

implementation achieved very similar results to the original model on a smaller dataset[11] (results not shown).

The mwNN was also implemented in Theano. Since there are not many details on model training in the corresponding work [8], we added elastic-net regularization combined with DropConnect [22] on the network weights and optimized the cost function using mini-batch adaptive gradient descent. We randomly initialized the weights by drawing from a zero mean normal distribution where we treat the standard deviation as an additional hyper-parameter. The corrupted triples were sampled with respect to the local closed-world assumption discussed in [8]. We fixed the amount of corrupted triples per training example to five.[12]

For RESCAL, we used the ALS implementation provided by the author[13] and our own implementation used in [10], but modified them such that they support a more scalable early stopping criteria based on a small validation set.

For hyper-parameter tuning, all models were trained for a maximum of 50 epochs and for the final evaluation on the holdout set for a maximum of 200 epochs. For all models, we sampled 5% of the training data and used the change in AUPRC on this subsample as early stopping criteria.

5   Experimental Results

In tables 2, 3 and 4 our experimental results for RESCAL, TransE and mwNN are shown. All of these tables have the same structure and compare different versions of exactly one of these methods on all three datasets. Table 2 for example shows the results for RESCAL and Table 4 the results of mwNN. The first column in these tables indicates the datasets the model was applied to (Freebase-150k, Dbpedia-Music or YAGOc-195) and the second column which kind of prior knowledge about the semantics of relation-types was exploited by the model. *None* denotes in this case the original model that does not consider any prior knowledge on relation-types, whereas *Type-Constraints* denotes that the model has exploited the curated domain and range constraints extracted from the KG's schema and *LCWA* that the model has exploited the Local Closed-World Assumption (Section 3.3) during model training. The last two columns show the AUPRC and AUROC scores for the various model versions on the different datasets. Each of these two columns contains three sub-columns that show the AUPRC and AUROC scores at different enforced latent embedding lengths: 10, 50 or 100.

5.1   Type-Constraints are Essential

The experimental results shown in Table 2, 3 and 4 give strong evidence that type-constraints as provided by the KG's schema are generally of great value for

---

[11] http://alchemy.cs.washington.edu/data/cora/

[12] We tried different amounts of corrupted triples and five seemed to give the most stable results across all datasets.

[13] https://github.com/mnick/scikit-tensor

Table 2. Comparison of AUPRC and AUROC result for RESCAL with and without exploiting prior knowledge about relations types (type-constraints or local closed-world assumption (LCWA)) on the Freebase, DBpedia and YAGO2 datasets. d is representative for the model complexity, denoting the enforced length of the latent embeddings (rank of the factorization).

RESCAL	Prior Knowledge on Semantics	AUPRC			AUROC		
		$d=10$	$d=50$	$d=100$	$d=10$	$d=50$	$d=100$
Freebase-150k	None	0.327	0.453	0.514	0.616	0.700	0.753
	Type-Constraints	0.521	0.630	0.654	0.804	0.863	0.877
	LCWA	**0.579**	**0.675**	**0.699**	**0.849**	**0.886**	**0.896**
DBpedia-Music	None	0.307	0.362	0.416	0.583	0.617	0.653
	Type-Constraints	0.413	0.490	0.545	0.656	0.732	0.755
	LCWA	**0.453**	**0.505**	**0.571**	**0.701**	**0.776**	**0.800**
YAGOc-195k	None	0.507	0.694	0.721	0.621	0.787	0.800
	Type-Constraints	**0.626**	**0.721**	**0.739**	0.785	0.820	0.833
	LCWA	0.567	0.672	0.680	**0.814**	**0.839**	**0.849**

the statistical modeling of KGs with latent variable models. For all datasets, this prior information lead to significant improvements in link-prediction quality for all models and settings in both, AUPRC and AUROC. For example, RESCAL's, AUPRC score on the Freebase-150k dataset gets improved from 0.327 to 0.521 at the lowest model complexity ($d = 10$) (Table 2). With higher model complexities the relative improvements decrease but stay significant (27% at $d = 100$ from 0.514 to 0.654). The benefit for RESCAL in considering type-constraints was expected due to prior works [7,10], but also the other models improve significantly when considering type-constraints.

For TransE, large improvements on the Freebase-150k and DBpedia-Music datasets can be observed (Table 3), where the AUPRC score increases e.g. for $d = 10$ from 0.548 to 0.699 in Freebase-150k and for $d = 100$ from 0.745 to 0.826 in DBpedia-Music. Also on the YAGOc-195k dataset the link-prediction quality improves from 0.793 to 0.843 with $d = 10$. Especially the multiway neural network approach (mwNN) seems to improve the most by considering type-constraints during the model training (Table 4). In case of the Freebase-150k dataset, it improves up to 77% in AUPRC for $d = 10$ from 0.437 to 0.775 and on the DBpedia-Music dataset from 0.436 to 0.509 with $d = 10$ and from 0.538 to 0.754 with $d = 100$ in AUPRC. In case of the YAGOc-195k dataset the link-prediction quality of mwNN also benefits to a large extent from the type-constraints.

Besides observing that the latent variable models are superior when exploiting type-constraints at a fixed latent embedding length d, it is also worth noticing that the biggest improvements are most often achieved at a very low model complexity ($d = 10$), which is especially interesting for the application of these models to large datasets. At this low complexity level the type-constraints supported models even outperform more complex counterparts that ignore type-constraints, e.g. on Freebase-150k mwNN reaches 0.512 AUPRC with an embedding length

Table 3. Comparison of AUPRC and AUROC result for TransE with and without exploiting prior knowledge about relations types (type-constraints or local closed-world assumption (LCWA)) on the Freebase, DBpedia and YAGO2 datasets. d is representative for the model complexity, denoting the enforced length of the latent embeddings.

TransE	Prior Knowledge on Semantics	AUPRC			AUROC		
		d=10	d=50	d=100	d=10	d=50	d=100
	None	0.548	0.715	0.743	0.886	0.890	0.892
Freebase-150k	Type-Constraints	**0.699**	0.797	0.808	**0.897**	0.918	0.907
	LCWA	0.671	**0.806**	**0.831**	0.894	**0.932**	**0.931**
	None	0.701	0.748	0.745	0.902	0.911	0.903
DBpedia-Music	Type-Constraints	**0.734**	0.783	0.826	**0.927**	0.937	0.942
	LCWA	0.719	**0.839**	**0.848**	0.910	**0.943**	**0.953**
	None	0.793	0.849	0.816	0.904	0.960	0.910
YAGOc-195	Type-Constraints	**0.843**	**0.896**	**0.896**	**0.962**	**0.972**	**0.974**
	LCWA	0.790	0.861	0.872	0.942	0.962	0.962

Table 4. Comparison of AUPRC and AUROC result for mwNN [8] with and without exploiting prior knowledge about relations types (type-constraints or local closed-world assumption (LCWA)) on the Freebase, DBpedia and YAGO2 datasets. d is representative for the model complexity, denoting the enforced length of the latent embeddings.

mwNN	Prior Knowledge on Semantics	AUPRC			AUROC		
		d=10	d=50	d=100	d=10	d=50	d=100
	None	0.437	0.471	0.512	0.852	0.868	0.879
Freebase-150k	Type-Constraints	**0.775**	**0.815**	**0.837**	**0.956**	**0.962**	**0.967**
	LCWA	0.610	0.765	0.776	0.918	0.954	0.956
	None	0.436	0.509	0.538	0.836	0.864	0.865
DBpedia-Music	Type-Constraints	0.509	**0.745**	**0.754**	0.858	**0.908**	**0.913**
	LCWA	**0.673**	0.707	0.723	**0.876**	0.900	0.884
	None	0.600	0.684	0.655	0.949	0.949	0.957
YAGOc-195	Type-Constraints	**0.836**	**0.840**	**0.837**	**0.953**	**0.954**	**0.960**
	LCWA	0.714	0.836	0.833	0.926	0.935	0.943

of 100 but by considering type-constraints this models achieves 0.775 AUPRC with an embedding length of only 10.

In accordance to the AUPRC scores, the improvements of the less meaningful and generally high AUROC scores support the conclusion that type-constraints add value to the prediction quality of the models. It can be inferred from the corresponding scores that the improvements have a smaller scale, but are still significant.

5.2   Local Closed-World Assumption – Simple But Powerful

From Tables 2, 3 and 4, it can be observed that the LCWA leads to similar large improvements in link-prediction quality than the real type-constraints, especially at the lowest model complexities ($d = 10$). For example, by exploiting the LCWA

TransE improves from 0.715 to 0.806 with $d = 50$ in the Freebase-150k dataset, mwNN improves its initial AUPRC score of 0.600 ($d = 10$) on the YAGO dataset to 0.714 and RESCAL's AUPRC score jumps from 0.327 to 0.579 ($d = 10$). The only exception to this observation is RESCAL when applied to the YAGOc-195k dataset. For $d = 50$, the RESCAL AUPRC score decreases from 0.694 to 0.672 and for $d = 100$ from 0.721 to 0.680 AUPRC when considering the LCWA in the model. The type-constraints of the YAGOc-195k relation-types are defined over a large set of entities, covering 22% of all possible triples It seems that a closed-world assumption is more beneficial for RESCAL in this case. As in case of the type-cnstraints, the AUROC scores also support the trend observed through the AUPRC scores.

Even though the LCWA has a similar beneficial impact on the link-prediction quality than the type-constraints, there is no evidence in our experiments that the LCWA can generally replace the extracted type-constraints provided by the KG's schema. For the YAGOc-195k dataset, the type-constraint supported models are clearly superior to those that exploit the LCWA, but in case of the Freebase-150k and DBpedia-Music datasets the message is not as clear. RESCAL achieves on these two datasets its best results when exploiting LCWA where mwNN achieves its best results when exploiting the type-constraints. For TransE it seems to depend on the chosen embedding length, where longer embedding lengths favor the LCWA.

6   Related Work

A number of other latent variable models have been proposed for the statistical modeling of KGs. [20] recently proposed a neural tensor network, which we did not consider in our study, since it was observed that it does not scale to larger datasets [7,8]. Instead we exploit a less complex and more scalable neural network model proposed in [8], which could achieve comparable results to the neural tensor network of [20]. TransE [5] has been target of other recent research activities. [24] proposed a framework for relationship modeling that combines aspects of TransE and the neural tensor network proposed in [20]. [23] proposed TransH which improves TransE's capability to model reflexive one-to-many, many-to-one and many-to-many relation-types by introducing a relation-type specific hyperplane where the translation is performed. This work has been further extended in [14] by introducing TransR which separates representations of entities and relation-types in different spaces, where the translation is performed in the relation-space. An extensive review on representation learning with KGs can be found in [17].

Domain and range constraints as given by the KG's schema or via a local closed-world assumption have been exploited very recently in RESCAL [7,10], but to the best of our knowledge have not yet been integrated into other latent variable methods nor has their general value been recognized for these models.

Further, latent variable methods have been combined with graph-feature models which lead to an increase of prediction quality [8] and a decrease of model complexity [16].

7 Conclusions and Future Work

In this work we have studied the general value of prior knowledge about the semantics of relation-types, extracted from the schema of the knowledge graph (type-constraints) or approximated through a local closed-world assumption, for the statistical modeling of KGs with latent variable models. Our experiments give clear empirical proof that the curated semantic information of type-constraints significantly improves link-prediction quality of TransE, RESCAL and mwNN (up to 77%) and can therefore be considered as essential for latent variable models when applied to KGs. Thereby the value of type-constraints becomes especially prominent when the model complexity, i.e. the dimensionality of the embeddings has to be very low, an essential requirement when applying these models to very large datasets.

Since type-constraints can be absent or fuzzy (due to e.g. insufficient typing of entities), we further showed that an alternative, a local closed-world assumption (LCWA), can be applied in these cases that approximates domain range constraints for relation-types on instance level rather on class level solely based on observed triples. This LCWA also leads to large improvements in the link-prediction tasks, but especially at a very low model complexity the integration of type-constraints seemed superior. In our experiments we used models that either exploited type-constraints or the LCWA, but in a real setting we would combine both, where we would use the type-constraints whenever possible, but the LCWA on the relation-types where type-constraints are absent or fuzzy.

In future work we will further investigate on additional extensions for latent variable models that can be combined with the type-constraints or LCWA. In the related-work we gave some examples were the integration of graph-feature models (e.g. the path ranking algorithm [12]) was shown to improve these models. In addition we will look at the many aspects in which RESCAL, TransE and mwNN differ. Identifying the aspects of these models that have the most beneficial impact on link-prediction quality can give rise to a new generation of latent variable approaches that could further drive knowledge graph modeling.

References

1. Bergstra, J., Breuleux, O., Bastien, F., Lamblin, P., Pascanu, R., Desjardins, G., Turian, J., Warde-Farley, D., Bengio, Y.: Theano: a CPU and GPU math compiler in Python. In: Proceedings of the 9th Python in Science Conference, pp. 3–10 (2010)
2. Bizer, C., Heath, T., Berners-Lee, T.: Linked data - the story so far. Int. J. Semantic Web Inf. Syst. **5**(3), 1–22 (2009)
3. Bizer, C., Lehmann, J., Kobilarov, G., Auer, S., Becker, C., Cyganiak, R., Hellmann, S.: Dbpedia - a crystallization point for the web of data. Web Semant. **7**(3), 154–165 (2009)
4. Bollacker, K., Evans, C., Paritosh, P., Sturge, T., Taylor, J.: Freebase: a collaboratively created graph database for structuring human knowledge. In: SIGMOD, pp. 1247–1250. ACM (2008)

5. Bordes, A., Usunier, N., Garcia-Duran, A., Weston, J., Yakhnenko, O.: Translating embeddings for modeling multi-relational data. In: NIPS, pp. 2787–2795 (2013)
6. Carlson, A., Betteridge, J., Kisiel, B., Settles, B., Hruschka, Jr., E.R., Mitchell, T.M.: Toward an architecture for never-ending language learning. In: AAAI. AAAI Press (2010)
7. Chang, K., Yih, W., Yang, B., Meek, C.: Typed tensor decomposition of knowledge bases for relation extraction. In: EMNLP, pp. 1568–1579 (2014)
8. Dong, X., Gabrilovich, E., Heitz, G., Horn, W., Lao, N., Murphy, K., Strohmann, T., Sun, S., Zhang, W.: Knowledge vault: a web-scale approach to probabilistic knowledge fusion. In: SIGKDD, pp. 601–610. ACM (2014)
9. Hoffart, J., Suchanek, F.M., Berberich, K., Lewis-Kelham, E., de Melo, G., Weikum, G.: Yago2: exploring and querying world knowledge in time, space, context, and many languages. In: WWW, pp. 229–232. ACM (2011)
10. Krompaß, D., Nickel, M., Tresp, V.: Large-scale factorization of type-constrained multi-relational data. In: DSAA, pp. 18–24. IEEE (2014)
11. Krompaß, D., Nickel, M., Tresp, V.: Querying factorized probabilistic triple databases. In: Mika, P., Tudorache, T., Bernstein, A., Welty, C., Knoblock, C., Vrandečić, D., Groth, P., Noy, N., et al. (eds.) ISWC 2014, Part II. LNCS, vol. 8797, pp. 114–129. Springer, Heidelberg (2014)
12. Lao, N., Cohen, W.W.: Relational retrieval using a combination of path-constrained random walks. Mach. Learn. **81**(1), 53–67 (2010)
13. Lassila, O., Swick, R.R.: Resource Description Framework (RDF) Model and Syntax Specification. W3c recommendation, W3C (1999)
14. Lin, Y., Liu, Z., Sun, M., Liu, Y., Zhu, X.: Learning entity and relation embeddings for knowledge graph completion. In: AAAI, pp. 2181–2187 (2015)
15. Miller, G.A.: Wordnet: a lexical database for English. Commun. ACM **38**(11), 39–41 (1995)
16. Nickel, M., Jiang, X., Tresp, V.: Reducing the rank in relational factorization models by including observable patterns. In: NIPS, pp. 1179–1187 (2014)
17. Nickel, M., Murphy, K., Tresp, V., Gabrilovich, E.: A review of relational machine learning for knowledge graphs: From multi-relational link prediction to automated knowledge graph construction. CoRR, abs/1503.00759 (2015)
18. Nickel, M., Tresp, V., Kriegel, H.: A three-way model for collective learning on multi-relational data. In: ICML, pp. 809–816. ACM (2011)
19. Nickel, M., Tresp, V., Kriegel, H.: Factorizing yago: scalable machine learning for linked data. In: WWW, pp. 271–280. ACM (2012)
20. Socher, R., Chen, D., Manning, C.D., Ng, A.Y.: Reasoning with neural tensor networks for knowledge base completion. In: NIPS (2013)
21. Swartz, A.: Musicbrainz: a semantic web service. IEEE Intell. Syst. **17**(1), 76–77 (2002)
22. Wan, L., Zeiler, M.D., Zhang, S., LeCun, Y., Fergus, R.: Regularization of neural networks using dropconnect. In: ICML, vol. 28, pp. 1058–1066. JMLR.org (2013)
23. Wang, Z., Zhang, J., Feng, J., Chen, Z.: Knowledge graph embedding by translating on hyperplanes. In: AAAI, pp. 1112–1119 (2014)
24. Yang, B., Yih, W., He, X., Gao, J., Deng, L.: Embedding entities and relations for learning and inference in knowledge bases. CoRR, abs/1412.6575 (2014)

Publishing Without Publishers: A Decentralized Approach to Dissemination, Retrieval, and Archiving of Data

Tobias Kuhn[1,2]([✉]), Christine Chichester[3],
Michael Krauthammer[4], and Michel Dumontier[5]

[1] Department of Humanities, Social and Political Sciences, ETH Zurich,
Zürich, Switzerland
tokuhn@ethz.ch
[2] Department of Computer Science, VU University Amsterdam,
Amsterdam, The Netherlands
[3] Swiss Institute of Bioinformatics, Geneva, Switzerland
christine.chichester@isb-sib.ch
[4] Yale University School of Medicine, New Haven, CT, USA
michael.krauthammer@yale.edu
[5] Stanford Center for Biomedical Informatics Research, Stanford University,
Stanford, CA, USA
michel.dumontier@stanford.edu

Abstract. Making available and archiving scientific results is for the most part still considered the task of classical publishing companies, despite the fact that classical forms of publishing centered around printed narrative articles no longer seem well-suited in the digital age. In particular, there exist currently no efficient, reliable, and agreed-upon methods for publishing scientific datasets, which have become increasingly important for science. Here we propose to design scientific data publishing as a Web-based bottom-up process, without top-down control of central authorities such as publishing companies. Based on a novel combination of existing concepts and technologies, we present a server network to decentrally store and archive data in the form of nanopublications, an RDF-based format to represent scientific data. We show how this approach allows researchers to publish, retrieve, verify, and recombine datasets of nanopublications in a reliable and trustworthy manner, and we argue that this architecture could be used for the Semantic Web in general. Evaluation of the current small network shows that this system is efficient and reliable.

1 Introduction

Modern science increasingly depends on datasets, which however are left out in the classical way of publishing, i.e. through narrative (printed or online) articles in journals or conference proceedings. This means that the publications that describe scientific findings get disconnected from the data they are based on,

M. Arenas et al. (Eds.): ISWC 2015, Part I, LNCS 9366, pp. 656–672, 2015.
DOI: 10.1007/978-3-319-25007-6_38

which can seriously impair the verifiability and reproducibility of their results. Addressing this issue raises a number of practical problems: How should one publish scientific datasets and how can one refer to them in the respective scientific publications? How can we be sure that the data will remain available in the future and how can we be sure that data we find on the Web have not been corrupted or tampered with? Moreover, how can we refer to specific entries or subsets from large datasets?

To address some of these problems, a number of scientific data repositories have appeared, such as Figshare and Dryad.[1] Furthermore, Digital Object Identifiers (DOI) have been advocated to be used not only for articles but also for scientific data [22]. While these services certainly improve the situation of scientific data, in particular when combined with Semantic Web techniques, they have nevertheless a number of drawbacks: They have centralized architectures, they give us no possibility to check whether the data have been (deliberately or accidentally) modified, and they do not support access or referencing on a more granular level than entire datasets (such as individual data entries).

Even if we put aside worst-case scenarios of organizations going bankrupt or becoming uninterested in sustaining their services, their websites have typically not a perfect uptime and might be down for a few minutes or even hours every once in a while. This is certainly acceptable for most use cases involving a human user accessing the data, but it can quickly become a problem in the case of automated access embedded in a larger service. Furthermore, it is possible that somebody gains access to their database and silently modifies part of the data, or that the data get corrupted during the transfer from the server to the client.

Below we present an approach to tackle these problems, building upon existing Semantic Web technologies, in particular RDF and nanopublications, and adhering to accepted Web principles, such as decentralization and REST APIs. Specifically, our research question is: Can we create a decentralized, reliable, trustworthy, and scalable system for publishing, retrieving, and archiving datasets in the form of sets of nanopublications based on existing Web standards and infrastructure?

2 Background

Nanopublications [11] are a relatively recent proposal for improving the efficiency of finding, connecting, and curating scientific findings in a manner that takes attribution, quality levels, and provenance into account. While narrative articles would still have their place in the academic landscape, small formal data snippets in the form of nanopublications should take their central position in scholarly communication [21]. Most importantly, nanopublications can be automatically interpreted and aggregated and they allow for fine-grained citation metrics on the level of individual claims. On the technical level, nanopublications use the RDF language with named graphs [4] to represent assertions, as well as their provenance and metadata. Conceptually, the approach boils down

---

[1] http://figshare.com, http://datadryad.org

to the ideas of subdividing scientific results into atomic assertions, representing these assertions in RDF, attaching provenance information in RDF on the level of individual assertions, and treating each of these tiny entities as an individual publication. Nanopublications have been applied to a number of domains, so far mostly from the life sciences including pharmacology [28], genomics [23], and proteomics [6]. An increasing number of datasets formatted as nanopublications are openly available, including neXtProt [5] and DisGeNET [25], and the nanopublication concept has been combined with and integrated into existing frameworks for data discovery and integration, such as CKAN [19].

Research Objects are a related proposal to establish "self-contained units of knowledge" [1], and they constitute in a sense the antipode approach to nanopublications. We could call them "megapublications," as they contain much more than a typical narrative publication, namely resources like input and output data, workflow definitions, log files, and presentation slides. We demonstrate in this paper, however, that bundling all resources of scientific studies in large packages is not a necessity to ensure reproducibility and trust, but we can achieve these properties also with strong identifiers and a decentralized server network.

SPARQL endpoints, i.e. query APIs to RDF triple stores, are a widely used technique for making linked data available on the Web in a flexible manner. While off-the-shelf triple stores can nowadays handle billions of triples or more, they require a significant amount of resources in the form of memory and processor time to do so, at least if the full expressive power of the SPARQL language is supported. A recent study found that more than half of the publicly accessible SPARQL endpoints are available less than 95% of the time [3], posing a major problem to services depending on them, in particular to those that depend on several endpoints at the same time. To solve these problems, alternative approaches and platforms — such as Linked Data Fragments [27], the Linked Data Platform [26], and CumulusRDF [17] — have been proposed, providing less powerful query interfaces and thereby shifting the workload from the server to the client.

Fully reliable services, however, can only be achieved with distributed architectures, which have been proposed by a number of existing approaches related to data publishing. For example, distributed file systems that are based on cryptographic methods have been designed for data that are public [10] or private [7]. In contrast to the design principles of the Semantic Web, these approaches implement their own internet protocols and follow the hierarchical organization of file systems. Other approaches build upon the existing BitTorrent protocol and apply it to data publishing [8,18], and there is interesting work on repurposing the proof-of-work tasks of Bitcoin for data preservation [20]. There exist furthermore a number of approaches to applying peer-to-peer networks for RDF data [9], but they do not allow for the kind of permanent and provenance-aware publishing that we propose below. Moreover, only for the centralized and closed-world setting of database systems, approaches exist that allow for robust and granular references to subsets of dynamic datasets [24].

Our approach is based on previous work, in which we proposed *trusty URIs* to make nanopublications and their entire reference trees verifiable and immutable by the use of cryptographic hash values [15,16]. This is an example of such a trusty URI:

`http://example.org/r1.RA5AbXdpz5DcaYXCh9l3eI9ruBosiL5XDU3rxBbBaUO7O`

The last 45 characters of this URI (i.e. everything after ".") is what we call the *artifact code*. It contains a hash value that is calculated on the RDF content it represents, such as the RDF graphs of a nanopublication. Because this hash is part of the URI, any link to such an artifact comes with the possibility to verify its content, including other trusty URI links it might contain. In this way, the range of verifiability extends to the entire reference tree.

Furthermore, we argued in previous work that the assertion of a nanopublication need not be fully formalized, but we can allow for informal or underspecified assertions [14]. We also sketched how "science bots" could autonomously produce and publish nanopublications, and how algorithms could thereby be tightly linked to their generated data [13], which requires the existence of a reliable and trustworthy publishing system, such as the one we present here.

3   Approach

Our approach builds upon the existing concept of nanopublications and our previously introduced method of trusty URIs. It is a proposal of a reliable implementation of accepted Semantic Web principles, in particular of what has become known as the *follow-your-nose* principle: Looking up a URI should return relevant data and links to other URIs, which allows one (i.e. humans as well as machines) to discover things by navigating through this data space [2]. We argue that approaches following this principle can only be reliable and efficient if we have some sort of guarantee that the resolution and processing of any single identifier will succeed in one way or another and only takes up a small amount of time and resources. This requires (1) that RDF representations are made available on several distributed servers, so the chance that they all happen to be inaccessible at the same time is negligible, and that (2) these representations are reasonably small, so that downloading them is a matter of fractions of a second, and so that one has to process only a reasonable amount of data to decide which links to follow. We address the first requirement by proposing a distributed server network and the second one by building upon the concept of nanopublications. Below we explain the general architecture, the functioning and the interaction of the nanopublication servers, and the concept of nanopublication indexes.

3.1   Architecture

There are currently at least three possible architectures for Semantic Web applications (and mixtures thereof), as shown in a simplified manner in Figure 1. The first option is the use of plain HTTP GET requests. Applying the follow-your-nose principle, resolvable URIs provide the data based on which the application performs the tasks of finding relevant resources, running queries, analyzing and

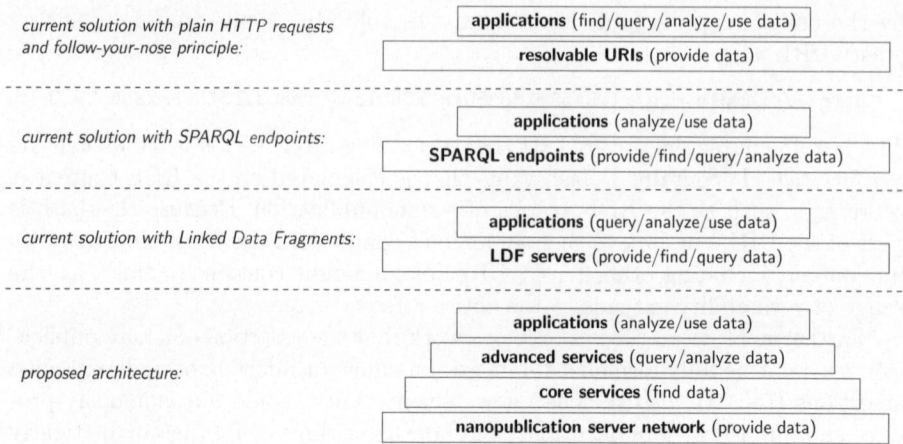

Fig. 1. Illustration of current architectures of Semantic Web applications and our proposed approach

aggregating the results, and using them for the purpose of the application. If SPARQL endpoints are used, as a second option, most of the workload is shifted from the application to the server via the expressive power of the SPARQL query language. A more reasonable approach, in our view, is the third option of Linked Data Fragments, where servers provide only limited query features and where the tasks are distributed between servers and applications in more balanced fashion. However, all these current solutions are based on two-layer architectures, and have moreover no inherent replication mechanisms. A single point of failure can cause applications to be unable to complete their tasks: A single URI that does not resolve or a single server that does not respond can break the entire process.

We argue here that we need distributed and decentralized services to allow for robust and reliable applications that consume linked data. At the same time, the most low-level task of providing linked data is essential for all other tasks at higher levels, and therefore needs to be the most stable and robust one. We argue that this can be best achieved if we free this lowest layer from all tasks except the provision and archiving of data entries (nanopublications in our case) and decouple it from the tasks of providing services for finding, querying, or analyzing the data. This makes us advocate a multi-layer architecture, a possible realization of which is shown at the bottom of Figure 1.

Below we present a concrete proposal of such a low-level data provision infrastructure in the form of a nanopublication server network. Based on such an infrastructure, one can then build different kinds of services operating on a subset of the nanopublications they find in the underlying network. "Core services" could involve things like resolving backwards references (i.e. "which nanopublications refer to the given one?") and the retrieval of the nanopublications published by a given person or containing a particular URI. Based on such core services for finding nanopublications, one could then provide "advanced services" that allow us to run queries on subsets of the data and ask for aggregated output. (These higher layers could of course make use of existing techniques such as SPARQL endpoints and Linked Data Fragments.) While the lowest layer would necessarily be accessible to everybody, some of the services on the higher level could be private or limited to a small (possibly paying) user group. We have in particular scientific data in mind, but we think that an architecture of this kind could also be used for Semantic Web content in general.

3.2   Nanopublication Servers

As a concrete proposal of a low-level data provision layer, as explained above, we present here a decentralized nanopublication server network with a REST API to provide and propagate nanopublications identified by trusty URIs.[2] The nanopublication servers of such a network connect to each other to retrieve and replicate their nanopublications, and they allow users to upload new nanopublications, which are then automatically distributed through the network.

Basing the content of this network on nanopublications with trusty URIs has a number of positive consequences for its design: The first benefit is that the fact that nanopublications are all similar in size and always small makes it easy to estimate how much time is needed to process an entity (such as validating its hash) and how much space to store it (e.g. as a serialized RDF string in a database). Moreover it ensures that these processing times remain mostly in the fraction-of-a-second range, guaranteeing quick responses, and that these entities are never too large to be analyzed in memory. The second benefit is that servers do not have to deal with identifier management, as the nanopublications already come with trusty URIs, which are guaranteed to be unique and universal. The third and possibly most important benefit is that nanopublications with trusty URIs are immutable and verifiable. This means that servers only have to deal with *adding* new entries but not with *updating* or *correcting* any of them, which eliminates the hard problems of concurrency control and data integrity in distributed systems. Together, these aspects significantly simplify the design of such a network and its synchronization protocol, and make it reliable and efficient even with limited resources.

Specifically, a nanopublication server of the current network has the following components:

- A **key-value store** of its nanopublications (with the trusty URI as the key)
- A **journal** consisting of a journal identifier and a list of the identifiers of all loaded nanopublications, subdivided into pages of a fixed size.
- Optionally, a **cache of gzipped packages** containing all nanopublications for a given journal page (but they can also be generated on the fly)
- A **list of known peers**, i.e. the URLs of other nanopublication servers
- **Information about each known peer**, including the journal identifier and the total number of nanopublications at the time it was last visited

---

[2] https://github.com/tkuhn/nanopub-server

Based on these components, the servers respond to the following request (in the form of HTTP GET):

- Each server needs to return general **server information**, including the journal identifier and the number of stored nanopublications
- Given an artifact code (i.e. the final part of a trusty URI) of a known nanopublication, the server returns the given **nanopublication** in a format like TriG, TriX, or N-Quads (depending on content negotiation).
- A **journal page** can be requested by page number as a list of trusty URIs.
- For every journal page (except for incomplete last pages), a gzipped **package** can be requested containing the respective nanopublications.
- The **list of known peers** can be requested as a list of URLs.

In addition, a server can optionally support the following two actions (in the form of HTTP POST requests):

- A server may accept requests to **add a given individual nanopublication** to its database.
- A server may also accept requests to **add the URL of a new nanopublication server** to its peer list.

Server administrators have the additional possibility to load nanopublications from the local file system. Together, these server components and their possible interactions allow for efficient decentralized distribution of published nanopublications.

The current system can be seen as an unstructured peer-to-peer network, where each node can freely decide which other nodes to connect to and which nanopublications to replicate. As the network is still very small, the present five nodes connect to all other nodes and replicate all nanopublications they can find. The current implementation is furthermore designed to be run on normal Web servers alongside with other applications, with economic use of the server's resources in terms of memory and processing time. In order to avoid overload of the server or the network connection, we restrict outgoing connections to other servers to one at a time. The current system and its protocol are not set in stone but, if successful, will have to evolve in the future — in particular with respect to network topology and partial replication — to accommodate a network of possibly thousands of servers and billions of nanopublications.

3.3 Nanopublication Indexes

To make the infrastructure described above practically useful, we have to introduce the concept of indexes. One of the core ideas behind nanopublications is that each of them is a tiny atomic piece of data. This implies that analyses will mostly involve more than just one nanopublication and typically a large number of them. Similarly, most processes will generate more than just one nanopublication, possibly thousands or even millions of them. Therefore, we need to be able to group nanopublications and to identify and use large collections of them.

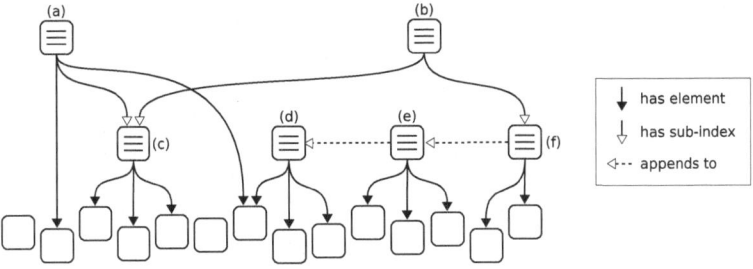

Fig. 2. Schematic example of nanopublication indexes

Given the versatility of the nanopublication standard, it seems straightforward to represent such collections as nanopublications themselves. However, if we let such "collection nanopublications" contain other nanopublications, then the former would become very large for large collections and would quickly lose their property of being *nano*. We can solve part of that problem by applying a principle that we can call *reference instead of containment*: nanopublications cannot contain but only refer to other nanopublications, and trusty URIs allow us to make these reference links almost as strong as containment links. To emphasize this principle, we call them *indexes* and not collections.

However, even by only containing references and not the complete nanopublications, these indexes can still become quite large. To ensure that all such index nanopublications remain *nano* in size, we need to put some limit on the number of references, and to support sets of arbitrary size, we can allow indexes to be appended by other indexes. We set 1000 nanopublication references as the upper limit any single index can directly contain. This limit is admittedly arbitrary, but it seems to be a reasonable compromise between ensuring that nanopublications remain small on the one hand and limiting the number of nanopublications needed to define large indexes on the other. A set of 100,000 nanopublications, for example, can therefore be defined by a sequence of 100 indexes, where the first one stands for the first 1000 nanopublications, the second one appends to the first and adds another 1000 nanopublications (thereby representing 2000 of them), and so on up to the last index, which appends to the second to last and thereby stands for the entire set. In addition, to allow datasets to be organized in hierarchies, we define that the references of an index can also point to sub-indexes. In this way we end up with three types of relations: an index can *append to* another index, it can contain other indexes as *sub-indexes*, and it can contain nanopublications as *elements*. These relations defining the structure of nanopublication indexes are shown schematically in Figure 2. Index (a) in the shown example contains five nanopublications, three of them via sub-index (c). The latter is also part of index (b), which additionally contains eight nanopublications via sub-index (f). Two of these eight nanopublications belong directly to (f), whereas the remaining six come from appending to index (e). Index (e) in turn gets half of its nanopublications by appending to index (d). We see that some nanopublications may not be referenced by any index at all, while others may belong to several indexes at the same time.

Below we show how this general concept of indexes can be used to define sets of new or existing nanopublications, and how such index nanopublications can be published and their nanopublications retrieved.

3.4 Trusty Publishing

Let us consider two simple exemplary scenarios to illustrate and motivate the general concepts, using the np command from the nanopub-java library[3]. Given, for example, a file nanopubs.trig with three nanopublications, we have to assign them trusty URIs before they can be published:

```
$ np mktrusty -v nanopubs.trig
Nanopub URI: http://example.org/np1#RAQoZlp22LHIvtYqHCosPbUtX8yeGs1Y5AfqcjMneLQ2I
Nanopub URI: http://example.org/np2#RAT5swlSLyMbuDO3KzJsYHVV2oM1wRhluRxMrvpkZCDUQ
Nanopub URI: http://example.org/np3#RAkvUpysi9Ql3it1c6-iIJMG7YSt3-PI8dAJXcmafU71s
```

This gives us the file trusty.nanopubs.trig, which contains transformed versions of the three nanopublications, now having trusty URIs as identifiers. We can now publish these nanopublications to the network:

```
$ np publish trusty.nanopubs.trig
3 nanopubs published at http://np.inn.ac/
```

We can check the publication status of the given nanopublications:

```
$ np status -a http://example.org/np1#RAQoZlp22LHIvtYqHCosPbUtX8yeGs1Y5AfqcjMneLQ2I
URL: http://np.inn.ac/RAQoZlp22LHIvtYqHCosPbUtX8yeGs1Y5AfqcjMneLQ2I
Found on 1 nanopub server.
```

This is what we see immediately after publication, but only a few minutes later the given nanopublication is found on several servers:

```
$ np status -a http://example.org/np1#RAQoZlp22LHIvtYqHCosPbUtX8yeGs1Y5AfqcjMneLQ2I
URL: http://np.inn.ac/RAQoZlp22LHIvtYqHCosPbUtX8yeGs1Y5AfqcjMneLQ2I
URL: http://ristretto.med.yale.edu:8080/nanopub-server/RAQoZlp22LHIvtYqHCosPbUtX8yeGs...
URL: http://nanopub-server.ops.labs.vu.nl/RAQoZlp22LHIvtYqHCosPbUtX8yeGs1Y5AfqcjMneLQ2I
URL: http://nanopubs.stanford.edu/nanopub-server/RAQoZlp22LHIvtYqHCosPbUtX8yeGs1Y5Afq...
URL: http://nanopubs.semanticscience.org/RAQoZlp22LHIvtYqHCosPbUtX8yeGs1Y5AfqcjMneLQ2I
Found on 5 nanopub servers.
```

Next, we can make an index pointing to these three nanopublications:

```
$ np mkindex -o index.nanopubs.trig trusty.nanopubs.trig
Index URI: http://np.inn.ac/RAXsXUhY8iDbfDdY6sm64hRFPr7eAwYXRlSsqQAz1LE14
```

This creates a local file index.nanopubs.trig containing the index, identified by the URI shown above. As this index is itself a nanopublication, we can publish it in the same way as described above, and then everybody can conveniently and reliably retrieve the given set of nanopublications:

```
$ np get -c http://np.inn.ac/RAXsXUhY8iDbfDdY6sm64hRFPr7eAwYXRlSsqQAz1LE14
```

This command downloads the content of the given index, i.e. the three nanopublications we just created and published.

---

[3] https://github.com/Nanopublication/nanopub-java

As another exemplary scenario, let us imagine a researcher in the biomedical domain who is interested in the protein CDKN2A and who has derived some conclusion based on the data found in existing nanopublications. Specifically, let us suppose this researcher analyzed five nanopublications from different sources, specified by the following artifact codes (they can be viewed online by appending the artifact code to the URL http://np.inn.ac/):

```
RAEoxLTy4pEJYbZwA9FuBJ6ogSquJobFitoFMbUmkBJh0
RAoMWOxMemwKEjCNWLFt8CgRmg_TGjfVSsh15hGfEmcz4
RA3BH_GncwEK_UXFGTvHcMVZ1hW775eupAccDdho5Tiow
RA3HvJ69n00mD5d4m4u-0c4bpX1xIWYN6L3wvB9jntTXk
RASx-fnzWJzluqRDe6GVMWFEyWLok8S6nTNkyElwapwno
```

These nanopublications can be downloaded from the network with the `np get` command and stored in a file, which we name here `cdkn2a-nanopubs.trig`. In order to be able to refer to such a collection of nanopublications with a single identifier, a new index is needed that refers to just these five nanopublications. This time we give the index a title (which is optional):

```
$ np mkindex -t "Data about CDKN2A from BEL2nanopub & neXtProt" \
  -o index.cdkn2a-nanopubs.trig cdkn2a-nanopubs.trig
Index URI: http://np.inn.ac/RA6jrrPL2NxxFWlo6HFWas1ufp00dZzS_XKwQDXpJg3CY
```

The generated index is stored in the file `index.cdkn2a-nanopubs.trig`, and our exemplary researcher can now publish this index to let others know about it:

```
$ np publish index.cdkn2a-nanopubs.trig
1 nanopub published at http://np.inn.ac/
```

There is no need to publish the five nanopublications this index is referring to, because they are already public (this is how we got them in the first place). The index URI can be used to refer to this new collection of existing nanopublications in an unambiguous and reliable manner, for example as a reference in a paper, as we do it for the datasets of this article [29–33].

4   Evaluation

To evaluate our approach, we want to find out whether a small server network run on normal Web servers, without dedicated infrastructure, is able to handle the amount of nanopublications we can expect to become publicly available in the next few years. At the time the evaluation was performed, the server network consisted of three servers in Zurich, New Haven, and Ottawa. Two new servers in Amsterdam and Stanford have joined the network since. The current network of five servers is shown in Figure 3, which is a screenshot of a nanopublication monitor that we have implemented. Such monitors regularly check the nanopublication server network, register changes (currently once per minute), and test the response times and the correct operation of the servers by requesting a random nanopublication and verifying the returned data.

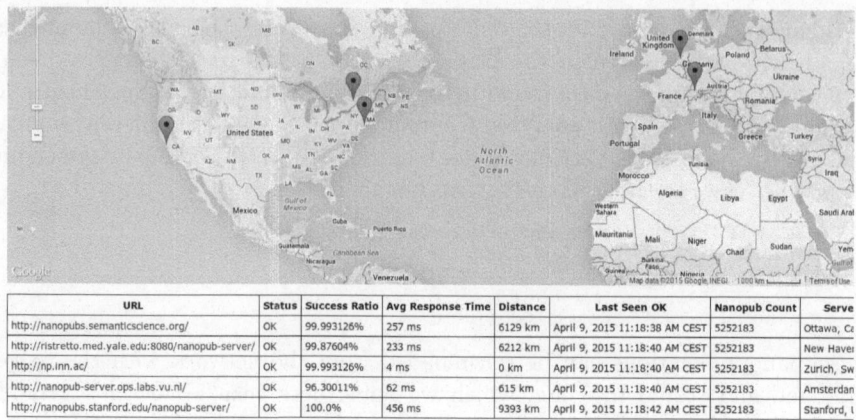

URL	Status	Success Ratio	Avg Response Time	Distance	Last Seen OK	Nanopub Count	Serve
http://nanopubs.semanticscience.org/	OK	99.993126%	257 ms	6129 km	April 9, 2015 11:18:38 AM CEST	5252183	Ottawa, Ca
http://ristretto.med.yale.edu:8080/nanopub-server/	OK	99.87604%	233 ms	6212 km	April 9, 2015 11:18:40 AM CEST	5252183	New Haver
http://np.inn.ac/	OK	99.993126%	4 ms	0 km	April 9, 2015 11:18:40 AM CEST	5252183	Zurich, Sw
http://nanopub-server.ops.labs.vu.nl/	OK	96.30011%	62 ms	615 km	April 9, 2015 11:18:40 AM CEST	5252183	Amsterdan
http://nanopubs.stanford.edu/nanopub-server/	OK	100.0%	456 ms	9393 km	April 9, 2015 11:18:42 AM CEST	5252183	Stanford, l

Fig. 3. This screenshot of the nanopublication monitor interface (http://npmonitor. inn.ac) showing the current server network.

Table 1. Existing datasets in the nanopublication format that were used for the first part of the evaluation.

dataset	# nanopubs index	# nanopubs content	# triples index	# triples content	initial location for evaluation
GeneRIF/AIDA [29]	157	156,026	157,909	2,340,390	New Haven
OpenBEL 1.0 [31]	53	50,707	51,448	1,502,574	New Haven
OpenBEL 20131211 [32]	76	74,173	75,236	2,186,874	New Haven
DisGeNET v2.1.0.0 [33]	941	940,034	951,325	31,961,156	Zurich
neXtProt [30]	4,026	4,025,981	4,078,318	156,263,513	Ottawa
total	5,253	5,246,921	5,314,236	194,254,507	

4.1 Evaluation Design

Table 1 shows the existing datasets that we use for the first part of the evaluation. This includes all datasets we are aware of that use trusty URIs, with a total of more than 5 million nanopublications and close to 200 million RDF triples, including nanopublication indexes that we generated for each dataset. The total size of these datasets when stored as uncompressed TriG files amounts to 15.6 GB. Each of the datasets is assigned to one of the three servers, where it is loaded from the local file systems. The first nanopublications start spreading to the other servers, while others are still being loaded from the file system. We therefore test the reliability and capacity of the network under constant streams of new nanopublications coming from different servers, and we use two nanopublication monitors (in Zurich and Ottawa) to evaluate the responsiveness of the network.

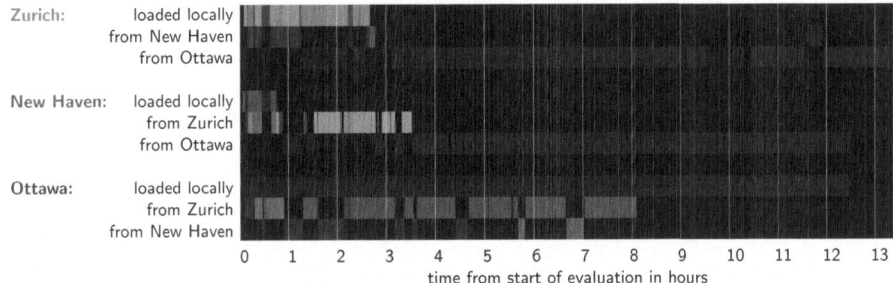

Fig. 4. The flow of nanopublications during the time of the evaluation. The colors indicate the *original* location of the respective nanopublications, and the brightness stands for the rate at which they are loaded (bright meaning high rate).

In the second part of the evaluation we expose a server to heavy load from clients to test its retrieval capacity. For this we use a service called Load Impact[4] to let up to 100 clients access a nanopublication server in parallel. We test the server in Zurich over a time of five minutes under the load from a linearly increasing number of clients (from 0 to 100) located in Dublin. These clients are programmed to request a randomly chosen journal page, then to go though the entries of that page one by one, requesting the respective nanopublication with a probability of 10%, and starting over again with a different page. As a comparison, we run a second session, for which we load the same data into a Virtuoso SPARQL endpoint on the same server in Zurich (with 16 GB of memory given to Virtuoso and two 2.40 GHz Intel Xeon processors). Then, we perform exactly the same stress test on the SPARQL endpoint, requesting the nanopublications in the form of SPARQL queries instead of requests to the nanopublication server interface. This comparison is admittedly not a fair one, as SPARQL endpoints are much more powerful and are not tailor-made for the retrieval of nanopublications, but they provide nevertheless a valuable and well-established reference point to evaluate the performance of our system.

4.2 Evaluation Results

The first part of the evaluation lasted 13 hours and 21 minutes, at which point all nanopublications were replicated on all three servers, and therefore the nanopublication traffic came to an end. Figure 4 shows the type and intensity of the data flow (i.e. the transfer of nanopublications) between the three servers over the time of the evaluation. The network was able to handle an average of about 400,000 new nanopublications per hour, which corresponds to more than 100 new nanopublications per second. This includes the time needed for loading each nanopublication once from the local file system (at the first server), transferring it through the network two times (to the other two servers), and for

---

[4] https://loadimpact.com

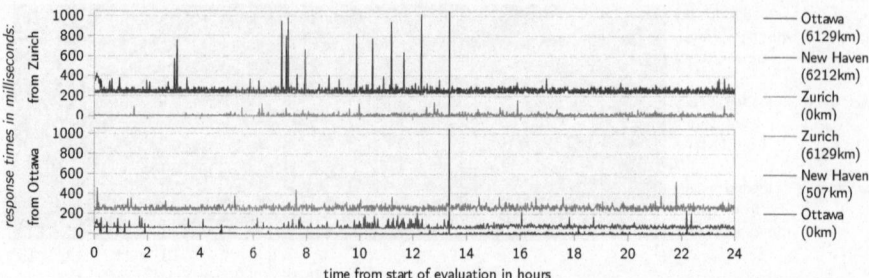

Fig. 5. Server response times as recorded during and after the first evaluation, which ended at 13 hours and 21 minutes, as indicated by the black vertical line.

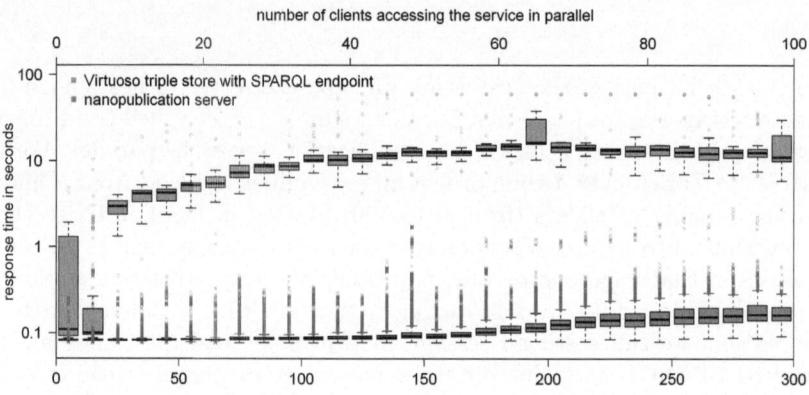

Fig. 6. Results of the evaluation of the retrieval capacity of a nanopublication server as compared to a general SPARQL endpoint (note the logarithmic y-axis)

verifying it three times (once when loaded and twice when received by the other two servers). Figure 5 shows the response times of the three servers as measured by the two nanopublication monitors in Zurich (top) and Ottawa (bottom) from the start of the evaluation until 24 hours later, therefore covering the entire evaluation plus an additional 10 hours and 39 minutes after its end. We see that the observed latency is mostly due to the geographical distance between the servers and the monitors. The response time was always less than 0.25 seconds when the server was on the same continent as the measuring monitor. In 99.86% of all cases (including those across continents) the response time was below 0.5 seconds, and it was always below 1.1 seconds. Not a single one of the 8636 individual HTTP requests timed out, led to an error, or received a nanopublication that could not be successfully verified. We see that the load put onto the network did not have much of an impact on the response times. Except for a handful of spikes, one barely notices the difference between the heavy-load and zero-load situations.

Figure 6 shows the result of the second part of the evaluation. The nano-publication server was able to handle 113,178 requests in total (i.e. an average of 377 requests per second) with an average response time of 0.12 seconds. In contrast, the SPARQL endpoint answering the same kind of requests needed 100 times longer to process them (13 seconds on average), consequently handled about 100 times fewer requests (1267), and started to hit the timeout of 60 seconds for some requests when more than 40 client accessed it in parallel. In the case of the nanopublication server, the majority of the requests were answered within less than 0.1 seconds for up to around 50 parallel clients, and this value remained below 0.17 seconds all the way up to 100 clients. As the round-trip network latency alone between Ireland and Zurich amounts to around 0.03 to 0.04 seconds, further improvements can be achieved for a denser network due to the reduced distance to the nearest server.

The first part of the evaluation shows that the overall replication capacity of the current server network is around 9.4 million new nanopublications per day or 3.4 billion per year. The results of the second part show that the load on a server when measured as response times is barely noticeable for up to 50 parallel clients, and therefore the network can easily handle $50 \cdot x$ parallel client connections or more, where x is the number of servers in the network (currently $x = 5$). The second part thereby also shows that the restriction of avoiding parallel outgoing connections for the replication between servers is actually a very conservative measure that could be relaxed, if needed, to allow for a higher replication capacity.

5 Discussion and Conclusion

We have presented here a low-level infrastructure for data sharing, which is just one piece of a bigger ecosystem to be established. The implementation of components that rely on this low-level data sharing infrastructure is ongoing and future work. This includes the development of "core services" (see Section 3.1) on top of the server network to allow people to find nanopublications and "advanced services" to query and analyze the content of nanopublications. In addition, we need to establish standards and best practices of how to use existing ontologies (and to define new ones where necessary) to describe properties and relations of nanopublications, such as referring to earlier versions, marking nanopublications as retracted, and reviewing of nanopublications.

Apart from that, we also have to scale up the current small network. As our protocol only allows for simple key-based lookup, the time complexity for all types of requests is sublinear and therefore scales up well. The main limiting factor is disk space, which is relatively cheap and easy to add. Still, the servers will have to specialize, i.e. replicate only a part of all nanopublications, in order to handle really large amounts of data, which can be done in a number of ways: Servers can restrict themselves to nanopublications from a certain internet domain, or to particular types of nanopublications, e.g. to specific topics or authors, and communicate this to the network; inspired by the Bitcoin system, certain servers could only accept nanopublications whose hash starts with a given number of zero bits, which makes it costly to publish; and some servers could be specialized to new nanopublications, providing fast access but only for a restricted time, while others could take care of archiving old nanopublications, possibly on tape and with considerable delays between request and delivery. Lastly, there could also emerge interesting synergies with novel approaches to internet networking, such as Content-Centric Networking [12], with which — consistent with our proposal — requests are based on content rather than hosts.

We argue that data publishing and archiving can and should be done in a decentralized manner. We believe that the presented server network can serve as a solid basis for semantic publishing, and possibly also for the Semantic Web in general. It could contribute to improve the availability and reproducibility of scientific results and put a reliable and trustworthy layer underneath the Semantic Web.

References

1. Belhajjame, K., Corcho, O., Garijo, D., Zhao, J., Missier, P., Newman, D., Palma, R., Bechhofer, S., García, E., Cuesta, J.M.G.-P., et al.: Workflow-centric research objects: first class citizens in scholarly discourse. In: Proceedings of SePublica 2012. CEUR-WS (2012)
2. Berners-Lee, T.: Linked data – design issues (2006). http://www.w3.org/DesignIssues/LinkedData.html
3. Buil-Aranda, C., Hogan, A., Umbrich, J., Vandenbussche, P.-Y.: SPARQL Web-Querying Infrastructure: Ready for Action? In: Alani, H., Kagal, L., Fokoue, A., Groth, P., Biemann, C., Parreira, J.X., Aroyo, L., Noy, N., Welty, C., Janowicz, K. (eds.) ISWC 2013, Part II. LNCS, vol. 8219, pp. 277–293. Springer, Heidelberg (2013)
4. Carroll, J., Bizer, C., Hayes, P., Stickler, P.: Named graphs, provenance and trust. In: Proceedings of WWW 2005, pp. 613–622. ACM (2005)
5. Chichester, C., Gaudet, P., Karch, O., Groth, P., Lane, L., Bairoch, A., Mons, B., Loizou, A.: Querying nextprot nanopublications and their value for insights on sequence variants and tissue expression. Web Semantics: Science, Services and Agents on the World Wide Web (2014)
6. Chichester, C., Karch, O., Gaudet, P., Lane, L., Mons, B., Bairoch, A.: Converting neXtProt into linked data and nanopublications. Semantic Web (2014, to appear)
7. Clarke, I., Sandberg, O., Wiley, B., Hong, T.W.: Freenet: a distributed anonymous information storage and retrieval system. In: Federrath, H. (ed.) Designing Privacy Enhancing Technologies. LNCS, vol. 2009, p. 46. Springer, Heidelberg (2001)
8. Cohen, J.P., Lo, H.Z.: Academic torrents: a community-maintained distributed repository. In: Proceedings of XSEDE 2014, p. 2. ACM (2014)
9. Filali, I., Bongiovanni, F., Huet, F., Baude, F.: A survey of structured P2P systems for RDF data storage and retrieval. In: Transactions on Large-Scale Data- and Knowledge-Centered Systems III, pp. 20–55. Springer (2011)
10. Fu, K., Kaashoek, M.F., Mazières, D.: Fast and secure distributed read-only file system. ACM Transactions on Computer Systems **20**(1), 1–24 (2002)
11. Groth, P., Gibson, A., Velterop, J.: The anatomy of a nano-publication. Information Services and Use **30**(1), 51–56 (2010)

12. Jacobson, V., Smetters, D.K., Thornton, J.D., Plass, M., Briggs, N., Braynard, R.: Networking named content. Commun. ACM **55**(1), 117–124 (2012)
13. Kuhn, T.: Science bots: a model for the future of scientific computation? In: WWW 2015 Companion Proceedings, pp. 1061–1062. ACM (2015)
14. Kuhn, T., Barbano, P.E., Nagy, M.L., Krauthammer, M.: Broadening the scope of nanopublications. In: Cimiano, P., Corcho, O., Presutti, V., Hollink, L., Rudolph, S. (eds.) ESWC 2013. LNCS, vol. 7882, pp. 487–501. Springer, Heidelberg (2013)
15. Kuhn, T., Dumontier, M.: Trusty URIs: verifiable, immutable, and permanent digital artifacts for linked data. In: Presutti, V., d'Amato, C., Gandon, F., d'Aquin, M., Staab, S., Tordai, A. (eds.) ESWC 2014. LNCS, vol. 8465, pp. 395–410. Springer, Heidelberg (2014)
16. Kuhn, T., Dumontier, M.: Making digital artifacts on the web verifiable and reliable. IEEE Transactions on Knowledge and Data Engineering **27**(9) (2015)
17. Ladwig, G., Harth, A.: CumulusRDF: linked data management on nested key-value stores. In: Proceedings of SSWS 2011 (2011)
18. Markman, C., Zavras, C.: BitTorrent and libraries: Cooperative data publishing, management and discovery. D-Lib Magazine **20**(3), 5 (2014)
19. McCusker, J.P., Lebo, T., Krauthammer, M., McGuinness, D.L.: Next generation cancer data discovery, access, and integration using prizms and nanopublications. In: Baker, C.J.O., Butler, G., Jurisica, I. (eds.) DILS 2013. LNCS, vol. 7970, pp. 105–112. Springer, Heidelberg (2013)
20. Miller, A., Juels, A., Shi, E., Parno, B., Katz, J.: Permacoin: repurposing Bitcoin work for data preservation. In: Proceedings of the IEEE Symposium on Security and Privacy (SP), pp. 475–490. IEEE (2014)
21. Mons, B., van Haagen, H., Chichester, C., den Dunnen, J.T., van Ommen, G., van Mulligen, E., Singh, B., Hooft, R., Roos, M., Hammond, J., et al.: The value of data. Nature genetics **43**(4), 281–283 (2011)
22. Paskin, N.: Digital object identifiers for scientific data. Data Science Journal **4**, 12–20 (2005)
23. Patrinos, G.P., Cooper, D.N., van Mulligen, E., Gkantouna, V., Tzimas, G., Tatum, Z., Schultes, E., Roos, M., Mons, B.: Microattribution and nanopublication as means to incentivize the placement of human genome variation data into the public domain. Human mutation **33**(11), 1503–1512 (2012)
24. Proell, S., Rauber, A.: A scalable framework for dynamic data citation of arbitrary structured data. In: 3rd International Conference on Data Management Technologies and Applications (DATA2014), 8 2014
25. Queralt-Rosinach, N., Kuhn, T., Chichester, C., Dumontier, M., Sanz, F., Furlong, L.I.: Publishing DisGeNET as nanopublications. Semantic Web – Interoperability, Usability, Applicability (2015, to appear)
26. Speicher, S., Arwe, J., Malhotra, A.: Linked data platform 1.0. Recommendation, W3C, February 26, 2015
27. Verborgh, R., Vander Sande, M., Colpaert, P., Coppens, S., Mannens, E., Van de Walle, R.: Web-scale querying through linked data fragments. In: Proceedings of LDOW 2014 (2014)
28. Williams, A.J., Harland, L., Groth, P., Pettifer, S., Chichester, C., Willighagen, E.L., Evelo, C.T., Blomberg, N., Ecker, G., Goble, C., et al.: Open PHACTS: semantic interoperability for drug discovery. Drug discovery today **17**(21), 1188–1198 (2012)
29. AIDA Nanopubs extracted from GeneRIF. Nanopublication index, 4 March 2015. http://np.inn.ac/RAY_lQruuagCYtAcKAPptkY7EpITwZeUilGHsWGm9ZWNI

30. Nanopubs converted from neXtProt protein data (preliminary). Nanopublication index, 10 March 2015. http://np.inn.ac/RAXFlG04YMi1A5su7oF6emA8m Sp6HwyS3mFTVYreDeZRg

31. Nanopubs converted from OpenBEL's Small and Large Corpus 1.0. Nanopublication index, 4 March 2015. http://np.inn.ac/RACy0I4f_wr62Ol7BhnD5EkJU 6Glf-wp0oPbDbyve7P6o

32. Nanopubs converted from OpenBEL's Small and Large Corpus 20131211. Nanopublication index http://np.inn.ac/RAR5dwELYLKGSfrOclnWhjOj-2nGZN_ 8BW1JjxwFZINHw, 4 March 2015

33. Nanopubs extracted from DisGeNET v2.1.0.0. Nanopublication index http:// np.inn.ac/RAXy332hxqHPKpmvPc-wqJA7kgWiWa-QA0DIpr29LIG0Q, 5 March 2015

Author Index